SARA JAPHET

I & II CHRONICLES

THE OLD TESTAMENT LIBRARY

Editorial Advisory Board

SARA JAPHET

I & II CHRONICLES

A Commentary

Westminster/John Knox Press
Louisville, Kentucky

Copyright © Sara Japhet 1993

First published 1993
by SCM Press Ltd,
26–30 Tottenham Road, London N1 4BZ

First American edition

Published in the U.S.A. by Westminster/John Knox Press, 100 Witherspoon Street, Louisville, Kentucky 40202-1396

This book is printed on acid-free paper that meets the American National Standards Institute Z39.48 standard. ∞

PRINTED IN THE UNITED STATES OF AMERICA

9 8 7 6 5 4 3 2 1

Library of Congress Cataloging-in-Publication Data

Japhet, Sara.
    I and II Chronicles : a commentary / Sara Japhet. — 1st American ed.
        p.   cm.
    Includes bibliographical references.
    ISBN 0-664-21845-8

    1. Bible. O.T. Chronicles—Commentaries. I. Bible. O.T. Chronicles. English. Revised Standard. 1993. II. Title. III. Title: 1 and 2 Chronicles. IV. Title: First and Second Chronicles.
BS1345.3.J374   1993
222'.6077—dc20   93-4666

CONTENTS

PREFACE

Commentary is a literary genre in its own right, and the writing of commentary is essentially different from all other types of writing, either creative or scholarly. For exegetes forgo all independence and consciously and willingly subordinate themselves to someone else's work. They do not write about what may interest and attract them, but rather assume total commitment to the work which they are interpreting: it dictates the subjects of their research, the order of priorities among these subjects and even the manner in which these subjects are presented. Hence not only are the subjects of the exegete's writing and the details of its content determined by the text being interpreted, but also the structure of the commentary and the choice of its components.

In addition to the inevitable yoking of the text and its interpreter, there is a third party. As it is said: 'a threefold cord is not readily broken!' (Ecclesiastes 4.12) This third party is the reader to whom both the text and its exegesis are addressed, and without whom they do not truly exist. The exegete, as the 'first reader', guides those who follow in his or her footsteps, so that they may see the text with their eyes and hear its voice.

This commentary was written primarily for the readers of the Old Testament Library. Therefore, although my own understanding of the book was acquired in the only way one can attain full understanding of the text, that is, by reading it in the original Hebrew language, my writing is intended not only for the reader who shares knowledge of Hebrew with me, but also for those whose access to Scripture is gained through the intermediary of an English translation. This orientation dictated the small number of notes regarding the Massoretic Text, although this is a topic of great scholarly interest with respect to Chronicles. In this area I have restricted myself to matters entailing interpretative conclusions. The commentary includes a special section of remarks on the RSV, the English translation which is used throughout this series, and thus also in the present commentary. Naturally all translation is a form of commentary, and, when necessary, I have called the reader's attention to interpretative questions that arise out of the decisions of the RSV. To clarify these issues I have used many other translations, but for the reader's convenience I have limited explicit references to two new translations, the NEB and the JPS.

Study of Chronicles necessitates dealing with various areas and a wide variety of issues. Because I wished to present the book in its full scope, and to make the reader aware of the broad foundation upon which understanding of the book is based, the commentary raises issues from many diverse fields, such as language and style on the one hand, and history, geography and archaeology on the other. However, attention has mainly been directed to two other areas, which are the heart of the book: the literary aspect, where my goal was to shed light upon the book as a historical composition and upon the methods and means chosen by the author to convey his ideas; and that of theology, where I meant to illuminate the author's goals, the comprehensive structure of his spiritual world as reflected in the book, and his message. Because of limitation of time and space I could not devote all due attention to the history of exegesis and research. What I omitted is worthy of inclusion, though this was not possible.

From my early remarks about commentary as a unique literary genre, and especially since we are dealing here not with mere commentary, but rather with the interpretation of scripture, it of course follows that this work cannot be entirely 'new'. Many generations of commentators and scholars have striven to understand the words of this book, and I stand upon the shoulders of my predecessors. Each commentator is, as it were, a new spotlight, illuminating new areas and colouring them with its light. Every interpretation is a guide escorting the reader and telling him: stop here, turn your head here, pay attention here. I hope that the present commentary, which joins a long, impressive and venerable series of readers of Scripture, will add something of its own, helping those who come after it, providing a new point of departure, and shedding additional light upon the message of Chronicles.

The writing of a commentary is also a path of study and of constantly increasing knowledge. Having reached this point, the publication of the commentary, I wish to thank all those who were partners in my labour, with and without their knowledge: teachers whose lessons I heard, authors from whose works I learned, colleagues from whose wisdom I benefitted, and students, of whom it is written, 'and from my students more than them all'. Without their contribution, this book could never have been written.

Special thanks are due to two of my research assistants over the years: Mrs Lea Mazor, with whom I took my first steps in research toward the formation of this work, and Mr Raphael Carse, who worked diligently with me to ensure accuracy in many details, and primarily in the precision and polish of my English. I also wish to thank Professor Peter Ackroyd, the editor of this series, with whom I consulted on many matters and who saw an earlier draft of this work, offering important comments. Responsibility for the book, both what it contains and what it lacks, is of course solely my own.

Over the years I have received material support from several institutions, and I wish to express my gratitude to them for the trust they placed in me, permitting me to devote my time to research and writing and to receive assistance from others. The Fund for Basic Research of the Israel Academy of Sciences supported my research in its early stages, in 1982–1983. The Rothschild Foundation awarded me a grant which supported me during a sabbatical year at Wolfson College in Oxford during 1983–84. The Paula and David Ben-Gurion Fund at the Institute for Jewish Studies of the Hebrew University enabled me to benefit from research and editorial assistance over a number of years. I express heartfelt gratitude to all of them.

Last but far from least, I give special thanks to the members of my family. The research and writing of this commentary became part of their lives and their daily bread, and they became full partners in the long and uneven journey, with its ascents and descents. I dedicate this book to them with love.

ABBREVIATIONS

AB	The Anchor Bible
AJSL	*American Journal of Semitic Literature*
ANEP	*The Ancient Near East in Pictures* (ed. J. B. Pritchard), Princeton 1969
ANET	*Ancient Near Eastern Texts* (ed. J. B. Pritchard), Princeton ³1969
ATD	Das Alte Testament Deutsch
AUSS	*Andrews University Seminary Studies*
AV	Authorized Version
B	Bombergiana
BASOR	*Bulletin of the American Schools of Oriental Research*
BCE	Before the Common Era
BDB	Brown, Driver, Briggs, *A Hebrew and English Lexicon of the Old Testament*
BH(K)	*Biblia Hebraica*, ed. R. Kittel
BHS	*Biblia Hebraica Stuttgartensia*
BJPES	*Bulletin of the Jewish Palestine Exploration Society*
BK	Biblische Kommentar
BN	*Biblische Notizen*
BR	*Biblical Research*
BS	*Biblical Studies*
BT	Babylonian Talmud
BTB	*Biblical Theology Bulletin*
BZAW	Beihefte zur Zeitschrift für die alttestamentliche Wissenschaft
CAT	Commentaire de l'Ancien Testament
CB	Cambridge Bible
CBC	Cambridge Bible Commentaries
CBQ	*Catholic Biblical Quarterly*
CE	Common Era
EB	Encyclopedia Biblica
EHAT	Exegetisches Handbuch zum Alten Testament
EJ	*Encyclopedia Judaica*
ET	English translation

ExpT	*Expository Times*
FOTL	Forms of the Old Testament Literature
FRLANT	Forschungen zur Religion und Literatur des Alten und Neuen Testaments
FS	Festschrift
HAT	Handbuch zum Alten Testament
HKAT	Handkommentar zum Alten Testament
HS	*Hebrew Studies*
HSAT	Die Heilige Schrift des Alten Testaments
HSM	Harvard Semitic Monographs
HTR	*Harvard Theological Review*
IB	The Interpreter's Bible
ICC	International Critical Commentary
IDB	The Interpreter's Dictionary of the Bible
IEJ	*Israel Exploration Journal*
JAAR	*Journal of the American Academy of Religion*
JANES	*Journal of the Ancient Near Eastern Society*, Columbia University, New York
JBL	*Journal of Biblical Literature*
JETS	*Journal of the Evangelical Theological Society*
JPOS	*Journal of the Palestine Oriental Society*
JPS	Jewish Publication Society Bible
JQR	*Jewish Quarterly Review*
JSJ	*Journal for the Study of Judaism*
JSOT	*Journal for the Study of the Old Testament*
JSOTS	Journal for the Study of the Old Testament Supplements
JT	Talmud Yerushalmi
KAT	Kommentar zum Alten Testament
KBL	L. Kohler and W. Baumgartner, *Lexicon in Veteris Testamenti Libros*
KHAT	Kurzer Handkommentar zum Alten Testament
KS	Kleine Schriften
LXX	Septuagint (Greek) translation of the Old Testament
LXX^A	Septuagint Codex Alexandrinus
LXX^B	Septuagint Codex Vaticanus
LXX^L	Septuagint Lucianic Recension
MS(S)	Manuscript(s)
MT	Massoretic Text
NCBC	New Century Bible Commentary

NEB	New English Bible
OLP	Oriental Library Publications
OLZ	*Orientalische Literaturzeitung*
OTL	Old Testament Library
OTS	*Oudtestamentische Studiën*
P	Peshitta (Syriac) translation of the Old Testament
PJB	*Palästina Jahrbuch*
RGG	*Die Religion in Geschichte und Gegenwart*
RSV	Revised Standard Version
RTK	*Realencyklopädie für Theologie und Kirche*
SJLA	*Studies in Judaism in Late Antiquity*
SJOT	*Scandinavian Journal of the Old Testament*
TBC	Torch Bible Commentaries
TDNT	*Theological Dictionary of the New Testament*
TDOT	*Theological Dictionary of the Old Testament*
TJ	Targum Jonathan
TQ	*Theologische Quartalschrift*
TR	*Theologische Rundschau*
TZ	*Theologische Zeitschrift*
UF	*Ugaritische Forschung*
USQR	*Union Seminary Quarterly Review*
V	Vulgate (Latin) translation of the Old Testament
VL	Vetus Latina (Old Latin) translation of the Old Testament
VT	*Vetus Testamentum*
VTS	*Vetus Testamentum Supplements*
WBC	Word Bible Commentary
WMANT	Wissenschaftliche Monographien zum Alten und Neuen Testament
WO	*Die Welt des Orients*
ZAH	*Zeitschrift für Althebraistik*
ZAW	*Zeitschrift für die alttestamentliche Wissenschaft*
ZDPV	*Zeitschrift der Deutschen Palästinavereins*

Titles cited in the text with * are in Hebrew

SELECT BIBLIOGRAPHY

The bibliography includes commentaries, handbooks which have been used extensively, major and influential monographs (either books or articles), and recent and relatively recent works with which the reader may not be familiar. For further bibliographical information the reader is referred to the commentary itself, to earlier commentaries and works on Chronicles, and to the bibliographical guide of Kalimi, mentioned below.

Commentaries

P.R. Ackroyd, *I and II Chronicles, Ezra, Nehemiah* (TBC), London 1973
W.E. Barnes, *The Books of Chronicles* (CB), Cambridge 1899
I. Benzinger, *Die Bücher der Chronik* (KHAT), Tübingen/Leipzig 1901
E. Bertheau, *Commentary on the Books of Chronicles*, ET Edinburgh 1857
R.L. Braun, *1 Chronicles* (WBC), Waco, Texas 1986
M. Cogan – H. Tadmor, *II Kings* (AB), New York 1988
R.G. Coggins, *The First and Second Books of Chronicles* (CBC), Cambridge 1976
E.L. Curtis and A.A. Madsen, *A Critical and Exegetical Commentary on the Books of Chronicles* (ICC), Edinburgh 1910
R.B. Dillard, *2 Chronicles* (WBC), Waco, Texas 1987
S.R. Driver, *Notes on the Hebrew Text and the Topography of the Book of Samuel*, Oxford ²1913
A.B. Ehrlich, *Randglossen zur Hebräischen Bibel*, Vol. 7, Leipzig 1914 (reprinted 1968)
—, *Mikra Ki-Pheshuto – The Bible according to its Literal Meaning*, 1899 (reprinted New York 1969, Hebrew)
W.A.L. Elmslie, *The Books of Chronicles* (CB), Cambridge 1916
—, *The First and Second Books of Chronicles* (IB), New York/Nashville 1954
K. Galling, *Die Bücher der Chronik, Esra, Nehemia* (ATD), Göttingen 1954
J. Goettsberger, *Die Bücher der Chronik oder Paralipomena* (HSAT), Bonn 1939
J. Gray, *I and II Kings* (OTL), London ²19170
H.W. Hertzberg, *I and II Samuel* (OTL), London 1964
T.R. Hobbs, *2 Kings* (WBC), Waco, Texas 1985
F.C. Keil, *The Books of Chronicles*, ET Edinburgh 1872

—, *Chronik, Esra, Nehemia und Esther* (BK), 1870, reprinted Giessen 1990

D. Kimhi, *Chronicles, Rabbinic Bible* (Hebrew)

R. Kittel, *Die Bücher der Chronik* (HKAT), Göttingen 1902

S. Langton, *Commentary on the Books of Chronicles*, ed. A. Saltman, Ramat Gan 1978

P.K. McCarter, *Samuel I–II* (AB), New York 1980–1984

F. Michaeli, *Les Livres des Chroniques, d'Esdras et de Néhémie* (CAT), Neuchâtel and Paris 1976

J.A. Montgomery, *A Critical and Exegetical Commentary on the Book of Kings* (ICC), Edinburgh 1951

J.M. Myers, *I and II Chronicles* (AB), New York 1965

M. Noth, *Könige* (BK), Neukirchen-Vluyn 1968

Pseudo-Rashi, *Chronicles, Rabbinic Bible* (Hebrew)

J.W. Rothstein – J. Hänel, *Kommentar zum ersten Buch der Chronik* (KAT), Leipzig 1927

A. Šanda, *Die Bücher der Könige* (EHAT), Münster 1911

W. Rudoph, *Chronickbücher* (HAT), Tübingen 1955

S. de Vries, *1 and 2 Chronicles* (FOTL), Grand Rapids 1989

—, *I Kings* (WBC), Waco, Texas 1985

T. Willi, *Chronik* (BK), Neukirchen-Vluyn, Fasc. 1, 1991

H.G.M. Williamson, *1 and 2 Chronicles* (NCBC), Grand Rapids and London 1982

General Bibliography

P.R. Ackroyd, 'The Chronicler as Exegete', *JSOT* 2, 1977, 2–32

—, 'Chronicles – Ezra – Nehemiah: The Concept of Unity', *ZAW* 100 (supplement, 1988), 189–201

—, *The Chronicler in his Age*, JSOTS 101, Sheffield 1991

Y. Aharoni, *The Land of the Bible*, Philadephia ²1979

W.F. Albright, 'The Date and Personality of the Chronicler', *JBL* 40, 1921, 104–24

—, 'The List of Levitic Cities', *Louis Ginzberg Jubilee Volume*, New York 1945, 49–73

—, 'The Judicial Reform of Jehoshaphat', *Alexander Marx Jubilee Volume*, New York 1955, 61–82

W. Alfink, '1 Chronicles 16.8–36 as Literary Source for Revelation 14:6–7', *AUSS* 22, 1984, 187–96

L.C. Allen, *The Greek Chronicles – The Relation of the Septuagint of I and II Chronicles to the Masoretic Text*, I–II, Leiden 1974

—, 'Kerygmatic Units in 1 and 2 Chronicles', *JSOT* 41, 1988, 21–36

Y. Amit, 'The Role of Prophets and Prophecy in the Teachings of Chronicles', *Beth Mikra* 28, 1983, 113–33 (Hebrew)

M. Anbar, 'La "Reprise"', *VT* 38, 1988, 385–98

P.M. Arnold, 'Hosea and the Sin of Gibeah', *CBQ* 51, 1989, 457–60

M. Augustin, 'Beobachtungen zur chronistischen Umgestaltung der deuteronomistischen Königschroniken nach der Reichsteilung', *FS H.W. Wolff*, Frankfurt 1982, 11–50

—, 'The Role of Simeon in the Book of Chronicles', *Proceedings of the Tenth World Congress of Jewish Studies*, Jerusalem 1990, 137–42

A.G. Auld, 'The "Levitical Cities": Texts and History', *ZAW* 91, 1979, 26–40

D. Barthelemy, *Critique Textuelle de l'Ancient Testament I*, Fribourg and Göttingen 1982, 427–521

W. Baumgartner, *Hebräisches und Aramäisches Lexikon zum Alten Testament*, I—IV, Leiden 1967–1990

C.T. Begg, 'The Death of Josiah in Chronicles: Another View', *VT* 37, 1987, 1–8

A. Bendavid, *Biblical Hebrew and Mishnaic Hebrew*, Tel Aviv 1971 (Hebrew)

—, *Parallels in the Bible*, Jerusalem 1972

G. Beyer, 'Das Festungssystem Rehabeams', *ZDPV* 54, 1931, 113–34

E. Bickerman, *From Ezra to the Last of the Maccabees*, New York 1962

J. Botterweck, 'Zur Eigenart der chronistischen Davidsgeschichte', *TQ* 136, 1956, 402–35

R.L. Braun, 'Solomonic Apologetic in Chronicles', *JBL* 92, 1973, 503–16

—, 'Solomon, the Chosen Temple Builder: The Significance of 1 Chronicles 22, 28, 29 for the Theology of Chronicles', *JBL* 95, 1976, 581–90

—, 'A Reconsideration of the Chronicler's Attitude toward the North', *JBL* 96, 1977, 59–62

—, 'Chronicles, Ezra and Nehemiah: Theology and Literary History', *VTS* 30, 1979, 42–64

T.A. Busink, *Der Tempel von Jerusalem, von Salomo bis Herodes*, Leiden 1970

T.C. Butler, 'A Forgotten Passage from a Forgotten Era (1 Chr XVI 8–36)' *VT* 28, 1968, 142–50

B.S. Childs, *Introduction to the Old Testament as Scripture*, London and Philadelphia 1979

M. Cogan, 'The Chronicler's Use of Chronology as Illuminated by Neo-Assyrian Royal Inscriptions', in J.H. Tigay, *Empirical Models for Biblical Criticism*, Philadelphia 1985, 197–209

F. M. Cross, 'A Reconstruction of the Judean Restoration' *JBL* 94, 1975, 3–18

D. G. Deboys, 'The Chronicler's Portrait of Abijah', *Biblica* 70, 1991, 48–62
A. Demski, 'The Genealogy of Gibeon (1 Chronicles 9:35–44): Biblical and Epigraphic Considerations', *BASOR* 202, 1971, 16–23
—, 'The Genealogies of Manasseh and the Location of the Territory of Milkah Daughter of Zelophehad', *Eretz Israel* 16, 1982, 70–5 (Hebrew)
—, 'The Clans of Ephrath: Their Territory and History', *Tel Aviv* 13–14, 1986/7, 76–89
B. J. Diebner, 'Überlegungen zum Brief des Elia (2 Chr 21,12–15)', *Henoch* IX, 1987, 197–228
R. B. Dillard, 'The Reign of Asa (2 Chr 14–16): An Example of the Chronicler's Theological Method', *JETS* 23, 1980, 207–18
S. R. Driver, *An Introduction to the Literature of the Old Testament*, Edinburgh 1891, ⁹1910
R. K. Duke, *The Persuasive Appeal of the Chronicler: A Rhetorical Analysis*, JSOTS 88, Sheffield 1990

D. Edelman, 'The Asherite Genealogy of 1 Chronicles 7:30–40', *BR* 33, 1988, 13–23
E. L. Ehrlich, 'Der Aufenthalt des Königs Manasse in Babylon', *TZ* 21, 1965, 281–6
T. C. Eskenazi, 'The Chronicler and the Composition of 1 Esdras', *CBQ* 48, 1986, 39–61
O. Eissfeldt, *The Old Testament – an Introduction*, ET Oxford 1965

M. Fishbane, *Biblical Interpretation in Ancient Israel*, Oxford 1984
D. N. Freedman, 'The Chronicler's Purpose', *CBQ* 23, 1961, 436–42
V. Fritz, 'The "List of Rehoboam's Fortresses" in 2 Chr 11:5–12 – A Document from the Time of Josiah', *Eretz Israel* 15, 1981, 46–53

I. Gabriel, *Friede über Israel, eine Untersuchung zur Friedentheologie in Chronik I, 10 – II, 36*, Klosterneuberg 1990
G. Galil, *The Genealogies of the Tribe of Judah*, Diss. Jerusalem 1983 (Hebrew with English summary)
H. Gese, 'Zur Geschichte der Kultsänger am zweiten Tempel', in *Von Sinai zum Zion*, München 1974, 147–58
W. Genesius, *Hebrew Grammar* (ed. E. Kautsch), ET Oxford 1909
J. Goldingay, 'The Chronicler as a Theologian', *BTB* 5, 1975, 99–126

K. H. Graf, *Die Geschichtlichen Bücher des Alten Testaments*, Leipzig 1866

M. P. Graham, *The Utilization of 1 and 2 Chronicles in the Reconstruction of Israelite History in the Nineteenth Century*, Atlanta 1990

S. Grébaut, *Les Paralipomènes livres I et II, Version Éthiopienne, Patrologia Orientalis* 23/4, Paris 1932, 525–771

B. Halpern, 'Sacred History and Ideology: Chronicles' Thematic Structure – Indications of an Earlier Source', in R.E. Friedman (ed.), *The Creation of Sacred Literature*, Berkeley and London 1981, 35–54

P. D. Hanson, '1 Chronicles 15–16 and the Chronicler's Views on the Levites', *FS S. Talmon*, 1992, 69–77

M. Haran, 'Studies in the Account of the Levitical Cities', *JBL* 80, 1961, 45–54, 156–65

R. E. Hoffmann, 'Eine Parallele zur Rahmenerzählung des Buches Hiob in 1 Chr 7:20–29?', *ZAW* 92, 1980, 120–32

A. Hurvitz, *A Linguistic Study of the Relationship between the Priestly Source and the Book of Ezekiel*, Paris 1982

—, 'Terms and Epithets Relating to the Jerusalem Temple Compound in the Book of Chronicles', *FS J. Milgrom* (forthcoming)

Z. Ilan, 'Jehoshaphat's Battle against Amon and Moab', *Beth Mikra* 53, 1973, 205–11 (Hebrew)

T. S. Im, *Das Davidbild in den Chronikbüchern*, Frankfurt, Bern and New York 1985

S. Japhet, 'The Supposed Common Authorship of Chronicles and Ezra-Nehemiah Investigated Anew', *VT* 18, 1968, 332–72

—, 'Conquest and Settlement in Chronicles', *JBL* 98, 1979, 205–18

—, 'Biblical Historiography in the Persian Period', in *The World History of the Jewish People*, Vol. VI, ed. H. Tadmor and I. Eph'al, Jerusalem 1983, 176–202 (Hebrew)

—, 'The Historical Reliability of Chronicles: The History of the Problem and its Place in Biblical Research', *JSOT* 33, 1985, 83–107

—, 'Interchanges of Verbal Roots in Parallel Texts in Chronicles', ET *HS* 28, 1987, 19–50

—, 'Law and "the Law" in Ezra-Nehemiah', *Proceedings of the Ninth World Congress of Jewish Studies, panel sessions*, Jerusalem 1988, 99–104

—, *The Ideology of the Book of Chronicles and its Place in Biblical Thought*, ET Frankfurt, Bern and New York 1989

—, 'The Relationship between Chronicles and Ezra-Nehemiah', *VTS* XLIII, 1991, 298–313

—, 'The Israelite Legal and Social Reality as Reflected in Chronicles: A Case Study', in *Sha'arei Talmon, FS S. Talmon*, 1992, 79–91

—, 'The Prohibition of the Habitation of Women', *FS Y. Muffs* (forthcoming 1993)

M. Jastrow, *A Dictionary of the Targumim, the Talmud Babli and Yerushalmi and the Midrashic Literature*, New York 1950

E. Jenni, 'Aus der Literatur zur chronistischen Geschichtsschreibung', *TR* 45, 1980, 97–108

W. Johnstone, 'Guilt and Atonement: The Theme of 1 and 2 Chronicles', *FS W. McKane*, JSOTS 42, Sheffield 1986, 113–38

—, 'Which is the Best Commentary? 11. The Chronicler's Work', *ExpT* 102, 1990, 6–11

I. Kalimi, *Recurrences of Literary-Historiographical Differences in the Parallel Texts Between the Book of Chronicles and the Books of Samuel–Kings*, Diss. Jerusalem 1989 (Hebrew with English summary)

—, *The Books of Chronicles, A Classified Bibliography*, Jerusalem 1990

M. Kartveit, *Motive und Schichten der Landtheologie in 1 Chronik 1–9*, Stockholm 1989

Y. Kaufman, *The History of the Religion of Israel*, Jerusalem 1960 (Hebrew)

J. Kegler – M. Augustin, *Synopse zum chronistischen Geschichtswerk*, *BEATAJ* 1, ²1991

K. A. Kitchen, *The Third Intermediate Period in Egypt*, Worminster 1973

R. W. Klein, 'Abijah's Campaign Against the North (2 Chr 13) – What were the Chronicler's Sources?', *ZAW* 95, 1983, 210–17

G. N. Knoppers, 'Rehoboam in Chronicles: Villain or Victim?', *JBL* 109, 1990, 423–40

—, 'Reform and Regression: The Chronicler's Presentation of Jehoshaphat', *Biblica* 72, 1991, 500–24

K. Koch, 'Das Verhältnis von Exegese und Verkündigung anhand eines Chroniktextes', *TLZ* 90, 1965, 659–70

A. Kropat, *Die Syntax des Autors der Chronik*, BZAW 16, 1909

E. Y. Kutscher, *The Language and Linguistic Background of the Isaiah Scroll*, ET Leiden 1974

R. Le Déaut – J. Robert, *Targum de Chronique*, Tome 1971

W. E. Lemke, 'The Synoptic Problem in the Chronicler's History', *HTR* 58, 1965, 349–63

J. Liver, 'So All Israel was Enrolled by Genealogies', in *Studies in Bible and Judean Desert Scroll*, Jerusalem 1971, 234–48 (Hebrew)

—, *Chapters in the History of the Priests and Levites*, Jerusalem ²1987 (Hebrew)
S. E. Loewenstamm and J. Blau, *Thesaurus of the Language of the Bible I–III*, Jerusalem 1957–1968 (Hebrew and English)

R. Mason, 'Some Echoes of the Preaching in the Second Temple?', *ZAW* 96, 1984, 23–49
—, *Preaching the Tradition, Homily and Hermeneutics after the Exile*, Cambridge 1990
D. Mathias, *Die Geschichte der Chronikforschung im 19 Jahrhundert*, Diss. Leipzig 1977
—, '"Levitische Predigt" und Deuteronomismus', *ZAW* 96, 1984, 23–49
B. Mazar, 'The Cities of the Priests and Levites', *VTS* 7, 1960, 193–205 (= *Biblical Israel, State and People*, Jerusalem 1992, 134–45).
L. Mazor, 'The Origin and Evolution of the Curse upon the Builder of Jericho', *Textus* XIV, 1988, 14–23
D. J. McCarthy, 'Covenant and Law in Chronicles – Nehemiah', *CBQ* 44, 1982, 25–44
S. L. McKenzie, *The Chronicler's Use of the Deuteronomistic History*, Atlanta 1985
R. Micheel, *Die Seher- und Prophetenüberlieferungen in der Chronik*, Frankfurt and Berne 1983
J. Milgrom, *Studies in Levitical Terminology I*, Berkeley 1970
J. M. Miller, 'The Korahites of Southern Judah', *CBQ* 32, 1970, 58–68
F. L. Moriarty, 'The Chronicler's Account of Hezekiah's Reform', *CBQ* 27, 1965, 399–406
R. Mosis, *Untersuchungen zur Theologie des Chronistischen Geschichtswerk*, Freiburg 1973

N. Na'aman, 'A New Look at the System of Levitical Cities', *Borders and Districts in Biblical Historiography*, Jerusalem 1986, 203–36
—, 'Hezekiah's Fortified Cities and the LMLK Stamps', *BASOR* 261, 1986, 5–24
—, 'The Date of 2 Chr 11:5–10 – A Reply to Y. Garfinkel', *BASOR* 271, 1988, 74–7
—, 'Sources and Redaction in the Chronicler's Genealogies of Asher and Ephraim', *JSOT* 49, 1991, 105–10
B. Neteler, *Die Bücher der Chronik der Vulgata und des hebraischen Textes*, Münster 1899
J. D. Newsome, 'Toward a New Understanding of the Chronicler and his Purposes', *JBL* 94, 1975, 201–17

J. S. Noble, *The Syriac Version to the Book of Chronicles*, Diss. New York 1943

R. North, 'Does Archeology Prove Chronicles' Sources?', *FS J.M. Myers*, Philadelphia 1974, 375–401

M. Noth, *Das System der Zwölf Stämme Israels*, Stuttgart 1930, reprinted Darmstadt 1980

—, 'Eine siedlungsgeographische Liste in 1 Chr 2 und 4', *ZDPV* 55, 1932, 97–124

—, 'Die Ansiedlung des Stammes Juda auf den Boden Palästinas', *PJB* 30, 1934, 31–47

—, *Überlieferungsgeschichtliche Studien*, Halle 1943, ³1967; ET 1. *The Deuteronomistic History*, JSOTS 15, Sheffield 1981; 2. *The Chronicler's History*, JSOTS 50, Sheffield 1987

—, 'Eine palästinische Lokalüberlieferung in 2 Chr 20', *ZDPV* 67, 1944/5, 45–71

M. Oeming, *Das Wahre Israel, Die 'Genealogische Vorhalle' 1 Chronik 1–9*, *BWANT* 128, Stuttgart 1990

J. B. Payne, 'Validity of Numbers in Chronicles', *BS* 136, 1979, 109–28, 206–20

D. L. Petersen, *Late Biblical Prophecy*, Missoula 1977

O. Plöger, 'Reden und Gebete im deuteronomistischen und chronistischen Geschichtswerk', 1957 = *Aus der Spätzeit des Alten Testaments*, Göttingen 1971, 50–66

K. F. Pohlmann, 'Zur Frage von Korrespondenzen und divergenzen zwischen des Chronikbüchern und dem Esra/Nehemia Buch', *VTS* XLIII, 1991, 314–30

R. Polzin, *Late Biblical Hebrew: Toward an Historical Typology of Biblical Hebrew Prose*, Missoula 1976

G. von Rad, *Das Geschichtsbild des chronistische Werkes*, Stuttgart 1930

—, 'The Levitical Sermon in I and II Chronicles', ET in *The Problem of the Hexateuch and other Essays*, Edinburgh, London and New York 1966, 267–80

—, *Holy War in Ancient Israel*, ET Grand Rapids 1991

M. Rehm, *Textkritische Untersuchungen zu den Parallelstellen der Samuel–Königsbücher und der Chronik*, Münster 1937

G. A. Rendsburg, 'The Internal Consistence and Historical Reliability of the Biblical Genealogies', *VT* XL, 1990, 185–204

H. Reviv, 'The Times of Athaliah and Joash', *Beth Mikra* 47, 1971, 541–8 (Hebrew)
—, 'The Pattern of the Whole-Kingdom's Assembly in Israel', *Eretz Israel* 15, 1981, 308–11 (Hebrew)

J.R. Shaver, *Torah and the Chronicler's History Work*, Atlanta 1989
K. Strübind, *Tradition als Interpretation in der Chronik*, BZAW 201, Berlin 1991
I.L. Seeligmann, 'From Historical Reality to Historiosophical Concepts in the Bible', *P'rakim* II 1969–1974, 273–313 (Hebrew)
—, 'Die Auffassung von der Prophetie in der deuteronomistischen und chronistischen Geschichtsschreibung', *VTS* 29, 1978, 254–84
—, 'The Beginnings of *Midrash* in the Books of Chronicles', *Tarbiz* XLIX, 1979/80, 14–32 (Hebrew)

D. Talshir, 'A Reinvestigation of the Linguistic Relationship between Chronicles and Ezra-Nehemiah', *VT* 38, 1988, 165–93
E. Talstra – A.J.C. Verhei, 'Comparing Samuel/Kings and Chronicles: The Computer Assisted Production of an Analytical Synoptic Database', *Textus* 14, 1988, 41–60
M. Throntveit, 'Linguistic Analysis and the Question of Authorship in Chronicles, Ezra and Nehemiah', *VT* 32, 1982, 201–16
—, *When Kings Speak: Royal Speech and Royal Prayer in Chronicles*, Atlanta 1987

E.C. Ulrich, *The Qumran Text of Samuel and Josephus*, HSM 19, 1978

P. Vannutelli, *Libri Synoptici Veteris Testamenti*, Rome 1931/1934
R. de Vaux, *The Early History of Israel*, London and Philadelphia 1978
A.J.C. Verhei, *Verbs and Numbers. A Study of the Frequency of the Hebrew Verbal Tense Forms in the Books of Samuel–Kings and Chronicles*, Assen 1990
S. de Vries, 'Moses and David as Cult Founders in Chronicles', *JBL* 107, 1988, 619–39

W.G.E. Watson, 'Archaic Elements in the Language of Chronicles', *Biblica* 53, 1972, 191–207
D.R. Weber, *Les anciennes versions latines du deuxième livre des Paralipomènes*, Rome 1945

J. P. Weinberg, 'Das Wesen und die Funktionelle Bestimmung der Listen in 1 Chr 1–9', *ZAW* 93, 1981, 91–114

—, 'Die Natur im Weltbild des Chronisten', *VT* 31, 1981, 324–45

—, 'Krieg und Frieden im Weltbild des Chronisten', *OLP* 16, 1985, 111–29

—, 'Die Soziale Gruppe im Weltbild des Chronisten', *ZAW* 98, 1986, 72–95

—, 'Königtum und Königreich im Weltbild des Chronisten', *Klio* 69, 1987, 28–45

A. C. Welch, *The Work of the Chronicler*, London 1939

J. Wellhausen, *De Gentibus et Familiis Judaeis*, Dissertatio Gottingen, 1870

—, *Prolegomena to the History of Israel*, ET Edinburgh 1885

—, *Der Text der Bücher Samuelis*, 1871

P. Welten, *Geschichte und Geschichtsdarstellung in den Chronikbüchern*, WMANT 42, Neukirchen-Vluyn 1973

—, 'Lade – Tempel – Jerusalem. Zur Theologie der Chronikbüchern', *FS E. Würthwein*, 1979, 169–83

W. M. L. de Wette, 'Historisch-kritische Untersuchung über die Bücher der Chronik', in *Beiträge zur Einleitung in das Alte Testament*, Halle 1823, reprinted Darmstadt 1971

T. Willi, *Die Chronik als Auslegung*, FRLANT 106, Göttingen 1972

H. G. M. Williamson, 'The Accession of Solomon in the Books of Chronicles', *VT* 26, 1976, 351–61

—, *Israel in the Book of Chronicles*, Cambridge 1977

—, 'Eschatology in Chronicles', *Tyndale Bulletin* 28, 1977, 115–54

—, 'The Origins of the Twenty-Four Priestly Courses: A Study of 1 Chronicles XXIII–XXVII', *VTS* 30, 1979, 251–68

—, 'Sources and Redaction in the Chronicler's Genealogy of Judah', *JBL* 98, 1979, 351–9

—, 'The Death of Josiah and the Continuing Development of the Deuteronomistic History', *VT* 32, 1982, 242–8

—, '"We are yours, O David": The Setting and Purpose of 1 Chronicles XII 1–23', *OTS* 21, 1982, 164–76

—, 'The Dynastic Oracle in the Books of Chronicles', in *FS I.L. Seeligmann*, Jerusalem 1983, 305–18

J. W. Wright, 'Guarding the Gates: 1 Chronicles 26:1–19 and the Roles of the Gatekeepers in Chronicles', *JSOT* 48, 1990, 69–81

—, 'The Legacy of David in Chronicles: The Narrative Function of I Chronicles 23–27', *JBL* 110, 1991, 229–42

S. Zalevski, 'The Revelation of God to Solomon in Gibeon', *Tarbiz* 42, 1972/3, 215–58 (Hebrew)

—, *Solomon's Ascension to the Throne. Studies in the Books of Kings and Chronicles*, Jerusalem 1981 (Hebrew)

A. Zeron, 'Tag für Tag kam man zu David, um ihm zu helfen, 1 Chr 12:1–22', *TZ* 30, 1974, 257–61

—, 'Die Anmassung des Königs Usia im Lichte von Jesajas Berufung', *TZ* 33, 1977, 65–8

L. Zunz, *Die Gottesdienstlichen Vorträge der Juden*, Berlin 1832

W. Zwickel, 'Über das ungebliche Verbrennen von Raucherwerk bei der Bestattung eines Königs', *ZAW* 101, 1989, 266–77

Introduction

A. Name of the book and its place in the canon

Chronicles is among the very few biblical books the name of which is actually a definition of genre: *dibrē hayyāmim* = 'the events (or: the words) of the days', that is, a history. Books by the same title are quite commonly referred to in the Bible, often qualified with their subject: 'the Book of the Chronicles of the Kings of Israel' (e.g. I Kings 14.19); 'the Book of the Chronicles of the Kings of Judah' (e.g. Kings 14.29); 'the Book of the Chronicles of the Kings of Media and Persia' (e.g. Esther 10.2); and 'the chronicles of King David' (I Chron. 27.24). The name is also attested, however, without qualification, in Esther 2.23, in Esther 6.1 (where it is more precisely presented as 'the book of memorable deeds, the chronicles'), and Neh. 12.23. However, as is the case for all biblical historical works – and many others – there is no evidence for its title in the book itself, the earliest attestations for its name being found in rabbinical sources: the Mishnah (Yoma 6.1), the Talmud (Meg. 13a; Kidushin 30a; Baba Bathra 14b–15a), and the Midrash (e.g., Leviticus Rabbah 1.3; Ruth Rabbah 2.1). Rabbinical tradition also attests another designation of the book, 'the Book of Genealogies', *sēper yōḥāsîn*, Pesahim 62b). In his prologue to the translation of Samuel and Kings, Jerome described the book as *chronikon*, while still preserving as its title the name prevalent in the Septuagint (*paralipomena* = 'things left out'). This view may have been a reflection of the earlier Jewish tradition, or his own discernment of the book's nature. The same approach is also attested in the heading of the Aramaic Targum, where it is conflated with the other rabbinic tradition to read: 'This is the book of genealogies, the words of the days from days of old.' It is probably through Jerome's suggestion and influence that 'Chronicles' was taken up by most modern translations of the Bible.

The Septuagint's designation of the book does not refer to its genre, but to what the translators regarded as its contents: *paraleipomena*, '[the book of] the things omitted' or 'left over'. This view of the book, which certainly confirms the book's sacred origin and authority, may carry negative connotations for its contents, an attitude which is manifested later in opinions expressed by some Syriac fathers, who posited that the book should be excluded from scripture (cf. Willi, 13). Except for these late voices, however, the canonicity of Chronicles is firmly established in all traditions. In his count of 'thirteen books' in which 'the prophets ... wrote the history of the events of their own times' (*Against Apion* 1.40), Josephus must have included Chronicles. The

Mishnah names Chronicles as one of the books which were read before the
high priest on the eve of the Day of Atonement to keep him from sleep (Yoma
1.6), and the remark of Matt. 23.35 and Luke 11.51 clearly alludes to a
canonical history which includes the book of Chronicles.

Already in the Talmudic Baraitha (BT, Baba Bathra 14b), the Book of
Chronicles appears at the end of the Writings, which is also the place it
occupies in the majority of manuscripts and printed editions. However, in a
major school of biblical transmission, manifested among others by the most
venerable manuscripts of Codex Leningrad B19a and the Aleppo Codex
(which form the basis of BHK + BHS, and the Jerusalem Bible Project
respectively), it appears at the beginning of the Writings. This order is also
reflected in the Massorah apparatus and books, where the notes on
Chronicles come first among the Writings, and according to the mediaeval
book *Adat Devorim* (1207 CE) this position reflects differences of tradition
between Palestine (Aleppo Codex; Leningrad B19a) and Babylon (cf. C. D.
Ginsburg, *Introduction to the Massoretico-critical Edition of the Hebrew Bible*,
²1966, 2–8). While preserving the order of Codex Leningrad B19a in all other
matters (the reversal of Job and Proverbs and the different ordering of the
five scrolls), the editors of BHK and BHS succumbed to the more dominant
Babylonian tradition in the case of Chronicles: 'The BHS, following the
BHK, deviates from the order of the Biblical books in L [Leningrad B19a]
only in placing 1,2 Chronicles at the end' (BHS, XI).

Earlier sources do not adduce explicit arguments for the position of the
book, but either of the two locations – at the beginning of the Writings or
their end – may be well justified. As a comprehensive history of the people of
Israel, beginning with Adam, it brings appropriate closure to the whole
canon which began with Genesis, while its position after the section of 'the
Prophets' on the one hand and before the Psalms on the other marks its
similarity in genre to the Former Prophets, and places the historical record
which emphatically accounts for the Temple's musical cult before the
Psalms. In the Septuagint, Chronicles is placed among the historical books
after Kings, and this order, as transferred to the Vulgate, influenced its
position in many modern translations.

Chronicles is a single book and is so counted among the 'Twenty-Four'.
The traditional Massoretic remarks regarding the count of its verses and its
middle point are found only at the end of II Chronicles. The division into two
parts was first made in the Septuagint and was maintained from then on in
the other translations. Beginning with the fifteenth century, the division was
introduced into Hebrew editions of the Bible.

B. *Scope and extent of the Chronicler's work*

In order to establish a precise frame of reference and unity of terminology, two preliminary matters, to which much attention has been given in the study of the book and which bear upon the very definition of 'Chronicles', must be clarified. Both issues challenge the equation of the canonical book of Chronicles with 'the work of the Chronicler'; the first involves the suggested extension of the 'Chronistic work' to include the book of Ezra–Nehemiah, while the other examines Chronicles itself, questions the originality of the canonical format, and attempts to reconstruct the various literary stages of the book's composition.

(*a*) The view that one author is responsible for both Chronicles and Ezra–Nehemiah is the traditional opinion of rabbinical Judaism and mediaeval Christianity; the composition of both is attributed to Ezra the scribe (BT, Baba Bathra 15a; for John of Salisbury and Ralph Niger, cf. Saltman, *Stephen Langton: Commentary on the Book of Chronicles*, Ramat Gan 1978, 23). This view was partly challenged by L. Zunz (1832), who found it difficult to regard the whole of Ezra–Nehemiah as the work of Ezra. Preserving as much as possible of the traditional view, Zunz suggested that it was not Ezra who composed Chronicles, but *vice versa* that it was 'the Chronicler' – the anonymous author of Chronicles – who composed both books (L. Zunz, *Die Gottesdienstlichen Vorträge der Juden*, 1832, 22). Zunz's view (proposed independently also by Movers, 1834) eventually gained general recognition, was adopted almost unanimously, and was sometimes presented as a sheer truism. Yet even during the time of its predominance it was in fact challenged by some scholars, and the matter was re-opened for discussion in 1968 (cf. S. Japhet, 'The Supposed Common Authorship of Chronicles and Ezra–Nehemiah Investigated Anew', *VT* 18, 1968, 332–72). Since then it has engaged the interest of scholars, and while Zunz's position has been restated in various forms, in particular by scholars whose work centres on Ezra–Nehemiah (cf. A. H. J. Gunneweg, 'Zur Interpretation der Bücher Esra–Nehemia',*VTS* 32, 1981, 146–61; id., *Esra* (KAT), Gütersloh 1985, 25–8; M. Haran, 'Explaining the Identical Lines at the End of Chronicles and Beginning of Ezra', *Bible Review* 2/3, 1986, 18–20; J. Blenkinsopp, *Ezra–Nehemiah*, 1988, 47–54; P. R. Ackroyd, 'Chronicles–Ezra–Nehemiah: The Concept of Unity', *ZAW* 100 (supplement), 1988, 189–201; K. F. Pohlmann, 'Zur Frage von Korrespondenzen und Divergenzen zwischen den Chronik-büchern und dem Esra–Nehemia Buch', *VTS* XLIII, 1991, 314–30), the view that the two books are independent literary works has become more widespread. Although the principal consequences of this view devolve on the study of Ezra–Nehemiah, it does have implications for the book of Chronicles as well, in particular when the two works are discussed together under the common term 'Chronistic history', or when issues pertaining to Chronicles (such as date, provenance, development of cultic institutions, literary method and theological and historical views) are determined by the testimony of Ezra–Nehemiah. I have dealt with this topic on several occasions ('The Supposed Common Authorship', *VT* 18, 1968; 'The Historical Reliability of Chronicles: The History of the Problem and its Place in Biblical Research', *JSOT* 1985; 'The Relationship Between Chronicles and Ezra–Nehemiah', *VTS* 1991, 298–313), and so have other scholars (cf. in particular H. G. M. Williamson in *Israel in the Book of Chronicles*, Cambridge 1977, 1–70, his introduction to the commentary on Chronicles, 5–11, and 'Did the Author of Chronicles Also Write the Books of Ezra and Nehemiah?', *Bible Review* III, 1987, 56–9; Willi, 37–8; Welten, 3–4; R. L. Braun, 'Chronicles, Ezra and Nehemiah: Theology and Literary History', *VTS* 30, 1979, 42–64; J. D. Newsome, 'Toward a New Understanding of the Chronicler and his Purposes', *JBL* 94, 1975, 201–17; T. Eskenazi, *In an Age of Prose*, 1988, 14–36; S. J. De Vries, *1–2 Chronicles*, 1989, 8–10, and more). With the aim of avoiding repetition, here I shall give only my general conclusion, and refer the reader to the specialized discussions of the subject.

Chronicles and Ezra–Nehemiah constitute two different works by two different authors. Not only do they illustrate an array of small and large differences – in language, style, literary method, etc. – and express different and often opposite views about central issues of biblical history and theology, but when considered in their totality they represent two varieties of biblical historical writing during the Persian-Hellenistic period. In its historiographic method and chronological substructure, the book of Ezra–Nehemiah is a new experiment, an attempt at a new form of historical writing, deviating from the historiographical model of the Deuteronomistic history which preceded it (cf. S. Japhet, 'Biblical Historiography in the Persian Period', *World History of the Jewish People*, Vol. 6, ed. H. Tadmor and I. Eph'al, Jerusalem 1983, 176–81*). Its motivation and theological point of departure, however, are a continuation of the Deuteronomistic historiography, since the two are aimed at coping with pressing realities, attempting to find justification and meaning for concrete and desperate situations: destruction and exile for the one, a limited restoration and despair of eschatological hopes for the other. Chronicles, on the other hand, is more traditional than Ezra–Nehemiah in the form of its history writing and continues to a great measure the literary tradition of earlier biblical historiography, in particular the Deuteronomistic, but at the same time deviates from its predecessor in its theological purpose and general understanding of the history of Israel. Chronicles is not a limited theodicy for a specific crisis, but an attempt to find the general principles which govern the history of Israel. 'History', according to Chronicles, is a series of concrete expressions of the Lord's rule of the world, determined by his divine attributes. Since these are founded in the concepts of divine providence and absolute justice, they indicate a positive and optimistic attitude to human existence in general and Israel's future in particular. The Chronicler has a much broader perspective of the fortunes of Israel, and his orientation is towards a promising future. The strongest conviction for the realization of this future is anchored in his particular understanding of history as divine revelation.

(*b*) The question of the unity and originality of Chronicles, and consequently of the very definition of 'Chronicles', has greater impact on the understanding and appreciation of the book. In its most general formulation this is the question whether all of Chronicles was composed by one writer, or whether it contains 'primary' and 'secondary' elements which should be distinguished and defined. The strongest motive for this question comes from one of the book's most conspicuous features, its heterogeneity, which attracts the reader's attention on first reading. This diversity applies to many aspects of the work. It is seen in the book's language and style (the classical style of its sources in some parts, late post-exilic expression in others); different modes of historical writing with a variety of literary genres; and even differences and contrasts in actual facts and details. This diversity, and in particular the combination of historical records on the one hand and lists of every kind and form on the other, is found by some scholars to be irreconcilable in one author and to suggest different author-personalities from the outset. From a different perspective, scholars have pointed to the alternating sources of influence exhibited by the final form of Chronicles. The existence of both Priestly and Deuteronomistic traditions and forms, for example, suggested to scholars a gradual literary process in which an 'original' work, composed in the vein of one school, was secondarily superimposed with the touches of an other school or schools (Hänel – Rothstein: Priestly original, later redacted under influence of the 'Hexateuch'; Welch: Deuteronomistic original, later reworked by a Priestly reviser; cf. J. Hänel – W. Rothstein, *Kommentar zum ersten Buch der Chronik*, 1927, xliv; A. C. Welch, *The Work of the Chronicler*, 1939, passim). With the aim of 'tailoring' the Chronicler's heterogeneity into a more uniform pattern, with greater affinity to earlier biblical literary phenomena or a more unified theological 'school', biblical scholarship employed the method of literary criticism to reach the 'original' Chronicles. This has been carried out along several lines, influenced by more general trends of biblical scholarship; the more influential proposals among them may be roughly classified as follows:

1. Under the influence of Pentateuchal criticism, Chronicles was viewed as composed of 'sources' (considered to number between two and four), i.e. complete and continuous documents, each with its own author. The Chronicler was viewed more as a compiler or a redactor than an author, and

later, 'post-Chronistic' revisions were also considered. This group is best
represented by the commentaries of Kittel and Benzinger (cf. Curtis, 21–6),
and received graphic expression in Kittel's contribution to P.
Haupt's poly-chrome Bible (*The Sacred Books of the Old Testament*, 1895).

2. From another point of view, certain sections of Chronicles, in particular the massive bulks of lists and registers, were regarded as alien to the
book. Following earlier suggestions, Welch claimed that all of I Chron. 1–9
and 23–27 should be excluded from the book at the outset. Welch also
regarded the original Chronicles as devoid of any Priestly influence, and
ascribed various further sections of the book to a 'Priestly reviser' (Welch,
The Work of the Chronicler, passim).

3. A trend with much influence in present biblical scholarship is that
initiated by M. Noth and followed by the influential commentary of W.
Rudolph (cf. also Willi). Within the method of 'tradition history', Noth
regarded Chronicles basically as a single composition based on earlier,
Deuteronomistic sources, but ascribed extensive sections in the book to
secondary, post-Chronistic additions and adaptations. In contrast to the
theory of sources, or to that of 'revisers', Noth and Rudolph did not make any
attempt to define continuous and coherent secondary layers or identify their
authors; rather, a conjectured original 'Chronicles' – very similar in fact to
the Deuteronomistic history – is viewed as overlaid with all manner of 'wild
growth' (M. Noth, *The Chronicler's History*, ET Sheffield 1987, 29–50;
Rudolph, VIII, 1–5).

4. An attempt to account for the heterogeneity of Chronicles in a more
orderly manner, by seeing its composition as evolving in well-defined stages,
has been undertaken in two different forms by Galling on the one hand and
Cross on the other. Galling saw the whole of Chronicles and Ezra-Nehemiah
as composed of two distinct strata, 'Chronist A' and 'Chronist B', which were
in fact very similar in many aspects of the literary work, including language
and theology. Their distinction, according to Galling, was based on literary-
critical arguments: repetition, conflation, contrasts, etc. (K. Galling, *Die
Bücher der Chronik, Esra, Nehemia*, ATD, Göttingen 1954, 8–12). F. M.
Cross, on the other hand, suggested a comprehensive and synthetic view,
which incorporated not only Chronicles and Ezra–Nehemiah but also
1 Esdras ('A Reconsideration of the Judean Restoration', *JBL* 94, 1975, 11–
14). This whole body of literature was seen as composed in a three-step
process, from an 'original' Chronicles in the sixth century (covering parts of
the canonical book of Chronicles and parts of a conjectured *Vorlage* of
1 Esdras), through second and third 'Chronicles' in the fifth and fourth
centuries. A later undefined stage saw the emergence of the extant works:
the canonical books of Chronicles and Ezra–Nehemiah and the apocryphal
1 Esdras.

As already mentioned, these attempts take their departure from the book's apparent heterogeneity and raise considerations of content, spheres of interest, literary genres, the use of sources, and the existence of contradictions, great or small, between different parts of the book. They are influenced, however, also by other arguments, like the question of dating, established presuppositions on the development and value of biblical literature and theology, strict application of preconceived methodological criteria, and the like. Thus, for example, gradual growth of complex literary works is a decisive presupposition in Noth's general method of 'tradition history', which he applied to biblical historiography in general. It also enables him (and Rudolph) to bring Chronicles as close as possible to the Deuteronomistic model that preceded it, with the lists – a more 'priestly' occupation – regarded as later 'wild growth'. For Welch, the existence of late elements in the book, either 'priestly' or post-exilic in general, is irreconcilable with his theory that Chronicles was composed after the exile of the northern kingdom; they must also be regarded as secondary when the book's composition is ascribed to the last quarter of the sixth century, against the background of the eschatological movement connected with Zerubbabel (D. N. Freedman, 'The Chronicler's Purpose', *CBQ* 23, 1961, 436–42; Cross, ibid.; and others). In the end, it seems that each of these approaches has come with its own, idiosyncratic 'Chronicler', ascribing to him political and theological goals which are not always evident in the actual 'Chronicles'; in many cases these attempts fail to take into sufficient account the book's special character, to cope with the problem of what are defined as secondary (or tertiary) elements in the book, or to account for the final emergence of the canonical reality.

In the commentary I have examined the most influential of these propositions, and could not concur with any. Even the most severe forms of literary criticism did not achieve meticulous harmony of the details, and the problems they raised were sometimes greater than those they solved. More problematic was the recognition of how arbitrary some of the arguments actually were. While the possibility of secondary elaboration during the course of transmission was not ruled out – in particular in the lists, which are most susceptible to change – it seemed that a better explanation of the book's variety and composition is the view that it is one work, composed essentially by a single author, with a very distinct and peculiar literary method. The author's penchant for citing existing texts, for expressing his own views through elaboration and change of such texts, and his being influenced by both the Pentateuch, the Deuteronomistic historiography and a plethora of earlier sources, yet going his own way, account best for the varieties of the book. It is doubtful whether a rational, meticulous harmony of all the possible details was ever aimed at by the Chronicler.

C. Contents and basic structure

Chronicles describes the history of Israel from beginning to 'beginning', that is, from the inception of human existence with Adam, through the destruction of the first commonwealth during the reign of Zedekiah, to the new commencement with the declaration of Cyrus. It thus constitutes a comprehensive parallel to the earlier biblical historiography from Genesis to Kings – commonly designated the 'Deuteronomistic history' – with its conclusion pointing toward a new era. This comprehensive work is composed of three parts, clearly distinguished by contents, literary features, and major historical and theological emphases:

I Chron. 1–9: Introduction;
I Chron. 10–II Chron. 9: the history of Israel under David and Solomon;
II Chron. 10–36: the history of the kingdom of Judah from the defection of the northern tribes.

(a) *I Chron. 1–9.* The common designation of this section as 'introduction' is based on both its contents and its literary nature. While the historical account proper begins with I Chron. 10, the first nine chapters, in fulfilment of the task of any conventional introduction to a work of history, prepare the necessary ground by presenting the ethnic, geographical and chronological setting of the following history, defining the people, their territory and the chronological point of departure. The introduction also relates in a cursory manner to the religious-institutional aspect of Israel's existence. A brief sketch of the cultic institutions and personnel, with their functions (6.31–32, 28–49 [MT 16–17, 33–34]; 9.19–34), lays the groundwork for this aspect in the following historical narrative. Rather than recording a successive chain of events – like the historical record – it reflects a static situation, portrayed mainly by genealogical and geographical lists. Even when certain events are included in the introduction, they serve to illustrate and enhance the static situation.

In general outline, the introduction is built of three sections: 1.1–2.2 portray the genealogical sketch from Adam to the twelve sons of Jacob-Israel; 2.3–9.2 present 'the people of Israel' in its composition by tribes; and ch. 9 ends with a list of the inhabitants of Jerusalem (9.3–34), followed by an appendix which presents the genealogy of Saul's house as an introduction for the historical story (vv. 35–44). The structure of ch. 1, in turn, is determined by a clear historiographical principle. Starting from a presentation of a genealogical basis with primary and secondary ramifications, the secondary ramifications are handled first, as if to clear the way, and then follows the primary descent, which constitutes the basis for the next phase in the genealogical development. In this process of election, the list ends with the sons of Israel; thus:

A. 1–4 From *Adam* to *Noah* and his sons

Sons of Noah $\begin{cases} \text{5–7 Japhet} \\ \text{8–16 Ham} \\ \text{17–23 } Shem \end{cases}$

B. 24–28 From *Shem* to *Abraham* and his sons

Sons of Abraham $\begin{cases} \text{29–31 Ishmael} \\ \text{32–33 Keturah} \\ \text{34a } Isaac \end{cases}$

C. 34b From *Isaac* to *Jacob-Israel*

Sons of Isaac $\begin{cases} \text{35–54 Esau} \\ \text{2.1–2 } Israel \end{cases}$

D. 2.3ff. *Israel*

The inner structure of chs. 2–8 is governed by a unique ordering of the tribal units, encompassing groups of tribes recorded in a geographical order. Beginning in the centre with the tribe of Judah, the first unit encompasses the 'southern tribes' Judah and Simeon (I Chron. 2.3–4.43). The geographical line then crosses the Jordan to the three Transjordanian tribes – Reuben, Gad and half of Manasseh – recorded from south to north, but also presented as one group (5.1–26). At this point, approximately midway through the lists, the tribe of Levi is introduced (6.1–81; MT 5.27–6.66). The following group consists of the northern tribes: Issachar, (Benjamin), Dan and Naphtali (7.1–13), and then the line comes back to the central tribes of Rachel, moving from the north southwards: Manasseh, Ephraim and Benjamin. This section (7.14–8.40) also includes the tribe of Asher (7.30–40), which traditionally belongs to the northern tribes (Josh. 19.24–31), but is here conceived as having its inheritance among the central tribes, adjacent to the 'house of Joseph'. The geographical circle ends in the centre where it started: after a general conclusion (9.1–2), it presents the inhabitants of Jerusalem. Quantitatively, the three major components of the kingdom of Judah consume the largest space: Judah is dealt with most extensively, followed by Levi and Benjamin.

In its general outlines, the structure of this unit may be sketched as follows:

A. 1.1–2.2   From Adam to Israel
              (for the details, cf. above)

B. 2.3–9.2   Israel
   (*a*) 2.3–4.43   Southern tribes   2.3–4.23 Judah

(b) *I Chron. 10 – II Chron. 9.* The reigns of David and Solomon are described in Chronicles as one period, in which Israel reached the peak, the climax of its virtues and achievements. The two kings, whose stories are adapted along the same lines, are described as both parallelling and complementing each other. David is the founder and initiator, while Solomon is the executor and culminator of their shared period.

The records of both David and Solomon are composed of smaller units, each revolving around one general topic. In the context of these topics and from their general perspective, additional matters are incorporated into each unit, as indicated by the Chronicler's earlier sources. The history of David is thus built of four sub-units while that of Solomon is built of three: (a) I Chron. 10–12: David becomes king over all Israel; (b) I Chron. 13–17: David's initiative to establish the Lord's worship in Jerusalem; (c) I Chron. 18–20: David's wars; (d) I Chron. 21–29: David's steps toward internal organization and stabilization: preparing for the building of the Temple, administrative organization of the state, securing his succession; (e) II Chron. 1: Solomon is confirmed as king over all Israel; (f) II Chron. 2–7: Building and dedicating the Temple; (g) II Chron. 8–9: Solomon's enterprises and achievements.

The first section of David's history begins with the death of Saul (I Chron. 10), which provides the background for the following narrative and creates a line of continuity for David's kingship. David's enthronement (chs. 11–12) also includes, in addition to his accession and the national celebrations, the conquest of Jerusalem, and extensive lists of all his supporters. The second unit is dedicated to David's first steps in his initiative to establish the Lord's worship in Jerusalem. These are presented in two major stages: the transfer of the ark from Kiriath-jearim to Jerusalem, followed by the establishment of the cult in both the tent of the ark in Jerusalem and the tabernacle in Gibeon (chs. 13; 15–16); and initial steps toward the building of the house by his approach to Nathan. The privilege of building the Lord's house is denied David and transferred to his son Solomon, but his dynasty is simultaneously confirmed 'for ever' (ch. 17). Other matters, taken from II Sam. 5, are incorporated in this context and presented as an intermezzo between the two stages of the transfer of the ark (ch. 14). Chapters 18–20 are a systematic presentation of David's military achievements, while the last section – the longest and most complex of chs. 21–29 – is devoted to David's internal policy and administrative achievements, centred upon three closely related topics: the building of the Temple, the consolidation of the organization of the kingdom, and the succession to David's throne. It begins with the census, the conclusion of which is the divine selection of the site of the Temple (21.1–22.1), and continues with David's preparations and his testament to Solomon and the people (22.2–19). It then turns to the administrative layout of the kingdom, referring first to the clerical system (chs. 23–26) and then to the people and the central government (ch. 27). This pericope ends with the public ceremonial undertaking to build the Temple and the accession of Solomon (28.1–29.25), concluded by a short Chronistic summary of David's reign (29.29–30).

Solomon's story is built of three clearly-structured units. It begins with the confirmation and consolidation of his reign by God's revelation in Gibeon (II Chron. 1), and moves directly to Solomon's execution of his father's testament, the building of the Temple (chs. 2–7). The process of building is followed step by step: from the preparations, through the correspondence with Hiram (ch. 2) and the building and furnishing of the house (3.1–5.1), to the dedication (5.2–7.22). The last unit is a systematic list of all of Solomon's worldly achievements – military, political and economic – as well as the final arrangements of the Temple cult (8.1–9.28), concluded by a brief Chronistic summary (9.29–31). In its general outlines, this section is structured thus:

I. I Chron. 10–29 David

A. 10–12 David becomes king of Israel
  (a) 10 Saul's death
  (b) 11.1–12.41 David's accession
      11.1–3 Enthronement
      11.4–9 Conquest of Jerusalem
      11.10–12.38 David's supporters
      12.39–40 Celebrations

B. 13–16 Establishment of worship in Jerusalem
  (a) 13 First transfer of the ark
  (b) [14 Intermezzo]
  (c) 15–16 Second transfer of the ark
  (d) 17 David's wish to build a house / the dynastic promise

C. 18–20 David's wars

D. 21–29 David's internal achievements
  (a) 21.1–22.1 Selection of the Temple site
  (b) 22.2–19 Preparations and testament
  (c) 23–26 Organization of the clergy
      23.1–32 (24.20–30) Levites
      24.1–19, 31 Priests
      25.1–31 Singers
      26.1–19 Gatekeepers
      26.20–28 Treasurers
      26.29–32 Judges and officers
  (d) 27.1–34 Organization of the people
      27.1–15 Divisions
      27.16–24 Leaders of the tribes
      27.25–34 Stewards and counsellors
  (e) 28.1–29.25 Public undertaking of the building, and Solomon's accession
      28.1–10 David's address
      28.11–21 Transfer of the Temple plan
      29.1–9 Contributions for the building
      29.10–20 Blessing the Lord
      29.21–25 Solomon made king
  (f) 29.26–30 Conclusion of David's reign

II Chron. 1–9 Solomon
E. 1 Confirmation of Solomon's reign
  (a) 1.1–13 Solomon's journey to Gibeon
  (b) 1.14–17 Solomon's riches and honour
F. 2–7 Building and dedicating the Temple

(*a*) 2.1–5.1 Building the Temple
    2.1, 16–17 Preparation of labour force
    2.2–15 Correspondence with Huram
    3.1–5.1 Building and furnishing the Temple
(*b*) 5.2–7.22 Dedicating the Temple
    5.2–6.2 Ceremonial transfer of the ark
    6.3–11, 12–41 Solomon's addresses
    7.1–3 Dedication of the Temple by divine fire
    7.4–10 Sacrificial and popular celebrations and
    7.11–22 The Lord's revelation to Solomon

G. 8–9 Solomon's enterprises and achievements
    (*a*) 8.1–18 Varia
    (*b*) 9.1–12 The visit of the queen of Sheba
    (*c*) 9.13–28 Solomon's riches
    (*d*) 9.29–31 Conclusion of Solomon's reign

(*c*) *II Chron. 10–36.* The history of the kings of Judah is also composed of smaller units, usually distributed one per king. It is prefaced, like the preceding part, by an introduction establishing its setting: the story of the revolt of the northern tribes (II Chron. 10.1–11.4). It then follows the historical order and the chronological framework of Kings. The most distinctive kings, to whom the longest units are devoted, are Asa, Jehoshaphat, Hezekiah and Josiah:

(*a*) 10.1–11.4 Revolt of the northern tribes
(*b*) 11.5–12.16 Rehoboam
(*c*) 13.1–14.1a Abijah
(*d*) 14.1b–16.14 Asa
(*e*) 17.1–21.1 Jehoshaphat
(*f*) 21.2–20 Jehoram
(*g*) 22.1–9 Ahaziah
(*h*) 22.10–24.27 Joash
(*i*) 25.1–26.2 Amaziah
(*j*) 26.3–23 Uzziah
(*k*) 27 Jotham
(*l*) 28 Ahaz
(*m*) 29–32 Hezekiah
(*n*) 33.1–20 Manasseh
(*o*) 33.21–25 Amon
(*p*) 34–35 Josiah
(*q*) 36.1–21 The last kings of Judah
(*r*) 36.22–23 The edict of Cyrus

D. *The sources and their use*

The issue of 'sources', should be approached from two different directions: the internal evidence of the book on the one hand, and the explicit statements of the author on the other. The relationship between the two should then be examined on its own.

(a) *The sources of Chronicles*

Like every historical work, Chronicles is dependent on sources, as confirmed even by a superficial reading of the book. The study of the sources and of the manner of their employment has been greatly influenced – probably even determined – by the fact that a major source of the Chronicler's work is available to the reader in the Bible itself. A synopsis of Chronicles *vis à vis* its biblical sources provides a graphic presentation of the passages which the Chronicler extracted from the biblical works; it may also suggest the guide-lines for selecting this material and the manner in which it was utilized to become the 'building blocks' for the new enterprise. The insights gained from this study may then direct scholars in their approach to the non-parallel sections, beginning with the most basic question of whether the Chronicler employed extra-biblical sources for these sections or wrote them all on his own. Confirmation of the first possibility would lead to a further inquiry into the nature and authenticity of these sources, as well as to the manner of their use. Did the Chronicler employ them similarly or differently from the biblical material?

From among the biblical works, the Chronicler's major sources are the historical compositions that preceded him: the Pentateuch, the Former Prophets, and Ezra–Nehemiah. These constitute not only a source of ex-tracts, cited in full or in a reworked form, but also the basis and framework for his own work. As for the other books of the Bible, while the influence of the prophets is seen in the Chronicler's views and concepts, and some citations of prophetic addresses are literally or almost literally incorporated into his own rhetorical compositions, no extensive literary excerpts are taken from the prophetic literature, and this includes the book of Lamentations, the influence of which may be traced in II Chron. 36. In addition to the historical works, only some Psalms are cited literally (I Chron. 16.6–36; II Chron. 6.41–42). Many synopses (most recently, by J. Kegler and M. Augustin, *Synopse zum Chronistischen Geschichtswerk*, Frankfurt [2]1991), have been promulgated by scholars to present and analyse the Chronicler's borrowings, and they also figure in many commentaries and various mono-graphs; they are dealt with in detail in the commentary.

The Chronicler's *modus operandi* for the use of these biblical extracts varies, being determined by his own purposes, historiographical methods, and theological concepts. He may cite them literally (or almost so); he may use them as a foundation into which additional material is set and from which a more elaborate picture is produced, or he may epitomize them with only their gist preserved in a highly condensed form. He may also simply allude to earlier traditions; a single comment or even a mere adjective may embrace the contents of an entire earlier passage. In his reliance on earlier biblical material, the Chronicler displays different degrees of acceptance and agreement, from a whole-hearted adoption of the testimony and message of the earlier document, through deviation in detail, to a wholesale polemic and retroversion. A careful study of the Chronicler's work would fully uncover his intricate attitude to these sources, displaying an interesting combination of servitude and freedom: on the one hand a basic adherence to his source text on all the levels of literary expression, and on the other a skilful blend of omissions, additions and changes along the way, which transforms the final composition into a story which is not only divergent, but sometimes contrasting. The Chronicler's most distinctive feature in the reformulation of the synoptic sections is probably that he casts his own work as emanating from a core of venerated traditional statements while reserving for himself a large measure of freedom.

Some of the general features of the Chronicler's actual use of biblical sources may be noted.

(*a*) Very rigorous principles guide the Chronicler's selection from the Pentateuch. As illustrated by his introductory chapter (I Chron. 1.1–2.2), the book of Genesis has been scanned systematically; all the lists which directly link Adam to Israel, including all the offspring of Abraham, Isaac and Jacob, have been sifted out, restructured and incorporated into the book. The only lists in Genesis which were excluded are those completely outside this line: Cain (Gen. 4.17–26), Terah (Gen. 11.26–32) and Nahor (Gen. 22.21–24). Chapter 1 is thus the Chronicler's own way of representing all of Genesis. Of the other parts of the Pentateuch, very little is included in Chronicles in literal citations. The stories revolving around the servitude in Egypt, the exodus and the wandering in the wilderness are not repeated, and only selected items find expression in the Chronicler's presentation. The legal sections of the Pentateuch are reflected in Chronicles in an eclectic manner, with either literal citations or paraphrastic allusions, in particular regarding the sacrificial system (cf. J. R. Shaver, *Torah and the Chronistic History Work*, 1990). Thus we find echoes of the tabernacle tradition, the descriptions of the priestly and levitical roles, the festivals, the sacrificial system, some genealogical material, and references to personages known from this period (such as Nahshon, Phinehas, Bezalel, Joshua, and others). One may confidently

state that while the Chronicler's picture of Israel's early history is emphatically different from that of the Pentateuch (cf. Japhet, 'Conquest and
Settlement in Chronicles', *JBL* 98, 1979, 205–18), he has surveyed all of
Exodus to Deuteronomy as source material for his own writing; both his
citations and his omissions are a function of his historiographical and theological plan.

(*b*) Of all the potential list material of Joshua, only two sections have
actually been cited: the Simeonite cities (Josh. 19.2–8 // I Chron. 4.28–33),
and the priestly and levitical cities (Josh. 21.10–39 // I Chron. 6.54–81 [MT
39–66]). The book of Joshua is, however also represented by polemic
references, such as to the cities of Manasseh (I Chron. 7.29 – Josh. 17.11–12)
and 'the land that remained' (I Chron. 13.5 – Josh. 13.2–5), and allusions
such as I Chron. 2.7 to Josh. 7.1ff.

The book of Judges is hardly represented in Chronicles at all, a fact which
readily conforms to the Chronicler's almost total silence regarding the period
of the judges. The historical story begins in I Chron. 10 with a reworked
citation of I Sam.31, but I Chron. 12 also retains explicit references to I Sam.
28–30, which forms the background of Saul's death. From this point onwards, the Chronicler's history is cast into the framework of Samuel–Kings;
it follows faithfully the order of the text – omitting and adding on the way –
and only rarely introduces changes of order. Two such changes are introduced into the history of David: the placement of II Sam. 5 after the material
taken from II Sam. 6 (I Chron. 14 following I Chron. 13), and of II Sam.
23.8–39 in the context of David's accession (I Chron. 11.11–41). When the
selection from II Samuel is viewed as a whole, a very clear procedure
emerges: the Chronicler borrowed all the beginning of the story in II Sam.
5.1–12.31 (with the deletion of the stories of Mephibosheth and Bathsheba:
II Sam. 9; 11.2–12.25), and three chapters from the end (II Sam. 21.18–22;
23.8–39; 24). He refrained from citing any part of the comprehensive
pericope known as the 'succession narrative' (II Sam. 9; 12.2–25; 13.1–20.23;
I Kings 1–2), and passed over a few other sections at the beginning (II Sam.
1–4) and end (II Sam. 20.23–26; 21.1–17; 22.1–23.7). All the borrowed
material, with some change of order and some additions, is placed in
Chronicles as the first part of his story (I Chron. 11–21). Beginning with I
Chron. 22 the Chronicler strikes out independently, with a comprehensive
presentation of the preparations for the Temple, David's administration, and
Solomon's accession. He returns to his biblical source only at the very end,
with I Chron. 29.26–30 being dependent on, yet elaborating, I Kings 2.10–
12.

The book of Kings is the most important of the Chronicler's biblical
sources. It is differently employed, however, for the description of
Solomon's reign and the reigns of the kings of Judah. More than for any other

section of Chronicles, Kings is the ultimate source for the Chronicler's history of Solomon: the order of the earlier text is faithfully followed except once, where an account of Solomon's wealth is joined to the revelation at Gibeon (II Chron. 1.14–17), and large sections are literally repeated. The Chronicler also adheres to his common practice of omission: large sections of Solomon's early story and the concluding chapter of his reign are not repeated (I Kings 1.1–2.9; 2.13–3.3; 3.16–28; 4.1–20, 22–36 [MT 5.2–14]; 8.54–61; 11.1–40). However, in contrast to other parts of the book, the Chronicler does not contribute much additional material to this story, and only elaborates on some episodes through the insertion of short passages (in general: II Chron. 1.1–5; 2.3–6, 11–13; 3.1; 4.1, 9; 5.11–13; 6.12, 41–42; 7.1–3, 13–14; 8.3, 12–15), most of which may be easily identified as his own composition. Thus, the portrayal of Solomon's reign is very clearly a shortened reformulation of 1 Kings 1–11.

The book of Kings also forms the basis for the Chronicler's history of the kings of Judah. The Deuteronomistic literary, historical and chronological framework constitutes the foundation on which the Chronicler's own story is constructed. The specific Deuteronomistic literary pattern, in which every king's history is presented, is transferred systematically into Chronicles; in the majority of cases it also has the same function of 'introduction' and 'conclusion' of the Chronistic record. The Chronicler follows to the letter the chronological statements of Kings and does not change its data even when they collide with his theological tenets. His own contribution to chronology is some additional details, with their own literary and theological functions, but never a change of the basic Deuteronomistic chronological pattern. The Chronicler also preserves all the elements of this Deuteronomistic framework – with various changes in detail and phraseology – except for the systematic omission of the synchronisms. Yet, with all this fidelity to his source, the general plan of the Chronistic work is different from the Deuteronomistic one. Rather than being a synchronistic history of two kingdoms, it is a record of only one, the only legitimate kingdom of Judah. For the Chronicler, the kingdom of north Israel is an illegitimate political entity, a temporary defection of some rebellious elements, and should not be accorded a separate record. Except for one instance at the beginning (II Chron. 13.1), he omits all synchronisms with Israel and simply skips the passages relating its history. Nevertheless, the Chronicler includes in his record *all* the passages of Kings in which the relationship between the two kingdoms is recorded, even when he himself may eventually judge these relationships negatively (cf. II Chron. 19.2), and supplements his record from extra-biblical traditions (e.g. II Chron. 28.6–15). The northern kingdom is thus not absent from Chronicles. It is presented – with everything that the Chronicler found in his sources – from the perspective of Judah.

18 INTRODUCTION

For the history of the kingdom of Judah the Chronicler borrowed from Kings as much as possible, ignoring only occasional passages relating to the first Judean kings (e.g. I Kings 14.22b–24; 15.3–6); larger omissions and more severe epitomization mark the borrowing from the time of Ahaz onward. The Chronicler's own contribution in this part, however, is characterized by extensive additions, which more than double the scope of his narrative. These include not only literary elaborations of existing narratives and isolated new episodes, but the introduction of topics which were not handled in the Deuteronomistic history: the military organization of the kingdom, records of economic achievements, administrative details, a systematic history of the Temple, etc. Only at the description of destruction and exile at the end of the period is the Deuteronomistic record greatly abridged – an abridgement entirely consistent with the Chronicler's historical view.

(c) The last source among the biblical historical works is the book of Ezra–Nehemiah, from which two sections are cited: the beginning of the edict of Cyrus (II Chron. 36.22–23 // Ezra 1.1–3a), and the list of the inhabitants of Jerusalem (I Chron. 9.2–17a // Neh. 11.3–19), which serves a different function in Chronicles. Here again, although the Chronicler's view of the history of Israel diverges greatly from that of Ezra–Nehemiah, the work itself is used as a source for his own extracts.

Did the Chronicler have sources for the non-parallel material? In the history of scholarship this question was often connected to the reliability and authority of the book (cf. D. Mathias, *Die Geschichte der Chronikforschung im 19 Jahrhundert*, Diss. Leipzig, 1977), and thus assumed an apologetic turn. The defenders of the historical reliability of the book felt that by regarding the bulk of the Chronicler's material as having been derived from authoritative sources, the book's claim to be reliable could face the most severe doubts and criticism. It is also in this context that the strongest denials of the sources of the book were voiced. The two questions, however, involve different considerations, and the problem of the Chronicler's sources should be discussed on its own, as a relevant issue for any historical work, with no apologetic disposition and in isolation from the question of 'reliability'. In the last analysis, even the existence of 'sources' does not guarantee the reliability of the book, since their antiquity or authenticity may then be questioned, and even authentic sources may be used in an uncritical or anachronistic manner. Each of these questions, then, should be dealt with on its own, in its relevant parameters.

The analysis of Chronicles as a literary work seems to leave no doubt that the Chronicler used extra-biblical sources. While this may have been suggested by his attitude towards the biblical material, where not only acceptance but also rejection are expressed *vis à vis* his source texts, this is actually confirmed by a careful study of the non-synoptic sections themselves. Many passages have distinct patterns and common topics, and can be identified as stemming from common specific sources. Certain tribal genealogies (e.g. I Chron. 2.25–33, 42–50a) or census records (e.g. 7.1–5, 6–11, 30–40), as well as passages from the monarchical period (e.g. I Chron. 27.25–34; II Chron. 11.6–10, 18–20; 21.2 – to mention only some of the least debated passages), point very clearly to their origin in earlier sources. It is also obvious that a major source for the Chronicler's non-parallel sections consisted of late, post-exilic materials. These relate to the legitimization and organization of the Temple personnel in its fourfold division into priests, levites, singers and gatekeepers, and in the rotatory structure of twenty-four divisions. Among these materials we may mention the genealogies of the chief levites and the chief singers (I Chron. 6.16–47 [MT 1–32]), and the division system as presented in I Chron. 23–26. A late source by its own historical definition is the genealogy of Jehoiachin's line (I Chron. 3.17–24).

The Chronicler's adherence to sources may also be seen, however, when these are missing. At certain points along the historical record the experienced reader expects some addition or elaboration which is indicated by the Chronicler's general presuppositions, but these are not provided. The absence of appropriate information is the best answer for these lacunae.

The existence of sources for the Chronicler's non-synoptic sections is thus firmly established, and is not denied even by some of the book's most severe critics (e.g. Wellhausen, 223). It is the nature, origin and reliability of these sources which remain problematic, and these should be investigated in each passage on a case-by-case basis. In the absence of comparative material, this frequently unrewarding effort may, in some instances, be influenced by circular arguments, but the more familiar we become with the Chronicler's literary methods, historical views and theology, the more refined our considerations may become, and the more credibility may be ascribed to our judgment.

(b) Sources mentioned in Chronicles

Another aspect of the Chronistic work is the Chronicler's explicit reference to written sources. By their position in the book and their titles these may be first divided into two groups: works mentioned in the conclusion formulas of the kings' reigns, referring the reader to additional sources by the repeated formula 'the rest of the acts of ... are written in ...' (e.g. I Chron. 29.29; II Chron. 9.29, etc.), and those mentioned outside this context.

1. All the references to sources within the conclusion formulas, except the one for David (I Chron. 29.29), are parallel to the Deuteronomistic notes of the same kind (e.g. I Kings 14.29, etc.) and have the same historiographical

purpose: to support and substantiate the historical work by reference to its sources. While the Deuteronomistic history mentions three such works, referring consistently to the same work for the kings of Israel ('the Book of the Chronicles of the Kings of Israel', I Kings 14.19 etc.), one for the kings of Judah ('the Book of the Chronicles of the Kings of Judah', I Kings 14.29 etc.), and one source for Solomon ('the Book of the Acts of Solomon', I Kings 11.41), the Chronicler replaces these remarks with less homogeneous references to eighteen works of various titles. These, in turn, are of two classes: six works bearing general titles, i.e. 'the Book of the kings of Israel and Judah' (e.g. II Chron. 27.7); 'the Book of the Kings of Judah and Israel' (e.g. II Chron. 16.11); the same book with a slightly different title in Hebrew (e.g. 25.26); 'the Book of the Kings of Israel' (e.g. 20.34); 'the Chronicles of the Kings of Israel' (33.18); and 'the Commentary (Heb. Midrash) on the Book of the Kings' (24.27); and twelve books, the authorship of which is ascribed to prophets, e.g., 'the Chronicles of Samuel the seer', etc. (I Chron. 29.29; II Chron. 9.29; 12.15; 13.22; 20.34; 26.22; 32.32; 33.19), including Samuel, Nathan, Gad, Ahijah, Jeddo, Shemaiah, Iddo, Jehu, Isaiah and Hozai, most of them known from the earlier Deuteronomistic history. These two groups of works are mutually exclusive in the Chronicler's presentation. When a work with a general title is referred to as a source, there is no reference to a prophetic work, and *vice versa*, and the works with general titles always appear alone; nowhere does the Chronicler refer to two of these works as the source for any one period. In two cases, however, we find a title consisting of double ascription: 'the chronicles of Jehu the son of Hanani, which are recorded in the Book of the Kings of Israel' (II Chron. 20.34); and 'the vision of Isaiah the prophet the son of Amoz, in the Book of the Kings of Judah and Israel' (32.32). These titles indicate that 'the chronicles of Jehu the son of Hanani' and 'the vision of Isaiah the son of Amoz' are not independent works but extracts from a comprehensive book on the history of the kings of Judah and Israel.

2. Several works are mentioned in Chronicles outside the concluding formulas. Some of these actually employ the same introductory formula as the above, and probably serve the same purpose: 'So all Israel was enrolled by genealogies; and these are written in the Book of the Kings of Israel' (I Chron. 9.1), and 'behold, they are written in the Laments' (II Chron. 35.25). In a number of cases it is reported that certain information was noted and committed to writing, without further clarification whether these documents actually served as the author's source. These include: 'These, registered by name, came in the days of Hezekiah' (I Chron. 4.41); 'All of these were enrolled by genealogies in the days of Jotham king of Judah, and in the days of Jeroboam king of Israel' (I Chron. 5.17); 'And the scribe ... recorded them in the presence of the king' (I Chron. 24.6); and in a negative statement: 'and the

number was not entered in the chronicles of King David' (I Chron. 27.24). In addition, there is a group of writings referred to as authoritative for several steps taken by the kings of Judah. These include foremost 'the book of the law of the Lord given through Moses' (II Chron. 34.14), referred to in various ways (e.g. I Chron. 16.40; II Chron. 25.4, etc.), but also 'the writing of King David of Israel and ... the document of his son Solomon' (35.4 JPS), and 'the words of David and of Asaph the seer' (29.30).

What are all these works, thus referred to in Chronicles, and how are they related to the Chronicler's actual sources as revealed by the analysis of the book? These questions have engaged biblical scholarship intensively for many years (cf. Mathias, 1977, *passim*), and the full spectrum of possibilities has been suggested. By way of summary, the following considerations may be pointed out.

Several of these titles may refer to canonical books, such as the Pentateuch for 'the book of the law', the Psalms for 'the words of David ... and Asaph', and probably Lamentations for 'the Laments'. These are, however, only a small fraction of the sources mentioned; how should all the others be viewed? The titles of the six general works would imply, at least on the face of it, that the Chronicler refers to six different works – a rather doubtful possibility in view of further consideration. Several of these works are mentioned only once, and none of them is very common; this would imply that some of these comprehensive works were hardly employed by the Chronicler, and even the more common were not extensively used, some supplying only very limited information. Moreover, the fact that the Chronicler never mentions any two of these works together may indicate that these titles are not exclusive but interchangeable – a possibility supported by the great similarity of the titles, sometimes differing only in the order of their components or in the definition of genre. In fact, these titles show clear signs of stylistic variety and inconsistent terminology; they differ in the definition of genre ('book', 'chronicles' and 'commentary'), of topic ('the kings', 'the kings of Israel', 'the kings of Judah and Israel', 'the kings of Israel and Judah'), and even of the order of the common elements ('Judah and Israel', 'Israel and Judah'). It is obvious that the term 'Israel' has various connotations; when juxtaposed with 'Judah' (as in 'the Book of the Kings of Israel and Judah'), it refers to the northern kingdom alone; when appearing alone (e.g. 'the Chronicles of the Kings of Israel'), it may apply to either the northern kingdom or the people of Israel in general. Since this is referred to as the source for the time of Manasseh (II Chron. 33.18), only the latter is tenable. Given the Chronicler's general stylistic inclination towards a variety of expression, and the difficulty in assuming that he actually had six comprehensive historical works at his disposal, the position suggested by many previous scholars (cf. Curtis, 22; Rudolph, XI; O. Eissfeldt, *The Old Testament: An Introduction*, Oxford 1965,

535; etc.), that all these titles actually refer to one work – a comprehensive history of Israel – seems to be the most compelling.

As for the prophetic compositions, here again the apparent testimony of Chronicles is that the author had at his disposal over ten works, in which the prophets of each generation wrote the history of their times. This testimony, too, raises severe doubts. The Chronicler's claim is not substantiated or supported anywhere; there is no evidence that the prophets were in fact the historians of their time and put on record the history of the kingdoms. More specifically, the chronological gap between the Chronicler and many of these prophets is very great; even assuming that the prophets did write history, would authentic works of Samuel, Nathan and Gad, for example, survive to the time of the Chronicler, without having left any traces in earlier literature? In the case of some specific names there are further difficulties: how could Samuel write the history of David's reign, if he died before David's accession to the throne (cf. the phrasing of I Chron. 29.29 with I Sam. 25.1)? These reservations are supported by three further considerations: the evidence of the two formulations mentioned above, in which the prophetic works are explicitly described as part of a general work (II Chron. 20.34; 32.32); the fact that the Chronicler cites as sources *either* prophetic works *or* general ones but never both, for any given king (for the case of Manasseh, cf. on II Chron. 33.18–19), except in the formula just mentioned; and the great stylistic variety which characterizes their titles, the works and the prophets being designated in every possible way: 'chronicles', 'prophecy', 'vision' and 'commentary'; 'prophet' (*nābī'*), 'seer' (*rō'eh*), and 'man of vision' (*ḥōzeh*).

It has thus been suggested (cf. Curtis, 23–4) that in referring to all these prophetical works, what the Chronicler actually had in mind was the same comprehensive work with a general title, 'the history of Israel'. The respective parts of this work are thus ascribed to contemporary prophets, a most concrete expression of the view that it was the prophets of Israel who wrote the history of their time – a view explicitly formulated by later authorities (cf. Josephus, *Against Apion* 1.40; BT Baba Bathra 14b–15a). The writing of history is thus seen as contemporary with the events, inspired and of absolute authority. The final implication of these considerations would be that in his explicit references to sources in the context of the concluding formulas, the Chronicler had in mind only one work, to which he referred in every possible way, a variety indicated by both his literary inclination and theological presuppositions.

What is this work? There are three possible answers to this question, and all have been actually proposed in the history of investigation (cf. the comprehensive survey of Mathias, ibid.). (*a*) The Chronicler refers to a non-canonical 'History of Israel', a book similar in form and content to the canonical book of Kings but different from it. It is from this work that he derived all his additional material. The nature of this work, its origin and authenticity, are likewise disputed among scholars (e.g. Curtis, 22; Eissfeldt, 533–5). (*b*) The Chronicler refers to the canonical books of the Former Prophets, which he prefers to designate in these changing terms, probably because of his literary tendencies (e.g. Williamson, 18). (*c*) The Chronicler does not have any concrete work in mind. The mention of sources is for him a 'mere show' (C. C. Torrey, 'The Chronicler as Editor and as Independent Narrator', *AJSL* XXV, 1909, 173), an imitation of the authentic references found in the book of Kings. They serve to support his claim of authenticity, but have no concrete reality behind them (Torrey, ibid, 192–6; cf. also R. H. Pfeiffer, *Introduction to the Old Testament*, New York 1957, 804–6).

Each of the three possibilities can be supported in some way, and none has reached the degree of certitude which would make it conclusive. It therefore seems best to leave the two aspects of the issue of 'sources' separate, and deal with each on its own merits. Even if we follow the more extreme possibilities suggested above – that all the Chronicler's references to sources are no more than a historiographical device, or that he is referring all along to various canonical books – the very fact that he used extra-biblical sources cannot be denied. These are evidenced by the work as such. The most we may say in this case is that the Chronicler's actual use of sources, and his technique of referring to various literary works, comprise two different aspects of his work, the one not necessarily reflecting on the other.

As for the actual extra-biblical sources which the Chronicler employed, these will be discussed in detail in the commentary. They seem to have included a host of various pieces, different in genre, scope and origin. Some of them display a unity of subject-matter and form and may have belonged to longer documents, either primary chronicles or secondary literary works, while others are isolated elements of divergent origin. When these extra-biblical materials are taken as a whole, they do not seem to display any comprehensive unity – of literary method, historical presuppositions or theology – which would justify their ascription to one work, analogous to the Deuteronomistic history. Rather, it is the Chronicler's historical method and philosophy which, together with the biblical extracts and his own writing, bind these written and oral pieces into a new comprehensive history.

E. The author and his time

Early statements regarding the authorship of Chronicles ascribe it to Ezra the scribe: 'Ezra wrote his book and the genealogies of the Book of Chronicles up to his own time ... Who then finished it? Nehemiah the son of Hacaliah' (Baba Bathra 15a). This view is also expressed by mediaeval writers, both

Jewish and Christian (cf. above, p.3), the consequences being twofold: a recognition of the book's lateness, at the last phase of the biblical period, and an affirmation of its canonicity, having been composed by the person acclaimed as the 'second Moses'. This view, however, was by no means the only one. The mediaeval Jewish exegete Kimhi (1160–1235) identified the book as 'the book of the Chronicles of the Kings of Judah' mentioned in the book of Kings, and thus relegated it to a much earlier period and attributed to Ezra only its later inclusion in the canon, by the prophets Haggai, Zechariah and Malachi (Kimhi, prologue). Some Christian exegetes, too, regarded the book as earlier than Ezra, viewing him as its editor (S. Langton and others, cf. Saltman, *Stephen Langton*, 23). The early critical impulse tended to date the book late. Since Ezra was proposed as the final author of all the 'nine books' (Genesis to Kings; cf. B. Spinoza, *Theological-Political Treatise* (1670), translated by R. H. M. Elwes, in *The Chief Works of Benedict de Spinoza*, New York 1957, 146), and later of the Pentateuch or the 'Priestly source' alone (cf. e.g. Wellhausen, 405–8), the composition of Chronicles had to be pushed to a much later date, and relegated as far as the Maccabean period. The identification of the book's author as Ezra was questioned in a more specific way by Zunz (ibid., 20–1; cf. above, p.3), who reversed the traditional position and regarded 'the Chronicler' as the author of both his book and Ezra–Nehemiah. Among modern scholars, only Albright returned to the traditional view, again suggesting the identification of 'the Chronicler' with Ezra (W. F. Albright, 'The Date and Personality of the Chronicler', *JBL* 40, 1921, 104–24).

Modern suggestions about the date and provenance of Chronicles have ranged from the first half of the sixth century, parallel to Ezekiel and the Deuteronomistic history (A. C. Welch, *The Work of the Chronicler*, London 1939, 155), to the second century, some time in the Maccabean period (Spinoza, *Treatise*, 146; A. Lods, *Israel*, London 1932, 14, and others), a range of over four hundred years (for a partial listing, cf. M. A. Throntveit, *When Kings Speak*, Atlanta 1987, 97). An early dating of the book must entail a very specific view of the literary work, with extensive parts of it regarded as secondary or of later editions (cf. above p.7). A very late date for the book's composition is very often commended by a scholar's general view of the chronology of the biblical literature (Pfeiffer, *Introduction*, 811–12), or, more specifically, by the literary appreciation of Chronicles as a sample of post-biblical genres (Zunz, *Gottesdienstliche Vorträge*, 32–8; Welten, 199–200). On the whole, however, the most common view is the middle one, with many scholars placing the book's composition some time in the fourth century BCE or towards its end (e.g. S. R. Driver, *Introduction to the Literature of the Old Testament*, Edinburgh 1913, 315; Eissfeldt, *The Old Testament*, 540; Curtis, 6; Rudolph, X; Williamson, 16).

Several lines may be considered in approaching the question of the book's date and provenance.

1. Several attempts have been made to tie the book of Chronicles to concrete historical events, a connection which would allocate it a well-defined chronological matrix. Among the more popular recent suggestions is the last quarter of the sixth century, with the eschatological expectations linked with the figure of Zerubbabel (Freedman, Cross, Newsome, Braun, Throntveit, etc.), or the wake of the Samaritan schism (Noth, *The Chronicler*, 100ff., Rudolph, VIII–IX). In fact, however, the actualities of the period, whether under Babylonian, Persian or Hellenistic rule, are not expressed in Chronicles in concrete references to events, and only a few may be more precisely pinpointed. Foremost among them are the edict of Cyrus, the list of the inhabitants of Jerusalem, both cited from Ezra–Nehemiah, and the genealogical list of Jehoiachin's line (cf. below). If other occasions are alluded to in the book (cf. for example Noth's interpretation of II Chron. 20, 'Eine palästinische Lokalüberlieferung in 2 Chr 20', *ZDPV* 67, 1944–5, 45–71), the state of our knowledge of this period precludes their disclosure. The date and provenance of Chronicles must thus be determined mostly on the basis of general considerations, with no support from reference to precise historical events.

2. The language of Chronicles is clearly 'Late Biblical Hebrew', with features common to late biblical and extra-biblical works such as Ezra–Nehemiah, Esther, Daniel, etc., on the one hand, and the Dead Sea Scrolls and the Samaritan Pentateuch on the other. Within this general phase of Hebrew, Chronicles displays a peculiar diction of its own (cf. Japhet, 'Common Authorship', *VT* 18, 1968), but no distinction has yet been proposed for a detailed diachronic or dialectic differentiation within this general linguistic stratum (but cf. A. Bendavid, *Biblical Hebrew and Mishnaic Hebrew*, Tel Aviv 1971, 60–94*; R. Polzin, *Late Biblical Hebrew*, Missoula 1976, 10, 159). These facts fix the upper limit of the composition of the book no earlier than the post-exilic period, and probably well into it.

3. As for the other extreme, Chronicles displays no sign of Greek-Hellenistic influence, in either language or theology (P. R. Ackroyd, *The Age of the Chronicler*, 7–8, Williamson, 16). In view of the strong Hellenistic impact on Judah from the third century BCE on (illustrated in the biblical texts by Qoheleth on the one hand and Daniel on the other), this absence may suggest the lower limit for the composition of the book, before the influx of Hellenistic influence. Here, however, another phenomenon should be pointed out, that is, the degree of Persian influence illustrated in the book. Contrary to Ezra–Nehemiah, no trace of the Persian administrative system is evidenced in Chronicles. Not only words of apparent Persian derivation

(such as פתשגן, אחשדרפן, תרשתא etc.), but also more neutral forms like פחה (found only once in a parallel text, II Chron. 9.14 // 1 Kings 10.15) and מדינה (cf. on I Chron. 9.2), are conspicuously missing from Chronicles. There are very few clear Persian words in the whole corpus of Chronicles (גנזך, I Chron. 28.11; פרבר, I Chron. 26.18; and probably אדרכן, I Chron. 29.7). This absence may be interpreted as a conscious effort to avoid anachronisms, or as a polemic against anything Persian, but it may also be a neutral reflection of a non-Persian provenance of the work. The latter would concur with other considerations pertaining to the book provenance, and would point to the end of the fourth century as its date.

In the attempt to fix a more precise date for the composition of the book there are several more relevant considerations.

(*a*) Most famous is the genealogy of Jehoiachin (I Chron. 3.17–24). Since the last names registered in this list must be either contemporaneous with or earlier than the book's author, it may serve as a useful means in establishing its upper chronological limit. In practice, however, this procedure is more problematical. The text of the list is faulty at several points, and no general consensus has been reached over its reading. Even on the assumption that Jehoiachin's line runs with interruption, the count vacillates from seven to fourteen generations after Jehoiachin. Assuming an average of twenty years per generation, this would put the last recorded generation between 140 and 280 years after Jehoiachin, that is, between about 460 and 320 BCE. More- over, even the employment of Jehoiachin's genealogy for the purpose of dating must reckon with the objection of scholars (foremost being those who place Chronicles at a much earlier date, but also others; cf. Rudolph, 26) who regard the genealogy as secondary to Chronicles.

(*b*) Of a more general character is the development of the cultic institu- tions, the organization of the Temple personnel and the integration of the non-priestly clergy into the levitical order. The Chronistic picture of these institutions reveals a great measure of stabilization and schematization. The priests are meticulously organized in a system of twenty-four divisions, the structure and even names of which are well established, to remain unchanged into the post-biblical period (cf. Japhet, *VT* 18, 1968, 346). With this structure as a model, a parallel organization of twenty-four units is conceived for all other clerical classes, Levites, singers and gatekeepers, an attempt with patently artificial features (I Chron. 23; 25; 26). On the whole, however, it represents a much more advanced stage in the development of the cultic organization than anything reflected in Ezra–Nehemiah, and this applies also to the independence of the singers as a distinct class and the integration of the gatekeepers into the Levites. Chronicles also attests an analogous structuring of the lay people into 'divisions', to be represented in the regular Temple service as a counterpart to the clerical 'divisions' (II Chron. 35.5, 12). Here again, several scholars would deny the argument from the development of the cultic administration, on the ground that I Chron. 23–27, together with other parts of the book pertaining to the organization of the cult, are secondary to Chronicles (cf. Welch, *The Work of the Chronicler*, passim; Noth, *Chronicler*, 29–35; Rudolph, 153ff.; Willi, 194–204). H. G. M. Williamson, on the other hand, would regard only a 'final layer' which deals more specifically with the 'divisions' as secondary ('The Origins of the Twenty-Four Priestly Courses: A Study of I Chronicles 23–27', *VTS* 30, 1979, 251–8; *Chronicles*, 14–15), and would make this literary-critical decision a basis for his own dating of the book. My analysis of these chapters does not support these literary-critical conclusions, which involve not merely the detailed presentation of the 'division system' in I Chron. 23– 26 but many other sections, large and small, throughout the book. The Chronicler's reflection of the cult constitutes an authentic and essential feature of his view of the Temple service (cf. Japhet, *Ideology*, 222–34), and could not be excised from Chronicles without our composing a whole new 'Chronicles'. In the absence of comparative material it is difficult to draw precise chronological conclusions from this general portrayal of the cult organization, but since a prolonged and complex process is involved, a late provenance, certainly later than the one assumed by Ezra–Nehemiah, must be presupposed.

(*c*) Another general consideration concerns the Chronicler's position *vis à vis* other biblical works. Because of his peculiar literary method of employing and citing earlier works, the 'library' which was available to the Chronicler may be easily reconstructed. The Deuteronomistic history is extant basically in its final canonical form (Willi, 55; cf. the different view of S. L. McKenzie, *The Chronicler's Use of the Deuteronomistic History*, Atlanta 1985, and the review by Williamson in *VT* 37, 1987, 107–14), but at the same time the Chronicler has no hesitation in deviating from the Deuteronomistic historical and theological concepts at significant points. Both these facts imply a certain distance between the Chronicler and his Deuteronomistic predecessor(s), their work being viewed as a stabilized historical work, the message of which can no longer be accepted as it is. Moreover, the influence on Chronicles of the whole Pentateuch on the one hand, and of Zechariah and Lamentations on the other, and the two passages cited from Ezra–Nehemiah (Ezra 1.1–3a; Neh. 11.3–19), all point to a date later than the composition of the latter, well into the fourth century. Here again, some scholars would deny the evidence of the latter by claiming that both these citations – the one included in the genealogical introduction of Chronicles (I Chron. 9.2–17), and the other concluding the book (II Chron. 36.22–23) – are secondary to Chronicles; this argument comes dangerously close to circularity.

My own conclusions, then, point towards a later rather than earlier date for the book's composition. I would place it at the end of the Persian or, more probably, the beginning of the Hellenistic period, at the end of the fourth century BCE.

F. Text and versions

The 'synoptic' nature of Chronicles – the fact that much of the book represents a literal citation of earlier biblical works – makes Chronicles a 'favourite' in textual criticism. Like other aspects of the book, the study of its text served as a kind of tool in basically two directions: the establishment of the text of its biblical sources, in particular Samuel and Kings, and the illustration of general features of biblical transmission. A comparison between Chronicles and its biblical sources will immediately reveal the many differences between the two texts. While many of these are caused by intentional editing of linguistic, literary or theological origin, not a few may be defined as 'textual variants', caused by the actual process of transmission. Chronicles would then be the most ancient 'witness' to the text of its sources, and instrumental for their reconstruction (cf. J. Wellhausen, *Der Text der Bücher Samuelis*, 1871, passim; S. R. Driver, *Notes on the Hebrew Text of Samuel*, 1889, passim; C. F. Burney, *Notes on the Hebrew Text of Kings*, 1903, passim, followed by all commentaries on these books). Generally speaking, the existence within the MT itself of two (sometimes more) versions of the same text can best illustrate the problems involved in the textual transmission and stabilization of the Bible, from the earliest stages to the later ones. The contribution of Chronicles to this field of study was acknowledged already by Kimhi, who demonstrated the interchangeability of letters which are orthographically or phonetically similar, by comparing the differences between Chronicles and Genesis (cf. his commentary on I. Chron. 1.6–7). The broader implications of the text of Chronicles for the process of textual transmission are illustrated in the works of G. Gerleman, *Synoptic Studies in the Old Testament*, 1948; F. M. Cross (cf. below), R. W. Klein, 'New Evidence for an Old Recension of Reigns', *HTR* 60, 1967, 93–105; id., 'Supplements in the Paralipomena: A Rejoinder', *HTR* 61, 1968, 492–495; L. C. Allen, 'Further Thoughts on an Old Recension of Reigns in Paralipomena', *HTR* 61, 1968, 483–90 and others.

The study of the synoptic texts disclosed very early that as far as the 'textual variants' go, Chronicles may reflect a better reading than the MT of its source, implying that the corruption or redactions of Samuel-Kings attested by the MT occurred either later than the Chronicler's use of his *Vorlage*, or in a different textual tradition. Thus, for example, Chronicles contains a series of the well-known pre-redacted forms (מריבעל ,אשבעל, ישמעאלי ,בעלידע, etc.) while Samuel has the edited ones (מפיבשת ,אישבשת, ישראלי ,אלידע cf. I Chron. 8.33, 34; 14.7; 2.17, etc. as compared with II Sam.

2.8, etc.; 4.4, etc.; 5.16; 17.25). This conclusion is supported by the fact that some of the Chronicler's readings concur with variant readings of the Septuagint, thus attesting to a common, different *Vorlage* for the Septuagint on the one hand and Chronicles on the other (cf. W. E. Lemke, 'The Synoptic Problem of Chronicles', *HTR* 58, 1965, 349–63). The conclusions reached by the study of Chronicles *vis à vis* the textual evidence of its sources have become fact with the discovery of fragments of Samuel at Qumran (cf. F. M. Cross, *The Ancient Library of Qumran* 1961, 41). Although these have not yet been published in full, the extant paragraphs in the synoptic texts reveal some clear matches between the deviating text of Samuel and Chronicles, and suffice to demonstrate that Chronicles reflects a *Vorlage* different from the MT (cf. e.g. W. E. Lemke, ibid., 355–7; E. C. Ulrich, *The Qumran Text of Samuel and Josephus*, 1978, 151–64; P. K. McCarter, *I Samuel*, 1980, 6–8; *II Samuel*, 1984, 131, 268, 506–17 and others). How far these reflect isolated incidental readings, or a defined textual 'edition', is still a matter of controversy (cf. F. M. Cross, 'The History of the Biblical Text in Light of Discoveries in the Judean Desert'; id., 'The Evolution of a Theory of Local Texts', in F. M. Cross and S. Talmon, *Qumran and the History of the Biblical Text*, 1975, 281–99; 306–20).

The preoccupation with the text of Chronicles in its synoptic sections also contributed to the study of its text in general, and hastened the eventual change of the 'auxiliary' approach (cf. M. Rehm, *Textkritische Untersuchungen* 1937). As has been recognized by all its commentators, the text of Chronicles has been preserved in fairly good condition (Curtis, 36; Rudolph, IV; Elmslie, *Interpreter's Bible*, 347), and some of its corruptions have already been emended by the Massoretic apparatus of Kethib and Qere and Sebirin (about eighty remarks of the former, many of them, however, referring to the change of ' and ו, or displaying grammatical editing, and about ten remarks of the latter). The only exception to this statement is represented by the list-material, where a host of textual variants and corruptions sometimes result in very difficult readings (cf. L. C. Allen, *The Greek Chronicles*, Leiden 1974, Vol. II, 81–162 passim).

Only a very small fragment of Chronicles has been found so far among the documents from Qumran (cf. F. M. Cross, *The Ancient Library of Qumran*, 1961, 41). The fragment has not yet been published, but according to the information provided by Randellini, of the six lines in two columns, only four complete words are legible, and they are devoid of any value for textual criticism ('Il Libro delle Cronache nel Decennio 1950–1960', *Rivista Biblica* 10, 1962, 137–8, 139). As for the contribution of the synoptic passages for the study of the Chronicler's text, it has been pointed out, and bears repeating, that 'these older books ... must be used with extreme caution ... the task of the textual critic of Chronicles is not to restore the original source reading ...

but only ... the text ... as it came from the hand of the Chronicler' (Curtis, 37).

Among the Versions, the most significant for the textual study of Chronicles is the Septuagint. In general, the study of the ancient Versions has undergone a process similar to that of Chronicles itself, from their study as an auxiliary tool for the textual criticism of MT to their acquiring the status of literary works in their own right, within a specific genre of 'translation'. It has become increasingly evident that the readings attested by the Versions cannot be taken at face value, nor can they be regarded as automatic variants of MT. Not only have inner-Greek mistakes through transmission and theological editing long been recognized, but also the various aspects of the translation process, more specifically approached as 'translation techniques', and the repeated revisions of the Greek text have also come to play an important role in the study of the Versions, with their contribution to the textual study of the Hebrew *Vorlage* becoming a secondary goal. This trend is seen very clearly in the comprehensive work of L. C. Allen on the Septuagint to Chronicles, where he deals with the problem of its origin, the state of its transmission as manifest by the various groups of MSS, the problems of its text, etc. His conclusion on the origin of this translation emphatically opposes that of Torrey (cf. C. C. Torrey, 'The Nature and Origin of "First Esdras"', *AJSL* XXIII, 1907, 121ff., and id., 'Apparatus for the Textual Criticism of Chronicles – Ezra – Nehemiah in the OT', *Harper Memorial Volume* II, 1908, 55–111), who was followed by Curtis (38–40), that the received translation of Chronicles is not the Old Greek but that of Theodotion – a judgment that would render its contribution to the study of the MT even more limited. Although Allen quotes Elmslie's claim that where the text of Chronicles is faulty 'the LXX does not help; for it was made from a manuscript virtually identical with the present Hebrew text' (*Interpreter's Bible*, 347, Allen, Vol. II, 166), he himself ends his study with another, more positive conclusion: 'Used with care Par [LXX to Chronicles] provides as it were in refrigerated form a Hebrew text which is a valuable witness to the state of the text of Chron in second century B.C. Egypt' (ibid., 168, cf. also Rudolph, VI). Of the many variants of this text form not a few still represent a better reading than MT (e.g. I Chron. 2.24; 4.15; 26.17; II Chron. 1.13; 14.6, 9; 19.8; 22.2; 30.22; 32.22 and many more).

The Vetus Latina of II Chronicles was preserved in full in a mediaeval MS, and edited by R. Weber, *Les anciennes versions Latines du deuxième livre des Paralipomène*, Rome 1945; fragments from both I and II Chronicles were collected by Sabatier (1751; cf. the list in Curtis, 41–2). Because of the nature of this translation, it is not especially significant for the MT, although Rudolph cites three cases in which, according to his view, the Old Latin may be the only witness to an ancient Hebrew text (II Chron. 4.17; 20.2; 32.31; cf.

Rudolph, VL and BHS). Its greater contribution is to the text of the
Septuagint, for which Rudolph and Allen together cite thirteen instances in
which the Septuagint text may be corrected by its reading (Rudolph, ibid.;
Allen, 108).

The Latin translation of Jerome, i.e. the Vulgate, the Syriac translation of
the Peshitta and the Aramaic Targum, are all of marginal value for the textual
study of Chronicles, although occasionally they may still contain an original
reading (cf. Rudolph, VII). Their main contribution, as has been recognized,
is to the history of exegesis. The Aramaic Targum of Chronicles has been
studied by several scholars, recently in the thorough work of R. Le Deaut – J.
Robert (*Targum de Chronique*, 1971), who conclude that although it does
have a relatively ancient core, the Targum of Chronicles did not receive its
final form before the eighth or ninth century (ibid., 24–7). N. E. Barnes (cf.
An Apparatus Criticus to Chronicles in the Peshitta Version, 1897) has demonstrated that the Peshitta was constantly and deliberately harmonized with the
text of Samuel-Kings in addition to its being of a midrashic nature; it has also
been preserved in a very faulty state. 'All these make the Peshito text of
Chronicles practically worthless for critical purposes' (Curtis, 43; somewhat
less harshly, Rudolph, VII; see also J. S. Noble, *The Syriac Version to the Book
of Chronicles*, Diss. New York 1943). For the Ethiopic version cf. S. Grébaut,
Les Paralipomènes livre I et II, Version Ethiopienne, Patrologia Orientalis 23,
Paris 1932, 525–771.

G. *Literary genre and forms*

For many generations of students, the book of Chronicles was regarded as
what it claimed to be: a history. Yet different definitions of its genre were also
proposed, long before 'form criticism' came to dominate the stage of biblical
research. Among the early scholars, Zunz related the book of Chronicles to
the midrashic activity of 'the people of the Great Assembly', finding in it the
connecting link between biblical and post-biblical literature (cf. Zunz,
Gottesdienstliche Vorträge, 34–8). In a similar direction but from a different
point of departure, Wellhausen also describes the book as 'midrash', which is
for him a sign of the utmost degradation: 'a wholly peculiar artificial way of
reawakening dry bones' (227), while Torrey regarded Chronicles basically as
a work of fiction, the fruit of the author's imaginative creativity ('by taste and
gift he was a novelist', 'Chronicler as Editor', *AJSL* XXV, 217). Again, without employing clear literary definitions, Barnes also described Chronicles as
'Midrash' (W. E. Barnes, 'The Midrashic Element in Chronicles', *Expositor*,
5th series 4, 1896, 426–39; cf. I. L. Seeligmann, 'The Beginnings of Midrash
in the Book of Chronicles', *Tarbiz* XLIX, 1979/80, 14–32*).

The question of the genre of the book was taken up more systematically with the flourish of 'form criticism' and 'traditio-historical criticism' in biblical studies, a trend which is still potent in today's scholarship. In his foundational and influential study, Noth (1943) defined Chronicles as a work of history, and studied it along the same guidelines which directed his study of the other comprehensive biblical histories, the Pentateuch and the Deuteronomistic History. Although Noth was as critical as his predecessors of the Chronicler's historical reliability, this consideration did not – as indeed it should not – affect his view of the genre of the book and its position in biblical literature. In the footsteps of Zunz and under the influence of Movers, Willi conceives of Chronicles as a 'commentary' (*Auslegung*) – an exegesis of written scripture characterized by midrashic features (53–66). M. D. Goulder proposed the view that Chronicles was composed for liturgical purposes: a collection of sermons, to be read along with the weekly Torah portions (*Midrash and Lection in Matthew*, London 1974, 202–4), while Welten defined the book as a 'free parabolic writing of history' which might be understood as a 'historical Midrash' (206). Ackroyd regards the Chronicler as a theologian, and his work as almost a theological essay ('The Chronicler as Exegete', *JSOT* 2, 24; cf. also Mosis, 14–16).

The results of my study bring me closest to the position taken by Noth. A consideration of the work's relevant features, such as aim, plan, form, and method, must lead to the conclusion that Chronicles is a history, an idiosyncratic expression of biblical historiography (cf. also E. Bickerman, *From Ezra to the Last of the Maccabees*, New York 1962, 20–31: De Vries, 15–16, etc.). It is a presentation of consequent events, focussed on the fortunes of a collective body, Israel, along a period of time within a defined chronological and territorial setting. The events do not constitute an incidental collection of episodes but are both selected and structured. They are represented in a rational sequence, governed by acknowledged and explicitly formulated principles of cause and effect, and are judged by stringent criteria of historical probability. The Chronicler wrote this history with full awareness of his task, its form and meaning.

Doubts regarding this definition of Chronicles often stem from a scholar's awareness that the work is different from what is broadly defined as 'history' in the modern sense. While this is certainly true, the difference does not exclude Chronicles (or other parts of biblical historiography, for that matter) from belonging to the general genre of 'history'. The nature of this difference should, however, be pointed out and clarified.

1. The most important element of difference is the essence of the *principles* which govern history and inform the historical process. While the modern concept of 'history' would regard only human and natural factors – either material or spiritual – as the governing forces of history, in Chronicles (and in biblical history in general) these principles belong to the realm of the super-

natural. Although natural factors are taken into consideration, history is determined by the divine attributes and is a consequence of the human-divine interaction. It is governed by the final and absolute supernatural entity God.

2. Ancient historians, like modern ones, are directed by the consideration of 'historical probability'; they may differ, however, in their judgment of what constitutes 'probability'. The scope and nature of available information, on the one hand, and theoretical and philosophical principles, on the other, may result in different evaluation of 'the probable'. By way of illustration we may consider the category of 'the miraculous', or the intervention of supernatural entities like 'angels' in human history. These would be denied *a priori* by a 'modern historian', but would be accepted as probable by other writers, either ancient or modern, of different theological presuppositions.

3. Every historical work – and Chronicles is no exception – is dependent on sources for its information. In this respect two facts are made very clear by the Chronicler's work: the actual employment of sources, attested in an unequivocal way by his use of earlier biblical works, and his need to point explicitly to his dependence on sources by constant references. Nevertheless, in the criticism of sources, one historian may differ from another. Thus, for example, a 'modern historian' would hesitate to accept genealogical lists and family-trees as legitimate historical sources, but they would be warmly accepted by the ancient one, for whom they constitute a conventional form of scientific knowledge, of ethnic, social and institutional content. From a different perspective, the element of eye-witnessing would very much influence a 'modern historian's' criticism of sources; for the ancient one, hearsay, as expressed by tradition, may be no less valid.

4. As for the literary format of their respective works, both a 'modern history' and an ancient one may contain not merely historical records proper, but other genres as well. Historians may cite archival documents, letters, speeches and the like, which they will carefully scrutinize for their authenticity. The Chronicler's initial awareness of this aspect of historical writing is evidenced by his reluctance to include 'prophetical stories' in his work, very much in contrast to the Deuteronomistic history (cf. Japhet, *Ideology*, 511–12). Nevertheless, he does include in his work a great variety of other genres, some of which may not be regarded as appropriate by a 'modern historian': lists, anecdotes, speeches, prayers, prophecies, psalms, etc., which give his work a very particular character.

5. And finally, there is the problem of authority. The authority of the modern historian rests entirely on natural talents and human abilities. Being aware of their limitations, historians may confess lack of information, weakness of argument, and inability to render judgment. The biblical historian, on the other hand, assumes an absolute authority: he knows and understands

all that there is to know and understand. What is the source of this authority? Does the biblical historian in general, and the Chronicler in particular, regard himself as inspired? Although there are no explicit statements to this effect in the Bible itself, a positive rather than a negative answer would seem to account better for the Chronicler's enterprise. Again by way of illustration, the Chronicler includes in his work many records of divine revelation and prophecies which are clearly his own composition; their ascription to prophets of old – which a modern critic may sometimes judge as flagrant spuriousness – is done innocently and straightforwardly. The licence the Chronicler uses seems to derive from his own self-understanding as inspired. Not only were the histories of old composed by prophets (cf. above p.22), but his own history-writing as well; it is an authentic expression of the divine will.

Taking all this into consideration, the best definition of Chronicles is that of a 'history' written not by a mere 'historian', but by an author who is fully aware of his task.

Another aspect of the problem of 'genres and forms' relates to the varieties of material included in the final work. Like all other examples of biblical historiography, Chronicles contains not only historical records, but other genres as well, the study of which has long lagged behind the other aspects of the book. This has now been rectified by two works. The first is the pioneering, systematic definition and classification of all the genres found in Chronicles undertaken by Kegler-Augustin (*Synopse*, 1984, 22–56, [2]1991). As pointed out by the authors, their attempt demanded at times totally new definitions of genres (ibid., 22). The second is the new commentary of S. De Vries, in the series of *The Forms of the Old Testament Literature* (1989). The expressed aim of the series in general (ibid, XII), and the commentary on Chronicles in particular, is to analyse the book in the context of a strict form-critical method, with 'extensive employment of an exegetical technique developed many decades ago by Gunkel' (XIV). It is thus directed to the study of 'structure', 'genre', 'setting', and 'intention' (ibid.). Unfortunately I have not been able to profit fully from this work, since my own work was virtually finished when the book appeared.

In studying the genres attested in Chronicles, one is immediately confronted by the methodological obstacles inhering in the application of a 'pure' form-critical method. Since the immanent relationship of 'genre' and 'setting' (*'Sitz im Leben'*), with all the consequent considerations and results, applies, according to Gunkel, to the original emergence of 'genre' from the living and recurring life-situations (cf. H. Gunkel, 'Literatur-geschichte, biblische', RGG[2], 1927, III, 1677–8; id., *What Remains of the Old Testament?*, New York 1928, 57-68), it would be applicable only when the *genre itself* – and not merely the individual literary piece – is identified as

'Chronistic'. This excludes the relevance of 'setting' when the genre is already an established literary form, illustrated by numerous individual pieces. The difficulty, then, lies in the dominant features of Chronicles – its being heir to a long literary tradition, and the fact that its greater part is taken from earlier sources – but the difficulty may be differently defined when applied to the biblical citations on the one hand, and extra-biblical ones on the other. While the Chronicler's position *vis à vis* his biblical sources in matters of 'genre' and 'form' may be elucidated through the comparison of the two texts, the original form of the material taken from extra-biblical sources remains unknown; it is left to the student to decide whether the Chronicler borrowed from his sources only the contents while the literary formulation was his own, or whether he transferred to his work form as well as contents. Only when the literary formulation is ascribed to the Chronicler are the questions of 'setting' and 'intention' applicable, at least according to the initial presuppositions of 'form criticism'. Thus it is not incidental that von Rad's 'form-critical' study of Chronicles yielded only one genre which he regarded as emanating from the living Chronistic *'Sitz im Leben'*, and that was the characteristic rhetorical passages in the work, which he defined as 'levitical sermons' (cf. below). Unless a thorough study is devoted to uncovering what is idiosyncratically 'Chronistic' in terms of genre and not in terms of the individual literary piece, a general comprehensive classification of the genres exhibited in Chronicles (cf. Kegler–Augustin, ibid.) must remain largely a descriptive endeavour, a classifying and labelling of the individual sections according to established literary genres.

There are, however, many aspects of 'literary form', in the broad and non-technical sense of the term, which are not attended to by classical 'form criticism'; these pertain to the literary formulation of individual units. Although I could not exhaust the discussion of this aspect of the book, in the commentary I have paid much attention to 'form' and its significance for the Chronicler's articulation of his message. I have pointed to a host of literary tools: inclusion and framing, *Leitmotivs* and chiastic structures, resumptive repetition and flash-back, anthological style and poetic parallelism, as well as to skilful and sophisticated methods of redaction, applied to textual elaboration, omission and change. They illustrate in the clearest way that 'the Chronicler was a person of much greater literary skill than is usually attributed to him' (Braun, xxv).

Of the many features of 'form' displayed by Chronicles, I wish to discuss here four features of general application, which give the Chronicler's work its particular literary character: the sense of 'composition', the rhetorical pieces, the descriptions of ceremonies, and the lists.

(*a*) As already indicated, and as will become evident throughout the commentary, the Chronicler has a very strong sense of composition, expressed in

his attention to a multitude of formal aspects of his work. It is expressed first
of all in the careful structuring of the book as a whole, and then in the
continuous attention to larger and smaller structural units (cf. above, pp. 8–
13). The Chronicler writes his history as a series of literary 'blocks', each of
which is a comprehensive unit revolving around a specific topic and marked
by formal features. As will be demonstrated in the commentary, within these
larger 'blocks' the smaller components, in turn, are carefully structured, with
a constant awareness of form (cf. now also L. C. Allen, 'Kerygmatic Units in
1 and 2 Chronicles,' *JSOT* 41, 1988, 21–36).

The compositional element is also frequently expressed quantitatively, a
fact to which I occasionally draw attention in the commentary. The literary
structure of larger and smaller units and points of emphasis may be expressed
by quantitative proportions and balance between the various components,
involving the abridgment or the elaboration of the source material.

(*b*) As late as the end of the nineteenth century, the particular status of the
speeches in the Chronicler's work was the subject of a debate between S. R.
Driver and V. French (S. R. Driver, 'The Speeches in Chronicles', *Expositor*,
5th series 1, 1895, 241–56; V. French, 'The Speeches in Chronicles:
A Reply', ibid., 2, 1895, 140–52; S. R. Driver, 'The Speeches in Chronicles',
ibid., 286–308). The former's view that these rhetorical pieces are all the
work of the Chronicler and express his views has since become a general
consensus, and the rhetorical pieces are regularly scrutinized for the light
they shed on the Chronicler's theology (cf. for instance, O. Plöger, 'Reden
und Gebete im deuteronomistischen und chronistischen Geschichtswerke',
1957, also published in *Aus der Spätzeit des Alten Testaments*, 1971, 50–66). It
was von Rad who approached the rhetorical passages from the more
methodologically controlled perspective of 'form criticism', in an attempt to
establish their '*Sitz im Leben*' and precise formal features. Von Rad defined
these works as 'levitical sermons' (G. von Rad, 'The Levitical Sermon in I
and II Chronicles' [1934] in *The Problem of the Hexateuch and Other Essays*,
Edinburgh 1966, 267–80), and his definition has been generally followed. As
has been shown by D. Mathias ('"Levitische Predigt" und Deuteronomismus', *ZAW* 96, 1984, 23–49; cf. also R. Mason, 'Some Echoes of the
Preaching in the Second Temple?', *ZAW* 96, 1984, 221–35), this definition
of genre is deficient, as these pieces are neither 'levitical' nor 'sermons'.
Their specific nature, however, and their significance for the Chronicler's
work cannot be overestimated (cf. also M. Throntveit, *When Kings Speak*,
1987; R. Mason, *Preaching the Tradition*, 1990).

The historical writing of Chronicles is interspersed with rhetorical
passages of every kind and genre: divine speeches, royal addresses, prophetic
exhortations and oracles, prayers, letters, dialogues, and more. Like other
features of the Chronicler's work, there is nothing new in this feature itself,

which is a quite faithful continuation of the literary tradition of biblical historiography. Similar to the procedure of the Deuteronomistic history, and in analogy to non-biblical historiography (cf. M. Dibelius, 'The Speeches in Acts and Ancient Historiography', in *Studies in the Acts of the Apostles*, 1956, 138–85; Japhet, *Ideology*, 14), speeches are placed at important points along the historical course and carry the heaviest burden of the book's theological cargo. However, the Chronicler's particular position may be seen in his strong inclination towards 'the rhetorical' in general, as illustrated by the preponderance of rhetorical elements in his work and their great variety.

The Chronicler cites from his Deuteronomistic sources many of their rhetorical sections, such as Nathan's prophecy and David's prayer (II Sam. 7.5–29 // I Chron. 17.4–27), Solomon's prayers and addresses at the dedication of the Temple (I Kings 8.12–50 // II Chron. 6.1–40), the negotiations between Rehoboam and the northern tribes (I Kings 12.4–17 // II Chron. 10.4–17), or the prophecy of Huldah (II Kings 22.15–20 // II Chron. 34.23–28), to name some of the representative examples. On other occasions the Chronicler takes his point of departure from his sources but further elaborates them (e.g. I Kings 5.3–9 [MT. 17–23] // II Chron. 2.2–15). However, not all the speeches found in his source are repeated in Chronicles; some are changed to a greater or lesser degree, some are replaced, and some are omitted altogether (cf. for instance David's psalms in II Sam. 22; 23.1–7; David's testament in I Kings 2.2–9; Isaiah's prophecy, in II Kings 19.21–34; the prophetic message to Manasseh, II Kings 21.11–15, etc.). The extent and significance of the rhetorical element, however, may be seen in the Chronicler's own rhetorical compositions, the origin of which may be traced not only to his literary inclination but to his most fundamental sociological, psychological and theological presuppositions.

A significant component of these rhetorical pieces may be defined as 'warnings', a mandatory element in the Chronicler's view of divine justice (cf. Japhet, *Ideology*, 176–91). Most of these warnings are formulated as prophetic speeches (e.g. II Chron. 12.5; 20.37; 24.20), but there is no equation between the two; 'warning' may also be expressed by persons other than a prophet, such as Joab, Abijah, a priest, or the Egyptian Necho (cf. I Chron. 21.3; II Chron. 13.4–12; 26.18; 35.21), while prophetic addresses may have such non-warning functions as a call for repentance (e.g. II Chron. 15.2–7) or an oracle of deliverance (II Chron. 20. 15–17).

While 'warning' forms part of the juridical process of divine justice, it may be seen also as one expression of a more pervasive feature of the Chronicler's philosophy, the existential significance of *dialogue*. It is founded on a firm belief in the power of reasoning and persuasion, appealing to the understanding and goodwill of the other party. These elements of dialogue, reasoning and persuasion are manifest in Chronicles in every form and level of inter-

relationship: God and people, king and people, etc. The dialogue between
the Lord and his people is expressed in an ongoing revelation of the divine
will and purpose through a continuous chain of prophets and messengers. It
is this ceaseless commissioning of prophets which manifests in Chronicles
the supreme expression of God's compassion (II Chron. 36.15). From the
human perspective, the dialogue is embodied in man's turning to the Lord –
in prayer (e.g. II Chron. 14.10), in the demand for justice (e.g. II Chron.
20.6–12), in thanksgiving (e.g. II Chron. 20.21), or in exaltation (e.g. I
Chron. 29.10–19). There is also a continuous dialogue on the human level,
between the king and his people. The king in Chronicles does not simply
command the people, but he solicits their co-operation by reasoning and
persuasion (cf. e.g. I Chron. 15.12–13; II Chron. 14.6; 19.6–11; 29.5–11;
30.6–9, etc.; also Japhet, *Ideology*, 420–7). There is also a dialogue between
the Chronicler and his audience, expressed in the Chronicler's own comments, intended to explain to the reader the covert principles underlying the
overt phenomena (e.g. II Chron. 12.2; 13.18; 17.3; etc.). This tone of
persuasion, then, permeates the whole work and grants it its 'rhetorical'
character.

The Chronicler's rhetorical works are all in prose, the only poetical items
being from Psalms (I Chron. 16.8–36; 6.41–42). They are characterized,
however, by an elevated style, achieved by various literary means: parallelism
of members, extensive use of quotations in the form of 'anthological style',
prevalence of *Leitmotivs*, the use of literary formulas, paranomasia and alliteration, and more.

(*c*) A prominent characteristic of the Chronicler's history is his penchant
for *public ceremonies*. Although again in principle there is nothing new in this
feature, a comparison of his work with other biblical texts may clarify his
peculiar disposition.

While descriptions of public ceremonies are also found in the Chronicler's
major source – the Deuteronomistic history in Samuel-Kings – they are
rather limited in number and scope. The most outstanding among them is
the complex literary work describing the dedication of the Temple in
Solomon's time, in which many rhetorical sections are incorporated (I Kings
8.1–66). Second to it is the public ceremony of transferring the ark (II Sam.
6.2–8, 12–19), a much shorter piece with no rhetorical component at all. A
few other ceremonies are included in the non-synoptic sections, e.g. I Sam.
7.5ff.; 12; etc. The Pentateuch is much richer in descriptions of ceremonies,
reflecting different styles and alternating origin (e.g. Gen. 15.9–21; Ex. 19–
24, etc.); the most outstanding Pentateuchal example, of course, is
Deuteronomy, cast as a whole in the framework of Moses' ceremonial
farewell and testament (Deut. 1.1–32.47). Even within this fundamental
framework, there are smaller units which also depict public ceremonies, such

as Deut. 26.1–11; 27–28, etc. Descriptions of ceremonies are also found in Ezra–Nehemiah: the laying of the Temple foundations (Ezra 3.10–13), the reading of the law (Neh. 8.1–12); the making of the covenant (Neh. 9.1–10.40) and the dedication of the wall (Neh. 12.27–43). The Chronicler, then, had abundant literary precedents and models upon which to draw; yet the scope and nature of his disposition are still his own; the following features may be noted:

1. The Chronicler elaborates extensively on the 'ceremonial' aspect of his sources. He cites all the ceremonies found in the synoptic texts and broadens their scope. This is particularly the case with the transfer of the ark, but even the comprehensive description of the dedication of the Temple is enlarged upon to include new elements. Furthermore, when a ceremony is merely referred to or simply implied in his sources (as at II Sam. 5.3; I Kings 3.4), this becomes the foundation upon which a full-fledged ceremony is built (I Chron. 11–12; II Chron. 1.2–6). And finally, the Chronicler introduces ceremonies to episodes in which the ceremonial element is altogether missing in his sources, such as the reform of Asa (I Kings 15.12–13 // II Chron. 15.1–15) or the passover of Josiah (II Kings 23.21–23 // II Chron. 35.1–19).

2. To the 'ceremonial core' taken from his sources, the Chronicler adds a variety of ceremonies which have no basis at all in the synoptic texts. These may have been found – in the same rudimentary state – in the non-biblical sources which he used (e.g. Hezekiah's passover, II Chron. 30), or they may be entirely his own creation.

3. The Chronicler turns 'ceremony' into a basic literary framework into which numerous different units of a variety of genres are incorporated. This is already the case in the dedication of the Temple which the Chronicler cites from his sources and elaborates, but it can also be seen elsewhere. Thus, major sections of Chronicles are explicitly described as ceremonies: the beginnings of David's reign, incorporated into the framework of his enthronement (I Chron. 11.1–3; 12.38–40); the transfer of the ark (I Chron. 13; 15–16); the registration of the clergy and their division (I Chron. 23.2; 24.3ff.); the enthronement of Solomon (I Chron. 28.1–29.25); the visit of Solomon to Gibeon (II Chron. 1.1–13); the dedication of the Temple (Chron. 5.2–7.10); the purification of the Temple by Hezekiah (II Chron. 29); and the celebration of the passover by Hezekiah and Josiah (II Chron. 29; 35).

4. The most 'Chronistic' feature of all, however, seems to be the Chronicler's way of colouring as 'ceremony' events which do not really belong to this category, either by adapting the accounts taken from his biblical sources, or composing passages which are peculiar to his work. This is illustrated, for example, in the changes which the Chronicler introduces into the story of Jehoiada's revolt (II Chron. 23 – II Kings 11.4–20). Rather

than being a conspiracy leading to a *coup d'état*, it is described as a public ceremony in the court of the Temple, with great crowds, strict observance of ritual, etc. It is even more obvious in the Chronicler's descriptions of wars (II Chron. 13.3–20; 20.1–30, etc.), which are stamped with Chronistic features and evade persistent scholarly attempts to define their genre (cf. De Vries, 434: 'Quasi-Holy-War Story'). Although these descriptions are clearly intended as war records, as indicated by their topic, subject matter, and some detail, what they depict is more like 'war ceremonies' than actual wars. Being loaded with rhetorical and ritual elements, the narratives' concrete action or plot retreats to the background.

The prevalence of the 'ceremonial' component in the Chronicler's work may very well reflect his historical setting, in which public ceremonies may have occupied an important place in the community's life. It may also reflect literary and theological characteristics of the Chronicler himself.

(d) Lists are a major component in the Chronicler's writing – almost all of I Chron. 1–9 and 23–27 – and extensive sections throughout the book, are comprised of lists (e.g. I Chron. 11.26–47; 12.24–37; 15.5–10, 17–24; 28.11–18; etc.). This great body of material may be further classified by topic and form (cf. Kegler-Augustin, 233–41) to include genealogical tables (e.g. I Chron. 1.5–23; 2.25–33), pedigrees (e.g. I Chron. 2.10–17; 36–41), kings' lists (I Chron. 1.43–51; 3.10–14), city lists (e.g. I Chron. 4.28–33; II Chron. 11.6–10), census lists (e.g. I Chron. 7.1–5, 6–11), lists of inhabitants of a city (I Chron. 9.3–17, 35–38), of officials (e.g. I Chron. 18.15–17; 27.25–34), of clerical orders (e.g. I Chron. 24.7–18; 26.1–11 etc.), of warriors (e.g. I Chron. 12.3–8, 10–14), of tribal leaders (I Chron. 27.16–22), of the king's sons (e.g. I Chron. 3.1–9; II Chron. 11.19–21), of materials (I Chron. 22.3–4; 29.2–5, 7–8), of the Temple's vessels and furnishings (e.g. I Chron. 28.14–18; II Chron. 4.12–22), of participants in certain occasions and undertakings (e.g. I Chron. 15.5–10; 16.5–6; II Chron. 17.7–8), and so on. Even in this respect, however, the Chronicler is not an innovator, his work differing in degree rather than in essence from earlier historiography.

Of all biblical historiography, only the book of Deuteronomy seems to avoid the genre of lists, probably because of its specific literary form as Moses' testament. Lists are also not common in the Deuteronomistic history of Samuel-Kings, although it does include several documents pertaining to different areas of the state's and Temple's administration, such as David's officers (II Sam. 8.16–18; 20.23–26), David's sons (II Sam. 3.2–5; 5.14–16), David's warriors (II Sam. 23.24–39), Solomon's officials (I Kings 4.2–19), the Temple's vessels and furniture (I Kings 7.41–50; 25.13–17), the conquests of Tiglath-pileser (II Kings 15.29), and others. On the other hand, 'lists' constitute a significant component of Genesis through Numbers, Joshua and Ezra–Nehemiah. They are integrated into the narrative sequence to provide the 'skeleton' of acknowledged facts which give the records their undeniable validity.

The Chronicler employs 'lists' in various literary capacities: from a systematic compilation of lists as a 'scientific' presentation of data without even a thread of narratory linkage (e.g. I Chron. 1; 2, etc.), to the incorporation of name lists into broader narrative contexts (e.g. II Chron. 17.7–8; 29.12–14). Thus, for example, when stating that Jehoshaphat sent officers, Levites and priests to teach the law in the cities of Judah, the Chronicler finds it necessary to supply the names of these individuals, thereby enhancing the reality and historicity of his report (II Chron. 17.7–8). The general information that 'Rehoboam ... built cities for defence in Judah' (II Chron. 11.5) is followed by a list of these cities and their description (II Chron. 11.6–10), and the idea that 'all Israel supported David' is not stated thus generally, but is meticulously reinforced with as many registered data as possible (I Chron. 11.10–12.38).

Although the modern scholar may find some lists more authentic than others, and may sometimes doubt whether their present function in the Chronicler's work (or in other biblical works, for that matter) faithfully reflects their original setting, their central literary function is not thereby affected. They constitute one of the Chronicler's most important methods of bolstering his account with the validity and authority of 'accurate fact'.

In this extensive use of 'lists', the Chronicler seems to adhere more to the model of the Pentateuch and Joshua than to that of Samuel-Kings. Although, as stated above, this genre is also attested in Samuel-Kings, from a form-critical point of view this propensity for lists is the Chronicler's most distinct deviation from the Deuteronomistic model of Samuel-Kings. It illustrates again, this time in the area of form, the Chronicler's most fundamental characteristic: the combination of faithful adherence to his sources with freedom to change. In his editorial activity he adopts genres from all earlier biblical historiography; the final combination of narrative, lists, and rhetorical works, however, as well as their distribution and manner of composition, are certainly his own.

H. Language and style

The peculiarity of the Chronicler's diction was observed very early, as can be seen in various handbooks like grammars (cf. Gesenius, §2 l–v, 12–17) and dictionaries (cf. *BDB, passim*), where many phenomena peculiar either to Chronicles alone or to other books as well are designated 'late'. It seems, however, that early interest in the Chronicler's language focussed mainly on its vocabulary (cf. S. R. Driver, *Introduction*, 535–40; Curtis, 28–34), and to a lesser extent on its syntax (Curtis, 34–6). A pioneering study in this area is that of A. Kropat (*Die Syntax des Autors der Chronik*, BZAW 16, 1909). In its early stages, the study of Late Biblical Hebrew in general and the Chronicler's language in particular was marked by a judgmental perspective. According to Curtis, for example, 'The many peculiarities ... indicate that the compiler and author ... either used Hebrew with some difficulty, or that the language itself was decadent in his day' (27). Late Biblical Hebrew was characterized mainly by the strong Aramaic influence (cf. Gesenius, 17), to the degree that F. Zimmerman suggested that Chronicles was a 'partially translated book' ('Chronicles as a Partially Translated Book', *JQR* 42, 1951/ 2, 265–82; 387–412). Although the impact of Aramaic on Late Biblical Hebrew is certainly very strong, this statement should be qualified in two ways: an Aramaic influence by itself can no longer be ascribed exclusively to the 'imperial Aramaic' of the Persian period; it may also point to earlier contacts with this language through, for example, the language of northern Israel. Secondly, there are many features of Late Biblical Hebrew which are not necessarily a result of Aramaic influence, and their source should be sought elsewhere, in inner-Hebrew processes or in the influence of other Semitic and non-Semitic languages (cf. for example C. H. Gordon, 'North Israelite Influence on Postexilic Hebrew', *IEJ* 5, 1955, 85–8; W. G. E. Watson, 'Archaic Elements in the Language of Chronicles', *Biblica* 53, 1972, 191–207; R. Polzin, *Late Biblical Hebrew*, 1976, 10–12; G. Rendsburg, 'Late Biblical Hebrew and the Date of P', *JANES* 12, 1980, 65–80; S. Gevirtz, 'Of Syntax and Style in the "Late Biblical Hebrew" – "Old Canaanite Connection"', *JANES* 18, 1986, 25–9).

Recent years have witnessed an increasing interest in Late Biblical Hebrew, of which Chronicles comprises the largest corpus. This interest may be attributed to three factors: the general development and refinement of linguistic study in recent decades; the accumulation of epigraphic material which has greatly increased and diversified our knowledge of the prevalent languages of the time (cf. W. R. Garr, *Dialect Geography of Syria-Palestine 1000–586 BCE*, Philadelphia 1985); and the discovery of the Dead Sea scrolls, the language of which belongs in its general characteristics to the same linguistic stratum (cf. E. Qimron, *The Hebrew of the Dead Sea Scrolls*, Atlanta 1986) – although a direct line of development from Late Biblical Hebrew to the language of Qumran has now been questioned (S. Morag, 'Qumran Hebrew: Some Typological Observations', *VT* 38, 1988, 148–64). It seems, however, that a systematic and comprehensive description of Late Biblical Hebrew, in its various synchronic and diachronic realizations, is now indicated. It should address itself to all pertinent questions, such as its survival as a living language in the post-exilic period, the extent and origin of the Aramaic influence, the simultaneous influence of other Semitic and non-Semitic languages, its position in relation to the transition from biblical to rabbinic Hebrew, and so on. The responses to these questions, which will take into full consideration the Chronistic material, will contribute to a clearer picture of this stage in the development of the Hebrew language.

Within the general linguistic phase of Late Biblical Hebrew, Chronicles displays linguistic and stylistic features all its own. A comparison of its language with other late corpora like Ezra–Nehemiah, Daniel or Esther might throw into relief the author's particular personal traits (cf. for example, Japhet, *VT* 18, 1968, 358–71). However, since what was very often described as the Chronicler's personal style has turned out to reflect general linguistic usage (cf. for instance, Williamson, *Israel in the Book of Chronicles*, 37–59), the distinction between peculiar Chronistic elements of style and general linguistic usage of his time has become very precarious and must be carried out with the utmost caution.

I. Aim and major theological themes

I have dealt with the Chronicler's theology in the past in great detail, first in my Hebrew dissertation (1973) and then in its published form which followed (1977), through which my views became known (sometimes anonymously) to the scholarly world; this monograph is now available to a more general readership in an English translation (1989), so I may limit myself here to a brief summary of the major issues.

That the Chronicler had strong historical and theological motives in writing his work is self-evident; why else would he bother to rewrite the history of a period which was already documented? The uncovering of these motives has continually engaged scholarly attention, culminating in the defining of the Chronicler's theological and historical position in the development of biblical literature and religion.

Several attempts have been made to ascribe the entire book to a single purpose or mood, which would account for all its features. Wellhausen claimed that 'the difference of spirit arises from the influence of the Priestly Code' (171). Some scholars, including Torrey, Noth and Rudolph, consider the book's aim to be to establish the exclusive legitimacy of the Jerusalem cultic institutions and of Judah as the only community of God, as a polemic against the Samaritans and their claims (cf. C. C. Torrey, *Ezra Studies* [1910], reprinted New York 1970, 208–9; Noth, *The Chronicler*, 100ff.; Rudolph, IX). Freedman, followed by several others, claims that the purpose of the book was to provide a basis for the legitimate claims of the house of David to rule in Israel, and in particular for its claims to authority over the Temple and the cult in the time of Zerubbabel ('The Chronicler's Purpose', *CBQ* 23, 1961, 436–42). It is doubtful, however, whether one single and unilateral purpose would account for such an enormous enterprise, with all its complexities of content and form. Chronicles is not a manifesto devoted to a specific political movement but a more general and comprehensive theological stock-taking, striving to achieve a new religious balance in the face of a changing world. For the Chronicler, 'the history of Israel' is the arena in which God's providence and rule of his people are enacted. By unveiling the principles which govern its history, a firm foundation is laid for the future existence of Israel. It is from this 'total' perspective that the grand historical and theological enterprise should be judged.

'History' being the concrete expression of God's and Israel's interrelationship, the book is centred upon two topics: the God of Israel and the people of Israel, each seen on its own, and in their interaction. Some of the basic concepts of biblical faith are taken for granted in Chronicles and are referred to only cursorily, such as the monotheistic idea, God's sovereignty and rule of the world, etc. The greater theological effort is invested in those themes in which the Chronicler wishes to make his own statement, and these may find expression in both explicit pronouncements and polemical silence.

The Chronicler displays a peculiar view of Israel's election, which would eventually be more explicitly expressed in some apocryphal works, as well as in some rabbinic sayings (cf. e.g. The Assumption of Moses 1.12–13; II Esdras 6.53–59; Mekilta to Exod. 14.15). The special relationship between the people and their God is viewed not as a 'new' creation, the result of a particular historical act at a given historical moment, like the covenant with Abraham or the Exodus from Egypt; rather, it is a 'given'; its origins do not lie in the sphere of history but are embedded in the very creation of the world itself. This is, then, an absolute relationship; it is not defined in terms of 'covenant' and its validity is akin to that between God and the universe.

God's rule of his people is expressed by his constant, direct and immediate intervention in their history. From among the divine attributes which govern God's rule of his people, the most prominent is 'justice'; the sovereign Lord 'is just' (II Chron. 12.6), and all that he does is characterized by the attribute of absolute justice. It is through the correct understanding of the human acts on the one hand and the Lord's just reaction to those acts, on the other, that the nature of the Lord's justice becomes manifest. The Chronicler's well-known theory of 'reward and punishment', which has been designated in various ways in the history of scholarship (cf. for instance, Dillard, 76–81), is in fact his way of portraying history as a concrete manifestation of divine justice. It is characterized by several features. Reward is mandatory, immediate and individual. Every generation is requited for its own deeds, both good and evil, with no postponement of recompense; there is no accumulated sin and no accumulated merit. The 'ultimate cause' of man's fortunes lies in man's free choice: God reacts to his behaviour, granting him what he deserves. Attending this free choice are two major factors: warning and repentance. Warning before punishment is regarded in Chronicles not merely as an option, but as a mandatory element in the judicial procedure. Man is always offered a chance to repent, and God does not fail to react to repentance; the gate remains open for man to return. This status of man as the master of his fate may lead to a certain limitation of God's free and sovereign acting; the Chronicler guards these essential divine attributes through the concepts of 'trial' and compassion applied to the human–divine relationship.

In several respects, the Chronicler's view of divine justice seems to develop from that of Ezekiel. The most important point of difference, however, lies in its perspective: the Lord's absolute just rule of his people is not a wish or a promise for the future (cf. Jer. 31.29–30; Ezek. 3.17–21; 18.1–32), but an established fact, proven by historical experience. These are the rules by which the fortunes of Israel have always been determined; their absolute validity forms the basis for faith in Israel's future.

The human side of this mutual relationship is expressed by worship, and the Chronicler advances the religious life of Israel as a major topic of his historical account. Chronicles provides a systematic history of Israel's worship, a description of the cultic institutions, and the establishment and functioning of the clergy. It presents the cultic forms of the Lord's worship as having been established in two stages: first, the Law, with its precepts and the details of the sacrificial cult, was given through Moses; then the place of worship, its order and organization were established as permanent institutions by David and achieved their complete realization under Solomon. The idea of a central, unique place of worship is expressed as a concrete historical reality, with the unwavering conviction that the only legitimate form of cultic worship is the central cult of the Jerusalem Temple. Of the Temple personnel, special attention is paid to the non-priestly classes: Levites, singers, and gatekeepers, conceived of as constituting sub-orders of 'the Levites'. Whether a reflection of the Chronicler's actual circumstances, or an expression of his own stand on controversial issues regarding the functions and status of the various cultic orders, Chronicles is one of the most important reflections of the changes which affected the structure and functions of the clerical orders during the Second Temple period.

Notwithstanding its significance, the cultic performance does not exhaust the obligation of the Israelites, both individual and corporate, toward their God. Being 'righteous', according to Chronicles, involves the whole human soul: knowledge of God, trust in God, humility and fear of God, are all part of correct conduct and attitude. Moreover, even the concrete religious act is incomplete unless it is performed with 'a whole heart', a totality which receives its main expression in 'joy', and in its cultic counterpart, music.

Chronicles devotes an important place to the prophets and displays a broad view of their function. In the wake of earlier views he presents the prophets as mediators between the Lord and his people. They appear before king and people to transmit the word of the Lord, rebuke them for their evil-doing, warn them of the consequences of their conduct, call for repentance and encourage faith in the Lord. They also act as intercessors, bringing the people's prayers to the Lord. Throughout the history of Israel they are represented by a continuous chain of such figures, including a priest (II Chron. 24.20), a Levite (II Chron. 20.14), many known figures like Jehu (II Chron. 19.2), Isaiah (II Chron. 32.20), Jeremiah (II Chron. 35.25), and others, and some unknown ones like Azariah the son of Oded (15.1), Oded (II Chron. 28.9) and more. Yet, they also act in other capacities. Their position as 'mediators' implies that they not only transmit the Lord's message in *ad hoc* matters, accompanying historical actualities, but also represent the Lord's will in matters of permanent standing. Stated in the most general way, it is 'through the prophets' that God's *commandment* reaches his people (II Chron. 29.25). The Chronicler also ascribes to the prophets the writing of history – a function for which there is no precedent in the Bible. Historio-graphy is an inspired task, and in each generation there are prophets who record the events of their period (cf. above, p. 22).

Inspiration, however, is not limited in Chronicles to figures which are identified as 'prophets'; the Chronicler also regards as prophets the founders of the Temple music – Asaph, Heman and Jeduthun (I Chron. 25.1–5; cf. D. L. Petersen, *Late Biblical Prophecy*, Missoula 1977, pp. 55–96), and ascribes direct communication with the Lord to the two founding kings of the Davidic dynasty – David (I Chron. 28.2, 6–7, 12, 19) and Solomon (I Chron. 1.7–12; 7.12–22). For the Chronicler, 'prophecy' is a vital and active institu-tion, the uninterrupted channel of God's will and purpose.

The Chronicler has a very special picture of the people of Israel in its ethnographic, geographical and political aspects. His dominant view is that of 'great Israel' in the broadest sense, applying to both its ethnographic definition and geographical expansion. The people of Israel are conceived of as a comprehensive, unified body comprised of tribes, which in turn are vital and active entities throughout the history of Israel. Not only in the introduc-tory nine chapters, when 'Israel' is introduced, and in the reigns of David and Solomon when Israel achieved its ideal existence, but also after the defection of the northern tribes, there is a process of return to this original unity, which culminates in the days of Josiah. The Chronicler is not confined by the traditional concept of the 'twelve tribes'; rather, he strives at encompassing every element in Israel, including the 'sojourners' (*gērīm*) the non-Israelite population of the land. According to the Chronicler's portrayal, there are no Gentiles in the land of Israel; all its dwellers are 'Israel', either through their affiliation with the tribes, or as the attached 'sojourners'.

The same broad concept applies to the Chronicler's view of the land and to the relationship of 'land' and 'people'. The borders of the land are presented as 'from the Shihor of Egypt to the entrance of Hamath' (I Chron. 13.5), a definition which exceeds the known borders of any actual historical period, and the people are viewed as actually settled in these broadest borders from the beginning of their history. The Chronicler presents a picture of undisturbed continuity of settlement stretching from 'the children of Israel', that is, the sons of Jacob, to the time of David's reign, when already in their earliest days the people are settled throughout their broadest territorial reaches (I Chron. 13.1–5). The period between Jacob's sons and David, which according to the conventional picture of Israel's history includes the sojourn in Egypt, the exodus, the wandering in the wilderness, the conquest, and the unstable period of the judges, is not included in the Chronicler's historical portrayal, but is rather 'bridged upon'. The undisturbed continuity of settlement is also expressed in the Chronicler's attitude towards the issues of 'destruction' and 'exile'. The scope and significance of these phenomena are reduced by cutting down the scope of the description and limiting the dimensions of the destruction. The Chronicler thus expresses a common historiographical concept which regards the original 'sojourn and exodus' and 'exile and restoration' as analogous phenomena, an analogy pronounced by the prophets and embodied in the understanding of the historical process in Ezra–Nehemiah (cf. Japhet, 'The Temple of the Restoration – Reality and Ideology', *USQR* 43, 1991, 213–14). The direction of this analogy, however, is in opposition to these earlier expressions. Rather than glorifying these events, both the exodus from Egypt and the destruction of the kingdom are muted; severance from the land, whether in the beginning of Israel's history or in its later phase, is reduced to the minimum. The tie with the land is an undisturbed continuity, and like the tie between the people and their God, is described as existing in its own right, without the need of assurances, explanations, or reasons.

The history of Israel also reflects their social and political existence, in which the most prominent feature is the institution of kingship. For the Chronicler, 'kingship' is a self-evident political order, but since the kingship of Israel is basically the Lord's, in the practical administration of the state 'the kingdom of the Lord' (*mamleket yhwh*, II Chron. 13.8) is entrusted to the hands of David and his dynasty; the Davidic king, chosen by the Lord, sits 'on the throne of the Lord' (I Chron. 29.23). Yet, notwithstanding this exalted status, the Davidic monarchs are conceived of as human in every aspect of their being, as human beings, in their relationship with the people, and in their relationship with God. Of particular interest is a thread of 'democratization' which runs through the Chronicler's portrayal of the people's status *vis à vis* their king; the king's exclusivity is limited through the people's active participation in the state's enterprises.

As for the portrayal of the persons and achievements of the individual kings, a clear distinction is made between David and Solomon on the one hand, and the rest of the Judaean kings on the other. The period of David and Solomon is a unified whole, according to the Chronicler's view, with the creation and consolidation of all the permanent institutions which would thereafter be binding upon the people and their kings; it is the zenith of Israel's virtues and achievements.

In portraying the figures of David and Solomon on the basis of his sources, three major guidelines direct the Chronicler's presentation: 1. the glorification of the king's figure – a feature which has received the greatest attention in the scholarly discussion; 2. a focus on the king's public figure rather than on his private life – a feature which, because of the nature of his sources, is applied more vigorously to David than to Solomon; and 3. a strong emphasis on the Temple, as the central interest of the two kings. David and Solomon appear in Chronicles in a much more positive light than in earlier biblical historiography, in both the political and the religious realms. Yet neither of them can be considered perfect or 'ideal'. Not all the shadows in David's career were in fact omitted: his rejection from building the Temple is justified by the fact that 'he shed blood' (I Chron. 22.7–8; 28.3), and he is twice described as committing a sin: during the transfer of the ark from Kiriath-jearim (I Chron. 15.13), and by undertaking the census (I Chron. 21.1, 3, 8). Solomon, on the other hand, is indeed flawless, and several positive qualities are appended to his figure, such as his personal election, his special relationship with God, and the achievement in his time of 'rest' and 'peace'. On the whole, however, the lustre of his image in Chronicles is tarnished by the fact that in many of his achievements he was anticipated by David, and there is a systematic understating of his wisdom. Neither David nor Solomon, then, is perfect, but they are both the elected kings, chosen by the Lord 'to sit upon the throne of the kingdom of the Lord over Israel' (I Chron. 28.5; also 29.23); their combined reign is the glorious period in the history of Israel.

In portraying the kings of Judah, the Chronicler's method differs from both the Deuteronomistic historian in the book of Kings, and his own procedure in the case of David and Solomon. In contrast to David and Solomon, there is no desire to fashion faultless figures. The kings' sins and transgressions are not omitted and may in fact be augmented. This is the case not only for the kings who are originally described as 'evil', but also for the 'righteous' ones. In comparison with the Deuteronomistic picture, the major difference may be seen in the non-schematic portrayal of the various kings, illustrated in every sphere. The addition of many details regarding the military, economical, political and religious activities of the kings, the description of their inconsistent religious conduct, and the more subtle and varied standards for the appraisal of the kings – all these result in a multi-faceted presentation which avoids simplistic or all-embracing judgments and reflects the Chronicler's sober realism and understanding of human limitations.

In summing up the theological meaning of the Chronicler's historical enterprise, I quote and somewhat rephrase what I have written before (*Ideology*, 515–16):

> Alongside the development of Israel's religion, together with the process of self-understanding, we find a constant process of elevating the past. History ... becomes a compelling standard or norm with eternal validity for the people and its religion. Early in Israel's history, the first historical stages ... were considered formative ... During the Second Commonwealth, this formative period was extended and came to include what might be termed, rather generally, the First Commonwealth – the period whose history, institutions, belief and experiences later generations saw reflected in a biblical corpus of divine origin, inspired by the 'holy spirit'.
>
> However, together with the increasing sanctification of the past by later generations, there developed a gap – which also steadily increased – between their own complex reality and the reality they found described in the Bible. A gap of this sort, the inevitable result of historical development, undermines the stability of both realities. First, early history becomes incomprehensible to the present generation and the norms of the formative period are in fact no longer appropriate to contemporary needs and aspirations. Second, present-day institutions, religious tenets, and ritual observance are severed from their origins and lose their authoritative source of legitimation.
>
> The book of Chronicles represents a powerful effort to bridge this gap. By reformulating Israel's history in its formative period, the Chronicler gives new significance to the two components of Israelite life: the past is explained so that its institutions and religious principles become relevant to the present, and the ways of the present are legitimized anew by being connected to the prime source of authority – the formative period in the people's past.
>
> Thus, Chronicles is a comprehensive expression of the perpetual need to renew and revitalize the religion of Israel. It makes an extremely important attempt to affirm the meaningfulness of contemporary life without severing ties between the present and the sources of the past; in fact, it strengthens the bond between past and present and proclaims the continuity of Israel's faith and history.

I Chronicles

1.1–2.2

1 1 Adam, Seth, Enosh; ² Kenan, Mahalalel, Jared; ³ Enoch, Methuselah, Lamech; ⁴ Noah, Shem, Ham, and Japheth.

5 The sons of Japheth: Gomer, Magog, Madai, Javan, Tubal, Meshech, and Tiras. ⁶ The sons of Gomer: Ashkenaz, Diphath, and Togarmah. ⁷ The sons of Javan: Elishah, Tarshish, Kittim, and Rodanim.

8 The sons of Ham: Cush, Egypt, Put, and Canaan. ⁹ The sons of Cush: Seba, Havilah, Sabta, Raama, and Sabteca. The sons of Raamah: Sheba and Dedan. ¹⁰ Cush was the father of Nimrod; he began to be a mighty one in the earth.

11 Egypt was the father of Ludim, Anamim, Lehabim, Naphtuhim, ¹² Pathrusim, Casluhim (whence came the Philistines), and Caphtorim.

13 Canaan was the father of Sidon his first-born, and Heth, ¹⁴ and the Jebusites, the Amorites, the Girgashites, ¹⁵ the Hivites, the Arkites, the Sinites, ¹⁶ the Arvadites, the Zemarites, and the Hamathites.

17 The sons of Shem: Elam, Asshur, Arpachshad, Lud, Aram, Uz, Hul, Gether, and Meshech. ¹⁸ Arpachshad was the father of Shelah; and Shelah was the father of Eber. ¹⁹ To Eber were born two sons: the name of the one was Peleg (for in his days the earth was divided), and the name of his brother Joktan. ²⁰ Joktan was the father of Almodad, Sheleph, Hazarmaveth, Jerah, ²¹ Hadoram, Uzal, Diklah, ²² Ebal, Abimael, Sheba, ²³ Ophir, Havilah, and Jobab; all these were the sons of Joktan.

24 Shem, Arpachshad, Shelah; ²⁵ Eber, Peleg, Reu; ²⁶ Serug, Nahor, Terah; ²⁷ Abram, that is, Abraham.

28 The sons of Abraham: Isaac and Ishmael. ²⁹ These are their genealogies: the first-born of Ishmael, Nebaioth; and Kedar, Adbeel, Mibsam, ³⁰ Mishma, Dumah, Massa, Hadad, Tema, ³¹ Jetur, Naphish, and Kedemah. These are the sons of Ishmael. ³² The sons of Keturah, Abraham's concubine: she bore Zimran, Jokshan, Medan, Midian, Ishbak, and Shuah. The sons of Jokshan: Sheba and Dedan. ³³ The sons of Midian: Ephah, Epher, Hanoch, Abida, and Eldaah. All these were the descendants of Keturah.

34 Abraham was the father of Isaac. The sons of Isaac: Esau and Israel. ³⁵ The sons of Esau: Eliphaz, Reuel, Jeush, Jalam, and Korah. ³⁶ The sons of Eliphaz: Teman, Omar, Zephi, Gatam, Kenaz, Timna, and Amalek. ³⁷ The sons of Reuel: Nahath, Zerah, Shammah, and Mizzah.

38 The sons of Seir: Lotan, Shobal, Zibeon, Anah, Dishon, Ezer, and Dishan. ³⁹ The sons of Lotan: Hori and Homam; and Lotan's sister was Timna. ⁴⁰ The sons of Shobal: Alian, Manahath, Ebal, Shephi, and Onam. The sons of Zibeon: Aiah and Anah. ⁴¹ The sons of Anah: Dishon. The sons of Dishon: Hamran, Eshban, Ithran, and Cheran. ⁴² The sons of Ezer: Bilhan, Zaavan, and Jaakan. The sons of Dishan: Uz and Aran.

43 These are the kings who reigned in the land of Edom before any king reigned over the Israelites: Bela the son of Beor, the name of whose city was Dinhabah. ⁴⁴ When Bela died, Jobab the son of Zerah of Bozrah reigned in his stead. ⁴⁵ When

Jobab died, Husham of the land of the Temanites reigned in his stead. [46] When Husham died, Hadad the son of Bedad, who defeated Midian in the country of Moab, reigned in his stead; and the name of his city was Avith. [47] When Hadad died, Samlah of Masrekah reigned in his stead. [48] When Samlah died, Shaul of Rehoboth on the Euphrates reigned in his stead. [49] When Shaul died, Baal-hanan, the son of Achbor, reigned in his stead. [50] When Baal-hanan died, Hadad reigned in his stead; and the name of his city was Pai, and his wife's name Mehetabel the daughter of Matred, the daughter of Mezahab. [51] And Hadad died.

The chiefs of Edom were: chiefs Timna, Aliah, Jetheth, [52] Oholibamah, Elah, Pinon, [53] Kenaz, Teman, Mibzar, [54] Magdi-el, and Iram; these are the chiefs of Edom.

2 1 These are the sons of Israel: Reuben, Simeon, Levi, Judah, Issachar, Zebulun, [2] Dan, Joseph, Benjamin, Naphtali, Gad, and Asher.

A. Notes to MT

[4] נח, LXX adds בני נח, cf. commentary; [6] דיפת, Gen. 10.3 ריפת, cf. commentary; [7] ותרשישה, Gen. 10.4 ותרשיש; ורודנים, Gen. 10.4 ודדנים; [12] ואת כפתרים: these words are already misplaced in Genesis 10; [17] וארם, add ובני ארם?, cf. commentary; ומשך, Gen. 10.23 ומש; [41b] דישון, Gen. 36.26 דישן; [50] הדד, Gen. 36.39 הדר; [2.2] דן, transfer after בנימן, cf. commentary.

B. Notes to RSV

[8] 'Egypt', MT מצרים (Mizraim, so NEB and JPS); [10, 11, etc.] note that the parallel texts in Genesis are differently translated; [33] 'these were', cf. v. 54, 'these are'; [44] '*When* Bela died, Jobab … reigned', Gen. 36: 'Bela died *and* Jobab reigned', the same difference up to v. 50; [48] 'Rehoboth on the Euphrates', MT 'Rehoboth on the River' (so NEB and JPS); [51] 'And Hadad died', better: 'When Hadad died …' (cf. above); 'chiefs Timna, Aliah, Jetheth, etc.', MT 'chief Timna, chief Aliah, chief Jetheth, etc.'

C. Structure, sources and form

1. In the framework of I Chron. 1–9, the Chronistic representation of the entire history of Israel prior to David (or to the death of Saul), I Chron. 1 represents the book of Genesis, from which all its material is taken.

The selection of passages from Genesis follows clear principles: the source used is the 'genealogical blocks' of Gen. 5.10–11; 25; 35–36; the recording of the material adheres as closely as possible to the original order, and its adaptation conforms to strict rules and methods. The Chronicler seems to have combed the book of Genesis for its genealogical material, from which he systematically borrowed. Genealogical lists and information found in Genesis outside the main genealogical blocks are thus not included in Chronicles: the sons of Cain (Gen. 4.17–22), the sons of Nahor (Gen. 22.20–24), and the offspring of Lot's daughters (Gen. 19.37–38).

2. Regarding the material which *is* incorporated, the Chronicler deviates from Genesis at several points:

(*a*) In summarizing Genesis 11, he names the 'descendants of Shem' down to Abram (Gen. 11.26). Then, by means of an explanatory note, 'Abram, that is, Abraham' (v. 27), the Chronicler moves directly to Gen. 17, where the change of Abram's name is recorded. He then proceeds with Abraham's sons, omitting the list of his brothers and the descendants of Terah (Gen. 11.26b–32).

(*b*) In two cases, the order of the material is reversed, in accordance with the new context. In Gen. 25 the sons of Keturah (vv. 1–4) precede the descendants of Ishmael (vv. 13ff.); in Chronicles this order is reversed. In the same way in Genesis the sons of Jacob (35.23–26) are recorded before the genealogy of the descendants of Esau (ch. 36). In Chronicles this order is reversed; the genealogical introduction culminates rather with the sons of Israel, as the focal point of the Chronicler's interest.

(*c*) The material from Genesis is much distilled and abridged. Headings, conclusions, territorial references, narrative passages, etc. are all omitted, as are the especially repetitious formulas of Gen. 5 and 10. Only the bare genealogical information, relevant to each context, is retained.

3. The only additions made by the Chronicler to the Genesis material are in two short verses: v. 27, which forms the concluding and transitional verse between the first section of the chapter and the second (cf. also below p. 60), and the words: 'and Hadad died' (v. 51), which is a connecting element of historiographical significance in the Edomite list. Of the Genesis material which is not strictly genealogical, three notes remain: (*a*) v. 10, 'he began to be a mighty man in the earth', which is a greatly condensed form of the story of Nimrod; (*b*) v. 12, 'whence came the Philistines'; (*c*) v. 19, 'for in his days the earth was divided'. Certain elaboration is retained only in the list of the kings of Edom, a fact accounted for by the general objectives of the genealogical introduction.

4. Chapter 1 is composed of three parts, clearly distinguishable by content and formal elements.

(*a*) 1–27 From Adam to Abraham
(*b*) 28–34a The descendants of Abraham
(*c*) 34b–2.2 The descendants of Isaac.

As we shall see below, the first part is an *inclusio*: a portrait of the post-diluvian world, framed by an introduction (vv. 1–4) and a conclusion (vv. 24–27). The other two parts open with headings, both of which follow the same form: 'The sons of Abraham: Isaac and Ishmael' (v. 28), 'The sons of Isaac: Esau and Israel' (v. 34b). The second part concludes with 'Abraham was the father of Isaac' (JPS 'Abraham begot Isaac', v.34a), while after the third part comes the opening of a new section presenting the sons of Israel (Jacob, 2.3ff.) In all this, Chronicles follows the content, order and structure of Genesis. The first part is based on Gen. 5 and 10–11, the second on Gen. 25, and the third on Gen. 35–36. The measure of this dependance can be demonstrated by the difference between v. 28 and v. 34b. In the first instance, the younger son is mentioned first: Isaac and then Ishmael; in the second it is the elder who precedes the younger: Esau and then Israel. This is accounted for entirely by reference to the material in Genesis: Gen. 25.9 and 35.29 respectively.

A single method is followed in the recording of the lists themselves: these genealogies record first of all the many figures whose histories will *not* be told and of whom no further mention will be made. By this 'concentric' process, the peripheral elements are dealt with first, to form the background upon which the main genealogical line may be developed. Thus, among the sons of Abraham, details are first given concerning the sons of Ishmael and Keturah and only then are Isaac's descendants recorded. Among the sons of Isaac it is to Esau's descendants that attention is first given. As the record approaches more closely 'the sons of Israel' (2.1), it becomes progressively more detailed, and the main genealogical line receives full treatment in chs. 2–9.

Another feature common to parts 2 and 3 is the inclusion in the list of elements not referred to in the heading: the sons of Keturah in the second section, the sons of Se'ir in the third.

5. The first section, vv. 1–27, is itself composed of three parts:

(a) 1–4 The generations of the world from the creation to the flood
(b) 5–23 An ethnic portrait of the world after the flood
(c) 24–27 The generations from Shem to Abraham.

This section is thus an *inclusio*: a framework enclosing a central passage. The framework is to be found in the two short passages (a) and (c), identical in form and composition, based on Gen. 5 and 11.10–26; these passages summarize human genealogy from Adam to Abraham. Set within this frame is a portrayal of the world, (b), adopted from Gen. 10 and describing the expansion of the descendants of Noah after the flood. The arrangement of this *inclusio* reveals the following internal structure: v. 4b forms the connecting link between the components; the names of Noah's sons, Shem, Ham and Japheth, appear in Genesis at the end of the first source (Gen. 5.32), and at the beginning of the second (Gen. 10.1). Following the example of Genesis, Chronicles names them as Shem, Ham and Japheth (v. 4), and then lists the descendants of each in reverse order: Japheth (vv. 5–7), Ham (vv. 8–16), and Shem (vv. 17–23). The concluding section (vv. 24–27) then opens with the last name, Shem (following Gen. 11).

6. The second part of the chapter also displays a clear inner structure:

(a) 28 Heading
(b) 29–31 The sons of Ishmael
(c) 32–33b The sons of Keturah
(d) 34a Conclusion.

Verse 28 introduces the two sons of Abraham, 'Isaac and Ishmael', in that order, as in Gen. 25.9. Details concerning the sons of Ishmael follow, according to the genealogy of Gen. 25.12ff. The citation from Genesis 25 is abridged: the introductory and concluding verses (12–13a, 16aα–18) are omitted, leaving only a bare list of names, beginning with 'The first-born of Ishmael' and concluding with 'these are the sons of Ishmael'. The following verses, following Gen. 25.1–4, record the sons of Keturah, although these were not included in the heading of v. 28. This is fully accounted for by the situation in the Genesis source; the same system is repeated for the record of the sons of Esau, into which the sons of Se'ir are introduced (v. 38), without being referred to in the heading of v. 34. Here, the descendants of Keturah are introduced with a rephrasing of Gen. 25.1; the list, which from the outset contained only names, is almost complete (v. 3b is missing, cf. the commentary); its summary, 'these were the descendants of Keturah' (v. 33b), follows Gen. 25.34. Finally the concluding reminder of v. 34a, 'Abraham was the father of Isaac', based on Gen. 25.19, refers back to the one son whose descendants have not been enumerated. The sons of Isaac will now be given special attention.

7. The last passage (vv. 34–2.2) is devoted to the descendants of Isaac. The structure is similar to that of the previous section:

(a) 34b Introduction
(b) 35–54 The sons of Esau
(c) 2.1–2 The sons of Israel.

The introduction, parallel to v. 28, names the two sons of Isaac in the order found in Gen. 35.29. The list proceeds directly to the sons of Esau. Their record has three components:

35–37 The sons of Esau
38–42 The sons of Se'ir
43–54 The rulers of Edom: kings (vv. 43–51a) and chiefs (vv. 51b–54).

The passage ends with a skeletal list of Jacob's sons, taken from Gen. 35.23–26.

As I have mentioned above, the unheralded introduction of the sons of Se'ir, not mentioned in v. 34, is accounted for by the arrangement of the material in Gen. 36, which opens with 'These are the descendants of Esau', followed by what is in fact a new list, 'These are the sons of Se'ir the Horite' in v. 20. In this context, the list of the sons of Esau is greatly abridged, to a mere three verses (35–37), and is immediately followed by the sons of Seir.

8. It is quite a common tendency among scholars to attribute the major part of the chapter to late glossators and interpolators. Rudolph, for example, would regard as authentic and original only those elements which further what he regards as the purpose of the chapter: the establishing of a direct linear genealogy from Adam to Israel. He thus views vv. 1–4a, 24–27, 28–31, 34–42 as Chronistic, and the rest as a disorderly array of interpolations, the provenance and aim of which are not clear.

Now the integrity of method and structure displayed by ch. 1 as a whole, and its preservation of the full and exclusive representation of the book of Genesis, would seem difficult to attribute to a chance compilation of accidental glosses. Moreover the purpose of each of the assumed glossators and interpolators remains entirely unaccounted for. Nevertheless, the detailed literary-critical arguments against authenticity should be more carefully scrutinized. They are as follows:

1. Lack of systematic recording: since vv. 1–4a and 24–27 follow a similar method of registration, while vv. 4b–23 deviate from this method, the latter passage is regarded as inauthentic.

2. Repetition: vv. 17–19 anticipate vv. 24–25 and are, therefore, an inauthentic repetition.

3. Incongruities with Chronistic interests and goals: since the Chronicler did not express any interest in Abraham's brothers, we should not expect him to do so in the case of Noah's descendants. Therefore vv. 4b–23 are inauthentic. And since one cannot find any reason for the inclusion of the list of the kings and chiefs of Edom, these lists too are inauthentic. The same would be said for the list of the sons of Keturah, which strikes the reader as unexpected.

There seems no need to elaborate on the refutation of these arguments; their subjective and prejudiced nature is so obvious that it is not clear which came first – the determination of the supposed purpose of the chapter or its literary analysis. I have amply demonstrated above that the material as it stands exhibits the Chronicler's literary-redactive methods and attests his theological goals, while all the 'inconsistencies', both formal and theological, are fully accounted for by the strict adherence of the chapter to its source in Genesis. Verses 1–4 and 24–27 have a common form because of their dependence on Gen. 5 and 11, which, alone in Genesis, share a common pattern. Verses 17–19 are repeated somewhat in vv. 24–25 because this is also the situation in Genesis 10 and 11, from which these passages were respectively drawn, the order of the original material kept also in Chronicles. From a formal point of view it should be realized that in genealogies variety is the rule, rather than the exception; all the more so in Chronicles, where it is fully accounted for by the sources.

As for theological points, the purpose of vv. 4b–23 in this context is irrefutably obvious: it is to provide an ethnic backdrop of the 'seventy nations' of the world against which the history of Israel is about to be described. It is a coherent part of the plan, both of the chapter and the book. As for the list of Edomite kings – this too sits in with the Chronicler's aims, as will be duly pointed out below.

The integrity of the genealogical material, reworking and summarizing the sources in Genesis, yet all the while maintaining the original data and order, is itself the purpose of this chapter. Its aim is to delineate human history as the stage for the enacting of the history of Israel. It also expresses a unique concept of the election of Israel (cf. Japhet, *Ideology*, 116–24) as beginning with Adam.

D. Commentary

[1–4] The list contains thirteen names: ten generations from Adam to Noah and the three sons of Noah. From the source in Gen. 5, the names alone have been reproduced, arranged in sequence, with no hint of the connection or relationship between them.

[4] This presents an exegetical problem. Instead of an enumeration of consecutive generations, the three sons of Noah are recorded in a similar form. To judge by the method of the list, one might assume that Ham and Japheth are the sons, rather than the brothers, of Shem. In LXX there is an addition in the verse, 'the sons of Noah', thus resolving the difficulty. Some scholars accordingly accept the words *bᵉnē nōaḥ* as part of the original text; they might easily have been omitted by parablepsis (e.g. Rudolph, 6; Williamson, 42). Consequently these scholars tend also to see the conclusion of the first list in vv. 3–4a: 'Enoch, Methushelah, Lamech, Noah' (so NEB). 'The sons of Noah' would then be the opening of the second list. Although this interpretation is possible, one can also account for the text as it stands. Genesis 5 in fact names 'Shem, Ham and Japheth' at the conclusion of the 'book of the generations of Adam'. In this context in Chronicles, the inclusion of these names in their present position serves to define the first list as a concise genealogy of humankind from creation to the flood. There follows, in

the next list, a portrayal of the world after the flood, described through the proliferation of the descendants of Shem, Ham and Japheth. In this case, LXX's addition of 'the sons of Noah' would be an interpretative gloss.

[5–23] This section is devoted to the descendants of Noah's three sons, and its inner structure is defined by the fixed formulas heading each of the respective parts: 'the sons of Japheth' (v. 5), 'the sons of Ham' (v. 8), 'the sons of Shem' (v. 17). Note that the order of the names is the reverse of v. 4b, thus reflecting the source of the section in Genesis 10. That this reversed order is an indication of the relative importance of the three lines is confirmed by the actual textual scope of each unit. Least important are the sons of Japheth, comprising a relatively small number of peoples, recorded as laconically as possible. Next are the Hamites, to whom the greatest part of the list is devoted, with additional details provided for each of the four Hamite families (excepting Put). Last and most important is Shem, and although the record of his line in this list is not the longest, it is in fact only a preface to the full genealogy, continued in Genesis 11 and, here, in v. 24.

[5–7] The list of the sons of Japheth follows faithfully the record in Genesis (10.2–4), except for the omission of the concluding note in v. 5. This adherence is so pedantic that even the appearance of the conjunctive *waw* (and its absence before *kittīm*) is strictly reproduced. On the other hand, there are small variations *vis à vis* the Genesis source in three of the names, changes to be attributed no doubt to scribal activity: Diphath (v. 6, Gen. Riphath), Tarshishah (v. 7; RSV adapts to the form in Genesis, Tarshish); and Rodanim (v. 7, Gen. Dodanim).

A general remark regarding these variations would be appropriate. In the whole of ch. 1 there are over thirty cases of name variations, all of which seem to be of scribal origin. For the most part they reflect changes in script (defective versus *plene* and final *he* versus final *alef*), interchanges of letters (mostly *yod* and *waw* and *resh* and *dalet*), and metathesis. These variants are augmented by the evidence of the MSS and the ancient Versions, which may reflect the version of Chronicles in Genesis, or *vice versa*, and at times reflect a different reading entirely. Although the orthographic development of these variations can be easily traced, it is not always certain what form the names originally bore. The appearance of the name in another context can serve as a guideline, but many of the names are unique, and no clear-cut decision can be made concerning them.

The form Tarshishah was probably introduced by analogy to the preceding Elishah. However, it should be mentioned that several names appear in Chronicles with a final *he* which has lost its locative connotation (thus Timnathah, Ephrathah, Ba'alathah, etc.).

For the historical-geographical identification of the various names and the actual historical-geographical context portrayed by this list, I refer the reader

to the thorough discussions in the commentaries on Genesis. This is because
the material as a whole is taken from Genesis without change or adaptation,
and such geographical and historical considerations are not integral to or
derived from the actual context of Chronicles (of also E. Lipiński. 'Les
Japhetites selon Gen 10.2–4 et 1 Chr 1.5–7', *ZAH* 3, 1990, 40–53).

A numerical structure is evident in the passage: seven sons of Japheth, for
two of whom (Gomer and Javan) the third generation is recorded. Here again
seven names appear: three sons of Gomer and four of Javan.

[8–16] Much more detail is provided for the Hamite families. For three of
the four sons (with the exception of Put), genealogies are cited to the third
generation, and in one case (Cush) to the fourth. The descendants of Cush,
including this fourth generation, are also seven, as are the descendants of
Mizraim (RSV 'Egypt'). The Canaanites, together with their father Canaan,
are twelve.

[9–10] In Gen. 10.7–12, the section on the sons of Cush contains two
distinct literary elements: a list of the descendants of Cush, similar to the
other sections of this pericope (v. 7), and a narrative passage (vv. 8–12)
relating the exploits of one individual, Nimrod the son of Cush, whose name
is not included in the preceding list. These elements are usually assigned to
two sources, P and J respectively. While this chapter in Chronicles preserves
the two elements, its version of the Nimrod narrative is limited to a very short
and slightly rephrased passage: '... he began to be a mighty one in the earth'.

Two points should be made regarding the sons of Cush. In contrast to the
general variety in the forms of the names throughout the genealogies, those of
the Cushites are markedly similar to each other: Seba and Sheba on one hand,
Seba, Sabta and Sabteca on the other. Furthermore, the names Sheba and
Dedan are also referred to the descendants of Abraham's concubine Keturah
(v. 32), and Sheba appears again, paired with Havilah, among the offspring of
Shem (vv. 22, 23). This repetition of identical names, in different genealogical contexts, is characteristic of these lists, and probably reflects ethnic
circumstances and developments (cf. especially the list of sons of Seir,
vv. 38ff.).

[11–12] Mizraim (RSV: Egypt) also has seven sons; the form of their
names is not proper but gentilic: *lūdīm*, *ᶜ°nāmīm* (Ludians, Anamians, etc.), a
point not clearly reflected in RSV. The gentilic form is of course the furthest
removed from a proper name, and is the best indication of the 'literary
fiction' of these genealogies. Gentilic names in the plural are restricted in this
list to the sons of Mizraim and to two sons of Javan: Kittim and Rodanim
(v. 7). The singular form (not preserved in RSV) is characteristic of the sons
of Canaan (vv. 14–16). All this variety of usage is found in Genesis 10 and
reproduced here unchanged.

The names of the sons of Mizraim follow three patterns: Ludians are a

class by themselves, then Anamians and Lehavians (*'^anāmīm, l^ehābīm*) are
similarly formed, and the last four names also follow one pattern: Naph-
tuhians, Kasluhians, etc. This conformity may point to the linguistic common origin of the names, although their present form is adapted to Hebrew
phonology.

The words 'and Caphtorim' in v. 12 seem to be misplaced; they must have
stood originally after 'Casluhim' and before the note 'whence come the
Philistines'. This would accord with the biblical tradition indicating Caphtor
as the origin of the Philistines (Amos 9.7); the whole genealogical passage
thus acquires a certain note of familiarity. Since, however, these words were
already misplaced in the Chronicler's source (Gen. 10.14), they should not be
amended.

[13–16] The list of the sons of Canaan is taken from Gen. 10.15–18a,
omitting vv. 18b–19 (the territorial expansion of the Canaanites), and v. 20
(a conclusion of the Hamites genealogy, parallel to that for the Japhethites
in 10.5, also omitted in Chronicles). Except for Sidon and Heth, the names
are in the singular gentilic form: 'the Jebusite, the Emorite, etc.' This list
contains the most comprehensive enumeration of the Canaanite peoples, who
together with Canaan himself number twelve, probably paralleling the
twelve sons of Israel (Pseudo-Rashi, Kimhi). Six of the names (Canaan,
Heth, Jebusite, Amorite, Girgashite and Hivite) are common to the list of the
'seven nations' (Deut. 7.1 etc.), five of these (with the exception of the
'Hivite') also belong to the list of the ten peoples in Gen. 15.19–20. The other
six peoples, all probably situated in the north of Israel, are peculiar to this list.

[17–23] The list of the sons of Shem is taken from Gen. 10.22–29; omitted
from Chronicles are the introduction (v. 21), the territorial expansion of the
Shemites (v. 30), the conclusion of the list (v. 31) and the final closing of the
pericope (v. 32) – in strict adherence to the principles of redaction demonstrated above.

The list comprises two parts: v. 17 names the sons of Shem, while vv. 18–
23 continue a single branch, that of Shem's third son Arpachshad. After
listing four generations in direct descent, to Eber and his two sons (Peleg and
Yoktan), a list is given of the sons of Yoktan. It is clear that a tribal federation
tracing its origin to Yoktan was attached to a linear genealogy beginning with
Shem.

[17] The list of Shem's descendants numbers ten names (including Shem
himself), and differs from its source in Gen. 10.22–23 on two counts: in
vv. 17 the words *b^enē '^arām* are omitted and subsequently a *waw* is added to
'Uz'. In Genesis, the first five names in the list identify the sons of Shem,
concluding with Aram; the next four are the sons of Aram. Here, all nine are
presented as the sons of Shem. The missing words 'the sons of Aram' are
found in LXX and viewed by many commentators as original (cf. BH). While

this omission can easily be explained by parablepsis, it could also result from a different view of the Aramaean peoples as directly descended from Shem.

The second difference is in the name Meshech, in Gen. 10.23 Mash. Commentators tend to take Mash as the original, viewing Meshech as an adaptation to v. 5. However, LXX reads *Mosoch* in Genesis, reflecting the Hebrew Meshech. We have already seen that multiple instances of certain names are attested many times in the lists, cf. Sheba (vv. 9, 22, 32), Dedan (vv. 9, 32), Ebal (vv. 22, 40) and more. It is therefore hard to determine what the original reading was.

[18–23] The genealogy of Arpachshad records four generations through the firstborn, but in the end focusses on the second son of Peleg – Yoktan. The genealogical line is parallel to Gen. 11.12ff. and in this chapter vv. 24–25a. It is possible that originally a linear genealogical record like that in Genesis served as a root on to which the 'sons of Yoktan' – a federation of Arab tribes from south Arabia – were grafted. Both of these elements were found in Gen. 10.24–30 and taken over by the Chronicler, who omitted the information about territorial expansion (v. 30) and the concluding formulas (vv. 31, 32).

[24–27] These verses parallel the opening list of the chapter (vv. 1–4), are drawn from a parallel source (Gen. 11.10–26a), and are similarly reworked. From his source the Chronicler drew only an unadorned series of names, with no indication of the relationship between them. The ten names in the list conclude with Abram. The Chronicler's additional remark 'that is Abraham' moves us from Gen. 11.26 to the changing of the patriarch's name in Gen. 17, thus omitting the genealogical data at the end of Gen. 11. This remark, however, constitutes more than a literary device. It marks the change from the 'Abram' of the extant genealogical lists to 'Abraham' – the forefather of the Israelites. In this respect one should note the difference in the Chronicler's treatment of Abraham and Jacob. Both were renamed by God as an act of special grace and symbolic blessing. However, while Abraham's original name is still cited and the change noted, Jacob is always called 'Israel' throughout Chronicles (with the exception of I Chron. 16.13, 17, where, in a passage quoted from Ps. 105, 'Jacob' is twice retained in parallelism to 'Israel'. Note also that in v. 13 'Israel' replaces 'Abraham' – a Chronistic touch ignored by RSV). In this chapter, Jacob is already called 'Israel' in v. 34, which in its original context (Gen. 35.29) has 'Jacob'. Among other things, this difference in treatment attests the superior significance of Israel, the actual father of the tribes, over Abraham, their more distant ancestor.

[28–34a] The introduction of the sons of Abraham in v. 28 is followed by the sons of Ishmael (vv. 29–31), the descendants of Keturah (vv. 32–33) and the reference to Isaac (v. 34a).

[28] This genealogical key-phrase, 'the sons of x', conforms to a common

made to the sons of Dedan. By means of these two slight changes, the list in Chronicles gains in uniformity. In Gen. 25, the offspring of two of Keturah's six sons are recorded: two generations of Jokshan's descendants and one of Midian's. Further, the sons of Jokshan are distinguished from the others by the narrative quality of their presentation. Just as these irregularities are missing in Chronicles, so the omission of the sons of Dedan, mentioned in Gen 25.3b, may not be a scribal corruption but the result of redaction.

The conclusion in v. 33b, 'all these were the descendants of Keturah', is taken from Gen 25.4b and parallels v. 31b above.

[34a] The phrase 'Abraham was the father of Isaac' is in fact the conclusion of the section concerning Abraham's sons, and prepares us for the 'genealogies' of Isaac which will follow in the next passsage. These words are based on Gen. 25.19, which parallels Gen. 25.12. In the Genesis context they open the history of Isaac; here they conclude the genealogy of Abraham.

[34b] The heading 'the sons of Isaac ...' opens a new section, similar in length to the first part of the chapter (vv. 1–27). In accordance with the method of the chapter, the passage refers in detail only to the descendants of Esau, while 'the sons of Israel' will be listed in 2.1–2 and treated at length from 2.3 onwards.

Although Esau was the firstborn, the Bible refers to them also as 'Jacob and Esau' (Gen 28.5), and some scholars would restore this order here as well (cf. Curtis, 76). However, the present order is again determined by the Chronicler's source (Gen. 35.29), and should not be altered.

It has already been mentioned that for Jacob the Chronicler uses exclusively the name Israel; in this case he deviates from his source in so doing. The significance of 'Jacob-Israel' as the father of the people who bear his name is thus emphasized.

[35–37] This list is a concise summary of Gen. 36.9–14, where Esau's sons are recorded according to their mothers: first Eliphaz, from Esau's first wife (36.10a), and Reuel, from his second wife (v. 10b), then the descendants of Eliphaz and Reuel, summarized in relation to their mothers (vv. 11–13), and finally the sons of Esau from his third wife (36.14). This emphasis on the mothers, a characteristic feature in the Genesis source, also recurring in the list of the 'chiefs' (36.15–19), is by contrast completely ignored in Chronicles. Here the sons' names are rearranged according to the order of their birth: the first generation of Esau's sons from all three wives (who are not named – v. 35), followed by the next generation: the sons of Eliphaz (v. 36) and Reuel (v. 37). The details of the list follow strictly the material found in Gen. 36.

Materially speaking, this new arrangement results in one major difference. In Gen. 36, after the enumeration of Eliphaz' five sons from his unnamed wife (v. 11), there is a short paragraph referring to his concubine 'Timna' and pattern (cf. above, vv. 5, 6, 7, 8, etc.). It is not found as it stands in Genes. but is forged by the Chronicler as a heading for the present passage – a fac. which clearly indicates his structural concepts. However, the presentation of 'Isaac and Ishmael' together and in that order as Abraham's sons is found in Genesis in the chapter which serves as source for the whole passage (25.8–9): 'Abraham ... died ... Isaac and Ishmael his sons buried him'. In the same way, Gen. 35.29 is the source of v. 34b, the heading of the next passage.

[29–31] The list of Ishmael's sons is drawn from Gen. 25.13–18 and the introductory formula 'These are their genealogies' (*'ēlleh tōlʿdōtam*) is an abridgment of the introduction in Genesis: *wᵉʾēlleh tōlʿdōt yišmāʿēʾl ... lᵉtōlʿdōtām* (vv. 12–13a). In the context of Chronicles these words may seem to refer to both Isaac and Ishmael, but the continuation shows that they more probably form a transition to the 'sons of Ishmael', as is made explicit only at the conclusion (v. 31b).

The list follows accurately Gen. 25.13b–16a, concluding with 'these are the sons of Ishmael'. The references to Ishmael's death and to Ishmaelite organization and territorial expansion are omitted (vv. 16a–18).

[32–33] In Gen. 25 the list of the descendants of Keturah precedes the sons of Ishmael, the logic of the sequence determined by the 'genealogies' (*tōlʿdōt*) of Genesis: first the sons of Abraham himself (in this case, by his concubine Keturah), then the offspring of his sons: Ishmael (25.12–18) and Isaac (25. 19ff.). The Chronicler, however, creates a different structure, in accordance with his specific goals. All of Abraham's descendants are recorded together, in an order determined by the source material and the specific structure of the pericope. Following the heading of v. 28 the sons of Ishmael are recorded first; since Isaac and his offspring are to be dealt with in detail at the conclusion of the genealogy, the sons of Keturah must be mentioned in the middle.

A certain syntactical difficulty is raised at the beginning of v. 32: the phrase *ubᵉnē qᵉṭūrāh pīlegeš 'abrāhām yālᵉdāh 'et* ('The sons of Keturah Abraham's concubine bore ...', RSV 'she bore') seems to result from the conflation of two parallel clauses: 'The sons of Keturah ...' and 'Keturah bore ...'. Indeed, following the Peshitta, Ehrlich would regard the words *yālᵉdāh 'et* as redundant (*Randglossen* VII, 326). However, the peculiar specific syntax can again be explained by the fact that this verse is actually a rephrasing of Gen. 25.1–2, with the change of 'wife' to 'concubine', following Gen. 25.6.

From the list in Gen. 25.2–4 the Chronicler omits all the accusative particles (*'et*), and combines the names by means of *waw* conjunctive. There are further variations as well: in place of the narrative style of Gen. 25.3 ('Jokshan was the father of ... The sons of Dedan were ...'), the Chronicler has recourse to the more formal pattern 'the sons of Jokshan'; no reference is

Amalek her son (v. 12). This concubine is mentioned later (v. 22) as the sister of Lotan the Horite, no doubt a reflection of the ethnic connections between 'Esau (that is Edom)' and 'the sons of Seir ... the inhabitants of the land'. In the list in Chronicles, Timna and Amalek are listed in one breath as Eliphaz' children, and Timna's status is changed from concubine to offspring, evidently a son. The change could result from one of three factors: a different understanding of the ethnic context of Esau, reflected here in genealogical terms; a stylistic distillation of the material, disregarding and thus altering some of the details; or a scribal corruption. The latter could result from a misreading of Gen. 36.11–12 and an attaching of the name Timna to the preceding list: *wayyihyū b^enē '^elipāz ... ūq^enaz w^etimna'*. Such a reading would append Amalek, Eliphaz' son by an unnamed concubine, to the end of the list in Chronicles (thus Curtis, 76).

[38–42] In Genesis the list of 'the sons of Seir the Horite' (Gen. 36.20–28) is extremely orderly and thorough. It first enumerates the seven sons of Seir (vv. 20–21) who are identified as the 'the chiefs of the Horites' (v. 21b), and then proceeds systematically to record the descendants of each, also including women: Timna, 'Lotan's sister' (v. 22), and Oholibamah, 'the daughter of Anah' (v. 25), earlier referred to as the third wife of Esau (v. 18). The section also includes a narrative note (v. 24).

The Chronicler cites this material concisely, omitting all unnecessary details: headings (v. 20), the related list of 'chiefs' (vv. 29–30), the narrative note concerning Anah, and the reference to Oholibamah. Thus, only a bare framework of names and their family relationship is retained.

Regarding the details, the list may seem confused at first glance because of the similarity between Seir's fifth son 'Dishon' and his seventh son 'Dishan', the further recurrence of the name 'Dishon' as a son of Anah (v. 41), and the repetition of the name 'Anah', first as Seir's son (v. 38), then as his grandson through Zibeon (v. 40b). When all these elements are sorted out, the regularity of the list becomes apparent.

As elsewhere in the chapter, there are several variations in the names, stemming from the interchanges of *waw* and *yod* (Homam – Heman, etc.), of *resh* and *daleth* (Hamran – Hamdan, etc.), *mem* and *nun* (Homam – Heman) etc., all due to the interchange of letters in the process of transmission or to different pronunciations of the names in various periods. The original forms of the names cannot, in most cases, be determined.

[43–54] The passage referring to the rulers of Edom, their kings (vv. 43–50) and chiefs (vv. 51b–54), taken from Gen 36.31–43, is unique in the present context in several ways:

1. In contrast to all the other lists in the chapter, the original heading of the passage in Genesis is cited in full: 'These are the kings who reigned in the land of Edom before any king reigned over the Israelites' (v. 43).

2. All the details concerning the rulers of Edom are repeated faithfully, without a significant abbreviation or alteration.

3. In Genesis 36 there are lists of chiefs of Esau (36. 15–19) and of Seir (29–30), attached to their respective genealogical records, and an additional, independent list of (probably twelve) 'chiefs of Esau' (40–43) appended to the 'kings of Edom'. While the first two lists are omitted completely in Chronicles, the last is retained in our passage and undergoes several changes: (*a*) The independent heading 'These are the names of the chiefs of Esau, according to their families and their dwelling places, by their names' (Gen. 36.40a) is omitted in Chronicles; 'the chiefs of Edom' are linked with the passage concerning 'the kings who reigned in ... Edom' by the statement 'when Hadad died, the chiefs of Edom were ...' (v. 51a–b). The list is thus conceived as the continuation of the preceding passage, the heading of which is found in v. 43. (*b*) The conclusion is retained but greatly shortened: 'these are the chiefs of Edom'.

All this testifies to a conscious redactional effort, which should therefore become the key for our understanding of the passage. The historical concept expressed here is that there were two phases in the political history of Edom: in the first, Edom was ruled by kings (eight in all) who established their own capitals and were succeeded one by the other. After the death of Hadad there were no more kings; Edom was ruled by chiefs (of which the list cites eleven), successively or simultaneously. This development should of course be understood in the light of the words 'before any king reigned over the Israelites' in the heading of the passage as a whole (v. 43). The transition from one political order to another is connected with the accession of a king in Israel, who was, according to Chronicles, David, with whom the history of kingship in Israel actually begins. Political circumstances of Edom were thus determined: kings reigning before the accession of David, and chiefs thereafter.

Moreover, as we shall see, the overall purpose of the genealogical introduction of I Chron. 1–9 is to portray the pre-Davidic background from which the history of Israel will unfold. The present passage in fact records the political history of Edom down to the same point: 'before there was a king in Israel'. In accordance with the method followed throughout the chapter, subjects of secondary importance are introduced and dealt with first, before the reader's attention is drawn to the main topic. Thus, the history and genealogy of Jacob's brother are treated here as fully as the state of the sources will allow, and only then do the chronicles of Israel's history proceed.

[43–51a] The passage concerning the kings of Edom follows a relatively fixed pattern: 'X died, Y of Z (place name) reigned in his place'. This formula is observed for four of the Edomite kings: Jobab (v. 44), Husham (v. 45), Samlah (v. 47) and Shaul (v. 48). For each of the other four, there is some deviation: an abbreviation through the omission of the place name (v. 49), a mention of the king's capital rather than his place of origin (vv. 43, 46, 50), and additions, referring in one case to the king's military exploit (v. 46) and in the other to his wife (v. 50). This formal variety is also expressed by the kings' names: four are identified by their proper names alone, while the other four bear a patronym as well. These variations on the basis of a strict formula are already evident in Genesis, and the Chronicler follows suit; this realization should serve as our guide in the study of these lists.

All the Edomite kings bear familiar names, attested elsewhere in the Bible. One should mention, however, the first king, Bela the son of Beor, whose name is so close to the famous 'Balaam the son of Beor' (Num. 22.5, etc.), and the recurrence of the name Hadad (vv. 46, 50, cf especially I Kings 11.14ff.). Of the points of origin, however, only Bazrah is well attested as an Edomite city (Isa. 63.1); all the other names (Dinhabah, Avith, Masrekah, Rehoboth on the River [RSV: Euphrates] and Pai/Pau) are peculiar to this passage.

[50] 'The daughter of Mezahab' is generally regarded as corrupt, and is mostly amended to 'the son of Mezahab' following LXX and P to Gen. 36.39, 'son' (*ben*) having been changed to 'daughter' (*bat*) by analogy to the preceding 'the daughter of Matred'. It can also be regarded as a corruption of 'of Mezahab' (*min mē zāhāb*), by the same analogy (cf. Skinner, *Genesis*, ICC, 1910, 436). Since the corruption is already attested in the Chronicler's source in Genesis (36.39) it should not be altered here (for the historical and geographical background of the list cf. J. R. Bartlett, *Edom and the Edomites*, JSOTS 77, 1989, 94–102).

[51b–54] The list of the chiefs contains eleven names, and it is probable that the original list contained one more. Indeed, many commentators following LXX would restore 'the chief of Sepho' in Gen. 36.43.

Two of the chiefs listed here have already been mentioned in an earlier list (Kenaz and Teman; Gen. 36.15); two others, Oholibamah and Timna, are cited beforehand as women: Timna the concubine of Eliphaz and Oholibamah the third wife of Esau (Gen. 36.12, 18). All the other names do not appear in the preceding Edomite lists and are peculiar to the present context.

[2.1–2] The enumeration of the twelve sons of Israel is both the conclusion of ch. 1 and an introduction to the detailed tribal genealogies of chs. 2–9. The list here is an abbreviated form of Gen. 35.23–26: the names themselves are retained, but all the other details are systematically omitted. In addition, the patriarch Jacob is introduced as 'Israel', in accordance with the Chronicler's views.

The sons are recorded according to their mothers: first the sons of Jacob's principal wives, Leah and Rachel; followed, in a reverse order, by the sons of the concubines, Bilhah and Zilpah. Only Dan deviates from the regular order; while several reasons have been suggested for his unusual position, accidental misplacement in the process of transmission still seems the most plausible.

2 3 The sons of Judah: Er, Onan, and Shelah; these three Bath-shua the Canaanitess bore to him. Now Er, Judah's first-born, was wicked in the sight of the Lord, and he slew him. [4] His daughter-in-law Tamar also bore him Perez and Zerah. Judah had five sons in all.

5 The sons of Perez: Hezron and Hamul. [6] The sons of Zerah: Zimri, Ethan, Heman, Calcol, and Dara, five in all. [7] The sons of Carmi: Achar, the troubler of Israel, who transgressed in the matter of the devoted thing; [8] and Ethan's son was Azariah.

9 The sons of Hezron, that were born to him: Jerahmeel, Ram, and Chelubai. [10] Ram was the father of Amminadab, and Amminadab was the father of Nahshon, prince of the sons of Judah. [11] Nahshon was the father of Salma, Salma of Boaz, [12] Boaz of Obed, Obed of Jesse. [13] Jesse was the father of Eliab his first-born, Abinadab the second, Shimea the third, [14] Nethanel the fourth, Raddai the fifth, [15] Ozem the sixth, David the seventh; [16] and their sisters were Zeruiah and Abigail. The sons of Zeruiah: Abishai, Joab, and Asahel, three. [17] Abigail bore Amasa, and the father of Amasa was Jether the Ishmaelite.

18 Caleb the son of Hezron had children by his wife Azubah, and by Jerioth; and these were her sons: Jesher, Shobab, and Ardon. [19] When Azubah died, Caleb married Ephrath, who bore him Hur. [20] Hur was the father of Uri, and Uri was the father of Bezalel.

21 Afterward Hezron went in to the daughter of Machir the father of Gilead, whom he married when he was sixty years old; and she bore him Segub; [22] and Segub was the father of Jair, who had twenty-three cities in the land of Gilead. [23] But Geshur and Aram took from them Havvothjair, Kenath and its villages, sixty towns. All these were descendants of Machir, the father of Gilead. [24] After the death of Hezron, Caleb went in to Ephrathah, the wife of Hezron his father, and she bore him Ashhur, the father of Tekoa.

25 The sons of Jerahmeel, the first-born of Hezron: Ram, his first-born, Bunah, Oren, Ozem, and Ahijah. [26] Jerahmeel also had another wife, whose name was Atarah; she was the mother of Onam. [27] The sons of Ram, the first-born of Jerahmeel: Maaz, Jamin, and Eker. [28] The sons of Onam: Shammai and Jada. The sons of Shammai: Nadab and Abishur. [29] The name of Abishur's wife was Abihail, and she bore him Ahban and Molid. [30] The sons of Nadab: Seled and Appa-im; and Seled died childless. [31] The sons of Appa-im: Ishi. The sons of Ishi: Sheshan. The sons of Sheshan: Ahlai. [32] The sons of Jada, Shammai's brother: Jether and Jonathan; and Jether died childless. [33] The sons of Jonathan: Peleth and Zaza. These were the descendants of Jerahmeel. [34] Now Sheshan had no sons, only daughters; but Sheshan had an Egyptian slave, whose name was Jarha. [35] So Sheshan gave his daughter in marriage to Jarha his slave; and she bore him Attai. [36] Attai was the father of Nathan and Nathan of Zabad. [37] Zabad was the father of Ephlal, and Ephlal of Obed. [38] Obed was the father of Jehu, and Jehu of Azariah. [39] Azariah was the father of Helez, and

Helez of Ele-asah. [40] Ele-asah was the father of Sismai, and Sismai of Shallum.
[41] Shallum was the father of Jekamiah, and Jekamiah of Elishama.

42 The sons of Caleb the brother of Jerahmeel: Mareshah his first-born, who was
the father of Ziph. The sons of Mareshah: Hebron. [43] The sons of Hebron: Korah,
Tappuah, Rekem, and Shema. [44] Shema was the father of Raham, the father of Jorke-
am; and Rekem was the father of Shammai. [45] The son of Shammai: Maon; and
Maon was the father of Bethzur. [46] Ephah also, Caleb's concubine, bore Haran,
Moza, and Gazez; and Haran was the father of Gazez. [47] The sons of Jahdai: Regem,
Jotham, Geshan, Pelet, Ephah, and Shaaph. [48] Maacah, Caleb's concubine, bore
Sheber and Tirhanah. [49] She also bore Shaaph the father of Madmannah, Sheva the
father of Machbenah and the father of Gibe-a; and the daughter of Caleb was Achsah.
[50] These were the descendants of Caleb.

The sons of Hur the first-born of Ephrathah: Shobal the father of Kiriath-jearim,
[51] Salma, the father of Bethlehem, and Hareph the father of Beth-gader. [52] Shobal
the father of Kiriath-jearim had other sons: Haroeh, half of the Menuhoth. [53] And
the families of Kiriath-jearim: the Ithrites, the Puthites, the Shumathites, and the
Mishra-ites; from these came the Zorathites and the Eshtaolites. [54] The sons of
Salma: Bethlehem, the Netophathites, Atroth-beth-joab, and half of the
Manahathites, the Zorites. [55] The families also of the scribes that dwelt at Jabez: the
Tirathites, the Shime-athites, and the Sucathites. These are the Kenites who came
from Hammath, the father of the house of Rechab.

A. Notes to MT

[6] זמרי, Josh. 7.1: זבדי; דרע, I Kings 5.11 (RSV 4.32) דרדע; [7] ובני, add ובני כרמי. ובני כרמי?
cf. commentary; [10] בני, LXX reads בית; [18] הוליד את עזובה, proposed הוליד מעזובה
את (so RSV), cf. commentary; [24] בכלב, proposed בא כלב (so RSV); אביה ... ואשת,
proposed אשת ... אביהו, cf. commentary; [25] אחיה, LXX אחיהו, proposed מאחיה
(haplography) or ואחיה (so RSV); [42] ובני מרשה, possibly מרשה [מישע] ובני, cf. commentary; [46] גזז (end), proposed יהדי; [48] ילד שבר, probably read שבר [ה את] ילד;
[49] ותלד, proposed ויולד or [X את] שעף or ותלד שעף [את] שעף (RSV); [50] כלב, put the
final accent here (thus RSV); בן, read בני with LXX and V; [52] הראה, probably ראיה,
cf. 4.2; המנחות, probably המנחתי, cf. v. 54; [55] ספרים, proposed ספרים.

B. Notes to RSV

[10–13, 36–41, 44, 46] 'was the father of', MT 'begot' (so JPS), cf. commentary on
v. 21; [42] 'Mareshah' (first), MT 'Mesha'; 'Hebron', MT 'the father of Hebron';
[52] 'Shobal ... had other sons', MT 'Shobal had sons'.

C. Structure, sources and form

Chapters 2.3–4.23 are among the most difficult and interesting chapters of the
genealogical introduction to Chronicles; they have already been given systematical
and thorough treatment by several scholars, most recently in the dissertation of G.

Galil, *The Genealogies of the Tribe of Judah*, Jerusalem 1983*; cf. also H. G. M. Williamson, 'Sources and Redaction in the Chronicler's Genealogy of Judah', *JBL* 98, 1979, 351–9.

1. The overall structure of the chapters is quite obvious:

(*a*) 2.3–55 Genealogies of the tribe of Judah
(*b*) 3.1–24 The house of David
(*c*) 4.1–23 Further genealogies of the tribe of Judah

The treatment of the descendants of Judah is quite simple: the house of David dominates the centre, framed by various genealogies. Thus, while chs. 2–9 intend to portray the entire people of Israel, some aspects receive more emphasis than others. Here, Judah is placed at the beginning, and within the tribe of Judah the house of David has pride of place. The structure thus expresses a theological concept, explicitly stated by David elsewhere: 'The Lord God ... chose Judah as leader, and in the tribe of Judah my father's house, and among my father's sons he took pleasure in me' (I Chron. 28.4).

2. On the basis of the broad pattern outlined above, the question must now be posed of the more detailed structure, sources and interpretation of the pericope. As in I Chron. 1, the questions of 'sources' and 'structure' are interrelated. However, while the first chapter drew all its material from biblical sources, thus making the structure and redactional activity of the chapter relatively easy to comprehend, the picture in 2.3–4.23 is much more complicated. In attempting to clarify this issue it seems best to proceed from the more obvious to the more problematic factors.

Of the source material of these chapters, some has biblical provenance or parallels, while the rest is peculiar to Chronicles. Each of these categories can be further analysed into material which is taken unchanged from its source and material which is reworked and reshaped. This last distinction is possible, at least at first, only for such passages which can be compared with their source. Thus, the whole could be categorized as follows:

A.1 Parts which have accurate biblical sources or parallels:
    I Chron. 2.10–12 (Ruth 4.19b–22a)
    I Chron. 3.1–8 (II Sam. 3.2–5; 5.5, 14–16).
A.2 Parts which are a reworked form of extant biblical material:
    I Chron. 2.3–7 (8?)
    I Chron. 2.13–17
    I Chron. 2.20
    I Chron. 2.49b
    I Chron. 3.9
    I Chron. 3.10–16
B. Parts which have no biblical source or parallel:
    I Chron. 2.9
    I Chron. 2.17–55 (except for vv. 20 and 49b)
    I Chron. 3.18–23
    I Chron. 4.1–23.

Within category B certain blocks of material can be distinguished and categorized.

(*a*) 3.17–21 – a genealogy of the house of David from Jeconiah (Jehoiachin) on.

(*b*) In the large block composed of 2.18–55 and 4.1–23, one may distinguish clearly the traces of a major source with distinct formal features, concepts and methods. This source includes three genealogical sections (2.25–33, 2.42–50a and 2.50b–55 + 4.2–4), each clearly framed by a heading and a conclusion, which are similar in all three cases: 'The sons of X ... These were the sons of X'. The sections record respectively the descendants of Jerahmeel, Caleb and Hur, 'the firstborn of Ephrath'.

Although in the present context the sequence between these passages is interrupted in 2.34 by the addition of a different list, and again in 3.1 by the house of David, they seem originally to have comprised one sequential source; in 2.42 Caleb is in fact explicitly identified as 'the brother of Jerahmeel' (cf. 2.33).

Outside the passages just mentioned, the material having no biblical parallels does not display any obvious coherence; some of it is probably compiled from various sources and some is editorial, as we shall see below.

From this perspective of sources, then, the whole pericope is a sophisticated weave of diverse elements, intertwined and reworked to form a meaningful composition. My innocent assumption, at least until there is convincing reason to think otherwise, is that the Chronicler should be viewed as the author of this composition. His hand, then, may be sought in the reworking of the various biblical and non-biblical material and its integration into the present composition, and in his own editorial additions, if any. Of course, the existence of 'post-Chronistic' elements is not ruled out, but my approach is first to exhaust the exegetical means at our disposal before having recourse to this possibility.

3. The genealogy of Judah follows a line of development which in principle is very similar to the treatment of the material in ch. 1. The 'secondary' genealogical ramifications are recorded in order to present as full and systematic a picture as possible. Soon, however, the material concentrates increasingly on the main line of election, which in the tribe of Judah focusses in the family of Hezron, the son of Perez, to whom the Davidic family traces its origin. A considerable portion of the genealogical material (2.9–4.20) is devoted to the Hezronites.

The main line of the Judahites is seen as developing from Perez and Zerah, Judah's sons by his daughter-in-law, Tamar. Of his other sons, Er and Onan are presented in v. 3 as completely extinct (cf. Gen. 46.12), while Shelah's descendants are relegated to a kind of appendix at the very end of the pericope (4.21–23). Of the main line, Zerah is dispatched with a brief and entirely artificial genealogy in 2.6–8 (cf. below). Even this is more than is provided for one of Perez' two sons, Hamul, who is completely ignored. In this way, after a summary treatment of the different branches of Judah, the genealogy focuses on Hezron, who will occupy the major part of the pericope. The fact that Zerah and Hamul received such different treatment may indicate that the Chronicler made an effort to make use of all the information he could find, but did not make up completely imaginary genealogies.

4. In 2.3–5 we have a short composition, the sources of which are in two biblical passages: Gen. 46.12 and Gen. 38, arranged according to a calculated method. The framework of this unit is taken from Gen. 46.12. Verse 3a is a literal repetition of Gen. 46.12a, 'The sons of Judah: Er, Onan and Shelah', and v. 5 is taken from the conclusion of the same verse, 'The sons of Perez were Hezron and Hamul'. In vv. 3b–4, however, the Chronicler replaces the short note of Gen. 46.12 ('but Er and Onan died in the land of Canaan') by his own composition, a concise but accurate summary

of Gen. 38. Verse 3a is an adequate summary of Gen. 38.1–5; v. 3b is a quotation from Gen. 38.7; and v. 4a is a summary of the rest of the chapter, 38.8–30. Only v. 4b is an addition, not found as it is in the sources, but clearly based on the evidence of the material.

The method of this passage is an outright indication that the Chronicler was not satisfied with the brief note found in Gen. 46.12b but wished to relate more fully the family circumstances of Judah, the father of the tribe (cf. also in the commentary).

5. The artificial nature of 2.6–8 is glaringly evident; this unit is a combination of all the biblical material which concerns, or is thought to concern, the offspring of Zerah:

(a) The first words of v. 6 ('the sons of Zerah, Zimri') and v. 7 reproduce the reference to Zerah in Josh. 7.1.

(b) From the words 'Ethan, Heman ... etc.', v. 6 repeats the reference to the 'Ezrahites' in I Kings 4.31 (MT 5.11), taking them to be 'Zerahites'.

(c) Verse 8 refers to a further branch, for the possible origin of which cf. the commentary.

The overall structure is simple: five sons of Zerah (parallel to the five sons of Judah) in v. 6, followed by a further generation of the first two: Zimri (Zabdi) in v. 7 and Ethan in v. 8.

6. With v. 9 the main genealogical corpus, that of the Hezronites, begins. Here, more than elsewhere in the pericope, one should distinguish between the structure and purpose of the present context and those of the source-material. As it now stands, the genealogy of Hezron intersects the original sequence of the genealogical block already discussed (2.25–33, 42–55; 4.2–4), and an even further intrusion is formed in the middle by the genealogies of the house of David.

The whole genealogy of the Hezronites is composed of two or three main blocks:

(a) 2.9–41 The descendants of Hezron

(b) 2.42–4.7 (with the exclusion of 3.1–4.1) The descendants of Caleb

(c) 4.8–20 Miscellaneous genealogies, the exact affiliation of which is unclear, and which may be viewed as the continuation of the second block.

7. The first block, vv. 9–41, deals with 'the sons of Hezron'. The introduction in v. 9 states the objective and basic presupposition of the genealogy: 'The sons of Hezron that were born to him, Jerahmeel, Ram and Chelubai'. This specific genealogical concept is peculiar to the final editing of this passage and contradicts to some extent the testimony of the original sources (cf. also below). It is the creation of the redactor who created the present structure, i.e. the Chronicler. The order of the various groups which follow the introduction is influenced by the demands of the new structure: vv. 10–17 Ram; vv. 18–24 Caleb; vv. 25–41 Jerahmeel. Each of the sections is composed from different source-material (as demonstrated already above p. 68) and is differently reworked.

8. The passage dedicated to the descendants of Ram has two parts: a genealogical tree leading from Ram to Jesse (vv. 10–12) and Jesse's family (vv. 13–17). The direct genealogical tree is different from all the other genealogies of Judah, the only similar passage being in vv. 36–41, at the conclusion of the Jerahmeelite genealogy. Ordinarily, the genealogies provide a horizontal composition of ethnic/social circum-

stances; here, however, there is a vertical progression from the family forefather Ram to Jesse, the father of David. Consequently, while the other genealogies are composed basically of eponyms, the record of the family of Ram refers to individuals, historical figures known to us from biblical sources, mainly historiography. This difference is highly significant, as we will presently see.

Verses 10–12 are also found, with some variations, in the appendix to Ruth (4.19–22), and this inevitably raises the question of origin. In both contexts the list serves to provide the direct lineage between Judah and David, counting ten generations from Judah to Jesse. While this purpose is central to the present context, in Ruth it comes rather as an 'afterthought'. It seems better to regard Chronicles rather than Ruth as the original context, although this is by no means conclusive; it may be that the list existed independently and was used by both compositions.

The structure and origin of this passage are best understood in the light of its purpose. Biblical sources provide no clear genealogical data confirming David's direct descent from Judah. One does find, interspersed throughout the scriptures, some details about certain individuals of the tribe of Judah. These details are: a genealogy of Judah which descends as far as Hezron and Hamul (Gen. 46.12; Num. 26.19–21); the name of 'Nahshon the son of Amminadab', a leader of the tribe (Num. 1.7; 2.3, etc.), and a genealogy found in Ruth 4.17 relating David to Boaz through Obed and Jesse. It is notable that only in the case of Achan (Josh. 7.1) is a direct descent from Judah (through Zerah) recorded. In the present context, two connecting links have been supplied to bring together these scattered data: on the one hand, Nahshon the son of Amminadab is linked to Hezron by the addition of Ram, who appears elsewhere (2.25, 27) as the son of Jerahmeel, and on the other hand he is related to Boaz by the addition of Salma/Salmon, known otherwise as 'the father of Bethlehem' (2.51). Whether these additions were made by the Chronicler himself or preceded him cannot be determined. The result is, all the same, a direct line leading from Judah to David.

Verses 13–17 record the family tree of Jesse with all its branches. Most of the details are found in biblical sources, especially Samuel, but there is also additional – and at one point contradictory – information. According to I Sam. 16.10–11 (and 17.12ff), David was the youngest of Jesse's eight sons, of whom the first three are mentioned by name. In these verses, David is the last of seven sons, and all the names are recorded. Also, that Zeruiah was the daughter of Jesse – making David and Joab first cousins – is apparently contrary to II Sam. 17.25 (but cf. the commentary).

It is therefore quite probable that the Chronicler had at his disposal some additional information regarding the family of David, which the author of Samuel seems to have neglected. As for 'seven' versus 'eight' sons, although these are sometimes harmonized by the addition of one more son (I Chron. 27.18), it is also possible that the numbers in I Sam. 16 (and 17) were guided by the literary pattern of 7+1, and that it is Chronicles which preserves the more original information.

As pointed out above, vv. 2–17 are composed mainly from biblical sources and follow an overall structural plan. This passage is also marked by a formal feature (which recurs in ch. 3), the inclination to numerical statements: sums (vv. 3, 4, 6, 16) and detailed enumerations (vv. 13–15). These give the unit some uniformity and should probably be attributed to the Chronicler.

9. In contrast to the coherence exhibited both in the preceding passage (vv. 10–17) and in the following one (vv. 25–33), the uneven character of vv. 18–24 is striking,

and is augmented by the possible textual corruptions of vv. 18 and 24. The topic is indicated by the opening phrase: 'and Caleb the son of Hezron begot . . .', and the pith is found in vv. 18–19 and 24: the sons of Caleb from his wives Azubah (v. 18) and Ephrath (v. 19), and the birth of Ashhur, the father of Tekoa (v. 24). The intervening section (vv. 21–23), referring to Caleb's father Hezron and to the settlement of Gilead, probably derives from a different source, as is indicated by the conclusion: 'all these were the descendants of Machir' (v. 23). Its inclusion in this context was probably occasioned by the allusion to 'the death of Hezron' in v. 24.

Verse 20 is no doubt the work of the Chronicler, illustrating his constant attempts to relate the various Judaean personalities to some point in the genealogies. Here his intention is to identify Hur, the grandfather of Bezalel (Ex. 31.1, also Ex. 24.14) with the son of Caleb.

10. The passage dedicated to the sons of Jerahmeel is clearly composed of two distinct parts: the genealogy of Jerahmeel (vv. 25–33), and the genealogical tree of one Jerahmeelite: Elishama the son of Jekamiah (vv. 34–41). The juxtaposition of the two parts is secondary; the common denominator is found in the name 'Sheshan' mentioned in the genealogy of Jerahmeel and regarded as the forefather of Elishama. The origin of the second part, reflecting thirteen generations, is of course much later than the first. This is the only Judahite genealogical tree, except for David's, and in both cases the family tree is appended to basic material of an ethnic nature.

The passage about 'the sons of Jerahmeel' (2.25–33) is a self-contained unit with its own heading and conclusion, and is marked by formal features. The family of Jerahmeel is traced to two wives, but it is the offspring of 'another wife' which is recorded in the greatest detail. Formally speaking, two patterns are applied: for the first two generations (Jerahmeel, Ram and Onam) one formula: X ויהיו בני (vv. 25, 27, 28), while from the third generation onwards (including only the family of Onam) another formula is used: X ובני (vv. 28b, 30–32).

11. The passage devoted to the sons of Caleb (2.42–55; 4.2–7) is composed of three parts: vv. 42–50a the sons of Caleb; vv. 50b–55, 4.2–4 the sons of Hur; vv. 4.5–7 the sons of Ashhur. Between the first two parts there is a strict formal connection (cf. above), but for neither Hur nor Ashhur is the genealogical relationship to Caleb stated. This subject is treated and explained in 2.18–24, where both Hur and Ashhur are presented as Caleb's sons (cf. the commentary). It is possible that the following lists in 4.8–20 actually belong in part to the 'sons of Ashhur', but in the absence of an explicit reference, this depends on the reconstruction of the unit.

The record of 'the sons of Hur the firstborn of Ephrathah' is interrupted after 2.55, to continue in 4.2–4, concluding with the summary 'These were the sons of Hur, the first-born of Ephrathah, the father of Bethlehem' (4.4). This original sequence was intentionally broken by the intrusion of ch. 3, with the formal signs of the interpolating process found in 4.1 (cf. A. Demski, 'The Clans of Ephrath: Their Territory and History', Tel-Aviv 13–14, 1986/7, 53). In 2.50b three sons of Hur are mentioned: Shobal, Salma and Hareph; these are followed by the sons of Shobal (vv. 52–53), including Haroeh (=Reaiah), and the sons of Salma (vv. 54–55). 4.2 resumes with 'Reaiah the son of Shobal, etc.', but since the original sequence has been disrupted, the exact genealogical position of Reaiah is explained in 4.1. Here, a direct line of descent, based on the preceding genealogies, leads from Judah to Shobal (thus: 'Judah, Perez, Hezron, Caleb [Carmi], Hur, Shobal'). The method here resembles the linear lists of I Chron. 1.1–4 and 24–27, with no reference to the relationship between the names. The genealogical presuppositions resemble 2.19, where Hur is presented as the son of Caleb (Carmi), and its purpose is to re-establish the genealogical context for 'Reaiah the son of Shobal' after the interruption occasioned by ch. 3. Both this interruption and the resumption of the sequence through the addition of 4.1 can be regarded as the work of the Chronicler.

12. Chapter 3, the genealogical history of the house of David, can be regarded as the continuation of 2.17. Why then, was it introduced in its present position?

The answer to this question is to be found in the overall genealogical structure. The genealogical framework for the development of the Judahite elements is outlined in 2.9: Hezron and his three sons. Each of these three branches is unfolded, probably until they attain the age of David. This is explicitly illustrated by the line of Ram, and the genealogies of Jerahmmel and Caleb were therefore bound to follow suit.

In addition, there are more positive considerations determining the present position of the Davidic material in ch. 3. As stated above, the genealogical connection of David to the tribe of Judah was not fully established in the book of Samuel. By contrast, his affiliation with Bethlehem and Ephrath is greatly emphasized, cf. *inter al.* I Sam. 17.12: 'Now David was the son of an Ephrathite of Bethlehem in Judah, named Jesse.' Chronicles, having already established David's link to Hezron through Ram (2.9–15), emphasizes his kinship to Ephrathah and 'Salma the father of Bethlehem' (2.50b, 54f.) by the present position of ch. 3 in the middle of the sons of Hur. Thus the Chronicler assigns to David his twofold affiliation in Israel.

(On the structure, sources and form of ch. 3 and 4.4ff, cf. under the respective headings of these chapters.)

13. While the Jerahmeelite families follow an obvious structure, this is not the case for the Calebites. The literary difficulties here arise from textual corruptions and from the fact that some paragraphs stand alone, with no connection to what precedes them. In addition, there is a lack of strict formal guidelines, except for the framework of headings and conclusions. It is also possible that the Calebite genealogies are an attempt to depict complicated ethnic and territorial developments in a laconic and somewhat cryptic manner. The gist of the matter is not always entirely clear, particularly since our knowledge of the peculiar code of the genealogies is not complete.

D. Commentary

[3–5] The tribal genealogies themselves open with Judah. As observed by many generations of scholars, 'he started with the genealogy of Judah because the kings of Judah are the centre of the book' (Kimhi on v. 1). For the Chronicler, very much more than for the Deuteronomist, Judah plays the central role in the history of Israel. The Chronicler is aware of the tension between the genealogical tradition in which the birthright passes from Reuben, the firstborn, to Joseph, with Judah occupying an insignificant fourth place among Jacob's sons, and the historical actuality of Judah's eventual supremacy. This tension is referred to in the context of Reuben's genealogy (5.1–2), where the superiority of Judah is attributed to two points: 'Judah became strong among his brethren' and 'a prince was from him'.

As pointed out above, vv. 3–4 are a combination of Gen. 46.12 and a concise summary of Gen. 38, enlarging upon the vicissitudes of Judah's early family history. The use of Gen. 38 is striking, as in general the Chronicler avoided the narrative material of Genesis and limited himself almost exclusively to the genealogies. A specific intention must have guided the Chronicler's choice here, and it is through the details of the material itself that it can be brought to light. The facts cited from Gen. 38 are: (*a*) Judah's first three sons were born of a Canaanite wife, Bathshua; (*b*) Judah's eldest son, Er, was 'wicked in the eyes of the Lord' and therefore slain; (*c*) Judah's other two sons were by his daughter-in-law, Tamar.

At first glance, these details seem selected precisely to reveal all the weak points in the early history of the tribe. They must, however, be evaluated in the light of the Chronicler's own theology.

(*a*) The Canaanite origins of Bathshua should be regarded as a positive rather than a negative point. The genealogies in general refer constantly to non-Israelite elements, both men and women, whose foreign origins are either mentioned explicitly (e.g. 4.8; 3.17), or learned from their names or titles ('another wife', 2.6; etc.). There is never any incrimination implied in these data. Indeed, one of the goals of these genealogies is the inclusion, rather than exclusion, of the non-Israelite elements in the people of Israel, by presenting them as an organic part of the tribes, mainly in the status of 'wives' or 'concubines'. It is geographical rather than ethnic affiliation which constitute the unifying element, especially in Judah.

(*b*) The fate of Er and Onan is described in Gen. 38 in order to justify the unconventional relationship between Judah and his daughter-in-law which brought about the birth of Perez and Zerah. In this context, the mention of Er's death serves to explain the twisting path of election which was eventually to reach the family of Jesse (I Chron. 28.5). Just as Reuben lost the right of first-born through his sin, so Er, who was 'wicked in the sight of the Lord', lost the same right within the tribe of Judah. Gradually the birthright is tending toward Hezron, the firstborn of Perez.

(*c*) The Chronicler systematically avoids idealization (of his heroes as well as of the history of Israel), a fact not fully recognized in the study of the book (cf. already Pseudo-Rashi: 'I wonder that he mentioned the flaws of David's grandmother'). Here, at the very beginning of the history of Israel, neither the firstborn position of Er nor the powerful status of Judah would guarantee them immunity from wrongdoing. At the same time, Judah's sin is pardoned and does not constitute a hindrance to his offspring. Here we first get a glimpse – as yet a silent one – of the Chronicler's concept of divine justice, which is one of his major theological convictions. Judah sinned unwittingly, and the story does not condemn him; from the moment that he learned Tamar's identity, 'he did not lie with her again' (Gen. 38.26).

The fate of Onan, Judah's second son, is passed over in silence. Some scholars would supplement it on the assumption of homoioteleuton (cf. BHS), but in view of the concise and selective nature of the passage the reference to Onan may simply have been omitted as irrelevant to the present context.

[6–8] Beginning with the 'subsidiary' branches of Judah, the Chronicler first extracts from his biblical sources everything he can find concerning the family of Zerah, Tamar's first-born (Gen. 38.28–30). The beginning of v. 6, and v. 7, are drawn from Josh. 7.1, where Achan (=Achar) is identified as 'the son of Carmi, son of Zabdi, son of Zerah'. The rest of v. 6 is dependent on I Kings 4.31 (MT 5.11), which mentions the wisdom of four men: 'Ethan the Ezrahite, and Heman, Calcol and Darda, the sons of Mahol.' Taking 'Ezrahite' to mean 'Zerahite' and ignoring the fact that these sages are explicitly called 'the sons of Mahol', the Chronicler adds them to Zimri (Zabdi), thus coming up with five sons of Zerah.

The chronological impossibility of this list is obvious. As the brothers of Zimri/Zabdi, the four sages must have lived during the wilderness period, while the book of Kings seems to regard them as Solomon's contemporaries. Since the names are all of individuals, regarding them as indications of families or clans is excluded. It is precisely these historical difficulties which emphasize the Chronicler's intentions: to establish some kind of genealogy for the Zerahites, and to weave into his genealogical fabric as many as possible of the historical figures appearing in his narrative sources but which he does not mention in his own narrative sections.

The main line of the Zerahites is through Zimri, Carmi and Achan (Achar), the rough transition from v. 6 to v. 7 arising from the omission of any reference to the fact that Carmi was the son of Zimri/Zabdi. This problem will confront us many times throughout the genealogies, where the sequence between the names is obscured because of the absence of connecting links. It is difficult to determine whether this is an authentic feature of the genealogies or a result of textual corruption. In this case, however, the missing link can be restored through reference to Josh. 7.1.

Achan is intentionally called 'Achar' ('ākār = 'the one who brought trouble'), thus developing further the word-play which in Josh. 7. 25–26 serves as a basis for Achan's fate: 'why did you bring trouble on us?' (māh ^{a}kartānū), 'The Lord brings trouble on you today' (ya'k^{o}r^{e}kā yhwh bayyōm hazzeh), and provides an aetiology for the place-name where his stoning took place: 'emeq 'ākōr ('Valley of trouble').

With this reference to Achan/Achar, the reader is presented with an additional negative element regarding the tribe of Judah. The allusion is enough as a reminder of the fate of Achan and his whole family, who were all executed together 'on that day' (Josh. 7.24–25). Again, the line of election does not abide with the Zerahites but must be sought elsewhere in the tribe of Judah.

Ethan and Heman are also mentioned in the headings of psalms: 'A Maskil of Heman the Ezrahite' (88.1), and 'A Maskil of Ethan the Ezrahite' (89.1). Since both are designated 'Ezrahites' they are usually identified with the men whose wisdom was rivalled by Solomon's. The book of Chronicles, however, reflects a different tradition, according to which the singers appointed by David to 'the service of song ... before the tabernacle' bear the same proper names as the wise men: Heman the son of Joel, of the Kohath family (I Chron. 6.33–38 [MT 18–23]), Asaph, the son of Berechiah, of Gershom (I Chron. 6.39–43 [MT 24–28]) and Ethan the son of Kishi, of Merari (I Chron. 6.44–47 [MT 29–32]). These leaders of the singers are clearly Levites, and are never referred to as 'Ezrahites'. Whatever the presuppositions of I Kings and the headings of the psalms, in Chronicles there are two different traditions: the 'wise men' of Solomon's time who are 'Zerahites' of the tribe of Judah, and the singers Heman and Ethan, connected with the Temple music, who are Levites.

The fifth among the sons of Zerah is called here 'Dara' and in I Kings 'Darda'. Neither form is attested elsewhere, either could be a corruption or variation of the other, and thus the original cannot be determined.

Verse 8 records the name of Ethan's son Azariah, not known from any other source. In view of the eclectic nature of the whole list, composed as it is of excerpts from extant biblical sources, one would expect to find another mention of Azariah. A possible candidate might be 'Azariah the son of Nathan' of I Kings 4.5, proposing a different tradition for his father's name (note the orthographic similarity of *nātān* to *ētān* and their phonetic similarity); however, this remains in the realm of conjecture.

[9] The heading of the Hezronites sums up in a nutshell the new understanding of their genealogies, and forms the 'blueprint' for all that follows. Linguistically, the hand of the Chronicler can be discerned in two points: the indefinite 'born to him' (*nōlad lō*, cf. I Chron. 2.3; 3.1, 4; also 3.5; 20.6, 8), and the introduction of the accusative particle *'et* before the names of Hezron's sons (cf. Kropat, 2–3).

Jerahmeel here retains the position of firstborn (cf. also v. 25); the second is introduced as Ram. Caleb is called here Chelubai (*kelūbāy*), but the synonymity is confirmed by v. 18: 'Caleb the son of Hezron'. These are probably variant forms of the name, to which 'Chelub' (4.11; 27.26) should be added. All these forms have parallels: Chelubai (the rarest) in Ahumai (4.2), Chelub in Segub (2.21) and many others, and Caleb in Hareph (v. 51) and others.

[10–12] The record of the Hezronites opens by tracing the origins of the house of David in a genealogical tree descending from Ram to Jesse.

As already mentioned, the list is a sophisticated composition, numbering ten generations from Judah to Jesse and purporting to depict the family of Jesse as rooted in the most ancient and venerated of Judean families. Seen against the historical picture of the Pentateuch (which is a similar attempt to 'historicize' and 'individualize' genealogical data), this list poses several chronological difficulties. On the one hand, Moses' contemporary Nahshon (Ex. 6.23) is placed in the sixth generation from Judah, while the common genealogical pattern of the Pentateuch usually takes the Exodus as the fourth generation, as illustrated for the tribe of Levi (Ex. 6.16–20, 21) and Reuben (Num. 26.5–9). Similarly, if we place Boaz somewhat at the end of the period of the Judges, the transition to David is plausible, but only one generation (Salma) would have to span the period from the Exodus to the last of the Judges. The solving (or: harmonization?) of such chronological difficulties is, however, outside the scope of this commentary (for a different stand on the matter see G. A. Rendsburg, 'The Internal Consistence and Historical Reliability of the Biblical Genealogies', *VT* XL, 1990, 185–204).

The title 'prince of the sons of Judah' assigned to Nahshon is another way in which the Chronicler explicitly identifies a historical figure known from biblical sources, notwithstanding the difficulties such an identification may incur.

[13–17] The data about the offspring of Jesse could not all have been taken from II Samuel. The names of the fourth to sixth sons (Nethanel, Raddai and Ozem) are not found there, and the view that Zeruiah and Abigail were Jesse's daughters contradicts II Sam. 17.25. Another contradiction is the statement that David was the seventh, rather than the eighth, of Jesse's sons (I Sam. 17.12). However, there is nothing in these additions that would render the record artificial or inauthentic. One may assume that the records of the king's family were kept in the royal archives, and in any case the names of David's brothers – omitted for literary reasons in Samuel – would have been common knowledge. Further, the assumption that Joab was David's cousin would explain their special relationship, as well as David's words to Amasa, 'you are my flesh and blood' (II Sam. 19.14) – although they may also have been meant metaphorically. As to the question of who fathered Zeruiah and Abigail, the Lucianic version of II Sam. 17.25 has, in fact, 'Jesse' for the MT 'Nahash'. The conflicting traditions of David as eighth or seventh of Jesse's sons have equal force; both are based on typological numerology.

The name of Joab's brother always appears in Chronicles as Abshai, while its form in Samuel is usually Abishai (except in II Sam. 10.10, MT). Chronicles is fully systematic in this regard, but the origin of the change is not clear.

Jether (II Sam. 17.25, Jethra) is designated here as an Ishmaelite, while he is called 'Israelite' in Samuel. This is one of many instances where Chronicles probably preserves the original version, changed in Samuel for apologetic reasons.

[18–24] These verses are heterogeneous and rather incoherent, and the text is corrupt at two crucial points – the opening and the conclusion. Consequently, several suggestions have been offered for understanding the sources, meaning and place of this passage in the Chronistic context.

The passage parallels v. 9 in that it aims to provide the basic framework of the sons of Caleb, connecting the two Judahite branches of Hur and Ashhur as sons of Caleb by the same wife, Ephrathah. At the same time, the union between Caleb and Ephrathah is presented explicitly as a second marriage for both: Caleb took Ephrath as wife only after the death of Azubah (v. 19), and Ephrath was apparently formerly the wife of Hezron (v. 24, cf. below). Viewed from an ethnological angle, these data lead to several conclusions. Her designation as 'wife' marks Ephrath as originally a non-Judahite ethnic element, only later connected with Judah. This connection was established in several ways: first through Hezron, to whom Hur was originally affiliated (cf. below), and only later through Caleb, in the clan of Ashhur (cf. below on v. 24). In this context, Hur's affiliation is also transferred to Caleb.

While most of the above seems evident, a problem does arise about the exact status of Hur and his position *vis à vis* Ashhur. Hur is presented in the lists as 'the first-born of Ephrathah' (2.50; 4.4), and this is also implied in v. 19. However, according to v. 24 (reading *bā' kālēb* in place of *bᵉkālēb* cf. below), Caleb took Ephrath to wife only after the death of Hezron. If, then, Ashhur was born at this time, when was the birth of Hur, and why is he termed 'the firstborn of Ephrathah'? The form and structure of the original source (above p. 69) seem to indicate that the status of 'Hur the firstborn of Ephrathah' was equivalent to that of Caleb and Jerahmeel, the three genealogies having been related in one sequence and in the same format. Judging from this sequence, Hur would appear to be Caleb's brother rather than his son, and indeed it is only here in v. 19 that a 'father-son' relationship is established for Caleb and Hur. It would seem, therefore, that originally the three branches of Judah, regarded as 'the sons of Hezron', were Jerahmeel, Caleb and *Hur*. Both the special status of the latter, as well as his secondary affiliation, were expressed by regarding him as the son of another wife, Ephrath, the 'firstborn of Ephrathah' whose father was, originally, Hezron. In addition, a less significant branch of Judah, Ashhur, living in Tekoa in the vicinity of Bethlehem, was also regarded as the offspring of the same Ephrath, but fathered by Caleb. However, this original picture was altered in the present context of Chronicles; here the position of Hezron's third son was taken by 'Ram', the supposed forefather of the family of Jesse (v. 9), and Hur was relegated to the position of 'the son of Caleb'. Verse 19 is therefore the Chronicler's restructuring of the genealogy of Caleb, following the similar treatment of the genealogy of Hezron (v. 9). This is then given expression again in 4.1, once more from the hand of the Chronicler (cf. further below). The alternative structures may be illustrated as follows:

Original structure

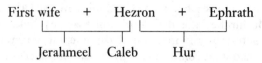

First wife   +   Hezron   +   Ephrath

Jerahmeel   Caleb   Hur

cf. 2.25 Jerhameel, the first born of Hezron
    2.42 Caleb, the brother of Jerahmeel
    4.5   Hur the first born of Ephrathah

Chronistic structure

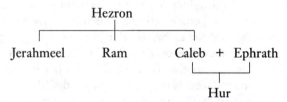

Hezron

Jerahmeel   Ram   Caleb   +   Ephrath

Hur

cf. 2.9   The sons of Hezron . . . Jerahmeel, Ram and Chelubai
    2.19 Caleb married Ephrath who bore him Hur

[18] The syntax of this verse is difficult, literally: 'Caleb ... begat Azubah, a woman, and Jerioth, and these are her sons ...' One solution is to regard *'iššāh* as a gloss, in which case both Azubah and Jerioth would be Caleb's daughters. However, the following phrase, '*her* sons', refers only to *one* woman. Many commentators would accept the version of the Peshitta, reading '*from* Azubah *his* wife' (*īštō*) thus: *hōlīd mēʿᵃzūbāh 'ištō 'et*. Accordingly, Caleb had one daughter by his wife Azubah, i.e. Jerioth, whose sons are then recorded (RSV, differently, implies that both Azubah and Jerioth were Caleb's wives; this, however, fails to account for '*her* sons').

The verse is probably a fragment of the Calebite genealogies, introduced here for the sake of the more important v. 19; the comprehensive record of Caleb's offspring, by several wives and concubines, is referred to in vv. 42ff. The branch recorded here seems a weak one: Azubah soon 'died' and even the offspring of her single 'daughter' are recorded for only one generation. This would be a marginal branch of the Calebites, of little significance.

[19] The Chronicler cites the circumstances of the birth of Hur: after the death of Azubah, Caleb married Ephrath. As it stands, the verse is a simple one; the difficulties arise from its juxtaposition with v. 24 (cf. above).

[20] Like vv. 7, 10b, 49b, etc., this is a clear example of the Chronicler's tendency to link the protagonists of the wilderness period to the genealogy of the tribe. Since Hur, the first-born of Ephrath, is viewed as Bezalel's grandfather, Hur of the Exodus becomes the fifth generation from Judah.

[21–23] These verses in fact belong to the genealogy of Machir, the son of Manasseh, as is demonstrated by the concluding words: 'All these were descendants of Machir the father of Gilead'. The passage is linked secondarily to the present context by the mechanical conjunction 'afterward'; this may originally have had some connection with the circumstances of Machir, but is completely out of context here. The introduction of the passage in the present position is probably because of the association with Hezron's old age and death in v. 24.

The passage gives genealogical expression to the ethnic connections between Judah and Manasseh, by describing a late marriage between Hezron and an unnamed daughter of Machir. Its main point is to claim a Judahite affiliation for large parts of Gilead, which was originally a Manassite and Machirite territory *par excellence*. For Jair, the son of Segub, the Judahite element takes precedence over the Machirite, as it is his father who comes from Judah and his mother from Machir. To Jair belong the twenty-three towns in Gilead, called Havvoth-jair (probably: 'the villages of Jair').

The testimony of the parallel passage in Num. 32.39–42 is of special interest. Jair the son of Manasseh, the equivalent to the main figure of our passage (Jair the son of Segub), figures there together with Machir and Nobah. Both contexts explicitly associate the settlements called 'Havvoth-jair' with Jair. However, although in Num. 32 he is called 'the son of Manasseh', he does not appear as such in the standard Pentateuch genealogies (cf. Num. 26.29). According to Num. 32.41, 'Jair ... went and took their [the Amorites'] villages and called them Havvoth-jair'; the towns were, then, taken from the Amorites after the Exodus, during the wanderings in the wilderness. A third tradition regarding the same settlements is attached to a judge, also named Jair, and also from Gilead: 'He had thirty sons ... and they had thirty cities called Havvoth-jair to this day, which are in the land of Gilead' (Judg. 10.4).

The basis of these passages is a strong tradition concerning a group of settlements called 'Havvoth-jair'. According to the Pentateuch they were taken by force from the Amorites, in connection with the Exodus, while in the Chronicles tradition they were founded by Jair, a Judahite branch of Hezron which settled in Gilead and mingled with the Machirite population there. These are two mutually exclusive concepts regarding these settlements: conquest from the Amorites, related to the tradition of the Exodus, on the one hand, and gradual expansion of Israelite elements, and sociological-ethnographical circumstances, on the other. Whatever conclusions one may reach regarding the historicity of these approaches, their points of departure are diametrically opposed.

At what time were Havvoth-jair and Kenath, sixty cities altogether, taken from the Israelites by Geshur and Aram? The short note to this effect in the present passage (v. 23) seems to reflect authentic circumstances of the monarchical period. 'Geshur' is known to be active in the time of David, who married Maacah, the daughter of Talmai the king of Geshur (II Sam. 3.3); it was there that her son, Absalom, later took refuge (II Sam. 13.38). According to II Sam. 10.6//I Chron. 19.6, Geshur did not join the Ammonite-Aramean attack on Israel, although its closest neighbour, Maacah, did so (II Sam. 10.8; Josh. 13.13). In I Kings 4.13 'the villages of Jair' are mentioned in the district of 'Ramoth-gilead' under Solomon's administrative system. We should therefore attribute this note to the waxing of the power of Aram in Transjordan, some time in the ninth century.

In 'Machir the father of Gilead' (*mākīr ʾᵃbī gilʿād*, v. 21) we encounter for the first time the pattern X the father of Y, a formula recurring abundantly in the genealogies of Caleb and Hur (vv. 42ff.). The specific formulaic usage is blurred in RSV, which also uses the same phrase, 'was the father of', as translation of *hōlīd* (JPS 'begot'). In the formula 'X the father of Y', Y is always a place name, while X is an ethnic element. Thus we are actually presented with the record of a double-affiliation: ethnic (family) origins and a specific geographic locale (town or territory). In this essentially technical terminology one 'son' may have several 'fathers', such as 'Hur ... the father of Bethlehem' (4.4) and 'Salma the father of Bethlehem' (2.51); the 'son', Bethlehem, remains the same, but is inhabited, synchronically or diachronically, by various ethnic elements. In the present case, the designation, 'Gilead', the territory in which the Machirites settled, is itself independent of and previous to that settlement.

[24] In the present Massoretic version the verse reads: 'After the death of Hezron in Caleb-Ephrathah, Hezron's wife Abiah bore Ashhur the father of Tekoa.' Accordingly, Ashhur, the son of Hezron and Abiah, was born after his father's death. However, the reference to Hezron's place of death, the unique place-name 'Caleb-Ephrathah', which is difficult from any point of view, together with the mention of another son of Hezron, unanticipated in this context, and the affiliation of Ashhur with Hezron rather than with Hur (I Chron. 4.5), all cast considerable doubt on this reading. It has been commonly accepted that *bᵉkālēb* should indeed be read *bāʾ kālēb*, following the Septuagint and the Vulgate (J. Wellhausen, *De Gentibus et Familiis Judaeis*. Dissertatio Göttingen 1870, 14–15, followed by many), and by means of the slightest alterations the next phrase is read by many as *ʾēšet ḥeṣrōn ʾᵃbīhū*. Following these reconstructions (both of which are already reflected in RSV's translation), the verse now relates the marriage of Caleb

and Ephrath after Hezron's death, and the consequent birth of Ashhur. However, Ephrath has already been mentioned previously as Caleb's wife, whom he married after the death of his first wife, Azubah (v. 19). One way out of this difficulty is to regard Hur and Ashhur as one person (the former name being an hypocoristic form of the latter), and v. 24 as an elaboration of v. 19 (Curtis, 92). Another suggestion is to regard w^e'ēšet ḥeṣrōn '^{a}bīyyāh ('the wife of Hezron Abiah') as a gloss; thus the births of Caleb's sons by Ephrath would be related to the death of his father Hezron, Hur born before and Ashhur after, with no connection to be seen between Ephrath and Hezron (Williamson, 53–4). This, however, is to suppose a unique procedure, never attested elsewhere in the lists, without accounting for the appearance of the gloss itself.

As suggested above, there is no intrinsic difficulty with the reconstruction of v. 24, which would relate both the origins of Ashhur from Caleb and Ephrathah, and the relatively late association of Caleb and Ephrath. The difficulties arise only from the juxtaposition of v. 24 with v. 19, the contradiction being a product of a new Chronistic understanding of the genealogical affiliation of Hur, who becomes not Hezron's son but Caleb's.

Ethnologically, Ephrathah would be a non-Judahite element, established in the area of Bethlehem and Tekoa, which was amalgamated with the already Judah-affiliated Hezronite and Calebite families to form the dominant ethnic factor in this area.

What is the origin and provenance of 'Ephrath'? From the usage and occurrences of the title 'Ephrathite' in the Bible one may assume that it is actually the gentilic form of 'Ephraim' (cf. *inter al.* Judg. 12.5; I Sam. 1.1; I Kings 11.26, MT '^{e}prātī. RSV obscures the similarity by representing the Hebrew '^{e}prātī, 'Ephra*th*ite', by 'Ephrai*m*ite)'. The strong connections between Ephraim and Bethlehem are illustrated in the story of Gibeah (Judg. 19), and it is therefore quite possible that Ephraimite families, settled in the surroundings of Bethlehem, were later absorbed into Judah as a result of the intensive expansion of Judaean elements, from the margins to the centre. In the traditions of the Pentateuch 'Ephrath' is already a place-name, identified with Bethlehem (Gen. 35.19 etc.); if, then, the above description of social developments is correct, they had reached a stage of completion and ethnographical abstraction already in ancient times.

[25–33] The list of the sons of Jerahmeel follows two lines: the one from his unnamed principal wife, reaching only the third generation, and the other, more detailed record, from Atarah (crown), 'another wife' ('*iššāh* '*aḥeret* – a unique term in the genealogical context, although found elsewhere, cf. Judg. 11.2 and I Kings 3.22). The ethnic development within Jerahmeel is described as both reduction and expansion: reduction by the extinction of certain branches, indicated – in this context only – by the genealogical terminology 'x died childless' (vv. 30, 32), and expansion by the assimilation of outside elements, designated 'wives'. The expansion indicated by the 'other wife' (of v. 26) became the major factor among the Jerahmeelites (vv. 28–33), while another element is added through Abihail, the wife of Abishur (v. 29).

Altogether the families tracing their origin to Jerahmeel number twenty-one or twenty-two, depending on whether we read 'Ahiah' (v. 25) as a proper name – in which case a conjunction should be added (thus RSV) – or (more unusually, following the Septuagint) 'his brother'. The list contains no hint of the geographical-historical circumstances pertaining to the Jerahmeelites, as all the appellations are proper names, to be understood in sociological terms as families or clans, not localitites or territories (cf. by contrast, the subsequent lists of Caleb and Hur). This may be construed (thus de Vaux, *The Early History of Israel*, 1978, 537) to indicate a nomadic existence with no attachment to fixed localities or towns (cf. the general 'the towns (RSV: cities) of the Jerahmeelites' in I Sam. 30.29, with no explicit place-names. The testimony of other sources indicates that the Jerahmeelites' territory was in the southern Judean hills and the Negev (cf. I Sam. 27.10; 30.29).

There is nothing in the list itself, or in the data found outside Chronicles, which would justify reference to Jerahmeel as 'the first-born of Hezron' (v. 25). It is possible that Jerahmeel was indeed a most ancient ethnic group in the Judean hills and a primary factor in the emergence of the tribe of Judah (I Sam. 30.26–28: 'The elders of Judah … in the cities of the Jerahmeelites' versus 27.10: 'Negeb of Judah, Negeb of the Jerahmeelites'); however, since Jerahmeel preserved the nomadic way of life in the more arid fringes of the hill-country and the Negev, the families affiliated with Caleb, who settled in the areas of Hebron and Bethlehem, eventually became stronger.

[34–41] The genealogical tree of Elishama the son of Jekamiah resembles that of Jesse (2.10–12), the high priests (6.4–14 [MT 5.30–40]), and others. It follows a strict formal pattern: X begot Y, and purports to establish Elishama's distinction (and/or legitimacy) by tracing his exact descent. While other sources shed no light on his identity, the Midrash equates him with the Elishama mentioned in II Kings 25.25 as grandfather of the man who slew Gedaliah at Mizpah: 'Ishmael the son of Nethaniah … of the royal family' (2 Kings 25.25; Jer. 41.1). Although this identification may well have been based merely on the fact that the names are identical, the period chosen for Elishama (thirteen generations after Sheshan, who himself is a rather late descendant of Jerahmeel) is quite plausible. Ehrlich suggests that the Nathan mentioned here as the son of Athai and the father of Zabad should be identified with the prophet of David's day, the reference being to I Kings 4.5: 'Zabud the son of Nathan was priest and king's friend' (*Mikra Ki-Pheshuto* II, 431–2*). This possibility, although tempting, is not conclusive.

The most interesting part of this section is the introduction in vv. 34–35, which tells how Sheshan, having no sons, gave one of his daughters in marriage to his Egyptian slave, by whom 'she bore him' a son. The syntax of v. 35 obviously indicates that it is to Sheshan that the pronoun 'him' refers. This is indeed the point of the whole episode: having no son of his own, Sheshan could secure the continuation of his line only by marrying his daughter to a slave; if she were given to a free man, their son would bear the name, not of Sheshan but of his natural father. In a much later generation such a story would provide a person bearing the patronym 'Sheshan' with a legitimate genealogy, although it was known that Sheshan had only daughters.

The sociological and legal presuppositions of this little story resemble those underlying some narratives in Genesis; in addition we have here an instructive illustration of the actual application of the law in Ex. 21.4: 'When you buy a Hebrew slave ... If his master gives him a wife and she bears him sons or daughters, the wife and her sons shall be her master's.' While the situation is basically the same, this account differs from the ruling in Exodus in that here the slave is an Egyptian and not a Hebrew, and the wife is not any woman but the master's daughter. In these circumstances, the offspring of this union does not become his master's 'house-born' (*yᵉlîd bāyit*), but actually 'his son'. In the Genesis narratives we encounter the same legal principles, but applied by the mistress rather than the master of the house. Thus, the Egyptian slave-girl Hagar is given to Abraham (Gen. 16.2 *'ûlay 'ibbāneh mimmēnnāh*, translated 'it may be that I shall obtain children by her'), and the maids Zilpah and Bilhah to Jacob. In all these cases the children of the maid belong to her mistress.

Also, as in Genesis, the attitude of the story is that there is nothing reprehensible about this marriage with an Egyptian slave or maid. The difference between the two sources lies only in the varying circumstances of the social problem being addressed: there a woman unable to bear children, here a man who begets only daughters.

Just as the offspring of Hagar, Zilpah and Bilhah are regarded in every way as the master's sons, so here the descendants of the Egyptian slave are fully-fledged Israelites, of unflawed Jerahmeelite descent. These are undoubtedly reflections of social circumstances which occasioned the absorption of foreign elements into Israel. The author takes a positive view of the phenomenon and, far from concealing it, makes a point of attributing just such an origin to the distinguished Elishama (cf. further S. Japhet, 'The Israelite Legal and Social Reality as Reflected in Chronicles: A Case Study', in *Sha'arei Talmon. Festschrift S. Talmon*, 1992, 79–91).

It might at first seem that there is a contradiction between v. 31, 'the sons of Sheshan: Ahlai', and v. 34 which declares that 'Sheshan had no sons'.

Some commentators would harmonize the two by assuming that 'Ahlai' was the name of a daughter (Curtis, 94) but this is hardly necessary. Originally, the two passages (vv. 25–33 and vv. 34–41) were distinct treatments of two different matters. The first records the families affiliated to Jerahmeel, while the second is a genealogical pedigree composed of individuals. There is no need strictly to identify the Jerahmeelite family 'Sheshan' of v. 31 with the individual 'Sheshan' (probably a real or fictitous member of that family) of v. 34, any more than one should identify the tribes of Israel with any individual bearing that name.

[42–50a] Despite difficulties in sequence, the heading and conclusion which form the framework of this passage establish clearly that it contains the ramifications of the Calebite family. The genealogies here abound in place-names and more than in any other section take the form 'X the father of Y' – where Y is a geographic appellation (cf. above on v. 21). The places thus indicated are: Ziph, Hebron (v. 42), Jorkeam (v. 44) Bethzur (v. 45), Madmannah, Machbenah, Gibea (v. 49). Some of these places are very familiar, some known less or not at all. Other place-names would be Mareshah (v. 42), Tapuah (v. 43), Maon (v. 45), etc., and the question arises whether the distinctive presentation here is merely a variation of literary convention in the genealogies, or points to a different concept in the process of settlement and expansion. We can give no conclusive answer, as both formulations may (although rarely) occur in the designation of one set of relationships. A case in point is that of Bethlehem, which appears in v. 51, 'Salma, the father of Bethlehem', but again in v. 54, 'The sons of Salma: Bethlehem'. Biologically speaking, these are of course two sides of the same coin, but in the formulaic language of the lists there would seem to be a certain difference between them. The designation of a locality as a 'son' would indicate a fuller identification between an ethnic group and the village or town bearing the same name. The group is regarded as either having founded this locale or as having ancient connections there. By contrast, in the formula 'X the father of Y', historical memory still preserves the identity of the place as independent of the present ethnic group. If this distinction is correct, the lists could reflect prolonged processes of expansion, absorption and dispersal, all expressed in the code of genealogical structures. In the present context, we could see the Calebite families expanding into towns like Ziph or Hebron, which were previously inhabited by others. This would also account for cases where one town is 'fathered' by several ethnic groups, such as 'Salma the father of Bethlehem' (v. 51) and 'Hur ... the father of Bethlehem' (v. 4.5), or 'Mesha (RSV: Mareshah) ... the father of Ziph' (v. 42) and 'the sons of Jehallelel: Ziph' (4.16), etc.

Of special interest in this context is the connection between the Calebites and the town of Hebron, which, notwithstanding the somewhat corrupt reading of v. 42b (cf. below), is firmly established. Hebron is the 'son' of Caleb's (grand)son, Mareshah, and the father of four other 'sons', of whom two (Tapuah and Shema) may also indicate place names. This could mean that the Calebites expanded to Hebron, and from there to farther areas in the territory of Judah. It was probably the weight of this tradition which also caused the Pentateuch and the Former Prophets to adopt and emphasize the connection of Hebron with Caleb (described in the Pentateuch sources as 'the son of Jephunneh', Num. 13.6, etc.). Caleb takes Hebron by force from its autochthonic population (Josh. 14.12–14; Judg. 1.10). Thus, what is expressed in the genealogical lists as sociological-ethnic processes of expansion and settlement ('Caleb ... the father of Hebron') is presented in the Pentateuch as an act of military conquest. The same phenomenon has been demonstrated earlier with 'Machir the father of Gilead' (v. 21), interpreted in Numbers as the military conquest of Gilead by the Machirites (Num. 32.39–40).

[42] In this introduction, Caleb is introduced as 'the brother of Jerahmeel', which emphasizes the stronger connection of these two elements, and may imply a weaker connection with their 'father' Hezron (cf. above).

The very unusually formulated second half-verse is probably corrupt. Pseudo-Rashi: 'Thus the whole genealogy is confused.' Several suggestions have been made for its reconstruction: to read 'Mareshah' in place of 'Mesha' at the beginning of the verse, and to omit 'the father of' before 'Hebron' (both changes reflected in RSV); to omit 'the sons of Maresha', taking Mesha as 'the father of' both Ziph and Hebron; to introduce 'Ziph' before Maresha, reading 'and the sons of Ziph: Maresha the father of Hebron'; or to add 'Mesha' in the same position: 'the sons of Mesha: Maresha the father of Hebron'. While all these are possible solutions, the last is orthographically the easiest to accept.

[46] 'Gazez' recurs as the name of both the son and the grandson of Caleb. This is in itself not impossible, as the family by that name could have traced its origin either directly to Caleb or through an intermediate stage, to Haran. Alternatively, there could have been two branches by the same name, differently recorded. Similar examples can be found in the case of Ram, who in our lists is both Hezron's second son (2.9) and his grandson as the first born of Jerahmeel (vv. 25, 27); or the Horite family of Dishon, who in one sequence appears as both the son and the brother of Anah (1.38, 41). However, in the case of 'Gazez', since the next words, 'the sons of Jahdai' (v. 47), appear so unexpectedly, it has been suggested that the second 'Gazez' should be read Jahdai. This would render the whole structure more coherent.

[47] Another possibility of integrating Jahdai into the context is suggested by the fact that the name 'Ephah' appears both among the sons of Jahdai and as Caleb's concubine (v. 46). It has been proposed to regard the genealogy of

Jahdai as a completely independent section, introduced here in order to account for the origins of Ephah. There is nothing in the verse itself to refute this possibility, except for the facts that 'wives' and 'concubines' are usually introduced with no record of their descent, and that the name Ephah could be either male or female.

[48] 'Maacah ... bore Sheber': the verb appears in the masculine form and the accusative conjunction *'et* is absent before 'Sheber' but found before the following name, Tirhanah. Both of these irregularities are restored by most scholars, although it has been pointed out that similar ones may also be found elsewhere (Rudolph, 20).

[49] The verse opens awkwardly in Hebrew: *wattēled ša'ap '^{a}bī madmannāh 'et š^{e}wā'*, literally, 'And Shaaph the father of Madmannah bore Sheva ...'. If the subject is 'Shaaph', the last son of Jahdai (v. 47), we would expect a verb in the masculine gender (*wayyōled*), and the verse should follow v. 47. However, it does not seem likely that the verse should be transferred, since it closes with the reference to Achsah, Caleb's daughter, and such references to daughters are more often than not placed, as in this case, at the very end of a genealogy. There are two other suggested reconstructions: one involves taking v. 49 as a direct continuation of v. 48, with the verb 'she bore' (*wattēled*) referring for its subject back to Maacah, Caleb's concubine, and having 'Shaaph the father of Madmannah' for its object (with or without the accusative particle *'et*). RSV reads in this way, emphasizing, 'she *also* bore Shaaph'. Alternatively, one may regard 'Shaaph' as the name of another of Caleb's concubines; assuming then that her son's name and her designation as Caleb's concubine have dropped from the text, we read: 'Shaaph bore [x] the father of Madmannah'. All these suggestions require only slight adjustments and are orthographically plausible.

Thus, the list of the Calebites includes Caleb's sons from his chief (unidentified) wife (vv. 42–45), from his concubines Ephah (v. 46) and Maacah (v. 48), and the additional, variously reconstructed, 'sons of Jahdai' and of 'Shaaph'.

In accordance with the method he follows elsewhere, the Chronicler appends 'Achsah the daughter of Caleb', known from Josh. 15.16–19 and Judg. 1.12–15, to the list of the Calebites, thus affiliating her to Caleb 'the son of Hezron' or 'the brother of Jerahmeel', rather than to 'the son of Jephuneh', as is the case in Joshua.

In spite of the indication of the Massoretic accents, the first words of v. 50, 'These were the descendants of Caleb', do not constitute an introduction to what follows but a conclusion to the genealogies we have just seen.

[50b–55] The list of the sons of Hur follows a systematic structure: the three sons of Hur (vv. 50b–51) are followed by their respective descendants (vv. 52–53, 54–55; 4.2; 4.3–4). The singular 'son of Hur' (v. 50) is rendered by the Versions in the plural (also RSV), and this is no doubt the meaning intended.

[51] Three families trace their descent to Hur, and each is presented as the 'father' of a significant locality: Shobal of Kiriath-jearim, Salma of Bethlehem, and Hareph of Beth-gader.

[52–53] The opening words in Hebrew (literally 'There were sons to Shobal, the father of Kiriathjearim' (RSV 'Shobal ... had other sons') are unusual. This resembles the forms of vv. 25, 27 and 28, but here there is an added emphasis, the reason for which is not specified. These 'sons' are 'Haroeh, half of the Menuhoth' and the 'families of Kiriath-jearim', whose names follow (v. 53) in the gentilic singular form (rendered plural in RSV).

The function of the genealogical record as a sociological code, the meanings and nuances of which were familiar to all concerned, comes to its strongest expression here. The reference to a 'son' as 'half of something' reflects a concept of ethnic development far removed from biological descent; the same is true of the listing of 'families' as 'offspring', especially when the names appear in their gentilic form (Ithrites, Puthites, etc.). The actual sophistication of the seemingly primitive registration should be kept in mind when dealing with this material.

As is often the case in these genealogies, most of the names are unattested elsewhere; the one exception being the Ithrites, a quite common family name, found also in the affiliation of two of David's mighty men: Ira the Ithrite and Gareb the Ithrite (II Sam. 23.38; I Chron. 11.40).

The first son (or the first of the 'other sons', RSV) of Shobal is here called 'Haroeh, half the Menuhoth', but in view of 4.2 (Reaiah), and 2.54 (half of the Manahathites), here, too one should probably read 'Reaiah, half of the Manahathites'. The territorial expansion of Shobal is clearly defined as including half the people of Manahath, four families of Kiriath-jearim, and their branches in Zorah and Eshtaol. The other half of Manahath is also affiliated with Hur, through Shobal's brother, Salma (v. 54).

It should be noticed that the names of both Shobal and Manahath, as father and son, are found among the descendants of Seir the Horite (1.38, 40). The similarity could hardly be accidental; the allusion may be to Horite components among the inhabitants of Manahath, who possibly affiliated themselves later with Judah through 'Hur'.

There is one more, also rather unusual, reference to the inhabitants of Manahath: Benjaminite elements who were exiled there (I Chron. 8.6). Thus the locale had a particularly mixed population, the result of complicated political and sociological circumstances, either synchronical or diachronical, of which we can only catch a glimpse.

Kiriath-jearim itself is known as one of the Hivite towns, on the border between Judah and Benjamin (Josh. 9.17), at the time of the conquest. Here again one may assume that Judaean elements moved northward and gradually gained control of Kiriath-jearim, or, *vice versa*, that the non-Israelite population of this town eventually affiliated itself with Judah. Since these processes reach as far as Zorah and Eshtaol (cf. also 4.2), originally regarded as Danite, the historical context should probably not be fixed any earlier than the migration of Dan to the north.

[54–55] The list of the 'sons of Salma' is in strict parallelism to the sons of Shobal: the names of sons (vv. 52//54) and the list of families (vv. 53// 55). Two of the recorded 'sons of Salma' are in fact place names, Bethlehem and Atroth-beth-joab, while the other two (or three) have a gentilic formulation: 'the Netophathites' and 'half the Manahathites the Zorites'. The enumeration of Bethlehem as a 'son' of Salma would probably mean that a fuller identification between the town and the ethnic entity of Salma is envisaged (cf. also above p. 85).

The double designation 'half the Manahathite the Zorite' is difficult. If *haṣṣorʿi* is to be identified with *haṣṣorʿāti* (v. 53; 4.2), referring to the town of Zorah, 'half the Manahathite' affiliated with Salma would be an additional element in the population of Zorah. It is also possible that 'the Zorite' is a different name, and that a *waw* should be restored before it.

The Netophathite refers to a well-attested Judaean town, in the vicinity of Bethlehem, from which come two of David's mighty men (II Sam. 23.28, 29; I Chron. 11.30) and one of the supporters of Ishmael the son of Nethaniah (II Kings 25.23, etc.); in the Restoration period it was settled by singers (Neh. 12.28; I Chron. 9.16; also Ezra 2.22).

[55] The relevance of this verse to the present context is confirmed by the way in which its registration parallels that of Shobal; by contrast, however, the 'families' mentioned here constitute the population of a town which was not referred to previously, Jabez. We may assume a certain connection between the families of v. 54 and v. 55, but that connection is not spelled out.

The families referred to here are given four designations: 'The families ... of the scribes', 'dwellers of Jabez', the gentilic plural 'Tirathites, Shumathites, Suchathites', and lastly 'The Kenites who came from Hammath, the father of the house of Rechab'. Some difficulties are inherent in each of these designations (mostly in the last), and in their combination.

1. The word translated 'Kenites' (in RSV and elsewhere) is actually vocalized with a *hireq* (*haqqinim*), which would affiliate these people to a place such as *qin* or *haqqayin* ('Kain', Josh. 15.57) or *qinah* ('Kinah', Josh. 15.22). These names, however, may have originally derived from their 'Kenite' population; in this case, most scholars prefer the reading 'Kenites', understanding this to mean the Kenite nomadic tribe, one of Israel's neighbours in the south, with whom there were several forms of contact (Judg. 1.16; I Sam. 27. 10; 30.29, etc.).

2. 'Who came from Hammath, the father of the house of Rechab': according to the registration-technique already mentioned (X the father of Y), 'the house of Rechab (Beth Rechab)' should be regarded as a place name (cf. '^{a}bī bēt-ṣūr, '^{a}bī bēt-leḥem, etc.), and 'Hammath' would be the ethnic group dwelling there. Beth-rechab could then be identified with bēt-hammarkābōt (Josh. 19.5; I Chron. 4.31) in the territory of Simeon, or any other plausible locale. The 'Kenites' would be the offspring of Hammath, who affiliated themselves secondarily with Judah, through the three families of Jabez. However, the phrase 'come from' (bā'īm min) is never used for genealogical derivation, but always in the sense of to 'come from somewhere'; 'Hammath' must then be a locality, in spite of the irregular mode of registration. Further, 'the house of the Rechabites' is known from Jer. 35.2, etc., as a distinct group with a strict nomadic anti-civilizational life-style. Their father is always alluded to in Jeremiah as 'Jehonadab the son of Rechab' (Jer. 35.6 etc.), and this would support the view that 'Hammath' is the name of a place with which the Rechabites were identified. In this case, a strong link between the 'Kenites' and the 'Rechabites' would be established.

3. Sōp^{e}rīm has commonly been translated as 'scribes', in accord with the common meaning of the word supported by the appearance of different professions in the lists (4.15, craftsmen; 4.21, linen workers; 4.23, potters). However, some scholars would prefer to read here 'Siphrites', the inhabitants of Kiriath-sepher (Ehrlich, Randglossen, VI, 327; Rudolph, 25; Williamson, 55). Such a rendering makes their genealogical affiliation so complex as to be nearly incomprehensible, and besides is refuted by the designation 'dwellers of Jabez'. The title 'dwellers of X' is found in the genealogical records only once more, in 4.23, also associated with professional craftsmen in the service of the king. It is therefore probable that these 'dwellers of Jabez' enjoyed a special status, thanks to their craft as 'scribes'; this distinction would account for the complicated way in which they are presented: according to their ethnic origin, their original geographical provenance, and their final settlement and affiliation with the families of Caleb.

It should be emphasized that these 'Kenites' (if that is the correct reading) are completely absorbed into the tribe of Judah, as one branch of the Calebites through Hur and Salma – although there is a missing link in the genealogical chain. The Kenites were originally non-Israelites (Gen. 15.19, etc.); their absorption is not related to a 'marriage' with a 'wife', but is conceived as a straight genealogical sequence. It is similar to the absorption of the Qenizites within Judah, and is one more characteristic of the Chronicler's approach.

3

3 1 These are the sons of David that were born to him in Hebron: the first-born Amnon, by Ahino-am the Jezreelitess; the second Daniel, by Abigail the Carmelitess, [2] the third Absalom, whose mother was Maacah, the daughter of Talmai, king of Geshur; the fourth Adonijah, whose mother was Haggith; [3] the fifth Shephatiah, by Abital; the sixth Ithream, by his wife Eglah; [4] six were born to him in Hebron, where he reigned for seven years and six months. And he reigned thirty-three years in Jerusalem. [5] These were born to him in Jerusalem: Shime-a, Shobab, Nathan, and Solomon, four by Bath-shua, the daughter of Ammi-el; [6] then Ibhar, Elishama, Eliphelet, [7] Nogah, Nepheg, Japhia, [8] Elishama, Eliada, and Eliphelet, nine. [9] All these were David's sons, besides the sons of the concubines; and Tamar was their sister.

10 The descendants of Solomon: Rehoboam, Abijah his son, Asa his son, Jehoshaphat his son, [11] Joram his son, Ahaziah his son, Joash his son, [12] Amaziah his son, Azariah his son, Jotham his son, [13] Ahaz his son, Hezekiah his son, Manasseh his son, [14] Amon his son, Josiah his son. [15] The sons of Josiah: Johanan the first-born, the second Jehoiakim, the third Zedekiah, the fourth Shallum. [16] The descendants of Jehoiakim: Jeconiah his son, Zedekiah his son; [17] and the sons of Jeconiah, the captive: She-altiel his son, [18] Malchiram, Pedaiah, Shenazzar, Jekamiah, Hoshama, and Nedabiah; [19] and the sons of Pedaiah: Zerubbabel and Shime-i; and the sons of Zerubbabel: Meshullam and Hananiah, and Shelomith was their sister; [20] and Hashubah, Ohel, Berechiah, Hasadiah, and Jushab-hesed, five. [21] The sons of Hananiah: Pelatiah and Jeshaiah, his son Rephaiah, his son Arnan, his son Obadiah, his son Shecaniah. [22] The sons of Shecaniah: Shemaiah. And the sons of Shemaiah: Hattush, Igal, Bariah, Neariah, and Shaphat, six. [23] The sons of Neariah: Eli-o-enai, Hizkiah, and Azrikam, three. [24] The sons of Eli-o-enai: Hodaviah, Eliashib, Pelaiah, Akkub, Johanan, Delaiah, and Anani, seven.

A. Notes to MT

[1] דניאל, II Sam. 3.3 כלאב, LXX דלאה, cf. commentary; [2] שני, prob. השני (cf. LXX and V); לאבשלום, omit ל? [6] אלישמע, II Sam. 5.11 אלישוע, prob. correct; אליפלט, absent from II Sam. 5, cf. commentary; [7] ונגה, absent from II Sam. 5; [8] אלידע, I Chron. 14.7 בעלידע, prob. correct, cf. commentary; [15] יוחנן, Lucianic Version יואחז; [17] אסר, proposed האסיר; בנו, omit? [19] פדיה, LXX reads שאלתיאל, cf. commentary; ובן, possibly ובני, following several MSS and the Versions; [20] חמש, read חמשה? [21] בני, read בנו with LXX and V; שכניה, add בנו; [22] ששה, cf. commentary; [23] ובן, possibly ובני, but cf. v. 19.

B. Notes to RSV

[2] 'whose mother was', MT 'the son of' ; [10] 'the descendants', MT 'the son'; [17] 'the captive', MT 'Assir'.

C. Structure, sources and form

1. The purpose of this chapter is to give a representative genealogical portrait of the Davidic house from David's own day to some time in the fourth century BCE. This record, however, is not intended to be comprehensive; it focusses on certain elements of this history.

The chapter is composed of three parts, distinguished by their topics, sources, structure and goals, but its structure can be conceived in two ways:

I. (*a*) 1–9 David's sons
    (*b*) 10–16 The kings of Judah
    (*c*) 17–23 The house of David after Jehoiachin
II. (*a*) as above
    (*b*) 10–14 The kings of Judah down to Josiah
    (*c*) 15–24 Josiah and his descendants.

According to the first, and more common, view (cf. Rudolph, 26–9; Williamson, 56–9, etc.), the second section is devoted to 'the kings of Judah'; the second view is based on formal distinctions, according to which the method of registration changes with the sons of Josiah (cf. J. Liver, *The House of David*, Jerusalem 1959, 8–19*, but also Curtis, 100, and cf. below).

2. The first section records the sons born to David by his principal wives; it is composed of two parts, each with a heading: v. 1 'These are the sons of David ... in Hebron'; v. 5 'These were born ... in Jerusalem'. The concluding formula for the passage is in v. 9, 'All these were David's sons'.

The section is drawn completely from biblical sources, adopted here either literally or in reworked form, thus:

3.1–4a = II Sam. 3.2–5 (the sons born in Hebron)
3.4b   = II Sam. 5.5 (reworked; duration of David's reign)
3.5–8   = II Sam. 5.14–16 (I Chron. 14.4–7, the sons born in Jerusalem)
3.9   = eclectic: I Sam. 5.13; 13.1.

Here again, the compositional element in the Chronicler's work is outstanding. In order to compose a complete record of 'the sons of David', a topic not found as such in II Samuel, he draws material from various places in his sources, combines them and gives them new function and meaning. Thus, II Sam. 5 as a whole is cited by the Chronicler in I Chron. 11.1–9 and I Chron. 14, but the specific II Sam. 5. 5 is reserved for use here in I Chron. 3, to form the transition from one list of sons to the other, explaining the locations 'Hebron' and 'Jerusalem' in the respective headings (vv. 4, 5). Verse 9, on the other hand, is the Chronicler's conclusion, based on II Sam. 5. 13, with the addition of a reference to Tamar. The Chronicler thus rounds off the genealogical lists by supplementing relevant material extracted from the historiographic sections.

3. The list of David's sons born in Jerusalem is found both here and in I Chron.

14.4–7. Such double use of genealogical material is a known literary phenomenon in Chronicles and is often regarded as a result of interpolation (according to Rudolph, 11, 26, the whole of ch. 3 should be therefore regarded as secondary), or multiple literary layers. This is not necessarily the case; the same list may be adduced for two different purposes, and reworked accordingly. In the present context, the list forms part of the genealogical picture of David's house, while in I Chron. 14 it is cited as an illustration of David's establishing his roots in Jerusalem. II Sam. 5.13, for example, is taken over in I Chron. 14.3, but not here.

In this passage, as in several others, the author's propensity for numbers is apparent: the numerical order of the sons of David (vv. 1–3, following II Sam. 3.2–6), and the introduction of sums: six (v. 4) and nine (v. 8).

4. The list of vv. 10–16 presents the kings of Judah consecutively in the form of a genealogical tree. Only at the end does the list broaden somewhat, introducing the four sons of Josiah and the two of Jehoiakim, although only three of these six were kings of Judah (formally reflecting at this point the same features as the following section, cf. below). The list is an extremely concise extract of the history of the kingdom of Judah, preserving only a sub-structure of names, connected by the word 'his son'. In principle, the technique here follows that of I Chron. 1.1–4 etc.: the simple names were extracted from a more elaborate presentation.

The question of the origin of the list cannot be answered conclusively. The list may have been composed by the Chronicler himself on the basis of the book of Kings (which he followed in the historiographic portions of his book), as it has no heading and is fully integrated into its present context. It could also have been available to the Chronicler in its present form. Similar records are found elsewhere in the genealogical material, e.g. the list of the high priests in I Chron. 6.4–15 (MT 5.30–41), where 'begot' is used to link the names instead of 'his son'. The main difference between these two lists is that while the actual history of the kings is found in the sources available to us, thus accounting for the data contained in the list, nothing of the sort is available for the list of priests.

As hinted above, 3.10–16 is not a full genealogical record of the house of David, but strictly a list of kings. The kings of Judah had numerous offspring, material on whom is preserved to some degree by the Chronicler himself: II Chron. 11.18ff., the sons of Rehoboam; II Chron. 21.2, the sons of Jehoshaphat. He does not, however, utilize this data here, as his focus is the direct line of the house of David, the full story of which will come later.

5. Verses 17–24 (or 15–24) outline, not comprehensively, the genealogical record of the house of David after Jehoiachin (or Josiah). Since v. 21 is probably corrupt, its reconstruction also bears upon the question of form. Basically, the reconstruction of the verse may be achieved in two different ways: by minor adjustments, which would preserve its deviant form, or by a more drastic adjustment to the prevailing structure of the whole passage. According to the first method, vv. (15–)17–24 would be composed of three parts, corresponding to the alternation in the mode of registration. In the first part (vv. [15–]17–20) and the third (vv. 22–24), several generations are recorded following one pattern: an enumeration of the sons of one father, continued in the next generation through one of these sons only. Thus: (Josiah and his sons, Jehoiakim and his sons); Jeconiah (Jehoiachin) and his sons; (Assir and his sons, cf. the commentary), Pedaiah and his sons; Zerubbabel and his sons; and, later, Shechaniah and his sons; Shemaiah and his sons; Neariah and his sons; Elioenai

and his sons. The intervening v. 21 would be construed either as a 'vertical' list of seven generations from Hananiah to Shechaniah, or a synchronic list of Hananiah's sons, recorded in a different manner. A severe reconstruction of v. 21 (cf. below), would regard it as recording one generation only, and the list as a whole would be completely homogenous.

Formally, the passage is also marked by the addition of numbers, which are attached systematically to the last part (vv. 22, 23, 24), and sporadically to the first (v. 20), in the same mode as the opening passage of the chapter.

The number of generations represented in the list (and consequently its date) are likewise determined by its form, i.e. by the restoration of the text. The two methods outlined above and further textual considerations would set the number of generations after Jehoiachin between seven and fourteen, which (giving twenty years for a generation) are equivalent to a period between 140 and 280 years. The list would thus reach from 460 to 320 BCE, and if we assume that this would be approximately the date of the author himself, we see that the reconstruction of the passage is of major significance in establishing a *terminus ad quem* of the Chronicler's composition.

Some scholars regard the passage as post-Chronistic, their arguments being mostly of a general nature, based on their general attitude toward the book rather than on intrinsic facets of the passage in question. In particular, an *a priori* assumption of an early date for the Chronicler will render impossible any attribution to him of this list.

D. Commentary

[1–4] The list of David's sons born in Hebron is taken almost verbatim from II Sam. 3.2–5. The changes are either textual and stylistic or alterations indicated by the different context. In II Sam. 3 the list is incorporated into the narrative: 'And David grew stronger ... and sons were born to David'; here, the context is dominated by lists, and so bears a different heading: 'These are the sons of David that were born, etc.' The same formula is used in I Chron. 2.33b and 50 for conclusions, but there is no apparent difference in the use of the formula in its different locations.

As in II Sam. 3, six sons are mentioned, and the list concludes explicitly 'six were born to him in Hebron' (note the Chronicler's touch: 'six' instead of 'these', and *nōlād lō* instead of *yull^{e}dū*). The heading and conclusion (vv. 1, 4) are problematical in two ways: first, it is doubtful whether the list includes *all* of David's sons born in Hebron. In fact, only the first-born of each mother is recorded, and the very first, Amnon, who is also the first-born of his father, is explicitly mentioned as such. It is hardly likely that none of David's wives bore him further children during those seven years in Hebron. Secondly, it is possible that some of the sons listed here were born previously, as the two first wives are mentioned already in relation to the period before David reigned in Hebron (I Sam. 25.43–44; 27.3; 30.5; II Sam. 2.2). It would seem, therefore, that originally the list had served another function, as a record of the first-born of each of the royal wives, information which probably had some bearing on status in the court hierarchy. Only secondarily was this list adduced to record all David's sons 'that were born to him in Hebron'.

Of the four wives whom David took in Hebron, Maacah seems to be the most distinguished, as her origins are cited in full. This is probably the first of the 'diplomatic marriages' which were to reach their zenith in Solomon's time. Both this list and its source avoid the mention of Michal, Saul's daughter (cf. further on I Chron. 15.29).

It should also be noticed that in spite of the simple subject-matter, the list reveals no uniform pattern. The sons are referred to their respective mothers, sometimes with 'by' (l^e), sometimes with 'the son of', while the fifth son is designated differently in Samuel from Chronicles. These variations point to a stylistic preference for variety rather than uniformity, and should serve as guidelines in our general literary approach to the lists.

David's second son, by Abigail, is called 'Chileab' in II Sam. and 'Daniel' in Chronicles. It is commonly accepted that one is the corruption of the other, the reading of LXX forming the intermediate link. In the stories of II Sam. the fate of three of these first-born – Amnon, Absalom and Adonijah – is told, while Chileab, David's second son, is ignored, probably because he did not survive.

The title of Abigail, 'the wife of Nabal the Carmelite' (II Sam. 3.3; also I Sam. 27.3; 30.5; II Sam. 2.2), is shortened here to 'the Carmelitess'. Whether this is in order to avoid the reference to the circumstances in which she became David's wife (I Sam. 25), or merely a stylistic abbreviation, cannot be determined.

Eglah is designated in II Sam. 'David's wife' and here 'his wife'; both appellations are equally peculiar, and have led to the Midrashic elaboration that this was in fact referring to Michal, David's most beloved wife (*Yalkut Shimeoni*, section 141).

[4aβ–b] This is of interest. In its present context it provides an explanation for the fact that some of David's offspring were born in Hebron and some in Jerusalem, and is therefore placed between the two lists of sons. The verse, taken from II Sam. 5.5, undergoes several changes. The words 'over Judah' and 'over all Israel and Judah' are omitted, in full accord with the Chronicler's characteristic view that David was, from the very beginning, king over 'all Israel'. However, the verse still presents some difficulty. The course of events as described in I Chron. 11–12 does not leave room for seven-and-a-half years of rule in Hebron. David's enthronment in Hebron was from the outset 'over all Israel' (I Chron. 11.3), and this was immediately followed by the conquest of Jerusalem, by the establishment of David's court there, and the transfer of the ark to its resting place. No hiatus is found for the more-than-seven-year reign in Hebron. A convenient way out of the difficulty is to regard this verse (alone, or as part of a longer unit) as 'post-

Chronistic', making a later interpolator responsible for the incongruity. However, the advantages of such a solution are dubious. Except for the chronological tension, there is no reason to regard the passage as non-Chronistic, while there are several indications – stylistic and theological – that the Chronicler is the author. Moreover, it is again stated in I Chron. 29.29, this time following I Kings 2.11, that 'he reigned seven years in Hebron and thirty-three years in Jerusalem'.

One might perhaps hazard the suggestion that the Chronicler was not fully sensitive to all the logical incongruities resulting from his own restructuring of the material, or to the tensions between his new emphases and the dry chronological framework which he had adopted unchanged. This is further evidence of the fact, which we will encounter later, of the stability of the chronological framework in Chronicles, from which he by no means deviates.

[5–9] The changes introduced in this passage, drawn from II Sam. 5.13–16, are required by the new context and the Chronicler's views. Since the context is genealogical, the Chronicler omits the opening of the list (II Sam. 5.13) and moves directly to the names themselves. An echo of this verse is found, however, in v. 9, where 'the sons of the concubines' are mentioned.

Unlike the former list, this passage does not refer the sons to their respective mothers, so we cannot determine whether it also purports to record only the 'first born' or all of David's sons born in Jerusalem. In v. 5 the first four sons are assigned to 'Bathshua the daughter of Ammiel', and since Solomon is one of the four, the reference is undoubtedly to 'Bathsheba the daughter of Eliam' (II Sam. 11.3). This is the only item of information not known to us from Samuel; can it be regarded as reflecting data from another source available to the Chronicler (thus Rudolph, 26)? The appearance here of Solomon as Bathsheba's fourth son, while according to all our sources he was clearly her first, is indeed difficult. Apparently the Chronicler drew the name of Bathsheba (=Bathshua) from the narrative material in Samuel – a technique he applies systematically – and ascribed to her not only Solomon but the first group of names in which he appears. In doing so the Chronicler followed the example of the opening passage, but since Bathshua is the only Jerusalem mother named in Samuel, he did not go on to provide maternal identification for the other sons. The same list appears in I Chron. 14.4ff. without the addition of Solomon's mother.

In the royal mother's name, the patronymic forms Eliam/Ammiel are interchangable (cf. Jeconiahu – Jehoiachin and more), while a close similarity also exists between 'Bathsheba' and 'Bathshua'. These could reflect alternative spellings or an adaptation of the original 'Bathsheba' to the name of Judah's first wife, following a general inclination to parallelism between David's household and that of Judah; note that both Bathshua and Tamar are explicitly mentioned in Judah's biography (I Chron. 2.3–4).

The list includes two names not found in II Sam. 5.14, 'Eliphelet and Nogah'. These are regarded by several scholars as the results of dittography: Eliphelet – of the same name in v. 8, and Nogah – of the proximate 'Nepheg'. However, both names do appear in I Chron. 14.5–6 as well. The sum 'nine' given at the end of the list (v. 8) takes these names into account. It seems unlikely that the presumed *double dittography* (in itself an extremly unusual phenomenon) was followed up by a corresponding change of 'seven' to 'nine'. All these points seem to support the originality of the names; their omission in Samuel could have resulted from a textual corruption. That David may have had two sons by the name Eliphelet is not in principle impossible, the children having been born to different wives; however, it may also be that an original distinction between the two names has been lost in transmission (in I Chron. 14 there is a slight difference between the two: 'Elpalet' and 'Eliphelet').

Two differences of detail in the names should be mentioned: 'Shimea' (v. 5) is a variant for 'Shamua' in the other two lists, and both are probably hypocoristic forms of 'Shemaiah'. 'Eliada' (v. 8) probably derives from the more original form preserved in I Chron. 14.7, Beeliada, which still retains the element 'Ba'al', so common in the onomasticon of the early monarchy.

[9] The conclusion of the list introduces two more details: a reference to the 'sons of the concubines', known from the heading of the list in II Sam. 5.13, and a reference to one of David's daughters, Tamar, who is familiar from the narratives of Samuel (esp. II Sam. 13), which were not included in Chronicles. Thus, all of David's family known to the Chronicler from the book of Samuel are assembled, to complete the list of royal offspring.

[10–16] The kings of Judah, in the order of their reign, are presented in the form of a genealogical tree as far as Josiah; there follows a list of the four sons of Josiah and two of Jehoiakim (vv. 15–16). Difficulties arise both from the names of the four sons of Josiah (Yohanan, Jehoiakim, Zedekiah and Shallum) and from the order in which they appear. According to the book of Kings Josiah had three sons, who were, in order of their reign: Jehoahaz (II Kings 23.31, twenty-three years old in 608 BCE); Eliakim–Jehoiakim (II Kings 23.34, 36, twenty-five years old in 608 BCE) and the much younger Mattaniah-Zedekiah (II Kings 24.17–18, twenty-one years old in 597 BCE). The order of their birth according to Kings would be Eliakim–Jehoiakim, Jehoahaz, Mattaniah-Zedekiah. A son of Josiah named Shallum is mentioned in Jer. 22.10–12, and it can be deduced from the circumstances described in the prophecy that this is none other than Jehoahaz. The list in Chronicles would bear out all this information, adding a son by the name of Johanan who was not mentioned in Kings because he never reached the throne. If the order of the list is that of birth, it may be assumed that for some reason he was not fit for kingship or simply did not survive. The appearance of Shallum

(Jehoahaz) at the end of the list might be due to accidental misplacement, or to chronological considerations: Zedekiah, whose age might have been misrepresented in II Kings 24.18, could in fact have been older than Shallum/ Jehoahaz (cf. also below). The reading in the Lucianic recension of LXX ('Joahaz' in place of 'Johanan'), reflecting the order of their appearance in Kings, is preferred by some scholars (Kittel, BH). Such a reading, however, would take Shallum and Joahaz as two different persons, and render the prophecy of Jer. 22 inexplicable. It seems preferable to regard the Greek reading as secondary, motivated by harmonization.

[16] Contrary to the information in II Kings 24, two sons of Jehoiakim are mentioned: Jeconiah (Jehoiachin), who according to the book of Kings reigned after his father's death, and another Zedekiah, who is not mentioned in Kings at all. This peculiar note is also reflected in II Chron. 36.10, where Zedekiah, the last king of Judah, is not introduced as the son of Josiah, the brother of Jehoiakim and Jehoiachin's uncle (II Kings 24.17), but as the son of Jehoiakim and Jehoiachin's brother. The tradition of Chronicles is thus consistent in its two expressions: only two, not three of Josiah's sons were kings; Jehoahaz the younger reigned first, followed by his older brother Jehoiakim; the order of their birth and not of their succession has been presented in v. 15. This may account for the place of Zedekiah before Shallum/Jehoahaz, as this Zedekiah is not to be confused with the much younger king by the same name. Following Jehoiakim, two of his sons were kings, Jehoiachin and Zedekiah the younger.

The alternative views may be illustrated as follows:

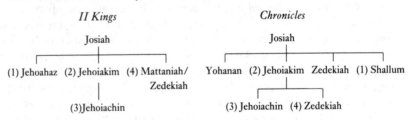

(1) etc. – the order of their reign

Should the tradition of Kings or of Chronicles be accepted as authentic? The impressive consistency of the Chronicler's view counts strongly in its favour. Moreover, the firmest support for II Kings 24.17 is to be found in Jer. 1.3 and 37.1, both of which are of an editorial nature; while Jeremiah himself always refers to Jehoiakim as 'the son of Josiah' (Jer. 22.18, etc.), he never uses the same designation for Zedekiah, but always 'the king of Judah' (21.7; 24.8 etc.) or 'the king' (37.18 etc.). However, in spite of these indications, one should still remember that the book of Kings was much closer to the events than Chronicles, and no reason has been shown why the author of Kings should change the original affiliation of the last king of Judah. General considerations, then, still make a better case for the tradition of Kings; the origin of the Chronicler's view is not fully clear (cf. also the other facts regarding the last kings of Judah, such as the deportation of Jehoiakim).

[17–24] This passage is our most detailed portrait of the Davidic house after the exile (for a detailed discussion of the data cf. J. Liver, *The House of David*, Jerusalem 1959, 8–19*). Elsewhere we find only 'Zerubbabel the son of Shealtiel', who according to Hag. 2.20 should be regarded as Davidide, and Hattush 'of the sons of David', who returned with Ezra (Ezra 8.2). The debate still goes on whether 'Sheshbazzar' of Ezra 1.7, 11, etc. is to be identified with 'Shenazzar' in this passage (v. 18), and some scholars would regard Nehemiah the son of Hachaliah as a Davidide, although there is no explicit basis for this either in his Memoirs or in this list (cf. U. Kellermann, *Nehemia, Quellen, Überlieferung und Geschichte*, BZAW 102, 1967, 158).

The authenticity of the list has not been questioned, and is supported by the reference to Jehoiachin and his five sons in a Babylonian document, thus establishing the continuity of the house of David after the destruction (cf. E. F. Weidner, 'Jojachin, König von Juda', in *Babylonische Keilschrifttexten, Mélanges R. Dussaud*, II, 1939, 923–8).

The list does not provide a full genealogy of the house of David, since only the descendants of one son are given in each generation (more often than not it is not the first-born). As it is hardly likely that all other members of the family died childless, this form should be regarded as intentional, possibly indicating the line of succession within the house of David. If correct, this would mean that the Davidic dynasty maintained a clear line of succession for many generations after the end of the monarchy; probably these Davidic scions held also a certain status within the community – although nothing of this is preserved in our sources.

[17] In the book of Kings, Jehoiakim's first son is always called Jehoiachin (II Kings 24.6, etc.), in Jeremiah always Coniah or Jeconiah (Jer. 22.24; 24.1, etc.), except in Jer. 52.31, which is parallel to II Kings 25.27. In Chronicles both names are found, probably depending on which sources were being used: thus 'Jehoiachin' in II Chron. 36.8, 9; 'Jeconiah' here and in v. 16. The structure of the verse, as well as the function of the word *'assir* ('Assir', RSV 'captive'), is problematical. Formally, the verse is parallel to v. 10, excepting the change in the first word, *ben, b⁶nē* thus:

ūben-š⁶lōmōh r⁶hab'ām, 'ᵃbiyyāh b⁶nō
ūb⁶nē y⁶kānyāh 'assir, š⁶'altī'ēl b⁶nō.

According to this parallel, Assir would be the name of Jehoiachin's son, and Shealtiel, together with the individuals in v. 18, would be the sons of Assir.

The plural 'the sons of Jehoiachin', followed by only one name, is a form abundantly attested in the genealogical material (*inter al.* I Chron. 2.31). Neither is there any difficulty in the name Assir itself (cf. Ex. 6.24; I Chron. 6.22, 23, 37 [MT 6.7, 8, 22]). However, the extra-biblical evidence that Jehoiachin had five sons, and the nevertheless uncommon structure here, have prompted many scholars to regard *'assir* as an adjective, i.e. 'captive' (thus RSV), regardless of the fact that such titles are not found elsewhere in these lists. In this case, Shealtiel and those mentioned in v. 18 would be Jehoiachin's sons, an understanding which poses difficulty in 'his son' after the name of Shealtiel. This form of registration is found in the lists either when only one son per generation is mentioned (cf. vv. 10bff.) or, less often, after each of the sons of one father (cf. v. 16), but I have not encountered 'his son' after only one son out of several. The word has been regarded either as a gloss or as a corruption of *b^ekōrō*, 'his first-born'.

[19] There is nothing intrinsically difficult in the phrase 'sons of Pedaiah', but its juxtaposition with other texts does pose a problem. The leader of the Judean community in the time of Darius is called in all sources either simply 'Zerubbabel' (Zech. 4.6, etc.; Ezra 2.2, etc.), or 'Zerubbabel the son of Shealtiel' (Hag. 1.1, etc.; Ezra 3.2, etc.); in Hag. 2.20 he is alluded to as a successor of Jehoiachin. In this list, the Davidic line of succession does indeed go through Zerubbabel, and in the appropriate chronological setting, but he is described here as a son of Pedaiah. Harmonizing comments have regarded this contradiction as an indication of a levirate marriage: Zerubbabel was in fact the son of Pedaiah, but was called by the name of Shealtiel, his childless brother (Rudolph, 29); or, less dramatically, he was the son of the one and brought up by the other (Ibn Ezra on Hag. 1.2). Others would find here two different persons, actually cousins, by the same name: the son of Pedaiah mentioned here, and the son of Shealtiel in all the other sources (W. F. Albright, 'The Date and Personality of the Chronicler', *JBL* 40, 1921, 108–9). Most scholars, however, would adopt the reading of the LXX, 'Shealtiel' for 'Pedaiah'.

The verse ends with the mention of 'Shelomith their sister'. As all the other daughters or sisters mentioned specifically in the lists are well-known historical figures (2.16, 49; 3.9), one would not go too far in assuming that Shelomith was a figure of some standing at the time of the Restoration, although no information to that effect has survived. Avigad would hazard the suggestion that it was this Shelomith who was the owner of the seal bearing the inscription 'Shelomith, the maidservant (*'mt*) of Elnathan' (N. Avigad, *Bullae and Seals from a Post-exilic Judean Archive*, Qedem IV, Jerusalem 1976, 11, 22).

[20] The actual affiliation of the five names recorded in this verse is not clear. If reference to a sister ordinarily determines the end of a list (cf. above,

v. 9), the children of Zerubbabel would be only three: Meshullam, Hananiah and Shelomith, their sister (v. 19); the following names would stand independently, as is also indicated by the number 'five' at the end of v. 20, which marks these as a distinct group. The more common approach is to supply here $b^e n\bar{e}\ m^e \check{s}ull\bar{a}m$, 'the sons of Meshullam' (cf. BH). This would, however, trace the line of descent through two of Zerubbabel's sons, counter to the general principle of the list. Others would see the two groups of names as belonging to two phases in Zerubbabel's life, in Babylon and in Judah, and Rudolph (p. 29) would even reconstruct the text in this way.

Five is in the masculine form in Hebrew ($h\bar{a}m\bar{e}\check{s}$), as if referring to daughters; nothing in the names, however, indicates that they are feminine. One should probably read $h^a mi\check{s}\check{s}\bar{a}h$.

[21] In the attempt to reconstruct this difficult verse, several approaches have been taken. The least radical is to regard the series of $b^e n\bar{e}$, 'sons of' , as corruption of $b^e n\bar{o}$, 'his son' (following the LXX and V). This reading raises some doubts regarding the punctuation of the verse. According to the Massoretic accentuation, the restored word $b^e en\bar{o}$, 'his son', would precede the name it describes and will necessitate reading 'the sons of Hananiah' in the plural at the beginning of the verse, following the ancient Versions (thus RSV). Such a mode of registration, however, is not attested elsewhere in the lists. Another possibility is to regard the word 'his son', disregarding the Massoretic accents, as following the name in each case, which would require the addition of 'his son' after 'Shecaniah' (again, following LXX). This arrangement would make only Pelatiah the son of Hananiah.

When all is said and done, the interpretation of the verse still depends on the exegete's understanding of the specific form yielded by his reconstruction. The list of names may be interpreted as a genealogical tree, numbering several generations from Hananiah to Shecaniah (as in vv. 10bff. above), or equally as recording five (or four) sons of one father, each name followed by the word 'his son' (as in v. 16 above). Since both ways are attested in the lists, no conclusive position can be taken. The position of Jeshiah, as either Pelatiah's brother or son, would have to be decided independently.

The more radical approach is to omit altogether the series of 'the sons' ($b^e n\bar{e}$) and replace them with waw conjunctive (Kittel, Rudolph, followed by BH and BHS). In addition, 'the son of' at the beginning would be changed to the plural, following multiple textual witnesses, and the verse would thus present the six sons of Hananiah. While this solution has the advantage of achieving complete uniformity in the method of registration throughout the passage, it offers no explanation for the supposed drastic corruption.

[22] As it stands, the verse records one son of Shecaniah, called Shemaiah, and five sons of the latter, the list of which, however, concludes with 'six'. This incongruity can be solved by assuming that a name has dropped from

the list, or that the number is wrong and should be 'five'. Most scholars, however, would resort to the more radical view, that 'the sons of Shemaiah' is a gloss, and should be omitted – resulting in six sons of Shecaniah. The suggestion is based on Ezra 8.2, where the reference to Hattush 'of the sons of Shechaniah' is restored to 'Hattush the son of Shecaniah'. In fact, there is no need for this double reconstruction. Both texts attest the same fact: that Hattush was 'of the sons' (namely: of the house) of Shecaniah, not his direct son, his exact relationship as the grandson of Shecaniah being suggested by this verse.

The reading 'and the sons of' , in the plural, at the beginning of the verse, while only one name follows, has been attested many times before (*inter al.* I Chron. 2.31).

Although the preponderance of the names in this genealogy is Hebrew, there are also three Babylonian names: Shenazzar (*sin-uṣur*), Zerubbabel (zer-babili) and probably Hattush, which, although of uncertain origin, is found in Assyrian and Babylonian documents.

In the light of all that has been said, can anything be determined about the provenance of this list? The meagre data at our disposal do not permit a conclusive reply, but the case for Babylon seems to be stronger than for Judah. The mention of Hattush among those who returned from Babylon in Ezra's caravan (Ezra 8.2) locates his birth-place, and therefore the residence of the house of Shecaniah, in Babylon. Shecaniah is a descendant of Zerubbabel, and if Zerubbabel of our list is to be identified with 'Zerubbabel the son of Shealtiel' of the time of Darius, this would mean that either all or some of Zerubbabel's sons stayed in Babylon or returned there. At the other end of the list, the line of descent does not proceed through Hattush but through the fourth son of Shemaiah, Neariah. This may again indicate Babylon and not Judah as the place of origin of the list. It has been suggested above that the form of the list implies a 'line of succession' in the house of David; it would be in Babylon, then, that this line was preserved and transmitted for generations.

4.1–23

4 1 The sons of Judah: Perez, Hezron, Carmi, Hur, and Shobal. [2] Re-aiah the son of Shobal was the father of Jahath, and Jahath was the father of Ahumai and Lahad. These were the families of the Zorathites. [3] These were the sons of Etam: Jezreel, Ishma, and Idbash; and the name of their sister was Hazzelelponi, [4] and Penuel was the father of Gedor, and Ezer the father of Hushah. These were the sons of Hur, the first-born of Ephrathah the father of Bethlehem. [5] Ashhur, the father of Tekoa, had two wives, Helah and Naarah; [6] Naarah bore him Ahuzzam, Hepher, Temeni, and Haahashtari. These were the sons of Naarah. [7] The sons of Helah: Zereth, Izhar, and Ethnan. [8] Koz was the father of Anub, Zobebah, and the families of Aharhel the son of Harum. [9] Jabez was more honourable than his brothers; and his mother called his name Jabez, saying, 'Because I bore him in pain.' [10] Jabez called on the God of Israel, saying, 'Oh that thou wouldst bless me and enlarge my border, and that thy hand might be with me, and that thou wouldst keep me from harm so that it might not hurt me!' And God granted what he asked. [11] Chelub, the brother of Shuhah, was the father of Mehir, who was the father of Eshton. [12] Eshton was the father of Bethrapha, Paseah, and Tehinnah the father of Irnahash. These are the men of Recah. [13] The sons of Kenaz: Othni-el and Seraiah; and the sons of Othniel; Hathath and Meonothai. [14] Meonothai was the father of Ophrah; and Seraiah was the father of Joab the father of Ge-harashim, so-called because they were craftsmen. [15] The sons of Caleb the son of Jephunneh: Iru, Elah, and Naam; and the sons of Elah: Kenaz. [16] The sons of Jehallelel: Ziph, Ziphah, Tiri-a, and Asarel. [17] The sons of Ezrah: Jether, Mered, Epher, and Jalon. These are the sons of Bithi-ah, the daughter of Pharaoh, whom Mered married; and she conceived and bore Miriam, Shammai, and Ishbah, the father of Eshtemoa. [18] And his Jewish wife bore Jered the father of Gedor, Heber the father of Soco, and Jekuthiel the father of Zanoah. [19] The sons of the wife of Hodiah, the sister of Naham, were the father of Keilah the Garmite and Eshtemoa the Maacathite. [20] The sons of Shimon: Amnon, Rinnah, Ben-hanan, and Tilon. The sons of Ishi: Zoheth and Ben-zoheth. [21] The sons of Shelah the son of Judah: Er the father of Lecah, Laadah the father of Mareshah, and the families of the house of linen workers at Beth-ashbea; [22] and Jokim, and the men of Cozeba, and Joash, and Saraph, who ruled in Moab and returned to Lehem (now the records are ancient). [23] These were the potters and inhabitants of Netaim and Gederah; they dwelt there with the king for his work.

A. Notes to MT

Preliminary remark: The main obstacle to the understanding of this chapter is a lack of sequence between the individual segments. With the help of some conjecture a measure of continuity may be found in vv. 1–7; another coherent unit, related to the original framework laid down in 2.3–5, is found in vv. 21–23. However, the main body of the genealogy of Judah (vv. 8–20) is composed of seemingly independent passages, the juxtaposition of which reveals no apparent pattern. As it stands, the text comprises the following units: vv. 8, 9–10, 11–12, 13, 14, 15–16, 17–18, 19, 20. In addition, the text of some of these passages seems hopelessly corrupt.

Two distinct *a priori* approaches to this material are possible. It may be considered to reflect what was originally a rather random accumulation of isolated data; in this case continuity between the passages would be sought only when the explicit genealogical structure they portray suggests such a link. The fact that two fragments stand juxtaposed would not necessarily imply inter-relationship, and no textual reconstruction would therefore be necessary (cf. *inter al.*, Curtis, 146; Rudolph, 10–14). The other approach is to regard the very arrangment of the material as implying an original connection between the passages; links between seemingly independent segments would then be discovered, either by deciphering hidden allusions, or by 'probable reconstructions'. Since 'probability' invariably attracts some degree of subjectivity, such reconstructions will inevitably give rise to debate. While I tend in principle to follow the second approach, I have endeavoured always to keep its limitations in mind. Foremost among these is the possibility that gaps between the individual segments may have been caused not only by textual corruptions (which would justify the exegete's attempt at reconstruction), but also by an originally non-sequential grouping of the material. An illustration of the latter is found in what we may call the 'archetype' of 1.38 ff., where the introduction of 'the sons of Seir' is indeed unconnected genealogically with the preceding verses – as is demonstrated by the parallel of Gen. 38.

[1] וכרמי, probably read וכלבי, cf. commentary; [3] ואלה, some words are probably missing, cf. commentary; הצללפוני, possibly corrupt; [7] ואתנן, proposed add וקוץ; [8] הצבבה, proposed יעבץ;אחרחל בן הרום, corrupt? [11] אחי, LXXᴸ אבי; [12] נחש, LXX אחי אשלון הקנוי +; רכה, LXX רכב, cf. commentary; [13] חתת, probably add ומעונתי, following LXX and V; [15] עירו אלה, read עיר ואלה;ובני אלה וקנז, proposed אלה בני קנז, cf. commentary; [17–20] cf. commentary; [22] וישבי לחם, proposed וישבו לחם or בית לחם.

B. Notes to RSV

[2] 'was the father of', MT 'begot' (so JPS), also vv. 8, 11, 12, 14, cf. on 2.21; [18] 'Jewish', MT Judean, or Judahite (thus JPS); [19] 'fathers', MT 'father'; [20] 'Ben-zoheth', probably 'the son of Zoheth'; [21] 'the house of linen-workers of Beth-ashbea', cf. commentary; [23] 'and inhabitants', better 'who were the inhabitants' (JPS 'who dwelt'); 'with the king for his work', better, with NEB and JPS, 'on/in the king's service'.

C. Structure, sources and form

1. It has already been noted that ch. 4 is the most difficult in the Judaean genealogy, because of both the textual corruptions, which sometimes seem incorrigible, and the lack of continuity between the individual passages. In the course of the commentary I shall propose several ways to discover the hidden ties between the lesser passages and reveal the larger units. Meanwhile the Judaean genealogy in ch. 4 apparently comprises the following units:

1 A connecting link to 2.55
2–4 close of the genealogy of Hur
5–7 (8) genealogy of Ashhur
9–10 the story of Jabez
11–12 genealogy of Chelub
13 sons of Kenaz
14 sons of Meonothai and Seraiah
15 sons of Caleb the son of Jephunneh
16 sons of Jehallelel
17–18 genealogy of Ezrah
19 sons of the wife of Hodiah
20 sons of Shimon and Ishi
21–23 genealogy of Shelah.

A more radical reconstruction reveals five larger units here, linked by v. 1 to the preceding Judaean genealogy: vv. 2–4 Hur; vv. 5–10, Ashhur; vv. 11–15, Kenaz; vv. 16–20, Jehallelel and Ezrah; vv. 21–23, Shelah.

2. The literary form of the various units is not uniform, but varies with the nature of the genealogical detail. From a literary point of view, one passage in the pericope, vv. 9–10, stands out in particular. It is an aetiological story with a double word-play on the root עצב, from which the name Jabez (in metathesis) is regarded as derived. Although the genealogical introduction contains aetiological elements or even explicit word-plays here and there (1.19, Peleg; 2.7, Achar; 2.22–23, Havvoth-jair; 4.14, Ge-harashim; and especially 7.23, Beriah), the Jabez passage is remarkable for its polished aetiology, more characteristic of the Genesis material than of Chronicles. For particulars, cf. the commentary.

3. The question of sources in this chapter should be considered in relation to the Judaean genealogy as a whole. Very little of the actual writing in the chapter can be attributed to the Chronicler, whose hand is to be discerned in the vertical genealogy of 4.1, which provided the connecting link between 2.55 and 4.2ff., after ch. 3 had been interposed (cf. above, p. 72). The idiom of the Jabez passage, while consonant with Late Biblical Hebrew, is not specifically Chronistic; the same is true of its theological message, which accords with the attitude of the Chronicler but is too general to be decisive in determining authorship. Another consideration is the genre of the story which, while not unheard of, is quite rare in Chronicles. It is therefore difficult to decide whether these verses reflect an original composition of the Chronicler, his reworking of an earlier source, or an unretouched record derived from later material of some kind.

The main body of the genealogies displays no specifically Chronistic features, linguistic or otherwise. They were most probably derived by the Chronicler from sources which reflected actual socio-historical circumstances of the families of Judah; the principal question is whether these were mainly pre-exilic (Noth, 'Die Ansiedlung des Stammes Juda auf den Boden Palästinas', *PJB* 30, 1934, 41ff.) or post-exilic (Rudolph, 14).

The genealogies are only lightly coloured by Late Biblical Hebrew (the word בַּץ in v. 21; the phrase בעלו למואב in v. 22), but this could be due to linguistic texture rather than the source of the material. Thus, it seems that a decision on origins cannot rely on the evidence of specific details. As for general considerations, one should note that the material is not dependent on any known convention – genealogical or other – and that there is no correspondence between this framework and the information about Judah found in Ezra-Nehemiah: the record of the Judean families (Ezra 2.3–35// Neh. 7.8–33), the list of the 'chiefs of the province' (Neh. 11.4–9), or the list of settlements in Neh. 11.25–30.

My conclusion, phrased negatively, would be that there is no reason to accept this genealogical framework as reflecting the conditions of the Restoration period or later. Certain considerations would support a positive statement of this position. For the 'sons of Shelah' (vv. 21–23) very little genealogical material has survived; in vv. 13–14 there is actual genealogical material for the ethnic segment of Kenaz, which eventually was absorbed into Judah; in v. 15, Caleb, the son of Jephunneh, who is so familiar from the Pentateuch traditions, is not affiliated to any major Judahite branch. All these indications would point to early conditions of the tribe and independent lines of tradition. In view of these considerations I incline to regard the present genealogical material as reflecting pre-exilic conditions; its exact chronological provenance seems, however, to elude us.

D. Commentary

[1] As already stated, this connecting verse traces the genealogical thread back to 2.50–55, after the insertion of ch. 3. While the opening words are 'the sons of Judah', the five names are not another version of 2.3–5, but a vertical genealogical tree, descending from Judah to Shobal, following the order of generations as recorded beforehand in 2.4, 5, 9, 19, 50. The composition of the verse is similar in principle to 1.1–4, 24–27, in which consecutive generations are listed in one sequence without the father-son relationship being formally indicated. Similar lists, following different literary patterns, may be found in 2.10–12, 3.10–14, and more.

Contrary to 2.9 and 19, Hezron's son, the father of Hur, is 'Carmi'. However, since all these verses are from one hand and reflect the Chronicler's specific understanding of the genealogical system, the form *karmī* reflects, not a deviating tradition or an early confusion (Williamson, 59), but simply a textual corruption of *kālēb*, or more possibly, of *kelūbāy* (2.9), as proposed by many (BH; BHS; Curtis, 104; Rudolph, 30; *et al.*).

[2] The genealogy of Reaiah the son of Shobal presents three sons, Jahath, Ahumai and Lahad (all unique names), as 'the families of the Zorathites'. The Shobal/'Zorathite' affiliation has already been recorded in 2.53. There, however, the Zorathites (and Eshtaolites) are linked to Shobal through the four families of Kiriath-jearim, connected to Shobal by the latter's identification as 'Shobal the father of Kiriath-jearim' (2.50, 52) rather than through Reaiah (= Haroeh in 2.52; cf. there). It would seem, therefore, that the two records express different views about these affiliations, the former (2.52–53) more territorial in nature, the latter more ethnic.

The fact that the inhabitants of Zorah, the 'Zorathites' (possibly also the

'Zorites' of 2.54), were the object of so much attention, while possibly only an incidental result of the state of our sources, may also reflect the uncertain status of the town of Zorah, originally belonging to Dan (cf. Josh. 19.41; Judg. 13.2) but eventually attached to Judah (Josh. 15.33). The lists may preserve traces of some of the socio-ethnic processes connected with these changes.

[3–4] The Massoretic text, with the plural $w^{e'}\bar{e}lleh$ (these) before the singular $'^{a}b\bar{\imath}$ (the father of), is certainly corrupt. The simplest solution is suggested by LXX (followed by RSV), which reads 'sons of' in place of 'father of', thus opening here the genealogy of a new figure, Etam. This solution, however, does not take into account the broader context of the list, which in its final phrase (v. 4b) implies that 'Etam' is somehow related to 'the sons of Hur'. Since the list provided genealogical detail about the first two sons of Hur, Shobal (2.52–53; 4.2) and Salma (2.54–55), the verses probably represent the genealogy of Hareph. I would therefore follow the suggestion to regard MT and LXX as corruptions of a longer original, such as 'These were [the sons of Hareph the father of Bethgader: X] the father of Etam, etc.' (cf. M. Noth, 'Eine siedlungsgeographische Liste in 1 Chr. 2 und 4', *ZDPV* 55, 1932, 103, followed by Rudolph, 30; Myers, 23).

In this reconstruction, the 'Harephite' element would be the largest among the Hurites, comprising four localities, indicated by the formula 'the father of': Bethgader, Etam, Gedor and Hushah; six ethnic groups: X (the father of Etam), Izreel, Ishma, Idbash, Penuel and Ezer; and an additional branch of 'their sister'.

The introductory phrase 'and the name of their sister was ...' is not very usual, her name 'Hazzelelponi' even less so. Several scholars have accordingly seen the clause as corrupt (restored radically by Noth, for example, to 'Jehallelel Hazephoni', ibid. 105), or as a gloss, also corrupt (Rudolph, 30).

However, the same pattern is attested elsewhere in the genealogies, cf. 1.19 ('and the name of his brother was Joktan'); 1.50; 2.29; and in particular 7.15: 'the name of his sister was Maacah'. Since reference to feminine figures – 'wives', 'sisters', etc. – is a common feature of the genealogies, there is no substantial reason to regard it as secondary in this verse. As for the name itself, its last four letters seem indeed to be a dittography from the following name (פנואל – פוני); what remains (הצלל) is a unique name. While it may reflect textual corruption, any restoration would be arbitrary.

[4] In 2.54 'the father of Bethlehem' is Salma, but here the same title refers to Hur, Salma's father. Some scholars, regarding this as a difficulty, read *hī' bēt-leḥem*, referring to Ephrathah (cf. Rudolph, 30). However, 'Ephrath' is introduced throughout as a 'wife' and not as a locality. In fact, the difficulty is more apparent than real. Since the designation is to be taken ethnically rather than biologically, there is really no difficulty in regarding either more

generally 'Hur' or more specifically 'Salma' as 'the father of Bethlehem'. This repeated reference to Bethlehem can be attributed to the prominence of David's house, and the gloss, 'the father of Bethlehem', should perhaps be attributed to the Chronicler, who introduced the Davidic genealogical material into the midst of the list of Hurites.

[5–7(8)] The genealogy of the Ashhurites is constructed of two main branches, descending from Ashhur's two wives, Naarah (v. 6) and Helah (v. 7). Their ethnic and territorial circumstances may be adduced from several data. Ashhur himself is introduced in 2.24 as the son of Caleb and 'Ephrathah', a detail which illustrates the expansion of the Calebites from the hills of southern Judah towards the north, intermingling there with 'Ephrathite' elements. The designation of Ashhur as 'the father of Tekoa' defines the Ashhurite territory very clearly. Tekoa was a town of some significance on the outskirts of the desert east of Bethlehem; it is well-known as the home town of the prophet Amos (Amos 1.1), and its surroundings are probably alluded to in 'the wilderness of Tekoa' (II Chron. 20.20). The affinity between the Hurites and the Ashhurites is thus demonstrated not only by their similar names, but also by their provenance and territory.

Hepher is quite a common name; it is better known in Manasseh (Num. 26. 32–33; 27.1; etc.), but also as one of David's warriors (I Chron. 11.36). Temeni and Haahashtari are actually gentilic names ('of Teman', that is, 'the southerner'; of Ahashtar – probably a name of Persian origin). Ethnan could probably be identified with Ithnan of Josh. 15.23, usually located in the Negev.

While v. 8 is phrased as a continuation of v. 7 ('*and* Koz begot'), it in fact has no antecedent in vv. 5–7 as they stand. The proposal of many scholars, that 'and Koz' should be supplemented at the end of v. 7, is orthographically plausible (haplography), and would make v. 8 a direct sequel to v. 7, recording the third generation of the Ashhurites through Koz.

All the names in v. 8 are unique, and rather unusual, the most difficult being 'Aharhel the son of Harum'. In general, the pattern 'the families of' is attached in the genealogies either to a place name (with or without a gentilic suffix, cf. 4.2 and 2.53 respectively), to an ethnic group (7.5), or to a guild of craftsmen (2.55; 4.21). This analogy would make the unique 'families of Aharhel the son of Harum' a major ethnic factor (cf. 'the families of Manasseh the son of Joseph', Num. 27.1). However, the formulation of this verse, 'Koz begot ... the families of Aharhel the son of Harum', remains unique and difficult, since it would have Koz 'father' a family whose patronym is in fact 'Harum'. In all probability v. 8b is corrupt, and no satisfactory emendation has so far been suggested.

[9–10] In form and genre, these verses differ from the rest of the chapter: rather than being a genealogy of some kind, they introduce an aetiological story revolving around one man, Jabez. No mention of this personality has been encountered before, and the passage stands unconnected to its context. It has been suggested that the present text has suffered some omission or corruption; one possibility of reconstruction is to regard the unusual 'Hazobebah' (RSV: Zobebah) of v. 8 as such an antecedent (cf. BH; Curtis, 107–108). However, in this case a broader textual omission is more likely.

Jabez is mentioned in 2.55 as a place-name. Although from a literary point of view there is no connection, these two passages may, in the present genealogical framework, be somehow related to the 'Ephrathite' element within Judah.

The story presents several interesting facets, first of which is the word-play on the name Jabez derived, as it were, from the root *ṣb*. Ostensibly this is a case of wrong etymology, since the conjectured root of the name is *ʿbṣ* (cf. Baumgartner, *Lexicon*, III, 735), and not *ṣb*. However, the derivation here is not only presumed but emphasized. The name recurs three times, and the word-play on the root *ṣb* is demonstrated twice: first in the words of Jabez' mother, 'I bore him in pain (*bᵉʿōṣeb*)', clearly alluding to Gen. 3.16, 'I will ... multiply your pain (*ʿiṣbōnēk*) ... in pain you shall bring forth children (*bᵉʿeṣṣeb tēlᵉdī bānîm*)'. The second is in Jabez' own prayer 'that it might not hurt me (*ʿoṣbī*)'.

This discrepancy, between the actual pronunciation of the name and its assumed root, is the implicit but probably the strongest illustration of the premise of the story: the potent force of the name! The fear of the potentially harmful effects of a 'wrong' name is such that two precautions are taken to forestall its action: first, an intentional mis-pronunciation, 'Jabez' rather than 'Jazeb', as if to fool the messengers of fate, and secondly, on a different level, an urgent plea to God to avert the name's inherent dangers.

The structure of the story is unusual. In general, an aetiology offers an explanation for a given datum (commonly, but not always, a name) by recounting the causes from which it arose and demonstrating a positive connection between datum and causes (Beer-sheba, because they swore, Gen. 21.34; Beth-el, because this was the house of God, Gen. 28. 17–19; etc., cf. H. Gunkel, *Genesis*, Göttingen 1910 [⁹1977], XXff.). While this story contains several aetiological elements, its core is contradictory rather than causal: how did it happen that a man by the name of 'Jabez' was, nevertheless, prosperous! The story's exposition first presents the situation to be accounted for: 'Jabez was more honourable than his brothers' (v. 9a). To the Israelite ear, accustomed to aetiological word-plays, this poses a paradox which demands a solution: how could anyone by the name of Jabez be 'honourable'? The narrative then develops an aetiological origin (v. 9b), how he was given this unfortunate name in the first place, and an aetiological motive (v. 10a), showing how he wisely averted its danger. The conclusion of the story, 'God granted what he asked', closing the circle, provides a theological explanation for the opening statement, that 'he was more honourable than his brothers'.

The literary structure is well balanced:

Exposition (vs. 9a)
Direct speech, the mother's words (v. 9b)
Direct speech, the prayer of Jabez (v. 10a)
Conclusion (10b).

The exposition and conclusion are equal in length; each is structured as a single sentence introduced by an imperfect with *waw* consecutive: 'and he was (*way^{e}hī*) ... and God brought (*wayyābē'*) ...' The enclosed portions of direct speech are presented thus: the first with *'immō qār$^{e'}$āh*, which should be translated 'and his mother *had called* him' (RSV, 'called his name'), continued by 'and Jabez *called*' (*wayyiqrā' ya'bēṣ*). The same root *qr'* is used, and both introduce the direct speech with 'saying' (*lē'mōr*). Jabez' 'calling on the God of Israel' is thus formally presented as antithesis to his mother's 'calling' him by such a dire name.

The most elaborate element in the story is the prayer (v. 10a). Irrevocably burdened with a name which was determined by his mother's experience and is now to determine his own fate, Jabez takes the only possible step: a prayer to his God. God's power alone is superior to and more effective than the potency of the name, and it may be activated by acknowledgment in prayer. The latent intrinsic force in the name is not denied, but is subordinated to the mightier power of God.

The language of the prayer is difficult, a fact which is not brought out by the translation. The details are too technical for a full discussion here but the point should be noted.

The prayer's opening *'im* ('if') is the most common conditional lexeme and could imply an oath or a vow: 'if ... then'. However, no apodosis follows. It is therefore either an implied vow, or a case of the word *'im* serving as a wish: 'Oh that ...' (so RSV). For this last usage Gesenius cites four more instances, but only two of these (Ps. 139.19; Prov. 24.11) seem convincing (Gesenius §151e p. 477).

The prayer has a poetic structure, with three wishes dependent on the first expectant plea: 'Oh that thou wouldst bless me'. Each wish opens with a verb in the perfect with *waw* consecutive: *w^{e}hirbītā, w^{e}hāy^{e}tāh, w$^{e'}$āśītā*, and the four lines are rhymed by the recurring first person pronominal suffix: *t^{e}bār^{a}kēnī, g^{e}būlī, 'immī, 'oṣbī*.

The dry, almost bureaucratic character of the genealogies does not usually allow room for religious views; there is hardly a mention either of God or of his relationship with man. However, when such elements do enter the pericope, as in the excellent example of Jabez's prayer, it is always in conformity with the Chronicler's religious concepts (cf. also 2.3; 5.20, etc.).

[11–15] In the Massoretic text these verses comprise four or five isolated lists, neither interconnected nor linked with the broader genealogical context: the sons of Chelub (vv. 11–12), the sons of Kenaz (v. 13), the sons of Meonothai and Seraiah (v. 14), and the sons of Caleb, the son of Jephunneh (v. 15). However, a closer look at these fragments, with the assistance of extraneous information, may reveal some common elements and a stronger coherence, even so far as to suggest that the whole section represents a rather large component within the tribe of Judah.

The more obvious signs of congruity are in vv. 13–15. In v. 14 we find the records both of the previously unmentioned Meonothai, and of Seraiah who has been referred to in v. 13. The Lucianic Version of LXX and V (followed by RSV) supply the missing link: the mention of 'Meonothai' at the end of v. 13, which was omitted as a result of haplography. The overall structure of vv. 13–14 would be: the sons of Kenaz, Othniel and Seraiah (13a); the sons of Othniel (13b–14a); the sons of Seraiah (14b).

Verse 15 stands independently, with the record of 'Caleb the son of Jephunneh'. The difficult 15b, $ūb^en\bar{e}$ '$\bar{e}l\bar{a}h$ $ūq^enaz$ (lit. 'and the sons of Elah and Kenaz') can be restored in several ways: (a) the omission of the *waw* before Kenaz, assuming that 'the sons' in the plural is followed by one name, 'the sons of Elah: Kenaz' (thus RSV), (b) the restoration of an unknown name, 'the sons of Elah: X and Kenaz'. After these emendations, v. 15 must clearly be transposed before vv. 13–14, where 'the sons of Kenaz' are now recorded. In this reconstruction, Kenaz is seen as a descendant of Caleb. However, Caleb the son of Jephunneh is alluded to elsewhere as a 'Kenizzite' (Num. 32.12; Josh. 14.6, 14), and Othniel as 'the son of Kenaz, the brother of Caleb' (Josh. 15.17; Judg. 1.13; 3.9). 'Kenizzites' are also viewed as a major ethnic element of Canaan in Gen. 15.16 – all of which would indicate the genealogical precedence of Kenaz and the better restoration of 15b as '$\bar{e}lleh$ $b^en\bar{e}$ q^enaz ('these were the sons of Kenaz'), the conclusion of a list to which the introduction has been lost. Such a reconstruction, which is orthographically plausible, would account for the recurring references to Othniel as 'the brother of Caleb', and both being 'the sons of Kenaz'. Much as we would like to know the exact ethnic affiliation of Caleb himself within the 'Kenizzites', this remains obscure.

While a fair measure of coherence may, then, be established within vv. 13–15, their continuity with the preceding vv. 11–12 is more problematical. Here we find an account of the 'the men of Recah', descendants of the unknown 'Chelub the brother of Shuhah'. The name 'Chelub' may suggest an affiliation with 'Caleb', through one particular element identified as the 'brother of Shuhah'. This last name may have been a metathesis of 'Hushah', mentioned in v. 4 (and cf. 'the Hushathite' in II Sam. 23.27 and I Chron. 11.29; 27.21). The LXX alteration to 'Caleb the father of Achsah' seems to be a harmonization.

In v. 12 the LXX has an addition after the name 'Ir-nahash', reading 'the brother of Eshlon the Kenizzite'. This could be a corruption of an original 'the brother of Eshton, Kenaz' (thus Curtis, 110). If original, it would provide a certain link between the 'Chelubites' of vv. 11–12 and the 'Kenizzites' of vv. 13–15.

Another relevant element is the LXX rendering 'Recab' for MT 'Recah'. There is no way of ascertaining the originality of this reading, but the affinity between 'Rechab' and the Kenites in I Chron. 2.55, and of the 'Kenites' with the 'Kenizzites' in Gen. 15.19, may point to the priority of LXX.

Whether we regard the whole of vv. 11–15, or only vv. 13–15 as introducing the genealogies of the 'Kenizzites', it is clear that they comprise a relatively independent element within the tribe of Judah. Contrary to the Jerahmeelites and Calebites, we find no formal integration of the Kenizzites into the tribe by means of affiliation with any of the traditional 'sons' of Judah.

It has been proposed (H. L. Ginsberg and B. Maisler, 'Semitised Hurrians in Syria and Palestine', *JPOS* 14, 1984, 258–9, but cf. R. de Vaux, *The Early History of Israel*, London and Philadelphia 1978, 136–7) that the Kennizites were originally a Horrite element in Palestine. Kenaz appears also as Esau's grandson by Eliphaz (Gen. 36.11; I Chron. 1.36), which may mean that Kenizzite elements which settled in the southern parts of the land of Israel were eventually assimilated into both Edom and Judah. While in Edom their complete integration is demonstrated by the official genealogy, this is not the case in the references we possess for the tribe of Judah – a fact which might indicate the relative antiquity of this material. The same argument is further supported by the independence of 'Caleb the son of Jephunneh' within the tribe of Judah. The genealogies of Judah present Caleb as one of the major components of the tribe (2.18–20, 42–50a; cf. there), but he is consistently identified as 'the son of Hezron' (2.18 etc.) or 'the brother of Jerahmeel' (2.42). Even Achsah, known from Joshua and Judges as the 'daughter of Caleb the son of Jephunneh' (Josh. 15.16–17; Judg. 1.12–13), is linked here to Caleb, the son of Hezron (2.49).

These literary phenomena may reflect the historical process by which the Kenizzites were absorbed into Judah. The traditions of the Hexateuch account for the strong Calebite element in the hills of Judah by presenting 'Caleb the son of Jephunneh' as the only one of the spies (in addition to Joshua) who entered the land of Canaan after the wandering in the wilderness, and received a special lot in the territory of Hebron (Num. 14.24; Josh. 15.13–15; 21.12). Chronicles, by contrast, differentiates between two

Calebite elements: the main body of the tribe is ascribed a full Judaean affiliation as a branch of Hezron; the second, represented by 'Caleb the son of Jephunneh' and 'his brother' Othniel, recorded separately, was not fully integrated into the tribe of Judah and probably retained a greater degree of independence. The differences between the Hexateuch and the Chronicler are reflections not only of literary approach, but also of socio-ethnic developments and historical circumstances. One may say that the material found in Chronicles has a stronger foothold in historical reality, and from the point of view of the history of tradition reflects an earlier stage in the development of the 'Calebite' tradition.

The genealogy of the Kenizzites offers very little in terms of geographical information. Some of the proper names are quite common (Seraiah, Joab), while others are unique (Mehir, Eshton, Hathath, etc.). Only three are clear geographical designations: Ir-nahash (the town of Nahash), Beth-raphah (the house of Raphah) and Ge-harashim (the valley of the smiths/craftsmen). None of these, however, is attested elsewhere. The possible derivation of *nāḥāš* from *nᵉḥōšet* (copper, bronze), the reference to 'smiths', the general affinity between the Kenizzites and the Kenites (Gen. 15.19), who are also known as smiths (Gen. 4.22), and certain possible identifications with later names, may all point to the copper-smelting sites in the Arabah, on the slopes of Edom (Z. Kallai, *Historical Geography of the Bible*, Jerusalem and Leiden 1986,117).

These rather marginal territories would account for the relative isolation of this Kenizzite element at the period reflected here, and would accord with the existence of Kenizzite elements in both Judah and Edom (cf. above).

[16–20] This is the most difficult of all the Judahite passages. Verses 16–18 may possibly be reconstructed into a relatively coherent unit by supplying a missing introduction, such as 'the sons of X: Jehallelel and Ezrah'. Verses 16 and 17–18 would then represent two branches of one family, but we are still ignorant of its identity and position within the broader Judean structure.

A more familiar reconstruction is that which relates 'Jehallelel' and 'Ezrah' of vv. 16–17 to 'Hazzelelponi' and 'Ezer' of vv. 3–4 (Noth, 'Siedlungsgeographische Liste', *ZDPV* 55, 1932, 105). The families registered here would then form a branch of the Hurites, either directly through Hur, or through his son 'Hareph' (cf. *ad loc.*). This proposition is attractively coherent; its one shortcoming is that it is impossible to prove. In any case, as a geographical identification of the names may show, they represent a rather scattered element within Judah.

The descendants of Jehallelel are four: 1. Ziph is presented in 2.42 as descending from Caleb's son 'Mesha (RSV "Mareshah")'. It is also well-known from the stories of David's wanderings in Judah (I Sam. 23.14, etc.). 2. Ziphah, a very similar name, may refer to a kindred group. Indeed, the lists of Judah mention two localities by the name of Ziph (Josh. 15.24, 55), a distinction which may be reflected here too. 3. For the famous identification of Tiria, Asarel and Epher (v. 17), cf. W. F. Albright, 'The Smaller Beth Shan Stela of Sethos I (1309–1290 BC)' *BASOR* 125, 1952, 30–1. Asarel is known also as a Manassite family, Asriel (Num. 26.31; Josh. 17.2; for I Chron. 7.14, cf. there). One wonders how far this similarity may be followed to detect further connections between Judah and Manasseh (cf. above, on 2.21ff.).

[17–18] Here the descendants of Ezrah are recorded in detail. MT reads literally: '(v. 17a) And the *son* of Ezrah: Jether, Mered, Epher and Jalon. (v. 17b) And *she* conceived Miriam, Shammai and Ishbah, the father of Eshtemoa.' The generally accepted reconstruction of these lines is that proposed by Curtis (111, following Berthau and others). The words 'These are the sons of Bithiah, the daughter of Pharaoh, whom Mered married' are transposed from v. 18b to after v. 17a, 'son' (17a) becomes 'sons' (following some MSS and the Versions), and in v. 17b *watteled* ('and she bore') is added, for the reading 'and she conceived and bore Miriam, etc.'

According to these emendations, all of which are reflected in RSV, v. 17a records four sons of Ezrah, and what follows is a record of the offspring of one of these sons, Mered, by his two wives, one Egyptian and the other Judahite. Thus:

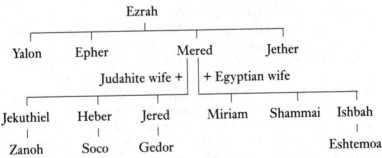

This text, as reconstructed above, testifies to a strong Egyptian factor in this Judahite segment, specifically in the family of Mered. It includes the common Judean element 'Shammai' (in 2.28–33 a descendant of Jerahmeel, in 2.44–45 of Caleb), the Judaean town of 'Eshtemoa' (cf. Josh. 15.50; 21.14; and esp. I Sam. 30.28), and also the unique 'Ishbah', and 'Miriam', familiar from an Egyptian milieu as the name of Moses' sister (Num. 26.59 etc.). This Egyptian component, introduced as 'the daughter of Pharaoh', is explicitly juxtaposed with a 'Judahite' (RSV 'Jewish') wife, the 'mother' of the remaining sons.

The name and title of this Egyptian wife, the unique 'Bithiah the daughter of Pharaoh', are both extraordinary. While the theophoric element in the name may be explained as a Hebraism, pinpointing her origin is more difficult. 'Pharaoh', according to biblical tradition, is not an Egyptian proper name but a royal title. That an undistinguished member of the tribe of Judah would marry a 'daughter of Pharaoh' is extremely unlikely, not only in the context of biblical tradition but for historical reasons as well. The marriage of Solomon to an Egyptian princess is presented in the book of Kings as an event of special significance (I Kings 3.1, etc.), and this is also the view of the modern historian, who regards such intermarriages as highly rare (A. Malamat, 'A Political Look at the Kingdom of David and Solomon and its Relations with Egypt', in T. Ishida, ed., *Studies in the Period of David and Solomon*, Tokyo 1982, 198–200). It is therefore no surprise that rabbinic tradition identified 'Mered' with Caleb, and regarded 'Bithiah' as the very daughter of Pharaoh mentioned in Ex. 2.7 (*Yalkut Shimeoni*, section 1074).

From a socio-historical point of view, it is of course highly probable that Egyptian elements may have mixed with the population of the Judaean Negev (cf. I Sam. 30.11, 13 – an Egyptian who is a slave to an Amalekite). In terms of the genealogies, such elements would be identified as 'wives'. It is rather the unusual name and title which make the reference so problematical.

The genealogy contains four explicit place-names, introduced by the formula 'X the father of Y': Eshtemoa, Gedor, Soco and Zanoah, all well-known Judean localities (cf. Josh. 15.34, 35, 48, 50, 58). Eshtemoa is in the southern part of the Judaean hills, Gedor is north of Hebron and Zanoah in the Shephelah. Soco may be identified either as the better-known town in the vicinity of Zanoah (Josh. 15.35; I Sam. 17.1, etc.), or with the town by the same name near Eshtemoa in the south (Josh. 15.48). In v. 19 Eshtemoa 'the son' of Ishbah is called 'Eshtemoa the Maachathite' and presented as a son (RSV a grandson) of 'the wife of Hodiah'. Similarly, Gedor, 'the son' of Jered, is according to 4.4 the son of Penuel, related to 'Hur'. These double affiliations may confirm the emendation mentioned above, or reflect the vicissitudes of the ethnic affiliation of these settlements during various historical periods.

[19–20] In MT, these verses contain three independent genealogical fragments: (*a*) v. 19 lists the two (or three) sons of 'the wife of Hodiah the sister of Naham', the father of Keila the Garmite (or the father of Keila, the Garmite), and Eshtemoa the Maacathite; (*b*) v. 20 lists first the four sons of Shimon, Amnon, Rinnah, Ben-hannan and Tilon, and then (*c*) the 'sons of Ishi', of which only one, Zoheth, is named. The list ends abruptly with the unfinished phrase 'and the son of Zoheth ...' (a lacuna not reflected in RSV, which takes 'Ben-zoheth' as a name).

Many of the elements in these fragments are unusual: the heading (the sons of the wife of X), the reference to 'the father of Keila' without a mention of his name, the abrupt ending with 'the son of Zoheth', etc.; all point to the corrupt state of this section, of which in fact, very little can be made. In LXX, v. 19 has an addition after the name of Naham which contains, among others, the name Shimon, and provides for a tighter connection between vv. 19 and 20a. Rudolph took the lead from this addition and proposed a rather complex reconstruction, which may provide solutions for several of the difficulties. It remains, however, entirely conjectural (Rudolph, 34, and BHS *ad loc*).

Of the names recorded here, the most familiar is Keila, known from the Judaean town list (Josh. 15.44), from the stories of David (I Sam. 23.1, etc.), and as 'half the district' in Neh. 3.17, 18. Eshtemoa has already been discussed above.

[21–23] With the exception of Neh. 11.5 (I Chron. 9.5), this section contains the only biblical data regarding the Judean branch of the Shelanites, which, according to the basic genealogical convention of the Pentateuch, is the most ancient Judaean element, descending from Judah's first wife, Bath-shua (or 'the daughter of Shua') of Gen. 38.5. The Shelanites are presented in these traditions as affiliated directly with the Canaanite families of Adullam (Gen. 38.1, also I Chron. 2.3).

This passage offers very little genealogical material; it contains neither vertical nor horizontal genealogies, and sheds very little light on the ethnic circumstances of the Shelanites. Instead, there are some general references to the main families of Shelah, mention of some individuals, and a relatively broad reference to their occupation.

The Shelanites mentioned here are:

(*a*) 'Er, the father of Lecah'. No Judean town by the name of Lecah is mentioned anywhere in the biblical sources, while the name 'Er' is known as the first-born of Judah (Gen. 38.3 etc.). 'Er' is thus represented as both Judah's extinct first-born and his grandson through Shelah. This double affiliation is similar to several other ethnic elements recorded in the lists, such as the case of Ram, presented as both the son of Hezron and his grandson through Jerahmeel (I Chron. 2.9, 25), or that of Dishon, who is both the son and the grandson of Seir (Gen. 36.21, 25; I Chron. 1.38, 41). It seems that the situation reflected in this verse, where 'Er' is the Shelanite first-born, if not taking precedence over the claim of Gen. 38.3 that 'Er died without sons', at least has a different concept of his affiliation and fate.

(*b*) 'Laadah, the father of Mareshah'. 'Laadah' is not mentioned elsewhere (but cf. the existence of Ladan in both Ephraim and Levi, I Chron. 7.26; 23.7, etc.), but Mareshah is a well-known Judaean town in the Shephelah (cf. Josh. 15.44, etc.), which has been previously affiliated to the Calebites (2.42). As is the case in all similar instances, such complicated ethnic developments are reflections of different periods and perspectives.

(*c*) Affiliated with the Shelanites are also the 'families of the house of linen workers of Beth-ashbea'. The free rendering of NEB reflects the meaning better: 'the clans of the guild of linen-workers at Ashbea'. It is not entirely clear whether 'the house of Ashbea' (*bēt-'ašbē'a*) stands for the town or the ethnic affiliation of the 'linen workers'.

(*d*) The list ends with a cryptic reference, pregnant with hidden implications, to three individuals (Yokim, Joash and Saraph) and a group ('the men of Cozeba'). They are all enigmatically described as having 'mastered (RSV "ruled in") Moab', and 'returned to Lehem', with the further remark that the 'records/matters are ancient'. The original coherence of these unique references and their possible allusion to well-known incidents of the past may be deduced from scattered information elsewhere. 'Cozeba' should probably be identified with 'Chezib', the place where Shelah is said to have been born according to Gen. 38.5. It is also to be identified with Achzib of Josh. 15.44, mentioned together with Mareshah. For us, however, these hints remain an enigma. (The Midrash applied them all to the incident of Rahab and the spies, of Josh. 2; cf. *Yalkut Shimeoni*, section 1074.)

(*e*) Verse 23 defines more precisely that 'these were the potters ...'. Since v. 21 ended with a reference to the linen workers, we may conclude that the potters are not the Shelanites at large, but only those mentioned above, in v. 22. We thus win a glimpse of the intricate history of this group: at present they are settled in 'Netaim and Gederah' and are enlisted for 'the king's service'; their past has been alluded to in v. 22.

The salient point of the laconic and abrupt list of the Shelanites is their designation as craftsmen. Such professional references are encountered sporadically in 2.55 and 4.14, but here they seem to occupy a more central place in the record. One may surmise that, as with the Kenites, it was through their occupations that the Shelanites were identified as a group.

It is not easy to say whether the fragmentary nature of the Shelanite material is due to the author's lack of interest or to the state of his sources – although the latter seems most likely. With this brief reference to the Shelanites, the circle begun in 2.3 is closed, and the genealogy of Judah comes to an end.

4 24 The sons of Simeon: Nemu-el, Jamin, Jarib, Zerah, Shaul; [25] Shallum was his son, Mibsam his son, Mishma his son. [26] The sons of Mishma: Hammu-el his son, Zaccur his son, Shime-i his son. [27] Shime-i had sixteen sons and six daughters; but his brothers had not many children, nor did all their family multiply like the men of Judah. [28] They dwelt in Beer-sheba, Moladah, Hazar-shual, [29] Bilhah, Ezem, Tolad, [30] Bethuel, Hormah, Ziklag, [31] Beth-marcaboth, Hazar-susim, Beth-biri, and Sha-araim. These were their cities until David reigned. [32] And their villages were Etam, Ain, Rimmon, Tochen, and Ashan, five cities, [33] along with all their villages which were round about these cities as far as Baal. These were their settlements, and they kept a genealogical record.

23 Meshobab, Jamlech, Joshah the son of Amaziah, [35] Joel, Jehu the son of Joshibiah, son of Seraiah, son of Asi-el, [36] Eli-o-enai, Ja-akobah, Jeshohaiah, Asaiah, Adi-el, Jesimi-el, Benaiah, [37] Ziza the son of Shiphi, son of Allon, son of Jedaiah, son of Shimri, son of Shemaiah – [38] these mentioned by name were princes in their families, and their fathers' houses increased greatly. [39] They journeyed to the entrance of Gedor, to the east side of the valley, to seek pasture for their flocks, [40] where they found rich, good pasture, and the land was very broad, quiet, and peaceful; for the former inhabitants there belonged to Ham. [41] These, registered by name, came in the days of Hezekiah, king of Judah, and destroyed their tents and the Me-unim who were found there, and exterminated them to this day, and settled in their place, because there was pasture there for their flocks. [42] And some of them, five hundred men of the Simeonites, went to Mount Seir, having as their leaders Pelatiah, Ne-ariah, Rephaiah, and Uzziel, the sons of Ishi; [43] and they destroyed the remnant of the Amalekites that had escaped, and they have dwelt there to this day.

A. Notes to MT

[33] מושבתם, proposed to transfer here the final pause (*soph pasuq*); [34] ומשובב, read ומשובב; [41] אהליהם, proposed אהלי חם.

B. Notes to RSV

[33] 'and they kept a genealogical record': for the verse division cf. above (A); NEB 'The names of their register were' (similarly JPS).

C. Structure, sources and form

1. In the basic genealogy of Jacob's sons, Simeon is the second and Judah the fourth. However, once the pericope has opened with Judah, it is natural for it to continue with Simeon. Not only do the two tribes share a common origin in Leah, but they are

geographical neighbours (Simeon's inheritance being south of and within the territory of Judah, cf. Josh. 19. 1–8), and function as partners throughout their history (Judg. 1.3). The genealogical material in fact refers to these links in stating the relative status of the two tribes (v. 27) and establishing the chronological framework in the reign of David (v. 31).

2. The section devoted to the tribe of Simeon differs in structure from that devoted to Judah, and is distinguished by two features: a paucity of actual genealogical material, and a clear interest in presenting a thorough depiction of the tribe's circumstances. The unity of the section is enhanced by its structural logic:

(a) 24–27 A genealogical sketch of the Simeonites
(b) 28–33 Their settlements
(c) 34–43 Two records of their history:
　　　　　(i) 34–41 Their expansion to the west
　　　　　(ii) 42–43 Their expansion to the east.

It may be noted that these three elements – genealogies, settlements and historical episodes – are attested for other tribes as well; the selection and scope of the components differ in each case.

3. The integrity of the passage, its logical thematic sequence, and the fact that the same elements appear in other passages of the genealogical introduction, all lead to the conclusion that the unit has retained its original structure. In this I differ from e.g. Rudolph, who regards the passage as a result of a complicated four-stage process: original Chronistic material (vv. 24–27); addition of geographical material (vv. 28–33); addition of historical events (vv. 34–43); glosses (vv. 30, 44). Rudolph's theoretical contention here is that the Chronicler had no interest in matters geographical (cf. Rudolph, 39); this, however, is refuted by the evidence of the book itself, which renders the argument a vicious circle (cf. also M. Kartveit, *Motive und Schichten der Landtheologie in I Chronik 1–9*, Stockholm 1989, 61–5).

4. Of the sources from which this passage was constructed, only two are available to us: the names of Simeon's sons in Num. 26.12–14, and the list of the Simeonite cities, in Josh. 19.1–9. As for the rest of the material, the question of sources should be approached in light of the following pertinent considerations:

(a) No specific Chronistic stylistic or theological tendencies are reflected in this non-paralleled material.

(b) The circumstances described here are not post-exilic; they hardly reflect the political realities of the Persian period, as by that time no defined entity 'Simeon' would appear on the historical stage. The tribal territory as described in this material clearly extended beyond the boundaries of the province of Jehud.

(c) In fact, as the commentary will show, the material fits best into its presumed context, the First Commonwealth.

I would conclude that some authentic sources have been used for the stories and genealogies of Simeon, although, like the biblical sources, they probably underwent some redaction (cf. below, and N. Na'aman, 'Pastoral Nomads in the Southeastern Periphery of the Kingdom of Judah in the 9th–8th Centuries BCE', *Zion* LII, 1987, 261–76*; for a different view see M. Augustin, 'The Role of Simeon in the Book of Chronicles', *Proceedings of the Tenth World Congress of Jewish Studies*, Jerusalem 1990, 137–42).

5. From the abundant geographical material of Josh. 13ff., the Chronicler applied himself to only three carefully chosen units: the levitical cities (Josh. 21//I Chron. 6), the Manassite cities (Josh. 17.11–13//I Chron. 7.28), and this list of the Simeonite cities. Levi and Simeon share a problematical status among the tribes of Israel: they were both cursed by Jacob (Gen. 49. 5–7) and in Moses' blessing the tribe of Simeon is missing, although his name (שמעון) is probably hinted at in the word 'hear' (שמע) of 'Hear, O Lord, the voice of Judah' (Deut. 33.7). That Levi 'has no portion or inheritance with his brothers' is repeatedly emphasized by Deuteronomy (Deut. 10.9 *et passim*). The Chronicler thus makes a point, with the help of earlier material, of locating the settlements of Simeon and Levi and demonstrating that they were full partners in the territorial structuring of the land. This is another of the Chronicler's expressions of the validity of the tribal system.

6. An interesting insight into the development of biblical genres is provided in the record of the Simeonites' westward expansion. It is composed in two distinct parts: vv. 34–38, a precise registration of the 'princes' of the families of Simeon; and vv. 39–41, a record of their exploit. This last has strong affinities, as has been recognized long ago (cf. Pseudo-Rashi, *ad loc.*; Curtis, 116), with the story of the conquest of Laish by the tribe of Dan (Judg. 18). The main similarity lies in the historical presuppositions: the conquest of a 'quiet and unsuspecting' people, whose 'land is broad', by Israelite raiders coming from afar, in urgent need of expansion or resettlement. The parallel is made explicit by the use of the same phraseology: compare Judg. 18.18 to I Chron. 4.40, והארץ רחבת ידים (somewhat differently translated in RSV), and Judg. 18.7, 27 (שקט ובטח, 'quiet and unsuspecting') to I Chron. 4.40 (שקטת ושלוה, quiet and peaceful).

In spite of this similarity, the differences in form are very clear. The complex narrative of Judg. 18 unfolds slowly, following two plot lines which eventually merge: the episode of the Levite and the conquest of Laish. Highly repetitous and rich in direct speech, the historical context of the tale remains vague and its characters anonymous, while it lacks a chronological anchor.

By contrast, this passage, while weak in literary embellishment, displays all the historical detail necessary in a 'chronicle' worthy of the name. First, there is an exact registration of the *dramatis personae*: thirteen family leaders recorded by name, then a clear chronological reference: 'in the days of Hezekiah king of Judah'. There are also geographical and ethnic details: 'the entrance of Gedor to the east side of the valley' (v. 39), a place occupied by 'Meunim' (v. 41), although 'the former inhabitants ... belonged to Ham' (v. 40). From a comparison between the two sources, one may assume that the literary development led from the 'chronicle' to the 'narrative', the story of Judg. 18 being a complex artistic elaboration of an original record which may have had the same form as our story in Chronicles.

D. Commentary

[24–27] Although this section opens with the general heading 'the sons of Simeon', it in fact has a more limited objective: the genealogical documentation of the family of Shimei (v. 27). It is around this family that all the material is structured, from the conventional listing of the sons of Simeon

(v. 24) to the genealogical tree which connects Shimei with Shaul, the son of Simeon (vv. 25–26).

The five sons of Simeon are recorded in v. 24 for the fourth time in the Bible (also Gen. 46.10; Ex. 6.15; Num. 26.12). Of these lists, the first two are identical, numbering six sons of whom the first is Jemuel, the third Ohad, the fifth Zohar and the sixth 'Shaul the son of a Canaanitish woman'. Both Num. 26.12 and this list have only five names, omitting Ohad; the first is called Nemuel, Zohar is presented as Zerah, and there is no reference to Shaul's mother. The third son in the list, Jarib, appears in all other sources as Jachin.

Verses 25–26 provide the link between the conventional scheme of the Simeonites and the family of Shimei. Here there are six names, appended mechanically to v. 24 in such a way as to imply (arbitrarily?) that 'Shallum' is the son of Shaul. The six names are in two groups of three, and each name is followed by the word *b⁵nō* ('his son'). The list distinguishes between the two groups by the interjection of the words 'the sons of Mishma' at the beginning of v. 26.

It is not clear whether each 'his son' denotes a new generation, the whole representing a genealogical tree of eight generations (Simeon – Shaul – Shallum – Mibsam – Mishma – Hammuel – Zaccur – Shimei), or whether some (or most) of the references are to sons of a common father, providing alternative genealogies of six or three generations (1. Simeon – Shaul – Shallum – Mibsam – Mishma; Hammuel, Zaccur and Shimei, the sons of Mishma; 2. Simeon – Shaul; Shallum, Mibsam and Mishma the sons of Shaul; Hammuel, Zaccur and Shimei, the sons of Mishma). Both possibilities are consonant with the patterns of the genealogies, but the first, with seven full generations between Simeon and Shimei, most closely approximates to the constructions of the genealogies of Judah.

A note of onomastic interest: the three highlighted points in the genealogy are occupied by Simeon, Mishma and Shimei, all different formulations of the root *šmᶜ*. This may signify that the family laid great stress on its affiliation as 'Simeonite'.

The pith of the passage is found in v. 27: the blessing of prolific offspring granted to Shimei is in explicit contrast to the infecundity of 'his brothers', and to the fortunes of the Simeonites as a whole, who did not 'multiply like the men of Judah'. The point is reinforced by the numbering of both male and female offspring for a round total of twenty-two. Cases of one branch of a family being more blessed in progeny than the others are illustrated several times in the genealogies (cf. 24.4; 25.5, etc.).

hirbū, 'multiply', is an elliptic phrase for *hirbū bānīm*, 'had many sons' (cf. 7.4; 8.40; 23.11 – all in the context of the genealogies).

It is difficult to place this list in any precise historical period. It reflects in a most practical way a process by which the tribe of Simeon decreased drastically, until only one family maintained, in a very loose form, the tribal lineage.

[28–33] 1. Lists of Simeonite cities as an integral part of Judah are also found in Josh. 15.21–32 and Neh. 11.25–29, but the Chronicler used Josh. 19.1–9 as his source, and his redaction is of significance.

(a) The first relevant difference between the two texts is the change of 'inheritance' (nah ^{a} lāh), to 'settlements' or 'dwellings' (mōš ^{e} bōtām). In the context of Josh. 19.1–9, the root 'inherit' is repeated emphatically seven times in the introductory and concluding verses: 'and its inheritance was in the midst of the inheritance of the tribe of Judah. And it had for its inheritance ... This was the inheritance of the tribe of Simeon ... The inheritance of the tribe of Simeon formed part of the territory of Judah ... the tribe of Simeon obtained an inheritance in the midst of their inheritance.' In Joshua, then, the cities are the Simeonites' 'inheritance', 'lot' and 'portion'. By contrast, in the Chronistic redaction, the word 'inheritance', in general very rare in Chronicles, has here been completely and pointedly excised. The introduction and conclusion of the Joshua passage are omitted altogether, and the opening of 19.2 and the conclusion of 19.8b are altered:

Josh. 19.2	I Chron. 4.28
And it had for its inheritance	They dwelt in (wayy ^{e} šbū)
Josh. 19.8b	I Chron. 4.33b
This was the inheritance of the	These were their
tribe of Simeon according to its	settlements (z'ōt mōš ^{e} bōtām)
families	

Even after this radical redaction, the dependence on Joshua is betrayed at the beginning of v. 33b by the singular 'this' (z'ōt, rendered as plural 'these' in RSV), a survival of 'this was the inheritance' (z'ōt nah ^{a} lat).

This systematic alteration is an expression of the Chronicler's different concept of the settlement: the Israelites, rather than receiving their land by 'lot' after a 'conquest', were simply 'dwelling' in the land from time immemorial (cf. S. Japhet, 'Conquest and Settlement in Chronicles', *JBL* 98, 1979, 205–18). The thematic 'they dwelt in ...' is furthermore echoed (in the Hebrew text) by the prefixing of the locative particle to eleven out of the thirteen place-names.

(b) Redaction is also evident in the restructuring of the list of cities. In Josh. 19 there are two groups of names, probably distinguished by their geographic location, each with its conclusion:

6b: 'thirteen cities with their villages'
7b: 'four cities with their villages'.

These notations are altered by the Chronicler, who replaces the first with

'These were their cities until David reigned' (v. 31b), and makes use of the words 'and their villages' (v. 32a) to introduce the second group:

Josh. 19.6b: 'thirteen *cities* with their *villages*'
I Chron. 4.31b: 'these were their *cities* ...', 32a: 'and their *villages* were ...'

The list of Chronicles thus preserves the two groups of names, but while Joshua does not specify the difference between them, Chronicles identifies the first as 'cities' (*'ārīm*), and the second as 'villages' (*ḥ*ᵃ*ṣērīm*). In this vein, the word *wᵉḥaṣrēhem* is omitted from v. 31, while 'cities' is retained.

We are again struck by the refined (yet never exhaustive) manner in which the Chronicler reworks his source, introducing a different view by means of the lightest changes. This observation should warn us against a simplistic restoration of our text to its form in Josh. 19, 'undoing' the Chronicler's redaction (see Rudolph, 40).

2. An additional difference between the two lists is in the names, where the discrepancies in details may be due to textual and linguistic factors (such as Balah/Bilhah; Bethul/Bethuel; Beth-Marcaboth/Hammarcaboth, etc.), or to a different tradition (as may be the case with Sharuhen/Shaarim, Baalath-beer/Baal). In the latter case, an actual historical geographical reality must be postulated for each of these lists, but it remains difficult to pinpoint their origins (cf. recently, Kartveit, *Motive und Schichten*, 155–7).

In Josh. 19.7 the second group of localities consists of four names, while in Chronicles there are five, the added name being 'Etam'. A further change is in the rendering 'Tochen' for 'Ether', which may reflect a double corruption of 'Atach', mentioned in Sam. 30. 30 (עתך עתר תכן). Some scholars would regard 'Ain' and 'Rimmon' as a secondary corruption of 'En-rimmon' (Neh. 11.29). As both Ain and Rimmon are legitimate, this is not necessarily the case, and even if so, the corruption did not originate in Chronicles, but is found already in Josh. 19.7 (MT: Ain, Rimmon, rendered 'En-rimmon' by RSV).

3. In the significant statement of v. 31b, 'These were their cities until David reigned', the Chronicler gives explicit expression to this introduction's ultimate chronological objective: the tribes of Israel on the eve of the Davidic monarchy. These 'cities of Simeon' continued to exist, according to Chronicles, throughout the monarchic period, to be referred to again in the time of Josiah (II Chron. 34.6).

[34–41] 1. With no introduction, a list of names is presented, then described as 'these mentioned by name [were] princes in their families'. The passage may have been derived from a more comprehensive context, the heading of which has been deleted. The genealogical depth differs for each of the thirteen individuals: ten are mentioned only by their names; for one there is also a patronymic (Joshah the son of Amaziah), for one (Jehu) four generations are recorded, and for the last person (Ziza), the longest genealogical tree of six generations is provided. The list is clearly not schematic; its structure probably points to a difference in the status of these individuals.

The author makes no attempt to affiliate these persons to any of the Simeonite's traditional families – another mark of the authenticity of the list. A possible connection to the preceding section may be obtained by the identification of Shemaiah of v. 37 with Shimei of v. 27 – a formal change quite common in the biblical onomasticon. The two passages would then reflect the same context: the proliferation of the house of Shimei (v. 27), and several affiliated families, leading eventually to the expedition: 'and their fathers' houses increased greatly, and they journeyed ... to seek pasture for their flocks' (vv. 38b–39). Ziza, the most distinguished of these Simeonites, would then trace his ancestry to Shimei.

2. The registration itself is referred to in two unique phrases: 'entered by names' (v. 38, *habbā'īm bᵉšēmōt*) and 'written by names' (v. 41, *hakkᵉtūbīm bᵉšēmōt*), rendered by RSV 'mentioned by name' and 'registered by name'. The first is often regarded as a corruption, but there is no apparent reason to think so. The more usual idioms are *qārā' bᵉšēm* and *nāqab bᵉšēm*, which refer originally to the oral designation of the name. Their having been 'written by name' may probably refer to some kind of census (cf. the Damascus Covenant, 14.3ff.), the traces of which may be found in the genealogies.

3. The incident described in vv. 38b–41 bears all the marks of historical probability in the socio-economic conditions, the course of events and the various details. In the opening phrase, 'and their fathers' houses increased greatly' (v. 38), the most basic motive for 'peacetime' immigration is provided: under the prevalent sociological and economic circumstances of Palestine, this would imply that some members of the family would have to leave their traditional locations and search for new living areas and pasture lands. The situation is well-illustrated in a different form in Gen. 13.6: 'the land could not support both of them'. Also in accord with authentic conditions is the view of the Simeonites as herdsmen, who 'seek pasture for their flocks' (v. 39), who 'found rich, good pasture' (v. 40) and who 'settled in their place because there was pasture there for their flocks' (v. 41). The incident is a graphic example of armed expansion as an outlet for accumulating economic pressure.

4. The Simeonites' actual destination cannot be exactly determined, since 'Gedor' is quite a common name (cf. Josh. 15.58; I Chron. 4.4, 18; 8.31), and may refer to 'grazing land' in general. LXX renders 'Gerarah', which seems plausible, although of course a textual variant is equally likely. The former inhabitants of the area are described as 'of the Hamites' (v. 40) and 'Meunim' (v. 41), which may indicate some location in the western Negev (cf. Na'aman,

ibid., differently E. A. Knauf, 'Mu'näer und Meuniter', *WO* 16, 1985, 114–22). The similarity of the passage to Judg. 18 may imply an isolated ethnic element, without strong political ties and protection.

The chronological setting is 'the days of Hezekiah', who, according to our sources, 'smote the Philistines as far as Gaza and its territory, from watchtower to fortified city' (Kings 18.8). While the Simeonites are credited with initiating this military raid, independent of the central government, it may have been a continuation of the earlier action of Hezekiah. In any case, the episode highlights the relative independence of the various groups, even within such a small state as Judah and after such a long period of stabilization. This may have been true particularly in the border areas, where the initiative of the local population would be felt more strongly (and cf. also in ch. 5).

5. The repetition of 'these registered by name' at the beginning of v. 41 (cf. v. 38) gives the impression of a conflation of two texts, but is not sufficient basis for seeing here a reference to two different groups. Another difficulty is in the uneven combination of 'their tents' and 'the Meunites who were found there'; Ehrlich's proposition (*Randglossen*, VII, 329) to render *'oh°lēhem* (their tents) as: *'oh°lē hām* (the tents of Ham) is very attractive, and would restore textual balance: 'and they destroyed the tents of Ham and the Meunites', with 'tents' a designation of a type of settlement. II Chronicles 14.14–15 (MT 13–14), uses the same phraseology: 'and they smote (*wayyakkū*) all the cities around about Gerar ... and they smote "tents of cattle"' (*'ōh°lē miqneh*; RSV 'the tents of those who had cattle'), meaning the herders' settlements, as contrasted to cities.

This precise description also provides us with some information regarding ethnic changes in the area. Originally (*l°pānīm*, in former times), it was inhabited by unspecified people of Hamite origin. Then, a Meunite element was added, and finally, these were all subdued by the Simeonites, who settled there with their flocks.

Although only a short chronicle, this passage nevertheless boasts a measure of literary completeness. It begins with 'they journeyed to seek pasture for their flocks' (v. 39), and ends on the same note: 'because there was pasture there for their flocks' (v. 41); the theme of 'pasture' is repeated three times.

[42–43] The second, even briefer episode, refers to another incident concerning the Simeonites, presented explicitly as a continuation of the first: 'And some of them ... of the Simeonites, went, etc.' Both the former incident and this one are based on the same assumptions, but here the facts are recorded in more general terms, without explanation or argument. The raid was undertaken for the sake of settlement (v. 43: 'and they have dwelt there to this day'), and its motive was probably a need for larger pasture areas to serve a growing population.

A round number of 'five hundred men' is given for the participants in this foray, and their destination is the general 'Mount Seir'. For a local incident, this seems to be a rather large military unit, and it might represent the entire immigrating group rather than merely the warriors. (David's band of fighters was of similar size: 'about four hundred', or 'six hundred', I Sam. 22.2; 22.13, which probably included whole families: 'every man with his household', I Sam 27.3). If 'Mount Seir' may be identified with the Edomite territory east of the Jordan (cf. Y. Aharoni, *The Land of the Bible*, Philadelphia and London [2]1979, 40 and 388), the incident would then involve a massive immigration of a large Simeonite group. Their leaders are mentioned by name: four men, 'the sons of Ishi'; but here again, there is no hint of their identity or of their genealogical relation to the more familiar Simeonite components.

The Simeonites are attacking a local population defined as 'Amalekites that had escaped', implying a prior disaster from which only a remnant survived, a situation which made it easier for the Simeonites to gain the upper hand. If this note alludes to Saul's major campaign against the Amalekites (the only such operation attested in the Bible, in I Sam. 15), the story would belong to the days of Saul or somewhat later, the same historical context explicitly mentioned in I Chron. 5.10. However, the reference may of course be to another military encounter, not recorded in our sources.

Both incidents are marked by the concluding formula 'to this day', and 'this day' may refer either to the time of the Chronicler or to that of the source on which he was relying. In the first case, the Simeonite occupation of Mount Seir is viewed as continuing to quite a late date in the Second Temple period, with Simeon surviving as a distinct Israelite tribe outside the territory and authority of the province of Jehud/Judah. That 'to this day' refers to a time in the First Commonwealth seems more likely, and not only from a historical point of view. The formula 'to this day' in Chronicles is restricted, almost exclusively, to parallel texts (cf. II Chron. 5.9//I Kings 8.8; II Chron. 10.19//I Kings 12.19, etc.). Besides this passage, there is only one other apparent instance of the formula being found in independent material, I Chron. 5.26; even this, however, may in fact be a reflection of II Kings 17.23. In all likelihood, then, the reference 'to this day' here is also derived from the Chronicler's source material; the vantage point of the narrative would be some period in the First Commonwealth.

The last point to be mentioned is the emphasis on the military disposition of the Simeonites, who take the initiative in securing their livelihood. Although these incidents are by no means the only examples of tribal belligerence in the genealogical introduction (cf. the Reubenites in I Chron. 5, and others), they indicate just how bellicose Simeon could be, very much in line with the tradition of Gen. 34.5ff. and 49.5–7. While in Genesis the references are to the eponyms Levi and Simeon, here the tribal groups take action within the context of the authentic circumstances of the period. The abstract Genesis tradition here receives socio-historical confirmation, and the sources are mutually supportive in providing a characterization of the historical tribe of Simeon.

5 The sons of Reuben the first-born of Israel (for he was the first-born; but because he polluted his father's couch, his birthright was given to the sons of Joseph the son of Israel, so that he is not enrolled in the genealogy according to the birth-right; ² though Judah became strong among his brothers and a prince was from him, yet the birthright belonged to Joseph), ³ the sons of Reuben, the first-born of Israel: Hanoch, Pallu, Hezron, and Carmi. ⁴ The sons of Joel: Shemaiah his son, Gog his son, Shime-i his son, ⁵ Micah his son, Re-aiah his son, Baal his son, ⁶ Beerah his son, whom Tilgath-pilneser king of Assyria carried away into exile; he was a chieftain of the Reubenites. ⁷ And his kinsmen by their families, when the genealogy of their generations was reckoned: the chief, Je-iel, and Zechariah, ⁸ and Bela the son of Azaz, son of Shema, son of Joel, who dwelt in Aroer, as far as Nebo and Baal-meon. ⁹ He also dwelt to the east as far as the entrance of the desert this side of the Euphrates, because their cattle had multiplied in the land of Gilead. ¹⁰ And in the days of Saul they made war on the Hagrites, who fell by their hand; and they dwelt in their tents throughout all the region east of Gilead.

11 The sons of Gad dwelt over against them in the land of Bashan as far as Salecah: ¹² Joel the chief, Shapham the second, Janai, and Shaphat in Bashan. ¹³ And their kinsmen according to their fathers' houses: Michael, Meshullam, Sheba, Jorai, Jacan, Zia, and Eber, seven. ¹⁴ These were the sons of Abihail the son of Huri, son of Jaroah, son of Gilead, son of Michael, son of Jeshishai, son of Jahdo, son of Buz; ¹⁵Ahi the son of Abdi-el, son of Guni, was chief in their fathers' houses; ¹⁶and they dwelt in Gilead, in Bashan and in its towns, and in all the pasture lands of Sharon to their limits. ¹⁷ All of these were enrolled by genealogies in the days of Jotham king of Judah, and in the days of Jeroboam king of Israel.

18 The Reubenites, the Gadites, and the half-tribe of Manasseh had valiant men, who carried shield and sword, and drew the bow, expert in war, forty-four thousand seven hundred and sixty, ready for service. ¹⁹ They made war upon the Hagrites, Jetur, Naphish, and Nodab; ²⁰ and when they received help against them, the Hagrites and all who were with them were given into their hands, for they cried to God in the battle, and he granted their entreaty because they trusted in him. ²¹ They carried off their livestock: fifty thousand of their camels, two hundred and fifty thousand sheep, two thousand asses, and a hundred thousand men alive. ²² For many fell slain, because the war was of God. And they dwelt in their place until the exile.

23 The members of the half-tribe of Manasseh dwelt in the land; they were very numerous from Bashan to Baal-hermon, Senir, and Mount Hermon. ²⁴ These were the heads of their fathers' houses: Epher, Ishi, Eliel, Azri-el, Jeremiah, Hodaviah, and Jahdi-el, mighty warriors, famous men, heads of their fathers' houses. ²⁵ But they transgressed against the God of their fathers, and played the harlot after the gods of the peoples of the land, whom God had destroyed before them. ²⁶ So the God of Israel stirred up the spirit of Pul king of Assyria, the spirit of Tilgath-pilneser king of Assyria, and he carried them away, namely, the Reubenites, the Gadites, and the half-

tribe of Manasseh, and brought them to Halah, Habor, Hara, and the river Gozan, to this day.

A. Notes to MT

[7] למשפחתיו, corrupted by analogy to the preceding word; read: למשפחתם; [9] ישב, proposed, וישבו; [12] ושפט, proposed, following LXX[BL] and T, שופט, cf. commentary; [14] אלה בני, probably omit; [15] אחי, absent from the LXX and P, cf. commentary; [16] בבשן, difficult. Proposed ביבש or בבשן בגולן etc.; cf. commentary; על probably עד; [18] וגדי, probably וגד (corrupted by analogy); [23] בארץ מבשן, difficult; proposed בארץ מבשן or מבשן [X] בארץ; [24] ועפר, omit *waw*; [26] והרא, corrupt?

B. Notes to RSV

[1]'He [Reuben] is not enrolled in the genealogy according to the birthright', better NEB 'Joseph ... could not be registered as the eldest son'; cf. commentary; [8, 9, 11, 23] 'dwelt'; better NEB 'lived' (vv. 8, 23), or 'occupied territory' (v. 9), 'occupied their encampments' (v. 10), 'occupied the district' (v. 11); [10] 'who fell by their hand', better 'who fell *into* their hand', cf. Judg. 15.18; II Sam. 24.14, etc., and RSV *ad loc.*; [18] 'ready for service', MT צצא יצא; rendered 'able to go forth to war' in Num. 1.3, 20, etc. and in various other ways in I Chron. 7.11; 12.33, etc.; [20] 'When they received help against them', extremely literal; JPS 'they prevailed against them'; [21] 'men alive', lit. souls; NEB, 'captives'; JPS 'people'; [23] cf. A, and commentary; [25] 'played the harlot', JPS 'going astray'.

C. Structure, sources and form

1. The unity of this chapter, devoted to one topic – the two-and-a-half tribes east of the Jordan – is inherent in its structure: it refers to these tribes first separately, and then together as a body. Moreover, the continuity of the individual paragraphs is emphasized by the fact that the subsections devoted to Gad and Manasseh do not open with the conventional presentation of the tribe's families, as is the case for Reuben at the beginning of the unit (v. 3), Judah and Simeon in the previous chapter, and almost all the tribes thereafter (7.1, 6, 13, etc.). Considering the material available to the author in Gen. 46.16 or Num. 26.5–17, 28–33, his digression here from his usual format is surely significant: the tribes east of the Jordan are formally defined as one unit.

2. The literary structure of the chapter is as follows:

(a) 1–10 Reuben
(b) 11–17 Gad
(c) 18–22 The war against the Hagrites
(d) 23–24 the half-tribe of Manasseh
(e) 25–26 transgression and exile.

The modern reader would expect a somewhat different structure, placing (d) before (c) so that the records of all the individual tribes would precede the two passages referring to them together. While this may have been the original sequence (that is,

vv. 23–24 following v. 18), the present structure also displays a certain literary logic, as it avoids the theological questions which might be raised by the juxtaposition of (c) and (e).

3. The introduction of the tribes in I Chron. 2.1–2 refers to Reuben, Joseph (implying Manasseh) and Gad, by their genealogical status: the first-born of Leah, the son of Rachel, and the son of Bilhah. By contrast, the principle which guides the composition of the present pericope is evidently geographical. The view of these tribes as a unit is determined by their common dwelling east of the Jordan, and their order – Reuben, Gad, Manasseh – follows the delineation of the tribal territories: after Simeon, the most southerly tribe west of the Jordan, comes Reuben, the most southerly tribe east of the Jordan, and then, proceeding northwards, come Gad and Manasseh.

4. Generally speaking, the unit includes the same elements which we found in the section devoted to Simeon (genealogy, settlement, historical episodes), but here they appear in a different order and have probably been taken from different sources. There is a more marked interpolation by the Chronicler's own hand, recognizable at the beginning, middle and end of the unit. A detailed analysis of the pericope reveals:

(a) Genealogies: vv. 3–8a for Reuben, vv. 12–15 for Gad, and v. 24 for the half-tribe of Manasseh.

(b) Records of settlement: vv. 8b–9, 10b for Reuben, vv. 11, 16 for Gad and v. 23 for the half-tribe of Manasseh.

(c) Records of wars: v. 10a for Reuben, vv. 18–22 for the two-and-a-half tribes, and an account of the exile – again for the whole group – in vv. 25–26.

(d) Editorial notes: vv. 1–2, the birthright; v. 17, indication of source material.

5. Only a very small part of the unit is taken from scriptural sources: v. 3 is a literal citation of Ex. 6.4 (cf. commentary), and vv. 1–2 and 25–26 are rewritings of biblical material. Taken together, these passages frame the beginning and end of the unit, the pith of which is peculiar to Chronicles.

A propos the problem of sources, it seems that a distinction should be made, even in the non-biblical material, between vv. 18–22 and vv. 4–17, 23–24. The latter verses constitute a collection of records and fragmentary data which are best understood as deriving from ancient sources of some kind. Although we may sometimes be unconsciously inclined to deny the possibility of authentic tribal records surviving to the Chronicler's day, it is still more difficult to assume that we are dealing with sheer literary fictions, or even that the Chronicler's own times are reflected.

The form – the fact that the material is fragmentary and inconsistent, with none of the passages complete – would indicate that dependence on authentic sources is more likely than fictitious composition. As for the possibility that the material reflects conditions contemporary to the Chronicler, this also must be ruled out. The text assumes that the circumstances described here had definitely terminated with the exile under Tiglath-pileser. Would any historian, even the most tendentious, project the conditions of his own day back in time, and describe them as extinct? The social, geographical and historical logic of the material also supports the view that the Chronicler had sources at his disposal, and although it is difficult to assess the scope of his editing, it does not seem to be very broad (cf. below).

6. The chapter contains notes and details of chronological significance: repeated allusions to Tiglath-pileser and the Exile (vv. 6, 22, 26), mention of the days of Saul

(v. 10) and the period of Jotham and Jeroboam (v. 17). Such notes are also occasionally found elsewhere (6.15 [MT 5.41] etc. and especially 4.31, 41), but they are most prominent in this chapter.

7. The subsection of vv. 1–10, opening with 'the sons of Reuben' is a literary continuum, its individual components forged together with no intervening headings or conclusions. It is an eclectic selection of various data regarding certain elements of Reuben:

(a) The conventional list of the four main families of the tribe (v. 3).

(b) The genealogy and settlement of the family of Joel, including the pedigree of a Reubenite prince who was exiled by Tiglath-pileser (vv. 4–6); his two brothers (v. 7); and the genealogy and territory of 'Bela the son of Azaz' (v. 8).

(c) A note about the eastern expansion of the tribe, relating to its victory over the Hagrites in the time of Saul (vv. 9–10).

Two matters concerning form should be pointed out: (a) the clause 'the sons of Reuben the first-born of Israel' (v. 1) is repeated verbatim in v. 3, after the digression (vv. 1b–2) on the intricacies of birthright – a classical example of *Wiederaufnahme* (resumptive repetition, cf. C. Kuhl, 'Die "Wiederaufnahme" – ein literarkritische Prinzip?', *ZAW* 64, 1952, 1–11; M. Anbar, 'La "Reprise"' *VT* 38, 1988, 385–98; see already the mediaeval exegetes Pseudo-Rashi and Kimhi, *ad loc.*). The artistic structure of the passage is a clear sign of its originality.

(b) Verses 1–2 comprise one of most distinct examples of Midrash in Chronicles. Its midrashic features are, first of all, the fact that the passage is formed as an interpretation of a given text. A citation from Ex. 6.14, 'the sons of Reuben the first-born of Israel', is followed by an interpretation, designed to account for the discrepancy between Reuben's nominal status as first-born and his actual historical position among the tribes. Secondly, this interpretation introduces a new theological concept, given form through a novel combination of existing biblical texts (cf. further in the commentary).

8. As already mentioned, the presentation of the Gadites in vv. 11–17 opens without the conventional list of tribal families. Rather, the section is chiastically connected with the preceding paragraph by an initial description of the settlements where 'the sons of Gad dwelt', presented explicitly as 'over against' those of the Reubenites.

9. The war of the eastern Israelite tribes against the Hagrites (vv. 18–22) is the longest and most complex piece of narrative found in the genealogical introduction. Its style, structure, concepts and motives, all remind us of the war stories found in the narrative part of the book (II Chron. 14.8–14; 20.1–30; etc.). A good starting point for clarifying its form is a comparison with v. 10a, which contains the same basic elements: war, Hagrites, Reuben, victory and settlement. It is immediately evident that most of v. 10a is incorporated, almost literally, into the longer story, thus:

v. 10: 'they made war on the Hagrites, who fell into their hand'
v. 19: 'they made war upon the Hagrites ...(20) and (they) were given into their hands'
v. 10: 'and they dwelt in their tents'
v. 22: 'and they dwelt in their place'.

In fact, only the chronological remark of v. 10, 'in the days of Saul', finds no parallel in vv. 18–22. However, the latter narrative is about five times longer than the former, as its scope is broadened through an elaboration of the already existing elements and the addition of a few more. While in v. 10 the combatants are only of the tribe of Reuben, in v. 18 the two-and-a-half tribes take part; their prowess, military qualifications and numbers are all described in detail. While in v. 10 the enemy are the Hagrites, in v. 19 these are supported by other Arab elements. The military outcome is recorded in v. 10 by a short clause, while vv. 20–21 depict not only the victory, but the numbers of captives and spoil. And finally, vv. 18–22 include remarks of a religious nature which serve both to lay down the postulate 'the war was of God' (v. 22), and to explain the course of events: 'for they cried to God in the battle, and he granted their entreaty, because they trusted in him' (v. 20).

One may recognize here a literary process by which a short chronicon has been elaborated into a historical narrative, and a local shepherds' skirmish has become a large-scale war involving combatants from all the Israelite tribes east of the Jordan – a fully-fledged and outfitted army of over forty thousand fighters. Their opponents are a coalition of several ethnic groups, and the fighting results not in the expelling of shepherds from their tents and pasturage, but in incredible quantities of prisoners and livestock captured, many fighters slain, and a total territorial occupation achieved. The combat is not placed at a specific historical point, but is integrated by its final remark into the general history of the people of Israel. Finally, the theological perspective becomes central, both in the behaviour of the fighters, who 'cried to God' and thereby secured the results of the battle, and in the philosophical stance of the author, who remarks that 'the war was of God'.

While the stylistic and ideological elaborations seem to be characteristic of the Chronicler, they provide a broader pattern for understanding the historiographic process leading from limited local traditions to national exploits in other contexts as well.

D. Commentary

[1–3] It has already been pointed out that v. 3a is a resumptive repetition of v. 1a; the central message of the passage is therefore to be found in v. 3, while vv. 1b–2 are an interpretative digression.

A list of the sons of Reuben is found three more times in the Bible: Gen. 46.8b–9; Ex. 6.14; and Num. 26.5–6. This version copies Ex. 6.14 so completely that the copulative *waw* is found precisely in the same places (preceding Pallu and Carmi), and both the name-forms and the phrasing of the heading are identical.

Verses 1b–2 contain a rather long Midrash on the problem broached by the heading: Reuben's status as first-born, a subject highlighted by the six-fold repetition of 'first-born' (*bᵉkōr*) and cognate nouns in vv. 1–3. The Midrash points out that Reuben's conventional title 'first-born of Israel/Jacob', in all the genealogies (in addition to the above references, also in Gen. 35.23; Num. 1.20; Gen. 49.3) is merely nominal. While Reuben is the biological oldest son, his corresponding rights of status were transferred to

Joseph. Yet, even Joseph realized this birthright only to a certain extent, since 'Judah became strong among his brothers'. The author here suggests, then, three levels of priority among the sons of Jacob: the biological first-born, the legally nominated elder, and the one who wielded actual authority.

In full accord with his general world-view, the Chronicler explains Reuben's loss of his birthright as a punishment for sin, a theological conviction which is presented as an interpretation of texts in Genesis. Gen. 35.22 records how Reuben 'went and lay with Bilhah his father's concubine', and ends with the neutral statement 'and Israel heard of it'. Gen. 49.3–4 refers to this deed as the sin for which Reuben is cursed: 'you shall not have pre-eminence because you went up to your father's bed; then you defiled it'. Here the Chronicler interprets the rather vague lost 'pre-eminence' as Reuben's first-born status.

The transfer of the birthright to Joseph is the second stage of the midrashic course. The legal implication of Jacob's words in Gen. 48.5, 'And now, your two sons ... Ephraim and Manasseh shall be mine, as Reuben and Simeon are', is that these sons of Joseph are raised to the status of full membership among the tribes of Israel. In terms of inheritance, Joseph's portion in Jacob's inheritance was increased from one part (which would have been divided among his descendants) to two. Joseph's other sons will now be registered under the names of their two elder brothers, Manasseh and Ephraim (Gen. 48.6). This is precisely the 'double portion' which is the inalienable scriptural prerogative of the first-born, 'for he is the first issue of his strength' (Deut. 21.17). The juxtaposition and strictly legal interpretation of Gen. 48.5 and 49.3 provide a basis for transferring the rights of first-born from Reuben to Joseph. *Pace* Rudolph, NEB and others, no corrections or alterations are called for here. 'He polluted his father's couch' is an unmistakable allusion to Gen. 49.4, somewhat obscured by the translations (cf. $ūb^eḥall^elō\ y^eṣu'ē\ 'ābīw$ to $'āz\ ḥillaltā\ y^eṣū'ī$).

MT $w^elō'\ l^eḥityaḥēṣ\ labb^ekōrāh$ is erroneously understood by RSV as referring to Reuben: 'so that he was not enrolled in the genealogy according to his birthright'. This interpretation, however, contradicts not only Hebrew usage, but all the genealogical records including I Chron. 2.1, where Reuben is enrolled first. NEB refers it correctly to Joseph, who 'could not be registered as the oldest son', although the status of first-born was in fact conferred on him. There is thus a discrepancy between the conservative character of the records and the actual legal situation.

Verse 2 re-emphasizes that although Judah surpassed all his brothers in strength and became the forefather of a great ruler, still the birthright belonged to Joseph. ($ūl^enāgīd$ is an example of the use of emphatic *lamed* to introduce the subject; it should not be omitted, cf. Kropat, 4–5.) For similar phraseology, cf. II Chron. 11.22; $l^enāgīd\ b^e'eḥāw$.

[3] In citing Reuben's genealogy, the Chronicler restricts himself to the four direct sons as known from the sources mentioned above, with no recourse to further information about Reubenite individuals known from the Pentateuch (such as Dathan and Abiram of Num. 26.9, On the son of Peleth of Num. 16.1, and others). While this procedure follows that applied to some other tribes in the genealogies, it contrasts sharply with the treatment of Judah, where every bit of information has been scrutinized and incorporated.

[4–8] The boundaries of the passage are problematic. RSV, taking v. 9 to be a direct continuation of v. 8, assumes that it is none other than 'Bela the son of Azaz' who 'dwelt to the east ...' It seems more likely, however, that v. 8 concludes the entire genealogical passage of vv. 4–8 with a reference to their settlements, and that vv. 9–10 then form a distinct unit, with a different, unspecified, subject.

Verses 4–8a present the record of several Reubenite families, claiming descent from a venerated ancestor by the name of 'Joel', for whom no affiliation is provided with any of the four conventional Reubenite families – a situation similar to the genealogy of Simeon but in contrast to that of Judah. The ancient Versions overcome the abrupt introduction of Joel in different ways. P reads 'Carmi' in place of 'Joel', while the Lucianic version of LXX reads 'Joel his son' rather than 'the sons of Joel', thus imitating the way in which the Simeonites are incorporated into the primary list (4.24–25).

Four individuals are registered here, but with difference of genealogical depth. Two are explicitly related to Joel: Beerah, a 'prince' (*nāśī*', RSV 'chieftain') of the Reubenites, with a genealogical tree of seven generations (vv. 4–6), and Bela, only three generations after Joel (v. 8). The other two, Jeiel 'the chief' and Zechariah, are described simply as 'his brothers' (RSV 'kinsmen'); they probably represent other branches of the tribe, for which no further information is given.

For Beerah a precise historical setting is also provided: exile by Tiglath-pileser, probably during the Assyrian king's campaign to Galilee and the eastern side of the Jordan, usually dated at 733–732 BCE. The description of this campaign in II Kings 15.24, however, sees the axis of the Assyrian invasion in northern Transjordan, and not in the territory of Reuben to the south (cf. further below).

The name of the Assyrian king is rendered 'Tiglath-pileser' in Kings, while in Chronicles it always appears as 'Tilgath-pilneser', a form arising from metathesis in the first component and dissimilation in the second (also v. 26; II Chron. 28.20). Beerah's title 'prince of the Reubenites' may suggest that the tribal system was in force at that time, as evidenced by further material in Chronicles.

After the very general reference to a 'reckoning of generations' at the beginning of v. 7, while the reader might expect a detailed genealogical record, only three names are in fact mentioned. This may indicate that the Chronicler chose to omit all but a fraction of the material at his disposal.

Formally, 'Bela the son of Azaz the son of Shema' of v. 8 is only three generations removed from Joel (Shema may represent a hypocoristic form of Shemaiah, of v. 4). However, this shorter genealogy does not necessarily imply an earlier date; the meaning may be that 'Bela the son of Azaz' belonged to the Reubenite family of 'Shema the son of Joel', with no chronological implications.

The description of Bela's territory implies that from their centre in Aroer they expanded 'as far as Nebo and Baal-meon'. Aroer, on the Arnon river, is repeatedly referred to in the context of the events east of the Jordan (Deut. 2.36; 3.12; Josh. 12.2; 13.16 etc.). It is mentioned specifically as having been built by the tribe of Gad (Num. 32.34), or as forming the border between Reuben and Gad (Josh. 13.16, 25). Our notice may indicate that the border between the two tribes fluctuated southwards or northwards in accordance with tribal fortunes. Nebo and Baal-meon are definitely Reubenite according to Num. 32.38, and the occupation of these territories by Israelite elements is already attested for the days of Saul, when David sends gifts to 'friends' who are referred to in I Sam. 30.28 as 'the elders of Judah ... in Aroer'. However, the three names Aroer, Nebo and Baal-meon also appear in the Mesha inscription of the ninth century, where the Moabite king boasts that after a long Israelite occupation he built them as Moabite towns. Without precise chronological links, all these details do not add up to a complete historical picture, but if Beerah of v. 6 and Bela of v. 8 indeed are of the same generation, the implication would be that this note belongs to the context of the eighth century: while one part of the family was taken into exile, the other remained settled, and thrived in its ancient territory.

[9–10] In v. 9 it would seem that the agent of the verb $y\bar{a}\check{s}ab$ (RSV 'dwelt', NEB 'occupied the territory') is no longer Bela (as implied by RSV 'he [Bela] also dwelt'), but rather the tribe of Reuben as a whole. The tribe is not only the subject of the following v. 10, but is also implied by the plural suffix of '*their* cattle' (v. 9b). This passage explains the expansion of the Reubenites eastwards, to 'the entrance of the desert (NEB 'the edge of the desert') this side of the Euphrates ...' as the result of an urgent need: 'their cattle had multiplied', a circumstance which would drive them to seek new pasture lands, and which is in accord with the characterization of the Reubenites as herdsmen in both Num. 32 and Judg. 5.16 (and cf. the description of Simeon in 4.38). The Reubenite hegemony of these territories is seen as the result of a war in 'ancient times' – 'in the days of Saul'.

The former inhabitants of the conquered area are designated as Hagrites – the descendants of Hagar. The main allusions to this Arabian group are found in Chronicles: in this chapter (again in vv. 19, 20), and in David's administration: Jaziz the Hagrite is 'over the flocks' (I Chron. 27.30), and Mibhar the son of Hagri is one of David's warriors (I Chron. 11.38; in II Sam. 23.36, Bani the Gadite). As a people they are mentioned only once more, in Ps. 83.6 (MT 83.7), which appropriately numbers them with Edom, Ishmaelites and Moab. They are absent, however, from the the the main traditions of the Pentateuch describing Israel's wanderings in the wilderness, and are represented in the traditions of Genesis by Hagar, Sarah's maid and Abraham's concubine, who, throughout the narrative, retains eponymic characteristics.

There is no further indication of any broader political affiliation of these Arabian tribes or of their status *vis à vis* the Transjordanian kingdoms of Edom or Moab, but neither is the action of the Reubenites supported by any central authority. These facts may indicate that independent military initiatives were taken by Israelite elements, especially on the desert borders, even during the period of the established kingdoms.

[11–17] Verses 11–13 record one Gadite family numbering eleven fathers' houses, which occupied the Bashan as far as Salecah, and the names of their four leaders. Of these, the first two bear the titles 'chief' and 'second' (*mišneh*). The title 'chief' is more common in the genealogies of chs. 23–26 (I Chron. 23.8, 11, 16, etc.) than in the genealogical introduction (5.7; 9.17), and 'second' is infrequent in both (I Chr. 15.18 *hammišnîm*, 'the seconds [in rank]'; I Chron. 16.5; II Chron. 31.12).

The somewhat repetitive 'in Bashan' at the end of v. 12 has prompted scholars to follow some of the Versions and read *šōpēṭ* in place of *wešāpaṭ*, resulting in 'and Janai was a judge in the Bashan'. Although orthographically it requires only a minor reconstruction, this correction would nevertheless introduce here the title and status of *šōpēṭ*, which is never mentioned in any of the tribal genealogies.

Salecah seems to be the traditional eastern province of the Bashan (Deut. 3.10; Josh. 12.5; 13.11), but according to Josh. 13.29–31 all Bashan fell to the lot of the half-tribe of Manasseh. The picture portrayed here of both Gad and Manasseh occupying the Bashan seems more in conformity with the actual vicissitudes of the tribes' fortunes.

[14–16] The passage is difficult in several ways. All of v. 14 is a heading, presenting a new family of Gad: 'the sons of Abihail'. The registration method is, however, unusual, as it presents a unique and artificial combination of two methods: a list of names headed by 'these are the sons of', and a genealogical tree in which a single person is introduced with the record of his ancestors. Thus, instead of the expected enumeration of 'the sons of Abihail', we have a long pedigree of eight generations of his forefathers. Then again, in v. 15, instead of the expected names of 'sons', we find the introduction of only one person, 'Ahi', with his own pedigree. Ahi's genealogy and status as 'chief in their fathers' houses' fail to reflect any connection with Abihail.

The inevitable conclusion is that the text is corrupt. There are two alternative approaches to its reconstruction. (a) A quite lengthy part of the section may have been irretrievably lost; it would have included the families who traced their origin to 'Abihail', as well as the name of the individual whose family tree is given in v. 14. (b) LXX does not have the name 'Ahi' at the beginning of v. 15. Taking this reading as a starting point and omitting the words 'these are the sons of' at the beginning of v. 14, we obtain a coherent section, which mentions first the eleven fathers' houses of Gad, and then the name of their chief (Abihail), with a genealogical tree of ten generations.

It has already been mentioned that there is no link between these families of Gad and the traditional Gadite branches (Gen. 46.16; Num. 26.15); however, some kind of link may be obtained if we regard Guni, the forefather of Abihail (or Ahi, as the case might be), as representing 'Shuni', one of Gad's main branches (Gen. 46.16).

Verse 16 goes on to define in more detail the territory of the Gadites in the Bashan. Two phrases here present some difficulty. The metaphorical term 'its daughters' (bᵉnōteyhā) is always used in reference to the small settlements around a central town or city (cf. Num. 21.32; 32.42, etc., RSV 'and its villages'), and this is its meaning in all the other occurrences in Chronicles as well (I Chron. 7.28, 29; 2.23, etc.). The text of this verse, if correct, would be the only use of bᵉnōteyhā in reference to a geographical region. Moreover, the possessive suffix is always in the feminine as it is understood to be governed by the noun 'ir (town, city); in this case, however, 'Bashan' is, as far as one can tell, masculine (Isa. 33.9; Nah. 1.4, etc.). The text may be corrupt, either by an erroneous reading of 'Bashan' for some city name such as Jabesh or the like, or by the omission of the city name 'Golan' after 'Bashan': wayyēšᵉbū baggil'ād babbāšān [baggōlān] ūbibᵉnōteyhā.

The second difficulty is in the term migrᵉšē šārōn, translated 'the pasture lands of Sharon' (NEB 'the common land of Sharon'). migrēš usually refers to the pasture lands around a city; these were probably common property (Ezek. 45.1, 2; 48.15, etc.), and are mentioned in particular in the context of levitical and priestly cities (Num. 35.3ff.; Josh. 21.2, etc.). Since 'Sharon' is usually understood as either a common noun or the name of a region, 'the pasture lands of Sharon' would appear to be a unique usage, unless the reference here is in fact to a city (cf. line 13 in the Mesha inscription: 'the men of Sharon').

[17] The synchronizing of Jeroboam the king of Israel and Jotham king of Judah has long been cited as an example of the artificial nature of the

Chronicler's work ('Jotham and Jeroboam ... make so impossible a synchronism that the partisans of Chronicles will have it that none is intended', Wellhausen, *Prolegomena*, 213). Indeed, according to I Kings 15.32, Jotham became king over Judah 'in the second year of Pekah', many years after Jeroboam's death. Considered utterly unhistorical, this juxtaposition has been traced to its source in the introduction to the book of Hosea, where the prophet is said to have prophesied in the days of 'Uzziah, Jotham ... and in the days of Jeroboam' (Wellhausen, ibid.). However, this very incongruity actually enhances the possibility that the note in Chronicles is based on an alternative source. That the reigns of Jeroboam and Jotham were at least partly synchronous has been confirmed by chronological studies of the period (cf. Tadmor, *EB* IV, 261, 270ff. 282ff.*), and since the Chronicler could not have known this from the book of Kings, another source is to be postulated (cf. Rudolph, 48–9).

The verse refers to an 'enrolment by genealogies', probably a census based on the registration of fathers' houses, as demonstrated by Num. 1; 3; and 26. The census records may have constituted one of the sources for these genealogies.

Chronology aside, the historical presuppostion of this note is more problematical. One finds it difficult to accept that the two rival kings initiated a joint census of a single tribal territory or of the two kingdoms. It is therefore possible that the Chronicler gave a broader historical significance to the synchronic facts which he found in his source.

[18–22] On the possible misplacement of the passage, see above, pp. 129–30. The concept of the Transjordanian tribes as one group, undertaking joint enterprises and sharing a common fate (cf. also I Chron. 12.37–38), is clearly Chronistic. In this respect the Chronicler may be seen as an heir to the traditions of the Pentateuch and Joshua (Num. 32; Josh. 1, etc.).

The literary elaboration of the passage has been mentioned above. Of the three different terms relating to the warriors' qualifications, the first, 'valiant men', and the last, 'ready for service' (*yōṣʾē ṣābāʾ*) are very common in Chronicles, while 'expert in war' (*lʿmūdē milḥāmāh*) is unique. This is also the first appearance of the form *lāmūd* in place of the more common noun *limmūd* (Isa. 54.13 etc.), but there is no reason to alter the vocalization.

The two phrases describing the military expertise of the fighters – 'who carried shield and sword and drew the bow' – are both within the literary tradition of Chronicles, but are illustrated in the genealogies only in the registers of Benjamin (I Chron. 8.40; also II Chron. 14.8). For the variations in Chronistic military idiom see especially the comments on I Chron. 12.

The enemy is also described as a comprehensive body: the Hagrites with three other Arab tribes. The first two are presented in Gen. 25.15 as Ishmael's sons, while the third is unique – a fact which would indicate an independent tradition here, the source of which is still debated (see I. Ephal, *The Ancient Arabs*, Jerusalem 1982, 65–7).

Under the supposed circumstances, the nature of the spoil is very appropriate: camels, sheep and asses. The numbers here, as throughout the tale, are greatly exaggerated and clearly typological – for the most part multiples of fifty thousand.

Verse 20 displays some very clear examples of Late Biblical Hebrew, as well as more specific Chronistic vocabulary and theological concepts. The Chronicler's favourite '*zr*, here in the Niphal *wayyē'āzrū*, denoting 'become strong, prevail' (I Chron. 12.21; II Chron. 26.7, 13, etc.), was already recognized by LXX. We also find the infinitive replacing a conjugated verb (*wᵉn'tōr*, cf. Kropat, 23); the omission of the pronoun governing a relative clause in *wᵉkōl šeʻimmāhem* (supplied in the translation by 'who were'); the conjunction of sentences with *kī*, in this verse translated once 'for' and once 'because'; and a presentation sequence in which results precede causes, a style also involving an increased use of simple tenses (*zāʻᵃqū, bāṭᵉḥū*, cf. Curtis, 125).

nepeš 'ādām, translated 'men alive' (NEB 'captives'; JPS 'people'), is a rather rare usage. It is restricted to priestly sources (Lev. 24.17; Num. 9.6; 19.11, 13; 31.35, 40, 46; Ezek. 27.13), and usually serves as a clear distinction between man and beast. Its only occurrence in Chronicles is in this passage, which may have been influenced by the story of Num. 31. It is also the only occurrence in Chronicles of *nepeš* alone denoting 'person', which is the more common usage in the priestly stratum.

Verse 22 again illustrates the Chronicler's characteristic traits already noted in v. 20 (the use of *kī* as conjunction, the increased use of simple tenses, the abundant use of nominal clauses), with the additional theological statement that 'the war was of God', the religious message of which is unmistakable: the outcome of a conflict is determined by God, who helps those who trust in him. The phrasing here is very similar to II Chron. 18.31, in the short Chronistic addition to the story taken from Kings: 'they turned to fight against him; and Jehoshaphat cried out, and the Lord helped him. God drew them away from him.'

How probable is the narrative in historical terms? As it stands, the story's premises are difficult: on the one hand, this campaign is a comprehensive project which united all the Israelites of Transjordan in an organized, almost professional army, to fight their Hagrite neighbours. On the other hand, the initiative is entirely limited to the local level, with no hint of any central government or leadership. The unity of the tribes and the kind of army they muster seem to exclude the pre-monarchical period. However, it is hardly likely that tribal co-operation on such a grand scale would have been possible during the monarchical period without central initiative or control.

The solution seems to lie in a distinction between the basic facts of the story and its elaborated form. From the incidents related above (I Chron. 4.39ff.; 4.42–43), we learn that local ventures, especially on the borders, could have been common throughout the monarchical period, although nothing of the kind is ever referred to in the book of Kings. Such raids would have been carried out in Israel without direct intervention of the central government – a point which may in turn cast light on the kind of government then existing and the measure of centralization then enforced. One may consider the possibility that a royal campaign into Transjordan is presented here as a joint project of the Transjordanian tribes, but it seems more plausible that a local, limited initiative has here undergone literary elaboration.

[23–24] Just as with the Gadites, here too the record of the half-tribe of Manasseh opens with their territory, with the omission of the traditional families, the 'sons' of Manasseh.

The Manassites are seen as occupying a vast territory, embracing the entire northern reaches of Transjordan. According to MT, followed by RSV, 'they settled in the land; from Bashan, etc.' It is commonly proposed to read 'they settled in the land *of* Bashan, to Baal Hermon, etc.', similar to 5.10. To the three landmarks Baal-hermon, Senir and Mount Hermon, LXX (followed by NEB) also adds Lebanon. It is difficult to see the historical context of an Israelite occupation of such a large area, coinciding with other ethnic elements, Aramaic in particular.

The isolated terms describing the same territorial expansion all appear in earlier texts like Deut. 3.8–10; 4.48–49; Josh. 12.4–5. However, the particular combination of terms here is unique and does not conform to any given formula. 'Senir' is regarded as another name for 'Hermon' in Deut. 3.9, but they are presented as two different mountains in Song of Songs 4.8 and may refer here to two points of the same ridge. Baal-hermon is mentioned only once more, in Judg. 3.3, as 'Mount Baal-hermon'. The non-formulaic character of the text may indicate an authentic historical situation for which we have no other information. The phrase 'they were very numerous' attributes the great expansion of the Manassites to population growth.

The genealogical record of the Manassites lists seven men with their full legal titles: 'men of property' (*gibbōrē ḥayil*, RSV 'mighty warriors'), 'men of repute' (NEB), 'heads of their fathers' houses', but with no indication of mutual affiliations, secondary developments, or ties to traditional family units or to localities. The list is therefore similar to those preceding it in the same chapter and to 4.34–37, and differs from the ethnically orientated genealogies of the tribe of Judah.

[25–26] This last section – the exile of the Transjordanian tribes – is the climax of the whole chapter, and has already been alluded to in vv. 6 and 22. In matter and scope it continues vv. 18–22, and like these was composed by the Chronicler.

The late provenance of the passage is revealed by phrases like 'stir up the spirit', which is found elsewhere in Chronicles (II Chron. 21.16, etc.); the proleptic pronominal suffix in *wayyaglēm*, 'he carried them away', the particular structure represented in the RSV by the addition of 'namely'; and the use of *lamed* as the accusative particle (*lār'ūbēnī*, etc.). Specific Chronistic phraseology is manifest in the use of the terms *m'l* and *znh* to describe Israel's transgression (cf. especially II Chron. 21.11; 36.14); the divine titles 'the God of their fathers' and the God of Israel' (cf. Japhet, *Ideology*, 14–20), and the form 'Tilgath-pilneser' for the Assyrian king (cf. above, v. 6).

An analysis of the literary method of the passage highlights its theological import. The information is taken from the book of Kings, which relates two distinct stages in the exile of the northern kingdom:

(*a*) The conquest of Galilee and Transjordan by Tiglath-pileser, in the time of Pekah, the son of Remaliahu. The conquered Israelite territory is described in detail in II Kings 15.29, but the exact locations in Assyria to which they were exiled are not recorded: 'In the days of Pekah ... Tiglath-pileser ... came and captured Ijon, Abel-beth-maacah, Janoah, Kedesh, Hazor, Gilead and Galilee, all the land of Naphtali; and he carried the people captive to Assyria.'

(*b*) The conquest of Samaria after the siege of Shalmanesser, and the exile of its inhabitants. This final destruction of the northern kingdom, ten years after the previous event, is described twice in the book of Kings: 'In the ninth year of Hoshea, the king of Assyria captured Samaria, and he carried the Israelites away to Assyria and placed them in Halah, and on the Habor, the river of Gozan, and the cities of the Medes' (II Kings 17.6; similarly in 18.11). Note that this time the conquered area is referred to very generally as 'Samaria', while the places to which the Israelites were exiled are enumerated in detail.

The Chronicler utilizes the two records. Drawing from each passage the details he prefers, he creates a completely new historical structure: (*a*) the subject of the passage is the first exile, that of Tiglath-pileser; however, the places to which the Israelites were exiled are cited from the record of the second exile. (*b*) While according to II Kings 15.29 the exile affected mainly the northern parts of the western tribes, with only 'the Gilead' being mentioned on the eastern side, here it affects exclusively the eastern tribes of Transjordan. The exile of Galilee, Dan and Naphtali, is completely ignored.

The 'transfer' of the second exile to the first is implemented also by its theological justification. The book of Kings provides a long review of sins in order to account for the final destruction of the northern kingdom (II Kings

17.7ff.), but nothing of the kind is found in the matter-of-fact report of the first exile in the time of Tiglath-pileser. The Chronicler recalls the sins of the Transjordanian tribes in order to justify their exile, and he uses harsh words, resembling those referring to the destruction of the Temple and Jerusalem in the time of Zedekiah. Compare v. 25 'but they transgressed (*wayyim'ᵃlū*) against the God of their fathers and played the harlot after the gods of the peoples of the land', with II Chron. 36.14: 'All the ... people ... were exceedingly unfaithful (*hirbū lim'al ma'al* – the similarity is lost in the translation) following all the abominations of the nations.'

Furthermore, the Chronicler closes the passage with the observation that the exiles were still settled in distant Assyria 'to this day'. The theological message of this note is obvious: for the three tribes of Transjordan there was to be no return; in punishment for their sin they were given up to exile.

With these far-reaching reformulations, the Chronicler has created a new historical and theological scene: although the north-western part of the land has suffered from some violent incursions, it underwent no fundamental change. In spite of temporary failure, the majority of the Israelites remained settled in their ancient territories and were expecting the return of their brethren (II Chron. 30.6–9, cf. in detail there). The only complete failure, an exile from which there was no reprieve, was that of the Israelites in Transjordan. This reconstruction presents an important expression of the Chronicler's attitude toward the fact of 'exile' in the history of Israel (cf. further Japhet, *Ideology*, 364–73).

Does the Chronicler regard 'Pul' and 'Tiglath-pileser' as two different kings? 'Pul' is Tiglath-pileser's name in neo-Babylonian sources, and is probably a hypocoristic form of some kind. Neither the meaning of Pul, nor the fact that Tiglath-pileser had two names, has been adequately explained so far. The appearance of both names in biblical sources (II Kings 15.19, 29) has been considered as the origin of 'the error of the Chronicler' (Curtis, 125). However, the verbs that follow the initial statements 'he stirred the spirit of Pul ... and the spirit of Tiglath-pileser' are in the singular and not in the plural: 'and *he* carried (*wayyaglēm*) and *he* brought (*wayy'ᵉbī'ēm*)', clearly referring to one king. One should therefore take the *waw* of *w'ᵉet* as interpretative, to be translated 'that is' (NEB; for another suggestion cf. M. Anbar, 'Poul Roi d'Assyrie et Tilgath-Pilnésser Roi d'Assyrie', *BN* 48, 1989, 7). With this additional allusion to II Kings 15.19 the Chronicler draws together all the principal data referring to the subordination of the northern kingdom, but limits it exclusively to that kingdom's eastern component.

6 The sons of Levi: Gershom, Kohath, and Merari. [2] The sons of Kohath: Amram, Izhar, Hebron, and Uzziel. [3] The children of Amram: Aaron, Moses, and Miriam. The sons of Aaron: Nadab, Abi-hu, Eleazar, and Ithamar. [4] Eleazar was the father of Phinehas, Phinehas of Abishua, [5] Abishua of Bukki, Bukki of Uzzi, [6] Uzzi of Zerahiah, Zerahiah of Meraioth, [7] Meraioth of Amariah, Amariah of Ahitub, [8] Ahitub of Zadok, Zadok of Ahima-az, [9] Ahima-az of Azariah, Azariah of Johanan, [10] and Johanan of Azariah (it was he who served as priest in the house that Solomon built in Jerusalem). [11] Azariah was the father of Amariah, Amariah of Ahitub, [12] Ahitub of Zadok, Zadok of Shallum, [13] Shallum of Hilkiah, Hilkiah of Azariah, [14] Azariah of Seraiah, Seraiah of Jehozadak; [15] and Jehozadak went into exile when the Lord sent Judah and Jerusalem into exile by the hand of Nebuchadnezzar.

16 The sons of Levi: Gershom, Kohath, and Merari. [17] And these are the names of the sons of Gershom: Libni and Shime-i. [18] The sons of Kohath: Amram, Izhar, Hebron, and Uzziel. [19] The sons of Merari: Mahli and Mushi. These are the families of the Levites according to their fathers. [20] Of Gershom: Libni his son, Jahath his son, Zimmah his son, [21] Joah his son, Iddo his son, Zerah his son, Jeatherai his son. [22] The sons of Kohath: Amminadab his son, Korah his son, Assir his son, [23] Elkanah his son, Ebiasaph his son, Assir his son, [24] Tahath his son, Uriel his son, Uzziah his son, and Shaul his son. [25] The sons of Elkanah: Amasai and Ahimoth, [26] Elkanah his son, Zophai his son, Nahath his son, [27] Eliab his son, Jeroham his son, Elkanah his son. [28] The sons of Samuel: Joel his first-born, the second Abijah. [29] The sons of Merari: Mahli, Libni his son, Shime-i his son, Uzzah his son, [30] Shime-a his son, Haggiah his son, and Asaiah his son.

31 These are the men whom David put in charge of the service of song in the house of the Lord, after the ark rested there. [32] They ministered with song before the tabernacle of the tent of meeting, until Solomon had built the house of the Lord in Jerusalem; and they performed their service in due order. [33] These are the men who served and their sons. Of the sons of the Kohathites: Heman the singer the son of Joel, son of Samuel, [34] son of Elkanah, son of Jeroham, son of Eliel, son of Toah, [35] son of Zuph, son of Elkanah, son of Mahath, son of Amasai, [36] son of Elkanah, son of Joel, son of Azariah, son of Zephaniah, [37] son of Tahath, son of Assir, son of Ebiasaph, son of Korah, [38] son of Izhar, son of Kohath, son of Levi, son of Israel; [39] and his brother Asaph, who stood on his right hand, namely, Asaph the son of Berechiah, son of Shime-a, [40] son of Michael, son of Ba-aseiah, son of Malchijah, [41] son of Ethni, son of Zerah, son of Adaiah, [42] son of Ethan, son of Zimmah, son of Shime-i, [43] son of Jahath, son of Gershom, son of Levi. [44] On the left hand were their brethren the sons of Merari: Ethan the son of Kishi, son of Abdi, son of Malluch, [45] son of Hashabiah, son of Arnaziah, son of Hilkiah, [46] son of Amzi, son of Bani, son of Shemer, [47] son of Mahli, son of Mushi, son of Merari, son of Levi; [48] and their brethren the Levites were appointed for all the service of the tabernacle of the house of God.

49 But Aaron and his sons made offerings upon the altar of burnt offering and

upon the altar of incense for all the work of the most holy place, and to make atonement for Israel, according to all that Moses the servant of God had commanded. [50] These are the sons of Aaron: Eleazar his son, Phinehas his son, Abishua his son, [51] Bukki his son, Uzzi his son, Zerahiah his son, [52] Meraioth his son, Amariah his son, Ahicub his son, [53] Zadok his son, Ahima-az his son.

54 These are their dwelling places according to their settlements within their borders: to the sons of Aaron of the families of Kohathites, for theirs was the lot, [55] to them they gave Hebron in the land of Judah and its surrounding pasture lands, [56] but the fields of the city and its villages they gave to Caleb the son of Jephunneh. [57] To the sons of Aaron they gave the cities of refuge: Hebron, Libnah with its pasture lands, Jattir, Eshtemoa with its pasture lands, [58] Hilen with its pasture land, Debir with its pasture lands, [59] Ashran with its pasture lands, and Beth-shemesh with its pasture lands; [60] and from the tribe of Benjamin, Geba with its pasture lands, Alemeth with its pasture lands, and Anathoth with its pasture lands. All their cities throughout their families were thirteen.

61 To the rest of the Kohathites were given by lot out of the family of the tribe, out of the half-tribe, the half of Manasseh, ten cities. [62] To the Gershomites according to their families were allotted thirteen cities out of the tribes of Issachar, Asher, Naphtali, and Manasseh in Basham. [63] To the Merarites according to their families were allotted twelve cities out of the tribes of Reuben, Gad, and Zebulun. [64] So the people of Israel gave the Levites the cities with their pasture lands. [65] They also gave them by lot out of the tribes of Judah, Simeon, and Benjamin these cities which are mentioned by name.

66 And some of the families of the sons of Kohath had cities of their territory out of the tribe of Ephraim. [67] They were given the cities of refuge: Shechem with its pasture lands in the hill country of Ephraim, Gezer with its pasture lands, [68] Jokmeam with its pasture lands, Bethhoron with its pasture lands, [69] Aijalon with its pasture lands, Gath-rimmon with its pasture lands, [70] and out of the half-tribe of Manasseh, Aner with its pasture lands, and Bileam with its pasture lands, for the rest of the families of the Kohathites.

71 To the Gershomites were given out of the half-tribe of Manasseh: Golan in Bashan with its pasture lands and Ashtaroth with its pasture lands; [72] and out of the tribe of Issachar: Kedesh with its pasture lands, Daberath with its pasture lands, [73] Ramoth with its pasture lands, and Anem with its pasture lands; [74] out of the tribe of Asher: Mashal with its pasture lands, Abdon with its pasture lands, [75] Hukok with its pasture lands, and Rehob with its pasture lands; [76] and out of the tribe of Naphtali: Kedesh in Galilee with its pasture lands, Hammon with its pasture lands, and Kiriathaim with its pasture lands. [77] To the rest of the Merarites were allotted out of the tribe of Zebulun: Riommono with its pasture lands, Tabor with its pasture lands, [78] and beyond the Jordan at Jericho, on the east side of the Jordan, out of the tribe of Reuben: Bezer in the steppe with its pasture lands, Jahzah with its pasture lands, [79] Kedemoth with its pasture lands, and Mephaath with its pasture lands; [80] and out of the tribe of Gad: Ramoth in Gilead with its pasture lands, Mahanaim with its pasture lands, [81] Heshbon with its pasture lands.

(The chapter division of the English translation follows LXX and differs from the Hebrew Bible, in which ch. 5 continues for another fifteen verses. We follow the English version, with cross-references to MT.)

A. Notes to MT

[9] (MT 5.35) עזריה, transfer here from v. 10 (MT 5.36) the words 'it was he who served, etc.', cf. the commentary; [22] (MT 6.7) עמינדב, LXX^A יצהר (cf. Ex. 6.18, 21), proposed עמרם; cf. commentary; [25] (MT 6.10)ואחימות, in v. 35 (MT 6.20) and II Chron. 29.12 מחת, proposed ואחיו מחת; [26] (MT 6.11) אלקנה (Qere אלקנה בנו (בני, read נחת;אלקנה בנו, v. 34 (MT 6.19)תוח; [27] (MT 6.12)אליאב, v. 34 (MT 6.19) אליאל; I Sam. 1.1 אליהוא;אלקנה בנו, add: שמואל בנו; [28] (MT 6.13) read ובני שמואל יואל הבכר והשני אביה ; cf. commentary; [40] (MT 6.25) בעשיה, read probably, with some MSS and Versions, מעשיה; [42/43] (MT 6.27–28) בן שמעי בן יחת, probably transpose the names, read בן יחת בן שמעי; [44] (MT 6.29) ובני, proposed ומבני;אחיהם, probably, following some of the Versions,אחיהם; [57] (MT 6.42) ערי, proposed עיר, also v. 67, cf. commentary, p. 162;חברון, Josh. 21.13 + ואת מגרשיה;יתר, add ואת מגרשיה; [58] (MT 6.43) חילז, Josh. 21.15 חלן; probably correct; [59] (MT 6.44) ואת מגרשיה, add ואת עשן ואת מגרשיה ואת יטה following LXX^B and Josh. 21.16; [60] (MT 6.45) בנימן, add את גבעון ואת מגרשיה; [61] (MT 6.46)ממחצית המטה ממשפחת, corrupt, read, following Josh. 21.5, ומחצי [אפרים וממטה דן] ממשפחת מטה , cf. commentary; חצי, dittography, omit; [65] (MT 6.50) transpose after v. 54, cf. commentary; [66] (MT 6.51)וממשפחות, read ומשפחות (ditt.);גבולם, Josh. 21.20 גורלם; [67] (MT 6.52) ערי, proposed עיר, cf. v. 57; [68] (MT 6.53) יקמעם, Josh. 21.22 קבצים; [69] (MT 6.54) insert וממטה דן למשפחת לבני ,read את אלתקה ואת מגרשיה ואת גבתון ואת מגרשיה, cf. Josh. 21.23;למשפחות; [70] (MT 6.55) ענר, probably read חענך, withJosh. 21.25;בלעם, read בלעם; [71] (MT 6.56) ממשפחת חצי, better למשפחתם מחצי; [72] (MT 6.57) קדש, Josh. 21.28 קשיון, probably better; [73] (MT 6.58) ענם,Josh. 21.29 עין גנים; [75] (MT 6.60) חוקק, read, withJosh. 21.31חלקת; [76] (MT 6.61)קריתים,Josh. 21.32קרתן; [77] (MT 6.62)זבולן, add את יקנעם ואת נהלל ואת מגרשיה ואת מגרשיה, cf. commentary;רמונו, probably רמון (Josh. 19.13).

B. Notes to RSV

[1] 'Gershom', MT 'Gershon', cf. commentary; [4] et passim 'was the father', MT הוליד ('begot', thus JPS), cf. on 1 Chron. 2.23; [31] 'put in charge', NEB 'appointed' (MT העמיד); [48] 'were appointed', MTנתונים (NEB 'dedicated'), Num. 3.9 'given'; [61] 'of the family of the tribe', etc., cf. commentary; [65] 'they also gave them', MT 'they gave'; [71] 'of the half-tribe', MT 'of the family of the half tribe'; but cf. on v. 56 in MT (A above); [77] 'were allotted', not in MT.

C. Structure, sources and form

1. Chapter 6, with its 81 verses devoted to the tribe of Levi, far surpasses in scope any other unit, with the exception of that of Judah. This is no coincidence, but reflects quantitatively the Chronicler's view of Levi's status among the tribes.

2. The similarity between this pericope and the other genealogies in regard to their components only serves to emphasize the essential difference. Because of the clerical nature of the chapter, no events of the tribe's life are recorded here, while the detailed registration of the fathers' houses is postponed to chs. 23–26. On the other hand, we find here an unprecedented emphasis on two matters:

(*a*) The levitical settlement. The list of the levitical cities is derived *in toto* from Joshua 21, although the Chronicler's own hand is evident in certain redactional features. We have already seen that the motif of 'dwelling' is of major significance for the Chronicler; the disproportionate emphasis it receives in regard to the Levites will be dealt with in the commentary.

(*b*) The genealogical affiliation of the three singers, Heman, Asaph and Ethan. Their registration, precise affiliation to the main levitical families Kohath, Gershon and Merari, and the historical circumstances of their establishment as singers, comprise seventeen verses (vv. 31–47).

3. The chapter is divided evenly into two parts: the first half (vv. 1–49) presents the genealogies of the tribe's three most significant groups – priests, Levites and singers – with a short description of the priestly and levitical duties; the second half, (vv. 50–81) provides a survey of their settlements. Analysed in greater detail, the components of the pericope are as follows:

(*a*) 1–15   The genealogical tree of the high priests
(*b*) 15–30   The genealogical trees of the three levitical branches
(*c*) 31–47   The genealogical trees of the three head singers
(*d*) 48–49   A summary of the levitical and priestly functions
(*e*) 50–81   Levitical and priestly cities (cf. further, below).

While obvious similarities and literal repetitions link these components, each has its unique and separate function within the overall context.

4. It has been suggested by several scholars that ch. 6 represents the final outcome of a prolonged process of growth, in which various sections of the first part and all of the second were gradually appended to an original, smaller or larger, core (cf. *inter al.*: Noth, *Chronicler*, 39–40; Rudolph, 51–64; Kartveit, *Motive und Schichten*, 75–86). However, the highly systematic structure of the pericope clearly indicates that it is not a haphazard composition (cf. also Williamson, 68–9, who conceives of the structure of the chapter in somewhat different terms). In addition to the general plan of the chapter (above, no. 3), each section is composed of two parts: some sort of introduction, followed by a list; the first half of the chapter is provided with a short conclusion (vv. 48–49), resulting in a coherent structure as follows:

1–49 Levitical genealogies
(*a*) 1–15 The high priests
  (i) 1–3   Introduction
  (ii) 4–15   Genealogical tree
(*b*) 16–30 The Levites
  (i) 16–19a Introduction
  (ii) 19b–30 Genealogical trees
(*c*) 31–47 The singers
  (i) 31   Introduction
  (ii) 32–47 Genealogical trees
  (iii) 48–49 Conclusion.

5. The second half of the chapter (vv. 50–81), the longest geographical unit in Chronicles, is a list of the levitical and priestly cities. Notwithstanding the contrary

claim of G. Auld ('Cities of Refuge in Israelite Tradition', *JSOT* 10, 1978, esp. 32–5; 'The "Levitical Cities": Texts and History', *ZAW* 91, 1979, 194–206), I hold to the generally accepted view that the Chronicler's version is dependent on that of Josh. 21. For all their differences, the versions of Chronicles and Joshua preserve two readings of the same document; while the Joshua text is the more dependable, Chronicles may in fact retain specific details of an original nature. An analysis of Josh. 21 is beyond the scope of the present discussion, but some remarks about its composition will help us understand the form and structure of the document in Chronicles.

Joshua 21 is composed of three parts: introduction (vv. 1–3), list (vv. 4–42), and conclusion (vv. 43–44). The list itself again comprises two parts: vv. 4–7 deal with the casting of lots, and record in *general terms* the distribution and number of the levitical cities within the individual tribes of Israel and their number; vv. 8–42 register the cities *in detail*, by levitical families and Israelite tribes. More specifically, the list may be analysed as follows:

(*a*) Verses 4–7, casting lots: v. 4, the family of Aaron and its allotment from the tribes of Judah, Simeon and Benjamin, thirteen cities; v. 5, the non-priestly Kohathites, their allotments from Ephraim, Dan and half of Manasseh, ten cities; v. 6, the family of Gershon, from the tribes of Issachar, Asher, Naphtali and half of Manasseh, thirteen cities; v. 7, Merari, from Reuben, Gad and Zebulun, twelve cities.

(*b*) Verses 8–42, the registration of cities, by levitical families and Israelite tribes: v. 8, introduction; vv. 9–19, a detailed list of the cities allotted to Aaron from Judah, Simeon and Benjamin; vv. 20–26, the cities of the Kohathites, from Ephraim, Dan and Manasseh; vv. 27–33, the cities of Gershon, from Manasseh, Issachar and Naphtali; vv. 34–40, Merari, and their cities from Zebulun, Reuben and Gad. This section is concluded by vv. 41–42.

A systematic structure of repeated forms and terminology links all these individual units.

The document in Chronicles, while containing essentially all the elements of Josh. 21, reflects a restructuring of the material. The Chronicler's version comprises two parts rather than three: an introduction (vv. 50–53) and the list itself (vv. 54–81), omitting the conclusion. In addition, the two-part structure of the list, while preserved, is based on a different principle, as we can see from the following analysis:

(*a*) Verse 54, followed by v. 65 (see commentary), 55–60: the allocation of the priestly cities, with all the information regarding their names, number, and the Israelite tribes from whose inheritance they are taken.

(*b*) Verses 61–81 (with the exception of v. 65): the cities assigned to the Levites. Unlike the first part, the original distinction between two stages in the recording of the cities is preserved, thus: vv. 61–63 outline the general distribution of the cities according to levitical families and respective Israelite tribes; v. 61 for the non-priestly Kohathites, v. 62 for the Gershonites, and v. 63 for Merari; vv. 64–81 (excepting v. 65) contain the detailed registration of the cities by levitical families and Israelite tribes: v. 64 is the introduction; vv. 66–69, Kohath; vv. 71–76, Gershon, vv. 77–81, Merari.

The main purpose of this reorganization, in which traces of the original list are still to be found, is to make a more definite distinction between the priests and the Levites (cf. also Auld, 'Levitical Cities', *ZAW* 91, 1979, 194). In Joshua 21, the priests form but one family, albeit the first, among the four tribal groups. Here they are given separate treatment, to be followed by the three levitical families.

6. A few more points should be made about the form of the list in Chronicles, which is basically an abbreviation, encompassing only about two-thirds of its original form in Joshua. The many textual corruptions (including the omission of six names – cf. section A above) of course contributed to the formation of this shorter version and they should be duly restored. However, the main factor is to be found in the redactional abbreviations, undertaken for the purpose of textual economy. One should include here systematic omissions, especially the way in which the conclusions, if not eliminated entirely, are at least severely curtailed. The concluding statement about the number of cities from each tribe (Josh. 21.16: 'nine cities out of these two tribes', and likewise in vv. 18, 22, 24, 29, 31, 35, etc.); the conclusions for each of the levitical families (Josh. 21.26, 33, 40); the conclusion of the list as a whole (Josh. 21.41–42), and the conclusion of the chapter (Josh. 21.43–44) – none of these is repeated in the Chronicles version. In addition, there are also occasional, less systematic omissions, which tend to use more concise language, for which cf. the commentary. It is therefore incumbent on the commentator to refrain from a blanket restoration of elements simply on the grounds that the missing detail is found in Joshua. Each of these cases should be examined in its own specific context, with an awareness of the general inclination to abbreviation in the Chronicler's version.

Another systematic change concerns the six cities of refuge, mentioned among the priestly and levitical cities. In Josh. 21, the city of refuge has three features: in all cases it is the first city mentioned for each tribe (Josh. 21.13, 21, 27, 32, 38), it is always stated that it is 'the city of refuge for the slayer', and its geographical location is always specified: 'Hebron in the hill country of Judah' (Josh. 21.11, etc. The only exception is the Reubenite city of refuge, v. 36, for which cf. below). In the version of Chronicles, only the first and last of these features are retained. The second is abbreviated to 'the city of refuge' for Hebron and Shechem (vv. 57, 67), and omitted altogether for the other four – Golan, Kedesh, Bezer and Ramoth (vv. 71, 76, 78 and 80). For these last, the specific geographical designations are the only remaining indications of distinction.

The careful manner of this abbreviation may reflect a specific Chronistic understanding of the cities of refuge, recognizing the existence of only two such cities rather than six: 'Hebron in the land (Josh.: "in the hills") of Judah' and 'Shechem in the hill country of Ephraim', that is, one city each for the southern and northern kingdoms.

Another systematic omission is the reference, in the context of Joshua, to 'the command of God through Moses' (21.2, 8). It is this command which inspires the Levites to apply to Joshua for property rights (v. 2), which are duly granted (v. 8). In the new context of Chronicles, both references are omitted.

7. Although the pericope as a whole was no doubt composed by the Chronicler, over fifty per cent of the material derives from extant biblical sources: the traditional genealogy of Levi and his sons (6. 1–3; 16–19), and the list of the levitical cities (6. 54–31); vv. 48–49 may also be seen as a reworking of Pentateuchal data. Even in vv. 4–15, 20–47, which alone are not directly borrowed from other sources, certain biblical elements can be found (as in the list of the Kohathites, in the genealogy of Samuel, etc.). The question of the identification and authenticity of the Chronicler's sources will be raised after a detailed study of the lists themselves. Here it will suffice to say that, in addition to the Chronicler's editing and redaction, the following passages

should be ascribed to his pen: vv. 31–32, 33–47, 48–49, 50–54a – the middle part of the chapter.

D. Commentary

[1–3] (MT: 5.27–29) Like the lists of Judah, Simeon and Reuben, the levitical pericope opens by introducing 'the sons of Levi' (MT 5. 27). Then, postponing the further development of the levitical genealogy to vv. 16–19, the text here focuses on the family of Kohath, with the objective of documenting a link between the levitical ancestors as known from the Pentateuch and the high priests of the monarchical period. Like the record of the sons of Jehoiachin which we have already noted (1 Chron. 3.17–24), the present list is then very systematically structured:

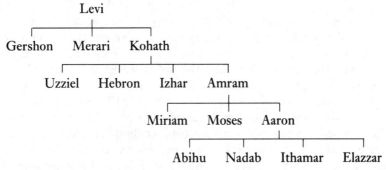

The data for the first generations of Levi are found in several Pentateuchal sources (Gen. 46.11; Ex. 6.16–25, and, most broadly, in Num.3. 17ff.; 26.57ff.), but the specific formulation of this passage has no parallel and is clearly an intentional reformulation of the levitical material, for the specific needs of the present context.

Here the name of Levi's first-born is (in spite of RSV) 'Gershon', a form repeated in I Chron. 23.6. Elsewhere in Chronicles, the name is always Gershom (6.16, 17, 20, 43, 62, 71; 15.7). Outside Chronicles, the form is consistently Gershon (Gen. 46.11 etc.), and the gentilic form always 'the Gershonites', even in Chronicles (I Chron. 23.7; 26.21, etc.). There is no doubt that the Chronicler prefers the final *mem* for the name, as is clear from 6.62, 71 [MT 6.47, 56]) as against the parallel passages of Josh. 21.6, 27. The two instances of Gershon may be due to the routine of copying given sources (in both cases the name is found in the same traditional formula), or may be an adjustment by later scribes, a phenomenon illustrated by the occasional change in the Peshitta from Gershom to Gershon in I Chron. 6.16, 17 – an adjustment to the Pentateuch tradition.

In v. 3 (MT 5.29) Miriam is included among the descendants of Kohath, in what may be regarded as the final stage of her absorption into the Amramites (cf. Ex. 6.20; Num. 26.59; and finally Micah 6.4).

[4–15] (MT 5.30–41) The passage depicts a genealogical tree deriving from Aaron's son Eleazar and concluding with Jehozadak, who is said to have been exiled by Nebuchadnezzar. Judging from the first and last personalities, from the bracketed note regarding Azariah, and from the few identifiable names, we have here a purported representation of the whole line of high priesthood from its origin with Aaron and Eleazar to the destruction of the Temple. The list thus parallels that of the Davidic monarchs (I Chron. 3.10ff.), but with two differences. First, the registration form employs 'X begot Y' instead of 'X, Y his son' which appears in 3.10ff. Second, and much more complicated, is the aspect of sources and authenticity. For want of historical data, we will deal with this problem with the help of the material itself.

The list records a genealogical tree of twenty-two names, descending from Eleazar. Allowing an average of twenty or twenty-five years for a generation, their lives would span 440 to 550 years, a reasonable period between the settlement and the destruction of the Temple. However, the internal chronology of the list follows typological rather than historical criteria. Incorporating the generally accepted emendation of vv. 9–10 [MT 5.35–36], so that the first-mentioned Azariah, and not the second, was priest in the Temple at its dedication, only ten generations remain between the dedication and the exile, implying that each priest ministered almost forty years. While the historical validity of such a chronology is doubtful, it is in full harmony with the historical framework suggested by I Kings 6.2 and regarded as characteristically Deuteronomistic (cf. Noth, *The Deuteronomistic History*, 18–57). According to this view, the building of the Temple took place 480 years after the Exodus, and the typological length of forty years per generation would indicate twelve generations of priests for that interim. Indeed, this is corroborated by the list, in which Azariah represents the thirteenth generation after Aaron.

Another doubt about the full historical authenticity of the list arises from the way in which certain names are included or excluded. Our sources in Samuel-Kings provide some information about the priests who were actually in office during the monarchical period. We know of Azariah, the son of Zadok, from Solomon's time (I Kings 4.2); Jehoiada, in the time of Athaliah and Joash (II Kings 11.4–12.10); Urijah in the time of Ahaz (II Kings 16.10–16); Hilkiah in the time of Josiah (II Kings 22.4–23.4); and Seraiah at the destruction (II Kings 25.18). In addition, the Chronicler mentions two other priests: Amariah in the days of Jehoshaphat (II Chron. 19.11) and Azariah in the time of Uzziah (II Chron. 26.20). Of all these priests, no hint is found in this list of Jehoiada, Urijah and Uzziah's contemporary Azariah, and it is only

possible that Amariah of v. 11 is the one mentioned in II Chron. 19. At the
same time, the list does contain other figures known to us from the biblical
sources: Eleazar, Phinehas, Ahitub, Zadok, Ahimaaz and the Azariah who
served under Solomon. All things considered, the list in its present format
can hardly be what it purports to be: a full and authentic record of the high
priests during the monarchic period.

Some light is shed on the form, source and authenticity of the list by a
comparison with its parallels, in particular with Ezra 7.1–5. (Since the
parallel of I Chron. 6.50–53 is just a segment of the list, it is of no help in this
case.)

Ezra 7.1–5 is ostensibly the genealogical tree of Ezra, who is recorded here
as the son of Seraiah, replacing Jehozadak, the last priest of I Chron. 6.14–15
(MT 5.40–41). The other major difference between Ezra 7.1–5 and this list
is that it consists of seventeen generations from Aaron, rather than twenty-
three. This shorter format is achieved, not by sporadic omissions but by the
absence of one continuous block of six generations appearing in the middle of
the Chronicles list (from Amariah in v. 7 to Johanan in v. 10). The first eight
generations and the last nine are transmitted without gaps or omissions.

This bulky lacuna in Ezra might be explained as the result of an editing
process or textual corruption (cf. F. M. Cross, 'The Priestly Houses of Early
Israel', *Canaanite Myth and Hebrew Epic*, Cambridge 1973, 196); however,
the nature of the missing names makes these solutions doubtful. The persons
appearing only in Chronicles but not in Ezra are: Amariah, Ahitub, Zadok,
Ahimaaz and Azariah – that is, the group including particularly those four
priests familiar to us from the book of Samuel (II Sam. 8.17; 15.27 etc.; I
Kings 4.2). As is known from the study of Samuel, the Aaronide origin of
Zadok has been questioned since Wellhausen's study in 1878 (*Prolegomena*,
121ff.; cf., however, Cross, 'Priestly Houses', 208–15). Can a coincidental
textual corruption be responsible for the omission from the genealogy of all
the names connected explicitly with Zadok? It is my tendency, then, to
regard the list of Ezra 7.1–5 as the more original and the list in Chronicles
as its elaboration; the investigation should, accordingly, first focus on the
former list.

It would seem that the need to establish an unequivocally legitimate
ancestry for the priests, including the high priest, arose in that transition
period between the destruction of the First Temple and the building of the
Second – more specifically, in the days of Jeshua the son of Jozadak and his
successors. This need was motivated by several factors:

(*a*) An increasing sensitivity to the purity of blood line, for the people in
general and the priests in particular (cf. Ezra 2.59–63).

(*b*) The lack of information from the First Temple period, as a result of the
destruction.

(c) The emergence of the view that all priests must be of Aaronide origin, a concept which inspired efforts to establish legitimate Aaronide genealogies in cases where these had been lost, or had in fact never existed.

The list found in Ezra 7.1–5 is a sample of such an effort to connect the last known priests of the First Temple (Hilkiah, Azariah, Seraiah) to Aaron. We lack the critical tools needed to establish whether or not this is an authentic list. Several points, however, should be made:

(a) Except for the last two figures (Seraiah and Hilkiah), the Ezra list contains none of the priests known to us from the pre-exilic period. After Phinehas, the son of Eleazar, the list goes blithely its own way, ignoring altogether priests known from the historical records. Even 'Zadok the son of Ahitub' occupies a position in the list which makes it very unlikely that the priest of David's time is meant. Thus, this attempt to create an Aaronide genealogy intentionally avoids any reference to the actual priesthood of the monarchic period.

(b) Between Phinehas and Hilkiah only ten generations are registered, a simplification which surely leaves room for gaps and omissions.

The 'short list' of Ezra is, then, an attempt to produce an 'Aaronide' genealogy for the last priests of the First Temple, to whom the priests of the Second Temple traced their ancestry, without making a full adjustment to the history of the monarchical period as portrayed in the historical books. In Chronicles, this list was subsequently adapted and elaborated: 'the house of Zadok' was integrated into the Aaronide line and finally legitimized, and the list as a whole was reworked to conform to the typological concept of I Kings 6.2. Since this elaboration was motivated by social and theological factors, the other details in the sacerdotal history were not affected and could be left out.

It is therefore likely that the context for the original promulgation of the list is to be sought in the figure of Jehozadak (v. 15) who now concludes it. The death of Seraiah, Jehozadak's father, is narrated in II Kings 25.18–21// Jer. 52.24–27, but the present passage is our only evidence, not only of Jehozadak's Aaronide ancestry, but also of his kinship to Seraiah. Here, then, we have the key to the levitical/Aaronide legitimacy of Joshua, the high priest of the Restoration period (Hag. 1.1, etc; Ezra 3.2, etc), and the missing link between the priesthood of the First and Second Temple.

This last item of information must, in spite of the possible artificiality of most of the list, derive from a dependable source. None of the testimonies of the period – Haggai, Zechariah and Ezra – raise any doubt about the right of Joshua the son of Jehozadak's claim to high priesthood; in a period so scrupulous about legitimacy the texts would hardly be so unanimous if his descent from Seraiah were in any doubt.

Verse 15 in this chapter and I Chron. 9.1 are the only references in Chronicles to the exile of Judah. In the relevant historical context (II Chron.

36), only the exile of Jerusalem is probably implied, and for I Chron. 9.1, cf. *ad loc*. In the spirit of 5.26; II Chron. 12.5–7; 28.5, etc., the exile 'by the hand of Nebuchadnezzar' is seen as the Lord's own doing.

[16–30] (MT 6.1–15) 1. This passage continues the levitical genealogical scheme by presenting the three central genealogies of the Levites: Gershon, Kohath and Merari. The two-part structure is then a reflection of the previous section: an introduction (vv. 16–19a), and the genealogical trees themselves (vv. 19b–30). While the introduction in vv. 1–3 was intended to introduce the line of the high priests and therefore recorded one member only in each generation, the focus of the verses before us is on the heads of all the levitical families, individuals whose status would parallel that of the high priest among the priests. The present introduction (vv. 16–19a) therefore develops in three parallel lines, recording the three levitical families.

Of the two texts which parallel this section, Exod. 6.6–19 and Num. 3.17–20, the introduction has probably been taken from the latter, with some abbreviations and changes in the function of the material. One example: 'These are the families of the Levites according to their fathers' serves as a conclusion in Num. 3.20, but as an opening in the present context (v. 19). Here, then, 'their fathers' (and not 'their fathers' houses', as in Num. 3.20) refer not to the forefathers 'Gershon, Kohath and Merari', but to the heads of the three levitical groups in each generation.

2. In its present form, the list betrays two literary stages (cf. also A. Lefèvre, 'Note d'exégèse sur les généalogies des Qéhatites', *RSR* 37, 1950, 287–92). The original consisted of three genealogical trees, tracing eight generations from the traditional forefathers:

(*a*) *Gershon* – Libni – Jahath – Zimmah – Joah – Iddo – Zerah – Jeatherai (vv. 20–21);
(*b*) *Kohath* – Amminadab (Amram?) – Korah – Assir – Tahath – Uriel – Uzziah – Shaul (vv. 22, 24);
(*c*) *Merari* – Mahli – Libni – Shimei – Uzzah – Shimea – Haggiah – Asaiah (vv. 29–30).

Accordingly, the last three 'fathers' of the Levites would be Jeatherai, Shaul and Asiah, nine generations removed from Levi. This genealogical scheme fully parallels that of the high priests in vv. 50–53, intended to provide a continuous line down to the time of David, like the other lists in the genealogies of Judah.

In the second stage, a genealogy of the prophet Samuel has been transplanted into the line of the Kohathites, in an attempt to provide Samuel with a legitimate levitical pedigree. The traces of this literary elaboration can be clearly discerned. To the genealogy of Samuel from I Sam. 1.1, the names of his sons are added from I Sam. 8.2, resulting in the pedigree: Zuph – Tohu – Elihu – Jeroham – Elkanah – Samuel – Joel and Abijah. This, too, is a genealogical tree of seven generations; its grafting into the levitical genealogy has been effected by sub-dividing the line of Kohath. After the reference to Assir in v. 22, the list in fact goes back to Korah and lists his three sons as if in brackets. Verse 23 should now be viewed as a horizontal rather than a vertical genealogy (cf. also Lefèvre, ibid.; also Williamson, 71–72):

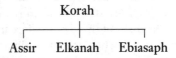

Taking its data from Ex. 6.24, v. 24 then proceeds with the descendants of Assir (cf. above), while vv. 25–28 go back to record the descendants of Elkanah, Korah's second son. To this second line the whole pedigree of Samuel has been linked, the result being a genealogy of Kohathites which does not balance the other levitical branches:

Gershon	*Kohath*	*Merari*
Libni	Aminadab (Amram?)	Mahli
Jahath	Korah	Libni
Zimmah	Assir, Elkanah, Ebiasaph	Shimei
Joah	Amasai, Ahimoth	Uzzah
Iddo	Elkanah	Shimea
Zerah	Zophai	Haggiah
Jeatherai	Nahath	Asaiah
	Eliab	
	Jeroham	
	Elkanah	
	Samuel	
	Joel Abijah	

A third literary stage, which further confirms my view here, is found in the genealogical trees of the three head-singers, in the following passage.

The most difficult textual problem of the lists is the appearance of an

'Amminadab' as Kohath's son in v. 22. At this stage in the consolidation of the levitical genealogical schemes, when traditional concepts have been established, the appearance of a 'new' son of Kohath is very unlikely. His role as father of Korah would seem to indicate an emendation of the name to 'Izhar' (cf. Exod. 6.21 etc.; Curtis, 131; Rudolph, 54), and this is indeed the rendering of certain LXX texts. However, a comparison with the other levitical lines suggests that the oldest of Kohath's sons is expected here, and Amram would be a better emendation (K. Mohlenbrink, 'Die levitischen Überlieferungen des Alten Testament', ZAW 52, 1934, 201), preferable also from an orthographic point of view. Thus, in addition to 'Korah the son of Izhar' (vv. 37–38; Ex. 6.21), the list would presume the existence of another Korah, the son of Amram, unattested by any other record. For this difficulty no fully satisfactory solution can be found, given the present state of our knowledge.

3. How should the sources, authenticity and authorship of these lists be viewed? The Chronicler could hardly have been sole author of all three discernible literary stages: he must either have worked out the last on the basis of the other two, or alternatively written either the first or the second, which subsequently were elaborated upon by later editors. The further possibility, that all three stages preceded the Chronicler's composition, cannot be excluded. It is not in the nature of lists to exhibit unequivocal linguistic or stylistic features which might betray the identity of their author; but if I should nevertheless venture a suggestion, it would be to ascribe to the Chronicler the special preoccupation with the singers, thus attributing to him the last stage of redaction, reflected in vv. 33ff.

It does not seem out of place at this point to draw attention to the fact that these lists are no mere literary compositions, and should be considered from a broad historical and sociological perspective. The energy invested in the production of levitical pedigrees answered a pressing need on the part of the Levites to legitimize their status as fully as possible. Their social position, like the pedigrees themselves, is based on the assumption (further elaborated in chs. 23–26) that the reorganization and reinstatement of the Levites in the Temple service were initiated by David. The forging of these lists, through a complex accumulation of details, is therefore not the literary effort of an individual, but the result of a prolonged collective process of legitimization within the levitical circles themselves.

4. One more detail which should be briefly discussed is the inclusion of the prophet Samuel among the Levites. Early presentation of Samuel's origins confronts later generations with a dilemma: he is described as an 'Ephrathite' (= Ephraimite, I Sam. 1.1) and yet, as 'ministering to the Lord under Eli' (I Sam. 3.1), a task which was by definition considered levitical. Here, then, an effort is being made to present Samuel as a Levite, a descendant of

Kohath. Since, however, Samuel is not a very significant figure in Chronicles, this effort is hardly a product of the Chronicler's own genealogical goals; it must have answered some contemporary need. And indeed, in the following section, the founder-singer 'Heman' is introduced as Samuel's grandson. It is for his legitimacy – a crucial prerequisite of his status – that this genealogical structure was created, in the two stages still visible to us in the present context.

[31–47] (MT 16–32) Verses 31–32 introduce the genealogical trees of the three head singers, and explain why, in addition to the three main lines of the Levites, the singers are recorded separately. This explanation is based on one of the Chronicler's fundamental concepts regarding the development of the clergy: with the permanent 'coming to rest' of the ark in Jerusalem, an overall transformation of the levitical functions was decreed by David. Freed now from the task of 'carrying the ark', the Levites were assigned other roles, the most important of which was the 'service of song'.

This introduction is in fact a summary of 1 Chron. 15.1–16.43, which describes the actual appointing of the three singers to their tasks, first on a provisional basis and then permanently. The terminology is carefully selected. The singers were entrusted from the outset with 'the service of song in the house of the Lord' (v. 31), but until the Temple was built, they would serve temporarily 'before the tabernacle of the tent of meeting'. This last title, as well as the shorter 'the tabernacle of the Lord', refers to the tent constructed by Moses in the wilderness (Ex. 39.32; 40.2, 6, 29). In employing the same titles for the Davidic tent as for that erected by Moses, the Chronicler anticipates the observance here of a full tabernacle cult. In the desert sanctuary of Moses, however, there was no place for music; the 'service of song' is an elaboration of the original ritual, made possible by the fact that the ark 'has come to rest'.

After the introductory words 'These are the men who served and their sons' (v. 33a), the three head singers are presented in the following order: Heman of Kohath (vv. 33b–38); Asaph of Gershon (vv. 39–43); and Ethan of Merari (vv. 44–47). The depth of the genealogical register is not uniform, but a major difference is evident between Heman and the other two. In fact, here again one may reconstruct a two-stage process in the development of the Kohathite list, which would parallel that in the preceding passage.

(a) Stage one reflects a balanced three-part list, in which the three head singers, Heman the son of Joel, Asaph the son of Berechiah and Ethan the son of Kishi, are affiliated to the three levitical ancestors Kohath, Gershon and Merari by genealogical trees of approximately equal length. In each case the affiliation is conceived as passing through the respective forefather's *second* son, just as the line of the head Levites in the preceding list passes through the *first* son.

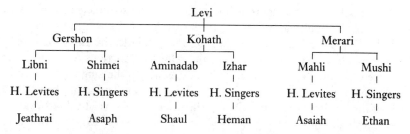

(*b*) For Asaph and Ethan, this original structure survived in the text. Heman, on the other hand, is identified as 'son of Joel the son of Samuel', and his pedigree is elaborated by mechanically appending of the genealogy of Samuel (vv. 26–28) to his own. The resulting genealogy is then simplistically presented as a linear series of names, where in addition, pairs of brothers are recorded as father and son – as with Mahath (Ahimoth) and Amasai (cf. v. 25), and Assir and Ebiasaph (cf. v. 23). Thus the genealogy of Heman reaches an unprecedented length of twenty-two names.

The detailed lineage of stage (*a*) is as follows:

> *Asaph* – Berechiah – Shimea – Michael – Baaseiah – Malchijah – Ethni – Zerah – Adaiah – Ethan – Zimmah – Shimei – Jahath – Gershon – Levi
> *Ethan* – Kishi – Abdi – Malluch – Hashabiah – Amaziah – Hilkiah – Amzi – Bani – Shemer – Mahli – Mushi – Merari – Levi
> *Heman* – Joel – Azariah – Zephaniah – Tahath – Assir – Ebiasaph – Korah – Izhar – Kohath – Levi

In spite of the great similarity between these genealogical trees and those of the heads of the Levites registered before, different genealogies were here conceived, the difference being most evident in the case of Merari.

The secondary development of Heman's line (stage *b*) would appear as follows:

> *Heman* – Joel – Samuel – Elkanah – Jeroham – Eliel – Toah – Zuph – Elkanah – Mahath – Amasai – Elkanah – Joel – Azariah – Zephaniah – Tahath – Assir – Ebiasaph – Korah – Izhar – Kohath – Levi.

The length of this list and the affiliation of Heman to the prophet Samuel both express the increasing prestige of the house of Heman among the singers. In addition, Heman is recorded first, although his ancestor Kohath was the second among the sons of Levi; in the liturgical ritual his post is in the centre, with Asaph standing 'on his right hand' (v. 39) and Ethan 'on the left hand' (v. 44). This decline of the Asaphites and rise of the Hemanites is most strikingly expressed in I Chron. 25.

All in all, these paragraphs illustrate an intense preoccupation with schematization and legitimization, in the circles of the levitical clergy.

[48–49] (MT 33–34) These two verses conclude the three preceding passages. They begin the account of the religious functions with 'and *their* brethren the Levites' (v. 48), referring explicitly to the singers' 'service in song', introduced above in vv. 31–32. The statements referring first to the role of the Levites (v. 48) and then to the priests (v. 49) relate chiastically to the genealogies of Levites (vv. 16–30) and priests (vv. 1–15), thus bringing this long unit to a conclusion.

The clear literary differentiation between the singers on one hand and the Levites and priests on the other reflects the traditional view of the history of these sacerdotal institutions. The singers are consistently presented as having been appointed by David: 'These are the men whom David put in charge' (v. 31), while the Levites and priests fulfil their more ancient calling 'according to all that Moses ... had commanded' (v. 49). This distinction is to be repeated in future chapters (e.g. II Chron. 8.14, etc.).

To sum up the levitical functions, v. 48 emphasizes that they were 'dedicated (RSV "appointed") for all the service of the tabernacle'. The tasks of the priests (v. 49) are much more detailed: they are responsible for the burnt offerings, incense, 'the work of the most holy place' and to make atonement for Israel. In general, these verses are constructed from fragments of Pentateuchal phrases: the allusion to the Levites as 'dedicated' (RSV 'wholly given', Num. 3.9; 8.16–19, etc.), the definition of their service as *ʿᵃbōdāh* (ibid., cf. J. Milgrom, *Studies in Levitical Terminology* I, Berkeley 1970, 60ff.), the reference to the priestly order as 'Aaron and his sons' (Num. 8.13, 22, etc.), and to their tasks as offering, incense and atonement (Lev. 16.17; 23.28, etc.). Yet, the phraseology is nevertheless tailored to the present context. In the Pentateuch, 'tabernacle' (*miškān*, literally: abode) is the term used for the tent erected in the desert, a connotation preserved in Chronicles (above v. 32, I Chron. 16.39, etc.). In v. 48, the unique conflation 'tabernacle of the house of God' (*miškan bēt hāʾᵉlōhīm*) makes *miškān* a general noun, defining that 'the abode (*miškan*) of the Lord' could be either a tent or a house.

The historical context presupposed here (by the juxtaposition of vv. 31 and 48–49) is the time of David. Although the Temple has not yet been built, a full liturgy is assumed to exist, with an 'altar of burnt offering' and an 'altar of incense', and all the ritual commandments of Moses being performed in the 'tabernacle of the house of the Lord'. The circumstances probably reflect those described in I Chron. 15–16 (q.v.), where the implied dichotomy of the divine service, with singers separated from the other cultic personnel, is fully explained.

[50–81] (MT 35–66)

[50–53] These verses serve to introduce the list of levitical cities and, like Josh. 21.1–3, to determine its precise historical context. The information presented here, which has already appeared in the list of the high priests (vv. 4–8), is here arranged to produce a direct line from Aaron to Eleazar and Pinehas, using a different formula, 'X, Y his son', instead of 'X begot Y'. The list ends pointedly with an inconspicuous figure among the priests, that of Ahimaaz, the son of Zadok, whose role in David's day is clear from II Sam. 15.36; 17.17–29; and 18.19–29.

Of course the establishment of a Davidic setting clashes starkly with the context in Joshua, in which the list represents the cities which 'the people of Israel gave to the Levites ... out of their inheritance' (v. 3), and which fell by lot to the future inheritance of the Levites. Whatever the original framework, it is evident that the list's position in Joshua aims to give concrete expression to the idea that the conquest and settlement were complete, as is then expressed in the conclusion of the chapter: 'Thus the Lord gave to Israel all the land which he swore to give to their fathers ... Not one of all the good promises ... had failed; all came to pass' (Josh. 21.43–45). The Chronicler, in transplanting the list from Joshua to the time of David, introduces a new element. These are no longer cities which 'fell by lot' to future levitical settlement, but rather the settlements actually occupied by priests and Levites. Consequently, the wording of the list is changed several times, as for example in the heading: 'These are their dwelling places (*mōš*ᵉ*bōtām*) according to their settlements (*l*ᵉ*ṭīrōtām*) within their borders (*bigᵉbulām*)' (v. 54). However, in this respect, the redaction is incomplete, and traces of the context of division by lot remain in the sporadic appearance of 'they gave' (v. 64, etc.).

[54–60] (MT 39–45) The information pertaining to the priestly cities is derived from Josh. 21.10–19, with some abbreviations (cf. above). The rough text of Josh. 21.11–12 and 13 (cf. commentaries on Joshua), which is probably due to some redactional process, is transferred unaltered to Chronicles. The present structure is as follows:

54 and 65 Introduction (see below)
55–56 Hebron
57–59 The cities in Judah and Simeon
60 The cities in Benjamin.

[54] (MT 39) The second part of the verse is taken from Josh. 21.10, with some omissions. The first part is a heading added by the Chronicler, introducing his own view of actual occupation of these cities by the priests. The plural *mōš*ᵉ*bōt* (settlements) is a distinct priestly term, occurring 17 times in Priestly texts (Gen. 36.43; Ex. 10.23; 12.20; 35.3; Lev. 3.17, etc.; Ezek. 6.6, 14; 37.23), translated as 'dwelling places', 'where they dwelt',

'dwellings', 'habitations', 'the land you are to inhabit' (Num. 15.2 *'ereṣ mōš'bōtēkem*), 'the places where they dwelt', etc. In addition it appears three times in Chronicles, in 4.33; 6.54 (MT 34); and 7.28 – all connected with the city lists taken from Joshua. Thus the Chronicler insists on his view regarding these cities.

ṭīrōtām (RSV 'their settlements') is a more poetic word, coupled with *mōš'bōtām* in Num. 3.10. This is its only occurence in Chronicles, adding emphasis to the idea of 'settlements'. The third word *g'būlām* (RSV 'their borders', NEB: 'districts'), although frequent in Priestly sources, cannot be defined as strictly confined to such material. It clearly belongs to a specific 'Chronistic' lexicon, and in three of its occurrences (I Chron. 6.54, 66 [MT 39, 51]; II Chron. 11.13) is used in reference to the levitical cities.

[55] (MT 40) The somewhat repetitious text of vv. 55 and 57a is already found in Josh. 21.10–11 and 13. It would seem that in Joshua 21 a kind of compromise pertains between two traditional views: Hebron as a city of refuge among the levitical cities, settled by the Aaronide priests (for further implications of this view cf. Cross, 'Priestly Houses', 206–15), and Hebron as belonging by special decree to Caleb the son of Jephunneh. It is characteristic of the Chronistic literary methods of 'global borrowing' that no attempt is made to adjust these traditions to those of I Chron. 2–4, where Caleb, to whom Hebron belongs, is not the son of Jephunneh but the son of Hezron and the brother of Jerahmeel (2.18, 42–43).

[65] (MT 50) (cf. below).

[59–60] (MT 44–45) The names 'Juttah' and 'Gibeon' should be restored, following Josh. 21.16, as implied by the number 'thirteen' here. Such omissions, caused by homoioteleuton, are frequent in the list.

[61–63] (MT 46–47) As discussed above, these verses, derived from Josh. 21.5–7, were transferred to this position as the list was restructured (above, p. 147).

In general, the allocation of tribal cities to the Levites follows a geographical rather than a genealogical logic, the families of Levites being grouped in defined geographical districts. This would be one of the elements which accentuate the schematic nature of the list. The priests are assigned cities in Judah, Simeon and Benjamin, the southernmost tribes west of the Jordan and what may be seen as the kingdom of Judah. The other Kohathites receive their cities in the central part of the land, from the tribes of Ephraim, half of Manasseh and Dan, who is here regarded as belonging to the central area according to his nominal inheritance (Josh. 19.40–48) rather than to his actual occupation (Judg. 18).

To the families of Gershon the cities are allocated in the north, on both sides of the Jordan – Issachar, Asher, Naphtali and Manasseh in the Bashan. The only exception to this strict geographical principle is found in the case of the Merarites, for whom Zebulun is added to the remaining Transjordanian tribes of Gad and Reuben; even here the guideline from south to north is not completely abandoned.

The distribution of the tribal cities to the levitical families is less schematic. A strictly schematic distribution would allocate four cities from each tribe and – regarding Kohath as entitled to 'two parts' (priests and the other Kohathite families) – twelve cities to each of the levitical components. In fact, only for the Merarites is this scheme preserved, as they receive twelve cities from three tribes, equally distributed. The Kohathites take twenty-three cities (13+10) while the Gershonites take thirteen. Deviations from the scheme also appear in the tribal 'contributions': nine cities are taken from Judah and Simeon while only three are taken from Naphtali.

[61] (MT 46) The text *mimmišpaḥat hammaṭṭeh mimmah^{a}sīt maṭṭēh ḥ^{a}sī m^{e}naššeh* is certainly wrong and should be restored with the help of Josh. 21.5: *mimmišp^{e}ḥōt (ham)maṭṭēh 'eprayīm ūmimmaṭṭēh-dān ūmēḥ^{a}sī maṭṭēh m^{e}naššeh*. It is possible that the Joshua text is also already corrupt, and in place of the present *mimmišp^{e}ḥōt maṭṭēh* originally read ... *l^{e}mišp^{e}ḥōtām, mimmaṭṭēh*, as in v. 7 and I Chron. 6.62, 63. However, the Chronicler's *Vorlage* seems already to have contained the faulty Joshua reading. RSV (rather untypically) preserves the MT with no emendation.

[64] (MT 49) The parallel in Josh. 21.8 serves to conclude the preceding unit, followed by a return to the priests. This verse, on the other hand, serves to introduce the subsequent register of the cities. In line with the general aims of the list in this context, the words 'by lot ... as the Lord had commanded through Moses' are omitted.

[65] (MT 50) Any view of the structure of the list must regard this verse as misplaced. Its origin is in Josh. 21.9, where it serves as the introduction to the registration of the priestly cities. The sequence of Josh. 21.8–9, logical enough in that context, has influenced the secondary placement of the verse in Chronicles, where it is completely out of place. (This difficulty is tackled by RSV with the addition of two words: 'they *also* gave *them*'; NEB employs brackets.)

However, the verse is not to be dismissed as a mere verbatim gloss from Josh. 21.9; there is the addition of 'the tribe of Benjamin' and a grammatical change from singular to plural in *yiqr$^{e'}$ū 'ethem b^{e}šēmōt* (literally 'they call them by names', RSV 'are mentioned by name'). If the verse is transposed after v. 54, it will serve to open the passage dealing with the priests, just as in Josh. 21.9. In fact, we now see that the information offered in Josh. 21.4 has been divided by Chronicles and transplanted into both this verse (with the addition of the tribe of Benjamin) and v. 60: 'all their cities throughout their families were thirteen'. The section referring to the priests is thus coherently restructured.

[66–70] (MT 51–55) This section deals with the cities of 'the rest of the families of the Kohathites', those who were not of the 'sons of Aaron', but Levites (cf. I Chron. 23.13–14). Their status is defined more precisely in Josh. 21.20: '... the rest of the Kohathites belonging to the Kohathite families of the Levites'. For the term 'the rest (*hannōtārīm*)', cf. I Chron. 24.20. The passage is taken, with the usual abbreviation of numbers and conclusions, from Josh. 21.20–26. The names of the Danite cities in Josh. 21.23 have fallen out of the text and should be restored.

[71–76] (MT 56–61) [77–81] (MT 62–66) Following Josh. 21.27–33, the first passage cites the cities of the Gershonites, located in the tribal territories of Manasseh (the eastern half), Asher and Naphtali, with the systematic omission of numbers, conclusions and references to the cities of refuge. Similarly, the cities of the Merarites in the tribes of Zebulum, Reuben and Gad, follow Josh. 21.34–40, with the same omissions.

An interesting glimpse into the process of borrowing and redaction is offered by vv. 78–79 (Josh. 21.36–37 in several editions). In Joshua these verses were evidently omitted at one stage, and reintroduced from the Chronicles text – cf. for instance, BH and Bombergiana, *ad loc*. They differ from the rest of the Joshua list by bearing the distinguishing marks of the Chronistic editing, which were noted above (p. 148).

The names

(Cf. W. F. Albright, 'The List of Levitic Cities', *Louis Ginzberg Jubilee Volume I*, New York 1945, 41–73; Y. Aharoni, *The Land of the Bible*, 301–5.) The names in the two parallel lists are relatively uniform. Six names have been omitted by corruption in the Chronicles text; of the remaining forty-two, twenty-seven are fully identical, with only slight variations in spelling (מְשָׁאֵל – מִשְׁעָל in v. 74; רָאמוֹת – רָמֹת, יְעֹזֵר – יְעֹזֵר, in vv. 80, 81 etc.). Among the remaining fifteen names the variations may be tentatively classified as follows:

(*a*) The change may result from textual corruptions, either in Joshua or in Chronicles. While in certain cases the preferable text may be indicated with relative confidence, in others only the nature of the change may be surmised. Taking into consideration the various biblical data and the geographical-historical information at our disposal, we may draw the following conclusions.

In five cases the version of Joshua seems preferable to that of Chronicles. These are Holon (Josh. 21.15) for Hilez (v. 58, RSV Hilen); Taanach (Josh. 21.25) for Aner (v. 70); Kishion (Josh. 21.28) for Kedesh (v. 72); En-ganim (Josh. 21.29) for Anem (v. 73); and Helkath (Josh. 21.31) for Hukok (v. 75).

In three cases the Chronicler's version of the names should be preferred to that of Joshua: Ashan (v. 59) for Ain (Josh. 21.16); Bileam (better Ibleam, v. 70) for Gath-Rimmon (Josh. 21.25), and Rimon(o) (v. 77) for Dimnah (Josh.21.35).

In one case, where Chronicles reads Tabor and Joshua Nahalal (v. 77/ Josh. 21.35), the texts should be regarded as complementary. An original list, which included Jokneam and Nahalal (now attested in Joshua 21), Rimmon and Tabor (now attested in Chronicles), has been eventually corrupted in both texts, two names out of the four having been omitted in Chronicles.

(b) A variation in a place name may also result from a different tradition or an alternative pronunciation, producing forms with equal claims to originality. These include Alemeth/Almon (v. 60/Josh. 21.18); Ashtaroth/ Be-eshterah (v. 71/Josh. 21.27), and Hammon/Hammoth-dor (v. 76/Josh. 21.32).

We must leave as undetermined the cases of Ramoth/Jarmuth (v. 73/ Josh. 21.29); Kiriathaim/Kartan (v. 76/Josh. 21.32) and Jokmeam/Kibzaim (v. 68/Josh. 21.22).

Historical origin and context

One of the questions most frequently raised regarding the list of levitical cities has been that of its historical origins: when and for what reason was it promulgated? The answers offered throughout the long history of the discussion are basically of two kinds:

(a) The list indeed reflects authentic historical-geographical-sociological circumstances. The precise period and specific function of the list must be decided by juxtaposing the data of the list with the known history of Israel.

(b) The list is a literary-theological construction. Here again, its origin and function are differently situated within the history of Israel.

Common to both views is the conviction that whatever the origin of this material, it cannot be accepted as what it claims to be – a list from the time of Joshua. Its situation in that context is regarded by virtually all as of theological significance: a final indication that all the goals of the conquest have been accomplished.

In Chronicles, the list is situated in a Davidic context, and given a different role. I have amply shown that the Chronicles version derives from that of Joshua. But does the new context also have a historical value? Does it shed light on the authentic origin and functions of the list? A whole school of scholars would answer this question in the positive. Albright, B. Mazar ('The Cities of the Priests and Levites', *VTS* VII 1960, 193–205 = *Biblical Israel, State and People*, Jerusalem 1992, 134–45) and their followers would regard the list as historical in origin and function and attribute it to the time of David, or, at the latest, to the 'united kingdom'. According to this view, in attributing the list to the period of David, the Chronicler preserves a historical fact, and his position should be adopted.

Whatever stand we may take regarding the historical origins of the levitical cities or the circumstances of the final list (cf. more recently N. Na'aman, 'A New Look at the System of Levitical Cities', *Borders and Districts in Biblical Historiography*, Jerusalem 1986, 203–6) it should be remembered that the Chronicler's version does not stand on its own nor was it taken as it is from an undefined 'original'. Its placement in the time of David is therefore not an original feature of the literary format, but a deliberate change of the framework of Joshua, involving an adjustment of the list to its new context. This is evident mainly in remnants of phrases relevant to the context of Joshua but not to that of Chronicles, especially references to the 'giving' of cities to the Levites: 'and they gave them Hebron' (v. 55); 'and they gave to Aaron' (v. 57); 'and the people of Israel gave to the Levites' (v. 64. etc.). This 'giving' of the cities is the point of the context of Joshua, but not of the new one in Chronicles.

Moreover, the placing of the list in the time of David is in full conformity with the general aim of the genealogies, which purport to portray the ethnic and geographical background of Israel at the time of David. This goal is the focus of the whole introduction of I Chron. 1–9 to such an extent that no specific historical value should be attributed to the Davidic context of the list. Whether or not the list was promulgated at the time of David (or, for that matter, at any point in the history of Israel) should be decided without the benefit of the Chronicler's testimony on the matter.

What, then, is the function of the list in Chronicles?

(*a*) As I have already stated, to describe the Israelite settlement in the time of David.

(*b*) Moreover, to present the tribe of Levi as 'settled' in the land to an extent equal to any other tribe. While the other tribes may have their territories, the Levites have their 'cities with their pasture land'.

(*c*) The list itself is a perfect reflection of the unity and completeness of the people of Israel. It contains all the tribal units – including the two half-tribes of Manasseh and the inner division of the Levites (cf. also I Chron. 12. 24–28) – 15 components altogether. It therefore serves one of the Chronicler's main aims – to depict the whole people of Israel in all its elements, settled in its land.

(*d*) The list emphasizes the status of the Levites *vis à vis* the priests; their rights are independent of those of the priests.

(*e*) The comprehensive picture of levitical settlement does not constitute a concrete demand for actual property rights; in the Persian period the great majority of the listed cities were out of the borders of the province of Judah. The focus here is rather a matter of principle: the unequivocal right of the sacerdotal orders to settle in the land.

7 The sons' of Issachar: Tola, Puah, Jashub, and Shimron, four. ² The sons of Tola: Uzzi, Rephaiah, Jeri-el, Jahmai, Ibsam, and Shemuel, heads of their fathers' houses, namely of Tola, mighty warriors of their generations, their number in the days of David being twenty-two thousand six hundred. ³ The sons of Uzzi: Izrahiah. And the sons of Izrahiah: Michael, Obadiah, Joel, and Isshiah: five, all of them chief men; ⁴ and along with them, by their generations, according to their fathers' houses, were units of the army for war, thirty-six thousand, for they had many wives and sons. ⁵ Their kinsmen belonging to all the families of Issachar were in all eighty-seven thousand mighty warriors, enrolled by genealogy.

6 The sons of Benjamin: Bela, Becher, and Jedia-el, three. ⁷ The sons of Bela: Ezbon, Uzzi, Uzziel, Jerimoth, and Iri, five, heads of fathers' houses, mighty warriors; and their enrolment by genealogies was twenty-two thousand and thirty-four. ⁸ The sons of Becher: Zemirah, Joash, Eliezer, Eli-o-enai, Omri, Jeremoth, Abijah, Anathoth, and Alemeth. ⁹ All these were the sons of Becher; and their enrolment by genealogies, according to their generations, as heads of their fathers' houses, mighty warriors, was twenty thousand two hundred. ¹⁰ The sons of Jedia-el: Bilhan. And the sons of Bilhan: Jeush, Benjamin, Ehud, Chenaanah, Zethan, Tarshish, and Ahishahar. ¹¹ All these were the sons of Jedia-el according to the heads of their fathers' houses, mighty warriors, seventeen thousand and two hundred, ready for service in war. ¹² And Shuppim and Huppim were the sons of Ir, Hushim the sons of Aher.

13 The sons of Naphtali: Jahzi-el, Guni, Jezer, and Shallum, the offspring of Bilhah.

14 The sons of Manasseh: Asri-el, whom his Aramaean concubine bore; she bore Machir the father of Gilead. ¹⁵ And Machir took a wife for Huppim and for Shuppim. The name of his sister was Maacah. And the name of the second was Zelophehad; and Zelophehad had daughters. ¹⁶ And Maacah the wife of Machir bore a son, and she called his name Peresh; and the name of his brother was Sheresh; and his sons were Ulam and Rakem. ¹⁷ The sons of Ulam: Bedan. These were the sons of Gilead the son of Machir, son of Manasseh. ¹⁸ And his sister Hammolecheth bore Ishhod, Abiezer, and Mahlah. ¹⁹ The sons of Shemida were Ahian, Shechem, Likhi, and Aniam.

20 The sons of Ephraim: Shuthelah, and Bered his son, Tahath his son, Eleadah his son, Tahath his son, ²¹ Zabad his son, Shuthelah his son, and Ezer and Ele-ad, whom the men of Gath who were born in the land slew, because they came down to raid their cattle. ²² And Ephraim their father mourned many days, and his brothers came to comfort him. ²³ And Ephraim went in to his wife, and she conceived and bore a son; and he called his name Beriah, because evil had befallen his house. ²⁴ His daughter was Sheerah, who built both lower and upper Beth-horon, and Uzzen-sheerah. ²⁵ Rephah was his son, Resheph his son, Telah his son, Tahan his son, ²⁶ Ladan his son, Ammihud his son, Elishama his son, ²⁷ Nun his son, Joshua his son.

CHAPTER 7   167

28 Their possessions and settlements were Bethel and its towns, and eastward
Naaran, and westward Gezer and its towns, Shechem and its towns, and Ayyah and
its towns; 29 also along the borders of the Manassites, Beth-shean and its towns,
Taanach and its towns, Megiddo and its towns, Dor and its towns. In these dwelt the
sons of Joseph the son of Israel.

30 The sons of Asher: Imnah, Ishvah, Ishvi, Beriah, and their sister Serah. 31 The
sons of Beriah: Heber and Malchi-el, who was the father of Birzaith. 32 Heber was the
father of Japhlet, Shomer, Hotham, and their sister Shua. 33 The sons of Japhlet:
Pasach, Bimhal, and Ashvath. These are the sons of Japhlet. 34 The sons of Shemer
his brother: Rohgah, Jehubbah, and Aram. 35 The sons of Helem his brother;
Zophah, Imna, Shelesh, and Amal. 36 The sons of Zophah: Suah, Harnepher, Shual,
Beri, Imrah, 37 Bezer, Hod, Shamma, Shilshah, Ithran, and Beera. 38 The sons of
Jether: Jephunneh, Pispa, and Ara. 39 The sons of Ulla: Arah, Hanniel, and Rizia.
40 All of these were men of Asher, heads of fathers' houses, approved, mighty
warriors, chief of the princes. Their number enrolled by genealogies, for service in
war, was twenty-six thousand men.

A. Notes to MT

[1] ולבני, proposed ובני; [4] גדודי, read גבורי with LXX? [6] בנימן, read בני בנימן with
some MSS and the Versions; [12] ושפם וחפם, gloss, cf. commentary; עיר, read דן; בני
אחר, read בנו אחד, cf. commentary; [13] בני בלהה, proposed אלה בני בלהה; [14] אשר ילדה,
dittography from ישראל? [15] ומכיר, proposed וגלעד; אשה, several words were
probably deleted; לחפים ולשפים, gloss? cf. v. 12; מעכה, read המלכת [המלכת] ושם אחתו,
transfer to the end of v. 14; [16] מכיר, probably גלעד; [18] מחלה, add ואת שמידע? For
the suggested reconstructions, cf. commentary; [25] ורשף, add בנו? [29] תענך ובנתיה,
probably add יבלעם ובנותיה; cf. LXX and Josh. 17.11; [30] ובריעה, proposed add ארבעה
(haplography); [32] שומר, v. 34 שמר; חותם, v. 35 הלם; [34] אחי ורוהגה, read אחיו רוהגה;
[35] ובן, read ובני; [36] וברי וימרה, probably read ובני ימנע; [37] יתרן, v. 38 יתר;
[39] עלא, probably שעא, cf. v. 32.

B. Notes to RSV

[2] 'of their generations', cf. commentary, p. 168; [4] 'units of the army', probably
'mighty warriors', cf. above (A); [14–18] cf. commentary; [27] 'Nun', MT 'Non';
[28] 'eastward, westward', NEB 'to the east', etc.; JPS 'on the east', etc.; [29] 'also
along the borders of the Manassites', this is the version of LXX; MT ידי ועל, cf.
NEB 'In the possession of Manasseh ...'

C. Structure, sources and form

1. Chapter 7 provides the genealogies of all the tribes of Israel which have not yet
been mentioned: Issachar, Benjamin, Dan, Naphtali, Manasseh, Ephraim and Asher.
Only Zebulun is absent, an omission which is probably to be attributed to textual
error (cf. also below).

2. The chapter's five sections differ from one another in length, structure, literary components and genres, although some common features can certainly be found. The structure of the chapter is as follows:

(a) 1–6   Issachar
(b) 7–11   Benjamin
(c) 12–13 The sons of Bilhah: Dan and Naphtali
(d) 14–29 The sons of Joseph
(e) 30–39 Asher

This bare skeleton may already imply that Issachar, Benjamin and Asher form one group. The similarities between these sections are indeed the greatest; they are of approximately equal length, and each is devoted to one tribe. The other units, (c) and (d), the shortest and the longest in the chapter, each refer to two tribes, from different points of view.

3. A closer study shows that the units on Issachar, Benjamin and Asher display more common features, which clearly distinguish them as a group:

(a) each of these genealogies opens with a record of the traditional 'sons' of the forefather in question, based on one or another Pentateuchal source (vv. 1, 6, 30).

(b) although not identical, the lines of the genealogical registration are similar, recording fathers' houses rather than individuals or genealogical trees.

(c) all these passages emphasize military terminology, which may indicate that they originated in the records of a military census. The most systematic genealogy in this respect is that of Benjamin.

(d) none of these passages provides any information about the 'settlements' of the tribes in question.

4. Although some military terms have already appeared in the genealogy of the tribes east of the Jordan (5.13), it is in this chapter that they are most dominant. In fact, such descriptions appear here seven times, three times each for Issachar and Benjamin, and once for Asher (vv. 2, 4, 5, 7, 9, 11, 40). In each instance the number of soldiers is given – a detail found elsewhere only in 5.18; they are further described as 'mighty warriors', numbered by 'fathers' houses', and 'enrolled by genealogies' (התיחש). The record is not stereotyped, and no one statement is fully identical to any other.

The two distinguishing terms of these registrations are התיחש (enrol by genealogy) and לתלדותם (by their generations). The latter is a recurring term in the census of Numbers 1 (vv. 20, 22, 24, etc.) and elsewhere (Gen. 10.32; 25.13, etc.). Without the suffix, it is a well-known feature of the Priestly records (Gen. 2.4; 5.1; 10.1; 11.10; etc.). Its use in Chronicles is appropriately restricted to the genealogies, mainly from ch. 5 onward (I Chron. 1.29; 5.7; 7.2; 4, 9; 8.28; 9.9, 34; 26.31), but is absent from the records of Judah and Levi. The translation 'their generations' highlights the connection with the census of Numbers 1 and other texts, but obscures any affinity with the other Priestly sources, where 'descendants' or 'genealogies' are employed.

By contrast, התיחש is characteristic of late Hebrew, its use attested only by Chronicles and Ezra-Nehemiah. Since, however, there is no equivalent early verb to express the same idea, it is difficult to say whether its present distribution depends on linguistic circumstances, implying that the verb was introduced into Hebrew only at a later phase, or whether its absence from the Priestly material is due to the latter's stylistic preferences.

5. The literary evidence points to a military census as the source of the material (J. Liver, 'So All Israel was Enrolled by Genealogies', in *Studies in Bible and Judean Desert Scroll*, Jerusalem 1971, 234–48*). While the Chronicler refers this census to 'the days of David' (v. 12), there are other historical candidates, such as Jeroboam the son of Joash, king of Israel (I Chron. 5.17), or Josiah the king of Judah. There is really no reason to doubt the existence of such a census or its registration, as is clear from II Sam. 24; the Chronicler may have obtained these data from an intermediate source.

I referred elsewhere to the order of the tribes in the genealogies; in this case the order of the three tribes seems also to correspond to the scope of their military force, with Issachar, the largest, placed first, and Asher, the smallest, last.

6. Almost all the elements characteristic of the sections devoted to Issachar, Benjamin and Asher are absent from the portion dealing with Manasseh and Ephraim. There is no listing of the traditional 'sons', no 'mighty warriors', no numbers of people 'ready for service'. By contrast, the passage contains a narrative unit (vv. 20–24), a genealogical tree (vv. 25–27), and a record of settlements (vv. 28–29).

7. Major questions raised by this chapter concern the absence of Zebulun, the apparent omision of Dan and the scant material about Naphtali. The generally accepted view since Klostermann (*RTK* 4, 94; cf. Curtis, 150; Noth, *The Chronicler*, 37–8, *et al*.), is that v. 12 still retains a reference to Dan (but cf. below, p. 174). Verse 13, with the most unusual reference to Bilhah, Jacob's concubine, points to the source of the two verses in Gen. 46.23–24, of which this passage is an almost literal repetition: 'the sons of Dan, Hushim. The sons of Naphtali ... these are the sons of Bilhah.' Curtis (145–9) has endeavoured to show that the list of Benjamin in this chapter is a corruption of an original record of Zebulun. The internal evidence, however, does not seem to support this view, and the list seems to be a solid, coherently structured Benjaminite document (Williamson, 77–8).

The three problematical tribes of Zebulun, Dan and Naphtali have a common denominator in their geographic location in the north of Israel. Given the fate of the northern tribes in the deportation by Tiglath-pileser (II Kings 15.29), one may well ask whether the existence of only scant material regarding these tribes is due to their historical circumstances, a consideration which would also set the date of the census after Tiglath-pileser's invasion in 733–732 BCE. If this was the case, it can be argued that the present form of the material is due to the Chronicler's effort to complete the genealogical picture and, for lack of better sources, to base his text on the bare skeleton borrowed from Pentateuchal data. However, as this interpretation does not account for the complete omission of Zebulun, it is more likely that an entire passage, perhaps a full column devoted to Zebulun, Dan and Naphtali, was lost from the Chronicler's original work (Williamson, 78). Later, the material for Dan and Naphtali was secondarily supplemented by a direct literal borrowing from Gen. 46.23–24, while Zebulun was completely overlooked.

8. These lists are far from stereotyped, as is best illustrated by a comparison of the concluding phrases of passages which belong basically to the same group (i.e. vv. 2, 4, 5, 7, 8–9, 11 and 40). Variety is manifest in every possible way. Although certain elements are common to most of these conclusions, only the number of warriors is found in all, usually – but not always (cf. vv. 4, 5, 11) – cited at the end. The textual length varies widely, from eleven words (v. 5) to twenty (v. 40). The number of the fathers' houses is sometimes recapitulated (vv. 3, 7); in other cases there is an opening

statement 'all these were the sons of' (v. 9 [MT 8b], 11, 40). Certain elements appear only once: the explanation in v. 4, the historical remark in v. 2, the titles 'approved' and 'chief of the princes' in v. 40. The phrase 'their number' is found for the first group (v. 2) and the last (v. 40). Even those elements which recur more frequently are phrased differently: thus, the definition of the men as 'warriors' (גבורי חיל) in vv. 2, 9; גבורי חילים in vv. 5, 7, 11, 40; and גבורי צבא מלחמה in v. 4) and their description as 'heads of fathers' houses' (ראשים לבית אבותם in v. 2; לבית אבותם ... ועליהם ראשים כולם in vv. 3–4; ראשי בית אבותם in v. 7; ראשי בית אבותם in v. 9; לראשי האבות in v. 11 and ראשי בית האבות in v. 40). No two expressions are the same, although one and the same status is meant throughout. This variety, which could be further demonstrated and which is to a great extent obscured by the translation, could not be a result of textual transmission, although corruptions are of course possible. It is certainly a function of the stylistic quality of the material, the aim of which is to present the same basic facts with a minimum of monotony. In such variations, even the quantitative element is of significance. Thus, for the tribe of Asher there is only one conclusion (v. 40), but it is the longest in every way. Its twenty words include almost all (but still not all) of the preceding elements, and the largest number of titles: 'heads of fathers' houses', 'approved', 'mighty warriors', 'chief of the princes'. The men are 'approved', then, not only by the meaning of these titles, but by their quantity and repetition. Second to this in length is the description of the family of Uzzi, of the tribe of Issachar, singled out as exceptionally blessed (vv. 3–4).

9. The centre of the chapter is occupied by 'the sons of Joseph the son of Israel' (v. 29). Although no explicit heading indicates that vv. 14–29 should be seen as one section, this is evident in the chiastic structure of the whole passage, concluding with the statement quoted above: 'the sons of Joseph the son of Israel'. The structure is as follows:

(i)   14–19   genealogy of Manasseh
(ii)   20–27   genealogy of Ephraim
(iii) 28   settlements of Ephraim
(iv)   29   settlements of Manasseh.

Unlike the other lists of the chapter, these genealogies do not open with the traditional sons of Manasseh and Ephraim – who are absent from Gen. 46.27 as well. Neither is there any indication of military terminology in either list. The genealogies as they stand may contain certain elements which are similar to details found elsewhere (cf. the commentary), but the text is not literarily dependent on any known source. By contrast, the lists of settlements, and especially v. 29, are clearly dependent on other biblical passages, such as Josh. 17.1ff. [MT 16.11ff.], Judg. 1.27ff., and more.

D. Commentary

[1–5] The passage devoted to the sons of Issachar is structured in four parts: v. 1, the conventional families of the tribe; v. 2, the sons of Tola; v. 3–4, the sons of Uzzi; v. 5, all the others. This genealogical registration is presented explicitly as the result of a census in the days of David.

The list of Issachar's four sons in v. 1 follows Gen. 45.13 and Num. 26.23 in almost identical terms, except for the different spelling of 'Puah'.

It has already been pointed out (H. W. Hogg, 'Issachar and Tola, Their Genealogies', *OLZ* 3, 1900, 366–8; cf. Curtis, 144), that the introduction in Judges of Tola from the tribe of Issachar is extremely similar to the list of Issachar's sons in Numbers; cf:

'Judg. 10:1: 'Tola the son of Puah ... and he lived ($y\bar{o}\check{s}\bar{e}b$) in Shamir ($\check{s}\bar{a}m\bar{\imath}r$)'.

Num. 26. 23f.: Tola, Puah, Jashub ($y\bar{a}\check{s}\bar{u}b$), Shimron ($\check{s}imr\bar{o}n$).

However this similarity may be explained, for the Chronicler it is already an established genealogical tradition.

The actual registration of Issachar is limited to only one branch of the tribe, Tola, while the others are referred to by the general term 'their kinsmen belonging to all the families of Issachar' (v. 5). Six fathers' houses are recorded in the family of Tola, of which one, that of Uzzi, is developed as an independent family, also consisting of four fathers' houses:

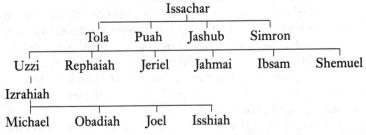

The fathers' houses of Tola numbered around 23,000 warriors, and those of Uzzi 36,000 – an unusual proliferation which is duly acknowledged by the statement 'for they had many wives and children'.

[3–4] Verse 3 begins with the plural 'the sons of', followed by one name – a recurring phenomenon in the lists (I Chron. 3.22, etc.). However, the notation 'five' after four names have been mentioned seems more difficult; the Peshitta indeed renders 'four', while Rudolph suggests that the phrase 'the sons of Izrahiah' is a gloss, and that all five names refer to 'the sons of Uzzi' (Rudolph, 64). However, since the list does not refer to the biological 'sons' of one 'father' but rather to the social affiliation of 'fathers' houses', the two difficult details, 'the sons of Uzzi' and the number 'five', may both indicate that the 'clan' of 'Uzzi' developed *via* the intermediate stage of 'Izrahiah', a unit which kept its independent status as a fathers' house. Thus, the last four names are at one and the same time 'the sons of Izrahiah' and, together with him, 'the sons of Uzzi'.

[5] The already unusually large families of Tola and Uzzi, when aug-

mented by 87,000 mighty warriors of 'their kinsmen', bring the total of the tribe's military force to almost 150,000 warriors, unparalleled by any detailed tribal record, either in I Chron. 1–9; Num. 26; or I Chron. 12.25–38. Even if the figure 87,000 is meant to *include* Tola and Uzzi (as may be suggested by the repetition of the word 'all'), the tribal unit of Issachar still remains the largest recorded anywhere – with the exception of Judah in II Sam. 24.9 and I Chron. 21.5.

[6–11] The list of Benjamin's sons is found here and in three other biblical texts (Gen. 46.21; Num. 26.38; I Chron. 8.1); the four lists differ from each other in almost every detail: the number of the sons, their names, and the relationship between the generations. The only feature they all share is the name of Benjamin's first-born – Bela.

Since Becher, Benjamin's second son in the list, also appears in Gen. 46.21, we may regard the Genesis list as nearest to this version, although there the third son is Ashbel (as in Num. 26.38 and I Chron. 8.1), while here it is Jediael. As in Num. 26.38 and I Chron. 8.3 (but not Gen. 46.21), the list records the third generation from Benjamin through Bela; the names of Bela's sons are, however, altogether different.

As a matter of fact, it is precisely these differences which confirm the authentic origins of the list. Rather than portraying the development of the ethnic units and their family affiliations, the list provides a 'horizontal' registration of the fathers' houses of Benjamin, at a given historical point, for the sake of a census. The number of the Benjaminite branches is here conceived as three, and taking Gen. 46.21 for comparison, it is clear that 'Jediael' has replaced 'Ashbel'.

The other points of difference between this list and the others may be understood in various ways. It is possible that, notwithstanding the heading of v. 6, the list does not record the full Benjaminite picture. Alternatively, it is more likely that the Benjaminite families not mentioned here had gradually lost their independent status, either becoming extinct or being absorbed by the families of the third generation.

2. The Benjamin registration is distinguished by its method, although here, too, as in the whole chapter, there is an inclination to stylistic variety rather than uniform terminology. The list begins with the names of Benjamin's sons, and their number ('three'), and proceeds in an orderly manner to the third generation: of Bela (v. 7a), of Becher (v. 8), and of Jediael (v. 10). In the case of Jediael – in the same way as for Uzzi of Issachar (v. 3) – an intermediate generation is recorded. The genealogical record of each family is concluded by a description and number (vv. 7b, 9, 11). This full Benjaminite record may come nearest to an original census registration:

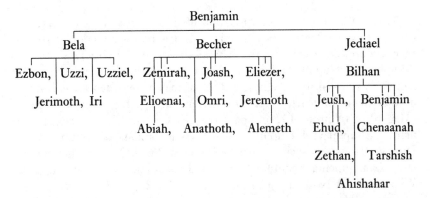

The total number of the Benjaminites is fifty-nine thousand, four hundred and thirty-four.

Several more details should now be clarified:

1. As far as one can tell, all the names are proper names with the exception of Anathoth and Alemeth (v. 8), which are known elsewhere as place names, and appear together in I Chron. 6.60 [MT 6.45]. We have already noticed that there is really no absolute distinction between family names and place names, not only because in practice localities were associated with the peoples or families who inhabited them and *vice versa*, but also because the whole genealogical conceptual system presents social and geographical circumstances in genealogical terms. Nonetheless, in the context of the Benjamin list as (probably) reflecting a census at a specific historical point, one would expect only designations of 'fathers' houses' – individuals who represent the social units within the tribe. 'Anathoth' and 'Alemeth' may be explained along one of two lines: as a literary irregularity, their appearance could simply be regarded as secondary; as a socio-geographical phenomenon, they may indicate the homogeneity of these localities, each regarded as comprising one fathers' house, and both tracing their origins to one eponym.

2. A grandson of Jediael, a fourth-generation descendant of Benjamin, also bears the name 'Benjamin'. It is true that some names of Jacob's sons are repeated in the Bible as regular proper names (Judah, Simeon and Benjamin in Ezra. 10.23, 31, 32; Issachar in I Chron. 26.5, etc.), and the absence of others is probably no more than incidental. This case, however, is the only one in which one rather small tribal segment has taken the name of the tribe itself, and the possibility of corruption should not be ruled out.

3. After the introduction in the plural, 'the sons of Jediael' (v. 10), only one name is cited: Bilhan; the following fathers' houses are then presented as Bilhan's sons. This structure follows identically the record of Uzzi in v. 3. With this parallel in mind, and counting Bilhan among the fathers' houses, the Benjaminite family heads reach the round sum of twenty-two.

[12–13] Whatever the interpretation of these verses, they are certainly corrupt to some degree. As it stands, v. 12 has no introduction at all, and therefore appears to continue the Benjaminite section with brief references to 'Shupim and Hupim the sons of Ir' and 'Hushim the sons of Aher'. The name 'Ir' is similar to 'Iri' of v.7, and 'Aher' may be regarded as a corruption of some Benjaminite name like 'Ehi' of Gen. 46.21, 'Ahiram' of Num. 26.38, 'Aharah' of I Chron. 8.1, or Adar/Ard of I Chron. 8.3; Gen. 46.21. The names 'Shupim and Hupim' are just vocal variants of 'Shupham and Hupham', sons of Benjamin according to Num. 26.38. One may therefore see in v. 12 a fragmentary continuation of the Benjaminite genealogy (H. G. M. Williamson, 'A Note on I Chronicles 7.12', *VT* 23, 1973, 375–9).

This interpretation, however, is difficult in two ways. First of all, the proposed continuation would contrast sharply with the systematic and comprehensive format of the Benjamin passage as a whole, which presents three sons of Benjamin with their respective offspring and relevant concluding remarks. Secondly, the incongruous plural of the phrase 'the sons of Bilhah' clearly implies that vv. 12–13 referred originally not only to Naphtali, but also to Bilhah's first son, Dan (cf. Gen. 30).

This last difficulty hints at another approach (proposed by Klostermann and generally accepted), that v. 12 represents a corrupt version of the genealogy of Dan. The reconstruction is based on the following observations:

(a) Hushim is the name of Dan's only son in Gen. 46.23.

(b) LXX reads 'his son' ($b^e n\bar{o}$) for 'sons of' ($b^e n\bar{e}$) in v. 12b.

(c) 'Shuppin and Huppim' are probably a gloss to v. 6 (based on Num. 26.38); their insertion here was the first of a series of scribal errors.

Assuming that 'Ir' ('*ir*) is a secondary correction for 'Dan', we can then posit an original version $b^e n\bar{e}$ *dān hušîm*, $b^e n\bar{o}$ *'ehād*, 'the sons of Dan, Hushim, his one son', certainly the briefest passage devoted to any tribe.

Verse 13 is a literal reproduction of Gen. 46.24, with three minor differences: the slightly variant vocalization of the first and last names (Gen. 46.24 and Num. 26.48 – Jahzeel, Shillem), and the omission of the word 'these' (*'ēlleh*), probably by corruption. The end of the passage, with the unique reference '[these were] the sons of Bilhah', clearly points to its origin in Gen. 46.23–25.

[14–19] In its present form, the passage seems incorrigibly corrupt (cf. the commentaries and A. Demski, 'The Genealogies of Manasseh and the Location of the Territory of Milkah Daughter of Zelophehad', *Eretz-Israel* 16, 1982, 70–5*). Textual reconstruction may provide the text with a modicum of logic, on condition that we do not lose sight of the conjectural nature of the results.

I shall begin the discussion by presenting the difficulties:

(a) Verse 14 mentions one son of Manasseh by the name of 'Asriel', who appears elsewhere only once, as the son of Gilead (Num. 26.31).

(b) The mention of Asriel is followed by the words 'whom she bore' ($^{a}\check{s}er$ $y\bar{a}l\bar{a}d\bar{a}h$), with no explicit subject governing the verb 'bore'. RSV deals with the difficulty by translating 'Asriel whom his Aramean concubine bore; she bore Machir ...', a reading which ignores the sense of the Massoretic accents and grammatical balance.

(c) In v. 15 we are told that 'Machir took a wife for Huppim and Shuppim'. These two have already been mentioned in v. 12, probably a misplaced gloss to the previous genealogy; they have no function in the present context, as is shown by the absence of any reference to children of these marriages.

(d) The passage continues 'the name of his sister was Ma'acah', but it is not clear whether 'his' refers to Machir, Shuppim or Huppim. The picture is further confused by the reference in v. 16 to Ma'acah as Machir's wife.

(e) Verse 15 says 'and the name of the second was Zelophehad', but does not specifiy how he fits into the context; nothing is said about his ancestry, nor who was 'the first', to whom Zelophehad was 'second'.

(f) Verses 16–17a record the descendants of 'Maacah the wife of Machir', but the conclusion of the list in 17b sums up with 'these were the sons of Gilead the son of Machir, etc.', implying that those mentioned in vv. 16–17a (and probably earlier) are the descendants of Gilead.

(g) Another sister, 'Hammolecheth', is mentioned in v. 18, where she is probably regarded as the sister of Gilead.

(h) Verse 19 lists 'the sons of Shemida', a note which appears utterly incongruous, although we know from Num. 26.29 that Shemida is one of Gilead's sons and therefore bears some (unspecified) relationship to our context.

My attempt at reconstruction is based on the relationship between v. 14b, 'His Aramaean concubine bore Machir the father of Gilead', and the formula of v. 17b, 'These were the sons of Gilead the son of Machir the son of Manasseh', a juxtaposition which may indicate that vv. 15–17 were initially intended to be the record of the 'sons of Gilead'. I further assume, with most commentators, that 'Shuppim and Huppim' are a misplaced gloss (originally intended to supplement v. 6 and secondarily inserted both here and in v. 12). In v. 14 many scholars would regard 'Asriel' as a dittograph of the following אשׂריל דה, and regard as original only one son of Manasseh, Machir, the father of Gilead, as in Num. 16.29 (e.g. Curtis, 152; Rudolph, 68; Williamson, 79; Braun, 110). However, the opposite reasoning is just as probable, namely, that the words $^{a}\check{s}er\,y\bar{a}l\bar{a}d\bar{a}h$ result from a dittograph of the original 'Asriel', or, for that matter, that a name has dropped after $y\bar{a}l\bar{a}d\bar{a}h$ (Demski, ibid.).

In my reconstruction I would try to make maximum use of the elements already found in these verses, introduce as few changes as possible, and complement only in accord with the internal logic of the existing details. The changes are:

(a) Omission of *'ašer yālādāh* (dittography); (b) a double change of 'Machir' to 'Gilead', in vv. 15, 16; (c) assumption of a lacuna after 'wife' (*'iššāh*) in v. 15; (d) transfer of the clause 'the name of his sister was Maacah' from v. 15 to the end of v. 14; (e) reading 'Hammolecheth' in place of 'Ma'acah' in the same clause; (f) omission of 'Huppim and Shuppim' in v. 15; (g) addition of 'and Shemida' at the end of v. 18.

Not all these suggestions are equally necessary. (For a different and more thorough reconstruction, which makes ample use of Num. 26.29–33, cf. Rudolph and BHS.)

My reconstruction would be as follows: 'The sons of Manasseh: Asriel. His Aramean concubine bore Machir the father of Gilead, and his sister's name was Hammolecheth. [Gilead] took a wife [and she bore him X (Hepher?). X had two sons; the name of the first was Y] and the name of the second Zelophehad. Now Zelophehad had only daughters. And Ma'acah [Gilead's] wife bore a son, and she called his name Peresh; the name of his brother was Sheresh, and his sons were Ulam and Rakem. The sons of Ulam: Bedan. These were the sons of Gilead the son of Machir, son of Manasseh. And his sister Hammolecheth bore Ishhod, Abiezer, Mahlah [and Shemida]. The sons of Shemida were Ahiam, Sechem, Likhi and Aniam.'

According to the Pentateuch genealogies, Manasseh is survived by only one son, Machir, who in turn has also only one son, Gilead. For Manasseh, then, the genealogical ramification begins, not in the first generation as with the other tribes, but in the third, and concludes not in the third but in the fifth generation. This difference in scope is probably due to the secondary integration of 'Gilead the son of Machir' into an existing, more ancient, genealogy of Manasseh which viewed 'Iezer, Helek, etc' as Manasseh's direct sons. The consequences of this integration are seen in the present genealogical picture of Num. 26.28, which would be as follows:

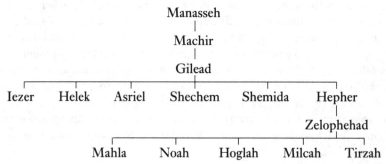

More significantly, the tribe as a whole is thereby attributed an 'eastern' origin; its western affiliation – expressed for example in the names of Zelophehad's daughters – is presented as secondary.

Note also that in Numbers no wives either of Manasseh or of his sons are mentioned.

The picture presented in this chapter, with the line of Manasseh developing through 'Machir the father of Gilead', is similar in its major points to that of Num. 26, a similarity apparent in the names recorded in the two lists. In fact, except for Hepher (whose name has probably fallen out) and three or four of Zelophehad's daughters, all the individuals of Num. 26 are represented in this list in one way or another: Asriel, Shechem, Shemida, Zelophehad and Mahlah are identical; Iezer (*'ī'ezer*) and Helek (*ḥēleq*) are represented as Abiezer (*'ᵃbī'ezer*) and Likhi (*liqḥī*) and Noah (*nō'āh*) may be represented by Aniam (*'ᵃnī'am*). The list therefore represents a different structure of the Manassites, with the old tribal components differently linked and new ones added. Following the reconstruction suggested above, the Chronistic genealogical scheme of Manasseh would be as follows:

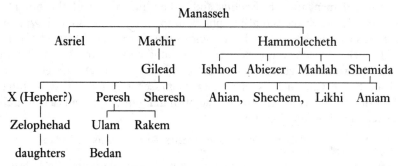

One aspect of the Chronicler's genealogical view is the special place of Asriel among the Manassite families. Rather than being a fourth generation to Manasseh, as one of Gilead's sons, he is presented as Manasseh's first-born, an offspring of his principal, unnamed wife, the most ancient element among the Manassites. Although his status has greatly declined, the tradition of his original supremacy is still preserved in our list. (For the name, and the possible consequences of its proximity to 'Israel', cf. A. Lemaire, 'Asriel, Sr'l, Israel et l'origine de la confédération israélite', *VT* 23, 1973, 239–43.)

Most significant in the Manassite genealogical picture is the strong Aramaean element in the Manassite families. The main branch of 'Machir the father of Gilead' is the offspring of an 'Aramean concubine'. Two women are then mentioned: Maacah, the wife of Machir (or rather, of Gilead), and 'his sister Hammolecheth', the two names bearing clear Aramaic associations. The unusual name 'Hammolecheth' (literally 'the reigning') is very similar to 'Milcah' (the daughter of Haran and the wife of Nahor, Gen. 11.29; 2.20), while Maacah as an Aramaean name is well-attested by the kingdom of the Maacathites (Deut. 3.14, etc.), David's wife (II Sam. 3.3), and one of the children of Nahor (Gen. 22.24). Thus, all the women mentioned in the Manassite line are either explicitly or implicitly Aramaean. In the ethnic code of the genealogies this would signify that the tribe of Manasseh is actually conceived as a mixture of primary, dominant, 'male' Israelite elements, with secondary, conventionally 'female', Aramaean components. The infiltration of Aramaean elements is regarded as very ancient, represented by Manasseh's own 'Aramaean concubine'. It is noteworthy that most of the offspring in the Manassite record are identified by their mothers (vv. 14, 16, 18).

All of these phenomena conform well to the historical-geographical situation of the Manassite tribe, settled on the north-eastern side of the Jordan, near the borders of the Aramaean kingdoms, where the actual ethnic and even political boundaries were undoubtedly not always clearly fixed. It should be noted that according to the Pentateuch's portrayal of the history of Israel, this Manassite-Aramaean ambience was actualized only during the tribal settlement after the Exodus, and had nothing to do with the individual figure 'Manasseh the son of Joseph', who spent his whole life in Egypt, and whose son Machir as well as his grandsons were born there (Gen. 50.23). The Chronicler, by contrast, conceives of the bond between the Manassites and the Aramaeans as going back to the person of Manasseh himself. In this respect, the Chronicler's picture of Manasseh resembles that of Judah; ignoring the intermediate phase of sojourn in Egypt, it presents a continuity of territorial occupation, thus:

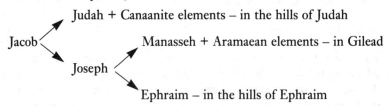

2. 'Machir the father of Gilead', the common title of Manasseh's son in Chronicles (I Chron. 2.21, 23), is also found in the 'remnant' of Josh. 17.1, which reflects similar attitudes, but is absent from the Pentateuch traditions. I have dealt in detail above with the construction 'X the father of Y', so common in the genealogies of Judah, which denotes the secondary occupation by an ethnic element (X) of a certain geographical area (Y). Its insistent appearance in this context would signify the occupation of Gilead by the ethnic group 'Machir'.

3. The general reference to the daughters of Zelophehad is an intentional allusion to the Pentateuch (Num. 26.33; 27.1–11); we have seen similar

allusions for Judaean personages (I Chron. 2.7, 20, 49). The names of the daughters are not explicitly recorded. 'Mahlah' does in fact appear in v. 18 as one of the offspring of 'Hammolecheth', but there is no indication if a 'son' or a 'daughter' is meant. It is also possible that 'Aniam' of v. 19 represents another daughter, Noah.

4. According to Josh. 17.2–3, the Manassite families which settled west of the Jordan were Abiezer (also Judg. 6.11ff.), Helek, Asriel, Shechem, Hepher and Shemida, and a specific reference is made to the five daughters of Zelophehad, the son of Hepher. The genealogical data of Num. 26.28ff. indicate that these families in fact represented the entire tribe – with the exception of Machir and Gilead, who are conceived in this list as earlier fathers of the same line. The majority of the Manassites, then, all descending from Machir and Gilead, are seen as settled in the west. The present list takes a different view of the matter. In vv. 18–19 almost the same western elements of Manasseh (Abiezer, Mahlah, Shemida, Shechem, Likhi (Helek) and Aniam) are presented, not as the offspring of 'Machir the father of Gilead', but as affiliated with 'his sister Hammolecheth'. In whatever way we view the genealogical affiliation of 'his sister Hammolecheth', this genealogical view accentuates the distinction between the two half-tribes of Manasseh, and limits the offspring of Machir more tightly to the east side of the Jordan. In addition, Asriel is set completely on his own, as related directly to Manasseh (cf. above).

The direct descendants of Gilead recorded in v. 16 are not known elsewhere as Manassites. Bedan (v. 17) is referred to again only in Samuel, as one of the judges (I Sam. 12.11; RSV follows the Septuagint and reads 'Barak'), but his appearance there between the two judges of Manassite origin, Jerubbaal (Gideon) and Jephthah (Judg. 6.11; 11.1), may indicate that he, too, was probably of Manassite stock. Ulam and Rekem both appear also in Benjaminite contexts (I Chron. 8.39–40; Josh. 18.27).

[20–27] While the section devoted to Ephraim has been structured as one continuous unit, it consists of different literary genres: a genealogy (vv. 20–21a), a narrative unit (vv. 21b–24) and finally the pedigree of Joshua the son of Non (RSV Nun, vv. 25–27). Of these units only the first is ambiguous, allowing several interpretations.

'The sons of Ephraim: Shuthelah, and Bered his son, etc.' illustrates a formula found elsewhere in the genealogies (e.g. I Chron. 3.10ff.; 6.20ff. [MT 6.5ff.]; 6.29ff. [MT 6.14ff.]); the indication is that only Shuthelah is regarded as Ephraim's son, while Bered is already his grandson. The question is whether we should regard the names which follow as a 'horizontal' genealogy, in which all are conceived as the sons of Shuthelah, or a 'vertical' genealogy, developing the line at least as far as the next 'Shuthelah'. There are precedents for both possibilities (cf. for instance in I Chron. 4.24–26), and they can be outlined as follows:

(a)

Ephraim
|
Shuthelah
|
| | | | | | | |
Bered Tahath Eleadah Tahath Zabad Shuthelah Ezer Elead

(b) Ephraim – Shuthelah – Bered – Tahath – Eleadah – Tahath – Zabad – Shuthelah.

In (b), the precise relationship of the last two names – Ezer and Elead – is undefined; they may be either brothers or sons of Shuthelah.

Each of these proposed genealogies has its exegetical virtues and weaknesses. The list (a) records eight sons of Shuthelah, in the third generation from Ephraim. This list may serve to introduce the following anecdote, which tells how they died and were mourned by 'Ephraim their father'. The difficulty lies in the repetition of certain names: is it likely that Shuthelah would have not only a son bearing his name but two sons by the name of Tahath and two sons by the name of Elead(ah) as well? This difficulty is dispelled if we understand the list as a genealogical tree. In doing so, however, we would lose all continuity with the story that follows, the point of which is that since all Ephraim's offspring perished at a blow, his line was continued through a new son, Beriah. This plot cannot be reconciled with a vertical genealogical tree proceeding from Shuthelah to Elead.

The difficulty seems to arise from the grafting together of two originally separate literary units. The tradition of vv. 21b–24 told of Ephraim's three sons: Shuthelah, Ezer and Elead. Verses 20–21a, on the other hand, present an independent, rather artificial, Ephraimite genealogy, constructed from traditional data regarding Ephraim's sons and augmented by secondary repetition of names. These two units were mechanically juxtaposed, with no real harmony created between them.

A more comprehensive literary solution is proposed by Rudolph (see also H. W. Hogg, 'The Ephraimite Genealogy (I Chron. 7.20ff.)', *JQR* XIII, 1900, 147–54), who regards vv. 20–21a (to the words 'Zabad his son') and vv. 25–27 as originally one list, containing the pedigree of Joshua, secondarily interrupted by the story in vv. 21b–24 (Rudolph, 71). However, it would seem more likely that vv. 25–27 represent an independent list and not a continuation of 21a (cf. below). However we explain these difficulties, it is clear that the seams in the literary fabric were not properly finished (cf. also N. Na'aman, 'Sources and Redaction in the Chronicler's Genealogies of Asher and Ephraim', *JSOT* 49, 1991, 105–10).

[20–21] In the Pentateuchal list of Num. 26.35ff., Ephraim is the father of three sons – Shuthelah, Becher and Tahan – and the son of Shutelah is Eran. Ephraim's second son Becher is somewhat problematical; he usually appears as Benjamin's second son, and his name is in fact absent in the LXX version. The list resembles Num. 26.35 only in the name and position of Shuthelah; the other names, while showing slight similarities (esp. Tahath – Tahan), are nevertheless basically different and of unknown origin. Elead/ Eleadah is unique; Bered is known only as a place name (Gen. 16.14); Tahath, Ezer and in particular Zabad are quite common proper names.

[21ab–24] This unique story is closer in genre to Pentateuch material than to the common Chronistic genealogies, although it does bear some similarity to the story of Jabez in I Chron. 4.10. The passage is structured around two unequal aetiological foci: the names of Beriah and Uzzen-sheerah. The dynamic of the first aetiology resembles that of Jabez: a name conceived as bearing a basically negative connotation explained by the circumstances of the man's birth. While the story of Jabez developed the idea of reversing the potential threat of the name, such a reversal of curse to blessing is not spelled out in this case. The 'evil' which prompted the choosing of Beriah's name is anchored in broader tribal rather than family circumstances, shedding light on the historical-sociological background of the Israelite tribes, as well as on the Chronicler's own views.

The tale is sketched with basic lines and few words, recording only essential actions and motives. Particular emphases are, however, expressed by the very few elaborative details not of a strictly essential nature. These are: 'who were born in the land', 'his brothers came to comfort him', and 'Ephraim their father'. They amount to an insistence on the geographical background of the events in the neighbourhood of 'Gath' and the conflict between 'the men of Gath who were born in the land' and the sons of Ephraim. The phrase 'came down' ($y\bar{a}r^e d\bar{u}$) is well-chosen: the Ephraimites descended from the hills to the lowlands in order 'to raid ... cattle', although, in contrast to the parallel raids of Simeon, Reuben and others, they are not successful. It is obvious that this aetiology represents recurring events in the life of the Ephraimite tribe in the hill country of Israel. However, actual circumstances notwithstanding, the story as a literary work deals with the individual Ephraim, the son of Joseph – an approach emphasized by 'their father', 'his brothers', 'his wife', etc. The events described transpired *in the land*; this is where the historical emphasis of the narrative lies. The depiction of Ephraim as a real individual, settled in the land, is not a passing remark here but a fundamental element, and this is true also of 'his brothers', whose coming to comfort Ephraim in his grief reminds the reader of the story of Job's friends (Job 2.11; cf. Rudolph, 73. R. E. Hoffmann, 'Eine Parallele zum Rahmenerzählung des Buches Hiob in I Chr. 7:20–29?', *ZAW* 92, 1980, 120–32, would go so far as to posit a literary dependence between the two texts with far-reaching literary consequences, but see Rudolph, 'Lesefrüchte 1', *ZAW* 73, 1981, 291–2). Furthermore Ephraim's daughter Sheerah is the builder of three cities, two of which are well-known Ephraimite localities. We should therefore distinguish carefully between the historical and the literary-theological aspects of the story. Historically, it may be harmonized with the Hexateuch traditions, as such events in the tribe's life could well have taken place after the conquest of Canaan. Cf. also the alternative Midrashic solution, attributing a premature exodus to the Ephraimites (BT, Sanhedrin 92.2; Targum, and more; and M. J. Moulder, 'I Chr 7.21b–23 und die rabbinische Tradition', *JSJ* VI, 1975, 141–66), and Albright's theory in the same vein ('New Israelite and Pre-Israelite Sites', *BASOR* 35, 1929, 6). This possibility is, however, expressly refuted by the presuppositions of the story itself. The individual Ephraim, his sons, brothers, wife and daughter, are all here in the land, and as a person he could not have lived in both Egypt and Israel. The close bond established between Joseph and the land should be regarded as the Chronicler's alternative to the Hexateuch tradition. It is probably no coincidence that this bond is so emphasized for the sons of Joseph – traditionally the most 'Egyptian' of the tribes, giving expression to the Chronicler's idiosyncratic views in this matter.

[23] The popular nature of this aetiology could not be more obvious. It is based on the noun *rā'āh* ('evil') from the root *r* ", while the name of Ephraim's son, Beriah, is in fact derived from a root like *br'* with an originally positive connotation (cf. Gen. 14.2 and Baumgartner, I, 150). The aetiology is made possible by viewing the initial *beth* as a preposition, but the syntax still remains awkward.

The story reflects inner sociological tribal processes: the emergence of the younger family of Beriah, a 'newcomer', which attains to a prominent position by in fact replacing or incorporating the original Ephraimite elements. The name 'Beriah' is also borne by the youngest son of Asher (Gen. 46.17; Num. 26.44, 45, etc.); it appears in Chronicles elsewhere as a Benjaminite element, linked with Gath (I Chron. 8.13, 16). These data may be explained in different ways. Beriah may be taken to represent a quite extensive ethnic element living in the central hill-country; portions of this entity were absorbed into and affiliated with the various surrounding tribes of Asher, Ephraim and Benjamin. Alternatively, one may assume that one and the same family altered its tribal affiliations with different historical situations (cf also on vv. 30ff. and 8.13, and Z. Kallai, 'The Settlement Tradition of Ephraim', *ZDPV* 102, 1986, 72–4).

[24] Here is recorded a remark of great interest concerning Sheerah, Ephraim's daughter (or Beriah's, for her parentage is not clearly defined). The Bible in several places narrates the construction of cities (Gen. 4.17; 10.11; Judg. 1.26; 1 Kings 16.34, etc.), but there is never a woman among the

builders. The author here credits Sheerah with founding not only the city which bears her name (Uzzen-sheerah) but two other important towns – upper and lower Beth-horon – in the hill country of Ephraim. Interpreted in the light of the genealogical code, this may reflect the incursion of Ephraimite elements into cities which are already established; seen from the point of view of their local autochthonic element they are ascribed to a 'female' eponym. Since, however, the story has no parallel, these surmises cannot be regarded as conclusive. (For a different reading of the verse and its possible consequences, cf., in great detail, L. Mazor, 'The Origin and Evolution of the Curse upon the Builder of Jericho', *Textus* XIV, 1988, 14–23.)

[25–27] The structure of the pedigree of Joshua the son of Non resembles that of David in I Chron. 2.10–15, except that the formula is 'X, Y his son', rather than 'X begot Y'. In the case of David, Nahshon the son of Amminadab, the prince of Judah known from the Pentateuch sources (Num. 1.7 etc.) is integrated into the genealogy. In the same way here, Elishama the son of Ammihud, known as a prince of Ephraim in the wilderness (Num. 1.10 etc.), is incorporated into the list before 'Non', the father of Joshua. Elishama, who according to the Pentateuchal tradition is a contemporary of Joshua (who is first mentioned in Exod. 17.9), has thus become his grandfather. The artificial nature of the list is also evident in other ways. While in David's genealogy 'Nahshon the son of Aminadab' represents the sixth generation from Judah, here Elishama is placed at least eight generations from Ephraim, Joseph's son. Also, the list as a whole seems to have extended the genealogy by a vertical restructuring of the Ephraimite figures known from the Pentateuch: Telah (=Shuthelah) and Tahan are both Ephraim's sons according to Num. 26.35, and Ladan may be a variant of 'Eran', Ephraim's grandson. Only the first two names (of which one – Resheph – is regarded by Rudolph, following Hogg, as a corruption, 72, cf. also BHS) were added, in order to reach the round number of ten and provide Joshua with a genealogical tree numbering ten generations from Ephraim.

The main difficulty here lies in the opening of the list. As the text now stands, Rephah may be the son of either Beriah of v. 23 or Ephraim of v. 22, and Joshua would be removed ten or eleven generations from Ephraim. The tension with Hexateuch traditions would be greater here than in other genealogies because of the large gap between Joshua and Ephraim.

As already stated, I prefer this understanding of the text, although the apparently more attractive option, from a literary-critical point of view, is Rudolph's suggestion that v. 25 was originally the continuation of v. 21a. This view has the drawback of assuming that the supposed original list was a combination of two different lists which made use of the same basic material but were structured differently: the first as a repetition, and the second as a vertical positioning of earlier horizontal genealogies. This view would also accentuate even more, without apparent reason, the gap between Ephraim and Joshua.

The tension between the list and the Pentateuch tradition lies not only in the genealogical views and chronological differences, but most significantly in the relationship of Joshua and Ephraim. Joshua, the hero of the conquest *par excellence*, is here only a rather distant descendant of the tribal chief Ephraim, who was firmly settled in Canaan from time immemorial. More than any other passage, this list emphasizes the Chronistic alternative concept of the beginnings of Israel in their land.

[28–29] The emphatically phrased heading defines the purpose of the passage as recording the 'possessions and settlements' – of Ephraim in v. 28 and of Manasseh in v. 29. Although the list of Ephraimite sites does not appear as such elsewhere, all the cities are known individually from other biblical texts. 'Naaran' is probably to be identified with 'Naarah' in the vicinity of Jericho (Josh. 16.7); Ayyah (or Aija, Neh. 11.31), as well as Aiath (Isa. 10.28), may be variants (or more original forms) of the better known 'Ai' (Josh. 7.2 etc.). The list follows a geographical principle: from Bethel in the south, moving to Naaran in the east, Gezer in the west, Shechem in the north, and back to Ayyah, again in the south. Bethel and Ai are better known as Benjaminite cities (Josh. 18.22; Neh. 11.31), while Bethel, Gezer and Naarah are, in Josh. 16.2–3, 7, landmarks on the border between Ephraim and Benjamin, and Shechem was situated between Ephraim and Manasseh (Josh. 17.7). The common denominator of the towns grouped here is that they are centres for the border provinces of Ephraim, a status expressed by the designations 'to the east' and 'to the west'. They probably reflect the expansion of Ephraim into the territory of neighbouring tribes.

The list of the Manassite cities in v. 29 is found also in Josh. 17.11 and Judg. 1.27–28, with the addition of 'Ibleam', which was probably omitted from the text by corruption. In Joshua the cities are described as the inheritance of Manasseh 'in Issachar and in Asher', and in both texts they are expressly designated as unconquered territory: 'Manasseh did not drive out the inhabitants of Beth-shean and its villages, or Taanach and its villages, or the inhabitants of Dor and its villages, or the inhabitants of Ibleam and its villages, or the inhabitants of Meggido and its villages, but the Canaanites persisted in dwelling in that land.' While the dependence of Chronicles on these sources is evident in the identity of the names, and in literal similarity, the list in its new context conveys a different message. Cities, and in fact whole districts ('Beth-shean and its villages, etc.') which in Joshua and Judges are distinctly Canaanite enclaves, which the Manassites never managed to dispossess ('when Israel grew strong they put the Canaanites to forced labour but did not utterly drive them out') are here emphatically described as the 'possessions and ... settlement (*mōšᵉbōtām*)' of Manasseh, an emphasis repeated in the concluding phrase: 'In these dwelt the sons of Joseph the son of Israel.'

The outright polemic of the Chronicler with his sources here comes to the surface, and the resulting picture harmonizes with the view expressed in the list of levitical cities, in which Shechem, Gezer, Taanach and Ibleam are listed as in fact occupied by Levites (I Chron. 6.67, 71 [MT 6.52, 56]).

[30–40] The list of the Asherites is again a census list; it opens with the conventional 'sons of Asher', as introduced in Gen. 46.17 and somewhat differently in Num. 26.44, but then goes its own way, with no further parallels to biblical texts. Differently from Benjamin but similarly to Issachar, the list ignores three of the 'sons' and proceeds only with Beriah, and even then only with his first-born, 'Heber'. Beriah's second son, Malchiel, is dismissed with the formula 'the father of Birzaith' from the Pentateuch sources already mentioned. These verses, then, amount to an extended and highly systematic registration of the line of Asher's grandson Heber, a clear picture of the ramification of the Heberite families. The distinctive method enables us to restore with confidence some of the list's textual corruptions.

I have already noted that Beriah has been presented as the son of Ephraim, born after the death of all Ephraim's other sons, and that there is also a major Benjaminite branch by the same name (I Chron. 8.13, 15–16). Heber, a more common name, is also introduced as a lesser family of Benjamin (8.17). Moreover, Heber's first-born according to the list, 'Japhlet', is unmistakably referred to on the south-western border of Ephraim (Josh. 16.3). With due caution and reserve, the following conclusions seem appropriate (cf. also F. M. Abel, 'Un Mention Biblique de Birzeit', *RB* XLVI, 1937, 217–24).

The geographical location of 'Heber' was probably the western outskirts of the hill-country of Ephraim, and not the north-west part of Israel, the traditional Asherite territory according to Josh. 19.24–31 (cf. D. Edelman, 'The Asherite Genealogy of I Chronicles 7.30–40', *BR* 33, 1988, 13–23; Na'aman, 'Sources and Redaction', *JSOT* 49, 1991, 100–5). The Heberite branch of Asher thus formed an enclave, adjacent to Ephraim and Benjamin. 7.23 and 8.13 indicate that the family, as a whole or in part, was eventually regarded as Ephraimite or Benjaminite. The city of Aijalon, with which Heber is connected in 8.13, is also alternatively designated as belonging to Dan (Josh. 19.42; 21.4). Heber's original distinction from Ephraim is marked clearly by the borders of Josh. 16.3.

The limited scope of this 'southern' Asher is evident in the relatively small number of tribal members. In spite of their numerous fathers' houses, the total roll of warriors is only 26,000, a unit not much larger than an average family of the other tribes.

A last point concerns the names in this section. Although the genealogies abound in what seem to be non-Semitic or non-Hebrew names, their preponderance in the context of Asher is striking. Not only the obviously Egyptian Harnepher, but also Suah, Zophah, Rohgah, Ashvath, Bimhal, Passach and many others bear a distinct foreign stamp; even Shua is a Canaanite name according to Gen. 38.2. This Asherite branch, with the common name Heber, may have comprised a thorough mixture of Israelite and originally non-Israelite elements, occupying the western parts of Ephraim.

The genealogical picture of Beriah, Asher's fourth son, would be as follows:

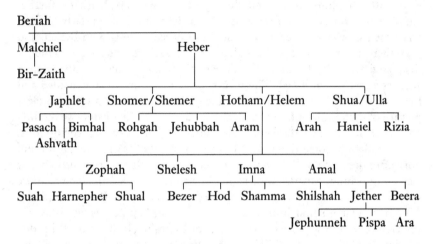

At it stands, the text of vv. 31–39 describes three complete generations of Heber, and then limits the genealogy to the line of Zophah. This outline, however, follows a reconstruction of v. 36 which indicates that further generations of Zophah and Imna are recorded (cf. below).

[33] Japhlet's prominence among the Asherites is illustrated by two features: the special concluding formula 'These are the sons of Japhlet', and the designation of Shemer (Shomer) and Helem (Hotham) as his brothers (vv. 34–35). Although the list in fact records the sons of Hotham in more detail, he is nevertheless presented as 'Helem his brother', thus retaining Japhlet's superiority.

[36–37] As the text now stands, there are eleven 'sons of Zophah', with a further generation recorded for one of them, Ithran/Jether. However, it is possible that the unusual absence of the copulative *waw* at the beginning of v. 37 implies that the words *ūbērī wᵉyimrāh* (RSV: Beri, Imrah) are a corruption of an original text reading: *ūbᵉnē yimnāʿ* ('and the sons of Imna …'; Rudolph, 74, following Noth); following this conjecture, v. 37 would be a record of the offspring of the Imna mentioned in v. 35.

[39] While Ulla, whose sons are here recorded, is not mentioned pre-

viously, it is very likely that this isolation is just a result of textual corruption. There are two possible lines of reconstruction. If 'Ulla' was one of Ithran's offspring, the name was omitted from v. 38, which would have read 'the sons of Jether ... Ara and Ulla'. Alternatively, 'Ulla' may be a variant of a name already recorded, e.g. Ara (v. 38), Shual (v. 36), or Shua (v. 32). I incline to regard the last as the more plausible in this case, because of the orthographic similarity of *'ullā'* and *šū'ā'*, the fact that the descendants of all of Heber's children are fully registered with the exception of Shua, and the observation that the registration of a 'sister's' offspring tends to be delayed to the end of a section (cf. 2.16–17; 7.18).

For the concluding summary of v. 40, see above, p. 170.

8 Benjamin was the father of Bela his first-born, Ashbel the second, Aharah the third,[2] Nohah the fourth, and Rapha the fifth. [3] And Bela had sons: Addar, Gera, Abihud, [4] Abishua, Naaman, Ahoah, [5] Gera, Shephuphan, and Huram. [6] These are the sons of Ehud (they were heads of fathers' houses of the inhabitants of Geba, and they were carried into exile to Manahath): [7] Naaman, Ahijah, and Gera, that is, Heglam, who was the father of Uzza and Ahihud. [8] And Shaharaim had sons in the country of Moab after he had sent away Hushim and Baara his wives. [9] He had sons by Hodesh his wife: Jobab, Zibia, Mesha, Malcam, [10] Jeuz, Sachia, and Mirmah. These were his sons, heads of fathers' houses. [11] He also had sons by Hushim: Abitub and Elpaal. [12] The sons of Elpaal: Eber, Misham, and Shemed, who built Ono and Lod with its towns, [13] and Beriah and Shema (they were heads of fathers' houses of the inhabitants of Aijalon, who put to flight the inhabitants of Gath); [14] and Ahio, Shashak, and Jeremoth. [15] Zebadiah, Arad, Eder,[16] Michael, Ishpah, and Joha were sons of Beriah. [17] Zebadiah, Meshullam, Hizki, Heber,[18] Ishmerai, Izliah, and Jobab were the sons of Elpaal. [19] Jakim, Zichri, Zabdi, [20] Eli-enai, Zille-thai, Eliel, [21] Adaiah, Beraiah, and Shimrath were the sons of Shime-i. [22] Ishpan, Eber, Eliel, [23] Abdon, Zichri, Hanan, [24] Hananiah, Elam, Anthothijah,[25] Iphdeiah, and Penuel were the sons of Shashak. [26] Shamsherai, Shehariah, Athaliah, [27] Jaareshiah, Elijah, and Zichri were the sons of Jeroham. [28] These were the heads of fathers' houses, according to their generations, chief men. These dwelt in Jerusalem.

29 Je-iel the father of Gibeon dwelt in Gibeon, and the name of his wife was Maacah. [30] His first-born son: Abdon, then Zur, Kish, Baal, Nadab,[31] Gedor, Ahio, Zecher,[32] and Mikloth (he was the father of Shime-ah). Now these also dwelt opposite their kinsmen in Jerusalem, with their kinsmen. [33] Ner was the father of Kish, Kish of Saul, Saul of Jonathan, Malchishua, Abinadab, and Eshbaal; [34] and the son of Jonathan was Merib-baal; and Merib-baal was the father of Micah. [35] The sons of Micah: Pithon, Melech, Tarea, and Ahaz. [36] Ahaz was the father of Jehoaddah; and Jehoaddah was the father of Alemeth, Azmaveth, and Zimri; Zimri was the father of Moza. [37] Moza was the father of Bine-a; Raphah was his son, Ele-asah his son, Azel his son. [38] Azel had six sons, and these are their names. Azrikam, Bocheru, Ishmael, She-ariah, Obadiah, and Hanan. All these were the sons of Azel. [39] The sons of Eshek his brother: Ulam his first-born, Jeush the second, and Eliphelet the third. [40] The sons of Ulam were men who were mighty warriors, bowmen, having many sons and grandsons, one hundred and fifty. All these were Benjaminites.

A. Notes to MT

[1] ואחרח, probably read ואחרם; [3] ואביהו, probably read אבי אהוד; [4] ואחוח, v. 7, ואחיה; [6] אחוד, read אהוד; [7] ואחיה וגרא, omit: dittography; [8] חורם, ושחרים or אחרם proposed; אתם, add את (haplography); [13] probably read at the beginning ובני עבר

ירמות, ואחיו LXX^B; ואחיהם :LXX^{AL} read ,ואחיו [14] ;שמעי .v 21 ;שמע ;ברעה ושמע
9.37 ,וזכר [31] ;9.36 .cf ,ונר add ,ובעל [30] ;9.35 .cf ,יעיאל add ,גבעון [29] ;ירחם 27 .v
ושעריה ועבדיה, ;Versions and MSS with ,בכרו read ,בכרו [38] ;ומקלות add ,וזכריה
LXX^L עזריה ועבדיה ושריה, probably correct.

B. Notes to RSV

[6] 'they were heads', etc. cf. commentary; [7] 'Heglam', extremely unlikely, cf. the
margin; probably read 'It was Naaman who carried them into exile'; [29–32] in v. 29
the text is restored with the help of 9.35, but not in the following verses, in which the
names 'Ner' and Mikloth' should be added, cf. above, A; [38] 'Bocheru', thus MT,
but cf. above, A.

C. Structure, sources and form

1. With the completion of the genealogies of the sons of Israel, the tribe of Benjamin is
reintroduced in ch. 8, which constitutes a kind of sequel to 7.6–11. If we consider the
geographical principle which governs the order of the tribes, this sequence is almost
self-evident: the circle began with Judah and now returns to the centre, with
Benjamin (ch. 8) and Jerusalem (ch. 9).

The material of ch. 8 differs substantially from that of ch. 7, and is probably taken
from other sources. The component elements are:

1. Tribal genealogies (vv. 1–6a, 7b–12a, 14–27, 29–32;
2. Very short episodes from the tribe's history (vv. 6b–7a, 12b, 13);
3. Details of settlement (vv. 6b, 8a, 28–29, 32b);
4. The genealogical tree of 'Ulam', leading back to Saul's family (vv. 33–40).

All these are blended together, and in spite of the rather damaged state of certain
passages a structural coherence can still be perceived.

2. The chapter is basically composed of two large sections: (*a*) vv. 1–32, the
expansion of the Benjaminites, and (*b*) vv. 33–40, the genealogy of the sons of Ulam.
The first section is composite, and the key to its structure is found in the recurring
clause 'These were heads of fathers' houses', as follows:

(i)   6: '... they were heads of fathers' houses of the inhabitants of Geba'
(ii) 10: 'These were his sons, heads of fathers' houses'
(iii) 13: 'These were the heads of fathers' houses of the inhabitants of Ayalon'
(iv) 28: 'These were the heads of fathers' houses ... These dwelt in Jerusalem'.

Verses 29–32 may be considered a supplementary list to (iv).

Taking as our point of departure this almost (yet not absolutely) stereotyped
formula, the structure of the first section may be viewed as follows:

(*a*) 1–2   Introduction
(*b*) 3–7   Genealogy and episode of the 'sons of Bela'

(c) 8–14 Genealogy and episodes of 'Shaharaim'
    8–11 In Moab
    12–14 West of the Jordan
(d) 15–28 Benjaminites living in Jerusalem
(e) 29–32 Benjaminites of Gibeon

The validity of this structure will become evident through details discussed in the commentary.

3. There are very few biblical parallels for the material of the chapter. In fact, only the genealogical details of Saul's near family (vv. 33–34) are known from the book of Samuel. The sources vary, as a closer look at the commentary will indicate, and no part of the chapter seems to bear any clear signs of the Chronicler's hand.

4. One of the major problems of the chapter, the repetition of its second part in 9.35–44, will be dealt with in ch. 9.

D. Commentary

[1–2] The recapitulation of Benjamin's sons, rather than signalling a new tribal record, is a limited introduction to the material which follows, cf. the same technique in 4.1 and 6.16 [MT 6.1]. Probably reflecting a variant source, the sons of Benjamin are introduced by a formula differing from that used in 7.6: 'Benjamin begot X his first born, Y his second, etc.'; five sons, rather than three, are listed.

This number five corresponds to Num. 26.38–39, and some of the names are also similar: Bela, who is attested in all texts as Benjamin's first-born, Ashbel, who appears in Gen. 46.21 and Num. 26.38 but not in I Chron. 7.6, and probably also Ahrah, whose name may be a corrupted form of 'Ahiram' of Num. 26.38, often restored also in Gen. 46.21 (cf. e.g. BH, BHS). The last two, Nohah and Rapha, are not known elsewhere as Benjamin's sons, although 'Raphah' appears again in the tribe's genealogy in v. 37.

Some scholars make the orthographically attractive proposition of seeing 'his first born' (bᵉkōrō) as the corruption of a proper name: beker (Becher, cf. e.g. Curtis, 157). The numbers attached to the sons (first, second, etc.) and the relative similarity of the list to Num. 26.38, which also lacks reference to Becher, incline me (with Rudolph, 76) against this view.

[3–7] This section is devoted to the 'sons of Bela'. The record here is very different from 7.7, not only in its method, but certainly also in its purpose, sources, and probably also in its historical context as well. The passage poses several difficulties:

1. Gera is mentioned twice (vv. 3 and 5),

2. The opening words of v. 6 are difficult, not only because Ehud has not been mentioned previously, but also because the heading 'These are the sons of Ehud' is *not* followed, as one would expect, by a list of names. To circumvent this last difficulty RSV (and NEB) brackets v. 6b, and omits

'and' before 'Naaman' in v. 7; in this way the names cited in v. 7 become the missing 'sons of Ehud'.

3. It is not clear how v. 7 fits into the context, although some connection with v. 4 can be assumed.

4. While the subject of v. 7 is plural – Naaman, Ahijah and Gera – the predicate 'he carried them into exile' (*heglām*) is in the singular. RSV renders this verb as a proper name: 'Heglam', but adds a footnote with the actual meaning. Finally, RSV renders *weʰhōlīd* ('*and* begot') as 'who was the father of' (an unusual reading for the conjunctive *waw*), implying that 'Heglam' had two sons, Uzza and Ahihud.

In view of all these difficulties, some measure of reconstruction seems indispensable – as already indicated by RSV. Several commentators have suggested that 'Abihud' at the end of v. 3 is a corruption of 'the father of Ehud' (*'ʰbī 'ēhūd*, cf. among others: Curtis, 158; Rudolph, 76; Williamson, 83), a change which would provide an obvious link with v. 6 (so NEB). Others would also transfer the heading 'These are the sons of Ehud' to the beginning of v. 4, applying to all the persons named in vv. 4–5 (cf. Rudolph, ibid.; Williamson, ibid.).

The 'Abihud' = *'ʰbī 'ēhūd* reading is not only orthographically very attractive, but also identifies one of Bela's sons with a person mentioned elsewhere in the biblical narrative: Ehud the son of Gera, the hero of Judg. 3.15ff. It has one shortcoming, which although weighty is not conclusive. The phrase 'X the father of Y' will be understood in its literal sense (as in Gen. 11.29; I Sam. 14.51, etc.), and not in the formulaic one, which is characteristic of its many occurences in the Chronistic genealogies. Transferring the heading 'these are the sons of Ehud' would have the advantage of providing a logical sequence, the persons named in vv. 4–5 being the subject of the narrative note of v. 6b. Also, the second 'Gera' (v. 5) would now be, more reasonably, the grandson, rather than the brother, of 'Gera' of v. 3. However, all this leaves the problems of v. 7 still unsolved, and has the added drawback of distancing the two major branches of Benjamin – Naaman and Shephupham – farther from their forefather than our Pentateuchal sources will countenance (cf. Gen. 46.21 and, somewhat differently, Num. 26.40).

Another line of restoration, which would require less textual intervention, would assume that a few names have been lost after the heading of v. 6, and that only one of the three names in v. 7 is original (the other two being additions influenced by vv. 4–5). Verses 3–7 would then read: 'And Bela had sons: Addar, Gera, the father of Ehud, Abishua, Naaman, Ahoah, Gera, Shephuphan and Huram. These are the sons of Ehud: [...]; they were heads of fathers' houses ... It was Naaman who carried them into exile, and he begot Uzza and Ahihud.'

[6–7] This first narrative episode of the chapter relates how the 'heads of

fathers' houses of ... Geba', affiliated with the house of Ehud, were exiled to
Manahath by 'Naaman'. The use of 'exile' to denote deportation from one
town to another within the borders of the land is also attested elsewhere (e.g.
in Ezek. 12.3). A similar incident is illustrated by II Sam. 4.2–3, which tells
how 'the Beerothites fled to Gittaim and have been sojourners there to this
day'. No reason is specified either for this 'flight' of the Beerothites from
their home or for the 'exile' of some of the 'heads of fathers' houses' here.
These are probably reflections of internal tribal struggles, which ended in
some of the member families finding refuge in Judah, outside their tribal
territory (on the mixed population of Manahath, cf. 2.52, 54). On the
possible historical background of this episode, cf. below on vv. 29–32.

[8–14] This passage refers to the fortunes of 'Shaharaim' and his family,
with all the vicissitudes of its various branches, and their expansion to east
and west. Before dealing with the content of these verses, we should sort out
some of their textual problems.

'Shaharaim' is not mentioned either in the preceding list, or elsewhere; he
may of course represent a Benjaminite family for which this passage is the
only surviving textual introduction. However, since this family dominates
the entire passage as far as v. 28, it must have been a major Benjaminite
element, and it is very unlikely that no attempt was ever made to link it to the
other Benjaminite lines. It is therefore more plausible that the unusual form
'Shaharaim' (*šahªrayim*) is just a variant of one of the preceding names,
hūrām (Huram) of v. 5 or *'ahrah / 'ªhirām* of v. 1 being the obvious candidates.
If this is the case, a great measure of coherence pertains throughout the
chapter.

Verse 8 seems to have suffered some corruption. Although *hušīm* is more
familiar as a man's name (cf. 7.12), there is no reason why it should not also be
a woman's, occurring twice in our passage (cf. also v. 11: 'and of Hushim he
begot'; RSV 'and by Hushim he had sons ...').

The syntax of the clause, ... *min šilhō 'ōtām, hušīm* ... (RSV 'after he had
sent away Hushim ...'), illustrates the use of the proleptic accusative pronoun *'ōtām*, which, while more often attested in post-biblical Hebrew, is also
found in the Bible (M. H. Segal, *A Grammar of Mishnaic Hebrew*, Oxford
1927, 192–3; S. Kogut, 'The Extra Pronominal Element in the Bible',
Lešonenu 46, 1982, 24–6*). However, this would require the addition of the
accusative particle *'et*, probably omitted by haplography. The RSV translation is basically correct, but ignores the unusual proleptic usage; its literal
rendition would be: 'after he had sent *them* away, Hushim and Baara his
wives ...'

In v. 11, *hōlīd* (RSV 'he also had sons') should be viewed as a past perfect
'he had had sons' (thus correctly NEB).

The whole passage is an example of literary economy. It relates the fortunes of the Shaharaim/Ahiram families, in particular as they expanded outside the boundaries of their original, unspecified territory. Shaharaim/ Ahiram is said to have had three wives: Hushim, Baarah and Hodesh; their offspring are introduced, for literary reasons, in reverse order. A reconstruction of the family movements in chronological order would be as follows. In his original location, Shaharaim/Ahiram had two sons by his wife Hushim: Abitub and Elpaal (v. 11), whose offspring and development are subsequently related in vv. 12ff. Then Shaharaim/Ahiram 'sent away' his two wives and, 'in the country of Moab', sired another seven sons by another wife 'Hodesh' (vv. 8–10). These remarks are enlightening, in that they very plausibly reflect an ethnic-sociological reality. Benjamin is described in the Bible as a warrior tribe (Gen. 49.27; Judg. 20) and at the same time as being confined to a rather small territory, between Ephraim and Judah. The need for expansion is reflected here in the movement of certain tribal elements eastwards to Moab and westwards to Lod and Ono. In the case of Moab the emigration is emphasized by reference to Shaharaim/Ahiram's 'divorce' from his earlier wives, that is, to actual uprooting. The name of his first wife is also highly instructive, for 'Hushim' is the only son of Dan in Gen. 46.23, a fact which has inclined scholars to regard *hūšīm* in this passage as a corruption (H. W. Hogg, 'The Genealogy of Benjamin', *JQR* XI, 1899, 104–5; Rudolph, 76). From an eponymic point of view, however, this is precisely the genealogical point being made: the only son of Dan is the 'wife' of a Benjaminite family, that is, its secondary component. The fathers' houses of 'Hushim' are associated here with the localities of 'Lod and Ono' (v. 12) and of 'Aijalon' (v. 13), the first two being in the nominal inheritance of Dan, quite far from the traditional territory of Benjamin, and the last being a major town of Dan (Josh. 19.42; 21.24). This genealogical structure actually indicates the absorption into westward-moving Benjaminite families of Danite elements which had remained in the Shephelah after most of the tribe had immigrated northward.

[13–14] Two more Benjaminite families, Beriah and Shema, are introduced here, without any explicit connection to the preceding names. Another problem is in the reading of *'aḥiō* in v. 14: is it a proper name ('and Ahio', so RSV), or a corruption of *'aḥēhem* ('their brothers'), as in LXX^AL? If it is indeed a name, it must be determined whether Ahio, Shashak and Jeremoth belong to the preceding list or to what follows.

RSV regards the remarks of vv. 12b and 13b as parenthetical clauses and sees vv. 12–14 as recording 'the sons of Elpaal', eight in all. NEB joins v. 14 to the following list, making 'Ahio, Shashak and Jeremoth' the sons of Beriah. These constructions both achieve a measure of coherence for the passage of vv. 12–14 (or 12–13); however, they have several short-comings. 1. There is really no indication in the text that the clauses mentioned should be considered parenthetic; in fact, their emphatic syntax denotes something like 'He is the one who built Ono ...' (RSV ignores the emphatic structure), and then 'It was these who were the heads etc ...' 2. The following lists of vv. 15–27 record the sons of Beriah, Elpaal, Shema/Shimei, Shashak and Jeremoth/Jeroham as independent lines, but 'Ahio' is missing.

Taking all this into consideration, I am inclined to adopt the view that some connecting link is missing at the beginning of v. 13, such as *ūb⁽ᵉ⁾nē 'eber* ('the sons of Eber'), and that 'Ahio' (*'aḥiō*) should be regarded as a corruption of *'aḥēhem* ('their brothers', cf. e.g. Curtis, 162; Rudolph, 178). Verses 13–14 would then be a direct continuation of the line of Elpaal through Eber, while v. 15 would belong to the following passage. Another seven sons of Elpaal are recorded in vv. 17–18 (cf. below), and the whole genealogy would be as follows:

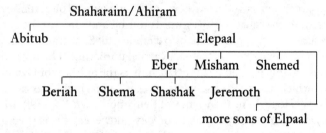

I have noted that Beriah and Shema as 'heads of fathers' houses of Aijalon' indicate a mixture of Benjaminite and Danite elements, although Beriah may reflect even more complicated ethnic circumstances (cf. above on 7.23).

Verse 13b attributes to these Benjaminites the expulsion of 'the inhabitants of Gath', i.e., both here and in 7.21, probably 'Gittaim' (as suggested by B. Mazar, 'Gath and Gittaim', in *Cities and Districts in Eretz-Israel*, 1975, 101–9*). The juxtaposition of II Sam. 4.2–3 and these two references yields a quite full history of the struggles over this town. Originally non-Israelite, and positioned outside the borders of Ephraim, Benjamin and Dan, Gittaim was the scene of the flight of the Beerothites, the death of the sons of Ephraim (7.21) and the invasion of the Benjaminites. After their expansion westwards, with the building of Lod and Ono, another arm of the tribe is stretched out, toward Gath/Gittaim. As in the case of Simeon, internal pressures compel the Benjaminites to overreach their borders.

What is the historical background of these remarks? One may see these migrations of the Benjaminites in the context reflected in the list of Neh. 11.31–35 or that of the returning exiles of Ezra 2.3ff. (where Lod and Ono are also mentioned), and ascribe all these circumstances to the late monarchic or even the Persian period (cf. Rudolph, 77; Williamson, 83). However, the series of episodes referring to the movements, resettlement and building enterprises of the Benjaminites, in the south (Manahath), east (Moab) and west (Lod, Ono, Gath), would be more indicative of a context in the monarchical period. A more precise decision is impossible, but note the insistence on the tribal affiliation and the local initiative – especially at the borders – throughout this period.

[15–28] The passage records systematically a number of Benjaminite 'heads of fathers' houses' affiliated with five larger families, who are described as 'having dwelt in Jerusalem'. Four names are identical with those already mentioned in vv. 12–14 (*šema'/šim'ī*, Shema/Shimei are variants), and it is most probable that the fifth (Jeremoth/Jeroham) would be of the same group; the name was transmitted at one point in a corrupt form.

Recorded here are six sons of Beriah (vv. 15–16), seven of Elpaal (vv. 17–18, in addition to the three mentioned above in v. 12), nine of Shimei (vv. 19–21), eleven of Shashak (vv. 22–25) and six of Jeroham (vv. 26–27) – altogether thirty-nine names of men 'settled in Jerusalem'.

Jerusalem is described in biblical sources as located on the border between Judah and Benjamin. Two statements are most instructive in this respect: Josh. 15.63, 'But the Jebusites, the inhabitants of Jerusalem, *the people of Judah* could not drive out; so the Jebusites dwell with *the people of Judah* at Jerusalem to this day', and Judg. 1.21, 'But the *people of Benjamin* did not drive out the Jebusites ... so the Jebusites have dwelt with *the people of Benjamin* in Jerusalem to this day'. The verses are the same, except for the identity of the Israelite tribe whose responsibility it was to conquer Jerusalem. While the Chronicler does not refer specifically to this matter, the general context may indicate that the objective of the passage, like that of the preceding ones, is to describe another expansion of the Benjaminites beyond their original borders. If this is indeed the case, then Jerusalem would be regarded essentially as being within the boundaries of Judah.

According to I Chron. 9.3ff., Jerusalem was inhabited by the descendants of many tribes, among them four 'heads of fathers' houses' of Benjamin, 'with their brothers', 956 men in all (9.7–9). None of the names, except the fathers' house of Jeroham (9.8; cf. 8.27), matches this list. It is difficult to determine the historical setting for these lists; they obviously reflect two altogether different situations and outlooks. It should be noted, however, that even in the capital of the kingdom, social position and registration were determined by tribal affiliation.

[29–32] The first part of the chapter ends with the Benjaminites who settled in Gibeon, as distinguished from those who lived in Jersualem. The contrast expressed in MT, 'These dwelt in Jersulem, and (or but) in Gibeon dwelt, etc.', is somewhat obscured by the translations.

The affiliation of 'Jeiel, the father of Gibeon' to the preceding Benjaminite families is not recorded. The formula 'X the father of Y' implies that the occupation of Gibeon by this Benjaminite family is actually a secondary process (cf. on 2.21), as is well borne out by other biblical evidence.

Gibeon was the centre of the Hivite population of the area (Josh. 9.3–7), and it is explicitly described as a foreign enclave within the Benjaminite territory. The Gibeonites were persecuted by Saul (II Sam. 21.1–2), but were not wiped out. It is very likely that Benjaminite elements gradually took possession of the Hivite/Gibeonite territory; three of its cities, Gibeon, Beeroth and Chephira, are listed as Benjaminite (Josh. 18.25–26, etc.), while the fourth, Kiriath-jearim, is described as Judahite (Josh. 15.60, etc.). The Gibeonite element itself was probably eventually absorbed into Benjamin, and these processes of conquest and ethnic absorption may be reflected in this passage.

The similarity between the names of Jeiel's sons and the nomenclature of the family of Saul (Kish, Baal, Nadab and Ner) may imply family affiliation, while the explicit reference to 'his wife Maacah' may allude to a non-Israelite element within the Benjaminites, properly described as a 'wife', that is, a secondary component of the family, of different ethnic origin.

The passage is repeated in 9.35–38, a text which provides enlightening emendations which make this passage clearer: the addition of the name 'Jeiel' in v. 29 (so RSV); the addition of the name 'Ner' as one more of Jeiel's sons in v. 30, and the addition of 'and Mikloth' at the end of v. 31.

Verse 32b is somewhat difficult. *neged '*ᵃ*ḥēhem*, 'alongside (NEB, cf. 5.11) their kinsmen', and '*im* '*ᵃḥēhem*, 'with their kinsmen', seem repetitious. Also, as the MT of v. 29 begins with 'And in Gibeon dwelt . . .', it is not clear who is the subject of 'these . . . dwelt in Jerusalem': all those mentioned in vv. 30–32, only those mentioned in v. 32, or any part of them? One may only say that some of the Benjaminites whose origin was in Gibeon were now dwelling in Jerusalem, together with their 'kinsmen'.

In addition to the genealogical information, this passage highlights another important feature: the juxtaposition of Jerusalem and Gibeon, which is first introduced in I Kings 3.4, 15; 9.2, and which is further emphasized in I Chron. 16.37ff. and II Chron. 1.3–6. Is the same juxtaposition – even rivalry – also implied in the structure of these passages?

[33–40] The passage introduces a genealogical tree from Ner (v. 33) to 'the sons of Ulam' (v. 40). It opens in vv. 33–34 with details of the family of Saul, known also from the book of Samuel; the relationship of the various sources needs some clarification.

Two passages in Samuel provide the genealogical circumstances of Saul: I Sam. 9.1 has the pedigree of Saul's father, 'Kish, the son of Abiel, son of Zeror son of Becorath, son of Aphiah, a Benjaminite', and I Sam. 14.50–51 offers the following details: 'And the name of the commander of his [Saul's] army was Abner the son of Ner, Saul's uncle; Kish was the father of Saul and Ner the father of Abner was the son of Abiel.'

How should this information be sorted out? Who was the father of Kish – Ner (v. 33), Abiel (I Sam. 9.1) or Jeiel (I Chron. 8.30 reconstructed; 9.36)?

There are two different approaches: one way is to read 'Abner' for the first 'Kish' in v. 33, thus: 'Ner begot Abner and Kish begot Saul' (cf. BH, BHS, etc.). This solution, which is orthographically plausible, would create a direct link between vv. 29–30 (as emended above) and v. 33, and would also conform with I Sam. 14.50–51. Its shortcomings are as follows: 1. Instead of being 'the son of Abiel' (I Sam. 9.1), Kish (and Ner) would be 'the sons of Jeiel'. 2. More significantly, instead of one continuous line presented by the common formula 'X begot Y' resumed further in the list, v. 33 would present two parallel lines, one of which ('Ner begot Abner') is abruptly curtailed. 3. A direct genealogical connection between vv. 29–30 and 33 would make Gibeon the origin of Saul's family, whereas the unmistakable tradition of I Sam. 10.26, etc. makes it Gibeah, or Gibeah of Benjamin. The similarity of the names may lead scholars to render Gibeah in v. 29 in place of Gibeon: another probable but rather arbitrary orthographic solution.

Another approach to these difficulties is to regard the text of vv. 33ff. as indepedent of the preceding vv. 29–30 (the similarity of names being a result of the ties between the two Benjaminite branches, or of the common genealogical material used by both lists), and to leave v. 33 unaltered, seeing 'Ner begot Kish' as authentic. This would create a certain tension with the statement of I Sam. 9.1 that Kish was 'the son of Abiel', but one may take this to mean that 'Abiel' was in fact the grandfather of Kish, or the name of the family to which he was affiliated (cf. also J. Marquart, 'The Genealogies of Benjamin', *JQR* XIV, 1902, 349). The family line would be as follows:

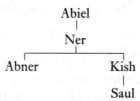

This view harmonizes all the genealogical facts; one may even conjecture (so BH) that in I Sam. 14.50 'the sons ($b^e n\bar{e}$) of Abiel' should be read in place of 'the son' (*ben*), which focuses the picture even more.

The present list proceeds only through the house of Saul, ignoring his uncle Abner as well as Saul's wives and daughters. It mentions Saul's four sons: Jonathan, Malchishua, Abinadab and Eshbaal. The first three, in a different order, are mentioned together in I Sam. 31.2 (=I Chron. 10.2); the fourth, Eshbaal, is introduced in Samuel by two other names: in I Sam. 14.49

he appears as the second son of Saul, 'Ishvi' (*yišwī*), and in II Sam. 2.8ff. as 'Ishbosheth' (*'īšbōšet*). It has long been recognized that Eshbaal is probably the original form, while the other two are corrections. *yišwī* would be a corrupt form of *yišyō*, in which the theophoric element *yō/yᵉhō* replaced Baal, and *bōšet* would be the more common replacement of *ba'al*, as also illustrated in the name of Jonathan's son Mephibosheth for the original Meribba'al (J. Wellhausen, *Der Text der Bücher Samuelis*, Göttingen 1871, 95). Note the frequency of the name Baal, either alone or in compounds, in the lines of both Saul and David (cf. also on I Chron. 3.8; 14.7). If the information in this passage was drawn from the book of Samuel, one should conclude that the Chronicler's borrowing preceded the editorial process by which these changes were introduced into Samuel. The Chronicler himself was not bothered by these, or other, non-Israelite theophoric names.

The information about Jonathan's offspring down to his grandson Micah (v. 34) is found in II Sam. 9.12, where Micah is depicted, at the time of David's reign, as a 'small boy'. From v. 35 the list has no biblical sources. Its form of registration is very methodical: for each generation the family line proceeds through one son, the descendants of the remaining sons not being mentioned. Until v. 36, the line of descent proceeds through the firstborn, recording his name alone. When the genealogy proceeds through a younger son, all those preceding him are mentioned first, before this son's descendants are listed:

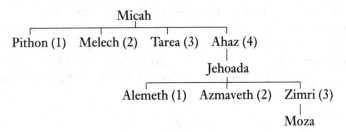

Verse 37 records only one son for each of the last generations: Moza – Bina – Rapha – Elaasah – Azel. That these represent generations and not the entire family line is demonstrated by v. 39. Here we find the genealogy of Eshek who is presented as Azel's brother, although he was not introduced in the genealogy of v. 37.

This method of registration clearly indicates a fact which is obvious from the conclusion of the list, that the ultimate aim of the list is the families of Azel and his brother Eshek (vv. 38–40). These were the 'mighty warriors (or 'men of substance', JPS), bowmen, having many sons and grandsons' (v. 40). This distinguished family derived its descent from no less than the royal family of Saul.

The provenance of the list can be determined by its genealogical line. From Micah in v. 35 the direct line counts ten generations; if we take Micah to be a contemporary of Solomon, it follows that Ulam would be living around the end of the seventh century, before the destruction of Jerusalem. We have already seen a similar span of time in the list of the high priests (6.1–15 [MT 5.27–41]), the Davidic kings (3.10–15), and a few individuals (cf. 4.36–41). At that time the descendants of Saul seem to have prospered greatly, proudly bearing their noble lineage.

9 So all Israel was enrolled by genealogies; and these are written in the Book of the Kings of Israel. And Judah was taken into exile in Babylon because of their unfaithfulness. [2] Now the first to dwell again in their possessions in their cities were Israel, the priests, the Levites, and the temple servants. [3] And some of the people of Judah, Benjamin, Ephraim, and Manasseh dwelt in Jerusalem: [4] Uthai the son of Ammihud, son of Omri, son of Imri, son of Bani, from the sons of Perez the son of Judah. [5] And of the Shilonites: Asaiah the first-born, and his sons. [6] Of the sons of Zerah: Jeuel and their kinsmen, six hundred and ninety. [7] Of the Benjaminites: Sallu the son of Meshullam, son of Hodaviah, son of Hassenuah, [8] Ibneiah the son of Jeroham, Elah the son of Uzzi, son of Michri, and Meshullam the son of Shephatiah, son of Reuel, son of Ibnijah; [9] and their kinsmen according to their generations, nine hundred and fifty-six. All these were heads of fathers' houses according to their fathers' houses.

10 Of the priests: Jedaiah, Jehoiarib, Jachin, [11] and Azariah the son of Hilkiah, son of Meshullam, son of Zadok, son of Meraioth, son of Ahitub, the chief officer of the house of God; [12] and Adaiah the son of Jeroham, son of Pashhur, son of Malchijah, and Maasai the son of Adi-el, son of Jahzerah, son of Meshullam, son of Meshillemith, son of Immer; [13] besides their kinsmen, heads of their fathers' houses, one thousand seven hundred and sixty, very able men for the work of the service of the house of God.

14 Of the Levites: Shemaiah the son of Hasshub, son of Azrikam, son of Hashabiah, of the sons of Merari; [15] and Bakbakkar, Heresh, Galal, and Mattani-ah the son of Mica, son of Zichri, son of Asaph; [16] and Obadiah the son of Shemaiah, son of Galal, son of Jeduthun, and Berechiah the son of Asa, son of Elkanah, who dwelt in the villages of the Netophathites.

17 The gatekeepers were: Shallum, Akkub, Talmon, Ahiman, and their kinsmen (Shallum being the chief), [18] stationed hitherto in the king's gate on the east side. These were the gatekeepers of the camp of the Levites. [19] Shallum the son of Kore, son of Ebiasaph, son of Korah, and his kinsmen of his fathers' house, the Korahites, were in charge of the work of the service, keepers of the thresholds of the tent, as their fathers had been in charge of the camp of the Lord, keepers of the entrance. [20] And Phinehas the son of Eleazar was the ruler over them in time past; the Lord was with him. [21] Zechariah the son of Meshelemiah was gatekeeper at the entrance of the tent of meeting. [22] All these, who were chosen as gatekeepers at the thresholds, were two hundred and twelve. They were enrolled by genealogies in their villages. David and Samuel the seer established them in their office of trust. [23] So they and their sons were in charge of the gates of the house of the Lord, that is, the house of the tent, as guards. [24] The gatekeepers were on the four sides, east, west, north, and south; [25] and their kinsmen who were in their villages were obliged to come in every seven days, from time to time, to be with these; [26] for the four chief gatekeepers, who were Levites, were in charge of the chambers and the treasures of the house of God. [27] And

they lodged round about the house of God; for upon them lay the duty of watching, and they had charge of opening it every morning.

28 Some of them had charge of the utensils of service, for they were required to count them when they were brought in and taken out. [29] Others of them were appointed over the furniture, and over all the holy utensils, also over the fine flour, the wine, the oil, the incense, and the spices. [30] Others, of the sons of the priests, prepared the mixing of the spices, [31] and Mattithiah, one of the Levites, the firstborn of Shallum the Korahite, was in charge of making the flat cakes. [32] Also some of their kinsmen of the Kohathites had charge of the showbread, to prepare it every Sabbath.

33 Now these are the singers, the heads of fathers' houses of the Levites, dwelling in the chambers of the temple free from other service, for they were on duty day and night. [34] These were heads of fathers' houses of the Levites, according to their generations, leaders, who lived in Jerusalem.

35 In Gibeon dwelt the father of Gibeon, Je-iel, and the name of his wife was Maacah, [36] and his first-born son Abdon, then Zur, Kish, Baal, Ner, Nadab, [37] Gedor, Ahio, Zechariah, and Mikloth; [38] and Mikloth was the father of Shimeam; and these also dwelt opposite their kinsmen in Jerusalem, with their kinsmen. [39] Ner was the father of Kish, Kish of Saul, Saul of Jonathan, Malchishua, Abinadab, and Eshbaal; [40] and the son of Jonathan was Merib-baal; and Merib-baal was the father of Micah. [41] The sons of Micah: Pithon, Melech, Tahre-a, and Ahaz; [42] and Ahaz was the father of Jarah, and Jarah of Alemeth, Azmaveth, and Zimri; and Zimri was the father of Moza. [43] Moza was the father of Bine-a; and Rephaiah was his son, Ele-asah his son, Azel his son. [44]Azel had six sons and these are their names: Azrikam, Bocheru, Ishmael, She-ariah, Obadiah, and Hanan; these were the sons of Azel.

A. Notes to MT

[4] בן בנימן, read, with some of the Versions בן בני מן; [5] השילוני read השלני; [10–11] ידעיה ויהויריב ויכין ועזריה, read ידעיה בן שריה בן עזריה, cf. Neh. 11.10 and the commentary; [13] חיל מלאכת, read חיל למלאכת (haplography); [15] ובקבקר וחרש וגלל, probably corrupt; בקבקר, in Neh 11.17 בקבקיה; גלל, dittography (v. 16); [24] מזרח, read מזרחה? [26] הם הלוים, probably read המה הלוים; האצרות, irregular, read האצרות or אצרות; [33] ואלה, proposed ואלם; [41] ותחרע, add ואחז, cf. 8.35; [42] יערה, probably יעדה; 8.36 יהועדה; [44] בכרו, read בְּכֹרוֹ, cf. commentary.

B. Notes to RSV

[2] 'again', not in the text; cf. commentary; [3] 'And some of the people ... dwelt in Jerusalem', better 'And in Jerusalem dwelt: of the people', etc. [4] 'the son of Bani, from'... thus the Versions (cf. A above), MT 'the son of Banimin'; [13] 'very able men', MT חיל גבורי: either 'men of substance' (NEB) or 'mighty men of valour' (RSV cf. Neh. 11.14); [17] 'and their kinsmen (Shallum being the chief)', MT 'and their kinsman Shallum was the chief' (NEB); 'the camp', MT 'the camps'; [20] 'ruler', MT נגיד, rendered in v. 11 'chief officer'; 'the Lord was with him', better 'The Lord be with him' (NEB). [25] 'from time to time', NEB 'in turn'; [26] 'were in charge', JPS 'were entrusted (באמונה) to be over' (cf. also NEB); [31] 'flat cakes', MT 'what is

baked on the griddle' (Lev. 2.5; 7.9); **[33]** 'Now these are the singers', better (NEB); 'These, the singers (or musicians) ...'; **[34]** 'who lived in Jersualem', better, 'these lived in Jerusalem'.

C. Structure, sources and form

1. Chapter 9 serves a double role: it brings to a conclusion the comprehensive introduction to Chronicles, and at the same time introduces the subsequent pericopes. Thus, after an explicit statement of introduction (v. 3), the first part of the chapter (vv. 3–34) completes the information of chs. 2–8, while vv. 35–44 already form a transition to what follows. The structure of the chapter is, therefore:

(a) 1–2   Conclusion of chs. 2–8
(b) 3–34   The inhabitants of Jerusalem
    (i)   3   Heading
    (ii) 4–9   Israel
    (iii) 10–13 Priests
    (iv) 14–34 Levites
        14–18 Registration
        19–33 Functions
        34   Conclusion
(c) 35–44 Benjaminite genealogy
    35–38   Genealogy of Jeiel
    39–44   The house of Saul

2. About sixty per cent of the chapter finds parallels in the Bible: vv. 2–17 reflect Neh. 11.3–9, and vv. 34–44 are almost identical to I Chron. 8.29–38. The middle section, vv. 18–33, provides new material concerning the Temple service, particularly the gatekeepers, and is probably based on an extra-biblical source. An examination of the chapter from the dual aspects of sources and structure will reveal that while heavily dependent on his sources, the Chronicler has restructured them according to his own line of composition. This tendency is best observed at the literary 'seams' between the sections (vv. 2, 17, 34).

3. The list of the inhabitants of Jerusalem (vv. 3–34) follows a very clear principle already stated in v. 2: Israel (vv. 4–9), priests (vv. 10–13) and Levites (vv. 14–34). It is based on a concept of the people which evidently emerged in the post-exilic era, setting the people's status *vis à vis* the Temple ritual, that is, 'laity' versus 'clergy'; the clergy is then classified in descending order: priests, Levites, etc., and a new connotation is implied for the name 'Israel': non-clerics, laity.

In Ezra-Nehemiah, this new view of the people governs the structure of all the lists, although the order of the clerical and lay (Israel) components may vary (cf. Ezra 2//Neh. 7.5ff; Ezra 8.2–14, Levites missing); 10.8–44; Neh. 10.2–30 [MT 3–30]). By contrast, the basic principle of registration in Chronicles is tribal, and the tribe of Levi (sometimes divided into priests and Levites) constitutes one of the units of 'Israel'. Thus the origin of the list, while certainly post-exilic, is not Chronistic. In preserving the distinction between 'Judah' and 'Benjamin', it resembles Ezra 1.5, where the general principle of classification is that of 'Israel, priests, Levites', but Judah and Benjamin are still distinct entities within 'Israel'. We may thus conclude

CHAPTER 9

that the Chronicler made use of an existing document, and the parallel list of 'the chiefs of the province' in Neh. 11.3–19 immediately comes to mind. A close comparison of the two texts leads to the following observations:

(i) In general, Neh. 11.3–19 constitutes a fuller and more authentic version of the document, while Chronicles is actually an abridgment.

(ii) Many variants between the two texts may be explained as either deliberate omissions on the part of the Chronicler or corruptions of his version.

(iii) Some differences indicate that the text of Neh. 11 is also corrupt, probably through transmission.

(iv) In certain cases, especially in I Chron. 9.16b, it seems that Chronicles represents a different *Vorlage* from Nehemiah; an additional stage between the two versions should be postulated, and this may account for some of the other differences as well.

4. According to Neh. 11.3 the list is to register 'the chiefs of the province who lived in Jerusalem', a purpose which is faithfully carried out. 'Chiefs' of each sector of the population of Jerusalem are mentioned by name and pedigree: Israel (Judah, Benjamin), priests, Levites (including singers) and gatekeepers, and their respective families or orders are then recorded by their numbers (vv. 6, 8, 12, 13, 14, 18, 19). In addition, the 'overseer' (פָּקִיד) or the 'chief officer' (נָגִיד) is mentioned in each case:

9: the overseer of 'Israel', Joel the son of Zichri;

11b: ruler (נָגִיד) of the house of God, Seraiah the son of Hilkiah;

14b: the overseer of the priests, Zabdiel the son of Haggedolim;

21: over the temple servants (עַל הַנְּתִינִם), Ziha and Gishpa;

22: the overseer of the Levites, Uzzi the son of Bani;

24: the general overseer (לְיַד הַמֶּלֶךְ), Pethahiah the son of Meshezabel.

In addition to all these, in v. 9b we have the 'second over the city', Judah the son of Hassenuah.

The sections dealing with the priests and Levites (vv. 10–14, 15–18) are the best preserved, and may offer an illustration of the original structure of the list.

For the Chronicler, the list has a different purpose; it is not a record of 'the chiefs of the province' but of 'those who dwelt in Jerusalem' (cf. the commentary). Consequently, all the 'overseers' are omitted, the pedigrees are abridged and the titles and conclusion are much more concise. In certain cases passages have been restructured in an attempt to reach a more economic presentation, reflecting different views of the subject matter.

The most extensive restructuring is applied to the list of the Levites. Of Neh. 11, vv. 20–24 have been completely omitted, the gatekeepers have been included among the Levites, and the whole unit of I Chron. 9.14–34 has been differently conceived. It would seem that much of the new material derives from a different source, the style of which may sometimes be recognized (cf. below).

In order to appreciate the new structure, we should first see how the parallel sections of Neh. 11.15–19, 21–23, were composed. Neh. 11.15–18 is devoted to the Levites, as is clear from the heading 'Of the Levites' (v. 15) and the conclusion 'All the Levites in the holy city …' (v. 18). Included in this group are three leaders of the 'Levites' in the stricter sense of the term, with a short description of their task (vv. 15–16), and the three head singers with their basic function (v. 17). This group is followed in v. 19 by the gatekeepers: the names of their heads and their number.

Verses 22–23 introduce 'the overseer of the Levites', with another reference to the singers.

In this passage in Nehemiah, the singers are explicitly included among the Levites, while the gatekeepers (and the 'temple servants', v. 21) are not. Thus the list occupies a very clear intermediate position in the process by which all the non-priestly clergy came eventually to be identified as 'Levites'.

The restructuring of this material in Chronicles clearly reflects a different concept, in which the gatekeepers are an integral part of the levitical order. The Chronicles version records first the Levites – including the singers – and then the gatekeepers (vv. 14–17). Only then does a long passage record the functions of the various orders, with particular elaboration of the gatekeepers' tasks and repeated insistence on their definition as 'Levites'. In a very unbalanced, but premeditated, chiastic manner, their functions are described as follows:

> vv. 18–29 gatekeepers
> v. 30 priests
> vv. 31–33 Levites and singers
> v. 34 conclusion.

The integration of all the temple clergy is thus completed, but the emphasis on the gatekeepers may imply that controversy is not yet silenced.

5. As will become clearer through the commentary, vv. 17b–33 derive from a different source and are joined to the preceding unit in order to provide a more comprehensive picture. The idiom of this passage is obviously Late Biblical Hebrew: nominal clauses are the rule (vv. 17b, 18a, 18b, 19a, 19b, 21, 22a, 22b, 23, 25, 26a, 26b, etc.); as far as verbs are concerned, there is only one with a consecutive *waw* (והיו, v. 26, although this feature may be due to the nature of the passage). We also find the frequent use of היה as copula (vv. 20, 24, 26c), and the infinitive with either a verbal or nominal function (התיחשם, להכין, לבוא). Regular repeated action is still expressed by the imperfect (v. 24, 27, 28). Another feature is the abundant and varied use of the prepositions ל (about fifteen times) and על (fourteen times).

However, it is mainly the syntax which evokes the sensation of a late idiom: the subject is placed at the beginning of the sentence when no emphasis is intended, and pronouns are employed repeatedly.

The passage is much too brief to identify its style as idiosyncratic; nevertheless, several features stand out:

(a) The use of the pronoun הם in its longer form המה, either alone, as in המה השוערים (v. 18) or in a distinctive structure, where it is repeated twice for emphatic force:

v. 22: המה בחצריהם התיחשם המה יסד
v. 26: המה ארבעת ... הם[ה] הלויים

(For other instances of this demonstrative use of המה, cf. I Chron. 2.55, המה הקינים; 4.23, המה היוצרים; 8.13, המה ראשי האבות ... המה הבריחו; cf. also the proleptic pronoun in 4.42, ומהם מן בני שמעון.

(b) The description of the gatekeepers' function as their 'trust' (אמונה) with the preposition ב is repeated three times in the passage (vv. 22, 26, 31), a specific usage found again in Chronicles only in II Chron. 31.12, 15, 18 (a context which resembles this passage in other points as well) and, differently, in II Chron. 19.9; 34.12.

(c) The recurring use of 'camp/s' (vv. 18, 19) as well as the designation 'the camps of the Lord' for the Temple precincts is found only here and in II Chron. 31.2 (cf. above (b)).

(d) The blessing 'The Lord be with him', expressed upon the mention of an honoured ancestor, is peculiar to this passage.

The accumulation of these stylistic features, together with the subject-matter indicated by the commentary, suggests that the Chronicler was working here with some source, which he endeavoured to combine with the preceding document.

6. The last passage of the chapter is a literal repetition of 8.29–44; vv. 35–38 record the descendants of Jeiel, the father of Gibeon, and parallel 8.29–32, while vv. 39–44 record the family tree of the Saulides, and parallel 8.33–38. For some scholars, the very fact of repetition is an indication that only one occurrence can be authentic, and their effort is directed towards identifying the original (cf. also A. Demski, 'The Genealogy of Gibeon (I Chronicles 9.35–44): Biblical and Epigraphic Considerations', *BASOR* 202, 1971, 16–23). Braun, for example, regards 8.29–38 as derived from ch. 9 (Braun, 122), while Rudolph would go so far as to suggest that both are secondary to the Chronicler's original work (75ff., 91ff.). It should not, however, be ruled out in principle that the Chronicler (or for that matter, any author) could make use of the same document more than once, for different purposes. The question which concerns us, then, is one of understanding the literary procedure.

The following observations are pertinent here:

(i) Both the lineage of Jeiel and the genealogy of Saul are integral to the Benjaminite passage in ch. 8 (cf. there). This is not the case here in ch. 9, where these passages lack an organic thematic link with the first part of the chapter. On the other hand, one should note that the words ובגבעון ישבו do provide a syntactic and stylistic bridge, as in ch. 8.

(ii) If I was correct in my analysis of the literary nature of ch. 8, the two passages 8.29–32 and 8.33–40 were originally independent and were juxtaposed by the Chronicler. Their appearance together in ch. 9 assumes the textual integrity of ch. 8.

(iii) The fact that the close of the list in ch. 9 is abridged, thus ending differently from ch. 8, may indicate that the present list has a different motive, concentrating on a genealogical portrait of the house of Saul rather than a legitimization of 'the sons of Ulam'.

(iv) Moreover, looking at the passage from a different perspective, a genealogy of the Saulides is a very appropriate introduction to ch. 10, where the narrative begins with the death of Saul and his sons.

(v) The real difficulty seems to be posed by the repetition of the Jeiel genealogy in vv. 35–38. This may have been introduced by the author for the sake of completeness, or inserted secondarily under the influence of ch. 8.

Taking all these factors into consideration, I tend to see a better case for the view that both passages are authentic; the same material (with or without vv. 35–38) is employed twice, in somewhat different formats, in order to provide a fitting introduction to ch. 10 and a transition between the genealogies and the historical narrative. In so doing, the Chronicler stands squarely in the tradition of ancient historiographers, who prelude their narratives with genealogies of the protagonists; examples would be the genealogy of Noah (Gen. 5.32) which precedes the narrative of the flood; the genealogy in Gen. 11.31–32 which introduces the story of Abraham, and more. Thus the reader has been well prepared for the next episode: the demise of Saul.

D. Commentary

[1–2] This is the conclusion of chs. 2–8, where the Israelites and their territories were registered, and as summed up in v. 1a, 'all Israel' was 'enrolled by genealogies'. The literary source given for this material, 'the Book of the Kings of Israel', is mentioned again in II Chron. 20.34 and, by a similar title, in II Chron. 33.18. As has been proposed by several scholars (already Pseudo-Rashi), the title of this work may have been 'the Book of the Kings of Israel *and Judah*', mentioned in II Chron. 27.7; 35.27; 36.8. This view may be based on a variant setting of the accents (cf. the Versions, *ad loc.*; Curtis, 169), or on the probable assumption of omission of 'Judah' by haplography (cf. BH, BHS). No definite stand can be taken on the book's original title, although surely one and the same book is intended in all these places, and the reference to 'all Israel' includes Judah.

The second part of the verse is difficult and, in fact, provocative. It refers to the 'exile of Judah', which is mentioned only once more in Chronicles, in I Chron. 6.15 [MT 5.41], and is very much at variance with the book's attitude towards exile. There is also an emphasis here on the dichotomy 'Israel'/'Judah', a concept which it is the Chronicler's policy to understate (cf. on 21). The juxtaposition of 1a and 1b raises a difficult question: as only 'Judah' (which in this context may denote either the kingdom or the tribe) is said to have been exiled, what about 'Israel' – was it exiled or not? The spontaneous response, based on our knowledge of the Deuteronomistic history, would be an emphatic yes; however, according to the attitudes pronounced in Chronicles, the answer would be in the negative. For Chronicles, only the two-and-a-half eastern tribes were exiled (cf. above, on 5.5, 22, and in particular 25–26), while 'Israel' continued to dwell in its territory, as described, for example, in II Chron. 30. As for Judah, whatever the scope of their deportation, their exile was temporary (cf. on II Chron. 36.20ff.), to be rescinded by Cyrus' decree. The description here of Judah's fortunes as essentially worse that those of the majority of Israel is unexpected, to say the least.

It is therefore possible that 1b, 'And Judah was taken into exile etc.', is in fact a gloss, intended to restore to the text a reality which the Chronicler had tried to avoid. To overstate this possibility, however, is to risk arguing in a vicious circle.

Verse 2 derives from the parallel document of Neh. 11.3ff; it is through the differences between these texts that their message comes to the fore. The heading of Neh. 11.3–4a is structured as a repetitive resumption; the main sentence introduces the topic of the passage: 'These are the chiefs of the province who lived in Jerusalem', to be resumed in 4a by: '... in Jerusalem lived ... of the sons of Judah and of the sons of Benjamin. Of the sons of Judah ...' Inserted into this main clause is the parenthetical note 'but in the towns of Judah everyone lived on his property in their towns: Israel, the priests, the Levites, the temple servants and the descendants of Solomon's servants'. Thus, the general theme of the heading is the 'dwelling' of Israel: the majority of the people dwell in the 'towns of Judah' (a term which reappears in 11.20), while the 'chiefs of the province' dwell in Jerusalem. It is only the latter which are then systematically recorded.

While the Chronicler adopts this heading, he deletes the first main clause, thus immediately omitting the 'chiefs of the province'; then he also removes the reference to 'the towns of Judah' (both here and in 11.20). In their place, the Chronicler introduces a new subject: 'the first dwellers' (RSV 'to dwell again'; cf. below). This is how the text was borrowed and changed:

Neh. 11.3: [These are the chiefs of the province who lived in Jerusalem; but in the towns of Judah] every one lived ($y\bar{a}\check{s}^e b\bar{u}$) on his property ($ba'^a huz\bar{a}t\bar{o}$) in their towns ($b^e `\bar{a}r\bar{e}hem$): Israel, the priests, the Levites, the temple servants [and the descendants of Solomon's servants].

I Chron. 9.2: Now the first dwellers ($w^e hayy\bar{o}\check{s}^e b\bar{i}m\ h\bar{a}r'\bar{i}\check{s}\bar{o}n\bar{i}m$) in their possessions ($ba'^a huzz\bar{a}t\bar{a}m$) in their towns ($b^e `\bar{a}r\bar{e}hem$): Israel, the priests, the Levites, and the temple servants.

The change of subject also results in the deletion of 'province' ($m^e d\bar{i}n\bar{a}h$), a basic term of the Persian era, which never occurs in Chronicles, thus eliminating any explicit indication of the provenance of the list in the Persian period.

The Chronicles heading also avoids reference to the dichotomy between 'the towns of Judah' and Jerusalem. The general subject is now 'the first dwellers', who live 'in their cities'; part of these people dwell in Jerusalem and are presently to be recorded.

An understanding of the topic and purpose of the lists depends entirely on the interpretation of this unique phrase: 'the first dwellers'. The more common view, already expressed by Kimhi (ad loc.: 'the first who came from Babylon'), is that this alludes to the community of the Restoration. This interpretation probably underlies the RSV translation 'the first to dwell again' and the NEB heading 'The restored community', which is then read into the translation 'the first to occupy their ancestral land, etc.' Rudolph would go one step further and emend the text to read 'the first returnees' ($ha\check{s}\check{s}\bar{a}b\bar{i}m\ h\bar{a}r'i\check{s}\bar{o}n\bar{i}m$, 84); Williamson's heading is 'The Post-exilic Community'.

From a theological point of view, this is a sound interpretation and would conform nicely with the Chronicler's stand. However, it in fact reflects information learned from other sources; it is not inherent in the text. If we take for granted that the verse has the same intention as Neh. 11.3, why did the Chronicler take so much trouble to rephrase and transform that text?

Nothing in the context in fact indicates a 'return' or 'restoration', and one wonders how 'the first dwellers' could be construed as 'the first to dwell *again*'. I have often noted that one of the main interests of I Chron. 2–9 is the 'dwellings' or territories of the tribes. The people of Israel have been systematically depicted as 'dwelling' in their towns, and the root *yšb* has occurred twenty-five times in these chapters. Thus, while here v. 1 sums up the genealogical sections of I Chron. 2–8, v. 2 deals with the territorial theme; both serve as a transition to a conclusion of the genealogies and a preparation for 'the dwellers of Jerusalem'. In order to understand the unique *hayyōš⁽e⁾bīm hār'īšōnīm*, one may compare it to Zechariah's *hannᵉbī'īm hār'īšōnīm* (RSV 'former prophets', NEB 'prophets of old', Zech. 1.4; 7.7), or Qoheleth's *hayyāmīm hār'īšōnīm* (RSV 'the former days', NEB 'the old days', Eccles. 7.10). *hayyōš⁽e⁾bīm hār'īšōnīm* should accordingly be understood as 'the old dwellers', or 'dwellers of old'. It is in line with this usage that Chronicles omits 'the towns of Judah' from the original document, leaving no hint in the list itself to a 'restoration'. After due reference to the 'old dwellers', attention is drawn to the 'dwellers of Jerusalem'.

A minor detail to be mentioned is Chronicles' omission of 'the descendants of Solomon's servants'. In general, the cultic organization of Chronicles includes neither these nor 'temple servants' (*nᵉtīnīm*), the lowest orders of the clergy in Ezra-Nehemiah (Ezra 2.43ff., etc). The reference to 'temple servants' in v. 2 is no more than the inadvertent survival of a textual detail from Neh. 11; the Chronicler does *not*, significantly, follow up with their registration from Neh. 11.21.

[3] The last clause of the introduction (cf. Neh. 11.4a) now turns, for the first time, to the 'dwellers of Jerusalem'; here 'the sons of Ephraim and Manasseh' are added to the original 'Judah and Benjamin'. For the Chronicler, Jerusalem has always been the centre of 'all Israel', where people from all the tribes have lived, both during and after the time of the united kingdom. A list of the inhabitants of Jerusalem should then naturally include Ephraim and Manasseh. This statement, however, remains a mere declaration, which can muster no support in the details of the list itself.

No chronological indications for the 'dwellers of Jerusalem' are found in the document taken from Neh. 11, and none are subsequently inserted. The material reproduced in vv. 19ff. clearly (and anachronistically) presupposes a provenance some time in the time of David, and internal textual evidence indicates that the Chronicler also wished to associate the 'inhabitants of Jerusalem' with the reign of David.

[4–6] The details now proceed according to the guidelines of the list as set forth in Neh. 11.3; the presentation of each group or order dwells first on their leader, and then the group is briefly alluded to. While there is obvious parallelism between this passage and Neh. 11.4b–6, neither text seems to represent faithfully the original version. The authentic heading, 'Of the sons of Judah', has been omitted in Chronicles, or rather is made to apply only to Perez (v. 4). Nehemiah mentions two Judahite leaders, Athaiah and Maaseiah, both with long genealogies. Athaiah is identified as 'of the sons of Perez' (Neh. 11.4), and the pedigree of Maaseiah traces back to the 'son of the Shilonite' (v. 5). The Nehemiah list ends in v. 6 with 'All the sons of Perez, etc ...'. Chronicles, on the other hand, lists three lines rather than two: 'the sons of Perez' (v. 4), 'of the Shilonites' (v. 5), and finally 'the sons of Zerah' (v. 6a). The list closes with a very short conclusion: 'and their kinsmen, six hundred and ninety'.

According to the general genealogical convention, the three principal branches of Judah were Shelah, Perez and Zerah (Num. 26.20), and 'the Shilonite' in v. 5 should be rendered 'the Shelanite', the head of the family of Shelah. We may also assume that Jeuel, named in Chronicles as 'of the sons of Zerah', although absent altogether in Nehemiah, is original to the list.

It is difficult to assess how systematic the list originally was, but if the following passages are to be taken as a model, it would seem that the text of Neh. 11 was corrupted by the omission of the Zerahite, and of the conclusions for each of the Judahite families. The passage in Chronicles seems to have been deliberately abridged, especially the pedigrees; the conclusion 'and their kinsmen, six hundred and ninety' may, however, be a corrupted form of a longer original (cf. v. 9 for Benjamin and v. 13 for the priests).

Many of the proper names of the parallel lists are similar; some forms seem to be variants (e.g. Uthai – Athaiah; Imri – Amariah), but there are others which are altogether different (Ammihud – Uzziah, etc.). The various names are affiliated to the line of the same personages in both texts – which would indicate either textual corruption or, more probably, different selections from still longer pedigrees, now lost.

The interchange of Uthai/Athaiah is similar to that of Meshullam/Meshelemiah (Neh. 12.25//I Chron. 9.21, cf. below); 'Asaiah' ($^{\prime a}\check{s}\bar{a}y\bar{a}h$) and 'Maaseiah' ($ma^{\prime a}\check{s}\bar{e}y\bar{a}h$) are certainly variants of the same name (cf. $m^e\check{s}elemy\bar{a}h/\check{s}elemy\bar{a}h$ of I Chron. 9.21 and 26.1ff.). The plural 'the sons of Perez' in v. 4 comes after the reference to a single person, Uthai; together with the unusual name 'Banimin' preceding it, this may point to a corruption of: 'Bani, from ($b\bar{a}n\bar{i}\ min$) the sons of Perez' (thus generally accepted; already RSV). As both 'the first born' $hab^e k\bar{o}r$ and 'his sons' ($\bar{u}b\bar{a}n\bar{a}w$) are completely out of place in this context, they might very well stand for $ben\ b\bar{a}r\bar{u}k$, 'the son of Baruch', as in Neh. 11.5. Jeuel is recorded without a pedigree.

[7–9] The same relationship noted between the Chronicles and Nehemiah texts for the preceding passage applies here as well: there is undoubtedly parallelism to Neh. 11.7–9, but neither of the two lists seems to be the original. In Neh. 11.7, 'And these are the sons of Benjamin' is followed by one name, Sallu, who is given an unusually long pedigree of seven generations. Then comes a numerical conclusion (v. 8, which seems to contain a corrupt phrase: 'and after him Gabbai Sallai') and the names of two officials, 'Joel the son of Zichri' and 'Judah the son of Hassenuah' (v. 9). The contrasting structure of Chronicles is abridged along two lines: the pedigrees are shortened, and the names and functions of officials are omitted. On the other hand, four heads of Benjaminites are mentioned first (vv. 7–8), followed by a conclusion (v. 9).

Of these four, the first has the same name as in Neh. 11.7: 'Sallu the son of Meshullam'; here, however, we find only a very short pedigree of two generations: 'the son of Hodaviah (*hōdāwᵉyāh*) the son of Hassenuah (*hassᵉnū'āh*)'. This can hardly be other than a different presentation of the name 'Jehudah (*yᵉhūdāh*) the son of Hassenuah (*hassᵉnū'ah*)', who according to Neh. 11.9 was the 'second over the city'. Since the document as found in Chronicles omits the names of all functionaries, we may conclude that this transformation was already found in the Chronicler's source, which may in turn suggest that the Chronicler was using a *Vorlage* different from the text in Neh. 11. Such a conclusion is supported by the names of the other three Benjaminite leaders, which find no parallel in Neh. 11.7–9.

The long conclusion of v. 9 comprises two parts: 9a sums up vv. 7–8 with the total number of the Benjaminites; 9b is the conclusion of the entire first part of the document (vv. 4–9), and introduces into the text the characteristically Chronistic 'heads of fathers' houses according to their fathers' houses', a terminology completely foreign to the document of Neh. 11.4ff.

[10–13] With the exception of the name of the first priest, 'Jedaiah', this passage seems to be the least damaged in both versions of the list, and may serve as a double sample of the document's original format.

The beginning of v. 10 is unusually out of balance: three unrelated names (Jedahia, Jehoiarib, Jachin) are followed by a fourth, Azaraiah, called 'the chief officer of the house of God' and linked to Ahitub by a pedigree of five generations. The names of two more priests then follow with their full pedigrees. The three unadorned names at the beginning of the list, and the appearance of the most distinguished priest of the house of Zadok in the fourth place, clearly indicate that the text is corrupt. The parallel in Neh. 11.10 reads: 'Jedaiah the son of Joiarib, Jachin ...', a different constellation (also secondary, it seems) in which the three first names represent only two persons. Further, 'the son of Joiarib, Jachin', also seems to be corrupt, and the name of the 'chief priest' in Neh. 11.11 is Seraiah rather than Azariah.

Following the brilliant proposition of Rudolph (p. 84), I think that in both Chronicles and Nehemiah, vv. 10–11 represent what was originally a single genealogy. Taking *yākīn* ('Jachin') to be a corruption of *ben* ('son of'), and regarding 'Azariah' and 'Seraiah' as two consecutive names in the official priestly genealogy (cf. Ezra 7.1; I Chron. 6.14 [MT. 5.40]), the text can be reconstructed as follows: 'Jedaiah, son of Joiarib, son of Seraiah, son of Azariah, son of Hilkiah, etc.' The whole priestly passage (vv. 10–13) thus records three priests: Jedaiah, Adaiah and Maasai. Their affiliation betrays the post-exilic provenance of the record: Adaiah and Maasai are affiliated with the houses of Pashur and Immer, two of the four priestly families of the Restoration (Ezra 2.37–38 = Neh. 7.40–41; Ezra 10.20, 22, etc.). As for Jedaiah, he belongs to the first of these priestly families, designated in Ezra-Nehemiah as 'the sons of Jedaiah of the house of Jeshua', or 'the sons of Jeshua the son of Jozadak and his brethren' (Ezra 2.35; 10.18).

If this list is regarded as faithfully representing the last generations of its genealogical structure, than Jedaiah would be a cousin of Jeshua the high priest:

```
                    Seraiah
          ┌────────────┴────────────┐
       Joiarib              Jozadak
          │                     │
       Jedaiah               Jeshua
```

In any event, these would be two branches of the main line, as illustrated by the ramification of the priestly divisions from the four original Restoration families (Neh. 12.2–7, etc.).

Of these families, only Harim (Ezra 2.39 etc.) is not represented. If in fact his name had originally been included but fell out of the list, this might account for the discrepancy in the total number of the priests: 1198 priests in Neh. 11 and 1760 in Chronicles; keeping in mind, of course, that numerical errors are among the most common in textual transmission, it is just possible that the difference of almost six hundred priests represent the 'lost' fourth family. This might also account for the additional phrase in the conclusion of the Chronistic version (v. 13, cf. below). It is also possibile that the family of Harim was not of equal status, or that it declined and was eventually absorbed by the other families; our knowledge is too poor to reach a conclusion.

Is 'the chief officer of the house of God' in fact the 'high priest' of the Temple? The evidence, which is not conclusive, can be summarized thus:

(*a*) Nothing can be learned from the word *nāgīd*, which denotes 'an officer' in various capacities: of the treasuries (I Chron. 26.24), of the gatekeepers (I Chron. 9.20), etc.

(*b*) In II Chron. 31.10 the high priest is called 'Azariah the chief priest (*hakkōhēn hār'ōš*) who was of the house of Zadok'. Somewhat later (v. 13), a priest by the same name is titled 'Azariah the chief officer (*n^egīd*) of the house of God'. If the same person is intended, then one priest carried both titles: 'chief priest' and 'chief officer'.

(*c*) II Chron. 35.8b speaks of three 'chief officers of the house of God', of whom the high priest, Hilkiah, is one.

(*d*) As far as we know from extant sources, no high priest by the name of Jedaiah is recorded from the Persian period.

It would seem that the 'chief officer' might have been the high priest, but not necessarily; he certainly was a person of distinction in the ranks of the clergy. Jedaiah is the only officer whose title was not omitted in the Chronicles version of this passage.

It has been already recognized (cf. Rudolph, 87) that the single concluding phrase of the list in Chronicles (9.13) in fact summarizes not only the numbers of the priestly families of Jedaiah, Adaiah and Maasai (1760, cf. above) but also the various titles found in the three separate descriptions of Nehemiah:

Neh. 11.12a: 'and their brethren who did the work of the house, 822'
Neh. 11.13a: 'and his brethren, heads of fathers' houses, 242 …'
Neh. 11.14a: 'and their brethren, mighty men of valour, 128 …'
I Chron. 9.13: 'and their brethren, heads of their fathers' houses, 1760, mighty men of valour, for the work of the service of the house of God' (my translation; RSV obscures the essential similarities).

The method by which the three Nehemiah phrases are combined into one sentence in I Chron. 9.13 leads us to the following conclusions:

(*a*) The Chronicler's source is undoubtedly the list of Neh. 11, or another version of it.

(*b*) The Chronicler restructured the material in order to render it stylistically more concise, and for the same reason abridged some of the pedigrees.

(*c*) The functionaries are generally omitted (cf. Neh. 11.14b).

The names in the first two pedigrees are in general identical in Nehemiah and Chronicles, but in the third, the following variants should be noted: Maasai/ Amashsai; Adiel/Azarel; Jahzerah/Ahzai.

[14–16] This passage parallels Neh. 11.15–18. Under the heading 'Of the Levites', two groups are recorded: (*a*) the Levites in the strict sense and (*b*) the singers, a division which is more obvious in Neh. 11 than in Chronicles. In Nehemiah, the names for each group – Shemaiah, Shabtai and Jozabad of the first, Mathaniah and Bakbukiah of Asaph and Abda of Jeduthun of the second – are followed by brief descriptions of their functions: 'who were over the … house of God' (v. 16), and 'who was the leader to begin the thanksgiving in prayer' (v. 17), descriptions which properly follow the precedent of the priests in v. 12. In Chronicles, however, the balance between the names has been upset and the role-references have been omitted altogether. Of the Levites listed in Nehemiah, Shemaiah alone remains, here affiliated to 'the sons of Merari'. The context would imply that the three names which follow, 'Bakbakar, Heresh, Galal', should also be regarded as Levites (but cf. below). The record then proceeds with three more names, presumably (but not explicitly) referring to leaders of the singers: Mattaniah of Asaph and Obadiah (Abda) of Jeduthun (vv. 15b–16a), who were mentioned as second and third among the singers in Nehemiah, and the unique 'Berechiah, the son of Asa, son of Elkanah, who dwelt in the villages of the Netophathites' (16b).

The mention of 'Bakbakar, Heresh, Galal' seems corrupt: Bakbakar is probably a misrepresentation of 'Bakbukiah' (Neh. 11.17), 'Heresh' may be a remnant of the name of a second Levite, and 'Galal' is probably a dittography from v. 16. As regards the singers, although both lists record three leaders, only two are the same. Several points should be made at this juncture:

1. Among the singers, the name Berechiah is documented twice as the father of Asaph (I Chron. 6.39 [MT 6.24]; 15.17), but his ancestry is presented differently from that of 'Berechiah' of this context.

2. Berechiah is not linked to any of the known families of singers.

3. His home is given as 'the villages of the Netophathites', immediately calling to mind Neh. 12.28, 'the sons of the singers gathered together from ... the villages of the Netophathites'.

4. The family of Heman is not recorded among the singers, either here or in Neh. 11.

5. The name 'Elkanah', Berechiah's grandfather, is extremely frequent in the genealogy of Heman in I Chron. 6 (vv. 33–36 [MT 18–21]).

It is therefore possible that during the chronological gap, as it were, between Neh. 11 and I Chron. 9, the family of Heman had made its first step into the order of the singers, challenging the monopoly of Asaph. While the Nehemiah list contains two singers related to Asaph and one to Jeduthun, Chronicles contains one each for Asaph and Jeduthun, and a third whose genealogy is not yet completely formulated, affiliated with this group of singers who would eventually be represented as Heman. The addition of Berechiah precedes the Chronicler, for whom Heman is an absolutely established reality.

Due to the restructuring of the list at this point, the Chronicler omitted, in contrast to all other sections, the numerical conclusions of the Levites (Neh. 11.8).

[17–18] After briefly paralleling Neh. 11.19a, the list goes its own way, mentioning four names, noting that 'their brother Shallum was the chief' (NEB) and explaining how his priority was expressed by a responsibility for the east gate of the Temple – the king's gate. Verse 18b is a conclusion, emphasizing unequivocally that the gatekeepers were part of 'the camp of the Levites'. This note, however, is the echo of a second source used by the Chronicler; with the literary transition from one source to another, a different view of the gatekeepers is introduced.

In order to clarify this difference, some general observations are in order:
Two major stages in the history of the gatekeepers can be discerned in biblical material, the one expressed mainly by Ezra-Nehemiah and the other by Chronicles. The first stage is characterized by the following features:
1. The gatekeepers constitute an independent order among the Temple personnel, usually registered between the singers and the temple-servants (Ezra 2.42, etc.).
2. The number of gatekeeper families varies from two (Neh. 11.19) to six (Ezra 2.42=Neh. 7.45); the more persistent of these is Talmon, repeated in all four lists (Ezra 2.42 = Neh. 7.45; Ezra 10.45; Neh. 11.9; 12.25), while Shallum/Meshullam and Akkub appear in three of them.
3. No levitical lineage for the gatekeepers' families is indicated.

The next stage of their history, as expressed in Chronicles, takes shape as follows:
1. The gatekeepers are included among the Levites (I Chron. 23.3–5, etc.).
2. All the family-names of Ezra-Nehemiah disappear, with the exception of Shallum, who becomes Shelemiah or Meshelemiah (I Chron. 26.1, etc.), and new families emerge: Obed-edom and the sons of Merari (I Chron. 26.8, 10).
3. The gatekeepers possess a basic genealogical tree linking them to the sons of Levi.

This text, with the transition from vv. 17–18 to v. 19, is a literary (rather than historical) attempt to harmonize the two systems. Verse 17a, taken from Neh. 11.19, introduces the system of Ezra-Nehemiah: four non-levitical families of gatekeepers. Verse 17b already introduces 'Shallum' as their chief, while v. 18b emphasizes a levitical affiliation. Verses 19ff. then focus on 'Shallum and his kinsmen' alone, highlighting in every possible way their levitical status. The other gatekeepers' families are implied in 'their brethren' and 'the four chief gatekeepers' (v.26), whose further description in I Chron. 26 differs from that of Ezra-Nehemiah.

[19–22] These verses may be regarded as the '*magna carta*' of the gatekeepers. From the answers provided here, we may surmise that their two fundamental problems were the legitimization of their functions within normative biblical traditions and the confirmation of their lineage as Levites. This passage and the following one describe in detail not only their tasks but also their legal and historical foundations and precedents. Stylistically, this is marked by an insistence on terminology connected with the 'tent', and the identification of 'tent' with 'house of God'. Following the method of 'halachic Midrash', this text provides the necessary link between the 'tabernacle' and the gatekeepers.

Verse 19 records the genealogy of the chief gatekeeper: 'Shallum the son of Kore, son of Ebiasaph, son of Korah'. We have already noted the lengthy pedigrees provided in I Chron. 6.33–47 [MT 6.18–32] for the head singers in the time of David, Asaph, Heman and Ethan, in the intensive effort to trace their levitical descent in full detail. Here, by contrast, the record could hardly be more brief, with a mechanical conjunction linking 'Shallum the son of Kore' himself to his most distant ancestor 'Ebiasaph the son of Korah'. No real effort has been invested in providing the intermediate stages, as was the case for the singers, the heads of the Levites (I Chron. 6.20–30 [MT 6.5–15]) and the priests (I Chron. 6.4–15; [MT 5.30–41]). Affiliated with 'Korah' and repeatedly called 'the Korahites' (vv. 19, 31), the gatekeepers are assigned a further removed descent from Kohath the son of Levi, through his grandson (Exod. 6.16–24).

The task of the gatekeepers is first described generally, 'in charge of the work of the service', and then more specifically as 'keepers of the thresholds of the tent'. This last, as well as their general title, indicates a duty as Temple guardians. Now according to random notices in biblical historiography, those who 'guarded the threshold' were priests (II Kings 12.9 [MT 10]; 23.4; 25.18; also Jer. 35.4; 52.24). The Chronicler makes clear, in no uncertain terms, that this function is reserved to the levitical gatekeepers; cf. II Chron. 34.9: '... the Levites, the keepers of the threshold ...' (also II Chron. 23.4). It is only the overall supervision which is invested in the hands of the high priest.

Verses 19b–21 continue with a comparison of the present functions of the gatekeepers with those of their ancestors. This is in fact the only instance where a description of cultic functions marks a distinction between generations: 'they' *vis à vis* 'their fathers'. The gatekeepers of 'today', the text implies, are those who have been appointed by David and Samuel the seer; their fathers are those of time past, of whom 'Phinehas the son of Eleazar was the ruler'. Thus the legitimization of the gatekeepers, while resembling to some extent that of the singers, still differs. The source of authority is the same, as both singers and gatekeepers were appointed by David to their service in the tent, and both are authorized by a divine decree, delivered by prophets. The establishment of the singers is attributed to the command of David together with 'Gad the king's seer and Nathan the prophet' (II Chron. 29.25), while that of the gatekeepers is seconded in this passage (v. 20) by 'Samuel the seer', who is, according to Chronicles, also a Levite (I Chron. 6.27–28 [MT 12–13]). The difference lies in the tradition within which singers and gatekeepers are respectively placed. The first function has no precedent in the wilderness tabernacle; it was David's innovation, intro-

duced after the ark had 'found rest' (I Chron. 6.31 [MT 16]), and the original
levitical task of carrying the ark had been abolished. Singers were therefore
ordinary Levites who underwent a professional change. The gatekeepers, by
contrast, were always directly connected with the tabernacle, as their ancient
fathers were 'in charge of the camp of the Lord, keepers of the entrance'.
David altered only their specific functions, in accordance with the changing
circumstances. It should be noted that according to the Pentateuch tradition,
the guarding of the tabernacle was assigned to all the Levites, and their
overseer was 'Eleazar the son of Aaron' (Num. 3.32); here, the task is limited
to one levitical branch, whose ancient 'ruler' was Phinehas, the son of Eleazar
(a probable influence of Num. 25.7ff.).

The passage employs ambiguous terminology in order to create a typological equation among three historical contexts: the ancestral 'past', in
which the role of the gatekeepers was initiated; the list's 'present', presumed
to be the time of David, with Shallum as chief gatekeeper, when all the
arrangements concerning the guarding of the 'tent' are established, with the
ultimate goal being the Temple service; and finally, implied in all these, the
time of the Chronicler (or the author of this document), who seeks, by
reference to Phinehas and David, to legitimize the gatekeepers' status in his
own days.

Accordingly, the vocabulary of the passage includes 'the camp of the
Lord', meaning here the sacred precincts, based on the idea of 'camp' in the
wilderness traditions (Exod. 16.13, etc.) and paralleled only by 'the gates of
the camp of the Lord' in II Chron. 31.2; also, the recurring allusion to the
tent: 'keepers of the thresholds of the tent' (v. 19), 'gatekeeper at the entrance
of the tent of meeting' (v. 21), and especially the paradoxical 'house of the
tent' (v. 23). The apparent self-contradiction in this last term is paraphrased
by NEB in v. 23: 'the tent dwelling'. But a similar term was also used in
the related context of I Chron. 6.48 [MT 33], 'the tabernacle of the house of
God', and both terms seem constructed with the deliberate purpose of fully
equating the two components, 'the house' and 'the tent', thus creating a
continuity between the two institutions and all that they entail. The terms
'entrance' (*mābō'*) and 'threshhold' (*sap*) both used elsewhere exclusively for
the Temple, and 'gate' (*ša'ar*) which is certainly more common in Temple
contexts, are all applied here to the tent. To complete the discussion of these
verses, a few more points should be made.

(*a*) The head of the gatekeepers, 'Shallum the son of Kore' (v. 19), and the
only other person named in this context, 'Zechariah the son of Meshelemiah'
(v. 21), would seem to be completely unrelated. However, according to
I Chron. 26.1–2 (cf. also v. 14), the head of the gatekeepers is 'Meshelemiah
(or 'Shelemiah') the son of Kore' and his firstborn is 'Zechariah'. Shallum
and Meshelemiah are then variant forms of the same name, the choice of

Shallum in v. 17 being dictated by the wish to link this list with the more established form of the name in the Chronistic material.

(b) The realities of the author's day are glimpsed through the statement that the main body of the gatekeepers dwelt outside Jerusalem 'in their villages' (v. 22, 25), another similarity to the singers, who 'built themselves villages around Jerusalem' (Neh. 12.29).

[23–29] This detailed exposition of the actual areas of the gatekeepers' responsibility is structured as a continuum, the items following one other, with no literary signs of subdivisions. It has two components: 1. vv. 23–26a, the arrangement of the guards at the Temple gates; 2. vv. 26b–29, specific items of responsibility.

The description of the organization of the gatekeepers, while systematic, is concise, and should be supplemented from I Chron. 26. The keepers man posts on all four sides of the Temple – east, west, north and south (v. 24) – assisted by their colleagues who come to Jerusalem from the villages for week-long shifts and lodge in the vicinity of the Temple (v. 27). Responsible for all the guards are the four *gibbōrē-haššō'arīm* (RSV 'chief gatekeepers'; NEB 'principal door-keepers'), who, according to I Chron. 26.14ff., divide their duties according to the four gates of the Temple court.

The specific areas of responsibility recorded in vv. 26b–29 include chambers, treasuries, daily opening of the gates, inventory and upkeep of the furniture and the holy utensils, and also guarding the supplies for the regular service, such as flour and oil for the bread offering, wine for the wine offering and frankincense and spices for the incense. While the responsibility for guarding all of these lay with the gatekeepers, their actual administration was probably in the charge of the Levites (cf. I Chron. 26.20–28; II Chron. 31.12–13).

The unique phrase (v. 25) *mē'ēt 'el 'ēt* (RSV: 'from time to time') is probably similar to Ezek. 4.10, 11 *mē'ēt 'ad 'ēt*, meaning from a certain point of time of one day to the same point of the next. Here, too, from the beginning of one week to the beginning of the next.

[30–33] This passage records certain Temple functions carried out by other orders of the clergy, but presented from the point of view of their relationship to those of the gatekeepers. Following the gatekeepers' charge over 'flour, wine, frankincense and spices', the text then continues in inverted order with the actual preparation of these items: the spices by members of the priestly class (v. 30) and the 'flat cakes' (probably the 'cereal offering' baked on the griddle according to Lev. 2.5; 6.21 [MT 6.14]) and the showbread by other Levites (vv. 31–32). For the sake of completeness there is also a reference to the singers, stating their exemption from any of the responsibilities just mentioned, in order to free them to attend to their own service, day and night.

The division of labour presupposed in this passage seems to deviate in certain details from the Pentateuch traditions. According to Num. 4.16, the charge 'of the oil for the light, the fragrant incense, the continual cereal offering, and the anointing oil, with the oversight of all the tabernacle ...' was entrusted to 'Eleazar the son of Aaron', that is, the high priest himself or his successor. It is not specified, however, if this general charge also included the preparation of these items. The initial preparation of the anointing oil, the incense and the bread of presence, is ascribed in the Pentateuch to Moses himself (Exod. 30.22–25, 34–36; Lev. 24.5–7). While no one is explicitly designated to follow him in this, the general division of charges in the Pentateuch makes it likely that these preparations were a priestly prerogative. According to this passage, however, only the preparation of the incense is a priestly monopoly, while the other tasks were transferred to the lower clergy, the Levites (cf. also I Chron. 23.29). The exemption of the singers may imply that all the work of the 'chambers' was carried out by 'Levites', the non-priestly members of the tribe.

[34] The conclusion of the passage is well balanced: v. 34a concludes the section dealing with the Levites (vv. 14–32), while v. 34b serves as a conclusion for the larger unit, beginning with v. 3. As we have already seen, in restructuring the levitical passage the Chronicler omitted the original conclusion of Neh. 11.18; he replaces it here, at the end of his own record, 'these were the heads of the fathers' houses of the Levites, according to their generations', a conclusion modelled after 8.28, adapted lightly to the present context.

The fine chiastic structure of references to Jerusalem in both vv. 3 and 34 – 'In Jerusalem dwelt', '... these dwelt in Jerusalem' (*'elleh yāš^{e}bū bīrūšālayim – bīrūšālayim yāš^{e}bū*), an artisitic touch obscured by the translations, rounds off the main body of the chapter.

[35–44] This passage, parallel to I Chron. 8.29–38, is a preliminary introduction to ch. 10 (cf. above, 205). Since the details of the list have been discussed in connection with ch. 8, I shall only summarize them here. The version here has the better rendering in three places, preserving names omitted from ch. 8: Jeiel in v. 35, Ner in v. 36 and Mikloth in v. 37 (8.29, 30, 31). On the other hand, 'Ahaz' is retained in I Chron. 8.35 and omitted here.

In the names themselves, the following variants are discernible: Zecher/ Zechariah; Shimeah/Shimeam; Merib-baal/Meribaal; Tarea/Tahrea; Jehoaddah/Jarah; Raphah/Rephaiah. Some of these variants reflect different forms of the same names, amply illustrated in the biblical ono-masticon (cf. Shema/Shemaiah for Zecher/Zechariah; Abiah/Abiam for Shimeah/Shimeam, etc.). Both synchronic and diachronic factors are at work here (cf. the weakening of the gutturals in the case of Tahrea/Taarea), and no conclusive 'history' of these changes is yet possible. In the case of

Jehoaddah/Jarah we probably have a combination of a variant form with a textual corruption (Ja'adah/Ja'arah). Since the two lists are closely dependent, their variations attest to an ongoing process of transformation of these names.

In v. 44, the second of Azel's sons is, as in 8.38, Bocheru ($bōk^e rū$). The unusual name has been recognized as a corruption of $b^e kōrō$, 'his first born', and emended accordingly, together with the addition of a sixth name to the list, following LXX. However, since the same corruption appears in both versions of the list, a possible conclusion would be that the author of 9.44 had already found the corruption in his *Vorlage*, implying, in turn, a secondary origin of the passage and prohibiting any emendation (cf. Rudolph, 90). However, one may also attribute the double appearance of the same corruptions more simply to the Massoretes harmonizing 9.44 to its earlier version in 8.38.

10   Now the Philistines fought against Israel; and the men of Israel fled before the Philistines, and fell slain on Mount Gilboa. ² And the Philistines overtook Saul and his sons; and the Philistines slew Jonathan and Abinadab and Malchishua, the sons of Saul. ³ The battle pressed hard upon Saul, and the archers found him; and he was wounded by the archers. ⁴ Then Saul said to his armour-bearer, 'Draw your sword, and thrust me through with it, lest these uncircumcised come and make sport of me.' But his armour-bearer would not; for he feared greatly. Therefore Saul took his own sword, and fell upon it. ⁵ And when his armour-bearer saw that Saul was dead, he also fell upon his sword, and died. ⁶ Thus Saul died; he and his three sons and all his house died together. ⁷ And when all the men of Israel who were in the valley saw that the army had fled and that Saul and his sons were dead, they forsook their cities and fled; and the Philistines came and dwelt in them.

8 On the morrow, when the Philistines came to strip the slain, they found Saul and his sons fallen on Mount Gilboa. ⁹ And they stripped him and took his head and his armour, and sent messengers throughout the land of the Philistines, to carry the good news to their idols and to the people. ¹⁰ And they put his armour in the temple of their gods, and fastened his head in the temple of Dagon. ¹¹ But when all Jabesh-gilead heard all that the Philistines had done to Saul, ¹² all the valiant men arose, and took away the body of Saul and the bodies of his sons, and brought them to Jabesh. And they buried their bones under the oak in Jabesh, and fasted seven days.

13 So Saul died for his unfaithfulness; he was unfaithful to the Lord in that he did not keep the command of the Lord, and also consulted a medium, seeking guidance, ¹⁴ and did not seek guidance from the Lord. Therefore the Lord slew him, and turned the kingdom over to David the son of Jesse.

B. Notes to RSV

[1] 'and fell slain', the subject in MT is 'slain' (חללים); probably best translated as 'and [some] fell slain'; [3] 'found him', or 'hit him' (cf. BDB, p. 598, מצא 3b); 'he was wounded by', or 'he was in fear of', cf. commentary; [7] 'that the army had fled and that Saul and his sons were dead': the translation is based on I Sam. 31.7; MT 'that Saul and his sons had fled and died', cf. commentary; [13–14] The phrasing and division of sentences is not compatible with the Hebrew syntax. Better 'for the trespass (or 'act of unfaithfulness') which he had committed against

the Lord, in that he did not keep the command of the Lord and also consulted a medium. He did not seek guidance ... therefore ...'

C. Structure, sources and form

1. With ch. 10 we reach the beginning of the principal part of Chronicles: the narration of the history of Israel from this juncture onward, until Cyrus' declaration in II Chron. 36.23. This is also a turning point from one mode of literary expression to another: from a compilation of lists and anecdotes organized according to their common subject, with the factor of time-sequence playing almost no role, to a narration of successive events, disposed along a vertical time sequence. The change of form at this point is an unmistakable indication of the author's conscious movement from the introduction of his work to its main body. The inevitable question is, therefore: why did he choose to begin at this exact point? Since the Chronicler is a very aware historian, highly attentive to his task, the choice of a beginning must be meaningful. The answer is made explicit in vv. 13–14; cf. the commentary.

2. Chapter 10 is also the first long section taken from the book of Samuel, which becomes a major source for the narrative from this point until the end of the history of David. The chapter is an almost literal parallel to I Sam. 31, and as such serves as an excellent example of one of the Chronicler's most characteristic literary methods: the literal transposition of a written source, with apparently minor changes of language, style and content. An examination of these alterations is an important key for understanding the Chronicler's literary methods and general outlook – historical and theological. Still, the full message of the chapter cannot be appreciated merely by comparison with its parallel in I Sam. 31; its place and role in its new context must be examined. I Sam. 31 forms part of a historical and narrative sequence which begins in I Sam. 9 with the election of Saul, and continues in II Sam. 2–4 with the divided kingdom. From this long sequence the Chronicler chose only one chapter, relating Saul's death, but omitted the long history of Saul on one hand and the divided kingdom on the other. For him, the death of Saul is followed by the enthronement of David, taken verbatim from II Sam. 5.1–3. Even assuming that the original context is known to the reader of Chronicles, the complete isolation of the chapter from its original context, and its placement in a new one, gives it a different meaning. Therefore, while the actual historical background and the geographical, political and social presuppositions of the events can be learned from the book of Samuel and its commentaries, the full meaning of the chapter, in general and in detail, can only be appreciated from its actual context in Chronicles.

3. The story of Saul's death is composed of three main parts:

1–7 the story of the war with the Philistines and its results;
8–12 the fate of Saul and his sons after their death;
13–14 summary and reflections.

The transitions between the parts are well marked: from the first to the second by a new beginning, 'On the morrow', and from the second to the third by a change of form and style. Verses 1–12 are taken from I Sam. 31, where they are continued by II Sam. 1. In Chronicles this original sequence is dismissed and the story is summarized by the addition of vv. 13–14, which form a connecting link between chs. 10 and 11. It might appear that the role of vv. 13–14 is similar to any of the concluding formulae for each of the kings of Israel: Saul died and David reigned in his place. However, in contrast to other basically neutral formulae, these verses contain in a nutshell the author's judgment and evaluation of the entire kingship of Saul (cf. below pp. 229–30), and provide a context in which the whole narrative will be integrated and best understood.

4. In spite of the changes introduced by the Chronicler into the story, it still preserves most of the literary qualities of the book of Samuel: a short, concise and condensed presentation; a dramatic chain of successive events; a prompt transition from one scene to the next; the use of dialogue to develop the plot; an indirect but sensitive expression of the psychological and emotional aspects of the story, etc. The Chronicler's own style can be found in the two concluding verses, which are characteristic examples of his own vocabulary and style.

5. Although many of the differences between this chapter and I Sam. 31 result from the Chronicler's careful reworking, either from his historical and theological views or his linguistic and stylistic preferences, one should always consider the possibility that some of these differences were already present in the text he used. Since we will not cover the whole field of textual transmission, these cases will be pointed out only occasionally.

D. Commentary

[1–7] The first part of the story has two components: vv. 1–5: a description of the battle, reaching a climax with the death of Saul; vv. 6–7: a summary of the battle, describing the immediate results in the field and the more general consequences for Israel.

Unity of time and place is not held to in v. 7, since the general consequences of the battle are a prolonged historical process connected with various locations: the Israelites leave their cities, which are then occupied by the Philistines. In the structure of the narrative, the verse provides a sort of pause between the two parts of the story. The second part, from v. 8 onwards, goes back to pick up again the narrative time sequence: 'On the morrow ...'

In his reworking of the story, the Chronicler interferes only slightly in vv. 1–5, and much more so in the summary in vv. 6–7. This already suggests that the Chronicler had views of the war and its consequences which differed from I Sam. 31.

[1] The verse opens with the war against the Philistines, paralleling I Sam. 31.1, but changing the tense of the opening verb: 'fought' (*nilḥ^amū*) in place of 'were fighting' (*nilḥāmīm*: this distinction disappears in the English translations). For Samuel, the war at Mount Gilbo'a is a continuation of previous events, and is directly connected with I Sam. 29.11, 'But the Philistines went up to Jezreel', and earlier with 28.4, '... and Saul gathered all

Israel and they encamped at Gilbo'a'. It is the insertion of I Sam. 30 which occasions a break in the narrative, requiring the author to recount the situation again in 31.1. In Chronicles the story has no connection anywhere, being an entirely new beginning; accordingly, 'fought' is much more suitable.

The literary isolation of course has historical consequences as well. In Chronicles the war with the Philistines stands on its own as an isolated event, unanticipated and unheralded by prior circumstances. It is bereft of any historical logic, and against the background of I Chron. 1–9 loses much of its weight in the history of Israel. This different appraisal of the war is part of the Chronicler's general approach, which will be further demonstrated throughout the course of the story.

Another change here is the omission of the article from the name of the mountain Gilbo'a, as also later in v. 8. Since these are the only occurrences of the name in Chronicles, it is difficult to determine what motive lies behind the change (on the topography of the war cf. Z. Kallai, 'The Wars of Saul', in J. Liver, *The Military History of the Land of Israel in Biblical Times*, Tel Aviv 1973, 141–4*).

[2] The description of the battle has the quality of a moving picture, coming ever closer to its focus in Saul. After the general defeat (v. 1) the Philistines wish to strike down the leaders of Israel, to complete their triumph. First they find Saul's three sons, whose importance is expressed by the mentioning of their names but whose death is reported only in general terms. Then the focus nears the story's centre: Saul.

[3] After the flight of his soldiers and the death of his sons, Saul remains alone on the field of battle; the war 'presses hard' upon him and he is wounded by the archers. Archery was one of the most common fighting tactics (cf. Y. Yadin, *The Art of Warfare in Biblical Times*, London 1963, 6–9, 80–3, 295–6), and the wounding of other kings is related in a similar way: Ahab (I Kings 22.34), Joram (II Kings 9.24), and Josiah (II Chron. 35.23). Still, as emphasized by pseudo-Rashi, in the wounding of Saul a direct and ironic act of providence is demonstrated. The pride of the Benjaminites was their skill with the bow (cf. below on 12.2), but when God was against him Saul became a victim of that very weapon.

The verb *wayyāḥel* is not an irregular form of *ḥlh* I (Rudolph, 92), but a regular form of *ḥyl*, denoting 'to tremble from fear, fear' (cf. *Thesaurus* I, 1968, 132). On the motive of fear in the whole story cf. the following verse.

[4] Instead of elaborating on Saul's feelings as he faces imminent death, the narrator records his last words; these express very clearly the fear which grips him: not of death, which he welcomes, but of torture, which he can expect at the hands of the Philistines. In this context Saul's fear is an isolated element, introduced without antecedent or preparation; in the original context of I

Sam. fear is a dominant emotion, which motivates many of Saul's actions and predestines his defeat in battle. According to I Sam. 28.5, 'when Saul saw the army of the Philistines, he was afraid and his heart trembled greatly', and his dread is intensified by his meeting with the spirit of Samuel: 'Then Saul fell at once ... filled with fear because of the words of Samuel' (v. 20). The outcome of the war substantiated his fears: the Philistines, failing to take Saul alive, took vengeance on his body.

Saul's suicide on the battlefield (together with his armour-bearer) is unique in the Bible, suicide in general being quite rare (Ahithophel, II Sam. 17.23; Zimri, II Kings 16.18). It is described in rather neutral terms and the author's attitude to it is not spelled out. Is it another manifestation of fear, dominating Saul's actions up to his very last moment, or is it an act of heroism, demonstrating Saul's return, at his death, 'to himself'?

[5] The death of the armour-bearer, who is after all not a participant in the main drama, emphasizes the bitter end of the battle: all the courageous warriors are dead; not Saul alone, not only his sons, but even the anonymous armour-bearer.

[6] The majority of the changes introduced by the Chronicler into the first section are to be found in vv. 6–7. These are significant as much for what they add as for what they omit. On the one hand the Chronicler's version broadens the scope of the defeat: not only Saul and his sons died on that day but 'all his house died together'. Williamson, following Rudolph, stresses correctly that 'the dynastic overtones of house are unmistakable' (93). After the defeat on Mount Gilbo'a there remained no living claimant to the throne of Saul. On the other hand the same version narrows the scope of the defeat as well: the Chronicler omits from the summary not only the armour-bearer, but what is more significant: 'all his men'. The result is clear: the overthrow of the house of Saul is utter and complete – but this is all. The death of 'all his men' is passed over in silence.

[7] The same line of reworking is followed also in v. 7. The first change is seemingly syntactic: the Chronicler omits the subject of 'had fled', thus disrupting the perfect syntax and the nice balance of the verse. This is probably what prompted the English translations to reintroduce the subject: RSV 'the army'; NEB 'their army'; JPS 'they'. However, the imbalance in structure emphasizes the change in meaning: it is not the 'men of Israel' who fled the battlefield but Saul and his sons; they had both fled and died (so also Mosis, 23).

Another alteration in this verse is to be accounted for in the same way. After the defeat, the people of Israel leave their cities, not 'on the other side of the valley and those beyond the Jordan' (I Sam. 31.7), but only those 'who were in the valley'. Here the consequences of the war for Israel are again minimized.

This particular manner of editing, in which the original story is taken over almost verbatim, with the introduction of only minor changes, gives rise to some incongruous results. The testimony of v. 1, 'and the men of Israel fled before the Philistines', is left untouched. Yet the general tendency of the reworking is obvious. In the book of Samuel the defeat is the fate of the whole people and as such is the fulfillment of the word of God through Samuel: 'The Lord will give Israel also with you into the hand of the Philistines; and tomorrow you and your sons shall be with me; the Lord will give the army of Israel also into the hand of the Philistines' (I Sam. 28.19). In Chronicles not only is the broader context of Samuel's prophecy absent; even the event itself is construed differently. The downfall is limited to Saul and his house; for Israel the blow of defeat is softened. This general attitude will be repeated in vv. 13–14, which are added by the Chronicler. The version of Chronicles confronts the reader with several questions. How should we interpret 'and all his house died together' (v. 6) in view of the fact that the rule of Ish-bosheth, Saul's son, is described in II Sam. 2–4 and was undoubtedly known to the Chronicler and his audience? And what are we to make of the two versions of a genealogical list of the house of Saul, registered in Chronicles itself and continuing many generations after Saul's death (I Chron. 8.33–40; 9.39–44)?

We can confidently say that the Chronicler actually ignored the kingship of Ish-bosheth, as well as David's rule over Judah alone. From his point of view the kingship of David *over all Israel* was a direct and immediate outcome of the battle of Gilbo'a. As far as his historical conception is concerned the kingdom of Ish-bosheth and the partial kingdom of David never existed. The explicit description in II Sam. could not alter this concept. Here is one of the cases in which the Chronicler's sense of 'historical probability' prompts him to provide a diametrical alternative to his sources in the Former Prophets: not merely a change in the details of the event or an elegant silence, but a full and conscious alternative (cf. also I Chron. 29.24 as against I Kings 1.15). This is an important aspect of his historical-theological attitude: he is subordinate to the literal presentation of his sources, but at the same time acts with full freedom when impelled by his convictions regarding the correct historical course.

Some scholars would conclude from this attitude of the Chronicler that he would have had no interest in genealogical lists of the house of Saul; they would regard both of the above-mentioned versions as late additions to the book (cf. Rudolph, 95; Willi, 56). It seems, however, that such an approach fails to solve the basic incongruity found in Chronicles, and at the same time leaves without adequate explanation the motives of the late interpolator(s) who are supposed to have added the lists. It should be noted that the genealogical list continues the family tree of Saul through Merib-ba'al, the son of Jonathan, whom neither David nor the Chronicler regarded as a claimant to the throne of Saul (II Sam. 4.4, 9; 21.7). Thus the genealogy actually reflects the Chronicler's historiosophy. Although the house of Saul continued genetically, and even flourished, its fate as a dynasty was sealed on Mount Gilbo'a.

[8–12] The second section of the chapter describes what befell the mortal remains of Saul and his sons after their death. It opens with one chronological statement, 'on the morrow', ends with another, 'seven days', and is divided into two parts: vv. 8–10 describing the behaviour of the Philistines; vv. 11–12 the acts of the people of Jabesh-gilead. These verses are reworked in a manner reminiscent of the first part (above p. 222): while vv. 8–10 are left basically parallel to I Sam. 31.8–10 (for details cf. below), a greater measure of change is introduced into the following vv., 11–12.

The intense interest in the fate of the bodies after the battle, and the detailed description of their exposure, is peculiar to the tale of Saul's death. An explicit reference to this story and a similar interest combine in II Sam. 21.9–14, where the fate of the remaining heirs of Saul is recorded. These accounts demonstrate the custom of degrading the dead by hanging them in public and preventing their decent burial – atrocities attributed in both cases to non-Israelites (Philistines and Gibeonites). It seems that, while both incidents refer to the particular fate of the house of Saul, we can see reflected in them the customs of the time. In the book of Chronicles the description is, once again, isolated from its more general context as the material in II Sam. 21.9–14 is omitted, and the details of the narrative are far removed from the original. It should be stated, however, that the subjects of death, internment, rites and place of burial etc., do occupy the Chronicler's interest and recur in his book on various occasions (II Chron. 16.14; 21.19–20, etc.).

[8–9] Verse 8 is an exact parallel of I Sam. 31.8, but from v. 9 onward various changes are gradually introduced into the text. Although the subject and many of the details remain unchanged, the final picture drawn in Chronicles is not the same. The phrasing of v. 9 is somewhat unclear. In place of I Sam.'s precise and well phrased 'they cut off his head and stripped off his armour', the Chronicler has 'they stripped him and took his head and his armour'. There is no explicit reference to the cutting off of the head, but this can be inferred from 'they took his head'. If *nś'* is explained as intentionally used for 'cutting the head', following Gen. 40.19, this verb would then have a different meaning for each of its objects, a usage which defies sound grammar. (On the general decrease in the use of *krt* in Chronicles for purposes other than *krt bᵉrīt*, cf. S. Japhet, 'Interchanges of Verbal Roots in Parallel Texts in Chronicles', *HS* 28, 1987, 19–20.)

Another matter is the use of *'ªṣabbēhem* (RSV 'idols') as an epithet for the gods of the Philistines, found also in II Sam. 5.21. In general, the Chronicler did not use abusive terms for the heathen deities and did not scruple to call them by their names or by the generic term 'gods'. Cf. the following verse, in 'the temple of their gods' and 'the temple of Dagon', and also I Chron. 14.12 against II Sam. 5.21. One would have to assume that 'idols' was either taken by the Chronicler from his source without change, or is a later adaptation to Samuel.

The double act of the Philistines – cutting off the head and stripping the armour – has its parallel in the story of David and Goliath. David 'took the head of the Philistine and brought it to Jerusalem; but he put his armour in his tent' (I Sam. 17.54). The parallelism is both literary and historical, reflecting the customs of the day as well as the literary techniques of the author of Samuel.

[10] The divergence of the text from its parallel increases gradually. In I Sam. 31.10 the final fate of the head is not recorded. After the head and the armour have made the round of the land of the Philistines the armour is deposited in the temple of Ashtaroth, but the head is not mentioned again. It might be assumed that, when it began to decompose, the head was simply disposed of. On the other hand, the verse does relate the fate of the headless corpse: it was fastened to the wall of Beth-shan. Thus there is only a partial correspondence between I Sam. 31.9 and 10. The armour is mentioned in both, the head only in v. 9 and the corpse in v. 10. I Chron. 10.10 has a more precise correspondence to v. 9 and refers to the same two objects: the armour is deposited in the 'temple of their gods' and the head is fastened to the 'temple of Dagon'. Thus, Chronicles presents a fuller account for the head, but avoids any reference to the bodies. The consequences for the story are obvious: the head is not disposed of and there is no display of the dead bodies on the walls of Beth-shan; rather, the story would imply that the bodies were left in the battlefield.

Does the Chronicler make use of another tradition (P. R. Ackroyd, 'The Chronicler as Exegete', *JSOT* 2, 1977, 5)? Does his version reflect another, preferable *Vorlage* (Rudolph, 92)? The reconstruction suggested by Rudolph, introducing the reference to the head into I Sam. 31.9, although apparently plausible, is totally arbitrary. It presupposes a theoretical text which is not evidenced elsewhere and of which each of the existing versions is a corruption. The actual texts would support a simpler solution: that the version of Chronicles is a sophisticated reworking of his source, in which the external similarity of the parallel texts is outstanding. Thus:

ואת גויתו   תקעו בחומת בית שאן
ואת גלגלתו תקעו   בית דגון

The choice of the unusual *gulgalat* for 'head', which deviates from the prevalent usage of the story, is clearly motivated by its similarity to $g^e wiyyātō$, while *bēt-dāgōn* is chosen for its literal closeness to Beth-shan (a similarity obscured by the translation). That the new picture of Chronicles is a deliberate reworking is proved also from its continuation in v. 12.

[12] In relating the heroic acts of the people of Jabesh-gilead the Chronicler omits three elements, which considerably affect the story: 'and went all night', 'from the wall of Beth-shan', 'and burnt them there'. The courageous act of the people of Jabesh-gilead is greatly elaborated in Samuel. In a series of verbs, 'arose ... went ... took ... etc.', without one word wasted on emotions, the author depicts in full their decisiveness, valour and devotion. The version of Chronicles is much paler. The people of Jabesh-gilead did not have to walk all night, and did not steal the bodies from the midst of a hostile Philistine stronghold. They simply repaired to the deserted battlefield on Mount Gilbo'a and gathered the corpses that were lying there. The Chronicler also omits the burning of the bodies, although he leaves the burial of the bones unchanged. These two elements, the burning of the bodies followed by the burial of the bones, are peculiar to the present story; they should be distinguished from death by fire, prescribed as a mode of execution and mentioned in several instances (Gen. 38.24; Lev. 20.14; 21.9; Josh. 7.15, 25). The burning of the bodies seems to be connected with the act of exposure by hanging, the deeper meaning of which is not explicit here. The law of Deut. prescribes that 'his body (of the hanged man) shall not remain all night upon the tree ... for a hanged man is accursed by God, you shall not defile your land ...' (Deut. 21.22–23). It is probably this danger of defiling the land (with the hanged bodies) which led the people of Jabesh-gilead to burn the bodies before burial.

In the narrative of Chronicles all this aspect of the story is greatly understated. The bodies are not displayed on the walls of Beth-shan, and therefore all the details which follow are altered. The Chronicler spared Saul and his sons this ultimate degradation.

Another aspect of the change is the replacement of Beth-shan (*bēt-šᵉ'ān*) with 'the temple of Dagon' (*bēt-dāgōn*) – the name of a place with the name of a temple. Besides the literal similarity, there may have been a further motive as well. According to the information found in Joshua and Judges, Beth-shan was one of the cities of which the sons of Manasseh could not take possession during the period of the conquest; they probably became Israelite only under David (Josh. 17.11–12; Judg. 1.27; I Kings 4.12). In Chronicles these cities had always been pronouncedly Israelite and could not have been Canaanite or Philistine. The head of Saul is placed, therefore, not in Beth-shan, but in an unspecified 'temple of Dagon', somewhere in the land of the Philistines.

All in all, the Chronistic reworking of the story smoothes the rough edges and moderates the extremes: the scope of the defeat, the disgrace of Saul and his sons, the geographical expansion of the Philistines and the heroic acts of the people of Jabesh-gilead are mitigated by carefully chosen changes, while interference with the original is kept to a minimum.

[13–14] This addition, composed by the Chronicler, provides the story with a general context, historical as well as theological. In I Sam. 31 the theological meaning is derived from the broader narrative framework. Taken by itself, the story is completely secular: God is not mentioned even once, and the military events have their own inner logic. However, the story is to be read against the background of ch. 28 and Samuel's words to Saul: 'Therefore the Lord has done this thing to you this day' (I Sam. 28.18). The defeat is the fulfilment of a decree of God which was given before the events. The 'double causality' is remarkable: on the external, superficial level the results of the war are decided by human, natural factors; beneath the surface these are the work of the word of God, realized through these very human factors. In Chronicles, where ch. 10 stands in isolation from its original context, the theological framework is absent. The addition of vv. 13–14 provides the story with a proper religious framework, not as prophetic anticipation but as concluding remarks of evaluation. These verses state explicitly that: 1. The death of Saul was a direct act of God, 'therefore the Lord slew him'. 2. The death of Saul is a punishment for his sins, 'for his unfaithfulness', which took two forms: he did not keep the command of the Lord and he consulted a medium and not the Lord. 3. Directly upon Saul's death, God turned his kingdom over to David.

The historiosophical view expressed in these remarks is actually no different from that of I Sam. 28, which they come to replace. Most of what is said here is found, in a different order, in Samuel's words to Saul: 'the Lord has turned from you and become your enemy ... for the Lord has torn the kingdom out of your hand and given it to ... David. Because you did not obey the voice of the Lord ... therefore the Lord has done this thing to you' (I Sam. 28.16–18). The actual addition of the Chronicler is only in one detail, that Saul 'did not seek guidance from the Lord', which is an unavoidable conclusion from some of his basic suppositions. According to I Sam. 28.6 it was only out of absolute distress that Saul turned to a medium, for 'when Saul inquired of the Lord, the Lord did not answer him'. According to Chronicles it was Saul's free choice. The possibility that God would not answer his seekers is inconceivable for the Chronicler. His general rule is expressed very clearly: 'If you seek him, he will be found by you' (II Chron. 15.2). Moreover, the principle of exclusivity in the worship of God (cf. Japhet, *Ideology*, 216) dictates that the worship of the Lord and any other form of worship are incompatible and mutually exclusive. The very seeking of the medium is by definition forsaking the Lord. Therefore Saul's sin is termed *ma'al*, 'unfaithfulness'. The root, which is used mainly in a limited technical meaning in the Priestly literature (cf. J. Milgrom, 'The Concept of

Ma'al in the Bible and the Ancient Near East', *JAOS* 96, 1976, 236–47), takes on a very general meaning in Chron., covering the whole range of man's sins against God, equivalent to 'forsaking God'. It was not a specific, occasional sin which caused Saul's misfortune, but his whole practice, a reference to which is mentioned again in I Chron. 13.3. As a parallel to *ma'al*, the root *drš* (seek) is also used in this context, with its double meaning: the limited one, denoting 'inquiring, consulting etc.' (cf. *BDB*, 205), but also the more general one implying the whole range of worship, a meaning which is abundantly demonstrated in Chronicles and characteristic of it (cf. Driver, *Introduction*, 536).

The significance of vv. 13–14 lies as much in what they do not say as in what they say. The tendency revealed in the reworking of the story, to play down the role of the people and to concentrate on Saul and his house, is developed even further here; the people are omitted altogether. This is all in sharp contrast to the Chronicler's general practice of emphasizing the people's role, which we will encounter again and again elsewhere (cf. for the time being, Japhet, *Ideology*, 416–28). Here the concluding remarks deal only with Saul, his sins and his fate.

For the Chronicler, ch. 10 serves as a turning point: from pre-Davidic Israel, as symbolized in Saul, to David. We may even say: from pre-history to history. The pre-history remains in the background, and the Chronicler will refer to it whenever the case may require, but it is not of interest as a topic in itself. At the same time it should be noted that the scope of the transition is rather limited: from one dynasty to another; from Saul who failed, to David whose kingdom will be established for ever. In two other aspects of Israel's existence, there is no change at all. First, there is no transformation of the political system as such. It was not with David that kingship was introduced, but rather it is 'Saul's kingdom' which is turned over to David. Saul is rejected but not his kingdom. Secondly – no real change is implied in the historical-geographical situation of Israel. We shall refer more broadly to this matter in discussing 13.1–5.

To sum up: with introductions completed and uncertainties solved, the proper history of Israel now begins. From David onward, the central factor of Israel's political existence, its royal dynasty, is established – soon to be followed by the implementation of all the religious institutions. This is surely in one sense a point of beginning; yet, in the continuum which is the life of Israel, it is merely a turning point.

11   Then all Israel gathered together to David at Hebron, and said, 'Behold, we are your bone and flesh. [2] In times past, even when Saul was king, it was you that led out and brought in Israel; and the Lord your God said to you, "You shall be shepherd of my people Israel, and you shall be prince over my people Israel."' [3] So all the elders of Israel came to the king at Hebron; and David made a covenant with them at Hebron before the Lord, and they anointed David king over Israel, according to the word of the Lord by Samuel.

4 And David and all Israel went to Jerusalem, that is Jebus, where the Jebusites were, the inhabitants of the land. [5] The inhabitants of Jebus said to David, 'You will not come in here.' Nevertheless David took the stronghold of Zion, that is, the city of David. [6] David said, 'Whoever shall smite the Jebusites first shall be chief and commander.' And Joab the son of Zeruiah went up first, so he became chief. [7] And David dwelt in the stronghold; therefore it was called the city of David. [8] And he built the city round about from the Millo in complete circuit; and Joab repaired the rest of the city. [9] And David became greater and greater, for the Lord of hosts was with him.

10 Now these are the chiefs of David's mighty men, who gave him strong support in his kingdom, together with all Israel, to make him king, according to the word of the Lord concerning Israel. [11] This is an account of David's mighty men: Jashobeam, a Hachmonite, was chief of the three; he wielded his spear against three hundred whom he slew at one time.

12 And next to him among the three mighty men was Eleazar the son of Dodo, the Ahohite. [13] He was with David at Pas-dammim when the Philistines were gathered there for battle. There was a plot of ground full of barley, and the men fled from the Philistines. [14] But he took his stand in the midst of the plot, and defended it, and slew the Philistines; and the Lord saved them by a great victory.

15 Three of the thirty chief men went down to the rock to David at the cave of Adullam, when the army of Philistines was encamped in the valley of Rephaim. [16] David was then in the stronghold; and the garrison of the Philistines was then at Bethlehem. [17] And David said longingly, 'O that some one would give me water to drink from the well of Bethlehem which is by the gate!' [18] Then the three mighty men broke through the camp of the Philistines, and drew water out of the well of Bethlehem which was by the gate, and took and brought it to David. But David would not drink of it; he poured it out to the Lord, [19] and said, 'Far be it from me before my God that I should do this. Shall I drink the lifeblood of these men? For at the risk of their lives they brought it.' Therefore he would not drink it. These things did the three mighty men.

20 Now Abishai, the brother of Joab, was chief of the thirty. And he wielded his spear against three hundred men and slew them, and won a name beside the three. [21] He was the most renowned of the thirty, and became their commander; but he did not attain to the three.

22 And Benaiah the son of Jehoiada was a valiant man of Kabzeel, a doer of great deeds; he smote two ariels of Moab. He also went down and slew a lion in a pit on a day when snow had fallen. ²³ And he slew an Egyptian, a man of great stature, five cubits tall. The Egyptian had in his hand a spear like a weaver's beam; but Benaiah went down to him with a staff, and snatched the spear out of the Egyptian's hand, and slew him with his own spear. ²⁴ These things did Benaiah the son of Jehoiada, and won a name beside the three mighty men. ²⁵ He was renowned among the thirty, but he did not attain to the three. And David set him over his bodyguard.

26 The mighty men of the armies were Asahel the brother of Joab, Elhanan the son of Dodo of Bethlehem, ²⁷ Shammoth of Harod, Helez the Pelonite, ²⁸ Ira the son of Ikkesh of Tekoa, Abi-ezer of An-athoth, ²⁹ Sibbecai the Hushathite, Ilai the Ahohite, ³⁰ Maharai of Netophah, Heled the son of Baanah of Netophah, ³¹ Ithai the son of Ribai of Gibe-ah of the Benjaminites, Benaiah of Pirathon, ³²Hurai of the brooks of Gaash, Abiel the Arbathite, ³³ Azmaveth of Baharum, Eliahba of Sha-albon, ³⁴ Hashem the Gizonite, Jonathan the son of Shagee the Hararite, ³⁵ Ahiam the son of Sachar the Hararite, Eliphal the son of Ur, ³⁶ Hepher the Mecherathite, Ahijah the Pelonite, ³⁷ Hezro of Carmel, Naarai the son of Ezbai, ³⁸ Joel the brother of Nathan, Mibhar the son of Hagri, ³⁹ Zelek the Ammonite, Naharai of Be-eroth, the armour-bearer of Joab the son of Zeruiah, ⁴⁰ Ira the Ithrite, Gareb the Ithrite, ⁴¹ Uriah the Hittite, Zabad the son of Ahlai, ⁴² Adina the son of Shiza the Reubenite, a leader of the Reubenites, and thirty with him, ⁴³ Hanan the son of Maacah, and Joshaphat the Mithnite, ⁴⁴ Uzzia the Ashterathite, Shama and Je-iel the sons of Hotham the Aroerite, ⁴⁵ Jedia-el the son of Shimri, and Joha his brother, the Tizite, ⁴⁶ Eliel the Mahavite, and Jer-ibai, and Joshaviah, the sons of Elna-am, and Ithmah the Moabite, ⁴⁷ Eliel, and Obed, and Ja-asiel the Mezoba-ite.

A. Notes to MT

[1] ישבעם, probably ישבעל, cf. commentary; השלושים, Kethib השלושים, Qere השלישים, II Sam. 23.8, השלשי, probably השלשה; [20] ולא, read ולו with many MSS, Versions and II Sam.; [22] שני אריאל, cf. commentary, proposed שני בני אריאל ממואב or שני אראלי מואב; [27] הפלוני, probably הפלטי; [34] בני, dittography; [46] המחוים, probably המחנימי or המחני (RSV המחוי); [47] המצביה difficult, probably מצבה (RSV המצבאי).

B. Notes to RSV

[8] 'in complete circuit', Hebrew difficult, translation approximate; [11] 'a Hachmonite', MT 'the son of Hachmoni'; [14] 'he took his stand', MT 'they took their stand', cf. commentary; [20, 21] 'thirty', MT 'three', cf. commentary; [21] RSV omits the word בשנים (among the two) in conformity with II Sam.; [26] 'The mighty men of the army', Heb. 'the mighty men', cf. commentary.

C. Structure, sources and form

1. Chapters 11–12 form one cohesive and comprehensive literary unit, dedicated to a single subject: the enthronement of David. Its major aim is demonstrated in its structure as much as in its contents: to give expression to the unity of the people of

Israel at the enthronement of David, which is the fulfilment of God's word to Israel. In addition, these chapters stress the unity of the army and the greatness of David's military force at his accession.

The components of this unit were drawn from various sources and joined together by means of the Chronicler's editorial notes. Some of his sources are biblical and some are not, but all the material, whatever its provenance, underwent reworking and derives its meaning from its new context.

2. The organization of the material within the comprehensive literary unit is worthy of note. The material drawn from biblical sources appears first, arranged consecutively; following this, and again in sequence, the non-parallel material is presented. All this reflects the procedure evident on a more comprehensive scale, in the overall framework of I Chron. 10–29, where all the parallel material is found at the beginning, in chs. 10–21, and from ch. 22 onward there is a continuous unit peculiar to Chronicles.

The components of the unit are as follows:

1. The enthronement of David in Hebron (11.1–3//II Sam. 5.1–3);
2. Conquest of Jerusalem (11.4–9//II Sam. 5.6–10);
3. List of David's mighty men who came to Hebron and their exploits (11.10–41a//II Sam. 23.8–31; and 11.41b–47);
4. List of men that came to David at Ziklag (12.1–7 [Heb. 1–8]);
5. Men of Gad that came to David in the stronghold (12.8–15 [Heb. 9–16]);
6. Men of Judah and Benjamin that came to David in the stronghold (12.16–18 [Heb. 17–19]);
7. Men of Manasseh that came to Ziklag (12.19–22 [Heb. 20–23]);
8. Divisions of the armed troops who came to Hebron (12.23–38 [Heb. 24–39]);
9. The celebrations in Hebron (12.39–40 [Heb. 40–41]).

3. Although the sequence of the material is determined by its source, the section as a whole is structured with purpose and artistry (cf. also H. Williamson, '"We are yours, O David": The Setting and Purpose of I Chronicles XII 1–23', OTS 21, 1981, 164ff.). Its historical and narrative focus is a point in the present – the accession of David as king over all Israel. While making constant reference to this focal point, the various components of the unit are unfolded by means of a 'flashback' technique. The method of this 'flashback' is as follows: the starting point is in Hebron, with the enthronement of David and the list of mighty men 'who gave him strong support' (11.1–47); the story then moves backward, first to the near past – the men who joined David in Ziklag (12.1–7), and then to the further past – those who joined him in the stronghold (12.8–18). The story then follows the same thread forward again: through Ziklag (12.19–22) back to the present, to the 'divisions of the armed troops', again in Hebron (12.23–39). The account concludes where it originated, with the celebrations in Hebron (12.39–40). Along this route, backwards and forwards the link with the present is maintained through editorial notes in 11.10 and 12.23.

4. In the whole unit there is one passage which does not fit smoothly into the overall structure: the description of the conquest of Jerusalem (11.4–9). According to II Sam. 5.6–10 the conquest of Jerusalem was one in a series of events following David's accession. The transfer of the ark to Jerusalem takes place, therefore, only after an unspecified time, when David had completed his preparations (II Sam. 6). According to Chronicles the conquest of Jerusalem takes place as part of David's

royal accession rather than some time later. After relating the story of the conquest (11.4–9), the tale continues with a description of the circumstances and events of the enthronement, reaching its climax with the celebrations (12.39–40). Moreover, the transfer of the ark to Jerusalem follows directly upon the enthronement, with no interim period elapsing (I Chron. 13, cf. the commentary).

From a historical point of view such a sequence is impossible; there is no need to elaborate on the difficulties it raises. Jerusalem could not have been conquered and built during the very event of the enthronement, and even the Chronicler reiterates that David first reigned in Hebron for seven years (I Chron. 3.4; 29.27).

It seems that the question cannot be solved from a historical point of view, and even the principle of the 'pressure of the sources', which is indeed an important factor in the Chronistic historiography, is not adequate in this case. The question arises from the new structuring of the material, the work of the Chronicler himself, in which he is not bound by any source. He could, for example, have placed the conquest of Jerusalem after ch. 12, thus avoiding many of the historical–chronological problems. It would seem, then, that the Chronicler's theological motivation in this instance greatly outweighed not only historical considerations, but even his own literary structuring. He wished to present the conquest of Jerusalem as the first and foremost act of David the king, and in clear sequence to his accession. The bond between David and Jerusalem, already emphasized by the Deuteronomistic historiography, has thus become inalienable.

5. The literary unit of chs. 11–12 demonstrates a common feature of Chronicles: the formation of a new composition, with its specific literary structure and historical and theological views, by the use of existing materials which are transferred almost verbatim from a different original context. The inevitable result is the emergence of tensions between the overall meaning of the new context and certain details of the adopted material which were not fully adjusted to their new role. These tensions may be clarified and explained, especially when the sources are available, but they cannot be completely smoothed out.

6. The recognition that chs. 11–12, in spite of some inner tensions, form one unified composition, rules out the possibility that much of its material is the fruit of more or less wild accumulation by later redactors (Noth, *The Chronicler*, 34–5; Rudolph, 103ff.). The problem of the material peculiar to Chronicles should, then, be centred upon two questions: (*a*) What part of the material was taken from additional sources which the Chronicler had at his disposal, and what part did he write himself? (*b*) What is the nature and reliability of the assumed sources? Because of the structure of the two chapters, these questions are more urgent for ch. 12 than for ch. 11; we will deal separately with each.

7. Chapter 11 has two major sections, which are themselves composite:

(a) vv. 1–9:   1–3   The enthronement of David
               4–8   The conquest of Jerusalem and its rebuilding
               9   Conclusion
(b) vv. 10–47: 10   Heading
               11–25 The heroic acts of David's mighty men
               26–47 List of the mighty men.

8. Three literary genres are demonstrated in this chapter, in three originally independent sections: historical narration (vv. 1–9); short anecdotes of heroic deeds

(vv. 11–25); and a list (26–47). Each of these components has had a longer or shorter literary history. The individual anecdotes were probably first compiled into a collection and only then joined to the list of the mighty men, which was of a different, more official, origin. This sequence is already found in II Sam. 23 and was taken as a unit by the Chronicler, who added to it only the last part of the list, vv. 41b–47. The combination of this complex with the historical narration is peculiar to the present composition.

9. The problem of sources is relevant only to 11.41b–47, for which there exists quite a wide range of suggestions and considerations. II Sam. 23.24–39, from which the main body of the list is drawn, is most probably a list of 'the thirty', a title mentioned with the first name (23.24). The list contains thirty-one names, and concludes with the phrase: 'thirty-seven in all', this number being reached by the addition of the five warriors whose deeds are previously described to the listing of the names, from which one has probably dropped out. (For another possibility cf. the commentary on v. 26.) In Chronicles the unifying principle of the list is different. The reference to 'the thirty' is replaced by 'the mighty men of the army' (11.26), the numerical conclusion is omitted, the list is lengthened by an additional sixteen names, and in v. 42, after the second new name, there is a new heading: 'a leader of the Reubenites and thirty with him'.

What, then, is the source and the nature of the additional section? Scholarly opinion on the subject runs the whole gamut between two extremes. On one hand is the claim that vv. 41b–47 are not an 'addition' at all but the original continuation of II Sam. 23.39 which was lost in Samuel but preserved in Chronicles (Rothstein, 220, 241). The difficulty in accepting this view arises not only from the differences in the forms of registration in the two parts of the list (K. Elliger, 'Die Dreissig Helden Davids', *Kleine Schriften*, Munich 1966, 78; Williamson, 103) but mainly from the fact that the list in Samuel was most probably intended to be a list of 'thirty'. At the other extreme stands the claim that the list is a late composition, from the time of the second commonwealth, composed either by the Chronicler or by some later author, for specific, social objectives (Noth, *The Chronicler*, 136; Elliger, 'Dreissig Helden', 78, 'a pure invention of the Chronicler's'). As far as one can argue from a bare list of names, this claim is not supported by any element in the list. It does not contain any name which can be surely identified as late. Moreover, the origin of many of the mighty men listed here is in Transjordan, some of them being of non-Israelite origin – a fact which does not conform to certain norms of the community and would hardly be expected in a freely composed list. The only support for such a claim is the general argument that the existence of authentic sources, especially from as far back as David's time, is inconceivable for the time of the Chronicler. This argument is axiomatic in nature and forces the discussion into a vicious circle.

If the list is indeed ancient and was not an original continuation of II Sam. 23.39, then the only possible assumption is that the Chronicler did have an additional source from which this list, among others, was drawn (cf. further on I Chron. 27.1 ff.). Several considerations make such an assumption seem likely. (*a*) The institution of the 'thirty', established as far as we know by David, endured for a considerable time and is last heard of at the very end of David's reign (I Kings 1.7). It would be logical to assume that a military group of this sort would have undergone some changes through the years, with old members being replaced by new ones. This would undoubtedly result in a constant updating of the lists, and the existence of various

236   I CHRONICLES

versions of it. (b) The manner in which the names are registered in the additional section of the list is very similar, though not identical, to the main part. It is an enumeration of consecutive names, identified by their families and/or place of origin. (c) All the identifiable locations are east of the Jordan, meaning that the list has a common geographical denominator and was organized around a guiding principle. Moreover, such an 'eastern' group of warriors is very plausible, especially for David's reign. (d) In this part of the list, as much as in its main part, there are some warriors of non-Israelite origin (Moab – v. 46; Zoba – v. 47, RSV 'the Mezobaite'). All these considerations seem to support the view, expressed by several scholars (cf. *inter al.*, Rudolph, 101; Williamson, 104) that vv. 41b–47 form an additional list of mighty men who belonged to the thirty at one stage or another. Its absence from Samuel should be dealt with from the point of view of that book.

D. *Commentary*

[1–3] Appropriately enough, the reign of David opens with his accession, the first part of the description being taken, with very slight changes, from II Sam. 5.1–3. However, in spite of the literal similarity between the two texts, their import is different in many ways, because of their different literary and historical presuppositions.

According to II Sam. 5.1–3 the anointing of David as king over all Israel takes place after a period of seven years, during which David reigned over Judah alone. His accession over all Israel is a direct result of the assassination of Ish-bosheth, which left the northern tribes kingless. 'All the tribes of Israel' who came to David to Hebron are, therefore, the northern tribes, and the emphasis in their statement 'we are your bone and flesh' is understandable in the circumstances. They are, therefore, the ones with whom 'king David made a covenant ... at Hebron'. By contrast, in Chronicles the anointing of David is a totally new beginning, and there is a direct transition from the death of Saul (ch. 10) to the accession of David. There is no such thing, in Chronicles, as a partial kingship of David over Judah. The adjustment of the passage to its new context occasions several changes, most important of which is the change of 'all the tribes of Israel' to 'all Israel'.

The great emphasis put on the fact that the kingdom of David was from its very first day onwards a kingdom over all Israel has been rightly recognized by all those who have studied the book of Chronicles, although their interpretations vary (cf., *inter al.*, Wellhausen, 172ff.; von Rad, *Geschichtsbild*, 35; Rudolph, 97; Willi, 161; Williamson, *Israel*, 95; Japhet, *Ideology*, 267ff). It should be emphasized, however, that the significance of the change is not to be looked for in its negative aspect, namely in the omission of 'the tribes of Israel'. This phrase is found in Chronicles in the parallel sections (II Chron. 6.5//I Kings. 8.16; II Chron. 12.13//I Kings. 14.21; II Chron. 33.7// II Kings. 21.7), as well as in the non-parallel ones (I Chron. 27.16, 22; 29.6;

II Chron. 11.16). The import of the change is rather in its positive aspect, in stressing that the historical starting point for the kingdom of David is 'all Israel'.

Another result of the new context is the fact that it was not only the northern tribes who 'made a covenant' with David on the occasion in question, but all the tribes, including Judah. This view does not depend on terminology but rather on the historical context: until this point David had not been king at all.

From a literary point of view the passage in II Sam. 5.1–3 is intrinsically connected with various parts of the preceding narrative. David's stay at Saul's court, his military exploits at that time, and Samuel's saying that God was going to seek 'a man after his own heart ... to be prince over his people' (I Sam. 13.14 etc.), all hark back to earlier stages of the narrative. These inner literary ties lose their original points of reference in the narration of Chronicles, where the event is presented as a new beginning, and their message should be understood, as far as possible, from the new context.

At various junctures in this literary unit the Chronicler provides new points of reference in place of those which he has dismissed. First, a connection has already been established between the unit and the preceding chapter, with the concluding words of I Chron. 10.14: 'Therefore the Lord ... turned the kingdom over to David the son of Jesse.' Secondly, the Chronicler describes the kingdom as the fulfillment of God's word to Samuel and in v. 3 adds the note 'according to the word of the Lord by Samuel'. As the story unfolds, reference is made to these two points, integrating the accession of David into a historical and theological sequence. In v. 10 the Chronicler again mentions that making David king was 'according to the word of the Lord concerning Israel', and in 12.23 he repeats that all this took place in order 'to turn the kingdom of Saul over to him, according to the word of the Lord'. The words of v. 2, 'even when Saul was king it was you that led out and brought in Israel', take their meaning in Chronicles not from the stories of the book of Samuel (which are not included in Chronicles), but from those episodes which the Chronicler introduces into the story. In this new context all the heroic deeds of David's mighty men took place in the time of Saul (cf. the commentary), as did the events described in ch. 12.

However, the text still contains several points which are fully accounted for only in their original context, and were not fully adjusted to the new one. The words of the people 'we are your flesh and bone' seem rather an overstatement in the present context, and the title 'king' in v. 3 is premature. It was a proper title in II Sam. where David had been king over Judah for seven years, but is not here, before the anointing. Rudolph tries to solve the difficulty by suggesting that the text of Chronicles was originally different, i.e. 'to make him king' (*l^ehamlīkō*), and was later adjusted to Samuel. There is no basis for this assumption except in the understandable wish to make the Chronistic editing of Samuel as systematic as possible. Here, as in many other instances, it would seem rather that the Chronicler was not aware of any difficulty, and left the text as it was. The same is true of a gap found in the narrative of II Sam. 5, between vv. 1–2 and v. 3. Between the presentation of the proposition vv. 1–2 and the actual coming of 'all the elders of Israel' to Hebron (v. 3), an intermediate phrase which would describe David's reaction and acceptance is missing. This hiatus in II Sam. 5 is reproduced without change in Chronicles.

The words concluding the passage, 'according to the word of the Lord by Samuel', connecting the enthronement of David directly with the prophecy of Samuel, present nothing new from a theological point of view but only make more explicit what is already referred to in v. 2. The words of the people, 'and the Lord your God said to you', are given their full significance: it was the word of the Lord, through a prophet, to the king and to all Israel.

The accession of David is followed in II Sam. 5 by some chronological data regarding David and his rule (vv. 4–5), omitted in Chronicles. The omission is usually regarded as the work of the Chronicler, who wished to avoid the reference to the kingship of David over Judah alone (cf. for example Rudolph, 97). This generally accepted theory has now to be re-examined, in view of the absence of these verses from 4QSam. (cf. E. C. Ulrich, *The Qumran Text of Samuel and Josephus*, HSM 19, 1978, 60–2). The other possibility which must now be considered is whether the absence of these verses from I Chron. 11 is due to the textual form of the Chronicler's *Vorlage* rather than to his own editing. To answer this we should not restrict our considerations to the texts at present before us. II Samuel 5.5 is indeed absent from this context, but is found in Chronicles in another place: I Chron. 3.4. There it is a part of a longer passage, the beginning of which is taken from II Sam. 2–5 and the continuation from II Sam. 5.13ff. (cf. the commentary *ad loc.*). The description of the duration of David's reign in Hebron as 'seven years and six months' is peculiar to these verses (otherwise I Kings 2.11; I Chron. 29.27), and makes it clear that for I Chron. 3.4 the Chronicler made use of II Sam. 5.5, and even then omitted the reference there to a separate kingship of David over Judah. It would seem, therefore, that the omission of II Sam. 5.4–5 from the present context of I Chron. 11 is the work of the Chronicler and not the precise reproduction of a *Vorlage*. The absence of these verses from 4QSam. could be explained as an independent phenomenon, either textual or editorial, or as already influenced by the text of Chronicles.

[4–6] The description of the conquest of Jerusalem is parallel to II Sam. 5.6–8, but the differences are many. The story of II Sam. contains some of scholarship's most famous cruxes, which naturally yield a rich crop of interpretations. The main difficulties are found in II Sam. 5.8, in the meaning of *ṣinnōr* and the role of 'the lame and the blind'. In Chronicles these very details are absent from the parallel verse, and the difficult words of David are replaced by a simpler statement and by a reference to the deed of Joab. The description of the conquest in Chronicles is thus much clearer, but somewhat general. The question to be asked seems self-evident: what is the origin of these changes? Do they reflect lost portions of the story of II Sam., which need to be re-integrated, or an alternative tradition of the conquest drawn from a different source? Were they introduced into the story, as taken from II Sam. 5, by the Chronicler himself? If the changes are ascribed to the Chronicler, what were his motives? Did he omit the obscure details because he did not understand them properly, or was it because he understood them all too well and was unwilling to accept their views?

A careful comparison of the parallel texts will show how the method followed in the omission of the various elements from the text demonstrates one form of editing characteristic of the Chronicler: a strict adherence to the literal sequence of the source, the transference of certain parts verbatim or with only minor changes, and the complete omission of other elements along the way. The following parts of the text are adopted literally, or almost so, from II Sam. 5.6ff., with no change in their sequence: 'and David ... went to Jerusalem ... where the Jebusites were, the inhabitants of the land. (They) said to David: You will not come here. Nevertheless David took the stronghold of Zion, that is the city of David. David said: whoever shall smite the Jebusites ... And David dwelt in the stronghold' (the literal similarity of the parallels is somewhat lost in the translation).

The characteristic method and the essential parallelism support the view that the changes, and especially the omissions, are the work of the Chronicler. However, because of the obscurity of his source in II Sam., it is uncertain whether the Chronicler's motive was only a wish to clarify a difficult story, or a more polemical stand *vis à vis* his source. A case in point is the complete omission from Chronicles of 'the lame and the blind', although in II Sam. 5.6 their appearance does not seem to raise difficulties (cf. lately, G. Brunet, 'Les Aveugles et Boiteux Jébusites', *VTS* 30, 1979, 65–72; R. Murray, 'The Origin of the Aramaic *'ir*, Angel', *Orientalia* 53, 1984, 312).

The story in Chronicles opens with 'And David and all Israel went to Jerusalem', a divergence from II Sam. 5.6, which has 'And the king and his men went to Jerusalem'. This change has rightly been emphasized by all commentators on Chronicles, and its significance relates to the two components of the statement. On the one hand it is stressed that David was king over all Israel and acted on behalf of all the people in the conquest of Jerusalem. On the other hand there is a reflection on the status of Jerusalem: its conquest is not a limited military foray with a small group of warriors, but concerns the people as a whole.

There is probably another point to the change. 'David and his men' is a very common phrase in the book of Samuel (*inter al.*, I Sam. 18.27; 23.2, 3, 8, etc.), and is almost a technical term. It reflects a certain reality of Saul's time and points very clearly to the origin of David's strength as chieftain of a military group. It is possible that this phrase reflects a historical reality which continued into the reign of David over all Israel until his rule was fully consolidated. Its appearance in II Sam. 5.6 and 5.21 could, therefore, reflect authentic circumstances. In both of his parallel passages the Chronicler has changed the wording; indeed, the phrase 'David and his men' is absent altogether from Chronicles. The reality reflected by the phrase is thus ignored, and an alternative view of Saul's times is presented in ch. 12.

In II Sam. 5.6 the inhabitants of Jerusalem are called 'the Jebusites, the inhabitants of the land'. Though the Chronicler preserves these two definitions, he adds two more. He identifies Jerusalem as 'Jebus' (v. 4), and defines those who opposed David as 'the inhabitants of Jebus' (v. 5). The importance of these additions is in the clear-cut definition of the extension of the Jebusites: they are not 'the inhabitants of the land' who also dwell, among other places, in Jerusalem – as is clearly the case in II Sam. – but they are only 'the inhabitants of Jebus', that is, Jerusalem. This limitation is a kind of compromise between the Chronicler's view of the ethnic population of the land at the beginning of David's reign (cf. further on 13.1–5) and the firmly established tradition that Jerusalem was conquered by David from the Jebusites.

The identification of Jerusalem as Jebus is found in a different order in Judg. 9.10 and Josh. 18.28. Whether the identification is historically valid or the result of a misunderstanding (cf. J. M. Miller, 'Jebus and Jerusalem; A Case of Mistaken Identity', *ZDPV* 90, 1974, 115–27) is irrelevant for the Chronicler. For him this is already an accepted tradition, which he passes on.

Of the conquered city only 'the stronghold of Zion' is explicitly mentioned (v. 5) and is later called 'the city of David'. In the course of history the name 'Zion' became one of the poetical epithets of Jerusalem, but in the Chronistic historiography, as in the Deuteronomistic literature in general, it is hardly used. It is found in Chronicles only once more, in II Chron. 5.2, which is parallel to I Kings 8.1.

[6] This verse deviates greatly from its parallel in II Sam. 5.8. David's words are different, and at the end there is a reference to Joab's role in the conquest of Jerusalem. Through this alteration, and the addition of v. 8b, the Chronicler makes Joab a major figure in the events concerning the conquest and rebuilding of Jerusalem. It is probable that the allusion to Joab's being 'chief' is provided in view of the succeeding list of 'the chiefs of David's mighty men', from which Joab is missing. His absence from the original context in II Sam. 23 was probably less conspicuous, as the list was placed at

the end of David's reign, after the multi-faceted character of Joab had received much attention. In Chronicles, where the list of the 'mighty men' is found at the beginning of David's reign, Joab's absence is conspicuous indeed. His role in the conquest of Jerusalem fills the gap and explains his position as 'commander'.

One should also note the twice-repeated pun based on the four-fold repetition of $r\bar{o}'\check{s}$: 'David said: whoever shall smite the Jebusite first ($b\bar{a}ri'\check{s}\bar{o}n\bar{a}h$) shall be chief ($r\bar{o}'\check{s}$); Joab ... went first ($b\bar{a}ri'\check{s}\bar{o}n\bar{a}h$) so he became chief ($r\bar{o}'\check{s}$).' Joab is, clearly, a chief among chiefs.

The historical significance of the conquest of Jerusalem, political and religious, was given its classic expression by A. Alt ('Jerusalems Aufstieg', *KS* III, 243–57) and elaborated by many (lately: J. W. Flannagan, 'The Relocation of the Davidic Capital', *JAAR* 47, 1979, 223–44). The geographical and military aspects of the conquest have also received much attention (cf. the commentaries on Samuel and elsewhere). In the context of Chronicles the conquest of Jerusalem, together with the accession of David, provides a turning point for the history of Israel: from various incomplete beginnings through a process of maturing to a fully-fledged political entity. The religious institutions, dependent for full existence on Jerusalem, will very soon take on complete form. (On the historical and literary difficulties which result from the Chronicler's placement of the conquest, cf. above, pp. 233–4).

[7–9] These are basically parallel to II Sam. 5.9–10 and relate the steps taken by David after the conquest: the establishing of his residence in the stronghold, and the rebuilding of the city. The establishment of David in Jerusalem was the beginning of a gradual consolidation of his strength, for 'the Lord of hosts was with him'.

There are, however, a few changes. From the linguistic point of view mention should be made of the word $m^e\bar{s}\bar{a}d$, which in v. 7 replaces the more common $m^e\bar{s}\bar{u}d\bar{a}h$ (which was left in vv. 5 and 16). $m^e\bar{s}\bar{a}d$ is probably an Aramaism, found only in Chronicles (cf. I Chron. 12.3, 16).

The naming of the city is attributed in II Sam. 5.9 to David, while in Chronicles the form is impersonal – a passive verb in the translation. Is this merely a linguistic-stylistic alteration of the Chronicler, or his *Vorlage*, to a more common aetiological formula, or does the impersonal phrasing reflect a different understanding of the renaming, not by David but as a result of a historical process?

[8] The rebuilding of the city is described in Chronicles in more detail than in II Sam. 5. The first change: 'and he built the city' ($wayyiben\ h\bar{a}'\hat{i}r$) in place of 'and David built' ($wayyiben\ d\bar{a}wid$) is also found in 4QSam. (Ulrich, 70), and probably reflects a different, preferable, *Vorlage*. The phrase $min\ hammill\bar{o}'\ w^e'ad\ hass\bar{a}b\hat{i}b$ (translated 'from the Millo in complete circuit') is difficult. On the one hand it is a unique appearance of $s\bar{a}b\hat{i}b$ ('around') as a

noun, but on the other hand the formula *min* ... '*ad* ('from ... to') is common
in geographical designations (cf. M. Saebø, 'Grenzbeschreibung und Land-
ideal im Alten Testament', *ZDPV* 90, 1974, 17ff.). It would seem that the
intention of the phrase is to describe the building of the city 'from the Millo
outward' (as opposed to 'from the Millo inward').

Another detail is the added reference to Joab's deeds. Attention has
already been paid to the unusual use of the verb *ḥyh* in reference to a city
(translated 'repaired'), and Neh. 4.2 [Heb 3.34] has been cited to confirm this
use. The appearance of *rp'* in the context of building belongs to the same
semantic field (I Kings 18.30, also translated 'repaired'). Joab's deeds therefore refer to the city and not to its inhabitants.

It is difficult to say if the varying details of the building of the city
represent a different tradition or were introduced by the Chronicler. On one
hand there is nothing specifically 'Chronistic' in these additions, and the
assumption of a different *Vorlage* for v. 8 may provide an excellent explanation for the Chronistic additions in v. 6 (cf. above). On the other hand, an
omission of these data from II Sam. 5 would be difficult to explain. Furthermore, there is an emphasized tendency in Chronicles to allude to the king's
officers and describe them as cooperating with the king and helping him in
his enterprises (cf. Japhet, *Ideology*, 417 ff.). The reference to Joab could be
explained in this way, and as a Chronistic continuation of v. 6.

Verse. 9 is taken over from II Sam. 5.10, with its solemn language,
preserving even the title 'Lord of hosts' for God, which is retained in
Chronicles in two more places, omitted in three others, and never used in the
specific Chronistic texts (cf. Japhet, *Ideology*, 24–5).

[10–47] Except for v. 10, which serves as a heading and determines the
place of this section in its context, and vv. 41b–47, whose origin was discussed
above (pp. 235–6), the whole section is taken over from II Sam. 23.8–39.

In II Sam. 23 the section forms part of an appendix to the history of David,
and stands isolated from what precedes (22.1–23.7) as well as from what
follows (II Sam. 24). Moreover, there is no intrinsic link between this section
and the main narrative of Samuel, a connection which could have clarified
the exact historical provenance of its data. The first exploits of the 'mighty
men' have the pressure of the Philistines and their domination over Israel as
their background (II Sam. 23.16//I Chron. 11.16). The encounters of David
with the Philistines could be ascribed on the one hand to the time of Saul
(I Sam. 18.27; 19.8; 23.1–5), and on the other hand to the period immediately
following his enthronement over all Israel (II Sam. 5.17//I Chron. 14.8). It
seems that as long as David was king over Judah alone there were no military
clashes with the Philistines, who probably took a favourable view of the
antagonism between Judah and the kingdom of Ish-bosheth. The second part
of the anecdotes, the protagonist of which is Benaiah, is completely detached

from any Philistine context and could have happened at any time during David's reign (cf. below, on vv. 22–25)

In the book of Chronicles the context of the section is very well defined: it is the list of mighty men who came to Hebron to make David king. All the heroic deeds of David's mighty men should consequently be thought of as belonging to an earlier time, the reign of Saul. This however, is not the unintentional result of a literary *faux-pas*, but rather an expression of a different historical view (cf. further on v. 10).

The original three-fold literary structure of the section is clear:

(*a*) The 'three' – the names and acts of each of the three warriors (II Sam. 23.8–12) and the acts of 'the three' as a group (II Sam. 23.13–17).

(*b*) The exploits of two more warriors of special status (II Sam. 23.18–23).

(*c*) A list of all the mighty men, without reference to their deeds (II Sam. 23.24–39).

In Chronicles, this basic structure is retained, but with two changes:

(*a*) Because of a textual corruption two of the anecdotes become one. The heroic deed of the second warrior, Eleazar the son of Dodo, and the name of the third warrior, Shammah the son of Agee, have been dropped from the text. Thus the act of the latter is now attributed to the former. The result for the structure of the section is a more balanced composition: one group of two heroes (Jashobeam and Eleazar) at the beginning, and a second group of two heroes (Abishai and Benaiah) at the end. However, the allusion to 'the three mighty men' (I Chron. 11.12) and the reference to the three as a group (vv. 15ff.) betray the original structure.

(*b*) The list of the mighty men is longer, because of the addition of vv. 41b–47, but this does not effect the literary structure.

[10] The new heading of the section is coined to comply with the Chronicler's concepts and style. The mighty men listed here are described as those who helped David 'to make him king'. But they do not act on their own initiative; rather, it is 'together with all Israel' and in order to fulfil 'the word of the Lord concerning Israel'.

The verse is connected to v. 2 on one hand and to 12.1 on the other. According to v. 2, 'even when Saul was king' the word of God to David was 'you shall be prince over my people Israel'. This divine dictum was the turning point which determined David's fate; from that point on the king-ship was his: it was only Saul who prevented him from realizing it. As is explicitly expressed in 12.1, in those days David was 'as yet held back because of Saul son of Kish' (translated differently by RSV). Therefore all the acts of the mighty men, who supported David and fought at his side, took place at the time of Saul, when David was the 'king designate', but not yet in fact.

[11] The original heading in II Sam. 23.8 'these are the names' is mechani-

cally changed to 'these are the account' (*mispar*) preserving the plural of 'these' before the singular noun (the translation makes the necessary grammatical adjustment). *mispār* ('account') is a common element in the Chronicler's vocabulary (over 25 times), while the formula 'these are the names' is omitted in several places (I Chron. 1.29, 35, 51) and preserved in a few others (I Chron. 6.2; 14.4).

In II Sam. 23.8, the name of the first warrior is 'Josheb-basshebeth Tachemoni' (RSV for the last component 'a Tachemonite'), but 'Jashobeam the son of Hachmoni' (RSV 'a Hachmonite') in Chronicles. It is generally accepted that the version of Samuel is corrupt, and Wellhausen's famous conjecture provides the basis for the evolution of the name and the patronym. The original was, accordingly, Ish-ba'al (*yišba 'al*), also evidenced for this period by I Chron. 8.33. In line with the general editing of Samuel, Ishba'al was changed to Ish-bosheth the Hachmonite, which through a dittography of the *beth* and the change of *he* to *taw* became in II Sam. 23.8 *yōšēb bašebet tahk'mōnī*. In Chronicles, through a change of one letter, Ishba'al became Jashobeam.

Some of David's mighty men are listed again in I Chron. 27.2–15. The first mentioned there is Jashobeam the son of Zabdiel. It is probable that his full name was originally Ishba'al, the son of Zabdiel, the Hachmonite (cf. also the name 'Hachmonite' in I Chron. 27.32).

The three: Heb. 'the thirty' or 'the captain' alternatively. The confusion between the 'three' and the 'thirty' runs throughout this chapter. There are repeated occurrences of *Kethib* and *Qere*, differences between II Sam. 23 and I Chron. 11, variations among the ancient Versions, and even cases of a straightforward text nevertheless amended by the commentators. The most generally accepted views for the verse are either the *Kethib* of Chronicles, 'the thirty', or 'the three' (so RSV).

To Jashobeam is ascribed the act of slaying three hundred at one time. Some commentators would regard Samuel's 'eight hundred' as more original, since 'three hundred' is the number of slain ascribed in v. 20 to Abishai, who was probably lower in rank than 'the chief of the three/thirty'.

[12–14] In II Sam. the second warrior is 'Eleazar the son of Dodo son of Ahohi', while here his name is 'Eleazar the son of Dodo the Ahohite'. The difference is formal only; it is to be found in other instances as well, and is not always reflected in the translation. In many instances the formula 'son of' is used generically, referring to the person's family rather than a patronym.

The deed which was originally that of Shamma the son of Agee is here ascribed to Eleazar (cf. above p. 243). In place of the obscure *behār'pām* (RSV 'they defied') the location of the fight is given, Pas Dammim. This is probably the more original reading, referring to the same place called Ephes-dammim in II Sam. 17.1, the locus of the battle between David and the Philistine (differently Willi, 151–2).

The exact circumstances of the deed are not clear. The background is represented in three elements: the Philistines gathered for battle, the plot of ground full of barley, the men fleeing from the Philistines. Since the actual heroic deed was in defending the plot, the background could be either an attempt by the Philistines to pillage the crops, or a battle in exceptionally difficult circumstances.

The meaning of the alteration from lentils to barley, or *vice versa*, is no longer clear. It may be a simple change from a rarer to a more common word, but this cannot be proved.

In v. 14 the verbs are in the plural – in contrast to the singular in II Sam. Since the change is executed consistently, this must be more than a textual version (as assumed by RSV, which adjusts the translation accordingly). In Chronicles the story is understood differently, with the deed performed by more persons; perhaps with David (v. 13)?

[15–19] This section, relating the exploits of 'the three', parallels II Sam. 23. 13–17, with only slight changes. The details of the incident are not all consistent; the difficulty lies in vv. 15–16, which describe a complicated military setting. According to v. 15 David is staying 'at the cave of Adullam', but according to v. 16 he is 'in the stronghold'. The army of the Philistines is first described as encamped in the valley of Rephaim, but immediately thereafter as at Bethlehem. 'The stronghold' and 'the valley of Rephaim' as the respective locations of the two armies are confirmed in II Sam. 5.17–18. The connection between this setting and the cave of Adullam is, however, problematical. Another difficulty is the 'going down' of the mighty men to David, which implies that they were not present at David's camp from the start.

These difficulties seem to indicate that v. 15a preserves the torso of an originally independent account, which was later combined with the story of the well at Bethlehem. The protagonists of both stories were 'the three'. While the first story related how these brave men joined David when he was still 'in the cave of Adullam' by 'climbing down the rock', the second, of which the beginning was lost, told how these three made their way through the heavy Philistine guard at Bethlehem to bring David water from the well 'by the gate'. It is possible that the word *rō'š* (v. 15), which is difficult in the present context (a difficulty disguised by the RSV translation – 'chief men'), is a remnant of the conjectured textual process. The plural 'these things' at the end of v. 19 points in the same direction.

If my reconstruction is correct, the first deed is evidently from the days of David as a commander of a band, wandering in the wilderness of Judah (cf. II Sam. 22.1); the second may be connected with the first years of David's reign, when the Philistines' domination reached its peak, with their garrison stationed deep in the area of Judah, at Bethlehem. It could be connected, not

just geographically but also historically, with the battle described in II Sam.
5.17ff. (I Chron. 14.8ff.).

Verse 19 is difficult in its two versions. In Samuel, the word *'ešteh* ('shall I
drink'), attested both in Chronicles and by LXX Sam. and supplied by RSV)
is missing from the MT of II Sam. 23.17. In Chronicles the original word
hahōlᵉkīm, 'who went', was changed, probably unintentionally, to *hā'ēlleh*,
'these', resulting in the disintegration of the phrase 'who went at the risk of
their lives' and the retaining of 'in their lives' alone. This is what necessitated
the explanation 'for at the risk of their lives they brought it', added quite
reasonably by the Chronicler or by someone who preceded him.

The water which is brought from the well of Bethlehem is likened to the
men's blood, for these people risked their lives in order to get it. Since 'the
blood is the life', the drinking of the water would be equivalent to drinking
the men's blood.

[20–21] These verses describe the deeds of Abshai, the brother of Joab,
and are parallel to II Sam. 23. 18–19. In v. 20, as elsewhere throughout
Chronicles, MT has Abshai for Abishai (cf. also I Chron. 2.16; 18.12; 19.11,
15).

The omission of 'the son of Zeruiah' is probably a matter of style, an
example of the Chronicler's economy of expression and his inclination to
avoid unnecessary details.

The deed of Abshai is identical with that of Jashobeam – the slaying of
three hundred at one time. His exact position remains unclear, because of an
obvious contradiction in the Hebrew text. According to v. 20 he was 'the
chief of the three', while according to v. 21 'he was the most renowned of the
three ... but he did not attain to the three'. There have been two ways of
interpreting these inconsistencies. One follows v. 25, which reads 'he was
renowned among the thirty' and amends 'three' to 'thirty' in both v. 20
and v. 21a (thus RSV). Accordingly, Abshai and Benaiah occupied a special
position among David's mighty men: they were awarded distinction among
the 'thirty' but were not exalted to the 'three'. The weakness of this interpretation lies in the need to introduce into the text an emendation which
would not otherwise be indicated. The second interpretation is based on the
assumption that there was more than one group of 'three' in David's military
organization, and that Abshai was the chief of the second group; although
much admired by his peers, he did not reach the status of the first 'three'.
The advantage of this interpretation – the historical basis of which is
probable although not explicitly attested – is its foundation in the biblical text
as it stands.

The word *baššᵉnayim* ('among the two') in the MT of v. 21 (omitted by
RSV) may point to some kind of relationship between the two warriors,
stressing Abshai's superiority to Benaiah.

[22–25] These verses introduce Benaiah in great detail. His full pedigree is given and three of his deeds are recorded; in addition there is the paragraph's concluding statement: 'And David set him over his bodyguard'. It is evident that whatever may have been the military rank and renown of the various other personages, the central figure for the compiler of the section was Benaiah, the son of Jehoiada. This could provide a point of departure for determining the time of compilation. It seems that Benaiah rose to prominence in the late part of David's reign. He is first mentioned in II Sam. 8.18 as the commander of the Cherethites and Pelethites; although not explicitly stated, it is reasonable to assume that with this military group he participated in the stormy events of David's reign (II Sam. 15.18; 20.7). His main role is in the accession of Solomon, after which he is appointed as Solomon's chief commander, replacing Joab (I Kings 1.8, 26, 32, 36, 38, 44; 2.35). The accounts of his exploits, which make no allusion to the pressure of the Philistines, seem to point in the same direction. It is possible, then, that the compilation was made in Solomon's time; this conjecture would also account for the complete absence of Joab from the present context.

Benaiah is described as *ben 'iš ḥayil*, which is probably a conflation of *'iš ḥayēl* and *ben ḥayil*. The title shows him to be a man of substance and the head of a family. A reference to his more personal qualities is found in the unique phrase 'a doer of great deeds'. His place of origin is also mentioned: Kabzeel, one of the Judaean towns in the Negev, on the border of Edom (Josh. 15.21).

Three exemplary deeds are ascribed to Benaiah. The first is the smiting of the two ariels of Moab (v. 22bα). This is a famous crux; while 'Ariel' appears to be a proper name (attested also in Ezra 8.16), the construct state and especially the number 'two' make the interpretation difficult. This is, however, the basis of the famous conjecture which assumes a double dittography and reconstructs the original *'ēt šᵉnē [bᵉnē] 'ᵃrī'ēl [mim]mō'āb* (the first of these dittographies is supported by LXX, cf. Driver, *Samuel*, 368). Another path taken by exegesis is the interpretation of 'ariel' as a common noun, meaning warrior (cf. Baumgartner, 80; Thesaurus, 270). This interpretation too implies a textual emendation, but less extensive: *'ᵉr'elē mō'āb*.

The story of the slaying of the lion, different from all the others, is closest to the feats of Samson. It is not connected with the wars of Israel and has no public repercussions; it is simply an act of valour which illustrates Benaiah's personal courage and daring.

The struggle with the Egyptian is similar in some of its features to the battle of David and Goliath (I Sam. 17), a likeness accentuated by the small additions found in its version in Chronicles. The original point of similarity is the fact that Benaiah opens the combat by confronting his already superior enemy with a much inferior weapon, a staff against a spear, and in the end overcomes his opponent with his own weapon. In Chronicles two more points appear: the measure of the Egyptian, 'five cubits tall', and the likeness of his spear to 'a weaver's beam' (cf. I Sam. 17.4, 7). (For the phenomenon of literary assimilation see Y. Zakovitch, 'Assimilation in Biblical Narrative', in J. H. Tigay, ed., *Empirical Models for Biblical Criticism*, Philadelphia 1985, 175–96.)

[24–25] These verses sum up Benaiah's deeds and position, more elaborately than the similar conclusion for Abshai. The final statement is peculiar to Benaiah.

[26–47] The list of David's mighty men opens with the heading *weᵍibbōrē hahᵃyālīm*: the mighty men. This is an example of Late Biblical usage which forms the plural of a construct phrase by rendering both of its components in the plural (i.e. *gibbōrē hahᵃyālīm* instead of *gibbōrē hahayīl*, cf. Kropat, 11). This linguistic peculiarity is not taken into account by RSV, in which the *nomen rectum hahᵃyālīm* is translated independently with the additional phrase 'of the army'.

In II Sam. 23.24 the heading 'of the thirty' appears after the name of Asahel. This has led some scholars to assume that Asahel did not belong to the thirty but to the group of warriors whose deeds were recorded previously, but that the account of his feats dropped from the text. If the list indeed begins after Asahel, it contains exactly thirty names (Elliger, 'Dreissig Helden', 76–7; Rudolph, 99–100). This view, however, is contradicted by the explicit conclusion of II Sam. 23.39, 'thirty-seven in all', which signifies that the original list of the 'thirty' contained more than thirty – either thirty-one or thirty-two, depending on the place of Asahel. This number is in fact obtained if we add to each version of the list one name that dropped out: Elika of Harod (II Sam. 23.25), who is absent from Chronicles, and Hefer the Mecherathite (I Chron. 11.36), who is absent from Samuel. Moreover, Asahel's place in the list is supported by the version of I Chron. 27.7, a different and independent testimony of the same list (cf. below, pp. 469ff). Since Asahel was killed during the struggle between David and Ish-bosheth (II Sam. 2.23), his inclusion in the list provides a kind of a chronological *terminus a quo* for the establishment – or at least the inception – of the 'thirty'. It may also explain the number: the list probably contains the names of men who were no longer members of the 'thirty'.

In Chronicles the whole framework of 'thirty' is abolished. The list is defined as 'the mighty men', a definition which is not necessarily identical with the 'thirty' (II Sam. 10.7; 16.6; 20.7; I Kings 1.8, 10; I Chron. 28.1); only in the addition to the list, in I Chron. 11.42, is there again a reference to 'thirty': 'Adina ... and thirty with him'.

2. It has been demonstrated by various scholars that the two versions of the list represent one tradition, with each of the versions undergoing textual

corruption in the process of transmission. Some of these corruptions can be recovered and the original reconstructed, while in other cases no decision can be made and the two different versions must remain as they are.

3. One of the outstanding features of the list is the lack of uniformity in the registration of the names, which are recorded according to the following formulas: 1. X the Y (Y = gentilic or a place name); 2. X the son of Y the Z (Z = gentilic or a place name); 3. X from Y (place name); 4. X son of Y from Z (place name); 5. X the son of Y; 6. X brother of Y.

One of the formulas peculiar to Chronicles is 'X the son of Y'. In three cases it replaces a different form in Samuel (I Chron. 11.35, 37, 38); it is found three times in the additional section (I Chron. 11.41, 43, 45) and once in the plural (I Chron. 11.46).

Another peculiar feature, unique to the additional section, is the conjunction of several names by 'and', indicating a family relationship: members of one family (v. 43); sons of one father (v. 44b, 46a) and brothers (v. 45). The kinship related in v. 47 is not clear.

[27] Shammoth of Harod (MT 'the Harorite'); II Sam. 23.25 Shammah of Harod; I Chron. 27.8 Shamhuth the Izrahite: the unusual name 'Shamhuth' can be interpreted as a conflation of the other two, Shammah and Shammoth. It is also possible, however, that the longer name is the original, of which each of the others is a shortened form. The man is described as 'the Harorite' in Chronicles and as 'the Harodite' in II Sam. RSV observes the accepted preference for the latter version. The following name in II Sam. 23.25, Elika the Harodite, has dropped from the list in Chronicles, and this omission could be easily explained as homoioteleuton if Shammoth, too, was 'the Harodite'. On the gentilic 'the Izrahite' cf. I Chron. 27.8.

Helez the Pelonite: so also in I Chron. 27.10; in II Sam. 23.26 the Paltite. The orthographic transition from one form to the other is simple. The name Pelet and its gentilic Paltite are quite common in the Bible, while 'Pelonite' is peculiar to the list in Chronicles, here and in v. 36 (also in I Chron. 27.10). Most commentators regard 'the Pelonite' as a corruption (NEB, however, renders: 'of an unknown place'!).

[29] Sibbecai the Hushathite; II Sam. 23.27 Mebunnai the Hushathite; I Chron. 27.11 Sibbecai: since Mebunnai is unique and since 'Sibbecai the Hushathite' is also mentioned in II Sam. 21.18//I Chron. 20.4 as one of David's warriors, the latter name is preferred by many. Now, however, a recently discovered seal with the name *mbn* testifies both to the existence of the name and to its antiquity (cf. A. Zeron, 'The Seal M-B-N and the list of David's Heroes', *Tel-Aviv* 6, 1979, 156–7). One wonders whether the process was not in the opposite direction: through the influence of II Sam. 21.18 the more rare Mebunnai was changed to Sibbecai.

Ilai; II Sam. 23.28 Zalmon: the transition between the names is not self-evident. Rudolph suggests that an intermediate form 'Zilai', a short form of Zalmon, was corrupted to 'Ilai'.

[30] Heled; in I Chron. 27.15 Heldai: these forms are preferable to Heleb, of II Sam. 23.29.

[32] Hurai; II Sam. 23.30 Hiddai: the two names are unique; either of them could have originated in the other.

Abiel – called in II Sam. 23.31 Abialbon: the name is unusual but not impossible. However, Wellhausen's proposal that the original name was 'Abi-ba'al' is rather attractive (Wellhausen, *Samuel*, 215). Abi-el would reflect the editorial practice, found elsewhere as well, of replacing the theophoric element 'ba'al' with some other element, theophoric or otherwise, in this case (cf. also I Chron. 14.7 Beeliada, as against II Sam. 5.16 Eliada). Since the Chronicler himself is not sensitive to the use of 'ba'al', the change was probably already found in his *Vorlage*. The name 'Abialbon' in II Sam. could then be explained as a result of the addition of the suffix 'on' to the form Abialab, itself an orthographic or intentional metathesis of Abi-baal (differently Driver, *Samuel*, 370).

[33] The Baharumite (RSV 'of Baharum') is probably from the town of 'Bahurim'.

[34] Benei Hashem (or 'the sons of Hashem') the Gizonite: the name seems a corruption, since 'Benei' (*bᵉnê*) is not a proper name. It is usually regarded as a dittography of the last consonants of the previous name *haššaʿalbōnî*. In II Sam. 23.32 'Hashem' is called 'Jashen'; both names are *sui generis*. His town is the unique 'Gizoh', regarded by some commentators as a corruption of 'the Gunite' or 'the Gimzonite'.

Jonathan the son of Shagee the Hararite: in II Sam. 23.32–33 the text is corrupt; 'the son' was omitted and the name Jonathan was appended to 'Jashen'. What was left was 'Shamma the Hararite'. A warrior by this name is mentioned, with the record of his deed, in II Sam. 23.11; his full name there is 'Shammah the son of Agee'. It is of course possible that 'Shagee' in Chronicles is a name in its own right, with no real connection between 'Jonathan the son of Shagee' and 'Shammah the son of Agee', except for their both being 'Hararites'. One should not, however, ignore the fact that the name 'Shagee' is a conflation of 'Shammah' and 'Agee'; it could have been a sort of abbreviation for Jonathan's forebears, Shamma and Agee. If this is the case then we have to deal here with a father and a son: Shammah the son of Agee, of the 'three'; and Jonathan his son, of the mighty men.

[35b–36a] For the two names in Chronicles, Eliphal the son of Ur and Hefer the Mecherathite, there is only one name in II Sam. 23.34: Eliphelet the son of Ahasbai the son of the Maachite (RSV: 'of Ma'acah'). This form of registration is exceptional in two ways: the genealogy reaches back to the third generation, and the gentilic name 'Ma'acaite' is preceded by 'the son of'. In addition, the name Ahasbai is unprecedented and difficult. The relationship between the two versions has been explained in several ways (cf. Curtis, 193); it seems, however, that the simplest textual process is presupposed if the original version is taken to be the one in Chronicles (otherwise Rudolph, 102; Williamson, 103). Of the two forms, Eliphal and Eliphelet, the second seems more plausible, while no decision can be made between 'the Ma'achite' and 'the Mecherathite'; they are much more similar in Hebrew.

Ahijah the Pelonite; in II Sam. 23.34 Eliam the son of Ahithophel the Gilonite (RSV 'of Gilo'): these data could be interpreted as retaining two altogether different names, one in each version; the full list of the mighty men would include both. Another approach is to regard one of the names as a corruption or transformation of the other; indeed, the name Ahijah the Pelonite could be explained as a corrupt form of 'Ahithophel the Gilonite', and in this case the name of Eliam himself was dropped from the list in Chronicles.

[37] Na'arai the son of Ezbai; in II Sam. 23.35 Pa'arai the Arbite: the transition from the form 'the + gentilic' to the form 'the son of + proper name' is found in several cases and could be stylistic. The differences between the names are plausible orthographic changes, but there is no way to decide between them. A town named 'Arab', mentioned in Josh. 15.52, makes the gentilic 'the Arbite' the more probable one.

[38] Joel the brother of Nathan, Mibhar the son of Hagri; II Sam. 23.36 Igal son of Nathan of Zobah, Bani the Gadite: the two versions are clearly interrelated (as is much more obvious in MT), one being either a corruption or an editing of the other. Each version has its own logic and plausibility. On the question of preference it should be pointed out that a decision regarding the relationship between 'Mibhar' (*mibhār*) and 'of Zobah' (*miṣṣōbāh*) would determine most of the other details.

The form 'the + gentilic (place)' is the rule in the list, the only exception being in cases of composite place names (of Gibeah of the Benjaminites, of the brooks of Ga'ash). So we would expect here 'the Zobathite' rather than 'of Zoba'. However, Zeron sees this as a characteristic designation of origin for a prophet (A. Zeron, 'The Lineage of the Prophet Nathan', *Teuda* II, 1982, 179*), implying that Nathan is none other than the prophet of David's time (cf. also Rudolph, 102). This might be substantiated by the designation 'brother of Nathan' in Chronicles, but in this version his origin is omitted altogether.

[42] This verse begins the second part, actually a new list with its own heading. It includes an explicit reference to the position of Adina the son of Shiza as 'a leader of the Reubenites', followed by a special opening: 'and thirty with him'. The description of Adina as 'a leader of the Reubenites' has no parallel in the list; this does not, however, raise doubts about its reliability

or antiquity. The additional version of the list, in I Chron. 27, contains many tribal designations: of the sons of Ephraim (v. 10), a Benjaminite (v. 12), and more. This element, the originality of which can hardly be doubted, has completely disappeared from the version of II Sam. 23.8–39 (cf. further on I Chron. 27, and Japhet, *Ideology*, 289–90). The source from which the personal details of Adina were taken had probably still preserved the tribal or national affiliation of the persons listed, and these were faithfully repeated by the Chronicler.

'And thirty with him': instead of the expected thirty names, the list which follows, probably truncated, contains only fourteen. It has already been observed that all the locations mentioned in the following verses are from the eastern side of the Jordan: Mattanah, Ashtaroth, Aroer, Moab, and probably also Ma'achah, Mahanaim and Zobah. It is possible that the context is an additional group of 'thirty', based on men recruited from the eastern tribes of Israel, established some time during the reign of David.

[43] The two names mentioned in this verse are connected by a copulative; it is therefore unclear whether the gentilic 'the Mithnite' refers to both. If this is the case the version should rather be 'the Mithnites'.

[46] The Mahavites (*hammaḥ^{a}wim*) is difficult (RSV singular); a place by that name is not attested anywhere. It could very plausibly be a corruption of 'Mahanaim'.

[47] The form, meaning and reference of 'the Mezobaite' (*hamm^{e}ṣōbāyāh*) are difficult. Most commentators would regard the word as a corruption from 'of Zobah', referring either to the last of the names mentioned or to all three.

12 Now these are the men who came to David at Ziklag, while he could not move about freely because of Saul the son of Kish; and they were among the mighty men who helped him in war. [2] They were bowmen, and could shoot arrows and sling stones with either the right or the left hand; they were Benjaminites, Saul's kinsmen. [3] The chief was Ahi-ezer, then Joash, both sons of Shemaah of Gibe-ah; also Jezi-el and Pelet the sons of Azmaveth; Beracah, Jehu of Anathoth, [4] Ishmaiah of Gibeon, a mighty man among the thirty and a leader over the thirty; Jeremiah, Jahaziel, Johanan, Jozabad of Gederah, [5] Eluzai, Jerimoth, Bealiah, Shemariah, Shephatiah the Haruphite; [6] Elkanah, Isshiah, Azarel, Jo-ezer, and Jashobe-am, the Korahites; [7] and Jo-elah and Zebadiah, the sons of Jeroham of Gedor.

8 From the Gadites there went over to David at the stronghold in the wilderness mighty and experienced warriors, expert with shield and spear, whose faces were like the faces of lions, and who were swift as gazelles upon the mountains: [9] Ezer the chief, Obadiah second, Eliab third, [10] Mishmannah fourth, Jeremiah fifth, [11] Attai sixth, Eliel seventh, [12] Johanan eighth, Elzabad ninth, [13] Jeremiah tenth, Machbannai eleventh. [14] These Gadites were officers of the army, the lesser over a hundred and the greater over a thousand. [15] These are the men who crossed the Jordan in the first month, when it was overflowing all its banks, and put to flight all those in the valleys, to the east and to the west.

16 And some of the men of Benjamin and Judah came to the stronghold to David. [17] David went out to meet them and said to them, 'If you have come to me in friendship to help me, my heart will be knit to you; but if to betray me to my adversaries, although there is no wrong in my hands, then may the God of our fathers see and rebuke you.' [18] Then the Spirit came upon Amasai, chief of the thirty, and he said,

> 'We are yours, O David;
>   and with you, O son of Jesse!
> Peace, peace to you,
>   and peace to your helpers!
> For your God helps you.'

Then David received them, and made them officers of his troops.

19 Some of the men of Manasseh deserted to David when he came with the Philistines for the battle against Saul. (Yet he did not help them, for the rulers of the Philistines took counsel and sent him away, saying, 'At peril to our heads he will desert to his master Saul.') [20] As he went to Ziklag these men of Manasseh deserted to him: Adnah, Jozabad, Jedia-el, Michael, Jozabad, Elihu, and Zillethai, chiefs of thousands in Manasseh. [21] They helped David against the band of raiders; for they were all mighty men of valour, and were commanders in the army. [22] For from day to day men kept coming to David to help him, until there was a great army, like an army of God.

23 These are the numbers of the divisions of the armed troops, who came to David in Hebron, to turn the kingdom of Saul over to him, according to the word of the Lord. [24] The men of Judah bearing shield and spear were six thousand eight hundred armed troops. [25] Of the Simeonites, mighty men of valour, for war, seven thousand one hundred. [26] Of the Levites four thousand six hundred. [27] The prince Jehoiada, of the house of Aaron, and with him three thousand seven hundred. [28] Zadok, a young man mighty in valour, and twenty-two commanders from his own father's house. [29] Of the Benjaminites, the kinsmen of Saul, three thousand, of whom the majority had hitherto kept their allegiance to the house of Saul. [30] Of the Ephraimites twenty thousand eight hundred, mighty men of valour, famous men in their fathers' houses. [31] Of the half-tribe of Manasseh eighteen thousand, who were expressly named to come and make David king. [32] Of Issachar men who had understanding of the times, to know what Israel ought to do, two hundred chiefs, and all their kinsmen under their command. [33] Of Zebulun fifty thousand seasoned troops, equipped for battle with all the weapons of war, to help David with singleness of purpose. [34] Of Naphtali a thousand commanders with whom were thirty-seven thousand men armed with shield and spear. [35] Of the Danites twenty-eight thousand six hundred men equipped for battle. [36] Of Asher forty thousand seasoned troops ready for battle. [37] Of the Reubenites and Gadites and the half-tribe of Manasseh from beyond the Jordan, one hundred and twenty thousand men armed with all the weapons of war.

38 All these, men of war, arrayed in battle order, came to Hebron with full intent to make David king over all Israel; likewise all the rest of Israel were of a single mind to make David king. [39] And they were there with David for three days, eating and drinking, for their brethren had made preparation for them. [40] And also their neighbours, from as far as Issachar and Zebulun and Naphtali, came bringing food on asses and on camels and on mules and on oxen, abundant provisions of meal, cakes of figs, clusters of raisins, and wine and oil, oxen and sheep, for there was joy in Israel.

A. Notes to MT

[3] השמעה, difficult; proposed יהשמע, haplography of *yod* and dittography of *he*; [7] מן הגדור, many MSS הגדוד, proposed dittography; [18] השלושים, add ויאמר (thus RSV) or ויאמר לדוד; [19] עזרם, read עזרם (thus RSV).

B. Notes to RSV

[1] 'could not move about freely', MT עצור, meaning 'prevented', 'held back' (cf. Baumgartner), cf. commentary; [3] Shema'ah, MT 'the Shema'ah', which is impossible. Possibly Yehoshama'; [8] 'Whose faces were like the faces of lions', extremely literal, JPS 'they had the appearance of lions'; [14] 'the lesser over a hundred ... over a thousand', preferably 'the least of them a match for a hundred, etc.' (NEB, also JPS); [15] 'all those in the valleys', MT 'all the valleys'; cf. commentary; [17] 'knit to you', cf. commentary; 'to betray me', MT 'to cheat me', cf. commentary; 'rebuke you', preferably 'judge' (NEB) or 'give judgment' (JPS); [20] 'chiefs of thousands', JPS 'chiefs of the clans'; [38] 'arrayed in battle order',

NEB 'bold men in battle'; 'with full intent', JPS 'with whole heart'; [40] 'neighbours', JPS 'relatives'.

C. Structure, sources and form

1. Chapter 12 is composed of two main sections:

A. Verses 1–22 [MT 1–23], those who joined David before he became king, consisting of four groups:

(a) 1–7 [MT 1–8]: of Benjamin, coming to Ziklag.
(b) 8–15 [MT 9–16]: of Gad, coming to the stronghold.
(c) 16–18 [MT 17–19]: of Judah and Benjamin, coming to the stronghold.
(d) 19–21 [MT 20–22]: of Manasseh, coming to Ziklag.
(e) 22 [MT 23]: conclusion.

B. Verses 23–40 [MT 24–41], the troops who came to David at Hebron:

(a) 23–37 [MT 24–38]: the divisions of the armed troops.
(b) 38–40 [MT 39–41]: summary, and description of the celebration in Hebron.

2. The chapter is a unified composition (cf. above pp. 232–3); its various parts are integrated into one whole, bearing the stamp of specific literary and stylistic features and dominated by characteristic historical and religious concepts. As a sequel to ch. 11 it depicts the strong support given to David by all the tribes of Israel, before he was made king and at his accession. Its focal point is the view that all were 'of a single mind' (literally 'one heart') to enthrone David 'king over all Israel', 'according to the word of the Lord'.

3. From the point of view of form the chapter is characterized by an interesting quality: while clearly displaying a unity of subject-matter, themes and style, it aims at variety of expression and form.

(a) A stylistic and thematic element, throughout the entire chapter, is the 'coming to David', expressed in various ways: in v. 1, 'who came to David'; v. 8, 'went over to David'; v. 16, 'came to the stronghold to David'; vv. 19–20, 'deserted to David ... deserted to him'; v. 22, 'men kept coming'; v. 23, 'who came to David'; v. 31, 'to come and make David king'; v. 38, 'came ... to make David king'.

(b) The unity of the chapter is also enhanced by uniformity of literary genres. The chapter consists mainly of lists, interspersed with descriptions (vv. 2, 8, etc.), short episodes (vv. 15, 16 etc.), and editorial notes (vv. 19, 20, 22, 23). The lists are then concluded by a broader narrative paragraph, which presents a synthesis of all the elements of the chapter and expresses its purpose in more elaborate language.

(c) Yet, contrary to what might be automatically expected from a series of lists – namely a use of uniform structure and stereotyped language – the chapter is characterized by a variety and richness of expression. The four episodes of the first section, relating how members of the tribes of Israel joined forces with David, are all cast in a similar mould: an opening, reference to the circumstances, and in most cases, a list of names, etc. However, each of the openings is phrased differently (vv. 1, 8, 16, 19); while in three of the episodes the names of the new recruits are given (vv. 3–7, 9–

13, 20), they are registered differently in each case; three of the four stories describe the courage and military skills of the men listed – but the descriptions vary; even the point in the story in which these eulogies are set is subject to change: at the beginning of the first (v. 2), at the end of the third (v. 21), and at both the beginning and the end of the second story (v. 8, 14–15). The third story is the most distinctive of all, with its greater part taken up by dialogue.

(d) The second part of the chapter (vv. 23–40) displays the same features. Although it is a list, enumerating 'the divisions of the armed troops', there are considerable variations in both expression and form. Generally speaking, each registration-unit contains four elements: 1. designation of the tribe; 2. the number; 3. a short description of the recruits; 4. an additional note.

An examination of these elements reveals the following:

(i) Only the first element, the naming of the tribe, recurs in the list with relative uniformity; there are two exceptions: the tribe of Levi is divided into three (cf. below, p. 267) and the tribes east of the Jordan are presented as one group. In addition, no one formula serves for presenting the names. They are introduced as 'the men of x' (v. 24); 'of the x (gentilic)' (v. 26, etc.); 'of the men of x' (v. 30, etc., not in RSV); 'of x' (vv. 31, 33, etc., not in RSV). Most of the names are proper names; for Levi, Dan, Reuben and Gad, however, the gentilic form is used (this difference is not systematically retained by RSV).

(ii) The element 'number' is found in each of the registration units, but the objects of enumeration differ. Zadok and the priests are represented by twenty-two commanders, while the number of the troops is not given; in Issachar only 'two hundred chiefs' are mentioned, and for Naphtali both the commanders and the troops are numbered. For all the other tribes the number of the troops alone is registered.

(iii) A description of the troops is found in nine units, mostly referring to their military skills, but with other qualities and details also noted (Benjamin, v. 29; Issachar, v. 32, etc.).

(iv) In seven registration units various additional notes are found, following the number.

(v) It is only for six tribes that we find all four of these elements of registration present.

Of course, all this results in a great variety of form and phrasing. When the list is read in continuous sequence, no two consecutive tribes are presented identically.

(e) An important factor for thematic variety is the great number of military terms employed in the list. Weapons, for example, are indicated both by the general designation 'all the weapons of war' (vv. 33, 37) and the specific phrases 'shield and spear' (v. 24), 'shield and lance' (v. 34; RSV 'shield and spear'). Each of these is known from other biblical contexts (such as Num. 25.7; Judg. 5.8; I Kings 10.16 etc.), but the specific pairing of 'shield (צנה) and spear (רמח)' is peculiar to Chronicles, recurring five times (I Chron. 12.8, 24; I Chron, 11.12; 14.7; 25.5). Also peculiar to Chronicles is 'shield and lance' (צנה וחנית), v. 34).

The fighters themselves are designated with almost every possible phrase: 'divisions of the armed troops' (v. 23); 'armed troops' (v. 24); 'mighty men of valour for war' (v. 25); 'young man, mighty in valour' (v. 28); 'mighty men of valour, famous men in their fathers' houses' (v. 30); 'chiefs' (v. 32); 'seasoned troops equipped for battle' (v. 33); 'commanders' (v. 34); 'seasoned troops ready for battle' (v. 36); 'men of war, arrayed in battle order' (v. 38); and more.

4. It is obvious, then, that the two sections of the chapter do not comprise official, formal lists; they are literary compositions. The question is, therefore, self-evident: who is their author and what are their sources?

As noted above, chs. 11–12 form one literary unit; while in ch. 11 most of the material is taken from the book of Samuel and the Chronicler's own writing is rather limited in scope, in ch. 12 his language, style and views are very much in evidence. More precisely, then, we should ask: was the chapter freely composed by the Chronicler or was he drawing on ancient source-material? This question must be discussed separately for each of the sections – vv. 1–22 on one hand and vv. 23–40 on the other – because of the nature of the material and the particular problems involved.

5. Verses. 1–22 describe a series of events which are historically highly probable: the desertion of men from various Israelite tribes to David during the reign of Saul. The fact of this desertion is not in doubt; it is repeatedly recorded in the book of Samuel, and accounts for the rise of David and the development of his career. This chapter diverges from the book of Samuel only in its attitude towards these people, an attitude expressed already in the method of presentation, and in the choice of details. According to I Sam. 22.1–2, 'when his brothers and all his father's house heard it, they went down to him. And every one who was in distress, and every one who was in debt, and every one who was discontented gathered to him and he became captain over them.' Although the attitude taken toward these 'malcontents' is unfavourable, the underlying social and political circumstances cannot be controverted. The escape of Abiathar to David after the massacre of the priests (I Sam. 22.20) sheds more objective light upon the nature of the political and social circumstances, which gave rise to 'distress' and 'discontentment'. As time went by David gained in strength and experience (I Sam. 23.13; 27.2), becoming more and more an alternative to Saul. The factual background for vv. 1–22 cannot, therefore, be doubted. But more than this, even some of the details seem trustworthy. Those who came to David are confined to four tribes, Benjamin, Gad, Judah and Manasseh, while the more accurate data of names and numbers refer only to three, excluding Judah. The bond between David and the tribe of Gad, in fact with the whole of Transjordan, seems to have been established early in his career and lasted to its end. In the face of Saul's persecutions he left his parents with the king of Moab (I Sam. 22.3–4), and at the end of his reign it is to Gilead that he escapes from his rebellious son, Absalom (I Sam. 17.24–29). These connections would account for the desertion of the Gadites; that of the Manassites, on the eve of Saul's last war, also seem very probable, while the desperate political situation and the one-sided policies of Saul could account for discontent even in Benjamin. Also basically trustworthy are the numbers, which are strikingly small: twenty-three people in the first group, eleven in the second and seven in the fourth.

The plausibility of the material focuses our attention on the question of sources, and here another consideration should be raised. One of the features of the Deuteronomistic historiography is its systematic neglect of a major source of historical data: the whole range of lists, geographical, genealogical, etc. The Chronicler, on the other hand, made ample use of such materials, of various forms and origins. The very existence of lists and their importance as a historical source cannot be doubted, and it is very likely that such lists were extant for the particular historical setting in question. When David eventually became king, those who supported him in his early days were, so it seems, rightly expecting to be duly rewarded. A list of their names would carry with it actual political and social significance. Such a consideration is particularly substantiated by the list of Benjaminites, whose origin is marked by both family affiliation and place of origin.

The sum of these considerations would support the view that the section is indeed based on ancient, authentic data, to which the Chronicler still had access and which he further reworked. In the absence of the source itself, however, no determination can be made regarding the form of the original and the degree of the Chronicler's interference with his source.

6. The second section of 12.23–40 is of a different nature. I have already pointed out its strikingly literary character. Additional considerations make its authenticity even more problematical.

The underlying presupposition of the list is the view that the accession of David was celebrated in an impressive, all-Israelite ceremony. Even if we disregard for the time being the huge numbers, which are in any case exaggerated, the whole view seems historically unlikely, and incongruous in the historical circumstances, as known from other sources. According to II Sam. 5.1–3, the enthronement of David in Hebron was performed almost in secret. Until that time David had been king over Judah under the patronage of the Philistines; very little had been left of Israel under the rule of Ishbosheth, who was obliged to establish his throne at Mahanaim, in Transjordan (II Sam. 2.9). The enthronement in II Sam. 5.3 is portrayed in the most modest of colours. Indeed, after the enthronement (and probably as its immediate result), the Philistines renew their military campaigns against Israel (II Sam. 5.17). In such circumstances the gathering of organized, armed troops, from all quarters of the land, is historically inconceivable. Moreover, the very idea of such an armed force at that time is highly improbable. If such an army ever existed, could it have remained so well organized immediately after the defeat at Mount Gilbo'a? And further, one of the basic problems of Saul's army was that of arms: 'Now there was no smith to be found throughout all the land of Israel ... so on the day of the battle there was neither spear nor sword found in the hand of any of the people' (I Sam. 13.19–22). The situation had probably gradually improved during Saul's reign, but it is still too much to assume that at the beginning of David's reign all the tribes of Israel, thousands of fighters, were properly equipped with 'shields and spears', as proposed by this passage. The absence of a grand enthronement festival is therefore a genuine reflection of the circumstances. For the Chronicler, however, the all-Israelite in-gathering was not only feasible, but indispensable. We have already noticed how he played down the consequences of the war with the Philistines; his geographical views will be demonstrated in ch. 13. In his opinion there was nothing that could justify the absence of a grand enthronement in the description of Samuel, and the ceremony, which for him was conspicuous by its absence, is fittingly supplemented (vv. 38–40).

It is clear, therefore, that the list as it stands is not an authentic reflection of a particular historical situation. The question to be asked is therefore whether any of its details could provide a foothold for determining its origin and date. In the absence of place names, specific events and historical allusions, the compilation of the list could be ascribed to almost any historical context. Of the few identifying marks a notable one is the division of the tribe of Levi into three components (vv. 27–28), especially the specific details of this division. According to prevailing views in biblical research the genealogical distinction between priests and Levites, the definition of the priest as 'the house of Aaron' and the placing of Zadok as head of twenty-two commanders, all point to a very late date, surely post-exilic. From the point of view of these verses the list should be regared as post-exilic, Chronistic or later. However, some scholars tend to regard vv. 27–28 as a late interpolation (cf. for example Rudolph, 109–11); such a possibility, and further considerations, make the post-exilic origin of the list less obvious.

An important factor in the list is its organization according to geographical principles. (cf. Noth, *Das System der Zwölf Stämme Israels*, Stutgart 1930, 20; Japhet, *Ideology*, 285–6). The tribes are listed not according to their traditional order of birth, but geographically. First, there is a clear distinction between the tribes west of the Jordan and those to the east; then, a geographical south–north direction is followed on each side. The list starts with the tribes constituting the kingdom of Judah: Judah, Simeon and Levi. Then it proceeds in a direct line northwards: Benjamin, Ephraim, Manasseh, Issachar, Zebulun, Naphtali, Dan and Asher. The Jordan is then crossed and the tribes are mentioned in a south–north direction: Reuben, Gad, and the half-tribe of Manasseh.

The numbers are another significant element. For the first four tribes the numbers are relatively small. Even taking the priests into account, we reach a total of 25,200 people. Most conspicuous is the small number of the tribe of Judah, which is outnumbered even by Simeon. From Ephraim onward, the numbers increase, until for the last four tribes they seem typological: 40,000 people per tribe.

The evidence of the list as it stands is therefore rather complicated. While the geographical outlook and the comprehensive view of all Israel would fit well with the Chronicler's general attitudes (cf. Japhet, *Ideology*, 278ff, 352ff.), the numerical concept, and especially the inconsequential representation from the kingdom of Judah, would hardly agree. The assumption that the list is a completely free composition of the Chronicler is therefore difficult. More probable is the supposition that the list was based on some kind of a source, of which the nature and delimitation can no longer be determined (so already Graf, 198–9, Rudolph, 108). The Chronicler used this source, elaborated on it, and incorporated it into his composition.

D. Commentary

[1–2] These verses form the opening of the first paragraph, providing the general framework: who came, to where, in what were they distinguished and in what circumstances they came. Particular emphasis is placed on these warriors' previous connections with Saul; they are defined not merely as 'Benjaminites' but as 'Saul's kinsmen' (v. 2), and the exact circumstances of their coming to Ziklag are set forth: 'while he was still held back (RSV 'could not move about freely') because of Saul, son of Kish' (v. 1).

The reference to the 'Saulic' background of the events recurs three more times in this chapter: v. 19 provides a condensed summary of the events immediately preceding Saul's last war with the Philistines; v. 23 repeats the fact that Saul's kingdon was turned over to David, and v. 29 refers again to the Benjaminites as 'the kinsmen of Saul ... of whom the majority had hitherto kept allegiance to Saul'. This repetition serves to emphasize Saul's position in the Chronicler's historical conception. Although the Chronicler does not describe Saul's kingdom, he dedicates to him the whole of ch. 10 and a detailed genealogical list (I Chron. 8.33–39; 9.39–44); his reign is the background of another episode, in I Chron. 5.10; he is mentioned seven times in this chapter, again in I Chron. 13.3; 26.28, and in the parallel paragraphs, I Chron. 11.2; 15.29. In contrast to the Chronicler's treatment of some aspects of the history of Israel, Saul is not passed over in complete silence; his figure and reign are significant for understanding the historical process that led to David.

Of great importance in this respect is v. 1aα, of which the translation does not adequately reflect the significance. *'āṣūr* means simply 'prevented, held back' (cf. the dictionaries), one of its usages also denoting to be kept in prison. RSV's translation, 'he could not move about freely', is a modification of the original meaning, possibly influenced by the latter usage. However, such a paraphrase is not necessary, the sense of the clause being more in line with the basic meaning of the root. According to the Chronicler's view David was the king of Israel since 'the word of the Lord by Samuel' (I Chron. 11.3) had been proclaimed to him. His belated accession to the throne was due to one factor: Saul; as long as Saul remained in power David was 'held back'. The struggle between Saul and David is, therefore, not between the legitimate king and an usurper, but quite the opposite: the kingdom has been taken from Saul by decree of the Lord, but the one to whom the royal power has passed is prevented from realizing it. According to Chronicles, then, the men who joined David were not social outcasts, eluding their oppressors and creditors (I Sam. 22), but rather 'mighty men who helped him in war', who 'kept coming to David to help him until there was a great army, like an army of God' (v. 22). The three aspects of this matter are presented in ch. 12: David was 'held back' from the kingship by the person of Saul (v. 1); yet, through the help of the people, who recognized his right to the throne, his power grew (v. 18, 22). With Saul's death, the kingship was finally turned over to David (v. 23).

The Benjaminites are described in v. 2 with the unique phrase 'helpers of war' (*'ōzrē hammilḥāmāh*, paraphrased by RSV as 'who helped him in war'). Synonymous expressions are *'orʿkē milḥāmāh* (vv. 33, 35; RSV 'equipped for battle'; JPS 'able to man a battle line') and *'ōdrē maʿʿrākāh* (v. 38, RSV 'arrayed in battle order', JPS 'manning the battle line'). The root *'zr* is a key-word in the first section of this chapter (vv. 1, 17, 18, 18, 19, 21, 22 – seven times in all), and its Aramaic variant *'dr* is found twice in the second section (vv. 33, 38). The overall usage is within its general semantic field, denoting help. The question regarding this idiom is whether it should be considered within the same semantic field (thus RSV), or as derived from *'zr* II, the equivalent of the Ugaritic *gzr*, meaning warrior (cf. Baumgartner, 767).

If the latter is the case, it would demonstrate the preservation of ancient linguistic elements as late as the Chronicler, side by side with late developments in language and style.

The military skills of the Benjaminites are in archery and slinging. Similar characterizations are found in Judg. 3.15; 20.16 (cf. also I Chron. 17.17; 14.17).

[3–8] These verses comprise the list itself, the names and origins of the Benjaminites. Verses 3b, 4, 5 are somewhat difficult in the MT, the gentilic designation at the end of each verse being attached, in the singular, only to the last name: ... Jehu the Anthothite (RSV 'of Anathoth'); ... Jozabad the Gederathite (RSV 'of Gederah'); ... Shephatiah the Haruphite. As a result the preceding names remain undefined, with no affiliation. It is possible that, notwithstanding the formal incongruity, the gentilic refers back to each of the preceding names, affiliating each of the Benjaminites with either a family (Azmaveth, the Korahites), a town (Gibeon, Anathoth, Gederah, Harif), or both (Shema'ah of Gibeah, Jeroham of Gedor). Most of the place-names are of well-known Benjaminite towns.

[4] Ishmaiah of Gibeon merits a special title, 'a mighty man among the thirty and a leader over the thirty', although he is not listed first and is not introduced as 'chief'. Ishmaiah is not included in any of the lists of the 'mighty men', but some scholars would identify him with Shimei, mentioned together with Rei and the mighty men in I Kings 1.8 (Zeron, 'Lineage of Prophet Nathan', 181). Thus, while in II Sam. only one or two warriors are assigned the role 'over the thirty', four or five are mentioned in Chronicles: Jashobeam the Hachmonite (I Chron. 11.11//II Sam. 23.8), Adina the Reubenite (I Chron. 11.42), Ishmaiah of Gibeon, Amasai in I Chron. 12.18, and according to some commentators, also Abishai (I Chron. 11.20//II Sam. 23.18). This certainly reflects a more variegated picture of this military institution; it is probable that there were several units known as 'the thirty'.

[5] Hariph (Qere: Haruph) is mentioned as a Benjaminite town in Neh. 7.25, close to Gibeah. In Neh. 10.19 it is the proper name of one of the chiefs who signed the covenant, together with Anathot and Nebai (Nebo?). It is the name of a family, a town, or both.

'The Korahites': Korah is a very common name, attested in Edom (Gen. 36.5, 14, 16, 18), the tribe of Levi (Exod. 6.21 etc.), and Judah (I Chron. 2.43). These could have been all branches of one ethnic group, a family of which had for some time also settled in Benjamin.

The warriors recorded in this list, although more numerous than from the other tribes, are still rather few – twenty-three in all. These men are not described as 'officers' or 'commanders' of troops, but as individuals, registered in a manner similar to the lists of the mighty men in ch. 11. The places of origin of these men seem to be incidental, with no intentional geographical scheme expressed in their selection – all of which points to the basic authenticity of the list.

[8–15] The passage about the Gadites adds to the substantial data and traditions relating to the east-Jordanian tribes, which are peculiar to Chronicles. These shed some light on the living reality of these tribes, so conspicuously absent from the Deuteronomistic historiography (cf. also Japhet, *Ideology*, 304–8).

[8] The portrayal of the Gadites is a strange admixture of military terms and poetic imagery. 'Mighty and experienced warriors, expert with shield and spear', and 'whose faces were like the faces of lions and who were swift like gazelles upon the mountains'. The comparison of man's courage and might to a lion's is a common motif, but this concrete simile is unique to this verse. The image of the gazelles is also quite common, but the combination of the two similes in one portrait is again unique.

The military prowess of the Gadites is also the leading motif in the two epigrams characterizing the tribe of Gad in Gen. 49.16 and Deut. 33.20. So, notwithstanding the late phrasing of the verse (exemplified mainly by the peculiar use of the infinitive with *lamed*, *l*ᵉ*mahēr*), the tradition reflected in it is most probably authentic.

[9–13] The names of the Gadites are followed by ordinal numbers: first (actually, the first in rank), the second, the third etc. A similar method is used in several other cases, mostly when enumerating a sequence of sons from one father (cf. I Chron. 3.1–3; 3.13–15; 8.39; 23.19; 26.2–5, 10–11, etc.). There is no way to determine whether the exact ordinal position serves any social purpose or whether it is just a literary technique or a mnemotechnic device. According to its number, the group of the Gadites could have formed a military unit: a 'ten' with their commander.

[14–15] The episode is brought to a conclusion in two ways: by further emphasizing the military prestige of these warriors, 'the lesser over a hundred etc.', and by recording in detail their courageous feat. Verse 15 describes how these Gadites crossed the Jordan in the first month, when the melting snows swell the river water to its limits. The crossing of the Jordan in the first month was one of the outstanding miracles in the history of Israel, as we read in Josh. 3–5 (cf. 5.10); there too the Jordan 'overflows all its banks' (3.15). However, while for the people of Israel 'the waters coming down from above stood and rose up … and those flowing down … were wholly cut off' (Josh. 3.16), the Gadites crossed the Jordan at the peak of its overflow, through the torrent, in a feat of human strengh.

The second half of the verse is somewhat obscure. After the parenthetic clause the subject of 'put to flight' should be the Gadites, and therefore the 'valleys' would refer to 'those in the valleys' (so RSV, cf. mainly Jer. 4.29). The Gadite warriors put to flight all the inhabitants of the Jordan valley

whom they met on their way, east and west of the river. This little episode
thus demonstrates the concrete meaning of '... like the faces of lions': they
spread fear and terror wherever they went.

[16–18] Of the four episodes in ch. 12, that concerning the 'men of
Benjamin and Judah' is the most abstract, and its literary and theological
reworking is the most thorough. Its focus is the dialogue between David and
Amasai, composed in poetic idiom with parallel colons, but reflecting a rather
late Hebrew, not of the linguistic stratum of David's time. The strong
religious tone of this passage is also obvious, especially in comparison with
the previous scenes, where it is completely absent.

There is hardly any doubt that the passage in question is a late composition; its affinity to the Chronicler's language, style and view makes him the
best candidate for its authorship. However, the possibility should not be
completely ruled out that even here the Chronicler made use of some source
– much shorter in scope – which he elaborated and reworked. (A similar
phenomenon can be seen in the relationship between I Chron. 5.18–22 and
5.10, although in this case the shorter passage is not at our disposal.)

The story is related in several ways to David's wandering in the Judaean
wilderness: by the reference to David's location 'at the stronghold in the
wilderness' (cf. I Sam. 23.14); by David's fear of betrayal by these men of
Benjamin and Judah and his doubts concerning their motives (cf. I Sam.
23.10); and by the appointment of the new recruits as 'officers of the troops'
(MT 'troop'). The historical difficulty of the story lies in the unexpected
combination of 'Benjamin and Judah', coming to David as one group. That
people of Judah would join David is to be expected, and is well attested; that
some individuals from Benjamin would do so is also reasonable. But an
organized group from the two tribes, under a common leader, is highly
unlikely in the circumstances presupposed here. This difficulty, together
with the mention of Amasai and his identification with Absalom's
commander-in-chief (II Sam. 17.25), have induced Zeron to propose a
different understanding of the passage. According to his view this episode, as
well as the whole of vv. 1–22, reflects the background of Absalom's revolt.
The Chronicler had access to authentic traditions about that event in David's
history, but, unwilling to record the revolt itself, attributed what he found
there to a similar but earlier situation (A Zeron, ' "Tag für Tag kam man zu
David, um ihn zu helfen", 1 Chr 12, 1–22', *TZ* 30, 1974, 257–61). However,
Zeron's presuppositions are not compelling. It is hardly necessary to limit
Amasai's activity to the Absalom revolt. Moreover, the consequences of the
story for the general portrayal of that revolt are rather dubious. The difficult
'Benjamin and Judah' in this passage can be solved by a simpler supposition,
based on the Chronicler's general literary methods: that the original element
of the story had only 'the men of Judah' as its subject. 'Benjamin' was added

by the Chronicler, to conform to his concept of 'Judah and Benjamin' as a common entity.

David's fear of being betrayed to his enemies is peculiar to the present episode and absent from the others. The fact is that David faced the danger of betrayal particularly when he wandered in the hills and wilderness of Judah (Keila, I Sam. 23.10–12; Zif, I Sam. 23.19ff; Nabal, I Sam. 25.10; Zif, I Sam. 26.1). Are David's words here based on an authentic situation, not recorded in the book of Samuel, or are they a literary expression, founded on the well-known tradition? The two views are equally possible.

[17] This verse and the following one are phrased in poetic language, for which the reader is prepared by the dramatic opening: 'and he spoke up, saying to them' (RSV, much more casual, 'and said to them', cf. U. Cassuto, *The Goddess Anath*, 1951, 32; cf. also F. H. Polak, 'Epic Formulae in Biblical Narrative and the Origins of Ancient Hebrew Prose', *Teudah* VII, 1991, 11–12*), a rare form in Chronicles (II Chron. 29.31; 34.15).

David's greeting is composed of two opposite conditional clauses: 'if ... in friendship ... but if to betray me ...' While this literary pattern occurs in Chronicles several times (I Chron. 19.12//II Sam. 10.11; I Chron. 28.9; I Chron. 15.12), it is more frequent in earlier literature (e.g. Gen. 13.9; 24.49; Ex. 1.16; I Kings 2.10, etc.). It serves to present a given situation in its two aspects, positive and negative, giving full expression to their respective consequences.

The first condition, 'if you have come to me in friendship' (or: in peace), is a late casting of the more classical idiom 'do you come peaceably' (*haŝālōm bō'ekā*, I Sam. 16.4; I Kings 2.13; the difference between the two is not fully reflected in translation). In the late phrasing the *he* interrogative is dispensed with (an additional example of the diminishing use of this particle, cf. A. Bendavid, *Biblical Hebrew and Mishnaic Hebrew I*, Tel Aviv 1967, 116–17*), the word 'peace' is preceded by a preposition, and the infinitive is replaced by a simple past tense. The idiom is further elaborated by the addition of 'to help me', which is the key-word of the whole section.

The second condition in such a literary pattern can in principle be implied from the first, as its opposition, and is therefore not always explicitly expressed (cf. for example Gen. 24.21: 'whether the Lord had prospered his journey – or not'). In this context the second clause is spelled out in full, as having special importance, providing the basis for David's declaration of his innocence. The phrasing of this part is rather complicated. It opens with an elliptical sentence, 'but if [you came] to cheat me, [to betray me] to my adversaries', which is elaborated by a further clause, 'although there is no wrong in my hands'. This last disturbs the metrical balance of the verse and even the sequence of the idea, but this very interference serves to emphasize the significance of the words. They carry David's, and the author's, declaration of David's innocence. His distress, his wanderings, his being 'held back', are not to be counted against him; they are neither the result of his own acts nor God's chastisement for his sins.

'My heart will be knit to you': the translation of JPS seems preferable, 'I will make common cause with you' (on the use of *yāḥad* here cf. S. Talmon, 'The Sectarian חד' – A Biblical Noun', *VT* 3, 1953, 136). The phrasing of this clause is, again, an excellent example of the Late Biblical diction.

The last clause leaves the decision with God. The problem which faces David, that of judging hidden intentions, can be resolved only by God, who 'sees into the heart' (I Sam. 16.7, JPS).

Stylistically, David's speech exemplifies a characteristic phenomenon of the poetic and semi-poetic sections of Chronicles, that is, the 'anthological style'. The author avails himself of already existing, ready-made poetical phrases and interlaces them, with minor changes, into his own literary expression. The phrase 'although there is no wrong in my hands' is almost an exact quotation of Job 16.7, and the words 'then may ... God ... see and judge' are a modified citation of Exod. 5.21: 'The Lord look upon you and judge' (the similarity of structure, tenses and roots is somewhat lost in the translation). The Chronicler's hand is felt in the slight changes, in the introduction of 'the God of our fathers', which is one of his favourite epithets (cf. Japhet, *Ideology*, 14–19), and by the interweaving process itself.

[18] David left the decision with God, and it was from God that the answer came: 'The spirit came upon Amasai', enabling him to convince David of the loyalty and good faith of his company.

The specific idiom 'and the spirit clothed Amasai' is found elsewhere in the Bible only twice: in Judg. 6.34 and II Chron. 24.20. In Judges, the 'clothing' (RSV 'possession') of the spirit impels Gideon to action; in the two occurrences in Chronicles it inspires speech.

Amasai's response consists of two parts, the first of which is an epigram of loyalty: 'We are yours, O David, and with you, O son of Jesse'. The declaration fits the situation well, but bears no linguistic or stylistic affinity to David's challenge. The second part of Amasai's response contains all the elements which made up David's words: peace, used three times by Amasai, echoing David in v. 17 (RSV 'friendship'); help, used twice; the reference to God; and the centrality of David's person, expressed by the personal pronouns 'to you ... your helpers ... your God ... helps you', answering David's 'me ... my heart ... my adversaries ... God of our fathers'. A rhetorical feature common to both short speeches is the inclusion of an apologetic or causal clause, in order to strengthen the argument. David explains his vulnerable situation and his turning to God for vindication should he be wrongly persecuted: for 'there is no wrong in my hands'. For his part, Amasai is not satisfied with a declaration of peace but justifies his blessing with a

2

266   I CHRONICLES

causal clause: 'for God helps you'. The two statements reflect one and the same idea: David's innocence and favour before God.

Williamson, following Ackroyd, is probably right in assuming that the present poetic structure is actually a superstructure, based on an ancient poetic nucleus (Williamson, '"We are Yours, O David"', *OTS* 21, 1981, 172ff.; Ackroyd, 55). The epigram 'We are yours, etc.', bearing a very loose connection to the stylistic and lexical environment, could have formed an ancient, authentic antithesis to the well-known 'We have no portion in David and ... no inheritance in the son of Jesse' (II Sam. 20.1). Around this epigram the Chronicler wove his own poetic fabric, which aims to display David's righteousness, and present God as his 'helper'. I have already posed the question of Amasai's identity (above, p. 263): is he the same as 'Amasa ... the son of a man named Ithra the Ishmaelite' (II Sam. 17.25 RSV; mentioned also in I Chron. 2.17)? On one hand Amasa/Amasai is quite a common name (I Chron. 6.25 (Heb. 6.10); 15.24; II Chron. 28.12; 29.12), and our Amasa could have been any outstanding officer in David's service, whose portrayal in this context was influenced by the later betrayal of the more famous Amasa, of Absalom's revolt. On the other hand, in both this story and Absalom's revolt Amasa is presented as a commander. From a historical point of view his appointment by Absalom prompts the supposition that he had already been an experienced officer, who had served David. If authentic, then, the data in this context would number Amasa among those who had joined David during his early wanderings, probably later than his kinsmen Joab and Abishai. Rivalry within both the family and the army, among other things because of his foreign origin, would explain his desertion to Absalom at a later stage.

[19–21] The fourth episode relates how David was joined by the men of Manasseh, who, like the Gadites, are described as changing their allegiance and going over from Saul's side to David's. 'Desertion' is indeed a key-word in this passage, repeated three times (vv. 19, 19, 20).

The passage is structured as a repetitive resumption (cf. above on 5.1–2), comprising the beginning of v. 19, 'some of the men of Manasseh deserted to David', and the beginning of v. 20, 'these men of Manasseh deserted to him'. Between these two statements a long parenthetical sentence supplies the following details:

1. David came with the Philistines for the battle against Saul.
2. He did not, however, help them.
3. The rulers of the Philistines sent him away.
4. They suspected that he would desert to his master Saul.
5. David then returned to Ziklag.

This complicated sentence is a condensed summary of I Sam. 28.1–2; 29, the words of the Philistines being nearly a direct citation of I Sam. 29.4. Verse 21, too, referring to 'the band of raiders', is an allusion to the same context (cf. I Sam. 30.8, 15, 23). For a similar structure cf. I Chron. 5.1–2.

[20] The Manassites are seven in number: their names are given, but not any further affiliation. They are described as 'chiefs of thousands', or, if '*elep* is interpreted as 'clan' (cf. Baumgartner, 58), they were 'chiefs of the clans of Manasseh', who deserted to David on the eve of the battle at Mount Gilbo'a.

[22] This verse is a conclusion of the whole section vv. 1–21, which is the Chronistic equivalent of I Sam. 28–30, and alludes to the even earlier history of David during Saul's reign. The aim of this verse is to describe the increasing support given to David and the gradual waxing of his strength. At the death of Saul he had at his side not only 'the chiefs of … mighty men', whose names are recorded in ch. 11, but the masses, who joined him 'until there was a great army, like an army of God'.

From this point the Chronicler moves back to Hebron, to the enthronement itself.

[23–38] The list of the 'armed troops' who came to David in Hebron is the most 'military' list in Chronicles. Not so much because of the large numbers, which are surpassed in other texts (II Chron. 13.3; 14.17; 17.14–18, etc.), but in the grandness of its lay-out: extremely detailed, rich in military vocabulary, and purposefully elaborated (cf. also above, p. 256). It seems that the Chronicler wished to display here the unified might of Israel at its zenith.

Another aspect of the list is the number of the tribes. Both Levi and the two sons of Joseph are enumerated, and Manasseh is regarded as two separate tribal entities. Thus the list indicates that there are fourteen tribes (with the inner division of Levi the number increases). The purpose of such an enumeration is to refrain from using the stereotyped number 'twelve', and embrace the people of Israel in its fullest and widest sense. At the same time it expresses the view, so different from that of Samuel, that monarchical Israel was a tribal society, the tribal system being a living, active reality (cf. further Japhet, *Ideology*, 278ff.).

[24] The heading of the passage is coined in the terminology characteristic of the entire context: 'came to David', 'to turn the kingdom of Saul over to him, according to the word of the Lord'. The kingdom is transferred not by strife and war, but peaceably and joyfully. The main expression of this peaceful transition is the ingathering of the whole army, declaring their allegiance to David from the very outset.

'Number' is found in this verse in the plural – a unique occurrence in the Bible and another example of the late linguistic tendency to turn abstract nouns into plurals (cf. Kropat, 10).

[29] The verse turns again to the problematical relationship: Saul–Benjamin–David. The armed troops of Benjamin are the smallest group,

three thousand in all. It is probably for this reason that the statement of the number is followed by an apologetic note: 'the majority had hitherto kept their allegiance ... to Saul'. The implication is twofold: this accounts for the small number of Benjaminites who joined David; at the same time Benjamin is seen as an exception among the tribes: they alone, because of their kinship, kept their loyalty to Saul. All the other tribes saw David as their king.

[32–33] These verses describe the northern tribes, Issachar and Zebulun, which of all the tribes receive the greatest attention. In contrast to all the other tribes, for Issachar not the whole army but only the number of the commanders is recorded (as with the Zadokites, v. 28). They are further characterzied by their unusual quality of 'understanding the times'. This last phrase seems to be a conflation of two others: $y\bar{o}d^{e'}\bar{e}$ $b\bar{\imath}n\bar{a}h$ as a synonym of wise men (Isa. 29.24; Prov. 4.1, Job 38.4 and especially II Chron. 2.11, 12) and $y\bar{o}d^{e'}\bar{e}$ $h\bar{a}'itt'\bar{\imath}m$ found elsewhere only in Esther 1.13, in 'the wise men who knew the times'. The continuation of the verse seems to indicate some kind of wisdom, astrological or other, the exact nature of which is not specified. Why this knowledge was ascribed to Issachar and whether this information has any historical basis are questions for which no satisfactory answers can be given. In the song of Deborah, Issachar is highly praised, but on different grounds, and in the characterization of the tribe in Gen. 49.15; Deut. 33.18 nothing similar to this reference is to be found.

The most distinguished tribe in this list is Zebulun, whose excellence is eulogized in every possible way. The passage referring to him is fully detailed and contains all the necessary items: his 'armed troops' are the largest in number, fifty thousand; his arms are described in the most comprehensive term, 'equipped for battle with all the weapons of war'; and most important, his integrity is praised in a unique phrase, 'with singleness of purpose' (JPS 'whole heartedly'). Here too, as with Issachar, the questions regarding the origin of these descriptions and their historical basis must remain unanswered. One should mention, however, the praises of Zebulun in the song of Deborah, 'Zebulun is a people that jeoparded their lives to the death' (Judg. 5.18), and the special role of Issachar, Zebulun and Naphtali in the war against the Canaanite Yabin (Judg. 4.6, 10; 5.15, 18).

[38–40] These verses, relating the celebrations in Hebron, form the climax of the whole literary unit. They bring to full expression all the objectives of the unit and provide an excellent example of the Chronicler's composition.

Verse 38a, 'all these, men of war ... came to Hebron to make David king', is a summary of the preceding listing, and in some ways is a repetition of the heading in v. 23. But in addition to the historiosophical elements already elaborated, another idea is brought to the fore: Israel came to make David king 'with full intent', or, preferably, 'with a whole heart'. The sequel of 38a is in v. 39; 38b forms a parenthetical clause, diverging momentarily from the syntactical sequence to make an extremely important point: not only those who actually came to Hebron but also 'all the rest of Israel' were likewise 'of one mind to make David king'.

I have already elaborated on the military character of the section; this leads us to a consideration of what is missing from the description. Those present at Hebron are all men of the army; terms such as 'the people', 'all the people', 'the assembly', 'the assembly of Israel' and the like, which are abundantly evidenced in other sections of Chronicles, are completely absent here.

[39–40] The continuation from v. 38a describes the celebration itself, the 'eating and drinking' lasting for three days. The passage contains a unique description of an ingathering of Israelites, from all parts of the country as far as Issachar, Zebulun and Naphtali. The people, bearing their provisions with them, are streaming to Hebron by every method of transportation. The motive and purpose for all this is stated at the very end: 'for there was joy in Israel' (cf. also Japhet, *Ideology*, 253; Y. Muffs, 'Joy and Love as Metaphorical Expressions of Willingness and Spontaneity', *FS Morton Smith*, III, 1975, 1–36; id., 'The Joy of Giving (Love and Joy as Metaphors of Volition in Hebrew and Related Literatures, Part II)', *JANES* 11, 1979, 91ff.).

Another aspect of the celebrations, which should be clearly qualified, is their secular character. There is no doubt that the enthronement itself was enacted with a religious rite – the anointing (II Sam. 5.3//I Chron. 11.3); the covenant with the people is also accomplished 'before the Lord' (ibid). In his own additions the Chronicler emphasizes that David is made king in fulfilment of the word of the Lord (I Chron. 11.3, 10; 12.18, 23). However, the festivities themselves are devoid of any religious or ritualistic element: no sacrifices, no praise or thanksgiving, no sermons and no prayers. The ceremony is not attached to any sanctuary, and 'priests and Levites', recorded among the armed troops, do not serve any cultic function. This aspect of the enthronement is even more conspicuous in comparison with other ceremonies, so abundant in Chronicles.

The enthronement of Solomon could serve as an appropriate example. I Chron. 29.22: 'and they ate and drank *before the Lord* on that day, with great gladness ... and they made Solomon ... king and they anointed him as *prince for the Lord and Zadok as priest*'. Three elements, peculiar to Chronicles, are common to both events: eating, drinking and being joyful. At the enthronement of Solomon these are all done 'before the Lord', not so for David.

All this, which at first glance seems so un-Chronistic, is really deeply rooted in the Chronicler's view of the history of worship in Israel. In Hebron, the scene of the enthronement, according to the Chronicler's view there was no sanctuary, and no ritual could have taken place there. Therefore the religious element is intentionally and consciously omitted from the picture. Another result of the same sensitivity is the inclusion of the conquest of

Jerusalem as synchronous to the enthronement, and the description of the transfer of the ark to Jerusalem as the first act of David the king (I Chron. 13.1ff.). The omission of the religious context of the celebrations at Hebron is very soon compensated for in the description of the transfer of the ark, which is a direct continuation of the enthronement. There, the religious and ritual aspects are by far the dominant factors, and are abundantly elaborated.

13

13 David consulted with the commanders of thousands and of hundreds, with every leader. [2] And David said to all the assembly of Israel, 'If it seems good to you, and if it is the will of the Lord our God, let us send abroad to our brethren who remain in all the land of Israel, and with them to the priests and Levites in the cities that have pasture lands, that they may come together to us. [3] Then let us bring again the ark of our God to us; for we neglected it in the days of Saul.' [4] All the assembly agreed to do so, for the thing was right in the eyes of all the people.

5 So David assembled all Israel from the Shihor of Egypt to the entrance of Hamath, to bring the ark of God from Kiriath-jearim. [6] And David and all Israel went up to Baalah, that is, to Kiriath-jearim which belongs to Judah, to bring up from there the ark of God, which is called by the name of the Lord who sits enthroned above the cherubim. [7] And they carried the ark of God upon a new cart, from the house of Abinadab, and Uzza and Ahio were driving the cart. [8] And David and all Israel were making merry before God with all their might, with song and lyres and harps and tambourines and cymbals and trumpets.

9 And when they came to the threshing floor of Chidon, Uzza put out his hand to hold the ark, for the oxen stumbled. [10] And the anger of the Lord was kindled against Uzza; and he smote him because he put forth his hand to the ark; and he died there before God. [11] And David was angry because the Lord had broken forth upon Uzza; and that place is called Perez-uzza to this day. [12] And David was afraid of God that day; and he said, 'How can I bring the ark of God home to me?' [13] So David did not take the ark home into the city of David, but took it aside to the house of Obed-edom the Gittite. [14] And the ark of God remained with the household of Obed-edom in his house three months; and the Lord blessed the household of Obed-edom and all that he had.

A. Notes to MT

[6] אֲשֶׁר נִקְרָא שָׁם, difficult; proposed אֲשֶׁר נִקְרָה שָׁם, cf. commentary; [9] שְׁמְטוּ, difficult; proposed שְׁמְטוֹ.

B. Notes to RSV

[2] 'land', MT plural, better 'territories'; [3] 'bring again', MT 'turn, bring round' (BDB, p. 686b); 'neglected it', MT 'did not seek it'; [5] 'entrance of Hamath' or Lebo Hamath (NEB), cf. commentary; [6] 'which is called by the name', MT difficult; RSV's translation is influenced by the parallel in II Sam. 6.2, cf. commentary; [11] 'was angry', NEB 'was vexed'.

C. Structure, sources and form

1. Chapters 13–17 form one literary unit, with a single central topic: the second stage in the transformation of Jerusalem into the political and religious centre of Israel. The unit opens with the transfer of the ark from Kiriath-jearim to Jerusalem and concludes with God's promise to establish in Jerusalem the house of God and the dynasty of David. Around this thematic focus the Chronicler creates a new literary complex, characteristically blending together variegated elements into a new structure. Some of these elements have been taken from biblical sources, mainly II Samuel; some have probably been drawn from non-biblical sources, while some he penned himself. All these are reorganized and put in a new historical and theological framework. As elsewhere in his book, the material is to be understood in reference both to its original setting – when possible – and to the new context from which its message is derived.

2. Chapter 13 is dedicated to the first attempt to transfer the ark of God to Jerusalem, paralleling II Sam. 6.2–11. While it is obvious that the Chronicler has taken his point of departure from the pericope of II Samuel as it stands, he introduced changes in the order of the material and made the present passage a direct sequel to II Sam. 5.6–10 (introduced in I Chron. 11.4–9). The issues related in II Sam. 5.11–25, which antedate the transfer of the ark both literally and historically, were moved *in toto* to a new context in I Chron. 14.1 ff., after the failure of the first attempt. A new historical and theological sequel is thus created, in which the transfer of the ark to Jerusalem is the first act of David as king. This act is also presented as a direct continuation of the celebrations in Hebron (cf. below). The failure of the first attempt led to an unexpected hiatus of three months, an interlude during which David initiated a series of actions, originally described as preceding the transfer of the ark.

3. The new structure is rife with chronological and historical difficulties. I have already mentioned (above pp. 233–4) the difficulty of ascribing a proper chronological setting to the conquest of Jerusalem, which is included in I Chron. 11 as an organic part of the enthronement ceremony itself. This difficulty is aggravated by ch. 13. From a purely liteary point of view there is actually no break between ch. 12 and ch. 13, no concluding formula at the end of ch. 12, and no new introduction for ch. 13. No passage of time is indicated; those 'who remain (הנשארים) in all the territories of Israel' (13.2) are identifiable with 'the rest (שרית) of Israel' of 12.38. Thus, while the transfer of the ark is described as a direct continuation of the celebrations in Hebron, the implied historical setting indicates that Jerusalem has already been conquered, and moreover that David has already settled there, cf. 13.13: 'So David did not take the ark home into the city of David.' On a superficial level this difficulty is accounted for by the reference to the rebuilding of Jerusalem in I Chron. 11.7–9, but from a historical-chronological point of view no real interval is provided for the events themselves. If we wish to attribute any historical plausibility to this aspect in the description of Chronicles, we have to assume that some time had elapsed between the events described in ch. 12 and those in ch. 13. Literarily, however, this interval must be supplied by the reader; it is not provided by the Chronicler himself. His theological motives lead him to situate everything concerning Jerusalem and the house of God at the very beginning of David's rule, the consequence of which is a literary structure which does not explain its improbable historical results.

4. As for sources, chapter 13 is composed of two parts. Verses 6–14 are taken

almost verbatim from II Sam. 6.2–11 (on the textual problems of this section and its relationship to the MT of II Sam. and 4QSam^a, cf. now Ulrich, 193–221). By contrast, vv. 1–5 have no biblical parallel and are a good example of the Chronicler's language, style and views. These verses comprise his own introduction to the whole unit, providing the narrative with a new context and perspective.

5. Structurally, the chapter is composed of two unequal parts: the introduction in vv. 1–4, which describes how the decision was taken, and vv. 5–14, which relate the actual events. This last section is composed of three smaller units:

5–6: the journey to Kiriath-jearim.
7–11: the transfer of the ark, ending tragically with Uzzah's death.
12–14: the removal of the ark to the house of Obed-edom.

There is a fine structural balance here, with the literary fulcrum in the middle unit, which is also the longest and ends with an aetiological formula which gives the unit finality and weight. The first and last sections, which are almost equal in length, comprise the exposition and the conclusion of the story. These two sections open with David, 'So David assembled' (v. 5), 'and David was afraid' (v. 12), while the middle unit concentrates on the activity of the whole gathering: 'they carried the ark'.

6. The borrowed and original elements in the chapter are easily recognizable. The literary style of the section from II Samuel is compressed: a series of scenes passes rapidly before the eyes of the reader. The protagonists of these scenes vary and the events take an increasingly dramatic turn, until finally the original plan for transferring the ark is abandoned entirely. At the end of the story the reader finds himself back very nearly where he started; the ark has been transferred, but only from one place outside Jerusalem to another. This narrative avoids dialogue throughout, the only quotation being David's short question 'How can I bring the ark of God home to me?', expressing his disappointment at the failure of his plans but also his full resignation to the will of God.

The section composed by the Chronicler himself (vv. 1–5) is quite different. The narrative is rather static, comprising in fact one major scene: the consultation at which it is decided to transfer the ark. Verse 5 describes in general terms the ensuing ingathering of the people. The protagonists are only two, David and 'all the assembly', and most of the section is devoted to David's speech. The rhetorical style of the Chronicler, poor in drama but rich in theological overtones, is clearly illustrated in this section.

D. Commentary

[1–4] According to II Sam. 6, the transfer of the ark is essentially David's concern, both in decision and execution. The language of the narrative reflects this unmistakably: 'David ... gathered ... and David arose and went ... and David was angry ... and David was afraid ... and he said ... So David was not willing ... but David took it aside ...' The people are mentioned in the story as being present at the occasion (II Sam. 6.2, 5 and again in vv. 15, 18–19), but their role is negligible. The focus of the story is David: his actions, feelings and words.

The Chronicler has a different attitude to this matter, expressed not only in the particular emphases of his introductory addition (vv. 1–5), but also in the tensions between this introduction and the story itself, taken verbatim from II Samuel.

According to the Chronicler's introduction, only the idea and the initiative are David's, while the actual decision is to be taken by the people as a whole. This necessitates a long, rather complicated process. First David takes counsel with the 'commanders of thousands and of hundreds, with every leader' (v. 1); then, he brings before 'all the assembly of Israel' (v. 2) his proposal, which includes not only the transfer of the ark but also the preliminary ingathering of the people. Finally the assembly is convinced and decides to accept David's proposal: 'all the assembly agreed to do so' (v. 4). Only then is the first step of action taken: the assembling of all Israel. Regarding the relationship between David and the people, there is a constant process of broadening: David – the commanders – the present assembly the people who remain in all the land of Israel – all Israel from the Shihor of Egypt to the entrance of Hammath.

In addition to this wish to portray the people of Israel, understood most broadly and as fully united, another feature comes into play, for which the term 'democratization' is probably the most appropriate. In Chronicles there is a changing attitude toward the people's role in the political life of Israel *vis à vis* the king. In this case the people are not limited to playing the role of accompanying crowd or the audience at a performance; rather, they are full partners – in consultation and decision-making. This is characteristic of the Chronicler's overall political and social views (cf. Japhet, *Ideology*, 416–27).

'Democratization' in the process of decision-making implies the presence of two elements: consultation and persuasion. The leader – whoever he may be – consults with others before taking action. It is for this reason that persuasion, the art of reasoning and explanation, plays such an important role in the social texture. The Chronicler does not, then, open his story with the ingathering of the people, which is delayed to v. 5, but with the long process leading up to it.

[2–3] Here David unfolds his plan, with two introductory conditional clauses: 'if it seems good to you', and 'if it is the will of the Lord'. However, the fulfilment of only one of these conditions is expressed in what follows: 'for the thing was right in the eyes of all the people' (v. 4). The second is left pending, and only at the last stage of the transfer is it fulfilled: 'and because God helped the Levites …' (15. 26). Still, God's basic approval of David's plans is also expressed in the interim, in 13.14 (cf. *ad loc.*)

The main purpose of David's proposal is the bringing of the ark to Jerusalem, but this is prefaced by a preliminary suggestion: an invitation to all the people of Israel to take part in this important event. Thus the two

objects of David's speech are similarly phrased: 'that they may come together
to us' (v. 2), and later: 'let us bring ... the ark ... *to us*' (v. 3).

The idiom '*im* "*lēkem tōb*, 'if it seems good to you' (recurring in Neh. 2.5,
7; Esther 1.19, 3.9, etc.), is undoubtedly late and inspired by Aramaic
parallels (cf. *BDB*, 758; *KBL*, 1078). Its earlier equivalent is *('im) tōb b*ᵉ*'ēnē*,
cf. I Kings 21.2; Jer. 40.4 etc.

'Let us send abroad' (*nipr*ᵉ*ṣāh niśl*ᵉ*ḥāh*): the adverbial use of two consecutive verbs is common in biblical Hebrew (Ges. §§120dff.) but the specific
occurrence of *prṣ* in this usage is unique. The root is already found in II Sam.
5.20 and 6.8, but in the Chronicler's composition it has become a more
pregnant element. Here, its first appearance evokes Gen. 28.14, 'and you
shall spread abroad to the west and to the east and to the north and to the
south'. Next comes the triple use of the same root in v. 11, the smiting of
Uzzah (= II Sam. 6.8), followed by David's defeat of the Philistines (14.11),
where *prṣ* is used four times (= II Sam. 5.20), and finally the same verb
expresses God's punishment for sacrilegious handling of the ark (I Chron.
15.13). The transfer of the ark and the wars with the Philistines are thus fused
together into one literary complex, in which Israel is understood in its
broadest sense (cf. also Williamson, 114).

'Our brethren who remain' (*'ahēnū hanniš'ārīm*): it is to them that David
addresses his call. The connection between this title and 'all the rest (*šērīt*) of
Israel' (12.39), seems self-evident. The use of these terms is regarded by
various scholars as an intentional or accidental anachronism, referring to all
the inhabitants of Israel at the time of David by a term borrowed from the
vocabulary of the Restoration. (cf. bibliography in Japhet, *Ideology*, 361
n. 361, 333 n. 243, already quoted by Williamson). However, the actual usage
of the Chronicler does not substantiate such a view. In both these cases the
verb refers to those who were 'left out' of the former gathering, the one in
Hebron; it bears no further theological connotations.

'The lands (RSV "land") of Israel': the use of '"*raṣōt* in the plural to
indicate either parts of the land or all of it is peculiar to Chronicles and
appears twice more, in II Chron. 11.23, 'all the districts (MT lands) of Judah
and Benjamin', and II Chron. 34.33, 'all the territory (MT lands) that
belonged to the people of Israel' (note that RSV uses three different
synonyms for its translation). It should also be pointed out that the land is
named 'the land of Israel' four times in Chronicles, out of ten in the Bible as a
whole (cf. also on I Chron. 22.2). It is possible that the use of the plural is
motivated not only by the general linguistic tendency to prefer the plural
form, but also by the historical-theological penchant to describe the territory
of the Israelites in its broadest possible scope (cf. further on v. 5).

'The priests and the Levites in the cities that have pasture lands': I have
already noted on I Chron. 6 (p. 164 above) that the reference to the levitical

cities reflects the Chronicler's views on the Israelite settlement in the land. According to him, the Levites and the priests were fully settled in their cities at the very beginning of David's reign (cf. S. Japhet, 'Conquest and Settlement in Chronicles', *JBL* 98, 1979, 210–12). The exact term used, *'ārē migrāš* (translated by RSV in a periphrastic manner, 'cities that have pasture land'), is found in post-biblical rabbinic literature as a technical term for a levitical city (cf. S. Japhet, 'The Supposed Common Authorship of Chronicles and Ezra-Nehemiah Investigated Anew', *VT* 18, 1968, 349). The priests and the Levites are not assigned any role in the first part of the narrative, which is taken from II Sam. In the second part of the story, however, they play a central role (cf. below on ch. 15).

[3] 'Bring again ... to us' (*wᵉnāsēbbāh ... 'ēlēnū*): This significant phrase used by David for the bringing up of the ark seems to imply that until David's time the ark was not in Israelite hands, and that David's wish is to retrieve the ark from some point outside Israel, not merely to transfer it from place to place. Since the location of the ark is mentioned later – 'Kiriath-jearim which belongs to Judah' (v. 6) –, 'to us' should be understood in a spiritual sense: 'let us make the ark "ours"'. This interpretation is substantiated by David's explicit argument: 'For we did not seek it (RSV 'neglected it') in the days of Saul'. The problem, therefore, is not the physical presence of the ark – it had been there in Kiriath-jearim all the time – but rather its role in God's worship, as an object of 'seeking'. Accordingly, the full conclusion of the 'bringing' of the ark is not seen in its placement 'inside the tent' (I Chron. 16.1// II Sam. 6.17), but in the establishment of a permanent liturgy of worship before it, as described in detail in ch. 16.

Verse 3 is orientated on the overall theological framework of Chronicles by the recurring motifs of 'seeking' and 'turning': Saul was condemned in that 'he did not seek ... the Lord', and therefore God 'turned over the kingdom to David'. After Saul's death the people undertook the first step: 'to turn (*lᵉhāsēb*) the kingdom of Saul over to him' (12.23). It was now for David to seek the Lord by 'turning' (*nāsēbbāh*) the ark over to Israel, establishing its abode as the place where God is to be sought. The structure of the whole is antithetically parallel:

> Saul fails to *seek* the Lord and the ark, is found deserving of death for himself and his house, and so his kingdom is *turned over* to David. David has the kingdom *turned over* to him, 'turns' the ark to himself and Israel's worship, *seeks* the Lord as is right, and merits life for himself and his house.

Chapter 17, in which an everlasting dynasty (house) is promised to David, is the climax of this dramatic development. Such a promise has become possible only after the seeking of God, verified through the restoration of the ark.

[4] The people react to David's initiative with complete approval. From this point onward, the transfer of the ark is not only David's responsibility but also that of the people, who are seen to enjoy an independent position *vis à vis* the king, both politically and theologically.

[5–14] In v. 5 the actual undertaking begins. The account opens with a reference to the increase in David's strength, paralleling II Sam. 6.1 'David again gathered all the chosen men of Israel, thirty thousand'. However, this reference is limited, strictly military, and not obviously relevant to what will follow. The Chronicler here refers instead to a grand popular assembly, and forms an excellent connecting link between the introduction in vv. 1–4 and the story itself.

'From the Shihor of Egypt to the entrance of Hamath', this is a classical boundary formula (cf. Saebø, 'Grenzebeschreibung', *ZDPV* 90, 1974, 17–31), referring to only two points of the circumscribed territory, Shihor of Egypt at the south-west and the entrance of Hamath at the north-east. Between these two points lies the Chronicler's 'land of Israel'.

The geographical picture drawn by these points is rather unusual (cf. also *JBL* 98, 1979, 208ff.). Shihor of Egypt is undoubtedly the Nile – according to all its other occurrences in the Bible (cf. Isa. 23.3; Jer. 2.18, but cf. recently N. Na'aman, 'The Shihor of Egypt which is in front of Egypt', *Teudah* II, Tel Aviv 1982, 205–11*, who claims that the word is used as a common noun denoting 'river' and therefore should not be interpreted as referring to the Nile) – while the northern point is either the general 'entrance of Hamath' or, as explained by several scholars, 'Labu of Hamath' (B. Mazar, 'Lebo-hamath and the Northern Border of Canaan', in *The Early Biblical Period: Historical Studies*, Jerusalem 1986, 189ff.; R. de Vaux, 'Le pays de Canaan', *Essays in Memory of E. A. Speiser*, New Haven 1968, 28–30: Japhet, 'Conquest and Settlement', *JBL* 98, 1979, 209). The combination of these two points in the delineation of boundaries is very rare, the more common one being 'from the brook of Egypt to Lebo (or: the entrance of) Hamath' (i.e. I Kings 8.6, also Num. 34.5; Ezek. 47.20, etc). Some scholars would therefore introduce this reading into this text as well (already LXX, cf. Curtis, 205). However, the same terminology is found elsewhere in the Bible (although only once), in Josh. 13.3–5, and a similar geographical concept, though differently termed, is found in Gen. 15.18: 'from the river of Egypt to the great river, the river Euphrates'. The points, Shihor of Egypt and Lebo (or: the entrance of) Hamath, are the boundaries of 'the land that yet remains' (Josh. 13.2), namely, of those parts of the land that Joshua could not conquer, according to the editorial framework of that book. Historically, some parts of the 'remaining land' were later conquered by David, while some parts, among others the

Philistine territories, were never conquered (on the whole problem, cf. Y. Aharoni, *The Land of the Bible*, Philadelphia and London [2]1979, 232–9). The Chronicler takes this very picture, the broadest boundaries of the land, to depict the territory in which the people of Israel are actually settled; not at the end of David's rule and after all his military campaigns, but at the very beginning of his reign. Moreover, since according to the Chronicler's view of history David's rule was a direct continuation of Saul's, the same boundary would have applied also to Saul's kingdom.

There is no need to elaborate on the lack of historicity in this geo-political picture. The change from 'Shihor of Egypt' to a conjectured 'brook of Egypt' may modify some detail, but not the overall view. This is an expression of the Chronicler's peculiar historical understanding of the beginnings of Israel, cast here in geographical terminology.

[6] The verse is parallel to II Sam. 6.2, with a change – pointed out by all previous commentators. 'David ... with all the people who were with him' (JPS 'and all the troops that were with him'), becomes 'David and all Israel'. For the Chronicler it is self-evident that 'all the people who were with him' are indeed 'all the people', described here as 'all Israel'. In this way the verse is integrated into the general Chronistic outlook, given full expression in the introductory verses.

'To Baalah etc.': the version of II Sam. 6, *mibba‘ᵃlē yᵉhūdāh*, is probably a corruption of either a short designation such as *mibba‘ᵃlāh ’ᵃšer lihūdāh*, or a longer one, such as *ba‘ālāh, hī’ qiryāt yᵉ‘ārīm ’ᵃšer līhūdāh* attested now by 4QSam4[a] (Ulrich, 194). Basically, Chronicles here reflects a better version than the MT of I Sam.

On the other hand, in Chronicles there seems to have been some corruption of the clause 'which is called name' (*’ᵃšer niqrā’ šēm*). RSV 'which is called by the name of the Lord' avoids the difficulty by replacing the Chronistic reading with that of II Sam. As it stands the phrase appears unfinished. It may also be misplaced, but this possibility is precluded by the absence in Chronicles of the word *‘ālāyw* (by), or a similar preposition. A more plausible interpretation would be that the Chronicler's version was originally different, resulting from his own editing or taken from a different *Vorlage*, reading 'which happened to be there', *’ᵃšer niqrāh šām* (so I. L. Seeligmann, 'Indications of Editorial Alteration and Adaptation in the Massoretic Text and the Septuagint', *VT* 11, 1961, 204–5). Through a corruption, the word *šām* was later vocalised as *šēm*.

II Samuel 6.2 has 'hosts', *ṣᵉbā’ōt*, which is absent from Chronicles, and probably also from 4QSamᵃ. As has been mentioned elsewhere (Japhet, *Ideology*, 24–5; Williamson, 101), the Chronicler omits the epithet in three out of its six occurrences in his sources, and never uses it in his own writing. This is no doubt a reflection of a much broader trend of thought regarding divine titles, also expressed in other biblical texts (cf. *inter al.* the text of Jeremiah with its LXX counterpart, and T. N. Mettinger, *The Dethronement of Sabaoth*, Lund 1982).

[7] The verse in Chronicles parallels II Sam. 6.3–4a but reflects a preferable reading in not containing the dittography *ḥʷdāšāh wayiśśāʼuhū mibbēt ʼʷbinādāb ʼʷšer baggibʼāh* found there at the end of v. 3 and beginning of v. 4 (this repetition is absent from most LXX MSS followed by RSV, cf. Driver, *Samuel*, 266). On the other hand the words 'with the ark of God, and Ahio went before the ark' (II Sam. 6.4b), which are attested by 4QSamᵃ (Ulrich, 195), are missing from Chronicles – another example of the Chronistic stylistic tendency to shorten the story and omit what might appear to be superfluous details.

[8] Paralleling II Sam. 6.5, this verse describes the great rejoicing which accompanied the transfer of the ark. The picture is that of a crowded procession – the ark in the middle surrounded by the people and the king, moving forward with singing and dancing.

The fundamental concept of the whole event, that the ark is the vehicle of God's presence in the midst of his people, comes to the fore in the linguistic usage of this verse. The people dancing and singing before the ark are 'making merry *before God*'. In the version of II Sam. 6 this identification of the ark with divine presence is repeated in vv. 14, 16, and is given an unequivocal and highly emphasized expression in David's rebuke to Michal: 'It was before the Lord, who chose me ... and I will make merry before the Lord' (II Sam 6.21). In the version of Chronicles this identification is somewhat modified. It is retained here and later in v. 10, 'and he died there before God'. II Samuel 6.7 reads '... besides the ark of God', but Chronicles preserves the better reading, as is now also attested by 4QSam.a (Ulrich, 196). However, in I Chron. 15.27, 29 (parallelling II Sam. 6.14, 16), 'before God' is not retained, and David's rebuke is omitted altogether.

In specific details, this verse differs from its parallel in two respects: (*a*) *bᵉkōl ʻōz ūbᵉšīrīm* (RSV. 'with all their might, with song') is represented in the MT of II Sam. 6.5 by *bekōl ʷšē bᵉrōšīm* ('with all fir trees'; for this, RSV introduces the reading of Chronicles). The dependence of one reading on the other is apparent, the differences stemming from the interchange of letters *y/w; ṣ/z* and metathesis. Most commentators give precedence to the reading of Chronicles (now supported by 4QSam.). (*b*) The Chronicler probably replaced the original *mᵉnaʻanᵉʻīm ūbᵉṣelṣᵉlīm* (RSV 'castanets and cymbals') with *mᵉṣilᵉttayīm wᵉhᵃṣōṣᵉrōt* (RSV 'cymbals and trumpets'). These last instruments are very common in the Chronicler's musical vocabulary ('cymbals' occurring eleven times, and only two more in Ezra-Nehemiah, 'trumpets' twenty-one times in Chronicles, but also elsewhere). The other two are quite rare, *mᵉnaʻanᵉʻīm* appearing only here and *ṣelṣᵉlīm* only twice more, in

Ps. 150.5. Is the variation here merely a matter of vocabulary, or are the presupposed musical instruments actually different? The latter would seem to be the case in the transition from $m^e na' an^{e'}im$, 'castanets', to $h^a s \bar{o} s^e r \bar{o} t$, 'trumpets', but no categorical decision can be made (cf. B. Bayer, *'Neginah vezimrah'*, *Encyclopaedia Biblica* V, 1968, 766–8*).

[9–11] With these verses the story reaches its turning point – the tragic crisis. The procession is unexpectedly and violently brought to a halt, and the tone turns from 'songs' to 'sorrow'. The tragedy originates in an accidental 'stumbling' (cf. below) of the oxen. Uzzah puts out his hand, God smites him, and David calls off the whole undertaking. The story crystallizes into a chain of action and reaction, expressed through by a refined use of ambiguous verbs: *šālaḥ yād* (RSV 'put out, put forth'), vv. 9, 10, *wayyiḥar* (RSV 'anger ... kindled, was angry'), vv. 10,11, and by the recurring use of causal clauses: 'for the oxen stumbled' (v. 9), 'because he put forth his hand' (v. 10), 'because the Lord had broken forth' (v. 11). *šālaḥ yād*, used twice in this context, has two slightly different meanings. The first is neutral, denoting simply 'to stretch out the hand' (cf. *BDB* שלח 3, 1018), and here applies to the description of Uzzah's act. The second meaning, with the preposition b^e, has a negative nuance, meaning 'to stretch out (the hand) against' (cf. Ex. 24.11; Ps. 138.7, *BDB*, ibid.). Uzzah's action is described in a neutral manner, as an instinctive impulse; this innocent motion, however, is regarded by God as a transgression, as 'stretching out the hand against the ark', for which the punishment is the severest – immediate death.

What is the nature of Uzzah's sin? This is not spelled out, and can be understood on different spiritual levels. The very touching of a sacred object is sacrilege, to be avenged either by the inherent force of the sacred object itself (according to a more primitive understanding of the event), or, as this text has it, by God, who reacts in the most implacable way to the desecration of the *sancta*. A sin of this kind is objective and absolute, the aspects of volition, intent and moral considerations playing no role (J. Milgrom, *Cult and Conscience*, Leiden 1976, 43). On a different level, Uzzah's sin can be interpreted as an expression of mistrust in the power of God, represented in the ark. It is for God and not for man to protect the ark, and any human action in this regard is a demonstration of disbelief.

David's emotional reaction is described with the same verb as God's: *wayyiḥar l^e dāwīd*. It seems, however, that here again the verb is used with certain nuances. *ḥārāh 'ap* means 'his anger kindled' (cf. *BDB*, 354), but ..., *ḥārāh l^e* may also denote 'to be annoyed, to grieve' (cf. Gen. 4.5; 34.7; 45.5; Jonah 4.1, 9 etc. and *Thesaurus* III, 244). David understands God's reaction as a sign for himself and therefore calls off the whole enterprise (cf. further below, on v. 13).

Chidon is the name of the place where Uzzah was struck, called 'Nacon' (*nākōn*) in the MT of II Sam. 6.6; 'Nodan' (*nōdān*) in 4QSamᵃ, and 'Nodav' in LXXᴮ of Samuel. All these readings are orthographically close, but the degree of proximity varies. Chronicles, 4QSamᵃ and LXXᴮ form one group (נודן ⟵ נודב), while the form of the MT of Sam. stands more apart (נודן ⟶ נכון). One could reconstruct the various possible orthographic processes, but no decisive preference can be established.

'Stumbled': the few occurrences of this root make a transitive meaning more likely (cf. II Kings 9.33). Therefore 'let it drop' (*šᵉmāṭō*) would probably be a better reading (cf. *BDB*, 1030, and Driver, *Samuel*, 267). Such a reading would make Uzzah's reaction even more understandable.

'Before God': II Sam. 6, 'beside the ark of God'. On the preferable reading cf. the commentary on v. 8.

[12–13] David's ensuing acts seem to demonstrate that he interpreted God's 'breaking forth' as an expression of divine displeasure with the project itself, namely with the actual transfer of the ark. David's words, 'How can I bring the ark of God home to me?', have been interpreted as reflecting his primitive fear of the sacred, even contagious power of the ark, which he now realized for the first time. This, however, seems to take a rather narrow view of the general issue, and to be an inappropriate interpretation of the context of II Samuel 6, and even more so of I Chron. 13ff. The holiness of the ark and its embodiment of God's presence were the very *raison d'être* of the transfer of the ark to Jerusalem, and it is hardly likely that David was unaware of the various traditions connected with its sacred power. It seems rather that the slaying of Uzzah was understood by David as God's active objection to the removal of the ark, which put the whole project in jeopardy. In his rhetorical question, David emphasizes his own inadequacy: 'How can I bring the ark ... to me?', implying that it had better stay where it was. If Uzzah, Abinadab's son, could not handle the ark, could anyone else? David's next step is understandable – he 'turns' the ark aside, probably to the nearest available place.

'Obed-edom the Gittite': by name and affiliation, Obed-edom seems to be a foreigner, probably a Philistine. This makes his choice rather problematical. Hertzberg concludes that he 'will hardly have accepted the ark of his own free will' (279), but this is hardly the point. Could we conceive of David 'unburdening himself' of the ark at the nearest house, as if it were only a dangerous embarrassment? The fact that Obed-edom is assigned a levitical pedigree (I Chron. 26.4ff.) is usually regarded as the Chronicler's own interpretation, but it could very well have been an earlier tradition. Whatever the case, the entrusting of the ark to Obed-edom is a clear sign of David's resignation to God's will.

[14] The significance of this verse, which serves as a conclusion to the first

stage of the transfer of the ark and is taken almost verbatim from I Sam., lies as much in what it does not report as in what it does. David faces a disastrous situation. 'All the house of Israel' (II Sam. 6.5), or 'all Israel from the Shihor of Egypt to the entrance of Hamath' (I Chron. 13.5), had been gathered for the event, and now this has turned into a failure. God has pronounced his displeasure and the ark has been turned aside quietly to the house of a 'Gittite'. However, both versions of the story ignore this subject altogether. The disappointment, the shameful dismissal of the people to their tents, the mourning which replaces rejoicing – all these receive no attention whatsoever. The verse relates only that 'the Lord blessed the household of Obededom and all that he had'.

As seen from the context of II Sam. 6, this blessing is not an 'automatic' result of the presence of the ark but a result of God's providence. It is also a purposeful sign, intended for David, sufficient to imply that the moving of the ark from the house of Abinadab was not a transgression, since the ark may dwell elsewhere with impunity. Therefore the continuation of the story in II Sam. 6.12–13 is: 'and it was told king David, "The Lord has blessed the household of Obed-edom ... because of the ark" ... So David went and brought up the ark.' David's response is not a sign of egocentricity – wishing the blessing for himself – but a direct response of trust in the sign given him by God. The wrath has passed and it was not a result of the removal of the ark. David may therefore go on with his original plan: to bring the ark to Jerusalem.

In Chronicles, the transition between the two phases of the transfer is differently conceived. II Sam. 6.12a, 'and it was told king David, etc.', is completely omitted, since for the Chronicler the blessing of Obed-edom is not sufficient. In place of this verse the Chronicler introduces a long section, comprising 14.1–15.24 (cf. below, pp. 284–5).

This verse, although very similar to II Sam. 6.11, shows some deviations, mostly of a linguistic/stylistic nature. The replacing of 'the Gittite' with 'in his house', could have other motives. The most obvious would be the Chronicler's wish to avoid the mention of Obed-edom's origin. However, this has already been specified in the previous verse, and in any case the Chronicler regards Obed-edom as a Levite, and would interpret the designation 'the Gittite' as referring to residence, rather than ethnic origin. It would seem, therefore, that the cause of the alteration (to the extent that it is more than textual) would be in the greater emphasis on 'in his house'. The translation of JPS, 'in its own abode', provides one possibility of explaining this emphasis.

14 And Hiram king of Tyre sent messengers to David, and cedar trees, also masons and carpenters to build a house for him. [2] And David perceived that the Lord had established him king over Israel, and that his kingdom was highly exalted for the sake of his people Israel.

3 And David took more wives in Jerusalem, and David begot more sons and daughters. [4] These are the names of the children whom he had in Jerusalem: Shammua, Shobab, Nathan, Solomon, [5] Ibhar, Elishu-a, Elpelet, [6] Nogah, Nepheg, Japhia, [7] Elishama, Beeliada, and Eliphelet.

8 When the Philistines heard that David had been anointed king over all Israel, all the Philistines went up in search of David; and David heard of it and went out against them. [9] Now the Philistines had come and made a raid in the valley of Rephaim. [10] And David inquired of God, 'Shall I go up against the Philistines? Wilt thou give them into my hand?' And the Lord said to him, 'Go up, and I will give them into your hand.' [11] And he went up to Baal-perazim, and David defeated them there; and David said, 'God has broken through my enemies by my hand, like a bursting flood.' Therefore the name of that place is called Baal-perazim. [12] And they left their gods there, and David gave command, and they were burned.

13 And the Philistines yet again made a raid in the valley. [14] And when David again inquired of God, God said to him, 'You shall not go up after them; go around and come upon them opposite the balsam trees. [15] And when you hear the sound of marching in the tops of the balsam trees, then go out to battle; for God has gone out before you to smite the army of the Philistines.' [16] And David did as God commanded him, and they smote the Philistine army from Gibeon to Gezer. [17] And the fame of David went out into all lands, and the Lord brought the fear of him upon all nations.

A. Notes to MT

[1] וחרשי קיר difficult (=4QSam.), II Sam. 5.11 וחרשי אבן קיר.

B. Notes to RSV

[2] 'and that his kingdom', adjustment to II Sam. 5.12, MT 'for his kingdom'; cf. commentary; [11] 'he went up', MT 'they went up'; [14] 'balsam trees', meaning of Hebrew uncertain; NEB 'aspens'.

C. Structure, sources and form

1. Chapter 14 is taken from II Sam. 5.11–25, with the introduction of slight changes and the addition of v. 17. However, as already recognized by earlier commentators (cf. mainly Mosis, 55ff.), the full understanding of this section in Chronicles depends on its new context.

In II Sam. this material is part of a collection of paragraphs all connected by one major theme: the transition of David's throne from Hebron to Jerusalem. Accordingly, II Sam. 5 contains the account of David's enthronment (vv. 1–3), followed by a summary of the general chronological data of his kingdom (vv. 4–5); the establishment of a new capital – the conquest of Jerusalem and its rebuilding (vv. 6–12); David's abiding in Jerusalem as seen from the perspective of progeny (vv. 13–16); and the Philistine wars, accounted for by the fact that 'David had been anointed king over Israel' (vv. 17–25). The organization of these data, of differing genres and origins, under one thematic roof, was undoubtedly the work of an author/editor. This raises the question of the original historical provenance and literary setting of each of the individual elements. Thus, for example, although the conquest of Jerusalem is related immediately after the enthronement, one may wonder if this is an authentic reflection of the historical sequence (cf. below, p. 287). Again, the building of a house for David by Hiram, king of Tyre, follows upon the conquest of Jerusalem – but would not a later date in the history of David be more plausible? Some passages such as the list of David's wives and children and the summary of his reign are certainly written from a much later vantage point. The collecting of all these pieces into one coherent composition was obviously guided by certain historical and thematic considerations, and its historical and chronological assumptions are not self-evident.

The Chronicler took from II Sam. the whole of ch. 5, but dissolved its original (editorial) sequence. He placed its first part at the beginning of David's story (11.1–9), and inserted its second part into the interval between the two stages of the transfer of the ark (14. 1–17). This did not entail a major change in the historical context, which is still the early years of David's reign. However, the thematic sequence has now been broken and the historical question has become more acute, since all the events related in this section are now confined to a period of three months. Of greater significance, however, is the role of this 'insertion' in the historical and theological world-view of the Chronicler. What made him deviate from the order of his sources, divide the original chapter in two, and use the three months interval, afforded by the story, for the insertion of this material?

2. The transfer of the ark has miscarried, and has met with disaster in the death of Uzzah. This is David's first failure and touches him in a most sensitive realm: that of his direct relationship with God. According to the Chronicler's most basic theological axioms, a failure of any kind is understood as God's punishment for man's sin. Therefore, Uzzah's death and the failure of the whole undertaking were a punishment for David as well as for Uzzah. With this fundamental assumption in mind, logic and structure of the whole story become lucid and meaningful.

As already mentioned, the transition from the first phase of the transfer of the ark to the second is presented in II Sam. 6 in one sentence: 'And it was told King David, "the Lord has blessed the household of Obed-edom and all that belongs to him, because of the ark of God"' (v. 12a). This one sentence is replaced in Chronicles by a long section comprising two components, 14. 1–17 and 15. 1–24, which follow a strict theological sequence. The role of ch. 14 is to demonstrate, in unequivocal terms, the blessing bestowed on David. According to Chronicles, the fact that Obed-edom and his household were blessed by the presence of the ark did not suffice to confirm David's favour, for the blessing inherent in God's presence in the ark was taken for granted. David needed a personal proof that it was not the transfer of the ark which caused God's anger, and that divine favour had not been taken away from him. As in the whole of Chronicles, God's beneficence is shown in practical-material matters, such as building operations, blessing of progeny, victories over enemies, etc. (cf. Welten, 4–5). These very elements were indeed found in the Chronicler's sources, but in another context; it only remained for him to transpose them to the present setting. As in II Sam. 5, all these activities express the establishment of David's rule, but they are his reward and a sign of God's favour. It is this, more than the blessing of Obed-edom, which prompts David to return to his original plan and bring the ark of God to the city of David.

If there was no sin in the removal of the ark, what, then, was the cause of the first failure? David's deduction was that the disaster was caused by faulty procedure; having learned a bitter lesson, he arranges for a strict, fully supervised, rite of transfer, which will guarantee the success of this second attempt. The new *modus operandi* is set forth in great detail in ch. 15, which forms the second component of this transitional stage and acts as a bridge between the initial failure of the first transfer and the eventual completion of the undertaking, described in 15.25ff.

3. Chapter 14 comprises five sections:

1–2 (II Sam. 5.11–12): The building of a house for David and the political and religious significance of this project.

3–6 (II Sam. 5.13–16): The children born to David in Jerusalem.

7–12 (II Sam. 5.17–21): The first war with the Philistines.

13–16 (II Sam. 5.22–25): The second war with the Philistines.

17: Conclusion: David's fame.

4. Most of the chapter belongs to the genre of historical narration. In addition, it contains a list, and a theological appraisal, found already in II Sam. 5.12. The religious import of the collection is also emphasized in Chronicles through the addition of the concluding v. 17.

D. Commentary

[1–2] Hiram sends to David both the building materials and the craftsmen to execute the work. In II Sam. 5.11 the exact historical setting of this event, which implies some kind of a treaty between David and Hiram, is not spelled out, nor are its economic conditions. One wonders how much light might be shed on this matter by the later negotiations between Solomon and Hiram (I Kings. 5.1ff; II Chron. 2.3ff). The building of David's house is placed in II Sam, 5 between two appreciative statements: the preceding v. 10; 'And David became greater and greater, for the Lord ... was with him', and the succeeding v. 12, 'And David perceived (NEB 'knew') that the Lord had established him king over Israel ...' This is all the more important when we note that David's house-building is the only matter which evokes such an appraisal, and which is regarded as proof that God had chosen him. It is not specified why the building of the house, above all other achievements, is a sign that God 'had established him' and that 'he had exalted his kingdom'. Is it the fact that David has been recognized by other kings? Is it the grandeur of the cedar house (II Sam. 7.2)? Or is it the more elementary fact of David's presence in Jerusalem, firmly established in his capital?

The Chronicler adopts the passage as it stands, but weaves it into a different context. The building of David's house follows immediately, not upon the conquest of Jerusalem, but rather upon the turning of the ark to the house of Obed-edom. The statement 'David perceived (NEB 'knew') that the Lord had established him king over Israel, etc.' (I Chron. 14.2) is connected most particularly with the transfer of the ark. After the initial failure, the building of the house was concrete proof that God had not withdrawn his favour from David, and that his kingdom was if anything more firmly established than ever.

The statement 'David perceived that the Lord had established, etc.' (II Sam. 5.12) is composed of a main sentence with two objective clauses. David knew that: (a) God had established him ... (b) God had exalted his kingdom ... In Chronicles the syntax of the statement has been slightly changed, by the omission of the copulative *waw*. Thus the sentence comprises only one objective clause followed by a causative clause: David knew that 'God had established him ... *for* his kingdom was highly exalted' (the peculiar syntax of Chronicles is not reflected in the RSV, which adapts its translation of II Sam. 5.12). This seemingly minor change opens up the possibility of a more specific expression of the theological message. It is a leading theme of the Chronicler's historical view that the exaltation of the kingdom, in political and material terms, is a sign of God's election. From the exaltation of his kingdom David learned of the enduring favour of God, 'that he had established him king'.

[3–7] In the list of David's sons born to him in Jerusalem there is an emphasis on 'more' – 'more wives ... more sons and daughters' (v. 3). The blessing of offspring is one of the most generally recognized signs of blessing in the OT, and Chronicles is no exception. The inclusion of the list here is another example of the Chronicler's method of employing a single list in two different roles. In I Chron. 3.5–9 it forms part of the comprehensive genealogy of the house of David, while in the present context it is a sign of God's benediction which is bestowed on David in Jerusalem. On the details of the list and its relationship to I Chron. 3.5ff. cf. above, pp.96–7.

[8–16] David's wars with the Philistines were of the greatest historical and political significance. The Davidic victories determined unequivocally his position as an independent king, completely free of any subordination to Philistine patronage. However, these victories were not final, and military encounters with the Philistines were to continue for some time (II Sam. 8.1//I Chron. 18.1, etc.).

In II Sam. 5 the two battles are presented in a similar fashion. Both are set in the same geographical location, and both are depicted from the point of view of David's actions, which follow a similar pattern. Two points are made very clear: one is David's flexibility in military strategy and practice, and his ability to make instantaneous decisions and to improvise different tactics for each of the battles, fought in the same locale. The other is that David is depicted as receiving direct and constant divine guidance. He does not take one step without consulting God, and carries out his instructions to the letter: 'and David did as God commanded him' (v. 16). The account of Chronicles is basically the same as in II Sam. 5.17–25. The significant differences will be pointed out in the course of the commentary.

[8] The catalyst for the Philistine aggression is stated very clearly: their realization that David has become king 'over all Israel'. It would seem that as long as David reigned over Judah alone, the Philistines saw no need to curtail his activity. They probably regarded him as their protégé, although the exact nature of their relationship cannot be more precisely determined for lack of information. David's enthronement over 'all Israel' made him a potential threat, for two reasons: he became Saul's heir, and therefore a rival and enemy, and his kingdom and power surpassed what the Philistines considered tolerable.

Already in II Sam. 5, and even more clearly in Chronicles, these wars are placed after the conquest of Jerusalem. This view is chronologically problematical. It is doubtful whether David could have conducted a military campaign against Jerusalem under the watchful eyes of the Philistines (cf. J. Bright, *A History of Israel*, Philadelphia and London [3]1981, 198–9). It would seem more likely, therefore, that in spite of the explicit time-sequence of our sources, the wars with the Philistines preceded the conquest of Jerusalem and were waged from a base at Hebron. The resulting historical order would then be: war with the Philistines, the conquest of Jerusalem, the transfer of the ark, etc.

If these considerations are sound, the opening statement in II Sam. 5.17 becomes clear: 'all the Philistines went up in search of David; but David heard of it and went down to the stronghold'. If David was already established in Jerusalem, there was no need 'to search for him', and no logic in David's 'going down'. David's automatic reaction to the Philistines' threat is to avoid the danger before calculating his next step. When the Philistines pitched their camp in the Valley of Rephaim, David attacked them.

Another question concerns the identification of the 'stronghold': is it 'the stronghold of Zion', namely, 'the city of David' (II Sam. 5.9//11.7), or is it identical with 'the stronghold' of David's wanderings in the desert of Judah (I Sam. 22.4, 5; 24.22)? The latter possibility would seem to provide a better explanation for the general setting especially for David's 'going down' to the stronghold after learning of the Philistines' approach. This, however, is less problematical in the version of Chronicles, which reads 'and David heard of it and went out against them'.

[9] In II Sam. 5.18 and 22 the Philistines' foray is described with the rather rare term *wayyināt⁽ᵉ⁾šū* (cf. also I Sam. 30.16; Isa. 16.8). In Chronicles the verb *wayyipš⁽ᵉ⁾tū* is used. It is characteristic of Chronicles to exchange a rare word for a more common one (S. Japhet, 'Interchanges of Verbal Roots in Parallel Texts in Chronicles', *HS* 28, 1987, 12–13), but here the Chronicler's choice has further implications. The Philistines' aggression is emphasized: not only 'spreading out' in the valley, but probably 'raiding' it as well.

[10] This verse is an excellent example of the Chronicler's stylistic-linguistic technique. II Samuel 5.19 is artistically structured; it begins with David's inquiry of the Lord phrased in two questions: 'Shall I go up against the Philistines?', 'Wilt thou give them into my hand?' The first question is the longer, containing an explicit reference to the Philistines, while the second is shorter, referring to them by means of an accusative pronoun. God's answer is an echo of David's questions, summed up in one compound sentence: 'Go up, for I will ...', identical terms being employed in both: 'go up', 'give into the hand', 'the Philistines'. In God's reply, however, the second statement is the longer, and also forms an independent, fully detailed assertion: 'I will certainly give the Philistines into your hand'.

In Chronicles, many of these finer points are lost. The question is phrased in one sentence, of a different *consecutio temporum* (this difference is not attested in RSV, where the translation of I Chron. 14.10 follows the MT of II Sam. 5.19), and God's answer is paraphrased and shortened. Although the subject matter and even the details are retained, along with the repetition of 'go up', 'I will give', there are enough changes to illustrate several Chronistic peculiarities: the Chronicler's tendency to be more laconic and avoid what may seem unessential (Willi, 92ff.); his stylistic inclination to equalization, the result of which would be a more accurate parallelism between question and answer (Willi, 146– 7); a replacement of the infinitive absolute attached to the finite verb (cf. also II Chron. 6.2 against I Kings 8.13 etc.), and the diminishing use the *he* interrogative (cf. above, on 12.19).

[11] In MT, the verb 'went up' is in the plural, and could therefore refer either to the Philistines (which would defy the spirit of the passage), or to a more general, impersonal subject: 'they went up'. RSV follows the ancient Versions and translates in the singular: 'he went'. However, since David is explicitly mentioned later as subject, this reading makes for rather awkward syntax.

The use in Chronicles of the verbal root 'to go up' (*'lh*) in place of 'came' (*wayyābō'*) of II Sam. 5.20 would seem to be the more original, since 'going up' against the Philistines is the *Leitmotif* of this episode, and a key-word in the whole passage (vv. 8, 10bis, 11, 14).

In place of 'the Lord has broken through ... *before me*' (II Sam. 5.20), the Chronicler reads: 'God has broken through ... *by my hand*', making the theological point more obvious. The victory is made possible not only through God's standing by David and helping him but also through David's role as an instrument of God's will in the war against the Philistines.

On the interchange of *qārā'-qār^e'ū*, cf. also I Chron. 11.7 against II Sam. 5.9.

[12] This verse is one of the best-known examples of the refined midrashic technique employed by the Chronicler in adjusting his sources to the laws of the Pentateuch (cf. recently, I. L. Seeligmann, 'The Beginnings of *Midrash* in the Book of Chronicles', *Tarbiz* XLIX, 1979, 19ff.*). Much of the impact of the verse lies in the economical yet clear-cut manner in which this particular midrashic procedure is applied.

In their flight from the Israelite army, the Philistines leave behind them the statues of their gods, and according to II Sam. 5.21 'David and his men carried them away' (NEB, JPS 'carried ... off'). Literally and historically the event is an antithesis of I Sam. 4.10–11, and is usually regarded as fully reliable. The spoil of the divine statues, adorned as they were with costly metals and precious stones, was not only of religious but also of economic significance: they were the 'crowning acquisition' of the victorious army (cf. also II Sam. 12.30). However, an incident which posed no problem for the author of Samuel had become an impossibility for the Chronicler. Such an act was definitely a transgression of an explicit command: 'you shall ... burn their graven images with fire' (Deut. 7.5). By means of a light textual change the Chronicler presents David as complying with this law: 'David gave command, and they were burned.'

The import of this adjustment is first and foremost for the development of midrashic exegesis, for the literary techniques it employed, and for the understanding of Chronicles as a stage within the emerging midrashic process. However, this generally accepted interpretation has been challenged from two angles. (*a*) Some scholars see no midrashic element in the verse but claim that adherence to the Deuteronomic law is found already in the version of II Sam. 5.21. They would interpret the verb as a synonym for 'burn', following rabbinic literature (cf. in detail, Seeligmann, ibid., n. 15). (*b*) For others, the change does indeed have midrashic significance, but this should be attributed not to the Chronicler but to his *Vorlage*. Some of the MSS of LXX II Sam 5.21 reflect the reading/interpretation 'burn', and according to W. E. Lemke ('The Synoptic Problem in the Chronicler's History', *HTR* 58, 1965, 351–2) this may indicate a deviant Hebrew reading. Such a view has a bearing upon the development of the midrashic process by antedating its inception to an era prior to Chronicles, but does not affect the basic understanding of this verse (cf. also Williamson, 118–19).

Another difference between this verse and its parallel in II Sam. 5 is the reading 'gods' in place of 'idols'. It is likely that the original version has been preserved by the Chronicler, who had no scruples about the names and epithets of the heathen deities, a sensitivity which is abundantly demonstrated in the editing of Samuel (cf. above p. 198 etc.).

[14–15] In both versions the account of the second battle is presented in a shorter format. Although there is a reference to David's inquiry of God, its actual phrasing is omitted, and God's answer follows immediately. Here, in contrast to the first occasion, instead of a general assurance of victory, David receives detailed tactical instructions: to avoid direct contact with the Philistines and to attack them from 'opposite the balsam trees'. The identification of *bᵉkā'îm* as trees, and more specifically as 'balsam trees', is uncertain (NEB 'aspens'). The word appears elsewhere only once, in the singular, in Ps. 84.7 (RSV 'the valley of Baca', v. 6). The exegetical tradition of 'tree' was probably inspired by 'the sound of marching in the tops of Bechaim', but this is far from being conclusive.

God's answer contains what may be interpreted as a strongly anthropomorphical element: 'the sound of marching' is a sign that 'God has gone out before you to smite the ... Philistines'. But the question remains: what is this 'sound of marching', and does it allude to some mythological context already lost?

[16] Victorious in this battle, David goes on to strike the Philistines in other regions of the land. The boundary mentioned here, 'from Geba/Gibeon to Gezer', relates to David's success in eradicating the Philistines' presence from the territories of Benjamin and Ephraim – a conclusive response to the people's confidence in making him king (II Sam. 5.2// I Chron. 11.2). Such an achievement was probably a result of a series of battles, of which the one mentioned may have been the first.

[17] The verse is not found in II Sam. 5. In its subject-matter and characteristic phrasing it is similar to other verses in Chronicles such as II Chron. 17.10; 20.29; 26.8, etc. The Chronicler thus places the consequences of the Philistine wars in a broader context: David's victories secure him from additional wars because 'the Lord brought the fear of him upon all nations'. David's greatness has reached its zenith: it is not only he who knows that 'the Lord had established him king' (v. 2), but all the nations around, for his 'fame went out into all lands'. This, indeed, was an appropriate point for David to turn his attention again to his most important project, which had been so abruptly interrupted – the transfer of the ark.

15 David built houses for himself in the city of David; and he prepared a place for the ark of God, and pitched a tent for it. ² Then David said, 'No one but the Levites may carry the ark of God, for the Lord chose them to carry the ark of the Lord and to minister to him for ever.' ³ And David assembled all Israel at Jerusalem, to bring up the ark of the Lord to its place, which he had prepared for it. ⁴ And David gathered together the sons of Aaron and the Levites: ⁵ of the sons of Kohath, Uriel the chief, with a hundred and twenty of his brethren; ⁶ of the sons of Merari, Asaiah the chief, with two hundred and twenty of his brethren; ⁷ of the sons of Gershom, Joel the chief, with a hundred and thirty of his brethren; ⁸ of the sons of Elizaphan, Shemaiah the chief, with two hundred of his brethren; ⁹ of the sons of Hebron, Eliel the chief, with eighty of his brethren; ¹⁰ of the sons of Uzziel, Amminadab the chief, with a hundred and twelve of his brethren. ¹¹ Then David summoned the priests Zadok and Abiathar, and the Levites Uriel, Asaiah, Joel, Shemaiah, Eliel, and Aminadab, ¹² and said to them, You are the heads of the fathers' houses of the Levites; sanctify yourselves, you and your brethren, so that you may bring up the ark of the Lord, the God of Israel, to the place that I have prepared for it. ¹³ Because you did not carry it the first time, the Lord our God broke forth upon us, because we did not care for it in the way that is ordained. ¹⁴ So the priests and the Levites sanctified themselves to bring up the ark of the Lord, the God of Israel. ¹⁵ And the Levites carried the ark of God upon their shoulders with the poles, as Moses had commanded according to the word of the Lord.

16 David also commanded the chiefs of the Levites to appoint their brethren as the singers who should play loudly on musical instruments, on harps and lyres and cymbals, to raise sounds of joy. ¹⁷ So the Levites appointed Heman the son of Joel; and of his brethren Asaph the son of Berechiah; and of the sons of Merari, their brethren, Ethan the son of Kushaiah; ¹⁸ and with them their brethren of the second order, Zechariah, Ja-aziel, Shemiramoth, Jehiel, Unni, Eliab, Benaiah, Ma-aseiah, Mattithiah, Eliphelehu, and Mik-neiah, and the gatekeepers Obededom and Je-iel. ¹⁹ The singers, Heman, Asaph, and Ethan, were to sound bronze cymbals; ²⁰ Zechariah, Azi-el, Shemiramoth, Jehiel, Unni, Eliab, Ma-aseiah, and Benaiah were to play harps according to Alamoth; ²¹ but Mattithiah, Eliphelehu, Mik-neiah, Obed-edom, Je-iel, and Azaziah were to lead with lyres according to the Sheminith. ²² Chenaniah, leader of the Levites in music, should direct the music, for he understood it. ²³ Berechiah and Elkanah were to be gatekeepers for the ark. ²⁴ Shebaniah, Joshaphat, Nethanel, Amasai, Zechariah, Benaiah, and Eliezer, the priests, should blow the trumpets before the ark of God. Obed-edom and Jehiah also were to be gatekeepers for the ark.

25 So David and the elders of Israel, and the commanders of thousands, went to bring up the ark of the covenant of the Lord from the house of Obed-edom with rejoicing. ²⁶ And because God helped the Levites who were carrying the ark of the covenant of the Lord, they sacrificed seven bulls and seven rams. ²⁷ David was

clothed with a robe of fine linen, as also were all the Levites who were carrying the ark, and the singers, and Chenaniah the leader of the music of the singers; and David wore a linen ephod. [28] So all Israel brought up the ark of the covenant of the Lord with shouting, to the sound of the horn, trumpets, and cymbals, and made loud music on harps and lyres.

29 And as the ark of the covenant of the Lord came to the city of David, Michal the daughter of Saul looked out of the window, and saw King David dancing and making merry; and she despised him in her heart.

A. Notes to MT

[18] בֶּן, omit, with several Hebrew MSS and LXX; אֱלִיאָב, add *waw*, with several MSS; וְיעִיאֵל, the name עוזיהו or עזזיהו should probably be added, with LXX, cf. v. 21; הַשֹּׁעֲרִים, probably a gloss; [23] gloss? [24] וִיחִיה, probably וְאַחִיו, cf. commentary; [25] הַהֹלְכִים, read הֹלְכִים, dittography of *he*; [27] הַשַּׂר, read שַׂר, dittography of *he*; הַמְשֹׁרְרִים, dittography? cf. commentary.

B. Notes to RSV

[1] 'David built houses', MT 'He built houses'; [2] 'David said, "No one ..."', etc., MT indirect speech, NEB 'David decreed that ...' (JPS 'David gave orders that ...'); [16] 'as the singers', MT 'the singers'; [22] 'for he understood it', better with JPS 'for he was a master'; [24] 'also', added to MT (adjustment to v. 23?).

C. Structure, sources and form

1. From the point of view of its sources, the chapter is divided into two distinct parts: vv. 25–29 are based on the continuation of the account of the transfer of the ark in II Sam. 6.12b–16, while there is no parallel to vv. 1–24 in any biblical source. The following questions naturally arise: What are the sources for this section? How and why were they integrated into the present context?

2. Verses 1–24 are devoted to one comprehensive subject: the preparations for the second transfer of the ark. No such passage is found in the original story of II Sam. 6; the subject is conspicuous by its absence. One may, however, deduce from the narrative as it stands not only the fact that these preparations took place but also some of their details.

(*a*) David had prepared a tent as a place to receive the ark (II Sam. 6.17 – note the past perfect of the verb נטה).

(*b*) The people were assembled for the occasion (II Sam. 6.15, 18–19).

(*c*) A different system of transporting the ark had been introduced: there is no mention of a cart, and II Sam. 6.13 speaks of 'those who bore the ark'.

(*d*) Sacrificial animals had been provided, and the necessary personnel for their sacrifice were prepared (II Sam. 6.13).

(*e*) Musicians for sounding the horn had also been put in readiness (II Sam. 6.15).

Although these details give a clear indication that David had made thorough preparations for every aspect of the transfer of the ark, the author of the narrative did not devote a special narrative-unit to that stage; the preparations are to be understood as implicit in the story of the transfer itself. Therefore, the two attempts to transfer the ark are structured as a literary sequence, separated only by one half-verse: 'and it was told David ... because of the ark of God' (II Sam. 6.12a), the strict sequence being, however, only in literary terms and not in the actual events.

In Chronicles, as I have already mentioned, the sequel of the story is conceived differently. For the Chronicler, the intermediate phase is of the utmost importance, and he divides it into two parts: a series of actions which prove David's blessedness (14.1–17), and a series of steps providing strictly for all the details of the second transfer attempt. Even after this detailed description, some matters (such as the sacrifices) do not receive full attention.

The details in this section refer basically to issues implicit in the narrative in II Sam., but here made explicit or extensively elaborated. These include the pitching of a tent for the ark (I Chron. 15.1) and the assembling of all the people (15.3), but greater attention is given to two other issues: the bringing of the ark 'in the way that is ordained' (כמשפט, v. 13), and the singing and playing which would accompany the procession.

The failure of the first attempt had resulted, according to the Chronistic view, from a wrong procedure in handling the ark, because of carelessness. This subject therefore demanded maximum attention (vv. 2, 4–15). In the same way, the singing and playing had to be attended to by professionals – priests and Levites; vv. 16–24 describe their organization. Quantitatively, these two major subjects are equally treated.

3. The principal functions involved in the transfer of the ark – carrying, singing and playing – are allotted to the Levites, who are, appropriately, divided into two groups: the bearers of the ark (vv. 5ff.) and the singers (vv. 17ff). Other functionaries are, however, also mentioned. In the organization and supervision of the undertaking, the two high priests Zadok and Abiathar are given a part (vv. 4, 11; cf. below p. 298). The priests are also allotted the exclusive function of sounding the trumpets (v. 24); the gatekeepers are also mentioned (vv. 23, 24, cf. below). Although it is not expressly stated, it may be assumed that the offering of sacrifices (15.26; 16.1) was regarded as being a priestly role as a matter of course.

4. The elements which are described in pedantic detail in the preparatory stage (vv. 1–24) are all later brought into play in the description of the transfer itself (vv. 25–28). The latter is taken basically from II Sam. 6.12b–16, but has been extensively reworked:

(a) It is not only David who is the subject of the account (cf. II Sam. 6.12b, 'So David went and brought up the ark'), but a much broader circle, representing all the people: 'So David and the elders of Israel, and the commanders of thousands went ... to bring up the ark' (I Chron. 15.25).

(b) It is emphasized that 'those who bore the ark' (II Sam. 6.13) are none other than 'the Levites who were carrying the ark' (I Chron. 15.26).

(c) The sacrifice (cf. II Sam. 6.13) is referred to in v. 26b.

(d) In place of 'David danced before the Lord with all his might' (II Sam. 6.4a), the singing and playing of the levitical singers is introduced (I Chron. 15.27b), and in addition to the 'shouting and ... the sound of the horn' (II Sam. 6.15//I Chron. 15.28a), the 'trumpets, cymbals, harps and lyres' (the same instruments mentioned in

vv. 19–24) are also introduced (16.28b). In short: the changes introduced into the Chronistic description of the transfer itself are calculated to conform to the letter with the implications of the broader section, introduced in vv. 1–24.

5. An examination of the section as a whole reveals that it is a literary unit, the parts of which form a unified whole, and adjust well into their actual context. Some unevenness is to be found only in the matter of the 'gatekeepers' mentioned in vv. 18, 23, 24 (cf. below).

This view of the unity of the section stands in opposition to the attitude of quite a few commentators, who would regard it as the product of a cumulative process of editing and glossing through which it reached its present form. Rudolph, for example, regards only vv. 1–3, 11–15, 25–29 as Chronistic, with vv. 4–10, 16–24 as later additions. Thus Rudolph sees only eight out of the twenty-four verses which do not parallel II Sam. 6.12b–16 as Chronistic, and even of these he would attribute some phrases to later hands, i.e. 'the priests Zadok and Abiathar' in v. 11, 'the priests' in v. 14, and the words 'as also were the Levites ... of the singers' in v. 27 (ibid., 115). Moreover, according to Rudolph, the additions themselves are varied, and within the secondary vv. 16–24, vv. 22–24 should be regarded as the latest stratum.

Rudolph's work seems to be guided by several presuppositions, the solidity of which is not always confirmed by actual findings in Chronicles. Thus, for example, the argument that vv. 4–10 are parallel to v. 11 is for him a sufficient proof that vv. 4–10 are a later, inauthentic, addition. This conclusion is evidently based on the unspoken assumption that no repetition whatsoever, even the interchange of generalizations with detailed descriptions, is to be expected from the Chronicler. As a result, not enough attention is given to the final format of the material, and a hasty recourse is taken to 'additions' before other, less radical, possibilities have been exhausted. Rudolph does not even try to investigate the meaning of such repetitions or their role in the literary structure. The more crucial question is, of course, why the Chronicler should be denied the use of repetition – one of the most common rhetorical and literary techniques. In the final analysis, Rudolph fails to handle satisfactorily the problems raised by his recourse to 'additions', such as the questions of their *raison d'être*, and of how a chain of accidental additions could ripen into an harmonious and well-adjusted whole.

These questions make one wonder whether there is more to the matter than the overt, explicit considerations. Thus, for example, an examination of ch. 15 from the point of view of genres would immediately reveal that the non-parallel material comprises two components: narrative sections, incorporating the shorter and longer speeches of David (vv. 1–4, 11–17a), and lists (vv. 5–10, 17–24). A synopsis of these data with Rudolph's analysis reveals at once the correlation between the two. Most of the narrative material is attributed by Rudolph to the Chronicler, but none of the lists. One wonders, therefore, whether this, and not the assumed repetition, is Rudolph's point of departure. Is this a result of his implicit wish to bring Chronicles closer to the Deuteronomistic historiography, making it more attractive to the modern reader?

A view similar to Rudolph's is also suggested by Willi (196) and Myers (110–13). Even Williamson, who ordinarily shows more restraint in these matters, follows Welch in detecting in this pericope a 'priestly editing' (Welch, 65–66; Williamson, 123). I shall refer to some of these matters in the commentary.

6. Whether we regard all of ch. 15 as written by the Chronicler, or whether we

attribute to him all or most of the narrative sections alone, there seems to be no doubt that the new narrative elements, including the speeches, are his own composition. They originate in the Chronicler's understanding of the events, and are the inevitable conclusions of his theological presuppositions. Not so the lists; for them the question of sources is much more pertinent. What is their provenance? Are they authentic? And, finally, by whom and for what purpose were they incorporated into the present context? The two lists contained in ch. 15 differ in essence and function. The first, in vv. 5–10, registers the names of six chiefs of the Levites, the heads of fathers' houses, with the number of their 'brethren'. It may reflect, then, a census taken of the central levitical families at some juncture. The more precise historical background of the list is difficult to ascertain, and we will discuss it in the framework of the levitical divisions (I Chron. 23). Generally speaking, however, it might reflect some real situation of the Second Commonwealth, before, after, or contemporary with, the Chronicler. The fact that v. 11 mentions the same chiefs, and in the same order, may indicate that the Chronicler made use of an already existing list.

The second list, in vv. 17–22, is of a completely different nature. It reflects a comprehensive system of cultic music, and has three components: 1. the names of the singers, both the 'heads' and those of the second order (vv. 17–18); 2. a classification of the singers according to their musical speciality – cymbals, harps and lyres (vv. 19, 20, 21, 22, respectively) and the name of their leader (v. 22); 3. the names of the priests appointed for blowing the trumpets (v. 24). In addition the list refers twice to gatekeepers (in vv. 23, 24b).

The list is firmly anchored in its present context. The leaders of the singers, Heman, Asaph and Ethan, all three presented as sounding the 'bronze cymbals', are the ones who figure elsewhere as the forefathers of the singers (cf. mainly I Chron. 6.31–47 [MT 16–32], and further below), and were regarded as the founders of the fathers' houses from whom all the singers claimed their descent. According to the prevalent biblical genealogical reconstruction, these 'heads' were active in David's time, and were appointed to their tasks by him (cf. I Chron. 25.1ff; II Chron. 29.25, etc.) The depiction of these eponymic fathers as actual historical figures, participating together in a specific contemporary event, is therefore a literary expedient of a historiosophical and theological nature, and not an authentic reflection of the historical situation. Consequently, the historicity of all the other names should also be questioned. The individual names, of course, or certain combinations of them, could very well have been authentic; however, the nominal organization of the list as a whole cannot have originated in the setting to which it claims to belong.

The historical data of this list are of consequence, therefore, not in determining specific names and a particular historical event to which they are connected, but rather in the information they contain about the general organization of the singers in the Second Temple: their division into three main 'fathers' houses', named Heman, Asaph and Ethan; the internal division of the singers into 'chiefs' and 'those of the second order'; the organization of the musical instruments: cymbals for the 'heads' and other instruments – harps and lyres – for the second order; the inclusion of priests as sounders of the trumpets; and the existence of a 'leader', responsible for the system as a whole. These elements, in their general form rather than in their expression in particular names, may reflect a certain stage in the development and organization of the singers, at a certain point in the Second Temple period. The question here is twofold: can we determine more precisely the place of this specific situation in the development of the Temple music, or position it *vis à vis* the Chronicler himself?

The only point of departure for such a discussion is in the names and order of the three fathers' houses into which the singers are divided. Several attempts have been made to reconstruct the development of the order of singers from the genealogical information in the Bible. According to H. Gese, 'Zur Geschichte der Kultsänger am zweiten Tempel', in *Von Sinai zum Zion*, Munich 1974, 147–58, the two last stages of this development are reflected in the book of Chronicles: in both stages the singers were affiliated to three fathers' houses, first to Asaph, Heman and Jeduthun, and later to Heman, Asaph and Ethan. The first of these affiliations was contemporaneous with the Chronicler himself, while the second was later.

Without going into details, one should remark that the relative placement of these two stages is not reached through a reconstruction of the history of the singers, but deduced from the literary analysis of Chronicles on which Gese is drawing. According to this analysis, 15.17–24 (as well as I Chron. 6.31ff.[MT 16ff.] and a large section in I Chron. 16) are post-Chronistic, and this leads the discussion in a vicious circle. Underlying all this is the presupposition that there is only one solution to the problem of discordant details found in Chronicles, and that is to assume that every incongruous detail should be attributed to later interpolators. However, the same discord could well originate in differing sources used by the Chronicler, and the same tolerance for incongruity in details attributed to the 'interpolator' could have been characteristic of the Chronicler himself. In this specific case, the material itself seems to indicate this approach.

The two last stages of the development of the singers are harmonized by the assumption that 'Ethan' and 'Jeduthun' were interchangable names for one person. This alone would enable a reasonable interpretation of the final form of the material, whether collated by the 'interpolator' or by the Chronicler. Since the incorporation of the singers into the narrative is carried out with a clear perspective of the overall context, and with refined literary skill, it is more difficult to attribute it to a secondary hand. Moreover, the list of the singers cannot be completely isolated as an independent element; it is fully integrated into the description. It is not, therefore, a 'bare' list, but a literary composition based on registrative material and used in the broader literary context, which also includes the following section of the narrative (v. 27). These considerations seem to support the conclusion that this material was not added in a secondary stage, but compiled and composed by the Chronicler himself, in the service of his literary and historical conceptions.

D. *Commentary*

[1] The subject matter of the verse is clear, but its phrasing in MT is not. Since the grammatical subject of the verse is left implicit (MT '*He* built houses'; RSV '*David* built'), the verse is taken to be a direct sequel of 14.17. There, however, the last explicit subject was the Lord. This difficulty can be overcome either by suggesting that a few words, or at least the subject, have dropped out of the text (so RSV), or by assuming that the Chronicler endeavoured to produce a text which was a cohesive continuation of what

preceded, but failed. The main point of the verse is the statement that David did not abandon the idea of transferring the ark; while carrying on with his building enterprises in Jerusalem, he also pitched a tent for the ark.

[2] The second act of preparation is in establishing how the ark shall be carried. The failure of the first transfer on one hand, and the blessing of David on the other, have brought David to the correct conclusion that the failure resulted from the mode of transfer; this now has to be given attention and changed.

I have pointed out above that a different manner of carrying the ark in the second attempt can already be deduced from II Sam. 6.13, which mentions 'those who bore the ark of the Lord'. It is clear that it is men who bear the ark and not an ox-drawn cart. However, in contrast to II Sam. the Chronicler greatly elaborates the matter. On the one hand, he follows the traditions of the Pentateuch, but on the other hand he is eager to assign important roles and positions to the levitical order.

The instructions for carrying the ark are phrased in affinity with Deuteronomic texts. The first phrase, 'No one but the Levites may carry the ark', follows Deut. 10.8, while the second, 'for the Lord chose them to carry the ark of the Lord and to minister to him for ever', follows Deut. 18.5. This is another example of the Chronicler's anthological style: selecting ready-made elements from various texts, he weaves them into one fabric, and uses the whole to express his own attitudes.

Although the phrasing is obviously Deuteronomic, formulated with the words of Moses as found in Deuteronomy, one still must ask about the origin of the instructions themselves. In fact, I Chron. 15 lends itself to two explanations for the origin of the prescription which authorized only Levites to carry the ark. The more orthodox attitude would regard this chapter as reflecting the tradition found in the Pentateuch, according to which it was Moses who initiated the institution: the Chronicler, by using Deuteronomic phraseology, depicts David as following the legal norms of the Pentateuch (cf. above, on 14.12). The other explanation, however, would place heavy emphasis on the opening of the verse, 'āz 'āmar dāwīd, which is probably best represented by NEB 'David decreed' or JPS 'David ordered'. This formulation may seem to imply that the restrictions on the carrying of the ark were decreed for the first time on that very occasion, by David, and were not based on previously known norms.

We do not have sufficient data for deciding between the two possibilities. On the one hand, the very attribution of solid, independent and, one may even venture to say, historical traditions to the Chronicler is highly problematical, in view of the strong theological colour of his work. On the other hand, the assignment of this decree to David, on the occasion of the transfer of the ark, has a strong base in Chronicles (cf. also II Chron. 35.3), and its corollaries for the whole system of the levitical roles are so central and significant (cf. also I Chron. 6.31ff. [MT 6.16ff.]), that one wonders whether a historical or ancient basis may underlie the tradition which attributes to David the establishing of a levitical prerogative of carrying the ark. (The transfer of a Davidic ruling to Moses could serve as an example of the back-projection of institutions as a general feature of biblical historiographical motivation, cf. E. Voegelin, *Order and History* I, Louisiana 1956, 174ff.)

[3] The actual preparations now begin, with the assembling of the people in Jerusalem. The verse opens in full parallelism to I Chron. 13.5, 'So David assembled all Israel', but then goes its own way: instead of the 'froms' there are the 'to's'; in place of the vast geographical regions from which the people are gathered, we have here their destination, 'to Jerusalem'; and instead of 'to bring the ark of God *from* Kiriath-jearim', which suited the previous context in spite of the failure, we have here 'to bring up the ark ... to its place which he had prepared for it' – perfectly suitable in the present context.

[4] In full parallelism to 13.2–5, David also gathers the priests and the Levites to Jerusalem.

Since in the following verses (5–10) only the chiefs of the Levites are mentioned by name, and in the whole undertaking of transferring the ark no mention is made of the priests; and since in general the Chronicler is regarded as being interested only in the Levites, some scholars would regard the words 'the sons of Aaron and' here and 'the priests Zadok and Abiathar and' in v. 11, as 'priestly additions' (Welch, 65–6; Rudolph, 115; Williamson, 123). However, there is little support for this suggestion. There is no doubt that the Levites play a more prominent role in Chronicles than the priests, and that their interests are closer to the Chronicler's heart. Nevertheless, there is no reason to assume that this observation should be pushed to an extreme 'all or nothing' position. It is hardly likely that the Chronicler would ignore the priesthood altogether, or deny its well-established rights. One need only recall the placing of the high priest by the king's side, a proximity greatly emphasized in I Chron. 29.22, at the accession of Solomon, the participation of the priests in the organization of the clergy (I Chron. 23.1ff., also in II Chron. 31.13), and the careful safeguarding of their rights in II Chron. 26.16ff. The fact that they play only a secondary role in the present context should not, therefore, imply their complete absence. The priests are in charge of well-defined tasks such as sounding the trumpets and offering sacrifices, roles reserved for them in 15.24 and 16.39–40. Therefore, the suggestion to omit the priests in vv. 4 and 11 must be deemed quite arbitrary, not only for lack of textual justification but in the light of the Chronicler's general approach.

[5–10] These verses list the Levites in six groups, presented in a fixed pattern, thus: 'of the sons of X, Y the chief, with Z of his brethren'. The numbers range from 80 (of the sons of Hebron) to 220 (of the sons of Merari), and amount to 862 in all. The stereotyped structure is conspicuous – in harmony with certain similar lists in Chronicles, and in contrast with others. The division of the Levites is peculiar. According to the traditional genealogical framework of the Levites, found in the Pentateuch and also demonstrated in Chronicles, the Levites consist of three families, headed by three 'fathers' – Gershom, Kohath and Merari. The present context has these in a different order – Kohath, Merari and Gershom – and adds the families of Elizaphan, Hebron and Uzziel. Of these, Hebron and Uzziel are presented in Ex. 6.16 as Kohath's sons (together with Amram and Izhar), while Elizaphan is Uzziel's son, Kohath's grandson. In the situation reflected in the list, the family of Kohath has been further divided, and some branches (regarded in certain texts as 'the rest of the Kohathites', Josh. 21.20) have been given an independent status. The families of Hebron and Uzziel are also referred to in I Chron. 23.19–20; 24.23–24, while Elizaphan (mentioned in Num. 3.30 as 'head of the fathers' house of the families of the Kohathites') is regarded as an independent levitical branch in II Chron. 29.13, where he alone is added to the three 'established' levitical families of Kohath, Merari and Gershom.

[11–24] The nature and order of David's preparations bring to mind several other events, the description of which is peculiar to Chronicles. Most important of these are the cleansing of the Temple by Hezekiah in II Chron. 29 and the celebration of the Passover by Josiah in II Chron. 35. Although the details vary from case to case, all these passages share common features and a common sequence. The central points of similarity are the initiation of a project by the king, the summons of the priests and Levites with an appeal for their co-operation, and a speech delivered by the king in explanation of the undertaking and the role of the clergy in it. Also common to these stories is the primary role of the Levites (versus a secondary role for the priests), and the sanctification of the participants.

After assembling the priests and the Levites (vv. 4–10), David summons and addresses only their leaders, that is, Zadok and Abiathar the priests and six Levites recorded by name. The delegation of authority and the order of action is clear: David first delivers exact instructions in preparation for the carrying of the ark (vv. 12–13), and the execution of these instructions is recorded (vv. 14–15). Further, David goes on with the instructions to appoint the singers (v. 16), and these too are meticulously carried out (vv. 17–24). At that stage everything is ready for the procession to begin.

Some scholars would prefer a different structure for the Chronicler's description and suggest an alternative arrangement of the material: first the instructions in full and then the execution in full. These scholars would like to see v. 16 follow v. 13, and since it does not they regard it as secondary (cf.

Rudolph, 115). However, no explanation is given why a certain literary structure, i.e. 'instruction a+b – execution a+b' is authentic and admissible, while a different literary structure, namely 'instruction a – execution a; instruction b – execution b', is not. I can understand that one might wish to have the Chronicler's literary taste conform with one's own, but this cannot be forced.

The close relationship between the two instructions is emphasized by their position in the story and their length. Concern for the proper carrying of the ark is the focus of David's speech and considered in detail. The appointment of the singers and musicians is a direct result and corollary of that concern.

The clergy, and even more so the Levites, occupy the central place of this section. Note the various forms of reference to them:

v. 4:   the sons of Aaron and the Levites
v. 11: the priests, Zadok and Abiathar and the Levites
v. 12: the heads of the fathers' houses of the Levites ...
v. 15: the Levites [MT the sons of the Levites]
v. 16: the chiefs of the Levites
v. 17: the Levites.

The term 'Levites' is used in this context in its two primary meanings, also attested elsewhere: the first use denotes those of the tribe of Levi who are not priests; this is surely meant in all cases where the priests are mentioned separately, in addition to the 'Levites' (vv. 4, 11, 14). The other reference is to all the members of the tribe of Levi including the priests, as in v. 12 (cf. v. 14). The double usage of the term causes ambiguity in some of the verses; in v. 15 the first meaning is probably intended, in v. 16 the second. A more homogenous terminology may be achieved by regarding all the references to the priests as secondary (vv. 4, 11, 14, cf. above, p. 298), but even then the reference to the Levites themselves would not be standardized. Moreover, the variations in the presentation of the priests – three terms of reference, all different – would suggest the hand of an author characterized by an inclination for stylistic variety, rather than stereotyped editing.

[12–13] David's speech is composed of two parts, the first relating to the things which must be done, and the second giving their explanation. Some points need attention:

1. David's words in these verses are accurately repeated in the execution of the orders, in vv. 14–15. The similarities and the differences should be pointed out.

12: sanctify yourselves	14: sanctified themselves
that you may bring up	to bring up
the ark of the Lord	the ark of the Lord
the God of Israel.	the God of Israel.

Thus v. 14 is almost an exact echo of v. 12, in the repetition required by 'command and fulfilment', while v. 15 provides the explanation of v. 13. One phrase in v. 12 is not repeated in v. 14: 'to the place that I have prepared for it'. This clause provides the verse with a connecting link, not to what follows, but to what came before: v. 1, 'and he prepared a place'; v. 3, 'to its place, which he had prepared for it'.

2. Another conspicuous feature in these verses is the emphasis on 'you', (*'attem*): 'you are ... yourselves ... you did not ... etc.' (the emphasis is not fully conveyed by the English translation). The point of this emphasis, and of the general use of persons is clear: 'when it was not *you* – the Lord smote *us*, therefore *our* way is to appoint *you*.'

3. The key-word of this passage is 'the ark of the Lord', repeated three times (vv. 12, 14, 15).

David's explanations in v. 13 are directly connected with the description of the preceding events. The words 'for we did not seek it (RSV 'did not care for it') in the way that is ordained' hark back to I Chron. 13.3: 'for we did not seek it (RSV 'neglected it') in the days of Saul'. The point of this similarity in phrasing is to indicate the stages of the people's approach to God. In the days of Saul they did not seek the ark at all; in the first attempt to transfer the ark they did not seek it 'as ordained'.

The first part of the verse, 'the Lord ... broke forth upon us', is connected with 13.11: 'the Lord had broken forth upon Uzza'. However, the shift from third person to first is significant: the death of Uzza was 'our' punishment. This is an admission of sin and an acceptance of full responsibility. It was not Uzza who sinned, but 'we'.

The correct way of carrying the ark is referred to here in general terms 'in the way that is ordained', but v. 15 defines this 'way' explicitly.

The clause *l*ᵉ*mabbāri'šōnāh lō' 'attem* is difficult in two ways. The predicate is missing – supplemented by the translations (RSV 'carry'; NEB 'present'; JPS 'were ... there'), and the form *l*ᵉ*mabbāri'šōnāh* is unique and difficult. The syntactic difficulty could have arisen from the late biblical Hebrew use of elliptic clauses (cf. Curtis, 34 and 117), and in this case the supplementation by the translations would be justified. The unusual form *l*ᵉ*mabbāri'šōnāh* has been interpreted mainly in two ways: 1. as a combination of 'why' (*lāmāh*) and 'at first' (*bāri'šōnāh*, Curtis, 214); 2. as an accumulation of prepositions *b*ᵉ, *min*, *l*ᵉ + *ri'šōnāh* (Rudolph, 116). However, in both cases the words *lāmāh* and *l*ᵉ*min* must be interpreted in an unusual way, if any logical meaning is to be wrung from them. It would therefore seem preferable to regard the first two letters *m*, *l*, as the result of some corruption, and go back to the more common adverb, *bāri'šōnāh*.

[14–15] Verse 14 parallels vv. 12–13, while v. 15 explains more specifically the general statement 'as ordained'. The explanation comprises two elements: the right way of carrying the ark, 'upon their shoulders with the poles', and the source of authority for this way of carrying: 'as Moses had commanded, according to the word of the Lord'.

The manner of carrying the ark 'upon the shoulders' is also mentioned in II Chron. 35.3: 'you need no longer carry it upon your shoulders', and conforms with the instructions of the Pentateuch, found only once: 'which had to be carried on the shoulder' (Num. 7.9). However, there is some discrepancy between the details of the text and the instructions of the Pentateuch. Here the ark is carried with *mōṭōt*, which, according to the Pentateuch, does not mean 'poles' but some 'carrying frame', used for the transport of the smaller and more precious vessels of the tabernacle, including the lamp (Num. 4.10, 12). The heavier furniture of the tabernacle – ark, table, altar – is indeed carried with 'poles', but they are called *baddîm*. The question regarding the Chronistic description is whether the difference in terminology is lexical alone. Does *mōṭōt* replace *baddîm* (the view taken by RSV, which translates *mōṭōt* 'poles'), or was a change in the actual manner of transport presupposed, with a 'carrying frame' rather than 'poles'?

It is evident, however, that there is no literal correspondence between the manner of carrying the ark and the practice established in the Pentateuch. The words 'as Moses had commanded' are therefore only of general import. They do not refer the reader to any specific precept or to any given text found in the Pentateuch, but only state that the transfer was carried out with legal precision, in full conformity with the will of God, as expressed in the Mosaic command.

[16] When the arrangements for a proper carrying of the ark are complete, David's attention is turned to another matter: the organization of playing and singing to accompany the ark. The very fact that the bringing of the ark was accompanied by music is also mentioned in II Sam. 6.12–15, but in Chronicles there is much more detail, and the task is entrusted to those who are best qualified for it – the levitical singers.

The task of appointing the singers is delegated by David to 'the chiefs of the Levites', who then appoint the 'heads' of the singers – Heman, Asaph and Ethan. These latter, then, are not regarded as 'chiefs' themselves, but are subordinate to the 'chiefs' and described as 'their brethren'. On the one hand this would indicate that the singers have been identified, and absorbed completely into, the Levites (in contrast to Ezra 2.41 etc., where they are still regarded as an independent, non-levitical class). On the other hand, notwithstanding their significance in Chronicles, these 'heads' are not regarded as 'chiefs', and they form only one sector in the overall levitical framework.

The musical instruments are carefully recorded: harps and lyres, and then cymbals (in vv. 19–21 in a different order: cymbals, and then harps and lyres). These are, of course, the purely 'levitical' instruments, excluding the 'priestly' trumpets.

The terminology here is characteristic of all passages which deal with cultic music: 'play loudly', 'raise sounds', 'joy' (cf. also 15.28; 16.5, 42; II Chron. 5.13, etc.)

[17] Just as v. 14 (execution) echoes v. 12 (instruction), so v. 17 echoes v. 16 'So the Levites appointed …' The heads of the singers are three, in the following order: Heman the son of Joel; Asaph the son of Berechiah; and Ethan the son of Kushaiah. Both the names themselves and their order establish a close affinity between this chapter and I Chron. 6.31–47 [MT 16–32]. Moreover, while the first two are mentioned without indication of family origins, Ethan is ascribed to Merari and defined as of the 'brethren' of the other two. A very similar phrasing is found also in I Chron. 6.31ff. [MT 6.16ff.], where, although the genealogical registration goes back to Kohath, Gershon and Merari, the terminology is similar: Heman … (v. 33) and his brother Asaph (v. 39) … their brethren the sons of Merari, Ethan (v. 44). These two texts, with the close affinity between them, reflect one view about the registration and organization of the singers, those whom David appointed 'after the ark rested' (I Chron. 6.31 [MT 6.16ff.]. The slight variation in the name of Kishi/Kushaiha may reflect alternative forms of the same name, quite a common phenomenon in the list material.

[18] Here the singers of 'the second order' are recorded, fourteen in all (omitting Ben with several Hebrew MSS + LXX and adding Uzziahu). The reference to the gatekeepers at the end of the verse seems to be a later gloss. As clearly demonstrated in v. 21, Obed-edom and Jeiel are included among the singers. However, a stronger tradition identifies Obed-edom with one of the major fathers' houses of the gatekeepers (I Chron. 26.4), probably claiming descent from Obed-edom the Gittite, in whose house the ark was placed. This is probably what prompted a glossator to identify Obed-edom, the singer, as a gatekeeper. The name itself, although characteristic of the gatekeepers, should not be regarded as exclusively so.

[19–21] Certain points in these verses repeat vv. 17–18, clearly demonstrating the author's intention to elaborate the description rather than to shorten it. In vv. 17–18 the Levites were presented by name, divided according to their heads, and 'those of the second order'. Verses 19–21 again introduce the Levites by name, but their division into three groups is based on their musical speciality. The first group consists of the three 'heads', all sounding the cymbals, while the rest are divided between the playing of harps 'according to Alamoth' and leading the lyres 'according to the Sheminith'. The organization of the cultic music is thus clearly portrayed: the head-singer was responsible for the cymbals, the playing of which was defined as 'sounding' (cf. also 16.5) and had probably some conducting role, while the other singers were divided between the two other instruments. Here there is probably a broad rank of singers, with all three heads and all those of the second order participating. Later on, in establishing the permanent arrangements, their number will be reduced.

The terms 'Alamoth', 'Sheminith' and 'lead' (*nṣḥ*), which also occur in the Psalms and belong to the realm of Temple musical functions, have not yet been fully clarified (cf. recently, B. Bayer, 'The Titles of the Psalms. A Renewed Investigation of an Old Problem', *Yuval* IV, 1982, 29–123). It would seem, though, that the unusual phrases here, combining the names of the musical instruments with the titles of the psalm headings, are evidence that their meaning had already become obscure and their use is archaistic (so Bayer, 78).

[22] The verse is difficult, as its terminology seems ambivalent. An additional 'leader' is presented here, with a special role in the transfer of the ark, defined as *maśśā'*. This word (from the root *nś'*) could refer either to the carrying of the ark (cf. vv. 2, 15, 26, 27 and the noun *maśśā'*, recurring in Num. 4.15, 24, etc.) or to the raising of the voice, probably also connected with 'prophecy' (cf. *BDB*, 672; Baumgartner, 604; Curtis, 216; Rudolph, 118). The second possibility is followed by RSV and indeed seems more relevant to the immediate context, although in the broader literary unit the root *nś'* is used for carrying. A context of singing and playing is also suggested by the description of the 'leader' as 'master' (*mēbîn*, RSV understood), which is mentioned again in I Chron. 25. 7–8.

[23] The allusion to Berechiah and Elkanah as 'gatekeepers for the ark' is difficult, for the following reasons: 1. Verse 24b mentions two other persons who also have the same function. 2. Verse 24a lists the names of the priests 'who should blow the trumpets' and who are therefore a part of the musical framework and a direct continuation of the singers. This is attested also by v. 28 and 16.5, where the trumpets form an integral part of the musical arrangement. The mention of gatekeepers interrupts the sequence between v. 22 and 24. 3. The permanent arrangements before the ark, which are connected with this text, mention Obed-edom as gatekeeper (16.38), and not Berechiah and Elkanah. It would seem, therefore, that v. 23 is a later gloss. The two names referred to are found in one genealogical sequence in I Chron. 9.16, but the exact purpose of the gloss can no longer be ascertained.

[24] After the singers, seven priests are listed, who 'should blow the trumpets'. The trumpets are described as a priestly instrument in the Pentateuch (Num. 10.2, 8, 9, 10; 31.6), but there are only two of them, and their use is restricted to specific situations. According to other texts, the trumpets served on additional occasions (II Kings 11.14; 12.14; Ps. 98.6, etc.). In the post-exilic texts the trumpets appear together with other musical

instruments in the Temple service, but their sounding is restricted to the priests (Ezra 3.10; Neh. 12.35, 41; I Chron. 16.6; II Chron. 5.12; 7.6; 13.12, 14; 29.26). Seven as the number of the priests is also evidenced at the dedication of the wall of Jerusalem in the time of Nehemiah (Neh. 12.33–35a, 41). Thus, this verse completes the arrangements for the procession.

At the end of the verse there is reference to 'Obed-edom and Jehiah, gatekeepers for the ark'. This clause raises some questions. 1. In the instructions of David (v. 16) there is no provision for the appointment of gatekeepers, and their appearance is unexpected. 2. What would be the role of gatekeepers in a procession transferring the ark; is not the carrying of the ark entrusted to Levites mentioned already? 3. In comparison to more than eight hundred Levites (vv. 5–10), and almost thirty singers (vv. 19–24), the two gatekeepers are conspicuously few. 4. While Obed-edom is a well-attested name for a gatekeeper, Jehiah is not, and does not appear in 16.38.

To begin with the final question: it would seem that the reading of the clause should actually be: 'Obed-edom and his brethren (*wᵉ'eḥāw* instead of *wîḥiyyāh*) gatekeepers to the ark' (cf. 16.38). This would settle several of the difficulties: account for the otherwise unknown 'Jehiah', postulate a larger, though unspecified number of gatekeepers, and provide a closer affinity with 16.38. As for the matter itself: it would seem that the Chronicler wished to include all the elements of the cultic system in this constitutional event of the transfer of the ark. He therefore introduced the gatekeepers, too, although they probably played no role in the actual transfer. In addition, a close connection was thus demonstrated between the fathers' house of Obed-edom and the man in whose home the ark had been kept.

[25] With this verse, the Chronicler refers back to his source in II Sam. 6, and follows the story of the transfer itself to its successful conclusion (on the differences in detail, cf. above). The main change here is the replacement of 'David went and brought ...' (II Sam. 6.12) with 'David and the elders of Israel and the commanders of thousands went to bring ...', a change which is firmly based on one of the Chronicler's most characteristic traits (cf. above pp. 293–4).

[26] The comparison of v. 26 with its parallel in II Sam. 6.13 shows that the verses are interdependent, one being a reworked form of the other. Still, the differences in detail and theological views are many. The first difference is in theological presuppositions. According to II Sam. 6, once the transfer was executed as it should have been, everything went well. Nevertheless, after six paces (or: after each six paces), David sacrificed an ox and a fatling, to please God and express thanksgiving. In Chronicles, in spite of all the meticulous preparations which are so minutely recorded, the transfer of the ark goes well only because 'God helped the Levites who were carrying the ark'. For the Chronicler, then, this was the difference between the two attempts to

transfer the ark. At the first attempt God 'broke forth upon Uzza'; at the second, he helped the Levites who were carrying the ark 'as ordained'. Nothing can be achieved without the help of God, which is granted to those who seek him 'as ordained'.

The sacrifices are also presented differently in Chronicles: not 'an ox and a fatling', but one sacrifice of 'seven bulls and seven rams'. The terminology of II Sam. 6.13 is non-priestly and is not taken from the specific realm of the Temple cult; it is also referred to in I Kings 1.9, 19, 25; Isa. 1.11. On the other hand, 'a bull and a ram' is distinctly priestly terminology, although it is to be found in non-priestly contexts as well. This change is found also in 4Q Sam., but the fragmentary state of the text does not support any conclusions about the extent of the change, in addition to the description of the sacrifices (cf. Ulrich, 136, 196). Even this alteration would indicate that editorial changes, and not just variant readings of a textual nature, might already have been found in the Chronicler's *Vorlage*.

Another difference between the parallel verses is in the plural 'they sacrificed' which replaces the singular 'he sacrificed' of II Sam. In Chronicles, the possibility of David having sacrificed in person is excluded; the impersonal subject refers probably to the priests.

[27] The verse is taken from II Sam. 6, but the many changes which have been introduced render it almost unrecognizable. However, the editorial process involved in the reworking of the verse is characteristic of the Chronicler. The continuous sentence in the source material is divided at some point into two parts; a section of some length is inserted at the point of the break, and then the sentence continues in its original sequence. Thus: 'And David danced (I Chron. = was clothed) – and David wore a linen ephod.' Therefore, the last clause, 'and David wore, etc.', cannot be regarded as a secondary, post-Chronistic gloss; rather, it constitutes part of the original, demonstrating the peculiar editorial method.

The choice of the word *mᵉkurbāl* ('clothed'), to replace *mᵉkarkēr* ('danced'), is again demonstrative of the Chronicler's method; the graphical similarity of the two words is striking.

būṣ (fine linen) is a late word (Ezek. 27.16; Esther 1.6, 8, 15; I Chron. 4.21; II Chron. 5.12 etc.), equivalent to the earlier *šēš* (cf. A. Hurvitz, 'The Usage of שש and בוץ in the Bible', *HTR* 60, 1967, 117–21). The question is whether the 'robe of fine linen' worn here by David is intended as a priestly garment. As a matter of fact, this is already the case in II Sam. 6, where David is wearing a 'linen ephod', similar to the priests (cf. I Sam. 22.18: 'and Do'eg ... fell upon the priests ... eighty five persons who wore the linen ephod'). The Chronicler retains this detail but adds 'a robe of fine linen', which is not necessarily priestly. The high priest's 'robe of the ephod' was made 'all of blue' (Ex. 28.31), or 'woven all of blue' (Ex. 39.22), while the lay priests wore 'coats woven of fine linen' (Ex. 39.27). The robe of fine linen was probably majestic attire, but not exclusively priestly. What the Chronicler describes here is a kind of 'uniform' of ceremonial white linen, worn by all those associated with the actual transfer of the ark – David, the Levites, the singers and the leader of music.

'(of) the singers' ($w^e ham^e \v{s}\bar{o}rr\bar{i}m$). This seems superfluous after the preceding mention of the singers, and is regarded by most commentators as either an explanatory gloss (cf. Curtis, 219), or a corruption of 'gatekeepers' – $ha\v{s}\v{s}\bar{o}^{ca}r\bar{i}m$ (cf. Rudolph, 119).

[28] 'David and all the house of Israel' of II Sam. 6.15 are presented here as 'David and all Israel'. David had been mentioned in the previous verse, together with all the 'professional' staff, bearing the ark. Here, the people of Israel are referred to, accompanying the ark with singing and playing. To 'shouting and ... the sound of the horn' the Chronicler adds the instruments he is accustomed to, the preparation of which he had previously mentioned: trumpets, cymbals, harps and lyres.

[29] This is one of the best-known verses in Chronicles, for which very many interpretations have been suggested. What is of essential interest is the very fact that it is retained in Chronicles. This issue has several aspects. 1. The Chronicler omits the dramatic episode between David and Michal, which is narrated in II Sam. 6.20–22 at the conclusion of the transfer of the ark, as well as the ensuing remark, 'Michal ... had no child to the day of her death' (v. 23). This verse prepares the way for this episode and therefore is superfluous in a context that omits it. 2. Since the whole episode is missing, the literary sequence would have profited from the omission of v. 29, with a direct transition from v. 28 to 16.1. 3. The contents of the verse are also not well adjusted to the context of Chronicles. In II Sam. 6.14 David is described as having 'danced before the Lord with all his might', and this is what inspired Michal's scorn (II Sam. 6.16). In Chronicles, however, the first mention of David's dance has been changed to read 'David was clothed with a robe of linen' (v. 27), so that here the words 'dancing and making merry' are only very loosely connected with the actual description of the festive procession.

It is obvious, then, that this verse has survived as a detached member. It is neither a preparation for what follows nor integrally connected with what came before, and actually hinders the fluent development of the story. In addition, in contrast to other verses in this section, v. 29 has been left almost untouched, with only slight alterations.

In principle the presence of this verse can be explained away in one of two ways. It may indeed have been omitted by the Chronicler himself, but supplemented later by a post-Chronistic editor, in order to harmonize it with II Sam. Or, it is an additional indication of the incomplete nature of the

Chronicler's reworking: 'a mark of the unskilful art of the Chronicler' (Curtis, 219). However, these two interpretations in effect avoid the main issue and do not account for the actual features of the verse, its transfer to Chronicles in its exact position in the narrative sequence and the minor changes introduced into it, which are indicators of the Chronicler's method. So it should not be ignored; quite the contrary, its meaning and message in the present context should be investigated (cf. mainly, Mosis, 26).

The episode in II Sam. 6 has an aetiological orientation, leading up to Michal's barrenness (v. 23), which in Samuel is relevant to the overall composition and the transfer of kingship from David to Solomon. In Chronicles, on the contrary, the matter is connected only with the present context, the transfer of the ark, and its corollaries. Michal, who is here described as 'the daughter of Saul', has never been introduced in Chronicles as David's wife, and the problem of 'David's succession' is dealt with in Chronicles from a quite different angle. Michal's attitude in this matter reflects the traditional position of the house of Saul: a negative stand toward the ark of the Lord (I Chron. 13.3). Even at the very last moment, when the ark arrives in the 'city of David', the living representative of the house of Saul sticks to this negative, despising attitude – in contrast to David, who does whatever is in his power to 'seek God'.

16

16   And they brought in the ark of God, and set it inside the tent which David had pitched for it; and they offered burnt offerings and peace offerings before God. [2] And when David had finished offering the burnt offerings and the peace offerings, he blessed the people in the name of the Lord, [3] and distributed to all Israel, both men and women, to each a loaf of bread, a portion of meat, and a cake of raisins.

4 Moreover he appointed certain of the Levites as ministers before the ark of the Lord, to invoke, to thank, and to praise the Lord, the God of Israel. [5] Asaph was the chief, and second to him were Zechariah, Je-iel, Shemiramoth, Jehiel, Mattithiah, Eliab, Benaiah, Obed-edom, and Je-iel, who were to play harps and lyres; Asaph was to sound the cymbals, [6] and Benaiah and Jahaziel the priests were to blow trumpets continually, before the ark of the covenant of God.

7 Then on that day David first appointed that thanksgiving be sung to the Lord by Asaph and his brethren.

8 O give thanks to the Lord, call on his name,
    make known his deeds among the peoples!
9 Sing to him, sing praises to him,
    tell of all his wonderful works!
10 Glory in his holy name;
    let the hearts of those who seek the Lord rejoice!
11 Seek the Lord and his strength,
    seek his presence continually!
12 Remember the wonderful works that he has done,
    the wonders he wrought, the judgments he uttered,
13 O offspring of Abraham his servant,
    sons of Jacob, his chosen ones!
14 He is the Lord our God;
    his judgments are in all the earth.
15 He is mindful of his covenant for ever,
    of the word that he commanded, for a thousand generations,
16 the covenant which he made with Abraham,
    his sworn promise to Isaac,
17 which he confirmed as a statute to Jacob,
    as an everlasting covenant to Israel,
18 saying, 'To you I will give the land of Canaan,
    as your portion for an inheritance.'
19 When they were few in number,
    and of little account, and sojourners in it,
20 wandering from nation to nation,
    from one kingdom to another people,
21 he allowed no one to oppress them;

he rebuked kings on their account,
22 saying, 'Touch not my anointed ones,
       do my prophets no harm!'
23 Sing to the Lord, all the earth!
       Tell of his salvation from day to day.
24 Declare his glory among the nations,
       his marvellous works among all the peoples!
25 For great is the Lord, and greatly to be praised,
       and he is to be held in awe above all gods.
26 For all the gods of the peoples are idols;
       but the Lord made the heavens.
27 Honour and majesty are before him;
       strength and joy are in his place.
28 Ascribe to the Lord, O families of the peoples,
       ascribe to the Lord glory and strength!
29 Ascribe to the Lord the glory due his name;
       bring an offering, and come before him!
   Worship the Lord in holy array;
30 tremble before him, all the earth;
       yea, the world stands firm, never to be moved.
31 Let the heavens be glad, and let the earth rejoice,
       and let them say among the nations
       'The Lord reigns!'
32 Let the sea roar, and all that fills it,
       let the field exult, and everything in it
33 Then shall the trees of the wood sing for joy
       before the Lord, for he comes to judge the earth.
34 O give thanks to the Lord, for he is good;
       for his steadfast love endures for ever
35 Say also:
   'Deliver us, O God of our salvation,
       and gather and save us from among the nations,
   that we may give thanks to thy holy name,
       and glory in thy praise.
36 Blessed be the Lord, the God of Israel
       from everlasting to everlasting!'

Then all the people said 'Amen!' and praised the Lord.

37 So David left Asaph and his brethren there before the ark of the covenant of the Lord to minister continually before the ark as each day required, [38] and also Obed-edom, and his sixty-eight brethren; while Obed-edom, the son of Jeduthun, and Hosah were to be gatekeepers. [39] And he left Zadok the priest and his brethren the priests before the tabernacle of the Lord in the high place that was at Gibeon, [40] to offer burnt offerings to the Lord upon the altar of burnt offering continually morning and evening, according to all that is written in the law of the Lord which he commanded Israel. [41] With them were Heman and Jeduthun, and the rest of those chosen and expressly named to give thanks to the Lord, for his steadfast love endures

for ever. [42] Heman and Jeduthun had trumpets and cymbals for the music and instruments for sacred song. The sons of Jeduthun were appointed to the gate.

43 Then all the people departed each to his house, and David went home to bless his household.

A. Notes to MT

[5] יעיאל, read יעזיאל as in 15.18; [15] זכרו, Ps. 105.8 זכר; [19] בהיותכם, Ps. 105.12 בהיותם; [31] ויאמרו בגוים ה' מלך, gloss? [35] וקבצנו, gloss? cf. LXX; [38] cf. commentary; [42] הימן וידותון, dittography?

B. Notes to RSV

[3] 'a portion of meat', JPS 'cake made on fire'; [5] 'were' or 'was', cf. commentary; [6] 'continually', better 'regularly', also vv. 37, 40, cf. NEB of vv. 37, 40, and JPS; [7] 'first', MT 'at the head' (as chief); [13] 'Abraham', MT 'Israel', RSV is an adaptation to Ps. 105.6; [15] 'He is mindful', MT 'be mindful, remember', RSV is an adaptation to Ps. 105.8; [19] 'when they were', MT 'when you were', cf. Ps. 105.12; [40] 'according to all that is written', MT 'and for everything that is written'; [43] 'went', better 'turned', or 'returned' (NEB).

C. Structure, sources and form

1. The structure of ch. 16 is as follows:

(a) 1–3: the conclusion of the transfer of the ark.
(b) 4–38: the arrangements for musical service before the ark, for that day and in the future.
(c) 39–42: the appropriate arrangements at the tabernacle in Gibeon.
(d) 43: conclusion, departure.

From the point of view of source-material, the structure of the chapter follows an interesting pattern: the sections marked above as (a) and (d) (vv. 1–3, 43) are drawn, with slight variations, from II Sam. 6.17–20a, and serve as a 'basic source' of the pericope. This originally continuous text is treated in the manner demonstrated above for 15.28: at a certain point the original sequence is cut in two, and a section of varying length is inserted at the point of the break; following the insertion, the narrative is resumed in its original form, from the exact point of the interruption. Graphically, this would look like this:

II Sam. 6:	17 – 18 – 19a				19b – 20
I Chron. 16:	1 – 2 – 3		4–42		– 43.

By means of this method, which recurs regularly in Chronicles, the verses taken from the 'basic source' form a kind of *inclusio*, providing the introduction and conclusion of the enlarged unit.

The structure of the inserted section (vv. 4–42) also follows a particular pattern, similar to that already described. Verses 4–6 on the one hand, and vv. 38–42 on the other, form a sequence, focussed on one subject. Verses 4–6 describe the permanent arrangements before the ark in Jerusalem; vv. 38–42 conclude this description and relate the same for the tabernacle in Gibeon. This sequence is interrupted by the insertion of a long section, vv. 7–37. This, too, is composite: its main part consists of a psalm (vv. 8–36), woven into its context by means of an introductory phrase (v. 7) and a conclusion (v. 37).

The structuring of this chapter reveals a sophisticated literary technique, which endeavours to combine two matters: the permanent arrangements for the ark and the psalm which was sung before the ark of God 'on that day'. The connection between vv. 7 and 37f. is evident, since both refer to 'Asaph and his brethren', the one relating to 'that day' (ביום ההוא) and the other, antithetically, to 'regularly' (תמיד). Verse 7 is linked to what comes before, v. 37 – to what follows. Graphically, this could be illustrated as follows:

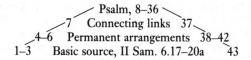

Since the literary construction of the unit is systematic, the final product cannot be regarded as a result of the chance 'growth' of haphazard additions.

The source material of vv. 4–42 is twofold: (*a*) a composite psalm, the parts of which are all found in the book of Psalms; (b) a description of the cultic arrangements peculiar to this context. Thus, with the exception of ten verses (4–7; 37–42) which are not paralleled in any other text, the major components of ch. 16 are all borrowed from various biblical sources and structured into a sophisticated literary unit.

2. The psalm of thanksgiving in vv. 8–36 constitutes a special literary pheno-menon. Its three parts are all found in Psalms: vv. 8–22//Ps. 105.1–15; vv. 23–33//Ps. 96.1–13; vv. 34–36//Ps. 106.1, 35–36. The middle section (vv. 23–33) forms in Psalms a full, independent work, while the other two parts are segments, joined here to form a complete psalmic composition.

This phenomenon, namely the construction of a new psalm by piecing together segments of existing ones, is already demonstrated in the book of Psalms itself, the most obvious example being Ps. 108, built upon Pss. 60 and 57. The same procedure is also evidenced in the Psalms Scroll from Qumran, where fragments of Ps. 118 are woven together to form a new psalm (J. A. Sanders, *The Psalms Scroll from Qumran Cave 11*, Oxford 1965, 37). However, the full scope of this literary practice cannot be brought to light in the absence of further comparative material, especially for the book of Psalms.

This synthetic practice of psalmodic composition should not be regarded as only a technical procedure; it surely involves literary considerations, regarding the selection and ordering of psalms, the points at which they are interrupted, etc. The question of authorship should therefore be asked: did the psalm under consideration ever exist as an independent work, eventually to be inserted into this context, or was it composed intentionally for its present role?

Several considerations seem to indicate that the Chronicler is responsible not only for the use of the psalm in the present pericope, but also for its composition. The most striking feature is the fundamental similarity in method between the compilation of this psalm and the general character of the Chronicler's literary activity: the joining, editing and reworking of existing materials into a new, extensive literary composition. This is not only a stylistic feature (Childs, *Introduction*, 514), but a mode of literary creativity. However, the Chronistic authorship of the psalm is expressed in two more specific features: on the one hand the exact adaptation of the psalm to the historical context immediately presupposed, and on the other hand its conformity with the Chronicler's theological and historical views, all of which will be discussed in the commentary (cf. also T. C. Butler, 'A Forgotten Passage From a Forgotten Era (I Chr. XVI 8–36)', *VT* 28, 1978, 142–50).

D. *Commentary*

[1–3] These verses are parallel (with minor changes) to II Sam. 6.17–19, but have a different role in the present context. In Chronicles, although their essence is unchanged, they show correspondence to the beginning of ch. 15, referring to the bringing of the ark to its tent (16.1a; cf. 15.1), and the cultic activity regarding the ark (16.1b; cf. 15.2) and the people (16.2–3; cf. 15.8).

The acts narrated in II Sam. 6.17–19 form the concluding stages of the transfer of the ark. David blesses all the participants and grants each of them a portion of food; the people then take their leave. While precisely the same facts are repeated in Chronicles, they constitute only an intermediate stage in the broader event: after the sacrifices, blessing and meal, the people do not depart but stay to thank God; a thanksgiving hymn is recited by the levitical singers and responded to by the people. This is followed by arrangements for the continuation of a regular worship; only then do the people depart to their homes.

This different concept of the events cannot be accidental. Just as the success of the project is assured only by God's help (15.26), so it is essential and self-evident that it conclude with 'thanksgiving, to be sung to the Lord' (16.7). Other major events depicted in Chronicles are concluded in the same way – II Chron. 20.26, 28; 29.30; 30.21, 27. Yet while in these cases only the fact of thanksgiving is mentioned, in this context the psalm of thanksgiving itself is cited in full. This should not surprise us, for according to Chronicles it was on this very occasion that the musical function of the singers in the framework of the cult had been initiated; the event is of constitutional significance for the Temple music, so it is related in full detail and with maximum grandeur.

[1] In addition to changes in the divine epithets and the word-order, the main way in which this verse differs from its parallel is in the transition from

the singular 'and David offered' (II Sam. 6.17) to the plural 'and they offered'. This has been interpreted as expressing the Chronicler's reluctance to depict David as offering sacrifices in person (cf. Myers, 119). This view is contradicted by the following verse, which continues in full correspondence to II Sam.: 'and when David had finished offering ...'. In spite of this phrasing, however, and that of I Chron. 21.26, it is difficult to assume that the Chronicler envisaged David as bringing the sacrifices in person; it seems more likely that in any case the Chronicler would interpret these statements as referring to David only as the person who authorized the offerings and on whose behalf they were offered. The intent of the change would therefore be to include the people ('they'): the 'burnt offerings' and the 'peace offerings' are brought not only on behalf of David, but for the whole people.

[3] The rather pompous phrasing of II Sam. 6.19 has frequently been noted. David's benevolence is spelled out to the letter, demonstrating that not a single soul has been deprived. The matter itself is retained in this verse, but the pompousness is mitigated by the more economical language. David is worthy of praise, but this no doubt is not the main issue.

[4–6] The arrangement of playing and singing before the ark is not recorded in II Sam. 6; there the story ends attractively with the departure of the people to their houses at the end of the celebrations. However, the conclusion of the narrative in II Sam. 6 seems incomplete from a historical point of view. It is difficult to imagine that David merely placed the ark in its tent, and thereafter forgot all about it! Some kind of cultic activity, not to mention a permanent guard, had undoubtedly to be established at the place. While the book of Samuel ignores this aspect of the story, Chronicles greatly elaborates it. The actual cultic details suggested by the Chronicler may very well be anachronistic, reflecting his own time and views, yet the historical standpoint reveals a concept compatible with historical writing, and an appropriate appreciation for the topics and matters which should be incorporated into a historiographical work (cf. further, Japhet, *Ideology*, 434 ff.).

The structure of the section is simple: after a general statement (v. 4), vv. 5–6 specify the names of the singers, all taken from the list of I Chron. 15.17–18, 19–21, 24. The division of the singers into sub-groups is based on the general supposition that the comprehensive body of priests and Levites has now been divided into two groups, one assigned to serve before the ark in Jerusalem, and the other at the tabernacle in Gibeon. Both groups consisted of singers, priests who blew the trumpets and gatekeepers; in Gibeon there were also priests in charge of sacrifices, and Levites.

From the standpoint of Chronicles, David's great innovation was not in the establishment of a 'high place' in Gibeon, but rather in the tent pitched for the ark in Jerusalem. According to his understanding of the history of the cult, the tabernacle had been placed in Gibeon from ancient times; its cult did not require elaboration. Not so the newly established Jerusalem tent of the ark, the cultic arrangements of which had yet to be fully recorded.

[4] The phrasing of the verse is carefully chosen. Those appointed by David are 'of the Levites', and not 'of the singers', the terms being clearly differentiated. Their role is described as 'to invoke, to thank and to praise the Lord', which is a combination of two distinct functions. 'To invoke' is a priestly role according to Num. 10.10: 'you shall blow the trumpets ... they shall serve you *for remembrance* before your God' (RSV 'for remembrance' translates *l^ezikkārōn*, derived from the same root as *l^ehazkir*, translated here in Chronicles 'invoke'). 'Thanks and praise' is a role of the Levites, or, more precisely, of the singers. 'The Levites' in v. 4, therefore, accurately introduce both Asaph and his brethren of v. 5 and the priests with their trumpets of v. 6; their acts are referred to chiastically.

[5] Ten singers are listed: the 'head', Asaph; second to him, Zechariah; and another eight. From the phrasing of MT it is not clear whether 'second to him' refers only to Zechariah, or to all the following names (as understood by RSV). As already demonstrated by 15.19–21, Asaph was responsible for the cymbals, while all the others were divided between the harps and the lyres. Although they are not listed here according to their specialization, this can be easily reconstructed by comparing this list with the one in 15.20–21. Six of the singers – Zechariah, Jeiel/Uzziel, Shemiramoth, Jehiel, Eliab and Benaiah – were playing the harps, while three – Mattithiah, Obed-edom and Jeiel – played the lyres.

[6] Of the priests, two are mentioned: Benaiah and Jahaziel. The latter is not found in 15.24, and since the number of priests in v. 24 is seven, it would be difficult to assume an omission. The only way to explain the name is as a corruption – either here or in the list of 15.24.

The phrasing of vv. 6 and 15.24bc is similar, almost repetitive, except for the addition of *tāmīd*. This should be translated (following NEB), as 'regularly'. 15.24 refers to the specific present ceremony, while this verse describes the enduring situation. The Chronicler returns here to two as the regular number of the trumpets (Num. 10.10).

[7] This verse, forming a new beginning and not a repetition of vv. 4–5, interrupts the description of the regular arrangements by the insertion of the events of 'that day'.

bārō'š is not 'first' (as represented by the English translations), since this usage is not attested in the Bible. It is the usual 'at the head of', referring to Asaph and his brethren who were to conduct the thanksgivings of 'that day'.

The psalm is defined as 'thanksgiving'; this is indeed specified at the beginning of the psalm: 'Give thanks to the Lord' (v. 8), repeated in the last section, 'O, give thanks to the Lord' (v. 34), and again in the final doxology, 'that we may give thanks to thy holy name and glory in thy praise' (v. 35b).

316

[8–36] 1. As it now stands, the psalm can be divided into two parts: a hymn of thanksgiving (vv. 8–33); thanksgiving and supplication (vv. 34–36). Each of the sections opens with the same phrase, 'O give thanks to the Lord' (vv. 8, 34), but while the first part is a general hymn, the second is more closely connected with the specific situation; it concludes with a doxology: 'Blessed be the Lord, the God of Israel, from everlasting to everlasting'.

2. All of the elements of this prayer are found in Psalms. There is, however, a difference between the components of the first part and those of the second. Verses 8–33 are composed of self-contained psalms, which were probably sung in the regular Temple cult, while vv. 34–36 are a 'mosaic' of smaller units. Verse 34 is a refrain, probably the people's response to the singing of the Levites. This antiphon opens and concludes several psalms (cf. Ps. 106.1; 107.1; 118.29 and especially 118.1–4; 136). Verses 35–36a are a doxology, probably also uttered by the participants in the cult, at the end of prayer. Such independent doxologies were included in Psalms in 72.18–19; 89.53 and this verse in Ps. 106.

3. Both Pss. 96 and 105, of which this psalm is composed, are psalms of thanksgiving, opening their address with a series of imperatives: 'give thanks, sing, glory, remember, etc'. (reflected here in vv. 8–12), and 'sing, honour, ascribe, etc.' (vv. 23–28), and continuing to praise God's mighty acts. Psalm 105 is a historical-thanksgiving psalm, praising the wondrous deeds of God for his people Israel. In its original framework, this psalm opens with a general introduction (vv. 1–6), followed by the main body of the psalm (vv. 7ff.): 'He is the Lord our God … He was (RSV 'is') mindful of his covenant for ever, of the word that he commanded for a thousand genera-tions.' The main theme of the psalm is, therefore, the faithfulness of God, the master of the universe, who remembered his covenant with the patriarchs and brought it to completion. Psalm 96 is a song of praise. It is sung by the world of nature (vv. 11–12), and proclaimed among the nations (vv. 3, 7, 10). The Lord is the only God, his reign secures the well-being of the world (v. 10), and he is coming to judge the world. These two different psalms were combined in Chronicles. Of Ps. 105 only the first part (vv. 1–15) was borrowed, while Ps. 96 was taken in its entirety, with some reworking. The result is a new literary piece, with its own emphases.

4. Chronicles has retained all the summons to praise and thanksgiving found in the original psalms: 'O give thanks, make known, sing, tell, glory, let the heart rejoice, seek, seek' (Ps. 105); 'Sing, tell, declare, ascribe, ascribe, bring offerings, worship, etc.', to the end of the psalm (Ps. 96). In addition, by a change of tense and person, from perfect singular (*zākar*) to imperative plural (*zikrū*), the Chronicler conforms Ps. 105.8, 'He (the Lord) was mindful of his covenant', to the same pattern of exhortation, making it a further summons to the people: 'remember his covenant for ever' (I Chron.

16.15: this change goes unnoticed in RSV, which introduces into Chronicles the version of Psalms).

5. With the transposition of Ps. 105.1–15 to this context, its theological-historical focus has shifted. The development of the theological theme in Ps. 105 has a specific premise: 'Give thanks to the Lord ... for he remembered his covenant ... To you I will give the land of Canaan.' From this vantage point, the psalm goes on to relate all the vicissitudes of Israel's history – the patriarchs, Joseph in Egypt, the plagues, the Exodus, the wanderings in the wilderness, and the climatic fulfilment: 'he gave them the land of the nations' (Ps. 105.44), so that 'they should keep his statutes and observe his laws' (105.45). This thematic development is lost in the present context. The record of historical events is very quickly interrupted before the reference to Joseph, so that only the patriarchs are mentioned. The strict connection between 'the covenant' at the beginning of the psalm and the fulfilment at the end is severed. Moreover, 'he remembered' (RSV 'is mindful') of Ps. 105.8 has been replaced by the imperative 'remember', addressed to the people (I Chron. 16.15).

In the present context, the psalm is connected with its actual historical setting, the transfer of the ark. It addresses the participating crowd, presented as the direct offspring of the patriarchs; the intermediate period between the patriarchs and David's contemporaries is obliterated. The promise 'to you I will give the land of Canaan' is being fulfilled in this present community which praises the Lord and thanks him for his marvels.

6. The second part of the psalm, taken from Ps. 96, is retained in full: a hymn of God's might, marvels, wondrous deeds. All of nature joins in the celebration, singing with the assembled throng.

Since Ps. 96 is cited in its entirety, the changes introduced into it are of special significance.

Verse 23, constructed of Ps. 96.1b and 2b, summarizes and shortens the opening praises of the psalm. However, since praise-giving is the heart of the psalm, this change could hardly have been intentional. It is more plausibly either a textual corruption or the reflection of a shorter *Vorlage*.

Verse 27b reads 'strength and joy are in his place' instead of 'strength and beauty are in his sanctuary' (Ps. 96.6), and v. 29 has 'bring an offering, and come before him' instead of 'bring an offering and come unto his courts' (Ps. 96.8). Both changes stem from the different context and presumed situation. It is not the 'sanctuary' with its 'courts' to which the people turn (at David's time these were not yet built), but the tent in 'its place', with *māqōm* denoting not merely 'a place' but probably 'a holy place' (cf. Baumgartner, 592–3). These changes testify to the refinement and sensitivity invested in the

reworking of the psalm. These, too, support the attribution of the composition of the psalm to the Chronicler himself.
Two clauses of Ps. 96 are absent from this context:

96.10: 'He will judge the peoples with equity';
96.13b: 'He will judge the world with righteousness, and the peoples with
his truth'.

Although not adjacent, these verses share a similar idea; their absence
should, therefore, be regarded as an editorial omission. It would seem to
result from the wish to link the psalm more closely to its new context. The
universal judgment of peoples, and the world at large, is not the immediate
concern of the psalm. We should probably interpret in the same vein the
displacement of Ps. 96.10a, 'Say among the nations the Lord reigns', which is
found in this context at the end of v. 31 rather than in the middle of v. 30.
Some scholars would restore it to its original place (cf. Rudolph, 124), but it
is possible that the clause was actually omitted by the Chronicler and re-
introduced by a later hand (so JPS).

[11] The exhortation to 'seek the Lord and his strength' seems to deviate
from the main flow of ideas. The context speaks about 'those who seek the
Lord' (v. 10) and the parallel colons call to 'seek the Lord' (*diršū yhwh* ...) and
'seek his presence' (*baqqšū pānāyw*). The mention of God's 'strength' therefore
seems out of place, and indeed, 'his strength' is represented in the Septuagint
by a verb: 'and be strong'. JPS, however, regards MT *'uzzō* as an epithet for
the ark, in parallelism to Ps. 78.61, where *'uzzō* (RSV 'his power') is
undoubtedly a reference to the ark, taken captive after the destruction of
Shiloh (cf. also Ps. 132.8 and its parallel in II Chron. 6.41).

The terminology of these verses, 'seek' (*bqš, drš*), 'seek his presence', and
the allusion to the ark, all anchor the psalm both in its immediate context and
in the terminology and views of the Chronicler.

[13] 'The seed of Israel (RSV 'Abraham!') his servant' is one of the
interesting variations between this text and Ps. 105. For the Chronicler, the
people 'Israel' are not the distant heirs of Abraham, but the direct offspring
of the patriarch Israel-Jacob (Williamson, *Israel*, 62; S. Japhet, 'Conquest
and Settlement in Chronicles', *JBL*, 98, 1979, 217). The affiliation of 'the
children of Israel' is to Israel and not to Abraham, and that is how they are
named (according to Willi, 163 n. 209, this, and not Ps. 105.6, is actually the
original reading). In the mention of the covenant, however, Abraham and
Isaac are retained, next to Jacob (v. 16).

[15] 'He is mindful', MT 'remember'. It is of interest that the perfect form
of the verb *zkr*, denoting a simple past, is translated by RSV in both Ps. 105
and here as present, 'is mindful'. We have already noted that RSV prefers the
reading of Ps. 105 to the MT of Chronicles.

[19] 'When you were', RSV 'When they are'. Again, the transition adjusts the text to Ps. 105.12. The same procedure had been followed by the ancient Versions of the LXX and V, while several MSS, the Peshitta and the Targum, adjust the reading of Psalms to that of Chronicles. The reading of Ps. 105.12, 'when they were', connects this verse to the succeeding one, while the reading 'when you were' connects it to what comes before, and the new theme begins only in the following verse, 20. The two interpretations are equally plausible.

[22] With Ps. 105 the patriarchs are called 'my anointed ones' and 'my prophets'. Among the patriarchs, it is only Abraham who is given the title 'prophet', and only once – in the context of his encounter with Abimelech (Gen. 20.7). This verse seems indeed to allude to this incident, but the example of Abraham is broadened to include the other two patriarchs as well. Moreover, 'my anointed ones' is most unusual. None of the patriarchs is ever referred to in this way; this is the only biblical reference to the title in the plural, and the only place where 'prophet' and 'anointed one' are found in parallel colons. The verb 'anoint' as a reference to the consecration of prophets is attested in the Bible in God's command to Elijah to 'anoint' Elisha in his place (I Kings 19.16), and in Isa. 61.1. The phrase 'anointed one', however, referred only to kings or priests. This context represents a twofold expansion in the application of the title: a full parallelism between 'prophet' and 'anointed one' (probably also in the Damascus Covenant, 5.21–6.1), and the inclusion of the three patriarchs in the category of prophets.

[23–33] On the changes in these verses, cf. above, pp. 317–18.

[34–36] Here the psalm moves to the actual situation. Following the refrain, 'O give thanks to the Lord, etc.', there is a direct address to the people, 'Say', to which the doxology is attached. The phrasing of the doxology differs in some details from Ps. 106.47, but the most conspicuous point is the return of the exiles, 'and gather and save us from among the nations'. Such a petition goes completely beyond the presupposed historical context, and since the overall reworking of the psalm has been so meticulous, one may wonder whether this obvious exception is at all original. The 'gathering of exiles' is also a quite uncommon concept in Chronicles in general; it is mentioned only once, in altogether different phraseology, in II Chron. 30.9, with reference to the people of the north. It is conspicuously absent from Solomon's prayer in II Chron. 6.39 (cf. *ad loc.*). That the original reading did not include the word 'gather us' is borne out by the version preserved in LXX: 'Deliver us O God of our salvation and save us from the nations.' This reading also exhibits better rhythm and a more balanced parallelism.

In v. 36b, the people are depicted as responding to the exhortation 'Then all the people said', in place of 'and let all the people say' of Ps. 106.47. Again, this is not a mere repetition of Ps. 106, but an accurate adaptation to the specific situation.

[37] With this verse we go back to 'that day', and to the more general circumstances: the appointment of Asaph and his brethren for the regular service. The verse itself gives us no new information, but serves as a connecting link between the psalm of 'that day' and the more general context. Returning to the project of the transfer of the ark, only one more thing need be mentioned: the gatekeepers, to whom v. 38 is devoted.

[38] The verse is difficult in several ways. 1. Obed-edom is mentioned twice, first with his sixty-eight brethren and then with Hosah. 2. MT reads 'their brethren' in place of the expected 'his brethren' (emended by RSV). 3. The descent of Obed-edom from 'Jeduthun' is new, Jeduthun himself being better known as a singer. 4. A new character, Hosah, is introduced.

A partial solution to the difficulties is offered by RSV, which regards v. 38a as a continuation of v. 37. This would make 'Obed-edom and his brethren' of 38a a contingent of the singers, while Obed-edom of 38b would be a different person, tracing his descent from Jeduthun; he is, with Hosah, in charge of the gatekeepers. However attractive this solution may appear, it leaves some points unaccounted for. From a syntactical viewpoint one would expect the mention of Obed-edom to follow that of Asaph rather than to be appended to the sentence as it is. Moreover, according to the overall literary structure, v. 37 refers back to v. 7, and accordingly, probably only 'Asaph and his brethren' are designated as singers.

Several other suggestions have been made. These either regard some elements of the verse as glosses or, alternatively, supplement it with conjectural haplographies. There seems to be no escape from the conclusion that the verse as it stands has undergone some interpolating, the purpose of which was to adjust the present context to other texts referring to the gatekeepers. A likely solution, although by no means conclusive, is to regard the repetition of 38b, 'and Obed-edom the son of Jeduthun and Hosah', as a gloss, in which case the text would read 'and Obed-edom and his brethren sixty-eight, were to be gatekeepers' (cf. also I Chron. 15.24 and the commentary *ad loc.*). Another solution, regarding as glosses v. 38a (under the influence of I Chron. 26.3), and 'son of Jeduthun' (under the influence of v. 42), would read: 'Obed-edom and Hosah were to be gatekeepers'. On the problems of the order of the gatekeepers cf. to I Chron. 26.

[39–42] In order to complete the depiction of the cultic arrangements of the kingdom after the transfer of some personnel to Jerusalem, the Chronicler refers to the sanctuary in Gibeon. The matter is presented abruptly, rather like an addendum to the main issue, introduced before its conclusion.

In the high-place of Gibeon, before the tabernacle of the Lord, a complete cult was to be observed, including all the ritual features. It comprised:

(a) A high priest and attendant priests, in charge of the sacrifices.
(b) Singers, responsible for the sanctuary's music.
(c) Gatekeepers, 'appointed to the gate'.

In this scheme only 'the Levites' are not mentioned, but this omission should probably be attributed to the brevity of the section and the fact that their tasks had already been presented in detail in I Chron. 9.31ff.

Of the priests, only Zadok the high priest is mentioned by name, while the others are called 'his brethren the priests'. Their role is also sketched without much elaboration: 'to offer burnt offerings to the Lord ... according to all that is written in the law of the Lord'. Of the singers, only the two masters are mentioned by name, while the others, who have already been recorded in I Chron. 15.20–21, are referred to only as 'the rest of those chosen and expressly named'. Their task, too, is mentioned briefly: 'to give thanks to the Lord'. There is also no specific indication that the blowing of the trumpets was reserved for the priests. This omission could be interpreted as representing a deviant tradition (so Williamson, 128, on v. 6), but it is difficult to imagine that a deviation in the case of such an obvious and systematic contingent of the musical service may be deduced only from silence. It is more likely that those whose names were not specified, and who were under the general charge of Heman and Jeduthun, included both the singers with 'instruments for sacral song' and priests with 'trumpets'.

At the very end of the passage, and again only briefly, the gatekeepers, 'the sons of Jeduthun', are alluded to.

The important question raised by these verses is that of the origin and value of the tradition about 'the tabernacle of the Lord in the high place that was at Gibeon'. Theoretically, three paths are open to the scholar, and all have actually been expounded in the scholarly literature.

1. The Chronicler 'devised' the whole story in order to provide a reasonable explanation for Solomon's going to the high place (I Kings 3.4ff.// I Chron. 1.3ff.), and a proper legitimization for the otherwise unknown Zadok (cf. already de Wette, 108–12; Wellhausen, 183; Curtis, 315).

2. The Chronicler made use of an ancient, authentic source (cf. H.W. Hertzberg, 'Mizpah', *ZAW* 47, 1929, 176–7; M. Görg, *Das Zelt der Begegnung*, Bonn 1967, 122–3, 131–37) or a variation of such a source (J. Milgrom, *Studies in Levitical Terminology* I, Berkeley 1970, 67–72).

3. The present passage, together with similar others, are post-Chronistic, products of the late priestly redaction (Welch, 30–41).

Whether or not we regard the Chronicler as responsible for the inclusion of this passage in the book, the main question is still that of the authenticity of the tradition itself. Is the reference to 'the tabernacle of the Lord ... in Gibeon' a late product of aetiological motives, created for the purpose of justifying existing institutions, or is it a reflection of an older tradition, which did not receive any expression in the existing biblical material?

Before addressing ourselves to the questions of the nature, sources, and reliability of the passage, let us clarify the presuppositions underlying it. These are:

1. The continuing existence and full functioning of the tabernacle is assumed beyond the period of the wilderness and after the conquest of Canaan, until the building of the Temple by Solomon.

2. The 'high place' in Gibeon was an Israelite sanctuary, as early as the time of the conquest, and surely afterwards.

3. Zadok, the high priest known from the times of David, was originally connected with Gibeon and its cult.

These presuppositions are combined into one concept: the existence and operation of the tabernacle of the Lord in the high place of Gibeon, under the ministry of Zadok.

A convenient starting point for discussing these views may be provided by the assertion, prevalent in biblical scholarship, that the very tradition of the 'tabernacle of the Lord' and 'the altar' which were created by Moses in the wilderness is a late Priestly projection with no historical basis. Therefore, the peculiar assertion of the Chronicler (or, for that matter, of a post-Chronistic author), that the cult of tabernacle and altar persisted in Gibeon, could only be an artificial construction with aetiological reasons, built on sand. However, a tradition about a 'tent of meeting', to which everyone 'who sought the Lord' must turn, and which was the place of Moses' encounter with God, is already found in earlier sources, outside the Priestly material (Ex. 33.7, 11, *et al.*). A distinction should be made, therefore, between the Priestly terminology, which might be late, and the ancient core of the tradition about the 'tent' in the wilderness.

A better point of departure is provided by the evidence on this matter of the Deuteronomistic historiography. On the one hand, the tent which was pitched in the wilderness disappears completely once the Jordan is crossed; not even a vague trace of such a tradition is to be found (cf. especially its absence from Shiloh, I Sam. 1–3, in contrast to II Sam 7.6 *wā'ehyeh mithallēk bᵉ'ōhel ūbᵉmiškān*). On the other hand, there can be no doubt that Gibeon was not an Israelite town (Josh. 9). It was the central town of the Hivite population, who are also called 'Gibeonites', even at the time of David (II Sam 21.1, 2, 3, 4 etc.). It is also evident that while there was already a sanctuary in Gibeon at an early date, it was not, at least initially, an Israelite one (Josh. 9.23, 27a). We may conclude, then, that although some of its elements may have been authentic (such as the existence of 'tent-sanctuaries', or the original connection of Zadok with Gibeon), the overall structure as presented in Chronicles could not reflect authentic historical conditions. Yet it is difficult to assume that only the narrow motive of justifying Solomon's journey to Gibeon could have inspired this complex structure. It would seem, rather, that broader theological and historical interests were the cause of both its creation and inclusion in the Chronistic work.

The main purpose of the tradition about 'the tabernacle at Gibeon' is to present a line of unbroken continuity in the cultic establishment of Israel from its inception by Moses to the kingdom of David and Solomon. Throughout this period, the worship of the Lord was performed in one central place, and in its full scope. This unbroken continuity of a central cult is an essential component of the Chronicler's general view of the history of the cult. In addition, by being made the location of tabernacle, Gibeon is immediately conceived of as Israelite, in obvious contrast to the evidence of Joshua. This polemical stand regarding the ethnic character of settlements in the land of Israel is characteristic of Chronicles and is demonstrated also by other sections, such as I Chron. 7.28–29. In addition to these two points, the passage provides answers to several questions in the history of Israel: the uncertain fate of the tabernacle and its furniture, which surely troubled the later reader, as the Deuteronomistic historiography refers only to the ark; the doubts concerning Solomon's sacrifice in the 'high place' and the need for their justification; and the obscure origins of Zadok, whose appearance on the historical stage in the book of Samuel seems rather abrupt. (This last element is regarded by many scholars as an authentic component of the whole.) It is possible that the whole structure was not an improvisation of the Chronicler but the final product of a prolonged midrashic process which gathered various originally independent elements under one theological roof. This collection was used by the Chronicler, like many other materials, for his own theological-historical purposes.

The main difficulty in the passage is the recurring of Jeduthun, both as a head of the singers and as a gatekeeper (vv. 38, 41, 42, 43). In the preceding story the singers were divided into three groups, headed by Heman, Asaph and Ethan (15.17, 19). Since Asaph has now been appointed to serve before the ark in Jerusalem, one would expect the other two to be mentioned here. Instead, Jeduthun and not Ethan appears next to Heman in v. 41. No fully satisfactory solution has hitherto been found for the difficulty (cf. also above, p. 296). Even the suggestion that 'Ethan' represents a later development of the singers' order does not solve the difficulty inherent in the text as it stands: the retaining of both names in one continuous context. We may solve our quandary either by assuming a different original reading in v. 41, such as

'Heman and Ethan', which was then corrupted into 'Jeduthun' (the orthographic similarity of the names is greater in Hebrew than in the English transcription), or alternatively, that for the Chronicler, Ethan and Jeduthun were indeed identical, and he chose to express this identity by using both names alternately.

As for the appearance of Jeduthun as gatekeeper (v. 42), it seems that this reflects a certain tradition of Jeduthun as a gatekeeper whose origin was in Gibeon. We have already noticed that the order of the gatekeepers has undergone many changes, and that there is no continuation of the original families, mentioned in Ezra. Most of these have disappeared and only Shallum, claiming its descent from Korah, survived (I Chron. 9.17). To this established family two more were added: Obed-edom (I Chron. 26.4), whose levitical affiliation is not recorded, and Chosah (I Chron. 26.10) descending from Merari. In the development of these orders there were probably transpositions from the singers to the gatekeepers and *vice versa*, and just as the 'Korahites', who are definitely singers according to Psalms 42.1; 44.1; 45.1 etc. (cf. M. D. Goulder, *The Psalms of the Sons of Korah*, Sheffield 1982, 77–84), eventually became gatekeepers, as reflected in Chronicles (I Chron. 9.19; 26.1ff.), so one may assume that 'Jeduthun' also had this double affiliation. Jeduthun's identification as a gatekeeper has been preserved only in this verse and in the gloss of v. 38.

[43] This is an exact parallel to II Sam. 6.19, with slight linguistic changes. After the extensive insertion of vv. 4–42, the story of II Sam. is resumed, at the precise point where the Chronicler left off.

As a concluding formula, 'and David went home to bless his household' is unique. In the context of II Sam. 6, the end of the story is in the more common concluding formula 'then all the people departed, each to his house' (v. 19, cf. I. L. Seeligmann, 'Hebräische Erzählung und biblische Geschichtsschreibung', *TZ* 18, 1962, 307–10), while the words 'and David returned to bless his household' actually form a new opening, introducing the episode with Michal. With the omission of the ensuing episode, the opening clause has become a conclusion, which is paralleled in Chronicles in II Chron. 30.27. In the present narrative it serves several purposes: the two stages of transferring the ark are now concluded with blessings, the first with the Lord's blessing of Obed-edom and his household (I Chron. 13.14), the second with David blessing his household after the successful accomplishment of the task he undertook. Furthermore, the verse serves as an excellent basis for the following chapter, which opens: 'When David dwelt in his house.'

17 Now when David dwelt in his house, David said to Nathan the prophet, 'Behold, I dwell in a house of cedar, but the ark of the covenant of the Lord is under a tent.' [2] And Nathan said to David, 'Do all that is in your heart, for God is with you.' 3 But that same night the word of the Lord came to Nathan, [4] 'Go and tell my servant David, "Thus says the Lord: You shall not build me a house to dwell in. [5] For I have not dwelt in a house since the day I led up Israel to this day, but I have gone from tent to tent and from dwelling to dwelling. [6] In all places where I have moved with all Israel, did I speak a word with any of the judges of Israel, whom I commanded to shepherd my people, saying, "Why have you not built me a house of cedar?"' [7] Now therefore thus shall you say to my servant David, 'Thus says the Lord of hosts, I took you from the pasture, from following the sheep, that you should be prince over my people Israel; [8] and I have been with you wherever you went, and have cut off all your enemies from before you; and I will make for you a name, like the name of the great ones of the earth. [9] And I will appoint a place for my people Israel, and will plant them, that they may dwell in their own place, and be disturbed no more; and violent men shall waste them no more, as formerly, [10] from the time that I appointed judges over my people Israel; and I will subdue all your enemies. Moreover I declare to you that the Lord will build you a house. [11] When your days are fulfilled to go to be with your fathers, I will raise up your offspring after you, one of your own sons, and I will establish his kingdom. [12] He shall build a house for me, and I will establish his throne for ever. [13] I will be his father, and he shall be my son; I will not take my steadfast love from him, as I took it from him who was before you, [14] but I will confirm him in my house and in my kingdom for ever and his throne shall be established for ever."' [15] In accordance with all these words, and in accordance with all this vision, Nathan spoke to David.

16 Then King David went in and sat before the Lord, and said, 'Who am I, O Lord God, and what is my house, that thou hast brought me thus far? [17] And this was a small thing in thy eyes, O God; thou hast also spoken of thy servant's house for a great while to come, and hast shown me future generations, O Lord God! [18] And what more can David say to thee for honouring thy servant? For thou knowest thy servant. [19] For thy servant's sake, O Lord, and according to thy own heart, thou hast wrought all this greatness, in making known all these great things. [20] There is none like thee, O Lord, and there is no God besides thee, according to all that we have heard with our ears. [21] What other nation on earth is like thy people Israel, whom God went to redeem to be his people, making for thyself a name for great and terrible things, in driving out nations before thy people whom thou didst redeem from Egypt? [22] And thou didst make thy people Israel to be thy people for ever; and thou, O Lord, didst become their God. [23] And now, O Lord, let the word which thou hast spoken concerning thy servant and concerning his house be established for ever, and do as thou hast spoken; [24] and thy name will be established and magnified for ever, saying, "The Lord of hosts, the God of Israel, is Israel's God," and the house of thy servant

David will be established before thee. [25] For thou, my God, hast revealed to thy servant that thou wilt build a house for him; therefore thy servant has found courage to pray before thee. [26] And now, O Lord, thou art God, and thou hast promised this good thing to thy servant; [27] now therefore may it please thee to bless the house of thy servant, that it may continue for ever before thee; for what thou, O Lord, hast blessed is blessed for ever.'

A. Notes to MT

[5] ואהיה מתהלך באהל ובמאכן, proposed ואהיה מאהיה מאהל אל אהל אל אהל וממשכן, corrupt: II Sam. 7.6; ואהיה באהל ובמשכן (LXX, NEB); ואהיה [מתהלך] מאהל אל אהל וממשכן [אל משכן] (so RSV) or ובמשכן באהל ואהיה; [18] את עבדך, proposed אויביך; ואויבי, ובית, read כי בית; [11] מלאו, read ימלאו; [10] אויביך, missing in LXX; transferred by error from v. 19? [19] להדיע, add את עבדך (cf. II Sam. 7.21 and v. 18); [21] אחד, LXX אחר.

B. Notes to RSV

[4] 'You shall not build', better 'It is not you who shall build' (NEB), or 'You are not the one to build' (JPS); [5] 'I have gone ... to dwelling', conjectural; [18] 'say to' supplemented from II Sam. 7.20; [21] 'other', MT 'one', cf. above; [27] 'may it please thee', an adjustment to II Sam. 7.29, MT 'thou hast been pleased to bless' (NEB); 'for what thou ... has blessed is blessed', better 'Thou it is who hast blessed it and it shall be blessed' (NEB), or 'For you ... have blessed and are blessed' (JPS), cf. commentary.

C. Structure, sources and form

1. With the exception of certain changes in detail, ch. 17 is taken as a unit and literally from II Sam. 7, and is presented in the same general context. As elsewhere, the changes introduced by the Chronicler are of major significance for understanding his attitudes and priorities. The study of these changes is rendered especially difficult by the textual condition of the chapter. While in both II Sam. 7 and Chronicles the chapter seems to have undergone textual corruptions, on the whole Chronicles seems to preserve a better textual tradition. In any case, the study of the chapter should be approached with special caution.

It is, moreover, generally accepted that II Sam. 7 does not contain the original literary form of Nathan's prophecy, but has undergone some Deuteronomistic redaction (cf. I. L. Seeligmann, 'From Historic Reality to Historiosophic Conception in the Bible', *Peraqim* II, 1969–1974, 282, 301ff.*; T. Veiola, *Die Ewige Dynastie*, Helsinki 1975, 68–79). While the analysis of the various literary strata is of major importance for the understanding of II Sam. 7, it should be borne in mind that, barring textual variations, the Chronicler had before him the literary unit of II Sam. 7 basically as it stands.

2. From a literary point of view the chapter is virtually unique in the book of Samuel. It comprises two rhetorical prose compositions: a prophecy and a prayer. There is a resemblance to I Sam. 12, although the rhetorical compositions there are of a different nature. Both chapters are placed at decisive turning points in the history of

Israel: I Sam. 12 at the retirement of Samuel and the final establishment of the monarchy as the political order of Israel; II Sam. 7 at the establishment of the house of David as Israel's 'kingdom for ever'.

Chronicles contains more compositions of this kind than Samuel and abounds in speeches, prayers and the like. The topic of the chapter, the dynastic house of David, also plays a more significant role in Chronicles. Chapter 17 is therefore a more organic element and less of a turning point in Chronicles.

3. Based as it is on II Sam. 7, the chapter is a direct sequel to the transfer of the ark, and its opening verses, 1–2, are parallel (with some changes) to II Sam. 7.1–3. Its place in the narrative sequence is nonetheless somewhat different. The transfer of the ark in II Sam. 6 concludes with the incident between David and Michal, which ends with: 'and Michal ... had no child to the day of her death' (6.23). The opening of II Sam. 7, 'Now when the king dwelt ... and the Lord had given him rest', far from reflecting obvious continuity with ch. 6, could have been introduced in any of several other contexts in II Sam. as equally or perhaps even more suitable. Not so in I Chronicles, where ch. 16 ends with: 'and David went home to bless his household (אל ביתו)', while ch. 17 opens with: 'Now when David dwelt in his house (בביתו)', the second half of the original verse ('and the Lord had given him rest ...') being omitted. A more coherent narrative flow is established with the repetition of the words 'his house' (ביתו) three times, leading the reader from one episode to the next.

This tighter narrative link is reflected not only in literary and chronological continuity but also in subject-matter: when the ark has been transferred to its tent (16.1), and David has gone to his house (16.43), the king becomes aware of the contrast between his own cedar house and the ark's humble abode.

Two further elements in I Chron. 16.43 find an echo in I Chron. 17: one is the reference to the 'people', who figure prominently both in Nathan's prophecy and in David's prayer, and the other is the 'blessing' which concludes ch. 17 as well. Chronicles 16.43, which was originally a fragment parallel to I Sam. 6.19b–20a, is in this context the point of departure for the whole of ch. 17.

4. The short introductory dialogue between David and Nathan (vv. 1–2) provides the basis for Nathan's prophecy (vv. 3–15) and David's prayer (vv. 16–27). The two compositions are of equal length in both their versions; this balance would appear to be intentional, since it is preserved in Chronicles in spite of the changes which are introduced.

In the rhetorical unit of vv. 3–15, Nathan's prophecy occupies the central place, while the circumstances of the vision are relegated to the short framework of vv. 3 and 15. Thus:

v. 3: introduction, describing the circumstances;
vv. 4–14: prophecy;
v. 15: conclusion.

In the next unit, v. 16a introduces the circumstances for David's prayer and constitutes its only 'narrative' component:

v. 16a: introduction;
vv. 16b–27: David's prayer.

D. Commentary

[1] David's approach to Nathan follows II Sam. 7.1, with the omission of the Deuteronomistic clause 'and the Lord had given him rest from all his enemies round about'. Although it is possible that the clause was missing from the *Vorlage* of Chronicles, it is still more likely that we can find the motivation for the omission in the Chronicler's own historical views. This clause establishes that David intended to fulfil the commandment of Deut. 12. 10–11: 'But when you go over the Jordan and live in the land which the Lord your God gives you to inherit, and when he gives you rest from all your enemies round about ... then to the place which the Lord your God will choose, etc.' Though Deut. 12 does not refer explicitly to the building of a house but only to the choosing of a 'place', it was interpreted as referring to the building of the Temple in Jerusalem (I Kings 3. 2–3). In Samuel, David is seen as saying that the time has come for establishing a permanent centre for the worship of the Lord, in conformity with the demands of Deut. 12. For the Chronicler, however, the 'rest' alluded to in Deuteronomy as the necessary condition for the building of the Temple will be achieved only at the time of Solomon: 'He shall be a man of peace (MT "rest"). I will give him peace (MT "rest") from all his enemies round about' (I Chron. 22.9). The description does not, therefore, suit the time of David and must be omitted (cf. further on v. 10). Consequently, 'house' remains as the only focus of the verse.

We should also notice the technique of the omission: a part of the text is extrapolated, and the text proceeds from the point of the break, precisely as it stood in the original, with nothing supplemented or changed.

In David's words 'I dwell in a house of cedar ... the ark ... of the Lord is under a tent', the implicit contrast suggests the question: should this situation endure? His words are phrased as an incomplete antithetic parallelism: 'I' against 'the ark of the covenant of the Lord', 'house of cedar' against 'tent' (JPS 'tent-clothes'), which contrasts the small and lowly 'I' with the great and mighty God; this is further emphasized in David's major speech, his prayer.

[2] Nathan, although he clearly understood David's intention, does not give it explicit expression, but only says, 'Do all that is in your heart'. Thus the actual subject of the short dialogue, the building of a house for the Lord, is not spelled out.

Nathan is presented as 'prophet' and in his answer he alludes to God's help: 'for God is with you'. Nevertheless, his words are not introduced by any indication that he speaks for the Lord; his answer is rather that of a counsellor who expresses his own thoughts.

[3–15] Each of the two parts of Nathan's prophecy has its opening: v. 4:

'Go and tell my servant David "Thus says the Lord"'; v. 7: 'Now therefore thus shall you say to my servant David, "Thus says the Lord ..."' Each of these parts serves a specific role in the framework of the prophecy. The first, relatively shorter, part conveys a negative message: the denial of David's request: 'You shall not build me a house.' The second and longer expresses the positive, principal burden of the prophecy: 'The Lord will build you a house.'

[3] God's response to the dialogue between David and Nathan is immediate: 'that same night ...' Although not presented as an answer to a specific appeal, God's words to Nathan should be understood as the divine response to David's question, addressed as it was to Nathan in his capacity as a prophet. As for Nathan's first answer, it is ignored completely; there is no attempt to explain the change of attitude, nor is Nathan rebuked for his hasty reply. The two answers do not fully integrate into one, coherent sequence.

[4–6] This portion of the prophecy is composed in three stages, with a gradual transition from one stage to the next and the *Leitmotiv* 'house' repeated in each: God declares that David will not build him a house (v. 4), that he has never dwelt in a house (v. 5), and that he has never desired a house or commanded that one be built (v. 6). Taken at face value, God's words may seem a harsh rebuke: David's wish to build a house is presented as contrary to both tradition and divine will. However, the literary form softens the impression of harshness. Most important is the opening, 'Go and tell *my servant* David', which determines the premise that God's words express an attitude of favour and not of rejection. Moreover, in II Sam. 7.5–7, the two main subjects are phrased as rhetorical questions, 'Would you build?' (v. 5) and 'Did I speak?' (v. 7), which lend the negation a softer tone. This point is, however, slightly altered in Chronicles (cf. further on v. 4). All this, together with the reference to Israel as the people of God ('my people', v. 6), supports the impression that while the content of God's response may be negative it still constitutes a moment of grace.

[4] In lieu of the rhetorical question of II Sam. 7.5, the phrasing in this verse is indicative: 'You shall not.' This change could be interpreted on a merely linguistic level in view of the diminishing use of the *he* interrogative in late Hebrew. Yet it would seem that here additional factors come into play. In II Sam. 7 the 'building of a house' is presented as a question of principle: 'would *you* build *me* a house?' No man is capable of building a dwelling for God, and therefore he never commanded one to be built! Only at a second stage and as a result of redaction in II Sam. 7.13 does this total rejection of David's idea become a question of precedence: first God will build a house for David by making his son king in his stead, and then this son will build a house for God. In Chronicles the emphasis is different. From the outset the determining factor is that of timing: not you but your successor will build a

house. The days of peace and 'rest' have not yet come; when they do my house shall be built.

[5] The general refusal is explained here, but although the words of II Sam. 7.6–7 remain mostly unchanged, they are given a different direction in the context of Chronicles, and their temporal aspect, 'until this day', becomes more prominent. It seems that even the change of 'I have been moving about in a tent for my dwelling' (II Sam. 7.6) to 'I have [gone] from tent to tent and from dwelling [to dwelling]' (I Chron. 17.5) should be interpreted from this point of view. II Sam. 7.5 emphasizes that God's dwelling is a tent, not a house, while the emphasis in Chronicles is on the mobile manner of God's abiding with his people; since the people have not yet settled down permanently, God accompanies them in their wanderings. What characterizes the period before the building of the Temple is that both the people and the ark of God 'have not as yet come to the rest and to the inheritance' (Deut. 12.9).

Notice the omission of 'Egypt' in v. 5 – one of the instances in which the Chronicler omits, or at least narrows, the role of the Exodus (cf. in detail, Japhet, *Ideology*, 379ff.).

[6] The climax of God's refusal is based on two arguments: the historical precedent, in that God has never asked for a house to be built; and the author of the initiative, the underlying assumption being that the initiative should come from God: 'Did I speak a word?', etc. This does not correspond to the Deuteronomistic view, which anticipated the 'choosing' of a 'place' immediately following the 'rest'. The rhetorical question which enquires about a specific 'word of God' demanding the building of a house is pre-Deuteronomistic in its basic assumption.

This chapter is the only instance in Chronicles in which the period of the judges is referred to explicitly (for an implicit reference cf. II Chron. 15.13ff., cf. *ad loc.*). In general, there are very few references in Chronicles to pre-monarchical times, and in these the period is represented by the figure of the prophet Samuel (I Chron. 26.28; II Chron. 35.18). This chapter, on the other hand, mentions the judges twice, in both parts of Nathan's prophecy (cf. also v. 10), and these references have been left unchanged by the Chronicler. This is a clear example of the problematics of a historiography based on ready-made building blocks rather than on the raw material of original composition, and of the working of divergent tendencies within one world-view. The major significance of this chapter in the Chronicler's historical-theological world-view leads him to introduce his source-material virtually unaltered. Thus, he retains some aspects of Israel's history which are played down elsewhere in his work.

The structure of the verse is of interest, for it contains two elements of direct speech, one within the other, conveying the intention in a rhetorical manner as a hypothetical query which was *not* directed to the judges: 'Did I speak ... why have you not built?' With this rhetorical technique this part of the prophecy is concluded.

[7–14] The second part of Nathan's prophecy opens with a new address, which, while essentially parallel to the first (v. 4), signifies a turning point: 'Now, therefore, thus shall you say, etc.'

The sequence of tenses in this part of the prophecy is difficult, as the verbs move from the past, expressed by the perfect forms (*l*^e*qaḥtīkā*) and imperfect with consecutive *waw* (*wā'ehyeh*, *wā'akrīt*), to the future, expressed by the perfect with consecutive *waw* (*w*^e*'āśītī*, *w*^e*śamtī*, *ūn*^e*ṭa'tīhū*, *w*^e*śākan*, *w*^e*hiknā'tī*, including forms of imperfect in the negative: *w*^e*lō' yirgaz*, *w*^e*lō' yōsīpū*), back to a declarative past as imperfect with consecutive *waw* (*wā'aggid lāk*), followed by the future, in the interchange of perfect + *waw* and imperfects, from v. 11 onwards (*w*^e*hāyāh*, *wah*^a*qīmōtī*, *wah*^a*kīnōtī*, etc; *yibneh*, *yihyeh*, etc.). All commentators on these passages have struggled with this sequence of verbal constructions – which constitutes the key to the understanding of the section.

Following the intricate tense structure, the argument of the section unfolds in three stages (as is understood and reflected in RSV):

1. Verses 7–8a portray God's favours to David in the past: 'I took you from the pasture and I have been with you ... and have cut off your enemies.'

2. Verses 8b–10a promise the future continuance of divine favour for David and the people of Israel: 'and I will make for you a name ... and I will appoint, etc.'

3. Verses 10b–14 present God's declaration (*wā'aggid lāk*) that he will build a house for David.

[7–8a] As God's past graces towards David are enumerated, the phrasing may incline the hearer toward a negative appreciation, in the mood of 'I have done all these things for you, but you ...', similar to a quite frequent pattern of prophetical sayings. However, the opening words 'my servant David', and the immediate sequel of God's future blessings, preclude such an interpretation. The implication of all these reminders is rather to be interpreted temporally: 'I have done all these things for you, and will do still more.'

The tradition that David was promoted to royalty from 'following the sheep' is very strong in biblical sources and there is no reason to doubt its authenticity. However, here it also serves a literary function, connecting v. 7 with the preceding v. 6. There the shepherd motif is used metaphorically of the judges: '... whom I commanded to shepherd my people.' For David, by contrast, the image is a concrete experience: once a shepherd he became a prince.

In v. 8a, God's saving acts for David are outlined in general terms: the allusions seem to be to the adversities and conflicts of David's life before he became king. In the framework of the book of Samuel these allusions direct the reader to the large section of I Sam. 16 – II Sam. 5; in Chronicles, where almost none of this material is actually included (but cf. on I Chron. 12), the references must remain undefined.

[8b–10a] The prophecy now moves from times past to the future, and the focus is now on political achievement: for David, of a great name; for the people of Israel, of a place where they may dwell in peace.

In the context of the promise of a firm future for the people, we find, by way of contrast, a reference to the period of the judges, when Israel had fallen to its historical nadir. 'Formerly' and 'from the time I appointed judges' are complementary phrases; the *waw* attached to *l⁽e⁾miyyāmîm* is explicative and thus is rightly omitted in translation.

The zenith of the people's well-being is presented here in the words 'I will plant them that they may dwell in their own place'. This specific metaphor not only accentuates the rooting and stability of the people, but reflects the beginning of the prophecy, where God is presented as one who wanders 'from tent to tent', etc. (v. 5). David's rule will be the turning-point in the destiny of his people: the beginning of enduring stability. Yet, through the change of 'and I will give you rest' (II Sam. 7.11) to 'I will subdue', the Chronicler avoids the motif of 'rest'; this is reserved for the time of Solomon (cf. above p. 328).

Although both II Sam. 7.11 and this verse read '*your* enemies', the suggestion made by Rudolph (130, following Benzinger) to read 'its enemies' (i.e. Israel's enemies) is very appealing. This involves only a slight change in MT and accords with the subject of the section, which is not David but the people. 'I will subdue' is the sequel of 'and be disturbed no more'.

Stylistically the section has no poetical structure, but its prose has a particular, formulaic character. A certain excitement can be sensed through the series of interpretative clauses: 'That they may dwell ... and be disturbed no more ... and violent men shall waste them no more, ... as formerly, from the time ... and I will subdue all your enemies ...'

[10b–14] In this last section the prophecy reaches its climax, returning to the topic of 'house', to God's great promise of a Davidic dynasty, 'a house' for David.

In the context of II Sam. 7 this is the only theme (excluding v. 13, which is probably of later Deuteronomic origin) which serves as a focus for all the details of the section. Like the preceding promise to the people, God's commitment to David is also contrasted to the past, to the withdrawal of divine grace from 'him who was before you': Saul. When David's days are fulfilled, one of his sons will reign after him, and so David's throne 'will be established for ever' (II Sam. 7.16). The Chronicler introduces into this section many changes, which reflect the differences in his historical assumptions. Since the negation of David's plan is not on principle but revolves around the questions of 'who' and 'when', attention is focused in this direction: 'not *you* but *your son* will build me a house'. The time sequence is transparent: I will build you a house (by establishing the kingdom of your son), and this son will in turn build a house for me. In II Sam. the promise is essentially for David's benefit: the founding of a Davidic dynasty and kingdom. In Chronicles the focus has shifted to the establishment of the son's 'house and kingdom'. David's time is the preparatory stage, the vestibule. The inner sanctum of peace, quiet and rest – with all that these imply – will be reached only in Solomon's day.

[10b] The special idiom of II Sam. 7.11, *bayit ya'ăśeh l'kā yhwh*, 'The Lord will "make you a house"', denoting the establishing of family and progeny (cf. *BDB*, 109), has become in Chronicles 'will build you a house'. Several factors, both linguistic and literary, are reflected in this change. With the use of 'build' instead of 'make' a tighter parallelism is achieved: 'the Lord will build you a house' echoes 'he shall build a house for me' (v. 12), and later 'I will confirm him in my house' (v. 14). Linguistically it would seem that the rare usage has been replaced by a more common one (S. Japhet, 'Interchanges of Verbal Roots in Parallel Texts in Chronicles', *HS* 28, 1987, 19–20).

[11] The solemn declaration of v. 10b is here made more specific. One of the well-remarked changes of this verse is the replacement of *'ăśer yēṣē' mimmaʿeykā*, 'who shall come forth from of your body' (literally – 'bowels', II Sam. 7.12), with *'ăśer yihyeh mibbāneyka*, 'who will be of your sons'. There is in fact no difference in meaning, the usage of Chronicles being probably a more euphemistic language (cf. II Chron. 32.21 with Isa. 37.38 and II Kings 19.37 and Isa. 39.7 in 1QIsaᵃ; Japhet, *Ideology*, 497–8). Yet one wonders whether a literary factor may also have been at play here. The change strengthens the link between this verse, 'one of your own sons', and v. 13, 'he shall be my son'.

[12] As many scholars justly claim, in Chronicles, as in II Sam. 7, the 'house of God' does not form the central element of the prophecy. II Sam. 7.13 is probably a redactional gloss; to a certain degree it causes a shift in the overall tendency of the prophecy, but its secondary nature is still felt. In Chronicles, which adopted the text of II Sam. 7, the matter is more organically integrated into the context by a tighter parallelism with v. 10 (cf. above).

[13] The conditional clause of II Sam. 7.14, 'when he commits iniquity I will chasten him with the rod of men, with the stripes of the sons of men', has been omitted from the verse in Chronicles. The editorial technique is already familiar: a segment of the source material is removed, and the text is resumed directly after the omission, with little or no changes or additions.

Many interpretations of this omission have been offered, but preference must go to those which take into account the function of the omitted clause in its original context, against the background of the Chronicler's views. In II Sam. 7.14 the clause is an assurance that God's steadfast love will not be taken from David's son. Even should he sin, he will be adequately punished, but not by the withdrawal of divine favour. This is the central contrast between the house of David and that of Saul, from whom God's steadfast love was turned away for ever. It is no coincidence that the root *swr* recurs in II Sam. 7.15 three times: *yāsūr, h^asīrōtī, h^asīrōtī* (RSV 'take ... from'; 'took ... from'; 'put away'; NEB 'withdraw' ... 'withdrew' ... 'removed'). This root is also a key to the understanding of the turning points in the whole of Saul's story. Thus, 'the Spirit of the Lord departed (*sārāh*) from Saul' (I Sam. 16.14); 'Saul was afraid of David because the Lord was with him but had departed (*sār*) from Saul' (I Sam. 18.12), and finally in I Sam. 28.15, 16: 'God has turned away (*sār*) from me ...' The fate of David's son is going to be different, even if he sins, for God's favour will not depart from him.

This is the core of the matter: the promise to David is not conditional on his son's behaviour. It is an act of grace towards David himself, for he is 'God's servant' and God is 'with him'; the possibility that David himself might sin does not even come to mind. Some scholars regard this clause as an intentional allusion to Solomon's sins; even if this is indeed the case, the main point remains the unconditional promise to David.

By omitting this clause the Chronicler avoids all its corollaries. 1. The hint of Solomon's sins, which in any case would not harmonize with the version of Chronicles, where the description of Solomon's transgressions (I Kings 11) is not reproduced. 2. The special emphasis on the contrast between Saul and David; with the omission of Saul's name the contrast is retained but in a somewhat weaker form. 3. Last and most important: the unconditional nature of God's promise is not retained. While the conditions themselves are not specified in this context but elsewhere (I Chron. 22.12; 28.7 etc.), the basic premise is also evident here. The Chronicler deviates from the central premise of II Sam. 7 and approaches more closely the Deuteronomistic redaction of I Kings, which does see God's promise as conditional (cf. Japhet, *Ideology*, 460ff.).

The phrase 'I will be his father and he shall be my son' has long been recognized as an adoption formula. The Chronicler makes abundant use of it, for Nathan's prophecy serves him as a 'treasury', from which he draws material for his other rhetorical compositions (cf. H. G. M. Williamson, 'The Dynastic Oracle in the Books of Chronicles', *I. L. Seeligmann Volume*, 1983, 305ff.). The formula has become an abstract expression of special favour, with no connotation whatsoever of 'deification'.

[14] The verse deviates at several important points from its parallel in II Sam. 7.16. There, the subject of the verse is David: because of all the

previously mentioned divine favours, David's house and kingdom 'shall be made sure for ever'.

Not so in Chronicles. Here the subject is no longer David, and the promise is transferred to Solomon. According to the rephrasing of the verse it is not the 'house' and 'kingdom' of David which 'shall be established'; rather, Solomon will be confirmed for ever in the 'house' and 'kingdom' of the Lord. These changes reflect two focal points in the Chronicler's views: his understanding of the institution of kingship (for which cf. on II Chron. 13.5 and Japhet, *Ideology*, 395ff.), and the role of David and Solomon in the history of Israel.

According to the Deuteronomistic view, expressed in both Samuel and Kings, David is the model king in the history of Israel. He is the measure both of righteousness and success, and the kings of Judah are repeatedly compared with him. In Chronicles, this evaluation has been modified. The fact that David did not build the Temple confronted the Chronicler with one of his most difficult theological problems. He coped with it in three ways: by augmenting David's role, attributing to him all the preparations for the actual construction of the Temple (cf. below on vv. 22ff.); by toning down the ideal image of David, stating that the time was not yet ripe for the building of the Temple, and refraining from comparing the kings of Judah with him; and by emphasizing that Solomon is the 'chosen' of the Lord, equal and complementary to David. The present verse reflects this new outlook: not David's day, indeed, but the combined reign of David and Solomon constitutes the climax of Israel's history, and it is in Solomon that the promise is fulfilled.

II Samuel 7.16 states 'your house ... shall be made sure' (*w⁽ne'man bēt⁽kā*). In Chronicles there is no 'sure house', and the verb *'mn* is transferred to David's prayer and to other contexts (cf. on v. 23). Sovereignty over Israel belongs to God, and it is in this 'house' that Solomon's throne will be established. The emphasis moves from the dynasty as a 'sure house' for David to the chosen ruler Solomon, whose throne will be made established 'for ever' in the 'house' of God.

Stylistically, the last portion of the prophecy emphasizes what I have already noted: the recurrence of key-words throughout the prophecy. In vv. 12–14 the following words or roots occur more than once, emphasizing the core of the prophetic message: throne (12, 14); kingdom (11, 14); house (12, 14), for ever (12, 14, 14); father (11, 12); establish (11, 12, 14); be (*hyh*, 11, 13, 13, 14); take from (*swr*, 13, 13).

[15] This transitional verse provides the necessary hiatus between God's address and David's response. This was made necessary by the choice of the author of Samuel to introduce the prophecy of II Sam. 7.5–16 (= I Chron. 17.4–14) as God's revelation to Nathan rather than Nathan's words to David

(as, for example, in I Sam. 12.1ff.). The phrasing of the verse emphasizes that Nathan delivered God's message fully and faithfully.

[16–27] At this point, David's prayer is the suitable means for him to express feelings which are rather complex. On the one hand, David's initiative to build a house for God has been rejected. The strong faith and devotion which led him to desire to do something for the Lord are met with silence. God does not even commend his initial wish (cf. differently in I Kings 8.18: 'but the Lord said to David ... "you did well that it was in your heart"'). On the other hand, the Lord now confers on David unasked-for honour and favour. This complexity receives full expression in the prayer.

Strikingly enough, this is not in fact a prayer of thanksgiving. It expresses no overflowing joy (such as is heard in Hannah's psalm in I Sam. 2, or even in the psalm of ch. 16), no summons to song and praise. The tone of the prayer is that of reconciliation. David expresses his recognition of the basic contrast between himself, an insignificant human being, and God's greatness. He reconciles himself to the divine will, for he regards himself as merely the servant of a great master. All that he asks for is that God's promise be fulfilled. This is a rather strange request, as if casting doubt on God's solemn declaration! It seems that this is what expresses David's mood most adequately: complete resignation to the will of God, accepting with equanimity both the refusal of his original wish and the promise of what he did not ask. 'Do as thou hast spoken' (v. 23) is the touchstone of his psychological attitude.

2. While the prayer is written in prose, without parallelism or poetic diction, there are still some stylistic features which should be noticed.

(a) The state of great excitement in which the prayer is uttered is reflected in the large number of addresses and invocations, ten in all, in the most variegated of phrases: O Lord God (vv. 16, 17); O God (v. 17); O Lord (vv. 19, 20); and thou, O Lord (vv. 22, 27); and now, O Lord (vv. 23, 26); for thou, my God (v. 25); for thou, O Lord (v. 27). Thus, rather than opening with one address followed by a continuous discourse, the prayer is a series of exclamations, each addressed anew to God. This exclamatory style alternates between rhetorical questions (vv. 16, 18a, 21) and prayerful interjections (vv. 17, 18b, 20 etc., until 27).

(b) Another element is that of repetition, which has two aspects. First, the prayer repeats all the major points of Nathan's prophecy: 'the house of thy servant David will be established before thee' (v. 24), 'thou wilt build a house for him' (v. 25), 'to bless the house of thy servant, that it may continue for ever before thee' (v. 27), etc. Secondly, the prayer contains many repetitions of certain phrases and motifs: the divine names, 'Lord', and 'God', recur in several variations twenty times; 'your servant' ten times; 'house' six times; 'for ever' five times, etc.

(*c*) After the first verse, the prayer uses the second and third person throughout; for the Lord on one hand, for David and the people on the other. Second-person pronominal suffixes recur over twenty times ('thy eyes', 'thy servant', etc.), and there are at least thirteen verbs in the second person. By contrast, 'I' is found only once, in the opening verse (v. 16), and there are only three pronominal suffixes of the first person singular: 'my house', 'brought me' (v. 16), and *ūrᵉ'ītānī* (RSV 'thou ... hast shown me', v. 17). There is also a single clause which is put in the first person plural in v. 20. Although David is the speaker, after the opening verse he refers to himself in the third person: 'What more can David say' (v. 18), 'thy servant has found courage' (v. 25). David throughout remains fully aware of his position as 'thy servant'; any reference to himself is dependent on his relationship with God, who alone is the focus of the prayer.

3. Since the prayer reiterates the basic themes of Nathan's prophecy, it is significant that it refrains from making reference either to Solomon (or 'the son') or to the building of the Temple. The essence of God's promise 'to build a house for David' is the confirmation of the kingdom of his son. Nathan's prophecy is adamant on this point: 'When your days are fulfilled ... I will raise up your offspring ... I will be his father, etc.' (vv. 11ff.). In his prayer David makes reference several times to 'thy servant's house' (vv. 17, 23, 24, 25, 27), but always in general and abstract terms, with no mention at all of his successor. The building of the Temple is implied in the introductory verses (vv. 1–2), rejected in God's response (vv. 5–6) and then referred to in the redactional layer of Nathan's prophecy (II Sam. 7.13//I Chron. 17.12). In David's prayer there is no mention of these elements – either of the plan initiated by David and rejected by God, or the assigning of the task to Solomon in the secondary stratum, which was not paralleled by a similar reworking of the prayer. Although the two versions of the prayer display the same features, the absence of these topics in Chronicles is especially conspicuous. We have seen that the Chronicler has introduced into Nathan's prophecy several changes which bring Solomon more to the fore, and the building of the Temple occupies a central position in his historical-theological view. Yet these themes were not followed up in David's prayer, which remained focused on David's sense of insignificance in comparison with God's benevolence, the greatness of God as revealed in the history of his people, and a supplication for the fulfillment of the promise.

4. The significant textual differences between II Sam. 7.18–29 and the text will be dealt with in the commentary, but one general phenomenon should be considered here in full: the numerous changes in the divine names. The following titles appear in the chapter in both versions: Lord (*yhwh*), O Lord God (*'ᵃdōnāy yhwh*), Lord of hosts (*yhwh ṣᵉbā'ōt*), O Lord God (*yhwh 'ᵉlōhīm*), God (*'ᵉlōhīm* or *hā'ᵉlōhīm*, both as proper name and as a common

noun), God of Israel. These titles stand either alone or as part of composite phrases: the ark of God, the word of the Lord, etc. They occur twenty-five times in Samuel and twenty-three in Chronicles; of these, only in eight cases is there an exact parallelism between the two versions. In all the other instances, while the changes and variations are not limited to one type and direction, some prominent features can still be distinguished.

In II Sam. 7 we find eight occurences (in certain MSS only seven), of the title *'ᵃdōnāy yhwh* (approximated in RSV by 'Lord God'), which is a common form of address in prayers and invocations and is demonstrated amply in David's prayer: II Sam. 7.18, 19, 19, 20, 28, 29, 22 (others *yhwh 'ᵉlōhīm*), 25 (not in all MSS). This form is never used by the Chronicler; when it appears in his sources it is replaced by various other titles: Lord, Lord God (*yhwh 'ᵉlōhīm*), God. This is true in all its occurrences in David's prayer, and also in 1 Kings 22.6, where it is replaced by 'God' in II Chron. 18.5. This systematic omission is undoubtedly a result of theological considerations, stemming from a reluctance to write down the form *'ᵃdōnāy* (literally 'my lords'). A certain sensitivity towards this title, although not a systematic reworking, is also evident in the Isaiah Scroll from Qumran (for a full discussion of the matter cf. Japhet, *Ideology*, 20–3).

A similar motive, though less systematically applied, is discernible in the omission of 'hosts' in I Chron. 17.25 (cf. in more detail above, pp. 278–9).

Another phenomenon which should be mentioned briefly is the interchange between the tetragrammaton and 'God' (*'ᵉlōhīm*), which has attracted much attention in the history of biblical research (cf. the accumulation of data in Rudolph's commentary, and the bibliographical references in Japhet, *Ideology*, 30–7). This interchange occurs in this chapter only in the first three verses, but altogether thirty-two times in Chronicles. To evaluate this, one should be aware of the fact that the tetragrammaton appears over five hundred times in Chronicles and is by far the dominant divine title. We should also note that the ancient Versions reveal a somewhat different picture, with fewer such changes to *'ᵉlōhīm*. The usage and meaning of these divine titles in Chronicles is clearly interchangeable and synonymous, and no theological conclusions can be drawn from the interchanges. The inevitable conclusion is that Chronicles cannot be counted a product of the 'Elohistic' school, which refrained for theological reasons from using the tetragrammaton, as demonstrated by Qoheleth and the Elohistic psalms. The incidental variations (which appear mostly in fixed phrases) should be interpreted as the result of a long history of textual transmission.

6. Although the prayer is structured as one continuum, three sections can nevertheless be discerned:

1. Verses 16–19: The nearest the prayer comes to thanksgiving.

2. Verses 20–22: Declaration of God's greatness and his rule over his people.
3. Verses 23–27: Supplication for fulfilment of the promise.

[16–19] David's opening words instantly and fully delineate the basic psychological approach of the whole prayer: 'Who am I and what is my house?'. This may, at first, appear nothing more than a convention, which we encounter in other places as well (cf. Judg. 9.28, 38). Yet, it is a genuine expression, borne out by all that follows. Moreover, the phrasing brings to mind Nabal's words. 'Who is David? Who is the son of Jesse?' (I Sam. 25.10); these are indeed David's own sentiments, concerning his relationship not with men, but with God. It is his appropriate response to and recognition of God's reminder: 'I took you from the pasture, from following the sheep ...' (v. 7).

As in Nathan's prophecy, David's words too move from the remembrance of God's help in the past to the present and forward to the promise of a distant future: *l^{e}mērāḥōq* (RSV 'for a great while'). In response to God's address 'my servant David' (v. 4), David repeatedly calls himself 'thy servant'. In David's mouth this appellation undergoes a shift in connotation: in God's words it is a sign of closeness and honour; in David's, an expression of humility. Fittingly, this part of the prayer ends with the recognition that all of God's great deeds were done 'according to thy own heart' and 'for thy servant's sake'.

Both the syntax and meaning of the phrase *ūr$^{e'}$ītānī k^{e}tōr hā'ādām hamma$^{'a}$lāh* (v. 17b) are difficult. The parallel in II Sam. 7.19, *w^{e}zō't tōrat hā'ādām*, is perhaps even more unclear (cf. the detailed discussion of Driver, *Samuel*, 276–7; Curtis, 231). RSV's translation 'thou ... hast shown me future generations' is based on a famous conjecture of Wellhausen (*wattar'ēnī dōrōt hā'ādām*), which combines elements from II Sam. and Chron., and is both substantially and orthographically weak. It would seem that in spite of all difficulties, the text may be understood basically as it stands, as reflected by the literal translations of NEB, 'and now thou lookest upon me as a man already embarked on a high career', or JPS, 'you regard me as a man of distinction'. These conform to the general atmosphere, in which David attributes all distinction, both his own and his people's, to God's benevolence.

Verse 18a is also difficult because of its elliptic structure (the word 'say', supplemented by RSV, is an adjustment to II Sam. 7.20), the unusual use of the preposition *l^e* (RSV 'for'; NEB 'of'; JPS 'regarding'), and the nominal structure of the last clause, translated approximately as 'honouring your servant'. All the translations have overcome these difficulties by making certain adjustments.

[20–22] This part of the prayer refers to God's uniqueness and greatness, revealed in his mighty deeds. God's uniqueness is stated in the indicative, 'There is none like thee, O Lord' (v. 20), while the uniqueness of Israel as God's people is expressed in a rhetorical question: 'What other nation on earth is like thy people Israel?' (v. 21). Here, then, as in Nathan's prophecy, the prayer focuses on the people alone, harking back to past days – not the unfortunate period of the judges but the great days of the Exodus, when the bond between the people of Israel and the Lord was established. The intermediate period in the history of Israel, from the Exodus to David's time, is epitomized in one clause: 'in driving out nations before thy people' (v. 21). As in v. 19, where God is exalted for 'making known all these great things', here, too, God has done all this for Israel, 'making for thyself a name for great and terrible things' (v. 21).

Here, too, as in other parts of the chapter, there are differences between the two versions: change of words, of word-order, omissions, etc. The following examples should be mentioned:

'God went' is phrased with a plural verb in II Sam. 7.23 ($hāl^eku$) but with the singular in Chronicles ($hālak$, v. 21). Although the text in Samuel is difficult and probably corrupt, its main message is understandable. Yet the precise rendering of 'went' is of significance for its interpretation, since a plural (as in MT) would render 'God' as a common noun, referring to the God of the 'other nation', while a singular would make it refer to the God of Israel (so RSV, following a common emendation; cf. in great detail Driver, *Samuel*, 277–8). In Chronicles, with the verb in the singular, whether the change reflects a better original version or the editing of the Chronicler, the matter is clear: the uniqueness of Israel is that their God has redeemed them in order to make them his people.

At the end of the verse, II Sam. 7.23 has 'nations and his gods' ($gōyīm$ $w\bar{e}'lōhāw$, RSV 'nation'), which joins the 'gods' to the 'driving away' of the nations. The reading in 4QSam^a for $w\bar{e}'lōhāw$ is $w'hlim$, which is also reflected in the ancient Versions. The word is not found in Chronicles, which may indicate that the Chronicler's *Vorlage* read $w\bar{e}'lōhīm$ (and gods), a phrase which he preferred to omit.

[23–27] Coming to the last part of his prayer with 'and now …', David resumes the main topic, which he had set completely aside in the intermediate section, i.e. God's promise to build him a house. I have already pointed out the complexity of David's psychological attitude, which finds full expression from the outset of this section: David is asking of God to accomplish what he has already promised: 'Let the word which thou hast spoken … be established.' The tone of David's supplication is apologetic and he justifies even the presentation of this request by pointing out that God has already made this promise; it is only because of this that 'thy servant has found courage ...' (v. 25), and even this request is made only for the sake of God's name: 'Thy name will be established.'

As in other parts of this chapter, here too we find many repetitions which serve a distinct literary function. The root *dbr* (speak) recurs four times; 'your servant' in each of the verses at least once, five in all; the root *brk* (bless) three times; 'house' four times; 'for ever' four times, etc.

Among the differences between the parallel texts, two should be pointed out. One is the introduction in Chronicles of the root *'mn* (translated as 'establish'), which is not found in the parallel verses in II Sam. 7. 'Let the word ... be established' (*yē'āmēn*) (v. 23), and 'thy name will be established (*w^eyē'āmēn*) and magnified' (v. 24). The introduction of this same verb in the two contiguous verses creates a tighter correspondence between the two ideas: the 'establishment' of God's word and of his name. Thus, while the verb *'mn* referring to David's 'sure house' is omitted in Chronicles from Nathan's prophecy (I Chron. 17.14//II Sam. 7.16), it is introduced here to emphasize the bond between God's faithfulness and God's glory.

The second difference is to be found at the conclusion of the prayer. In II Sam. 7 the prayer concludes with a supplication: 'may it please thee to bless ... for ... with thy blessing shall the house of thy servant be blessed for ever' (v. 29). In Chronicles, the conclusion opens from an opposite angle: David regards himself not as someone who is still to be blessed, but as someone who has already received blessing through the very word of God! David, there-fore, ends his prayer fully recognizing the grace which he has already received, and blessing God in turn: 'For you O Lord have blessed and are blessed for ever' (JPS). The Chronicler thus concluded David's prayer with a new element: a direct blessing of God. A fuller version of such a benediction can be found in other contexts, such as: 'Blessed be the name of the Lord' (Ps. 113.2; Job 1.21).

18

18   After this David defeated the Philistines and subdued them, and he took Gath
and its villages out of the hand of the Philistines.
2 And he defeated Moab, and the Moabites became servants to David and brought
tribute.
3 David also defeated Hadadezer king of Zobah, toward Hamath, as he went to set
up his monument at the river Euphrates. [4] And David took from him a thousand
chariots, seven thousand horsemen, and twenty thousand foot soldiers; and David
hamstrung all the chariot horses, but left enough for a hundred chariots. [5] And when
the Syrians of Damascus came to help Hadadezer king of Zobah, David slew twenty-
two thousand men of the Syrians. [6] Then David put garrisons in Syria of Damascus;
and the Syrians became servants to David, and brought tribute. And the Lord gave
victory to David wherever he went. [7] And David took the shields of gold which were
carried by the servants of Hadadezer, and brought them to Jerusalem. [8] And from
Tibhath and from Cun, cities of Hadadezer, David took very much bronze; with it
Solomon made the bronze sea and the pillars and the vessels of bronze.
9 When Tou king of Hamath heard that David had defeated the whole army of
Hadadezer, king of Zobah, [10] he sent his son Hadoram to King David, to greet him,
and to congratulate him because he had fought against Hadadezer and defeated him;
for Hadadezer had often been at war with Tou. And he sent all sorts of articles of
gold, of silver, and of bronze; [11] these also King David dedicated to the Lord,
together with the silver and gold which he had carried off from all the nations, from
Edom, Moab, the Ammonites, the Philistines, and Amalek.
12 And Abishai, the son of Zeruiah, slew eighteen thousand Edomites in the Valley
of Salt. [13] And he put garrisons in Edom; and all the Edomites became David's
servants. And the Lord gave victory to David wherever he went.
14 So David reigned over all Israel; and he administered justice and equity to all his
people. [15] And Joab the son of Zeruiah was over the army; and Jehoshaphat the son of
Ahilud was recorder; [16] and Zadok the son of Ahitub and Ahimelech the son of
Abiathar were priests; and Shavsha was secretary; [17] and Benaiah the son of Jehoiada
was over the Cherethites and the Pelethites; and David's sons were the chief officials
in the service of the king.

A. Notes to MT

[6] Insert נציבים after הרמשק, following the ancient Versions and II Sam. 8.6; [10] וכל,
difficult, II Sam. 8.10 ובידו היו, proposed בכל (Rudolph, cf. BHS); [12] ואבשי בן צרויה
difficult, II Sam. 8.13 בשבו מהכותו את ארם probably also corrupt, proposed בשבו מצובה
(Rudolph, cf. BHS); [16] ואביםלך, read with some MSS, all the Versions and II Sam.
8.17 ואחימלך, cf. commentary.

B. Notes to RSV

[1] 'After this', JPS 'Sometime afterwards'; [2] 'servants ... tribute', JPS 'tributary vassals'(!), also v. 6; [3] 'toward Hamath', incomprehensible, read 'Zobah-Hamath', cf. commentary; [5] 'Syrians', the LXX rendering for MT אֲרָם, read 'Aramaeans' throughout (cf. v. 6), so NEB and JPS; [10] 'and he sent', supplement to MT, possibly 'with'.

C. Structure, sources and form

1. Chapters 18–20, all taken from II Sam., are dedicated to David's wars. The source-material is carefully selected: I Chron. 18 = II Sam. 8; I Chron. 19 = II Sam. 10; I Chron. 20 = II Sam. 11.1 + 12.26, 29b–31 + II Sam. 21.19–22. It is obvious that these three short chapters in Chronicles actually represent, or 'cover', the whole of II Sam. 8–21. This is emphasized by the nature of ch. 20, a 'mosaic' constructed of bits and pieces from II Sam. 11, 12 and 21, and also by the fact that these chapters are bare of peculiar Chronistic material, as nothing has been added by the Chronicler. Our attention should therefore be drawn not only to the Chronicler's omissions (which have been abundantly noted in the history of exegesis) but to what he retained from the original pericope of II Sam. 8–21.

It has been amply demonstrated that the Chronicler's omission of the major part of II Sam. 9–20, a unit known in biblical scholarship as 'the succession narrative', serves to enhance and even idealize David's image by completely ignoring the flaws in his personal behaviour and the compromising of his position highlighted in the succession narrative. Exegetes have even regarded this idealization as a primary motive in the Chronistic reworking of David's history (cf. with persistent emphasis, Pseudo-Rashi, e.g. on I Chron. 3.6: 'for the whole book was written to honour David and his seed'). However, some of the material omitted (e.g. II Sam. 9) portrays David in a favourable light. To account for this fact we must add to the Chronicler's overall historical motivation another element: his reluctance to relate the private affairs of his protagonists, and his preference to stress the public and political aspects of their lives.

2. As demonstrated above, the Chronicler retained from the 'succession narrative' only certain excerpts, that is: II Sam. 10; 11.1; 12.29b–31; and 21.19–22. Thus, except for II Sam. 21.15–17, which depicts the threat to David's life, the Chronicler incorporated into his version all the material pertaining to David's military activities. The precision with which he picked out the details of the Ammonite war through the combination of II Sam. 11.1 with 12.26, 29b–31 is instructive. It shows that he was particularly interested in describing all of David's campaigns and political connections. This general principle is discernible elsewhere in the portrayal of David's history. The Chronicler gathered from II Sam. all references to the conquest of Jerusalem and to the wars with the Philistines (II Sam. 5) and did not omit even the episodes concerning David's warriors from II Sam. 21, 23. Only a very few of the other sections of the book of Samuel are transferred to Chronicles with the same thoroughness. Moreover, because of the Chronicler's new view of the history of David, some of this material, while fully preserved, is put in historical contexts which differ from those of II Sam. At the same time the Chronicler does not add anything to these descriptions, but cites them basically as they stand. The significance of these facts is mainly in the realization of the Chronicler's general historiographical

approach and motivation. He makes a literary effort to preserve (and later even to add) political aspects in the description of Israel's history.

3. While in the book of Samuel David's wars are scattered throughout the narrative, in Chronicles they are all gathered into this one pericope. This immediately presents David as 'the great warrior' of Israel's history. It should be emphasized, however, that in Chronicles, and for that matter also in Samuel, this is but one aspect of David's multi-faceted character, and does not diminish his role as the king who prepared for the building of the Temple and ruled over all Israel in justice.

4. Chapters 18–20 comprise three distinct literary units: ch. 18; 19.1–20.3; and 20.4–6. Chapter 18 is basically a collection of individual passages of annalistic origin, briefly relating several of David's wars. The individual components, including certain uniform but not fully standardized phrases, probably existed independently before being collected into the present context. 19.1–20.3 constitutes the story of one war recorded in the artistic narrative style of Samuel, of which there are only three more samples in Chronicles (I Chron. 10; 13+15; 21). Finally, 20.4–8 is a collection of three episodes, relating the exploits of David's mighty men, parallel to those included in I Chron. 11.10ff. (from II Sam. 23).

Each of these literary units opens with the stereotyped formula כן אחרי ויהי (18.1; 19.1; 20.4), represented by RSV as 'after this' but better by NEB at 19.1 'some time afterwards'. This is a conjunctive formula which joins the various elements rather loosely, while at the same time conferring on these three chapters a mark of uniformity, accentuated by the fact that the formula is unique in Chronicles to these three instances. It is of interest that the formula is already found in the Chronicler's source in Samuel (II Sam. 8.1; 10.1; 21.18), but serves no unifying literary role there. In Samuel, the formula is not unique to these passages but can be found elsewhere as well (I Sam. 24.6; II Sam. 13.1; 15.1); furthermore, the three sections which are here linked by the Chronicler do not add up in Samuel to a literary sequence.

5. All of the above indicates the Chronicler's careful, one might even say meticulous, editorial technique. In the structuring of this unit he selected passages from different contexts in Samuel, preserved their basic sequence, but bestowed on the composition a coherence all its own. This he achieved (a) through the common topic of David's wars; (b) by the position of the unit as a distinct and self-contained element between two literary pericopes relating to the building of the Temple (I Chron. 17 and I Chron. 21); (c) by the recurrent opening formula: 'some time afterwards', the distinguishing mark of the unit.

6. Chapter 18 is composed of several unequal parts, the formulation of which discloses both their origin in annalistic material and their redaction. The material of ch. 18 is of three types:

(i) War records, enumerating, in similar terms, the wars with the Philistines (v. 1), Moab (v. 2), Zobah (vv. 3–4), Damascus (vv. 5–6), and Edom (vv. 12–13).

(ii) Records of international relations, booty and tribute (vv. 7–8; 9–10; 11).

(iii) A list of David's officials (vv. 15–17).

The basic annalistic formula could be reconstructed approximately as follows: 'And David defeated X, and he placed garrisons in X; then X became tributary vassals of David.' This formula recurs, with slight variations, in the record of the wars with Moab, Damascus and Edom. It is absent from the description of the wars with Zobah and the Philistines because it would not accord with the outcome of these campaigns.

There is another formula which recurs twice in the chapter: 'and the Lord gave victory to David wherever he went' (vv. 6b, 13b). In v. 13b this clearly marks the end of the larger unit, and therefore could be regarded as a concluding formula. One may deduce, then, that the record of the war with Damascus was originally an independent passage, distinguished by its basic annalistic formula and its conclusion. If this was the case, then the story of Hadadezer, king of Zobah, originally formed one literary sequence (vv. 3–4, 7–8); this, together with the story of To'u king of Hamath, formed one narrative block, the central topic of which was booty.

Thus, the composition and redaction of the chapter can be traced in the following elements:

1. The combination of several annalistic elements taken from different sources into a single, more comprehensive, narrative context (vv. 3–10).
2. The addition of editorial notices, referring to general aspects of David's reign, of a historical (v. 11) and theological nature (vv. 6b; 13b–14).
3. The addition of the list of David's officials.

The literary history of the material, of which I have sketched only the most conspicuous lines, is pre-history as far as Chronicles is concerned. The Chronicler adopted the chapter basically as it stands, introducing only slight changes in detail which did not affect the general structure. The one important addition in Chronicles is the anachronistic remark of v. 8b, to which we will return in the commentary.

D. Commentary

[1] David's first campaign is against the Philistines, who pose the most imminent threat to his hegemony. The opening words, 'after this ...', do not imply a chronological link with ch. 17 but serve rather as a literary conjunctive formula.

The many campaigns and recorded victories notwithstanding, David did not completely dispel the Philistine menace. The Philistines remained entrenched in their coastal settlements. The precise borders of Philistine territory, and the nature of their eventual subordination to David, are not made clear in our sources. This verse speaks of 'subduing' (NEB 'conquered') the Philistines, with no further elaboration. We obtain some idea of these matters from two important allusions to the Philistines during the reign of Solomon:

(a) The borders of Solomon's kingdom extended 'from the Euphrates to the land of the Philistines and the border of Egypt' (I Kings 5.21 [MT 5.1]), that is, the 'land of the Philistines' remained a territorial and political entity, not included in Solomon's kingdom.

(b) At the outset of Solomon's rule there was a Philistine king in Gath, 'Achish son of Ma'acah king of Gath' (I Kings 2.39), whose precise status is not specified.

In contrast to the obscure text of II Sam. 8.1, 'and David took Metheg-ammah out of the hand of the Philistines', where the problematic *meteg hā'ammāh* of MT is understood as a place name, the text in Chronicles reads: 'he took Gath and its villages out of the hand of the Philistines'. The fact that the obscure 'Metheg-ammah' is also found in 4QSam[a], and the reference to 'Achish king of Gath' in I Kings 2.39, may support the view that Gath was not in fact conquered by David. In this case, the text of I Chron. 18.1 (*wayyiqqaḥ 'et-gat*) would be regarded as a simplification of the original of II Sam. (*wayyiqqaḥ ...'et meteg hā'ammāh*) and its rendering by an orthographically similar phrase. On the other hand, the subjugation of 'Gath and its villages' to David is not historically improbable; in this case the text would preserve an independent, authentic piece of information concerning this event. The fact that the recurring formula 'and X became tributary vassals' is not found in this context may indicate the non-formulaic and basically authentic nature of this information, but the limits of our knowledge and the nature of the material do not permit us to draw any definite conclusion about its historical value.

[2] The war with Moab is recorded here in an abbreviated form, omitting David's decimation of the captive Moabites (II Sam. 8.2b). Since victory in battle is an important element in the Chronistic world-view, it would be difficult to ascribe this omission to him on theological grounds. It could have resulted from textual corruption or literary preferences.

[3–4] It emerges in the course of the story itself, as well as from the following chapter, that David did not subdue the kingdom of Zobah, but only dealt it a severe blow in one engagement. At this historical juncture, when the two 'world powers' seem to have withdrawn for internal reasons, both Zobah and Israel were in the process of expansion. David's justification for his attack is the fact that Hadadezer 'went to set up his monument at the river Euphrates', which would imply a declaration of sovereignty to which David was evidently opposed.

Hadadezer is described in Chronicles as *melek ṣōbāh ḥ"mātāh*, rendered by RSV as 'king of Zobah, toward Hamath'. However, the locative function of final *he* is often lost in Chronicles, the longer form simply constituting an alternative form of the place name, e.g. Ephrathah (I Chron. 2.50; 4.5; etc.). 'Zobah-Hamatha' has probably the same meaning as 'Hamath-Zobah', in II Chron. 8.3. If, then, according to Chronicles, Hadadezer ruled both in Zobah and in Hamath, To'u king of Hamath must have been not only Hadadezer's sworn enemy (v. 9) but his rebellious subordinate or vassal.

The captives taken by David in this campaign are described in Chronicles in a different way from that in Samuel, in II Sam. 'a thousand and seven hundred horsemen', here 'a thousand chariots and seven thousand horsemen'. The explicit reference to 'chariots' is supported by 4QSam[a] and LXX of II Sam., and should be preferred. As for the numbers, without establishing their actual historicity, it would seem that from a textual point of view Chronicles preserves the better reading; after the word 'chariots' had fallen from the text, the original 'seven thousand' was adjusted in II Sam. to 'seven hundreds'.

David's disposal of the war horses indicates that he is not yet ready to integrate such a large contingent of chariots into his army. Only later, during the reign of Solomon, will a great chariot force also be deployed in Judah.

[5–6] It seems that the war with Damascus was originally described as an independent campaign, later incorporated into the account of the war with Hadadezer. This is demonstrated by the concluding formula in v. 6b, which is completely out of sequence in the present context. Thus, while from a historical point of view the two engagements could have been fought during one military campaign, from a literary point of view the passage comprises two originally independent units.

The defeat of Damascus is more total than that of Zobah: David stations his garrison there and makes the Aramaeans his vassals ('servants' as a translation of the MT *ʿăbādīm* is much too general for the present context. NEB is more precise: 'and they became subject to him and paid him tribute'. It seems, however, that a specific political status is denoted by the recurring Hebrew term *ʿăbādīm nośʾē minḥāh*).

The narrative concludes with a formula (v. 6b) which recurs in 13b. It may very well be that such a formula concluded each of the original accounts, but it has been preserved only in this context. In content and phraseology it resembles 'and the Lord wrought a great victory that day' found in II Sam. 23.10, 12 and I Chron. 11.14. Its origin may have been either in the original record of the event, or in its redactional phase.

darmeśeq is the standard form in Chronicles for the earlier *dammeśeq* (II Chron. 16.2; 24.23; 28.3, 23), cf. Y. Kutscher, *The Language*, 3–4.

[7–8] The spoils, of which David brings to Jerusalem only the precious metals, represent another aspect of the military activity. *šilṭē hazzāhāb* is translated by RSV as 'shields of gold', while, following Jer. 51.11, NEB renders it 'gold quivers' (R. Borger, 'Die Waffenträger des Königs Darius', *VT* 22, 1972, 385–98). Whatever the original meaning, the interpretation of the word as 'shields' is probably evidenced as early as 4QSam[a] and LXX of Samuel, both of which contain a similar addition, at this point (on II Sam. 8.7), 'And Shushak King of Egypt took them when he went up to Jerusalem in the days of Reboboam son of Solomon', clearly referring to I Kings 14.26, where the 'shields of gold' (*māginnē hazzāhāb*) which Shishak took from Jerusalem are mentioned. It would seem that the interpretation of *šᵉlāṭīm* as 'shields' prompted the interpolator of 4QSam[a] to identify the 'shields' of Hadadezer as part of the spoil taken by Shishak. For the textual problem involved in this addition, cf. below on v. 8.

348 I CHRONICLES

[8] This verse contains the first reference to the 'bronze' (or copper) which played such an important role in the preparation of the vessels of Solomon's Temple. It may be inferred from the text that David's control of the cities of Hadadezer was temporary, and was capitalized on by exploiting their bronze deposits as efficiently as possible.

The names of the cities vary in the different sources: Betah and Berothai in II Sam. 8.8, Tibhath and Cun in Chronicles. The transition from Betah to Tibhath, or *vice versa*, is most probably due to a textual corruption, Tibhath being the more plausible reading (cf. Gen. 22.24: Tebah, which is probably the original version of II Sam.). Berothai is attested in Ezek. 47.16 as situated near Hamath, while Cun is evidenced in extra-biblical sources (Willi, 120). The change of Berothai to Cun cannot be explained on textual, literary or theological grounds and probably reflects an inclination to 'modernize' the historical testimony.

Verse 8b is the only addition in Chronicles to the text of II Sam. 8, and is clearly an anachronistic remark, indicating that the bronze (or copper) which was taken from the cities of Hadadezer was later used by Solomon in the preparation of the bronze vessels for the Temple. The general tendency here conforms perfectly with the Chronicler's inclination to ascribe to David as many of the actual preparations for the building of the Temple as possible, in complete contrast to the attitude of Kings (cf. further on I Chron. 22.3, 14), as well as to the significance assigned by the Chronicler to the consecration of war-booty to the Lord (cf. also I Chron. 26.26–28). On the other hand, such a 'proleptic' remark, referring to a matter which will be brought up only further on in the story, is not characteristic of Chronicles; the question of its origin should then be posed. Because of its general importance, this question should be discussed in some detail.

The textual circumstances in this matter are as follows:

(*a*) In the MT of II Sam. 8.7–8 there are no 'proleptic' remarks.
(*b*) In LXX of II Sam. 8.7–8 there are two: one in v. 7, anticipating the campaign of Shishak in the time of Rehoboam; and one in v. 8, anticipating the building of the Temple in the days of Solomon.
(*c*) 4QSam[a] undoubtedly contains the first remark of v. 7, but the fragmentary state of the text does not allow for any conclusion regarding the second.
(*d*) The text in I Chron. 18.8 contains the second remark alone.

The textual evidence thus reflects three or four different situations: the MT of II Sam. 8 has the shortest version, LXX of II Sam. the longest, Chronicles containing one remark (of v. 8) and 4QSam[a] containing both remarks (as in LXX of II Sam.), or only one (of v. 7).

It is obvious that 4QSam[a] did not serve as the textual *Vorlage* of

Chronicles. It is also likely that the LXX of II Sam. was following a Hebrew *Vorlage* (the possibility of this being 4QSam^a should not be completely ruled out). The question, therefore, concerns the origin of the addition in v. 8: was it first introduced into an as yet unknown edition of II Sam. and transported from there both to LXX and to Chronicles? Or was it, conversely, introduced first into Chronicles and secondarily into a Hebrew version of II Sam. 8.8, which eventually served as the *Vorlage* of LXX?

In principle, the two possibilities are equally valid. The remark could have originated in the redactional activity of the Chronicler, then to be transposed through a process of harmonization into the text of Samuel, or it could have originated in Samuel, as the work of some anonymous redactor of the same school and theological inclinations as the Chronicler, transferring to David the main burden of preparing for the building of the Temple. If this was the case, we have here a demonstration that viewpoints regarded as 'Chronistic' were in fact the property of broader circles.

[9–11] From a syntactical and literary point of view this is one continuous passage, but its topics are in fact two:

(*a*) the relations with Hamath (vv. 9–10).
(*b*) the consecration of the spoils of war to God (v. 11).

The diplomatic rapprochement with Hamath is described as a unique event: the king of Hamath sends his compliments to David on his victory over Hadadezer, by a delegation of the highest rank headed by his son. In accordance with international etiquette, the delegation comes bearing gifts. The motive for this international achievement of David's is stated very clearly: the defeat of Hadadezer was of immediate advantage to Hamath. The episode is thus tightly connected with the war against Zobah, and is the only such delegation which is recorded in David's reign.

Can we learn more about the status of Hamath in David's kingdom? The arrival of the good-will delegation can be evaluated as either an isolated gesture or the indication of a permanent subordination. The text itself is not clear, especially in regard to the former relationship between Hamath and Zobah. If Hamath had been subordinate to Hadadezer, then David's victory over Zobah may have implied a transfer of vassal allegiance to David; however, if the preceding situation was only that of war between the two rivals, this passage would refer to a one-time delegation and no more. The reading of v. 3 as referring to Hadadezer 'the king of Zobah-Hamath' would support the first possibility, but this seems too narrow a basis for drawing historical conclusions.

The king of Hamath is called To'u in Chronicles and To'i in II Sam. A similar variation of an Aramaic 'i' also occurs in the name of Hiram, which is always vocalized 'Hiram' in I Kings but 'Huram' in Chronicles. These variations could reflect not just scribal errors (which in the case of Hebrew *w* and *y* are extremely common), but actual dialect forms of these names.

[11] While this is syntactically a continuation of v. 10, it introduces, by way of association, a new topic: the dedication of spoils of war to the Lord. The nations enumerated here include Edom (which will only be mentioned later in the chapter), Ammon (which is not included in the present chapter) and Amalek (which is not mentioned at all in the present pericope; the allusion may have been to I Sam. 30 or to some unknown record). This is therefore a summary of some kind, based by the author on general information available to him and not on the events described in the present literary context alone. The emphasis is on the fact that the gains from the wars are dedicated to God, not to be profaned by vulgar use.

The text deviates from II Sam. 8.12 in two details: Edom is referred to instead of Aram, and there is no mention of 'the spoil of Hadadezer the son of Rehob king of Zobah'. The variant Edom/Aram implies such a common orthographic change that the original version cannot be determined on textual grounds alone. It is also difficult to determine the preferable reading in the case of 'the spoil of Hadadezer ...', although an addition in II Sam. 8.12 would seem to be the most plausible explanation.

This verse suggests that David dedicated *all* the spoil of his wars to God, while a different phrasing is found in I Chron. 26.27, indicating that only a portion of the booty is meant: 'from spoil won in battles, they dedicated gifts'. The view reflected in this chapter is in line with the concept of the holy war, in which 'all silver and gold and vessels of bronze and iron are sacred to the Lord, they shall go into the treasury of the Lord' (Josh. 6.19).

[12–13] The war with Edom and the war with Aram are described in similar terms; nevertheless, the historicity of either conflict could hardly be doubted. The respective texts in Chronicles and Samuel open differently. II Samuel 8.13 (in MT) reads: 'When he returned from smiting eighteen thousand of Aram.' However, the continuation of the story referring to Edom, and the site of the battle in the 'Valley of Salt', make it likely that the subject was Edom all along, as indicated in the RSV translation, and as is indeed the case in the parallel version of Chronicles. Still, while the subject of the opening clause in II Sam. is David, in Chronicles it is Abishai. This raises both textual and historical questions: which text is the superior, and, historically, who was it who waged war against the Edomites and smote them? The next clause, 'and he put garrisons in Edom', clearly implies that the subject is David; moreover, although it is possible that Abishai was the commander of the army, it is hardly likely that the campaign would be associated with his name (cf. mainly II Sam. 12.26–28). In Ps. 60.2 the smiting of Edom is attributed to Joab, and similar evidence is found in I Kings 11.15–16. It seems, therefore, that here too textual corruption should be considered, the most attractive reconstruction being that of Rudolph: 'when he returned from Zobah' (*bᵉšubō miṣṣōbāh* becoming *'abšay ben ṣerūyāh*). If this is the case, then the two parallel texts would be corrupted versions of the original, while LXX of II Sam. still preserves a clearer rendering.

[14] This is a theological remark concluding David's reign, and stressing two of its very important aspects: his rule 'over all Israel' (an idea which is greatly elaborated in Chronicles), and his administration of 'justice and equity (JPS 'true justice') to all his people'. This last is the confirmation that David had satisfied the people's expectations of the ideal, just ruler. This is most closely paralleled by the reference to Josiah in Jer. 22.28: 'did not your father ... do justice and righteousness' (on the terminological aspect of this phrase and its place among ancient Near Eastern social and religious attitudes, cf. M. Weinfeld, *Justice and Righteousness in Israel and the Nations*, Jerusalem 1985, 12–25*).

[15–17] The evaluation of David's conduct also serves as an introduction to the list of David's officials, who include: (*a*) The commander of the army; (*b*) the recorder (*mazkīr*); (*c*) the priests; (*d*) the scribe-secretary (*sōpēr*); (*e*) the commander of the special groups of Cherethites and Pelethites; (*f*) David's sons.

The list is a laconic and schematic expression of the extensive administrative development in the royal court (cf. by contrast I Sam. 14.50, where only the commander of the army is mentioned). A similar list is found in II Sam. 20.23 and a still more detailed one for the reign of Solomon in I Kings. 4.3–19. These last, however, are absent from Chronicles, which supplements the picture of David's administration with a detailed record in I Chron. 27, cf. *ad loc*.

Two details in the list deserve further attention:

(a) II Sam. 8.17 reads 'Zadok the son of Ahitub and Ahimelech the son of Abiathar'; consequently (cf. also below) 'Ahimelech' should also be read in this text. However, the assertion that the priestly companion of Zadok during David's reign is Ahimelech the son of Abiathar stands in glaring contrast to the testimony of the other list in II Sam. 20.25, as well as to the narrative material of Samuel, where Abiathar himself plays a dominant role even at the end of David's reign (cf. *inter alia* I Kings. 1.7ff.). Moreover, the name of Zadok's father actually derives from the genealogical tree of Abiathar, who is, indeed, 'the son of Ahimelech, the son of Ahitub' (cf. I Sam. 22.20). It has been suggested, therefore, that the original reading, later corrupted into the present form of our text, was: 'Abiathar the son of Ahimelech the son of Ahitub and Zadok' (cf. for example, Driver, *Samuel*, 283). Although this is probably the correct historical concept, it hardly seems likely that a structure so lacking in balance, and not attested in any other source, could actually represent the original text. It seems more plausible that the designation of

Ahitub as the father of Zadok was intentionally introduced into the list, in order to afford him more dignity and to create a balance between him and the distinguished Abiathar; the reversing of the order of Ahimelech and Abiathar could result from a textual corruption. Whatever the case, the different order already stood in the Chronicler's *Vorlage* of II Sam., and was taken further in I Chron. 24.3, 6; there Ahimelech and not Abiathar is the chief priest, together with Zadok.

(b) The sons of David are described as 'priests' in II Sam. 8.17, and as 'chief officials' in Chronicles. It seems quite obvious that the Chronicler would not be able to accept the designation of the sons of David as priests, even if in Chronicles some cultic functions may be attributed to David and Solomon. At the same time, however, the very designation of David's sons as 'priests' is open to doubt and is never repeated for any of the other kings. In general, the priests are well-known individuals, referred to by their full names and never in such a general and collective manner (cf. I Kings 4.4, 5). It is therefore likely that the rendering of II Sam. 8.17 is already a corruption of some original text, for which the Chronicler has introduced his 'chief officials'. A suggestion for an original reading *sōkᵉnīm*, which was corrupted into *kōhᵃnīm* in II Sam. and rendered as 'chiefs' by the Chronicler, has been made by G. J. Wenham, 'Were David's Sons Priests?', *ZAW* 87, 1975, 79–82.

19 Now after this Nahash the king of the Ammonites died, and his son reigned in his stead. [2] And David said, 'I will deal loyally with Hanun the son of Nahash, for his father dealt loyally with me.' So David sent messengers to console him concerning his father. And David's servants came to Hanun in the land of the Ammonites, to console him. [3] But the princes of the Ammonites said to Hanun, 'Do you think, because David has sent comforters to you, that he is honouring your father? Have not his servants come to you to search and to overthrow and to spy out the land?' [4] So Hanun took David's servants, and shaved them, and cut off their garments in the middle, at their hips, and sent them away; and they departed. [5] When David was told concerning the men, he sent to meet them, for the men were greatly ashamed. And the king said, 'Remain at Jericho until your beards have grown, and then return.'

6 When the Ammonites saw that they had made themselves odious to David, Hanun and the Ammonites sent a thousand talents of silver to hire chariots and horsemen from Mesopotamia, from Aram-maacah, and from Zobah. [7] They hired thirty-two thousand chariots and the king of Maacah with his army, who came and encamped before Medeba. And the Ammonites were mustered from their cities and came to battle. [8] When David heard of it, he sent Joab and all the army of the mighty men. [9] And the Ammonites came out and drew up in battle array at the entrance of the city, and the kings who had come were by themselves in the open country.

10 When Joab saw that the battle was set against him both in front and in the rear, he chose some of the picked men of Israel, and arrayed them against the Syrians; [11] the rest of his men he put in the charge of Abishai his brother, and they were arrayed against the Ammonites. [12] And he said, 'If the Syrians are too strong for me, then you shall help me; but if the Ammonites are too strong for you, then I will help you. [13] Be of good courage and let us play the man for our people, and for the cities of our God; and may the Lord do what seems good to him.' [14] So Joab and the people who were with him drew near before the Syrians for battle; and they fled before him. [15] And when the Ammonites saw that the Syrians fled, they likewise fled before Abishai, Joab's brother, and entered the city. Then Joab came to Jerusalem.

16 But when the Syrians saw that they had been defeated by Israel, they sent messengers and brought out the Syrians who were beyond the Euphrates, with Shophach the commander of the army of Hadadezer at their head. [17] And when it was told David, he gathered all Israel together, and crossed the Jordan, and came to them, and drew up his forces against them. And when David set the battle in array against the Syrians, they fought with him. [18] And the Syrians fled before Israel; and David slew of the Syrians the men of seven thousand chariots, and forty thousand foot soldiers, and killed also Shophach the commander of their army. [19] And when the servants of Hadadezer saw that they had been defeated by Israel, they made peace with David, and became subject to him. So the Syrians were not willing to help the Ammonites any more.

20 In the spring of the year, the time when kings go forth to battle, Joab led out the army, and ravaged the country of the Ammonites, and came and besieged Rabbah. But David remained at Jerusalem. And Joab smote Rabbah, and overthrew it. [2] And David took the crown of their king from his head; he found that it weighed a talent of gold, and in it was a precious stone; and it was placed on David's head. And he brought forth the spoil of the city, a very great amount. [3] And he brought forth the people who were in it, and set them to labour with saws and iron picks and axes; and thus David did to all the cities of the Ammonites. Then David and all the people returned to Jerusalem.

A. Notes to MT

[8] צבא, proposed צבא, following MSS and Versions (so RSV), others הצבא והגברים; [17] ויערך דויד לקראת ארם, II Sam. 10.17 reverses לקראת דוד ארם; [20.3] וישר, וישם ,II Sam. 12.31, probably better; במגרות, II Sam. 12.31, במגזרות probably better.

B. Notes to RSV

[2] 'came to Hanun ... Ammonites', better, 'came to the land of the Ammonites, to Hanun' (JPS, similarly NEB); [4] 'and they departed', the division of verses deviates from MT, where וילכו forms the beginning of the next verse, cf. commentary; [6] 'Mesopotamia', actually 'Aram-Naharaim' (so NEB and JPS), 'Aram of the two rivers'; [10] 'Syrians', MT 'Aramaeans' (so NEB, the same also applies to vv. 12, 14, 15, 16, 17, 18, 19); [20.1] 'In the spring of the year', MT 'At the turn of the year' (NEB); [20.2] 'a precious stone', probably 'precious stones' (JPS).

C. Structure, sources and form

1. It has already been pointed out that 19.1–20.3 form one independent literary unit, taken from II Sam. 10.1–11.1; 12.26, 29b–31, relating the war with the Ammonites. The major difference between the parallel versions is of course the omission of the episode of David and Bathsheba (II Sam. 11.2–12.25). Except for that omission and II Sam. 12.27–29a, the section has not undergone major redaction.

2. The unit, which focuses on the war with Ammon but also tells of the victory over the Aramaean forces, comprises five parts:

19.1–5: the background: the fate of David's delegation of condolence.
6–8:   the mustering of the armies.
9–15:   the first battle with the Aramaeans and Ammonites.
16–19: the comprehensive war of Israel against the Aramaeans.
20.1–3: the final war with Ammon.

According to this scheme, Israel's challengers change in each of the stages: Ammon, Ammon+Aram, Aram, Ammon. Thus, Aram enters the picture in the second scene and departs in the third.

3. Of all David's wars, this one most attracted the attention of the historiographer of II Samuel, who portrayed it with the greatest detail. Although the political and

military significance of the engagement should not be underplayed, there was another motive for this treatment. As part of a comprehensive literary composition, this campaign provides the background and premise of many subsequent events. In contrast to the description of wars in II Sam. 8//I Chron. 18, the narrative style of this pericope does not preserve any traces of the annalistic material which might have served as its origin.

4. This is also, with the exception of the exploits of David's mighty men against the Philistines and others (II Sam. 21 and 23), the last of David's wars described in II Samuel. There follow descriptions of internal matters, with no allusion to military campaigns or international political activity. One may wonder whether this was indeed a reliable presentation of the historical situation, or merely a result of the literary arrangement of the material in II Samuel. (According to Malamat the wars described in II Sam. 8 are later than this one; cf. A. Malamat, *Israel in Biblical Times*, Jerusalem 1983, 197–200*.) However, the questions regarding the tension between the circumstances of the material dictated by literary demands, and the reconstruction of the actual course of David's career, apply only to Samuel. Chronicles has simply reproduced the chronology he found there. Following the war with Ammon, but before embarking on a broad description of internal matters pertaining to David's reign, the Chronicler concludes by introducing the exploits against the Philistines, taken from II Sam. 21 (I Chron. 20.4–8).

5. Although this chapter has not undergone theological redaction, it contains only very few verses which are accurate literal reproductions of II Sam. 10. A comparison of vv. 5–8 with the text of 4QSam[a] supports the view – previously based only on the correspondences between the LXX of Samuel and Chronicles – that some of these changes are not the work of the Chronicler but reflect a different *Vorlage* of II Sam. (cf. Ulrich, 152–6).

However, care should be taken not to let the argument swing to the opposite extreme. Notwithstanding the divergencies between the various texts and the growing tendency to refer to independent 'textual traditions', there are still clear signs of interdependence and a direct textual development.

D. Commentary

[1] In II Sam. 10.1 only the name of the Ammonite king's son is recorded; in Chronicles only the name of the father. Verse 2, in both versions, supplies both names.

[2] In the source material at our disposal there is no clarification of the 'loyalty' of the king of Ammon. This may be a reference to the pre-monarchical adventures of David, when he was forced to move his family to Transjordan, although I Sam. 23.3–4 mentions 'the king of Moab', not of Ammon.

The verse records David's thoughts and the considerations which motivated his sending of a delegation – a clear indication that we are dealing here not with annalistic records but with narrative. In a parallel manner, contrary thoughts of the princes of Ammon are then quoted in v. 3, in anticipation of their actions depicted in v. 4. Most probably, the sending of condolences was not merely a personal gesture of 'loyalty' but also a political act of recognition and a declaration of peaceful intentions.

[3] From the point of view of the narrator, whose sympathies of course lay with David's court, the explicit suspicion of the Ammonite officials was a flagrant error, in stark opposition to the sincerity of David's motives. The full historical picture is of course no longer attainable.

The situation depicted in this verse and the serious results for the Ammonites are strikingly parallel to another story – the division of the kingdom in I Kings 12. In both cases a young king, in the aftermath of his father's death, is exposed by his lack of experience to the advice of his officials, whose wrong reasoning and lack of insight bring disaster on him and his kingdom. In both cases the young king's actions are motivated by rashness, a sense of power, arrogance, and a wish to display authority and humiliate the other party. This last is very obvious in both cases. Even if the ultimate motive of David's envoys was indeed 'to spy out the land', Hanun might well have found more diplomatic ways to deal with the situation. The humiliating treatment given David's envoys was above all a demonstration of spite, self-confidence and superiority on Hanun's part. The deed itself must have been interpreted by David as an outright provocation and declaration of war, and a failure to react accordingly would rightly have been taken as a sign of weakness. The episode is therefore not a personal misunderstanding, but a 'test of power', an intentional provocation. This is made clear in what follows, where the Ammonites start immediately with actual preparations for war.

[4] The steps taken by Hanun are a series of well-calculated humiliations, to be understood against the background of the norms and standards of the time. While II Sam. refers to shaving 'half the beard of each', Chronicles has shaving 'them', which probably implies both the beard and hair. In cutting their garments to their middle, their flesh was exposed – to their utter shame (Isa. 47.2–3; Nahum 3.5; etc.). This treatment was a sharp contrast to the hospitality due to distinguished envoys in a foreign country.

In MT the next verse opens with *wayyēlᵉkū wayyayyīdū*, *wayyēlᵉkū* added to the version of II Sam. 10.5. RSV, following earlier commentators (cf. Rudolph, 136) transfers the word to the end of v. 4, thus creating the common formula *wayšallᵉhēm wayyēlēkū* (cf. *inter al.* Exod. 18.27; Judg. 2.6; II Sam. 3.21; Josh. 22.6 etc.). However, MT is just as probable, as is attested by Judg. 9.6, 7; 19.10; II Kings 5.5 etc. and especially II Sam. 17.21. No change is therefore indicated.

[5] The section ends with David's instructions to his servants, 'remain at Jericho'. Just as in v. 2, David is motivated by humane sentiments: he acts compassionately towards these men as he did towards Hanun. His instructions betray no political overtones, nor any reference to Hanun's behaviour.

The purpose of the narrator is very clear: to indicate by David's restraint that the initiative for the war is the Ammonites'. David is a man of peace, and even in such grave circumstances he does not seek revenge.

[6–8] The second section opens with the first of Ammon's preparations for war – the hiring of the Aramaeans.

The extant Qumran text shows similarity to that of Chronicles, but I differ from Ulrich on the method for a synoptic presentation of the texts. The correct approach will enable us to reconstruct both the original text and the processes of reworking in all the extant versions.

Let us examine the details.

In both II Sam. 10 and here, v. 6b opens with '[Hanun and] the Ammonites sent'; this is followed in the MT of Samuel by *'and hired'*, while in Chronicles it is followed by a more detailed text: 'a thousand talents of silver to hire chariots and horsemen from Aram-naharaim, from Aram-maacah and from Zobah; *and [they] hired ...*'

The broader text in Chronicles clearly incorporates additional material. Parts of these additional clauses are, however, attested in 4QSam^a, and this demonstrates that the text in Chronicles in fact reflects a different *Vorlage* of Samuel. Is it, then, a case of secondary expansion in 4QSam^a and Chronicles, or of omission in the MT of Samuel?

The next verse demonstrates the opposite phenomenon: a longer version in the MT of II Sam. 10.6b and a shorter in 4QSam^a and Chronicles. Thus:

II Sam. (MT) *and hired* the Aramaeans of Beth-rehob, and the Arameans of Zobah, twenty thousand foot soldiers, and the king of Maacah with a thousand men, and the men of Tob, twelve thousand men.

I Chron. *and hired* thirty-two thousand chariots and the king of Maacah with his army ...

Here it is clear that the text in Chronicles is an intentional abbreviation of the original as found in II Samuel, since the number 32,000 is the sum of the two numbers found separately in Samuel, 20,000 and 12,000. The governing noun is then altered from 'footmen' to 'chariots'. This is also the text reflected in 4QSam^a.

While in the first instance the text of Chronicles (and 4QSam^a) probably reflects an original longer version, abbreviated in the MT of Samuel by an omission (or a homoioteleuton) of a full sentence, in the second case the original is reflected in the MT of Samuel, abbreviated and slightly changed in Chronicles.

In v. 7b in Chronicles we find once more an expanded text, containing the additional lines: 'and they came and encamped before Medeba. And the Ammonites were mustered from their cities and came to battle.' This passage is again absent from the MT of II Sam.; there are traces of its presence in 4QSam^a.

Again, in v. 9, there is a summary in Chronicles, 'and the kings who had come were by themselves', in place of a much longer version in the MT of II Sam. 10.8b: 'and Aram of Zobah and of Rehob and the men of Tob and Maacah were by themselves'.

To sum up:

(a) It seems that none of the existing texts reflects the original story fully and accurately.

(b) While the texts of II Sam. and Chronicles are more or less of equal length, they differ in the extent to which they preserve the original material.

(c) It would seem that both texts display an abbreviated form of the original, but a different manner of reworking has been adopted in each text. In the MT of II Sam. the text is abbreviated by actual omissions of certain sections. Thus, in the present text of II Sam. two quite long passages are simply absent, leaving no trace. By contrast, MT of Chronicles (and also 4QSam^a) is reached through abbreviation by summary: two sections in the original are represented in a summarized form.

(d) As I pointed out, 4QSam^a and Chronicles reflect the same textual tradition.

[6] From the beginning of the engagement it is clear that Hanun's show of strength was a false pretence; the Ammonites do not dare to fight alone but must hire the help of various Aramaean groups. According to the description, this joining of forces is not dependent on a previous treaty or agreement between the parties; the Aramaeans are simply acting as hired mercenaries. This is demonstrated again, in different political circumstances, when Asa king of Judah hires the force of Aram against Israel (I Kings 15.18–20). The common element, which may be an authentic historical feature, is the readiness of the Aramaeans to take up arms as mercenaries, in conflicts not their own. It is 'chariots and horsemen' which the Ammonites seek, and these were indeed the backbone of the Aramaean military superiority.

Four kingdoms are mentioned in Samuel, but only two of these are repeated in Chronicles: Aram-maacah and Zobah. Tob is omitted altogether, while Aram of Beth-rehob is replaced by Aram-naharaim.

Thirty-two thousand is indeed an extravagant number of chariots, cf. I Chron. 18:4; II Sam. 8.4; and v. 18. below. On the other hand, according to II Sam. 10.6 there were only 32,000 'footmen', with no chariots. Although such a number seems more reasonable, the absence of chariots is unlikely. Taking into account the numerous changes undergone by the original text, one may assume that it included both footmen and chariots; the precise numbers of each can no longer be reconstructed.

While v. 7b is not found in II Sam., there is no reason to regard it as secondary, since it perfectly suits the course of the narrative. However, the mention of 'Medeba' is problematical. This was a city in Moab, south of the land of Ammon (Num. 21.30; Josh. 13.9, etc.), and it is not likely that the war was fought so far to the south. At the same time, the fact that the battle took place in front of a fortified city is evident from the story. The Israelites were engaged 'both in front and in the rear' – with the city before them and the 'kings ... in the open country' behind. For the difficult 'Medeba' Rudolph has suggested the reading 'Me-Rabbah' ('the water of Rabbah'), following II Sam. 12.27. This is orthographically an excellent conjecture, assuming the quite common change of one letter, resh, to dalet (myrbh – mydbh). However, there is no evidence that Rabbah, the Ammonite capital, was designated Me-Rabbah and, more importantly, it is hardly plausible that the Ammonites, who had themselves initiated the hostilities, would choose their own capital as the battle ground, even if they were sure of their victory. Some other city, probably closer to the Israelite border, would be more likely.

[8] David's response to the Ammonites' military initiative is immediate. He sends to battle 'Joab and the army of the mighty men', that is, the regular army, clearly distinct from 'all Israel' of v. 17, or 'all the people' of II Sam. 12.29. Even at this stage, the action is not regarded as a total war against the Ammonites, but only as a limited engagement, which the regular army could handle.

[9–11] The battle lines are described precisely and briefly. The Ammonites took up their position at the entrance to the city (II Sam. 'at the gate'); the Israelites were facing them, and the Aramaean armies were stationed in the open country. In fact, Joab and his army were trapped between the two camps. Joab, however, rather than being daunted by this situation, turns it to his advantage. He divides his army, arrays the 'picked men of Israel' against Aram, and 'the rest of the people', under the command of his brother Abshai, against the Ammonites. From a potential trap he moves to a double-fronted offensive (v. 14). At the same time the two formations are interconnected, providing mutual support.

[12–13] The gravity of the situation for the Israelites is expressed not only through the strategic details, but also in the words of Joab. These play a central role in the narrative, and in the version of Chronicles actually occupy the central place.

Until this point, the whole episode had been presented in political and military terms alone. All the events took place away from Israel's territory, the people within the land were not involved in any way, and the name of God was never mentioned. Yet, in the moment of crisis the true significance of the events becomes manifest: this is a struggle 'for our people and for our cities'; a war waged not by mercenaries but by the people for themselves. The spirit which permeates the age of David is faithfully expressed in Joab's exhortation: while it is incumbent on man to do all that is in his power, his real help is God, in whose providence he puts all his trust: 'and the Lord will do what he deems right' (JPS). Granted the significance of the political, economic and sociological factors which determined the rise of David and his success, one should not ignore the human and religious elements which turned the political options into reality.

[14–15] The results of the war are actually determined by Joab's words. The battle ends with the utter flight of Aramaeans and Ammonites alike, emphasized by the triple use of the verb 'to flee'. Then the episode is closed with the abbreviated and concise note: 'Then Joab came to Jerusalem.'

From a military point of view Joab's move may seem a retreat; he does not exhaust the potential of his victory by pursuing Aram or trying to conquer the city. He simply breaks off fighting and returns to Jerusalem. However, these steps reflect his military acumen and sobreity: they are only an interlude. The small force at his disposal was not intended for a general war; this must now be waged on two separate fronts, first against Aram and then against Ammon, with David's full force engaged in each. Only thus will David be able to overcome his main enemy in the east.

[16–19] According to the present story it is the Aramaeans who rally first from the defeat at the hands of Joab, as they see themselves threatened by David's potential advance. What had been a mercenary enterprise has now become the subject of Aramaean self-interest: to neutralize David's strength as soon as possible.

Although the narrator presents the war as an Aramaean initiative, historical logic would suggest that it was in David's best interests to engage the Aramaeans, eliminating the threat on that front – just as Joab had done in the battle before the city gate – before turning to combat the Ammonites. The broad muster of Aramaean forces, headed by 'Shophach the commander of the army of Hadadezer', and including troops from 'beyond the Euphrates', is summoned to an all-out war with Israel. It now is clear that we are dealing not with independent elements rallied together to face a temporary exigency, but with a sort of federation, in which the supremacy is that of Zobah, and the other kings referred to as 'the vassals of Hadadezer' (v. 19 JPS).

David has three objectives in this war: to diminish the threat of Aramaean might; to challenge the supremacy of Hadadezer by throwing Aramaean unity into disarray; and to prevent a pact between Aram and Ammon. The accomplishment of these goals is described in vv. 18–19: 'And the Aramaeans fled ... and David slew ... and when all the vassals of Hadadezer saw that they had been defeated ... they made peace with David and became subject to him. So the Aramaeans were not willing to help the Ammonites any more.'

The army is gathered from 'all Israel', under David's personal command. The name of the battlefield is given in II Sam. 10.15, 16 as 'Helam', but the two allusions are missing in Chronicles. It seems however, that the conflated text of v. 17 *wayyābō' '^alēhem wayya'^arōk '^alēhem* is a result of a corruption, and may originally have preserved the name of the battle-site, Helam, which is not known from other biblical sources. It seems that the war is conducted in Aramaean rather than Israelite territory, somewhere east of the Jordan.

In II Sam. 10.17 it is the Aramaeans who take the intiative to 'array themselves' against David, while in I Chron. 19.17 it is David who 'set the battle in array' against the Aramaeans. We should not attribute too much significance to this change, however, since the rendering of the verse in Chronicles seems corrupt.

[18] The Aramaean casualties are recorded differently: in II Sam. '700 chariots and 40,000 horsemen'; in Chronicles '7000 chariots and 40,000 foot soldiers'. The two texts are obviously interdependent. The problem of their relationship is more on the level of historiographical and literary priority than historical accuracy. The comparison with II Sam. 8.4 and I Chron. 18.4 would tend to support the reading 'foot soldiers' as preferable to 'horsemen', while the number of the chariots cannot be verified in any way.

The difference between 'Shobach' in II Sam. and 'Shophach' in Chron. is due to either dialect or orthography; the latter form is generally accepted as the more original (cf. Willi, 82).

[19] The major significance of the war lies in the abrogation of the supremacy of Zobah, and the subjection, in some way, of the Aramaean kingdoms to David. It seems, however, that Hadadezer himself was not killed and that his rule did not terminate. Further relationships between David and Zobah are not recorded, but the conquest of 'Hamath Zobah' is attributed to Solomon in II Chron. 8.3. The problematical relations with Aram are also evidenced by I Kings 11.23–25: the rebellion of Damascus and the overthrow there of Israelite rule (cf. also in the time of Asa, I Kings 15).

The passage (and the chapter) concludes with emphasis on the full accomplishment of David's primary objective: an end to the pact between Ammon and Aram, and the disintegration of the threat on the major eastern front.

[20.1–3] This section is one of the striking examples of the problems which now confront the exegete because of the reworking method which the Chronicler followed. The first part of v. 1 is transferred (with changes that will be discussed later), from II Sam. 11.1. There the verse concludes 'but David remained in Jerusalem', a statement which plays a cardinal role as an exposition for the story of David and Bathsheba which follows. Joab and 'all Israel' are fighting in Amnmon, while David remains in Jerusalem. This not only provides an ironic backdrop for subsequent events, but from a literary point of view also serves as point of departure: the setting for the Bathsheba episode alternates between Jerusalem and the battlefield. The narrator finally brings David from Jerusalem, by the explicit invitation of Joab, to complete the siege of Rabbah: 'and Joab sent ... to David ... So David gathered all the people ... and went to Rabbah' (II Sam. 12.27–29).

In Chronicles, the whole of the Bathsheba episode is omitted from the story, but the preparatory words '... David remained in Jerusalem' are retained (cf. also H. G. M. Williamson, 'A Response to A. G. Auld', *JSOT* 27, 1983, 36). Having lost their original expositional function these words now bear a different meaning: it was not David who besieged and smote Rabbah, but Joab! Moreover, since Joab's invitation to David is omitted, there is no proper preparation for vv. 2–3a: 'and David took the crown ... and he brought forth the spoil ... and he brought forth the people, etc.' How could David do all this if he had 'remained in Jerusalem'? Lastly, the words from II Sam. 12.31: 'Then David and all the people returned to Jerusalem', which were such a proper conclusion to II Sam. 11–12, are completely inexplicable here in v. 3.

Clearly this problematical situation is the result of a literary method in which the narrative is based on existing sources, the reworking and adaptation of which the author regards as his main task. A strict adherence to the original text and at the same time its adaptation according to various tendencies may result in internal incoherence, as demonstrated in the present case. Even the assumption that the readers were acquainted with the original story and were therefore undisturbed by this incoherence, while easing the problem on the informative and historical level, does not in fact account for the literary inconsistency of the unit as it stands.

The exegete, confronted with such a method, may proceed in two ways:

(*a*) The exegete may assume that, in spite of the contradictory elements in the editing process, the author succeeded in producing a fully coherent story, and that the present text is therefore a result of corruption and does not faithfully represent the Chronicler's original composition. On the basis of such an assumption Rudolph complements the story with a conjectured passage which was presumably omitted because of homoioteleuton. Thus:

'And Joab smote *Rabbah* [and he sent messengers to David saying: come and take Rabbah, etc ... So David gathered all the people together and went to *Rabbah*] and overthrew it.'

The inserted passage is a summary of II Sam. 12.27–29. Its addition has three significant advantages: it is orthographically plausible and can be fully accounted for as a homoioteleuton (cf. BH[3] with BHS); it removes the literary difficulty stated above; and finally it is also attested by similar complementary material in some minor MSS of LXX.

However, the weakness of this emendation lies in that it supplies precisely what the exegete so urgently seeks without giving adequate weight to the consideration that this same need could well have prompted the scribes of these LXX MSS to make the same emendation. The fact that it is so desirable from a literary point of view, and so plausible orthographically, does not make the addition a literary fact.

(b) The exegete may also adopt a less interventive mood, and accept the present text as authentic, observing that its adaptation did not reach perfection because of the natural mutual interference of the two tendencies: literary adherence and theological adaptation. Such an approach will regard the text before us, with all its literary weaknesses (excepting, of course, obvious textual corruptions), as the Chronicler's composition, the literary framework within which his work must be understood.

The two alternative approaches are open to the exegete, who will choose between them on exegetical presuppositions.

[1] The decisive engagement with Ammon does not follow immediately upon the war with Aram. It is at a tactically chosen time, 'the turn of the year', that Joab sets out with the express mission of besieging the Ammonite capital.

While in I Sam. 11.1 David plays a central role ('David sent Joab and his servants with him ...'), in Chronicles an unexpected change in the phrasing omits David entirely, and the initiative is Joab's: 'Joab led out the army.' Further, in II Sam. the verbs are in the plural, 'and they ravaged ... and besieged', and the campaign is a major one, involving 'all Israel', while in Chronicles they are in the singular, referring to Joab, 'and [he] ravaged ... and came and besieged', and the combatants are limited to 'the army'.

The question which poses itself is this: do the two versions of the story differ as a result of an adaptation in Chronicles, with the focus of the story transferred from David to Joab, or is the original preserved in Chronicles while the adaptation appears in II Samuel? A decision here is not easy, since the relevant considerations are applicable both ways. However, it seems that in this case it is the Chronicler who still preserves the original version of the story. This is supported by the continuation of the story in II Sam. 12.26 itself: 'Now Joab fought ... and took ... and ... sent ... and said: I have fought etc.' Here too the siege of Rabbah is attributed to Joab and not to 'all Israel', and Joab's words to David, 'gather the rest of the people' (II Sam. 12.28), would be meaningless if 'all Israel' had already been mustered to battle with Joab himself at the inception of the war. Another consideration concerns the relationship between this adaptation and the well-attested tendencies of the Chronicler. It has been repeatedly demonstrated that the Chronicler tends to broaden the scope of the events he describes, and to redact his sources in this mood, ascribing an increasingly important role to 'all Israel'. It is therefore rather unlikely that he would, with no apparent reason, rework a story in the opposite direction.

In II Sam. 12.26–29 Rabbah is conquered in two stages, the first conducted by Joab and the second by David. Verse 1b here is the Chronicler's parallel to II Sam. 12.26–29, but the credit goes to Joab alone (on suggested textual emendation cf. above, p. 362).

[2] From this point the narrative parallels II Sam. 12.30ff exactly, and the subject has become David. The greatest part of the verse is dedicated to the description of a single item, 'the crown of their king', while all the rest of the spoil is described laconically as: 'a very great amount'.

Whose was this crown? The seemingly natural reference to 'their king' entails some difficulties: the plural suffix 'their' has no antecedent, as the city and not the people were previously referred to, and the weight of the crown, explicitly recorded as 'a talent of gold', would make the crown too weighty to be worn by a human monarch. An alternative exegetical tradition regards *mlkm* as a proper name of the Ammonite god, usually called Milkom (I Kings. 11.5, 33; II Kings 23.13), but also Malkam (Jer. 49.1). The LXX of both II Sam. 12.30 and this text represents a conflation of both interpretations: 'Melchol their king'.

One wonders whether David's unusual act should be interpreted only as an act of triumphant boasting, or whether the wearing of the crown conveys some symbolic meaning in determining David's status as the ruler of Ammon. Without additional data no decisive answer can be given.

[3] The attention of scholars has been attracted to the question of David's treatment of the Ammonites. Does the verb *wayyāśar* denote 'sawing' and refer to acts of torture, or does it indicate hard labour? From a linguistic point of view the evidence is inconclusive. The root *śwr* denoting 'saw' is attested in the Bible only once as a noun (*maśśōr*, Isa. 10.15) but the possibility of a verbal usage cannot be ruled out. The exegetical tradition of 'sawing' goes back as far as the Septuagint, but the question still remains whether such an interpretation is actually probable, or conforms with David's methods of rule. The parallel in II Sam. 12.31 reads 'and he put' (*wayyāśem*), and the same verb in I Sam. 8.11, 'and he would put them in his chariots and horsemen', was taken as a technical term for conscription to the king's service. Most exegetes (including RSV, NEB) interpret the text as referring to hard labour, taking 'saw', 'iron pick' and 'axes' as various tools.

The conquest of the capital was followed by a systematic subjugation and thorough plunder of all the cities of Ammon. It seems that David took full advantage of his opportunity to take revenge for Hanun's humiliating provocation.

The story ends with a narrative conclusion, 'Then David and all the people returned to Jerusalem', with no reference to some basic details which may have been of interest to the historian: the status of Ammon after the conquest, the fate of Hanun the king, etc. Even the standard formulas which recurred in ch. 18, regarding Moab, Aram and Edom, are absent in this context. It is significant, however, that Solomon's first queen, Rehoboam's mother, was to be an Ammonite – a matter which no doubt should be interpreted politically.

20 4 And after this there arose war with the Philistines at Gezar; then Sibbecai the Hushathite slew Sippai, who was one of the descendants of the giants; and the Philistines were subdued. [5] And there was again war with the Philistines; and Elhanan the son of Jair slew Lahmi the brother of Goliath the Gittite, the shaft of whose spear was like a weaver's beam. [6] And there was again war at Gath, where there was a man of great stature, who had six fingers on each hand, and six toes on each foot, twenty-four in number; and he also was descended from the giants. [7] And when he taunted Israel, Jonathan the son of Shime-a, David's brother, slew him. [8] These were descended from the giants in Gath; and they fell by the hand of David and by the hand of his servants.

B. Notes to RSV

[2] 'the giants', better 'the Rephaim' (so NEB, JPS); [6] 'descended from the giants', better 'descended from the Raphah' (JPS), also v. 8.

C. Structure, sources and form

1. From a literary point of view, this section is distinguished by its opening 'some time after' (v. 4), and by its summarizing conclusion 'these were descended … and they fell …' (v. 8). The section was taken from II Sam. 21.18–22, where it stands (from v. 15 on) independently, as one component of the 'appendix' of the book of Samuel, devoid of any immediate literary or historical setting. By contrast, in Chronicles it is integrated into a coherent sequence relating David's wars. This latter context would seem preferable, although it is impossible to determine precisely the historical-chronological background of the events described. It should be pointed out, however, that the relative merit of the version in Chronicles is not due to more accurate data which the Chronicles may have possessed, but rather to the specific manner of reworking which he applied.

2. The section is devoted to one specific topic: the combats with the descendants of Raphah (RSV: 'giants'). In II Sam. 21.15ff. four such incidents are recorded, but only three are cited by the Chronicler. The first was omitted 'out of respect for David' (pseudo-Rashi on 20.4), and thus the mention of 'four' has been struck from the concluding verse (v. 8). The section is thus composed of these units: v. 4, Sippai; v. 5, Lahmi, the brother of Goliath; v. 6–7, 'a man with great stature'; v. 8, conclusion.

3. The material found in this pericope is similar in literary form and subject matter to II Sam. 23.8–23 (I Chron. 11.11–24). Both are collections of small literary units, describing the military exploits of individuals mainly against the Philistines during the early days of David's reign. The difference between the two collections lies in the principle which determined the compilation of the material: in the present collection

the common denominator is the identity of the enemies, all descendants of 'the Raphah', while in the other collection it is the identity of the Israelite fighters, all David's mighty men. These 'literary guidelines' determining the anthologizing of smaller literary units into larger compositions are of historiographical significance. They testify to the early existence not only of isolated records but of collections of material already clearly classified by subject. A similar conclusion can be reached on the basis of ch. 18 (II Sam. 8), of which the focal point is David's wars. Other collections are presented in II Sam. 22.1–23.5 (poems); II Sam. 21 + 24 (originally connected, calamities), but their origin as units is probably later than that of the present passage.

D. Commentary

Regarding the Philistine warriors, the terminology of II Sam. 21.15ff. is consistent: they are described as 'the descendants of Raphah' (vv. 16, 18), or 'born to Raphah' (vv. 20, 21). The 'matronym' is spelled with a final *he* and is also always preceded by a *he* (i.e. *hārāpāh*), which is usually interpreted as an article. This prefixed *he* is, however, never omitted, even after a preposition (v. 20). If a proper name is indeed intended, this cannot be regarded as an article but is rather part of the name – Haraphah; the four giants would be the sons of one mother. The general designation 'from the descendants of (literally: born to) Haraphah' may indicate, however, that the name is in fact a common noun, of unknown provenance and meaning, which represents the giants' common origin by the conventional genealogical phrase 'born to'.

This consistent terminology is not retained in the present section in Chronicles. First, the matronym is spelled with a final *alef* (vv. 6, 8). Moreover, in v. 4 the text is altered to read 'one of the descendants of the *Rephaim*' (RSV 'giants'), thus creating an explicit connection between the three Philistine warriors and the 'Rephaim', described explicitly as 'giants' in Deut. 2.11, 20–21; 3.11–13. Although the actual identification of these gigantic Philistines with the 'Rephaim' (as reflected in RSV) is not self-evident, this was undoubtedly the view of the Chronicler.

[4] The change from 'there was again' (*wattᵉhī 'ōd*) in II Sam. 21.19 to 'there arose' (*watta'ᵃmōd*) is probably because this verse is a beginning and not a continuation. Yet, even in this small detail the Chronicler's technique is evident: a graphically and phonetically similar word is chosen to replace the original; furthermore, the chosen verb is a very common element in the Chronistic vocabulary.

Chronicles locates this first combat at 'Gezer', a geographically plausible replacement for Gob, found only in II Sam. 21.18, 19. However, according to I Kings 9.16, Gezer was at the time a Canaanite, not a Philistine, city. This may be another case of the Chronicler replacing an unknown name with a more common one with some orthographic similarity.

Although this combat is described as 'war with the Philistines', its outcome is limited (in II Sam.) to the slaying of Saph/Sippai. The question
must be left open whether this is an authentic historical characteristic of
these 'wars', or a reflection of the specific interest of this collection in the
slaying of the giants. In Chronicles, the killing of Saph/Sippai is the first
blow in a more comprehensive military accomplishment: 'and they (RSV
'the Philistines') were subdued'. Such a view could have been influenced by
the story of Goliath (also a descendant of Haraphah, I Sam. 17.5), whose
death at the hands of David signalled a general defeat of the Philistines
(I Sam. 17.52–53). (On the use of *nkn'*, 'to be subdued', in Chronicles cf.
S. Japhet, 'The Supposed Common Authorship of Chronicles and Ezra-
Nehemiah Investigated Anew', *VT* 18, 1968, 359–60, and Williamson,
141–2).

[5] This verse and its parallel in II Sam. 21.19 figure prominently in any
discussion of tradition and redaction history. Although the text of II Sam is
probably corrupt (the word *'ōrᵉgîm* being a dittography), it clearly reflects a
tradition parallel to I Sam. 17. In both traditions the Philistine warrior is
introduced by his full name, Goliath the Gittite; his weapon is similarly
described ('the shaft of whose spear was like a weaver's beam'), and the
Israelite hero who fought him is identified as 'X son of Y' of Bethlehem:
David the son of Jesse in one tradition, Elhanan the son of Ya'are/Yair in the
other.

The existence of two parallel traditions for such a crucial incident should
not surprise us; a problem arises only when these traditions are pressed into
service as historical sources for the reconstruction of the period. In this case
only one of them can be authentic, but a rejection of either tradition greatly
weakens the reliability of the material in general.

Two basic approaches to the problem can be discerned in the history of
interpretation. One is the attempt to harmonize the two traditions by providing some explanation for the one deviating detail, the name of the warrior.
The rabbinic way, expressed also by the Targum, was to regard the two
names as being in fact two appellations for the same person. This principle
was followed by several scholars; it has been suggested that 'Elhanan' was a
proper name and 'David' an appellative (cf. J. J. Stamm, 'Der Name des
König David', *VTS* 7, 1960, 165–83), or differently, that one name was
merely a corruption of the other (cf. R. Weiss, 'Ligatures in the Hebrew
Bible', *JBL* 82, 1963, 194). The other, and opposite, way of interpretation
was to create maximum differentiation between the two traditions, emphasizing their independence. The earliest representative of this approach is
this text in Chronicles, which presents the tradition of II Sam. 21.19 as
completely distinct from I Sam. 17. This is accomplished by the slightest of
alterations, which may even seem at first glance to be accidental textual

corruptions: *bēt* is changed to '*et* and the article before *laḥmī* is omitted; as a result, the appellative 'the Bethlehemite' becomes a proper name Lahmi. Then further the accusative particle '*et* is changed into the very similar '*ᵃḥi*, 'the brother of'. Thus:

II Sam: *wayyak 'elḥānān ben ya'rē ('or'gīm) bēt hallaḥmī   'et golyāt haggittī*
I Chron: *wayyak 'elḥānān ben yā'ir   'et   laḥmi '*ᵃḥī golyāt haggittī.*

In this way the bonds between the stories are severed: David killed Goliath; Elhanan killed Lahmi, Goliath's brother. Such an adaptation of the tradition should not be viewed as necessarily Chronistic. Although prompted by an awareness of the historical consequences of the conflicting traditions, it has no theological motives. It could therefore have originated earlier, in the Chronicler's *Vorlage*.

The description opens with a formula which in Samuel is repeated four times (II Sam. 21.15, 18, 19, 20), and twice in Chronicles (vv. 5, 6): 'and there was again war'.

[6–7] These verses relate the third episode: the slaying by David's nephew (probably Jonadab's brother – II Sam. 13.3) of 'a man of great stature', who (unlike the previous warriors) remains anonymous. The episode has two points of affinity with the story of David and Goliath: the unusual and frightful size and form of the Philistine, in this case the number of his fingers and toes; and his arrogance, expressed by 'taunting' (cf. I Sam. 17.10, 25, etc).

[8] As mentioned above, since Chronicles has omitted one of the stories of combat recorded in II Sam. 21 (vv. 15–17), the number 'four' is also dropped from the summary verse.

21.1–22.1

21 Satan stood up against Israel, and incited David to number Israel. [2] So David said to Joab and the commanders of the army, 'Go, number Israel, from Beer-sheba to Dan, and bring me a report, that I may know their number.' [3] But Joab said, 'May the Lord add to his people a hundred times as many as they are! Are they not, my lord the king, all of them my lord's servants? Why then should my lord require this? Why should he bring guilt upon Israel?' [4] But the king's word prevailed against Joab. So Joab departed and went throughout all Israel, and came back to Jerusalem. [5] And Joab gave the sum of the numbering of the people to David. In all Israel there were one million one hundred thousand men who drew the sword, and in Judah four hundred and seventy thousand who drew the sword. [6] But he did not include Levi and Benjamin in the numbering, for the king's command was abhorrent to Joab.

[7] But God was displeased with this thing, and he smote Israel. [8] And David said to God, 'I have sinned greatly in that I have done this thing. But now, I pray thee, take away the inquity of thy servant; for I have done very foolishly.' [9] And the Lord spoke to Gad, David's seer, saying, [10] 'Go and say to David, "Thus says the Lord, Three things I offer you; choose one of them, that I may do it to you."' [11] So Gad came to David and said to him, 'Thus says the Lord, "Take which you will: [12] either three years of famine; or three months of devastation by your foes, while the sword of your enemies overtakes you; or else three days of the sword of the Lord, pestilence upon the land, and the angel of the Lord destroying throughout all the territory of Israel." Now decide what answer I shall return to him who sent me.' [13] Then David said to Gad, 'I am in great distress; let me fall into the hand of the Lord, for his mercy is very great; but let me not fall into the hand of man.'

[14] So the Lord sent a pestilence upon Israel; and there fell seventy thousand men of Israel. [15] And God sent the angel to Jerusalem to destroy it; but when he was about to destroy it, the Lord saw, and he repented of the evil; and he said to the destroying angel, 'It is enough; now stay your hand.' And the angel of the Lord was standing by the threshing floor of Ornan the Jebusite. [16] And David lifted his eyes and saw the angel of the Lord standing between earth and heaven, and in his hand a drawn sword stretched out over Jerusalem. Then David and the elders, clothed in sackcloth, fell upon their faces. [17] And David said to God, 'Was it not I who gave command to number the people? It is I who have sinned and done very wickedly. But these sheep, what have they done? Let thy hand, I pray thee, O Lord my God, be against me and against my father's house; but let not the plague be upon thy people.'

[18] Then the angel of the Lord commanded Gad to say to David that David should go up and rear an altar to the Lord on the threshing floor of Ornan the Jebusite. [19] So David went up at Gad's word, which he had spoken in the name of the Lord. [20] Now Ornan was threshing wheat; he turned and saw the angel, and his four sons who were with him hid themselves. [21] As David came to Ornan, Ornan looked and saw David and went forth from the threshing floor, and did obeisance to David with his face to the ground. [22] And David said to Ornan, 'Give me the site of the threshing floor that I

may build on it an altar to the Lord – give it to me at its full price – that the plague may be averted from the people.'[23] Then Ornan said to David, 'Take it; and let my lord the king do what seems good to him; see, I give the oxen for burnt offerings, and the threshing sledges for the wood, and the wheat for a cereal offering. I give it all.'[24] But King David said to Ornan, 'No, but I will buy it for the full price; I will not take for the Lord what is yours, nor offer burnt offerings which cost me nothing.'[25] So David paid Ornan six hundred shekels of gold by weight for the site.[26] And David built there an altar to the Lord and presented burnt offerings and peace offerings, and called upon the Lord, and he answered him with fire from heaven upon the altar of burnt offering.[27] Then the Lord commanded the angel; and he put his sword back into its sheath.

28 At that time, when David saw that the Lord had answered him at the threshing floor of Ornan the Jebusite, he made his sacrifices there.[29] For the tabernacle of the Lord, which Moses had made in the wilderness, and the altar of burnt offering were at that time in the high place at Gibeon;[30] but David could not go before it to inquire of God, for he was afraid of the sword of the angel of the Lord.

22   1 Then David said, 'Here shall be the house of the Lord God and here the altar of burnt offering for Israel.'

A. Notes to MT

[12] נֹסְפָּה, read נִסְכָה with the ancient Versions.

B. Notes to RSV

[1] 'Satan', cf. commentary; [2] 'commanders of the army', probably adjusted to II Sam. 24.2; MT, 'commanders/officers of the people' (NEB, 'public officers'); [3] 'why should he bring guilt', better 'why should it be a cause of guilt' (JPS, NEB, 'I will only bring guilt'); [12] 'decide', better 'consider' (NEB, JPS); [15] 'when he was about to destroy it', NEB 'but as he was destroying it', cf. commentary; [18] 'Then the angel ... commanded', cf. commentary; [20] the acts are differently ordered in MT; [24] 'I will buy *it* for the full price', better 'I will buy *them* ...' (JPS), or 'I will pay' (NEB); [26] 'peace offerings', NEB 'shared offerings'; JPS 'offerings of well-being'.

C. Structure, sources and form

1. While ch. 21 is taken from II Sam. 24, its import is determined, to an even greater extent than usual, by its new context: the tenor of the Chronistic history of David in general, and the immediate narrative context in particular.

II Samuel 24 constitutes one component of the appendix of II Sam. 21–24, a literary unit of some complexity. Originally, ch. 24 formed the sequel to II Sam. 21.1–14, but the sequence was interrupted when the unit was structured through the 'inserting' process of one section into the other, thus:

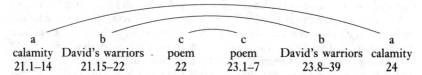

a	b	c	c	b	a
calamity	David's warriors	poem	poem	David's warriors	calamity
21.1–14	21.15–22	22	23.1–7	23.8–39	24

Thus, II Sam. 24 is a chapter of relatively little significance in the book of Samuel. It deals with one of the calamities which beset David's rule: the circumstances of the plague which was visited upon Israel and the way in which it was averted. It is also an aetiological story, accounting for the existence of an altar at the threshing floor of Araunah, but the role of the altar itself is assigned only marginal and *ad hoc* significance.

The Chronicler completely disrupts the original literary context. 21.1–14; 22; 23.1–7 are omitted altogether; the tales of David's mighty men are distributed between the beginning of David's reign (I Chron. 11.10–41) and the account of David's wars (I Chron. 20.4–8), and ch. 24 is transposed in the Chronistic context to serve as an introduction to the last stage of the history of David, the preparations for the building of the Temple.

2. The centre of gravity of the chapter is in the concluding passage added by Chronicles to the original narrative, relating the dedication of the altar and the assignment of the sacred precinct as the future site of the Temple. This initial act of preparation is here ascribed to David. In Chronicles the chapter also forms an important transition between the material taken from Samuel and that peculiar to Chronicles, either taken from extra-biblical sources or composed by the Chronicler himself. This chapter is the last literary passage based on II Sam. and is followed, from 21.27 to the end of the history of David, by non-parallel material.

3. The strong resemblance of this chapter to II Sam. 24 leaves no doubt that one text is dependent upon the other. Yet there are numerous differences between the two: additions, omissions and alterations which give to each of the narratives a direction of its own. The discussion of the relationship between the parallel chapters has for a long time been based on the assumption that the Chronicler had made use of the same (or practically the same) text which is represented in the MT of II Sam. 24, and that all the deviations of one version from the other should be attributed to views and tendencies of the Chronicler – except for small details which could be accounted for as originating in the process of transmission. Following the discovery of 4QSam^a, and the publication of a small section of the scroll's version of this chapter (cf. W. E. Lemke, 'The Synoptic Problem in the Chronicler's History', *HTR* 58, 1965, 355–7; Ulrich, 156–7), the question has become more complicated, in particular because of the appearance, in 4QSam^a, of the description of the angel with his drawn sword (I Chron. 21.16). The assumption that this image was a reflection of the 'angelological tendencies' of the Chronicler (Rothstein, xiv–xv; von Rad, *Das Geschichtsbild des Chronistischen Werkes*, Stuttgart 1930, 9) had now to be questioned and revised (Japhet, *Ideology*, 137–45; P. E. Dion, 'The Angel with the Drawn Sword (I Chr. 21, 16)', *ZAW* 97, 1985, 114–17).

However, without attempting to play down the significance of 4QSam^a, in particular in providing a factual basis for the text, the questions about the development of the chapter are already dictated by the very existence of the two deviant versions in II Sam. 24 and I Chron. 21. The difficulties in the narrative sequence, the occurrence of doublets, etc., compel us to the conclusion that neither of the versions represents the original form of the story, and that each has undergone certain processes of reworking. It is therefore impossible to determine *a priori* the form of the Chronicler's *Vorlage*. Each of the relevant matters will be dealt with individually in the commentary.

4. The chapter is constructed as one lengthy presentation, in which each matter is a direct continuation of the preceding one, with no literary signs of inner structuring. Still, the following pattern can be discerned:

1–6:   The census (II Sam. 24.1–9)
7–14:   The punishment (II Sam. 24.10–15)
15–22.1: The averting of the plague (II Sam. 24.16–25)
         15–21:   David's arrival at the threshing-floor
         22–25:   Negotiations with Ornan/Araunah
         26–22.1: Building of the altar, averting of the plague and dedication of
                  the site.

The third section is the longest and most complex, as in II Sam. 24. In Chronicles, however, the proportions are made even more uneven by the diminishing of the first part and the augmenting of the last. Thus, the significance of the final section is expressed not only by the structure and content of the story, but also quantitatively – a common feature of the Chronicler's manner of reworking.

D. *Commentary*

[1] This is one of the most discussed and interpreted verses in Chronicles, due to the appearance of 'Satan'. The concept directly engages our attention, all the more so when we note that it is introduced as an alteration of the text in II Sam.

The narrative opens in II Sam. 24.1, 'Again the anger of the Lord was kindled against Israel, and he incited David against them'. By this opening the story is linked with II Sam. 21.1–14, where the previous 'anger' of God against Israel, expressed by the famine, is recounted. This opening also sets the theological framework of the story: the census is presented from the outset as a transgression to which David was incited by God himself in his anger against Israel. However, while in II Sam. 21.1 the reason of God's anger is explicitly stated ('There is blood guilt on Saul and his house because he put the Gibeonites to death'), no such justification is provided for the divine anger in ch. 24, which led to the incitement of David; Israel's sin remains unspecified. This theological presupposition reduces in great measure – but does not altogether remove – David's responsibility.

The Chronicler detached the story from its former context and altered its opening in two ways: the anger of God was omitted, and the incitement to count Israel was attributed not to God but to another agent. The result of the first alteration is that David himself is presented as exclusively responsible for the events which follow. The second change, for which the verse has attracted so much attention, demands a detailed discussion: an examination of the meaning of šāṭān, and of the change in the overall presentation of Chronicles caused by its introduction.

The English translations (AV, RSV, NEB, JPS, Jerusalem Bible) all follow a long exegetical tradition, according to which šāṭān serves as a proper noun, and read 'Satan'. The interpretation is based upon several assumptions and considerations. Satan, as a member of the divine entourage, appears in the Bible in Zech. 3.1ff. and in Job 1–2. In the visionary trial of the high priest Joshua, he figures as the supernatural accuser in the divine court: 'and Satan standing at his right hand to accuse him' (Zech. 3.1). Also in Job (1.6ff.), Satan is one of the 'sons of God' who incites God against Job. In both these cases the noun is prefixed by the article, in contrast to this verse in Chronicles, where it is indeterminate. This difference has prompted scholars to regard the noun as a proper name: Satan. The ramifications of this seemingly linguistic decision have been far-reaching: the claim has been made that in this case the appellation has completely lost its general meaning as 'adversary' and has become a fully-fledged proper noun, the name of 'evil' as an autonomous entity. Accordingly, I Chron. 21.1 has been taken to represent the ultimate stage in the development of the figure of Satan as the embodiment of evil, and the nearest in the Bible to a dualistic concept of the divine.

This generally accepted view needs reconsideration. It should be remarked at the outset that from a linguistic point of view the course by which a common noun becomes a proper noun in Hebrew is different from the one presupposed above. In general, the transition is effected in Hebrew by the *addition* of the article; examples can be abundantly cited (cf. Gesenius, §126e, p. 405). The same route is followed in post-biblical Hebrew: *qādōš* is a general adjective 'holy', *haqqādōš*, *'the'* holy, refers to God; *raḥ^amān* means gracious, *hāraḥ^amān/raḥmānā'*, *'the'* gracious, is God, etc. Only when the noun had completely and absolutely lost its original meaning could it be found as a proper noun without the article; this, however, is not the case under consideration. The meaning of *šāṭān* as a common noun still continues to exist, denoting 'adversary' (cf. *BDB*, 966). It is, therefore *with the article* that evil as a specific divine being had to be represented – as is indeed demonstrated by the occurrences of the noun in Zechariah and Job. In post-biblical literature, where Satan does function as the embodiment of evil, the name is still used with the article (cf. Jastrow II, 1554). From a purely linguistic point of view it is in fact the absence of the article which should raise doubts about understanding it as a proper noun.

Other considerations should be added. In the generally accepted view the figure of Satan is conceived of as the most far-reaching stage in the development of the idea of evil, in comparison to Zechariah and Job, and the closest to rabbinic Judaism. However, this is not attested by the actual unfolding of the story. While in Zechariah and Job Satan is one of the 'sons of God', acting within the circle of the divine court where he accuses man and incites God against him, in the present context this figure is fully anchored in the human sphere. There is no reference to any activity in the divine realm and his incitement is against David, not God.

Moreover, if indeed such a significant theological development in the concept of evil and its origin were expressed by I Chron. 21.1, we would expect to find it elsewhere in the book as well. The dilemma of evil, as one of the aspects of God's justice, is one of the most difficult theological problems for the Chronicler. Yet nowhere in the whole book do we find any allusion to Satan, or even the slightest implication of the independent existence of evil. Evil, like good, originates in God, according to the general attitude of Chronicles.

Furthermore, such a reconstructed development in the concept of evil and its understanding as an independent entity are basically part of a more comprehensive angelology, in which angels play a dominant role as intermediaries between the divine and the human. Such a developed angelology is missing from Chronicles, which records the appearance of angels only for contexts in which they also appear in the Chronicler's sources. The text from Qumran may indicate that the augmenting of the role of angels in the present story had already been introduced in the Chronicler's *Vorlage* (cf. also below on v. 16).

In view of all these considerations, theological as well as linguistic, my conclusion is that the figure of 'Satan' which has been ascribed to the Chronicler is very far from his religious and psychological concepts. The word *sátán* still serves in I Chron. 21.1 as a common noun, similar to I Kings 11.14, 23, 25, or Ps. 109.6, and refers to 'an adversary', who acts against Israel by inciting the king to take the wrong action. From a literary point of view, this anonymous schemer is the antithesis of Joab, who tries hard to dissuade David from his plan. Whether this figure is indeed 'Chronistic' is difficult to determine.

The phrasing of the clause 'to number Israel' demonstrates the Chronicler's manner of reworking his sources. First, there is a linguistic change: a shift from direct to indirect speech, another example of which is to be found in v. 18 ('that David should go'). Although both direct speech and imperative forms are still found in Chronicles, there is a general preference for indirect speech. Secondly, the verse exhibits a theological modification: not 'Israel and Judah' but 'Israel' – an expression of the unity of the people, which is developed even in the smallest details of the Chronistic adaptation. In contrast to II Sam. 24.1, Israel does not designate the northern tribes but the people as a whole (cf. also the following verse).

[2] In place of 'the king' of II Sam. 24.2 the verse reads 'David'. Such changes recur in this chapter several times (v. 5, II Sam. 24.9; v. 21, II Sam. 24.20), and in the non-parallel sections of the book David is generally (but not exclusively) called by name. The same phenomenon is also attested in I Chron. 17, against II Sam. 7. It seems that this stylistic change belongs to the book of Samuel rather than to Chronicles; i.e. in reading 'David' the Chronicler simply adheres to his *Vorlage*, while in certain parts of Samuel MT had undergone such alterations, either changing 'David' into 'the king' or broadening it to 'David the king'. This is confirmed by chapters like II Sam. 8 (which has 'David' almost exclusively), II Sam. 10, etc. In certain cases the Chronicler omits such references altogether (vv. 3, 4), following his stylistic inclination to shorter phrases.

David's words to Joab in this verse are also phrased more briefly and simply. There are two main differences between the two versions: 1. 'Israel' in Chronicles in place of 'the tribes of Israel' in II Sam. 24.2; 2. the inversion of 'from Dan to Beer-sheba'. The view that the people of Israel is composed of tribal units is common and even characteristic of Chronicles, and therefore the omission here cannot be interpreted as deriving from a tendency to underplay the role of the tribes; rather, it was probably motivated by the wish to emphasize the unity of the people, in the light of the previous verse. Regarding the reading of 'from Beer-sheba to Dan', instead of the more common order, the question is one of approach: should the change be explained on theological grounds, as reflecting a specific Chronistic trait, denoting for example the increasing significance of the south *vis à vis* the north (Williamson, 144), or should it be interpreted on linguistic-stylistic grounds with, for example, Hurvitz, who claims that the reversed order is a linguistic phenomenon (A. Hurvitz, '"Diachronic Chiasm" in Biblical Hebrew', *J. Liver Memorial Volume*, Tel Aviv 1971, 253–4*), and is not necessarily Chronistic? The same alternative should be considered in many other cases of inverted word order.

[3] The two versions of Joab's answer differ in many details, but their main point remains: an attempt to convince the king to reverse his decision. On the historical level – whether or not his words and conduct are accurately reproduced – this could reflect the status of Joab in David's court. The author regards a dispute between Joab and David and an attempt by Joab to change the king's mind as historically plausible. When this attempt fails, Joab proceeds to carry out his mission, although reluctantly, and according to the reading of Chronicles, leaving certain aspects of it to his own discretion (cf. on v. 6).

In II Sam. 24.3 Joab's objections are phrased quite generally. Expressing a wish for the increase of the people and casting doubt on the necessity of the census, he implies that 'numbering the tribes' may cause calamity. In

Chronicles, although basically taken from II Sam., Joab's words are more specific and more severe. In place of 'while the eyes of my lord the king still see it' (RSV; NEB 'and your majesty should live to see it'), Chronicles reads: 'Are they not, my lord the king, all of them my lord's servants?', which refers to David's unspoken but evident objective in ordering the census. In Joab's view it would be superfluous to plan improvement and centralization of the kingdom's administration by a census of the population; they are already without exception 'the king's servants', loyally mustered to David's cause.

The additional clause in Chronicles, 'why should he bring guilt upon Israel', is a key to the Chronicler's specific mode of reworking. Although II Sam. suggests that the census may cause a disaster, it is not defined explicitly as a sin. This is done in Chronicles, which sees the census as a cause of 'guilt'. Moreover, the incurring of the guilt 'upon Israel' anticipates a theological difficulty raised by the story in its present form. Already in David's words in II Sam. 24.17, the question of the people's responsibility is raised: 'I have sinned ... but these sheep, what have they done?' A full response is not given in the version of Samuel, although v. 1, which depicts the census as a result of 'God's anger', might be regarded as such an attempt. In Chronicles the answer is given here: by his decision David makes transgressors of the people as well, for to submit to a census is in itself a sin!

Joab's words have another major purpose in the framework of the story, to which we will return in greater detail later. This is the role of *warning*, so central to the Chronicler's view of Providence (Japhet, *Ideology*, 176–80). One must be aware of one's sin before becoming liable to punishment. In Chronicles, Joab's words are therefore explicit – David's act will make all the people deserving of punishment! The emphasis on David's responsibility follows in the same vein as the changes introduced to v. 1 – a heavier shadow cast on David's character which should be taken into consideration in evaluating his figure in Chronicles (cf. further on ch. 29).

[4] This is a short summary of II Sam. 24.4–8. The inclusion of the details of Joab's itinerary indicates that the objectives of the story are many. Beyond a description of the plague and its outcome, the author intends to present a complete account of the whole census episode, the details of which were apparently based on authentic records. Not so in Chronicles, where the census itself is actually outside the scope of the story. For the Chronicler, having noted that a census was taken, the decisive factors are its results, and its theological ramifications.

[5] The figures are problematical – as pointed out by many commentators. In the parallel of II Sam. 24.9 the numbers are recorded separately for Israel, the north, and Judah, the south. In Chronicles the verse opens with the number of 'all Israel', including both 'Israel' and 'Judah'. Yet at the end of the verse, a separate figure for Judah is recorded. There are various aspects

here which are difficult. (*a*) In the Chronicler's version, Israel is presented from the outset as a unity, the division into two components being minimized or abrogated. In this verse this tendency is expressed by the change of 'Israel' into 'all Israel'. (*b*) The numbers given for the census are understandable on the basis of the same assumption: 1,100,000 is the sum of the two figures of II Sam. 24.9 (500,000 + 800,000) minus 200,000 for the two tribes that were not counted. The return to a specific number for 'Judah' at the end is therefore counter to both the numerical data and the theological trend of the story. So it has been suggested that the last clause of the verse is a later gloss, inspired by the parallel in II Sam. 24.9 (cf. Curtis, 250; Rudolph, 144; Williamson, 145). One may be inclined to regard the exact number given by the Chronicler – 470,000 against 500,000 in II Sam. 24.9 – as a sign of authenticity, but to retain this clause would leave the difficulties of the verse unsolved.

[6] The verse is not found in II Sam. 24 and has probably been added by the Chronicler, as an adaptation required by his theological concepts. The exclusion of Levi and Benjamin from the census is suggested to the Chronicler by the unfolding of the story. The common denominator of these two tribes is their connection with Jerusalem: Jerusalem is included in the territory of Benjamin according to certain geographical concepts (e.g. Josh. 18.28; also Deut. 33.12), while the tribe of Levi is linked to the cultic activity in the Temple. The exemption of Jerusalem from the horrors of the plague is explained in II Sam. 24 by a change in God's will: 'the Lord repented of the evil' (II Sam. 24.16). In Chronicles, this explanation is prepared for and given substance in our verse, which theologically speaking is the sequel of v. 3. Benjamin and Levi were in fact free from guilt. The 'guilt upon Israel' caused by the census justified God's punishment but also warranted the exclusion of Jerusalem. According to the immanent logic of the story the opportunity for saving Jerusalem was created by Joab, whose discretion prompted him to countermand the king's orders.

The bond between Joab and Jerusalem is also reflected in his personal role in the conquest and rebuilding of the city (I Chron. 11.6, 8), a detail which is peculiar to Chronicles and not found in II Sam.

[7–8] According to II Sam. 24.10, 'David's heart smote him ...' immediately after the census; he repents and turns to God for forgiveness: 'I have sinned greatly ... But now, O Lord, I pray thee, take away the inquity of thy servant.' However, his remorse goes unheeded. David's belated recognition of his sin, his repentance and his readiness to admit his failure surely add a certain colour to his image, but they have no consequences in the unfolding of the story. God's only response is to send David's seer, Gad, with three alternatives of punishment from which David must choose. God did not forgive.

In Chronicles events follow a different course. The words 'but David's heart *smote* him' (*wayyak lēb dāwīd 'ōtō*) are replaced by the graphically similar 'But God was displeased ... and he *smote* Israel' (*wayyak 'et yiśrā'ēl*). Thus, the general statement of David's immediate remorse is omitted and replaced by a punishment. The narrative then continues, paralleling II Sam., with David's words of repentance. In the new sequence the Chronicler reveals his view that repentance must be catalysed by some active factor, explicitly referred to in the course of the story: a prophetic message, divine punishment or the like. David's unmotivated repentance calls for motivation, and this is provided by the smiting of the Israel in v. 7 (cf. also the repentance of Rehoboam following the words of Shemaiah in I Chron. 12.6; Manasseh, after his exile, II Chron. 35.12, etc.).

From a literary point of view, however, the change introduced by the Chronicler did not contribute to a smoother story, as this verse does not fully integrate into the narrative sequence. The people of Israel are presented as doubly punished: first here, after the census, and then by the plague, following David's choice. The nature of the first punishment, 'the smiting', is not specified.

[9–12] Gad's mission is to present David with the choice between three options: famine, war or plague. Since the message is transmitted first from God to the prophet (v. 9) and then from the prophet to David (v. 11), we would expect, in theory, the entire message to be repeated, pronounced by each speaker. In practice, however, and already in II Sam. 24, the author adopts a different literary tactic. Only one half of the message is reported in God's words to Gad, while the other half is cited as Gad's words to David. In the facts of the story Gad does not quote God's words as found in the text but goes on with their sequel. The result is one single sequence of God's words, interrupted by the address: 'So Gad came to David and said to him' (v. 11).

While the essence of Gad's mission and the structure of the description is basically the same in the two versions, there are still several textual divergencies between them, as well as differences in subject-matter and changes of a linguistic and stylistic nature.

In v. 9 Gad is designated 'Gad, David's seer', while in II Sam. 24.11 he is called 'the prophet Gad, David's seer'. At first glance it would seem that the Chronicler abbreviated the longer title of II Sam. 24, an abbreviation to which several interpretations can be provided (R. Micheel, *Die Seher- und Prophetenüberlieferungen in der Chronik*, Frankfurt 1983, 18–19). It seems, however, that this is not the case. In I Sam. 22.5 Gad is called 'the prophet Gad' and in II Sam. 24 (except for the verse under consideration), always by his name without title (vv. 13, 14, 18, 19). Moreover, the title 'seer' (*ḥōzeh*) is never found in the book of Samuel, though another word, *rō'eh*, does appear.

By contrast, Gad is always described as 'seer' (*ḥōzeh*) in Chronicles (I Chron. 29.22; II Chron. 29.25), and the title 'seer' is more common in Chronicles than in all other biblical books together – ten times in Chronicles (I Chron. 25.5; II Chron. 9.29; 12.15; 19.2, etc.) in comparison to six times elsewhere. It would therefore seem that the two versions emerged differently. The original designation of II Sam. 24.11 was 'the prophet Gad', in accord with I Sam. 22.5. This was replaced by the Chronicler with his title 'Gad the seer'. The present rendering of II Sam. 24.11 is therefore a conflation of the original 'the prophet Gad' with its replacement in Chronicles. This implies that the influence of the parallel texts was bilateral, and that one should take into account an influence of Chronicles already on the MT of Samuel (for a different interpretation of the double designation, cf. Z. Zevit, 'A misunderstanding at Bethel, Amos VII 12–17', *VT* 25, 1975, 783–90).

The same phenomenon can be detected once more in the present passage. Chronicles reads: 'So Gad came to David and said to him' (v. 11), while the parallel in II Sam. reads: 'So Gad came to David and told him and said to him' (v. 13). Here, the original 'told him' was replaced in Chronicles by the paler phrase 'and said to him', while the MT of II Sam. is a conflation of the two.

Another difference between the parallel texts is in the duration of the famine: 'three years' in v. 12 against seven years in II Sam. 24.13. It is commonly accepted that Chronicles preserves the original reading, in view of the pattern 'three years', 'three months' and 'three days', in descending order.

I shall mention only a few linguistic details. 1. The Chronicler omits from v. 9 the words 'When David arose in the morning' (*wayyāqom dāwīd babbōqer*, II Sam. 24.11), and replaces the perfect construction of 'the word of the Lord came ...' (*ūd⁽ᵉ⁾bar yhwh hāyāh*) with the imperfect 'and the Lord spoke to Gad' (*way⁽ᵉ⁾dabbēr yhwh 'el gād*). With these changes the peculiar construction of the past-perfect in II Sam. (not evidenced in RSV, but cf. the commentaries, i.e. Driver, *Samuel*, 375; McCarter, 502) is obliterated and a regular temporal sequence is created. 2. The infinitive absolute which functions as imperative (*hālōk*), is replaced by a regular imperative (*lēk*, v. 10), following the general inclination of the Chronicler (Kropat, 23; G. Gerlemann, *Synoptic Studies in the Old Testament*, Lund 1947, 18). 3. Gad's address is prefaced with a new introduction, 'thus says the Lord, "Take which you will" ' (v. 11), containing the late root *qbl*. 4. In Gad's words the *he* interrogative is dropped. 5. Also the double imperative 'consider and decide' (II Sam. 24.13) is replaced by the single: decide (v. 12). All these details demonstrate how even such a short passage displays clear signs of various linguistic adaptations.

Another matter which finds expression here, as well as later in the chapter, is the concept of the plague. In II Sam. 24.13 the plague is presented briefly as 'pestilence in your land'. In the present version (v. 12) the reference is longer and combines three elements: 'the sword of the Lord; pestilence upon the land; the angel of the Lord destroying all through the territory of Israel'. What is the relationship between the various concepts of the plague, in particular between 'the sword of the Lord' and 'the angel of the Lord destroying'?

The view of the plague as a destroying angel already appears in II Sam. 24 (only in vv. 16–17), while the concept of the plague as 'the sword of the Lord' is restricted to Chronicles, where it is further developed to become 'the sword of the angel'. Several stages can be reconstructed in the development of the concept.

In the basic layer of the story the plague is presented simply as God's blow, coming from 'the hand of the Lord', as phrased in II Sam. 24.13–15 (I Chron. 21.13–14). In the following stage the plague is identified as a 'destroying angel' (II Sam. 24.16–17). The concept itself reflects an implicit struggle between two approaches to the pestilence: a demonic divine figure, of some autonomy (cf. Hab. 3.5), as against a lesser divine being, subordinate to God and operating as his messenger (cf. Exod. 12.13 against v. 23). II Sam. 24.16 seems to reflect a certain compromise, although the sudden appearance of the angel in v. 16 with the words 'and ... the angel stretched forth his hand toward Jerusalem' still preserves some independence of action for the angel. In Chronicles a new factor is added: the plague as a sword. This is introduced as a metaphor in Gad's words and influences their phrasing. While in II Sam. 24 three separate choices are given (famine, war and plague), in Chronicles the last two are posed as antithetical: 'The sword of your enemies', or 'the sword of the Lord'. This metaphor is, however, broadened into the concrete image of the 'angel of the Lord' holding a sword (vv. 16, 27, 30). Thus the pestilence is a destroying angel, or God's sword, or a combination of the two – an angel with a sword.

Which of these developments should be attributed to the Chronicler? I have already mentioned that the image of the angel with the drawn sword is also found in 4QSam[a] and therefore could be regarded as pre-dating the Chronicler. Such a possibility would conform to the Chronicler's general lack of interest in the world of angels: he accepts their existence when found in his sources but makes no additions of his own (cf. Japhet, *Ideology*, 137–45). In this case the Chronicler would only follow his sources by certain adjustments of his story, that is, the addition of v. 27 (on v. 30 see below) and the rephrasing of Gad's words in v. 12. His actual reworking would be reflected in the adjustment of v. 15 (cf. below). This view seems more probable and does more justice to the textual facts than the alternative theory (which should not be completely excluded), that the origin of the scene was in the version of Chronicles, and that its appearance in 4QSam^a was due to the influence of Chronicles on the version of Samuel.

In another addition to Gad's words the choice of pestilence is phrased to indicate already the plague's scope: 'throughout the territory of Israel' (v. 12). In II Sam. 24.15 the plague is described as striking 'from Dan to Beersheba', corresponding to the scope of the census (II Sam. 24.2). In v. 12 the Chronistic addition has preserved the same correspondence, although not in the precise parallel position. Thus:

II Sam. 24	I Chron. 21
2. the census	4. the census
'from Dan to Beersheba'	*'throughout the land'*
13. the choice of plague	12. the choice of plague
'in your land'	*'throughout all the territory of Israel'*
15. the plague	14. the plague
'from Dan to Beersheba'	*'upon Israel'*.

We should also notice the way in which the words of God are restructured. In II Sam. 24.12 they comprise three short questions, similar in length and formulation (the words 'while they pursue you' could already have been a gloss). This implies that the suggested punishments are of equal severity. By contrast, in Chronicles the propositions themselves are not equal but lengthen progressively. Thus, by the order in which the choices are presented, and even by their length, a certain gradation is created, the last being the most severe. This literary structure determines, as it were, the unavoidable choice: the last, the most severe, the punishment which comes directly from God.

[13–14] Here David's answer is repeated accurately and fully and in a context which has an advantage of clarity over the narrative context of II Sam. There, David's justification of his choice is not completely clear. The statement 'let us fall into the hand of the Lord' may refer equally to any of the three propositions, especially the first and last, as God is author of them all. In Chronicles David's reasoning is made absolutely plain by the contrast between 'the sword of your enemies' and the 'sword of the Lord' (v. 12). David chooses what seems the most terrible punishment – but directly from God.

The words of David do full justice to his image as manifested throughout the book of Samuel: a man who holds direct discourse with God, and whose faith is the motivating force of his personality and deeds.

In contrast to the full citation of David's words in Chronicles, the plague itself is described only briefly. Its duration 'from the morning until the appointed time', and its geographical range 'from Dan to Beer-sheba' are omitted, and in place of 'there died of the people' the text reads: 'and there fell of Israel'. The verb (fall) and the designation of the people (Israel) are the same words already used by David. Such a matching of linguistic details is one of the outstanding stylistic features of the Chronicler's editing.

[15] With this verse the scene is set for the central episode of the narrative: the averting of the plague from Jerusalem and the events that lead to the choice and dedication of the Temple site.

The beginning of the verse in II Sam. 24.16, 'and when the angel stretched forth his hand', still preserves a certain autonomy of action for the angel: once given the signal to begin, he was to continue his task independently of God's will. Only when the angel approaches Jerusalem does God repent of the evil and command him to stop. However, there is some tension between this view of the averting of the plague and the sequel of the story, in which the plague ceases only with the building of the altar and the sacrifice at the threshing floor of Araunah. Such is David's explicit explanation to Araunah (II Sam. 24.21), and so the story concludes (v. 25). By contrast, in v. 16 God's decision to stop the plague is not connected with the building of the altar; it even precedes it. This internal roughness in the story of II Sam. 24, which is created there by the secondary interpolation of vv. 16–17, is reworked in Chronicles in two ways:

(a) The opening words, 'and the angel sent (RSV stretched forth) his hand' are replaced in Chronicles by 'and God sent the angel' (wayyišlaḥ yādō hammal'āk/wayyišlaḥ hā'ᵉlōhīm mal'āk). The obvious textual similarity between the two versions has induced scholars to regard the change as a textual corruption, in either II Samuel or Chronicles (cf. Rudolph, 146), but it is more probably deliberate. Even the slight degree of angelic autonomy implied here is unacceptable to the Chronicler, for whom the angel is only the Lord's messenger, completely subordinate to God's sovereign rule. Such a view can be demonstrated from the only other passage in Chronicles where angels play a role, II Chron. 32.21. In place of 'And that night the angel of the Lord went forth, and slew ...' (II Kings 19.35), the Chronicler reads 'And the Lord sent an angel, who cut off ...'

(b) The second change is a corollary of the first: the addition of 'but when he was about to destroy it' is indicated by the logic of the situation. Since God himself sent the angel, a certain lapse of time and change of circumstances had to occur before he repented of his action.

[16–17] These verses are an interesting elaboration of the data of II Sam. 24. I have pointed out above that there is some tension between II Sam. 24.16–17 and their context; David's words are not really integrated into the story. His request to transfer God's wrath to himself and his father's house has in fact no point at this stage of the story. The punishment of the people has already been executed, and a divine decision has just called a halt to any further chastisement. Further, God's command to Gad in the following verse shows no relationship, either in its contents or wording, to David's request.

In the Chronicles version, already attested in 4QSam[a], an attempt is made to integrate these verses more fully into the fabric of the story. In place of the parenthetic clause 'when he saw the angel', in v. 16 there is an independent description: 'And David lifted his eyes and saw ...'. David and the elders who accompanied him are here presented as standing, all clothed in sackcloth, at the place where the angel halted. Upon seeing the angel poised with sword in hand, they fall on their faces, overwhelmed by the theophany. This is a whole new scene in the literary structure. While the characters and setting are indigenous to this context, some literary components are borrowed: 'the elders clothed in sackcloth' from the story of Sennacherib's siege (II Kings 19.2, cf. 4QSam[a], where the identical verbal form makes the similarity even more striking), and the angel with the drawn sword is from Josh. 5.13. The expression 'to fall upon one's face' is found in several biblical texts: Ezek. 1.28, etc. Ezekiel also attests to the phrase 'between heaven and earth' (8.3), but this passage is more similar to Zech. 5.9, where the precise phrase 'between earth and heaven' appears. Beyond exemplifying the intensive use of anthological style, the threshing-floor scene is a new creation, forged from previously isolated elements.

To David's words of supplication, the Chronicler adds two clauses: first an explicit reference to his sin; 'Was it not I who gave command to number the people?', and in conclusion an emphasis on the necessary implication, 'but let not the plague be upon thy people'. These words provide a link between the divine decision to end the plague at Jerusalem (v. 15), to which David's supplication gives added weight, and the sacrificial expiation ordered at the threshing floor (v. 22).

Two words in v. 17 have attracted much attention: *hārē'a h[a]rē'ōtī* (RSV 'have ... done very wickedly'; JPS 'have caused severe harm'), against *he'[e]wētī* (I have done wickedly) in II Sam. 24.17. The attention to these variants was initially triggered by the variant reading of the LXX at II Sam. 24.17: 'I, the shepherd did wrong' (followed by NEB), which was recognized as based on a Hebrew *Vorlage*, and could be reconstructed as *hārō'eh h[a]rē'ōtī*. This conjectured reading has now been confirmed by 4QSam[a]. The affinity between the three readings is obvious: *hārō'eh* (of 4QSam[a] and the LXX of II Samuel) and *hāre'a* (of Chronicles) depend on each other, through either dittography or haplography of one letter: the final *he*. The MT of II Samuel (*he'[e]wētī*) is clearly a later development, a replacement of one expression for 'I have done wickedly' by another. In determining the original reading several points are to be considered:

1. The reading of 4QSam[a] and LXX is much more poetic and provides for a more complete literary metaphor: 'I, the shepherd ... but these sheep.'

2. The Chronicler usually avoids the use of the infinitive absolute before the finite verb (cf. II Chron. 8.13 with I Kings 6.2, etc.); the existence of such a form in his text may indicate that it appeared in his source.

3. It is easier to regard the MT of II Sam. 24.17 as evolving from Chronicles (because of the tendency to replace a more difficult word or expression with a more common one – cf. Japhet, *HS* 28, 1987, 10–16) than from the text attested by 4QSamᵃ and LXX.

One may therefore suggest the following course of development: *hārō'eh hᵃrē'ōtī → hārē'a hᵃrē'ōtī → he'ᵉwītī*. This would be another case of Chronicles preserving an earlier stage of transmission than that of the MT of II Sam.

[18–19] In spite of the similarity of these verses to II Sam. 24.18–19, the development of the story here should be interpreted differently.

According to the preceding verses (15–17), David and the elders were already present at the threshing floor. Accordingly, v. 18 is not phrased as a continuation with the imperfect + *waw* consecutive (so in II Sam. 24.18, 'And Gad came that day to David etc.'), but with the perfect, functioning in this case as a past perfect, to be translated 'and the angel of the Lord *had* commanded'. The verb in Chronicles reflects not simply a change in tenses but a different understanding of the course of events. As a result, the imperative was replaced by an infinitive construct, and the phrase 'on that day' was completely omitted. Verses 18–19 are then not a continuation of v. 17 but a parenthetic clause (the events they refer to had taken place some time between those described in vv. 15 and 16); the sequel of v. 17 is to be found in v. 20.

These verses emphasize, to a greater extent than the parallel in II Samuel, that the command came to David from God, through his angel.

[20-21] The structuring of these verses is very interesting. Although they are basically parallel to II Sam. 24.20, the specific method of their redaction actually introduces into the story a new scene, which forms the basis for many aspects of the following narrative.

According to II Sam. 24.20 Araunah is in his house. He 'looks down', probably from a window, sees the king and his servants and comes 'forth' to meet them. According to Chronicles Araunah/Ornan is not in his house but at the threshing floor, together with his four sons, threshing wheat. Like David and the elders, he saw the angel, in utter fear of whom his sons hid themselves. Therefore he did not 'look down' (*wayyašqēp*) to see David, but just 'looked'. Verses 20–21 are, therefore, an interesting elaboration of II Sam. 24.20, *wayyašqēp ' ᵃrawnāh wayyar' 'et hammelek*, 'and Araunah looked down and saw the king'. This reading was developed in the text of Chronicles in two variants: *wayyāšōb 'ornān wayyar' 'et hammal'āk* (v. 20); *wayyabēṭ 'ornān wayyar' 'et dāwīd* (v. 21). Thus, the verb 'looked down' (*wayyašqēp*) was first modified to 'turned' (*wayyāšob*, v. 20), then changed to 'looked' (*wayyabbēṭ*, v. 21). 'The king' (*hammelek*) became 'the angel' (*hammal'āk*, v. 20) and in v. 21 was explicitly termed 'David'. With stylistic expertise, II Sam. 24.20 has thus been expanded and a whole new Chronistic verse introduced (v. 20). (For a different view on this and other matters in the chapter cf. A. Rofé, '4QSam in the Light of Historic-literary Criticism, 2 Sam. 24 – I Chr 21', *Paolo Sacchi Festschrift*, 1990, 109–20.)

The words of II Sam. 24.20, 'and his servants, coming toward him', are of course omitted from v. 21 in Chronicles. David and the elders were already present, together with Ornan.

[22–24] Again, in spite of the basic similarity to II Sam. 24.21–24a, a new understanding of the events is introduced here. In II Sam. 24.21, Araunah opens the conversation by addressing David with a polite question, 'Why has my lord the king come to his servant?', to which David replies, 'to buy the threshing floor ... to build an altar to the Lord, that the plague may be averted ...' In Chronicles it is David who opens the conversation, by a direct command: 'Give me the site ... that I may build ...' The change is anchored in two factors. On the literary level the question is made superfluous by the preceding course of events: since Araunah had been present at the threshing floor and seen the angel, he knows why David has come to him. On the level of content, there is a different understanding in Chronicles of Araunah's status *vis à vis* David (cf. below).

In addition to the omission of the opening question, there are numerous changes in the negotiation itself (vv. 23ff.). According to II Sam. 24.21–23 Araunah refuses, albeit politely, to sell the site to David. With full oriental decorum, he invites the king to build an altar and offers to supply all that is needed for sacrifice, but does not indicate that he will sell the threshing floor. In this spirit of compromise he also wishes David success: 'May the Lord your God accept you' (v. 23). In response to Araunah's proposal David insists that he must buy the threshing floor, and indeed does so (v. 24). According to Chronicles, David already states at the outset that he is willing to pay a 'full price' for the site, and this alone is the starting point of the negotiation. With the response 'Take it ...', Araunah already confirms the sale; in addition, however, he offers to donate his own oxen, the threshing sledges and the wheat. The ensuing negotiation, therefore, affects only these items, concerning which David replies: 'I will not take for the Lord what is yours, nor offer burnt offerings which cost me nothing' (RSV does not catch this nuance: both in II Sam. and Chron. *qānōh 'eqneh* is translated 'I will buy *it* (i.e.: the threshing floor) ...'

In Chronicles there is also a major change in Araunah's status. In II Sam. 24.23 he is designated 'Araunah the king'; even if the originality and meaning of this title be questioned (cf. McCarter, 508) his negotiations with David are presented as conducted between equals. In Chronicles, Araunah's title is missing; it is not he but David who speaks first (in the form of a command!), and his blessing of David is omitted. Ornan of I Chron. 21 is no more than a local farmer bringing his harvest to his threshing floor, together with his sons.

It has already been noticed that the reworking of the passage is also influenced by the story of the purchase of the cave of Machpelah, in Gen. 23. Much of the similarity is accounted for by the common subject and by the cultural milieu. Additional equalization is achieved by the use in Chronicles of the phrase 'full price', which is otherwise peculiar to Gen. 23. (On the assimilation of narratives see Y. Zakovitch, 'Assimilation in Biblical Narratives', in J. H. Tigay, *Empirical Models for Biblical Criticism*, Philadelphia 1985, 176–96).

From a stylisitic point of view it is interesting to follow the use made by the Chronicler of 'give' (*ntn*). The verb appears in the pericope of II Sam. 24 only once (v. 23), but five times in I Chron. 21.22–25, with three connotations: sell (JPS v. 22), give – donate (JPS v. 23), pay (v. 25: on its formulaic use see F. H. Polak, 'Epic Formulae in Biblical Narrative and the Origins of Ancient Hebrew Prose', *Teudah* VII, 1991, 21*).

[25] This verse, depicting the conclusion of the purchase, deviates from its parallel in II Sam. 24.24b in every detail. 'And David bought' (*wayyiqen dāwid*) is replaced by 'and David paid' (*wayyitēn dāwid*). Even in this minute change the Chronicler's characteristic method is manifest: the slightest orthographic and phonetic alteration (*wayyiqen/wayyitēn*) nevertheless serves a literary purpose in the repetition of the key-verb: give (*ntn*).

The purchased property is not 'the threshing floor and the oxen' but 'the site' (*māqōm*), a change already anticipated by v. 22, which reads 'the site of the threshing floor' in place of 'the threshing floor' alone. These changes certainly allude to the double significance of the place in question. It is indeed 'a site' for the future Temple, but also a 'holy place', following another connotation of the word *māqōm* (cf. Baumgartner, 592; Welch, 24; Williamson, 148–9).

Thirdly, the price is not 'fifty shekels of silver' but 'six hundred shekels of gold'. The purpose of the change to the typological number 'six hundred' through multiplication by twelve, and of 'silver' to 'gold', is obvious: to increase the value of the property and to demonstrate that it was indeed bought for a 'full price'.

[26–27] The first part of v. 26 is parallel to II Sam. 24.25, but serves a different role. In II Sam. 24 the concluding words 'and the plague was averted from Israel' are linked to v. 21, 'that the plague may be averted from the people'. David accurately followed Gad's instructions and so the goal was achieved. The clause 'So the Lord heeded supplications for the land' is

connected with II Sam. 21.14, linking the story of the plague with that of the
famine. The whole verse then serves as a summary and conclusion of two
examples of God's wrath and forgiveness.

In the context of Chronicles the verse is differently conceived. According
to the logic of the story in II Sam. 24, God's response to David follows
immediately upon the sacrifice – there is a tight sequential relationship
between the two. In Chronicles God responds only after David has 'called
upon the Lord'. Moreover, the response is not limited only to the averting of
the plague. First comes a description of the favourable acceptance of the
sacrifice itself: 'and he answered him with fire from heaven upon the altar';
only then is the deliverance from the plague referred to, depicted here in a
much more personal manner: 'the Lord commanded the angel; and he put his
sword back into its sheath'. The additional elements in Chronicles are thus
connected to the cultic act of sacrifice: 'calling upon the Lord' on the one
hand and an explicit reference to the answer 'with fire' on the other. This
'fire from heaven' is a confirmation that the altar itself, and the sacrifices
offered up on it, are favourable to the Lord. Indeed, it constitutes the
dedication of the altar and the basis for David's declaration in 22.1.

The description itself is most probably influenced by Kings 18.37–38, in
which the same two elements appear: a call to the Lord and an answer by fire.
The same topic, displaying a clearer influence of Lev. 9.24, is added by the
Chronicler to the dedication of the altar in Solomon's Temple (II Chron.
7.1). For Chronicles, then, this is an obligatory element in the legitimization
of a divinely-ordained cultic site.

[28–30] The major question raised by these verses regards their
provenance: do they belong to the original Chronistic sequence or are they a
later interpolation? The syntactic, literary and contextual sequel of v. 27 is
found in 22.1. As a matter of fact, 22.1 matches most perfectly 21.26
(although it is likely that v. 27 too belongs to the same sequence). This tight
connection is also expressed in the phraseology: God answered David 'upon
the altar of burnt offering' (v. 26), which is then declared to be 'the altar for
burnt offering for Israel' (22.1). By contrast, vv. 28–30 interrupt the narrative sequence between 21.26–27 and 22.1 on several counts: they contain a
twice-repeated special opening 'at that time' (vv. 28, 29); they refer to an
altogether new topic, the tabernacle at Gibeon, which appears to be only
marginally relevant to the present narrative; and above all, they exhibit an
apologetic tone, which contradicts the tenor of the main story. David's
actions are presented as requiring justification, and this is found in the cultic
exigencies of the moment and an allowance for human limitations.

There is therefore no doubt that vv. 28–30 constitute a self-contained
passage which can be interpreted in one of two ways: as a parenthetical
element in the Chronistic composition itself (thus Curtis, 254; Rudolph, 148;

Williamson, 150–1), or as a later interpolation. This latter view is upheld not only by Welch, who attributes the section to what he regards as the 'priestly redaction' of Chronicles (Welch, 31, regarding vv. 29–30), but also by others (*inter al.*, von Rad, *Geschichtsbild* 101, regarding the whole of 21.27–22.1; Willi, 174 etc.).

The purpose of this parenthetic passage is to answer an implicit question: at a time when the tabernacle of God was enshrined at Gibeon, how did David offer sacrifice at the threshing floor of Araunah? Behind this question stands a presupposition which is not immanent to the present story but comes from outside: the comprehensive concept of the centralization of the cult. There cannot be two places of worship in Israel; at that time the altar at Gibeon was the only 'natural' place for the king to make his offerings. A reasonable explanation had to be provided for his failure to do so, and this is introduced in our passage in the reference to his terror of the angel. The tenor of these verses is diametrically opposed to that of the story itself, the purpose of which is to show that the assignment of the threshing floor as the site of the future Temple was a divine decision. It was God, through his prophet Gad, who gave instruction for the building of an altar on the site and offering sacrifices there. It was God who confirmed the choice by answering David 'with fire'. If we adopt the cultic presupposition of the parenthetic passage, the narrative context itself loses focus and meaning.

At the same time, the theme and phrasing of this parenthetic passage are harmonious with other material in Chronicles. The tabernacle and altar at Gibeon are mentioned in other peculiarly Chronistic passages (I Chron. 16.39–40; I Chron 1.3ff.); the emphasis on the centralization of the cult finds explicit expression in the whole cultic plan of I Chron. 16, where singing and the playing of instruments are performed in Jerusalem, while sacrifices are restricted to Gibeon.

Moreover, the phrase 'at that time' (*bāʿēt hahîʾ*) is more common in Chronicles than in any book except Deuteronomy; of its ten occurrences, only two are taken from the sources (II Chron. 7.8/I Kings 8.65; II Chron. 21.10/II Kings 8.22, and further, II Chron. 13.18; 16.7, 10; 28.16; 30.3; 35.17). Also from a literary point of view, there is some affinity between v. 29 and 22.1, the same objects being mentioned in both: 'the house of the Lord' and the 'altar of burnt offering'. The affinity between those two verses and the antithesis they propose are obvious (cf. Curtis, 254), but the question still remains whether this antithesis was originally Chronistic, or was formulated secondarily as a reaction to 22.1.

It would seem, therefore, that the difficulty in ascribing vv. 28–30 to the Chronicler does not stem from matters of language, style, literary structure, subject matter or theological views. From all these aspects the passage can be regarded as a parenthetic statement which tries to account for a difficult theological problem evoked in the story. The difficulty lies in the most fundamental approach to the determination of the Temple site: should it be viewed, in the spirit of the narrative context, as a divine choice and act of grace, or should it be regarded, as in the parenthetic passage, as a concession to human limitation and weakness? The question is, rather, can these two concepts coexist in one author, or should we attribute the deviant one to a later redactor, who based his interpolation on the general standpoint of the Chronicler himself?

[28] The sacrifices referred to in this verse are probably not those already mentioned in v. 26: those offerings provided the opportunity for God's answer with fire, the very answer which David sees (in v. 28) as the motive for 'his sacrifices' here. These are therefore additional, subsequent offerings. It is, however, doubtful whether this passage indicates that the threshing floor of Araunah had already become a permanent place of sacrifice in the time of David: Solomon would still go to Gibeon, to bring his offerings there (II Chron. 1.3ff.). Curtis (254) regards the whole verse as the protasis of 22.1.

[29–30] These verses are dependent on II Chron. 1.3–6, and reflect the strictest views regarding the centralization of the cult, as a binding principle for the whole of Israel's history.

Verse 30 is the most difficult in this context. It attributes the sacrifice at the threshing floor to David's fear, and from the literary point of view it regards the 'sword of the angel' as an independent element, completely detached from the metaphor of the plague, and somewhat reminiscent of the 'flaming sword' of Gen. 3.24.

'Was afraid' is expressed by the rather unusual *nib'at*. The root is found in the *nif'al* only twice more, in Esther 7.6 and Dan. 8.17, but it appears earlier in the *pi'el* (I Sam. 16.14, 15; II Sam. 2.5; and often in Job).

[22.1] This is the climax and, according to the Chronistic context, the dénouement of the story: God has chosen the threshing floor as 'the holy place'. The declarative style of David's words is emphasized by the twice-repeated 'this' (MT *zeh*, RSV 'here'). The declaration is given metrical form and parallel structure:

Here shall be the house of the Lord God
and here the altar of burnt offering for Israel.

The house is God's, the altar is for the people.

22.2–19

22 2 David commanded to gather together the aliens who were in the land of Israel, and he set stonecutters to prepare dressed stones for building the house of God. [3] David also provided great stores of iron for nails for the doors of the gates and for clamps, as well as bronze in quantities beyond weighing, [4] and cedar timbers without number; for the Sidonians and Tyrians brought great quantities of cedar to David. [5] For David said, 'Solomon my son is young and inexperienced, and the house that is to be built for the Lord must be exceedingly magnificent, of fame and glory throughout all lands; I will therefore make preparation for it.' So David provided materials in great quantity before his death.

6 Then he called for Solomon his son, and charged him to build a house for the Lord, the God of Israel. [7] David said to Solomon, 'My son, I had it in my heart to build a house to the name of the Lord my God. [8] But the word of the Lord came to me, saying, "You have shed much blood and have waged great wars; you shall not build a house to my name, because you have shed so much blood before me upon the earth. [9] Behold, a son shall be born to you; he shall be a man of peace. I will give him peace from all his enemies round about; for his name shall be Solomon, and I will give peace and quiet to Israel in his days. [10] He shall build a house for my name. He shall be my son, and I will be his father, and I will establish his royal throne in Israel for ever." [11] Now, my son, the Lord be with you, so that you may succeed in building the house of the Lord your God, as he has spoken concerning you. [12] Only, may the Lord grant you discretion and understanding, that when he gives you charge over Israel you may keep the law of the Lord your God. [13] Then you will prosper if you are careful to observe the statutes and the ordinances which the Lord commanded Moses for Israel. Be strong, and of good courage. Fear not; be not dismayed. [14] With great pains I have provided for the house of the Lord a hundred thousand talents of gold, a million talents of silver, and bronze and iron beyond weighing, for there is so much of it; timber and stone too I have provided. To these you must add. [15] You have an abundance of workmen: stonecutters, masons, carpenters, and all kinds of craftsmen without number, skilled in working [16] gold, silver, bronze, and iron. Arise and be doing! The Lord be with you!'

17 David also commanded all the leaders of Israel to help Solomon his son, saying, [18] 'Is not the Lord your God with you? And has he not given you peace on every side? For he has delivered the inhabitants of the land into my hand; and the land is subdued before the Lord and his people. [19] Now set your mind and heart to seek the Lord your God. Arise and build the sanctuary of the Lord God, so that the ark of the covenant of the Lord and the holy vessels of God may be brought into a house built for the name of the Lord.'

B. Notes to RSV

[2] 'aliens', thus here and II Chron. 2.16 for MT הגרים, I Chron. 29.15 'strangers' (JPS 'sojourners'), I Chron. 30.25 'sojourners' (JPS 'resident aliens'), NEB is consistent in this respect, cf. commentary on II Chron. 2.16; [9] 'peace' (twice), MT 'rest' (so JPS), cf. also v. 18.

C. Structure, sources and form

1. Chapters 22–29 comprise the longest unit which has no parallel in other biblical texts; except for the final few verses all the material is peculiar to Chronicles. Here the question of sources is posed more acutely than in any other section of the book: what portion of this extensive section was taken from extra-biblical sources and what was composed by the Chronicler himself? How did he rework the 'borrowed' material, and how should the section – as a whole and in its details – be evaluated? From the viewpoint of biblical research and exegesis it is interesting to note that quite a few commentators, particularly in the last century, have tended to regard only a small part of this section as authentically 'Chronistic', while most of the material has been defined as 'post-Chronistic additions' of various kinds (cf. Noth, *The Chronicler*, 33–4; Rudolph, 2–3; Galling, 10–11; Willi, 194–5, and, to a lesser degree, Williamson, 158 and 'The Origins of the Twenty-Four Priestly Courses: A Study of I Chronicles XXIII–XXVII', *VTS* 30 1979, 251–68). I shall refer in more detail below (pp. 406–9) to the literary-critical analysis on the basis of which the material is defined as primary or secondary. Here I would point out that this analysis has broader consequences for the understanding and evaluation of the Chronistic composition as a whole. If this unit is regarded as nothing more than a compilation of various literary layers or fragments, it loses much of its significance for the understanding of the literary-historiographic methods of the Chronicler and his views of major aspects of the history of Israel. Scholars who view the unit in this way thus exempt themselves from a close examination of the internal structure of the unit and its role in the broader context of Chronicles, and are free to follow their own literary suppositions in selecting those elements which seem to them to contribute to our understanding of the Chronicler's style and views. Since ch. 22 – as a whole or in its major part – is usually regarded as 'Chronistic', I shall discuss the problem of 'additions' in the introduction to ch. 23.

2. The unit of I Chron. 22–29 is devoted to one theme: the steps taken by David 'before his death' (22.5) to ensure the smooth continuation of his enterprise. The subject matter of this unit is a continuation of what immediately precedes, in ch. 21, but its theme provides the answers for two matters which were raised in I Chron. 17: the establishment of David's dynasty with the enthronement of his son, and the building of the house of God. The influence of I Chron. 17 is evident in this section in phraseology, style and subject-matter (cf. Williamson, 'The Dynastic Oracle in the Books of Chronicles', in *FS I. L. Seeligmann*, Jerusalem 1983, 311ff.). However, this unit goes far beyond the statements and presuppositions of II Sam. 7//I Chron. 17.

Two topics are focused on in ch. 17: (*a*) after David's death, God will raise up his offspring and establish him on David's throne (I Chron. 17.11); (*b*) this son will build a house for the Lord (v. 12). These same themes constitute the heart of the present unit, but in neither case is the script of I Chron. 17 followed. David does not sit idly waiting for his death, but initiates his own preparations towards the fulfilment of the divine decree: he himself makes Solomon king and undertakes all possible preliminary steps for the building of the Temple.

3. As it stands, this unit has a specific concentric structure. Around the overall theme of David's preparatory actions, the first activity to be indicated is that which touches most closely the king himself: his personal address to Solomon and to the leaders of Israel (ch. 22). From here the preparations extend to the more complex matter of organizing the cult personnel. Against the background of the succession of Solomon, the gathering, numbering and organizing of the clergy is described: the Levites (ch. 23); the priests (24.1–19 with an appendix relating to the Levites, 24.20–31); the singers (ch. 25); the gatekeepers (26.1–19); and the treasurers and others (26.20–32). The organization of the inner circle of cult personnel is followed by the disposition of the people: the twelve divisions (27.1–15); the tribes (27.16–24), and the administration (27.25–34). When all these preliminaries are duly handled, the time is ripe for the enthronement of Solomon, which is related at length in chapters 28–29. Finally, in 29.26–30, comes the conclusion of David's reign.

4. Chapter 22 is composed of three parts, their common topic being the building of the Temple:

2–5   David's own preparations;
6–16 his personal address to Solomon;
17–19 his personal address to the leaders of Israel.

Each of the three parts is woven around a rhetorical core: the first part around David's reflections (v. 5); the second around David's words to Solomon (vv. 7b–16); and the last part around his words to the leaders (vv. 18–19). Thus, three-quarters of the chapter is taken up by speeches; only a quarter is narrative, and that is intended mainly to accompany the speeches.

5. The basically uniform pattern of the chapter is also evident in the relationship between narrative and direct speech. The two main speeches are introduced by opening statements which anticipate briefly their main contents, with the same verb (צוה) used in both: 'and charged him (ויצוהו) to build a house for the Lord' (v. 6), and 'David commanded (ויצו) ... to help Solomon his son' (v. 17).

Another literary feature of the chapter, which we have already encountered before, is the constant interplay of variety and uniformity. In contrast to the simple statement about the function of the Temple (cf. below, p. 403), here we encounter a great variety of idiom. The Temple is mentioned ten times in the chapter – a direct and most telling continuation of David's declaration in 22.1 – in almost as many variations: 'the house of God' (v. 2), 'the house that is to be built for the Lord' (v. 5), 'a house for the Lord the God of Israel' (v. 6), ' a house to the name of the Lord my God' (v. 7), 'a house to my name' (vv. 8, 10), 'the house of the Lord your God' (v. 11), 'the house of the Lord' (v. 14), 'the sanctuary of the Lord God', (v. 19), 'a house built for the name of the Lord' (v. 19). Thus the description of this one concept deliberately draws on many and various conceptual sources.

Side by side with this variety we find the rhetorical device of repetition: certain

key-words recurring throughout the chapter. In addition to the word 'house' (בית)
mentioned above, we also find repetition of the root for 'build' (בנה, vv. 2, 5, 6, 7, 8,
10, 11, 19), the verb 'prepare' (הכין, vv. 3, 5, 10, 14); the name 'Israel' (vv. 2, 9, 10, 12,
13, 17), the words 'much' (לרב, vv. 3, 4, 5, 14), 'son' (vv. 5, 6, 7, 9, 10, 11, 17), etc. By
accumulation, the combination of these items creates a strong rhetorical impression.

6. The uniform pattern of the chapter, the prevailing genres and their relationship,
the specific literary techniques, all point to the Chronicler as author. This is also
supported by the only new information contributed by the chapter: the fact that
David prepared building materials for the Temple (vv. 3–4, 14) and organized the
labour force (vv. 2, 15–16a). These observations are perfectly anchored in the
Chronicler's view of the respective roles of David and Solomon in the building of the
Temple.

D. Commentary

[2–5] Actual preparations for the building begin with the task of locating
craftsmen and accumulating building materials.

[2] The ingathering of aliens (gērîm) and the appointment of hewers are
presented in MT (followed by RSV) as two separate projects. Some translations, however, following I Chron. 2.16, combine them into one sequence:
'and set them' (NEB); 'and assigned them' (JPS). This is the first occurrence
of the two terms 'aliens' and 'the land of Israel' in one context; for the
meaning and significance of the terms, cf. on I Chron. 2.16.

[3–4] Most striking in these verses are the enormous quantities of the
materials. The adverb 'much' (lārōb) is thrice repeated: barzel lārōb, ʿᵃṣē
ᵃrāzîm lārōb, nᵉḥōšēt lārōb, translated variously by RSV 'great stores of iron
... bronze in quantities ... great quantities of cedar'. In addition the metal is
described as 'beyond weighing' and the timbers 'without number'. These
two phrases are then repeated in vv. 14–16, which return to the same theme.
They are peculiar to this context: 'without number' recurs in Chronicles only
once more (II Chron. 12.3), while 'beyond weighing' does not reappear in the
Bible at all.

[5] This verse sums up the first passage in two ways: by introducing the
motives for David's action (5a) and by a recapitulation of the preparations
(5b). The first part opens with wayyō'mer dāwîd (literally 'David said'), which
is better rendered 'David considered /reflected /thought'. David's lack of
confidence in Solomon's ability to cope with the grand project constitutes the
driving force for the whole section and is greatly elaborated in chs. 28–29.
His words open with an antithesis: 'Solomon ... is young ... and the house ...
must be exceedingly magnificent'. The conclusion is inevitable: 'I will
therefore make preparation for it.'

The phrasing of this short speech is characteristically Chronistic: the
protasis is a nominal clause with a sequence of infinitive constructs with

lamed: libnōt, lᵉhagdīl (to build, to be magnificent); there is an emphasized repetition of one preposition: *libnōt, layhwh, lᵉhagdil, lᵉma'lāh, lᵉšēm, lᵉtip'eret, lᵉkol, lō, lārōb*; characteristic phrases appear: *kol ha'ᵃraṣōt, hākīn, lārōb, lᵉma'alāh*; and there is the familiar repetition of key-words, here *hākīn* (make preparation, provide).

The description of Solomon as 'young and inexperienced' (NEB, 'a boy of tender years'; JPS, 'untried youth') is of interest. In the books of Kings there is no record of Solomon's age when he ascended the throne (but only of the length of this reign, I Kings 11.42 = II Chron. 9.30). His completely passive role in the events recorded in Kings 1–2 may support the impression that he was still a young man at the time, leaving centre-stage to the older and more experienced protagonists. Also in the account of his dream at Gibeon he portrays himself with 'I am but a little child; I do not know how to go out or come in (I Kings 3.7). Again in Chronicles, David introduces Solomon to the people of Israel in the same vein: 'Solomon my son ... is young and inexperienced' (I Chron. 29.1). Should these repeated references to Solomon's youth be taken literally, or regarded as mere literary conventions? Several scholars indeed accept the literal consequences of these statements and conclude that Solomon did not reach 'good old age' as David had before him (cf. for instance. S. Zalevski, *Solomon's Ascension to the Throne*, Jerusalem 1981, 182–5*). Although the persistence of the theme is impressive, we should also consider the evidence relating to the only other king who is described in Chronicles in similar terms: 'when Rehoboam was young and irresolute' (II Chron. 13.7), which according to the biblical chronological data applies to a man of forty-one years of age (I Kings 14.21//II Chron. 12.13).

David's desire that the Temple should be 'exceedingly magnificent, of fame and glory throughout all lands' lays down the guidelines for the whole section. The building is to be an enormous, formidable project which no one individual or single section in Israel could cope with alone, and for which no private contribution of materials could ever suffice. Only the full co-operation and joint effort of every part of the people will make it possible (cf. further, pp. 506ff.).

[6–16] David's next step is the initiation of Solomon into his future task as royal successor. This episode is depicted as a private meeting between the two, and the initial designation of Solomon as 'my son' (v. 5) is kept throughout the section (vv. 6, 7, 11; echoed by 'his son' in v. 17).

The passage is composed of two unequal parts: one verse of introduction, which summarizes the gist of the section (v. 6), and a long discourse (vv. 7–16). No response or reaction of any kind on the part of Solomon is recorded.

The discourse is composed of three parallel parts, distinguished by their content and by some literary devices:

1. Verses 7b–10: (*a*) introduction: 'My son'; (*b*) content: David transmits to Solomon the words of the Lord.
2. Verses 11–13: (*a*) introduction: 'Now, my son'; (*b*) content: delegation of the task of building the Temple; (*c*) conclusion: 'Be strong and of good courage. Fear not; be not dismayed.'
3. Verses 14–16: (*a*) introduction: 'See' (*wᵉhinnēh*, not in RSV); (*b*) content: David brings to Solomon's attention all that he has already done; (*c*) conclusion: 'Arise and be doing! The Lord be with you!'

The first part of the speech (vv. 7b–10) is the basis on which the following two parts stand. It is also the longest and of the greatest theological significance. The next two parts, which are of equal length, present the practical conclusions drawn from the theological premises of the first, regarding Solomon (vv. 11–13) and David himself (vv. 14–16).

[7b–10] This is the clearest and fullest statement of the Chronicler's views of the fact that the Temple was built by Solomon and not by David. This problem had already disturbed earlier historiographers, but in Chronicles it became a major issue. The portrayal of David as *the* greatest of Israel's kings and the object of future hopes, the establishment of the Temple as the centre of Israel's religious experience, and the inalienable bond between the house of David and the city of Jerusalem with its Temple – all these had become theological cornerstones. The irrefutable historical fact that the Temple was built by Solomon rather than David did not cease to challenge theological thinking and demand an explanation.

II Samuel 7 and I Chron. 17 state the facts and present them as God's will, but do not really provide an explanation. In the Deuteronomistic redaction of Kings we find a historical rationalization rather than a theological solution, which stands in some tension with II Sam. 7 and I Kings 8.18. It is found in Solomon's letter to Hiram: 'David my father could not build a house for the name of the Lord his God because of the warfare with which his enemies surrounded him' (I Kings 5.3 [MT 5.17]). The postponement of the building is conceived here as caused by historical exigencies rather than a predetermined decision of God. In this passage, the Chronicler seeks to provide a fuller theological argument and introduces it as God's word to David.

The structure of the argument is interesting. David recites to Solomon the events which are already familiar from II Sam. 7//I Chron. 17: his wish to build a house for the Lord and the revelation of God's word which postponed the building from his own reign to Solomon's. However, only the last part of the 'word of the Lord' (v. 10) is a quotation from II Sam. 7 (cf. below); the contents of vv. 8–9 are not found in Nathan's prophecy or anywhere else. One may conjecture that the Chronicler made use of an additional source, but this seems unlikely. Verses 7b–10, with their words of introduction (v. 7) and conclusion (v. 10), clearly reflect the sequence and phraseology of II Sam. 7. It seems, therefore, that the portion in question, vv. 8–9, contains the Chronicler's own interpretation of Nathan's prophecy, his understanding of history as a 'word of the Lord'.

The centre of gravity of these verses is in the postulate that the Temple can be built only at a time of 'rest' and by 'a man of rest' (*'iš mᵉnūḥāh*), a title applicable only to Solomon (cf. also R. L. Braun, 'Solomon the Chosen Temple Builder: The Significance of I Chronicles 22, 28, 29 for the Theology of Chronicles', *JBL* 95, 1976, 582–4). The nucleus of this idea is found in Deuteronomy 12, but the Chronicler has expanded it and assigned to it broader theological connotations. Deuteronomy 12 states that the establishment of a centralized cult will follow the achievement of 'rest from all your enemies round about' (v. 10). Indeed, these very words open II Sam. 7 and serve as a justification for David's wish to build a house. We have already seen that the clause is omitted from the parallel of I Chron. 17.1, for according to Chronicles David's time was not yet one of 'rest'. In this context (22.9), the idea is now transferred to Solomon: 'he shall be a man of rest (RSV peace). I will give him rest from all his enemies round about.' However, as it stands in Deut. 12, the condition of 'rest' as the basic prerequisite for the building of the Temple can be interpreted in purely historical terms (cf. I Kings 5.3 [MT 5.7]). The Chronicler's contribution to the development of the concept lies in seeing the connection between 'rest' and 'Temple building' not as circumstantial but as essential: he who is not a 'man of rest' is 'a man of war' (cf. 28.3), and as such is prevented not only in practice but *on principle* from building a house for the Lord. This is a further theological development of I Kings 6.7: 'nor any tool of iron was heard in the temple while it was being built', and especially of Exod. 20.25, where the prohibition against building an altar of hewn stones is explained by the 'profanity' caused by the 'sword' (Heb. *ḥarbᵉkā*, ET 'tool'). The clear statement that the use of force is incompatible with the building of altar or temple is the Chronicler's main theological contribution, repeated three times in v. 8: 'you have shed much blood'; 'waged great wars'; '... shed so much blood before me upon the earth'. From this theological premise, David's problematical situation can be conceived as the tragedy of his life. From whichever angle one chooses, whether the rational-historical or the theological, David's wars were God's wars – and we cannot accept Micheel's harmonizing claim that the Chronicler regards David as shedding 'clean blood' (cf. Micheel, *Seher- und Prophetenüberlieferungen*, 16). The Davidic wars were waged at God's command, with his explicit help and blessing. Moreover, through these very wars Israel achieved the condition of 'peace and quiet', the required state of 'rest'. Yet, the force of absolute concepts is stronger than any logic: however necessary these wars may have been for the fulfilment of God's plan for

Israel, the objective fact remained that blood was shed; this, according to Chronicles, was David's paradoxical and tragic flaw.

How is this to be interpreted in the context of the Chronicler's attitude toward the phenomenon of 'war'? Does he voice anti-war sentiments and a negative moral stance (Rudolph, 151) or does he see a ritualistic limitation, the warrior being ritually unclean and therefore unfit to build the Temple (Williamson, 154)?

We may question whether the Chronicler himself would adopt such distinctions and value-judgments. On the one hand, he regards victory in war as one of the clearest signs of God's aid and support, and he devotes great attention to military matters. 'War' and 'victory' are surely theological 'topoi' for him, and all the 'good' kings were marked for their military activity and success (cf. Welten, 166ff.). On the other, and notwithstanding, war is still presented *per se* in a negative light (II Chron. 16.9) and the true ideal is that of 'peace and quiet'. The opposition between 'war' and 'Temple' is absolute, and the qualifications of 'cultic', 'moral', etc., seem hardly to be relevant.

[9] The verse is a continuation of and antithesis to v. 8. Following the introduction 'Behold, a son shall be born to you', the attributes of the son are described in two clauses: 'he shall be a man of rest' (RSV peace), and 'his name shall be Solomon'. Each of these attributes is validated through God's statement that he will ensure their endurance: 'I will give him rest from all his enemies around about'; 'I will give peace and quiet to Israel in his days'. Thus a literary balance is achieved in the description of Solomon's attributes, and the theme is repeated three times (cf. v. 8): 'He shall be a man of rest; I will give him rest ... I will give peace and quiet.' The word-play 'Solomon' (*šᵉlōmōh*) – 'peace' (*šālōm*) is not found elsewhere in the Bible. Solomon's reign is indeed characterized as peaceful in I Kings 4.24 [MT 5.4], 'and he had peace on all sides round about him', but here in Chronicles the connection becomes essential. Solomon's very name, assigned to him by God before his birth, has its root in peace, the predetermined nature of his kingship.

[10] The verse is very nearly a literal quotation of II Sam. 7.13–14 (I Chron. 17.12–13). There, Nathan's words contain four elements: (*a*) 'he shall build a house'; (*b*) 'I will establish the throne of his kingdom'; (*c*) 'I will be his father'; (*d*) 'he shall be my son'. The present verse contains all these elements, with only a change of order: (*a*) (*d*) (*c*) (*b*).

Some phraseological details demonstrate that the quotation is based on the version of Nathan's prophecy in II Sam. 7, and not on that of I Chron. 17. The slight changes which the Chronicler introduced in ch. 17 are not in evidence here. Thus 'for my name'; 'the throne of his kingdom' follow the version of II Sam. 7.13–14; the change to *hᵃkīnōtī*, and the addition of 'on Israel', are peculiar to the passage in I Chron. 22.

[11–13] In the second part of this discourse, David entrusts Solomon with the task of Temple-building, the success of which will be possible only through the fulfilment of three interrelated conditions: (*a*) God's assistance, referred to as the most basic prerequisite, 'the Lord be with you', and further, 'may the Lord grant you discretion and understanding'; (*b*) observance of God's commandments, also referred to twice, 'that ... you may keep the law', and further, 'You will prosper if you are careful to observe the statutes ...'; (*c*) finally, personal steadfastness: 'Be strong and of good courage.'

At first glance these conditions may seem a compilation of stereotyped phrases, yet they give expression to a clear religious and psychological concept. The general, rather conventional, premise that a man may prosper only by God's assistance, available only to one who observes the divine commandments, implies in this particular case that God's help has not been guaranteed for Solomon by Nathan's prophecy or by the promise made to David; Solomon himself must earn it by keeping 'the statutes and the ordinances'.

Yet, even in order to keep God's commandments, Solomon needs divine assistance in the form of 'discretion and understanding'. Here the Chronicler greatly intensifies the concept of man's dependence on divine grace, a concept expressed even more emphatically in I Chron. 29.19: 'As to my son Solomon, give him a whole heart to observe your commandments' (JPS; RSV 'Grant to Solomon my son that with a whole heart he may keep thy commandments'). However, the factor of human responsibility is not exhausted merely in the observance of divine precepts. It also includes a man's general psychological disposition: trust in God and determination to proceed with the ordained undertaking. David relates to both: 'You will prosper – if you are careful to observe the statutes', and if you are 'strong and of good courage'.

[12] The verse as it stands presents a syntactical difficulty. The opening clause, 'Only, may the Lord grant you discretion and understanding', is followed by 'and put you in charge of Israel' (JPS); here, however, there is an awkward transition to the third part: *wᵉlišmōr 'et tōrat yhwh 'ᵉlōhēkā* (literally: 'and to keep the law ...'). One may assume either that the second clause is a corruption (cf. BHS) or that the last clause is linked, not to the second but to the first. In this case 'May the Lord grant you discretion ...' would be followed by two separate clauses, each referring back to it: 'and give you charge over Israel'; 'to keep the law'. RSV overcomes the difficulty by making the second part a temporal condition of the third: 'that *when* he gives you charge ... you may keep the law ...'

This section of David's discourse, like the previous one, is constructed of the building blocks of conventional phrases or existing verses. 'The Lord be with you' is a common formula of blessing. In this chapter it is repeated in

v. 16, where it concludes the exhortation. The formula recurs in the Bible in all possible variations, but the Chronicler gives it a significant twist in II Chron. 15.2: 'The Lord is with you – while you are with him.'

'Be strong and of good courage. Fear not; be not dismayed' is again a common formula, recurring in the Bible either in full or with one of its components. Also, 'to observe (and to do) the statutes and the ordinances' is a common expression, recurring mainly in the Deuteronomistic literature. However, only in one other context do all these elements come together, that is, in God's address to Joshua in Josh. 1 (cf. Braun, 'Solomon, the Chosen Temple Builder', *JBL* 95, 1976, 586–8; H. G. M. Williamson, 'The Accession of Solomon in the Books of Chronicles' *VT* 26, 1976, 351–61). We find there the following elements: 'as I was with Moses I will be with you' (v. 5); 'Be strong and of good courage' (v. 6); 'only be strong and very courageous . . . to do according to all the law' (v. 7 – the similarity between the texts being somewhat obscured by the different translations); 'then you shall prosper' (v. 8); 'be strong and of good courage . . . for the Lord is with you' (v. 9). In a similar way, but to a lesser degree, the words of David in this passage reflect his address to Solomon in I Kings 2.2ff. Thus, David's discourse as a whole is formulated as an adaptation of existing models: Nathan's prophecy to David in the first place and God's words to Joshua in the second.

[14–16] David reminds Solomon of all that he himself has done so far. His exhortation, 'arise and be doing', is based on his personal precedent: he himself had taken an active initiative.

An interesting facet of this section is to be found in the quantities and numbers. The Chronicler repeats the phrases he had already used: 'much', 'abundance' (*lārōb*, vv. 14, 15), 'beyond weighing' (v. 14), 'without number' (v. 16), but in addition he records the exact quantities, which indeed seem unimaginable: a hundred thousand talents of gold and a million talents of silver! In view of these exaggerated numbers and the contrast between them and those of I Chron. 29, Rudolph proposes that the passage should not be ascribed to the Chronicler (151; Braun, ibid., 582, etc.). However, the essential problem of the passage is the irrationality and improbability of the numbers cited; this is not really solved by a literary–critical proposal which simply relieves the Chronicler of the burden of responsibility by ascribing the passage to a different author. It would seem, rather, that what we read here should be understood in view of the spirit which permeates the entire pericope – an impression of the grandeur and exaltation of the house of God, beyond the power of humans to conceive. In the words attributed to Solomon: 'The house . . . will be great, for our God is greater than all gods' (II Chron. 2.5 [MT 2.4]), 'for the house . . . will be great and wonderful' (ibid., v. 9 [MT 8]). The degree to which these numbers present an idea rather than a practical reality is demonstrated in verse 14, where David commands

Solomon: 'To these you must add'. Is there any need to add to such incredible quantities? Indeed there is, because it is not in human power to supply adequately for the Lord's house.

The description of materials and craftsmen in vv. 14–16 differs somewhat from that of vv. 2–4. In v. 14 the materials appear in descending order of value: gold, silver, bronze, iron, timber and stones – the first two added to the list of vv. 3–4. In v. 15 the craftsmen are listed as stone-cutters, masons, carpenters and all kinds of craftsmen – as against the stonecutters alone, mentioned in v. 2.

Verse 16a is difficult. The verse division of the MT separates 'gold, silver, bronze and iron without number' from v. 15, making the clause a repetition of v. 14. By disregarding the Massoretic verse division, v. 16a becomes a direct continuation of v. 15 (thus RSV), the final 'without number' being a description of the craftsmen. If this reconstruction is correct, the extravagant tendency of the passage is even more evident. Not only are the metals 'beyond weighing', but the craftsmen are 'without number'.

The discourse ends with an energetic exhortation of Solomon: 'Arise and be doing! The Lord be with you.' Rationally speaking such an admonition is a bit premature: Solomon has not yet become king and he is not even about to begin. But from a literary and psychological point of view this is the necessary conclusion of all that has been said so far. 'Arise' is a common phrase of admonition, but the absolute 'be doing' without an object is peculiar to this context.

[17–19] From the narrative-sequence point of view this passage is not connected to what precedes it, since it has not been recorded that David gathered or invited the leaders. In some way the passage might be regarded as a doublet of the assembling of all the leaders, mentioned just below in 23.1 and later in 28.1, and of the gathering of the freewill offerings described in I Chron. 29. Some scholars would therefore conclude that the passage is a non-Chronistic interpolation, based on I Chron. 29 (cf. *inter al.*, Noth, *The Chronicler*, 31–2; Rudolph, 151–2, etc.). However, the passage is not really a 'doublet'. The circumstances differ from those recorded in 23.1ff., for here David's discourse is delivered in a preliminary and private gathering, before the enthronement of Solomon and the assembling of the whole people. Moreover, the king does not address the leaders with any call for actual assistance, and no response similar to the one described in 29.6–8 is required. David is only preparing the ground, persuading the leaders that the time is ripe for building the Temple and for the efforts this will entail.

Moreover, the position of the leaders as an independent constituent of the political system is in full accord with one of the more characteristic features of Chronicles. It would therefore be rather surprising if these 'leaders' were not active participants precisely in the most important project of which the

Chronicler knows. Furthermore, David's command to help Solomon is anchored in the spirit of the whole context, which presents Solomon as 'young and inexperienced' (v. 5). David enlists every possible support, naturally including that of the leaders. This passage is also a perfect example of the Chronicler's approach in its manner of enlisting co-operation by reasoning and persuasion.

The passage harmonizes with the Chronicler's views from another aspect as well. One of the salient features of the Chronistic narrative is the polemical portrayal of the enthronement of Solomon, in such a way as to reject the picture of I Kings 1–2 (cf. I Chron. 28.21 and in particular 29.24). In the context of this polemic the passage presents both the enthroning of Solomon and the enlisting of the people's support for it as having been planned and prepared for a long time in advance. In contrast to the old and weak king David portrayed in I Kings 1, manipulated by the intrigues of Nathan and Bathsheba, we are here confronted with an energetic ruler, who 'before his death' takes every necessary step for the transfer of his kingdom and royal functions to his son.

[18–19] David actually entrusts the leaders with the building of the Temple, 'Arise and build the sanctuary of the Lord God', but his address to them takes a different approach from his exhortation of Solomon. His point of departure is the premise that the leaders share his own sense of responsibility for the obligations dictated by the historical circumstances, and once initiated into the meaning and implications of the historical moment, will unwaveringly follow his lead. The focus of his short speech is therefore a historical-theological explanation that the time was ripe for building the Temple.

Theologically, the underlying theme of David's speech echoes that of Deut. 12: when the people of Israel have reached the state of 'rest', the time will have come for building the Temple. His claim is that this time has now arrived. The phrases used in v. 18 are all taken from the conventional terminology of the conquest: 'has he not given you rest round about' (RSV 'on every side'); 'he has delivered the inhabitants of the land into my hand'; 'and the land is conquered' (RSV 'subdued'). These phrases have close affinities with verses like Deut. 12.10; Josh. 21.44; Exod. 23.31; Num. 32.22; Josh. 18.1. This is the only instance in Chronicles where an explicit reference to the conquest of the land is to be found: 'so that the land *lies conquered* before the Lord and before his people' (JPS; RSV 'subdued'; NEB 'and they will be subject').

However, the terminology originally connected with the conquest, as understood by the Pentateuch and the book of Joshua, is here transposed to the time of David. 'The conquest of the land' is the enterprise of David, who fought 'the inhabitants of the land' until they were given into his hand.

Neither the accumulation of terms and phrases from the 'conquest' milieu nor the shift in their application (which may well have prompted the translators of RSV and NEB not to adhere to the original terminology) are results of accident or carelessness. In the Chronicler's historical conception there is no place for 'the conquest' in the terms of the Pentateuch and the book of Joshua. According to his most basic understanding, the people of Israel simply continued to multiply in the land where they were settled from the time of Jacob onwards. The 'conquest' according to Chronicles is the realization of the people's ownership of the land by seizing complete domination of its whole territory. 'Conquest' is therefore equivalent to 'rest', which the people achieve through the victorious completion of their wars.

David's explanation to the leaders that the time has come to build the Temple, is, however, also rational: the energy which had been invested in wars has now been freed for other endeavours. As pointed out above, v. 18 presents the theological motive, v. 19 reaches the conclusion, and in parallelism to David's address to Solomon, David now addresses the leaders: 'Arise and build.' Their sense of obligation to build the Temple should stem from their gratitude to the Lord for all that he has done for them.

Stylistically, vv. 18 and 19 illustrate two of the Chronicler's literary techniques. Verse 18 is emphatically anthological, with all its components having been taken from existing texts. This technique is best illustrated by the phrase $w^e nikb^e šāh hā'āreṣ lipnē yhwh$, a literal quotation of Num. 32.22. While in Numbers the form is clearly a perfect with waw consecutive, the verb pointing to the future, '*until* the land is subdued' (RSV), in this text it is clearly a regular perfect with copulative waw, pointing to a completed act: 'the land *is* subdued' (cf. Y. Kutscher, *Language*, 350ff.).

Another difference between this phrase and Num. 32.22 is the addition in Chronicles of 'and [before] his people'. One of the emphasized elements of Num. 32.20–22 is that everything is done 'before the Lord', repeated five times. By the addition of 'before his people', the Chronicler integrates it with the attitudes of Num. 32.29 and Josh. 18.1.

Verse 19 reflects the phraseology and terminology of the Chronicler himself: 'set your mind and heart to seek the Lord your God', 'the sanctuary of the Lord God', etc.

The chapter is concluded with a statement of the purpose of the building: 'So that the ark ... may be brought'. The statement is dependent on I Kings 8.4//II Chron. 5.5, which is usually regarded as a gloss in that context. Here again, the anticipation in David's day of matters actually belonging to the time of Solomon (cf. I Chron. 18.8) is expressed in the smallest details. Solomon was merely to bring to realization the enterprises already planned to the letter and fully prepared by David.

The statement of purpose also serves to emphasize that the primary role of the Temple will be as a permanent dwelling for the ark. This view is also implied in the description of the dedication of the Temple in I Kings 8.1–9, but is not explicit in the broad context of I Kings 6–9. By contrast, it is one of the most basic concepts of the Chronicler regarding the Temple (cf. also on I Chron. 28.2 and Japhet, *Ideology*, 75–9).

23

23 When David was old and full of days, he made Solomon his son king over Israel. 2 David assembled all the leaders of Israel and the priests and the Levites. [3] The Levites, thirty years old and upward, were numbered, and the total was thirty-eight thousand men. [4] 'Twenty-four thousand of these,' David said, 'shall have charge of the work in the house of the Lord, six thousand shall be officers and judges, [5] four thousand gate-keepers, and four thousand shall offer praises to the Lord with the instruments which I have made for praise.' [6] And David organized them in divisions corresponding to the sons of Levi: Gershom, Kohath, and Merari.

7 The sons of Gershom were Ladan and Shime-i. [8] The sons of Ladan: Jehi-el the chief, and Zetham, and Joel, three. [9] The sons of Shime-i: Shelomoth, Hazi-el, and Haran, three. These were the heads of the fathers' houses of Ladan. [10] And the sons of Shime-i: Jahath, Zina, and Jeush, and Beriah. These four were the sons of Shime-i. [11] Jahath was the chief, and Zizah the second; but Jeush and Beriah had not many sons, therefore they became a father's house in one reckoning.

12 The sons of Kohath: Amram, Izhar, Hebron, and Uzziel, four. [13] The sons of Amram: Aaron and Moses. Aaron was set apart to consecrate the most holy things, that he and his sons for ever should burn incense before the Lord, and minister to him and pronounce blessings in his name for ever. [14] But the sons of Moses the man of God were named among the tribe of Levi. [15] The sons of Moses: Gershom and Eliezer. [16] The sons of Gershom: Shebuel the chief. [17] The sons of Eliezer: Rehabiah the chief; Eliezer had no other sons, but the sons of Rehabiah were very many. [18] The sons of Izhar: Shelomith the chief. [19] The sons of Hebron: Jeriah the chief, Amariah the second, Jahaziel the third, and Jekameam the fourth. [20] The sons of Uzziel: Micah the chief and Isshiah the second.

21 The sons of Merari: Mahli and Mushi. The sons of Mahli: Eleazar and Kish. [22] Eleazar died having no sons, but only daughters; their kinsmen, the sons of Kish, married them. [23] The sons of Mushi: Mahli, Eder, and Jeremoth, three.

24 These were the sons of Levi by their fathers' houses, the heads of fathers' houses as they were registered according to the number of the names of the individuals from twenty years old and upward who were to do the work for the service of the house of the Lord. [25] For David said, 'The Lord, the God of Israel, has given peace to his people; and dwells in Jerusalem for ever. [26] And so the Levites no longer need to carry the tabernacle or any of the things for its service' – [27] for by the last words of David these were the number of the Levites from twenty years old and upward – [28] 'but their duty shall be to assist the sons of Aaron for the service of the house of the Lord, having the care of the courts and the chambers, the cleansing of all that is holy, and any work for the service of the house of God; [29] to assist also with the show-bread, the flour for the cereal offering, the wafers of unleavened bread, the baked offering, the offering mixed with oil, and all measures of quantity or size. [30] And they shall stand every morning, thanking and praising the Lord, and likewise at evening, [31] and whenever burnt offerings are offered to the Lord on sabbaths, new

moons, and feast days, according to the number required of them, continually before the Lord. [32] Thus they shall keep charge of the tent of meeting and the sanctuary, and shall attend the sons of Aaron, their brethren, for the service of the house of the Lord.'

A. Notes to MT

[3] שלשים, cf. commentary; [5] עשיתי, cf. commentary; [9] שמעי; probably corrupt, cf. commentary; [10] זינא, LXX and V read זיזה here, cf. MT v. 11; [16] שבואל, LXX reads שובאל, cf. MT 24.20.

B. Notes to RSV

[1] 'was old and full of age', MT, 'grew old', etc. (JPS, 'reached a ripe old age'); [2] 'David assembled', MT, 'he assembled' (NEB, 'he gathered together', cf. commentary); [3] the phrase 'by their heads' (לגלגלתם, JPS 'the head count') is omitted; [4] 'David said', conjectural addition, cf. commentary; [6] The division of the verse affects its translation, cf. commentary; 'Gershom', MT Gershon, also in v. 7; [7] 'the sons of Gershom', MT 'to the Gershonite' (so margin); [13] 'to consecrate the most holy things', MT 'to be hallowed as most sacred' (NEB margin), or 'to be consecrated as most holy' (JPS); [24] 'of the individuals', MT 'heads' (NEB), 'by heads' (JPS); [25] 'peace', MT 'rest' (cf. also 22.9, 18); [28f.] there is no indication in MT that these verses are David's words (cf. NEB); [31] 'continually', better 'regularly' (JPS).

C. Structure, sources and form

1. The view that 23.3–27.34 is secondary to Chronicles has found expression in several ways in the course of research, also involving different opinions on the origin of the material and the process by which it was interpolated. The literary-critical arguments advanced in favour of this view are basically three:

(a) 28.1 is a repetition, or even a 'resumptive repetition' of 23.2; all the intermediate material is then classified as an interpolation (cf. Noth, The Chronicler, 31ff., followed by others).
(b) The material found in chs. 23–27 shows neither unity of form nor coherence of content; rather, it is full of internal contradictions (Welch, 81–96, referring to chs. 23–26; Rudolph, 152ff.)
(c) Some of the details either contradict outright or exhibit some tension with characteristic Chronistic views and concepts.

These arguments, of which the first is usually considered the most conclusive, should be examined further.

A certain similarity of theme and content between 23.2 and 28.1 cannot be denied: both refer to the assembling of the leaders of Israel. However, except for this similarity in the broadest outlines of the narrative, the verses differ in almost every detail and from every point of view. The only identical element is the very common phrase כל שרי ישראל, 'all the leaders of Israel'. A simple synopsis of the two verses will suffice to demonstrate the striking differences, which are even more obvious in the Hebrew original.

23.2 '[and he (RSV David)] assembled all the leaders of Israel and the priests and the Levites'.

28.1 'David assembled at Jerusalem all the officials of Israel, the officials of the tribes, the officers of the divisions that served the king, the commanders of thousands, the commanders of hundreds, the stewards of the property and cattle of the king and his sons, together with the palace officials, the mighty men, and all the seasoned warriors.'

(a) In 23.2 the subject is not explicit but implied, '[and he] assembled', following the introduction of the subject (David) in the preceding verse (23.1). In 28.1 the explicit subject is presented in the opening of the sentence (cf. NEB). In each case the structure is determined by the immediate context.

(b) The Hebrew verb is different in each of these two verses: ויאסף, in 23.2 and ויקהל in 28.1 (this difference finds expression in NEB: 'gathered together' in 23.2, 'assembled' in 28.1; not so in RSV).

(c) It is a different group which is 'assembled' in each of the cases. In 23.2 the 'leaders of Israel' are mentioned in the most general terms, accompanied by 'the priests and the Levites'; by contrast, in 28.1 the priests and Levites are ignored, while the list of the 'officials' is the most elaborate presentation found anywhere in Chronicles. This record clearly draws on the preceding chapters, mainly 27.

(d) The locus of the assembly, stated ceremonially at the end of 28.1 – 'to Jerusalem' (RSV transposes to the beginning of the verse) – is not found in 23.2, which is organically followed by 23.3.

The third of the above points, the striking difference in the description of the summoned officials, has been accounted for by Rudolph with the claim that 28.1 (and 29.6 as well) have been rephrased under the influence of the large interpolation, and therefore only the basic framework of the verse should be regarded as original, e.g.: 'David assembled at Jerusalem all the officials of Israel, together with the palace officials, the mighty men and all the seasoned warriors', 185). However, this is a perfect example of 'circular argumentation', based entirely on the scholar's own presupposition, and furthermore, even the reconstructed verse is very far from being similar to 23.2, which it supposedly repeats.

The claim of a 'repetitive resumption' and the conclusions drawn from it should be examined from the general viewpoint of methodology as well. First, even where a literal repetition is ascertained, it does not necessarily follow that the repetition is 'resumptive', implying that the material between the two recurring phrases is of a secondary, interpolative nature. Repetition is a common stylistic feature in any literature, serving many purposes; it is also an extremely popular literary tool with the Chronicler. Should the above proposition be systematically followed and every repetition regarded as 'resumptive', with the intermediate material condemned as 'secondary', 'Chronicles' would become much shorter, and each scholar would possess his own peculiar version. An example could be brought from the repetition of

I Chron. 13.5, 'So David assembled all Israel ... to bring the ark of God', in I Chron. 15.3, 'and David assembled all Israel at Jerusalem to bring up the ark of the Lord'. Although not absolutely literal, this repetition is even closer than the one we are discussing between I Chron. 23.2 and 28.1. Would this mean that the whole of 13.6 – 15.2 is an 'interpolation'? In the same way one might claim that the whole of I Chron. 18 (and/or 19.1–20.3) is an interpolation in view of the repetition of ויהי אחרי כן in 18.1; 19.1 and 20.4, and so forth.

Furthermore, although the phenomenon of 'resumptive repetition' is common in the Bible and already pointed out in Chronicles by pseudo-Rashi (cf. his commentary on II Chron. 6.12–13 etc., Welten, 190–1, and Williamson, e.g. 122), two reservations have to be made: (a) nowhere in the Bible do we find a resumptive repetition which embraces such a huge body of interpolated material as that assumed in our context. (This could, of course, be countervened by the claim that the scope of the material was originally more limited and underwent several stages of 'growth'.) (b) Basically, even a 'repetitive resumption' is not an absolute sign of 'secondariness'. It can be, and in fact is, used by the author himself, especially in a composition like Chronicles, in which the method of composition entails the adoption of 'redactional' techniques (cf. for example on I Chron. 5.2).

The first literary-critical argument is founded, therefore, both on a rather 'loose' examination of the text and on a series of working hypotheses which can hardly be sustained independently, let alone when combined.

As for the two other arguments concerning internal contradictions and the presumed insoluble contrasts with the general outlook of the Chronicler, these should be examined following the common method of literary-critical analysis, each case on its own merits. The options of regarding certain passages as 'glosses', 'interpolations', or later redactional adaptations should not, of course, be excluded, but these cannot justify the indiscriminate exclusion of the material en bloc.

Two more factors, mentioned in the introduction, should also be taken into account: the very use of varying sources in the composition, which could give rise to many discrepancies, and the threshold of tolerance for such incompatibilities of detail, certainly much broader for the Chronicler than for the modern reader.

Thus far I have discussed the explicit arguments; it seems, however, that other considerations should also be brought up. From the point of view of form criticism, chs. 23–27 are not of the same genre as 28–29. They consist mainly of lists of every kind and origin, and some scholars may be disturbed by the absence of uniform guidelines in the structure of the lists or in the pericope as a whole (cf. Welch, 81ff.). I have already observed that the same scholars who advocate the 'secondariness' of 23–27 would pronounce the same verdict for all or most of I Chron. 1–9 or certain sections of I Chron. 15–16 which share the same literary characteristics. One wonders, therefore, whether behind the explicit arguments there might not be an unconscious tendency to adapt the literary figure of the Chronicler to a preconceived model; to free him from responsibility for 'non-systematic' list-material; to bring him closer to the image of the Deuteronomistic historiographer, and distance him as far as possible from the Priestly material. In the same spirit, although from a different source, would be the subliminal desire to play down the Chronicler's interest in the cult, either in its priestly vestiges alone (Welch) or in general (Willi) – a desire which would be served by the omission of all or most of chs. 23–27.

An unprejudiced consideration of chs. 23–27 will reveal that they exhibit a transparent structure, integrate nicely with the literary methods of the book, voice the same views as and have close affinities with the other parts of Chronicles.

2. The question of sources concerns first the origin of the lists: were they extant as they stand, and available to the Chronicler (or whoever incorporated them into the book), or is he himself responsible for their composition? From another point of view, one should ask: did the lists draw on authentic source-material, or were they free literary compositions, devoid of any authenticity? If authentic, what was the nature of these sources, the period in the history of Israel which they reflect, and the relationship between their origin and their actual function in our context? We will examine each passage on its own merits.

3. 23.1 serves as the introductory verse for the whole pericope, chs. 23–29 (cf. below), and the point of departure for chs. 23–27. David makes his son Solomon king over Israel and on this occasion transfers to Solomon a meticulously organized kingdom, the system of which is divided into two spheres, the secular and the religious. The secular organization in turn is formulated along three lines: military divisions, tribal units and central administration (ch. 27, cf. below). The clerical organization is based on a primary differentiation between priests and Levites, and a secondary division of the Levites into four sub-units: singers, gatekeepers, officers and judges. While the brief reference to the secular organization does not mention its inception, the present picture describes the clerical organization as a novelty, having its origin in these very circumstances. In anticipation of the building of the Temple, David takes the necessary steps to organize the Temple personnel in accordance with his vision of the future cult.

4. In their general topic, chs. 23–29 constitute a parallel to the enthronment of David, when the kingdom was 'turned over' to him as Saul's successor. On that occasion the author referred in great detail to the military, and to the way in which the various martial groups joined David, presenting the broadest military picture in the history of Israel (I Chron. 11.10–12.39, cf. above, p. 267). The occasion of the enthronement of Solomon is taken to provide the broadest 'organizational' picture, both secular and clerical. This is one expression of the 'changing times': a transition from 'a time of war' to 'a time of peace'.

5. Certain basic common elements recur in each, or most, of these chapters: twenty-four units/divisions, the casting of lots, registration according to fathers' houses, attribution of all the arrangements to David, etc., but there are actually no two chapters which follow identical lines. As in Chronicles in general, we do not find here one standard mould in which all the details are cast. On the contrary, the same general principles receive specific forms for each of the clerical orders, determined by the available source-material, the actual historical circumstances of the author's time, and his own literary contribution.

6. The first passage of ch. 23 constitutes a point of departure for the structure of the whole pericope, and its literary analysis is therefore of great significance. According to Curtis, for example, vv. 1–5 are a carefully sketched 'blue-print' of four topics (the enthronement of Solomon, the leaders of Israel, priests and Levites) which are repeated later in great detail and chiastic order: Levites (ch. 23), priests (ch. 24), leaders (ch. 27) and enthronement (chs. 28–29; cf. Curtis, 260). This is a rather interesting scheme, but it is impaired by the interference of chs. 25–26. Williamson,

on the other hand, regards vv. 1–6a as an introduction, composed of two parts: vv. 1–2 prelude the whole final pericope (chs. 23–29), while vv. 3–6a suggest a pattern for chs. 23–27 in particular. Williamson then proceeds to assume a strict, even absolute, conformity to this scheme: whatever in chs. 23–27 accords with vv. 3–6a is of Chronistic origin (23.6b–13a, 15–24; 25.1–6; 26.1–3, 9–11, 19–32), while all the rest constitutes later, post-Chronistic additions (23.13b–14, 25–32; 24; 25.7–31; 26.4–8, 12–18; 27; cf. H. G. M. Williamson, 'The Origins of the Twenty-Four Priestly Courses: A Study of I Chronicles XXIII–XXVII', *VTS* 30, 1979, 251–68; Williamson, 157–8). However, Williamson's literary analysis is not conclusive; the passage lends itself to a different approach, which also seems to do better justice to the pericope in general.

7. One of the difficulties in the overall structure of chs. 23–27 is posed by the position of ch. 24, concerning priests. At first glance it appears to be out of order: not only would we expect the priestly divisions to be recorded before the levitical, but their introduction here actually interrupts the presentation of the levitical orders. Indeed, since Williamson regards only vv. 3–6a as introducing chs. 23–27, he deems the chapter secondary, both in subject (priests) and theme (organization by lot). However, the position of ch. 24 is fully accounted for by the Chronicler's explicitly pronounced views regarding the tribe of Levi. In vv. 13–14 the Chronicler distinguishes, within the tribe of Levi, between the lines of Amram's two sons, Aaron and Moses, and elucidates the double meaning of the term 'Levite' which determined the structure of these chapters. On the one hand, a genealogy of the 'Levites' includes the priests who are 'the sons of Aaron, the son of Amram the son of Kohath the son of Levi'. On the other hand a functional genealogy would exclude them, for they 'were separated' for a special role. Thus, 'Levites' are presented first of all in vv. 6ff. in the most comprehensive sense as the 'descendants of Levi' with genealogies recorded according to the primary families: Gershon, Kohath and Merari. In passing, it is pointed out (v. 13) that the sons of Aaron, because of their priestly role, were not 'named among the tribe', although certainly Levites. Only when this general genealogy of levitical fathers' houses is complete are the secondary affiliations recorded: priests from Aaron; singers from Asaph, Heman and Jeduthun; gate-keepers from Korah, Obed-edom and Merari; and lastly – the additional functions of treasurers, judges and officers.

8. The structure of ch. 23 is as follows:

I 1–5: Introduction. The subject 'David' stands in the initial (and emphatic) position; the introduction as a whole comprises one stylistic sequence of continuous sentences. Within this continuation three progressively narrowing introductory functions are expressed:
  (a) 1: Exposition for the whole pericope, which ends in 29.25;
  (b) 2: Ensuing introduction to chs. 23–27, in which the priests, Levites and leaders (or officials, שׂרים) are recorded;
  (c) 3–5: Introduction to the actual levitical divisions, found subsequently in chs. 23 and 25–26.

II 6–24: This section opens with a new introduction: 'And David organized them in divisions ...', followed by a record of the genealogies and divisions of the Levites.

III   24–32: The tasks of the Levites (on the double function of v. 24 cf. the commentary).

D. Commentary

[1] This verse, as mentioned above, forms a general introduction to chs. 23–29. The words 'he made Solomon ... king' refer to the general fact of Solomon's succession and not to a specific event, which will be described later. The verse cannot therefore be made to support the supposition that there were two stages in the succession, or alternatively two acts of the enthronement of Solomon (cf. also on 29.22). The verse states in general terms that when David reached the 'fullness' of his life he undertook on his own initiative to ensure the fulfilment of God's word, laid down in I Chron. 17. The details of his enterprise are now to follow.

The idiom 'old and full of days (or years)' is found in the Bible several times (Gen. 25.8 of Abraham; 35.29 of Isaac, Job 42.17 of Job and I Chron. 29.28 of David). In the last instance the Chronicler uses the formula with a slight change, while in the present verse (and somewhat differently in II Chron. 24.15) he creates his own idiom by expressing the same idea with finite verbs in the perfect rather than an adjectival form (śāba‘ rather than śᵉba‘). Literally, his expression should be rendered: 'David has grown old and has become full of days (or: years)'. In its formulation it thus comes closer to I Kings 1.1: 'David grew old and advanced in years' (translated differently by RSV), but in place of 'advanced in years' (bā’ bayyāmīm) the present text reads 'full of years' (śāba‘ yāmīm), thus removing the negative tone which accompanies the description of David's old age in I Kings 1–2. In the verse as it stands, and the following chapters in general, the Chronicler depicts in a most sympathetic light David's activities at this stage in his life, clearly contravening the negative picture of his sources in Kings.

[2] The record of the 'gathering' is precise: from Israel only the 'leaders' (NEB 'officers'), while the priests and Levites are all present. This is already an indication that the subsequent record will focus on the priests and Levites.

[3–5] These verses record the census of the Levites and their classification according to clerical function. The Chronicler's attitude to the numbering of the Levites is similar to that of the Priestly sources in the Pentateuch. When numbering the people in the wilderness, Moses is explicitly instructed to exclude the Levites (Num. 1.49), justified by the argument that they are not part of those 'who are able to go forth to war' (yōṣē’ ṣābā’, Num. 1.3); their service (literally ṣābā’, army) is dedicated to the tabernacle. Consequently, the Levites are to be numbered only in connection with their specific tasks: 'Number the sons of Levi, by their father's houses and by families; every male from a month old and upward' (Num. 3.15). Their exact numbers, in several different age-brackets, are then recorded (Num. 3.39; 4.1ff., 48). A different attitude toward the census in general is exhibited in II Sam. 24; the Chronicler, however, in his reworking of that source (I Chron. 21) and in the levitical genealogy here, outlines an attitude similar to Numbers: he describes Joab as refraining from numbering the tribe of Levi as part of the general census (I Chron. 21.6), but here, before assigning them their tasks, shows no scruples about their counting.

The age of the Levites at their initiation into service is given here as 'thirty'. In this matter three different traditions are attested in the Bible. Most common in the book of Numbers is the age of thirty (Num. 4.3, 23, 29, etc.), but we also find the ages of twenty-five (Num. 8.24), and twenty (Ezra 3.8; I Chron. 23.24, 27 and II Chron. 31.17). From a historical point of view the different ages can be easily explained: the raising or lowering of the age requirement was probably determined by changing circumstances and the availability of Levites. The difficulty lies in the literary sphere: how to account for the existence of two different numbers in one chapter in Chronicles: 'thirty' in v. 3, 'twenty' in vv. 24,27. A possible solution is to posit different literary sources: the Chronicler in v. three and other authorities in vv. 24, 27; differently, the Chronicler in vv. 24, 27 and other sources, perhaps earlier, in v. 3; or alternatively, various non-Chronistic authors.

However, because of the textual proximity of these statements, which makes the deviation so glaring, the possibility of a textual corruption should also be seriously considered. Orthographically such a corruption can easily be accounted for, and 'thirty' could be regarded as influenced by the 'thirty-eight thousand' which immediately follows. I would take v. 24 as reflecting the Chronicler's stand on this matter (on v. 27 cf. below).

The total number of the Levites is exceedingly large, much more than the total given for the Levites in the Pentateuch (Num. 4.58, 'eight thousand five hundred and eighty'), and its typological character is obvious; all the numbers are multiples of four and six: four thousand; six thousand; twenty-four thousand. It would seem that the Chronicler's intention is to portray the levitical orders in their broadest possible scope, both in number and organization.

[4–5] The record of the census is unusual. In contrast to all precedents, the starting-point for both the numbering and the registration of the Levites is not in the traditional system of 'father's houses' or families, but in a functional division. This summary 'master-plan' of the levitical orders is unique, and although the following passages will return to the traditional system of counting the Levites by their 'fathers' houses', the overall structure of levitical orders will be maintained throughout. We may therefore distinguish between an actual registration, based on the principle of 'fathers' houses', and a (supposedly) previous 'numbering' initiated by David, which bears a theoretical and abstract stamp.

In contrast to the more prevalent tripartite classification of the levitical orders (Levites, singers and gatekeepers), the present passage mentions four (adding the 'officers and judges'). The unusual sequence (Levites, officers and judges, gatekeepers and singers), is also expressed by the decreasing numbers of each order: 24,000; 6000; and twice 4000.

In v. 5, 'the instruments which *I* have made for praise' raises a textual difficulty. In the Hebrew, all the preceding verbs are in the third person, and there is no indication of transition to a first person speaker. LXX in fact renders this verb, too, in the third person, perhaps reflecting a Hebrew variant reading such as: *'sh ly[hwh]* in place of MT *'syty*. Some commentators resolve the difficulty by introducing 'David said' into v. 4 or 5 (Rudolph, 154; Myers, 158, etc. So also RSV. NEB follows LXX).

[6–23] This comprehensive unit presents an organization of the whole tribe of Levi into 'divisions', registered according to their 'fathers' houses', beginning with the ancestral triad: Gershon, Kohath and Merari. In spite of some difficulties in the details of the list, it is easily seen that it contains twenty-four such fathers' houses: ten of Gershon, nine of Kohath and five of Merari. The number twenty-four is integral to the list and is not secondarily imposed on it. This accords with the heading, 'David organized them in divisions'. However, in contrast to the priestly divisions in ch. 24, the levitical divisions are not registered by ordinal number, and the parallelism with the priests is not made clear.

There are several approaches to the literary position and function of v. 6: it may conclude the preceding passage (RSV, NEB); it may introduce the following one (Curtis, 263; Galling, 72); or it may have a double function: the first half of the verse forming a conclusion to what comes before, while the second half serves to introduce the next passage (MT; JPS; Rudolph, 152–4; Williamson, 157). I tend to adopt the second of these views, for the following reasons:

(*a*) The verse begins with a restatement of the subject, 'David', after a long passage (vv. 1–5) in which the subject had been only implied (but supplied several times by RSV).

(*b*) 'David organized them in divisions' indicates clearly and directly the topic of the following passage (vv. 7ff.).

(*c*) This 'division' introduces the second stage of David's measures for organizing the cult personnel, after the completion of the preliminary census.

The phenomenon of 'divisions' in the organization of the clerical system is peculiar to Chronicles; only some traces of its beginnings are to be detected in Ezra-Nehemiah (cf. S. Japhet, 'The Supposed Common Authorship of

Chronicles and Ezra-Nehemiah Investigated Anew', *VT* 18, 1968, 344ff.). Its origins are most probably to be traced to the circumstances of the Second Temple, at first applied only to the priests and secondarily to the other orders as well. Since the principles, development and application of 'divisions' are connected with the priesthood, I shall deal with them in more detail in ch. 24.

[7–11] The depiction of the Gershonites here differs somewhat from the same father's house attested elsewhere in biblical sources. In the more common view the two main branches of the Gershonites are Libni and Shimei (Exod. 6.17; I Chron. 6.17 [MT 6.2]), while here the first and major branch is Ladan, and Libni disappears (vv. 9–10). From a historical-sociological point of view this shift should be viewed as the result of changing social circumstances and a shift in the balance of power within the family – phenomena amply demonstrated in the genealogical lists. The difficulty posed by these data stems only from the literary aspect of the matter, that is, the deviation from the traditional-conventional pattern and the existence of the two different testimonies in one literary composition. The question is therefore that of evaluating the Chronicler's need to harmonize the details of his source-material. The recognition that such shifts were amply recognized in actual circumstances and recur quite commonly in the regular genealogical systems would make the preservation of both registrations less problematic. The solution adopted by later Jewish exegesis, of regarding the two as alternative names for the same person (thus Kimhi, *ad loc.*), may well have applied earlier than the extant literary documentation; this solution may have resulted from the interplay between the development of actual traditions and the final establishment of convention.

[9] The heading 'the sons of Shimei' presents some difficulty. It cannot refer to Shimei the son of Gershon, the second main branch of the Gershonites, for two reasons: (*a*) v. 9 concludes with 'these were the heads ... of Ladan', which indicates that all those mentioned in vv. 8–9, including these 'sons of Shimei', were the sons of Ladan. (*b*) The sons of Shimei are in fact recorded in an orderly manner in v. 10.

Observing the registration methods in general, we may conjecture that the names listed in v. 9 constituted a further development of one of the families mentioned previously in v. 8. i.e. Jehiel, Zetham or Joel. In this case 'Shimei' would be a corruption, under the influence of v. 10, of one of these names.

Ladan's descendants constitute the largest group among the levitical class – six families in all: Jehiel the chief, Zetham, Joel, Shelomoth, Hasiel and Haran.

[10–11] The registration of the second branch of the Gershonites, Shimei, contains a reference to the vicissitudes of their destiny. The households of Shimei originally numbered four: Yahath, Zina/Ziza, Jeush and Beniah. Biological and social circumstances caused the last two to dwindle, until they were reckoned as one father's house. This would indicate that a different father's house, more prosperous than these two, would eventually bifurcate and fill the position left vacant by this merger. This replacement is not yet recorded in the present list; v. 11 is actually an 'afterthought', the consequences of which have not yet been actualized in the formation of the list. The Shimeites are still recorded as 'four', bringing the total number of the Gershonites to ten fathers' houses.

[12–20] After a schematic presentation of the four sons of Kohath (v. 12), their fathers' houses are detailed: Amram (vv. 13–17), Izhar (v. 18), Hebron (v. 19) and Uzziel (v. 20).

[13–14] The role of these verses is to make clear the differentiation, within the tribe of Levi, between the lines of Amram's two sons, Aaron and Moses. Although the 'sons of Aaron' are Levites by descent, they possess a special status and therefore are not included in the present registration. By contrast, although Moses himself was 'a man of God', his sons have not acquired any special status, but 'were named among the tribe of Levi', that is: their father's houses form part of the levitical divisions.

Aaron's line is described as 'set apart ... to be hallowed as most holy' (NEB margin; RSV 'to consecrate the most holy things'). Although this is not explicitly stated, the whole tribe of Levi is considered as 'holy' (*qōdeš*) while the priests are 'most holy' (*qōdeš qᵒdāšîm*). This is a unique use of the phrase, for although 'holy of holies' is descriptive of several objects (such as the altar, Exod. 29.37 etc.; the tabernacle and its vessels, Ex. 30.29, etc.), it is never applied to humans (this is probably the rationale for the non-literal translation of RSV). Its use here seems to result from the homiletic nature of v. 13, which is a midrash on Exod. 30.29–30. In Exod. 30.22ff. God instructs Moses to prepare 'a sacred anointing oil' with which he is to anoint the tent of meeting and all its vessels on one hand, and Aaron and his sons, on the other. The anointing of the tent and its vessels is described as follows: 'you shall consecrate them that *they may be most holy*' (v. 29), and that of the priests: 'you shall anoint Aaron and his sons and consecrate them, that *they may serve me as priests*' (v. 30). The Chronicler combines these two ideas, projecting the meaning of the one on to the other: just as the tent and its vessels have become 'most holy' through the anointing oil, so also Aaron and his sons are 'most holy'. In addition, the short phrase 'serve me as priests' is elaborated into 'to burn sacrifice before the Lord, to serve him, and to give the blessing in his name for ever' (NEB).

The first words of v. 13, 'Aaron was set apart to be hallowed as most holy', are clothed entirely in Priestly phraseology, while the second part is cast in a Deuteronomistic mould, the main sources for which are in Deut. 10.8 and 21.5. In forging his own definitions of the priestly and levitical roles the Chronicler bases himself on Deut. 10.8: 'At that time the Lord set apart the tribe of Levi to carry the ark of the covenant of the Lord to stand before the Lord to minister to him and to bless in his name to this day.' From here he proceeds to differentiate between the role of the Levites and that of the priests, thus:

> I Chron. 15.2: '... for the Lord chose them [the Levites] to carry the ark of the Lord and to minister to him for ever';
> I Chron. 23.14: 'Aaron [the priest] was set apart ... to make burnt offerings, to minister before him and to bless ... in his name' (JPS).

Both Levites and priests were chosen to 'minister before the Lord', but the former were 'to carry the ark' while the latter were 'to stand before the Lord' (Deut.), a role made more specific by the Chronicler: 'to make burnt offerings' (RSV 'burn incense') and 'to bless in his name'. Verse 14 is therefore a combination of Exod. 30.29–30 and Deut. 10.8, producing a clear view of the distinctive status and functions of the priests.

[15–17] Following the reservation voiced in vv. 13–14, the record of the Amramites is restricted to the families descending from Moses, through his two sons, known from the narratives of the Pentateuch (Exod. 18.3–4). Judges 18.30 makes explicit mention of a priest descending from Moses, 'and Jonathan the son of Gershom, son of Moses, and his sons were priests to the tribe of the Danites', but with the exception of this detail, the family of Moses is referred to only here and in the related verses in I Chron. 26.24–25. The proximate I Chron. 24.20–21 traces the genealogical tree of the same levitical branch directly from Amram to Shubael, ignoring Moses.

The precise genealogical constructions by which the levitical families of Shubael and Rehabiah traced their origins to Moses' sons Gershom and Eliezer have not survived. We may conjecture that if they ever existed they would have resembled those of the head-singers, in I Chron. 6.

The second of the Amramite families is described as highly prolific: '... the sons of Rehabiah were very many', undoubtedly an etymological midrash on the name 'Rehabiah', *kī hirḥīb yhwh lō* ('for God has made room for him', cf. in particular Gen. 26.22). This proliferation, however, did not influence the number of fathers' houses belonging to Rehabiah, just as the infecundity of Jeush and Beriah (v. 11) did not diminish theirs.

[18–20] Of the Izharites only one father's house is recorded, that of 'Shelomith', described nevertheless as 'the chief' (cf. also vv. 16, 17). The same genealogy is repeated in I Chron. 24.22 (Shelomoth) followed by a son – Yahath. A father's house by the same name is found also among the Gershonites (23.9), but the two should not be confused.

With the four sons of Hebron and the two of Uzziel the number of the Kohathites thus reaches nine fathers' houses in all.

[21–23] There are five fathers' houses of Merari: two of Mahli (Eleazar and Kish), and three of Mushi (Mahli, Eder and Jeremoth). Of special interest is v. 22, which presents – very briefly – an application of the 'law of inheritance' found in the Pentateuchal precedent of the daughters of Zelophehad. The case as told in Num. 27 deals with a specific situation, in which a man's only offspring are daughters. The argument brought forth by the daughters of Zelophehad is perfectly cast in biblical terms and concepts: 'Why should the name of our father be taken away from his family because he had no son?' (Num. 27.4), and God's ruling in response follows suit: 'you shall give them possession of an inheritance among their father's brethren' (v. 5). Our text does not deal with concrete inheritance of land or property but involves only the problem of 'the name', that is: the right to retain the status of an independent fathers' house when there are no surviving male claimants to it. In order to reach a decision in this matter the precedent from Numbers is interpreted as a legal Midrash: although the daughters of Eleazar were married to their kinsmen of the family of Kish, this did not effect a merging of the fathers' houses of Kish and Eleazar into one house of Mahli. Rather, following the 'law of inheritance', the daughters maintained an independent house of Eleazar. The roots of this legal midrash in Num. 27 are made clear by the similar phrasing: 'Eleazar died having no sons' (cf. Num. 27.3).

The total of twenty-four divisions of the Levites is thus reached. Even the bare data incorporated in the list of names and the short interpretative notices demonstrate that the list is a formal crystallization of sociological and political developments of the levitical order. Certain matters of principle had to be clarified in the process of this development, such as the reduction in the numbers of the Shimeites (v. 11), the increase of the father's house of Rehabiah (v. 16) and the marital affinity of the houses of Eleazar and Kish (v. 22). In the present list these matters did not alter the format and rigid framework of the system of divisions.

[24] The verse serves a double role in the chapter: a detailed conclusion of the preceding list and an introduction of the following section (vv. 25–32). The phrasing here, as in vv. 13–14 and 22, is based on scriptural precedents and is therefore revealing of the Chronicler's methods and views.

The technical 'census phraseology' of the verse is immediately striking, bringing to mind texts like Num. 1.2ff., 'Take a census of all the congregation of the people of Israel ... etc.' The verse is dependent in almost every detail on Numbers, as is apparent in the many recurring elements: 'fathers' houses', 'as they were registered' (pᵉqūdēhem, Num. 1.21ff.), 'according to the number of the names', 'head by head' (lᵉgulgᵉlōtām, RSV 'of the individuals'); 'from twenty years old'. Moreover, some of these elements are restricted to both or one of these contexts, thus:

(a) *gulgōlet* is found several times in the Bible for 'head' (Judg. 9.53; Exod. 16.16, etc.), but in this specific idiom *l^egulg^elōtām* it is peculiar to Num. 1 (RSV 'head by head', vv. 2, 18, 22, 26) and this chapter (vv. 3 [RSV omits], 24 [RSV 'of the individuals']).

(b) The form *p^eqūdēhem*, 'the number of', is dominant in the records of the census in Numbers (1.21, 23, etc.), but is found in Chronicles only once, here (RSV 'as they were registered').

(c) 'According to the number of the names' (*b^emispar šēmōt*), which is also very common in the census material in Numbers (1.2, 18, 20, etc.), is found in Chronicles only once – here.

(d) This verse displays some parallelism with v. 3 above, which contains the phrases 'head by head' and 'their males' (*lig^ebārīm*), reflecting 'every male' (*kol zākār*) of Num. 1.2ff. Thus, vv. 3ff. and 24 form the framework which encompasses the whole unit.

Within this pedantic 'census phraseology', the Chronicler has substituted several elements. The term 'by families' has been replaced by the more common Chronistic phrase 'the heads of fathers' houses', and more important, 'all ... who are able to go forth to war' (*kol yōṣē' ṣāba'*) has been replaced by 'who were to do work for the service of the house of the Lord'. Thus the Chronicler chose to conclude the numbering of the Levites with terminology taken from the census of the people, but with a shift of the objective from military registration of the whole people to a cultic division of the Levites.

A corollary of this discussion is the conclusion that the phrase 'from twenty years old and upward' should be regarded as an integral part of the text. It aims to harmonize the census-age of the Levites with that of all the Israelites.

[25–32] These verses form one unit, introduced as a direct continuation of v. 24 and describing the functions of the Levites. Except for the gloss in v. 27 the unit is coherent, revolving around two issues: a preliminary and theoretical justification of the extension of the levitical functions beyond what is prescribed in the Pentateuch (vv. 25–26), and a description of the functions themselves (vv. 28–32). While v. 24 is based on Num. 1, vv. 25–26 are connected with Num. 3–4 and the whole is an adaptation of Num. 1–4, portraying the census and arrangements of David in contrast to those of Moses.

[25–26] The premise underlying the development and amplification of the levitical functions has been stated in I Chron. 15 and will appear again in I Chron. 35. According to Chronicles, a change of historical circumstances had dictated a reform of the levitical system, and full institutional conclusions are drawn from this change, clothed in traditional vocabulary. The change itself is the one anticipated in Deut. 12: as a consequence of the last stage of 'inheritance and rest'; when once the people 'live in safety' (Deut.

12.10), their cultic procedures will have to be readjusted. The peculiar Chronistic elaboration of this idea lies in a different concept of 'conquest' and in the application of this cultic change to the specific tasks of the Levites.

As mentioned above, Num. 3–4 describe in detail the role of the Levites in carrying the tabernacle and its vessels (3.25, 31, 36–37; 4), as well as the division of responsibilities between the priests and the Levites (4.25–26). These verses in Chronicles have as their premise the declaration, couched in Deuteronomistic phraseology, that 'the Lord ... has given peace to his people and he dwells in Jerusalem for ever'; that is, 'rest' has been achieved and the place 'which the Lord ... will choose, to make his name dwell there' (Deut. 12.11) has been chosen. The evident conclusion is that all the levitical functions of Num. 3–4 have terminated. This serves as a theological basis for the justification and promotion of certain aspects of the cultic system. The Deuteronomistic idea, together with the Deuteronomistic terminology, is applied to a cultic-legal situation within the Chronicler's different understanding of the 'conquest' and with broader cultic consequences than envisaged in Deuteronomy.

[27] This seems to be a gloss, as it disturbs the sequence of vv. 25–26 and 28, both in syntax and in subject-matter. The motive for its interpolation seems obvious: another emphasis repeating v. 24 and echoing the census of all Israel in Num. 1, that the Levites were numbered from 'twenty years old and upward'. The intent is probably to smooth out the contradiction between vv. 3 and 24, stressing that v. 24, taken from the 'last words' of David, is the correct version, as against the hypothetical 'first words' of v. 3.

[28–32] A clear and gradated description of the ways the Levites 'assist the sons of Aaron' is framed by an opening and a conclusion containing the same basic formula:

v. 28a(a): 'for the service of the house of the Lord'
v. 32: '... for the service of the house of the Lord'.

The levitical duties are relegated to three distinct realms: guarding the Temple's precincts and taking responsibility for their cleansing, 'the care of the courts ... the cleansing of all that is holy' (v. 28a); assisting the priests in tasks relating to the sacrifical cult; preparing the showbread and the cereal offerings etc., '... and all measures of quantity and size' (vv. 28b–29); accompaniment in song of the regular service, 'they shall stand ... thanking and praising ... regularly before the Lord' (vv. 30–31).

These are, of course, the respective tasks of the three sub-orders of the Levites: gatekeepers, Levites and singers. In comparison with the traditions and ordinances of the Pentateuch material, all these tasks are completely new. None has existed 'in the wilderness'; they all stem from the fact that 'the Levites no longer need to carry the tabernacle' (v. 26).

The order of the Levites in this passage deviates from the more common one, in placing the gatekeepers at the head. Yet, this order has its own logic. The role of the gatekeepers is the closest to the levitical role as described in Num. 3–4 (indeed, one view in I Chron. 9.20 connects them with the period of the wandering and with the supervision of Phinehas, the son of Eleazar). The gatekeepers are thus the first to be mentioned in connection with 'the tabernacle and its vessels'.

Verse 29 refers to the second realm, that of sacrifices, in which the Levites are responsible for all the flour-products included in the regular cult: show-bread, flour of the cereal offering, unleavened bread, baked offering and the offering mixed with oil, some of which were also mentioned in I Chron. 9.31–32. In this sphere, more than in any other, the penetration of the Levites into the priestly realm is clearly evident, although the Pentateuch does not specify whose role it was to prepare the baked offerings. It is also interesting that the Levites are made responsible for 'all measures of quantity and size', which is close to their role as treasurers (I Chron. 26.20) and to the identification of some scribes as 'Levites' (J. Liver, *Chapters in the History of the Priests and Levites*, Jerusalem [2]1987, 24*). There seems to be an indication here of a learned background for the Levites.

[30–31] The third role is singing, a task which is also dependent on exemption from the work of 'carrying' the ark, as already indicated in I Chron. 6.31–32 [MT 6.16–17]. What has been described in I Chron. 15–16 as a specific historical event is here a general institutional legitimization and, as might be expected in Chronicles, the singing is described at the greatest length and minutest detail. The presentation follows a line from the least to the most detailed – no doubt denoting an increase in significance.

The particular emphasis of this passage is neither on the act of singing, the instruments or forms of performance, nor the individual participants – all subjects which either have already been or will eventually be referred to – but rather on the status of music as an integral part of the sacrificial cult. The singers 'thank and praise the Lord' on all the occasions in which sacrifices are offered, and these are detailed in full: morning and evening (the regular daily sacrifice), sabbaths, new moons and feast days. This is then summed up in the word *tāmīd* ('regularly', RSV 'continually') – the terminological mark of the regular service.

In RSV the words 'according to the number required of them' (*b^emispār k^emišpāt*) refer to the singers. While this is not impossible, their attribution to the offerings seems more in line with the common usage (cf. Num. 28.18, 21, 24, etc.). This is the only occurrence of the phrase in Chronicles, and it clearly refers the reader to its frequent recurrence in the pericope dedicated to the regular sacrificial service in Num. 28–29.

[32] This verse summarizes the areas of levitical responsibility. The

general definition of their role is 'they shall keep charge' (*wešām'rū 'et-mišmeret*), and the word *mišmeret* is repeated three times, in reference to the tent of meeting (*'ōhel mō'ēd*), the sanctuary (*haqqōdeš*), and the sons of Aaron. All these terms are taken from the tabernacle service and have affinity to texts from the book of Numbers, probably in particular from Num. 3.5–8 and 18.2–7. In Chronicles, the anachronistic 'tent of meeting' is retained and identified as 'the house of the Lord'.

Several scholars regard vv. 25–32 as secondary to their context and post-Chronistic in origin (although the date of the subject-matter is not necessarily so late). On the arguments in favour of this view cf. Rudolph, 155–6; Williamson, 158. In reply to these claims the following points should be made:

(*a*) The passage is linked to its context by several threads: the continuation of v. 32 in 24.1 (which incidentally leads Rudolph to regard 24.1, too, as secondary, ibid., 159); the contact between v. 32 and 24.31; and, in turn, the connection between 24.31 and 24.6. One may of course take the extreme position that all these texts are secondary as well (Williamson, 158).

(*b*) The passage is pregnant with characteristic Chronistic ideas and views, such as: 1. the division of the Levites attached to Temple service into three sub-orders, Levites, singers and gatekeepers; 2. the gradual appropriation of priestly functions by the Levites; 3. the presentation of the singing as a precise accompaniment of the sacrifices (cf. also I Chron. 8.14; 'to praise and to serve alongside the priests according to each day's requirement'; 4. a favourable view of the Levites who are 'the brethren' of the priests, assigned 'to attend' them; 5. and above all, the basic notion that the new system of levitical roles finds its justification in the fact that the people have reached their 'rest', and the role of carrying the ark has been abolished.

(*c*) In a peculiar literary form both Priestly and Deuteronomistic phraseology are pressed into the service of a new system, based on certain homiletic interpretations of these verses.

In view of the above it is difficult to deny the authenticity of the passage on the basis of arguments which seem rather technical and formalistic.

24 The divisions of the sons of Aaron were these. The sons of Aaron: Nadab, Abihu, Eleazar, and Ithamar. [2] But Nadab and Abihu died before their father, and had no children, so Eleazar and Ithamar became the priests. [3] With the help of Zadok of the sons of Eleazar, and Ahimelech of the sons of Ithamar, David organized them according to the appointed duties in their service. [4] Since more chief men were found among the sons of Eleazar than among the sons of Ithamar, they organized them under sixteen heads of fathers' houses of the sons of Eleazar, and eight of the sons of Ithamar. [5] They organized them by lot, all alike, for there were officers of the sanctuary and officers of God among both the sons of Eleazar and the sons of Ithamar. [6] And the scribe Shemaiah the son of Nethanel, a Levite, recorded them in the presence of the king, and the princes, and Zadok the priest, and Ahimelech the son of Abiathar, and the heads of the fathers' houses of the priests and of the Levites; one father's house being chosen for Eleazar and one chosen for Ithamar.

7 The first lot fell to Jehoiarib, the second to Jedaiah, [8] the third to Harim, the fourth to Se-orim, [9] the fifth to Malchijah, the sixth to Mijamin, [10] the seventh to Hakkoz, the eighth to Abijah, [11] the ninth to Jeshua, the tenth to Shecaniah, [12] the eleventh to Eliashib, the twelfth to Jakim, [13] the thirteenth to Huppah, the fourteenth to Jeshebe-ab, [14] the fifteenth to Bilgah, the sixteenth to Immer, [15] the seventeenth to Hezir, the eighteenth to Happizzez, [16] the nineteenth to Pethahiah, the twentieth to Jehezkel, [17] the twenty-first to Jachin, the twenty-second to Gamul, [18] the twenty-third to Delaiah, the twenty-fourth to Ma-aziah. [19] These had as their appointed duty in their service to come into the house of the Lord according to the procedure established for them by Aaron their father, as the Lord God of Israel had commanded him.

20 And of the rest of the sons of Levi: of the sons of Amram, Shuba-el; of the sons of Shuba-el, Jehdeiah. [21] Of Rehabiah: of the sons of Rehabiah, Isshiah the chief. [22] Of the Izharites, Shelomoth; of the sons of Shelomoth, Jahath. [23] The sons of Hebron: Jeriah the chief, Amariah the second, Jahaziel the third, Jekameam the fourth. [24] The sons of Uzziel, Micah; of the sons of Micah, Shamir. [25] The brother of Micah, Isshiah; of the sons of Isshiah, Zechariah. [26] The sons of Merari: Mahli and Mushi. The sons of Ja-aziah: Beno. [27] The sons of Merari: of Ja-aziah, Beno, Shoham, Zaccur, and Ibri. [28] Of Mahli: Eleazar, who had no sons. [29] Of Kish, the sons of Kish: Jerahmeel. [30] The sons of Mushi: Mahli, Eder, and Jerimoth. These were the sons of the Levites according to their fathers' houses. [31] These also, the head of each fathers' house and his younger brother alike, cast lots, just as their brethren the sons of Aaron, in the presence of King David, Zadok, Ahimelech, and the heads of fathers' houses of the priests and of the Levites.

A. Notes to MT

[3] ויחלקם, unusual vocalization, cf. also 23.6; [5] ובבני, probably ומבני, with MSS and some of the ancient Versions; [6] ואחז אחז, probably read אחד ואחד with MSS and Versions; [23] ובני יריהו, corrupt, LXX ובני חברון, probably read ובני חברון ירִיהו, לחברוני, cf. 23.19; [26] בני, difficult, probably delete; [27] ושהם, omit *waw*, following LXX; [28] לקיש, read וקיש, cf. commentary; [31] אבות, difficult, elliptical for בית אבות?

B. Notes to RSV

[4] 'chief men', better 'male heads' (NEB, JPS); [5] 'they organized', better 'they divided'; 'officers of the sanctuary', NEB 'sacred officers'; [26] 'Beno', not a proper name but a noun, 'his son' (NEB, JPS), so also the next verse (JPS), cf. commentary.

C. Structure, sources and form

1. Chapter 24 is the direct sequel to ch. 23, with 24.1 continuing 23.32. The main part of the chapter, vv. 1–19, is a detailed and organized description of the priestly divisions, and assignment of their duties by the casting of lots among them. The second part, vv. 20–31, is a list of Levites, similar to 23.16–23, under the heading 'of the rest of the sons of Levi'.

In the present context this heading is problematical: if we understand the term 'the rest of the sons of Levi' as referring to those members of the tribe who are not priests (as attested by Josh. 21.5, 20, 26), these were already recorded in 23.6ff.; if, however, we refer it to those of the Levites who were not mentioned before (as in Josh. 21.34, 40, also Josh. 17.2, 6), this is contradicted by the actual contents of the list, as most of the fathers' houses have already been mentioned in the previous list of ch. 23. In addition, the position of the list between the priests (24.1–19) and the singers (25.1ff) disrupts the systematic arrangement of chs. 23–27. Yet v. 31 is closely connected both to 24.3–6 and to the overall subject-matter and phraseology of chs. 23–27. It would seem, therefore, that the main body of the list, vv. 20b–30, comprises an independent unit, with its own conclusion (v. 30b). It was interpolated after the phrase 'the rest of the sons of Levi' (v. 20a), disrupting the original sequence of vv. 20a+31, 'And the rest of the sons of Levi, those also, the head of each father's house … cast lots, etc.', in which, as proposed above, the reference is to those of the Levites who are not priests, and are appointed by lot following the example of the priests. Verses 20b–30 constitute an independent list of Levites, of which the beginning is missing, reflecting later conditions than those depicted in 23.6ff. The interpolated list was intended to update and correct the previous one.

2. The focus of the chapter is on the establishment and detailed application of the system of divisions attributed to David: first of the priests, and then, following suit, of the 'rest of the Levites'. However, the Chronicler's claim of a 'Davidic' origin for the divisions does not seem to be historically substantiated. It seems more probable that the roots of the system are to be traced to the circumstances of the Second Temple period. The introduction of divisions, primarily of priests only, provided a solution for a problematical situation at the beginning of the Restoration period. As evidenced from the earliest lists of that time, the number of available priests

completely outweighed the needs of the single Temple. The numerous priests were in fact competing for the right to conduct the divine service and enjoy the ensuing privileges of the clergy. The system of 'divisions' was introduced as an expedient for the situation, a time-sharing device by which all the priests were enabled to serve in the Temple, but not all the time; each group of priests served for a limited time, on a rotation basis.

In the first lists of those returning from Babylon during the Restoration, four families of priests are registered: Jedaiah, Immer, Pashhur and Harim (Ezra. 2.35, etc), and this division is still reflected in I Chron. 9.10–13, taken from Neh. 11.10–14. Other lists in Neh. 12 reflect a division into twenty-two fathers' houses. Thus in Neh. 10.2b–9; 12.1b–7, 12–20, where the names of the fathers' houses are being standardized. The process by which the twenty-two divisions developed from the earlier four is not documented in our sources, and the larger number is very soon projected back to the beginning of the Restoration (cf. Neh. 12.1 with Ezra. 2.36).

The culmination of the process is reflected in this chapter: the groups are defined as 'divisions' (מחלקות), their number is twenty-four, and all the fathers' houses trace their descent to Eleazar and Ithamar, Aaron's sons. Their designations (of which ten out of twenty-four are identical with those of Ezra-Nehemiah) were to remain without change throughout the history of Judaism, even into the post-biblical era. The stabilization of the orders and terminology of the sacerdotal system had been achieved.

However, the historical exigencies which motivated the process were limited to the priests and did not obtain for the other clerical orders. The list of Ezra 2, which records 4289 priests, lists only 74 Levites, 128 singers (148 in Neh. 7.44) and 139 gatekeepers (138 in Neh. 7.45). The major problem in these orders was not too many members but too few (cf., in particular, Ezra 8.15–20), and their development followed different lines. Yet the inner dynamic of the institutional system initiated a process of schematization and parallelization which resulted in the artificial creation of divisions where none were in fact called for. This process converged with contemporary development in the definition, legitimization and role-casting of the other orders, reflected in the integration into the ranks of the Levites of the singers and the gatekeepers through detailed genealogical constructions, and the disappearance – through absorption or rejection – of the 'Nethinim' (RSV 'temple servants') and the sons of the servants of Solomon (Ezra 2.43–58; Neh. 7.46–60). The process of integration was probably more prompt for the singers than for the gatekeepers, but eventually all the fathers' houses of the two orders were ascribed levitical lineage, through the attribution of kinship to the main families of the Levites (cf. also above on chs. 6 and 9).

The accumulated evidence on the priestly divisions leaves no doubt that an authentic social development is reflected in the list of I Chron. 24. On the other hand, the actual social motivation behind the schematic presentation of the other cultic orders is disputable. While in the following chapters an attempt is made to establish a parallel system of divisions for all the orders, based on their full genealogical legitimization in their registration as Levites, the artificial character of this is still manifest, and the historicity of the evidence should be discussed in each case on its own merits.

3. Chapter 24 serves as an excellent illustration of the peculiarly Chronistic attitude toward the priests:

(a) In the overall cultic system (chs. 23–26), the record of the priests follows the registration of the Levites in the second place. This structure, prepared for and theologically justified by 23.13–14, indicates in the most emphatic way that the priests comprise only one branch of the tribe of Levi.

(b) Of all the levitical groups, the priests receive the least attention. The information concerning them is limited to their organization into divisions, and their appointment to cultic duties by the casting of lots. While for all the other levitical orders there is a more or less detailed description of their tasks (23.28–32; 25.1–6; 26.14–18, together with various elements in 26.20–32), there is no similar description of the priests.

(c) At the same time, there can be no doubt that the priests are the highest order of the cultic personnel, designated by the deferential title 'officers of the sanctuary and officers of God' (v. 5).

All of these points combine to reflect both historical conditions and the Chronistic attitude. The primacy of the priests at the apex of the cultic hierarchy is solidly established; the order and function of the priestly divisions, as well as the procedures for their rotation, have also reached stability and consolidation, to serve as the foundation and pattern for the organization of all the other cultic offices. The definition of the priestly roles, rights and authority is so apparent as to require no elucidation. The Chronicler takes cognizance of all this – yet his sympathy still lies with the Levites.

4. The structure of the chapter is as follows:

(a) 1–19: The priests
1–6: the procedures of organization;
7–18: the names of the divisions;
19: conclusion.
(b) 20a+31: Organization into divisions of the non-priestly Levites
(c) 20b–30: Interpolated list of Levites
20b–25: Kohathites;
26–30a: Merarites;
30b: conclusion.

5. The material of ch. 24 is peculiar to Chronicles, with no biblical parallels. It seems, however, that both the priestly (vv. 7–18) and the levitical (vv. 20b–30) lists comprise authentic material, reflecting actual historical situations in the development of the cult personnel in Second Temple times. The relationship between vv. 20b–30 and 23.6b–23 clearly indicates the dynamic process which preceded the consolidation of the levitical orders (cf. the commentary). The source material is inserted by the Chronicler into an adequate framework (vv. 1–6; 19–20a; 31) of his own composition.

D. Commentary

[1–6] The unit is a remarkably concise description of the origins of the priests and their organization into divisions, but it is not arranged as a genealogical structure (Liver, *Chapters in the History of the Priests and Levites*, 33). The system moves from the most ancient ancestors, the actual sons of Aaron, Eleazar and Ithamar, to the supposed 'heads of fathers' houses' at the time of David, without attempting to bridge the gap by a genealogical construction. Even the affiliation of the 'heads of fathers' houses' to either Eleazar or Ithamar (as in the levitical lists) is missing. It is in fact only for the line of the high priest that there is a full genealogy in Chronicles (I Chron. 6.1ff. [MT 5.27ff]).

[1–2] The heading in v. 1a is continued in v. 3, while vv. 1b–2 serve as a parenthetic note explaining the subsequent absence of any mention of Nadab and Abihu (cf. also I Chron. 5.1–2 for similar notes). The designation 'the sons of Aaron' is used twice in this verse, with its two different connotations: the priestly order in general (also 23.32; 24.31 etc.), and the actual sons of Aaron, known to us from the Pentateuchal tradition (Exod. 6.23; Num. 3.2–4; 26.60–61. In LXX Abihu is always Abihud).

The parenthetical note vv. 1b–2 serves to explain how the line of Aaronic priesthood came to by-pass Aaron's two eldest sons, to be continued by his two younger offspring. The note is dependent on Num. 3.2–4, but the Chronicler excises the whole of Num. 3.3 and the description of the sin of Nadab and Abihu in v. 4. In addition, the Chronicler reads 'before their father' (denoting 'in the lifetime of the their father'), in place of 'before the Lord' of Num. 3.4 (cf. also Lev. 10.3). Thus in Chronicles the Pentateuchal allusion to sacrilege becomes a neutral obituary remark.

The view that the Israelite priesthood traced its origins to Aaron's two sons is founded on the Pentateuch. Ithamar is mentioned in Exod. 38.21; Num. 4.28, 33; 7.8; with the exception of Chronicles, the only other reference is in Ezra 8.2, which refers to him as a counterpart of Phinehas: 'Of the sons of Phinehas, Gershom. Of the sons of Ithamar, Daniel.' His name is not attested in the Former Prophets, or in any other evidence from the monarchical period. By contrast, the affiliation of the high priesthood with Eleazar is a strong element of tradition and is repeated, not only in the Pentateuch (Num. 3–4; 20.25–26, 28; 26.1, 3, 63, etc.; Deut. 10.6), but also in Joshua and Judges (Josh. 14.1; 19.51; 21.1; 22.13; 24.33, etc.; Judg. 20.28). Whatever the historical realities reflected by these traditions, for the Chronicler they are firmly established facts, which need no support.

[3–6] Some points should be made on the organization of the divisions:

(a) It is clear from the passage that the initiative, authority and responsibility for the whole project are David's; he is not, however, alone. His collaborators in the enterprise are on the one hand 'the princes' (*śārîm*), who witness the registration 'in the presence of the king and the princes ...' (v. 6), and on the other 'the heads of the fathers' houses of the priests and the Levites'. Here again we encounter a characteristic Chronistic feature in presenting the political system: the existence of 'officers', who share with the king the responsibilities of the realm. In this respect v. 6 is parallel to 23.2, where David assembles the 'officers of Israel' as a preliminary step for the ensuing project.

(*b*) While the general responsibility falls on the 'officers'/'princes' and the 'heads of fathers' houses', the practical aspects of the organization are attended to by David, with the assistance of the two priestly 'princes': Zadok of Eleazar and Ahimelech of Ithamar. The affiliation of Zadok, the prominent priest of the time of David and Solomon, to the branch of Eleazar, is repeated in several biblical sources, all of them late (Ezra 7.1–5; I Chron. 6.4– 12 [MT 5.30–34]; I Chron. 6.50–53 [MT 6.35–38]). However, the artificiality of the genealogical tree and additional considerations have for long cast doubts on this assumed lineage (cf. Rudolph, 52–3). Even more dubious is the connection of Ahimelech with Ithamar. Ahimelech is not further identified in the text, but his appearance with Zadok would most probably indicate a point of origin in II Sam. 8.17 (I Chron. 18.16, MT Abimelech), where he is presented as 'the son of Abiathar'. Although it is generally accepted that the text of II Sam. 8.17 is corrupt and should actually read 'Abiathar the son of Ahimelech [the son of Ahitub]', it would seem that the corruption predated the Chronicler, for whom 'Ahimelech' and not 'Abiathar' is Zadok's counterpart in David's time. In any case, according to the evidence of the book of Samuel, Abiathar was a direct descendent of Eli, the priest of Shiloh (I Sam. 14.3; 22.20), who for his part was very likely a descendant of the central priestly line in Israel, that of Eleazar. However, the genealogical picture which eventually crystallized must be regarded as a reflection, not of biological processes, but of social ones. Since the main priestly line was that of Zadok, it was he who was to be affiliated with Eleazar; for the sake of symmetry the other priestly house, that of Abiathar, had to be traced to Ithamar.

(*c*) The artificial literary nature of the text is evident, and the 'historical' event described in it is totally theoretical. The Chronicler, in full conformity with his literary and historiographical method, transforms a conviction about the origin of the priestly divisions into a specific historical event.

[4] The primary of the Eleazarites among the priests is presented as a result of biological prolificness; they were more numerous than the Ithamarites, and the divisions were thus proportionally determined. However, the procedure envisaged here is very unusual: the 'fathers' houses' are not presented as organic social units developing from within, but as an external grouping of related persons, based on a preliminary counting of 'the male heads'. The Eleazarites constituted more 'fathers' houses' only after they were counted and found more numerous by 'male heads'; that is, a certain conventional number was expected to form an average 'father's house' or, more appropriately, a 'division', and not an inherent affiliation.

This too, adds to the impression of the 'posterior' nature of the account, rationalizing existing arrangements, for which the original causes were utterly different.

The fact that no attempt is made to construct a detailed genealogical system, to demonstrate the descent of the priestly fathers' houses from Eleazar and Ithamar respectively seems to indicate that this affiliation remained theoretical and abstract. The system of the twenty-four divisions had already become stable and fixed at an early date, with no need for further legitimization.

[5] The verse emphasizes that lots were cast on a basis of an absolute equality of the two priestly branches: 'all alike' (JPS 'both on an equal footing'). The honorary titles used for the occasion are ascribed to both branches: 'officers of the sanctuary', which recurs in Isa. 43.28 (RSV 'the princes of the sanctuary'), and the unique 'officers of God'. The use of *qōdeš* without the article supports the rendering of NEB, 'sacred officials', which would then be a qualification of 'the officers of God'.

These unusual titles probably derive from the analogy in Chronicles between the king and the high priest: on the occasion of the anointing of Solomon as 'prince for the Lord', Zadok the high priest is also anointed 'as priest' (I Chron. 29.22). Parallel to the king's entourage, then, the high priest is also surrounded by officers, responsible for 'all matters of the Lord' (*d'bar yhwh*, II Chron. 19.11). They are therefore 'the officers of God', dealing with all sacred matters.

The Chronicler specifies the casting of lots as the method employed in the organization of the priestly divisions, and also of the Levites (24.31), singers (25.8) and gatekeepers (26.13). There is no additional explicit evidence to support this claim, but the practice of casting lots in matters pertaining to the Temple is testified to by Neh. 10.34 [MT 35], 'we have likewise cast lots ... for the wood offerings', and for other matters in Neh. 11.1, 'and the rest of the people cast lots ... to live in Jerusalem' (cf. also Esther 3.7; 9.24, etc). The lot was, therefore, a prevalent and plausible technique for collocation in the Chronicler's time.

[6] The divisions are ordered according to a principle of alternation: one father's house from Eleazar and one from Ithamar, and so on up to the sixteenth division. The last eight are all of the sons of Eleazar, who cast lots between themselves to determine their order. Another possibility of alternation (followed by Rudolph, 160 and JPS among others; cf. also L. Dequeker, 'I Chronicles 24 and the Royal Priesthood of the Hasmoneans', *OTS* 24, 1986, 98–9) is that the lots were cast from the outset for two divisions of Eleazar and then one of Ithamar, and so on. My preference for the first alternative is substantiated by the similar arrangement of the singers, for which cf. ch. 25.

The ordering of the divisions by lots was immediately recorded by 'the scribe Shemiah ... a Levite'. This recording was a very public affair, attended by the king, his 'princes'/officers, the chief priests, and the heads of fathers' houses of priests and Levites. The presence of all these was not required by the actual circumstances: indeed, in the determining of cultic-sacral issues of this nature, the 'officers' seem out of their element. Their attendance, as pointed out above, would be a result of the Chronistic tendency to involve these officers in all matters of government. The presence of the 'heads ... of the Levites' may be accounted for by their active role in casting lots, after the priestly houses, for the ordering of the Levites, including the singers and the gatekeepers (v. 31).

[7–18] The list of the twenty-four divisions follows a stereotyped formula. Syntactically, it is one sentence, dependent on the opening in v. 7, 'the [first] lot fell', followed in this verse by 'to Jehoiarib'. The following divisions are recorded simply with the preposition 'to' (l^e), followed by the ordinal number: 'to Jedaiah the second, to Harim the third, etc.'. From the eleventh division onward (except for 'the twentieth'), the numbers are cardinal, literally: 'to Eliashib eleven, to Jakim twelve, etc.').

The list of names established on this occasion continued to exist, unchanged, for many generations. All the available extra-biblical evidence testifies to the same structure (Liver, *History of the Priests and Levites*, 34–7).

Ten of these names are found also in the parallel lists of Neh. 12. These are divisions nos. 1, 2, 3, 5, 6, 8, 10, 15, 16, 24. Of the others, some are unique (nos. 4, 13, 14, 18, 22), some are found elsewhere for different persons and only here as priestly names (nos. 17, 19, 23), and others are known as individual priests elsewhere (nos. 7, 9, 12, 20, 21).

One can theoretically posit how the names of the twenty-two groups in Neh. 12 developed into the present twenty-four: some large fathers' houses have split, with one section adopting a new name; some small fathers' houses have been united, with one of the names being abolished; names of secondary family branches have replaced the name of the previously major branch, etc. Such processes are all confirmed from the overall list-material in Chronicles, and conform well with the function of these genealogical constructions. None, however, can actually be reconstructed for lack of evidence and documentation.

Some of the names deserve special consideration.

[7] *Jehoiarib*. The position of Jehoiarib at the head of the divisions has led to some far-reaching speculations on the date of the list as a whole, based on the fact that the priest Mattathiah, the father of the Hasmonaeans, belonged to this division (I Macc. 2.1). A scholar making the double assumption that the list is arranged in order of precedence, and that the division of Jehoiarib attained primary status only after the Hasmonaean revolt, will inevitably

conclude that the whole list is post-Hasmonaean. In accordance, then, with his other literary presuppositions, he will determine the date of the Chronicler, or of the later redactor responsible for the list.

However, none of the above assumptions is substantiated by available sources. There is neither proof nor even indication that the order of the list reflects any hierarchical rank. It seems more likely that the festivals were regarded as the most highly significant time for the priestly service, and that the priestly duties during the festivals would therefore be more valued and point to some scale of rank (cf. Liver, *History of the Priests and Levites*, 36, and J. T. Milik, 'Le travail d'éditions des manuscrits du Desert de Juda', *VTS* IV, 1957, 25 for the list from Qumran). Nor is there any proof that the division of Jehoiarib was initially of inferior status, coming to prominence only after the rise of the Hasmonaeans. The opposite seems rather more likely – cf. below. Finally, even were the above assumptions true, there would be nothing easier for a redactor than to change the position of one name in the list; no such far-reaching conclusions can be based on the present order of names alone (cf. in more detail, Liver, 35–8).

Regarding the name itself, in Neh. 11.10 a priest 'Jedaiah the son of Joiarib' is mentioned, and if my reconstruction is correct (cf. on I Chron. 9.10), he holds the position of 'chief officer of the house of God'. This would mean that 'Joiarib/Jehoiarib' was already an important priestly family in the early stages of the Restoration period. The same name also attests a close relationship between 'Jedaiah' and 'Joiarib', and as 'Jedaiah' belongs to the four major priestly families (Ezra 2.36), it probably implies that Joiarib was a branch which developed from the house of Jedaiah. This relationship may be supported by the proximity of the names in Neh. 12.6, 19.

Jedaiah. 'The sons of Jedaiah' are mentioned as the first priestly family in the list of the returnees (Ezra 2.36//Neh. 7.39), bearing there the additional title 'of the house of Jeshua' – probably a reference to Joshua the son of Jehozadak, the high priest (Ezra 3.2 etc.). It was, then, an ancient priestly family, whose designation remained unchanged from the early days of the Restoration. The name appears in all the relevant lists of Ezra-Nehemiah except among those who set their seal to the 'firm covenant' (Neh. 9.38 [MT 10.1]). This omission could reflect a political stance rather than an omission (Liver, 41–2).

[8] *Harim.* Both Harim and Immer (the sixteenth division) are among the four priestly families of the returnees (Ezra 2.39, 37 respectively). They may be regarded as the founders of the Jerusalemite priesthood. The two names are repeated in all the relevant lists in Nehemiah (including the signatories of the 'firm covenant'), Ezra 10.20, 21; Neh. 10.3 (Amariah=Immer), 5; 12.2, 3 (Rehum=Harim), 13, 15. Like Jehoshua/Jeshua, the high priest of the 'sons of Jedaiah', these two traced their origin to the period of the monarchy. The

fourth and largest family of the returning priests, that of Pashhur (Ezra 2.38
//Neh. 7.41; Ezra 10.22; Neh. 10.3 [MT 4] is not mentioned in the list or in
Neh. 12. It is hardly likely that this large family, mentioned right up to the
time of Ezra (Ezra 10.22), has utterly disappeared. It would seem rather, that
the one family was divided into smaller units, which appear in the list under
their newly assumed names, without reference to their earlier designation.
[10] *Hakkoz*. In Ezra 2.61ff. this family is referred to as 'the sons of
Hakkoz' who 'sought their registration among those enrolled in the genealogies, but they were not found there, and so they were excluded from the
priesthood as unclean'. Among those who participated in the building of the
wall of Jerusalem and undertook a double load, was 'Meremoth the son of
Uriah, son of Hakkoz' (Neh. 3.4, 21), and the priest who received and
weighed the money brought by Ezra from Babylon is called 'Meremoth ...
the son of Uriah' (Ezra 8.33), very likely the same man. Thus, in spite of its
uncertain beginnings, the family of Hakkoz had gradually assumed recognition and power.
[11, 12] *Jeshua, Eliashib*. These are also the names of two distinguished
priests of the period: Joshua the son of Jehozadak who was high priest at the
beginning of the Restoration (Haggai 1.1, etc.; Zech. 3.1, etc.; Ezra 2.2, etc.),
and Eliashib who served as high priest in the time of Nehemiah (Neh. 3.1,
etc.). Whether there is any connection between these individual priests and
the divisions designated by the same names, or whether these were simply
common priestly names, is a question we must leave unanswered for lack of
information.
[13] *Jeshebeab*. This name is unique in the Bible. Some of the LXX MSS
have Ishba'al, and some scholars would prefer this reading (cf. BH). However, it is difficult to accept that at a such a late date in the Second Temple
period the element 'Ba'al' still survived in proper names, and there is no
epigraphic evidence to that effect. It would seem that the LXX reading is
either influenced by other texts, or reflects an inner-Greek corruption.
[15] *Hezir*. The name is found in the Bible only once more (Neh. 10.20
[MT 21]) as one of the 'chiefs of the people', but is familiar from the
inscription of the 'tomb of the sons of Hezir' found in the Valley of Kidron
(cf. *Encyclopaedia of Archeological Excavations* II, Jerusalem 1976, 629–30).
[19] The conclusion of the list follows the regular formula, *'elleh*, RSV
'These had...' (also v. 30; 26.19; 27.2, etc., variably translated). The focus of
the conclusion is in the second half: 'the procedure established ... by Aaron
their father, as the Lord ... had commanded him.'
The inauguration of the priestly service is thus ascribed to Aaron himself,
in obedience to God's command. In the Pentateuch, the more prevalent
concept is that the instructions pertaining to the priests were transferred to
Aaron by Moses, e.g. 'the Lord said to Moses: command Aaron and his

sons...' (Lev. 6.8 [MT 6.1]), 24–25 [MT 17–18]; 16.2; 17.1, etc.). Alternatively, both Moses and Aaron are the recipients of the word of God (Lev. 11.1; 13.1, etc); very rarely is it Aaron alone (Exod. 4.27; Lev. 10.8; Num. 18.1, 8, 20). In this verse there is no indication whether God's command came to Aaron directly or through the mediation of Moses; in any case his authority is restricted to the procedures of the priestly service. In all matters of sacrifice, it is the jurisdiction of Moses which is specifically referred to (cf. II Chron. 8.13; 23.18, etc.).

[20a + 31] (For the justification of this combination, cf. above, p. 423)

Once the arrangements for the priests have been established, it is the turn of the 'rest of the sons of Levi' that is, those who were not priests. These verses conclude the issue introduced in 23.6ff., completing a full circle.

The organization of the Levites is presented as completely analogous to the priests: 'these also ... just as their brethren the sons of Aaron'. However, contrary to the priests, the levitical divisions are not listed by ordinal position; it is in fact very likely that no such 'parallel' arrangement ever did obtain within the cultic orders. In the everyday life of the Temple the Levites did not reach the same degree of stability and regularity as the priests; the strict analogy of v. 31 is more theoretical than practical.

'ābōt hārō'š is difficult. The rendering of RSV ('the heads of fathers' houses') presupposes a Hebrew text hār'ōš l'bēt 'ābōt, which is indeed possible (JPS refrains from translating the word 'ābōt; NEB paraphrases, following RSV).

[20b–30] 1. In its present state this is a fragmentary and corrupted list of Levites, 'according to their fathers' houses' (v. 30). As has been pointed out by many (cf. Curtis, 272–3; Welch, 83–4), this passage is closely related to I Chron. 23.7ff., a connection which affords much assistance in reconstructing some corrupt readings and understanding the purpose of the list.

The heading of the list, as well as the first part which contained the families of the Gershonites, is missing. It is unlikely that the Gershonites – the largest levitical branch in 23.7ff. – have suddenly disappeared (cf. also 26.21–22), or that what purports (according to v. 30) to be a comprehensive levitical list would overlook them. Also probably missing is the preliminary introduction of the Kohathites.

2. The original purpose of the list was probably to update a previous one. The genealogical structure and terminology for some of the fathers' houses reflect a situation one generation later than that described in I Chron. 23.7ff.; e.g. Issiah succeeds Rehabiah, Jahath succeeds Shelomoth, etc. One should not exclude the possibility that biological and genealogical factors – such as the proliferation of certain families and the degeneration of others – influenced the development of the fathers' houses; it is clear in any case that the change is not a chronological matter of one generation but the result of

immanent social developments within the system of fathers' houses, in each case spanning differing lengths of time. A comparison of the two lists clarifies the nature of these developments: the affiliation of some of the fathers' houses remains unaltered; their names, and therefore their basic social structure, are unchanged. These are the sons of Hebron (v. 23) and of Mushi the son of Merari (v. 30) – seven fathers' houses in all. Other fathers' houses assume a new name but are regarded as 'sons' of the original houses, i.e. they represent a later generation. In this case the fathers' houses have undergone social changes and the balance of power has shifted, but they still recognize – and probably benefit from – their earlier affiliation. Here belong the two Amramite families (vv. 20b–21), the Izharites (v. 22), the Uzzielites (vv. 24–25) and the family of Kish the son of Mahli – six in all. The greatest transformation, however, is introduced by the complete abolition of one father's house (Eleazar the son of Mahli, v. 28) and the emergence of three completely new ones (Shoham, Zaccur and Ibri; for 'Beno' see below on v. 26), tracing their descent from Merari through a completely unknown son, Jaaziahu. Thus the Merarites have now become seven (Shoham, Zaccur, Ibri, Kish, Mahli, Eder and Jeremoth), which brings the total of fathers' houses in the list to sixteen. One may conjecture that the missing Gershonites composed the eight remaining fathers' houses, bringing the total to the presupposed twenty-four, and presenting an alternative, or rather a corrective, to the list in 23.7–23.

[20b–21] The list as it stands opens with the Amramites; its two fathers' houses Shubael and Rehabiah are descended from Moses, although neither he nor his sons are named. Shubael is succeeded by Jehediahu and Rehabiah by Isshiah; the condensed nature of the presentation shows that it is initially conceived as an 'appendix' to an already existing record.

[23] A comparison with 23.19 makes it clear that the verse records the Hebronites and should therefore be restored to read 'Of the Hebronites, Jeriah the chief etc.' (as indeed followed by RSV's 'the sons of Hebron', and others). The Hebronites remained the largest and the most stable of all the levitical branches, with the number of families unchanged (four, cf. the Shimeites in 23.10–11), and all their names retained.

[24–25] The registration of the Uzzielites is somewhat different from the preceding groups. First the elder son is mentioned and then the other is introduced as his brother. A similar manner of registration is found sporadically in other parts of the genealogical material as well (for example 7.16), but it is quite rare and its sociological significance unclear. The names of two Uzzielite families are replaced by two others, their 'sons': Shamir and Zechariah.

[26] An interesting phenomenon is exhibited by the list of the Merarites. Contrary to all other levitical genealogies, both in the Pentateuch and

Chronicles, Merari is depicted as having a third son, Jaaziah. The three fathers' houses which trace their origins from him are recorded first among the Merarites. This novelty is of course conspicuous mainly in comparison to I Chron. 23.21, and it should be clear that the phenomenon cannot be explained in biological–genealogical terms. It is hardly possible that a new 'son' had suddenly been born to Merari. In the sociological terms represented by these genealogical structures we can only conclude that in the interval between I Chron. 23.21–23 and I Chron. 24.26–30 the structure of the Merarites has undergone far-reaching changes. The fathers' house of Eleazar, the son of Mahli, the status of which had already been unsure (I Chron. 23.22), was completely abolished; the house of Mushi remained unchanged, and three new houses were established. Their actual provenance is not spelled out, and their affiliation to a new 'son' of Merari, rather than to 'sons' of subsequent generations on the list, may shed some light on the binding conventions of the genealogical system. However, the process by which the number of the Merarite families increased from five to seven should be viewed as rather long and complicated, and could not have been completed and consolidated in the span of one generation.

Verses 26b and 27b constitute a doublet; we may regard this as either a conflation or a dittography, or alternatively, either of the components may be a corruption. This second possibility is followed by Rudolph, whose suggestion (for v. 26b) 'of his sons ($b^e b\bar{a}n\bar{a}w$) Jaaziahu', while tenable from a linguistic point of view, is not attested elsewhere in the lists. In any case, 'Beno' is not a proper name (as in RSV and NEB) but a transcription of $b^e n\bar{o}$, 'his son'.

[28–29] The structuring of these verses is elliptical, as the precise affiliation of Kish (v. 29) is not stated. However, the structure parallels that of vv. 20b–21. The name of the father (Amram) is given first, followed in turn by his first son with his descendant (Shubael – Jehediahu). Then, the father's second son is recorded (Rehabiah), without any allusion to the relationship between him and those who precede. In the case of vv. 20b–21 this relationship can be supplemented from the data of 23.13–17, which presents Shubael and Rehabiah as the descendants of Gershom and Eliezer (the sons of Moses, the son of Amram) respectively. A synopsis of 20b–21 and these verses will illustrate their similar structure:

20b: ... of the sons of Amram, Shubael; of the sons of Shubael, Jehdeiah.
21: Of Rehabiah: of the sons of Rehabiah, Isshiah the chief.
28: Of Mahli: Eleazar, who had no sons.
29: Of Kish, the sons of Kish: Jerahmeel.

The difference between the parallels lies in the fact that instead of recording the name of Eleazar's son, the text mentions that Eleazar was childless. Thus, in the same way that Shubael and Rehabiah are Amramites, so are Eleazar and Kish Mahlites (as in 23.21).

This mode of registration emphasizes the nature of the present list as 'complementary notes' appended to existing records. In recognizing this, we also see that the reading of the MT is correct and should not be changed in accordance with LXX.

[30b] This is the original conclusion of the list with the statement of its purpose: 'These were the sons of the Levites according to their fathers' houses.' The title 'sons of the Levites' is rare, recurring only in I Chron. 15.15. This, however, is enough to show that no specific meaning for the present context is intended.

25 David and the chiefs of the service also set apart for the service certain of the sons of Asaph, and of Heman, and of Jeduthun, who should prophesy with lyres, with harps, and with cymbals. The list of those who did the work and of their duties was: [2] Of the sons of Asaph: Zaccur, Joseph, Nethaniah, and Asharelah, sons of Asaph, under the direction of Asaph, who prophesied under the direction of the king. [3] Of Jeduthun, the sons of Jeduthun: Gedaliah, Zeri, Jeshaiah, Shime-i, Hashabiah, and Mattithiah, six, under the direction of their father Jeduthun, who prophesied with the lyre in thanksgiving and praise to the Lord. [4] Of Heman, the sons of Heman: Bukkiah, Mattaniah, Uzziel, Shebuel, and Jerimoth, Hananiah, Hanani, Eliathah, Giddalti, and Romamti-ezer, Joshbekashah, Mallothi, Hothir, Mahazi-oth. [5] All these were the sons of Heman the king's seer, according to the promise of God to exalt him; for God had given Heman fourteen sons and three daughters. [6] They were all under the direction of their father in the music in the house of the Lord with cymbals, harps, and lyres for the service of the house of God. Asaph, Jeduthun, and Heman were under the order of the king. [7] The number of them along with their brethren, who were trained in singing to the Lord, all who were skilful, was two hundred and eighty-eight. [8] And they cast lots for their duties, small and great, teacher and pupil alike.

9 The first lot fell for Asaph to Joseph; the second to Gedaliah, to him and his brethren and his sons, twelve; [10] the third to Zaccur, his sons and his brethren, twelve; [11] the fourth to Izri, his sons and his brethren, twelve; [12] the fifth to Nethaniah, his sons and his brethren, twelve; [13] the sixth to Bukkiah, his sons and his brethren, twelve; [14] the seventh to Jesharelah, his sons and his brethren, twelve; [15] the eighth to Jeshaiah, his sons and his brethren, twelve; [16] the ninth to Mattaniah, his sons and his brethren, twelve; [17] the tenth to Shime-i, his sons and his brethren, twelve; [18] the eleventh to Azarel, his sons and his brethren, twelve; [19] the twelfth to Hashabiah, his sons and his brethren, twelve; [20] to the thirteenth, Shuba-el, his sons and his brethren, twelve; [21] to the fourteenth, Mattithiah, his sons and his brethren, twelve; [22] to the fifteenth, to Jeremoth, his sons and his brethren, twelve; [23] to the sixteenth, to Hananiah, his sons and his brethren, twelve; [24] to the seventeenth, to Joshbekashah, his sons and his brethren, twelve; [25] to the eighteenth, to Hanani his sons and his brethren, twelve; [26] to the nineteenth, to Mallothi, his sons and his brethren, twelve; [27] to the twentieth, to Eliathah, his sons and his brethren, twelve; [28] to the twenty-first, to Hothir, his sons and his brethren, twelve; [29] to the twenty-second, to Giddalti, his sons and his brethren, twelve; [30] to the twenty-third, to Mahazi-oth, his sons and his brethren, twelve; [31] to the twenty-fourth, to Romamti-ezer, his sons and his brethren, twelve.

CHAPTER 25 437

A. Notes to MT

[1] הנביאים, read הנבאים with *Qere*; [2] ואשראלה, probably אלה, ואשראל, but cf. v. 14; [3] וצרי, proposed ויצרי, cf. v. 11; וישעיהו, add ושמעי with Versions and v. 17; בכנור הנבא, inverse (cf. BHS); [6] אסף וידותון והימן, probably a gloss; [8] לעמת, insert משמרת with some MSS and Targum.

B. Notes to RSV

[1] 'certain of the sons of', MT 'the sons of' (*lamed* accusative, cf. NEB, JPS); 'who should prophesy', MT 'who prophesy'; [3] 'who prophesied with the lyre' renders MT in inverse order (cf. above); [5] 'to exalt him', MT 'to exalt', but the emendation is common; [6] read 'for the service of the house of God under the order of the king' (the three names Asaph, Jeduthun and Heman are probably a gloss); [7] 'all who were skilful', JPS 'masters', also in v. 8 (there also NEB); [8] 'for their duties', MT is understood in reverse order (so also NEB, JPS).

C. Structure, sources and form

1. Chapter 25 records the origins of the singers and their organization by lot, according to their divisions. The context is evident: the singers follow the Levites and priests and precede the gatekeepers. The structure, mode of registration and organization of this list are most similar to 24.1–19, with the clearest parallelism being between 24.2–18 and 25.9–31.

2. The chapter is composed of two equal parts: vv. 1–7 constitute a general introduction of the singers, their respective descent from the three 'fathers', a short description of their tasks, and their number; vv. 8–31 introduce the casting of lots and a stereotyped registration for the twenty-four divisions. This basic plan results in a certain duplication, as all the names (with slight variations caused by transmission) occur twice: first according to their origin in the three main branches (vv. 2–4), and again in the ordering of the divisions (vv. 9ff.). This structure is peculiar to the singers, as the Levites and gatekeepers are listed only by their descent (chs. 23, 26) and the priests only by their divisions (ch. 24).

3. In addition the chapter has other peculiar features:

(*a*) The references to the singer's ancestors emphasize their unusual merits and special status: 'prophesy', 'the king's seer', 'under the order of the king', etc. – an emphasis much stronger than for the other orders ('officers', 26.29ff., priests, 23.13).

(*b*) The singers' units are not defined as 'divisions', and the root meaning 'divide' (חלק) is entirely absent from the chapter. Since this term is prevalent throughout the pericope (24.1; 26.1 etc.), and the singers are in fact organized into twenty-four groups, the absence of the term is surprising and most probably intentional (cf. below p. 445).

(*c*) The list of the singers is unique in that the artificial element is so obvious that it has been recognized by almost all scholars. Of the sons of Heman, the nine last names seem to be fictitious, and no serious effort has been made to conceal this artificiality, which emphasizes the literary-polemic function of the lists and their weaker connection with actual conditions.

(*d*) While all of the lists are characterized by a stereotyped structure and phraseology determined by their nature and function, this is true in different measure for each list. The present chapter is especially marked in this respect, particularly in the fixed formulas of vv. 9–31, and this uniformity is also discernible in the typological numbers: twenty-four divisions of twelve singers each.

4. Very little connection exists between the present list and other source-material regarding the singers. With the exception of the three 'fathers' and a very few other names (Zaccur, Shimei, Bukkiah/Bakbukiah and Mattaniah, cf. Liver, *History of the Priests and Levites*, 61), none of those listed are mentioned anywhere else as singers.

5. The inevitable conclusion from all the above is that ch. 25 is to a great degree an artificial construction. It is based on certain presuppositions – historical or theoretical – and is guided by literary and social motives. It may be going too far to deny any historical nucleus for the chapter, but the composition as a whole is surely of a literary nature (cf. also below p. 443f.). In contrast to the levitical and priestly lists – which do reflect actual fathers' houses of the Second Temple period, even if their genealogical connections may be overworked – the record of the singers does not seem to reflect an actual operating system. In this respect the outstanding contrast to the list of singers is found in the most similar list: that of the priests, which probably served as a model for the structure of this passage. The theological motivation was the wish to provide a full analogy, down to the smallest detail, between the service of sacrifices and the service of song (cf. also on 23.30–31), but there is no evidence that such a perfect parallelism actually existed at any time in the liturgy of the Second Temple.

6. The detailed structure of the chapter is as follows:

(*a*) 1–7: 1   introduction
        2–6 the registration of the singers:
          2   the Asaphites;
          3   the sons of Jeduthun;
          4–6   the Hemanites;
        7   conclusion.

The structure is clear and straightforward, the phrasing of the opening having affinities with the conclusion:

1: 'the list of those ... was'
7: 'the number of them ... was'

These are two renderings of the same Hebrew phrase used in both cases: ויהי מספרם. The translation, while correctly indicating the different connotations of the phrase, obscures the great similarity between the two verses.

A certain degree of uniformity also obtains in the basic structuring of the smaller sections. Note the recurring phrases:

2: Of the sons of *Asaph* ... (their names) under the direction of *Asaph*.

3 Of ... the sons of *Jeduthun* ... (their names) under the direction of their *father Jeduthun.*
4 Of ... the sons of Heman ... (their names).
6 ... under the direction of their *father.*

Other recurring terms include prophesying (vv. 1, 2, 3); 'under the direction (or order) of the king' (vv. 2, 6); reference to the musical instruments (vv. 1, 3, 6).

In contrast to the great uniformity of this overall framework, there are differences of style and subject-matter between the smaller units, the most outstanding of which is their gradually increasing length. This is a characteristically Chronistic synthesis of intrinsic significance and literary elaboration. Heman is distinguished not only by his unique description in the present context as the 'king's seer', and as the most prolific of the fathers' houses (fourteen divisions as against ten for the other two), but also by the fact that the passage describes both him and his offspring in great detail. Thus, the author's favour and preference is expressed not only explicitly, but also through the code of literary elaboration.

(*b*) 8–31:   8   introduction
             9–31   the list of divisions.

With the exception of v. 9, which forms the syntactical basis of the unit, the structure follows throughout a stereotyped formula; for details cf. below.

D. *Commentary*

[1] Some features of this introduction are peculiar. First is the word *wayyab-dēl* ('set apart') used to describe David's act. This verb is employed (among other usages) for the 'separation' of the priests or Levites from the rest of the people, and their assignment for the service of God (Num. 16.9; Deut. 10.8; Num. 8.14). The 'setting apart' of the priests is found also in Chronicles, in I Chron. 23.13. By using this particular verb the Chronicler alludes to the actual initiation of the singers to their task, analogous to the 'setting apart' of the priests and Levites. Here, then, is another expression of the view, recurring in Ezra-Nehemiah and Chronicles, that is was David who introduced and established the cultic music.

Another unusual term in this context is 'the officers of the host' (*śārē haṣṣābā'*, RSV 'the chiefs of the service'; NEB 'chief officers'). It is unlikely that this refers to 'the officers of the army' (JPS) in their military capacity, as in I Chron. 26.26 or II Chron. 33.11. Rather, as recognized by the commentators, 'host' (*ṣābā'*) is the term used in the Pentateuch for the service of the Levites (Num. 4.3, 23, 30, 35; 8.24, 25), and 'the officers of the host of the service' would be the Chronicler's designation for the levitical officers, similar to 'the chiefs of the Levites' (*śārē hallewiyyim*, I Chron. 15.16). Being in charge of the levitical service, they co-operate with David in the 'setting-apart' of the singers.

The singers' function is described with the unusual term 'to prophesy', so also in the description of the three head-singers as 'prophets': Heman in v. 5, Asaph in II Chron. 29.30 and Jeduthun (or all three) in II Chron. 35.15. Several points should be made concerning this difficult issue:

(*a*) The title *ḥōzeh* ('seer') which designates the singers as prophets is common in Chronicles, being also attached to Gad, Jedo (RSV Iddo), Iddo, Jehu, and the prophets in general (I Chron. 21.9; 29.29; II Chron. 9.29; 12.15; 19.2; 33.18).

(*b*) The verb which describes their activity, the Nif'al of *nb'*, seems to be used in reference both to them (vv. 2, 3) and to their 'sons', that is, the singers in general (v. 1, cf. below).

(*c*) An obvious question concerns how the Chronicler conceives of the singers' activity as 'prophecy'. The available evidence, although too scarce to make possible an unequivocal answer, may still provide some insights (cf. also D. L. Petersen, *Late Israelite Prophecy*, Missoula 1977, 62ff.; R. H. Wilson, *Prophecy and Society in Ancient Israel*, Philadelphia 1980, 292–7).

The singers are called 'seers' first of all because they are regarded as composers of the Temple psalmody, probably already seen as the product of divine inspiration (Liver, *History of the Priests and Levites*, 87). Thus in II Chron. 29.30: 'to sing praises to the Lord with the words of David and of Asaph the seer'. Moreover, according to one of the concepts of Chronicles, it is the prophet who transmits to the people not only God's commands in *ad hoc* matters but also his will as expressed by lasting commandments and institutions (cf. Japhet, 'Law and "the Law" in Ezra-Nehemiah', *Proceedings of the Ninth World Congress of Jewish Studies, panel sessions*, Jerusalem 1988, 99–104). The clearest expression of this view is found in II Chron. 29.25: 'for the commandment *is* (RSV was) from the Lord through his prophets' (cf. the commentary, *ad loc.*). This important general statement is attached to the preceding appointment of the singers: 'and he stationed the Levites ... with cymbals, harps and lyres according to the commandment of David and of Gad the king's seer and of Nathan the prophet'. Here the prophets referred to are David, Gad and Nathan, but the statement should be compared to II Chron. 35.15: 'the singers ... were in their place according to the command of David, and Asaph, and Heman, and Jeduthun the king's seer' (cf. the commentary *ad loc.*). It would seem, then, that the appointment of the singers to their tasks was in accordance with God's command, delivered by the prophets, among whom the singers' fathers are included.

In addition, vv. 2–3 make it clear that the singers' actual performance, i.e. the singing and playing which are always combined, is called 'prophesying'.

This view is probably connected to earlier phenomena, such as the one described in I Sam. 10.5: 'you will meet a band of prophets ... with harp, tambourine, flute and lyre before them, prophesying'. Some scholars have regarded this facet of the singing as a continuation of the supposed 'cultic prophecy' of the first Temple (cf. S. Mowinckel, *Psalmenstudien* III, Amsterdam 1961, 1–105; A. R. Johnson, *The Cultic Prophet and Israel's Psalmody*, Cardiff 1979; Petersen, *Late Biblical Prophecy*, 62ff., and Myers, 171–2). Did the Chronicler regard as 'prophecy' only the activity of the three head-singers whom he sees as David's contemporaries, or did he regard the Temple singing of his own day as 'prophesying', and if so, in what specific manner?

I Chronicles 25.1 is the only instance where the verb 'prophesy' (in the version of the *Qere*) is attached to the 'sons of Asaph, Heman and Jeduthun', and on the evidence of this verse the Temple music as such, throughout the generations, is depicted as prophecy. Such a view would indicate that 'prophecy' is not ascribed to isolated, unique phenomena, but to the permanent singing establishment, which is part of the cultic framework. Yet it should also be noted that the singers are described in the same context as 'those who did the work' (*'anšē mᵉlā'kāh*), a title which is similar to that used for the Levites in general (I Chron. 23.24 etc.), and others as well. The exact manner in which the performing of sacred music is regarded as prophecy is not made clear by the references in Chronicles. It seems that this term is meant to ascribe to the Temple music a special significance as the most elevated function of the cult, rather than indicate the continuation of an earlier phenomena. One wonders whether this view led to the creation of the version of the *Kethib* 'the prophets' (*hannᵉbī'īm*), which can properly be a reference to the three head-singers alone, and not to the establishment as a whole.

The three instruments mentioned here (and in reverse order in v. 6) are lyres, harps and cymbals – the actual instruments of the time, recurring in Chronicles in all the relevant contexts.

[2] The position of the Asaphites at the head of the list is probably a sign of their priority among the singers. In other lists the singers as a whole are regarded as 'the sons of Asaph' (Ezra 2.41), and the special position of Asaph is emphasized also in II Chron. 29.30; 35.15. Yet in spite of their seniority, they comprise only four fathers' houses and form the smallest group among the singers. This means that in the actual Temple establishment the families ascribed to Asaph formed only a minority while the house of Heman was gaining momentum (cf. also I Chron. 15.17, etc.).

The first of the Asaphites, Zaccur, also appears with the same affiliation in other lists of singers (Neh. 12.35; I Chron. 9.15 as Zichri); in I Chron. 15.18,

20 and 16.5, Zechariah (probably to be identified with Zaccur) is 'of the second order' to Asaph. All the other Asaphite families – Joseph, Nethaniah and Asharelah – are found only in this context. On the other hand, in the present list Mattaniah and probably also Bukkiah (if we identify him with Bakbukiah), who are affiliated with Asaph in Ezra-Nehemiah (Neh. 11.17, 22; 12.35; and 12.8 without reference to Asaph), are related to Heman. This may indicate the ramification of original Asaphite families to form an independent fathers' house, identified as Heman, which gradually acquired equal, and eventually superior, status.

The name 'Asharelah' is difficult because of the unusual ending -elah. Since the number of the sons of Asaph is missing in this verse, in contrast to the totals for the other families given in vv. 3 and 5, and since the words 'the sons of Asaph' are unaccountably repeated, it has been suggested that the text be regarded as corrupt and reconstructed as 'and Asarel [four. These were] the sons of Asaph' (cf. Rudolph, 164). A simpler reconstruction is also possible (cf. above, p. 437). The same name, however, with slight variation, recurs in v. 14.

[3] Five sons of Jeduthun are listed, but the total given is 'six'; the missing name 'Shimei' (or Shemaiah), mentioned in v. 17, should be restored here (following one MS and some Versions). Shimei (Shemaiah, Shammua) is also, of all the six, the most strongly affiliated with Jeduthun (Neh. 11.17; I Chron. 9.16). Jeduthun is distinguished from the other singers by a special reference to his musical instrument and performance (v. 4). I have already pointed out the gradual increase in detail in this passage, which reaches its climax with Heman.

The main questions regarding Jeduthun concern the meaning of his name and his relationship with Ethan, who replaces him in I Chron. 6.44 [MT 6.29] and I Chron. 15.17, 19. Gese has suggested ('Zur Geschichte der Kultsänger am Zweiten Tempel', in *Von Sinai zum Sion*, Munich 1974, 147–58, followed by Williamson, 121), that the branch of Ethan replaced that of Jeduthun, and this is the latest stage in the development of the singers' order in Chronicles representing either the standpoint of the Chronicler himself or a post-Chronistic view. Although Gese's suggestion is basically correct, it seems to require certain qualifications.

The phenomenon exhibited by the interchange of 'Jeduthun' and 'Ethan' should not, to my mind, be regarded as reflecting a historical-sociological process in which a new branch of singers took the place of a degenerate one. This should rather be viewed as a literary phenomenon of a homiletic nature, to be ascribed to the Chronicler himself. The origin of the singers of 'Jeduthun', as well as the meaning of the name, are unclear. It already appears as a levitical family, probably of singers, in Neh. 11.17, 'and Abda the son of ... Jeduthun', and again in I Chron. 9.16. In the earlier lists of Ezra-

Nehemiah all the singers are described as 'the sons of Asaph' (Ezra 2.41; 3.10; Neh. 7.44), but Neh. 11.17 already testifies to the division of the singers into three components, represented here by 'Mattaniah ... the son of Asaph', 'Bakbukiah, the second among his brethren' and 'Abda ... the son of Jeduthun'. The first two apparently belong to Asaph, the third to a new element, Jeduthun. As for the name, it has been suggested, following the evidence of Psalms, that at a certain stage what was originally a musical term became the designation of this family of singers (Liver, *History of the Priests and Levites*, 84ff.; B. Bayer, 'The Titles of the Psalms. A Renewed Investigation of an Old Problem', *Yuval* IV, 1982, 77–81).

Alongside this setting of the actual singing establishment, there probably existed an independent tradition of the 'forefathers of the singers', the clearest expression of which is found in the headings of the Psalms. Next to Asaph we find there the names 'Heman the Ezrahite' (Ps. 88.1) and 'Ethan the Ezrahite' (Ps. 89.1). Thus, at a certain stage of the development two parallel situations obtained: an actual establishment of singers, consisting of three branches affiliated with Asaph and Jeduthun, and a literary tradition of the 'three forefathers' of David's time, who were Asaph (the strongest element), Heman and Ethan. These forefathers were affiliated (according to Chronicles at least), with Levi, and traced their origin to Gershom, Kohath and Merari. The subsequent stage was an inevitable corollary of the previous ones, and consisted of a full intergration of the parallel lines, facilitated by the common element: Asaph (cf. the analogy of the symmetry between Zadok as Eleazarite and Abiathar as Ittamarite in I Chron. 24). The three branches of singers were affiliated to the three 'forefathers', first by the addition of Heman and then by 'Hebraizing' the inexplicable name 'Jeduthun' into 'Ethan', a change which was also graphically and phonetically extremely simple (איתן – ידתן). The two came to be regarded as one.

[4] The sons of Heman are fourteen, but it was noticed long ago that only the first seven bear names which actually conform to the practices of the biblical onomasticon, while the last seven are unusual in their formulation (four are verbs, one an invocation, *'elī 'ātāh*, and two are of extremely irregular form). Some of these have remained completely unaccountable. The verse has attracted a great deal of attention (cf. the bibliography in Liver, 58–61 and Williamson, 167), and it has been shown that from 'Hananiah' onward the names actually join to form short poetical verses. Several attempts have been made to reconstruct them as an opening part of a psalm; indeed, the first part can be smoothly read as such: *ḥānnēnī yāh ḥānnēnī, 'ēlī 'attāh* ('Be gracious to me, O Lord, be gracious; thou art my God ...'), but this clarity deteriorates as we proceed. It has been suggested recently that the words do not add up to a continuous lyric piece but to 'incipits of hymns sung by the Levitical singers' (Myers, 173).

How should this unusual phenomenon be accounted for? Theoretically it can be explained from two opposite angles. One sees the list as indeed a reflection of historical circumstances; at one stage or another in the development of the singers, some fathers' houses were actually named by the opening verses of a certain psalm. This psalm could have been one attributed to their 'father' or characteristic of their music. According to this view, the present text is no more than a reflection of an unusual, but still probable, historical situation. From the opposite angle, these names are regarded as a literary fiction, which never had any actual basis, but was adduced in order to set up a full system of twenty-four divisions of singers. Since no actual antecedent was found, an artificial technique had to be followed.

There are inherent difficulties in each of these solutions; in either case the phenomenon remains amazing. It seems, however, that the second angle reflects in a better way the literary inclinations of the Chronicler and his ways of integrating his theological and historical views into his source-material. We have here a 'programme', the essentials of which are the establishing of a system of singers parallel in every detail to that of priests and Levites, with the emphasis on the Davidic initiative for this parallel system. In the absence of actual genealogical data and a well-developed tradition, the Chronicler formulates his programme according to a stereotyped system, and supplies the missing elements by repeating the names twice: in the preliminary listing according to their 'fathers', and in the allocation of their divisions in numerical order.

[5] The purpose of this verse is to substantiate what could already have been inferred from the bare list – the unusual proliferation of Heman, to whom fourteen out of the twenty-four divisions are ascribed. In order to give this honour a natural setting, the verse states that 'God had given Heman fourteen sons and three daughters'. Daughters do not regularly form fathers' houses and therefore are unnecessary for the present context, but their appearance somehow grants the unusual blessing of Heman a tone of probability. The numbers, however, are certainly typological, and are identical with those of Job's children after his restoration, when 'the Lord gave Job twice as much as he had before' (Job 42.10), that is: 'he had fourteen (NEB margin; RSV seven) sons and three daughters' (42.13).

A certain difficulty is raised by the phrase 'according to the promise of God to exalt *him*' (*l^eharim qeren*). The accusative pronoun 'him' is supplied by the translation, and 'the promise of God' is literally 'the words of God'. The difficulty is illustrated by the alternative translation of JPS: '[who uttered] prophecies of God for His great glory'. The stand taken by JPS puts the clause in better parallelism to 2b, 3b; on the other hand, the phrase *l^eharim qeren*, which is peculiar to the psalmodic idiom, usually has a human object: the righteous man, the people, etc. (Ps. 89.17 [MT 18]; 148.14, I Sam. 2.1, etc.; so also the Midrash, Yalkut Shimeoni II, 81). If indeed the phrase refers to Heman, no attempt is made to derive the blessing from his name by way of midrashic interpretation (cf. by contrast Rehabiah). Note also the way in which the Chronicler makes use in his prose of phrases which are exclusively characteristic of poetry.

[6] The verse opens with a repetition of the introductory words from v. 5, 'all these' (*kol 'ēlleh*, obscured by the different translations), followed by a detailed reference to the specific roles of Heman's sons: they are under the supervision of their father; they are occupied in 'song' (RSV music); they play specified instruments; and their appointment is by the king. (This last note is obscured by RSV, which, ignoring the Hebrew word order, regards *'al y'dē hammelek*, 'on the order of the king', as describing, not the sons of Heman but Asaph, Jeduthun and Heman. These last three names, however, are probably a gloss). This detailed conclusion is indeed appropriate for the singers as a whole, but the words 'all these' and the gradually increasing detail indicate that the author has a special interest in the house of Heman, according to him the dominant factor among the singers.

[7] The first part of the chapter is concluded by a numerical summary, making it clear that although the preceding names were presented as individuals, 'sons of so-and-so', from the outset they were intended to designate groups, although the prevalent term, 'father's house', is absent from the singers' pericope. Just as the four 'sons' of Asaph, six of Jeduthun and fourteen of Heman are technically regarded as 'brothers', so are the members of each individual group termed 'brethen' (RSV) or 'kinsmen' (NEB and JPS), and later 'brethren and sons' (vv. 9bff.).

The schematic number 288 anticipates the following list, in which twenty-four divisions contain twelve members each (vv. 9ff.). In spite of its typological nature, the number is comparable to the count of the singers in the list of the returnees: 128 (Ezra 2.41) or 138 (Neh. 7.44), as against over four thousand priests. Although more than double these figures, the number in Chronicles is still rather small; cf. also below.

[8] Although the syntax links this verse to what has gone before, it in fact opens a new section, concerned with the organization of the divisions by lot. The system is similar to the one used for the other orders, but the term 'divisions' is absent; instead we find *mišmeret* (correctly translated as 'duty') in what seems to be a somewhat corrupted text, *mišmeret l''ummat*. RSV 'for their duties' reverses the order, but perhaps the Targum should be preferred in reading 'duty against [duty]'.

We have seen that the casting of lots among the priests was to decide the order of the fathers' houses/divisions, and these were set 'all alike' (24.5, literally 'these against these'). For the Levites the lots were cast 'against their brethren', the priests (*l^e'ummat* *'^{a}hēhem*), and the fathers' houses among (*l^e'ummat*, literally 'against') themselves (24.31). By contrast, for the singers the lots are cast 'for their duties' or 'duty against duty', and those who participate are 'small and great, teacher and pupil alike' (v. 8). This may mean that the matter determined by lot in this case is not the same: it is not the rotating order of the 'divisions', but the composition and division of labour within the singers' groups themselves, each of which was to perform its tasks according to its appointed 'duty'. This could also account for the relatively small number of the singers: while each of the priestly divisions served two weeks per year, the divisions rotating every week, there seems to be no parallel rotating system amongst the singers. They are grouped in a general, overall arrangement according to 'duties', for which the given number is quite sufficient. This would again emphasize the artificial nature of the following list, creating a forced analogy between the priests and the singers.

Yet some kind of flexibility of function should also be considered for the singers. According to Neh. 12.28–29, the singers lived outside Jerusalem and were summoned to the city for the special occasion of the dedication of the wall. It might be that on certain public occasions, such as the festivals, additional singers would be recruited to assist the regular Temple staff.

[9–31] From a syntactical point of view the whole passage is one sentence, governed by its opening: 'The [first] lot fell to'. The list itself is a different presentation of the names already recorded. For each of the groups the details given are very specific, similar to the record of the military divisions in ch. 27. They are: the ordinal number, the name of the group (determined by the head singer of the group), the composition of the group, and the number of its members.

The literary method adopted by the author is of interest. Since the list follows a stereotyped formula, it could have been contracted into a concise passage, giving first the list of names and ordinal numbers and then concluding with a single summarizing sentence, such as: 'each group consisted of the head, his brothers and sons, twelve in all'. (Such a technique, with the actual phrasing determined by the context, is followed in 24.31.) Instead, the author chose to present again the twenty-four names mentioned already, and to repeat the clause 'his sons and his brethren, twelve' twenty-three times, demonstrating again that repetition and quantitative elaboration are mustered to the service of emphatic expression.

[9] This verse, although it opens the stereotyped list, deviates from the set mould in almost every conceivable way. Syntactically it is a complete sentence: 'the first lot fell for Asaph to Joseph'. It refers to the forefather Asaph, but omits any reference to the composition and size of the group (supplied, as a matter of fact, in LXX). The second half of the verse ('the

second to Gedaliah, etc.') is more in line with the formulaic mould, but still deviates from it in certain details: the name is followed by the ordinal number (literally 'Gedaliah the second'), and not the reverse as in the succeeding names; it contains an additional pronoun $h\bar{u}$' (RSV 'to him'), and the order of 'sons' and 'brethren' is reversed. All these variations are more likely expressions of premeditated stylistic technique than the result of textual corruption in the process of transmission. Their aim is to give the opening of the list a form of its own, adapted to – and yet deviating from – the fixed formula. As it stands, the opening is a narrative sequel to the preceding verse, and therefore $l^{e'}\bar{a}s\bar{a}p$ ('for Asaph') is not a dittography of $l^ey\bar{o}s\bar{e}p$ ('to Joseph') or a secondary addition, but an authentic component. In the same way, the omission of 'his brethren and and his sons, twelve' after 'Joseph' should be interpreted as stylistic. The first line as it stands, with its peculiar additional details and omissions, is equal in length to all the following lines, and thus a certain rythmical balance is achieved.

The number of singers in each group, twelve, is also documented in the Mishnah for one setting of musicians: 'There were never less than twelve Levites standing on the Platform, and their number could be increased without end' (Arakhin, 2.6). The standard twelve were composed of nine lyres (ibid. 2.5), two harps (ibid. 2.3), and one cymbal (ibid. 2.5). The same number is obtained also in I Chron. 16.5–6, although in a different way: nine harps and lyres, two trumpets and one cymbal, to be sounded by the head of the group (cf. I Chron. 15.19). It should be asked whether the Mishnah is an authentic reflection of the musical arrangements at a given time in the Second Temple period, or just a reasonable adaptation of the given number, twelve.

[10ff.] The order of the groups is of interest:

(a) Although the first lot is given to the sons of Asaph, it falls not to Zaccur his eldest son but to Joseph his second. There is no way to determine whether or not the order bears any hierarchical significance (cf. also on ch. 24).

(b) A comparison of the order of names in this part of the chapter with that of the first part affords some insights into the method of casting lots. It demonstrates that in each case the lots were cast among members of two given groups and singled out one member of each group. In the first four rounds the branch of Asaph constituted one of the two groups; its counter-parts were Jeduthun in the first, second and fourth rounds, Heman in the third. After the four members of Asaph were chosen, the lots alternated between the sons of Heman (beginning with Mattaniahu) and the remaining sons of Jeduthun, up to the fourteenth round. From the fifteenth round on, the sons of Heman cast lots among themselves; the first two come out according to their genealogical order (Jeremoth, Hananiah), but the remaining groups have been interchanged in some way.

Asaph	*Jeduthun*	*Heman*
1. Joseph	2. Gedaliah	
3. Zaccur	4. Izri	
5. Nethaniah		6. Bukkiah
7. Jesharelah	8. Jeshaiah	

	10. Shimei	9. Mattaniah
	12. Hashabiah	11. Azarel/Uzziel
	14. Mattathiah	13. Shubael

15. Jeremoth	16. Hananiah
17. Joshbekashah	18. Hanani
19. Mallothi	20. Eliathah
21. Hothir	22. Giddalti
23. Mahazioth	24. Romamtiezer

If we assume that the same method was followed for the choosing of the priestly divisions, then the first sixteen would have been arranged alternately, one name for Eleazar and one for Ithamar. From the seventeenth division onwards, the Eleazarites would have cast lots among themselves.

(*c*) Although the mould is firmly set, a certain variation appears in the use of the *lamed*, denoting 'to'. RSV supplies 'to' for all the names, but in fact it is found only for part of them, attached either to the proper names alone (Joseph, Izri, Hashabiah), to the ordinal number alone (thirteenth, fourteenth), or to both (from the fifteenth name to the end). There is thus an increasing use of the *lamed*, which affords variety even in this strictly uniform framework.

(*d*) Unlike other chapters, the list of the singers ends without any conclusion.

26 As for the divisions of the gatekeepers: of the Korahites, Meshelemiah the son of Kore, of the sons of Asaph. ² And Meshelemiah had sons: Zechariah the first-born, Jedia-el the second, Zebadiah the third, Jathni-el the fourth, ³ Elam the fifth, Jeho-hanan the sixth, Elie-ho-enai the seventh. ⁴ And Obed-edom had sons: Shemaiah the first-born, Jehozabad the second, Joah the third, Sachar the fourth, Nethanel the fifth, ⁵ Ammi-el the sixth, Issachar the seventh, Pe-ullethai the eighth; for God blessed him. ⁶ Also to his son Shemaiah were sons born who were rulers in their fathers' houses, for they were men of great ability. ⁷ The sons of Shemaiah: Othni, Repha-el, Obed, and Elzabad, whose brethren were able men, Elihu and Semachiah. ⁸ All these were of the sons of Obed-edom with their sons and brethren, able men qualified for the service; sixty-two of Obed-edom. ⁹ And Meshelemiah had sons and brethren, able men, eighteen. ¹⁰ And Hosah, of the sons of Merari, had sons: Shimri the chief (for though he was not the first-born, his father made him chief), ¹¹ Hilkiah the second, Tebaliah the third, Zechariah the fourth: all the sons and brethren of Hosah were thirteen.

12 These divisions of the gatekeepers, corresponding to their chief men, had duties, just as their brethren did, ministering in the house of the Lord; ¹³ and they cast lots by fathers' houses, small and great alike, for their gates. ¹⁴ The lot for the east fell to Shelemiah. They cast lots also for his son Zechariah, a shrewd counsellor, and his lot came out for the north. ¹⁵ Obed-edom's came out for the south, and to his sons was allotted the storehouse. ¹⁶ For Shuppim and Hosah it came out for the west, at the gate of Shallecheth on the road that goes up. Watch corresponded to watch. ¹⁷ On the east there were six each day, on the north four each day, on the south four each day, as well as two and two at the storehouse; ¹⁸ and for the parbar on the west there were four at the road and two at the parbar. ¹⁹ These were the divisions of the gatekeepers among the Korahites and the sons of Merari.

20 And of the Levites, Ahijah had charge of the treasuries of the house of God and the treasuries of the dedicated gifts. ²¹ The sons of Ladan, the sons of the Ger-shonites belonging to Ladan, the heads of the fathers' houses belonging to Ladan the Gershonite: Jehieli. 22 The sons of Jehieli, Zetham and Joel his brother, were in charge of the treasuries of the house of the Lord. ²³ Of the Amramites, the Izharites, the Hebronites, and the Uzzielites – ²⁴ and Shebuel the son of Gershom, son of Moses, was chief officer in charge of the treasuries. ²⁵ His brethren: from Eliezer were his son Rehabiah, and his son Zichri, and his son Shelomoth. ²⁶ This Shelomoth and his brethren were in charge of all the treasuries of the dedicated gifts which David the king, and the heads of the fathers' houses, and the officers of the thousands and the hundreds, and the commanders of the army, had dedicated. ²⁷ From spoil won in battles they dedicated gifts for the maintenance of the house of the Lord. ²⁸ Also all that Samuel the seer, and Saul the son of Kish, and Abner the son of Ner, and Joab the son of Zeruiah had dedicated – all dedicated gifts were in the care of Shelomoth and his brethren.

29 Of the Izharites, Chenaniah and his sons were appointed to outside duties for Israel, as officers and judges. [30] Of the Hebronites, Hashabiah and his brethren, one thousand seven hundred men of ability, had the oversight of Israel westward of the Jordan for all the work of the Lord and for the service of the king. [31] Of the Hebronites, Jerijah was chief of the Hebronites of whatever genealogy or fathers' houses. (In the fortieth year of David's reign search was made and men of great ability among them were found at Jazer in Gilead.) [32] King David appointed him and his brethren, two thousand seven hundred men of ability, heads of fathers' houses, to have the oversight of the Reubenites, the Gadites, and the half-tribe of the Manassites for everything pertaining to God and for the affairs of the king.

A. Notes to MT

[1] לשערים, probably read השערים (cf. vv. 12, 19 and commentary); אסף, LXX^B and 9.19אביאסף/אביסף; [6] הממשלים, probably read המשלים (dittography) or המשלים;אביהם;הם משלים, אביותם? [7] אלובד, read ואלזבד;אחיו, probably ואחיו; [16] לשפים, delete, dittography of האספים;שלכת, LXX reads לשכה, proposed הלשכות. שער [17] למזרח הלוים,למזרחה ליום,read הלשכות, following LXX, cf. commentary; [17end-18beginning] שנים לפרבר, dittography of the end of v. 18, delete; [20] אחיה, read אחיהם, with LXX; [21] corrupt, cf. commentary; [22] בני יחיאלי, gloss? [26] לשרי, read ושרי?

B. Notes to RSV

[12] 'corresponding to their chief men' (לראשי הגברים), NEB 'the male heads of families', cf. also 24.4; [15] 'storehouse', NEB 'gatehouse', JPS 'vestibule'; [20] 'Ahiah', NEB 'their fellow Levites', cf. above.

C. Structure, sources and form

1. Chapter 26 comprises two distinct parts, dedicated respectively to the gatekeepers (vv. 1–19) and to an additional group of Levites: treasurers, officers and judges (vv. 20–32). While both parts are composite, they differ in their general character, manner of registration and sources, and each should be dealt with separately.

2. The structure of vv. 1–19 may be viewed in two ways, depending on our understanding of the role of v. 12. If that verse is regarded as a conclusion of the list of gatekeepers, then we have two distinct sections:

1–12: the list of gatekeepers
13–19: their organization by lot.

Each of these sections would have its own introduction (vv. 1a, 13) and conclusion (vv. 12, 19).

On the other hand, however, the whole pericope may constitute a single section, framed by v. 1a and v. 19, which are clearly related by repetition. In this case, vv. 12–13 are a syntactical sequence with a single subject, 'the divisions of the gate-keepers', and form an intermediate link between the list of gatekeepers and their organization by lot. Thus:

1a: heading
1b–11: list of gatekeepers
12–13: transition section, both conclusion and introduction
14–18: organization by lot
19: conclusion.

Exactly the same structure is also found in ch. 25, where vv. 7–8 may serve the same function and have the same syntactical sequence as vv. 12–13 here.

The short heading (1a), containing only two words, is similar to those of the Levites (23.6a), and the priests (24.1).

3. It has been proposed that since the conclusion of v. 19 refers to only two families of gatekeepers, and since the family of Obed-edom is not explicitly connected to any levitical branch, vv. 4–8 should be regarded as a later interpolation. A corollary of this basic view would also regard as secondary vv. 14–18, which must be from the same origin as or later than vv. 4–8, since they depict Obed-edom as an integral component (cf. Rothstein, 465; Welch, 91ff.; and recently Williamson, 169).

However, a closer examination of the literary structure will render this view highly improbable. Two themes are developed in vv. 1–11: the enumeration of the gate-keepers' 'sons' (or fathers' houses), and the recording of the number of individual gatekeepers in each group; these are presented as follows:

I. (a) Genealogy of Meshelemiah (vv. 1b-3)
   (b) Genealogy of Obed-edom (vv. 4–7)
   (c) Number of gatekeepers of Obed-edom (v. 8)
   (d) Number of gatekeepers of Meshelemiah (v. 9)
II. (e) Genealogy of the Merarites (vv. 10–11a)
   (f) Number of the Merarites (v. 11b).

The two groups, I and II, follow a basic pattern: 'genealogy' first and 'statistics' second. However, since the first group is composite, its unity is expressed by an inner chiastic structure, with the last verse referring back to the first (ad, bc). One should not then regard v. 9 as the continuation of v. 3 (which in fact is a rather clumsy sequence): the original order is exactly as it stands.

In addition there are clear elements in the section which demonstrate its original literary unity. Each of the three enumerations opens in the same way: 'And x had sons' (v. 2 for Meshelemiah; v. 4 for Obed-edom; v. 10 for Hosah), and – in a surprisingly systematic manner unprecedented in any of the former chapters – the sons of each of the branches are identified by ordinal numbers: first-born, second, third, etc. (vv. 2–5, 10–11; for vv. 6–7, which are the exception which proves the rule, cf. below). The unity of the literary framework should therefore be the key for understanding the gatekeepers' respective affiliations: the major component 'the Korahites' consists of two sub-branches, Meshelemiah and Obed-edom, while the Merarites are represented only by Hosah.

Consequently, there is no reason to assess vv. 14–18 as secondary. They are already connected to vv. 4–8, and the two passages together conform to the general pattern of this pericope, which deals both with the divisions and with their organization by lot.

4. As demonstrated already (see p. 410), the genealogical link between the cultic orders and Levi's three sons (Gershom, Kohath and Merari) is portrayed differently in each case. This variety is also retained in the case of the gatekeepers. The largest and most dominant branch, according to the present context, is the family of Obed-edom; however, their link with 'Korah', their levitical 'father', is not explicitly worked out. Obed-edom himself is probably identified with 'Obed-edom the Gittite', in whose house the ark rested after the crisis of Uzzah (II Sam. 6.6–12//I Chron. 13.9–14), that is, a personality known from the history of David. His 'anchor' in history is thus established (as in the case of Zadok and Ahimelech the priests in ch. 24) more firmly than that of the head singers, whose activity in the time of David is not attested in the book of Samuel. However, the precise link between this Obed-edom and Levi is nowhere developed – in contrast to Zadok (I Chr. 6.1ff. [MT 5.27]) and the three head singers (I Chron. 6.15ff [MT 6.1ff.]).

The family of Meshelemiah traced its ancestry to Asaph (v. 1), who should most probably be identified with 'Ebiasaph' (I Chron. 9.19 and 6.23, 37 [MT 8, 22]). Since in I Chron. 9.19 'Ebiasaph' is presented as 'the son of Korah', the genealogical tree can be more fully reconstructed in this case, although the gap between Korah and Levi must be filled from other sources. According to Exod. 6.16–24, the line is Levi – Kohath – Izhar – Korah (cf. also I Chron. 6.37–38, [MT 22–23]), but other genea-logical traditions could equally have existed in this regard, cf. mainly II Chron 20.19.

The third family, Hosah, is linked to Levi's son Merari, but only by the general phrase 'of the sons of Merari' (26.10), with no further genealogical detail.

The significance of this manner of registration of the gatekeepers – which amounts in fact to their legitimization – should be understood in the light of the actual traditions regarding them. The family which displays the greatest persistence is that mentioned first: Meshelemiah. Six families of gatekeepers are recorded in the lists of returnees in Ezra 2//Neh. 7, the first of which is 'Shallum' (Ezra 2.42//Neh. 7.45). In I Chron. 9.17 he is titled 'the chief', and his genealogy is provided: 'Shallum the son of Kore, the son of Ebiasaph, son of Korah' (v. 19). Since the alternating forms Shallum/Shelemiah are fully consonant with the practice of this period (cf. Zechariah/Zaccur; Shemaiah/Shammua; Jedaia/Jaddua, etc.), Shallum should be identified with Meshelemiah and the family regarded as having its origins in the earliest days of the Restoration. Second in prestige is the family of Obed-edom, not yet mentioned in Ezra-Nehemiah, but recurring in Chronicles. The least known or most loosely rooted family, also in this context the smallest, is Hosah, mentioned again only once: I Chron. 16.38.

What are the general conclusions to be drawn from these data of tradition and genealogy? It is generally accepted that the initial status of the gatekeepers (reflected in Ezra-Nehemiah) was not regarded as levitical. Their integration into the Levites was a slower and less dynamic process than with the singers. The view prevailing in Chronicles was that the gatekeepers were Levites, but not enough effort had been invested in producing the exact genealogies. The main family of Shallum/Meshelemiah was defined as 'Korahite', and its transposition from the time of the Restoration to David's day left many gaps in the genealogical tree; the family of Obed-edom, only vaguely and abstractly linked to 'the Korahites', had no genea-logical tradition at all, while its eponymic father was found in one of the historical figures of David's time. The last and weakest tradition obtains for Hosah, whose sole identification is the undefined 'of the sons of Merari'. Thus, although the order of the gatekeepers had become well established, and their duties clearly delineated, no convincing effort had been made to supply genealogical detail to confirm their levitical descent.

5. The father's houses of the gatekeepers number twenty-four: seven of Shelemiah, thirteen of Obed-edom and four of Hosah. The system of the gatekeepers is thus described as parallel to all the other cultic orders. At the same time, twenty-two or twenty-four is also the number of individuals in each watch. This raises the obvious question of authenticity: to what degree are the systems presented here authentic representations of Second Temple arrangements? For lack of supporting evidence the answer cannot be definite, but it seems that a distinction should be made between the numbers 22/24 for each watch (vv. 14–18) and the total of twenty-four fathers' houses (vv. 1–11). While the latter does seem to contain artificial elements, it is difficult to doubt the authenticity of the former (for more detail cf. the commentary).

6. The second part of the chapter (vv. 20–32) is composite. To judge from the heading 'And of the Levites', or 'And the fellow-Levites', this is a supplementary list to 23.6–23 (and 24.20b–30). Some details in the present passage are indeed similar, yet it lacks precisely those elements which are common to all the previous material, and incorporates many original features. The section contains only a minimum of genealogical records, and even these relate to individuals rather than to fathers' houses, although some of these individuals are provided with genealogical trees. There is no trace in this section of the number twenty-four as the basis of any kind of organization, nor is there any casting of lots. Most tellingly, there is no introductory definition of the group as a whole. Only in v. 29 is the title 'officers and judges' mentioned, linking the section to 23.4. We seem to have here a compilation, the various components of which have not reached full integration.

7. The section has two major components: a list of treasurers and their responsibilities (vv. 20–28) and a record of officers and judges and their spheres of duty (vv. 29–32). While these two are not intrinsically related, some kind of connection is provided by the interpolated v. 23, which introduces the four sons of Kohath, thereby suggesting a genealogical relationship between the Amramites on one hand (vv. 24–28) and the Izharites and Hebronites on the other (vv. 29–32). Since the introduction of the Amramites in v. 23 follows a branch of the Gershonites in vv. 21–22, a certain external continuity is achieved. In the overall context of chs. 23ff., the passage as a whole defines the fourth levitical order, that of 'officers and judges'.

8. The very concept of such an 'order' in the framework of the 'Levites' is peculiar; its existence is never mentioned in any of the descriptions relating to the cultic establishment in Israel, including Chronicles itself. We do find in the Bible explicit allusions to 'officers and judges' (or 'judges and officers') together, but always in the context of political leadership or bureaucracy, never connected with the cultic personnel in general or the Levites in particular. Separating the two components of the phrase, we find the view that the 'officers' are Levites, or *vice versa*, that the Levites are officers, but this too is peculiar to Chronicles, found in the present context (23.4; 26.29; perhaps also 27.1) and twice more (II Chron. 19.11; 34.13). The identification of 'judges' as Levites, likewise limited to Chronicles, is still more tenuous, found only here and in II Chron. 19.8.

454 I CHRONICLES

9. The peculiar testimony of Chronicles should be further considered from a historical perspective. In the present context, David, in the fortieth year of his reign, appoints 'officers and judges' over Israel, on both sides of the Jordan, as part of the preparations for Solomon's succession. All of these 'officers and judges', whose responsibility was 'for all the work of the Lord and for the service of the king' (v. 30), were of levitical descent, belonging to either the Izharites or Hebronites, and in appointing them the system of 'officers and judges' had been established. Finally, this act is one aspect of the overall organization of the levitical orders. In the Former Prophets, however, the limited references to 'officers and judges' are confined to the book of Joshua (8.33; 23.2; 24.1), the phrase itself probably being Deuteronomistic in origin (cf. Deut. 16.18). 'Judge/s' alone are mentioned, of course, in the book of Judges (passim), and a few times in Samuel-Kings (I Sam. 8.1, 2; II Sam. 15.4; II Kings. 15.5).

When the separate components of the Chronicler's portrait are analysed in isolation from their overall framework, some probably historical elements emerge. The possibility that David may have organized a comprehensive administrative system to consolidate his rule in all the corners of his kingdom is actually granted by all historians. The difficulty lies in accepting the Chronicler's definition of this system as 'levitical' and the use of the Deuteronomistic term 'officers and judges' in describing its role. It is also hard to imagine that this broad bureaucratic system was based on a small number of families, all belonging to one tribe.

It is possible, therefore, that the Chronicler did have at his disposal certain historical sources, containing details on the administration of the kingdom in David's time (cf. also on ch. 27). He integrated these data into his own comprehensive system according to which David inaugurated the state's organization in his fortieth year, as part of the transmission of the kingdom to Solomon. However, instead of relegating this material to the 'secular' system presented in ch. 27, he 'created' a new levitical order of 'officers and judges', to whom he attributed these tasks. This choice could have been influenced by the actual circumstances of his time, when the Levites probably were 'the officers' of the courts, and the role of the judges was becoming increasingly close to the clerical administration. In spite of the high esteem for this group expressed by their prominent position in 23.4, the Chronicler neither embellishes description of them nor returns to them in his historical account.

10. The first part of this passage (vv. 20–28), draws from different sources. The names here do relate to those of levitical families in the previous chapters, and the section seems to reflect actual conditions of the Second Temple period – although of course transposed to the time of David. The role of the Levites is not organically connected to any of those previously mentioned, though they do form part of the Temple's administration. This probably explains why the Chronicler linked these individuals or groups to the 'officers and judges', and not to the 'Levites' or the gatekeepers.

The view that the Levites were charged with the administration of the Temple treasuries and property recurs in II Chron. 24.11; 31.12; etc., and is consonant with their responsibility for 'all measures of quantity or size' (23.29). Still, one should ask whether this is a reflection of concrete conditions or rather an attempt to encroach upon a priestly prerogative in the administration of the Temple (cf. Neh. 13.13: 'and I appointed as treasurers ... Shelemiah the priest, Zadok the scribe and Pedaiah of the Levites'). Again, no definite answer is possible.

To sum up: the relationship of 26.20–32 to 23.4 leaves no doubt that this section originates with the Chronicler and reflects a Chronistic concept of levitical 'officers and judges'. The passage is composed of two parts, of which the second may have been based on ancient sources, although the association of these officers and judges with the Levites in general, and particularly as presented in Chronicles, is a programmatic construction. The first part, which ascribes to the Levites a role as treasurers, with citation of levitical names previously mentioned, may reflect conditions and views contemporary with the Chronicler, with the distinction between practice and theory no longer attainable.

D. Commentary

[1] The verse contains three elements: a short heading for vv. 1–19, 'the divisions of the gatekeepers'; a heading to the list of vv. 1–9, 'of the Korahites'; and the name of the first branch, 'Meshelemiah'.

The first ancestor of the gatekeepers, Meshelemiah, is mostly designated in Ezra-Nehemiah as Shallum (Ezra 2.41, etc.), but also as Meshullam (Neh. 12.25); in Chronicles the name is Shallum in texts taken from Ezra-Nehemiah (I Chron. 9.17, 19), and otherwise Shelemiah/Meshelemiah (I Chron. 9.21 and in this chapter). This is an important clue to the onomasticon of the period and the mutability of the names. It may also indicate the Chronicler's tendency, which was not, however, systematically applied, to replace the prevalent dialect forms (Shallum, Meshullam) with normative classical ones (for another example cf. S. Japhet, 'The Supposed Common Authorship of Chronicles and Ezra-Nehemiah Investigated anew', *VT* 18, 1968, 338–41).

[2–3] To designate Meshelemiah's seven sons, ordinal numbers are used consistently: first-born, second, third, etc. Only Zechariah 'the first-born' is known to us from elsewhere (called 'a shrewd counsellor' in v. 14, and referred to in 9.21). All the other names, except for the unique Jathniel, are more or less common, but not used to identify gatekeepers.

[4–5] Although Obed-edom's sons are eight, 'for God blessed him', the figure seven remains dominant. Shemaiah his first-born is not numbered among the fathers' houses, for he has further ramified. There are, therefore, seven fathers' houses who are Obed-edom's 'sons', and six who are his 'grandsons'. These last again form a unit of seven, with their father Shemaiah.

The words 'for God blessed him', referring to proliferation, allude to I Chron. 13.14: 'the Lord blessed the household of Obed-edom', 'blessing' denoting first and foremost abundant offspring. The same motif is reflected in the names of Obed-edom's sons, at least three of which explicitly denote Obed-edom's divine 'reward': Sachar (*śākār*), Issachar (*iśśākār*), and Peullethai (probably *pᵉ'ullātī-yāh*). One cannot but sense the association with Jer. 31.16, cited in I Chron. 15.7: *kī yēš śākār lipᵉ'ullatkem*, 'for your work shall be rewarded'. The same motif is also present in names such as Jehozabad (the Lord has bestowed), Nethanel (God has given), and probably Amiel (my kinsman is God). This consistent and complete expression of gratitude for God's blessing may indicate the literary origin of the list, but in the absence of additional source material we should not pursue this hypothesis too far.

[6–7] In the third generation from Obed-edom, the sons of Shemaiah are introduced differently from the other groups. Instead of the usual 'and x had sons' (vv. 2, 4, 10), the opening reads 'the sons of Shemaiah' (v. 7); the names are not followed by ordinal numbers, and the special status of these 'men of great ability' as 'rulers in their fathers' houses' is expressly justified (v. 6). Their number, six, brings the total of the gatekeepers' houses to twenty-four. It would seem that an original list which was structured along a fixed pattern has been secondarily enlarged, in order to obtain the number twenty-four, in conformity with the overall system of the pericope.

hammimšālīm (RSV 'who were rulers') is difficult in the present context, being the plural of an abstract noun denoting 'dominion' (*mimšāl*, Dan. 11.3, 5). LXX reflects the reading 'chiefs of their father's houses', *rāšīm lᵉbēt ᵃbīhem*. This designation is common in the genealogical records and is sometimes followed by the phrase 'men of great ability', which appears also here (*gibborē ḥayil*, cf. I Chron. 5.24; 9.13; also with certain variations, 7.2, 7, 9, 11, 40). As LXX^B reflects both a translation of *rā'šīm* and its transliteration, it should be regarded as a variant reading. The rendering of RSV is based on the reconstructed text, *hēm mōšlīm* or *hammōšlīm*, which would be unique. In any case, the purpose of this clause is clear: to explain how one father's house, that of Shemaiah, has ramified into six branches, thanks to the exceptional ability of its sons. The names, again, are not attributed elsewhere to gatekeepers.

[8–9] Verse 8, which summarizes the family of Obed-edom, is greatly elaborated, especially in comparison to the summaries of the families of Meshelemiah and Hosah which follow (vv. 9, 11b). A look at the components of each reveals the pattern:

Obed-edom	Meshelemiah	Hosah
(sixteen words, six components)	(seven words, four components)	(six words, three components)
(*a*) all these	——	——
(*b*) of the sons of Obed-edom	Meshelemiah	of Hosah
(*c*) themselves (not in RSV) with their sons and brethren	had sons and brethren	all the sons and brethren

(d) able men qualified for the service	able men	——
(e) sixty two	eighteen	were thirteen
(f) of Obed-edom	——	——

This is another striking example of the literary method whereby the Chronicler expresses and emphasizes his priorities, not only by content and phrasing, but by purely technical factors of length, detail, and repetition versus brevity. (Cf. for example 25.2–6, where the relative eminence of Asaph, Jeduthun and Heman is expressed by the increasing length of their respective descriptions.) This deliberate elaboration and eloquence in the very midst of seemingly stereotyped formulae is a significant literary device.

The numbers here invite a separate study. The list has 62 men of Obed-edom, 18 and 13 of Meshelemiah and Hosah respectively, 93 in all. This is by all accounts a modest number. The list of the returnees (Ezra 2.42) mentions 139 gatekeepers (138 in Neh. 7.45). In I Chron. 9.22 there are 212 gate-keepers and the comparable number of singers is 288. The number 93 would allow for an average of less than 5 for each family of Obed-edom, still less for the others, and exclude any reasonable rotation system of 'divisions' amongst the gatekeepers. Cf. further on v. 14.

Verses 6, 8, 9, describe the gatekeepers as 'men of great ability' or 'able men' (*gibbōrē ḥayil, bᵉnē ḥayil*), terms which refer in Chronicles to various individuals and groups (priests, I Chron. 9.13/ Neh. 11.14; I Chron 12.28 [MT 29]; II Chron. 26.17; officers and judges, 26, 30, 31; and, of course, warriors, I Chron. 7.2; 8.40, etc.). Yet it would seem that the more detailed reference of v. 8, *'iš ḥayil bakkōaḥ laᵃbōdāh*, 'strong and able men for service' (JPS), may refer more specifically to the task of the gatekeepers, which demanded actual physical strength.

[10–11] The first member of the family of Hosah is introduced as 'Shimri the chief', rather than 'the first born' as in vv. 2 and 4. However, the deviation is justified in the following parenthetic phrase; the alteration of the fixed pattern was necessitated by the particular situation.

The explanation attached to Shimri's status is of significance, not only in the family sphere where it is introduced, but also at the level of the Merarite system to which it is applied. It is made clear that juristically there is no *de facto* equation between 'first-born' (*bᵉkōr*) and 'chief' (*rō'š*); *rō'š* therefore indicates not merely 'first' (*ri'šōn*), but a certain status. The distinction between *bᵉkōr* and *rō'š* derives from the definition of 'first-born' as biological, involving a man's relationship to his father or mother; as 'chief' his status *vis à vis* the whole family is defined. In most cases the two would no doubt overlap, but it seems that the father was entitled to appoint the chief at his own discretion (cf. also II Chron. 11.22). The causes and conditions for depriving the first-born of his rights as chief, and the conclusions to be drawn from it in other legal spheres (mainly of inheritance), cannot be learned from the present context (cf. in detail, J. Greenfield, 'Two Biblical Passages in the Light of Their Near Eastern Background', *H. M. Orlinski Volume, Eretz Israel* 16, Jerusalem 1982, 57–61). Since, however, the genealogical picture is a metaphorical abstraction of the ordering of the father's houses, the appointment of Shimri would mean that the leadership of Hosah, originally exercised by some other father's house, was transferred to Shimri, for either biological or political reasons. Although the earlier history of the family is not documented, this hint would suffice to imply that the present source reflects an already developed situation, after the family had undergone various changes.

The names themselves, like the majority of those already encountered, are not associated elsewhere with gatekeepers (Tebaliah is unique).

[12] Although syntactically connected with v. 13, this verse refers mainly to what precedes. Its opening, 'The male heads of families constituted the divisions' (NEB), relates to the two topics already raised: 'divisions', and the number of members in each group. The 'duties, just as their brethren ...' (cf. also 24.31) – i.e. parallel to the other cultic orders of priests, Levites and singers – may imply that their service is conceived as a rotating function of defined groups. However, as with the Levites, there is no ordinal listing of the gatekeepers according to their divisions, and their small number makes such a weekly alternation of divisions almost impossible. It would seem, therefore, that while the idea of such a parallel system may underlie the composition of the section, it is doubtful whether such a system was ever actually implemented (cf. below).

[13–18] The assignment to the gatekeepers of their respective responsibilities is described in two distinct stages: allocation of guardposts to the various families (vv. 14–16), followed by the manning of each post by the necessary number of watchmen (vv. 17–18). From the introduction in v. 13 it is not clear whether both arrangements were decided by lots, or only the first.

The responsibilities of the gatekeepers are described in great detail, with a full list of their posts and the exact number of guards in each watch. Another detailed description is given in I Chron. 9.29–33. It seems that there can be no doubt that actual conditions of the Second Temple period are reflected in these data (cf. also J. W. Wright, 'Guarding the Gates: I Chronicles 26.1–19 and the Roles of the Gatekeepers in Chronicles', *JSOT* 48, 1990, 69–81). However, the material was adjusted to the Chronicler's general terms of reference, that is: the levitical descent of the gatekeepers, their organization according to father's houses, the twenty-four divisions for all cultic orders, and the casting of lots. It is difficult to say how much of these reflect actual developments among the gatekeepers, and how much are an expression of theoretical systematization.

[13] The appointment of the guards to the Temple gates is decided by the casting of lots, to determine two issues: the composition of the respective watches ('small and great alike'; NEB 'young and old') and the distribution of the various posts between the gatekeepers' three major branches (vv. 14–16). The concept of twenty-four divisions seems to recede.

[14] As the three families were to be charged with the four sides of the Temple courts, the family of Meshelemiah/Shelemiah was allocated two portions, Meshelemiah being allotted the east and Zechariah his son the north. As pointed out above, Meshelemiah was the senior branch among the gatekeepers, in genealogical terms of reference 'first-born'. This basic analogy is observed by the application of the inheritance laws to the sphere of social rights and privileges: 'giving him a double portion ... the right of the first-born is his' (Deut. 21.17).

It is difficult to regard the two aspects of this allocation as decided by the chance casting of lots. The 'east gate' was of particular significance (cf. Ezek. 40.6ff.; 43.1ff., etc. and the references to the 'king's gate on the east side' – I Chron. 9.18), and it 'happened' to fall to the portion of Shelemiah, the veteran family among the gatekeepers; the same family, in its two branches, also supplied almost half of the guarding force. It seems more probable that these arrangements were the end-result of extended processes among the gatekeepers, catalysed by social and political factors.

In striking contrast to the status and functions of the family of Meshelemiah, their number as given in this section is very small. They total eighteen (v. 9), while according to v. 17 they would need ten men for one watch alone. The simplest solution, to regard the number given in v. 9 as corrupt, seems the best.

Zechariah is distinguished by the unique title *yōʿēṣ bᵉśekel*, translated 'a shrewd counsellor'. In I Chron. 9.21 he is described as 'gatekeeper at the entrance of the tent of meeting'. The meaning and implications of these titles are not spelled out in the available data.

[15] The two additional posts which follow are 'the south' and *bēt hā-ʾᵃsuppīm*, both assigned respectively to Obed-edom and 'his sons'. This indefinite 'his sons' may refer to the house of Shemaiah (vv. 6f.), which, unlike the family of Shelemiah, is not explicitly mentioned. *bēt hā ʾᵃsuppīm* (in v. 17 only *ʾᵃsuppīm*) is rendered by RSV 'store-house', by NEB 'gatehouse' and by the JPS 'vestibule'. The word has been recognized as an Akkadian loan-word, which probably entered Hebrew through Aramaic (Baumgartner, 72). Nehemiah 12.25 refers to *ʾᵃsuppē haśśᵉʿārīm* as the guards'

positions at the gates, which would support the meaning suggested by the Akkadian: vestibule.

[16] This verse, dealing with the appointment of Hosah to the western side, presents some difficulties. (a) The unexpected name 'Shuppim' has not been mentioned earlier, and is probably a dittography of the preceding *ᵃsuppīm. (b) 'The gate of Shallecheth' (*šlkt*) is peculiar; the name, which is itself unusual, is the only one given to a gate in the present context. LXX probably reads *liškat* with the first two letters reversed; some scholars have doubted the very existence of a gate on the western side (cf. Liver, *History of the Priests and Levites*, 115). Verse 18 also assumes two posts on the west side, but describes them as 'the road' and 'the parbar' (a Persian loan-word, cf. Baumgartner, 905–6; JPS 'colonnade').

Verse 16b refers back to the passage as a whole and relates the stationing of all the guards, each at his posts, 'watch corresponding to watch'.

[17–18] The daily total of the gatekeepers in their respective posts is twenty-two: six to the east, four to the north, four to the south and another two for the 'vestibule'; six to the west: four for the road and two for the 'parbar'.

The reading of v. 17b and 18a is somewhat difficult. The number of guards at the 'storehouse' is given as *šᵉnayim šᵉnāyim*, which has usually been interpreted as 'two and two' (RSV: NEB two at *each* gatehouse), with no explanation for this deviation from the usual form. The mention of 'parbar' at the beginning of v. 18 is also repetitious. These difficulties are removed by regarding *lapparbār* as a dittography of the same phrase at the end of v. 18 (cf. Rudolph, 172).

In spite of the great detail, the picture of the gatekeepers which emerges from the data is incomplete. Questions concerning the number of watches per day, the length of each watch, etc., are left unanswered. Some additional aspects of the gatekeepers' service are specified in I Chron. 9.17ff.; among these we note the weekly rotation of the watches (I Chron. 9.25). Cf. the commentary *ad loc*.

[20–28] The presentation of the treasurers follows a genealogical pattern, as follows: Introduction (v. 20); the Gershonites (vv. 21–22); and the Amramites (vv. 23–28). This literary structure is not completely consonant with the actual hierarchy among the treasurers. According to this passage, the 'treasuries' comprise two different establishments: 'the treasuries of the house of God' (or 'the Lord', vv. 22, 26) and 'the treasuries of the dedicated gifts' (vv. 20, 26). The person given authority over both establishments was 'Shebuel the son of Gershom the son of Moses' (v. 24) whose title was *nāgîd* (RSV chief officer). Under him were the Gershonites, responsible for 'the treasuries of the house of the Lord' (vv. 21–22), and another Amramite family, that of Shelomith of the line of Eliezer, in charge of the 'treasuries of the dedicated gifts' (vv. 25–26). The first of the two treasuries seems to have been connected with the regular functioning of the Temple, while the second was assigned for more unusual gifts and dedications.

The passage reflects the claim of certain of the Levites, mostly affiliated with 'the sons of Moses', to authority over the Temple treasuries. This claim, like that advanced by the singers, is grounded in David's establishment, but the actual circumstances reflected here can no longer be ascertained.

[20] Since the verse serves as an introduction to the whole section, the actual enumeration of the 'treasurers' beginning in v. 21 with the Gershonites, the reading of LXX 'their brothers' (*'ªhêhem*) should be preferred to 'Ahiah' (*'ªhiyyāh*) of MT (so NEB).

[21–22] The text, in which the heading is repeated in three different formulations, seems corrupt. Those wielding authority are referred to as 'the sons of Ladan', 'the sons of the Gershonites belonging to Ladan', and 'the heads of the fathers' houses belonging to Ladan the Gershonite'. Orthographically, the soundest solution would be to regard the middle component as a superfluous dittography of *bªnê la'dān*, which was then expanded in order to make some sense (cf. differently BHS, which takes the third component of the heading as a variant). The continuation of the text after the heading also seems corrupt. The plural 'heads of the fathers' houses' is referred to a single man, Jehieli. A new heading – 'the sons of Jehieli' – serves to introduce his two sons. The evidence of textual corruption is strengthened by the reference in 23.8, where Jehiel, Zetham and Joel are all brothers. Although changes in status within the fathers' houses are to be taken for granted, the accumulated difficulties in this case seem to call for a different reading, such as: 'Jehiel, Zetham and Joel his brothers'.

The Gershonite family of Ladan is peculiar to Chronicles. I Chron. 23.7 identifies the two sons of Gershon as 'Ladan and Shimei', in contrast to all other traditions (found in Chronicles as well, e.g. I Chron. 6.16 [MT 6.1], where Gershon's first born is Libni; cf. I Chron. 23.8–9).

[23] The Gershonites are followed by the four Kohathite families, without their descent from Kohath being explicitly mentioned. From among these families, the Amramites are referred to later among the treasurers, the Izharites and the Hebronites are the subject of the passage concerning officers and judges (vv. 29–31), and the Uzzielites are not mentioned again. Usually, an introduction of this sort would form an intermediate heading within a longer genealogical list (cf. for example 23.12), but this is not the case here. Only one branch of the Gershonites and three of the Amramites are actually enumerated, while the Merarites are completely absent. Also, the connection between vv. 20–28 and vv. 29–32 seems quite secondary. The whole passage should not then be seen as a 'torso' of a fuller levitical list, but as a combination of two independent units, brought together under one

'genealogical roof' by means of v. 23, a literary addition devised to bestow some inner unity on the section.

[24] Originally a continuation of v. 22, this verse refers to Shebuel (or Shubael), also mentioned in 23.16 and 24.20.

[25] The interpretation of the genealogical record of the Eliezerites depends on our understanding of 'his son', repeated five times. The names from Rehabiah to Shelomoth may be regarded either as appellations of five brothers, sons of Eliezer, or as a 'genealogical tree' spanning five generations. In the first case Shelomoth/Shelomith, the treasurer of the 'dedicated gifts', would be the youngest son of Eliezer and, like Shebuel, the third generation from Moses and sixth generation from Levi. This interpretation probably underlies the vocalization in the plural of 'and his brethren' (w^e'*eḥāyw*) at the beginning of the verse. The second possibility is supported by LXX, which reads 'his brother' in the singular (w^e'*āḥîw*). While both possibilities are attested in the genealogical lists of Chronicles, the second is in general more common, and is borne out in this case by 23.17, which claims that Eliezer had only one son, Rehabiah (followed by RSV, NEB, etc.).

The genealogical pedigree of Shelomoth provides his full line, from Moses to the time of David, making him a tenth generation from Levi (Levi – Kohath – Amram – Moses – Eliezer – Rehabiahu – Jeshaiahu – Joram – Zichri – Shelomith). This is another example of the genealogical system which counts ten generations from the sons of Jacob to David, also demonstrated in the cases of Zadok (I Chron. 6.1ff. [MT 5.27ff.]), Joshua (I Chron. 7.20ff.), David (I Chron. 3.3ff.), and others.

[26–28] Unlike the 'treasures of the house of the Lord', the 'dedicated gifts' are referred to in detail. The passage recalls in general terms David's dedication of the spoil of his campaigns (cf. also I Chron. 18.8, 11), the purpose of this dedication being 'the maintenance (NEB upkeep) of the house of the Lord' (v. 27). As there is no Temple in David's time, this is clearly an anachronism, but it conforms to the Chronicler's view of David's actions as focussed entirely on the 'house of the Lord'. The king is not, however, presented as acting alone. He is joined, first of all, on the contemporary plane, by the 'heads of the fathers' houses and the officers of the thousands and the hundreds and the commanders of the army', that is, all the leaders of war. This exemplifies once more the consistent tendency of the Chronicler to remove the exclusive burden of responsibility from the king, by attributing a measure of initiative to the 'officers'. This passage may reflect a literary influence as well, from the 'captains of thousands and the captains of hundreds' who bring their special offerings in Num. 31.48, 52, 54. From another, more vertical perspective, the Chronicler extends the theme of military offerings to include the spoils once dedicated by historical leaders preceding David (v. 28). He thus provides a chronological sketch of pre-

Davidic Israelite history, the significance of which is enhanced by the fact that this period is not explicitly described in Chronicles. In this sketch the pre-Davidic period opens with 'Samuel the seer', who represents the period of the Judges (cf. II Chron. 35.18: 'since the days of Samuel the prophet', with II Kings 23.22: 'Since the days of the judges who judged Israel'). Samuel is regarded here as a war leader, a view which may be based on I Sam. 7.7–14. He is followed by 'Saul the son of Kish', whose wars are described in I Sam. 11 (Ammon); 13–14 (Philistines); 15 (Amalek); and in a general sketch in 14.47. However, nowhere in any of these descriptions is there mention of the spoil being dedicated to God. The Chronicler thus 'corrects' the incomplete picture in his sources by supplying the missing detail.

In addition the Chronicler mentions the two commanders of the army: Abner the son of Ner and Joab the son of Zeruiah. The order of the list being chronological, this should be interpreted as alluding to the period of the divided kingdom (II Sam. 2–4). The king of Israel at that time was in fact Ish-bosheth, Saul's son, but his kingship is never recognized by the Chronicler.

True to his general historical method the Chronicler transforms his convictions into historical fact: this time in the realm of war. It was axiomatic that the spoils of war had always been dedicated to God (the root $qd\check{s}$ is repeated five times), and these offerings had always been under the supervision of a Levite. The introduction, 'This Shelomoth and his brethren', of v. 26 is emphatically repeated at the end (v. 28).

[29–32] This last paragraph, referring explicitly to 'officers and judges', connects the present unit with 23.4. It describes the levitical functions of this order in three different ways:

29: 'outside duties for Israel, as officers and judges';
30: 'for all the work of the Lord ($m^e le'ket\ yhwh$) and for the service of the king ($w^e la\,^{'a}\bar{b}odat\ hammelek$)';
32: 'for everything pertaining to God ($l^e kol\ d^e bar\ h\bar{a}'^e l\bar{o}h\bar{\imath}m$) and for the affairs of the king ($\bar{u}d^e bar\ hammelek$)'.

The last two, although differently phrased, seem to refer to the same functions of responsibility for the entire land, on both sides of the Jordan, assigned to the two Hebronite families, Hashabiah and Jerijah. The Izharites, on the other hand, seem to stand alone in their task as 'officers and judges for Israel'. At first glance there seems to be no connection between the role of the Izharites and that of the Hebronites who follow (vv. 30–32). There is, however, a similar case in Chronicles using the same terminology, which may shed light on this matter.

In his judicial reform, Jehoshaphat appoints 'judges' (II Chron. 19.5ff.), assigns to them 'officers' (v. 11), and the system is designated for 'all matters of the Lord' ($d^e bar\ yhwh$), and 'all the king's matters' ($d^e bar\ hammelek$, v. 11).

The force of this analogy is that it is the 'judges and officers' who attend the 'matters of the Lord and the matters of the king'. In the present context, the division between the 'Izharites' and 'Hebronites' would be artificial; both would attend to the same task, described in different terms. As the Hebronites 'cover' the entire geographical territory of Israel, we must assume some kind of hierarchy within the system, not explicitly expressed.

The system as described is not connected with the Temple cult but with the royal administration. In the sphere of $d^e bar$ $hammelek$ ('affairs of the king'), the system was probably intended to handle matters of conscription, labour, taxes, etc. It was, however, simultaneously assigned responsibilities for 'matters of the Lord'; in other words, it dealt with both secular and religious administration. Of the two levitical families, the Hebronites are described in detail, including their numbers (1700, 2700), while the Izharites are referred to only briefly and no numbers are provided. In 23.4 the number of 'officers and judges' is recorded as 6000, and this is the only case in which there is, at least in principle, a measure of correspondence between the introduction in 23.4 and the list itself.

The most difficult question posed by this section is that of authenticity: do we have here a reflection of actual conditions, or merely a literary fiction? On the one hand, the unlikelihood of a 'levitical order' like the one described here, affiliated with the cult, the artificial distinction between the Izharites and the Hebronites, and the date ('the fortieth year of David's reign') all seem to militate against authenticity. On the other hand, the passage does not seem to serve any of the Chronicler's established objectives, and what is more, the system of priests and Levites would have been clearer and more organically complete without it. The poor integration of the section would support the possibility of its being a reflection of actual conditions. The realistic elements here include kingship, a combination of the secular and religious administrations in one bureaucratic system, and a geographical-political reality which spans the two banks of the Jordan. The only period to which all these could coincide is that of David. It would seem, therefore, that some ancient source, the full import of which is no longer clear, was adopted by the Chronicler, and was included, in a reworked form, as part of the 'levitical system' at the very end of David's reign.

[29] The Izharite family of Chenaniah is not known elsewhere (Exod. 6.21; I Chron. 23.18; 24.22), although the name itself recurs several times for individual Levites (I Chron. 15.22, 27; II Chron. 31.12; 35.9). The term 'outside duties' ($m^e l\bar{a}'k\bar{a}$ $hahi\d{s}\bar{o}n\bar{a}h$) reappears in the Bible only once as $hamm^e l\bar{a}'k\bar{a}h$ $hahi\d{s}\bar{o}n\bar{a}h$ $l^e b\bar{e}t$ $h\bar{a}'^e l\bar{o}h\bar{\imath}m$ (RSV 'outside work of the house of God', Neh. 11.16; the verse is omitted in the parallel of I Chron. 9). Its exact implication is unclear.

The Izharites are described as 'Chenaniah and his sons', while the following Hebronites are described as 'x and his brethren' (vv. 30, 32): both of these two modes of recording, as well as their combination, are to be found in the lists.

[30–32] This passage refers to the two Hebronite families in a parallel structure, as follows:

30:      Of the Hebronites, Hashabiah and his brethren
31–32: Of the Hebronites Jerijah … and his brethren

30:      one thousand seven hundred men of ability
31–32: two thousand seven hundred men of ability …

30:      had the oversight of Israel westward of the Jordan
31–32: to have the oversight of the Reubenites the Gadites and the half
         tribe of the Manassites

30:      for all the work of the Lord and for the service of the king
31–32: for everything pertaining to God and for the affairs of the king.

The parallelism demonstrates that although Hashabiah was given responsibility over all the western bank of the Jordan and Jerijah of the eastern, the Chronicler puts greater emphasis on the latter, in his usual method of elaborating a given pattern. The main emphasis is found in 'search was made and men of great ability among them were found' (on the 'seek-find' motif in Chronicles, especially in religious contexts, cf. below, p. 718). It is of significance that the levitical branch suddenly 'found' in Jazer is a Hebronite family. The relationship between the levitical family of Hebron (son of Kohath son of Levi) and the Judahite family of the same name (I Chron. 2.42–43), which is clearly connected with the town of Hebron (cf. the technical term 'the father of Hebron'), is not clarified in the available sources. However, in I Chron. 2.21–22 there are clear allusions to genealogical bonds between Hezron of Judah and Gilead. The same Hezron is regarded as the father of Caleb (I Chron. 2.9), who in turn was the ancestor of the Hebronites in I Chron. 2.42. It does not seem too much to assume that Judahite families living in Gilead had formed the basis of David's royal administration, and later had come to be regarded as 'Levites', their genealogical connection with Levi never reaching full elaboration. Since the present text cannot be closely linked to either the Second Temple conditions or the obvious tendencies of the Chronicler, it must contain some authentic nucleus.

The inclusion of the city of Jazer – designated only in this context as 'Jazer in Gilead' – among the levitical cities (Josh. 21.39; I Chron. 6.81 [MT 66]), has made this passage a key one for B. Mazar, who based upon it his whole view about the origin of the Levites in the Davidic administration and their development (cf. in detail B. Mazar, 'The Cities of Priests and Levites', *Biblical Israel, State and People*, Jerusalem 1992, 138–9).

'The Reubenites, the Gadites and the half tribe of the Manassites' is one comprehensive unit for the Chronicler, the phrase being used as the term for the territory and people east of the Jordan (cf. I Chron. 5.18; 12.38). The origin of the phrase is probably Deuteronomistic (Deut. 29.7; Josh. 1.12; 12.6; 24.1, 9, 10, etc.).

27 This is the list of the people of Israel, the heads of fathers' houses, the commanders of thousands and hundreds, and their officers who served the king in all matters concerning the divisions that came and went, month after month throughout the year, each division numbering twenty-four thousand: 2 Jashobeam the son of Zabdi-el was in charge of the first division in the first month; in his division were twenty-four thousand. [3] He was a descendant of Perez, and was chief of all the commanders of the army for the first month. [4] Dodai the Ahohite was in charge of the division of the second month; in his division were twenty-four thousand. [5] The third commander, for the third month, was Benaiah, the son of Jehoiada the priest, as chief; in his division were twenty-four thousand. [6] This is the Benaiah who was a mighty man of the thirty and in command of the thirty; Ammizabad his son was in charge of his division. [7] Asahel the brother of Joab was fourth, for the fourth month, and his son Zebadiah after him; in his division were twenty-four thousand. [8] The fifth commander, for the fifth month, was Shamhuth, the Izrahite; in his division were twenty-four thousand. [9] Sixth, for the sixth month, was Ira, the son of Ikkesh the Tekoite; in his division were twenty-four thousand. [10] Seventh, for the seventh month, was Helez the Pelonite, of the sons of Ephraim; in his division were twenty-four thousand. [11] Eighth, for the eighth month, was Sibbecai the Hushathite, of the Zerahites; in his division were twenty-four thousand. [12] Ninth, for the ninth month, was Abi-ezer of Anathoth, a Benjaminite; in his division were twenty-four thousand. [13] Tenth, for the tenth month, was Maharai of Netophah, of the Zerahites; in his division were twenty-four thousand. [14] Eleventh, for the eleventh month, was Benaiah of Pirathon, of the sons of Ephraim; in his division were twenty-four thousand. [15] Twelfth, for the twelfth month, was Heldai the Netophathite, of Othni-el; in his division were twenty-four thousand.

16 Over the tribes of Israel, for the Reubenites Eliezer the son of Zichri was chief officer; for the Simeonites, Shephatiah the son of Maacah; [17] for Levi, Hashabiah the son of Kemuel; for Aaron, Zadok; [18] for Judah, Elihu, one of David's brothers; for Issachar, Omri the son of Michael; [19] for Zebulun, Ishmaiah the son of Obadiah; for Naphtali, Jereemoth the son of Azriel; [20] for the Ephraimites, Hoshea the son of Azaziah; for the half-tribe of Manasseh, Joel the son of Pedaiah; [21] for the half-tribe of Manasseh in Gilead, Iddo the son of Zechariah; for Benjamin, Ja-asiel the son of Abner; [22] for Dan, Azarel the son of Jeroham. These were the leaders of the tribes of Israel. [23] David did not number those below twenty years of age, for the Lord had promised to make Israel as many as the stars of heaven. [24] Joab the son of Zeruiah began to number, but did not finish; yet wrath came upon Israel for this, and the number was not entered in the chronicles of King David.

25 Over the king's treasuries was Azmaveth the son of Adi-el; and over the treasuries in the country, in the cities, in the villages and in the towers, was Jonathan the son of Uzziah; [26] and over those who did the work of the field for tilling the soil was Ezri the son of Chelub; [27] and over the vineyards was Shime-i the Ramathite; and

over the produce of the vineyards for the wine cellars was Zabdi the Shiphmite. [28] Over the olive and sycamore trees in the Shephelah was Baal-hanan the Gederite; and over the stores of oil was Joash. [29] Over the herds that pastured in Sharon was Shitrai the Sharonite; over the herds in the valleys was Shaphat the son of Adlai. [30] Over the camels was Obil the Ishmaelite; and over the she-asses was Jehdeiah the Meronothite. Over the flocks was Jaziz the Hagrite. [31] All these were stewards of King David's property.

32 Jonathan, David's uncle, was a counsellor, being a man of understanding and a scribe; he and Jehiel the son of Hachmoni attended the king's sons. [33] Ahithophel was the king's counsellor, and Hushai the Archite was the king's friend. [34] Ahithophel was succeeded by Jehoiada the son of Benaiah, and Abiathar. Joab was commander of the king's army.

A. Notes to MT

[2] ישבעם, proposed ישבעל, cf. commentary; [4] ומקלות, read מקלות, dittography of the *waw*; [5] ראש, possibly הראש (BHS); [6] השלשים, many MSS בשלשים; preferable; [8] היזרח, probably read הזרחי (cf. vv. 11, 13); [24] במספר, LXX בספר: preferable.

B. Notes to RSV

[1] 'the list', NEB, JPS 'the number'. [3] 'chief of all the commanders of the army for the first month', better 'chief of all the commanders, [he served] for the first month', cf. commentary; [5] 'as chief', cf. above, better 'the chief priest' (NEB, JPS); [32] 'he and Jehiel', in MT 'he' belongs to the preceding phrase ([he was] ... a scribe) and Jehiel starts a new clause.

C. Structure, sources and form

1. After the detailed record of the cult officials, the Chronicler complements the administrative picture of Israel on the secular side: military and economic. David's officers and ministers are introduced in four lists, in two categories: officers in charge of the people, and ministers responsible for the central administration, attached to the king.

2. Several scholars regard ch. 27 as secondary and post-Chronistic, either because of their attitude to the whole section chs. 23–27 (Noth, Rudolph, Willi and others) or because ch. 27 deviates from the programme laid down in 23.3ff. (Williamson, 174). I have expressed my attitude on these literary-critical questions in detail above (cf. pp. 406ff.), but at this juncture several further points should be made.

(*a*) 23.2 states that 'David assembled all the leaders of Israel and the priests and the Levites'. Since the last two groups were greatly elaborated upon in the previous chapters, the reader now expects a return to the first group, the leaders of Israel.

(*b*) 28.1 refers at length and in great detail to all the officers mentioned in ch. 27; it is a sequel to this chapter and is based on the information presented here. In a different way these officers are again referred to in 29.6 and mentioned generally in 28.21; 29.24.

(*c*) The ascription to David of the administrative organization of the kingdom of Israel is in line with the Chronicler's general tendency to transfer to David's reign actions which are otherwise attributed to Solomon (cf. in detail on chs. 28–29). As a corollary of this tendency, the Chronicler omits from his story I Kings 4, which describes the Solomonic administrative system.

(*d*) 'Officers' were an important element in the history of Israel, according to a view well attested in Chronicles. Their detailed introduction would be one expression of what we have recognized as the 'democratizing' tendency of the Chronicler.

(*e*) Various details in phraseology, style and literary method, as well as of concept and viewpoint, combine to prove that the chapter is perfectly integrated into its immediate context, as well as into the Chronistic composition as a whole.

3. Chapter 27 is composed of five units, four of which are lists:

(a) 1–15   the organization of the military divisions
(b) 16–22 the officers of the tribes
(c) 25–31 David's stewards
(d) 32–34 David's counsellors.

Each of the four lists has its peculiar form, structure and origin.

The fifth unit of the chapter comprises a historical-theological comment (vv. 23–24), the topic of which deviates from the general context of the chapter and clearly contrasts with other parts of the book. It is probably a later interpolation; cf. below.

4. Of the lists, the longest and most detailed is the first, which presents the military divisions. It is structured very simply, as follows: v. 1, a heading; vv. 2–15, the list.

As has been pointed out before, this list shows great similarity to the list of the singers (25.8–31), which also has no conclusion.

The most intriguing questions raised by this section concern origin and authenticity. It has been rightly pointed out that the names of the officers are all found, with only slight variations, in the list of David's warriors (II Sam. 23.8ff.//I Chron. 11.10ff., cf. pp. 278ff. and below p. 470). Therefore, whatever may be the verdict regarding the unit as a whole, the names it contains are certainly ancient and authentic. The historical picture portrayed by the section is a more complicated issue. A military organization in which all Israel is mustered in a comprehensive reserve-army is ascribed to the time of David. Each unit is recruited for one month per year, but there is no description of the actual tasks incumbent on the forces. We may conjecture that in time of peace these reserves would be given the duty of guarding the kingdom's borders, doing police service and maintaining order in conquered territories, manning strongholds and castles, attending to the weapons and equipment – chariots, horses, etc. Although twelve in number, the divisions are not related to the tribal structure, and this fact enhances the plausibility of the system. That each division incorporated members from various tribes (and other elements in the realm) is more likely than that each tribe was allocated one month of service. While the number for each division is given (24,000), we are told nothing of their recruitment, nor if all their members were called up each year. The army commanders are also presented as part of the 'reserve force', each serving one month yearly. However, as David's 'mighty men' they actually belonged to the professional army.

Is this picture an authentic reflection of historical conditions under David? An affirmative answer is given by Yadin, who reconstructs David's conscript army with the help of this document (Y. Yadin, 'The Army Reserves of David and Solomon', in J. Liver, *The Military History of the Land of Israel in Biblical Times*, Tel Aviv 1973, 355–9*). Most scholars, however, challenge its authenticity, mainly on two grounds:

(a) No supporting evidence is available for any period of Israel's history. This is, in fact, an argument from silence, but scholars tend to regard it as valid since not even the slightest hint of such a system is to be found in extant sources. Moreover, a military system of this kind presupposes a degree of centralization and sophistication which most scholars would deny was possible during David's régime. One should also add that many are reluctant to accept the possibility that authentic documents of David's time were still available to the Chronicler.

(b) The system conforms to the broader idea of 'divisions' which dominates the administrative concepts of the Chronicler (or, for others, the 'post-Chronistic' editor). Although the divisions number twelve rather than twenty-four, the principle of rotation applied to the king's service parallels that of the priests and Levites in the Temple. Many, therefore, regard the system as a Chronistic (or later) reconstruction, based on the Chronicler's own views. This parallelism between the two systems, although certainly tenable to some extent, should be further scrutinized.

The description of the organization of the priests and Levites into divisions certainly contains unhistorical elements, especially in its projection back to the time of David; however, there can be no doubt that it does reflect the basic historical conditions of the Chronicler's time. By contrast, it is absolutely impossible to assert that a parallel contemporary military organization of Israel served him as a model for the Davidic system. Also, while the Chronicler's interest in matters military is well-attested, it seems rather much to assume that the whole description of David's armed forces is a product of sheer imagination. Such considerations have led some scholars to argue that this description, although standardized for literary purposes, authentically reflects the monarchical period, e.g. the reign of Josiah (cf. E. Junge, *Der Wiederaufbau des Heerwesens des Reiches Juda unter Josia*, BWANT 5, Stuttgart 1937, 65–9), with only the names of the commanders being replaced, in order to project it back to David's time. The discussion of the historical issue has not yet reached conclusive results.

The names themselves are, as I have mentioned, parallel to the list of David's warriors in its two versions (II Sam. 23//I Chron. 11), with only minor variations. Of the names in the list, six are identical in all three places (Benaiah, Asahel, Ira, Abiezer, Maharai, Benaiah of Pirathon), two are identical here and in I Chron. 11 (Helez, Sibbecai) but somewhat different in II Samuel. The four names (Jashobeam, Dodai, Shamhuth, Heldai?) which deviate from both sources are discussed in the commentary. Generally speaking, then, in the form of the names the present list is closer to the version in I Chron. 11.10ff., than to II Sam. 23.8ff.

There are, however, some general differences:

(a) The list contains three names which do not appear at all in the other two, and these identify men who were 'second in command'. These are 'Mikloth the chief officer (*hannāgīd*)' (v. 4, omitted by RSV), Amizabad (v. 6) and Zebadiah (v. 7).

(b) For most of the military commanders a tribal or family affiliation is given; this is never the case in the list in II Samuel, where only the home town of the 'mighty men' is sometimes recorded (Harod, Tekoa, etc.). Such references are found in our list for eight of the commanders: three of the Zerahites/Izrahites (the fifth, eighth and tenth commanders), two of Ephraim (the seventh and eleventh), and one each of Perez, Benjamin and Othniel (the first, ninth and twelfth respectively). The picture that emerges is quite homogeneous, in that all the commanders come from the central regions of Israel: Judah, Benjamin and Ephraim. We might add Benaiah the son of

Jehoiada from Kabzeel (cf. Josh. 15.21; II Sam. 23.20); Asahel, Joab's brother; and Ira of Tekoa – all of Judah. Dodai the Ahohite is possibly connected with Benjamin, through Ahoah (I Chron. 8.4).

It is difficult to regard the origin of these tribal references as secondary and late; there is no reason to doubt their accuracy and no apparent ulterior motive is served by their addition. The Chronicler's source-list, then, probably included these references – an observation which has significant implications in regard to the list of warriors in II Sam. 23.8ff. (adopted by I Chron. 11.10ff.), in which the tribal/family indications have been removed. Indeed in the additional list of warriors, found in Chronicles alone (I Chron. 11.41bff.), there is one such reference (the Reubenite, v. 42); however, the state of the text there is far from perfect; there may originally have been more (cf. above, p. 235). These observations bring into focus the tendency of the book of Samuel to silence evidence of tribal society (cf. also Japhet, *Ideology*, 307–8).

From a formal point of view the list follows basically one stereotyped pattern. However, in its adherence to this formula three stages may be discerned: From the sixth division onward (vv. 9–15) the pattern is strictly stereotyped: 'Sixth, for the sixth month, was Ira ... in his divisions were twenty-four thousand', and so forth, repeated seven times. These clauses are syntactically governed by the opening of the third division (v. 5), which reads 'The third commander, etc.', followed, although with some variation of style and content, by the fourth and fifth in vv. 7 and 8. The first two divisions (vv. 2–4) are the most elaborate; it is clear (as amply demonstrated by other sections of the book) that the stylistic variation is intentional and serves to emphasize the author's preferences by literary means. It would naturally follow that no reconstructions can be suggested merely on the basis of the pattern which dominates from the sixth division onwards.

5. The short list of tribal leaders, vv. 16–22, has a simple, coherent structure:

16aα: heading
16aβ–22a: the list of leaders according to their tribes
22b: conclusion.

Two tribes are missing, Gad and Asher. While some scholars would regard this omission as a result of textual corruption or negligence, others would tend to see it as intentional, the purpose perhaps being to bring the number of leaders to twelve (cf. Rudolph, 182–3). However, the fact that even after the omission the number remains thirteen, together with the disorder of the second part of the list in regard to the sons of Bilhah and Zilpah (cf. below), and the general preference of the Chronicler for a comprehensive view of the tribes of Israel rather than the stereotyped number twelve, would all make textual corruption a more likely cause for the omission (cf. also M. Noth, *Das System der Zwölf Stämme Israels*, Stuttgart 1930, 20–1).

The order of the tribes follows strictly that of Num. 1.5–15: the sons of the major wives are mentioned first (Levi is omitted because of the specific context); among the sons of Rachel, Joseph is represented by his sons, and Ephraim appears before Manasseh. These are followed by the offspring of the maids: first Dan the son of Bilhah; then the two sons of Zilpah, Gad and Asher; and finally the other son of Bilhah, Naphtali. The present list differs from that in Numbers only in the unusual place of Naphtali, who is transferred from the end of the list to his geographical location next to Zebulun. This change probably followed the omission of Gad and

Asher. (The list in Gen. 35.24–26 is similar, but not identical.) Contrary to Num. 1.5–15, the present list contains a leader for the tribe of Levi (v. 17) and Manasseh is represented as two independent tribal entities.

The origin of the list cannot be definitely established. Although most of the names are very common in the Bible, they do not appear specifically as appellations of tribal leaders elsewhere. Since material of this kind is so poorly documented in the Bible, this silence may not be considered of great importance. The attitude adopted toward the origin and authenticity of the list would seem to depend in this case primarily on one's presuppositions about the tribal system in general. If we accept the basic biblical premise that Israelite society was organized along tribal lines, unified by some kind of central bond, then the list can be regarded as an authentic expression of historical–social conditions, without determining its precise provenance, such as in Num. 1.5–15.

The one, but major, flaw in the reliability of the list is found in v. 17. The difficulty concerns both the tribe of Levi itself and the priests as a separate entity within that tribe. Biblical evidence of the historicity of Levi as one of the tribes is meagre and its origin problematical (cf. mainly V. Kaufmann, *The History of the Religion of Israel*, Jerusalem 1960, 171–6*). The lists of tribal leaders or representatives found in the book of Numbers do not include Levi (Num. 1.5–15; 2.3ff.; 7.12ff; 13.4–15; 26.4–51). Even more artificial is the division of Levi into two separate entities, each having its own leader. Such a concept is linked only to another portion in Chronicles (I Chron. 12.27–29). It would seem, therefore, that although it is basically an authentic record of tribal leaders, the present list in its present, interpolated form, reflects the characteristic Chronistic view of the people of Israel, that is: a comprehensive unity composed of smaller social units, to be identified with the tribes, which existed as such all through the monarchical period. The tribes themselves are presented in the broadest, primarily geographical context, with the two tribes of Manasseh regarded as two independent factors. The number twelve no longer plays any role, and Levi is regarded as two units.

6. The list of David's stewards (vv. 25–31), introduced abruptly without a heading, does, however, have a conclusion: 'All these were stewards of King David's property.' The pattern of the list is uniform and simple: each of the twelve sections comprises a nominal clause of two components, following a fixed formula: (*a*) the sphere of responsibility, introduced by the preposition 'over' with the *waw* copulative (וְעַל), and (*b*) the name of the steward identified by his patronym (son of Adiel, Uzziah, etc.), or his place of origin (the Ramathite, the Shiphmite, etc.). Only one figure, Joash (v. 28), is assigned no further affiliation.

Although there is no explicit allusion to the origin of the list there is no reasonable cause to doubt its authenticity. The agricultural branches enumerated here reflect accurately the economic conditions of ancient Israel; neither here nor in the names is there any sign of stereotypic or artificial presentation. Some of the names seem particularly appropriate to that person's special field such as 'over the camels ... the Ishmaelite; ... over the flocks ... the Hagrite'. Moreover, there is nothing in the passage which reflects the Chronicler's phraseology, style or peculiar views.

An ascription to the time of David also seems to be affirmed by the data in the list. The few geographical allusions are not restricted to the kingdom of Judah; the inclusion of 'Sharon', 'the valleys' and 'the Shephelah' may indicate the historical context of the united kingdom.

7. The list of the king's staff in vv. 32–34 is the least structured; it is appended to that of the stewards with neither a heading nor a conclusion. There are two lists of David's ministers in II Samuel (8.16–18; 20.23–26), of which the first recurs in I Chron. 18.15–17 and includes six functionaries and a mention of David's sons. Of those six figures, the only one to reappear in the present list is Joab. This list is, then, an additional or supplementary record of court officials, and not a parallel to or replacement of I Chron. 18.15–17. For details, cf. the commentary.

8. Verses 23–24 comprise an interpolation, loosely linked to its context. Different in both genre and subject matter, it disturbs the sequence of the lists and deviates from the overall structure of the chapter, as well as from the Chronicler's historical and theological views.

(a) The passage is ostensibly linked to what precedes it by the possessive pronoun 'their number' (מספרם), not rendered by the translations. Syntactically, this possessive pronoun is governed by 'the leaders of the tribes of Israel' in v. 22, but vv. 23–24 concern a 'numbering' of Israel, with no reference to leaders. The connection is, therefore, a forced one, introduced secondarily in order to create an impression of continuity (and therefore ignored by all the English translations).

(b) The passage is a note of reservation regarding a census which David did not take, the results of which were not recorded 'in the Chronicles of King David'! The context does not refer to any census of David which could serve as a basis for this note.

(c) The passage introduces several factual and judgmental details, both positive and negative. In principle it expresses a critical attitude toward the census of the people, which is expressed in two ways: implicitly, by contrasting the 'numbering' to 'making Israel as many as the stars of heaven', and explicitly by stating that the census brought 'wrath upon Israel'. However, this reservation is directed not against census-taking in general, but only against numbering those below the age of twenty, the implication being that only this was reprehensible. The present passage is an attempt at coming to terms with David's census as described in I Chron. 21/II Sam. 24, but the justification of David is based on premises and distinctions not found in the original narratives.

The second claim of the passage is that 'Joab ... began to number but did not finish'. Taken out of context, this would accord with the facts of the narrative of I Chron. 21 (but not II Sam. 24!), where Joab refrains from numbering Levi and Benjamin. However, this harmonizing of the two accounts is only superficial, since the narrator's judgment of the participants in each case is diametrically opposed. According to I Chron. 21, Joab numbered the people (of unspecified age) in obedience to David's command but against his own better judgment. Joab's reluctance to comply with David's destructive and ill-conceived command, and his express contravention of the census order in regard to Levi and Benjamin, are points of light in a dark episode, and in fact make possible the eventual deliverance of Jerusalem (cf. above p. 378). The present passage also introduces a difference of opinion between David and Joab. But here the roles are reversed: the census which Joab 'began ... but did not finish', implicitly against David's will, brought wrath on Israel.

(d) In spite of the brevity of the passage and its general consonance with late biblical Hebrew, the Chronicler's idiom, it contains some peculiar linguistic features. The phrase 'those below twenty years of age' (למבן עשרים שנה ולמטה), a formula which is antithetical to the common 'from twenty years old and upward' (Num. 1.3 etc.), is unique. So also the phrase נשא מספרם (literally 'bear their number'); the common phrase is נשא ראש (Exod. 30.12; Num. 1.2 etc.), a certain shift being found in the unique שא את מספר שמתם (Num. 3.40). The usage here could be regarded as a further development of this phrase. לא עלה המספר for 'the number was not entered' is also unique.

The present passage, then, is a 'theological corrective' of a midrashic nature based on I Chron. 21. Its purpose is to present the census narrative in a new light and offer a new evaluation of David's image. How this passage found its way into the present context is unclear.

D. Commentary

[1] The heading of the first section presents general systematic principles: the structure of each division, composed from the 'people of Israel' as registered according to their fathers' houses (demonstrated in the genealogical lists of I Chron. 2–9); the commanders and officers of 'thousands and hundreds'; the operation of the system by monthly rotation; and finally, the number of men in each division. The actual manner of mobilization is not specified, but it is likely that it involved all the tribes, and was not governed by definitions of fathers' houses or social groups.

The terminology of the section and the identity of the division commanders indicate the military nature of the system. At the same time its thorough organization and comprehensive scope indicate a permanent institution, designed to endure in time of peace. The underlying principle is similar to the one attested in the list of Solomon's officers, 'who provided food for the king ... each man ... for one month in the year' (I Kings 4.7ff.), but the two systems are not by definition exclusive. One provides for the maintenance of the king and his household, while the other handles the military tasks of the kingdom. It seems, however, that the Chronicler did link the two, as he omitted any reference to Solomon's system after incorporating that of David.

[2–3] While v. 2, introducing the first commander, is only somewhat fuller than the stereotyped pattern, the details added in v. 3 serve to emphasize his origin and status.

Here, the first commander is Jashobeam, the son of Zabdiel; the first warrior in I Chron. 11.11 is called 'Jashobeam the son of Hachmoni', and the name reconstructed from the corrupt text of II Sam. 23.8 could be 'Ishba'al the son of Hachmoni'. Apparently, at least two different persons are meant: the mighty man Ishba'al the son of Hachmoni and the commander of the divisions, Jashobeam the son of Zabdiel. However, the close connection between the two lists in both details and order may support the conclusion that one individual is intended, each of the names being a partial rendering of the full appellation: 'Ishaba'al the son of Zabdiel the Hachmonite'. The 'chief of the thirty' would thus be also 'the chief of all the commanders of the army', claiming special prominence and status in David's military system. Stylistically, this is emphasized by the four-fold repetition of the element *rō'š* (head), three in the adjective 'first' (*ri'šōn ri'šōnāh*), and once in the noun 'chief' (*rō'š*).

[4] The commander of the second division is 'Dodai the Ahohite'. The second name in the list of mighty men is 'Eleazar the son of Dodo, the Ahohite' in I Chron. 11.12 (or 'son of Ahohi' in II Sam. 23.9). Are these father and son, or was the text corrupted by the addition of 'Eleazar the son of'? The charge of the second division is in fact entrusted to two leaders: Dodai the Ahohite and Mikloth the chief. From the similar arrangements described in vv. 6 and 7 one may deduce that either a replacement or a shared responsibility is envisaged in these cases; this would support the retaining of the commander's name as 'Dodai' and the view that he was the father of Eleazar – in addition to the fact that there is no obvious indication of a textual corruption.

The name 'Mikloth' is unique and its meaning unclear; a comparison with v. 6 supports MT against LXX (followed by RSV), which omits his name altogether. In fact, only the *waw* conjunctive before the name Mikloth should be omitted as dittography, thus: *wᵉ'al maḥᵃloqet haḥōdeš haššēnī dōday hā'ᵃḥōhī ūmaḥᵃluqtō miqlōt hannāgīd. wᵉ'al maḥᵃluqtō 'eśrīm wᵉarbā'āh 'ālep*, to be translated as: 'Dodai the Ahohite was in charge of the division of the second month; Mikloth the chief was in charge of his division. In his division were 24,000', the word 'division' being repeated three times.

[5–6] The words 'the third commander' govern the syntax of all the following sections, which refer in abbreviated form to 'the fourth, the fifth, etc.' (cf. also 25.9ff.). The commander is 'Benaiah' introduced as 'the son of Jehoiada the chief priest' (*hakkōhēn rō'š*). In this designation, two elements should be distinguished. One is the name of the commander himself, taken from a source like II Sam. 23.20 (I Chron. 11.22), where he is described as 'a valiant man of Kabzeel, a doer of great deeds'. The other is the view, peculiar to Chronicles, that Jehoiada, Benaiah's father, was a priest, also mentioned in I Chron. 12.27: 'the prince (or chief) Jehoiada of the house of Aaron (*wīhōyādā'ᵃ hannāgīd lᵉ'ahᵃrōn*)'. The Chronicler's deduction of the sacerdotal origin of Jehoiada was probably based on the title in II Samuel *ben 'īš ḥāyil* (literally 'the son of a valiant man', which in that context is peculiar to Benaiah), which was interpreted as referring to a priest (cf. the similar titles for priests in I Chron. 12.29, *na'ar gibbōr ḥāyil*, and in II Chron. 26.17, *kōhanīm lāyhwh šᵉmōnīm bᵉnē ḥāyil*), and also on the prevalence of Jehoiada as a priest's name, especially in the Second Temple period (cf. Neh. 12.10, 11, 21).

It is of interest that the Chronicler saw no difficulty in the fact that the son of a priest, in fact of the 'chief priest', was a military leader, a member and commander of the 'thirty'. This last information is peculiar to the present list.

(On the phrase *kōhēn hār'ōš*, literally 'priest, the head', as characteristic of the Chronicler's style, cf. II Chron. 19.11; 24.6, 11; 26.20; 31.10, and Japhet, 'The Supposed Common Authorship of Chronicles and Ezra-Nehemiah Investigated Anew', *VT* 18, 1968, 343–4).

The last clause would indicate that Benaiah's position as commander was formal or honorary; it was his son Amizabad who was actually in charge of the division. Note that three of the names peculiar to this list contain the element 'Zabad': Zabdiel (v. 2), Amizabad here, and Zebadiah in v. 7.

[7] The commander of the fourth division is recorded as Asahel, the brother of Joab. The difficulty this raises is obvious. According to the familiar story in II Sam. 2, the reliability of which has never been questioned, Asahel was slain by Abner in the struggle between the followers of Ish-bosheth and David, before the latter's enthronment over all Israel (II Sam. 2.18–23). The inclusion of Asahel among David's warriors in II Sam. 23.24 can be explained by the wide chronological scope of this list, and his appearance in I Chron. 11.26 by the fact that this list was borrowed from II Samuel and was not harmonized with the new historical context (cf. I Chron. 11.10). But his introduction in the present context, at the end of David's reign, is an outright anachronism. Undoubtedly the phrase 'his son Zebadiah after him' is intended to correct this, but it still leaves Asahel in charge of a division for a certain time during David's reign – an incongruity which is one of the weightiest arguments against the claim that the section is historically authentic.

[8] Except for the honorific title 'the commander' (*haśśar*) for Shamhuth, the section conforms to the regular pattern. The name itself seems to be a conflation of two other forms, Shamah/Shamoth, or alternatively, the latter names may be abbreviations of Shamhuth. This warrior is called either 'the Harorite' in I Chron. 11.27 or 'the Harodite' in II Sam. 23.25 (the latter probably being a corruption, influenced by the following 'Elika the Harodite'). The full name was probably 'Shamhuth the Harotite of the Zerahite' (cf. above A).

[9–15] The names of the following seven commanders are all taken from the list of David's mighty men. There are some changes in order, but whether these were coincidental, or dictated by some principle (such as the casting of lots), cannot be ascertained.

Two of the commanders – the tenth and the twelfth – come from the Judahite town of Netophah (Ezra 2.22; Neh. 12.28, etc.), but one of them is a Zerahite while the other is 'of Othniel'. In I Chron. 2.54 Netophah is related to 'Salmah the son of Hur' (v. 50). All these are indications of the mobility and intermingling of the Judaean families. In the genealogies of Judah in

I Chron. 2–4 the only passage which even mentions the family of Zerah, the son of Judah, is an artificial compilation of biblical notices (I Chron. 2.6–8). By contrast, three of the commanders in the list are described as Zerahites (vv. 8, 11, 13), an indication of the vitality of the branch among the families of Judah (for the days of the restoration cf. I Chron. 9.6).

[16–22] The list of tribal leaders follows a strict pattern: the designation of the tribe preceded by the preposition 'for' (l^e), and then the name of the leader, in most cases including a patronym as well, with two exceptions: Elihu, described as 'one of David's brothers' (v. 18), and Zadok, who appears without family affiliations. The names of the tribes also follow a fixed pattern, except for three cases: (a) and (b) the first two are gentilics, 'for the Reubenites', 'for the Shimeonites'; (c) the tribe of Ephraim is termed 'the children (sons) of Ephraim' (not noted in RSV) as elsewhere in Chronicles (I Chron. 27.10, 14, etc.).

The first leader is introduced at some length, as 'chief officer' (v. 16, nāgīd). This title is then implied for the other leaders as well (cf. 24.7ff.; 27.5ff.).

The names themselves are not stereotypic and do not follow any known source; they are mostly common biblical ones (except for Ido, yiddō, v. 21, which is unique).

[17] Only in I Chron. 18.16 (parallel to II Sam. 8.17) is Zadok identified with a patronymic, 'the son of Ahitub'; elsewhere he is always referred to by his proper name alone (I Chron. 12.28; 15.11; 16.39; 24.3, 6, 31; 29.22), although his descent is well-known. This brevity should therefore be regarded as a sign of distinction, as in reference to David, Solomon, etc.

[18] Most commentators are of the opinion that 'Elihu' should be regarded as an actual brother of David, and since no sibling by this name is mentioned in I Sam. 16 or I Chron. 2.13–15, one of two solutions is suggested: either 'Elihu' is identical with 'Eliab', David's eldest brother (thus already LXX), or that Elihu had been the eighth brother of I Sam. 16.10, omitted by I Chron. 2. It seems, however, that the phrase should be interpreted in its general sense, similar to mē'aḥē šā'ūl in 12.2 (RSV 'Saul's kinsmen'), also 12.29 etc.

[21] 'Gilead' is used to denote the whole territory of Transjordan (cf. Num. 32.1ff., especially vv. 29–30, where 'the land of Gilead' and 'the land of Canaan' are juxtaposed), but also the more limited territory of the Manassites (Num. 32.39–40). The same double meaning is retained in Chronicles.

[23–24] Cf. above pp. 473–4.

[25–31] The next list records the stewards of the king's private property (cf. also I Chron. 28.1). There are twelve officials, with three main spheres of responsibility: the first two are responsible, respectively, for the king's treasuries in Jerusalem and in the country; five stewards are in charge of the various field crops, vineyards and orchards; and five oversee the livestock. In general, these responsibilities were apparently state-wide. Only in one case is there an additional geographical distinction: 'over the herds ... in Sharon' and 'over the herds ... in the valleys' (v. 29).

No inner hierarchy is evident in the list, no mention is made of any special authority delegated to the first two officers, and we are not told whether the stewards were responsible to any of the government ministers or directly to the king.

The acquisition and origin of this vast agricultural property – land, vineyards, groves of olives and sycamore, cattle, sheep, camels and asses – are nowhere documented. The incidental geographical terms, Shephelah, Sharon and 'the valleys', probably indicate that these estates came to David as a result of his wars, when he lay claim to the royal property of conquered Canaanite states and cities, but this conclusion should be adopted only with caution.

The concept of the king as proprietor of large landed estates, and as intensively occupied in economic and agricultural development, is found in II Chron. 26 in regard to Uzziah. The picture portrayed there is similar to the one emerging from the list of David's stewards, and the same agricultural occupations are found in both: livestock, crops and vineyards. Uzziah's list, however, aims to be more comprehensive, and includes additional geographical detail.

Is it possible to draw further historical conclusions from the list? According to I Kings 4, Solomon introduced an elaborate economic system, in which twelve officers, appointed according to a geographical division of the country, were each responsible for the king's maintenance one month per year. A special official, Azariah the son of Nathan, was in charge of the twelve and therefore of the operation of the system as a whole. It is reasonable to assume that Solomon's elaborate system was a further development of David's simpler one, with more of the burden of maintaining the royal court being transferred to the people.

The claim of the list to antiquity is supported by the names themselves, which betray no sign of artificiality and bear the stamp of authenticity. Azmaveth is a well-attested Benjaminite name, of the alleged period and otherwise (e.g. II Sam. 23.31); Jonathan is probably the most common name of the period, occurring in the families of Saul, David and others. Three names take an abbreviated form: Ezri (for Azariah), Shimei (for Shemaiah) and Zabdi (for Zebadiah), the last two being attested from approximately that period (II Sam 16.5, etc.; Josh. 7.1, etc.). The name of the Ishmaelite is most probably a Hebraized form of the Arabic Wabil (cf. Baumgartner, 20), and the same probably holds true for the unique Jaziz of the Hagrites. Chelub is probably a variant form of Caleb (cf. I Chron. 2.9). The ethnic or the local origins, when mentioned, are also appropriate and plausible: an Ishmaelite and a Hagrite responsible for the camels and the flocks respectively; a Sharonite in charge of the cattle there, and a Gederite in the Shephelah.

The Chronicler's special interest in economic matters is characteristic of his approach as a historian (cf. Japhet, *Ideology*, 428ff., 510); this should not, however, put the reliability of this material in doubt.

[25] The contrast between 'the king's treasuries' in general and those scattered throughout the land may indicate that the treasuries mentioned here were located in the capital, Jerusalem. Another question pertains to the scope of the treasurers' responsibility: was it restricted to the king's royal estates and his own economic affairs, or did it also include the people's contributions *via* taxation? The second possibility is supported by the fact that the king's 'produce of the vineyards for the wine cellars' (v. 27) and 'stores of oil' (v. 28) were managed by special officials; 'the treasuries' in general may therefore have had a broader scope.

[32–33] Four counsellors, closely attendant upon David, are mentioned in these verses:

1. Jonathan, 'David's uncle', is described as 'a counsellor ... a man of understanding and a scribe'. It is uncertain whether he should be identified with 'the son of Shimea, David's brother' who slew 'a man of great stature' (I Chron. 20.7//II Sam. 21.21), or with some other Jonathan of David's family, such as the brother of Jonadab, who is also described as a 'a very wise (RSV crafty) man' (II Sam. 13.3).

2. 'Jehiel the son of Hachmoni, attended the king's sons'. Another 'son of Hachmoni' is Jashobeam, one of David's most outstanding warriors (I Chron. 11.11). Since we find in David's court the phenomenon of members of the same family occupying various positions (the three sons of Zeruiah, the sons of the priests Zadok and Abiathar, II Sam. 15.36; 18.19ff.; the prophet Nathan and his sons, I Kings 4.5, etc.), one may regard Jehiel and Jashobeam as brothers or kinsmen.

The scant information about the role of 'attending to the king's sons' does not permit us to determine whether a tutor or a counsellor is intended (for the latter, cf. I Kings 12.6ff.).

3.4. Ahithophel and Hushai are mentioned together, the first as counsellor and the second as 'friend'. This last term has for some time been interpreted as a title, rather than a simple noun (H. Donner, 'Der Freunde des Königs', *ZAW* 73, 1961, 269–77; T. N. Mettinger, *Solomonic State Officials*, Lund 1971, 63–9; cf. further I Kings 4.5, where the king's 'friend' is also a priest (but these Egyptian connections of the term have recently been denied). The positions of Ahithophel and Hushai as 'counsellor' and 'friend' respectively are exploited as a major constructive theme in the story of Absalom's revolt (II Sam. 15.12, 31; 16.23, etc., and 15.37; 16.17, etc.). The present passage seems to be independent of this story, and in fact supplies the basic information for the narrative's superstructure there.

[34] Two more counsellors who come after Ahithophel are Jehoiada the son of Benaiah and Abiathar; the commander of the royal army, Joab, concludes the list. These names pose many questions of origin and authenticity. From the available sources, 'Benaiah the son of Jehoiada' is well known (cf. above, pp.247f.). The person alluded to in this verse could be Benaiah himself, if the components of his name are regarded as having been misplaced. If we accept the text as it stands, this Jehoiada could be either a son of Benaiah, named after his grandfather, or possibly Benaiah's father himself. The latter is indeed viewed elsewhere in Chronicles as a priest (I Chron. 12.27; 27.5), but we do not know his father's name. Nor is the Benaiah who is familiar to us from II Sam. 8, etc. reputed to have a son named Jehoiada. Moreover, one should point out that while the system of papponymy is very well attested for the Second Temple period (cf. F. M. Cross, 'A Reconstruction of the Judean Restoration', *JBL* 94, 1975, 4–8), this is not the case for the time of the monarchy.

The name Abiathar is also problematical. As David's priest, he is mentioned in II Sam. 20.25 together with Zadok (probably also on the basis of II Sam. 8.17). In Chronicles it is Abiathar's son Abimelech/Ahimelech who was Zadok's peer (I Chron. 18.16; 24.3, 6), and Abiathar himself plays no role whatsoever. His appearance here as Ahithophel's successor is probably intended to compensate for his former omission by alloting him some role in David's court. Such a consideration would render this piece of information void of historical value.

The reference to Joab as commander of the royal forces is also incongruous in a list which concentrates on David's personal advisors. At the same time one should recall that both Abiathar and Joab were among the earliest and most faithful of David's supporters, accompanying him through all the vicissitudes of his life. They co-operated in the attempt to enthrone Adoniahu, and both were persecuted by Solomon. Their appearance together in this verse, among those closest to David, could reflect this special relationship.

The total number of persons in this short section, including Joab, is seven. Is this coincidental? Could the Chronicler's efforts to record in one passage seven men who were close to David be influenced by the fact that the Persian emperor had seven counsellors? Or is this another example of the biblical concept whereby seven indicates wholeness or completion? If the latter be accepted, would it reflect actual conditions or a literary inclination? A definite answer is unfortunately not possible.

28 David assembled at Jerusalem all the officials of Israel, the officials of the tribes, the officers of the divisions that served the king, the commanders of thousands, the commanders of hundreds, the stewards of all the property and cattle of the king and his sons, together with the palace officials, the mighty men, and all the seasoned warriors. 2 Then King David rose to his feet and said: 'Hear me, my brethren and my people. I had it in my heart to build a house of rest for the ark of the covenant of the Lord, and for the footstool of our God; and I made preparations for building. 3 But God said to me, "You may not build a house for my name, for you are a warrior and have shed blood." 4 Yet the Lord God of Israel chose me from all my father's house to be king over Israel for ever; for he chose Judah as leader, and in the house of Judah my father's house, and among my father's sons he took pleasure in me to make me king over all Israel. 5 And of all my sons (for the Lord has given me many sons) he has chosen Solomon my son to sit upon the throne of the kingdom of the Lord over Israel. 6 He said to me, "It is Solomon your son who shall build my house and my courts, for I have chosen him to be my son, and I will be his father. 7 I will establish his kingdom for ever if he continues resolute in keeping my commandments and my ordinances, as he is today." 8 Now therefore in the sight of all Israel, the assembly of the Lord, and in the hearing of our God, observe and seek out all the commandments of the Lord your God; that you may possess this good land, and leave it for an inheritance to your children after you for ever.

9 'And you, Solomon my son, know the God of your father, and serve him with a whole heart and with a willing mind; for the Lord searches all hearts, and understands every plan and thought. If you seek him, he will be found by you; but if you forsake him, he will cast you off for ever. 10 Take heed now, for the Lord has chosen you to build a house for the sanctuary; be strong, and do it.'

11 Then David gave Solomon his son the plan of the vestibule of the temple, and of its houses, its treasuries, its upper rooms, and its inner chambers, and of the room for the mercy seat; 12 and the plan of all that he had in mind for the courts of the house of the Lord, all the surrounding chambers, the treasuries of the house of God, and the treasuries for dedicated gifts; 13 for the divisions of the priests and of the Levites, and all the work of the service in the house of the Lord; for all the vessels for the service in the house of the Lord, 14 the weight of gold for all golden vessels for each service, the weight of silver vessels for each service, 15 the weight of the golden lampstands and their lamps, the weight of gold for each lampstand and its lamps, the weight of silver for a lampstand and its lamps, according to the use of each lampstand in the service, 16 the weight of gold for each table for the showbread, the silver for the silver tables, 17 and pure gold for the forks, the basins, and the cups; for the golden bowls and the weight of each; for the silver bowls and the weight of each; 18 for the altar of incense made of refined gold, and its weight; also his plan for the golden chariot of the cherubim that spread their wings and covered the ark of the covenant of the Lord.

[19] All this he made clear by the writing from the hand of the Lord concerning it, all the work to be done according to the plan. 20 Then David said to Solomon his son, 'Be strong and of good courage, and do it. Fear not, be not dismayed; for the Lord God, even my God, is with you. He will not fail you or forsake you, until all the work for the service of the house of the Lord is finished. [21] And behold the divisions of the priests and the Levites for all the service of the house of God; and with you in all the work will be every willing man who has skill for any kind of service; also the officers and all the people will be wholly at your command.'

A. Notes to MT

[2] אני עם לבבי, probably אני היה עם לבבי, cf. I Chron. 22.7; [8] have some words been lost? cf. BHS; [11] ואת בתיו, cf. commentary; [18] לפרשׂים, add כנפים?, thus BHS; [19] עלי, probably read עליו; [20] אלהים, dittography; cf. commentary.

B. Notes to RSV

[3] 'warrior', better 'a man of war', NEB 'a fighting man'; [4] 'leader', NEB 'ruling tribe', JPS 'ruler'; [11] 'of the temple', not in MT (also added by NEB); 'the room for the mercy seat', MT literally 'the place for the ark cover' (cf. NEB and JPS); [18] their wings, not in MT, cf. above; [19] cf. commentary.

C. Structure, sources and form

1. Chapters 28.1–29.25 form one unit, relating the enthronement of Solomon and focusing on one ceremonial occasion, as in the enthronement of David (I Chron. 11–12). Each of these pericopes is characterized by the extensive use of a specific literary genre: in David's case the narrative is dominated by lists of all the warriors who had supported him and who have now come to offer their support at his accession; the present unit by its rhetorical compositions, addressed to all of those present: the people, Solomon, and God himself. The stylistic mark of the pericope is the wealth of detail with which every topic is described: Solomon's divine election, the Temple plan, the contributions, etc.
2. The structure of these chapters is as follows:

(a) 28.1:   Introduction: assembly of the people at Jerusalem
(b) 2–10:   David's address
      (i) 2–8:   to the people
      (ii) 9–10:   to Solomon.
(c) 11–21: David entrusts the Temple plan to Solomon
      (i) 11–19:   specifications of the plan
      (ii) 20–21:   David's exhortation on the occasion.
(d) 29.1–9: The people's contribution
      (i) 1–5:   David's address
      (ii) 6–9:   the freewill offerings.
(e) 10–20: Blessing the Lord
      (i) 10–19:   David pronounces his blessing

(ii) 20:   The people worship.
(f) 21–25: Conclusion: the solemn festivities and enthronment.

The literary structure is carefully organized: the introduction and conclusion provide the narrative framework of the unit, and each of the other four paragraphs is devoted to a single topic. These paragraphs, almost equal in length, are similarly composed of two units each, and in three cases the first of these is longer than the second. Each of the paragraphs contains rhetorical pieces of varying length.

3. The topic of these chapters parallels I Kings 1–2, but the two pericopes otherwise have nothing in common; if there is any affinity between them, it is polemical. This is in fact one of the few cases in which the Chronicler refers to a subject recorded in Samuel/Kings without making any use of the material available there. Only one verse, I Kings 2.11, the formulaic conclusion of David's reign, is taken over and duly changed (I Chron. 29.26–27), and echoes of the Deuteronomistic portions of the Davidic testament (I Kings 2.2–4) are heard in David's words to Solomon, with differences in message and phrasing. This, then, is a specific feature of the Chronistic composition: while regarding the subject as significant and worthy of full attention, the Chronicler finds himself unable to accept the source material as found in I Kings 1–2. He therefore composes an entirely new piece, either ignoring the existing narrative or reacting to it polemically. A completely new alternative is thus offered to the reader.

4. The central figure in this literary pericope is David, and this is expressed through the style and syntax which places him as subject at the beginning of all the major units: 28.1, David assembled; 28.2, King David rose to his feet; 28.11, David gave; 29.1, David the king said; 29.10, David blessed; 29.21, they (LXX: David) sacrificed. Some of the sub-paragraphs open in the same way (28.20; 29.20).

Next in importance are the people themselves. By contrast, in I Kings 1–2 the people play almost no part, being referred to in only one verse at the end of the ceremony: 'Then they blew the trumpet; and all the people said "Long live King Solomon!" And all the people went up after him, playing on pipes and rejoicing with great joy' (I Kings 1.39b–40). This verse has no antecedent in the preceding narrative. Who were these 'people', how is their presence accounted for, and what was their role? From a literary point of view it is only the loud sound of their rejoicing which has any function in the narrative, serving as a kind of synchronous literary link between Solomon's company and Adonijah's camp at En-rogel, where the revellers are suddenly sobered up by the news of Solomon's anointing (I Kings 1.41–45).

In Chronicles, the issue of the people's role is approached from an opposite viewpoint:

(a) The enthronement takes place in the presence of all the people; nothing is done in secret. More than in any other context, the assembly of people is described in maximum detail, with mention of all the leaders from first to last.

(b) The bulk of David's words are addressed to the people (28.2ff.; 29.1ff.; 29.20ff.) and to God (29.10–19), with Solomon occupying only third place.

(c) David's disposition may be described as 'people-orientated'; not only does he directly address them, but he feels the need to explain his actions, justify his choice and gain their support. And in the end it is the loyalty and skill of the people which David places at Solomon's disposal (28.21).

(d) There is special emphasis on the people's participation in the matter of the freewill offering. David describes the enormous amounts of every necessary item: gold, silver, copper, timber etc. (29.1) which he himself has already provided. Yet this will not suffice; the people must also contribute, for the project is also theirs. And indeed, they made their offerings 'with whole heart'.

(e) The people also participate in the blessing of the Lord (29.20) and in the cultic celebration and festivities (29.21–22).

In contrast to the participation and rejoicing of the people, Solomon's role is completely passive: he neither does nor says anything. Only in one verse at the very end of the pericope are we told that 'Solomon sat on the throne ... and he prospered' (29.23), immediately followed by a renewed focus on the 'leaders and mighty men'. And yet, the justification of Solomon's succession by reference to divine election is one of the major theological concerns of the unit. A certain imbalance is thus evident between Solomon's theological importance and his actual role in the narrative.

5. After the introduction in 28.1, David's first discourse is composed of two parts (vv. 2–8, 9–10), which follow a similar pattern. Each opens with an address in the second person, emphasizing the hearers' relationship to David by the possessive pronoun: 'hear me *my* brethren and *my* people' (v. 2); 'And you, Solomon *my* son' (v. 9). These addresses conclude with an exhortation, phrased in the imperative: 'observe and seek out' (v. 8); 'Take heed ... be strong and do it' (v. 10).

The discourse itself is given coherent unity by recurring phrases: 'if he continues resolutely' (v. 7: אִם יֶחֱזַק לַעֲשׂוֹת, literally 'if he is strong to do [it]'), 'be strong and do it' (v. 10: חֲזַק וַעֲשֵׂה, a parallel obscured by the translation); 'seek out' (v. 8: דְּרֹשׁ); 'searches' (v. 9: דּוֹרֵשׁ); 'seek him' (v. 9: תִדְרְשֶׁנּוּ); 'to choose' (vv. 4–6: בָּחַר ... וַיִּבְחַר ... וַיִּבְחַר, v. 10: יְהוָה בָּחַר בְּךָ בָחַרְתִּי); 'to build a house' (vv. 2, 3, 6, 10).

6. David's speech has long been recognized as characteristically Chronistic. Although evidently a prose composition, it aspires to an elevated style. It also illustrates the Chronicler's anthological method of combining ready-made phrases, which have undergone some changes in form and detail, with conventional statements, integrating them into a new, coherent literary sequence.
The following are some of the characteristics of the discourse:

(a) It contains epigram-like sayings, such as: 'for the Lord searches all hearts//and understands every plan and thought' (v. 9a); 'if you seek him he will be found by you // but if you forsake him, he will cast you off for ever' (v. 9b).

(b) Many sections are phrased in parallel colons, of varying length, which contribute to the production of a rhythmic balance: 'for the ark of the covenant of the Lord//and for the footstool of our God' (v. 2); 'for you are a warrior //and have shed blood' (v. 3); 'I have chosen him to be my son//and I will be his father' (v. 6); 'in the sight of all Israel, the assembly of the Lord//and in the hearing of our God' (v. 8); 'with a whole heart//and with a willing mind' (v. 9); also the two sayings of paragraph (a) above.

(c) Whole phrases in vv. 3, 6, 7 are taken from II Sam. 7: cf. the commentary.

(d) The discourse incorporates phrases of Deuteronomistic origin, the wording of which is sometimes precise, sometimes approximate: 'Observe and seek out all the commandments of the Lord that you may possess this good land and leave it for an inheritance to your children after you for ever' (v. 8).

(e) The pattern of v. 8 is similar to that of one of the Decalogue commandments, the proximity in form probably being motivated by the similarity of the promised blessing:

Exod. 20.12: 'Honour your father ... that your days may be long in the land ...';
v. 8: 'observe and seek ... that you may possess this good land ...'

Also characteristic of the discourse is the development of one coherent argument through a constant change of speaker. While the discourse is formally David's, he develops his theme by interspersing his own words with citations from the words of God, as follows: v. 2b, David's words; v. 3, God's words; v. 4, David's words; vv. 6–7, God's words; v. 8, David's words. In the proclamation of v. 8, 'in the ears of our God', the actual presence of the Lord is indeed felt, as he has been invoked by David throughout his address.

7. The last part of the chapter, dealing with the plan of the Temple (vv. 11–21), is also divided into two unequal sections: vv. 11–19, the giving of the plan to Solomon, and vv. 20–21, David's exhortation concerning the building. Syntactically, vv. 11–19 constitute one sentence (not adhered to by RSV; for similar examples cf. I Chron. 24.7ff.; 25:9ff.), governed by its opening clause: 'David gave Solomon ... the plan of the vestibule, etc. (v. 11) ... and the plan of all that he had in mind, etc. (v. 12) ... all this in writing' (v. 19). Cf. the commentary.

The topic of the section, the plan (תבנית), is referred to explicitly four times: twice at the beginning (vv. 11, 12) and twice at the end (vv. 18b, 19), and is also the final word of the section. The detailed enumeration of the elements which David 'had in mind' in fact provides the Chronicler's architectural portrayal of the Temple.

The short exhortation of vv. 20–21, especially v. 20, displays the same stylistic features mentioned above for vv. 2–10: anthological style, parallelism of members, etc. Verse 20 is composed of Deuteronomistic formulas, in particular 'Be strong and of good courage' (Deut. 31.7, 23; Josh, 1.6, etc.); 'Fear not, be not dismayed' (Deut. 1.21; 31.8; Josh. 8.1, etc.); 'He will not fail you or forsake you' (Deut. 31.6, 8), and more. These are all concentrated in Deut. 31.1–8, which also contains 'God ... is with you', found in this verse. All these, in different order and with slight variations, are set in the context of the final goal: 'until all the work ... is finished'.

D. Commentary

[1] The verse describes in great detail David's assembling of the people at Jerusalem. This detail is the literary expression of the comprehensive nature of the occasion also indicated by the explicit 'all', and the actual contents of the verse. The nine elements mentioned constitute the most detailed description of the people of Israel in Chronicles. The enumeration of the assembled dignitaries is divided stylistically into three parts by a lengthening of the reference for the third and sixth items ('the officers of the divisions, etc.', and 'the stewards of all the property, etc.') and a new preposition at the beginning of the seventh: 'together with the palace officials, etc.' The dominant term is śārīm, repeated here six times in one verse, recurring in all the definitions of the first two groups (variously translated as officials, officers, commanders, stewards), but not once in the third group.

This verse is in a way a summary, especially of the preceding chapter (27), as the officials mentioned here include all those whose names were listed there. In addition, three more groupings, not defined as *śārīm*, are introduced: eunuchs (NEB; RSV 'palace officials'), mighty men, and 'all the men of substance' (JPS; RSV 'all the seasoned warriors'). This last group, introduced again by 'all', constitutes a different and independent category: 'David assembled ... all the officials (i.e., of the tribes, of the divisions, etc.) and all the men of substance.' The distinct independence of the latter is expressed by the emphatic *lamed* (*ūlᵉkol*, cf. Kropat, 4–7; on the translation of *gibbōr ḥāyil* as 'man of substance', cf. Z. Bendor, *The Israelite Bet-Ab*, PhD thesis, Jerusalem 1982, 199–202*).

The contradiction between these comprehensive references and the absence of special reference to the priests and Levites is only apparent. The particular point of view of this pericope makes such a reference unnecessary: the priests and Levites, like everyone else, are represented by their 'tribal leader', by any 'officers' appointed from their number, and by their 'men of substance' (cf. also II Chron. 1.2 for the same absence of sacerdotal ranks). They do, however, have a role in the Temple plan given to Solomon (v. 13) and a responsibility for the sanctuary cult (v. 21), and are duly mentioned in these contexts.

[2] The opening of the verse is somewhat unusual. The phrase 'rose to his feet' is used in biblical texts to describe the dead being raised to life (cf. mainly II Kings 13.21; Ezek. 37. 10), and to 'stand on one's feet' is the opposite of to fall prostrate (Ezek. 2.1, 2 as opposed to 1.28; 3.23–24, etc.; the same phrase in Zech. 14.12 indicates a tormented victim who is still alive). In this verse LXX reads 'and he rose in the assembly' (*wayyāqom baqqāhāl*), probably to overcome the difficult idiom.

It would seem, however, that even in this detail, as in many others which we will encounter, there is a note of polemic against I Kings 1–2, where the salient features of David's figure are his advanced age and helplessness. Feeble and venerable, David conducts the matter of his successor from the hidden recesses of his chamber. With one stroke of the pen, this verse presents a diametrically opposed portrait: having assembled at Jerusalem an enormous multitude, David 'rises to his feet' and, full of vigour, addresses the assembly. It is also possible that the Chronicler models his portrayal of David on the example of Moses, whose 'eye was not dim nor his natural force abated' (Deut. 34.7).

The address itself is introduced with the characteristic Chronistic 'hear me' (*šᵉmā'ūni*), found outside Chronicles only in Gen 23.8 (cf. II Chron. 13.4; 15.2; 20.20; 28.11; 29.5). The tone of the address is most familial: 'my brethren and my people'.

The speech revolves around three themes: the building of the Temple, the divine election of Solomon, and an appeal to keep God's commandments. Although the actual occasion is Solomon's enthronement, the main topic is the building of the Temple, to which the election of Solomon (vv. 4–5) is presented as subordinate.

Another point of interest is the depiction of the initiative for the Temple building. While it is God who is described as rejecting David's plan, and as electing Solomon to build in his stead, the original initiative to build the Temple is depicted not as being an observation of God's commandment, but as purely the will of David himself: 'I had it in my mind to build a house.'

The Temple is defined, uniquely, as 'a house of rest for the ark of the covenant'. This is an idiosyncratic development of the concept of 'rest' (dealt with extensively by G. von Rad, '"There Remains Still a Rest for the People of God": An Investigation of a Biblical Conception', in *The Problem of the Hexateuch and Other Essays*, Edinburgh and New York 1966, reissued London 1976, 94–102), applied in the Pentateuch both to the people of Israel and to the ark. Deuteronomy, and the Deuteronomistic literature in general, tell of the rest which God will provide for his people: 'He gives you rest from all your enemies round about' (Deut. 12.9, cf. also above p. 328, Japhet, *Ideology*, 391–2 and Mosis 95ff.). This rest will be realized only after the conquest of the land and the establishing of peace. The 'rest' of the ark, however, is defined in different terms. It is attained when the ark returns from battle, and bears no connotation of temporal or local permanence. 'And whenever the ark set out, Moses said, "Arise, O Lord" ... and when it *rested* he said: "Return, O Lord, to the ten thousand thousands of Israel"' (Num. 10.35–36). This ancient idea is further developed in the concept which combines the 'rest' of the ark with God's permanent repose in the 'tent' or Temple. Thus in Ps. 132: 'Arise O Lord, and go to thy resting place, thou and the ark of thy might' (v. 8), and 'This is my resting place for ever' (vv. 14). The same idea, but with a polemical edge, is found in Isa. 66.1: 'What is the house which you would build for me and what is the place of my rest?'

This verse can be regarded as a further refinement and correction of this idea, especially as expressed in Ps. 132.8. It is not God himself, but the ark alone, which comes to its rest in the Temple, described only as 'a house of rest for the ark' (cf. also I Chron. 6.31 [MT 16]).

This emphasis on the ark is underlined in the title 'the foot-stool of our God'. Elsewhere this phrase is used for the Temple (Japhet, *Ideology*, 76–8), e.g. Ps. 132.7: 'Let us go to his dwelling place//Let us worship at his footstool.' The close affinity of this verse to Ps. 132 gives it a polemic edge: it is the ark, and not the Temple, which is God's footstool; and the Temple itself is a place of rest, not for God but for the ark.

[3] We find here the same elements as in 22.8 (q.v.), in reverse order: (*a*) you may not build, (*b*) for you are a man of war, (*c*) and have shed blood (in 22.8 the order is c-b-a). The introductory phrase 'God said to me' is difficult to accept at face value; no such divine communication is to be found in the

Bible. The 'word of the Lord' rejecting David's plans to build the Temple is found in II Sam. 7, but the rejection there is grounded on entirely different reasons. It seems that the principle argument of II Sam. 7.6, 'I have not dwelt in a house ... but I have been moving about in a tent', does not, in the Chronicler's opinion, provide a solid enough theological basis for either the rejection of David or the eventual election of Solomon for the same task. The Chronicler feels the need for an explanation based on factors expressly distinguishing between David and Solomon, and since the rejection was God's, the explanation must also be his (cf. on I Chron. 22.8). The addition of the 'man of war' / 'man of peace' motif testifies both to the Chronicler's need to understand, explain and convince and to his freedom in creating an unattested 'word of God' as a vehicle of his convictions.

[4–5] These verses, although subordinate in the speech to the theme of the building of the Temple, contain some of the book's most important views on the concepts of the Israelite monarchy in general and the Davidic dynasty in particular. They are pregnant with characteristic Chronistic phrases and concepts.

The theological corner-stone of the 'election' theme is laid in the choosing of David, 'the Lord God of Israel chose me ... to be king over Israel for ever', repeated at the end of v. 4, in its right chronological place in the process of election: 'He took pleasure in me to make me king over all Israel'. The validity of this choice is both exclusive and comprehensive: 'over Israel' at the beginning of the verse is clarified by 'over all Israel' at the end, and the duration of the dynasty is unlimited: 'for ever'.

After affirming his election at the outset, David goes on to describe chronologically the whole election process (in detail, Japhet, Ideology, 445–52). Contrary to the assertions of the book of Samuel, the election was not confined to David alone, but was the result of a prolonged historical process, one choice following and delimiting another: Judah – the family of Jesse – David. This concept, although not found in the book of Samuel, is not completely new. The designation of Judah for rulership is found elsewhere (Gen. 49.8, 10; Ps. 78.67–69); immanent significance is already ascribed to the house of Jesse, although without the use of the verb 'choose', in Isa. 11.1. The present context combines all of these inchoate traditions into a view of the election as a process of gradual delimitation, formally resembling the technique of casting lots.

What is entirely new in Chronicles is the divine election of Solomon, repeated four times (I Chron. 28.5, 6, 10; 29.1). The significance of this idea lies in the fact that the process of divine choice is finalized not in David but in his son. Solomon and David are equals here, each personally and individually elected, as opposed to all the subsequent kings of Judah, who reign by virtue of God's promise to David.

By introducing the concept of Solomon's election, the Chronicler is able to provide a comprehensive theological framework for the historical circumstances of his accession, described in Samuel-Kings as the outcome of a long process, motivated by political and personal factors, in which all the candidates for kingship (Amnon, Absalom and Adonijah) had gradually been eliminated. The last stage in this process, the actual designation of Solomon, was achieved through the court intrigues of Nathan and Bathsheba – even if we accept at face value the appeal they make to David's prior promise to make Solomon his heir. According to Chronicles this whole process is framed differently: Solomon had been chosen for kingship from the outset, even before his birth: 'Behold, a son shall be born to you ...' (22.9). The narrative of Samuel-Kings at most reflects the external process by which Solomon's election was revealed.

Another point stressed here is the Chronicler's concept of 'kingship over Israel' (Japhet, *Ideology*, 395–400). Although this idea is mentioned in David's speech only in vv. 4–5, it recurs here three times: 'to be king over Israel / to make me king over all Israel / to sit upon the throne of the kingdom of the Lord over Israel'. The three forms are parallel and mutually interpretative. 'Israel' is 'all Israel'; 'to be king over Israel' is 'to sit upon the throne of the kingdom of the Lord over Israel'. While this last concept appears in Chronicles five times with variations (von Rad, *Geschichtsbild*, 125–6; Japhet, *Ideology*, 395ff.), this is the only occurrence of the phrase 'the kingdom of the Lord'. The dominion over Israel is in fact God's, and the actual Davidic ruler is seen as 'sitting on the throne of the kingdom of the Lord'. This peculiar Chronistic view is a synthesis of two originally contrasting views: the kingdom as belonging to God himself, and the kingdom as that of the Davidic dynasty.

The style of the passage is marked by the 'repetition with variation' so characteristic of Chronicles. The same words are repeated several times, with or without some variation, and with different points of reference. Words and roots which recur three times or more are *bḥr* (choose), *byt* (house), *'b* (father), *bn* (son), *yhwh* (the Lord), *yśr'l* (Israel), *mlk* (king/rule), *kl* (all).

[6–7] Both the syntax and the subject-matter of these verses mark them as a sequel to v. 5; at the same time they provide an antithetical sequel to v. 3, resuming the topic of 'building': 'You may not build ... It is Solomon who shall build'. Here, the speech resumes direct citation of God's words, which were parenthetically interrupted by David's interpretation in vv. 4–5. The views of vv. 6–7 are based almost completely on Nathan's prophecy in II Sam. 7, the echoes of which we have already noticed in I Chron. 22.10.

In contrast to II Sam. 7, however, the order of the respective components of the passage is more closely related to I Chron. 22.10: 'He (Solomon) shall build ... he shall be my son ... I will be his father ... I will establish ...'. In three respects the phrasing of these verses differs not only from II Sam. 7 but to a lesser degree from I Chron. 22.10ff. as well.

(a) The reference to the building of the Temple explicitly includes 'my courts'. In general, wherever the issue of building the Temple is discussed, 'house' is used as a comprehensive term; here the addition of 'the courts', although apparently a marginal matter, has special significance. It reflects the evolving religious atmosphere of the period. It was in the courts, and not the Temple itself, that the people celebrated the festivals. For the people, the essence of Temple worship was experienced through entering and celebrating in the Temple courts: 'My soul longs, yea faints, for the courts of the Lord' (Ps. 84.2, [MT 3]; Isa. 62.9; cf. also the addition in II Chron. 23.5 to II Kings 11.5–6). This, then, was the setting for living, popular religious life.

(b) 'I have chosen him to be my son' in place of 'he shall be my son'. It has repeatedly been pointed out that an ancient adoption formula is reflected in these phrases: 'I shall be his father/ he shall be my son', which already in II Sam. 7 should be understood metaphorically. In Chronicles, the original order of the elements is reversed, and 'he shall be my son' becomes 'I have chosen him to be my son'. This change has two aspects: the intensive use of the root *bḥr*, 'choose', in order to emphasize Solomon's election, and the further distancing of the adoption formula.

(c) The addition of a condition, closely linked to the promise. 'I will establish ... if he continues resolute ...' In Chronicles the divine promise to Solomon is definitely conditional: his kingdom will be established for ever only 'if'. We have already noted that the clause which makes the promise unconditional in II Sam. 7 has been omitted in the parallel version of I Chron. 17. In I Chron. 22 the conditional clause is included in David's exhortation to Solomon (v. 13), but not immediately attached to the divine promise (v. 10). Here the two are bound inseparably.

[8] The opening words, 'Now, therefore', clearly indicate that the speech has reached its conclusion. In a way, David's exhortation in this last section deviates from the general flow of the discourse, which is resumed in v. 9. Yet, in spite of this incongruity, this verse well summarizes the people's role in the matter, and concludes David's address to his 'brethren and people' before turning to Solomon in the final passage (vv. 9–10).

As it stands, the first sentence is elliptical. The vocative clause 'in the sight of Israel ... and in the hearing (lit. the ears) of our God', designates both the people and God as witnesses of this last exhortation, but both subject and predicate are missing. Since it is followed by a direct address in the second person plural, the missing words would seem to be an introductory formula, restored by NEB, 'I bid you all', and by JPS (in parenthesis), 'I say'. Whether such a formula should actually be restored, or only parenthetically implied, cannot be determined conclusively.

It is both the people of Israel and God himself who are called to witness, in two parallel statements, a double appeal dictated by the actual message of David's words: if the people for their part will keep God's commandments,' God will respond with an assurance of the inheritance of the land.

This verse is the only instance in Chronicles in which the people are called 'the assembly of the Lord'. The use of *qāhāl* (assembly) is itself very common in Chronicles (seven verbal forms, over thirty noun forms), and in the construct state we find 'the assembly of Israel' (mainly in parallel verses, II Chron. 6.3, 12, 13, but also in I Chron. 13.2) and 'the assembly of Judah' (II Chron. 20.5; 30.25). 'The assembly of the Lord', clearly implying 'all Israel', lends special colour to the occasion.

Another important point is the promise of the land (cf. also Japhet, *Ideology*, 389), clearly woven from Deuteronomistic phrases. This is the only occurrence of 'the good land' outside Deuteronomistic texts; the combination of 'possess' and 'inherit' is also characteristically Deuteronomistic (cf. *inter al.* Deut. 15.4; 25.19, etc.). The actual import of this verse is, however, determined by a major shift in context. In Deuteronomy these formulas are all relevant to the context of the conquest, which was to follow the unsettled period of wandering in the wilderness. Here, by contrast, at the end of David's reign and on the threshold of Solomon's, war is a thing of the past. At this point, the idea of 'possession' and 'inheritance', as the ultimate aim and hope for the people, is seen as a permanent task confronting each generation. It is precisely the use of terms and phrases connected traditionally with the conquest in a different historical and theological setting which emphasizes the absence of 'the conquest of Canaan' in Chronicles (cf. also S. Japhet, 'Conquest and Settlement in Chronicles', *JBL* 98, 1979, 205–18). The survival of Israel in its land is conditional upon the keeping of God's commandments, which is the people's responsibility as well as their king's.

[9–10] David addresses Solomon directly and encourages him in his future undertakings, reference to which is confined here to building 'a house for the sanctuary'. The address is formulated forcefully in a series of imperatives: 'Know ... serve ... take heed ... be strong and do it.'

The first imperative is twofold, 'know and serve', with 'knowing' the prerequisite for 'serving'. Although this is the unique occurrence of this poignant phrase in Chronicles, the same religious idea is demonstrated in the repentance of Manasseh: 'Then Manasseh knew that the Lord was God ...' (II Chron. 33.13). In this context, however, Solomon is not instructed 'to know *that* the Lord is God' nor, in fact, to know any of the divine attributes, but 'to know God' (cf. Isa. 11.9; Jer. 22.16; Hos. 6.6. etc., cf. G. J. Botterweck, ידע, *TDOT* V, 1986, 469–70).

The unusual title 'God of your father' occurs elsewhere in Chronicles only once in a somewhat different form: 'the God of David your father' (II Chron.

21.12). In this verse, LXX in fact reads 'the God of your fathers', which is a common usage in Chronicles. The authenticity of the unusual title seems to be supported by the immediate literary context. The emphasis with which Solomon is regarded as 'the son of David' is one of the characteristic features of I Chron. 22; 28 and 29. Of twelve references to Solomon in chs. 28–29, only two – both *after* his accession – fail to make any reference to his father David ('Solomon my son', 28.5, 9; 29.1, 19; 'Solomon your son', 28.6; 'Solomon his son', 28.11, 20; 29.28; 'Solomon the son of David', 29.22; '... king instead of David his father', 29.23). This stylistic feature is an eloquent expression of the view that the source of Solomon's power and authority is in David. The divine title 'the God of your father' defines the relationship between David and the Lord as so close as to be almost familial. This intimacy will be transferred, after David's death, to Solomon.

The phrase 'with a whole heart and with a willing mind' is parallel in meaning and form to the better-known Deuteronomistic phrase 'with all your heart and with all your soul' (Deut. 4.29; 6.5, etc.), but is peculiar to Chronicles. 'A whole heart', although attested by other texts, mainly Deuteronomistic (I Kings 8.61; 11.4; 15.3, 14; II Kings 20.3), is a favourite phrase in the Chronicler's vocabulary (I Chron. 12.38; 29:9, 19; II Chron. 15.17; 16.9; 19.9; 25.2).

In Isa. 66.3, 4, *ḥpṣ* is used as parallel to *bḥr*: 'a willing mind' is one fully committed to the deed in hand. There is no point in the external act alone, because 'the Lord searches all hearts'.

David's personal address to Solomon is here interrupted by two epigrammatic statements: '... for the Lord searches all hearts, etc.', and 'if you seek him he will be found by you, etc.' The phrase 'plan and thought' (*yēṣer maḥašābōt*; NEB, 'invention of men's thoughts'; JPS, 'the design of every thought'), is borrowed by the Chronicler from Gen. 6.5, and used to construct his own epigrams, both here and in 29.18, where the similarity to Genesis is even greater. In the same way he makes use of one of his own favourite verbs, *drš* (seek). Here, God is not the object of 'seeking', but the subject: 'he seeks (RSV searches) all hearts'. The idea itself is common in the Bible, and is found, in a different formulation, in Proverbs: 'The Lord weighs the spirit' (Prov. 16.2; 21.2; 24.12). The Chronicler's unique *kol lᵉbābōt dōrēš yhwh* is determined by the context of vv. 8–10, in which the verb 'seek' is used three times, and in particular to harmonize with the following phrase: 'If you seek him – he will be found by you'. In using the same verb, *drš*, the passage gains completeness and coherence.

The third part of the verse is an antithetical parallelism, comprising two opposed conditional clauses: 'If you seek him, he will be found ... but if you forsake him he will cast you off ...' The word-pair seek/find is found in the Bible several times, although the more common pair is search/find. In some contexts all three verbs are found, with a variety of nuances (cf. Jer. 29.13–14, etc.; also Deut. 4.29, which combines the two themes 'with all your heart' and 'seek/find': 'you will seek the Lord ... and you will find him, if you search after him with all your heart and with all your soul'). These usages are also characteristic of the Chronicler, cf. mainly II Chron. 15.2, 4.

David's words to Solomon now conclude with a short summary of the theological message: '... the Lord has chosen you ... be strong and do it.' David stresses not the privileges of the election, but its obligations: to seek the Lord and to build the Temple sanctuary.

[11–21] Two general features characterize the plan of the Temple:

(a) As explicitly mentioned in v. 19, the plan is divinely inspired and given to Solomon in writing, a view which contrasts with the implications of I Kings 6–7. There are three detailed plans for sanctuaries in biblical sources outside Chronicles: the tabernacle in Exod. 25ff.; Solomon's temple in I Kings 6–7; and Ezekiel's future temple in Ezek. 40ff. Both the tabernacle and Ezekiel's visionary temple are explicitly described as following a divine plan. Thus in Exod. 25.9: 'According to all that I show you concerning the pattern (*tabnīt*) of the tabernacle and of all its furniture, so you shall make it' (also 25.40; 26.30; 27.8, etc.), and in different terms in Ezekiel's vision: 'Son of man, look with your eyes, and hear with your ears, and set your mind upon all that I shall show you, for you were brought here in order that I might show it to you' (Ezek. 40.14). On the other hand, in sharp contrast to the version in Chronicles, the account in I Kings 6–7 gives no hint that Solomon's Temple was built according to any divine model or inspiration. In one stroke Solomon constructs the Temple, his palace (I Kings 7.1) and several other buildings, without any allusion to the plan or its source. Moreover, Hiram the craftsman, who creates the bronze vessels, is described in a neutral way as 'full of wisdom, understanding and skill for making any work in bronze' (I Kings 7.14). While the description of the actual construction in Chronicles (II Chron. 3–4) was taken essentially unchanged from the book of Kings, the Chronicler supplements what he considered a substantial lacuna: the reference to the Temple plan as divinely revealed to David, who then communicated it to his son.

This matter has a further aspect: God's promise to David that his son will build the Temple is most emphatically confirmed by the communication to David of the actual plans through divine inspiration. The Chronicler, who has described David as the one responsible for making all the preparations for the building of the Temple, here goes one step further: God himself was a partner to David's preparations.

Although the word *tabnīt* is used here, there is no indication that David was actually 'shown' the plan, as in Exod. 25 and Ezek. 40. Both v. 12 ('for the plan of all that he had in mind'; JPS 'he had by the spirit') and v. 19 (cf. below

494   I CHRONICLES

p. 498) refer to an inspiration rather than a visible model. There is, however, a strong connection with Ezekiel's vision in the transmission of the plan in writing, cf. Ezek. 43.11: 'and write it down in their sight', an idea which has no parallel in the description of the tabernacle. Thus the Chronicler has taken the term *tabnīt* from the tabernacle context, integrated it with Ezekiel's concept of a 'written' plan, and introduced both together into the context of Solomon's Temple, where formerly no plan appeared.

(*b*) The second characteristic of the Temple plan is its detail. In literary structure, this again is akin to the account in Exodus, where the construction of the tabernacle follows two parallel stages: the command (Exod. 25.1–31.11) and the execution (Exod. 35.4–40.33), the two being almost identical. (I refer, of course, to the final composition and not to its possible development.) The details are thus described twice, first as planned and then as realized. The same duality is also anticipated in Ezekiel's vision, but because of the special circumstances the details are introduced only in the framework of the plan, the building itself remaining a thing for the future. No such double pattern, however, obtains for Solomon's temple in I Kings, as no plan is mentioned, and the details are introduced only through the building process. The Chronicler makes good this omission by introducing the 'plan', the general structure of which is assimilated to that of the tabernacle. However, he does not go so far as to anticipate here the full description of the Temple construction (later found in II Chron. 3–4), but confines himself to an enumeration of the elements to be included when the work would begin.

[11] The first component of the plan is the architectural sketch of the Temple itself. There is some difficulty at the beginning of the verse, as the possessive pronoun of 'and its houses' is governed by 'the vestibule', while 'vestibule' (or 'porch', NEB) itself forms a part of the house, which also includes the 'nave of the house' (*hēykal habbayit*, I Kings 6.3) and the inner sanctuary (*dᵉbīr*) or 'holy of holies' (I Kings 6.16). The difficulty has been overcome in several ways, including the introduction of an actual or implied supplement, for example: 'the vestibule *of the temple*' (RSV), thus understanding the 'houses', 'treasuries', etc. as governed by 'the temple' (so also NEB). Another solution presupposes a textual corruption which may be restored; thus Rudolph; cf. BHS. It seems, however, that the text should be left as it stands, since in Chronicles *'ūlām* carries a connotation broader than 'vestibule', and is actually used as a synonym for 'house' (cf. II Chron. 8.12; 15.8 (*'ūlām yhwh*); and especially II Chron. 29.7, 17). Indeed, LXX consistently translates *'ūlām* as *naos*, i.e. sanctuary.

Some other terms used in this verse are also of interest. The innermost sanctuary of the tabernacle, described in Exod. 25ff. as *qōdeš qᵉdāšīm* (lit. 'the holy of holies', cf. Exod. 26.33, etc.), appears in Solomon's Temple (I Kings 6.16) with the same designation or, more frequently, as *dᵉbīr* (I Kings 6.19,

20, etc.). In this context in Chronicles the same chamber is called, uniquely, 'the room for the mercy seat' (lit. 'the place of the ark-cover'). This ark-cover (*kappōret*) is mentioned only in connection with the tabernacle (Exod. 25.18ff.), never with Solomon's Temple; moreover, the term does not recur in Chronicles and does not belong to the Chronicler's peculiar vocabulary. The designation serves a double purpose in our context: to equate the Solomonic Temple with the desert tabernacle, and to emphasize the role of the Temple as a resting-place for the ark, an emphasis repeated with special reference to the Cherubim in v. 18. (On the Chronistic usage 'the house of X' cf. now A. Hurvitz, 'Terms and Epithets Relating to the Jerusalem Temple Compound in the Book of Chronicles', *FS J. Milgrom*, forthcoming.)

The term used here for 'treasuries' is *ganzak*, a Persian loan-word; the reference to 'inner chambers' is unique and the 'upper rooms' (*ʿaliyyōt*) appear again only in II Chron. 3.9. Altogether it would seem, then, that this collection of infrequent terms reflects the late usage of the Chronicler's time.

[12–13] The second stage of the plan consists of elements outside the main building, including the arrangements for the Temple service. Of the items which are enumerated here, the courts, the surrounding chambers and the treasuries are all probably part of the construction; the divisions of priests and Levites refer to the liturgical arrangements, while the vessels are for the practical implementation of the Temple service.

[14–18] This long and tedious passage is governed by the last item of v. 13b and makes clear that David informed Solomon of the specific quantities of precious metal needed for the vessels. Verse 14 opens with a general introduction of the subject, while vv. 15–18 proceed with the details.

The contents of the list raise an interesting question, for the detailed enumeration is unusual: on one hand it seems that special significance is attached to the 'weight' of precious metal specified for each of the Temple vessels, and this technical reference is repeated for each object in turn. On the other hand, we are only told that the information concerning the weight was conveyed to Solomon; there is no record of the weight itself. The various Temple vessels are thus enumerated, not for their own sake but in order to state that the specifications of their weight were communicated to Solomon. It seems that a certain legitimation of the Temple vessels is sought in this context, although the actual problem is by no means clear.

The gold and silver Temple vessels are listed as follows: 1. golden lampstands and their lamps; 2. silver lampstands and their lamps; 3. golden tables for the showbread; 4. silver tables; 5. golden forks, basins and cups; 6. golden bowls; 7. silver bowls; 8. golden altar of incense; 9. golden chariot of the Cherubim.

The list is peculiar, as it is not identical with any other 'plan' found in the Bible.

(*a*) The first point is the materials. In both the tabernacle and Solomon's Temple (cf. I Kings 7.15–50) the vessels were made either of gold (the table, the incense altar, etc.) or of bronze (the altar and its vessels, the 'molten sea' etc.), but not of silver. By contrast, not only are silver vessels included in the present list, but they seem almost to parallel the golden vessels, such as 'lampstands, tables and bowls'. Although the use of silver vessels for the Temple's service is actually quite probable (cf. II Kings 12.13; 25.15; Ezra 1.9–11), there is nothing to support the claim that in addition to the smaller implements there were also 'lampstands' and even 'tables' of silver.

(*b*) A second point is the numbers. Except for the single altar and ark (lit.: the chariot ... that covered the ark), all the other items are referred to in the plural: 'lampstands', 'tables', etc. The tabernacle had one golden lampstand and one golden table for the 'bread of the Presence' (Exod. 25.23–30, 31–39). Solomon's Temple had ten golden lampstands (I Kings 7.49) but only one table (7.48). This list, therefore, mentions lampstands and tables, both of gold and silver, which are not attested in the other biblical sources. The existence of such objects in the second Temple cannot be verified, nor can we determine whether the picture reflects a concrete reality or only a tendency to systematization and idealization.

(c) Bowls (*k*ᵉ*pōrīm*) are mentioned only in this context and in Ezra 1.10. The term is probably late, referring either to a new object or, more possibly, a new definition of an existing one.

(*d*) The passage makes no mention of either the bronze vessels common to the tabernacle and the Temple (the altar, etc.) or of those peculiar to Solomon's temple (the 'sea', the pillars, etc.). Here, too, the reason for the omission can only be surmised. The lesser value of bronze vessels, in comparison to gold and silver, or their placement outside rather than within the Temple, may have made the mention of their weight seem less dignified. There is a possibility that bronze vessels did not feature in the Second Temple at all, and were anachronistically omitted from the plan of the Solomonic temple.

[18] The two single objects, the golden altar of incense and the chariot (*merkābāh*) of the cherubim, are mentioned at the end of the list, singled out also to some degree by the manner of their description: the altar is made of 'refined gold' (*zāhāb* *m*ᵉ*zuqqāq*), a term not repeated in Chronicles – and the chariot is described elaborately and given special signfficance by a return to the term 'plan' (*tabnīt*).

How did the Chronicler envisage the ark and its relation to the cherubim? Two main traditions of this image may be discerned in the biblical sources. In Solomon's Temple, the two large golden cherubim were built in the inner sanctuary (*d*ᵉ*bīr*) independently of the ark (I Kings 6.23–28). Upon the completion of the Temple, the ark was brought into the 'most holy place' and

CHAPTER 28 497

esconced 'underneath the wings of the cherubim' (I Kings 8.6). The Priestly tradition of the tabernacle presents a different picture. The cherubim are integral components of the ark-cover (*kappōret*, translated as 'mercy-seat') which covers the ark: 'of one piece with the mercy-seat shall you make the cherubim ... and you shall put the mercy seat on top of the ark' (Exod. 25.19–21). The phrasing of this verse in Chronicles, the unique term 'chariot', and the previous description of the holy of holies as *bēt hakkappōret* (v. 11, the only occurrence of this term outside the Priestly source), all indicate that the Chronicler saw the cherubim as in the tabernacle, an integral part of the ark. In this, as in other matters, his own image differs from the one portrayed by his source in Kings – which he follows almost verbatim in II Chron. 4.9–13).

This verse is the only description of 'the cherubim that spread their wings and covered the ark' by the term 'chariot' (*merkābāh*), a concept of great significance in post-biblical literature. How should this term be interpreted? Is its single occurrence accidental? Is it a new term only, or a completely new theological concept?

The view of the ark and the cherubim as God's chariot may be construed from the ancient title 'the Lord of hosts who sits enthroned on the cherubim' (II Sam. 6.2 and more), a phrase probably connected with the ark. A certain idea of God's presence between the two cherubim is also assumed in the priestly material, where the ark-cover is described as the place of God's revelation to Moses: 'There I will meet with you, and from above the mercy seat, from between the two cherubim that are upon the ark ... I will speak with you' (Exod. 25.22; also Num. 7.89). God's actual presence, however, is in the cloud covering the tabernacle (Exod. 40.34ff., etc.). The chariot image seems to retreat in these more sophisticated references.

Ezekiel's visions (Ezek. 1; 10) give us a graphic portrayal of a chariot-like vehicle, supported by four (not two) 'living creatures' (*ḥayyōt*, also called 'cherubim' in Ezek. 10.3ff., cf. v. 20). They bear up the throne on which God's presence leaves the Temple (Ezek. 10.18–19; 11.22–23). The term 'chariot', however, is never used in this vision and no reference to the ark is made.

Post-biblical literature endowed the term 'chariot', used as a title for Ezekiel's vision (*maʿaseh merkābāh*), with great mystical import (G. Scholem, *Major Trends in Jewish Mysticism*, Jerusalem 1941, 39ff.). In the Bible, however, this verse in Chronicles is the first and only instance in which 'chariot' is used explicitly in connection with the ark and its cherubim. Is this usage neutral and descriptive only? Was the Chronistic term 'chariot' applied only by later generations to the elaborate vision of Ezekiel, or should this allusion already be interpreted as having a polemical edge? The investigation of these subjects is beyond the scope of this commentary.

[19] Although the general meaning of the verse seems clear, the details of

v. 19a are rather difficult, and their exact message debatable. The nature of the difficulty can be illustrated by the respective translations of RSV, NEB and JPS. While suggesting at times a common solution for certain details, these versions in the end offer three completely different interpretations.

(*a*) The first difficulty is the first person pronoun suffix of *'ālay*, 'upon me, concerning me', which assumes a citation of direct speech of which there is no hint in the passage. NEB and JPS do regard the verse as a quotation, NEB adding the necessary 'said David'. RSV assumes a textual corruption and, following LXX, renders the pronoun in the third person (*'ālāw*, 'concerning it').

(*b*) Our next difficulty concerns the division of the verse, as dictated by the same preposition 'upon me'. NEB follows the Massoretic punctuation and translates the phrase *'ālay hiśkîl* as 'my part was to consider', paraphrasing 'upon me' to mean 'it was (laid) upon me'. JPS, opting against the Massoretic punctuation, joins the preposition to the preceding phrase and sees the whole as one idiom, 'by his hand on me' (*miyyad yhwh 'ālay*), while RSV follows the same punctuation but refers the preposition to the Temple (of v. 11), reading 'concerning it'.

(*c*) To whom is the 'writing' attributed? According to both RSV and NEB the writing is 'from the hand of the Lord' (more emphatically in NEB: 'the Lord's own hand'), while for JPS it is the writing of David: 'I give you in writing'.

(*d*) The meaning, the subject and the object of *hiśkîl* are all problematical. The usual meaning is transitive: 'teach, cause to understand', etc. This is followed by RSV: David made it clear to Solomon, and JPS: God made David understand. NEB gives the verb an intransitive connotation: David had to consider.

It may seem superfluous to suggest another solution, but I would like to make my own view clear. It seems, first, that *miyyād*, the original meaning of which was 'from the hand of', eventually deteriorated into a mere preposition, denoting 'from' (cf. II Chron. 30.6; Ps. 141.9; Job 5.20; Mal. 1.9, etc.). Secondly, the idiom 'the hand of the Lord upon x' (II Kings 3.15; I Kings 18.46; Ezek. 1.3 etc.) is never found with the preposition 'from', which indeed is incongruent with it. Thirdly, *hiśkîl* should be understood as transitive and the Massoretic punctuation retained. Our reading would, then, be: 'All this in writing, from God, as he had made me/him understand', thus completing the sentence which began in v. 11: 'Then David gave Solomon his son the plan ...'

[20–21] David's words to Solomon on this specific occasion open with traditional exhortations: 'Be strong', etc. These same formulas appear at the transfer of leadership from Moses to Joshua (cf. mainly Deut. 31. 6, 8; Josh. 1.5); this affinity, among other considerations, led Williamson to the conclu-

499

sion that the Chronicler modelled the Davidic transferral of authority on the Mosaic (H. G. M. Williamson, 'The Accession of Solomon in the Book of Chronicles', *VT* 26, 1976, 351–3, also R. L. Braun, 'Solomon, the Chosen Temple Builder: The Significance of I Chronicles 22, 28, 29 for the Theology of Chronicles' *JBL* 95, 1976, 581–90).

The similarity between the two situations, already found in the original sources, is greatly augmented by the Chronicler's treatment of the figures of David and Solomon. In addition to the actual transfer of leadership, there are other common elements: the first leader is the great founder, who established enduring institutions: Moses – the people, the covenant, the Law; David – the monarchy, the dynasty. The first leader did not live to realize what he regarded as the peak and climax of his mission (for Moses, the conquest of Canaan; for David, the building of the Temple) and had to leave the stage to his successor in obedience to God's command. Yet, while denied actual attainment, the first leader undertook many of the preparatory steps: Moses by fighting the east Jordanian kings and bringing the people to the threshold of Canaan; David by making all the necessary preparations for the Temple. In both cases the younger leader derives his power and authority from his predecessor, and a conscious attempt is made to describe the former in terms reminiscent of the latter.

There are, however, some basic differences between the two accounts, not only in the evidently different situation, but also in general attitudes, which should not be overlooked. In Deut. 31 and Josh. 1, Joshua alone is given responsibility to conquer the land: 'for you shall go with this people into the land ... and you shall put them in possession of it' (Deut. 31.7). Although the people, too, are addressed to some extent (Deut. 31.1–6), they passively follow their leader. The emphasis of the present context is that not only God but the people will stand with Solomon, to help him in his endeavour. In v. 21 the people are presented not as passive witnesses or bystanders, but as active partners in the work. This matter has already been mentioned in 22.17 and will be repeated shortly in 29.5.

[20] The phrase 'the Lord God, even my God' (*yhwh ᵉlōhīm ᵉlōhay*) seems awkward, although the title 'the Lord God' does appear in Chronicles several times (Japhet, *Ideology*, 37–41), and is no doubt a divine epithet in its own right. One wonders whether the text might be a result of dittography, the original being 'the Lord my God' (so LXX). David emphasizes throughout his special relationship with God: here 'the Lord *my* God', and in v. 9, addressing Solomon, 'know the God of your father'.

[21] The people's participation is three-fold: the divisions of the priests and Levites in the service of the Temple, craftsmen in 'any kind of service', and the officers and all the people 'wholly at your command'. Thus, David makes clear that he has provided not only for everything necessary in the

construction of the Temple, but also for its full operation once completed. David's words refer back to ch. 22 and chs. 23–27, summarizing the human aspect of his preparations, which even now are not complete, but will be returned to in ch. 29.

The term used for a craftsman, *nādīb baḥokmāh* (RSV 'willing man who has skill'), is a unique idiom, but the root *ndb* is common in the Temple context, especially in ch. 29 (vv. 5, 6, 9, 14, 17), as well as in the context of the tabernacle. It is probably an elliptic expression, as illustrated by the translation.

29

29 And David the king said to all the assembly, 'Solomon my son, whom alone God has chosen, is young and inexperienced, and the work is great; for the palace will not be for man but for the Lord God. [2] So I have provided for the house of my God, so far as I was able, the gold for the things of gold, the silver for the things of silver, and the bronze for the things of bronze, the iron for the things of iron, and wood for the things of wood, besides great quantities of onyx and stones for setting, antimony, coloured stones, all sorts of precious stones, and marble. [3] Moreover, in addition to all that I have provided for the holy house, I have a treasure of my own of gold and silver, and because of my devotion to the house of my God I give it to the house of my God: [4] three thousand talents of gold, of the gold of Ophir, and seven thousand talents of refined silver, for overlaying the walls of the house, [5] and for all the work to be done by craftsmen, gold for the things of gold and silver for the things of silver. Who then will offer willingly, consecrating himself today to the Lord?'

6 Then the heads of fathers' houses made their freewill offerings, as did also the leaders of the tribes, the commanders of thousands and of hundreds, and the officers over the king's work. [7] They gave for the service of the house of God five thousand talents and ten thousand darics of gold, ten thousand talents of silver, eighteen thousand talents of bronze, and a hundred thousand talents of iron. [8] And whoever had precious stones gave them to the treasury of the house of the Lord, in the care of Jehiel the Gershonite. [9] Then the people rejoiced because these had given willingly, for with a whole heart they had offered freely to the Lord; David the king also rejoiced greatly.

10 Therefore David blessed the Lord in the presence of all the assembly; and David said: 'Blessed art thou, O Lord, the God of Israel our father, for ever and ever. [11] Thine, O Lord, is the greatness, and the power, and the glory, and the victory, and the majesty; for all that is in the heavens and in the earth is thine; thine is the kingdom, O Lord, and thou art exalted as head above all. [12] Both riches and honour come from thee, and thou rulest over all. In thy hand are power and might; and in thy hand it is to make great and to give strength to all. [13] And now we thank thee, our God, and praise thy glorious name.

14 'But who am I, and what is my people, that we should be able thus to offer willingly? For all things come from thee, and of thy own have we given thee. [15] For we are strangers before thee, and sojourners, as all our fathers were; our days on the earth are like a shadow, and there is no abiding. [16] O Lord our God, all this abundance that we have provided for building thee a house for thy holy name comes from thy hand and is all thy own. [17] I know, my God, that thou triest the heart, and hast pleasure in uprightness; in the uprightness of my heart I have freely offered all these things, and now I have seen thy people, who are present here, offering freely and joyously to thee. [18] O Lord, the God of Abraham, Isaac, and Israel, our fathers, keep for ever such purposes and thoughts in the hearts of thy people, and direct their hearts toward thee. [19] Grant to Solomon my son that with a whole heart he may keep

thy commandments, thy testimonies, and thy statutes, performing all, and that he may build the palace for which I have made provision.'

20 Then David said to all the assembly, 'Bless the Lord your God.' And all the assembly blessed the Lord, the God of their fathers, and bowed their heads, and worshipped the Lord, and did obeisance to the king. [21] And they performed sacrifices to the Lord, and on the next day offered burnt offerings to the Lord, a thousand bulls, a thousand rams, and a thousand lambs, with their drink offerings, and sacrifices in abundance for all Israel; [22] and they ate and drank before the Lord on that day with great gladness.

And they made Solomon the son of David king the second time, and they anointed him as prince for the Lord, and Zadok as priest. [23] Then Solomon sat on the throne of the Lord as king instead of David his father; and he prospered, and all Israel obeyed him. [24] All the leaders and the mighty men, and also all the sons of King David, pledged their allegiance to King Solomon. [25] And the Lord gave Solomon great repute in the sight of all Israel, and bestowed upon him such royal majesty as had not been on any king before him in Israel.

26 Thus David the son of Jesse reigned over all Israel. [27] The time that he reigned over Israel was forty years; he reigned seven years in Hebron, and thirty-three years in Jerusalem. [28] Then he died in a good old age, full of days, riches, and honour; and Solomon his son reigned in his stead. [29] Now the acts of King David, from first to last, are written in the Chronicles of Samuel the seer, and in the Chronicles of Nathan the prophet, and in the Chronicles of Gad the seer, [30] with accounts of all his rule and his might and of the circumstances that came upon him and upon Israel, and upon all the kingdoms of the countries.

A. Notes to MT

[11] ובארץ, V + לך, omitted due to haplography? [21] ויזבחו, LXX ויזבח דוד; [22] שנית, missing in part of LXX MSS, gloss; וימשחו, follow Versions and read וימשחוהו.

B. Notes to RSV

[4] 'house', thus LXX, MT houses (+JPS; NEB 'buildings'); [6] 'heads of', MT 'officers of'; [9] 'these', literally 'they' (so NEB; JPS); [11] 'thou art exalted as head above all', JPS 'to You … belong … pre-eminence above all'; [15] 'no abiding', JPS 'with nothing in prospect'; [19] 'Grant to Solomon … that with a whole heart he may keep', MT 'Grant Solomon … a whole heart to keep', etc.; [20] 'worshipped', literally 'bowed low', prostrated (וישתחוו); 'did obeisance', not in MT; [24] 'pledged their allegiance', literally 'gave their hand in support' (so JPS). [25] 'gave … great repute', MT 'made … stand high' (NEB), or 'made … great' (JPS).

C. Structure, sources and form

1. The first part of the chapter, vv. 1–25, continues and concludes the larger pericope which began in 28.1. It comprises three sections, two of which are themselves composite:

1–9:   The freewill offerings
    1–5:   David's invitation
    6–9:   The people's response

10–20: The prayer
    10–19 David's prayer
    20   The people's worship
21–25: The enthronment of Solomon.

The chapter, and the history of David, are summed up in the concluding vv. 26–30.
2. The structure and style of vv. 1–9 are determined by their subject-matter. In contrast to the other speeches we have seen, the main topic is introduced only at the end, as a question: 'Who then will offer willingly?' The whole speech is structured in view of and in preparation for this final invitation.

It has already been pointed out that the theme of freewill offerings is taken from the description of the tabernacle in Exod. 25ff. There the project is financed exclusively from the contributions of the people, a stipulation laid down in the first divine command given to Moses: '... Speak to the people ... that they take for me an offering ...' (Exod. 25.1ff.). This was, then, the first command communicated by Moses to the people (Exod. 35.2), and their actual response follows (Exod. 35.21–29). By contrast, here in David's speech the Chronicler's different sociological and psychological point of view is clearly manifested. While Moses simply commanded the people, David endeavours to persuade them: with exhortations, *ad hominem* explanations, displays of personal example, etc. To this end David uses the following rhetorical means: (*a*) emphasis on the enormity of the task, much beyond the ability of any one person; (*b*) reference to Solomon's inadequacy – although he was the man chosen for the task – to cope with it; (*c*) demonstration of exemplary devotion: David's own contributions extended his duty, so fully was he aware of his responsibility; (*d*) great detail in the presentation of the necessary items, thus both stressing the generosity of David's offering and at the same time providing a guideline for the people's emulation; (*e*) the emphatic final position of the appeal itself, and its solemn language pregnant with expectation: 'who ... will offer ... consecrating himself today to the Lord'. This same psychological attitude continues after the appeal, in David's reaction of rejoicing (v. 9) and praise (v. 17).

Stylistically, the section is governed by the root נדב (to give freely, willingly), first presented in the appeal (v. 5), then in the response (v. 6), and finally in v. 9.

3. Verses 10–19 constitute the great prayer of David, an appropriate conclusion to the series of David's addresses. It is defined as 'benediction' and opens with the address 'Blessed art thou, Lord God of our father Israel', which recurs (with some variations) as a fixed formula at the end of the collections of Psalms: 41.13; 72.18; 89.52 [MT 53]; 106.48. This part of the ceremony is concluded by the people's blessing, responding to that of the king. Such doxologies are also referred to in II Chron. 20.26 and 31.8, but without recording their content.

In order to examine this literary genre, and its particular execution here, this text should be compared to other prayers. First of all, the blessing is firmly anchored in its actual historical and narrative context – the building of the Temple and the freewill offering. Although containing strong notes of praise for the greatness of divine might, it is not a general hymn, exalting God's deeds in nature and human affairs. Rather, it is linked to a specific time and place, and in this respect resembles the prayer of Neh. 9.5ff., which begins as a blessing in a defined historical context. However, this resemblance between the two compositions attracts our attention to a major difference: the prayer, like all the Chronistic speeches and prayers, with very few exceptions, contains no historical survey, either of God's deeds (contrast Neh. 9.7–15) or of the people's sins and punishments (Neh. 9.10b, 16ff.). Even the most universal of God's acts – the creation of the world – goes unmentioned. The divine might and glory are referred to in the most general terms, followed by an application to the immediate circumstances.

The elevated style and conventional idioms of the prayer bring to mind the psalms of thanksgiving, yet it remains essentially prose, in spite of occassional recourse to parallelism. Although the Chronicler could have made use of extant psalms, ready to hand, or at least might have woven together psalm segments (cf. e.g. I Chron. 16.8ff.), he chose to compose this prayer in his own vocabulary and style. This is all the more conspicuous for the first part, which resembles in nature and function the hymns of the psalter. This choice may shed light on the Chronicler's attitude to the place and function of psalmody. It seems that for the Chronicler's generation, psalmodic singing was tightly linked to the regular Temple service and entrusted exclusively to the levitical singers. A psalm of thanksgiving is therefore sung by Asaph and his brethren in I Chron. 16.8ff., and similarly in II Chron. 20.21: 'He appointed singers to the Lord (RSV those who were to sing)'. The formulaic-cultic chanting of psalms is the privilege of 'singers', mentioned many times with no citation of the text of their songs; cf. also Neh. 9.5ff., where the great prayer is recited by the Levites. The Chronicler thus expresses a distinction between the institutional Temple psalms, performed by cult professionals, and the prayer of the layman (even the king), which is not psalmody but prose.

4. The prayer is composed of three parts:

10b–13: doxology
14–17: presentation and dedication to God of the freewill offering
18–19: supplication.

Stylistically, the prayer demonstrates the characteristic Chronistic technique of adopting ready-made phrases and weaving them with the necessary contextual adaptations into his own literary web. This is clearly demonstrated in v. 15, which is almost a verbatim quotation of Ps. 39.12 [MT 13]: 'For I am thy passing guest, a sojourner, like all my fathers'. The similarity of the Hebrew texts is blurred by the variations in the respective translations:

כי גר אנכי ימך תושב ככל אבותי
כי גרים אנחנו לפניך תושבים ככל אבותינו

The following phrase, 'our days on the earth are like a shadow', quotes Job 8.9 כי צל ימינו עלי ארץ, and even 'there is no hope' (אין מקוה), RSV 'abiding') probably reflects a common idiom (cf. Ezra 10.2, יש מקוה, 'there is hope'). In the same way, 'blessed art thou', etc. is a fixed formula; the phrases בחן לבבות (v. 17, 'triest the heart', cf. Ps. 7.10; 17.3; Jer. 11.20; 12.3; 20.12) and יצר מחשבות, (Gen. 6.5) are established idioms, and v. 14, 'But who am I and what is my people', is modelled on II Sam. 7.18 (I Chron. 17.16). It should be emphasized, however, that these borrowed phrases and verses are not literary fossils; they are sensitively modulated and adapted to the new context, from which they derive their specific relevance.

Another stylistic feature of the Chronicler's rhetorical compositions is the prevalence in his prose of parallelism, of both small and larger units, some of which is lost in translation.

Smaller units:

1. who am I / and what is my people (v. 14)
2. for all things come from thee / and of thy own have we given thee (v. 14)
3. comes from thy hand / and is all thy own (v. 16)
4. thou triest the heart / and hast pleasure in uprightness (v. 17).

Longer units:

1. For all that is in the heavens and in the earth is thine / thine is the kingdom O Lord/ and thou are exalted as head above all.
2. Both riches and honour come from thee / and thou rulest over all / In thy hand are power and might / and in thy hand it is to make great and to give strength to all.
3. We thank thee / and praise thy glorious name.
4. For we are strangers before thee/ and sojourners as all our fathers were.

At times the parallelism is not expressed so much in the content as in the rhythm of the verses alone, e.g. v. 12.

The focal point of all parts of the blessing is to be found of course in God, a centrality expressed in both style and syntax:

(*a*) The prayer abounds in direct address to God: 'Blessed art thou, O Lord' (v. 10); 'Thine, O Lord' (v. 11, twice or three times); 'Now, our God' (v. 13); 'O Lord our God' (v. 16); 'I know, my God' (v. 17); 'O Lord, the God, etc.' (v. 18) – seven invocations in all.

(*b*) God is addressed in various epithets: Lord, God of Israel, our God, my God, the God of Abraham, Isaac and Israel – the longest title coming last (v. 18).

(*c*) God is constantly referred to by the possessive or accusative pronouns: thine, from thee, thee, etc.

(*d*) Verbs are in the second person.

The prayer contrasts the two partners in the relationship: God, whose alone is 'the greatness and the power', and the people, who are 'strangers, sojourners', whose life is 'like a shadow', who give to the Lord only what is already his. At the same time, they are never depicted in isolation: they are '*thy* people' (vv. 17, 18), who live 'before thee' (v. 15), who keep 'thy commandments, thy testimonies and thy statutes', and who are bound, by a series of possessive pronouns, not only to 'their God', to the God of their king (v. 17), but above all to 'the God of Abraham, Isaac and Israel, our fathers' (vv. 10 and 18).

The message of the prayer is thus expressed through a full accord between content and literary method.

D. Commentary

[1–5] David exhorts the people to contribute towards the building of the Temple, an appeal modelled basically on the example of the tabernacle (cf. above p. 503). As I have noted, in the book of Kings 'the house which king Solomon built for the Lord' (I Kings 6.2) is first and foremost Solomon's enterprise, in which the people have no share, with even the craftsmen alluded to only briefly. Nor is there reference in Kings to the question of the enormous economic burden of funding confronting Solomon. It is taken for granted that the financial responsibility was shouldered by the king alone. By contrast, Chronicles stresses repeatedly the heavy expense, quite beyond the ability of Solomon to meet alone, and the crucial assistance supplied both by David and by the people. At the same time, the Chronicler maintains the silence of the book of Kings over Solomon's own contribution. However, while in Kings this silence reflects an assumption of Solomon's exclusive responsibility, in Chronicles he is in fact exempted from this burden by the preparations of his father, except for the vague reference of David, 'To these you must add' (I Chron. 22.14).

[1] The opening words are actually a continuation of the previous addresses, and therefore the subject, the 'building of the Temple', is implicitly understood. The verse presents Solomon as 'young and inexperienced' and, on the other hand, 'the one chosen by God'. To aid the young king thus becomes mandatory.

The task at hand is so formidable mainly because the Temple of God must be more perfect than any other dwelling; this idea is expressed still more emphatically in II Chron. 2.5: 'The house which I am to build will be great, for our God is greater than all gods.' This aspiration is in fact the proper context for an appeal to all the people; but before asking directly 'who will offer willingly ...', David first takes care to develop his rhetorical persuasion.

Solomon, again presented as 'my son', is referred to only twice in this section, both times in the third person: once here and once at the end, in v. 19. The two formal references frame a section in which Solomon is completely absent, with all addresses made only to 'God' and 'the people'.

[2] The relationship between v. 2 and vv. 3–5a seems to indicate that David sees his donations as belonging to two categories: one prepared in his capacity as king, and the other donated from his private property, $s^eg ull\bar{a}h$. The former are enumerated in a list, the detail of which is unparalleled in the whole context, but which does not specify quantities. In the second category only gold and silver are mentioned, including their respective quantities (vv. 3–5a).

The list in v. 2 presents some difficulties over the meaning and order of the items:

(a) The metals are enumerated first, in decreasing order of value (gold, silver, bronze, iron), and then wood. There follows, however, instead of the anticipated 'building stones' (cf. 22.14, 15), a reference to gems and semi-precious stones, which would hardly have been used for the construction.

(b) In fact, however, there is apparently a reference to stone used for building in 'precious stones and marble' at the end of the verse. It is true that 'eben $y^eq\bar{a}r\bar{a}h$ is usually a term for a gem (e.g. II Sam. 12.30; I Kings 10.2, 10;

Ezek. 27.22, etc.). However, in I Kings 5.17 (MT 31); 7.9–11, the plural *'ªbānîm y⁴qārōt* (RSV 'costly stones') is descriptive of the great stones quarried for the building. II Chronicles 3.6 uses the singular , *'eben y⁴qārāh* for the stone facing of the house. Although the RSV translation 'he adorned the house with … precious stones' is a possible choice, it is not conclusive.

šayiš, marble, is unique, but is usually identified with *šēš*, mentioned in Esther 1.6 and Song of Songs 5.15 (RSV alabaster).

(*c*) The term *'abnē pūk m⁴riqmāh* is obscure. While *riqmāh* is used exclusively for coloured textiles, *pūk* is known in biblical texts for eye-cosmetic (II Kings 9.30; Jer. 4.30). It is used metaphorically in Isa. 54.11, *hinnēh 'ānōkî marbîṣ bappūk 'ªbānayik*, RSV 'I will set your stones in antimony' (NEB 'in the finest mortar'). It has been suggested that *pūk* should be read *nōpek*, while *riqmāh* and *šēš* should be interpreted as referring to textiles rather than stones (cf. Curtis, 303). It would seem, however, that in the process of idealization, metaphor (under the influence of Isa. 54.11) has taken the place of concrete terminology.

[3–5a] *s⁴gullāh* denotes the private property of the king (Baumgartner, 701), from which David donates 3000 talents of gold and 7,000 of silver. These quantities, which are relatively modest in comparison to 22.4, are still extravagant; the numbers themselves, and their sum (10), are clearly typological. The enormous quantities of gold and silver have two purposes: the panelling of the walls (v. 4b) and as material for all the work of the craftsmen (5a). The interior of Solomon's Temple was indeed overlaid with gold (I Kings 6.20–22); for the more common verb *ṣph* in the book of Kings, the Chronicler has substituted *ḥph* (II Chron. 3.4, cf. S. Japhet, 'Interchanges of Verbal Roots in Parallel Texts in Chronicles', *HS* 28, 1987, 19–20). The present context (v. 4) is the one instance in Chronicles of the verb *ṭwḥ*, found elsewhere only in Leviticus (14.42, 43, 48, RSV 'plaster') and Ezekiel (13.10–15; 22.28; RSV 'daub').

The appearance of the plural *bātîm* ('houses') is an example of one of the Chronicler's linguistic traits. The plural (RSV 'house') refers to all the chambers of the Temple (cf. 28.11), just as elsewhere 'lands' denotes all parts of the land (I Chron. 13.2; II Chron. 11.23).

'Gold of Ophir' is, for the presumed historical context, an anachronism; according to I Kings 9.26–28; 10.11 (paralleled in II Chron. 8.18–19; 9.10) it was only as a result of Solomon's alliance with Hiram that gold from Ophir was imported to Judah. Is this, however, merely another anachronism, quite insignificant in view of the chronological gap? Might it not rather be another expression of the Chronicler's tendency to put David and Solomon on an equal footing, making David anticipate some of the achievements otherwise attributed to Solomon – in this case neutralizing the novelty of Solomon's expedition to Ophir?

[5b] The whole passage tends towards this clause, and the idiom here is appropriately metaphorical and elevated. The term 'to fill the hand' (*l'mallē' yād*) actually denotes 'consecrating onself for a task'; used with 'to God' it is always 'to consecrate oneself to God's service', mainly applied to the priesthood (Exod. 28.41; 29.9, 29, 33; Lev. 8.33; 16.32; Judg. 17.5, 12; I Kings 13.33, etc.; also Exod. 32.29 used metaphorically, but referring to the Levites). Only in Chronicles is the sacerdotal term applied to the whole people, when they, and not the priests, 'consecrate themselves to the Lord' (cf. also II Chron. 29.31). This transfer does not indicate an equating of the Temple with the tabernacle (where the consecration was a priestly affair); might it not rather imply that the people themselves are virtually 'a kingdom of priests' (Exod. 19.6)?

[6–9] The title *śārē hā'ābōt*, literally 'the officers of the fathers' [houses]', is found in Chronicles only in this text, and elsewhere only in Ezra 8.29. RSV overcomes the difficulty of interpretation by ignoring the 'officers' and reading, in both passages, 'the heads of the fathers' houses' (similarly NEB). This may very well have been the meaning. However, a comparison of the categories of officers here with 28.1 may indicate that the reference is in fact to 'the officers of the divisions' missing here. In any case, it is through their 'officers' that all the people make their contribution for the Temple. The metals recorded in v. 7, gold, silver, bronze and iron, specify the quantities in ascending order, as the value of the metals decreases. The total contribution of the people exceeds that of David.

Anachronistically, 'darics' are mentioned in v. 7 (cf. H. G. M. Williamson, 'Eschatology in Chronicles', *Tyndale Bulletin* 28, 1977, 123–6). These are Persian gold coins first minted by Darius, towards the end of the sixth century.

The metals are followed by 'stones' (*'ᵃbānīm*). While these may refer either to building stones or to gems (RSV, NEB), the latter seems more likely, since these were given to the 'treasury of the house of the Lord'. We must note, however, that we have no other instances of precious stones being called simply *'ᵃbānīm*.

Jehiel the Gershonite is also mentioned in I Chron. 26.21–22. In both passages he is assigned the same role in the 'treasury of the house of the Lord', distinct from 'the treasuries of the dedicated things' (I Chron. 26.20). Although the literary link between the two texts is obvious, this distinction may reflect authentic circumstances of the Chronicler's times.

[9] One of the most significant aspects of the Chronicler's concept of 'religiosity' is his view that true service of the Lord – in fact, every religious act – should entail full participation of body and soul, a harmony which he defines as 'with whole heart' (Japhet, *Ideology*, 250–3, and also Y. Muffs, 'Joy and Love as Metaphorical Expressions of Willingness and Spontaniety',

SJLT 12/3, 1975, lff.; id., 'The Joy of Giving (Love and Joy as Metaphors of Volition in Hebrew and Related Literatures, Part II)', *JANES* 11, 1979, 91–111, esp. 108ff.). This wholeness of intention also has an external expression, which is 'rejoicing'. When a person performs any act with 'rejoicing' (*śimḥāh*), his heart is surely in it. The Chronicler's identification of 'a whole heart' with 'rejoicing' is given an explicit expression in this verse, which is in fact constructed of phrases all denoting good-will, readiness and joy: three times the root 'rejoice' (*śmḥ*), twice 'give willingly' (*ndb*), and in the focal position 'whole heart'. This concluding verse also mentions all three of the participants in this joyful occasion: the people, David and the Lord.

[10–19] Verse 10 introduces David's great prayer with a precise definition: 'David blessed the Lord'; that is, David pronounced a benediction opening with the words 'Blessed art thou, O Lord', etc. The emphasis on David's recitation of this blessing in the presence of all the assembly (literally 'before the eyes of all the assembly') continues the image of 28.2: a vigorous ruler, in control of all his faculties.

In two small details the opening words deviate from the common formula: (*a*) The blessing is not addressed, as is more usual, in the third person (cf. Ps. 41.14; 72.19; 89.53, etc.); rather, a second-person invocation is inserted: 'Blessed art *thou*, the Lord' etc. (elsewhere only in Ps. 119.12) – a change which immediately determines the disposition of all that follows. (*b*) To the title 'the God of Israel' is added 'our Father', thus defining 'Israel' not as the people in general, but as their common forefather Jacob/Israel. This allusion brings to mind the more personal relationship between God and the people's forefathers, thus setting the tone for the blessing and supplication on the people's behalf, culminating in v. 18.

[11] The benediction opens with a description of God's greatness and splendour, marked by a particular stylistic feature (which becomes predominant in post-biblical liturgy), that we might call accumulation (*gibūb*). This is a manner of listing a series of words – more or less synonymous – with the conjunctive *waw*: 'greatness and power and glory, etc.' This is a concrete, quantitative, stylistic expression of the very 'greatness' being extolled, the comprehensive nature of which is also expressed by the ten-fold repetition of the word *kol*, 'all'. That the number ten is meaningful is clear from the seemingly unnecessary 'performing all' of v. 19 (*wela'ašōt hakkōl*).

The text is marked by an unusual accumulation of nouns (greatness, power, glory etc.), rather than verbs or adjectives. This gives the description a certain abstract quality, peculiar to the Chronicler.

For the Hebrew *nēṣaḥ* RSV suggests 'victory' (JPS 'triumph'); the root, however, reflects this meaning only once in biblical Aramaic (Dan. 6.3 [MT 4]), and never in biblical Hebrew. In the light of passages like I Sam. 15.2; Isa. 63.6 (cf. the word-play with v. 3), NEB 'splendour' should be preferred.

The structure of the second part of v. 11 is not immediately obvious, and especially the status of 'all that is in the heavens and in the earth' (*kī kōl baššāmayim ūbā'āreṣ*), which in MT lacks a predicate. The Vulgate adds here 'is thine', followed by most commentators (also RSV; NEB); the omission of *lᵉkā* from the Hebrew could be easily attributed to haplography. Alternatively, one may regard *kī* ('for') as an emphatic rather than causative particle, in which case the verse would be regarded as a parallel structure of two rather than three parts: 1. 'Thine, O Lord, is the greatness ... indeed all that is in heaven and in the earth'; 2. 'Thine, O Lord, is the kingdom, etc'.

In the last clause the participle *hammitnaśśē'* is translated by RSV as 'exalted' (also NEB), but this implies the express introduction of 'thou art' into the present syntactical structure, and the intrusion of a verbal form into a list composed entirely of nouns. The participle here seems to be better understood as an abstract noun, a usage which is sometimes attested in biblical Hebrew (Isa. 1.21). We recognize the peculiar form here as demonstrating the struggle of the Chronicler with the limitations of his language. *hammitnaśśē'* should be translated as the last in a series of divine attributes: '... the glory, the victory, the majesty ... the kingdom and the *exaltation* as supreme over all' (JPS 'pre-eminence above all').

It is at this emphatic juncture that the Chronicler proclaims 'Thine is the kingship, O Lord ...', an axiom found differently elsewhere (cf. II Chron. 13.8, 'the kingdom of the Lord in the hand of the sons of David'). The stress on God's reign in the precise context of David's transfer of the kingdom to Solomon is significant: this is the right time to affirm that sovereignty is God's, while the human king is his chosen regent.

[12] From the enumeration of the divine attributes, David goes on to describe God's ways among men. This is done, however, in a very general way, depicting all of mankind as subject to God's rule.

The focus of this verse is again power. Both of the factors, strength and property, which constitute wordly power are given to man by God: 'In thy hand it is to make great and to give strength', and 'riches and honour come from thee'. God rules the world, and it is from that rule that man derives any potential he might have.

kābōd would probably be better translated by a synonym for 'wealth' rather than 'honour'; cf. *BDB*, 458.

[13] This is the conclusion of the introduction of the blessing, opening with 'and now'. David's prayer now moves gradually from general abstractions to the actual situation, in referring to the assembled people ('*we* thank thee ...'), who praise God for his glory.

After the address 'and now, our God', the verse is structured in parallel members, following the pattern abc/a'c', with c' (*lᵉšēm tip'artekā*) as a ballast-variant of c (*lāk*).

[14–17] The focus of the benediction now shifts to the actual context: not the general themes of Solomon's enthronment or the building of the Temple, but the specific subject of the freewill offering. The terms and concepts here reflect v. 9, of which v. 17 is almost an echo. Thus the root *ndb* recurs in this passage three times; also repeated are *ntn* (give, v. 14) and *hākīn* (provide, v. 16), echoing vv. 2, 3, 7, and 8.

The particular emphases of this passage are of interest. First and foremost is the unworthiness of man, which is given expression in several ways:

(*a*) 'We are strangers ... and sojourners' on earth, and, to pursue the metaphor, therefore possess no claim to permanence in the land of the living.

(*b*) Life itself is like a shadow – a phenomenon with only slight resemblance to concrete substance.

(*c*) Man can have neither hope (*miqweh*) nor confidence in his transient state in this world.

(*d*) The conclusion of all this must be: 'Who am I and what is my people?'

From another angle the emphasis lies in man's utter dependence upon God for all his possessions. This was generally stated in v. 12, but is now repeated in a more direct and personal way: '... of thine own have we given thee' (v. 14); '... all this abundance that we have provided ... comes from thy hand' (v. 16).

And yet, David does not belittle the great effort made by the people and himself: in spite of their nothingness, and having nothing of their own, they have taken upon themselves a tremendous project: to build a house for the Lord. 'All this abundance' (v. 16) which king and people have contributed reflects their 'uprightness', their worthy intention to offer 'freely and joyously to thee' (v. 17).

[18–19] The blessing ends with a petition in the same vein. David does not appeal for power, victory or riches, nor for the establishment and endurance of Solomon's kingdom, but only that the spiritual perfection which the people have reached may endure 'for ever', and that Solomon may be granted a 'whole heart' with which to proceed, 'performing all'.

The view that God 'directs hearts', and that in order to reach perfection in the service of God, man needs divine help, is found several times in Chronicles (cf. I Chron. 22.12; II Chron. 30.12, and probably also II Chron. 29.36; Japhet, *Ideology*, 254–5 and n. 182), and is presented here in a special way. David's assertion is that at this point in the people's history they have indeed reached the desired goal, the ideal state of 'wholeness of heart'; it is a climactic moment in the history of Israel, not in material but in spiritual terms, with the thoughts and hearts of all Israel directed to God. In order to maintain this ideal the people need God's assistance, and this is David's only request. All the rest – success, prosperity, establishment of the kingdom, etc. – are corollaries of this spiritual disposition and will surely follow. This is an expression of the Chronicler's deep religious conviction, and of the way in which he understands man's task in relation to God and his responsibility for his own life and deeds. Confidence in God's justice and benevolence is so complete that it is only man's part in the relationship which needs to be assured.

[20] This part of the ceremony ends with the people's benediction, in response to David's exhortation. It is very possible that this description of the ceremony reflects actual forms of the regular service in the Second Temple, especially in the people's vocal worship and bodily prostration in response to the prayer of the officiators in the cult, represented here by the king. A similar picture is also presented in I Chron. 16.36; the psalm recited by the Levites concludes with a doxology: 'Blessed be the Lord, the God of Israel', and the people's response is explicitly mentioned: 'then all the people said "Amen", and praised the Lord'. In this context, while the exact words of the people are not recorded, one may conjecture that their blessing was identical or similar to David's in v. 10b, or to any of the doxologies concluding collections of psalms (cf. above, p. 319).

After pronouncing the blessing, the people bowed low and prostrated themselves before both 'the Lord and the king'. Such a close conjunction of God and king in an act of worship (avoided in RSV by the addition of a second verb) is not found elsewhere in the Bible, although the divine and earthly rulers are mentioned together in several contexts (Prov. 24.21, 'Fear the Lord and the king'; I Kings 21.10, 13, etc.). The question is: should this allusion be construed as a reflection of actual contemporary custom in the Second Temple, i.e. an obeisance to the king in addition to a prostration 'before God'? If so, then the demand spelled out in Ezra 6.10, 'that they may offer pleasing sacrifices to the God of heaven, and pray for the life of the king and his sons', might be regarded as fully incorporated and thoroughly established in the cult. Our texts, however, provide far too meagre a basis for confident conclusions; cf. Mordecai's attitude to the Persian officials: 'but Mordecai did not bow down' (Esther 3.2).

[21–25] In these verses the enthronement of Solomon is described; there is no similiarity to I Kings 1–2, the only relationship to which is polemical.

[21] The people's first act following the speeches and prayers is to offer sacrifice. The phrasing of the verse is somewhat difficult, as it introduces in addition to the burnt offerings ('ōlōt), two different types of sacrifice (zᵉbāḥîm): 'to the Lord' and 'for all Israel'. RSV avoids the difficulty by distributing these sacrifices between the day in question, when 'they performed sacrifices to the Lord', and 'the next day', when they offered 'burnt offerings' and 'sacrifices for all Israel'. But since the phrase 'on the next day' is difficult in other ways as well, this seemingly smooth solution is not decisive. It would seem that the verse should be interpreted as a general

statement: 'and they performed sacrifices to the Lord', followed by the two specific types: 'burnt offerings to the Lord' and 'sacrifices ... for all Israel'.

The burnt offerings are enumerated: bulls, rams and lambs – the common combination in the priestly sacrificial system (cf. e.g. Num. 28–29). The term 'their drink-offerings' (niskēhem) also belongs to the priestly vocabulary, this being its only appearance in Chronicles. The description thus adapts priestly terminology to the occasion.

The extravagant number of the burnt-offerings, a total of three thousand bulls, rams and lambs, is a concrete expression of the grandeur of the event. By way of comparison, Solomon is said to have sacrificed only a third as many offerings during his visit to the shrine in Gibeon (I Kings 3.4//II Chron. 1.6).

As I have noted, the words 'on the next day' pose a variety of difficulties. The narrative sequence and inner logic of the event all lead to the culmination of the ceremony with the enthronement of Solomon. Indeed, v. 22 explicitly states that 'they ate and drank before the Lord on that day', which refers naturally to the same great day on which the people had been assembled to hear David's solemn addresses and benedictions. The transition of the climax – the sacrificial offerings and celebration – to 'the next day' is surprising. These words would seem to be a gloss, introduced by an editor who was not satisfied with the fact that in the original order of the events the sacrifices preceded Solomon's enthronement. By this addition the sacrifices are 'transferred' (without changing their actual position in the text) to the day following the enthronement, which itself took place 'on that day', i.e. on the day of the benedictions and feastings.

[22] Here is described the actual anointing of Solomon, followed in the next verse by his accession to the throne. The order and phrasing of the events are surprising: the enthronement is described only after the rejoicing and feasting 'before the Lord'. Thus Solomon's accession is a continuation of the celebrations, not their cause.

Furthermore, in this verse (as in the previous one), all the verbs are in the third person plural, either with an indefinite subject or referring to the people in general (as in v. 20). This is especially unusual for the first and the last verbs in the series: 'and they sacrificed ... and they anointed'.

We note, too, that the verse describes the anointing of Zadok to the priesthood, which is surprising in several ways. Except for the initial anointing of Aaron and his sons by Moses in the wilderness, which was to be 'a perpetual priesthood throughout their generations' (Exod. 40.15, cf. also Lev. 8), there is no biblical evidence from either the First or the Second Temple of the consecrating of priests by anointing. Moreover, in contrast to Solomon, who was only now ascending David's throne, Zadok was only continuing the priestly role already conferred upon him previously.

514   I CHRONICLES

It would seem, therefore, that the reference to the consecration of Zadok is intended to signify that on one and the same day the two hereditary lines of Israel's leadership were irrevocably determined for all time, with Solomon representing the house of David, and Zadok the house of Aaron. Zadok is thus given extremely significant status, as a counterpart of Solomon, a phenomenon which is well illustrated in the period of the restoration, when the secular and religious leaders cooperated in guiding the people (Zerubbabel and Joshua, Nehemiah and Ezra).

The last question in this verse concerns the word *šānīt*, 'the second time'. The view of the enthronement here as a 'repeat' of the event related either in 23.1 or in I Kings 1–2 (Williamson, 187) contradicts the inner dynamic of the whole unit. The words 'and Solomon sat on the throne of the Lord' (v. 23), which express the climax and purpose of the whole event, in fact lose all meaning if Solomon has already been anointed king. It is more reasonable to assume that *šānīt*, too, is a gloss, by the redactor who understood 23.1 as an actual description of the coronation, and viewed this section as describing a 'second' ceremony.

[23–25] These verses demonstrate the clearest affinity, both affirmative and polemical, to the story of Solomon's accession in I Kings 1–2. Verse 23a repeats, with variations, I Kings 2.12:

23a: 'Then Solomon sat on the throne of the Lord as king instead of David his father.'
I Kings 2.12: 'So Solomon sat upon the throne of David his father.'

The main change between these passages is the replacement of the 'throne of David' with 'the throne of the Lord'. 'The throne of David' occupies an emphatic position in the conceptual terminology of I Kings 1–2. It is alluded to repeatedly by David himself ('he shall sit upon my throne', 1.13; also vv. 17, 24, 30, 35) or by the other participants ('who shall sit on the throne of the lord the king', 1.20; also 27, 37, 47), culminating in the passage cited above (2.12). By contrast, Chronicles never refers to 'the throne of David'; instead it has 'the throne of the Lord' in this verse, or 'the throne of the kingdom of the Lord over Israel' (I Chron. 28.5), or 'the throne of Israel' (II Chron. 6.10, 16//I Kings 8.20, 25), or simply the 'royal throne in Israel' (I Chron. 22.10; II Chron. 7.18// I Kings 9.5). In I Chron. 17.14, 'his throne' refers to Solomon. The change in this verse, then, reflects the Chronicler's view of the nature of the Israelite kingship.

The polemical tendency of vv. 23b–24 is expressed first of all by their position at this precise point in the narrative. There is no literary or political justification for the unique 'all the leaders ... pledged their allegiance to King Solomon'. This remark's *raison d'être* is its polemic reference to I Kings 1–2. There, the struggle between the camps of Adonijah and Solomon culminate in the latter gaining the upper hand, but Solomon's enthronement was surely not the unanimous act of 'all the leaders'. I Kings 1 in fact remarks explicitly that 'the sons of the king' pledged their allegiance, not to Solomon but to Adonijah ('... he invited all his brothers, the king's sons' – v. 9, also vv. 19, 25), while it was 'the mighty men', under the command of Benaiah the son of Jehoiada, who joined Solomon (I Kings 1.8, 10). The Chronicler, on the other hand, stresses not only the consent of the entire people, but even more their active support in the accession of Solomon, by carefully including here members of both camps: 'the mighty men' and 'all the sons of king David'.

Furthermore, the narrative in Kings elaborates on the events which followed Solomon's accession until his kingdom was firmly established. These are described in detail, first in David's testament (I Kings 2.5–9) and subsequently in its execution (2.13–45). Only at 2.46 can the author write: 'So the kingdom was established in the hand of Solomon'. All these events are passed over in silence by the Chronicler, who relegates them to one short clause: 'and he prospered, and all Israel obeyed him' (23b). From the moment that he ascended the throne, Solomon's kingdom was prosperously established.

Verse 25 already anticipates Solomon's actual reign in describing his 'great repute' and 'royal majesty', right at the beginning. This again is literarily and theologically linked to Kings. In I Kings 1.37, Benaiah pronounces this wish: 'May the Lord ... make his [Solomon's] throne greater than the throne of my lord king David'. Cf. also v. 47: 'Your God make the name of Solomon more famous than yours'. This verse, 'and the Lord made Solomon exceedingly great' (JPS), refers back both to these wishes and to David's own prayer: 'in thy hand it is to make great and to give strength' (v. 12). The immediate fulfilment of all these majestic hopes is irrefutable evidence of Solomon's divine election.

[26–30] The last paragraph is devoted to a summary and general evaluation of David's reign. Such epitomes, strictly structured and of Deuteronomistic origin, are regular features of the historiography of the book of Kings, beginning with Solomon, and are ordinarily adopted, with slight changes, by the Chronicler (cf. p. 644). The summary of David's reign in I Kings 1.10–12 is peculiar. It contains some but not all of the elements of the Deuteronomistic pattern, and is more organically connected with the narrative in which it is embedded: the formulaic note concerning David's death and burial, and the data about the duration of this reign, are followed by a remark, not formulaic in idiom, about Solomon's succession – a connecting link with the ensuing narrative.

The Chronicler adjusts the unit more closely to the Deuteronomistic formula by adding an observation on his sources: 'Now the acts of David ... are written in the Chronicles of Samuel the seer, etc.' (v. 29), and by referring to Solomon's succession with the formal phrase 'and Solomon his son reigned in his stead' (v. 28b). In several other points, however, he deviates from the literary pattern:

(*a*) The Chronicler opens his summary with a programmatic declaration: 'Thus David the son of Jesse reigned over all Israel' (v. 26). With this he refers us to the only other instance, immediately after Saul's death, where he solemnly identifies David by his full name: 'Therefore the Lord ... turned the kingdom to David the son of Jesse' (I Chron. 10.14). Furthermore, the indication that David's reign was 'over all Israel' is a point of great significance in the Chronicler's understanding of the Davidic kingdom (cf. above pp. 236–7).

(*b*) In place of the common formula 'slept with his fathers', the Chronicler describes David's death in a more poetic style: 'Then he died in good old age, full of days, riches and honour' (v. 28). In this way David is compared to Abraham (Gen. 25.8), Isaac (Gen. 35.29), Gideon (Judg. 8.32), and Job (Job 42.17). The formula in this verse is, however, the longest. David goes to his rest, not only 'full of days' but also of 'riches and honours' – the very blessings bestowed on Solomon according to I Kings 3.13–14.

In Chronicles, the time and manner of a king's death constitute a kind of criterion for the evaluation of the king as either righteous or wicked. The elaborate phrasing of this verse would certainly indicate that David surpassed any other king. In addition, it also serves the Chronicler's purpose of setting David and Solomon as far as possible on an equal footing: all of Solomon's achievements were matched by David's own.

(*c*) This passage contains no reference to a burial place, as is customary in such summaries and is explicitly found concerning David in I Kings 2.10b. It is possible, therefore, that the reference was simply dropped from the text, by a parablepsis, thus: *'ōšer wᵉkābōd [wayyiqqābēr bᵉʿîr dāwîd] wayyimlōk šᵉlōmōh.*

(*d*) The reference to the literary sources on David's reign is augmented by the addition of v. 30, intended to glorify David by mentioning the abundant 'circumstances' of his reign, which influenced not only Israel but the known world – the only case in Chronicles where the scope of such a summary is broadened to include 'all the kingdoms of the countries' (RSV; JPS 'the kingdoms of the earth'). The structure of the verse weaves a concentric pattern around David himself: 'the circumstances that came upon him, and upon Israel, and upon the kindoms of the earth', making David's kingdom the focus of universal rule and influence.

The Chronicler mentions three works as sources for David's reign: the Chronicles of Samuel the seer, of Nathan the prophet and of Gad the seer, the three prophets active during David's lifetime. Their order here follows that of their appearance in the narrative of Chronicles: Samuel is already mentioned at David's accession (I Chron. 11.3), Nathan in his prophecy of the Davidic dynasty (I Chron. 17), and Gad only at the census, in I Chron. 21.9.

Each of the prophets has his own particular title: Samuel is 'the seer' (rō'eh), Nathan 'the prophet', and Gad 'the seer' (a different term, ḥōzeh). The title 'seer' for Samuel (cf. also I Chron. 9.22; 26.28) is probably based on I Sam. 9, where Samuel is repeatedly referred to as a 'seer' (I Sam. 9.11, 18 19), but never formally titled 'Samuel the seer'. The joining of this title to a prophet's name is peculiar to Chronicles, applied not only to Samuel but also for Hanani the father of Jehu (I Chron. 16.7, 10). The other term for 'seer' (ḥōzeh) attributed to Gad, is also found in I Sam. 24.11, but is more characteristic of Chronicles (cf. on I Chron. 21.9), and is repeated in II Chron. 29.25. The Chronicler also adds this title to the name of other prophets, cf. II Chron. 9.29; 12.15; 19.2, etc. By contrast, 'the prophet' is a quite common appelation, and not only for Nathan. It would seem, therefore, that by analogy to this more common phrase, the Chronicler constructed the two others, in an effort to achieve stylistic variation.

A major question about the Chronicler's reference to sources concerns their authenticity. In addition to the difficulties arising from the general aspects of this question, a problem is posed in this particular case by the highly dubious reference to the 'Chronicles of Samuel'. According to information from the book bearing his name, Samuel died during Saul's reign, while David was still a fugitive in the desert of Judah or among the Philistines (I Sam. 25.1). It is doubtful whether Samuel had recorded David's activities during that period. Moreover, the Chronicler passed over this period of David's life, beginning his narrative with David's accession, when Samuel was no longer among the living.

At the same time we must admit that the Chronicler had at his disposal some documents referring to David's time which are not included in the canonical book of Samuel. Even a minimal assessment will indicate that some of this additional material should be regarded as authentic, e.g. the second part of the list of the mighty men (I Chron. 11.41b–47), or the list of David's stewards (I Chron. 27.25–31). Thus, while it seems difficult to presume the use of an authentic work entitled 'The Chronicles of Samuel the Seer', the Chronicler's recourse to additional sources cannot categorically be denied. Some of these sources were undoubtedly post-exilic and late, but some earlier and even authentic.

As the 'chronicles' mentioned here by name can hardly be regarded as actual sources, their titles should be viewed as part of the Chronicler's historiographical and theological outlook. By describing his sources as composed by prophets, and as written contemporaneously to the events in question, the Chronicler declares their ultimate validity.

II Chronicles

1

1 1 Solomon the son of David established himself in his kingdom, and the Lord his God was with him and made him exceedingly great.

2 Solomon spoke to all Israel, to the commanders of thousands and of hundreds, to the judges, and to all the leaders in all Israel, the heads of fathers' houses. 3 And Solomon, and all the assembly with him, went to the high place that was at Gibeon; for the tent of meeting of God, which Moses the servant of the Lord had made in the wilderness, was there. 4 (But David had brought up the ark of God from Kiriath-jearim to the place that David had prepared for it, for he had pitched a tent for it in Jerusalem.) 5 Moreover the bronze altar that Bezalel the son of Uri, son of Hur, had made, was there before the tabernacle of the Lord. And Solomon and the assembly sought the Lord. 6 And Solomon went up there to the bronze altar before the Lord, which was at the tent of meeting, and offered a thousand burnt offerings upon it.

7 In that night God appeared to Solomon, and said to him, 'Ask what I shall give you.' 8 And Solomon said to God, 'Thou hast shown great and steadfast love to David my father, and hast made me king in his stead. 9 O Lord God, let thy promise to David my father be now fulfilled, for thou hast made me king over a people as many as the dust of the earth. 10 Give me now wisdom and knowledge to go out and come in before this people, for who can rule this thy people, that is so great?'

11 God answered Solomon, 'Because this was in your heart, and you have not asked possessions, wealth, honour, or the life of those who hate you, and have not even asked long life, but have asked wisdom and knowledge for yourself that you may rule my people over whom I have made you king, 12 wisdom and knowledge are granted to you. I will also give you riches, possessions, and honour, such as none of the kings had who were before you, and none after you shall have the like.' 13 So Solomon came from the high place at Gibeon, from before the tent of meeting, to Jerusalem. And he reigned over Israel.

14 Solomon gathered together chariots and horsemen; he had fourteen hundred chariots and twelve thousand horsemen, whom he stationed in the chariot cities and with the king in Jerusalem. 15 And the king made silver and gold as common in Jerusalem as stone, and he made cedar as plentiful as the sycamore of the Shephelah. 16 And Solomon's import of horses was from Egypt and Kue, and the king's traders received them from Kue for a price. 17 They imported a chariot from Egypt for six hundred shekels of silver, and a horse for a hundred and fifty; likewise through them these were exported to all the kings of the Hittites and the kings of Syria.

A. Notes to MT

[5] שם, BH שָׁם; many MSS, LXX and V שם ; [6] לפני יהוה, transpose after שם? cf. commentary; [13] לבמה, read מהבמה with the Versions; [16] מקוא, transfer the pause here? Cf. I Kings 10.28 and commentary.

B. Notes to RSV

[5] 'was there', so LXX, MT 'he placed', cf. commentary; 'sought the Lord', better 'resorted to it' (NEB, JPS; cf. commentary); [6] 'went up', or 'offered'; [16] 'received', better 'would buy' (JPS); [17] 'Syria', MT 'Aram' (NEB; JPS).

C. Structure, sources and form

1. II Chronicles 1–9 are devoted to the reign of Solomon, paralleling I Kings 2.12–11.43. In his own record, the Chronicler has made intensive use of his sources in Kings. The guiding principles for editing the borrowed material are in general similar to those of the history of David, with the difference that for Solomon's history the Chronicler's amplification of his sources and redactive activity are both relatively limited. The sum of omissions and additions leaves the final scope of Solomonic material in Chronicles shorter than in Kings, an 'abbreviation' which creates a new balance in the description of the figure of Solomon.

(a) The following passages in I Kings are cited, either reworked or verbatim, in the Chronicler's story: I Kings 3.4–15; 4.21, 26 [MT 5.1, 6]; 5.2–11, 15–16 [MT 5.16–25, 29–30]; 6.1–27; 7.15–51; 8.1–50, 52, 54, 62–66; 9.1–28; 10.1–29; 11.41–43.

(b) The texts in Kings not paralleled in Chronicles are: I Kings 2.13–46; 3.1–3, 16–28; 4.1–20; 22–25 [MT 5.2–5]; 4.27–5.1 [MT 5.7–15]; 6.28–37; 7.1–15; 8.52–53, 55–61; 11.1–40.

(c) Additions to the Kings text are: II Chron. 1.1b–5; 3.3–6, 8, 11–13; 5.11–13; 6.13, 41–42; 7.1–3; 8.2–3, 13–15.

With the exception of elaborations in Solomon's correspondence with Hiram (II Chron. 2.13–16 [MT 12–15] cf. there), only nineteen verses of the Chronicler's story are new. Of these, in one case the Chronicler seems to preserve a better text (II Chron. 6.13) and in another he is borrowing from a different biblical source (6.40–41 = Ps. 132.8–10); three other passages deal with matters of worship and cult and seem to be distinctly Chronistic. Only for two of the Chronistic additions (1.1b–5 and 8.2–3) is the problem of extra-biblical sources of any relevance; cf. the respective chapters.

2. II Chronicles 1 parallels the introduction of Solomon's reign in I Kings 3.1–28. The passage in Kings opens with the prefatory verses 1–3, followed by two parts which together form one composition: vv. 4–15 describing God's revelation to Solomon in Gibeon, and vv. 16–28 presenting Solomon's judgment of the two harlots. Following this model, II Chron. 1 is also composed of two parts, at first glance unrelated: vv. 1–13, Solomon's journey to Gibeon, and vv. 14–17, Solomon's wealth. The focus of Solomon's visit to Gibeon is, in both versions, his request for wisdom. In I Kings, then, the episode of the two harlots (I Kings 3.16–28) concludes the pericope with a final affirmation of Solomon's wisdom, a proof that God indeed granted his request: 'and all Israel heard of the judgment which the king had rendered and they stood in awe of the king, because they perceived that the wisdom of God was in him, to render justice' (I Kings 3.28).

From the Chronicler's point of view, this conclusion is inadequate. First, he understands the essence and scope of Solomon's wisdom differently (cf. also M. Garsiel, 'Solomon's Journey to Gibeon and his Dream', *Ben-Yehudah Festschrift*,

1981, 206ff.*). The root שפט, 'judge', is used differently in the context of Chronicles (cf. below), and the practical evidence of Solomon's discernment is not an act of judgment, but the construction of the Temple: 'a wise son, endued with discretion and understanding, who will build a temple for the Lord' (II Chron. 2.12 [MT 11]). The story of the two harlots, as well as other texts related to Solomon's wisdom, are therefore omitted from the Chronicler's version (cf. Japhet, *Ideology*, 482–4). God's gift of wisdom is then illustrated in II Chron. 1.14–17 not by Solomon's acumen as arbitrator (as in I Kings 3.16–28), but by his wealth and honour, matters which play a much greater role in the Chronicler's version of God's promise (cf. the commentary).

3. Verses 1–13 employ an intricate reworking of I Kings 2.46b and 3.4–15, to produce a passage of equal scope, an instructive example of the Chronicler's literary technique. The conclusion of David's reign in II Kings 2.10–12 is transferred with some changes to I Chron. 29.23, 26–30. Following faithfully the sequence of his source, the Chronicler now bypasses I Kings 2.13–46a, and moves on to 46b, which he uses as a cornerstone for the following passage. Compare:

I Kings 2.46b: והממלכה נכונה ביד שלמה, 'So the kingdom was established in the hand of Solomon';
II Chron. 1.1: ויתחזק שלמה בן דויד על מלכותו, 'Solomon the son of David established himself in his kingdom'.

Then, still tracing the line of his source, the Chronicler skips I Kings 3.1–3 and moves directly to borrow the whole passage of vv. 4–15, complete with structure and plot. A synoptic study of the texts will soon reveal that in the process of borrowing, additions and omissions affected not only the wording but the literary format as well.

The focus of the story in Kings is clearly God's revelation to Solomon, to which ten of the passage's twelve verses are dedicated (I Kings 4.5–14). This is framed by a brief introduction concerning Solomon's journey to Gibeon and the sacrifices he offered there (v. 4), and a short conclusion relating his return to Jerusalem (v. 15). In Chronicles, the narrative is composed of two nearly equal parts: vv. 2–6 tell of Solomon's journey to Gibeon, while vv. 7–12 are dedicated to God's revelation. This new structure, with its double focus, is achieved by (*a*) a lengthy addition (vv. 2–6) which makes the original one-verse introduction a unit in its own right, (*b*) a new introduction (v. 1), and (*c*) omissions which considerably shorten the main body of the story (I Kings 3.6b, 7b, 10, 14 are deleted, besides several words and phrases). The final structure of the Chronicler's narrative of course expresses a new understanding of the events (cf. the commentary):

1:     Introduction
2–6:   Solomon's journey to Gibeon and his worship there
7–12: God's revelation to Solomon
13:    Conclusion.

4. The second part of the chapter (vv. 14–17) is taken from Kings 10.26–29, the last passage of Solomon's history before his transgressions and decline (I Kings 11, omitted in Chronicles). The passage recurs – although in a different adaptation – in the Chronistic parallel to the context of Kings, in II Chron. 9.25–28 (cf. there). The common literary-critical inclination is to regard any repetition as redundant. This tendency, together with the observation that a given passage may be explained as a secondary complementary gloss when appearing in the same context of its source,

much more readily than when appearing in a new context, has led many to regard II Chron. 9.25–28 as secondary to Chronicles (cf. Rudolph, 221– 3). However, aversion to repetition should not be regarded as a compelling literary-critical principle; the same passage may serve different purposes in different contexts. This passsage is certainly an example in point:

(a) A closer examination of the two Chronicles passages will reveal that they are not really identical. While both are dependent on I Kings 10.26–29, each has been specifically adjusted to its new setting, the more reworked form being the text of II Chron. 9.25–28.

(b) While the appearance of this passage in II Chron. 9.25–28 is determined by the sequence of the Solomon narrative in Kings, its logic in II Chron. 1 follows the Chronicler's own particular emphases. Here it is the Chronicler's alternative for I Kings 3.16–28, presenting Solomon's riches as the fulfilment of God's promise.

5. Verses 1b–5 introduce information not found elsewhere in the Bible; the language and style bear signs of the Chronicler's hand, or at least of late biblical Hebrew. What, then, is the origin of the passage? Since it is a coherent literary unit with unmistakable marks of late Hebrew, and – as will be shown below – the literary structure is a response to and elaboration of the material in Kings, it seems quite improbable that the Chronicler was employing an independent literary source. The question of sources should therefore be further qualified to apply only to the new data in the passage relating to the 'tabernacle of the Lord' and 'the bronze altar'. Do these reflect an ancient, authentic tradition underlying the subsequent literary formulation, or are they *a priori* late and inauthentic? As this question is very much connected with the interpretation of the passage, I shall deal with it in the commentary.

D. Commentary

[1] The verse is an appropriate introduction to the story of Solomon's reign. In the book of Kings, the beginning of Solomon's reign is marked by his efforts to consolidate his rule, and these episodes (I Kings 2.13–46a) are framed by the following relevant comments:

2.12: 'and his kingdom was firmly established',
2.46b: 'So the kingdom was established in the hand of Solomon'.

As a result of this structure, the conventional Deuteronomistic introduction is missing; some of its elements are postponed to the Deuteronomistic conclusion (I Kings 11.41–43) and some are omitted altogether.

The Chronicler, following the structure of his source, does not provide an equivalent to the Deuteronomistic introduction. Having omitted all the material of I Kings 2.13–46a, which may have put Solomon's early career in a negative light, he composes a longer, rather solemn three-part introduction of his own, bearing all the marks of his style: Solomon the son of David established himself (*wayyithazzēq*) in his kingdom; God was with him and made him exceedingly great (*wayʿgaddʿlēhū lʿmāʿʿlāh*).

The phrasing of this introduction echoes David's blessings in I Chron. 22.11, 'The Lord be with you ...', and 28.20, 'be strong and of good courage ($ḥ^azaq\ we'^emaṣ$) ... for the Lord God ... is with you', as well as I Chron. 29.12: 'in thy hand it is to make great ($l^egaddēl$) and to give strength ($ūl^eḥazzēq$) to all'. David himself has been described as one whose greatness derives from God's presence with him (II Sam. 5.10 = I Chron. 11.9); now David's prayers are answered: 'The Lord was with Solomon'.

As in I Chron. 29.22 and II Chron. 13.6, Solomon is intentionally designated here 'the son of David', an emphasis on continuity, affinity and legitimacy.

[2–6] These five verses represent the Chronicler's parallel of I Kings 3.4, thoroughly reworked along literary and theological lines.

The Chronicler here employs the literary technique of a careful elaboration of his one-verse source. I Kings 3.4 has three parts: (i) 'And the king went to Gibeon to sacrifice there, (ii) for that was the great high place; (iii) Solomon used to offer a thousand burnt offerings upon that altar.' All three clauses are faithfully represented: the first in II Chron. 1.3a: 'And Solomon, and all the assembly with him, went to the high place that was at Gibeon'; the second, explaining Solomon's journey, in vv. 3b–5: 'for the tent of meeting ... was there ... Moreover the bronze altar ... was there'; and the last in v. 6: 'and Solomon offered (RSV 'went up') there ... a thousand burnt offerings ...'. In point of fact each word in I Kings 3.4 has its equivalent in Chronicles, with the exception of 'the great' (cf. below). The Chronicles text adds only the introduction (v. 2), which broadens the event to include not only Solomon himself but the whole people (cf. below), the explanatory note of vv. 3b–5, and the precise specification of 'that altar' in v. 6. These additions, of course, reveal the Chronicler's new insights into the historical setting and theological meaning of the event, which may be summarized as follows:

(a) In I Kings 3.4, Solomon's journey to Gibeon is described as a private venture; his entourage is not even mentioned until his return to Jerusalem, and even then the focus is still Solomon himself, who 'made a feast for all his servants' (I Kings 3.15). In Chronicles, the pilgrimage is conceived as a public event from the beginning. Solomon proposes the idea to 'the commanders ... to all the leaders ... the heads of fathers' houses', and they all go together to Gibeon. While Solomon's vision is still his private encounter with God, it is seen in a grander context of national worship; needless to say there is no need here for a special feast for Solomon's servants!

(b) Although the precise time of this journey is not given in Kings, the development of the narrative indicates that it is certainly not Solomon's first royal initiative. Not so in Chronicles, where the journey is tightly linked with the enthronement itself. We have already been told in I Chron. 29.23 and

526

II CHRONICLES

II Chron. 1.1 that Solomon was king, yet v. 13 repeats that 'he reigned over Israel'. The phrasing of the verse is probably influenced by the similar I Kings 4.1: 'King Solomon was king over all Israel'. Here, however, the observation concludes rather than opens the pericope, a fact which is doubly significant. Like David before him, whose first act after his accession was to gather all Israel to bring the ark to Jerusalem (I Chron. 13.1ff.), so Solomon's first act is to seek 'the tent of meeting of God' with 'all the assembly' – an act of worship before the Lord. The link between the two episodes is in fact explicit in the reference to the ark in v. 4. The revelation at Gibeon is the final confirmation of Solomon's accession.

(c) The need to account for Solomon's major sacrifices at Gibeon, already felt in Kings, is evident here as well, although the explanation offered is different:

I Kings 3.4: '*for* that was the great high place'
II Chron. 1.3: '*for* the tent of meeting ... was there'.

This is the innovation in the passage – the claim that the wilderness tent of meeting and the bronze altar were situated in Gibeon. In addition, the Chronicler cites facts already known from II Sam. 6//I Chron. 13.15: that the ark was transferred by David from Kiriath-jearim to a tent in Jerusalem, information which also appeared in I Chron. 16.39–42 and 21.29.

The importance of this matter for the Chronicler is expressed here by the literary form. The same matters are repeated several times: a reference to 'the tent of meeting' (v. 3), an explicit distinction between the two tents (v. 4), and two descriptions of tent and altar together (vv. 5, 6). This repetition is augmented by the varied terms used in these same verses for the wilderness tent: 'the tent of meeting of God' (*'ōhel mō'ēd hā'elōhīm*), 'the tabernacle of the Lord', (*miškan yhwh*), and 'the tent of meeting' (*'ōhel mō'ēd*). And finally, there is a strong emphasis on the origin and authenticity of both 'the tent which Moses, the servant of the Lord, had made in the wilderness' (v. 3), and 'the bronze altar that Bezalel, the son of Uri, son of Hur, had made' (v. 5).

Considering that the Chronicler does not repeat the wilderness traditions, and that Chronistic allusions to Moses are almost restricted to the 'Law of Moses', all of the wilderness terminology here has special significance. It will appear only in II Chron. 24.6, 9, again in connection with the tabernacle tradition. This, then, is an important feature of Chronistic theology: the continuity linking the desert tabernacle with Solomon's temple. Gibeon, where the Aaronide Zadok was officiating, is seen as a transitional stage.

I have raised the question of sources: what is the origin of the information cited here by the Chronicler? Having observed the tendency here to 'justify' Solomon, the reader is inclined to relegate the passage to the category of theological apologetics. However, this does not exempt us from asking whether the information itself is a 'free invention' of the Chronicler (cf. Curtis, 315–6; Rudolph, 197), or the faithful transmission of an existing tradition.

The 'literary invention' view would seem to find strong support in the Chronicler's historical and religious convictions, according to which it was unthinkable that Solomon sacrificed at a 'high place'. The assertion in Kings that he did just that is justified in I Kings 3.2 by the statement 'no house had yet been built for the name of the Lord', based on the assumption of Deut. 12.8–14 that multiplicity of cult-places was regarded as legitimate until the Temple was constructed. For the Chronicler, this whole complex is erroneous, and an alternative historical structure had to be suggested.

The central cultic tradition of the Former Prophets is that of the ark (Josh. 3–4; 6; I Sam. 4–6; 7.1–2; II Sam. 6). Although it is provided with some kind of abode, this is afforded little significance; the ark is an object of reverence in its own right. The central tradition of the Pentateuch, by contrast, is that of the tent. The Priestly version describes the Tabernacle itself in great detail; together with the bronze altar in its courtyard, it is an obvious Temple prototype. In the Priestly description the ark does play a role as the most important object within the tabernacle; in the Former Prophets, however, the tabernacle tradition is negligible, referred to only in Josh. 18.1; 22.19, 29 and in the more obscure text of I Kings 8.3–4.

Speaking very generally, we may regard the evidence of the Pentateuch and of the Former Prophets as expressing diverging theological attitudes to the history of the cult. One view regards the ark as Israel's primary cult object: prior to the building of the Temple it was placed in some kind of a shrine, and according to I Kings 2.28 there was also an altar attached to it; after the building of the Temple, the ark was situated inside the Temple, and its independent status was virtually lost. Besides the ark, there were in Israel other cult centres, differently conceived in the various biblical traditions; according to the Deuteronomic theology their legitimacy was secured until the building of the Temple.

The Priestly theology presents a full-fledged portable temple, with all the required furnishings, including a bronze altar, already in the wilderness. The only expression of this view in the historical narrative, in Josh. 22, is based on the assumption that sacrifices to the Lord may be offered only at the one altar, standing before the tabernacle; any other altar is a sign of mutiny. The location of the single legitimate altar is not specified, but it may have been Shiloh (Josh. 18.1; 22.9).

Prior to the Chronicler, no serious attempt was made to harmonize the ark-centred view of the Former Prophets with the tabernacle-centred picture of the Pentateuch (but cf. I Kings 8.4 and its parallel in II Chron. 5.5). This text, and the related I Chron. 16, express the Chronicler's effort to forge a unified and coherent theology from the distinct lines of tradition presented above. This effort presumes, first of all, that in the early history of the cult there were two different tents rather than one: the priestly tabernacle built by Moses in the wilderness, and the tent pitched by David upon the arrival of the ark in Jerusalem. Secondly, notwithstanding this duality, there was always an absolute centralization of cult in Israel. At first, a full cultic ritual was conducted before the 'tabernacle of the Lord'; concurrently in the tent of the ark in Jerusalem, only a 'service of song' was performed. When the Temple building was complete, the full sacrificial rite was transferred exclusively to it. Thus, in the Chronicler's view, the cultic difference between pre- and post-Temple times is not – as in the Deuteronomic view – the passage from many legitimate cult-places to one exclusive site, but rather from one *temporary* cultic tabernacle, at Gibeon, to the *permanent* setting of the Jerusalem sanctuary.

It is therefore evident that the 'tabernacle of the Lord in Gibeon' plays an important theological role in the Chronistic history of the cult (cf. Japhet, *Ideology*, 226 ff.), along the lines of Joshua 22 and very much in opposition to the well-known Deuteronomistic approach. The question of 'origins' must therefore be more precisely defined: is the setting of the central cult at the 'tabernacle of the Lord', in Gibeon of all places, an innovation of the Chronicler, designed to answer pressing theological problems, or does it reflect earlier traditions?

Several scholars have suggested that this element of the tradition is authentic (cf. Williamson, 130–1). One should note that Gibeon was indeed a venerable shrine and may already be alluded to in Josh. 9.27. It alone is designated 'the great high place', where Solomon's regular sacrifices amount to 'a thousand burnt offerings'; it was there, and nowhere else, that Solomon experienced God's revelation. According to I Kings 2–3, the religious significance of this high place at Gibeon probably surpassed that of the tent of the ark in Jerusalem. Our question therefore, concerns only the claim that Gibeon actually housed 'the tabernacle of the Lord and the bronze altar' and was conceived as a continuation of the wilderness institutions. It is not an easy matter to decide whether Chronicles presents us here with historical tradition or a theological structuring. One wonders how the complete silence of the earlier sources should be interpreted: the only 'tabernacle theology' in the historical context of the conquest claims Shiloh as the site – as is to be expected there (I Sam. 3). The traditions after the destruction of Shiloh belong to the 'ark-centred' theology and keep silence about any other major shrine. The Chronicler, then, is striving toward a twofold goal: to give historical expression to his theological conception of the nature of the divine worship prior to the building of the Temple, and to provide a legitimization for the prestigious shrine of Gibeon. Since the juxtaposition of these aims does not conceal a historical core, it is really immaterial whether it originated with the Chronicler, or antedated him.

Several points of detail should be discussed:

(a) We have noted several times the Chronicler's stylistic inclination toward variety; v. 2 may serve as a case in point. The Chronicler wishes to describe how all the people's leaders accompanied Solomon to Gibeon. A similar purpose underlies the portrayal of David's convocation in I Chron. 28.1. However, except for the phrase 'commanders of thousands and of hundreds' (also with a light variation), all other titles in the two passages differ: 'judges', 'leaders in all Israel', 'heads of fathers houses' in II Chron. 1; 'officials', 'officers', 'stewards' 'palace officials', etc. in I Chron. 28.1.

(b) The 'assembly' which accompanies Solomon is significant in other ways as well. The king does not 'assemble' the people (as in I Chron. 23.2, wayye'ⁿsōp; 28.1, wayyaqhēl); rather, he only proposes the idea: wayyō'mer šⁿlōmōh. The verbal content of his proposal is not recorded, but the people's consent and co-operation are expressed in action: 'And Solomon, and all the assembly with him, went to the high place ...'. The 'assembly' is thus mentioned three times (vv. 2, 3, 5): first as individual components addressed by Solomon, then as proceeding to the shrine, and finally as 'seeking the Lord'. Popular participation is the major innovation in the Chronicler's view of the event.

(c) The phrasing of v. 4 is elliptical in two ways. The phrase bahēkīn, joining a preposition or an article to a conjugated verb, is an illustration of late Hebrew usage. It replaces a fuller relative clause: '[the place that] David had prepared' (so correctly RSV). Secondly, the preposition bⁿ ('in', or 'at') implies a missing sentence: '[and put it] at the place etc.', a nuance which is not expressed by the translation.

(d) Bezalel the son of Uri is mentioned in v. 5 as the craftsman who created the tabernacle's furnishings and in particular 'the bronze altar'. He is thus the precursor of Huram, who will fill the same role for Solomon (cf. on II Chron. 2.13).

(e) The word šm in v. 5 is vocalized in the Hebrew MSS in two different ways: śām (BH; Bombergiana) or šām (many MSS, and cf. LXX and V). The first form is a verb ('put, placed'), with David as subject: 'the bronze altar ... [David] placed before the tabernacle, etc.'. The second, adverbial rendering, adopted by RSV ('the bronze altar ... was there') is supported by the persistent use of 'there' (šām) in reference to Gibeon, also in vv. 3 and 6.

(f) Since v. 5 is in fact a single compound sentence, the object of wⁿyyidrⁿšēhū ('sought') is the subject of the opening clause, i.e. 'the altar'. 'Seeking' the altar thus parallels 'seeking the ark' in I Chron. 13.3. In this verse, the NEB rendering 'resorted to it' is the preferable one.

(g) Verse 6 parallels I Kings 3.4b, but elaborates 'that altar' to 'the bronze

530 II CHRONICLES

altar which was at the tent of meeting'. The elaboration is accentuated by its parenthetic position between two repetitions of the verb *wayya 'al* ('he offered'); the verse should be translated 'and Solomon offered there – on the bronze altar before the Lord, which was at the tent of meeting – he offered on it a thousand burnt offerings'. RSV circumvents this by taking the first appearance of *wayya 'al* to mean 'he went up' and translating 'on' (*'al*) as 'to' (so also NEB. JPS goes a bold step further and translates 'there Solomon *ascended* the bronze altar', thus attributing a fully-fledged priestly role to the king).

The Chronicler, by his choice of syntax, has also caused a change in the verb tenses: the imperfect *ya ''leh* of I Kings has been replaced by a repeated imperfect consecutive *wayya 'al*, with an obvious change of meaning from regular, repeated practice ('used to offer') to a single act: 'he offered upon it a thousand burnt offerings'.

[7–13] Although this passage follows I Kings 3.5–14 in structure, subject-matter and even wording, refined reworking and modification lend new focus and emphasis to the material. Here, as in Kings, God's revelation at Gibeon is presented as a regular dialogue: God's question (I Kings 3.5b = v. 7b), Solomon's answer (I Kings 3.6–9 = vv. 8–10), and God's reaction and response (I Kings 3.10–14 = vv. 11–12). In each case Chronicles abbreviates to some degree, cutting the unit to half its size. The statement 'it pleased the Lord that Solomon had asked this' (I Kings 3.10) is omitted, as well as the conditional promise of long life (I Kings 3.14) and many other items (cf. below).

[7] The verse relates God's appearance and address very concisely. Note that while the divine words are quoted verbatim from I Kings 3.5, the circumstances differ: 'in a dream by night' (*bah''lōm hallāylāh*) has become 'in that night' (*ballaylāh hahū'*). Another reference to the dream in I Kings 3.15 is also omitted by the Chronicler, an indication that his polemic is directed not toward the revelation 'at night' (cf. also I Kings 9.2 with II Chron 7.12), but more precisely against 'the dream' – a resistance shared by other biblical texts (cf. Jer. 23. 25–32). How significant this point is for the Chronicler's religious outlook is difficult to say, as no further dreams appear in his sources; the Chronicler himself makes no reference to dreams anywhere in his book.

God's question is concise, 'Ask what I shall give you' (*š''al māh 'etten lāk*), and these four words completely govern the following passage. In I Kings 3.6–14 'ask' occurs seven times, of which five are in v. 11; 'give' appears four times, and 'to you' (*lāk*) five times, all in God's answer. In Chronicles, these three elements appear four times each in vv. 8–12.

[8–10] Solomon's elaborate response in I Kings 3.6–10 has here been abridged to almost half its length; an examination of the parallel versions is therefore instructive. The main difference seems to be stylistic: the Chronicler omits much oratorical and figurative material which seems irrelevant to the issue at hand; the resulting tone is much more matter-of-fact. Among the omissions are: the description of David's righteousness (I Kings 3.6aβ: 'because he walked before thee in faithfulness, in righteousness, and in uprightness of heart toward thee'); the repetitious note 'and thou hast kept for him this great and steadfast love' (I Kings 3.6b); the reference to Solomon's limitations (3.7b: 'I am but a little child; I do not know how to go out or come in'); and the election of the people (3.8: 'and thy servant is in the midst of thy people whom thou hast chosen'). The request for wisdom is also a drastic abbreviation of I Kings (3.9 – II Chron. 1.10a). In sum, the Solomon of Chronicles is more decisive and to the point, qualities expressed by the Chronicler's more pithy turn of phrase, e.g. 'has made me king in his stead' (v. 8b, $w^e himlaktan\bar{\imath} tahtayw$) in place of 'thou ... hast given him a son to sit on his throne this day' (I Kings 3.6), thereby omitting the mention of 'the throne of David'.

The Chronicler also has a different concept of Solomon's wisdom. In Kings, the main task anticipated by Solomon upon his accession to the throne, is to 'judge the people'. The verb $\check{s}pt$ ('judge'), recurring in Kings six times, may also mean 'rule, govern', but clearly here the focus is on 'discernment ($l\bar{e}b\ \check{s}\bar{o}m\bar{e}^c a$) in administering justice' (I Kings 3.9 NEB), rather than to 'to govern' (RSV). Indeed, the story culminates in Solomon deciding the case of the two harlots 'And all Israel heard of the judgment which the king had rendered ($hammi\check{s}p\bar{a}t\ ^{a}\check{s}er\ \check{s}\bar{a}pat\ hammelek$)', and 'perceived that the wisdom of God was in him, to render justice ($la\ ^{a}s\bar{o}t\ mi\check{s}p\bar{a}t$)'. In Chronicles, the more specific connotation of 'judgment' is entirely omitted; the episode of the two harlots is deleted, and the root $\check{s}pt$ occurs only twice, with the sense of 'rule, govern'. The 'wisdom and knowledge' which Solomon seeks, and the importance of which for successful leadership is underlined by the triple repetition (vv. 10–12), is in fact granted by God, 'that you may rule my people' (v. 11).

In both versions Solomon frames his request in references to God's 'steadfast love ($hesed$)' to David his father. In Chronicles these references are fewer. In view of the general abridgment of the text, the one addition in v. 9 is all the more striking: 'O Lord God, let thy promise to David ... be now fulfilled' (NEB 'confirmed'), a clear allusion to I Chron. 17. 23–24, with the double repetition of 'mn ('be established').

[11–12] Like Solomon's request, God's response here is not only shortened but given different emphases. According to I Kings 3.13, the essence of God's answer is that because Solomon has asked well, he will be granted not only what he requested, but also what he did not: 'both riches and honour'. The conditional promise of long life which follows (v. 14) deviates from the general style; its authenticity has been questioned by many (either in its entirety or in part, cf. Montgomery, *Kings*, 108), and its absence in Chronicles may in fact reflect a shorter *Vorlage*. Some scholars, however, would see in the Chronicler's omission of 'long life' a reflection of historical fact (cf. Garsiel, ibid., 217 n. 62; S. Zalevski, 'The Revelation of God to Solomon in Gibeon', *Tarbiz* 42, 1972/3, 255–8*).

While I Kings 3.13 states that Solomon will be unrivalled in wealth during his lifetime, it is his incomparable wisdom which will distinguish him from all other kings, both past and future (I Kings 3.12): 'none like you has been before you and none like you shall arise after you'. In Chronicles, by contrast, while Solomon's wisdom is barely indicated ('Wisdom and knowledge are granted to you', v. 12), his material wealth and honour are boundless: 'such as none of the kings had who were before you, and none after you shall have the like' (v. 12). Solomon's greatest fame, and God's choicest gift, is therefore not Solomon's wisdom but his wealth – a feature which characterizes all of the narrative which follows.

[13] The first part of the chapter here comes to an end in a verse which parallels I Kings 3.15, although the Chronicler's drastic editing has preserved from the original only the words 'Solomon came … to Jerusalem'. Having omitted the reference to a dream, the Chronicler now has no literary device to mark the end of the revelation. There is also no reference to 'burnt offerings and peace offerings' offered by Solomon upon his arrival in Jerusalem. As we have already seen in v. 4, according to the Chronicler's view the service conducted at the tent of the ark in Jerusalem was exclusively musical (I Chron. 16.37). It is for this reason that, in the Chronicler's version, when Solomon moves from the high place at Gibeon to Jerusalem, he comes not '*to*' but '*from*' the tent of meeting; the further ceremony and feasting described in Kings are no longer necessary; they are replaced with a final statement that Solomon 'reigned over Israel'. Having received the promise of God's assistance and the required 'wisdom and knowledge, richness, possession and honour', Solomon is now ready to set about his kingly duties.

[14–17] The function of this passage is to conclude and confirm the account of the divine revelation at Gibeon – a role played in Kings by the judgment of the harlots. In the Kings narrative, Solomon's greatness and wealth are described only near the end (I Kings 9.15–10.29), while the early chapters describe in broad terms his administration (I Kings 4.1–28 [MT 4.1–5.8]), wisdom (4.9–34 [MT 5.9–14]) and the building of the Temple (5.1–9.9 [MT 5.15–9.9]). While the Chronicler will omit the remarks about Solomon's wisdom and administration and will proceed directly to the building of the Temple (II Chron. 2.1ff.), the subject of Solomon's wealth – the axis of God's promise – is briefly related here.

Verses 14–17 are taken from I Kings 10.26–29 with only a negligible amount of editing, in strong contrast to the thorough reworking afforded the first part of the chapter. Most of the changes are of a textual and linguistic nature, of which I would mention two. (*a*) In *wayyanihēm* (v. 14, RSV 'whom he stationed'), the Chronicler preserves a better reading than *wayyanīhēm* of I Kings 10.26; RSV actually adopts the Chronicler's reading also in Kings. (*b*) The verbs in the *qal* conjugation (I Kings 10.29, *watta*ʿ*leh wattēṣēʾ*), having 'chariot' as subject, are replaced by verbs in the *hiphil* conjugation (*wayya*ʿ*lū wayyōṣīʾū*), with the indefinite 'they' as subject. This alteration represents the Chronicler's predilection for the use of the *hiphil* conjugation, also expressed on other occasions.

For greater emphasis on Solomon's wealth, the Chronicler has added 'gold' to the silver which the king made as common in Jerusalem as stone (v. 15//I Kings 10.27). As with other examples of Chronistic reworking, this addition is not introduced into the same verse when it reappears in II Chron. 9.27.

This passage juxtaposes three subjects which are not intrinsically connected and which have different historical significance. The metaphorical description of Solomon's extravagant wealth (v. 15) is flanked by precise reports regarding his great chariot force and his trade in horses and war vehicles. The common denominator in all these is to be found in grand dimensions, foreign fascination, and a sense of the novelty of Solomon's reign compared to David's. These attractions were accrued gradually in the course of Solomon's career, and from a historical point of view the more correct position for them is near the end of his reign (9.25–28) rather than at the beginning. However, as has been pointed out above, these data are cited here as an illustration of Solomon's wealth, a fulfilment of God's promise.

The information of vv. 14, 16–17 (I Kings 10.26, 28–29), is generally taken to reflect solid historical fact. Solomon's chariot force, cavalry and 'chariot cities' are mentioned in Kings in several contexts (I Kings 4.26 [MT 5.6]; 9.19), and although the numbers appear to have been rounded, there is no reason to doubt their basic authenticity (cf. J. A. Soggin, 'The Davidic–Solomonic Kingdom', in J. H. Hayes – J. M. Miller, *Israelite and Judaean History*, 1977, 374–5). The introduction into Israel of this chariot force was a definite innovation on Solomon's part; it marks the change of generations: David had no use for such a grand force and so 'hamstrung all the chariot horses' captured in his war with Aram, leaving only 'one hundred' (II Sam. 8.4 = I Chron. 18.4). Solomon, by contrast, made great efforts to develop a large chariot force, although to what extent he ever made use of it is debatable (cf. also on II Chron. 8.3)

Another matter altogether is the depiction of Solomon as a trader of horses and chariots (cf. I. Ikeda, 'Solomon's Trade in Horses and Chariots in its International Setting', in T. Ishida, *Studies in the Period of David and Solomon*, 1982, 215–38). This passage has been regarded as a corner-stone for understanding how Solomon controlled a monopoly on horse and chariot trade, as one of the main sources for his great wealth. The horses originated in Egypt to the south and Cilicia to the north (although the identification of 'Que' and 'Mizraim' is a controversial issue: cf. among others, H. Tadmor, 'Que and Muṣri', *IEJ* 11, 1961, 143–50; A. D. Crown, 'Once Again, I Kings 10: 26–29', *Abr Naharaim* 15, 1974–5, 35–8), while the chariots come from Egypt alone. However, observing correctly the parallelistic structure of v. 16, regarding the Massoretic separation of 'Que' from 'Mizraim' as of exegetical significance, and viewing the word-order in v. 16 as more original than its parallel in I Kings 10.8, Schley has recently claimed that the text is nothing but a eulogy, celebrating Solomon's magnificence, and 'does not afford a historically precise portrayal of his era' (D. G. Schley, 'I Kings 10: 26–29: A Reconsideration', *JBL* 106, 1987, 601). Schley rightly points to the literary and stylistic qualities of the text, and his attention to the Massoretic accents is well advised. However, it is of interest that while he translates extensively from the other texts he cites, he fails to do so for the crucial verses 16–17 (I Kings 10.28–29). One can hardly ignore the technical terminology of the passage – the king's traders, buy, price, import and export – or the explicit reference 'through them' and the precise geographical points. All these cannot be passed over as references to a 'legendary enterprise' (ibid., 600) simply because the text is written in a pleasant, balanced prose. And yet, the precise geopolitical setting in which Solomon's traders are operating is not further specified in the text.

2 Now Solomon purposed to build a temple for the name of the Lord, and a royal palace for himself. [2] And Solomon assigned seventy thousand men to bear burdens and eighty thousand to quarry in the hill country, and three thousand six hundred to oversee them. [3] And Solomon sent word to Huram the king of Tyre: 'As you dealt with David my father and sent him cedar to build himself a house to dwell in, so deal with me. [4] Behold, I am about to build a house for the name of the Lord my God and dedicate it to him for the burning of incense of sweet spices before him, and for the continual offering of the showbread, and for burnt offerings morning and evening, on the sabbaths and the new moons and the appointed feasts of the Lord our God, as ordained for ever for Israel. [5] The house which I am to build will be great, for our God is greater than all gods. [6] But who is able to build him a house, since heaven, even highest heaven, cannot contain him? Who am I to build a house for him, except as a place to burn incense before him? [7] So now send me a man skilled to work in gold, silver, bronze, and iron, and in purple, crimson, and blue fabrics, trained also in engraving, to be with the skilled workers who are with me in Judah and Jerusalem, whom David my father provided. [8] Send me also cedar, cypress, and algum timber from Lebanon, for I know that your servants know how to cut timber in Lebanon. And my servants will be with your servants, [9] to prepare timber for me in abundance, for the house I am to build will be great and wonderful [10] I will give for your servants, the hewers who cut timber, twenty thousand cors of crushed wheat, twenty thousand cors of barley, twenty thousand baths of wine, and twenty thousand baths of oil.'

[11] Then Huram the king of Tyre answered in a letter which he sent to Solomon, 'Because the Lord loves his people he has made you king over them.' [12] Huram also said, 'Blessed be the Lord God of Israel, who made heaven and earth, who has given King David a wise son, endued with discretion and understanding, who will build a temple for the Lord, and a royal palace for himself.

[13] 'Now I have sent a skilled man, endued with understanding, Huramabi [14] the son of a woman of the daughters of Dan, and his father was a man of Tyre. He is trained to work in gold, silver, bronze, iron, stone, and wood, and in purple, blue and crimson fabrics and fine linen, and to do all sorts of engraving and execute any design that may be assigned him, with you craftsmen, the craftsmen of my lord, David your father. [15] Now therefore the wheat and barley, oil and wine, of which my lord had spoken, let him send to his servants; [16] and we will cut whatever timber you need from Lebanon, and bring it to you in rafts by sea to Joppa, so that you may take it up to Jerusalem.'

[17] Then Solomon took a census of all the aliens who were in the land of Israel after the census of them which David his father had taken; and there were found a hundred and fifty-three thousand six hundred. [18] Seventy thousand of them he assigned to bear burdens, eighty thousand to quarry in the hill country, and three thousand six hundred as overseers to make the people work.

A. Notes to MT

Verse 1 of MT is v. 2 in RSV.

[10, MT 9] מכות, read מכלת with Versions.

B. Notes to RSV

[1, MT 1.18] 'purposed', NEB 'resolved'; [2, MT 2.1] 'assigned', in v. 17 [MT 16] 'took a census', MT ויספר; [3, MT 2] 'so deal with me', not in MT; cf. commentary; [4, MT 3] 'continual offering of the showbread', JPS 'for the regular rows of bread'; [6, MT 5] 'except ... to burn incense', NEB 'except ... to burn sacrifices', also JPS; [10, MT 9] 'crushed wheat', NEB 'provisions ... wheat', cf. commentary; [13, MT 12] 'Huram-abi', not a compound name in MT.

C. Structure, sources and form

1. The topic of this chapter is preliminary preparations for the building of the Temple, beginning with the correspondence between Solomon and Huram, king of Tyre, guaranteeing an adequate supply of timber for the building project. The Chronicler follows strictly the literary sequence of Kings, but – as already mentioned – moves directly from I Kings 3.15 to I Kings 5.2 [MT 5.16], and only then faithfully continues the original narrative pattern.

The Chronicler's omission of several passages in Kings establishes a new order for Solomon's enterprises: the building of the Temple is juxtaposed as closely as possible to his enthronement; it is in fact the *raison d'être* for Solomon's accession and his first priority of action. Since the Chronicler retains the information of I Kings 6.1, that the actual construction of the Temple began in Solomon's fourth year (II Chron. 3.2), the intermediate period is occupied by the correspondence with Huram, the preparation of timber and the mustering of a labour force.

2. With the deletion of these passages (of which I Kings 4.21, 26 [MT 5.1, 6] are later 'rescued') the Chronicler passes over in silence Solomon's judgment (I Kings 3.16–28), his high officials (4.1–6), his twelve officers (4.7–19), the peaceful tranquility of his reign (4.20, 25 [MT 5.5]), his daily provisions (4.22–23, 27–28 [MT 5.2–3, 7–8]), and his outstanding wisdom (4.29–34; 5.9–14). Consequently, Solomon's image suffers on three counts: his wisdom (as already mentioned in ch. 1), his state administration (the Chronicler's view is that this has been taken care of by David – cf. on I Chron. 27), and the emphasis on 'peace and quiet' in his day. This last point is most surprising in view of the explicit divine promise transmitted to Solomon by David (I Chron. 22.9), the fulfilment of which is not really related.

3. The Chronicler himself introduces his new approach to the material in v. 1, composed in view of the following narrative, to the end of chapter 7. After this introduction, the chapter comprises two unequal parts, which parallel, with a great measure of adaptation and reworking, I Kings 5.2–18 [MT 5.16–32]:

3–16 correspondence with Huram
17–18 preparation of the labour force.

4. The description of the contacts between Solomon and Huram is thoroughly reworked. I Kings 5.1–18 [MT 15–32] presents a narrative sequence in which Huram takes the initiative by sending his congratulations to Solomon at his accession; this is followed by Solomon's response, Huram's reaction, and his answer to Solomon. The story ends with the realization of the issues which were discussed: Huram's part (5.19 [MT 24]), Solomon's part (5.10 [MT 25]), and the treaty between them (5.12 [MT 26]). Finally there are remarks about Solomon's expedition of forced labour sent to Lebanon (5.13–14 [MT 27–28]), the levy of hewers and burden-bearers (5.15–16 [MT 29–30]), and the actual preparation of timber and stones (5.17–18 [MT 31–32]).

In Chronicles, the narrative aspect of the passage is much reduced. With the exception of one action, at the end (I Chron. 2.17–18//I Kings 5.15–16 [MT 29–30]), the chapter is composed entirely of oratorical passages: the two letters of Solomon (vv. 3–10) [MT 2–9]) and of Huram (vv. 11–16 [MT 10–15]). This literary transformation is achieved both by omission and by intentional restructuring of narrative passages in Kings: some details of the actions in I Kings 5 are here incorporated as part of the correspondence, differently presented in the two letters. The actual realization of these proposals is not related but taken for granted. After this thorough reworking, two elements remain unchanged, the general subject and the quantitative aspect of the unit: the letters occupy precisely the same textual space as the whole narrative in Kings. The literary method here greatly resembles the procedures applied in ch. 1.

5. The style and language of these passages bear clear marks of the Chronicler's pen. Segments of various biblical portions are employed in an anthological mosaic. Some are associated with contexts which deal with the same matters, such as v. 3, which calls to mind II Sam 5.11 (= I Chron. 14.1), where Hiram sends David cedar trees for his house. The phrase 'a house to dwell in' (הבית לשבת) relates to I Chron. 17.4, 'Thus says the Lord: you shall not build me a house to dwell in', and the whole context of that chapter. 'As you dealt with David my father' echoes II Chron. 1.8 (= I Kings 3.6) – a similarity obscured by the translation. 'Heaven, even highest heaven, cannot contain him' is a citation of Solomon's exaltation in I Kings 8.27 (= II Chron. 6.18), and Huram's words in v. 11, of the address of the queen of Sheba (I Kings 10.9 //II Chron. 9.8); the description of Huramabi (vv. 7, 13–14) is greatly influenced by Pentateuchal sections devoted to the artists who built the tabernacle (cf. the commentary). The similarity to David's rhetorical questions in I Chron. 29.14 was already pointed out by Pseudo-Rashi.

One should also note the linguistic peculiarities of these passages, of which three may be mentioned here: (a) the abundance of words, phrases and forms which are Chronistic 'favourites' (cf. Curtis, 28–38), such as הכין, RSV 'provide, prepare' (vv. 7, 9); לרב, 'in abundance' (v. 9); עצר כח, 'able' (v. 6); etc.; (b) the use of the infinitive in place of a conjugated verb (v. 9); and (c) the abundant use of explicative clauses, opening with כי, represented as 'for', 'since', 'except' (vv. 5, 6a, 6b, 8, 9).

D. Commentary

[1, MT 1.18] This introductory verse opens the pericope and, together with the conclusion 'thus Solomon finished the house of the Lord and the kings' palace' (7.11), comprises the framework of the unit. Interestingly, while the

introductory verse is not found (or in fact needed) in Kings, its phrasing links
it to the context of I Kings 9.1 (reflected in II Chron. 7.11) more than to the
Chronicler's edited form of the narrative, which pointedly omits references
to Solomon's palace (as in I Kings 7.1–12 not paralleled in Chronicles), in
order to emphasize the importance of the Temple. In fact, this verse, the
reference in 7.11, and the echo of both in Huram's letter (2.12 [MT 11]) are
the only Chronistic references to the building of Solomon's 'house'.

[2] (MT 1) Having decided to implement his building plans, Solomon
conducts a census (*wayyispōr*, RSV 'assigned'), in order to prepare his labour
force. This information, derived from I Kings 5.15–16 [MT 29–30]), is
repeated in our chapter in vv. 17–18 [MT 16–17] in a context closer to the
Kings' record, i.e., after the correspondence with Huram. Neither of the
Chronicles passages is, however, a verbatim replica of the original. Verses
17–18 are a reworked form, brought into accord with the Chronicler's
specific views, and this verse is closer to a summary form of vss. 17–18 than to
I Kings 5.15–16 [MT 29–30]. The literary development would therefore be
I Kings 5.15–16 [MT 29–30] – II Chron. 2.17–18 [MT 16–1] – II Chron. 2.2
[MT 2.1].

The question arises whether the repetition of this passage represents
another case of double employment of the same material by the Chronicler
himself (cf. Curtis, 320), or whether it is a secondary gloss (Rudolph, 201;
Williamson, 198). The literary dependence of v. 2 on vv. 17–18 and the fact
that its introduction here does not literarily enhance the plot or the message
of the narrative incline me to regard our verse as a gloss. It could have been
motivated by two factors: Solomon's reference to his own servants in his
letter to Huram (v. 8), or the influence of the story of David, in which the
gathering of the 'aliens' follows the assignment of the Temple site (I Chron.
22.1–2). For the interpretation of the verse, cf. below on vv. 17–18.

[3–10] (MT 2–9) According to I Kings 5.1 [MT 15], it is Huram who takes
the initiative in the relationship, but here it is Solomon who takes the first
step. Solomon's letter here is longer and more complicated than in Kings; in
fact, the two versions actually share only two details: Solomon's request for
cedars, and the reference to remuneration (vv. 8, 10//I Kings 5.6 [MT 20]).

The structure of the letter of Solomon resembles that of an oration; it
progresses through well defined points, marked by introductory phrases.
The proposition (vv. 3b–6) and the central issue (vv. 7–10) each develop in
two stages, relating to two aspects of the subject. The proposition introduces
first in v. 3b [MT 2b] the precedent 'As you dealt with David ...' and then
moves to the present situation, 'Behold, I am about to build ...' The central
issue opens with v. 7 [MT 6], 'So now send me ...', focusses on Solomon's
request, and moves, in conclusion, to the price he is willing to pay: 'Behold I
will give you ...' (v. 10 [MT 9]). This structure is lost in RSV; the pro-

position of v. 3 is complemented prematurely with 'so deal with me', and the final 'behold' in v. 10 is omitted.

The structure of I Kings is completely different, and may still preserve some epistolary elements (cf. D. Pardee, *Handbook of Ancient Hebrew Letters*, 1982, 182).

[3] (MT 2) Both versions of the letter open with a reference to David. In Kings this has an apologetic tone, in a double sense: for Huram it is an appeal to his tolerant judgment, 'you know that ...' (5.3 [MT 17]), accentuated by the modest note of the conclusion: 'for you know that there is no one among us', etc., both allusions by Solomon to some shortcoming or failure on the Israelite side. In reference to David, the letter explains David's inability to build a house for the Lord by the circumstances of his reign which have now changed.

None of this apologetic is found in Chronicles. The problem of David's inability to build the Temple has been dealt with by the Chronicler in a more appropriate context: in a conversation between David himself and Solomon his son (I Chron. 22.7–10, cf. there). In this verse, the reference to David simply establishes a political precedent: Huram should do the same for Solomon as he had for David. The allusion is to I Chron. 14.1 (II Sam. 5.11) and also to I Chron. 17.1 (II Sam 7.1–2), in which the connection is made between the cedar house of David and his desire to build a house for the Lord.

It should be noted that in Chronicles the name of the Tyrian king (as well as that of the master craftsman) is always Huram (2.3, 11, 12; 8.2, 18, etc.); even when 'Hiram' appears (*Kethib*), the *Qere* requires 'Huram' (I Chron. 14.1; II Chron. 4.11 [BH]; 9.10). Elsewhere in the Bible, the name is either Hiram (II Sam. 5.11; I Kings 5.1 [MT 5.15], etc.) or Hirom (only in MT: I Kings 5.24, 32; 7.40; not RSV: 5.10, 17; 7.40). The systematic distribution is clearly a sign of different pronunciation of the name in the Chronicler's time. The cases of *Qere* and *Kethib* may indicate that the Massoretes were aware of this uniformity and indicated the deviating forms.

[4–6] (MT 3–5) Solomon's explanation of the need to build a Temple focusses on two points: first its role as the setting for regular cultic services, as summarized in v. 6b, 'that I may burn sacrifices before him' (NEB), and later in God's response to Solomon's prayer: 'I ... have chosen this place for myself as a house of sacrifice' (II Chron. 7.12). To reinforce this idea, v. 4 lists the elements of the daily and annual regular service: incense, showbread, daily burnt offerings, sacrifices of the sabbaths, new moons, and the festivals. This is a concise and accurate summary of the Temple worship, drawn from the priestly material of the Pentateuch. The order of the elements is interesting, as it follows precisely that of their appearance in the Pentateuch: incense in Exod. 30.1–8, showbread in Lev. 24.5–9, and sacrifices in Num. 28–29.

Although similar references are found elsewhere (in particular II Chron. 8.13; 13.11; Neh. 10.33ff. [MT 34.ff]), this passage is unique in its comprehensive summary of the regular cult.

The last statement, *le'ōlām zō't 'al yiśrā'ēl* ('[as ordained] for ever for Israel') calls to mind the recurring priestly emphasis on the binding nature of the cultic regulations, ordained 'for ever' (Exod. 12.17; Lev. 3.17, etc.); the wording, however, is peculiar to this context.

[5–6] (MT 4–5) These verses cope with another question: why costly cedars, luxurious materials and grandeur? Here the argument is complex and apologetic, and the repetitive style clearly indicates that the author was confronted with a theological problem; his talent for abstraction is sorely taxed.

The first statement is simple: the house has to be 'big', RSV 'great', or 'big and wonderful' (v. 9), for 'our God is greater than all gods'. However, a simplistic understanding of this logic might conclude that the 'greatness' of the Temple and of God are of the same concrete nature, and even that the great God is to dwell in the great house! In order to shun any possibility of such reasoning, the author hurries to explain that since even the heights of heaven cannot contain God, much less an earthly temple, it is beyond any man, even Solomon himself, to build the Lord a house.

This complex argument is given literary form in two rhetorical questions: the first of a more general nature: 'who is able ...', the second more personal: 'who am I'. Each of these is substantiated by an explicative clause, introduced by *kī*: 'since (*kī*) heaven ... cannot contain him', and 'except (*kī 'im*) as a place of sacrifice' (NEB). Together with the preceding *kī*, 'for (*kī*) our God is greater ...', these phrases illustrate the intense effort by which the Chronicler attempts to resolve the tension between divine transcendence and the human religious need for a cultic 'locus' for mankind. The Temple's greatness symbolizes God, but for God the 'house' is a place of sacrifice.

[7] (MT 6) Solomon's request, which in I Kings 5.6 [MT 20] is as short as possible, 'Now ... command that cedars of Lebanon be cut for me', has an additional aspect here: that the king of Tyre should send a master craftsman for all the artistic works of the Temple. The great detail with which v. 7 treats this issue is reflected in Huram's answer as well (vv. 13–14).

What are the sources of this note? According to v. 13, the person meant is Huram (RSV 'Huramabi', cf. below on vv. 13–14), who is mentioned in I Kings 7.13–14 (by the variant name 'Hiram') as the master craftsman of Solomon. The Chronicler, by already introducing this figure during the initial stages of preparations, and as someone of great importance, thereby changes the information derived from Kings in several ways:

(*a*) In I Kings 7 the circumstances of the craftsman's arrival in Jerusalem are not specified; we are only told that '... he came to king Solomon, and did all his work'. These are among the many verses omitted in the parallel context of Chronicles. The Chronicler regards the sending of Huram as the king of Tyre's response to a special request of Solomon. The precise historical context of the statement in I Kings 7.13, 'king Solomon sent and brought Hiram from Tyre', is not known to us; it may well have been as the Chronicler describes. But by emphasizing the active role of the king of Tyre, the Chronicler creates a stronger analogy with the precedent of David, already alluded in v. 2: 'Hiram king of Tyre sent ... cedar trees, also carpenters and masons who built David a house' (II Sam 5.11//I Chron. 14.1). It was only appropriate that Solomon should be afforded the same service.

(b) By early reference to the master craftsman, the Chronicler also evokes a stronger affinity to the construction of the tabernacle as described in Exodus: there, the preparation of the necessary materials (Exod. 35.4–29) is immediately followed by the introduction of artisans (Exod. 35.30–36.1).

(c) The talents of Huram the craftsman are described differently. In Kings his speciality is work in bronze: 'full of wisdom, understanding and skill for making any work in bronze' (I Kings 7.14, etc.). In Chronicles, he is a versatile artist, capable of working any material – that this expertise is detailed twice in our context indicates how significant it was for the Chronicler. It has been pointed out by many commentators that the figure of Huram in Chronicles is influenced by those of Bezalel the son of Uri and Oholiab the son of Ahisamach, who realized the work of the tabernacle (Exod. 35.30–35; already Pseudo-Rashi on v. 13; cf. Rudolph, 199; Mosis, 136–8; Williamson, 199–201). As the description is fuller in v. 14, I shall deal with it there.

(d) Another matter which is peculiar to Chronicles is the insistence that here, as in all other aspects of the preparation, Solomon only complements and finalizes what David has already begun. What has been stated by David himself in I Chron. 22.15–16 and 28.20 is here repeated, both by Solomon, 'to be with the skilled workers ... whom David my father provided' (v. 7), and by Huram 'with your craftsmen, the craftsmen of my lord, David your father' (v. 14).

[8–9] (MT 7–8) Here, in contrast to the Kings' version, it is only as a second request that Solomon asks for timber, and here too his words are rephrased: in addition to 'cedar', Solomon askes for 'cypress and algum timber'. In Kings, cypresses are mentioned in Hiram's reply (5.8, 10 [MT 22, 24]), and the Chronicler has simply included them in the early stage of negotiation. The algums, however, are to appear in Kings only much later, as 'almug wood', among the precious items which were brought to Israel by a joint expedition of Huram and Solomon (I Kings 10.11–12 = II Chron. 9.10–11). The form 'algum' found here and in both Chronicles passages is a variant of 'almug' found in Kings. For the problems involved in the derivation of the name and the identification of the tree, cf. J. C. Greenfield – M. Mayrhoper, 'The Algummim/Almuggim Problem Reexamined', *VTS* 16, 1967, 83–9). It is not likely that the Chronicler regarded the algum as among the 'trees of Lebanon'; rather, they are included – like many other aspects of this correspondence – to augment and elaborate the description, with probably no clear idea as to what these 'algums' really were.

We have already noted the apologetic tone of I Kings 5.6 [MT 20], 'for you know that there is no one among us who knows ...'. In Chronicles, essentially the same statement is made, using the same verbal root, but the tone is assertive: 'for I know that your servants know ...'.

[10] (MT 9) The last item on the agenda of Solomon's letter is the remuneration for the provisions. In Kings, Solomon states his willingness to pay, but leaves the sum to the discretion of Huram: 'and I will pay you ... such wages as you set' (5.6 [MT 20]); this is explained by Solomon's complete confidence in Huram's know-how and good will. Here the Chronicler takes a different view of the negotiations: Solomon's letter already includes all the ramifications of the agreement, including the exact amounts of goods to be given in payment, phrased in a way quite independent of the remark about the Tyrians' professional expertise. The terms of payment, inserted here from the continuation of the story in I Kings 5.11 [MT 25], are in fact more generous in Chronicles. In addition to the 'wheat' and 'oil' of Kings, the Chronicler mentions 'barley' and 'wine' in the same proportions. These may be survivals of an original text, omitted in Kings through homoioteleuton, or additions introduced by the Chronicler to augment the dimensions of the agreement. An even greater contrast is found in the duration of the payment. According to Kings, the remuneration was to be delivered on schedule 'year by year'; in Chronicles there is no mention of an annual supply, and even Hiram's stipulation of 'food for my household' (I Kings 5.9, 11), is not repeated. The payments, following Huram's insistence, precede the delivery of the timber.

As pointed out by many commentators, the MT *makkōt* in v. 10 (literally blows) is very awkward in this context, and is an obvious corruption of *makkōlet* of I Kings 5.11, rendered there 'food'. RSV follows a long exegetical tradition (cf. also pseudo-Rashi) which regards the noun as a passive participle, hence '*crushed* wheat'.

[11–16] (MT 10–15) In Chronicles, Solomon's letter is longer than in Kings, and Huram's answer here is extended proportionately: from two verses to six. Except for some change of word-order near the end, it follows the content of Solomon's request; at the same time it is strongly affected by its source in Kings.

Huram's letter has two introductions, which – from a literary point of view

– are not fully integrated: 'Then Huram the king of Tyre answered ...'
(v. 11), and 'Huram also said ...' (v. 12). The rough transition between
Huram's two statements is perfectly explained by the way in which the
Chronicler's text tightly accompanies that of Kings. In I Kings 5.7 [MT 21],
after receiving Solomon's letter, Huram makes a congratulatory statement:
'Blessed be the Lord, etc.'; he then proceeds with a letter to Solomon. As the
Chronicler in restructuring the whole sequence omits every component of
the pericope except for the letters, and inserts this originally independent
congratulation as an epistolary preamble.

The letter, then, after this preamble, opens with a blessing (v. 12, see
below) followed by concise answers to Solomon's requests, introduced in two
stages by the formulaic 'Now' (vv. 13–14; 15–16). The response to
Solomon's request for a craftsman is the unconditional dispatch of Huramabi
to Solomon's court. On the other hand, reference to the shipment of the
required timber is preceded by, and therefore made conditional on, the
matter of payment. The letter thus anticipates the order in which the
contract will be executed: having received the request, Huram is sending a
master craftsman; Solomon will now dispatch the provisions he has
promised, and finally Huram will ship the requested timber.

It is noteworthy that the explicative *kī* ('for'), repeated in Solomon's
address five times, is absent from Huram's response. Here there is no need
for theological or practical justification; facts and procedures are sufficient.

In analysing the style of the letter, Pardee expresses the opinion that 'it is
unlikely that the author of Chronicles was citing an actual tenth-century
document' (ibid., 180). We may add to this prudent conclusion that the
Chronicler was citing no document at all.

[11] (MT 10) The opening congratulation is not dependent on the parallel
verse of I Kings 5.7 (MT 21) – which will be quoted presently – but rather
comprises two literal citations from the admiring address to Solomon by the
queen of Sheba (II Chron. 9.8//I Kings 10.9).

[12] (MT 11) Huram's blessing is an elaboration of I Kings 5.7 [MT 21].
We have already encountered the specific literary technique employed here,
which is as follows.

The Chronicler takes Huram's words as a base and transmits them almost
literally, with only two omissions: 'this day' and 'to be over his great people'.
He then elaborates each of the elements, thus:

(i) 'Blessed be the Lord' [+ Chronistic elaborations]:
(ii) '... who has given king David a wise son' [+ Chronistic elaborations].

These elaborations include three points:

(*a*) the epithets of the Lord: 'God of Israel, who made heaven and earth';

(*b*) the description of Solomon's wisdom: 'endued with discretion and understanding';
(*c*) the issue under discussion: 'who will build a temple for the Lord and a royal palace for himself'.

(i) Although a conventional blessing formula, this precise phrasing is not attested elsewhere in the Bible. 'Blessed be the Lord, the God of Israel' is found many times (I Kings 1.48; 8.15; Ps. 41.13, etc.); the reference to the Lord as the 'maker of heaven and earth' is also a conventional phrase (Ps. 115.15; 121.2; 124.8, etc.), but the combination is unique.

(ii) This text in Chronicles enlarges upon Solomon's wisdom in accord with the prediction of David, who said: 'may the Lord grant you discretion (*śēkel*) and understanding (*ûbînāh*)' (I Chron. 22.12). Here, God has fulfilled David's request, and the very same virtues are attributed by Huram to Solomon. The most significant point is mentioned last: 'who will build a temple, etc.' While in Kings, Solomon's wisdom is valued in its own right and associated with God's revelation at Gibeon ('... an understanding mind to govern thy people', 3.9), here the goal of that wisdom is the Temple building project.

Huram mentions 'a temple for the Lord, and a royal palace for [Solomon]', although Solomon's letter contained no hint of intentions to build himself a residence. The same words are found in 2.1 [MT 1.18], where the author introduces us to Solomon's plans. One could hardly find more convincing evidence than this that these letters are the fruit of the Chronicler's own pen.

[13–14] (MT 12–13) Huram notifies Solomon that he is sending a craftsman, whose name is somewhat problematic. MT *ḥûrām 'ābî* is formed of two distinct elements, literally 'Huram my father'. As the element 'my father' is not attested in any proper name in the Bible, and since the name is not a compound form (RSV's hyphen is not supported by the Massoretic signs), the element '*abî*' is taken by some scholars as a title, in which the suffix has lost its possessive force (like *rābî*; cf. Rudolph, 200). Hence the translation of NEB as 'Master Huram'. Although this proposal is attractive, a usage of this kind is not attested in the Bible itself. Another possibility is that the element *'ābî* is a dialectic form of *āb*, and that the name was originally a compound: 'Huram-ab' (like Ah-ab; Jesheb-ab; Oholi-ab, etc,). This possibility is adopted by RSV's representation of the name, 'Huram-abi'. The Chronicler introduced this form, whether on his own initiative or following his sources, in order to distinguish between the king of Tyre and the craftsman of the same name. In II Chron. 4.16 we find *ḥuram 'ābîw* in place of the simple *ḥiram* of I Kings 7.45, but MT *'ābîw* (literally '*his* father'), is probably a textual corruption, as indicated by the Versions. (For a more elaborate explication of this addition, cf. Williamson, 201.)

The ancestry of Huram the craftsman is presented differently here from Kings. Both texts agree that 'his father was a man of Tyre'; I Kings 7.14, however, has it that his mother is a 'widow of the tribe of Naphtali', while here she is 'a woman of the daughters of Dan'. Both views are historically viable, as both Dan and Naphtali were settled in the north of the country, in the neighbourhood of Tyre. The question is historiographic: did the Chronicler have an alternative tradition, which he preferred to that of Kings, or did he introduce the change himself? For lack of external evidence consideration of this point is inconclusive. It would seem, however, that in view of the thorough reworking of the correspondence, motivated by literary and theological factors, and in view of the author's inclination to create an analogy between this text and Exod. 35, it is most likely that the change was influenced by the figure of 'Oholiab the son of Ahisamach of the tribe of Dan', Bezalel's chief assistant in building the tabernacle.

The Chronicler, influenced, as I have said, by Exod. 35.31–35, presents Huram as a master in every craft. His expertise is first in metals: gold, silver, bronze and iron. Exodus 35.32 has only the first three metals; the series of four, including iron, characterizes the texts in Chronicles (I Chron. 22.16; 29.2, 7). He also works in stone and wood (Exod. 35.33; I Chron. 22.15; 29.2), and in textiles: purple, blue and crimson fabrics and fine linen. These last are also mentioned in Exod. 35.35, but in place of *tola 'at-haššānī* the present text has the Persian *karmīl* and the Egyptian word *šeš* is replaced by *būṣ*. In addition, Huram is skilled in engraving (Exod. 28.11; 39.6) and artistic design (cf. Exod. 35.32–35).

In spite of the similarity between Huram and his spiritual forbears Bezalel and Oholiab, a major difference stands out. Exodus emphasizes divine inspiration as the source of all the craftsman's extraordinary talents: 'and I have filled him with the Spirit of God, with ability and intelligence, with knowledge and all craftsmanship ... I have given to all able men ability ...' (Exod. 31.3–6; also 35.31, 34, 35; 36.1, 2). This feature is absent from I Kings 7.13–14, and also from Chronicles. Just as in the above texts from Exodus, the craftsmen are indeed titled *ḥākām* ('wise'), and their ability is *ḥokmāh* ('wisdom'). This context in Chronicles designates as *ḥākām* not only Solomon (v. 12), following I Kings 5.7 [MT 21], but everyone involved in the Temple project: Huramabi (v. 6, 13), David's artists (vv. 7, 14), and those of Solomon (v. 14) – these last two groups are confused in RSV. Huram himself is 'a skilful and experienced craftsman' (NEB), who is 'trained to work' (*yōdē'a la'ᵃśōt*), but there is no hint that he is inspired. In view of the great influence of Exod. 35–36 on the present text, this omission cannot be coincidental. According to Chronicles, craftsmanship is certainly 'wisdom', but definitely not divine inspiration.

Concluding this part of his letter, Huram echoes exactly Solomon's expectation that Huram the master would do work in co-operation with the other craftsmen who are already in Jerusalem. Here, a slight stylistic change is felt which will become more tangible in v. 15.

[15–16] (MT 14–15) Huram, then, has reviewed first Solomon's part in the agreement, recounting his obligations in detail, and now he turns to his own. Verse 15 introduces a different style as Huram resorts to the third-person address: 'Now ... the wheat ... of which my lord has spoken, let him send to his servants'. This, together with the explicit 'my lord' and 'his servants', indicates that Solomon and Huram do not share an equal status, as already hinted in Huram's words in v. 14: 'my lord, David your father'. Gradually, towards the end of the unit, the relationship between Solomon and Huram is depicted as that of a sovereign and his dependent. No hint of this Solomonic superiority is to be discerned in Kings. We might regard this passage as a stylistic refinement without political significance if it were not for the tendentious changes which the Chronicler introduced in his reworking of I Kings 9.11–13 (II Chron. 8.2, and cf. there).

[16] (MT 15) At the conclusion of his letter Huram details how the timber will reach Jerusalem – a note similar in substance to I Kings 5.9 but differently phrased. Huram's responsibility includes delivery to Joppa; it is Solomon's responsibility to transport the timber from there to Jerusalem. In I Kings, the vague destination is 'the place you direct' (5.9 [MT 23]), but the role of Joppa as an important port on the Mediteranean is well illustrated by Jonah 1.3 and Ezra 3.7. It is in fact the only port which gave its name to the sea: 'the sea of Joppa' (also Ezra 3.7, not reflected in RSV). It may be the Chronicler himself who specified the name of the port here, but as this would serve no specific purpose, it may as well have already been found in his *Vorlage* in Kings.

[17–18] (MT 16–17) As already mentioned, the Chronicler skips the passages in Kings which follow the correspondence. He has incorporated I Kings 5.10–11 [MT 24–25] into the letters, omitted I Kings 5.12–14 [MT 26–28], and proceeds now to present I Kings 5.15–16 [MT 29–30] in his own reworked form. In so doing he makes use of I Kings 9.20–23, which is also found in II Chron. 8.7–10.

I Kings 9.20–23 relates 1. how all those who were left from the 'seven nations' were recruited for forced labour; 2. that of the people of Israel Solomon made no slaves; and 3. that there were officers who 'had charge of the people who carried on the work'. As the latter are mentioned in identical terms in I Kings 5.16 [MT 30], it is easy to connect the two passages and to conclude that the 'seventy thousand burden bearers and eighty thousand hewers of stone' (I Kings 5.15 [MT 29]) were those 'who were left of the Amorites, the Hittites, etc.' (I Kings 9.20ff). This probable interpretation of the texts in Kings becomes explicit in Chronicles, but the principal innovation here is the manner in which the Chronicler conceives of this group. For him, those 'who were left of the Amorites ...' are designated 'the aliens (gērīm) who were in the land of Israel'. In this, the Chronicler enunciates one of the postulates of his concept of Israel: in the land of Israel there are no foreign peoples. Those who survived from the 'seven nations' are 'aliens' (gērīm), attached to the people of Israel and sharing their destiny (cf. in more detail, Japhet, *Ideology*, 334–51).

The second point is that for Chronicles, all the workers designated here belong to the same group. In I Kings 5.15–16 [MT 29–30], the officers are recorded separately, 'besides ... chief officers', and it is obvious that they have a different status. In Chronicles, a unit first presented as one comprehensive body of 153,600 workers is then subdivided into three groups: burden bearers, hewers and officers.

Another innovation in Chronicles *vis à vis* the text of Kings is the view – which we have encountered so many times – that even in this matter Solomon is only following in the steps of David. The Chronicler has already related how David took measures to gather these people and train them as stonemasons: 'David commanded to gather together the aliens who were in the land of Israel and he set stonecutters to prepare dressed stones for building the house of God' (I Chron. 22.2). In addition, Solomon is here explicitly described as emulating David: 'Solomon took census ... after the census of them which David had taken'. It should be noted that the terms 'the aliens who were in the land of Israel' are peculiar to these two contexts (and II Chron. 30.25, cf. there). The census, and the assignment of these people to the building project, were both initiated by David; Solomon only completed the task.

The number of 'officers' is given as 3300 in I Kings and 3600 here. Both are round numbers, but it seems that the corruption by analogy happened in the text of Kings. I Kings 9.23 with 550 officers and II Chron. 8.10 with 250 probably reflect different views of their role in the labour force.

3 Then Solomon began to build the house of the Lord in Jerusalem on Mount Moriah, where the Lord had appeared to David his father, at the place that David had appointed, on the threshing floor of Ornan the Jebusite. ² He began to build in the second month of the fourth year of his reign. ³ These are Solomon's measurements for building the house of God: the length, in cubits of the old standard, was sixty cubits, and the breadth twenty cubits. ⁴ The vestibule in front of the nave of the house was twenty cubits long, equal to the width of the house; and its height was a hundred and twenty cubits. He overlaid it on the inside with pure gold. ⁵ The nave he lined with cypress, and covered it with fine gold, and made palms and chains on it. ⁶ He adorned the house with settings of precious stones. The gold was gold of Parvaim. ⁷ So he lined the house with gold – its beams, its thresholds, its walls, and its doors; and he carved cherubim on the walls.

8 And he made the most holy place; its length, corresponding to the breadth of the house, was twenty cubits, and its breadth was twenty cubits; he overlaid it with six hundred talents of fine gold. ⁹ The weight of the nails was one shekel to fifty shekels of gold. And he overlaid the upper chambers with gold.

10 In the most holy place he made two cherubim of wood and overlaid them with gold. ¹¹ The wings of the cherubim together extended twenty cubits: one wing of the one, of five cubits, touched the wall of the house, and its other wing, of five cubits, touched the wing of the other cherub; ¹² and of this cherub, one wing, of five cubits, touched the wall of the house, and the other wing, also of five cubits, was joined to the wing of the first cherub. ¹³ The wings of these cherubim extended twenty cubits; the cherubim stood on their feet, facing the nave. ¹⁴ And he made the veil of blue and purple and crimson fabrics and fine linen, and worked cherubim on it.

15 In front of the house he made two pillars thirty-five cubits high, with a capital of five cubits on the top of each. ¹⁶ He made chains like a necklace and put them on the tops of the pillars; and he made a hundred pomegranates, and put them on the chains. ¹⁷ He set up the pillars in front of the temple, one on the south, the other on the north; that on the south he called Jachin, and that on the north Boaz.

A. Notes to MT

[1] נראה, add יהוה with LXX; במקום, transfer after אביהו? Cf. commentary; [2] בשני, omit with the Versions, dittography; [3] הוסד, proposed יסד; [4] על פני הארץ, proposed על פני [הבית הרחב אמות עשר ו] הארך read ;על פניו, הארך or על פני הבית, הארך, cf. commentary; מאה ועשרים, read אמות עשרים with some of the Versions; [8b–9] חפה זהב ... לככרים, transfer after 7a, cf. commentary; [12] האחד probably read האחר with the Versions; [14] עליו, read עליה; [15] ראשו, proposed ראשם; [16] בדביר, proposed כרביד.

B. Notes to RSV

[4] 'the nave of the house', not in MT, taken from I Kings 6.3; 'equal to the width', NEB 'spanning the whole breadth', cf. RSV v. 8 'corresponding to the breadth'; 'a hundred and twenty cubits', better 'twenty cubits' (so NEB, cf. A above); [9] 'of the nails was one shekel to fifty' reconstructed, better 'and the weight of gold for the nails fifty shekels'; [10] 'of wood', MT עֲצַמִּים, uncertain, NEB 'images', JPS 'sculptured'.

C. Structure, sources and form

1. Chapters 3–4 parallel I Kings 6–7 and are devoted to the building itself. Here we are confronted with an interesting fact: although the Chronicler has so far displayed an unusual interest in the Temple – as the subject of David's extensive preparations, the central topic and first concern of Solomon's reign, and the *mise en scène* of the organization and management of the cult – the attention he gives to the actual architecture, concrete form and furnishings of the Temple is far less here than in the parallel account of I Kings. These chapters are therefore characterized by a drastic abridgment and literary restructuring, whereby the Chronicler, while basically faithful to his source in Kings, extracts only the main points, rephrasing them in his own, much shorter, presentation.

2. However, this observation requires some qualification. To be precise, I Kings 6.1–7.39 (i.e. seventy-seven verses) are paralleled in Chronicles by 3.1–4.10 (twenty-seven verses); some of these passages were omitted entirely (I Kings 6.4–18, 29–38; 7.1–12), while others were greatly abridged. By contrast, the text of I Kings 7.40–51 is reproduced almost verbatim in Chronicles (4.11–5.1, for which cf. the commentary there). We have already encountered examples of such treatment by the Chronicler of his sources.

3. The structure of the present record in I Kings 6–7 is as follows:

6.1 Introduction
6.2–10, 14 General data concerning the Temple
6.15–22 Internal panelling with wood and gold
6.23–28 The cherubim
6.29–35 Internal decorations and doors
6.36 The inner court
6.37–38 Conclusion
7.1–12 Various buildings in Jerusalem
7.13–14 The summoning of Hiram from Tyre
7.15–22 The bronze pillars
7.23ff. The other furnishings (cf. II Chron. 4).

Broadly speaking, the same topics are dealt with in these chapters as well, with the exception of the other buildings in Jerusalem, the notice about the arrival of Huram from Tyre (transferred to ch. 2), and I Kings 6.11–13, obviously a secondary elaboration in the Deuteronomistic idiom. The absence of this last may be due to the Chronicler's lack of interest in this Deuteronomistic 'word of the Lord', or – equally likely – to its absence from his *Vorlage*.

The same topics, then, are presented here in very different sequence, detail and scope. The structure of the present chapter is as follows:

1–2 Introduction
3–7, 8bβ –9 General data on the Temple and its panelling.
8a–bα, 10–13 'The Most holy place' and the cherubim
14 The veil
15–17 The bronze pillars

From the ensuing detailed discussion it will become clear how the Chronicler, while employing entire verses from I Kings, restructured his material in a much more concise presentation.

D. Commentary

[1–2] While this introduction is similar in scope to its source in I Kings 6.1, it is significantly different in content and style. The Kings passage is central to the Deuteronomistic historiography, marking as it does the chronological position of the construction of the Temple: 'In the four hundred and eightieth year after the people ... came out of ... Egypt'. The juxtaposition of the Exodus and Solomon's Temple-building – two great turning points in the history of Israel – implies a third, silent association: just as the Exodus was the debut, an act of constitution for Israelite nationhood and religion, and the building of the Temple was the climax, providing a focus to Israel's history and its relationship with God, so the destruction would be the nadir, the eclipse of Israel's history. And these three pivotal points are related by the typological chronology of 480 years: twelve generations of forty years each (cf. the Midrash, which regards Solomon's kingship as the watershed in Israel's history, Exodus Rabbah 15.26 on Exod. 12.2; Noth, *The Deuteronomistic History*, 18–25).

This theological pattern is absent from Chronicles. We have already seen how the Chronicler plays down the significance of the Exodus, especially its constitutive function in the history of Israel, and so here the relevant reference is omitted.

The centrality of I Kings 6.1 in its context is also suggested by its elevated, declarative style, marked by intentional and even ceremonial repetitions (a sense somewhat lost in the translation): 'It was in the four hundredth year and eightieth year after the children of Israel had come out of the land of Egypt, in the fourth year of Solomon's reign over Israel, in the second month of that year, that he began to build the house of the Lord' (NEB with small changes). In Chronicles, nothing is left of this ceremonial introduction: the facts are narrated simply and the date is drastically abridged: 'Solomon began to build ... in the second month of the fourth year of his reign'.

The themes which the Chronicler does highlight in his introduction are his own: a detailed indication of the site of the Temple and the role of David (cf. M. Cogan, '"The city that I chose" – The Deuteronomistic view of

Jerusalem', *Tarbiz* 55, 1986, 301ff.*). The record in Kings omits altogether any indication of the place of the Temple, an omission only emphasized by the extreme attention given to the date. One may attribute this silence either to the author's lack of interest in the subject, or to the problematic position of the site within the sacral traditions of Israel. The significance of this matter for the Chronicler is evident in the reference to the site from four different angles: 1. geography, 'In Jerusalem, on Mount Moriah'; 2. theophany, 'Where the Lord had appeared to David his father'; 3. authority, 'At the place that David had appointed'; and 4. tradition, recalling the *hieros logos* of the Temple, connected with 'the threshing floor of Ornan the Jebusite'. This effort to bring together independent lines of tradition and fully to exploit their theological significance aims to grant legitimization and prestige to the Temple site.

Three separate *locus* traditions appear in earlier biblical sources, each having its own foothold in the context of the Israelite cult: a mountain in the land of Moriah, where Abraham bound Isaac (Gen. 22); a threshing floor in Jerusalem where the plague was halted and David built an altar (II Sam. 24); and the Temple in Jerusalem, built by Solomon at an unspecified place (I Kings 6). The name 'Mount Moriah' is not found in the Genesis account (nor elsewhere in the Bible), but here the allusion to the mountain on which Abraham was bidden to sacrifice his son is unmistakable. That the place of Abraham's trial is already identified with the Temple Mount in the aetiology of Gen. 22.14 is taken for granted, for example, by later traditional exegesis (cf. TJ on Gen. 22.14; the Midrash, Rashi on Gen. 22.2, etc.); whether this is the correct interpretation is still a debated point. However that may be, the Genesis passage makes no mention of Jersualem, and I Kings 6.1 does not refer to 'the mountain in the land of Moriah' as the site of the Temple; the identification is made explicit for the first time in this verse in Chronicles.

The same is also true of the other designations of the site. According to the original story of David's census in Samuel, the precise location of Araunah's threshing floor, although certainly in Jerusalem (II Sam. 24.16), is not known, nor is there any indication that this was to be the site of the future Temple; correspondingly, I Kings 6.1 does not position the Temple on 'the threshing floor of Araunah'. The whole context in fact views the 'threshing floor' as unrelated to other 'holy sites'. The first step in the direction of designating Araunah's threshing floor as the site of the Temple is made by the Chronicler at the end of the plague narrative (I Chron. 22.1), when David proclaims 'here shall be the house of the Lord'. The present verse goes one step further by claiming that this same place is none other than 'Mount Moriah', where Isaac was bound, to be sacrificed by Abraham.

This final identification of all three sites with the Temple Mount is a result of a midrashic process, following characteristic midrashic paths. As no other traces of this process are found in the Bible, the question of its origin is unavoidable: was this midrashic structure the work of the Chronicler himself, or was he bringing to the surface existing developments, to which he gave expression in his own language and style? Pending further evidence, no definite answer may be given. However, from this point onward, the identification of the place becomes an unquestioned datum of post-biblical tradition.

The second point which the Chronicler makes is the role of David in 'choosing' this site, a point passed over in silence in the book of Kings. This is all the more significant in view of the theological import in the Deuteronomistic complex of 'the place which ... God will choose' (Deut.12.11): the 'choice' is reserved for the city of Jerusalem and does not refer to a more specific Temple site (cf. also on II Chron. 6.6). The Chronicler, by contrast, emphasizes the 'chosenness' of the place itself – a decision made originally by David, following a divine revelation, thus ruling out any possibility of arbitrary selection of the site. For the history of tradition, this insistence is interesting from another point of view. It would seem that for legitimization of the Temple site, an identification with 'Mount Moriah' would suffice; this was, after all, the place where God appeared to Abraham and the ram was sacrificed. And yet, in the present text this site is authorized not by the precedent of Abraham, but by the 'appointment' (hēkīn) of David, who is emphatically mentioned twice: 'where the Lord had appeared to David his father, at the place that David had appointed'. Clearly this hints at the relative status of tradition elements – either in the general development of Israelite traditions or in the more idiosyncratic view of the Chronicler. Not only does David anticipate Solomon, as we have seen, in everything concerning the preparations for the Temple construction, even the actual choice of the site; Davidic authority also superseded the ancient traditions of the Abrahamic cult.

[3–7 + 8b –9] The description of the construction of the Temple centres on two topics: the measurements (vv. 3–4a, based on I Kings 6.2–3), and the panelling and decoration (vv. 4b–7, 8b–9, based on I Kings 6.15–18; 21–22). Separate measurements are given for the building itself (v. 3) and the vestibule (v. 4a), i.e. the length of the house (sixty cubits), its width (twenty); as for the height, according to I Kings 6.2 this was thirty cubits, although in the present passage a figure is given (an impossible 'hundred and twenty') only in v. 4, after the reference to the vestibule. Verse 4a as it stands gives the measurements of the vestibule in only one figure, probably the length: 'twenty cubits'; the text is clearly corrupt. Even if we accept that the other measure 'ten cubits deep' mentioned in I Kings 6.3 has been deliberately omitted, still in order to make any sense the verse should be complemented by reading habbayit ('the house') or hēkal habbayit ('the Temple sanctuary') after 'al pᵉnē (cf. Curtis, 326, followed by RSV). It seems more likely, however, that there was a more lengthy omission, which may be restored with the help of I Kings 6.3. The text would read: (cf. very similarly, Rudolph, 202 and BHS): *wᵉhā'ūlām 'ᵃšer 'al pᵉnē [habbayit hārōḥab 'ammōt 'ēšer wᵉ] hā'ōrek 'al-pᵉnē rōḥab habbayit 'ammōt 'ešrīm*, 'and the vestibule in front [of the house was ten cubits deep and] its length 'was twenty cubits, equal to the width of the house'.

The reference to the height, coming as it does after the mention of the vestibule, is taken by RSV to relate only to the vestibule. Not only this, but the improbable number of 'one hundred and twenty' (*mē'āh wᵉ'ešrīm*) is surely a corruption, generally regarded as standing for 'twenty cubits' (*'ammōt 'ešrīm*; cf. NEB). If we understand this height as referring to the whole Temple and not merely to the vestibule, then it is less than the overall height in I Kings 6.2 and equal to that of the inner sanctuary in I Kings 6.20, 'twenty cubits', a figure absent in the parallel text of v. 8. This would reflect a different understanding of the Temple's structure, lower and of uniform height for the entire building. We cannot determine whether this might in fact describe the Second Temple, as the dimensions of Ezra 6.3 ('its height ... and its breadth sixty cubits'), are certainly corrupt. Another possibility is that the original Chronicles version ignored the height altogether (cf. also vv. 3, 8, 12–13), and it was introduced secondarily at this point.

The measurements are said to be 'in cubits of the old standard', which was somewhat shorter than the new (cf. Deut. 3.11; Ezek. 40.5; 43.13).

A few more linguistic remarks are necessary at this point.

1. *hūsad* is difficult. Formally, it is *a hophal* form of the verb *ysd* in the singular, with the subject *'ēlleh* in the plural; the word 'Solomon': which follows may be construed to mean 'by Solomon': 'These were [the dimensions] established by Solomon'. However, since there is no evidence of the *hiphil* form of *ysd*, the *hophal* is dubious. The form is generally regarded as a corruption of the active *yāsad* or *yissad*, having Solomon as subject and 'these [dimensions]' as object, and employed here with the general connotation of 'lay down, establish' (cf. especially Esther 1.8; I Chron. 9.22).

2. The word order for the numerals differs systematically from that of Kings; cf. literally:

I Kings 6.2: sixty cubits its length, and twenty its width
II Chron. 3.3: the length – cubits sixty, and the width – cubits twenty.

This change is observed throughout the Chronistic parts of the chapter (and cf. A. Kropat, 50–3). Compare, by contrast, 4.1 and the commentary on ch. 4.

3. For 'height' the book of Kings uses consistently the term *qōmāh* (literally 'stature'), thirteen times in this context (I Kings 6.20; etc.). In Chronicles the treatment varies: the term 'stature' is retained on three occasions (II Chron. 4.1, 2; 6.13); other terms are used elsewhere (vv. 4, 15),

and in other instances the reference to the height is omitted (for the inner sanctuary, I Kings 6.20; for the cherubim, I Kings 6.23, 26).

[4b–7, 8b–9] These verses describe the interior panelling of the house and its decorations. Verse 4b is taken from I Kings 6.21a; vv. 5–7 are the Chronicler's own summary of details roughly parallel to I Kings 6.15–18, 21b–22; 29–35; vv. 8b–9 have additional data peculiar to Chronicles, regarding the gold overlay.

According to I Kings 6.15, 18, the Temple interior was lined with cedars and the floor was covered with cypress boards. The Chronicler describes the interior panelling as cypress and ignores the floor. This is rather curious, as Chronicles agrees with Kings that cedar was the principal timber used for the Temple construction and the central issue of the agreement between Solomon and Hiram, and goes on to describe how David had already made preparations to receive 'cedar timbers without number; for the Sidonians ... brought great quantities of cedar to David' (I Chron. 22.3), a supply to be augmented by Solomon's agreement with Huram (II Chron. 2.2,7). It is also said twice of Solomon that he 'made cedar as plentiful as the sycamore in the Shephelah' (II Chron. 1.15; 9.27). However, when it comes to the actual building, cedar is never mentioned in Chronicles, quite belying the claim of I Kings 6.18 that 'all was cedar'. Even while agreeing that the Temple was adorned with interior panelling, the Chronicler systematically omits all mention of cedar; this could hardly be coincidental. Although the motives for this remain unknown, the fact remains that, in the end, the Temple is not 'a house of cedar' (I Chron. 17.1, 6; II Chron. 6.2, 7).

The timber is overlaid with gold, decorated with palms, chains and settings of precious stones. The 'chains' are mentioned in I Kings 7.7 only as decoration of the bronze pillars; here they adorn the walls of the house as well. The precious stones appear only in Chronicles.

In sum, the Chronicler's description of the house is redulant with gold, for which he uses the adjectives 'pure' ($t\bar{a}h\bar{o}r$, v. 4), 'fine' ($t\bar{o}b$, v. 5) and 'of Parvaim' ($z^e hab parw\bar{a}yim$, v. 6). Elsewhere he uses the earlier $z\bar{a}h\bar{a}b s\bar{a}g\bar{u}r$ (I Kings 6.20, 21; 7.49, 50; 10.21; II Chron. 4.20, 22, NEB 'red gold', RSV 'pure gold'), and also 'beaten gold' ($z\bar{a}h\bar{a}b \check{s}\bar{a}h\bar{u}t$, I Kings 10.17; II Chron. 9.15, 16). Peculiar to the Chronicler are 'refined gold' ($z\bar{a}h\bar{a}b m^e zuqq\bar{a}q$, I Chron. 28.18), and 'gold of Ophir' ($z^e hab \check{}\bar{o}p\bar{\imath}r$, I Chron. 29.4; others $ketem \check{}\bar{o}p\bar{\imath}r$, Isa. 13. 12, etc.). The difference between these terms is no longer clear to us. The art of overlaying described earlier by the root sph is now indicated by the later root hph as well.

Another unique term introduced by the Chronicler is $habbayit hagg\bar{a}d\bar{o}l$ ('the big house'), translated by the NEB as 'the large chamber' (RSV 'the nave') probably intended to define the main part of the Temple building, otherwise called $h\bar{e}k\bar{a}l$ (I Kings 6.5, etc., RSV 'nave', NEB 'sanctuary'). In this unique designation the Chronicler actually restores the original meaning of the Sumerian *é-gal* = 'big house', from which the Hebrew *hēkāl* is derived (Baumgartner, 234). May we deduce that the Chronicler was aware of this original connotation, or does his choice of 'the big house' merely echo his view that 'the house … will be great' (literally 'big', 2.5)?

[8b–9] The information concerning the total amount of gold, the weight of the nails and the decoration of the upper chambers is not found in the record of Kings. As the text now stands, these details would seem to belong to the description of the 'most holy place', but this context is problematic.

In the first place, it would be strange if this information was provided only for the 'most holy place' with no equivalent for the Temple in general; secondly, six hundred talents of gold would seem extravagant indeed for the relatively small chamber here described; and thirdly, it is hardly likely that the 'most holy place' had any 'upper chambers'. (RSV smooths over this last difficulty by making the reference to the upper chambers a completely new sentence.) It would seem, therefore, that vv. 8b–9 relate to the Temple in general and not to the 'most holy place'. In the process of transmission these lines probably fell out as a result of homoioteleuton (*zāhāb … zāhāb*). Later they were supplemented in the margin and when interpolated back into the text they were misplaced, after another mention of 'gold'. The original sequence may be restored, placing this passage most probably after v. 7a:

ויחף את הבית ... זהב [לככרים שש מאות ומשקל למסמרות לשקלים חמשים זהב
והעליות חפה זהב] ופתח כרובים על הקירות. ויעש את בית קדש הקדשים ...
ויחפהו זהב טוב ( ). ויעש בבית קדש הקדשים ...

'So he lined the house, beams, thresholds, walls and doors, with six hundred talents of fine gold; and the weight of gold for the nails was fifty shekels; and he overlaid the upper chambers with gold, and carved cherubim on the walls. And he made the most holy place … and overlaid it with fine gold. In the most holy place he made …, etc.'

At first glance, fifty shekels of gold for the nails hardly seems sufficient for fastening six hundred talents of overlay. LXX in fact regards 50 shekels as the weight of one nail. This version, while not very realistic (much too heavy!) has provided scholars, in the word 'one', a basis for reconstruction of MT (cf. BH, followed also by RSV): 'one shekel to fifty shekels of gold'. Since, however, the nails were made of iron (I Chron. 22.3) and probably only plated with gold, the amount may be reasonable (cf. Rudolph, 203), and no emendation is required (thus NEB and JPS).

The 'upper chambers' are not mentioned in Solomon's temple in I Kings 6–7; regarding the Temple, the term is unique to Chronicles (also I Chron. 28.11), and the reference is probably to parts of the building which were differently designated before.

[8a–ba, 10–13] From the 'big house' the Chronicler turns to the 'most holy place'. The first stage refers to its construction (v. 8a) and its gold overlay (v. 8b, without the reference to 'six hundred talents', cf. above), following I Kings 6.20 with the omission of the height. The second stage (vv. 10–13) is a lengthy description of the cherubim (based on I Kings 6.23–28), in which the richness of detail immediately indicates that here is a topic of significance.

The inner shrine is described in biblical sources by two terms: 'the inner sanctuary' (*d^ebīr*), peculiar to Solomon's Temple (I Kings 6.5, 16, etc., and once in Ps. 28.2), and the general Priestly term: 'the holy of holies' (*qōdeš haqq^odāšīm*, translated by RSV 'most holy place'; Exod. 26.34, etc.), used for both the tabernacle and for Solomon's Temple (I Kings 6.16; 7.50; 8.6, regarded by many scholars as later additions). The Chronicler follows the extant text of I Kings and has both terms: II Chron. 3.16 MT; 4.20; 5.7, 9, 11. He also uses a term of his own, *bēt qōdeš haqq^odāšīm* (also translated 'the most holy place' in RSV), which distinguishes this part of the house as a separate shrine (vv. 8, 10).

[10] In describing the cherubim, the Chronicler follows I Kings 6 in more than usual detail, but in accord with his method elsewhere, he omits the height of the cherubim (repeated three times in I Kings 6.23, 25, 26) and the wood of which they were made. In place of this last he uses the unique phrase *ma^aśēh ṣa^aṣu'īm*. LXX understands ṣa^aṣu'īm as '*ēṣīm* (followed by RSV), while the Vulgate translates 'images' (= NEB).

[11–12] These verses describe in great detail (completely restructuring the source in Kings) the precise measure and position of the cherubim's wings. The main point is that four wings, each five cubits long, span the whole breadth of the inner sanctuary: the outside wings of the two cherubim touch the opposite walls, while the inside wings touch each other at the tip.

[13b] This verse adds two more details about the cherubim: they stand on their feet and face the main chamber ('nave'). These remarks seem intended to distinguish the cherubim of the Temple from those of the ark. According to Exod. 25.10–21 the latter was covered by a structure (*kappōret*, RSV 'mercy-seat'), which incorporated two cherubim: 'of one piece with the mercy seat shall you make the cherubim on its two ends ... *their faces one to another*, toward the mercy seat shall the faces be' (vv. 19–20). It is not clear, however, how the whole setting of this same ark in the context of the inner Temple sanctuary is envisaged; even II Chron. 5.8 (I Kings 8.7) is not much help.

In the second Temple the 'most holy place' held neither cherubim nor ark (cf. BT Yoma 21b). The data in these verses, then, are not a reflection of conditions contemporary with the Chronicler, but represent traditional knowledge which there is no reason to doubt, but no way to verify.

[14] The veil is not mentioned in I Kings – unless the text there is

reconstructed after the model of Chronicles (cf. Šanda and others) – since it was made for the desert tabernacle, as a portable partition between the main chamber and the inner sanctuary (Exod. 26.31–33). In Solomon's Temple the two parts of the structure were separated by an olive-wood door covered with gold and decorated with carvings (I Kings 6.31–32). The Second Temple had a veil (Josephus, *Jewish War* V, 5, 5) and it is this veil which the Chronicler describes anachronistically, in terms accurately taken from Exod. 26.31 – with the changes mentioned in connection with II Chron. 2.7, 14.

[15–17] Using the same verb 'and he made' (vv. 8, 10, 14, 15, etc.) in a single narrative sequence, the Chronicler now moves to the bronze Temple items – the first being the pillars (I Kings 7.15ff.). In Chronicles, then, there is no grammatical change of subject and it is Solomon who 'makes' the pillars. In the parallel text of I Kings, the transition from the actual building to the bronze furnishings is preceded by the summoning of Huram from Tyre (I Kings 7.13–14), who is the subject of the following passages and therefore maker of the pillars.

Here we are faced again with the same feature of unbalanced restructuring which we have already encountered. Huram the craftsman is given greater significance in Chronicles than in Kings: his appointment is the first of Solomon's requests of the king of Tyre, and his talents are so highly lauded that he becomes a second Bezalel (II Chron. 2.7, 13–14 [MT 2.6, 12–13]). However, when it comes to the actual crafting of the Temple furnishings, the Chronicler's literary restructuring actually relegates Huram to more obscurity: from 3.8 to 4.10 the repeated verb *wayya'aś* ('and he made') refers to Solomon (3.3); Huram is explicitly mentioned only in 4.11.

In a radical abridgement of his source, the Chronicler devotes only one verse to the casting and measure of the pillars, one to their decoration, and the last to their erection and names. His lack of real interest in the subject is evident in the mechanical way in which he derives the measurements of the pillars. It has long been recognized (cf. Rudolph, 204; Curtis, 328) that the height of thirty-five cubits is a sum of all the figures in I Kings 7.15–16: eighteen cubits height, twelve cubits circumference, and five cubits the height of the capital. Whether or not the five cubits of the capital mentioned here in Chronicles (v. 15) are seen as included in the thirty-five is really not of great significance.

The more common term for the capital is *kōteret*, used in the Bible exclusively for Solomon's bronze pillars (I Kings 7.16 etc.; II Kings 25.17; Jer. 52.22). Chronicles reproduces this term in the passage taken literally from Kings (II Chron. 4.12, 13), but the Chronicler himself uses the unique *ṣepet*, a word not attested in the Hebrew lexicon until the Middle Ages, when its usage is probably dependent on the Bible (but cf. the detailed discussion in Ben Yehuda's *Thesaurus*, Vol. 11, 5610–11*).

Of all the plethora of pillar decorations of I Kings 7.20, the Chronicler here retains only the chains and the pomegranates, and even these in smaller number. Here, too, the Chronicles text in II Chron. 4.12–13, taken verbatim from Kings, retains the original number and the 'networks'.

The text which positions the chains 'in the inner sanctuary' (*badd^e bîr*) is certainly corrupt, perhaps nothing more than a misplaced gloss. Another common proposal is the inversion of the letters to read *k^e rābîd*, a word occurring in the Bible only twice more (Gen. 41.42; Ezek. 16.11), for a reading reflected in RSV and elsewhere: 'like a necklace'.

The position of the pillars is here described twice, 'in front of the house' (v. 15) and 'in front of the temple' (v. 17), and I Kings 7.21 places them 'at the vestibule of the temple'. These three references do nothing to specify the precise location of the pillars. While the function of the pillars – which were architecturally independent of the Temple structure itself – and meaning of their names have inspired numerous midrashic and modern interpretations, they remain a mystery.

4 He made an altar of bronze, twenty cubits long, and twenty cubits wide, and ten cubits high. [2] Then he made the molten sea; it was round, ten cubits from brim to brim, and five cubits high, and a line of thirty cubits measured its circumference. [3] Under it were figures of gourds, for thirty cubits, compassing the sea round about; the gourds were in two rows, cast with it when it was cast. [4] It stood upon twelve oxen, three facing north, three facing west, three facing south, and three facing east; the sea was set upon them, and all their hinder parts were inward. [5] Its thickness was a handbreadth; and its brim was made like the brim of a cup, like the flower of a lily; it held over three thousand baths. [6] He also made ten lavers in which to wash, and set five on the south side, and five on the north side. In these they were to rinse off what was used for the burnt offering, and the sea was for the priests to wash in.

[7] And he made ten golden lampstands as prescribed, and set them in the temple, five on the south side and five on the north. [8] He also made ten tables, and placed them in the temple, five on the south side and five on the north. And he made a hundred basins of gold. [9] He made the court of the priests, and the great court, and doors for the court, and overlaid their doors with bronze; [10] and he set the sea at the south-east corner of the house.

[11] Huram also made the pots, the shovels, and the basins. So Huram finished the work that he did for King Solomon on the house of God: [12] the two pillars, the bowls, and the two capitals on the top of the pillars; and the two networks to cover the two bowls of the capitals that were on the top of the pillars; [13] and the four hundred pomegranates for the two networks, two rows of pomegranates for each network, to cover the two bowls of the capitals that were upon the pillars. [14] He made the stands also, and the lavers upon the stands, [15] and the one sea, and the twelve oxen underneath it. [16] The pots, the shovels, the forks, and all the equipment for these Huramabi made of burnished bronze for King Solomon for the house of the Lord. [17] In the plain of the Jordan the king cast them, in the clay ground between Succoth and Zeredah. [18] Solomon made all these things in great quantities, so that the weight of the bronze was not ascertained.

[19] So Solomon made all the things that were in the house of God: the golden altar, the tables for the bread of the Presence, [20] the lampstands and their lamps of pure gold to burn before the inner sanctuary, as prescribed; [21] the flowers, the lamps, and the tongs, of purest gold; [22] the snuffers, basins, dishes for incense, and firepans, of pure gold; and the sockets of the temple, for the inner doors to the most holy place and for the doors of the nave of the temple were of gold.

5 Thus all the work that Solomon did for the house of the Lord was finished. And Solomon brought in the things which David his father had dedicated, and stored the silver, the gold, and all the vessels in the treasuries of the house of God.

A. Notes to MT

[3] עשר באמה, difficult, thus already in I Kings 7.24; [10] מכתף, add הבית, with MSS, LXX and I Kings 7.39; [12] והגלות והכותרות, read וגלות הכותרות, cf. v. 13; [13] ... לכסות העמדים, dittography; already in I Kings 7.42; [14] עשה ... עשה, proposed עשר עשרה ..., cf. I Kings 7.43; [16] המזלגות, I Kings 7.45 המזרקות; כליהם, proposed הכלים, I Kings 7.45; אביו, read אבי; [17] צרדתה, read צרתנה, cf. I Kings 7.46 and commentary; [19b] ואת מזבח הזהב, read את מזבח הזהב, with I Kings 7.48; [21] הוא מכלות זהב, difficult.

B. Notes to RSV

[2] 'he made the molten sea', better 'he made the sea of cast metal' (NEB, JPS); [3] gourds, MT 'oxen' (בקרים); cf. I Kings 7.24 (פקעים); [5] 'over three thousand', MT 'three thousand' (NEB, JPS); [6] 'south, north', MT 'right side, left side'; also vv. 7, 8; 'what was used for the burnt offering', better JPS 'the parts of the burnt offering'; [10] 'he set the sea, etc ...', MT + 'on the right [side]' (cf. JPS); [17] 'in the clay ground', MT בעבי האדמה, NEB 'in the foundry', JPS 'in moulds dug out of the earth'; 'Zeredah', MT 'Zeredathah'; [18] 'so that', MT 'for' (כי, RSV is harmonized to I Kings 7.47); [18, 19] 'things', MT: 'vessels', or 'furnishings' (NEB; JPS); [22] 'sockets', MT 'entrance' (פתח, so NEB, JPS).

C. Structure, sources and form

1. Chapter 4 proceeds to detail the furnishings of the Temple. The structure of the passage is, however, rendered somewhat irregular in comparison with its source in I Kings 7.23–51, mainly by the insertion of vv. 7–10 into the sequence describing the bronze furnishings:

(a) 1–6 Bronze items:
   (i) 1 The altar
   (ii) 2–5 The sea
   (iii) 6 The lavers
(b) 7–8 The golden lamps, tables and basins
(c) 9–10 The courts
(d) 11–18 Summary of the bronze furnishings
(e) 19–22 Golden vessels inside the house
(f) 5.1 Conclusion.

2. The chapter is characterized by lengthy verbatim citations, with only minor changes, from Kings:

4. [1] 2–6a = I Kings 7.23–26 + 38a–39a;
4.10–5.1 = I Kings 7.39b–51.

An exception is found in the more free and less elaborate style of vv. 6aβ–10 (which, as we have already noted, break the original sequence).

This stylistic quality of the chapter is all the more apparent in comparison with the preceding narrative of II Chron. 1–3. There, while the Chronicler is definitely dependent on his sources in I Kings, he has thoroughly reworked and restructured each of the subjects: Solomon's journey to Gibeon and God's revelation there (II Chron. 1), the correspondence with Huram (II Chron. 2), and the first section dealing with the building of the Temple (II Chron. 3.1–17). Verses 6aβ–10 here adopt the same method, while the rest of the chapter faithfully reproduces the sources.

3. This double approach, in particular in ch. 3 as opposed to ch. 4, results not only in variations of style, linguistic usage and literary method, but also in contrasts in subject matter between the two parts of the Temple narrative:

(a) In ch. 3 there is no mention of Huram, the craftsman. The recurring verb 'he made' would seem to refer throughout to Solomon, initially mentioned in 3.1, 3 – and this would include the 'making' of the bronze pillars. From 4.11ff., however, material taken verbatim from Kings, Huram reappears, and all the bronze furnishings, including the pillars, are credited to him.

Furthermore, we have seen that according to I Kings 7.14, Huram is exclusively a 'master in bronze'. The Chronicler (in ch. 2) has presented him as a master of all crafts. Since II Chron. 4.11–16 duplicates the text of I Kings 7.40–45, here Huram appears – as in Kings – as a master of bronze alone. While the complete silence of ch. 3 over Huram does not explicitly contradict ch. 2, the text in 4.11ff. stands in tension with both.

(b) In the passage describing the bronze lavers (4.6), the Chronicler has omitted their 'stands' (I Kings 7.27–37). By contrast, in the general summary (4.14), taken verbatim from I Kings 7.43, the stands reappear.

(c) In describing the construction of the Temple, the Chronicler does not include any reference to the doors (I Kings 7.31–35); it is possible that he understood the entrance between the main chamber and the inner sanctuary to be covered by a veil (3.14). And yet, all the Temple doors, including that to the most holy place, are mentioned in the literal summary in 4.22b (= I Kings 7.50).

(d) The pillars, as well, are differently conceived. In the summary, the original 'network' and 'four hundred pomegranates' reappear (4.12–13 = I Kings 7.41–42).

(e) For marked stylistic differences, compare, for example, the measurements as they appear in a reworked text in II Chron. 3.3, as against their appearance in a verbatim reproduction in 4.1. For the sake of clarity the texts are presented in a literal translation:

I Kings 6.2: sixty cubits its length, and twenty its width and thirty cubits its height
II Chron. 3.2: the length (in cubits of the old standard) cubits sixty and the width cubits twenty,

as against

II Chron. 4.1: twenty cubits its length, and twenty cubits its width and ten cubits its height.

Words like קוֹמָה (height, literally, stature), זהב סגור ('complete' gold), כתרות (capitals), גֻלּוֹת ((bowls), שבכה (network), which were omitted or replaced in the Chronicler's rephrasing in ch. 3, all reappear here, in ch. 4.

4. A very tempting solution to all these irregularities is to view much of ch. 4 as an expanded version of a shorter Chronistic original, here complemented by a later author with verbatim passages from Kings. Some scholars would confine the application of this solution to the actual contradictions, and regard only vv. 10–22 as secondary (cf. recently Williamson, 211–12, citing earlier commentaries). Rudolph would see as additions all the passages cited literally from I Kings, and regard only vv. 2a, 3a and 6–9 as originally Chronistic (205–9).

The obvious advantage of this solution is that most of the problems of the chapter seem to be immediately solved. What has not been explained is the motive behind the later glossator's work. These long passages of rather technical details are of historical, or even archaeological, interest, and have no theological or contemporary relevance. Rudolph's analysis postulates an extremely sophisticated glossing, with no apparent motive.

5. In fact, a closer analysis of the chapter, with special attention to the use of the sources and the literary methods of omission and elaboration, reveals that these are the identical methods used consistently by the Chronicler.

(*a*) The source of this Chronicles text is clearly I Kings 7.15–38: the order of the various items is strictly kept, while items of lesser interest are omitted, thus: pillars, [altar], sea (stands), lavers.

(*b*) Into this 'basic text' insertions are made by cutting the source-text at a certain point, introducing a new passage at the point of the cut, and then proceeding with the original text with no regard for the logic of the new sequence. In the same way, omissions are made by simple extraction of passages from the original text, which then continues without any linking material or supplementary notes.

If we take I Kings 7.15ff. for our base, we realize this technique in two passages in Chronicles. The first is the omission of the description of the bronze stands:

I Kings 7.23–26	27—37	38
II Chron. 4.2–5		6

The second is the addition of vv. 6b–9. Here the Chronicles text follows the order and idiom of I Kings 7.38–39, with the omission of v. 38b (which relates to the stands); then, between v. 39a and v. 39b the text is interrupted by the insertion of a lengthy passage (4.6b–9), only to proceed once more with the original text of Kings (7.39b). In translation, a natural re-ordering of the text sequence obscures this procedure; a literal rendering of the Hebrew text of Chronicles would be: (v. 6a = I Kings 7.38a+39a) 'He also made ten lavers, and set five on the right side and five on the left side [insertion 4.6aβ–9: 'for washing. In these they were to rinse off the parts of the burnt offering etc.... and overlaid their doors with bronze]. (v. 10 = I Kings 7.39b): 'and he set the sea at the ... corner of the house'. This can be illustrated thus:

I Kings 7.38+39a		39bff.
II Chron. 4.6aα	6aβ–9	10ff.

(*c*) Although the passage taken literally from I Kings has been changed very little, several features are still best explained as deriving from the Chronicler:

(i) The enumeration of the golden furnishings (4.19–22) is borrowed from the

CHAPTERS 4.1–5.1 563

summary of I Kings 7.48–50. Notice, however, how Chronicles' reference to the golden lampstands differs:

I Kings 7.49aα: 'the lampstands of pure gold, five on the right side and five on the left before the inner sanctuary ...'
II Chron. 4.20a: 'the lampstands and their lamps of pure gold to burn before the inner sanctuary as prescribed'.

The information about the position of these lampstands is not in fact missing in the narrative of Chronicles; it has been provided earlier in 4.7, to which v. 20a is actually only a supplement. Such correspondence between the Chronicler's own composition and the verbatim citation from Kings can hardly be attributed to an incidental harmonizer.

(ii) The same applies in 4.19bβ, where Chronicles carefully emends I Kings 7.48bβ: 'the golden table for the bread of the presence', to read, in the plural: 'the tables for the bread, etc.'. According to the Chronicler there were ten tables, as is clear from his own insertion in 4.8: 'He also made ten tables etc.' (cf. also I Chron. 28.16).

(iii) Although the references to the lamps are divided between two passages, in both the Chronicler emphasizes their function with his characteristic phrase: כמשפטם, 'as prescribed' (4.7, 20).

All of the above makes it rather difficult to regard the sections literally parallel to I Kings 7 as no more than secondary additions, accidentally 'filling out' the 'original' Chronistic composition. Another approach would seem to be indicated by the textual facts.

Chapter 4 marks a transition between two different approaches to the source material, both of which are amply demonstrated in Chronicles. In fact, the faithful, even slavish adherence to the source text has been illustrated in passages like I Chron. 11.11–40; also chs. 14, 17, 18, etc. In these cases, the Chronicler's basically word-for-word transmission of his sources is peppered with shorter or longer passages from his pen, clearly marked by his style and theology (cf. I Chron. 10.13–14; 11.10; etc). In the history of Solomon we have so far found this phenomenon only in II Chron. 1.14–17, but from this point on this will be the dominant, if not the exclusive, method. The two approaches require different measures of editorial energy, but both are characteristic of the Chronicler's work.

If we are indeed to consider the chapter as a whole as Chronistic, we must take a more tolerant stance vis à vis its stylistic differences and contradictions; the literary method chosen by the Chronicler is not conducive to complete harmony.

6. An important stylistic feature, and one that clearly marks this chapter as a continuation of ch. 3, is the consistent repetition of the verb ויעש ('and he made') to open a paragraph (3.8, 10, 14, 15, 16; 4.1, 2, 6, 7, 8a, 8b, 9, 11, 18, 19; cf. Willi, 96–8; Williamson, 208). While some of these passages are no more than reproductions of the source in Kings (I Kings 6.23; 7.23, 38, 40, 48), the overall usage and role of ויעש in Chronicles is much more extensive. While the term is natural, and therefore expected in a context of building and craftsmanship, and thus appears in I Kings 6–7 sporadically throughout the narrative, in Chronicles it becomes a *Leitmotif*, lending the pericope a touch of uniformity. The three kinds of passages already noted in the Chronicles narrative – those taken verbatim from Kings, those abridged and re-worked, and a passage written by the Chronicler himself – are presented as a

continuum, all opening with the initial ויעש. Note in particular how the verbs ויצר ('he cast') and וינח ('he left') in I Kings 7.15, 47 are superseded in II Chron. 3.15; 4.18 by ויעש ('he made'), to say nothing of its frequency in 4.7–9.

D. Commentary

[1] Although there is no reference to the bronze altar in the parallel text of Kings, there is every reason to regard that text as corrupt, either by homoioarkton (similar beginning – 'and he made ... and he made'), or intentional editing (cf. below). The style and terminology of this verse are identical to other descriptions in I Kings, and different from the presentation peculiar to Chronicles: all three dimensions are given, the order of the numerals is the one followed in Kings, and the word $q\bar{o}m\bar{a}h$ is used for 'height'. What is more, there is explicit reference to a bronze altar among the Temple furnishings later, in I Kings 8.64 and II Kings 16.14. The Chronicler, in introducing the altar in this context, is probably citing his *Vorlage*, now either corrupt or secondarily abridged.

Note the impressive dimensions of the altar: 20×20×10 cubits, with sixteen times the surface area and more than three times the height of the bronze altar of the tabernacle (5×5×3 cubits). There is a possibility that these dimensions apply to the podium alone, upon which the actual altar stood – but explicit details are not provided in the brief description (cf. also T. A. Busink, *Der Tempel von Jerusalem, von Salomo bis Herodes*, Leiden 1970, 323–4). As the term 'cast'($m\bar{u}\bar{s}\bar{a}q$) is not used in reference to the altar, one may infer that it was actually built of wood and only overlaid with bronze.

[2–5] The description of the sea is taken verbatim, with a few exceptions, from I Kings 7.23–26. The sea was made $m\bar{u}\bar{s}\bar{a}q$ ('of cast metal', v. 2), forged together with all its decorations (v. 3), and its diameter was ten, its height five, and its circumference thirty cubits. According to I Kings 7.24, it was decorated with two rows of gourds ($p^e q\bar{a}'\bar{i}m$) just under the brim. Here, the Chronicler has 'figures of oxen' ($d^e m\bar{u}t b^e q\bar{a}r\bar{i}m$), which many scholars retrovert to 'gourds' (also RSV; NEB). While this variant may indeed have originated in a textual corruption ($p^e q\bar{a}'\bar{i}m - b^e q\bar{a}r\bar{i}m$), it is noteworthy that in the Chronicler's version the two occurrences of $p^e qa'\bar{i}m$ in I Kings 7.24 are both changed: one is rendered as indicated above and the other is represented by $habb\bar{a}q\bar{a}r$, 'the oxen' (v. 3). For the Chronicler, then, the sea not only stood upon twelve oxen (v. 4) but was also decorated with their images. It is possible that this different portrayal occasioned the omission in v. 3 of the reference to the 'brim' of the sea: the decoration did not 'run under its brim' but 'under it'.

Commentators understand 'ten cubits' as referring to the length of the decoration, and since the circumference of the sea is explicitly given as thirty cubits, the words 'ten cubits' are not accepted as original. Some would regard them as a gloss on the text of I Kings 7.24 (cf. BHS), while others would correct ten to 'thirty' (thus RSV). The Chronicler may have understood the phrase literally, as 'ten *in* a cubit' – in spite of the slight grammatical irregularity – and see it as referring to the dimensions of the gourds/oxen themselves (cf. Curtis, 333; Rudolph, 206).

Verses 4–5 follow I Kings 7.25–26, to describe how the sea was positioned on the oxen, its thickness, the artistic form of its brim, and its capacity. For this last, Kings has 2000 baths, Chronicles 3000, and while interesting attempts have been made to attribute the discrepancy to different concepts of the shape of the sea (cylinder versus hemisphere, cf. C. C. Wylie, 'On King Solomon's Molten Sea', *BA* XII, 1949, 86–90), the most plausible suggestion is still to regard one of the two numbers, probably the larger, as an error (cf. Busink, *Tempel*, 328).

[6] The description now turns, very concisely, to the lavers. The omission both of the detailed measurements of I Kings 7.38–39, and of the preceding reference to 'stands', is an indication that the subject evokes little interest here. The combination of I Kings 7.38a and 39a, with omission of various details [ ], produces a new sequence: 'He also made ten lavers [of bronze, etc., etc.]. And he set [the stands] five on the south side [of the house] and five on the north side [of the house].'

The Chronistic editorial technique, which combines faithful adherence to the source with radical textual pruning, is very much in evidence here. With the omission of 'of the house', 'left' and 'right' (RSV 'north' and 'south') do not give the concrete location of the lavers.

On the other hand, the Chronicler adds, regarding the sea and the lavers, notes which are not mentioned in Kings and reflect his own need to understand their function: concerning the lavers, 'in which to wash', and 'in this they were to rinse off what was used for the burnt offering' (RSV; JPS: '... rinse off ... the parts of the burnt offering'), and concerning the sea, 'for the priests to wash in'.

Now, these notes could hardly reflect the original functions of the sea and the lavers. What degree of mythological-symbolic meaning they had in Solomon's day is difficult to say; practically speaking they seem to have served as huge reservoirs in the Temple courts. The advantages of such large open reservoirs are not at all clear; it is at any rate doubtful that the priests would have actually washed themselves and rinsed the 'burnt offerings' there. A much more plausible procedure is described in Ezek. 40.38, where the burnt-offering is rinsed in the chambers adjacent to the court, near the place where the beasts were killed.

It would seem, therefore, that the Chronicler's understanding of the role of sea and lavers is influenced by, and harmonized with, the desert tabernacle, where there is 'a laver of bronze, with its base of bronze for washing ...

and you shall put water in it. And from it (RSV 'with which') Aaron and his sons shall wash their hands and their feet' (Exod. 30.18–19). Notice that it is clearly stated that the priests will wash 'from it' and not 'in it'; although the measurements are not given, the laver seems to have been all in all rather small. In the light of this association, the Chronicler may have omitted the measurements of the 'lavers' and their enormous stands as described in his source, assuming a set of smaller basins which were indeed used for washing and would reflect something more similar to the arrangement of his own time.

A few linguistic notes: the Chronicler's addition here comprises only a few, rather technical clauses at the end of v. 6; nevertheless, marks of late or, more specifically, Chronistic Hebrew may immediately be recognized. Most obvious is the placement of the numerals: in the four instances of numbering in vv. 6–8, the numbered noun always preceeds the numeral, as is the rule in over a hundred instances in Chronicles (for the full analysis cf. Kropat, 51.) One should not, however, leap to the opposite conclusion, that the Chronicler's sources always follow the alternative system; for a similar method in this context cf. the list of I Kings 7.40–50 = II Chron. 5.11–21.

[7–9] The second item in the Chronicler's addition is the making of the golden lampstands. Compared to the bronze vessels, the golden items receive only cursory attention in I Kings 7.48–50; their making is described very briefly, actually after the summary of the bronze furnishings, with no specifications of measurements or decoration. That the Chronicler was dissatisfied with this lack of proportion is evident in his restructuring of the narrative at this point: before going on with the placement of the sea and the summary of the bronze objects, he refers to three items: the golden lamps (v. 7), the tables, and the basins (v. 8); all three are also enumerated in a more original position in v. 19. The Chronicler then incorporates this insertion into the original text sequence, by referring to the making of the courts (v. 9). The order of the golden objects here deviates from that of the summary in vv. 19–22, but resembles that of the Chronicler's own enumeration in I Chron. 28.15–18: lampstands, tables, small vessels and the golden incense altar. As the latter item is mentioned in v. 19 and also in I Chron. 28.18, it is possible that it was referred to in this verse as well, but was omitted by corruption.

Here (v. 7), as in I Kings 7.49, the lampstands are ten and made of gold. In this detail, too, Solomon's Temple differs from the Mosaic tabernacle, in which there was only one lampstand (Exod. 25.31–38). Our information on the tables (v. 8) is broader. In I Kings 7.48 only one 'golden table for the bread of the Presence' is mentioned, just as in the tabernacle (cf. Exod. 25.23–30). In this context there are ten, specifically situated, 'five to the right side and five to the left side', and in v. 19 'table' is made plural: 'tables, and on *them* the bread'. Moreover, in neither of the chapter's references to the tables is it explicitly stated that they were made of gold, although the source of v. 19 in I Kings 7.48 expressly mentions the fact. On the other hand, in I Chron. 28.16, in recording the materials prepared by David, the Chronicler does include the tables among the 'golden vessels'. How then did the Chronicler view these tables? His insistence may indicate that in the Second Temple the bread of the Presence was arranged in ten settings rather than one, and it is possible that the tables were not made of gold.

The last items here are the 'court of the priests' and the 'great court', and their doors. In Kings, three courts are mentioned: 'the inner court' (I Kings 6.36; 7.12), 'the great court' (7.12, *ḥaṣer haggᵉdōlāh*), and the 'other court' (7.8), probably a part of the complex of palace buildings. The court mentioned in 8.64 (II Chron. 7.7), 'the court that was before the house of the Lord', is probably identical with 'the inner court'. Of all the texts from I Kings just cited as referring to the courts, not one is repeated in Chronicles; this verse is in fact the only reference to the courts in the building context of Chronicles. It would seem that the architectural picture is the same, with the two courts having somewhat different designations: 'the court of the priests' (which may refer to the 'inner court'), and 'the great court' (*haᵃzārāh haggᵉdōlāh*).

The term for 'court', *ᵃzārāh*, recurs in II Chron. 6.13. The same word appears several times in Ezekiel (43.14, 17, 20; 45.19), but there it seems to have some technical connotation in relation to the altar. The Chronicler's specific use of this term reflects its regular usage in post-biblical literature, as a strictly technical designation for the Temple courts (cf. A. Hurvitz, *A Linguistic Study of the Relationship between the Priestly Source and the Book of Ezekiel*, Paris 1982, 78–81).

I Kings does not mention that the doors of the courts were overlaid with bronze, but the information is very plausible, at least for the inner court, since all the vessels there were of the same metal. However, it is impossible to know whether this comment is the Chronicler's transmission of a lost source, a tradition, or an educated guess.

[10–11a] The Chronicler now reverts to his source in I Kings 7.39b, which he follows continuously to its end. Literarily speaking, this rather mechanical return to the original sequence of the source disrupts the coherence of content and syntax; the placement of the sea is not anticipated at this point, and the sequence of verbs is awkward. Originally, the whole section had a chiastic structure: the making of the sea (I Kings 7.23–26) – the making of the stands and lavers (I Kings 7.27–38) – the placement of the stands (I Kings 7.39a) – the placement of the sea (I Kings 7.39b). This structure is now completely abandoned, and the present sequence can be accounted for only on the basis of its source.

Verse 11a refers, finally, to the lesser bronze vessels; the mention of

Huram is of course a result of the Chronicler's return to his source (I Kings 7.40).

[11b–18] This summary of all the bronze objects made for the Temple follows I Kings 7.40b–47 faithfully. It includes (after the introduction, 11b) the enumeration of the objects, i.e. the pillars, the lavers and stands, the sea and oxen, and smaller utensils, all of 'burnished bronze' (vv. 12–16), the location of their casting (16b–17) and a general conclusion (v. 18).

The bronze altar is lacking in both texts, notwithstanding the list of smaller utensils for its function: pots, shovels and forks (v. 16). We have already seen that the information about the altar was preserved only in II Chron. 4.1 with no parallel in the MT of I Kings. Its omission in the conclusion of I Kings is fully in line with that narrative; its omission in Chronicles, however, may illustrate the shortcomings of the Chronicler's editing methods: rendering literally his source in I Kings, he fails to mention the altar, and on the other hand does include the 'stands'; in both cases tension is created with his own earlier account. In the same way, the reference to the pillars in this summary includes details completely absent at their construction in 3.15–16, e.g. bowls, capitals and networks, and the number of the pomegranates, a hundred according to 3.16, is here given as four hundred, following I Kings 7.42.

The text of v. 14 reads 'made' (עשה) twice in place of the original 'ten' (עשר, עשרה), a textual corruption which should be restored (NEB), or a stylistic variation which should be respected (RSV) – both suggestions are plausible.

Verse 15 has 'under it' (taḥtāw), in place of 'under the sea' (taḥat hayyām) of I Kings 7.44. Such small differences in phrasing abound. They express the Chronicler's stylistic inclination towards more brevity, and his linguistic preference for the suffixed pronoun.

For 'burnished' bronze, I Kings 7.45 has m‘mōrāṭ and v. 16 here mārūq. The two words are unique; verbal forms of the same roots have the same connotation, but are quite rare, especially the latter (cf. Ezek. 21.14, 15 etc.; Jer. 46.4). Note the Chronicler's technique of replacing one word with another which is orthographically and phonetically proximate.

[17] With the location of the casting, the subject is again 'the king', and the place is given, following I Kings 7.46, in 'the plain of the Jordan'. There is a discrepancy between 'Zarethan' of Kings and 'Zeredathah' (RSV 'Zeredah') here. According to biblical evidence, the latter was a town in Ephraim (I Kings 11.26), sometimes identified with 'Zererah' of Manasseh (Judg. 7.22). As for 'Zarethan', it is connected with the 'plain of the Jordan' in both Josh. 3.16 and I Kings 4.12. It would seem that here too, the original is preserved in Kings; the text in Chronicles probably read 'Zarethanah' – the longer form for which the Chronicler has a predilection (cf. also in v. 10, negbāh for I Kings 7.39 negbāh, and others). Textual corruption resulted in the present

form 'Zeredathah' (the last syllable, understood as locative, is omitted by the RSV).

[18] The concluding verse adds nothing of substance, except an explicit emphasis on the hitherto implicit enormous quantities of bronze used. By the introduction of the conjunction 'for' (*kī*), the two sentences now have a causal link: Solomon could make all these objects *because* the quantities of bronze at his disposal were 'beyond reckoning' (NEB). The allusion is to the preliminary preparations of David, who gathered bronze 'beyond weighing' (I Chron. 22.3, 16; 29.7), for this very purpose (I Chron. 18.8).

[19–22] Following I Kings 7.48–50, the passage now cites a summary enumeration of the golden objects: the golden altar (19a), the tables (19b), the lampstands with their decorations and utensils (vv. 20–21), the smaller service utensils (v. 22a) and the Temple doors (v. 22b).

As already mentioned, in I Kings 6–7 there is a lack of proportion between the bronze and golden vessels. Each of the bronze vessels is first described in great detail, including its design, measure and decorations (I Kings 7.15–40), and then all are listed in one summary (vv. 41–46); the golden vessels, on the other hand, are mentioned in the summary for the first time – except perhaps for the cursory remark about 'an altar of cedar' (I Kings 6.20), which may refer to the golden altar. This imbalance is all the more amazing when we consider the essential significance of the golden vessels, which were all used for the actual ritual inside the Temple, and the rather ornamental, secondary importance of the bronze objects (except for the altar, for which cf. below), which were placed in the court. A similar lack of proportion exists between the detailed description of the Temple building and the minimal reference to its inner furnishings. To these general observations, two more should be added, which may hint at the correct solution:

(a) In the summary regarding the lampstands in I Kings 7.49, some details of its design are nevertheless mentioned: 'the flowers, the lamps and the tongs, of gold' – a remark resembling in style the summary regarding the bronze objects, which may hint that the craftsmanship of the lampstands had originally been described in much broader detail.

(b) Of the many bronze items in the Temple, one is conspicuous by its absence in Kings: the bronze altar of offering. A partial description of this altar, consisting mainly of its measures, has been preserved in II Chron. 4.1.

Taking these facts into consideration, I suggest that the original account of I Kings which related to the furniture of the Temple has undergone a thorough editing, and that the source text contained, as with the bronze objects, a full and detailed description of the golden items, as well as of the bronze altar. Of all this material only the summary remains, and in the case of the altar, not even that. The result is the present unbalanced composition of I Kings 7.

The motive for such a thorough redaction is not difficult to find. For the common denominator of all the objects thus omitted is that they each have an explicit parallel in the furnishings of the Exodus tabernacle! When we compare the elements of Solomon's Temple with those of the desert shrine, it is immediately clear that the golden altar, the lampstand, the golden table and the bronze altar, all with their service utensils, are common to both sanctuaries (Exod. 25.23–29; 37.10–38.10); the bronze objects, on the other hand, the description of which is found in I Kings 7 – the pillars, the sea, the basins and their stands – are all peculiar to Solomon's Temple. Since these bronze items did not contradict anything known from the desert tradition, their description remained; the detailed descriptions of the gold items and the bronze altar, however, were so different from their counterparts in the tabernacle that they were completely excised from the Kings text.

The Chronicler restored some measure of proportion in several ways: by a considerable abridgement of his descriptions of the house and the details of the bronze objects, by a short reference to the bronze altar, and by his earlier and explicit mention of some of the golden objects (vv. 7–8).

I shall complement discussion of this summary (cf. above p. 563) with a few more points:

(a) The phrase 'as prescribed' (*kamišpāṭ*, here and v. 7) associates an element of legitimacy with the lampstands, and may represent a conscious attempt to account for the difference between the praxis of Solomon's Temple and that of the tabernacle, which had only one such stand (Exod. 25.31–38).

(b) In v. 21 two of the details, 'the flowers and the lamps', represent parts of the lampstand itself, while 'the tongs' refer to its utensils. All three were mentioned in Exod. 25.31, 37, 38, referring to the tabernacle lampstand, but other parts and implements mentioned there are not repeated here.

(c) The attribute of the gold here is *miklōt zāhāb* (v. 21), a unique and obscure phrase. It is generally interpreted as 'purest gold' (RSV) or 'solid gold' (NEB), based probably on its supposed derivation from *klh*, denoting 'complete'. It may be interpreted differently, as equivalent to *zāhāb sāgūr*, because of the semantic proximity of the respective roots: *kl'* and *sgr* (cf. Rudolph, 208). While the linguistic derivation may be clear, the precise quality of gold it denotes is not known.

(d) In conclusion, the Temple doors are mentioned. The obscure *pōtōt* of I Kings 7.50 (*pātu* in Accadian meaning 'forehead', cf. Isa. 3.17 and Baumgartner, 924, is difficult in this context) is replaced here (v. 22) by the more common *petaḥ* (= entrance), either the more authentic text or its replacement by the Chronicler.

The singular *petaḥ* is a collective noun, as is immediately clear: 'the doors of the house and of the most holy place'. According to I Kings 6.31–35 these doors were made of olivewood, decorated and overlaid with gold. As discussed above, the Chronicler elsewhere omitted the passage relating to the making of the doors, and introduced 'the veil' (cf. above, pp. 555–6). Here, however, the text follows I Kings 7.50b, without adjustment to these new views.

[5.1] The concluding verse copies I Kings 7.51 verbatim, with only minor linguistic differences in word-order, use of prepositions and word-replacements. The costly dedications of David – which were mentioned in Chronicles twice before (I Chron. 18.10–11 = II Sam. 8.11–12; I Chron. 26.26–27) – now find their place in the treasuries of the house of God. With this, the first stage of the Temple project, its construction, comes to an end. The second part of the narrative – the ceremonial dedication of the Temple – will begin presently.

5 2 Then Solomon assembled the elders of Israel and all the heads of the tribes, the leaders of the fathers' houses of the people of Israel, in Jerusalem, to bring up the ark of the covenant of the Lord out of the city of David, which is Zion. [3] And all the men of Israel assembled before the king at the feast which is in the seventh month. [4] And all the elders of Israel came, and the Levites took up the ark. [5] And they brought up the ark, the tent of meeting, and all the holy vessels that were in the tent; the priests and the Levites brought them up. [6] And King Solomon and all the congregation of Israel, who had assembled before him, were before the ark, sacrificing so many sheep and oxen that they could not be counted or numbered. [7] So the priests brought the ark of the covenant of the Lord to its place, in the inner sanctuary of the house, in the most holy place, underneath the wings of the cherubim. [8] For the cherubim spread out their wings over the place of the ark, so that the cherubim made a covering above the ark and its poles. [9] And the poles were so long that the ends of the poles were seen from the holy place before the inner sanctuary; but they could not be seen from outside; and they are there to this day. [10] There was nothing in the ark except the two tables which Moses put there at Horeb, where the Lord made a covenant with the people of Israel, when they came out of Egypt. [11] Now when the priests came out of the holy place (for all the priests who were present had sanctified themselves, without regard to their divisions; [12] and all the Levitical singers, Asaph, Heman, and Jeduthun, their sons and kinsmen, arrayed in fine linen, with cymbals, harps, and lyres, stood east of the altar with a hundred and twenty priests who were trumpeters; [13] and it was the duty of the trumpeters and singers to make themselves heard in unison in praise and thanksgiving to the Lord), and when the song was raised, with trumpets and cymbals and other musical instruments, in praise to the Lord,

'For he is good,
for his steadfast love endures for ever,'
the house, the house of the Lord, was filled with a cloud, [14]so that the priests could not stand to minister because of the cloud; for the glory of the Lord filled the house of God.

6 Then Solomon said,
'The Lord has said that he would
dwell in thick darkness.
2 I have built thee an exalted house,
a place for thee to dwell in for ever.'

A. Notes to MT

[5] הלוים, proposed והלוים, following I Kings 8.4, MSS and Versions; [9] ויהי, proposed ויהיו, following I Kings 8.8, MSS and Versions; [13] בית, probably read כבוד, with LXX^AB.

B. Notes to RSV

[5] 'the priests and the Levites', thus I Kings 8.4; MT has no 'and', and would be translated 'the levitical priests'; [8] 'For the cherubim', thus I Kings 8.7; MT without כ ('for'), 'The Cherubim spread, etc ...' (NEB); [9] 'from the holy place', thus I Kings 8.8; MT 'from the ark' (NEB omits); 'they are there', thus I Kings 8.8; MT '*it* is there' (cf. A above, and commentary); [10] 'there', thus I Kings 8.9, not in MT; [12] 'Asaph, Heman, and Jeduthun', MT 'of Asaph, of Heman, of Jeduthun'; [6.1] 'I built', MT '*and* (or *but*) I built'; 'a place', MT '*and* a place'; in both cases the translation reflects I Kings 8.12.

C. Structure, sources and form

1. II Chron. 5.2–7.22 constitutes one literary unit, paralleling I Kings 8.1–9.8, devoted to the dedication of the Temple. The size of this pericope may already signify that the focus of the Chronicler's interest is the dedication and not the construction of the Temple: while the sections devoted to the building were considerably abridged, here the Chronicler adopts the material from I Kings with only very few omissions, and these are compensated for by the few additions so that the overall scope remains the same. Thus, while in Kings the two topics received equal treatment, here the description of the dedication is nearly twice as long as that of the building.

2. I Kings 8.1–9.8 certainly does not represent an original literary unity. Its primary core attracted several stages of elaborations, resulting in a broad collection of speeches and prayers. The Chronicler, however, has adopted the unit basically in its final form and in its entirety. Minor details aside, the sections which the Chronicler has omitted are I Kings 8.50aα–53, 54aβ–61, the first replaced by II Chron. 6.40–42 and the second by 7.1aβ–3. Also additional in Chronicles are 5.11b–13a; 6.13 (an addition perhaps made before the Chronicler); 7.6; 7.12bβ–15. These additions complement some essential points in the narrative, the absence of which in I Kings is probably not accidental; they can therefore be regarded as 'correctives'.

3. The comprehensive unit has six sections:

5.2–6.2 The introduction of the ark into the Temple
6.3–11 Solomon's address following this event
6.12–42 Solomon's prayer
7.1–11 Conclusion of the ceremonies and celebrations
7.12–22 God's revelation to Solomon.

4. In Kings, the most outstanding feature of the whole pericope is the preponderance of rhetoric: Solomon is shown giving one address after another. These include his declaration when the cloud descends (I Kings 8.12–13); the recapitulation of the Temple construction (8.15–21); his major prayer concerning the function of the Temple (8.23–53); his address to the people (8.56–61). God's answer (9.3–9) continues the rhetorical tone. The narrative sections are no more than links connecting these oratorical pieces (I Kings 8.1–11, 14, 22, 54–55, 62–66; 9.1–2). One may regard the Temple dedication as a magnet which attracted to its original format one Deuteronomistic piece after another.

In the book of Kings, this is the first and major cluster of oratorical sections. In Chronicles, by contrast, we have seen the similar style in I Chron. 28–29, probably modelled on this pericope. Here again, David's history anticipates that of Solomon, the two made equal in as many aspects as possible.

Although the Chronicler omits only one of the speeches found in I Kings (I Kings 8.56–61), his story on the whole has somewhat more narrative and action than the Kings version, contrary to what we usually find in Kings-Chronicles parallels.

5. I Chron. 5.2–6.2, taken almost verbatim from I Kings 8.1–13, tell how the ark of the covenant is brought from the city of David into the Temple and how a numinous cloud confirmed the dedication of the 'house of the Lord'. Two remarks should be made about the Chronicler's treatment of his source:

(a) Near the end of the passage, a rather lengthy section of the Chronicler's own (11b–13aβ) is inserted, elaborating on the ceremonial aspects of the installation of the ark. We have already encountered this method: the source-text is divided at a certain point, the new passage is inserted, and the source text continues where it left off, unaffected by the literary process:

I Kings 8.10a		10b
II Chron. 5.11a	11b–13a	13b

'Now, when the priests came out of the holy place [II Chron. 6.11b–13ab] the house ... was filled with the cloud.'

6. The result of this elaboration is a shift in the structure of the narrative and a modified balance of its components. The single continuous presentation of Kings here becomes two units of approximately equal scope:

(a) the transfer of the ark from the city of David to its place in the Temple (5.2–10);

(b) the sacerdotal ceremony, and the confirmation of God's presence (5.11–6.2).

The first stage relates a series of acts – the assembly of the elders and leaders, the 'taking up' of the ark and its positioning in the Temple – with some explanatory remarks. The second stage describes a three-phase ritual: a liturgy, beginning with the exit of the priests from the Temple, the descent of divine glory into the Temple, and Solomon's solemn proclamation: 'I have built thee an exalted house'.

D. Commentary

[2] Solomon's removal of the ark from the city of David to the Temple precincts is a sequel to his father's expedition to bring the ark from Kiriath-jearim to Jerusalem; now the wanderings of the ark have come to an end. This view, however, receives such explicit expression only in Chronicles (cf. the commentary on 6.41–42).

The double title of 'the city of David, which is Zion' – already found in I Kings – links this story with Sam. 5.7; it may indicate that the name 'stronghold of Zion' was not entirely replaced by the new title 'city of David'.

It should be mentioned, however, that except for the narrative about its conquest (II Sam. 5.7/I Chron. 11.5) and the present verse, the name 'Zion' is restricted to the poetic sections of the Bible (especially in the Prophets, Psalms and Lamentations).

The assembly initiated by Solomon in Jerusalem is in fact a gathering of the representatives of the people: 'the elders of Israel and all the heads of the tribes'. 'The elders of Israel', or simply 'the elders' are mentioned (though not frequently) in certain sections in Kings (I Kings 12; 20–21; II Kings 6.10). On the other hand, neither 'the heads of the tribes' (*ra'še hammaṭṭōt*) nor 'leaders of the fathers' houses' (*nᵉśī'ē hā'ābōt*) ever appear in Kings. This identification of 'tribes' with 'fathers' houses' is characteristic of certain Priestly sections of the Hexateuch (cf. Num 1.4, 16; 7.2; 17.17; Josh. 19.51; etc.). A certain lack of proportion emerges here, with the twelve tribal leaders juxtaposed with a much larger group of 'elders'. It would seem, therefore, that the original version of I Kings 8.1 referred only to 'the elders of Israel' (cf. also in v. 3), glossed later through Priestly influence, the impact of which can be also seen further in the text.

Even with the tribal heads, as a representative assembly this group is relatively small. Other phrases of the narrative, like 'all the men of Israel' (*kol 'īš yiśra'ēl* v. 3), 'all the congregation of Israel' (*kol "dat yiśrā'ēl*), etc., indicate a much more popular gathering of enormous crowds in Jerusalem (cf. in particular 7.8). To what extent the various strata of the story can still be restored – with or without the help of the shorter version of LXX MSS A and B – is still problematical. In any case, neither of the two titles is characteristically Chronistic; in both cases the Chronicler merely followed faithfully the already complex text of I Kings 8.

[3] Here the Chronicler omits 'the month Ethanim' – the ancient Canaanite name for the seventh month. The now isolated remark 'which is the seventh month' renders this part of the verse somewhat obscure; the translations harmonize by rendering 'the feast which is *in* the seventh month'.

[4] This verse contains one of the best-known cases of intervention by the Chronicler in the phrasing of his source. The 'priests' who bore the ark in I Kings 8.6 are replaced by 'Levites', a change which harmonizes with the Pentateuch Priestly traditions, with their more marked differentiation between the roles of priests and Levites, the latter being responsible for the ark (Num. 3.31). This distinction also figures in Chronicles (cf. also on I Chron. 23.13–14). However, even in the Chronicler's version, while the Levites carry the ark from the city of David, the priests are still entrusted with the major task of actually installing the ark in the inner sanctuary, where the Levites were strictly prohibited (cf. also II Chron. 29.16).

[5] This verse parallels I Kings 8.4, which is often regarded as another

gloss since it interrupts the original continuity of vv. 3 and 5 and broadens the ceremony to include not only 'the ark' but 'the tent of meeting' and 'the holy vessels' as well. What precisely is 'the tent' mentioned in this note? If the reference is to the tent which David pitched for the ark in Jerusalem, this would imply that when the ark was transferred to its final location, the tent which housed it was dismantled and deposited in the Temple. As for the 'vessels', there must certainly have been some in the Davidic tent (although never mentioned elsewhere), since earlier testimony attests to sacrifices and ritual being conducted there (I Kings 1.50–51; 2.28ff.; 3.15). Such an interpretation would render the gloss a historical 'corrective' to the earlier narrative. A more traditional-historical interpretation would see here an allusion to the wilderness tabernacle. This would imply that the glossator was endeavouring to renew the neglected tradition of the tabernacle, view the ark as merely one of the furnitures of the tabernacle and cast the whole scene in Priestly terminology.

The Chronicler designates the two tents, the Mosaic and Davidic tabernacles, by the same titles: 'the tent of meeting' (I Chron. 6.32 [MT 17]; 9.20; II Chron. 1.6) and 'the tabernacle' (I Chron. 6.32 [MT 17]; II Chron. 1.5). In his view, Israel's cultic activity was divided between these two centres until they were in fact superseded by the establishment of the final cultic institutions in Jerusalem. Although the Chronicler does not explicitly identify the 'tent of meeting' in our context, the reference seems to suit the wilderness tabernacle more than David's 'tent of meeting'.

Is the gloss in I Kings 8.4 Chronistic? It is tempting to think so; 'the tent of meeting' and 'the holy vessels' are both terms found in his composition (cf. the above references and I Chron. 9.29; 22.19), and the view expressed in the gloss accords with the Chronistic view of the development of the cult. However, a close look at this verse in Chronicles reveals three deviations from the text of Kings: 'the ark' replaces 'the ark of the Lord', 'levitical priests' replace 'the priests and the Levites', and the tense of the last verb is changed from imperfect with *waw* consecutive (*wayya*$^{a}l\bar{u}$) to perfect (*he*$^{e}l\bar{u}$). While the second point might represent a textual corruption, the other two are in full accord with the Chronicler's stylistic and linguistic preferences. The implication is that in this verse the Chronicler is reworking the Kings version; if the latter is a gloss, then it could hardly have originated with the Chronicler himself.

The difference between 'the levitical priests' and 'the priests and the Levites' is only one *waw*; either reading is possible. Although the two terms may originally have represented a certain development in the understanding of the priestly order (cf. C. Steuernagel, *Das Deuteronomium*, HAT 1923, 119–20), in Chronicles the two forms are interchangeable, and equally appropriate. It seems, then, that here the Chronicler has simply copied his

Vorlage. Whether the addition (or omission) of the *waw* is editorial or textual is impossible to determine.

[6] The sacrifices on behalf of Solomon and the people call to mind the similar practice during the transfer of the ark from Kiriath-jearim to Jerusalem by David and the people of Israel (II Sam. 6.13//I Chron. 15.26). However, there full details of the ceremony are given, while here the reference is simply to sacrifices 'that could not be counted or numbered' (cf. the same idiom in I Kings 3.8).

The term *'ēdāh* has long been the subject of dispute. Is it strictly a priestly term? Is it a late idiom? (For a summary, cf. A. Hurvitz, *Linguistic Study*, 65–7). In any case, it is not part of the Chronicler's vocabulary; here, its unique occurrence in 'the congregation of Israel' (*"dat yiśrā'ēl*) is taken from I Kings 8.6.

[7] This verse, ceremonial and precise, marks in progression the four exact coordinates of the ark's new location: 'its place, in the inner sanctuary of the house, in the most holy place, underneath the wings of the cherubim'. The climax of the transfer of the ark has now been reached, and the symbol of God's very presence has found its home.

The continuation of the narrative is found in v. 11 (I Kings 8.10), where the exit of the priests signals the entrance of divine glory. The three intervening verses contain explanatory remarks about the ark: the precise position of the ark in relation to the cherubim (v. 8), the poles (v. 9), and the ark's contents (v. 10). While the first two are linked both to each other and to the general context, v. 10 deviates from the rest in style and content. Here again, we may observe gradual stages in the composition of I Kings 8.1–11 (cf. for example M. Noth, *The Deuteronomistic History*, 60; Montgomery, *Kings*, 187–8), adopted as they were by the Chronicler.

[8] As may be learned from the fashioning of the cherubim (I Kings 6.23–28; II Chron. 3.10–13), their most impressive dimension was the wings, which together stretched twenty cubits from one side of the inner sanctuary to the other, ostensibly to cover and overshadow (*sōkᵉkīm*) the ark. However, according to the Priestly description (Exod. 25.17–21), the ark itself was provided with a 'cover' (*kappōret*, RSV 'mercy seat'), and on this 'cover' two cherubim were made to overshadow the ark. Whether the ark which was brought into the Temple was envisaged as having such a 'cover' is difficult to say. On one hand, there is no hint of this element in any of the texts in the Deuteronomistic history which refer to the ark (Josh. 3–5; I Sam. 4–6; II Sam. 6); on the other hand, there is in fact reference to 'the ark of God … who sits enthroned on the cherubim' (II Sam. 6.2), whatever the image intended by this phrase. It would seem that the priestly portrait of the 'ark with the cover' in the tabernacle in fact represented an analogy to the inner sanctuary of the Temple, in which the two huge cherubim overshadowed the ark. This

is no doubt the view of the Chronicler, who describes the whole setting as the 'chariot': 'the golden chariot of the cherubim that spread their wings and covered the ark' (I Chron. 28.18).

If this analogy is correct, it may be carried further in viewing the cherubim as the *locus par excellence* of God's presence, a view explicitly stated in reference to the tabernacle: 'There I will meet with you, and from above the mercy-seat, from between the two cherubim that are upon the ark ... I will speak with you' (Exod. 25.22; also Lev. 16.2, 'for I will appear in the cloud upon the mercy-seat'; Num. 7.89). God's presence in Solomon's Temple is thus confirmed by the combination of two elements: the ark, and the cherubim who 'cover and overshadow' it. The fashioning of the cherubim themselves in the inner sanctuary was not sufficient; only when the ark had reached its place 'under the wings of the cherubim' did the glory of God fill the house.

[9] Although the wings were intended to cover all the ark, the protruding poles were visible: to what extent this was according to plan is difficult to say. The poles were originally provided to carry the ark, and most likely were superfluous once the ark was put in the Temple. By that time, however, the poles had probably acquired independent sanctity; the inherent conservatism of the cult ensured their preservation.

The essential link between the poles and the ark is illustrated in the descriptions of the tabernacle: while for all other furnishings poles were inserted only when they were actually being carried, regarding the ark Moses is instructed that 'the poles shall remain in the rings of the ark; they shall not be taken from it' (Exod. 25.15, but differently Num. 4.6).

How the poles 'were seen' is not too clear. According to the reading of I Kings 8.8, they were seen 'from the holy place before the inner sanctuary (i.e. from the main hall of the Temple) but they were not seen from outside'. In practice, the inner sanctuary had a door, which was generally closed. In Chronicles we read: 'the poles were seen *from the ark* in the inner sanctuary' (RSV adjusts the translation to the version of Kings). This would make better sense: the poles protruded from the ark and were not fully covered by the cherubim, but could not be seen from outside the inner sanctuary where the ark stood.

The verse ends in I Kings 8.8 with 'they are there to this day', referring to the poles. Some scholars (cf. BH) propose to transfer this clause to after v. 9, referring to the 'two tables' which Moses placed inside the ark. The text in Chronicles renders the subject in the singular rather than the plural, '*it is* there' (again, not represented by RSV), referring to the ark. It is hardly likely that this change was introduced by the Chronicler, in whose day there were neither ark nor poles in the Temple; it should be attributed rather to a previous editor, or regarded as a corruption.

[10] Strong emphasis is placed on the observation that the ark contained the two tablets. The negative phrasing 'there was nothing in the ark except …' has a strong polemical edge, which may be directed against either pagan or popular concepts of the ark, which attributed certain magical powers to it or viewed it as containing ritual objects or images, or against other traditions which regarded the ark as holding other holy artefacts such as 'the jar of manna' (Exod. 16.33) or the 'rod of Aaron' (Num. 17.10 [MT 17.25], cf. Gray, *Kings*, 210; Curtis, 338).

The phrasing of the polemic – in particular in the LXX version of I Kings 8.9, which also has the words 'of the covenant', not found in MT but implied by the verb (*kārat*) – is very similar to the wording of Deut. 9.9, 11. The Deuteronomistic idiom is minimized in Chronicles, which lacks not only the words 'of the covenant' but also 'of stone'. Nevertheless, the distinctively Deuteronomistic 'where the Lord made [a covenant] with the people of Israel, when they came out of Egypt' is retained, alluding to two matters which the Chronicler usually understates: the Sinai covenant and the Exodus (cf. Japhet, *Ideology*, 102–5, 379–86).

It would be very tempting to regard the whole verse as originally omitted by the Chronicler and secondarily re-introduced into it (a solution adopted by some scholars in similar contexts, cf. for example Rudolph on ch. 4), but this would be to argue in a circle. There is no avoiding the conclusion that this is another instance in which the Chronicler has fallen short of completely reworking his source and has retained matters which he is otherwise inclined to omit.

[11–13] We have already noted that after the first part of v. 11, which is a faithful repetition of I Kings 8.10a, the Chronicler has inserted, in his own distinctive idiom, an entirely new passage, for a purpose consonant with stock Chronistic attitudes. The text of Kings does not describe the entrance of the priests into the inner shrine, the positioning of the ark and their safe exit as accompanied by any sort of ceremonial effect, with the exception of Solomon's poetic proclamation honouring the descending of divine glory (I Kings 8.12–13). The Chronicler, quite to the contrary, regards this moment as the climax of the whole event and embellishes it with an impressive ceremonial perfomance of music, involving all the singers, Levites as well as priests. The magnitude and grandeur of this choir are emphasized in several ways:

(*a*) In v. 11 the Chronicler reports that 'all the priests who were present had sanctified themselves, without regard to their divisions'.

(b) The participation of each and every singer is made quite explicit by a detailed record: the names of the three orders of singers, of Asaph, of Heman and of Jeduthun, the insistence on 'all', and the technical reference (recalling I Chron. 25.9–31) to 'their sons and kinsmen'. If we take the list of I Chron.

25 as our standard, the participation of all the singers would bring the company to 288 musicians.

(c) The singers performing with cymbals, harps and lyres are accompanied by one hundred and twenty priests sounding the trumpets. This number, too, is not incidental. Each shift of trumpeters consisted of five priests, as is evidenced by the settings of I Chron. 15–16. During the transfer of the ark from Kiriath-jearim to Jerusalem, seven priests were appointed to sound the trumpets (I Chron. 15.24); of these, two were then mentioned as ministering at the tent of the ark (I Chron. 16.6), which indicates that the other five were attached to the regular cult of the tabernacle at Gibeon (I Chron. 16.39–42). In the grand ceremony described here, when the ark is carried to its final resting place in the Temple, the trumpeter priests, from all of the twenty-four divisions, join in the music.

(d) All of the participants, priests and Levites alike, are attired in fine linen. While this was in fact the standard priestly apparel, it is expressly specified also for the Levites on this very festive and unique occasion.

From the point of view of syntax, the insertion opens with a parenthetic clause: 'for all the priests who were present ...' (marked by the RSV with brackets). Scholars are divided over where this clause ends. Some would adopt the maximal view that the main sentence resumes only with 'and when the song was raised' (thus Rudolph, 210; Galling 88, and others, followed also by RSV). This view regards the final clause 'the house ... of the Lord was filled with a cloud', as preceded by two protases (1. 'when the priests came out ...' and 2. 'when the song was raised') as well as a long parenthetical clause – a burden which is unparalleled in biblical Hebrew. The minimal view (represented by NEB and JPS) limits the parenthetical clause to v. 11; in this case, however, the sequence of tenses in the Hebrew (*way^{e}hī b^{e}ṣē't ... 'ōm^{e}dīm*) would be awkward.

It would seem better to adopt a middle way, extending the parenthetical clause as far as the end of v. 12. The main sentence would then describe the musical performance itself: (11a) 'Now when the priests came out of the holy place [... (11b–12)...] (v. 13) it was the duty of the trumpeters and singers to make themselves heard in unison in praise and thanksgiving to the Lord. And when the song was raised ... the house was filled, etc.' The parenthetical clause (vv. 11b–12) would refer to the preparation of the setting: the sanctification of all the priests, the attire, musical instruments and position of the singers and the 120 trumpeter-priests.

It is only 'when the song was raised' – which punctually accompanies the exit of the priests – that the house is filled with the cloud. This musical accompaniment includes not only a vocal hymn of praise (in the conventional formula – 'praise to the Lord for he is good, for his steadfast love endures for ever'), but also string instruments, the sounding of trumpets and cymbals.

Such a precise description probably reflects the musical ceremonies of the Chronicler's own day, and the significance of music in the ritual of the Second Temple.

In v. 13b, the text of I Kings 8.10b is resumed, but in a somewhat different version with a change of subject from 'the cloud' in Kings to 'the house' here. The words *bēt yhwh*, 'the house of the Lord', seem to be corrupt; they are either misplaced (as assumed by RSV, and more literally by JPS), a gloss (cf. BHS), or a corruption of *kᵃbōd yhwh* (thus LXX, followed by NEB).

[14] The degree to which the 'house was filled' by the cloud is demonstrated by the fact that the priests could no longer pursue their assigned duties there; the cloud permeated the Temple's main hall, as well as the inner shrine.

While this description vividly recalls the divine visitation in Exod. 40.34–35, there is also a distinct difference in that Exod. 40 distinguishes very clearly between the 'cloud' and the 'glory' of God. The cloud dwells *on* the tabernacle from without, is visible to the whole people and with its arising signals the time to break camp and resume the journey. The glory, on the other hand, fills the tabernacle from within, and even Moses himself cannot then enter it (cf. Exod. 40.35 *et al.*; also Ezek. 10.4). In the present text, the 'cloud' and the 'glory' seem synonymous, and the cloud has a similarity to another line of tradition: the 'pillar of cloud' in Num. 12.5; Deut. 31.15, etc. The text as it stands makes use of priestly texts and is influenced by priestly concepts – without expressing them precisely.

[6.1–2] The whole ceremony culminates with Solomon's poetic proclamation, which gives expression to the most basic concept of the Temple: 'a place ... to dwell in for ever'. In I Kings, the Vatican and Lucianic MSS of LXX have a fuller version of this statement, and it is positioned after I Kings 8.53. Many scholars would adopt the LXX version of Kings in part or in full (cf. also RSV *ad loc*), but this is no more relevant to the text in Chronicles.

Solomon's words relate poetically to the preceding description: 'the cloud' is the 'thick darkness' (*ᵃrāpel*, cf. Baumgartner, 840–1) in which God had chosen to dwell. As for the 'exalted (NEB 'lofty') house', and 'a place for thee to dwell', these will later be the subject of the polemic in Solomon's long prayer (I Kings 8.27–53//II Chron. 6.18–42), where the place of God's dwelling is repeatedly designated as 'heaven', and the rhetorical questions are fraught with theological overtones: 'But will God indeed dwell ... on the earth? Behold heaven and the highest heaven cannot contain thee; how much less this house which I have built!'

6   3 Then the king faced about, and blessed all the assembly of Israel, while all the assembly of Israel stood. [4] And he said, 'Blessed be the Lord, the God of Israel, who with his hand has fulfilled what he promised with his mouth to David my father, saying, [5] "Since the day that I brought my people out of the land of Egypt, I chose no city in all the tribes of Israel in which to build a house, that my name might be there, and I chose no man as prince over my people Israel; [6] but I have chosen Jerusalem that my name may be there and I have chosen David to be over my people Israel." [7] Now it was in the heart of David my father to build a house for the name of the Lord, the God of Israel. [8] But the Lord said to David my father, "Whereas it was in your heart to build a house for my name, you did well that it was in your heart; [9] nevertheless you shall not build the house, but your son who shall be born to you shall build the house for my name." [10] Now the Lord has fulfilled his promise which he made; for I have risen in the place of David my father, and sit on the throne of Israel, as the Lord promised, and I have built the house for the name of the Lord, the God of Israel. [11] And there I have set the ark, in which is the covenant of the Lord which he made with the people of Israel.'

12 Then Solomon stood before the altar of the Lord in the presence of all the assembly of Israel, and spread forth his hands. [13] Solomon had made a bronze platform five cubits long, five cubits wide, and three cubits high, and had set it in the court; and he stood upon it. Then he knelt upon his knees in the presence of all the assembly of Israel, and spread forth his hands toward heaven; [14] and said, 'O Lord, God of Israel, there is no God like thee, in heaven or on earth, keeping covenant and showing steadfast love to thy servants who walk before thee with all their heart; [15] who has kept with thy servant David my father what thou didst declare to him; yea, thou didst speak with thy mouth, and with thy hand hast fulfilled it this day. [16] Now therefore, O Lord, God of Israel, keep with thy servant David my father what thou hast promised him, saying, "There shall never fail you a man before me to sit upon the throne of Israel, if only your sons take heed to their way, to walk in my law as you have walked before me." [17] Now therefore, O Lord, God of Israel, let thy word be confirmed, which thou hast spoken to thy servant David.

18 'But will God dwell indeed with man on the earth? Behold, heaven and the highest heaven cannot contain thee; how much less this house which I have built! [19] Yet have regard to the prayer of thy servant and to his supplication, O Lord my God, hearkening to the cry and to the prayer which thy servant prays before thee; [20] that thy eyes may be open day and night toward this house, the place where thou hast promised to set thy name, that thou mayest hearken to the prayer which thy servant offers toward this place. [21] And hearken thou to the supplications of thy servant and of thy people Israel, when they pray toward this place; yea, hear thou from heaven thy dwelling place; and when thou hearest, forgive.

22 'If a man sins against his neighbour and is made to take an oath, and comes and swears his oath before thy altar in this house, [23] then hear thou from heaven, and act

and judge thy servants, requiting the guilty by bringing his conduct upon his own head, and vindicating the righteous by rewarding him according to his righteousness. 24 'If thy people Israel are defeated before the enemy because they have sinned against thee, when they turn again and acknowledge thy name, and pray and make supplication to thee in this house; 25 then hear thou from heaven, and forgive the sin of thy people Israel, and bring them again to the land which thou gavest to them and to their fathers. 26 'When heaven is shut up and there is no rain because they have sinned against thee, if they pray toward this place, and acknowledge thy name, and turn from their sin, when thou dost afflict them, 27 then hear thou in heaven, and forgive the sin of thy servants, thy people Israel, when thou dost teach them the good way in which they should walk; and grant rain upon thy land, which thou hast given to thy people as an inheritance. 28 'If there is famine in the land, if there is pestilence or blight or mildew or locust or caterpillar; if their enemies besiege them in any of their cities; whatever plague, whatever sickness there is; 29 whatever prayer, whatever supplication is made by any man or by all thy people Israel, each knowing his own affliction, and his own sorrow and stretching out his hands toward this house; 30 then hear thou from heaven thy dwelling place, and forgive, and render to each whose heart thou knowest, according to all his ways (for thou, thou only, knowest the hearts of the children of men); 31 that they may fear thee and walk in thy ways all the days that they live in the land which thou gavest to our fathers. 32 'Likewise when a foreigner, who is not of thy people Israel, comes, from a far country for the sake of thy great name, and thy mighty hand, and thy outstretched arm, when he comes and prays toward this house, 33 hear thou from heaven thy dwelling place, and do according to all for which the foreigner calls to thee; in order that all the peoples of the earth may know thy name and fear thee, as do thy people Israel, and that they may know that this house which I have built is called by thy name. 34 'If thy people go out to battle against their enemies, by whatever way thou shalt send them, and they pray to thee toward this city which thou hast chosen and the house which I have built for thy name, 35 then hear thou from heaven their prayer and their supplication, and maintain their cause. 36 'If they sin against thee – for there is no man who does not sin – and thou art angry with them, and dost give them to an enemy, so that they are carried away captive to a land far or near; 37 yet if they lay it to heart in the land to which they have been carried captive, and repent, and make supplication to thee in the land of their captivity, saying, "We have sinned, and have acted perversely and wickedly"; 38 if they repent with all their mind and with all their heart in the land of their captivity, to which they were carried captive, and pray toward their land, which thou gavest to their fathers, the city which thou hast chosen, and the house which I have built for thy name, 39 then hear thou from heaven thy dwelling place their prayer and their supplications, and maintain their cause and forgive thy people who have sinned against thee. 40 Now, O my God, let thy eyes be open and thy ears attentive to a prayer of this place.

41 'And now arise, O Lord God, and go to thy resting place,
    thou and the ark of thy might.

Let thy priests, O Lord God, be clothed with salvation,
and let thy saints rejoice in thy goodness.
⁴² O Lord God, do not turn away the face of thy anointed one!
Remember thy steadfast love for David thy servant.'

A. Notes to MT

[18] שמים, read השמים with I Kings 8.27, haplography; [19] לפְנִיךְ, I Kings 8.28 adds היום;
[22] ונשא, MSS ונשׁא, cf. commentary; אלה, already in I Kings 8.31 proposed ואלה or
באלה; [26] תַעֲנֵם, so I Kings 8.35, proposed there and here (following the Versions)
תֵעֲנֵם; [28] אויביו, read אויבו with I Kings 8.37; בארץ, thus I Kings 8.37, LXX באחד;
[38] שבים, I Kings 8.48 איביהם; ולבית, probably read והבית with I Kings 8.48 and the
Versions; [42] משיחיך, many MSS משׁחך, cf. commentary.

B. Notes to RSV

[3] 'faced about', better NEB 'turned round'; [12] 'Solomon stood', MT 'he stood';
'in the presence of', JPS 'in front of' (MT נגד); [14] 'showing', not in MT;
[15] 'didst declare', NEB 'thy promise' (MT דברת); [22] 'is made to take an oath',
JPS 'an oath is exacted from him'; [24] 'turn again and acknowledge', better JPS,
'once again acknowledge'; [26] 'afflict', thus the Versions, MT 'answer', cf. A above;
[28] 'any of their cities', thus the Versions, MT 'the land of their cities', cf. A above;
[30] 'and render to each whose heart thou knowest, according to all his ways', NEB
'And as thou knowest a man's heart, reward him according to his deeds'; [32] 'he
comes and prays', MT 'they come and pray'; [35] 'maintain their cause', NEB 'grant
them justice'; [40] 'a prayer', better 'the prayer' (NEB); [41] 'saints', better 'faithful', or 'loyal ones' (cf. Ps. 149.1, 5, etc.); 'thy goodness', MT 'goodness'; [42] 'turn
away the face', better 'reject' (NEB, JPS), cf. commentary; 'anointed one' or
'anointed ones' (cf. above, A); 'steadfast love', NEB 'loyal service', JPS 'loyalty'; 'for
David' or 'of David' (NEB; JPS), cf. commentary.

C. Structure, sources and form

1. Chapter 6 as it stands comprises two rhetorical passages with their narrative
introductions: vv. 3–11 and vv. 12–42. In both, Solomon addresses God and refers to
the building of the Temple, and in both the style and theology are Deuteronomistic.
However, the separate introductions (v. 3, vv. 12–13) mark these as distinct
addresses; for their respective origins and literary development cf. further below.
2. The first unit opens with an introductory verse (v. 3) followed by an address
(vv. 4–11), which probably belongs to one of the later Deuteronomistic strata of
Kings. The transition from the introduction to the speech is not self-evident; the
first refers to Solomon's blessing 'all the assembly of Israel', but what follows is not a
'blessing' and is not concerned with the people. Solomon in fact addresses God,
emphasizing again that the building of the Temple was a realization of God's promise

to David, and that Solomon himself has fulfilled the role assigned him. A study of this passage in its original setting in Kings (I Kings 8.15–21) seems to indicate that there the verses in question were secondary additions to or replacements of part of the original text. While this literary history is also clearly discernible in Chronicles, its main relevance is for the context of I Kings 8; the Chronicler transmitted basically what he found there. Of the few differences between the two versions, the most notable is the later omission in Kings of II Chron. 6.5b–6a because of homoioteleuton and the dropping of the last clause in 11b; for both cf. the commentary.

After the introduction (v. 3), the speech itself is structured as follows:

(a) 4 Opening doxology
(b) 5–9 Citation of the divine promise:
     5–6 concerning the election of Jerusalem and David
     7–9 concerning the building of the Temple
(c) 10–11 The fulfilment of the promise.

3. Solomon's long prayer in vv. 12–42 is taken literally from I Kings 8.22–53, except for two significant differences at the beginning and end, framing a series of smaller changes. The complex literary history of the prayer, which is of interest to the commentator on the book of Kings, is relevant here in that it clarifies problems of structure and literary sequence. Our attention, however, should be mainly directed to the significance of the prayer in this context and the changes introduced in its Chronistic version.

4. The main body of the prayer begins in v. 18 (I Kings 8.27), with the rhetorical question 'But will God dwell indeed with man on the earth?' From this point on, the function of the Temple as a focus of prayer is increasingly stressed. However, neither this emphasis nor the strong polemic of v. 18 are logical or literary continuations of the prayer's opening in vv. 14–17 (I Kings 8.23–26). There, the subject is rather a request that God will fulfil his promise to David and establish Solomon's throne for ever – a natural continuation in both theme and vocabulary to Solomon's first address in vv. 4–11. What seems to have been an original sequence is now interrupted by a new opening (vv. 12–13), which in turn is followed in vv. 18ff.

The literary development of this unit may then be conceived in one of two ways:

(a) verses 4–17 (I Kings 8.15–26) originally comprised one Deuteronomistic speech, which was secondarily interrupted by I Kings 8.22 (or by its fuller version in II Chron. 6.12–13).

(b) The Deuteronomistic speech indeed concluded with v. 11 (I Kings 8.21), but a later author, feeling the lack of something very important – God's promise to David to establish his line, and Solomon's wish to walk in God's ways – added this material after the new introduction of v. 12 (I Kings 8.22).

The consequences of this analysis for the discussion of the chapter – whichever of the two literary possibilities we adopt – would be:

(a) Verses 14–17 (I Kings 8.23–26) should be regarded as a continuation (original or added) of the speech of vv. 4–11.

(b) Verses 12–13 (I Kings 8.22) should be seen as an introduction to the main body of the prayer, now opening in v. 18 (I Kings 8.27).

(c) Some kind of introduction, now lost, seems to have preceded v. 18 (I Kings 8.27).

5. As mentioned above, the major differences of the Chronistic version are the

addition of v. 13 at the beginning and the replacement of the original conclusion (I Kings 8.50aβ–53) with II Chron. 6.40–42, which contain a different version of I Kings 8.52.

The words '... in the presence of all the assembly of Israel, and spread forth his hands [toward heaven]', original to v. 12 (taken from I Kings 8.22), reappear in v. 13 as a verbatim resumptive repetition, creating an *inclusion* for the interpolation of v. 13a–bα. This passage, which deals with the precise position and posture of Solomon as he makes his prayer, is a parenthetic clause, as is immediately clear in the repetition and the sequence of verbal forms (ויעמד ... כי עשה). As such, however, it may equally have been original to the Kings text (later omitted), or have been added at any of several later stages – pre-Chronistic, Chronistic, or post-Chronistic. Nothing in the language, style or views here are, however, characteristically Chronistic.

The possibility that this verse was originally part of I Kings 8 may be supported by two arguments (cf. Rudolph, 213):

(*a*) Solomon is here described as having 'knelt upon his knees in the presence of all the assembly of Israel', a posture which is in fact referred to in Kings at the conclusion of the prayer: '... Solomon ... arose from before the altar of the Lord where he had knelt with his hands outstretched' (I Kings 8.54).

(*b*) The sequence of the platform measurements ('the length ... the width ... the height ...') resembles the way in which the book of Kings records the measurements of the Temple and its furnishings (cf. I Kings 6.2, etc.)

Against the claim of originality one may argue:

(*a*) The precise structure of the resumptive repetition, and in particular the way in which the word השמים ('toward heaven' – from I Kings 8.22) is avoided in v. 12, only to reappear in v. 13, marks the text of Chronicles as secondary to that of Kings.

(*b*) The designation of the Temple court as עזרה is late (cf. above on 4.9).

(*c*) The reference to Solomon's kneeling may indeed reflect the inspiration of I Kings 8.54, and it may have been missed in v. 12 by a glossator; on the other hand, the contrary is also possible: that I Kings 8.54b is a secondary element there, inspired by this text or the difficulties inherent in the original.

Although no unequivocal decision can be made, it seems to me that v. 13 is indeed an interpolation, but pre-Chronistic, appended to a text of I Kings 8 which served as the Chronicler's *Vorlage* (cf. further in the commentary).

The second change is more significant: the original conclusion of the prayer is replaced by vv. 40–42, which are, for the most part, a quotation of Ps.132.8–10. In this way, the Chronicler alters both the literary character and the subject and outlook of the conclusion – for which see in detail in the commentary.

6. The overall structure of Solomon's prayer is as follows:

(*a*) 12–13 Introduction
    [14–17 Continuation of 4–11]
(*b*) 18–39 The prayer
    (i) 18–21 An appeal to God to listen to supplication
    (ii) 22–23 *Of the individual*: in the case of an oath
    (iii) 24–31 *Of the people*: in cases of
        24–25 War
        26–27 Drought

28–31 Any affliction
(iv) 32–33 *Of the foreigner*
(v) 34–39 *Of the people at war*
(*c*) 40–42 Conclusion.

7. The style of the chapter, with the exception of a few verses, is markedly Deuteronomistic; it is pervaded by a paraenetic tone, characteristic vocabulary and specific theological maxims (cf. M. Weinfeld, *Deuteronomy and the Deuteronomic School*, 1972, 35–7). The commentary will indicate more specific expressions of tendencies within the broader Deuteronomistic school. As a text-book example of the Chronicler's method of faithful adherence to his source, even if at certain points his own views certainly differ, this chapter invites special attention to the details which are omitted or changed.

D. Commentary

[3] From his orientation towards the procession accompanying the ark to its place in the sanctuary, Solomon now 'faces about' to bless the people. Such a benediction is illustrated in other instances, especially II Sam. 6.18 (I Chron. 16.2). There, when the ark has been placed in its tent and sacrifices offered, David blesses the people and then turns (RSV 'returned') to bless his household. In neither episode are the words of the blessing cited. In this case, the blessing may originally not have been cited at all; later, the following speech was added by the connecting phrase 'and he said', and a benediction supplemented in I Kings 8.55ff.; or, an original blessing may have been replaced by the discourse which immediately follows (vv. 4–11).

[4–11] I shall now illustrate, at least in part, the marked Deuteronomistic style of this chapter. The most distinct example of Deuteronomistic vocabulary is the reference to the Temple as 'a house for the name of the Lord', an idea repeated in this short paragraph from every possible perspective (vv. 5–10):

'I chose no city ... to build a house, that my name might be there ... but I have chosen Jersualem that my name may be there ... to build a house for the name of the Lord ... Whereas it was in your heart to build a house for my name ... your son ... shall build the house for my name ... I have built the house for the name of the Lord.'

These quotations already illustrate the extremely elaborate, detailed and explicit style of the passage. So likewise the reference in vv. 7–8 to David's desire to build the Temple:

Now it was in the heart of David my father to build a house ... but the Lord said ... whereas it was in your heart to build a house ... you did well that it was in your heart.'

It is therefore an inherent feature of this style that each word and phrase is repeated almost beyond tolerance: 'Israel' eight times (my people Israel, God of Israel, the tribes of Israel, the throne of Israel, and the children of Israel); 'David' five times; 'my people' three times, etc. In the same manner, each item is characterized in some way: my people Israel; David my father; your son who shall be born to you; his promise which he made, etc. Thus, the leading ideas and terms of the speech are hammered home and engraved on the listener's mind.

[4] The opening of Solomon's address lays down the plan for the structure of his following words. This is best seen in the syntax of the Hebrew text, where the clauses can be literally rendered: 'Blessed be the Lord ... who what he promised with his mouth with his hand has fulfilled'. The order 'promise – fulfilment' is then maintained in vv. 5–9 (God's promise) and vv. 10–11 (the fulfilment).

This 'promise – fulfilment' antithesis is expressed by a particular chiastic idiom (*dibber b^{e}pîw ... ûb^{e}yādāyw millē'*). To 'fulfil with the hand' (*mallē' b^{e}yad*) should be clearly distinguished from the more common 'fill the hands' (*mallē' yad*), an expression which came to mean to consecrate or appoint, in particular relating to sacral functions (in Chronicles: II Chron. 13.9; 29.31, etc.). The present idiom, on the other hand, is found in the Bible only three times, always in an antithesis of word and deed: in this verse, again in v. 15 (and the parallel I Kings 8.24), and finally in Jer. 44.25 ('you and your wives have declared with your mouths and have fulfilled it with your hands').

[5–6] Solomon first quotes God as declaring that since the day he brought Israel out of Egypt he chose no city as an abode for his name, and no man as 'prince over my people Israel'; now he has chosen Jerusalem as that city and David as that ruler. It has long been recognized that the shorter version of I Kings 8.16 has been corrupted due to homoioteleuton (cf. BH; differently Montgomery, *Kings*, 195; Noth, *Könige*, 183). However, in the reconstruction of the Kings text there, some commentators would prefer the version of LXX^B, which is fuller than MT but shorter than the version in Chronicles (cf. Gray, *Kings*, 214). My view is that the full exposition of these verses, with the double antitheses and the Deuteronomistic style, accords well with the verbosity of the passage as a whole and should be preferred (also Rudolph, 211; BHS).

This seemingly conventional declaration is loaded with very specific theological views:

(*a*) First, the retrospect to the time of the Exodus implies that the genesis and origin of Israel as a people lay there. This conjunction of the Exodus as the debut and the election of David and Jerusalem as the climax of Israel's story is indeed a characteristic Deuteronomistic concept, which we have already encountered in the chronology of I Kings 6.1, omitted in the parallel text of II Chron. 3.1.

(*b*) The juxtaposition of the choosing of David with that of Jerusalem is also Deuteronomistic: the city and the dynasty are two aspects of one comprehensive promise. 'The city of David', originally a name for Jerusalem or a certain part of it (II Sam. 5.9), is taken to express a theological maxim (I Kings 11.32, 36; 15.4, etc.).

(*c*) Above all, these two acts of election – Jerusalem as the 'city in which to build a house' and David as a 'prince over Israel' – are seen as unique and unprecedented.

There is, however, a certain imbalance in representing these two choices as the first and exclusive. The singling out of Jerusalem as the ordained sanctum of Deut. 12 ('the place which the Lord ... will choose') is indeed primary and unique. Even if historically one may define it as a post-eventum theologoumenon, 'election' is not imputed to any other city in the Bible. The election of David, however, was definitely not the first, as it was preceded by the election of Saul (I Sam. 9.16; 10.24). In this respect, Solomon's words indeed reflect a theological rather than a historical perspective.

(*d*) Solomon cites a supposed divine statement: '... I chose no city ... and I chose no man as prince ... but I have chosen Jerusalem ... and I have chosen David ...' – a statement which is not extant in the Bible. Moreover, even the approximate terminology of David's election in I Sam. 16.12b ('Arise, anoint him for he is he'), is not paralleled by any formula for the election of Jerusalem. Solomon's words are therefore an expression of Deuteronomistic theology in this respect as well: the course of history is a realization of God's explicit word (cf. von Rad, *Studies in Deuteronomy*, 1953, 78–82). The cycle 'prophecy – fulfilment' is viewed as absolute in both directions: a prophecy determines its fulfilment, and fulfilment presupposes an explicit 'prophecy', even if none is actually extant.

[7–9] Solomon continues his discourse with a narrative section describing David's will to build a house (v. 7), moving us to the next historical stage and introducing a divine quotation (vv. 8–9), which in general transmits the contents of Nathan's prophecy in II Sam. 7//I Chron. 17. However, the quotation of God's verbal confirmation of David's will, 'you did well that it was in your heart', does not appear in Nathan's prophecy; it is in fact more of an exegesis in the spirit of Nathan's words than a quotation.

[10–11] The fulfilment of God's promise is none other than the actual unfolding of history. Solomon sits 'on the throne of Israel' and builds 'the house for the name of the Lord'.

In contrast to II Sam. 7 and I Kings 1–2, Solomon inherits not 'the throne of David', but 'the throne of Israel'; this is probably an intermediate concept leading from 'the throne of David' to 'the throne of the kingdom of the Lord over Israel' (I Chron. 28.5). The Temple's role as shrine for the ark and the covenantal tablets is repeated at the end; this is an echo of the original inspiration of the project in 2 Sam. 7.2 and a proper conclusion for this part of the ceremony (5.7): David's original wish is fulfilled. The fact that the ark contains the tablets of the covenant signifies a continuum in Israel's history and the integration of its traditions: the covenant of Sinai represented by the ark is blended with the Jerusalem Temple and the Davidic dynasty.

While all these central axioms of the Deuteronomistic philosophy of history are brought out fully by the Chronicler, his own views of history differ, especially on two points: the role of the Exodus as a constitutive act in the history of Israel and the relationship of God and Israel as established by a specific historic 'covenant' (cf. Japhet, *Ideology*, 104–5). However, since the election of Jersualem and of the Davidic line, and the realization of that election in the building of the Temple, are of great significance for his own theology, the Chronicler cites this speech in full, only limiting somewhat the centrality of the Exodus by omitting the words 'when he brought them out of the land of Egypt'.

[12–13] In I Kings 8.22, repeated here in v. 12, Solomon is described as speaking in a standing position; in v. 13 – unparalleled in Kings – the standing is followed by kneeling. Neither of the versions is completely smooth: I Kings 8.54 has it that Solomon 'arose' from a kneeling position, although in I Kings 8.22 he began to pray while standing, while the Chronicler's version indeed tells of Solomon's initial kneeling, but does not refer to him rising (cf. II Chron. 7.1).

Verse 13 also differs from v. 12 in another point. In the latter (and cf. also I Kings 8.22, 54a), Solomon prayed 'before the altar of the Lord', namely, in the inner court. It was inconceivable to a later generation that a public address of any type could have been in that area, and therefore the reference 'before the altar' is replaced by the more general *"zārāh*, probably (although not explicitly) the outer court.

If the insertion of the 'bronze platform' is, as it seems to be, an intentional correction, with the point of changing the place of Solomon's addressing the people, then both I Kings 8.54 and v. 13 would be secondary to the original narrative of Kings (cf. BH *ad loc.*). This change of place is combined with the practical point of providing the kneeling Solomon with an elevated position, 'above the people'.

[14–17] As already stated, these verses are in fact an original continuation or an elaboration of the Deuteronomistic speech of vv. 4–11, focusing on three issues: praise of God, the 'keeper of the covenant', a prayer that the Davidic dynasty may not fail, and a description of God's promise as conditional upon the human fulfilment of divine law.

The progressive structure of the passage opens with an elaborate expression of praise (vv. 14–15); this is followed by two successive addresses to God, each opening with 'now, therefore' (vv. 16, 17): the first Solomon's specific request for the occasion, and the second, a more general prayer that God's word 'be confirmed'.

The great doxology of v. 14 first lauds God's incomparable essence ('there is none like thee in heaven or on earth'), then his general faithfulness to the 'covenant and steadfast love', and finally the more specific promise to 'thy servant David'. The first element, especially as more eloquently worded I Kings 8.23, is a combination of two conventional phrases: 'there is none like thee' (II Sam. 7.22, etc.), and 'in heaven above and on earth beneath' (Exod. 20.4; Deut. 4.39; Josh. 2.11; etc.); the second is based on Deut. 7.9, rephrased in the Deuteronomistic style of Kings: 'to thy servants who walk before thee with all their heart'; the third is an echo of v. 4, and provides the basis for the following prayer (v. 16).

The establishment of the Davidic dynasty is peculiarly phrased here in the negative: 'There shall never fail you a man before me to sit upon the throne of Israel'; this idiom is restricted to very specific Deuteronomistic sections, and is also found in I Kings 2.4; 9.5 (and its parallel in II Chron. 7.18) and Jer. 33.17 (cf. Japhet, *Ideology*, 461–3).

The condition laid down for this dynastic continuity, absent from II Sam. 7, is also found in the same Deuteronomistic stratum (I Kings 2.4; 9.4), from which it has been adopted by the Chronicler as a basic tenet. The phrase 'to walk before me/you' as a description of devotion to God's demands, referring in v. 14 generally to 'thy servants' (cf. I Kings 8.23) and particularly in v. 16 to David's descendants (cf. I Kings 8.25), is also peculiar to this Deuteronomistic stratum (I Kings 2.4; 3.6, 14; 8.25; 9.4; II Chron. 6.14, 16; 7.17). For Solomon, then, God's original promise to David was conditional: 'there shall never fail you ... if only your sons take heed to their way ...' – a theological premise not based on Nathan's words in II Sam. 7 or elsewhere; cf. also on I Chron. 28.7.

Verse 16 introduces a change in the Deuteronomistic idiom, as was emphasized by von Rad (*Geschichtsbild*, 41), I. L. Seeligmann ('The Beginnings of *Midrash* in the Books of Chronicles' *Tarbiz* 49, 1979/1980, 19–20*), and Willi (125–6). While, as we have just seen, the Chronicler usually retains the original 'to walk before me/you', in v. 16b he renders it 'to walk in my law', found elsewhere in Jer. 26.4; Dan. 9.10 and Neh. 10.30 [MT 29]. It would seem, however, that rather than offering a major theological innovation, the Chronicler here simply replaces one Deuteronomistic idiom by another, giving the general and rather rare 'walk before the Lord' a more precise meaning, i.e. keeping God's commandments. The same vein is pursued in I Kings 9.4 and its parallel in II Chron. 7.17: 'if you walk before me ... keeping my statutes and my ordinances'.

Solomon's final request, 'let thy word be confirmed', is taken from I Kings 8.26, but here alludes more clearly to David's own prayer and to Solomon's earlier words in I Chron. 17.23 and II Chron. 1.9.

I have amply, though not exhaustively, demonstrated the strongly Deuteronomistic idiom of this passage. Verses 14–17 are also marked by constant repetition of all the key terms which develop the ideas to the fullest, as noted above for vv. 4–11. Thus, for example, God is addressed three times as 'Lord, God of Israel' (echoed in the following passages by a constant insistence on 'my/your people Israel'). 'Keep' (*šmr*) appears four times, in the context of covenant faithfulness (RSV once renders it 'take heed'). 'Speak' (*dbr*) is repeated five times, three of them in the identical verbal form *dibbartā* (and variously translated 'declare', 'speak', 'promised', 'word', 'hast spoken'). Other key words such as 'walk', 'before me/you', 'your servant David', are repeated three times, and 'my father' twice. This rather monotonous form (relieved to a certain degree by the variegated translation) gives clearest expression to the theological message of the passage.

[18–21] The main portion of Solomon's prayer, as already mentioned, was probably originally linked differently to the context of the dedication. These four verses constitute the present introduction to the prayer, stating the purpose for which the Temple was built. It proceeds from a complex negative statement to a positive conclusion: the Temple is by no means an actual dwelling for God, but as it is the place where God has decided 'to set his name', it is here that Solomon and the people will pray. When God attends the prayers of his people and grants their requests, the *raison d'être* of the Temple will be realized.

The purely polemical style of v. 18 differs considerably from the following passage. The argument develops in two stages, having in fact two different, and perhaps unconnected, theological goals, neither of which is specifically relevant only to Solomon's Temple. The first is set out in v. 18a: 'Will God dwell indeed with man on the earth?' The question is of course rhetorical, but the polemical edge is directed as a challenge to any concept of God's abode on earth, expressed by the simplest and most common titles of the Temple as 'dwelling (*miškān*) of God' (*bēt yhwh*), or 'the house of God'. The fact that this very image is given poetic expression in Solomon's own words in 6.1 (I Kings 8.12), 'I have built thee an exalted house / a place for thee to dwell for ever', is a striking illustration of the composite literary history of the pericope.

The second point of polemic is expressed in 18b: 'heaven and the highest heaven cannot contain' God – how much less an earthly house! While the prayer as a whole suggests that the question of 'dwelling' may be met with a relative negative – God dwells *not* on earth, but in heaven – the question of 'containing' evokes an absolute denial: no form of nature can encompass God.

Only the first of these two issues is actually pursued in the prayer itself, where constant repetition hammers home the point that God's abode is *only* in heaven: 'hear thou from heaven thy dwelling place' (vv. 21, 30, 33, 39). The second statement, if brought to its logical conclusion, would undermine the theological coherence of the first. For, if God dwells in heaven, although 'heaven and the highest heaven' do not contain him, it is logical to reason, in the same way, that God may dwell in the Temple although no temple can contain him. This view, however, is strongly refuted by the main body of the prayer.

It would seem that the original polemic between the views of God's dwelling as 'earthly' or 'heavenly' is here overshadowed by a different theological reflection: is God contained anywhere? The answer expresses a general biblical assumption: God's presence does not exhaust his existence!

Verses 19–21 contain the gist of the long prayer, summed up in the opening and closing words (vv. 19, 21), 'have regard to the prayer of thy servant ... and when thou hearest, forgive'. What follows is just a series of illustrations of occasions on which the people pray and God 'listens and forgives'. One pattern, and the recurring formula (with certain variations) 'they pray ... then hear from heaven ... and forgive' (vv. 24–25, 26–27, 29–30, 32–33, 34–35, 38–39), determine the composition of the literary fabric throughout.

The rhetorical tone of the introduction is fully evidenced in its repetitiousness, extreme particularity and dependence – once again – on key-words. In these three verses the words 'pray' and 'prayer' are repeated six times, together with 'supplication' and 'cry'; 'hear' or 'hearken' five times, 'this house/place' five times, and 'your servant' four times. Thus, all details aside, the heart of the passage is 'hearken to the prayer which thy servant offers in this place', now and always.

In this passage, 'this house', which is 'the place' in which God 'sets his name', is clearly distinguished from the divine 'dwelling place' in heaven. *Here* the people and the king pray; from *there* God will hearken. The 'house of prayer' (Isa. 56.7) means not only the place where the prayer is uttered, but the portal through which prayer finds its way to God. Any petition is therefore made either 'in this house' or 'toward this house' (vv. 24, 26, 29, 32, 33, 38).

The common designation of the Temple in the following passages is 'this house' (v. 22, 24 etc.//I Kings 8.31, 33, etc.) while 'this place' appears only in vv. 21 and 26. It is in v. 20 that the two are explicitly identified: 'this house, the place which ...'. The echo of 'the place which ... God will choose' of Deut. 12.5ff. is probably intentional, but only serves to emphasize the theological distance between these two Deuteronomistic passages. While 'the place' in Deut. 12 is primarily a *locus* of sacrifice (Deut. 12.6, etc.), there is not even a hint of this function here; 'the place' is exclusively one of prayer. Secondly, while the most important feature of 'the place' in Deut.12 is its being 'chosen' by God (vv. 5, 11, 14, 18, 21, 26), this term is never used in II Chron. 6 of 'the house', but is reserved exclusively for the city of Jerusalem (vv. 34, 38//I Kings 8.44, 48). The prayer here is therefore a somewhat distant reflection of the 'place theology' as expressed in Deut. 12, presupposing that 'the place' of Deut. 12 refers to the Temple of Jerusalem, but developing this identification differently.

[22–23] With this passage Solomon begins to list all the occasions on which the people may petition God's attention. The first example given, however, deals not with man's relation to God, but with that of a man to his neighbour. The *Leitmotif* of the prayer, 'hearken ... and forgive', is then absent here, for God appears not as one who 'hearkens to the prayer of the sinner' but as one who 'judges his servants'. God's intervention is expressly requested in the context of an 'oath', a matter from the broad realm of legal practice, which cannot be left to human discretion, but only to God's decision. To open this prayer with divine justice as the guarantee of the social order is very much in line with Solomon's image as arbitrator.

The social situation described here is of the same kind as those cited in Exod. 22.7–11. In cases of transgressions of an inter-personal nature which cannot be settled through the regular judicial system, the damaged party requires the other to take an oath concerning his innocence. This oath by nature requires divine intervention, 'God do so to me and more if ...', and there is no way to ascertain the truth of the sworn statement except through God's response. Solomon makes this his first request: that God may answer this human need and reveal his judgment.

The terms 'righteous' and 'guilty' are seen in this case in their juridical context: they serve to distinguish between the person who takes an oath and is indeed blameless and the other who uses the oath as a cover for his wickedness.

Since the oath is sworn 'before thy altar', some kind of accompanying sacrifice seems to be implied. It seems, however, that this offering should not be identified with Lev. 6.1–7 [MT 5.20–26]. There, the sinner is required to make a guilt-offering in addition to restitution of the actual loss, but nothing is said of how his guilt was proven. This is the only mention of the altar in Solomon's prayer; the passage probably reflects ancient customs and is important direct evidence of the existence and significance of this juridical procedure.

The text of v. 22 (*wᵉnāšā'bō 'ālāh*) should be understood 'and he *exacts* an oath from him' (assuming an exchange of *he* and *alef* in the verb *nšh*), the subject being the damaged party, 'the neighbour'. (In order to avoid the awkward change of subject, the translations render the active verb as passive;

RSV 'is made to take an oath'; JPS 'an oath is exacted from him'). As the damaged party cannot 'exact' anything concrete, he is entitled to demand an oath, an occasion for God's intervention on his behalf.

Another linguistic point concerns the change from I Kings 8.32 'condemn the guilty' (*l^eharšī'a rāšā'*), to 'requite the guilty' (*l^ehāšīb l^erāšā'*) in Chronicles. This was necessitated by a shift in the general connotation of the *hiphil* conjugation, so that *haršī'a* (= condemn) came to mean simply 'be wicked' (cf. Japhet, *HS* 28, 1987, 25; for more about the phenomenon, cf. M. Moreshet, 'The Hiphil in Mishnaic Hebrew as equivalent to the Qal', *Bar Ilan* XIII, 1976, 250–8*). The Chronicler guards against possible misunderstanding by replacing the juridical term *haršī'a* (Deut. 25.1; Prov. 17.15; Exod. 22.8 etc.) with a more general 'to requite'.

[24–25] Here begins the series of national catastrophes: defeat in war, drought (vv. 26–27), etc. The full theological cycle which the prayer illustrates (sin – punishment – prayerful repentance – and forgiveness) constitutes one of the more familiar assumptions of the biblical view of divine justice. In fact, the whole period of the judges is portrayed along the same constant cycles (cf. Y. Kaufmann, *History of the Religion of Israel* II, 1960, 363–5*). Against this background, it is the particulars of the context which draw our attention.

Solomon's examples do not open with sin but with punishment, the burden of which inspires prayer: 'If thy people ... are defeated', 'when heaven is shut', 'if there is famine', etc. Thus, the literary form is fully adapted to the function of the prayer: there is no rebuke or call to repentance, but rather a description of the human need of prayer in times of distress. The emphasis on the fact that catastrophe is itself a punishment for human sin (vv. 24, 26, 36) has, in this context, a positive theological direction: just as misfortune is God's response to man's evil acts, so he may grant relief in response to repentance. This is man's opportunity for redemption.

Repentance is conceived as having two aspects, an acknowledgment of God's sovereignty and a prayer for forgiveness: 'then once again (JPS) they acknowledge thy name and pray and make supplication ...' (vv. 24, 26// I Kings 8.33, 35). 'Acknowledgment of God's name' is found elsewhere only in poetry (Isa. 25.1; Ps. 44.9; etc.).

Throughout the prayer, God's pardon is expressed by a divine act of restoration: 'bring them again to the land' (v. 25), 'grant rain upon thy land' (v. 27), etc. The Chronicler rephrases the reference to 'the land which thou gavest to their fathers' (I Kings 8.34) to read: 'the land which thou gavest *to them* and *to their fathers*' (v. 25). This slight alteration reflects a very Chronistic view (Japhet, *Ideology*, 386ff.): the land was not given at one time to 'the fathers', to be automatically inherited by later generations; each Israelite receives the inheritance anew, and must prove himself worthy of it.

[26–27] The second catastrophe is the common affliction – drought (Gen. 12.10, etc.; I Kings 17–18, etc.). The passage develops along the same lines as the preceding one: affliction (because of sin), prayer, forgiveness, recompense (renewed rain). It is interesting, however, that in spite of the set pattern and the repetition of certain catch-phrases, each passage is different; as the prayer develops, elaboration and detail increase. This passage even introduces a sensation of rhythm and parallelism:

> when heaven is shut up / and there is no rain
> if they pray toward this place / and acknowledge thy name
> they turn from their sin / when thou dost afflict them
> and grant rain upon thy land / which thou hast given to thy people
> as an inheritance.

A completely new element in this passage is the didactic function of divine forgiveness, as God teaches the people 'the good way in which they should walk' (cf. also vv. 31, 33).

Although not so heavily marked, the Deuteronomistic origin of this prayer is nevertheless clear. One should mention the extraordinary parallelism between our passage and I Sam. 12.23: 'far be it from me that I should *sin* against the Lord by ceasing to *pray* for you; and I will *instruct* you in *the good and the right way*'. Also strongly Deuteronomistic are the references to 'the land which you gave', and 'inheritance' – not required by the context of the prayer or by its leading ideas but by its general Deuteronomistic setting, with its insistent view of the land as God's greatest gift (cf. vv. 25, 27, 31, 38).

[28–31] Here Solomon concludes the first part of the prayer with its series of seven disasters which prompt the people to pray for relief: famine, pestilence, blight, mildew, locust or caterpillar, an enemy in any of the cities – all common hazards of daily existence in the land of Israel. As befits the context, however, the descriptions are more moderate and reserved than the similar collections of Lev. 26.16ff. or Deut. 28.16ff. The list is summed up with the generalizing words 'whatever plague, whatever sickness there is' (v. 28).

These verses, too, have poetic traits. Rhythm is created by balanced repetition, with the threefold 'if there is' (*kī yihyeh* – one is omitted in RSV), completed by the fourth 'if' (*kī*): 'if there is a famine in the land ... if there is a pestilence ... [if there is] blight or mildew or locust or caterpillar ... if their enemies besiege them in any of their cities ...'. Parallel pairs are also created, through a series of six *kol* (represented in the translations by 'whatever', 'any' and 'all'): whatever plague / whatever sickness; whatever prayer / whatever supplication; by any man / or by all thy people.

This passage reveals a special degree of sensitivity to human suffering, and the distinct features of the retribution cycle, 'because they have sinned against thee' and 'acknowledgment of thy name', are omitted. The passage refers explicitly both to personal and public distress ('by any man ... all thy people Israel'), those whose pain is apparent and those whose pain is hidden: 'each knowing his own affliction, and his own sorrow'. Even for 'prayer', ordinarily termed *t^epillāh* and *t^eḥinnāh*, a more concrete personal description is given: 'stretching out his hands toward this house'.

God's response to prayer also has some new elements in this passage. The set pattern, 'then hear ... and forgive and render to each ... according to all his ways', is supplemented by divine attention to the hidden sphere of the human heart: 'and render to each whose heart thou knowest' (NEB 'as thou knowest a man's heart'), 'for thou, thou only, knowest the hearts of the children of men.'

The passage ends with another new element: a further appeal as if to persuade God to answer man's prayer for reasons of instruction: 'that they may fear thee and walk in thy ways ...' (cf. also v. 33). A similar tactic is very common in the Deuteronomistic paraenetic style, where the target of persuasion is the people: 'that you may live ...' (Deut 4.1), 'that your days may be prolonged' (Deut. 5.16), 'that you may fear the Lord your God' (Deut. 6.12), etc. Here, while the fruit of God's expected act would ultimately be seen in man's behaviour, the persuasive address is directed – unusually – to God.

Finally, the addition after 'all the days' of two consecutive relative clauses, 'that they live in the land which thou gavest', emphasizes that this is indeed the conclusion, not only of the last passage, but of the entire prayer until this point. God's ultimate purpose in his response is not only the deserved reward of the individual and the people, but to make them 'fear the Lord', know his ways, trust his justice and follow his commandments.

[32–33] After the ceremonial conclusion of the last passage, this section has the nature of an afterthought: Solomon requests a very unusual kind of divine attention, not connected with the righteousness and well-being of Israel. This is the prayer of the foreigner (*hannokrî*). Unlike the previous passages, these verses do not specify what distress brings the stranger to the Temple in Jerusalem. Obviously, the pattern of sin – punishment – repentance is absent in this passage. The foreigner's prayer is prompted not by 'cause' but by 'effect': he comes to Jerusalem '*for the sake of* (*l^ema'an*) thy great name, and thy mighty hand, and thy outstretched arm', and God is asked to respond '*in order that* (*l^ema'an*) all the peoples of the earth may know thy name and fear thee', and 'that they may know that this house ... is called by thy name'.

The two goals of knowledge, 1. of God's name and 2. of the divine sanction of the Temple, frame a third purpose, less neutral and more far-reaching: that the foreigner 'may fear thee as do thy people Israel'. Is this the kind of general 'fear of God' which is also demanded of pagans and denotes common moral standards (Y. Kaufman, *The History of Israelite Religion*, II, 1960, 438–41*), or should the comparison 'as do thy people Israel' imply a stronger commitment on the part of 'all the peoples of the earth'? With all due caution it might be said that Solomon's prayer understands the role of the Temple in the same spiritual terms as Isa. 56.7, 'for my house shall be called a house of prayer for all peoples', in both the designation of the Temple as 'a house of prayer' and its being open to 'all the nations'. To 'fear thee as do thy people Israel' of the prayer is defined in Isa. 56.7 as the foreigner's commitment 'to minister to him, to love the name of the Lord and to be his servants'.

Certain details should be discussed further. The precise definition of 'the foreigner, who is not of thy people Israel, [who] comes from a far country' clearly reflects the author's view of national identity: a 'foreigner' must come from afar; there is no foreigner in the land of Israel itself.

The phrasing of v. 32 deviates in certain points from its parallel in I Kings 8.41–42. The words 'for they shall hear of thy great name' may have fallen out of this verse accidentally through homoioteleuton, but may as well have been removed by the Chronicler's stylistic tendency to conciseness – an omission which caused a certain change of emphasis.

In another change, from the singular 'he comes and prays' to the plural 'they come and pray', the Chronicler makes explicit the collective meaning of the singular 'foreigner' – each and all of the non-Israelites who come to pray in 'this house'.

[34–39] This complex passage may be seen either as presenting one subject in two consecutive stages, or encompassing two closely related subjects. Two different contexts of prayer are here described: the first is when the people go to war, and beseech their God to 'maintain their cause'. Here there is no question of having suffered defeat, nor any confession of sin or prayer of repentance; the reference seems to be to an integral, although unspecified, part of war procedure. The second context is entirely different: the national distress of captivity. In contrast to all preceding passages this one opens with an explicit mention of sin and God's anger: 'If they sin against thee … and thou art angry with them, and dost give them to an enemy' (v. 36). In this last episode, there is special emphasis on the fact that the calamity is God's doing. This has indeed been implied in previous passages ('because they have sinned against thee'), but there the actual misfortune is portrayed in a neutral fashion: 'If thy people … are defeated' (v. 24), 'When heaven is shut' (v. 26), etc. Here, defeat and captivity are presented as a direct act of God: 'thou art angry with them, and dost give them to an enemy'.

Conflict between Israel and its enemies has already been mentioned (vv. 24–25, 28), but the issue here is not an enemy invasion of the land, but rather a war in which 'thy people go out to battle' (v. 34), an offensive campaign not determined by human considerations, but fulfilling a divine directive: 'by whatever way you shalt send them'. The people's position 'outside' is expressed also in the presentation of their prayer: the prayer is offered not 'in' or 'to' the house but from afar – 'through (*derek*, RSV 'toward', JPS 'in the direction of') this city which thou hast chosen and the house which I have built' (v. 34, also 38). This phrasing marks very precisely the various points along the way:

'through' the land – which thou gavest to their fathers (v. 38); the city – which thou hast chosen (vv. 34, 38); the house – which I have built for thy name (vv. 34, 38).

Out of the three, the city alone is conceived as 'chosen'; the land is God's gift, while the Temple is Solomon's achievement.

The urgency of the situation and the restrained emotions involved in its description are evident not only in the content of the verses, but also in their rhetorical quality. Certain elements, such as verbal roots, key topics, etc. are untiringly repeated. As the essential misfortune is 'captivity', the root *šbh* (take as captive) recurs in this short passage six times, strengthened by three appearances of the phonetically similar root *šwb*: 'They are carried away captive (*wešābūm sōbēhem*) ... yet ... they lay it to heart (*wehēšībū 'el-lebābām*) ... in the land to which they have been carried captive (*bā'āreṣ 'ašer nišbū šām*) ... and repent (*wešābū*) ... in the land of their captivity (*be'ereṣ šibyām*) ... if they repent (*wešābū 'ēleykā*) ... in the land of their captivity (*be'ereṣ šibyām*), to which they were carried captive (*'ašer šābū 'ōtām*).'

Another emphasis is upon 'the land'; here an antithesis is established between a 'land of their captivity' whether 'far or near', 'to which they have been carried captive' (vv. 36, 37, 38), and '*their* land, which thou gavest to their fathers' (v. 38).

Lastly, repentance is described again and again, in every possible way: 'they lay it to heart ... and repent, and make supplication to thee ... saying "We have sinned, and have acted perversely and wickedly" ... they repent with all their mind and with all their heart ... and pray ... their prayer and their supplication'. The confession of the repenting people is cited in the conventional confessional style, found in a very similar form in Dan. 9.5, 15 and Ps. 106.6.

All these emphases highlight the significance of this passage and may point to its actual context. The term constantly employed, however, is 'captivity', not 'exile', and this is hardly accidental (cf. Jer. 30.10). Note its recurrence in a Chronicles passage clearly dependent on this: 'For if you return to the Lord ... your brethren and your children will find compassion with their captors, and return to this land. For the Lord ... will not turn away his face ... if you return to him' (II Chron. 30.6–9).

[40–42] After v. 39, the faithful adherence to the Kings text ends; the completion of the long prayer in I Kings 8.50aβ–53 is replaced by the Chronicler's own conclusion in vv. 40–42. As the prayer is otherwise transmitted intact, these omissions and supplement are significant for the Chronicler's views.

First of all, the Chronicler omits the emphatic reference to Israel's sin and God's merciful restoration in I Kings 8.50aβ–b. He thus leaves unresolved the question of how God's forgiveness will be realized in captivity; this is probably because he regards as insufficient the kind of restoration proposed in Kings. It is interesting that the omitted verse is found elsewhere in Chronicles almost verbatim, with the final step of redemption spelled out: 'your children will find compassion with their captors, and return to this land' (II Chron. 30.9).

More radical is the omission of I Kings 8.51 and 53, verses which provide the theological basis for Solomon's appeal, by defining the relationship between God and the people of Israel, and the corner-stone of God's responsibility for his people's fate. Note the standard Deuteronomistic formulas: 'for they are thy people, and thy heritage, which thou didst bring out of Egypt, from the midst of the iron furnace' (I Kings 8.51); 'for thou didst separate them from among all the peoples of the earth ... when thou didst bring our fathers out of Egypt' (v. 53). These statements are in full harmony with Deuteronomistic theology, which regards the Exodus as the constitutive act in the history of the people of Israel, who henceforth become 'thy people and thy heritage'. This, however, is precisely the theology which the Chronicler cannot accept; accordingly he omits the reference, just as he handled I Kings 6.1. Whatever his attitude toward the Exodus, he cannot accept that the people of Israel became the people of God through a single act at a particular point of history.

[40] This verse provides the Chronicler's version of I Kings 8.52a – the one clause from the conclusion of Solomon's prayer which remains. The phrasing here is more parallelistic and concise, and lends a tone of finality to the prayer. The verse opens with an invocation, which marks its function as conclusion: 'Now, O my Lord'. The next phrase, 'Let thy eyes be open', is taken from I Kings 8.52a; it is found also in the introduction to the prayer (I Kings 8.29//II Chron 6.20), and its appearance here completes a cycle. The next words, 'and thy ears attentive, etc.', are peculiar to Chronicles. There are, however, several indications that the phrase belonged to the original text of I Kings 8.52.

(a) The extant metaphor of God's 'open eyes' is quite fitting in I Kings 8.29, 'that thy eyes may be open night and day toward this house', but becomes somewhat incongruous in 8.52, 'Let thy eyes be open to the supplication ...'. One would expect here a reference to the sense of hearing, in particular as the verse continues 'to hearken to them' (RSV harmonizes and renders: 'giving ear to them'). In fact, the general spirit of the prayer strongly emphasizes God's 'hearing'.

(*b*) The LXX version of I Kings 8.52 has: 'Let thy eyes *and ears* be open, etc.'.

(*c*) The prayer of Nehemiah (Neh. 1.6), strongly influenced by the formulations of Solomon's prayer, also contains the double metaphor: 'let thy ear be attentive, and thy eyes open, to hear the prayer of thy servant'.

The importance attached by the Chronicler to this verse, as an expression of God's attentive attitude toward his people's prayer, is evident in his reiteration of its statements in the first person in his addition to God's answer in II Chron. 7.15: 'Now my eyes will be open and my ears attentive to the prayer that is made in this place.'

[41–42] The Chronicler here provides his own conclusion for the prayer. Quite uncharacteristically, he does not compose his own passage but employs a segment of an existing psalm – a procedure followed elsewhere only in I Chron. 16.7–36: the ceremony of transferring the ark to Jerusalem is concluded by a complete psalm, sung by Asaph. This literary parallelism (utterly absent in Kings) highlights the relationship between the two stages of the transfer of the ark: by David to the tabernacle in Jerusalem, by Solomon to its final place in the Temple. Moreover, the psalm gives the conclusion a more elevated form than the parallel prose of I Kings 8. It will be followed by the song of the Levites mentioned in II Chron. 7.6; the last words of Solomon's prayer form a kind of prelude to the full musical ceremony that is to ensue. The citation from the Psalms on both occasions seems to reflect the Temple service of the Chronicler's time, when 'prayer' and 'psalm' were so closely identified.

The selection of the psalm is telling; the Chronicler chose very successfully from Ps. 132, so suitable for the occasion. It should be remembered, however, just as in any other instance of Chronistic borrowing from an existing literary piece, that the thought of the psalm is not the Chronicler's expression of his own views. How then are the views of the psalm linked to this context, changed, and adopted as a vehicle for the Chronicler's own ideas?

The main purpose of this passage is to bring Solomon's prayer back to the point of departure: the transfer of the ark to the Temple. The theological point of departure of Solomon's long prayer in Kings is the Temple not as the ark's abode, but as 'a house of prayer' for all Israel. Even the aspect of the Temple as representing God's presence in the midst of his people is not fully expressed in Solomon's prayer; in accord with Deuteronomistic 'name-theology', the divine presence is represented by 'the name of God' which God 'has set' there, and even this is expressed in a rather formulaic manner (I Kings 8.29, 43, 44, 48 // II Chron. 6.20, 33, 34, 38). For the Chronicler, all this calls for complementation. The prayer must end with a return to the *raison d'être* of the event: God's presence enters the Temple as the ark at last comes to its resting place – with all due implications for the well-being of Israel. The Chronicler then explicitly describes God's presence in a passage inserted in 7.1–3, which completes another cycle, begun in 5.13–14.

A further result of this addition is the change of tone. The recurring supplication, that God may hear the people's prayer, almost necessarily made Solomon's prayer centre on distress, sin, repentance and forgiveness, rather melancholy themes. The Chronistic conclusion is much more optimistic and elevated, represented by words like 'might', 'salvation', 'rejoice', 'goodness', never mentioned in the original prayer.

Although this segment undoubtedly derives from Ps. 132.8–10, there is not even one of the psalm's three lines which has been left intact, and it is evident that a great effort was made to make the psalm a proper vehicle for different ideas.

Ps. 132.8–10
Arise, O Lord ...
... to thy resting place (*lim⁽ᵉ⁾nūḥāteka̱*)
Let thy priests be clothed
with righteousness
thy saints shout for joy

For thy servant David's sake.

II Chron. 6.41–42
And now arise, O Lord *God* ...
... to thy resting place (*l⁽ᵉ⁾nūḥe⁽ᵉ⁾ka̱*)
Let thy priests *O Lord God*
be clothed with *salvation*
thy saints *rejoice in thy goodness,*
O Lord God
Remember thy servant David's loyal service (NEB).

The change which makes the greatest literary impression on the psalm is the addition and emphatic repetition of the explicit address 'O Lord God', in place of the psalm's shorter invocation 'O Lord' (Ps. 132.1, 8). The threefold addition of this invocation impairs the rhythm and parallelism of the psalm's strophes and is placed each time in a somewhat different position in the line, which further emphasizes its significance. The literary technique reflected here is found elsewhere in the Psalms themselves: a certain *Leitmotif* – idiom or formula – is regularly repeated as a kind of refrain – as in 'his steadfast love endures for ever' (Ps. 136), 'Praise him' (Pss. 148, 150), or 'Bless the Lord' (Ps. 135.19–21). In the Chronistic invocation, the solemn threefold repetition of 'O Lord God' takes on the implied connotation of an emphatic declaration: 'The Lord is God, the Lord is God, the Lord is God!'

It is difficult to evaluate the significance of the change of 'thy resting (place)', *m⁽ᵉ⁾nūḥāteka̱*, to the variant form *nūḥeka̱* (which may be either a noun or an. infinitive). There is some difference in the concept of God's rest between Ps. 132 and Chronicles. It is evident in Ps. 132 that God's own rest is meant, and the temple as 'a dwelling place of the mighty one of Jacob' (v. 5).

'For the Lord has chosen Zion / he has desired it for his habitation / This is my resting place ... / here I will dwell' (vv. 13–14). The second colon of verse 8, 'you and the ark of your might', may reflect the psalmist's interpretation of God's rest, if the 'and' is seen as being interpretative or instrumental, i.e. 'you – that is, through your ark of might'. In Chronicles, the idea of 'rest' relates throughout to the rest of the ark and not of God: 'a house of rest for the ark of the covenant of the Lord' (I Chron. 28.2, cf. there; also I Chron. 6.31 [MT 16]).

The title 'the ark of thy might' still preserves some ancient connotations of the ark as the emblem of Israel's wars, and the invocation 'Arise, O Lord' derives from the original battle cry, as preserved in Moses' proclamation whenever the ark set out: 'Arise, O Lord, and let thy enemies be scattered' (Num. 10.35). A certain paradox is thus created by this literary borrowing: God is called forth with the same old formula, 'arise,' not now to war or wandering but to 'his resting place'. It is possible that the change of $m^e n\bar{u}h\bar{a}tek\bar{a}$ to $n\bar{u}hek\bar{a}$ is occasioned by this association to Num. 10.36: 'when it rested' ($b^e nuh\bar{o}h$), referring to the ark.

Psalm 132 refers to two groups of people, clothed with justice, joy and salvation. These are 'your priests' and 'your saints' (132.9), the pronoun referring to God, and 'her priests, her saints', the pronoun referring to Jerusalem (v. 16). On the other hand, the 'people' as such are not mentioned. As the context of the psalm is not specifically cultic, but envisages general well-being, it would seem that here, as in other psalm $h^a s\bar{\imath} d\bar{\imath} m$ ('thy saints' or 'faithful ones') refers not to any particular group but to the people at large; cf. 'all who fear him', 'all who call him' (Ps. 145.18, 19), and 'the people of Israel who are near to him' (Ps. 148.14; also 149.1–5). 'His priests' may therefore also refer by extension to the whole people, in the sense found in Isa. 61.6: 'you shall be called the priests of the Lord ... / the ministers of our God'. In the context of Chronicles, however, where the psalm is indeed set in a cultic context, 'priests' may have its original sacerdotal meaning, complementing the 'saints' of the next colon of the verse.

In the change of 'righteousness' to 'salvation', this verse is probably influenced by Ps. 132.16. As 'shouting with joy' is many times coupled and synonymous with 'rejoicing' (Ps. 5.11; 32.11; 67.4, etc.), the present version simply seems to be referring specifically to the people's well-being, echoing Deut. 26.11: 'and you shall rejoice in all the good which the Lord your God has given to you'.

[42] Who is, or are, 'your anointed one/s'? The text has $m^e \bar{s}\bar{\imath}h\bar{e}k\bar{a}$, in the plural, as in Ps. 105.15//I Chron. 16.22, where 'my anointed ones' ($m^e \bar{s}\bar{\imath}h\bar{a}y$) is parallel to 'my prophets', both referring to the whole people of Israel. Following the text of Ps. 132.10 and 17, however, it seems that the singular $m^e \bar{s}\bar{\imath}hek\bar{a}$, 'thy anointed one', should be preferred here, a reading supported

by other major MSS. In Ps. 132.17, where the parallelism between 'David' and 'my anointed one' is synonymous, the title surely refers to David, and probably (although not unequivocally) also in 132.10. This is not the case in the present context in Chronicles. The entreaty 'do not refuse your anointed one', coming as it does at the end of the king's long prayer, surely indicates that Solomon himself is meant. The same conclusion is also indicated by the change of order in the colons of the verse, making this verse the last, final appeal. The narrative sequence also confirms this interpretation: as soon as Solomon concludes his prayer, God responds favourably to his request: 'When Solomon had ended his prayer, fire came down from heaven and the glory of the Lord filled the Temple' (7.1).

The Hebrew *hāšēb pānīm* is represented in the RSV by 'turn away the face of ...'. However, the general meaning of this idiom is 'refuse' (cf. I Kings 2.16, 17, 20; II Kings 18.24//Isa. 36.9, and Baumgartner, 887); 'turn (away) the face' actually renders another idiom, *hāseb pānīm*, which in general has a more concrete connotation (cf. I Kings 8.14//II Chron. 6.3; I Kings 21.4; II Kings 20.2//Isa. 38.2; etc.). The translation of the NEB 'reject' should therefore be preferred.

The more controversial phrase is *zokrāh lᵉḥasdē dāwīd 'abdekā*, which replaces *baᵃᵇūr dāwīd 'abdekā* of Ps. 132.10. Here all hinges on the interpretation of the phrase *ḥasdē dāwīd* (A. Caquot, '"Les Graces de David", à propos d'Isaie 55/3b', *Semitica* 15, 1965, 45–59; H. G. M. Williamson, 'The Sure Mercies of David', *JSS* 23, 1978, 31–49). The phrase itself is certainly taken from Isa. 55.3, where its meaning is already debated. In principle there are two interpretations of the construct *ḥasdē dāwīd*: 1. the common meaning of a construct in biblical Hebrew, that of a subjective genitive, would indicate a meaning 'the *ḥᵃsādīm of David*'; 2. a more exceptional use of the construct, the objective genitive, would render 'the *ḥᵃsādīm for David*'. Many scholars would explain Isa. 55.3 in this last manner, in particular because of the general context and the parallelism with 'covenant' (cf. *inter al.* J. L. McKenzie, *Second Isaiah*, AB, 141; C. Westermann, *Isaiah 40–66*, OTL, 280). Whatever the meaning of the phrase in Isa. 55.3, the question of its connotation in the Chronistic context nevertheless remains; both interpretations have a certain degree of probability. Adopting the objective genitive (thus RSV), Solomon's request is that God may not forget his steadfast love for David, probably referring to the dynastic promise, one of the themes of Ps. 132 (v. 11). This interpretation is rather difficult. The theme of God's promise to David is different in its tone and attitude from the general atmosphere of the prayer's conclusion. Moreover, all instances of the plural form *ḥᵃsādīm* either as construct or with the possessive pronoun have the meaning of subjective genitive. God's 'steadfast love' is consistently expressed by the phrase *ḥasdī yhwh* (Isa. 63.7; Ps. 89.2; 107.43; Lam. 3.22), or with the possessive pronoun *'thy* steadfast love' (*ḥᵃsādēkā*, Ps. 17.7; 25.6; 89.49 [MT 50]; 106.7; 119.41), or 'his steadfast love' (*ḥᵃsādaw*, Isa. 63.7; Ps. 106.45; Lam. 3.32). To view *ḥasdē dāwīd* as 'the Lord's steadfast love *for* David', i.e. an objective genitive, is to force upon the idiom a unique and exceptional usage. Moreover, the whole clause, *zokrāh lᵉḥesdē dāwīd* has a very clear parallel in Neh. 13.14, 'Remember (*zokrāh*) me, O my God ... and wipe not out my good deeds (*ḥᵃsāday*)'. Cf. also the use of *ḥᵃsādīm* in II Chron. 32.32 and 35.26, translated as 'the good deeds' of Hezekiah or Josiah respectively.

In conclusion, then, *ḥasdē dāwīd* would mean 'the good deeds (NEB 'loyal service', JPS 'loyalty') of David'. In this specific context, Solomon is probably referring to the main theme of Ps. 132, David's unflagging efforts to bring the ark to its resting place: 'Remember, O Lord, in David's favour, all the hardships he endured, how he swore to the Lord ... I will not enter my house ... I will not give sleep to my eyes ... until I find a place for the Lord, a dwelling place for the Mighty One of Jacob' (Ps. 132.1–5). These persistent efforts of David and Solomon have now borne fruit, and here in his inaugural prayer Solomon sums up in one concise phrase the long and complex enterprise now completed.

7 When Solomon had ended his prayer, fire came down from heaven and consumed the burnt offering and the sacrifices, and the glory of the Lord filled the temple. ² And the priests could not enter the house of the Lord, because the glory of the Lord filled the Lord's house. ³ When all the children of Israel saw the fire come down and the glory of the Lord upon the temple, they bowed down with their faces to the earth on the pavement, and worshipped and gave thanks to the Lord, saying, 'For he is good,
    for his steadfast love endures for ever.'
4 Then the king and all the people offered sacrifice before the Lord. ⁵ King Solomon offered as a sacrifice twenty-two thousand oxen and a hundred and twenty thousand sheep. So the king and all the people dedicated the house of God. ⁶ The priests stood at their posts; the Levites also, with the instruments for music to the Lord which King David had made for giving thanks to the Lord – for his steadfast love endures for ever – whenever David offered praises by their ministry; opposite them the priests sounded trumpets; and all Israel stood.

7 And Solomon consecrated the middle of the court that was before the house of the Lord; for there he offered the burnt offering and the fat of the peace offerings, because the bronze altar Solomon had made could not hold the burnt offering and the cereal offering and the fat.

8 At that time Solomon held the feast for seven days, and all Israel with him, a very great congregation, from the entrance of Hamath to the brook of Egypt. ⁹ And on the eighth day they held a solemn assembly; for they had kept the dedication of the altar seven days and the feast seven days. ¹⁰ On the twenty-third day of the seventh month he sent the people away to their homes, joyful and glad of heart for the goodness that the Lord had shown to David and to Solomon and to Israel his people.

11 Thus Solomon finished the house of the Lord and the king's house; all that Solomon had planned to do in the house of the Lord and in his own house he successfully accomplished. ¹² Then the Lord appeared to Solomon in the night and said to him: 'I have heard your prayer, and have chosen this place for myself as a house of sacrifice. ¹³ When I shut up the heavens so that there is no rain, or command the locust to devour the land, or send pestilence among my people, ¹⁴ if my people who are called by my name humble themselves, and pray and seek my face, and turn from their wicked ways, then I will hear from heaven, and will forgive their sin and heal their land. ¹⁵ Now my eyes will be open and my ears attentive to the prayer that is made in this place. ¹⁶ For now I have chosen and consecrated this house that my name may be there for ever; my eyes and my heart will be there for all time. ¹⁷ And as for you, if you walk before me, as David your father walked, doing according to all that I have commanded you and keeping my statutes and my ordinances, ¹⁸ then I will establish your royal throne, as I covenanted with David your father, saying, "There shall not fail you a man to rule Israel."

19 'But if you turn aside and forsake my statutes and my commandments which I

have set before you, and go and serve other gods and worship them, [20] then I will pluck you up from the land which I have given you; and this house, which I have consecrated for my name, I will cast out of my sight, and will make it a proverb and a byword among all peoples. [21] And at this house, which is exalted, everyone passing by will be astonished, and say, "Why has the Lord done thus to this land and to this house?" [22] Then they will say, "Because they forsook the Lord the God of their fathers who brought them out of the land of Egypt, and laid hold on other gods, and worshipped them and served them; therefore he has brought all this evil upon them."'

A. Notes to MT

[18] כרתי, I Kings 9.5 דברתי; [20] ונתשתים, Versions ונתשתיכם; להם, Versions לכם.

B. Notes to RSV

[3] 'When all the children of Israel saw the fire ... they bowed down', etc., contradicts the syntax of MT; better NEB 'All the Israelites were watching as the fire came down ... and they bowed low'; or JPS 'All the Israelites witnessed the descent of fire, etc.'; 'pavement', NEB, JPS, 'ground'; [6] 'whenever David offered praises by their ministry', JPS 'by means of the psalms of David', cf. commentary; [10] 'the goodness that the Lord had shown', NEB 'the prosperity granted by the Lord'; [11] the division into paragraphs is adjusted to I Kings 9.1, the new paragraph actually begins with v. 12; [20] 'the land', thus I Kings 9.7, MT '*my* land'; [21] 'which is exalted', MT 'which *was* exalted'.

C. Structure, sources and form

1. Chapter 7 is devoted to one topic: the conclusion of the dedication of the Temple. It is composed of two equal parts: vv. 1–11, the climax of the ceremonies and festivities; vv. 12–22, God's appearance to Solomon.

2. The source of the passage is I Kings 8.54–9.9. There, the structure was determined not by a preconceived literary plan, but by literary history. The present form of the Kings passage comprises three parts: a narrative section, relating the dedication festivities (8.62–66), framed by two rhetorical pieces: Solomon's blessing of the people (8.54–61) and the divine revelation to Solomon (9.1–9). As the unit now stands, 9.1–9 in particular gives the impression of a Deuteronomistic appendix to the original conclusion of the great event in 8.66.

While retaining the sequence and general scope of the Kings text, the Chronicler has introduced new structure and proportion through a series of omissions and additions:

(a) Solomon's blessing (I Kings 8.54aβ–61) is omitted from the original rhetorical material, while three passages are added to the narrative section (II Chron. 7.1aβ–3, 6, 9), and one to the remaining rhetorical piece (II Chron. 7.12bβ–15). The end-result is a balanced unit of two nearly equal sections, one narrative (vv. 1–11), the other rhetorical (vv. 12–22).

(b) The method for omissions and additions has been demonstrated several times. For additions, the source text is cut at a certain point and the new passage inserted. The original text is then resumed exactly (or nearly) where it left off:

1. I Kings 8.63 _ _ _ _ 64
   II Chron. 7.5   6   7

2. I Kings 8.66aα _ _ _ _ _ _ 66ab–b   שלח את העם | ביום השמיני
   II Chron. 7.9aα   9b–10aα   10aβ   עצר כמשפט ... לחדש השביעי

3. I Kings 9.3a _ _ _ _ _ 3b
   II Chron. 12a   12b–15   16

Omissions follow precisely the same method, in reverse. The omitted passage having been removed, the original sequence of the text is preserved as the gap is bridged. In this case, the space created by the omission of 54ab–61 serves for the insertion of 7.1–3, thus:

I Kings 8.54aα   54aβ–61 _ _ _ _ _ 62
II Chron. 7.1a   [+vv. 1–3]   4

3. The unit in Chronicles shows a stronger connection to its context, and serves better its function as the final stage of the dedication pericope.

(a) The first addition (7.1–3) is closely related – in content and wording – to the pericope's earlier phases, and refers back to 5.14. Solomon's three former addresses, in 6.1–2, 3–11, and 12–42, are now set within a general framework; 7.1–3 is also an organic sequel to the ceremony, naturally followed by 7.4ff. (I Kings 8.62ff.).

(b) The second addition (v. 6) is also linked to the preceding narrative section, in 5.11b–13. In this case both passages are composed by the Chronicler, and demonstrate the structural continuity of the ceremony.

(c) The same continuity is enhanced by the addition of 7.12b–15, in which God's recognition of Solomon's prayer, originally only briefly mentioned and rather isolated from its context, becomes a faithful reflection of Solomon's words, and a better conclusion for the dedication event.

(d) 7.11 is now a conclusion of the first section rather than an introduction to the next (as in 9.1).

4. The three new elements in the first part of the chapter represent three different literary types:

(a) Verses 1–3, the description of fire descending from heaven to consume the sacrifices, is heavily dependent on Lev. 9.23–24 and influenced by the Priestly style and views.

(b) Verse 6, the addition of music to the ceremonial aspect of the festivities, is parallel to 5.11–13, and is markedly Chronistic.

(c) Verses 9b–10aα are a homiletic interpretation of the source material, adjusting the text to the Pentateuchal laws and late concepts of the feast.

The first part of the chapter is thus structured as follows:

(*a*) 1–3 The dedication of altar and Temple with fire and glory
(*b*) 4–7 The sacrifices
(*c*) 8–11 The celebration of the feast, and departure.

5. With the insertion of 7.12b–15, which enlarges upon God's acceptance of Solomon's major prayer, the second section also receives new structure and proportion. God's words are now composed of two parts rather than one, their structure differently conceived:

(*a*) 12–16 (I Kings 9.2–3)   Positive acceptance of Solomon's prayer
(*b*) 17–22 (I Kings 4–9)   Exhortation of Solomon and the people.

Although the original Deuteronomistic tone of the passage is preserved, some lesser elements shift toward Chronistic views and emphases.

D. Commentary

[1–3] God's response to Solomon's prayer receives much greater attention in Chronicles than in Kings. In the latter context, that response is expressed in words: 'I have heard your prayer' (I Kings 9.3). In Chronicles, the first and essential answer is 'in fire', an actual outpouring of flames upon the altar and a descent of divine glory into the Temple (v. 1; cf. also I Kings 18.38; I Chron. 21.26: 'he answered him with fire from heaven upon the altar of burnt offering'). This conflagration is not only the final confirmation of all the steps so far taken by David and Solomon, but also accentuates the continuity between the wilderness tabernacle and the Temple.

In the Pentateuch account, the dedication of the tabernacle itself is depicted as the filling of the tabernacle with divine glory (Exod. 40.34–35); the consecration of the altar is described separately in Lev. 9.23b–25. In Kings, the Temple is filled with the glory (I Kings 8.10–11), but there is no specific event of dedication for the altar (cf. 8.65). In Chronicles, the dedication of the Temple has already been depicted in similar terms (II Chron. 5.13–14); the missing element is now added with the consecration by fire of the sacrificial altar (v. 9).

In Lev. 9.23–24 'the glory of the Lord appeared to all the people ..., fire came forth ... and consumed the burnt offerings ... and when all the people saw it ... they fell on their faces'. All three elements are found here in Chronicles: the fire, the glory, and the people of Israel witnessing both and prostrating themselves.

The juxtaposition of the two ceremonies highlights the identification of the two establishments, tabernacle and Temple. The 'cultic site', always one, nevertheless moved and was transformed: the tabernacle with its 'bronze altar that Bezalel ... had made' (II Chron. 1.5) is succeeded now by the Temple, and 'the bronze altar that Solomon had made' (v. 7).

In his eagerness to continue the story at the point indicated by his source-material, the Chronicler fails to mention a stage which must be presumed: the preparation of the sacrifices now consumed by fire (cf. Lev. 9.1–23; I Kings 18.33–35; I Chron. 21.6).

In vv. 1b–2 the almost verbatim repetition of 6.13–14 expresses the continuity of the two texts; the divine glory is a continuous state: it entered the Temple with the ark and still abides there, preventing the priests from entering to perform their service. From a literary point of view, we have the opportunity to witness here the process of resumptive repetition, intended to express simultaneity of events (cf. S. Talmon, 'The Presentation of Synchroneity and Simultaneity in Biblical Narrative', *Scripta Hierosolymitana* 27, 1978, 9–26; B. O. Long, 'Framing Repetitions in Biblical Historiography', *JBL* 106, 1987, 390–2).

The details of v. 3 attest significant points in the Chronicler's concept of religion. An important theological statement is made in the words 'all the Israelites were watching as the fire came down with the glory of the Lord on the house' (NEB). In Lev. 9.23–24 a similar experience is phrased in passive terms, as if to create a sense of distance: 'the glory of the Lord appeared' (literally 'was seen') ... and fire came from before the Lord'. Here the phrasing is in the active mood: 'all the people were watching as the fire came down' (NEB); a similar attitude is in Exod. 20.18: 'now ... all the people perceived the thunderings... .' (the same root is used in all three cases). Here, however, in contrast to the Sinai theophany, the people are not driven by fright to shun the experience; rather their religious awe prompts them to bow down with their faces to the ground and praise God. Their reaction illustrates in the best way their profound experience of and absolute trust in God's presence. It is not the priests or king alone, but 'all the children of Israel' who share this moment of worship: 'For he is good, for his steadfast love endures for ever.'

[4–6] A multitude of sacrifices is the principal and in I Kings 8.62–63 (the source of vv. 4–5) the only expression of popular festivity. The Chronicler's addition (v. 6) complements the ritual with due splendour.

The enormous number of sacrificial beasts, 22,000 oxen and 100,000 sheep, does not stand in proportion to any other Chronistic ceremonies (I Chron. 29.21; II Chron. 1.6; 29.32; 30.24), even the popular passover of Josiah's reign (II Chron. 35.7–9); reasonable or not, these are the numbers which appear in the Chronicler's source in Kings.

The ceremonial aspects of v. 6 are related to the Chronicler's addition in 5.11b–13, accentuating the continuity which has already been expressed in the mention of the cloud of divine glory. The people here are divided into the three classes, characterizing the Second Temple ritual: priests, Levites and 'Israel' (cf. on I Chron. 9). In this triple division, the singers are designated by the more general term, Levites. All the participants are standing, as is clear from the opening and closing phrases of v. 6: 'the priests stood at their posts ... and all Israel stood'.

The priests play a double role: 'at their posts' they perform their regular duties in presenting the sacrifices, and 'opposite' the Levites they sound the trumpets (for a precise description of this procedure cf. II Chron. 29.27). The greatest detail is reserved for the liturgical music, especially its connection with David, who according to Chronicles made 'the instruments for music for the Lord', and wrote 'the praise song of David', or perhaps, 'the psalms of David' (JPS).

[7] The verse is taken from I Kings 8.64, with only slight linguistic and stylistic alterations. More significant is the description of 'the bronze altar Solomon had made', replacing 'the bronze altar which was before the Lord', thus establishing an analogy with the ancient altar of the tabernacle, 'which Bezalel had made' (II Chron. 1.5).

The omission of the words 'the cereal offering' in the first part of the verse may be due to corruption, as they are retained at the end of the verse.

[8–10] The celebrations continue with the observance by the king and 'all Israel' of '*the* feast' (*heḥāg*, NEB 'the pilgrim-feast'), i.e. the autumn Festival of Booths, in Jerusalem. The relationship between the dedication of the Temple and the Feast of Booths is not made completely clear in the present version of I Kings 8. It seems that one should distinguish between an original view and a secondary adaptation. According to the original version, the dedication of the Temple coincided with the Festival of Booths. The celebrations open in I Kings 8.1–2, 'all the men of Israel assembled to king Solomon *at the feast* in the month Ethanim', and close in vv. 65–66, 'So Solomon held the feast at that time ... seven days. On the eighth day he sent the people away; and they ... went to their homes.' It was astute of Solomon to set the dedication ceremony at the Festival of Booths; he thus established the first precedent of pilgrimage to the new Temple in Jerusalem on the occasion of the most important of the three pilgrim feasts. This original text was secondarily glossed in I Kings 8.65 with the interpolation of the words 'and seven days, fourteen days' (omitted by RSV *ad loc.*), implying two distinct consecutive celebrations of seven days each.

A further adjustment was made in the Chronicler's version of the event (vv. 8–9). Here an explicit distinction is made: 'for they had kept the dedication of the altar seven days and the feast seven days'. Through a very fine interpolation of I Kings 8.66 the passage is made to convey the new idea.

The motive for this change seems to be two-fold. A minor difficulty was posed for later generations by the statement 'on the eighth day he sent the people away', a point which could be, and indeed was, harmonized by the alteration in v. 9: 'on the eighth day they held a solemn assembly' (cf. below).

A more weighty point is the complete dissociation of the Feast of Booths from the dedication celebrations, which reflects more serious motivations.

As the feasts were becoming increasingly established and their ritual forms more well-defined (cf. Neh. 8.14–18), each feast could be expected to display certain familiar features. Nothing of the kind is evidenced in Solomon's celebrations as described in I Kings 8. Except for the date, the name, and the length of the festival, there is no affinity at all between this event and the Feast of Booths in any of the biblical sources. For the learned reader, the conclusion must have been that this was in fact not a pilgrim festival; taking all the other details of the story into consideration, a clear-cut distinction has been made: a Temple dedication followed by a traditional Feast of Booths. This new understanding is given brief expression in the gloss on I Kings 8.65; the Chronicler develops it in a more systematic manner, with three additions: the holy convocation on the eighth day, an explicit statement about the two distinct festivals, and another on the date of departure.

A Feast of Booths of seven days is the law in Deut. 16.13–15, the phrasing of which is of relevance here: 'You shall keep the Feast of Booths seven days … For seven days you shall keep the feast to the Lord your God at the place which the Lord will choose.' Solomon's is in fact the first such feast celebrated in accordance with this injunction: for seven days, in the chosen place. Indeed, the feast is celebrated in the proper fashion at the earliest possible juncture – with the very dedication of the 'chosen place', the Temple.

Another view of the feast is reflected in the composite text of Lev. 23.34–36, in which an additional day is appended to the basic seven: 'for seven days is the Feast of Booths … on the eighth day you shall hold a holy convocation'. For the Chronicler, this law renders impossible the statement of I Kings 8.66, that Solomon dismissed the people 'on the eighth day' of the feast. He therefore retains the beginning of the verse, 'on the eighth day', but complements it with his own conclusion: 'they held a solemn assembly'.

The Chronicler also inserts a statement clearly separating between 'the dedication of the altar seven days' and 'the feast seven days'. As the dedication comes first, the assembly of the people to Jerusalem cannot now be placed 'at the feast'; it must have been at least seven days earlier, the plan being to celebrate the two events consecutively. This new view, however, is not developed consistently to its logical conclusion, for the beginning of the pericope in 5.3 still preserves the reading of I Kings 8.2: 'and all the men of Israel assembled … at the feast'. As for the dedication itself, v. 9 here refers it only to 'the altar', while v. 5 specifies 'the house of God' (cf. I Kings 8.63). This verse, then, again accentuates the role of the altar in accord both with the context of sacrifices, and the Chronicler's general attitude (cf. 7.12).

Finally there is the date of departure. In order to rule out any possibility of doubt, the Chronicler states that the celebrations ended 'on the twenty-third day of the seventh month' (v. 10a). This remark clearly establishes the exact sequence of dates according to the Chronicler's view: the gathering of the people was on the 8th of the month, the Feast of Booths on the 15th, the solemn assembly on the 22nd, and finally the dismissal.

In v. 10aβ, the Chronicler returns to his source in I Kings 8.66, reproducing it with some changes. First he omits the reference there to the people blessing the king, following his favourite technique: four words, *way^ebār^ekū 'et hammelek wayyēlekū*, are simply excised from the text, which then continues with its original wording. The motive of this omission is unclear. One may attribute it to the Chronicler's general inclination to conciseness. It must be noted, however, that both I Kings 8.54b–61 and 8.66 describe 'blessings' directed towards human recipients (the king blessing the people and *vice versa*), and both are omitted by the Chronicler. And while the words in I Kings 8.14, 'the king faced about and blessed all the assembly of Israel', are retained in II Chron. 6.3, they are in fact followed by a blessing addressed to God, not to the people.

It has been suggested that to bless the people is seen by the Chronicler as an exclusively priestly prerogative (cf. II Chron. 30.27 and Curtis, 347; differently Rudolph, 217), and that this motivated the omission of Solomon's blessing in I Kings 8.55–61. This position is refuted by other Chronistic texts (I Chron. 16.2; II Chron. 31.8); even if it were accurate, this would not account for the omission of the people's blessing of the king.

In another change, the Chronicler sees the 'goodness' of the Lord shown not only to David and Israel, but also 'to Solomon'. This is another illustration of the way in which the Chronicler constantly put Solomon on a par with David: the period of 'goodness' in the history of Israel is the combined era of David and Solomon. Moreover, this portrayal refers not only to a generation of the past ('David his servant'), but to the present as well: 'David, Solomon and the people.'

[11] In the narrative structure of I Kings this verse (9.1) marks the beginning of a new section, 'When Solomon had finished', etc. Here, the same phrase concludes the entire first section (vv. 1–11); the verbal tense is therefore changed: 'And Solomon finished' (the new structure is blurred at this point by RSV's paragraph division). I Kings 9.1 refers not only to 'the house of the Lord' and 'the kings' house' but also to the more general 'all that Solomon desired to build'. This last phrase is changed in Chronicles: 'all that Solomon had planned to do in the house of the Lord and in his own house'. Even this limited view of Solomon's building enterprises goes beyond the Chronicler's own narrative elsewhere, where all Solomon's projects except the house of the Lord have been omitted (cf. above, on 1.18; 2.11).

The Chronicler adds that Solomon accomplished everything successfully

– a characteristic Chronistic idiom. 'Success' is a mark of some of the righteous kings, such as Asa, Uzziah and Hezekiah (II Chron. 14.7 [MT 6]; 26.5; 31.21, etc.); its absence indicates sinfulness (II Chron. 12.12; 24.20, etc.). Solomon is twice blessed with a wish for 'success' by David (I Chron. 22.11, 13); his achievements are thus characterized both here and in I Chron. 29.23.

[12–22] This second section of the chapter, relating God's nocturnal revelation to Solomon, is based on I Kings 9.2–9 with certain changes. The most significant of these is the addition of vv. 12b–15, yielding a different literary structure and attitude toward the matters at hand (cf. also Williamson, 225).

The opening of the vision (v. 12a) is taken from I Kings 9.2, with 'a second time, as he appeared to him at Gibeon' replaced by the brief 'in the night'. There are three salient points to this change: 1. the first revelation in Gibeon is not cited as a precedent, a fact which indicates its diminished role in the Chronicler's view; 2. the chronological setting is more strongly linked to the dedication of the Temple – the implication seems to be that this was the night of the twenty-third of the month, immediately following the festivities; 3. the reader is naturally reminded of another revelation 'in the night' – God's injunction to Nathan forbidding David to build the Temple (I Chron. 17.3). In this latter passage a contrast is introduced: 'by day' David's will to build a Temple is confirmed by Nathan (I Chron. 17.1–2), but 'that same night' God rejects this plan and suggests another. Here, on the other hand, night complements day – God's revelation both answers and confirms Solomon's prayer.

The Chronicler's version of God's answer opens with a straightforward statement: 'I have heard your prayer, and have chosen this place for myself as a house of sacrifice'. One might conclude from this that the main point of Solomon's request was indeed the choosing of 'this place' as 'a house of sacrifice'. This, however, is not the case; in both Kings and Chronicles, Solomon's request had been that God might heed the prayers offered toward the sanctuary and grant them. The verse presents the Chronicler's own intepretation: that sacrifice is the primary role of the Temple, and that 'a house of prayer' is essentially a 'house of sacrifice' – compare in particular Isa. 56.7: 'their burnt offerings and their sacrifices will be accepted on my altar, *for* my house shall be called a house of prayer for all peoples'. The term 'a house of sacrifice' is itself unique to this context, but the view it represents is found implied in Ezra 6.3: '... the place where sacrifices are offered and burnt offerings are brought'.

We have already noted that the terminology of 'choosing' (*bḥr*) is never used in Solomon's prayer for the Temple, but is reserved for the city of Jerusalem and David (I Kings 8.16, 44, 48//II Chron. 6.5–6, 34, 38). Even in the present passage, the source in I Kings 9.3 has 'I have consecrated this house'. In the short passage inserted in Chronicles, 'I have chosen' is added twice to the text of Kings: 'I ... have chosen this place ... I have chosen and consecrated this house' (vv. 12, 16).

Here we have a new interpretation of the references in Deuteronomy to 'the place which God will choose' (Deut. 12.5, 11, 14). The Deuteronomistic literature identified 'this place' with the city of Jerusalem, while the present text, in vv. 12 and 16, focusses more specifically on the Temple. This theological turn presumes a precise semantic interpretation of māqōm ('the place'), meaning a sanctuary.

[13–16] God proceeds with a direct reference to the actual words of Solomon's prayer. This positive aspect is limited in the original version to one short and rather general verse (I Kings 9.3) which refrains from relating to the main point of Solomon's request: the heeding of Israel's prayer in times of distress. In the passage added here God's response is formulated in words taken from the prayer, and relates explicitly three of the calamities mentioned by Solomon, all of which might threaten the people's well-being on the land: drought, locust and pestilence. These are described, however, not in the neutral, passive manner of Solomon's prayer, but as initiated by God himself: 'When I shut up the heavens ... or command the locust ... or send pestilence ...'

The way from distress to salvation has been shown in Solomon's prayer separately for each case. Here (v. 14), this way is outlined in a more abstract, generally applicable form: repentance, prayer, return to virtue – leading to God's response, forgiveness and restoration. There are, however, certain terms which are peculiar to this passage. First, the people will 'humble themselves' (as the initial stage of any repentance – a very typically Chronistic concept (cf. Japhet, *Ideology*, 260–1); the honour of being 'called by God's name', which in Solomon's prayer is referred to the Temple ('this house which I have built is called by thy name', I Kings 8.43//II Chron. 6.33), is here applied endearingly to the people of Israel. Repentance is needed not 'because they have sinned' (I Kings 8.35//II Chron. 6.26), but because of their 'wicked ways'. Finally, God's relief is described, not in the details of the removal of the calamities, but in the general phrase 'I will heal their land'.

As already mentioned, II Chron. 6.40 is repeated (in the first person) in 7.15. Both verses are Chronistic: one concludes Solomon's prayer, and the second marks the end of the Chronicler's insertion. With v. 16 the Chronicler resumes the original sequence of I Kings 9.3, which now serves to elaborate on v. 15. Solomon's request has been granted, as God has emphasized: 'my eyes will be open and my ears attentive'. And now comes an added dimension of divine commitment: 'my heart will be there for all time'.

[17–22] Here begins the second part of God's address, which is primarily a theodicy – i.e. an explanation of the destruction of the Temple and the land. In Kings, this section is not really linked to its narrative context; it is rather a general Deuteronomistic observation, focussed on three topics: the future of the Davidic dynasty, the inheritance of the land, and the fate of the Temple.

After the opening phrase 'And as for you', which indicates a new direction of thought, come two conditional sentences in sequence: vv. 17–18 (I Kings 9.4–5), 'if you walk before me ... then I will establish your royal throne',; and vv. 19–22 (I Kings 9.6–9), 'But if you turn aside ... then I will pluck you up ...' The two conditions form a finely composed literary balance: each has a different address and centres upon a different subject. The first (positive) condition relates only to the royal conduct and the fulfilment of God's promise to David, which are viewed here as Solomon's own responsibility. The second (negative) condition is directed to the people of Israel; if they disobey the Lord, they will be driven from the land and the Temple destroyed. The juxtaposition of the two conditions sums up the three centres of Israel's existence: kingship, land and Temple. Israel's entire history is viewed here as a permanent state of condition and consequence, and this is expressed not only explicitly, but also through the literary structure. The people of Israel are responsible for their own fate: if they fulfil the condition, they will prosper, if not – they are doomed.

Although the passage is derived directly from I Kings 9.4–9, there are some changes, particularly omissions, which amount to a shift in the theological message.

(*a*) I Kings 9.4 refers to David's 'integrity of heart and uprightness'; here in vv. 17 these words are omitted. One might regard this as another illustration of the Chronicler's stylistic inclination to brevity, were it not for the similar omission in I Chron. 1.18 of David's virtues as described during the revelation of Gibeon: 'because he walked before thee in faithfulness, in righteousness and in uprightness of heart toward thee, and thou has kept for him this great and steadfast love' (I Kings 3.6). In general, the Chronicler restricts – without excising completely – comparisons to David.

(*b*) The Chronicler also omits or changes several words in vv. 18, 19 and 20, partly to limit the perspective and in particular the chronological scope of the passage. The characteristic theodicy of I Kings 9.4–9, which reviews the whole history of kingship, land and Temple, and was probably written after the destruction, is limited in its Chronistic version more specifically to Solomon and his generation. Here, then, God's promise to David is applied not to the entire Davidic dynasty, but to Solomon alone. To strengthen this impression the Chronicler omits 'on Israel for ever' and the phrase 'or your children'; the references are reduced to the present generation alone. In fact, with the latter omission the word 'you' becomes redundant; its survival in the text creates an unintentional emphasis. Thus the original characteristically

Deuteronomistic justification of the final destruction of the Temple becomes in fact an answer to Solomon's prayer, addressed to Solomon's generation alone: the monarchy, Israel's inheritance of the land, and the survival of the Temple are all dependent on this generation's religious behaviour.

Several further points in these verses should be mentioned:

(a) Verse 18 reads 'a man to rule Israel' (*'īš mōšēl bᵉyiśrā'ēl*), while I Kings 9.5 reads 'a man upon the throne of Israel' (*'īš mē'al kisse' yiśrā'ēl*). Commentators have regarded this text as influenced by Micah 5.2 [MT 1]: 'from you shall come forth for me one who is to be ruler in Israel' (*mōšēl bᵉyiśrā'ēl*, cf. von Rad, *Geschichtsbild*, 124). In view of the many scriptural influences on Chronicles and its anthological style, this is of course very likely. However, the LXX reading of I Kings 9.5 may indicate that the Chronicler merely represented an original *Vorlage* which was eventually corrupted in the MT. This of course does not exclude the influence of Micah's prophecy, but transfers it from Chronicles to the original passage in Kings.

(b) In I Kings 9.7–8 there is a full literary balance between 'Israel' and 'the house':

'I will cut off Israel ... and the house ... I will cast out'
'and Israel will become a proverb ... And this house will become a heap of ruins ...'.

Finally, both Israel and the Temple will become a 'byword'; it will be said: 'Why has the Lord done thus to this land and to this house?'.

In Chronicles (vv. 20–21), this balance is disrupted, and the Temple is given the central place. For 'Israel will become a proverb' v. 20b reads 'I will make it (i.e. the Temple) a proverb'. Thus, except for a short anonymous reference to the people, 'I will pluck you (them) up from the land', all references are now to the Temple: 'this house I will cast out ... and make it a proverb ... everyone passing by will be astonished'. This feature links the passage more closely to its context: the dedication of the Temple.

(c) The reading of I Kings 9.8 has attracted much attention and the proposal to read *lᵉ'īyyin* ('heap of ruins') in place of *'elyōn* ('exalted') is accepted by many (thus RSV and NEB). However, it seems that the Chronicler received the text in its present form *'elyōn* (so RSV; differently NEB), and duly changed 'will be' (*yihyeh*) to 'was' (*hāyāh*).

At the end of God's address, the Chronicler retains the standard Deuteronomistic formulas and the reference to the divine intervention which delivered the ancestors of the people from Egypt. It is the sheer ungratefulness of a generation forsaking the God of their fathers which is envisioned as the ultimate justification for the terrible potential punishment.

8 At the end of twenty years, in which Solomon had built the house of the Lord and his own house, [2] Solomon rebuilt the cities which Huram had given to him, and settled the people of Israel in them.

3 And Solomon went to Hamath-zobah, and took it. [4] He built Tadmor in the wilderness and all the store-cities which he built in Hamath. [5] He also built Upper Beth-horon and Lower Beth-horon, fortified cities with walls, gates, and bars, [6] and Ba'alath, and all the store-cities that Solomon had, and all the cities for his chariots, and the cities for his horsemen, and whatever Solomon desired to build in Jerusalem, in Lebanon, and in all the land of his dominion. [7] All the people who were left of the Hittites, the Amorites, the Perizzites, the Hivites, and the Jebusites, who were not of Israel, [8] from their descendants who were left after them in the land, whom the people of Israel had not destroyed – these Solomon made a forced levy and so they are to this day. [9] But of the people of Israel Solomon made no slaves for his work; they were soldiers, and his officers, the commanders of his chariots, and his horsemen. [10] And these were the chief officers of King Solomon, two hundred and fifty, who exercised authority over the people.

11 Solomon brought Pharaoh's daughter up from the city of David to the house which he had built for her, for he said, 'My wife shall not live in the house of David king of Israel, for the places to which the ark of the Lord has come are holy.'

12 Then Solomon offered up burnt offerings to the Lord upon the altar of the Lord which he had built before the vestibule, [13] as the duty of each day required, offering according to the commandment of Moses for the sabbaths, the new moons, and the three annual feasts – the feast of unleavened bread, the feast of weeks, and the feast of tabernacles. [14] According to the ordinance of David his father, he appointed the divisions of the priests for their service, and the Levites for their offices of praise and ministry before the priests as the duty of each day required, and the gatekeepers in their divisions for the several gates; for so David the man of God had commanded. [15] And they did not turn aside from what the king had commanded the priests and Levites concerning any matter and concerning the treasuries.

16 Thus was accomplished all the work of Solomon from the day the foundation of the house of the Lord was laid until it was finished. So the house of the Lord was completed.

17 Then Solomon went to Ezion-geber and Eloth on the shore of the sea, in the land of Edom. [18] And Huram sent him by his servants ships and servants familiar with the sea, and they went to Ophir together with the servants of Solomon, and fetched from there four hundred and fifty talents of gold and brought it to King Solomon.

A. Notes to MT

[9] אשר, delete, with the Versions and I Kings 9.22; ושרי ושלישיו , LXX[AB] and I Kings
9.22 ושריו ושלישיו [11] בבית דויד, LXX בעיר דויד; [13] לשבתות, probably read, ולשבתות;
[15] מצות, read ממצות with the Versions (haplography); [16] עד היום probably read מן
היום with the Versions.

B. Notes to RSV

[9] 'his officers', MT differently, cf. A above and NEB; [12–13] 'Then Solomon
offered ... before the vestibule, as the duty, etc.', better 'Then Solomon offered ...
before the vestibule. And as the duty, etc.' (cf. commentary); [14] 'for the several
gates', better 'at each gate' (NEB; JPS 'gate by gate').

C. Structure, sources and form

1. Chapter 8 is based on I Kings 9.10–28; while it retains the sequence and essential
points of the original, it nevertheless introduces several alterations, additions and
omissions. The primary result is the complete disruption of the original structure.
    The basic literary structure of I Kings 9.10–28 is an inclusion: the overall
framework is provided by Solomon's relationship with Hiram the king of Tyre (9.10–
14 and 26–28). An inner framework is found in the levies of slave-labourers and
overseers, the context of which is outlined in v. 15: 'and this is the account of the
forced labour', while vv. 17–23 supply the details. The centre of the section is
occupied by a note on the conquest of Gezer (v. 16).
    The whole inclusion may be illustrated as follows:

    10–14 ———— Hiram
        15 ———— Forced labour for building projects
            16 ———— Conquest of Gezer
        17–23 ———— Forced labour for building projects
    26–28 ———— Hiram

Only vv. 24–25, although showing some affinity to several passages, do not fit into
this general structure (cf. below).
    The symmetrical scheme of Kings is lost in Chronicles; here various details of the
material are omitted, amplified or altered without any attempt at a comprehensive
restructuring. The verses omitted are I Kings 9.14–17a and other minor details. The
added verses are 3, most of 4b–5, 11b, 13–16a. An alteration is found in the
remodelling of I Kings 9.11–13 in v. 2. A new structure is displayed at two points:
vv. 1–4, Solomon's enterprises on the northern borders of his empire, and vv. 12–16,
which summarize the topic of the Temple.
    2. In Chronicles, the chapter thus comprises the following passages:

    (a) 1–6   Solomon's building projects:
                    1–4 enterprises on the northern border
                    5–6 other construction projects

(*b*) 7–10   Matters of administration:
            7–8 forced labour
            9 Israelites
            10 officers
(*c*) 11   The residence for the daughter of Pharaoh
(*d*) 12–16   Inaugurating the Temple ritual
(*e*) 17–18   Expedition to Ophir via Eloth

3. The question of sources and authenticity is posed in this chapter by the first passage (vv. 1–6). Verse 2 exposes one aspect of the relationship between Solomon and Hiram and may be regarded as the Chronicler's representation of I Kings 9.11b–13, while vv. 4–6 are closely related to I Kings 9.17–19; v. 3 alone is an addition. The reworking procedure of the new literary structure may be fully appreciated through a synopsis of the parallel texts, of which I shall begin with the second part.

I Kings 9.17–19: 'So Solomon built (וַיִּבֶן, RSV 'rebuilt') Gezer and Lower Beth-horon and Baalath and Tamar in the wilderness, in the land (RSV 'of Judah'), and all the store cities that Solomon had'.

II Chron. 8.4–6aα: 'He built Tadmor in the wilderness, and all the store cities which he built in Hamath. He (also) built Upper Beth-horon and Lower Beth-horon ... and Baalath and all the store cities that Solomon had.'

Let us consider the differences between the two versions;

(*a*) 'Tamar in the wilderness' is rendered 'Tadmor in the wilderness';
(*b*) Tadmor is separated from the other cities by its placement at the beginning;
(*c*) There are two additions: 'store cities which he built in Hamath' and 'Upper Beth-horon';
(*d*) The reference to Gezer is omitted.

In I Kings, it is the 'forced labour' (9.15) which provides the context for the details of vv. 17–19. The Chronicler omits I Kings 9.15, and here provides a different unifying factor. A subtitle for vv. 1–4 might be 'Solomon's enterprises in the northern part of Israel'. This theme accounts for the various changes I have indicated, and the Chronicler's text is then not 'the best reconstruction he could make' of a corrupt or divergent *Vorlage* (Williamson, 228–9, following Willi, 75–8), but a well-planned composition having a definite goal: the systematic description of Solomon's settlement, development and fortification of the northern border of his kingdom. While remarks on the conquest and building of Gezer are omitted, and with the deletion of I Kings 9.15 the building of Hazor and Megiddo is not repeated, as far as the north is concerned, to Solomon are ascribed the rebuilding and resettling of cities given by Hiram (v. 2), the conquering of Hamath (v. 3), the building of store-cities there, and the building of Tadmor (Palmyra) in the desert. Together with vv. 5–6, cited from I Kings 9.17b–19, vv. 1–6 may now be entitled 'Solomon's building and fortifying enterprises'.

How should this additional information be evaluated historically? Many scholars would deny it any authenticity, an attitude exemplified by some 'histories of Israel', where the matter is passed over in complete silence (cf. *inter al.*, M. Noth, *The History of Israel*, 1958, 203–15; J. A. Soggin, 'The Davidic–Solomonic kingdom', in J. H. Hayes and J. M. Miller, *Israelite and Judaean History*, 1977, 373–6). My literary analysis, illustrating the transformation of the extant material in I Kings 9, may be cited to support this view. On the other hand, several aspects of the new material may stand the test of historical probability, as I shall indicate in the commentary.

4. Another example of lucid restructuring is found in vv. 12–16. These verses are based on I Kings 9.25, as is clear from the parallel opening and closing phrases:

I Kings 9.25: שלמה והעלה, 'Solomon used to offer...'
II Chron. 8.12: אז העלה שלמה, 'Then Solomon offered ...'
I Kings 9.25: ושלם את הבית, 'so he finished the house'
II Chron. 8.16: שלם בית יהוה, 'so the house ... was completed'.

Modified references to 'three times a year' and 'the altar which he built to the Lord' are also included in vv. 12 and 13. However, in Chronicles an extensive section (vv. 13–16a) replaces 'burning incense before the Lord'. This interpolation, thoroughly Chronistic in method, content, terminology and views, transforms the passage into a significant statement about the Temple ritual.

D. Commentary

[1–2] A temporal clause states how long it took Solomon to complete the Temple and the palace (cf. I Kings 6.37–7.1), and then the main issue is addressed: the cities. Verse 2, which parallels I Kings 9.11b–13, is often cited as a prime example of how Chronicles can transmit material in a manner diametrically opposed to its original presentation. According to I Kings 9.11b–13 Solomon gave Hiram 'twenty cities in the land of Galilee', for which the latter expresses his explicit disapproval. The Chronicler states the opposite: Huram donates to Solomon cities which the latter resettles. Since the specific number and location, 'twenty cities in ... Galilee', are not repeated in this text, the two notices could be seen as complementary, reflecting a territorial exchange between the two rulers (cf. Kimhi, *ad loc.*). However, both the place of this note in the sequence and the Chronicler's general view of the relationship between Solomon and Hiram would indicate that the Chronicler intended to replace rather than complement his source-text.

It seems that the best way to interpret this remark, with its non-explicit negation of the earlier evidence, would be along the principle of 'historical probability' underlying the Chronicler's reasoning (cf. E. J. Bickerman, *From Ezra to the Last of the Maccabees*, 1962, 23). Throughout his narrative, the Chronicler views the relationship between Solomon and Huram as one of superior and subordinate (cf. II Chron. 2.14 and further below). That Solomon would have given Huram part of his territory, and moreover that Huram would have expressed dissatisfaction, is for the Chronicler grossly improbable, and must be 'corrected'.

Solomon's resettlement of cities with the people of Israel is unique in biblical literature. Intentional policies of colonization, implemented by a

central government, are attributed in the Bible to the Assyrian kings (II
Kings 17.16, 24; Ezra 4.9–10), but always in the context of warfare and exile.
It seems likely that the depiction here of the same policy as a routine peace-
time activity is conditioned by the Chronicler's own historical experience.

[3–4] With the exception of the reference to Tadmor (from I Kings 9.18),
the verses were composed by the Chronicler. The joining of 'Hamath' and
'Zobah', regarded as an unhistorical reflection of the Chronicler's own
circumstances (cf. II Sam. 8.3–7 with vv. 9–10), the information about
peaceful relations between the kingdom of Hamath and David (cf. II Sam.
8.9–10//I Chron. 18.9–10), the location of Hamath in the extreme north, the
image of Solomon as a 'man of peace' who did not initiate military expeditions, and the decline of Solomon's political strength towards the end of his
reign (cf. I Kings 11.14–25) – all these have led scholars to regard a military
conquest of Hamath as flatly impossible or at best a presentation of a corrupt
Vorlage. However, while an unequivocal decision cannot be reached, fairness
demands that other points should also be considered.

When the facts are examined, an expedition against Hamath does not seem
so improbable. We were told that Tou, the ruler of Hamath, sought the
support of David against Hadadezer the king of Zobah (II Sam. 8.9–10//
I Chron. 18.9–10), but we are given no idea how long the relative independence of Hamath persisted. In I Chron. 18.3, Hadadezer is actually called
'the king of Zobah- Hamathah' (RSV 'toward Hamath'), similar to this verse.
It is quite probable that Hamath changed – or was forced to change – its
attitude towards Israel at a later stage, making an expedition against it
essential for the stability of the northern border. This may have occurred in
an earlier phase of Solomon's rule, the Chronicler's note 'at the end of twenty
years' being dictated by literary considerations. The northern border of
Solomon's empire is described as 'from the entrance of Hamath' (or, according to a different interepretation, 'from Labu of Hamath', I Kings 8.65/
II Chron. 7.8; cf. Y. Aharoni, *The Land of the Bible*, [2]1979, 72), and this
presupposes conquests at this far end of the kingdom. At a later date, when
Jeroboam, the son of Joash, '*restored* the border of Israel ... from the entrance
of Hamath as far as the sea of Arabah' (II Kings 14.25), the implication is
clearly that Israel had always retained its claim to Hamath as the northern
border.

Another point to be considered is the uncharacteristic portrayal here of
Solomon's military initiative, against all sources, and particularly the
Chronicler's own emphasis on the image of 'a man of peace' (I Chron. 22.9).
Two approaches are possible: the very unexpected nature of this portrayal
may argue for its authenticity; alternatively, one may see here another
attempt by the Chronicler to present David and Solomon as equals.

In the final analysis, the information is not as improbable as it seems at first, especially if seen as originally placed in the earlier part of Solomon's reign. One may further assume that the notice concerning the conquest of Hamath provided the basis for the overall reworking of this passage.

Verse 4 relates to the building of 'Tadmor in the wilderness' and 'store cities' in Hamath. I have noted already that the first is a reproduction of I Kings 9.18: 'So Solomon built . . . Tamar in the wilderness in the land'. The RSV rendering, 'in the land of Judah', accepts the authority of the *Kethib* of I Kings 9.18; the city then is identified with Tamar of Ezek 47.19; 48.28, marking the south-eastern limit of the land, in the vicinity of the Dead Sea. Ba'ala, mentioned with Tamar in I Kings 9.18, is a common name (for Kiriath-jearim in Josh. 15.9; for a city in Dan in Josh. 19.44); here, however, it seems to refer to a city in the territory of Simeon (Josh. 15.29). Together, the two cities fortify the south-eastern limit of Solomon's kingdom. However, the *Qere* of I Kings 9.18 and all the Versions already render 'Tamar' as 'Tadmor', not attested elsewhere in the Bible but known to refer to the oasis of Palmyra, a key point of the caravan route through the north Arabian desert. It seems most likely that the Chronicler already found the reading 'Tadmor' in his *Vorlage*; his own contribution was to separate it from Baalah, and to specify the location 'in Hamath' of the anonymous store-cities of I Kings 9.19a. Such an addition would be inspired not only by the previous reference to the conquest of Hamath, but also by the explicit mention of Solomon's building 'in Lebanon' (I Kings 9.19b).

This passage portrays Solomon in a light not found in the rest of the narrative. Here, he is more than the heir of a great conqueror, who first consolidated his father's achievements and eventually began to lose them; rather, he is a man of enterprise in his own right, expanding and fortifying the northern territory of his kingdom.

[5–6] The Chronicler omits the Kings heading 'this is the account of the forced labour', very much in harmony with the similar omission of I Kings 5.13–14 (MT 5.27–28) and I Kings 11.27–28. As for the cities, only Baalath and Lower Beth-horon are mentioned in Kings, but it is likely that Upper Beth-horon too was originally in the Chronicler's *Vorlage*, and fell out of the MT text of I Kings by oversight.

Upper and Lower Beth-horon, situated north-west of Jerusalem on the road leading from the coastal land through the Shephelah to the hill-country, are described as 'fortified cities, with walls, gates and bars'; in fact, they are not included among Rehoboam's fortified cities in II Chron. 11.6–10. The Chronicler's standard formula for fortified cities (cf. mainly II Chron. 14.6–7) is probably based on a more general convention (cf. Deut. 3.5, where the cities of Og in Bashan are 'fortified with high walls, gates, and bars').

All references to Gezer, its conquest, its being given to Solomon and its fortification (I Kings 9.15b–17a), are passed over in silence. The Chronicler takes at face value the information that Gezer belonged to Ephraim (I Chron. 7.28) and was a levitical city, actually occupied by Levites already in David's time (I Chron. 6.67 [MT 6.52]); its capture by Pharaoh at this time would be an impossibility.

From v. 6, the Chronicler's faithful adherence to and careful adaptation of his source can be seen in the smallest details. From the original text (I Kings 9.18) the Chronicler deletes 'Tamar in the wilderness in the land' (already represented in v. 4), and the remainder of the Kings text is then reproduced, carefully keeping to the original sequence: 'and Baalath, and all the store cities ...'.

The juxtaposition of 'Jerusalem' and 'Lebanon' in I Kings 9.18 is awkward from both literary and historical points of view. It is the only name mentioned here besides Jerusalem, and it is rather unlikely that Solomon undertook building projects at such a far remove from his capital. It would seem rather that the reference to Lebanon already appeared in the Chronicler's *Vorlage* as a secondary expansion of the original 'in Jerusalem', influenced by the account of Solomon's expeditions referred to in I Kings 5.13–14 [MT 5.27–28].

[7–8] The 'forced levy' of foreign workers here stands on its own, not explicitly connected (as in I Kings 9.20–21) with the building projects. This connection is implied by the context, as well as by the link with II Chron. 2.17 [MT 16]: 'Solomon took a census of all the aliens who were in the land of Israel'. Two small changes in the present version may reflect a certain moderation in the Chronicler's view of the matter. Instead of 'their descendants' (I Kings 9.20), the text has 'from their descendants', implying a more partial levy from among the non-Israelites. The replacement of 'were unable to destroy utterly' by the somewhat more neutral 'had not destroyed' avoids the extreme verb *lᵉhaḥᵃrīmām*.

The note 'so they are to this day' has nothing to do with the Chronicler's time, but is copied from his source in Kings; the chronological reference remains unspecified.

[9] The apologetic tone of this verse is obvious, as it was already in I Kings 9.22: 'Solomon made a forced levy of slaves ... But of the people of Israel Solomon made no slaves ...'. The reason for this remark is to be found in explicit references in the history of Solomon to 'a levy of forced labour out of all Israel' (I Kings 5.13 [MT 27]), and 'forced labour of the house of Joseph' employed in the building of the Millo (I Kings 11.28). Alleviation of this burden is the sole demand made of Rehoboam by the Israelite delegation (I Kings 12.4//II Chron. 10.4). In view of these data, I Kings 9.22 presents a rather unhistorical, idealistic picture of Solomon's rule.

In the Chronicles version, however, the same information stands in less tension with the general context. The Chronicler has systematically omitted all references to the forced levy of Israelites; twice it is stated that David and Solomon recruited 'aliens' for the building projects (I Chron. 22.2; II Chron. 2.17–18). Only the notice from Jeroboam's time is retained (II Chron. 10.4), and in isolation seems less explicitly to refer to slave labour. The development of the apologetic process may thus be traced in the historiography of Solomon's reign:

(a) Historical fact with no apologetic twist, reflected in I Kings 5.13–14 [MT 27–28]; 9.20–21; and 11.27–28: Israelites, as well as aliens, are recruited for forced labour.

(b) Apologetic remark in I Kings 9.22: only non-Israelites were enslaved; Israelites had only administrative tasks.

(c) The Chronicler's reformulation of the entire historical narrative on the basis of the apologetic point of view: all notes regarding Israelite forced labour are omitted, and the recruiting of 'aliens' for the various tasks is elaborated. There is no contradiction between this verse and the narrative as a whole.

[10] I Kings 9.23, from which this verse is taken, reads like a heading for a new sequence, but this does not follow. This impression is faithfully reproduced in Chronicles as well.

Who are the 'chief officers' of this verse? The Hebrew text in I Kings 9.23 has *śārē hanniṣṣābīm* and here, as everywhere in Chronicles, *śārē hanᵉṣībīm* (*Kethib*). According to I Kings 4.5, 7 'Solomon had twelve officers' (*niṣṣābīm*) appointed to authority over the districts of Israel and responsible for the monthly maintenance of the court. The reference here, however, is to a different group, whose task is described as having 'charge of the people who carried on the work', and their numbers vary from 3300 in I Kings 5.16 [MT 5.30] to 250 in I Kings 9.23 and 550 here. Since *niṣṣāb* itself means 'officer, someone who is in charge' (cf. Ruth 2.5, 6, Baumgartner, 675), *śārē hanniṣṣābīm* may either mean 'those in charge of the officers' (i.e. 'chief officers') or be an apposition: 'the officers, that is, those in charge' (Gesenius, §131, 423ff.). The numerical discrepancy in the passage is probably due to textual corruption, in either of the two texts.

[11] Verse 11a paraphrases I Kings 9.24, to which 11b is added. Solomon's marriage to the daughter of Pharaoh is referred to in the narrative of Kings four times (I Kings 3.1; 9.16, 24; 11.1) as a special indication of Solomon's greatness. In the same way, the queen's special residence distinguishes her among all Solomon's wives; the emphasis is heightened by the reference to her temporary domicile (I Kings 3.1), followed in 9.24 by her entry to permanent residence in her palace.

In Chronicles, this whole matter undergoes a thorough editing (for the revision of the Septuagint, cf. D. W. Gooding, 'The Septuagint's Version of Solomon's Misconduct', *VT* 15, 1965, 325–31). Of all the references to the daughter of Pharaoh, only that of I Kings 9.24 is retained. For the Chronicler, however, her removal to a special house is not a sign of privilege; on the contrary, it indicates reservations about the propriety of her very presence in the city of David. The reasoning of this passage is interesting in several ways.

The MT of the verse (followed by RSV) reads 'my wife shall not live in the house of David', the reason given being that David's abode had been sanctified by the ark's presence. This, however, is contrary to all other sources, none or which make any connection between 'the house of David' and 'the tent of the ark' (II Sam. 6.17; I Kings 3.15; I Chron. 15.1). Commentators therefore tend to prefer the LXX reading 'my wife shall not live in the *city* of David' (cf. Curtis, 353). However, this rendering, too, is problematical. If the queen's living in proximity to the ark in the city of David constituted a transgression, why is this never mentioned in reference to Solomon's initial decision to bring her 'into the city of David until he had finished building his own house ...' (I Kings 3.1)? The rationale given in this verse is also difficult. It is not human residence in a holy precinct *per se*, nor the fact that the queen is a foreigner, which prohibits her dwelling within a certain proximity to the ark, but an implication of impurity, specific to her *as a woman*. This view is not expressed elsewhere in the Bible; it seems, however, that a similar concept is found in the instructions of the sectarian (Essene) literature of which this verse may be regarded as an early precursor (cf. in particular the laconic injunction of the Damascus Covenant 12.1–2: 'No man shall lie with a woman in the city of the Sanctuary, to defile the city of the Sanctuary', Temple Scroll LXV, 11–12 and XLVII, and Y. Yadin, *The Temple Scroll*, I, 1983, 288, 306–7; S. Japhet, 'The Prohibition of the Habitation of Women', *Festschrift Y. Muffs* [forthcoming].

The issue of Solomon's wives is also presented differently in Chronicles. According to I Kings 11.1–3 Solomon had 'seven hundred wives ... and three hundred concubines', many of whom were Moabite, Ammonite, Edomite, etc. As Chronicles omits I Kings 11 entirely, the actual information repeated in Chronicles concerns only two wives, the daughter of Pharaoh and Naamah the Ammonitess, Rehoboam's mother (II Chron. 12.3). Solomon, then, according to Chronicles, had fewer wives than either his father (I Chron. 3.1–6) or his son (II Chron. 11.21).

[12–16] Following the Chronicler's characteristic method, I Kings 9.25 is here greatly elaborated. The new passage deals with the final inauguration of the Temple through the establishment of the regular ritual.

I Kings 9.25 can in several ways be defined as a 'literary torso', without a normal structural context. It disrupts the otherwise smooth narrative of the chapter, and its topic – Solomon's seasonal offerings together with their indicated incense, and the completion of the Temple – belongs elsewhere.

The Chronicler approaches this passage with a mixture of freedom and servile fidelity. On one hand, he does not transfer the passage to a more logical position after II Chron. 7.22, nor does he completely rephrase it. He does, however, greatly elaborate it and changes the topic, and makes it a standard description of the regular Temple worship, a definitive stage in the history of the cult.

We have noted in the context of the transfer of the ark to Jerusalem that the regular cult was conducted in two centres: the musical liturgies in the tent of the ark in Jerusalem (I Chron. 16.4–7, 37–38), and the full worship at 'the tabernacle' in Gibeon (39–42). Solomon's plans for the Temple, as outlined in his letter to Hiram (II Chron. 3.3), were orientated on the sacrificial cult; the present passage provides a sort of counterpart to those plans, as Solomon establishes the observances he envisaged. This text in fact provides more details of the cultic system than 2.3, as it includes the division of functions between the clerical orders. Here, then is a culmination and consolidation of all David's earlier preparations (I Chron. 23–26).

[12] In Chronicles, the new cultic beginning is emphasized with the words 'Then Solomon offered' in place of 'Solomon used to offer' (cf. also v. 17 with I Kings 9.26). The reference here is not to the thrice-yearly offerings of I Kings 9.25, but first to a single sacrifice making the final dedication of the Temple (v. 12). The daily and festal rituals, at their appointed times, are dealt with separately (v. 13). Verse 12 should conclude, then, not with a comma but with a full-stop.

The verse also adds the words 'before the vestibule' to the description of the altar. As 'vestibule' ('ūlām) is used by the Chronicler as a synecdoche for the Temple, this is just a reference to the exact position of the altar 'before the house' (cf. also II Kings 16.14).

[13] The full sacrificial cult consists of; 1. the regular daily sacrifice ('the duty of each day'), and 2. the additional sacrifices for the Sabbaths, the New Moons and the three pilgrim festivals. This distinction is obscured in RSV, which does not take into account that $l^e ha^{\,(a}l\bar{o}t$ should be interpreted as a conjugated verb (cf. JPS), and 'for the sabbaths' be preceded by a copulative waw: 'and for the sabbaths', etc. Although the matter is completely standardized, the wording of this passage nevertheless differs from that of II Chron. 2.3 – another indication of the Chronicler's stylistic inclination to variegated expression and presentation.

The terminology of this verse is basically Priestly (cf. Lev. 23.17 and Ezek. 45.17); the full scope of the arrangements, however, is concisely referred to only in Neh. 10.33 [MT 34]. The final clause 'the three annual feasts – the feast of unleavened bread, the feast of weeks and the feast of tabernacles' is a quotation from the commandment of Deut. 16.16 (cf. Curtis, 356). The verse is thus a combination of Priestly and Deuteronomistic terminology, focussing on the sacrificial cult, and probably reflecting the actual circumstances of the Second Temple.

[14–15] Concurrently, the clergy are installed according to their orders and divisions. I have already mentioned that the systematic account of this aspect of the cult is entirely an innovation of Chronicles: in the Deuteronomistic historiography matters relating to the clergy are always a footnote to some other topic (cf. Japhet, *Ideology*, 224–5). The Chronicler devoted a great deal of attention to this subject in the context of David's preparations; now he records the realization of those plans.

There is a double reference to the Davidic authority of the organization of the clergy: 'According to the ordinance of David his father he appointed the divisions ... for so David the man of God had commanded.' It is a juxtaposition of 'the command of David' with 'the command of Moses' of v. 13 (a similarity blurred by the translations) which embodies the Chronicler's distinct view of the development of the cult (see also S. de Vries, 'Moses and David as Cult Founders in Chronicles', *JBL* 107, 1988, 619–39). While the full sacrificial system – the most ancient element in the Israelite ritual – is the 'command of Moses', the administrative aspects, like the differentiation of the levitical order into sub-orders of Levites, singers and gatekeepers, the initiation of the liturgical song, and the organization of the clergy by divisions, are all 'the command of David'. This differentiation between the clerical orders and its attribution to David are also partially visible in Ezra-Nehemiah (Ezra 8.20; Neh. 12.24, 36, 45–46). It is probably the end-result of a long process of the legitimization of Second Temple institutions, guided by a historical assumption, that with the transition to a solidly established lifestyle with the consolidation of the monarchy and the building of the Temple, new and more complex arrangements were needed for the management of the national cult. These are attributed to David; in fact, 'the command of David' may be an invocation of legitimacy for prolonged historical processes during the First and Second Temple periods.

It should be noted that the term *miṣwāh* (command, commandment) is repeated three times in vv. 13–15, corresponding to the three authorities which the Chronicler recognizes for any cultic ordinance (cf. Japhet, *Ideology*, 234–9); Moses, as the authority for the sacrificial system; David, responsible for clerical reorganization and the introduction of liturgical music; and the reigning king, as *ad hoc* authority in situations requiring intervention, most notably in the times of Hezekiah and Josiah. Here, at the most relevant point, when the regular ritual is established in the Temple for generations to come, all the three are mentioned together.

David is here called 'the man of God', as also in Neh.12.24, 36. This is also Moses' title in I Chron. 23.14; II Chron. 30.16 and Ezra 3.2. The appellation is not very common in Chronicles; it appears elsewhere only for Shemaiah (II

Chron. 11.2//I Kings 12.22) and one anonymous prophet of the time of
Amaziah (II Chron. 25.7, 9). For David, the concept is supported by his place
among the prophets in II Chron. 29.25 (cf. also J. D. Newsome, 'Toward a
New Understanding of the Chronicler and His Purposes', *JBL* 94, 1975,
203–4; differently, D. L. Petersen, 'The Role of Israel's Prophets', *JSOTS*
17, 1981, 40–51, for David, 41, 43).

The details of the cult arrangements are as follows: the clergy – in their
three orders of priests, Levites and gatekeepers – are positioned by their
'divisions', that is, according to their shifts. For the priests, the general term
'service' (*ᵃbōdāh*) describes their functions; for the Levites 'praise' (*lᵉhallēl*)
and 'ministry (*lᵉšārēt*) before the priests' – i.e. Temple music and practical
assistance, referring respectively to the 'singers' and 'Levites' (in the more
restricted sense). Last mentioned are the gatekeepers, responsible 'for each
gate'. Verse 15 concludes with the declaration that whatever Solomon
decreed was faithfully done, and also reminds us of the fourth responsibility
of the Levites as viewed in I Chron. 26.20ff.: 'the treasuries'.

[16] Resuming the narrative sequence of I Kings 9.25b, this verse is a
ceremonial conclusion of Solomon's work on the Temple: all has now been
accomplished, from the foundations to the finishing. The term carefully
chosen for Solomon's projects is *mᵉl'ākāh* (= work, cf. v. 9), phonetically near
malkūt, kingdom. The result is a clear echo of David's blessing in I Chron.
28.20: 'the Lord ... is with you ... until all the work for the service of the
house of the Lord is finished (*likᵉlōt kol mᵉle'ket ᵃbōdat bēt-yhwh*)', but also a
variant repetition of I Kings 2.12. *wattikkōn kol mᵉle'ket šᵉlōmōh* echoes
wattikkōn malkutō mᵉ'ōd: 'and his kingdom was firmly established'.

[17–18] The chapter ends with Solomon's expedition to Ophir. These
verses are parallel to I Kings 9.26–28, and have the same general message:
Solomon, with Hiram's help, imported great quantities of Ophir gold. The
exact wording of the Kings text is, however, slightly, sometimes minutely,
changed throughout the passage, resulting in a different view of the matter in
some major points. In Kings (9.26–28), the course of events is as follows:
Solomon built a fleet of ships at his Red Sea port (v. 26); Hiram sent him
'seamen who were familiar with the sea', and together with Solomon's
servants they sailed to Ophir and returned with gold. All of this seems very
plausible. The Tyrians, Hiram's 'servants', were experts in seamanship, a
profession in which the Judaeans could boast no proficiency. On the other
hand, Solomon had the actual control of the easiest route to Africa *via* the
important port of Ezion-geber. Mutual co-operation would be in the best
interests of both sides.

In Chronicles the matter is differently conceived. Solomon repairs his port
at Ezion-geber, but does not build a fleet there; Huram provides not only
expert seamen, but also the vessels themselves. This change has an evident

purpose: what was a joint operation of two equal rulers (with even some superiority credited to Huram) is now portrayed as an enterprise in which a fully subordinate Huram provides everything for Solomon. The same tendency to suppress Huram's independent position may be traced in all other instances in which the matter is brought up. Thus:

(*a*) I Kings 10.11: '*the fleet of Hiram* which brought gold from Ophir ...'
   II Chron. 9.10: '*the servants of Huram and the servants of Solomon*, who brought gold from Ophir ...'
   (*b*) I Kings 10.22: 'For the king had a fleet of ships of Tarshish at sea, *with the fleet of Hiram*'
   II Chron. 9.21: 'For the king's ships went to Tarshish *with the servants of Huram* ...'.

To what extent was the Chronicler aware of the practical ramifications of this ideological change? If the ships for the expedition were sent by Huram from Tyre, did the Chronicler envisage them voyaging around Africa to reach the Red Sea port at Eloth, or did he imagine an overland transport of the vessels? Did he have a different idea of the locations of 'Ezion-geber' and 'Eloth'? As in the case of the 'twenty cities' exchanged between Solomon and Huram, it seems that here it is not the actual circumstances which were significant to the Chronicler, but the light which the episode sheds on the relationship between the two states and their monarchs.

9   Now when the queen of Sheba heard of the fame of Solomon she came to Jerusalem to test him with hard questions, having a very great retinue and camels bearing spices and very much gold and precious stones. When she came to Solomon, she told him all that was on her mind. [2] And Solomon answered all her questions; there was nothing hidden from Solomon which he could not explain to her. [3] And when the queen of Sheba had seen the wisdom of Solomon, the house that he had built, [4] the food of his table, the seating of his officials, and the attendance of his servants, and their clothing, his cupbearers, and their clothing, and his burnt offerings which he offered at the house of the Lord, there was no more spirit in her.

5 And she said to the king, 'The report was true which I heard in my own land of your affairs and of your wisdom, [6] but I did not believe the reports until I came and my own eyes had seen it; and behold, half the greatness of your wisdom was not told me; you surpass the report which I heard. [7] Happy are your wives! Happy are these your servants, who continually stand before you and hear your wisdom! [8] Blessed be the Lord your God, who has delighted in you and set you on his throne as king for the Lord your God! Because your God loved Israel and would establish them for ever, he has made you king over them, that you may execute justice and righteousness.' [9] Then she gave the king a hundred and twenty talents of gold, and a very great quantity of spices, and precious stones: there were no spices such as those which the queen of Sheba gave to King Solomon.

10 Moreover the servants of Huram and the servants of Solomon, who brought gold from Ophir, brought algum wood and precious stones. [11] And the king made of the algum wood steps for the house of the Lord and for the king's house, lyres also and harps for the singers; there never was seen the like of them before in the land of Judah.

12 And King Solomon gave to the queen of Sheba all that she desired, whatever she asked besides what she had brought to the king. So she turned and went back to her own land, with her servants.

13 Now the weight of gold that came to Solomon in one year was six hundred and sixty-six talents of gold, [14] besides that which the traders and merchants brought and all the kings of Arabia and the governors of the land brought gold and silver to Solomon. [15] King Solomon made two hundred large shields of beaten gold; six hundred shekels of beaten gold went into each shield. [16] And he made three hundred shields of beaten gold; three hundred shekels of gold went into each shield; and the king put them in the House of the Forest of Lebanon. [17] The king also made a great ivory throne, and overlaid it with pure gold. [18] The throne had six steps and a footstool of gold, which were attached to the throne, and on each side of the seat were arm rests and two lions standing beside the arm rests, [19] while twelve lions stood there, one on each end of a step on the six steps. The like of it was never made in any kingdom. [20] All King Solomon's drinking vessels were of gold, and all the vessels of the House of the Forest of Lebanon were of pure gold; silver was not considered as

anything in the days of Solomon. [21] For the king's ships went to Tarshish with the servants of Huram; once every three years the ships of Tarshish used to come bringing gold, silver, ivory, apes, and peacocks.

22 Thus King Solomon excelled all the kings of the earth in riches and in wisdom. [23] And all the kings of the earth sought the presence of Solomon to hear his wisdom, which God had put into his mind. [24] Every one of them brought his present, articles of silver and of gold, garments, myrrh, spices, horses, and mules, so much year by year. [25] And Solomon had four thousand stalls for horses and chariots, and twelve thousand horsemen, whom he stationed in the chariot cities and with the king in Jerusalem. [26] And he ruled over all the kings from the Euphrates to the land of the Philistines, and to the border of Egypt. [27] And the king made silver as common in Jerusalem as stone, and cedar as plentiful as the sycamore of the Shephelah. [28] And horses were imported for Solomon from Egypt and from all lands.

29 Now the rest of the acts of Solomon, from first to last, are they not written in the history of Nathan the prophet, and in the prophecy of Ahijah the Shilonite, and in the visions of Iddo the seer concerning Jeroboam the son of Nebat? [30] Solomon reigned in Jerusalem over all Israel forty years. [31] And Solomon slept with his fathers, and was buried in the city of David his father; and Rehoboam his son reigned in his stead.

A. Notes to MT

[4] ומלבושיהם, omit one occurrence, absent in I Kings 10.5; ועליתו, I Kings 10.5 ועלתו, proposed ועלותו; [11] מסלות, I Kings 10.12 מסעד; [12] מלבד אשר הביאה אל המלך, I Kings 10.13 מלבד אשר נתן לה כיד המלך שלמה, Targum מלבד אשר נתן לה תחת אשר הביאה אל המלד; [14] התרים difficult, already in I Kings 10.15, proposed התגרים or הערים; [18] וכבש, MSS וכבס; בוהב וכבש, transfer after מאחזים.

B. Notes to RSV

[4] 'his burnt offerings', MT differently (cf. above A and commentary); [6] 'the report', thus I Kings 10.7; MT 'their report' (דבריהם); [16] 'shekels', not in MT; [18] 'footstool', MT כבש = 'ascent, grade, landing bridge', cf. commentary; [29] 'from first to last', JPS 'early and late.'

C. Structure, sources and form

1. In ch. 9, the last chapter in Solomon's history, the Chronicler draws from his source in Kings: vv. 1–24 are appropriated from I Kings 10.1–25 practically unaltered; vv. 25–28 are based on I Kings 10.26–29 with both omissions and additions; and vv. 29–31 parallel I Kings 11.41–43. The whole is thus a fairly faithful reproduction of the Deuteronomistic source, the main difference being the omission of I Kings 11.1–40 – the summary of all the negative aspects of Solomon's reign, which the Deuteronomistic author presented at the end of his narrative.

The inclination to glorify Solomon, praising his greatness, splendour, wisdom, etc., is characteristic of Solomon's history in I Kings. The reprehensible aspects of his reign are limited to two focal points, the circumstances of his accession and early rule (I Kings 1–2) and the transgressions and grievances assembled in I Kings 11, both pericopes drawing most probably on sources other than 'the book of the acts of Solomon' (cf. J. Gray, *I and II Kings*, 1970, 14ff., 25). The specific structure of his source makes the Chronicler's task of adaptation especially easy: he replaces I Kings 1–2 with his own account of Solomon's accession (I Chron. 29), and omits I Kings 11.1–40 altogether; what remains of Solomon's history is well suited to the Chronicler's own views.

In Chronicles, the omission of negative aspects of a king's reign characterizes only the histories of David and Solomon, and is most thoroughly applied for the latter. After the two blocks of I Kings 1–2 and 11.1–40 have been deleted, not a single defect can be found in Solomon; even the mildest implications of disapproval have been excised. For all other kings of Judah, the Chronicler not only cites negative aspects in full, but at times augments them, going beyond his source in the Deuteronomistic historiography.

2. The literary structure of ch. 9 is as follows:

(*a*) 1–12 The visit of the queen of Sheba
(*b*) 13–28 Solomon's wealth, wisdom and international fame
(*c*) 29–32 Conclusion of Solomon's reign

The first section is a continuous narrative, the obvious sequence of vv. 9 and 12 interrupted by vv. 10–11 – a misplacement already evident in I Kings 10.11–12. The second section is a collection of shorter miscellaneous passages, showing some signs of literary structuring, and unified by the tendency to laud Solomon's unusual achievements. Finally, the summary of Solomon's reign is a somewhat rephrased version of the Deuteronomistic framework of I Kings 11.41–43.

3. The regal visit described in vv. 1–12 has a fine symmetrical structure, its axis in vv. 5–8 being the queen's speech. Because of some light changes in v. 1, the literary distinction between the proposition (I Kings 10.1) and the first scene (I Kings 10.2–3) is lost; other than that, the narrative structure is unchanged, its paragraphs marked by new allusions to the 'queen of Sheba':

(a) 1–2 The queen comes to Jerusalem for an interview with Solomon
(b) 3–4 The queen views the grandeur of Solomon's court
(c) 5–8 The queen's address
(d) 9, 12 Exchange of gifts and departure

Although the theme of the story is Solomon's wisdom and fame, the literary protagonist is the queen, whose movements open and conclude the story, and who is the subject of most of the verbs: 'the queen heard ... she came ... when she came... she told', etc. Solomon is the subject of only two clauses, the content or form of which display their secondary nature: a response to the queen (v. 2), and the reciprocation of the queen's gifts (v. 12). In the latter phrase Solomon's action is presented in a parenthetic clause: ותהפך ותלך ... והמלך שלמה נתן ... והמלך למלך ויתתן (the fine syntax is lost in the translation). Moreover, in spite of the reference to Solomon's perspicacity (v. 2), it is the queen alone whose words are actually quoted, and generously so. Solomon is certainly the object of this wisdom tale, but he is merely a secondary figure in the story.

4. The second part of the chapter exhibits some signs of organization, especially inclusion, but its unity is achieved by its theme rather than by its structure:

(i) 13–21 Gold and curiosities in Solomon's possession:
    13–14 ——— the yearly income
     15–16 ——— implements made of gold
      17–19 ——— the throne
    20 ———vessels of gold
    21 ———sources of wealth
(ii) 22–24 Solomon's international status and its economic implications
(iii) 25–28 Miscellaneous information:
    25 ——— horses and chariots
    26 ——— extent of Solomon's kingdom
    27 ——— affluence
    28 ——— importing horses

5. I Kings 10 is also marked by its style, preserved here in vv. 1–28. The narrative is peppered with exclamatory statements, often phrased in a rhetorical negative: 'there was nothing hidden from Solomon' (v. 2); 'there was no more spirit in her' (v. 4), 'half the greatness ... was not told me' (v. 6); 'there were no spices such as those' (v. 9); 'there never was seen the like' (v. 11); 'silver was not considered as anything' (v. 20).

D. Commentary

[1–12] Two of Solomon's international contacts are described in I Kings in great detail: Hiram of Tyre to the north, and the queen of Sheba to the south. The first is referred to several times, in the context of a long-term treaty with far-reaching consequences for the economy and politics of the two states. Nevertheless, no visit of Hiram to Jerusalem is documented. On the other hand, the contact with the queen of Sheba, described as a one-time event, bears a more personal and direct character.

The record of the queen's visit has a literary, even popular tone; while Solomon's wisdom, wealth and international status are praised, no attention is paid to the political aspects which might interest the historian. It is small wonder that this story has attracted all kinds of Aggadic supplements.

In the Chronistic framework, the episode takes on new significance. As several examples of Solomon's wisdom were not repeated in Chronicles (I Kings 3.16–28; 4.29–34 [MT 5.9–14]), the present story and its supplements constitute a major demonstration of Solomon's political and economic sagacity.

[1–2] The motive proposed by the narrator for the royal visit is the fame of Solomon's wisdom; this is affirmed in the queen's own words (vv. 5–6). This may then be regarded as one example of the more general phenomenon alluded to in v. 23: 'And all the kings of the earth sought the presence of

Solomon to hear his wisdom' (cf. I Kings 10.24, also 4.34 [MT 5.14]). So also for the precious gifts (v. 9) which accompany the royal visit: 'Every one of them brought his present, articles of silver and of gold, garments, myrrh, spices, horses and mules' (v. 24 = I Kings 10.25). This story is thus one detailed, literary elaboration of what the historiographer regarded as a constant of Solomon's reign: royal visits, motivated by the wish to enjoy Solomon's wisdom, and accompanied by precious, extraordinary gifts. This particular visit probably fired the imagination of the narrator because of its esoteric features.

Two unusual features distinguish the queen's gifts: they are carried by camels, and they include, in addition to gold and precious stones, large amounts of spices which prompt the narrator to take special note: 'there were no spices such as those which the queen of Sheba gave to King Solomon' (v. 9).

In v. 2, the nearly omniscient quality of Solomon's responses is emphasized with excitement by the author through positive and negative rhetorical expressions: 'Solomon answered all her questions, there was nothing hidden … which he could not explain to her.'

These verses seem to provide a good example of one of the Chronicler's stylistic inclinations. In I Kings 10.1–2 the fact that 'the queen of Sheba came' is repeated three times with gradual specification and slight nuance of meaning: 'Now when the queen of Sheba heard … *she came* to test him with hard questions' (v. 1); this general proposition is followed by two stages of the actual journey: '*she came* to Jerusalem … and when *she came* to Solomon she told him all that was on her mind' (v. 2). The Chronicler, inclined to be more concise but reluctant to make needless changes, omits only one 'she came', with the result that vv. 1–2 form a single action sequence: 'when the queen … heard … she came to Jerusalem to test him', etc. While there are several other features revealing the Chronicler's hand, the general style is that of his source.

[3–4] What the queen saw in Jerusalem, and the impression it made, are described in great detail. Foremost was the unusual grandeur of Solomon's court, conceived not as an indication of mere material wealth but rather as a sign of Solomon's wisdom: 'the queen … had seen the wisdom of Solomon …' It is to this quality that she refers in her admiring words: 'The report was true … of your affairs and of your wisdom … and behold, half the greatness of your wisdom was not told me; you surpass the report' (vv. 5–6). This is indeed the concept traditionally held in the circles of ancient sages: practical skills of speech, wit, craftsmanship and statesmanship – all these are 'wisdom' (cf. G. v. Rad, *Old Testament Theology* I, 1963, 429–37). The queen's reaction is expressed in a strong metaphor: 'there was no more spirit in her', a phrase which appears once more, in Josh. 5.1, describing the reaction of the local Canaanite and Amorite kings to the miracle of the Jordan: 'their heart melted, and there was no longer any spirit in them'. This is an amazement which may inspire either fear or supreme respect.

In biblical Hebrew the word '*ᵃliyyāh* always denotes 'an upper room' (Baumgartner, 787), which in this context makes no sense and probably prompted RSV's translation, adopted from the parallel text in I Kings 10.5: 'his burnt offerings which he offered'. It is possible, however, that the word is already used in its later, rabbinic connotation meaning 'going up', or that it is a scribal error for the infinitive (*ᵃlōtō*) having the same meaning. This is probably the rationale of JPS, which reads: 'the procession with which he went up to the House of the Lord' (cf. also NEB).

[5–8] The queen's address, phrased in the best courtly tradition, is the focus of the story; it is taken from I Kings 10.6–9, with only light alterations, and more significant changes are introduced in v. 8, reflecting the Chronicler's own view of certain issues. The address develops in three stages: the queen's wonder at the surpassing wisdom of Solomon, her blessing on the king's fortunate household, and her praise of the God of Israel who has favoured his people with such a worthy monarch. The *Leitmotif* 'wisdom' is likewise repeated three times.

In v. 7, some commentators (and thus RSV) propose to follow LXX^L and some of the Versions of I Kings 10.8, reading 'your wives' (*nāšēkā*) for MT 'your men' (*ᵃnāšēkā*, cf. Curtis, 358). There seems to be no convincing justification for this correction. The queen's compliments are intended as from one ruler to another and not as a woman's admiration of domestic success; the diplomatic context and courtly style do not warrant personal references. It would seem that the reading 'wives' already reflects later homiletic elaborations on the story.

In v. 8, in place of 'and set you on the throne of Israel', the Chronicler reads: 'and set you on his [the Lord's] throne as king for the Lord your God'. This change expresses the alternative motives, negative and positive, of redaction: a tendency to avoid certain phrases and ideas on one hand, and on the other hand to transform the borrowed text into a vehicle for the writer's own views. 'The throne of Israel', which appears in the Chronicler's sources five times (I Kings 2.4; 8.20, 25; 9.5; 10.9), is repeated only twice in Chronicles (II Chron. 6.10, 16; for II Chron. 7.18, cf. there); nowhere is the phrase introduced by the Chronicler on his own initiative. By contrast, 'the throne of the Lord' as an expression for rule over Israel is peculiar to Chronicles, and is repeated five times (cf. in more detail on I Chron. 29.23–25).

A less significant change in the same v. 8 is the addition of 'and would establish them' (*lᵉhaᵃmīdō*). This *hiphil* conjugation of '*md* is a favourite element of the Chronicler's vocabulary (cf. Curtis, 32); its introduction here entails a certain shift of meaning. It is for the purpose of establishing his people for ever that the Lord has provided them with a monarch endowed with 'justice and righteousness'. That the reign of Solomon is a sign of God's love for Israel is a view more emphasized in Chronicles than in Kings. It appears in the Chronicler's version of Hiram's letter to Solomon (II Chron. 2.11), thus creating a neat literary framework, highlighting this theme at the beginning and end of Solomon's reign, in the words of the two foreign rulers with whom he had special contacts.

The pursuit of 'justice and righteousness' (JPS 'righteous justice') is a moral ideal, the same 'way of the Lord' which Abraham would require his descendants to follow (Gen. 18.19), and the characteristic feature of Josiah, the ideal king (Jer. 22.15), and the future scion of David (Jer. 23.5; 22.15). In the historiographical literature only two kings are honoured with this attribute: David (II Sam. 8.15//1 Chron. 18.14, RSV 'justice and equity') and Solomon in this verse. One may of course attribute its absence for the other kings to the literary idiom of Deuteronomistic vocabulary which has other phrases for describing righteous rulers, e.g. 'he did what was right in the eyes of the Lord' (II Kings 18.3, etc.), while the evaluations of David and Solomon are of a non-Deuteronomistic origin. We have noted several times the Chronicler's tendency to make David and Solomon equals, and see their joint reigns as the climax of Israelite history. This is expressed to some extent in earlier historiography, by the characterization of their reigns as periods of 'justice and righteousness' (for an institutional interpretation of the phrase, cf. M. Weinfeld, *Deuteronomy and the Deuteronomic School*, 1972, 153–7; and recently, id., *Justice and Righteousness in Israel and the Nations*, 1985*).

[9, 12] The visit ends with an exchange of gifts. The queen presents Solomon with a great amount of gold (equivalent to the amount obtained from Hiram according to I Kings 9.14, not transmitted by the Chronicler in that context), precious stones, and 'a very great quantity of spices', the like of which was never before seen. Following I Kings 10.13, Solomon's gifts are described, very generally, as a response to the queen's requests: he gave her 'all that she desired'. In principle, the narrator's approach here is the same as with the theme of Solomon's wisdom: while the queen's words are actually cited, Solomon is merely said to have 'answered all her questions' (v. 2).

The king's extraordinary generosity is stressed in I Kings 10.13: 'all that she desired, whatever she asked, *besides* what was given her by the bounty of King Solomon'. In Chronicles, only the first part is reproduced, while the second is rephrased: 'besides what she had brought to the king'. In this construct, 'besides' makes absolutely no sense; we can only assume either that the Chronicler was so anxious to describe Solomon as the recipient rather than the donor that he mechanically reversed the sentence without regard for the syntax, or that the text is corrupt. The Targum contains a few more words, which might easily have been omitted from an original text due to homoioteleuton: *mill⁽ᵉ⁾bad* [*ᵃšer nātan lōh taḥat*] *ᵃšer hēbîʾāh*: 'besides [what he gave her freely in return for] what she had brought ...' (cf. also Rudolph, 222).

In a tidy dénouement, the story ends with the remark that the queen 'turned and went back to her own land'.

[10–11] These verses are an obvious interpolation, interrupting the natural sequence between vv. 9 and 12; their more appropriate place was probably after v. 21. Whatever the cause of the textual corruption, it was evidently already found in the Chronicler's *Vorlage*, which he faithfully followed.

There is no doubt that the joint expeditions of Huram and Solomon excited the imagination of Solomon's chronicler, who refers to these episodes, as if with special delight, three times (I Kings 9.27; 10.11, 22; II Chron. 8.18; 9.10–11, 21). Although the main object of these journeys was evidently gold, other exotica are also mentioned; here precious stones and algum wood, and in v. 21 silver, ivory, apes and peacocks (or baboons, RSV).

We have noted how the Chronicler rephrased the description of Solomon's expedition with Huram (cf. on 8.17–18). Here, too, it is not his fleet which fetched gold from Ophir, but 'the servants of Huram and the servants of Solomon'. The 'algum wood' was used to fashion unprecedented musical instruments and other objects. The same wood has already been mentioned in II Chron. 2.8 [MT 7], undoubtedly under the influence of this text, and appears in the form 'almug' in the parallel of I Kings 10.11–12. As the use of transliteration in the translations indicates, it is not clear what sort of wood is meant; the 'almug' shipments were indeed a one-time marvel; both name and origin were foreign (cf. J. Greenfield and M. Mayrhoffer, 'Algummin-Almuggim', *VTS* 16, 1967, 83–9).

Verse 11 mentions 'steps (*m⁽ᵉ⁾sillōt*) for the house of the Lord and for the king's house'. *m⁽ᵉ⁾sillāh* usually means 'road' or 'way' (cf. Baumgartner, 573); the precise connotation here is unclear. The interpretation of the term as 'gateway' in all three Chronistic occurences (also I Chron. 26.16, 18) was suggested by D. Dorsey, 'Another Peculiar Term in the Book of Chronicles: מסלה "Highway"?', *JQR* 75, 1984–5, 385–90 and followed by Dillard, 70.

The enthusiasm of Solomon's historiographer is moderated somewhat by the Chronicler's more sober expression 'there never was seen the like of them before in the land of Judah'.

[13–28] The general topic of this section is Solomon's superlative wealth and fame. The unifying key-word is 'gold', repeated thirteen times; even silver, which 'was not considered as anything' (v. 20), is mentioned four times. Again and again the incomparable quality of Solomon's acquisitions is emphasized: the spices of the queen of Sheba (v. 9), the algum wood (v. 11), the throne (v. 19); likewise, objects elsewhere considered precious, like silver and cedar (v. 20, 27) are comparatively common here.

A summary inventory of the chapter contains, then, the following items:

1. spices, gold and precious stones (v. 1)
2. 120 talents of gold plus spices and precious stones (v. 9)
3. gold from Ophir (v. 10)
4. algum wood and precious stones (v. 10)
5. 'steps', lyres and harps, made of algum wood (v. 11)
6. a yearly income of gold – 666 talents (v. 13)
7. gold and silver from Arabia (v. 14)
8. two hundred large shields of worked gold, and three hundred regular shields (v. 15)
9. an ivory throne, with steps, 'footstool' and lions (v. 17)
10. golden drinking vessels (v. 20)
11. golden vessels for the House of the Forest of Lebanon (v. 20)
12. gold and silver from Tarshish (v. 21)
13. ivory, apes and peacocks (baboons?, v. 21)
14. articles of silver and gold (v. 24)
15. yearly donations of garments, myrrh, spices, horses, mules (v. 24)
16. four thousand stalls for horses and chariots (v. 25)
17. twelve thousand horsemen (v. 25)
18. silver like stones and cedar like sycamore (v. 27)
19. horses imported from all lands (v. 28).

It was in fact superfluous for the author to note that 'King Solomon excelled all the kings of the earth in riches and in wisdom' (v. 22) when the bare enumeration of all this wealth and the untiring repetition of its origin is enough to create the desired impression. Nevertheless, such explicit elaborations also appear, both here and in the admiring words of the queen of Sheba (vv. 6–8).

While this chapter follows its source in I Kings 10 very closely, it nevertheless reflects an authentic feature of Chronistic theology. Great wealth is one sign of God's blessing. David dedicated his affluence to the building of the Temple (I Chron. 22.3–4, 14–16; 29.2–5) and thus died 'full of days, riches and honour' (I Chron. 29.28). Solomon's extreme wealth is therefore not only an indication of his wisdom, but also a concrete expression of divine favour and blessing. It is noteworthy that the only other king for whom the Chronicler gives details of riches is Hezekiah (II Chron. 32.27–29; on the similarity between Hezekiah and Solomon in Chronicles, cf. Williamson, *Israel in the Book of Chronicles*, 1977, 119–25); a very vague term, 'great riches and honour', is used for Jehoshaphat (II Chron. 17.5; 18.1).

[13–14] Repeating I Kings 10.14–15, this passage records Solomon's yearly income of gold – 666 talents. The meaning of the text in Kings is ambiguous: the yearly revenues are reported in v. 14, while v. 15 reads 'Besides (l^{e}bad) that which came from the traders and from the traffic of the merchants, and from all the kings of Arabia and the governors of the land'. Should the word l^{e}bad be rendered 'besides', referring to additional gold coming to Solomon indirectly from international trade conducted by others, or does it imply an 'exception' of gold which only passed through the land, not reaching Solomon's coffers? RSV in I Kings 10.15 counters this ambiguity by adding explicitly: 'besides that *which came from*, etc.' (NEB goes even further in this direction). This unequivocal understanding is also that of the Chronicler, who twice adds the verb 'brought' (m^{e}bī'īm) to the wording of his text. The more specific phrasing of Chronicles indicates that there are actually three sources of gold: the yearly income, the traders, and the kings of Arabia and the governors of the land.

[15–16] Here begins a list of unusual objects made or acquired by Solomon. The great weight of 200 larger and 300 smaller shields made of pure gold makes it doubtful that they were prepared as practical weapons; they were probably intended from the outset for court ceremonies and the king's personal guard. These shields are again referred to in I Kings 14.25–28 (II Chron. 12.9–11), where the story of Shishak's invasion is focussed on the plundering of the golden shields, and their replacement by bronze shields used by the guard whenever the king entered the house of the Lord.

Although the unit of weight is not given in MT, RSV is probably correct in reading six hundred *shekels* for each large shield and three hundred *shekels* for the smaller ones. The particular quality of gold is termed zāhāb šāḥūt (RSV 'beaten gold'), a term peculiar to this context and thus still obscure.

A description of the House of the Forest of Lebanon is not found in Chronicles, but in I Kings 7.2–5: an impressive structure 100 cubits in length, 50 cubits in width and 30 cubits in height. Its function, not indicated in the record of its building, is now specified in this text, i.e. an arsenal (cf. also Isa. 22.8, 'you looked to the weapons of the House of the Forest').

[17–19] The splendour of Solomon's ivory throne justly fired the imagination of later generations. In I Kings 10.18–20 the throne is very concretely portrayed as a kind of a high 'armchair' ('on each side of the seat were arm rests', I Kings 10.19). Six steps, each with two decorative lions, approached the seat itself, which formed a seventh stage and was also flanked by two lions – for the total of fourteen. The Hebrew text for I Kings 10.19 reads 'at the back of the chair was a round head' (rō'š 'āgōl). The last two words, however, are unanimously regarded as a scribal correction for 'calf's head' (rō'š 'ēgel, cf. LXX, and A. Geiger, *Urschrift und Übersetzungen der Bibel*, 1857, 343); the translations simply make the correction without further remark (cf. both RSV and NEB of I Kings 10.19). The throne itself is said to have been made of ivory plated with gold; since no special reference is made to the steps, it is likely that they were made of the same material.

While the Chronicler took no exception to the decorating of the throne with lions' images, he replaces 'at the back of the chair was a calf's head' with *m^ekebeš... lakkissē'. kebeš* does not recur in the Bible, but is very common in Rabbinic Hebrew and may have belonged to an earlier Hebrew vocabulary. The word means 'an ascent, landing bridge ... especially the inclined plane leading to the altar ...' (Jastrow, 611); often it appears together with or replacing 'steps' (cf. Mishna, *Middoth*, 3.3 etc). It would appear that Chronicles implies two different ways of approaching the throne: steps and an 'inclined ascent'.

Here again, the author can hardly contain his admiration for Solomon's unique throne: 'the like of it was never made in any kingdom' (v. 19).

[20] Next in the list of marvels are Solomon's drinking vessels and the unspecified 'vessels of the House of the Forest of Lebanon' – all made of gold.

[21] While the particle 'for' (*ki*) would seem to indicate that this verse is an explanation for v. 20, the subject of the periodic excursions to Tarshish for exotica is in fact an unrelated one. As in other mentions of these expeditions, the Chronicler introduces several changes: I Kings 10.22 twice has the designation 'a fleet of ships of Tarshish', referring to the type of vessel rather than the destination; the expeditions referred to there are probably the same as those mentioned before, following the route to Ophir. The Chronicler changes *'^onī* ('fleet of ships') to *'^oniyyōt* ('ships') and replaces 'the fleet of Hiram' with the 'servants' of Huram', ensuring that the expedition is Solomon's alone. Further, the generic designation 'ships of Tarshish' is changed to read 'the king's ships went to Tarshish', indicating that, while previous expeditions headed south through the Red Sea, those told of here have a destination in the western Mediterranean. Thus the Chronicler not only extends the political and territorial expansion of Solomon's realm northwards (II Chron. 8.1–4), but increases the scope of his maritime power in the west as well.

Since the ships of Tyre actually dominated the Mediterranean, Solomon may have broadened the terms of his agreement with Tyre to include the shipping on the Mediterranean coast. There is a historical plausibility to such a development, but whether the idea originates with the Chronicler's historiography, or also had a concrete factual basis, remains unclear (cf. also K. Galling, 'Der Weg der Phöniken nach Tarsis im literarische und archäologische Sicht', *ZDPV* 88, 1972, 1–18; 140–81; S. B. Hoenig, 'Tarshish', *JQR* 69, 1979, 181–2; M. Elat, 'Tarshish and the Problem of Phoenician Colonization in the Western Mediterranean', *Orientalia Louvaniensia Periodica* 137, 1982, 55–69).

The exotic curiosities imported in this context have names which do not appear elsewhere in the Bible: *šenhabbīm* for ivory, *qōpīm* for apes, and *tūkkīyyīm* for either peacocks or monkeys (Albright, *Archeology and the Religion of Israel*, Baltimore 1942, 212 n. 16).

[22–24] The author approaches Solomon's international prestige just as in the preceding passages, both glorifying the king and highlighting his material acquisitions. These verses may provide the framework for the story of the visit of the queen of Sheba, as one specific example illustrating what is described here as the general rule.

Are 'the kings of the earth' Solomon's subordinates in one way or another, or friendly rulers outside the orbit of his influence? The phrase 'Every one of them brought his present ... year by year' may indicate some regular obligation of allegiance. On the other hand, the example of the queen of Sheba suggests the autonomy of these other rulers; in this case, 'year by year' in v. 24 refers to Solomon's annual income rather than return visits of each individual king.

No precise political data can be extracted from these verses, as the effort to glorify Solomon has given them a vague and general tone. There are visits of all categories: single appearances like that of the queen of Sheba, envoys of subordinate rulers, and various diplomatic missions. On the whole, although our chapter focusses on Solomon's economic ventures, the present passage depicts his court as a centre of international diplomatic activity.

Among the gifts recorded here, there are a few new items: garments, myrrh, horses and mules. The word *nēšeq* (usually 'weapons') is taken here (as in LXX) to mean 'myrrh' or 'perfumes' (NEB), derived from a different root (cf. Baumgartner, 690).

While horses and chariots appear frequently in Solomon's history (cf. also on vv. 25ff.), this is the only place where mules are also mentioned. These are generally beasts of burden (Isa. 66.20; II Kings 5.17; Ezra 2.66, etc.); at least in the period referred to here they seem to have served as the royal mounts (cf. II Sam. 13.29; 18.9; I Kings 1.33, 34, 38, and Y. Yadin, *The Art of Warfare in Biblical Lands*, 1963, 287).

[25–28] The main source of this passage in I Kings 10.26–29 concludes there the topic of Solomon's wealth and fame, and the Chronicler has already cited the passage in II Chron. 1.14–17 with minimal alterations. On the other hand, while our verses serve the same concluding role as the Kings *Vorlage*, they deviate from it in structure and wording. How should these facts be interpreted? Rudolph, followed by Williamson, would regard only vv. 25–26 as original to the Chronicler, an eclectic collection from I Kings 4 [MT 5], probably intended to end the Chronistic narrative of Solomon; vv. 27–28 are seen as a secondary amplification, as they repeat material already used by the Chronicler (Rudolph, 221–3; Williamson, 236). This view is tempting, but does not take fully into account the careful literary technique which marks the passage as Chronistic rather than a chance addition by a 'glossator'.

Verse 25 is not, in fact, a reproduction of a single source but an artistic combination of two separate verses from the book of Kings, where the subject of Solomon's horses and chariots is presented from two different angles. I Kings 4.26 [MT 5.6] focusses on a reference to 'stalls of horses', while 10.26 centres on the 'chariot cities'; both verses include the information about Solomon's 'twelve thousand horsemen'. The Chronicler has omitted the entire context of I Kings 4.1–34 [MT 4.1–5.14]; however, here he 'salvages' I Kings 4.25 [MT 5.6] by combining it with 10.26b and presenting it as v. 25 here. The reference to the 'twelve thousand horsemen' is the connecting link:

And Solomon had four thousand stalls for horses
and chariots and twelve thousand horsemen
whom he stationed in the chariot cities and with the king in Jerusalem.

The Chronicler now employs another procedure, which we have encountered numerous times: here he interrupts the original continuity of I Kings 10.26–27, interpolates a passage (taken from I Kings 4.21 [MT 5.1], and then continues the original source sequence:

I Kings 10.26b	I Kings 4.21 [MT 5.1]	I Kings 10.27
II Chron. 9.25b	II Chron. 9.26	II Chron. 9.27.

Verse 26, then, in citing another remnant from I Kings 4, delineates the borders of Solomon's kingdom, which, like that of David, extended from the Euphrates to the border of Egypt. The geographical extent of Solomon's reign is an important issue for the Chronicler (cf. on I Chron. 13.5); the original emphasis on 'the kings' themselves, over whom Solomon held control, is moderated in Chronicles by the omission of the words 'they brought tribute and served Solomon all the days of his life' (I Kings 4.21 [MT 5.21]).

The Chronicler now proceeds in faithful adherence to his source material: v. 27 cites in full the admiring reference to the splendour and prosperity of Jerusalem in I Kings 10.27, while v. 28 summarizes briefly I Kings 10.28–29. The final scope of the new passage, with its omissions and additions, remains equivalent to I Kings 10.26–28 – a textual phenomenon we have also encountered before.

As with any case of a text in Chronicles which parallels another version, there are some differences in detail. Of these, both the number 'four thousand' and the reading 'whom he stationed' represent a better reading than the parallels of I Kings 4.26 [MT 5.6] and 10.26.

Finally, in place of a full inventory of the trade in horses and chariots (which the Chronicler has transferred to II Chron. 1.16–17), v. 28 refers only to the 'importing' (not mentioning any purchase prices) of horses 'from Egypt and from all the lands' – the implication, appropriate to the tone of the chapter as a whole, being that horses were included among the gifts presented to Solomon by foreign rulers. On this note the history of Solomon draws to a close.

[29–31] The conclusion of Solomon's reign is taken from I Kings 11.41–43. In general, the set pattern of the Deuteronomistic framework of the book of Kings, with its introductory and concluding components, is appropriated by Chronicles, with certain changes; some of these are made consistently throughout the book, others appear only in specific sections. This passage, for instance, has some peculiar features.

Reference is made to the following details: (a) sources for further information concerning Solomon (v. 29); (b) the duration of the king's reign (v. 30); (c) Solomon's death and burial, and the accession of his son (v. 31). In the books of Kings, the length of a king's reign appears in the introductory rather than the concluding part of the Deuteronomistic framework, Solomon's case being the only exception. In Chronicles, however, this information is transferred to the concluding section also for Rehoboam (II Chron. 12.13), Asa (II Chron. 16.13), Jehoshaphat (II Chron. 20.31), and Jehoram (II Chron. 21.20) – all the kings for whom the Deuteronomistic introduction was not preserved in Chronicles. In this instance, the Kings text in reference to Solomon may have served as the Chronicler's model for all the others.

In place of 'all that he did, and his wisdom' (I Kings 11.41), the Chronicler has 'the first and the last' (RSV 'from first to last'; JPS 'earlier and later'), a formula which is repeated for nine of the kings of Judah: David, Solomon, Rehoboam, Asa, Jehoshaphat, Amaziah, Uzziah, Ahaz and Josiah. This is one more example of the common biblical technique of merismus, i.e. an expression of totality by reference to two extremes or two components.

The Chronicler omits 'and his wisdom'; this is certainly surprising but not unprecedented: while Solomon was certainly 'wise' in the Chronicler's view, this was not his most significant feature.

The author of I Kings 11.41 refers the interested reader to 'the book of the acts of Solomon'. In place of this source, the Chronicler cites three other works: 'the history of Nathan the prophet', 'the prophecy of Ahijah the Shilonite' and 'the visions of Iddo the seer concerning Jeroboam, the son of Nebat'. These data are interesting in several ways.

Two of the prophets whose books are mentioned are known as contemporaries of Solomon: Nathan, who began his prophetic career in David's court (II Sam. 7; 12) and played a central role in Solomon's enthronement (I Kings 1), and Ahijah, of Shiloh in Ephraim, who was active at the end of Solomon's reign (I Kings 11.29ff.). The third name, Jeddi or Jeddo, is not known from the book of Kings, and may be identical with Iddo of II Chron. 12.15.

Several arguments support the impression given by the names themselves that the Chronicler is here drawing from some extra-biblical tradition:

1. Although the history of many of the rulers of Judah was recorded – according to Chronicles – by prophets, this claim is not made for all the kings of Judah, a fact which may suggest that the Chronicler did not feel that it was necessary to 'invent' undocumented figures.

2. For those of the prophetic chroniclers who may be identified, there is a full correlation between their time as known from the Bible and the king whose history they are supposed to have written.

3. In the specific case of the history of Solomon, the Chronicler would certainly have been content to mention the prophets named in his sources in Kings, had he not known of a *bona fide* tradition for the third.

4. There are recurring references in Chronicles to 'Iddo' in the context of the end of Solomon's reign. The similarity between Jeddo and Iddo cannot be ignored; both may be hypocoristic forms of a longer name, such as Jedaiah or Adaiah – cf. the alternative forms in Neh. 12.16 and I Chron. 6.21 [MT 6.6] as opposed to I Chron. 6.41 (MT 6.26). In this passage, Iddo is related to Jeroboam, Solomon's successor; in II Chron. 12.15 'the chronicles of Iddo the seer' is referred to as one source for Rehoboam's reign, and a 'story of the prophet Iddo' is attributed to the time of Abijah (II Chron. 13.22).

It is therefore likely that the Chronicler had at his disposal some tradition – written or oral – of a prophet by the name of Iddo who saw the end of Solomon's rule, and was a contemporary of Rehoboam and Abijah (i.e. during the reign of Jeroboam in northern Israel). Josephus names the 'man of God' of I Kings 13.1 'Iadon' (*Antiquities* VIII, 4.5), and the identification of this same figure with Iddo is also attested in Rabbinic sources (cf. *inter al.* Tosephta, Sanhedrin 14.15 – 'a prophet who transgressed his own teaching, like Iddo'; *Pesikta de Rav Kahana*, Shekalim 82–5). Possibly, however, rather than reflecting an independent tradition, Josephus is simply applying information from Chronicles to I Kings 13. Whether or not we identify Iddo with this man of God, the existence of a tradition about him should not be denied.

As for the titles attributed both to the prophets and to their works, here the Chronicler's stylisitic inclination to variety comes very much to the fore. Consistently, an effort is made to give each prophet his own distinct title, especially as here when a group of prophets is mentioned together. In I Chron. 29.29 we have a seer (*rō'eh*), a prophet (*nābī'*) and again a seer, with a different Hebrew word (*ḥōzeh*). In this case, Nathan is called prophet (*nābī'*), Iddo a seer (*ḥōzeh*), and Ahijah is identified by his place of origin, following I Kings 11.29; 12.15; 15.29. The same is also true of the titles of the books: the work of Nathan is described as 'chronicles' (*dibrē*), of Ahijah as 'prophecy' (*nᵉbū'at*), and of Iddo as 'vision' (*ḥᵃzōt*).

What were these works? The question of the Chronicler's alleged sources has been studied intensively for years (cf. recently D. Mathias, *Die Geschichte der Chronikforschung im 19. Jahrhundert*, Diss. Leipzig 1977, *passim*), and there seems to be no new breakthrough (cf. in the introduction). For this context, there are certain specific considerations:

1. As we have seen throughout, the history of Solomon as related in II Chron. 1–9 is faithfully and totally dependent on its source in I Kings 1–11, the only exceptions apparently being one piece of information regarding the conquest of Hamath, and at most an oral tradition regarding the location of the tabernacle in Gibeon. If any alternative source existed, its influence is nowhere in evidence.

2. Williamson has recently proposed that the remark 'the rest of the acts of Solomon, etc.', while 'imitating the notion of citation as a literary device', refers to those parts of the book of Kings which the Chronicler did not utilize (cf. Williamson, 236–7). This view is challenged by the observation that the Chronicler did not cite the passages in question – especially I Kings 1–2; 11 – precisely because the historical picture he wished to portray demanded their omission. It seems rather doubtful that he would direct his readers to the very material he had intentionally avoided.

3. Obviously, in citing these prophetic names and titles, the Chronicler wishes to make a point of great significance for his contemporaries: the recording of history was the responsibility of each period's prophets, who were in fact diligent in fulfilling their role (Josephus, *Against Apion*, I, 8). Here, then, is another example of the Chronicler's historization of a theological concept. Since he views historiography as a prophetic task, he ascribes the actual writing of historical documents to known prophetic figures. What actual literary compositions the Chronicler had in mind when he made these references remains a problem.

[30] Following I Kings 11.42, this verse states that Solomon reigned over 'all Israel'. In the Deuteronomistic historiography, Solomon is the only monarch who is thus honoured, while David is described as ruler 'over all Israel and Judah' (II Sam. 5.5) or 'over Israel' (I Kings 2.11). In Chronicles, this is another feature which the two monarchs, and they alone, have in common (cf. I Chron. 29.26).

[31] The frequent, though not fully consistent, change in Chronicles of the Kings formula 'he was buried' (*wayyiqqābēr*) to 'they buried him' (*wayyiqbᵉruhū*) has been amply noted. For a possible, though inconclusive, explanation, cf. Kropat, 14–15.

10 Rehoboam went to Shechem, for all Israel had come to Shechem to make him king. [2] And when Jeroboam the son of Nebat heard of it (for he was in Egypt, whither he had fled from King Solomon), then Jeroboam returned from Egypt. [3] And they sent and called him; and Jeroboam and all Israel came and said to Rehoboam, [4] 'Your father made our yoke heavy. Now therefore lighten the hard service of your father and his heavy yoke upon us, and we will serve you.' [5] He said to them, 'Come to me again in three days.' So the people went away.

[6] Then King Rehoboam took counsel with the old men, who had stood before Solomon his father while he was yet alive, saying, 'How do you advise me to answer this people?' [7] And they said to him, 'If you will be kind to this people and please them, and speak good words to them, then they will be your servants for ever.' [8] But he forsook the counsel which the old men gave him, and took counsel with the young men who had grown up with him and stood before him. [9] And he said to them, 'What do you advise that we answer this people who have said to me, "Lighten the yoke that your father put upon us"?' [10] And the young men who had grown up with him said to him, 'Thus shall you speak to the people who said to you, "Your father made our yoke heavy, but do you lighten it for us"; thus shall you say to them, "My little finger is thicker than my father's loins. [11] And now, whereas my father laid upon you a heavy yoke, I will add to your yoke. My father chastised you with whips, but I will chastise you with scorpions."'

[12] So Jeroboam and all the people came to Rehoboam the third day, as the king said, 'Come to me again the third day.' [13] And the king answered them harshly, and forsaking the counsel of the old men, [14] King Rehoboam spoke to them according to the counsel of the young men, saying, 'My father made your yoke heavy, but I will add to it; my father chastised you with whips, but I will chastise you with scorpions.' [15] So the king did not hearken to the people; for it was a turn of affairs brought about by God that the Lord might fulfil his word, which he spoke by Ahijah the Shilonite to Jeroboam the son of Nebat.

[16] And when all Israel saw that the king did not hearken to them, the people answered the king,
'What portion have we in David?
We have no inheritance in the son of Jesse.
Each of you to your tents, O Israel!
Look now to your own house, David.'
So all Israel departed to their tents. [17] But Rehoboam reigned over the people of Israel who dwelt in the cities of Judah. [18] Then King Rehoboam sent Hadoram, who was taskmaster over the forced labour, and the people of Israel stoned him to death with stones. And King Rehoboam made haste to mount his chariot, to flee to Jerusalem. [19] So Israel has been in rebellion against the house of David to this day.

11 When Rehoboam came to Jerusalem, he assembled the house of Judah, and Benjamin, a hundred and eighty thousand chosen warriors, to fight against Israel, to restore the kingdom to Rehoboam. [2] But the word of the Lord came to Shemaiah the man of God: [3] 'Say to Rehoboam the son of Solomon king of Judah, and to all Israel in Judah and Benjamin, [4] "Thus says the Lord, You shall not go up or fight against your brethren. Return every man to his home, for this thing is from me."' So they hearkened is the word of the Lord, and returned and did not go against Jeroboam.

A. Notes to MT

[5] אלהם, add לכו, following the Versions and I Kings 12.5; [14] אכביד, read אבי הכביד with some MSS; [16] ישראל, add ראו, with some MSS and Versions.

B. Notes to RSV

[4] 'upon us', MT 'which he laid upon us' (NEB); [11.1] 'The house of Judah, and Benjamin', better 'the house of Judah and Benjamin' (= I Kings 12.23).

C. Structure, sources and form

1. The chapter is adopted from I Kings 12.1–24 with certain linguistic and stylistic modifications. Some remarks on its literary development are in order:

(a) One of the difficult problems of I Kings 12 is the exact role of Jeroboam in the narrative; the inconsistencies in this respect are usually approached with the aid of evidence gleaned from the two LXX accounts (cf. Montgomery, *Kings*, 248; Gray, *Kings*, 299–301; also D. Gooding, 'The Septuagint's Rival Versions of Jeroboam's Rise to Power', *VT* 17, 1967, 180–1). We read in I Kings 12.1–3 that when Rehoboam departs for Shechem, Jeroboam is summoned by 'all the assembly of Israel'; he returns from Egypt and takes part in the negotiations with Rehoboam. Nevertheless, when these negotiations eventually fail, Jeroboam's return is again mentioned, as if for the first time: 'and when all Israel heard that Jeroboam returned, they sent and called him to the assembly and made him king over all Israel' (I Kings 12.20). The participation of Jeroboam in the initial approach to Rehoboam is difficult from another point of view as well. According to I Kings 11.40, Jeroboam was sought as a rebel, and this was the reason for his flight to Egypt. It is therefore hardly probable that he would have been permitted (or have dared) to come to Shechem and confront Rehoboam openly on the very day of his accession. It seems much more likely that Jeroboam indeed returned from Egypt upon hearing that Solomon had died but that the negotiations with Rehoboam were conducted without him; only after the failure of these negotiations was Jeroboam summoned and declared king by the assembly. This course of events may be discerned as the original view of I Kings 12. When several words in vv. 3 and 12 are recognized as secondary ('and they sent and called him', 'and Jeroboam' in v. 3, 'Jeroboam and' in v. 12), all the literary and historical difficulties disappear.

What is the origin of this redaction? Most likely the Chronicler's revision of the story, a revision motivated by historical and theological considerations and marked by several clear features:

(i) The record of Jeroboam's rebellion against Solomon in I Kings 11.26–40 is not retold, but only given a general and ambiguous expression in II Chron. 13.6: 'Yet Jeroboam ... a servant of Solomon ... rebelled against his lord'.

(ii) I Kings 12.20, which tells how the people of Israel called Jeroboam and made him king, is not repeated.

(iii) Jeroboam is introduced earlier in the story of the schism, and joins the negotiations with Rehoboam from the very outset.

(b) Another element in the story, often regarded as secondary in Kings, may also have originated with the Chronicler; this is I Kings 12.16b–17//II Chron. 10.16b–17. In its present form, this passage in Kings interrupts the original connection between v. 16a and v. 18; it raises prematurely the topic of Rehoboam's kingship over Judah, which is more properly noted in v. 20b. There is also a certain contrast of terminology and meaning between 'the people of Israel who dwelt in the cities of Judah' (v. 17) and 'the tribe of Judah only' (v. 20.)

This difficulty, too, is absent from Chronicles: with the omission of I Kings 12.20 the statement in v. 17 that Rehoboam remained king of the southern kingdom seems more natural. The choice of terms also gives authentic expression to the Chronicler's peculiar view, that the schism was not a confrontation between the ten tribes and the one tribe, Judah, but a defection of 'the people of Israel' who are 'in Israel' from 'the people of Israel' who are 'in Judah'. For the Chronicler, the political schism is essentially geographic, not ethnic or tribal.

(c) A further apparently secondary element of I Kings 12 is Rehoboam's attempt to restore his sovereignty over the north (I Kings 12.21–24; cf. Seeligmann: 'Almost the only point in I Kings 12, regarding which there is some kind of unanimous scholarly opinion, is the view that vv. 21–24 ... are a very late addition. ...', 'From Historic Reality to Historiosophic Conception in the Bible', P'rakim II, 1969–1974, 312*). Certain features of this passage are unusual: the term 'your kinsmen' (lit. your brothers) as defining the relationship between the Judahite and Israelite kingdoms is never found in Kings (but cf. II Chron. 28), and the view of the southern kingdom as 'Judah and Benjamin' (vv. 21, 23) rather than 'Judah alone' (v. 20) makes it clear that we are dealing here with a literary stratum distinct from the original story. However, in spite of its echoes of characteristic Chronistic attitudes, it seems that the present text was already found in the Chronicler's Vorlage, as can be seen mainly by the Chronicler's alterations introduced into the story, especially in the presentation of the people, to bring it more into harmony with his concepts. For 'all the house of Judah and the tribe of Benjamin' (v. 21) the Chronicler has 'the house of Judah and Benjamin' (II Chron.11.1), and in place of 'all the house of Judah and Benjamin' he reads 'all Israel in Judah and Benjamin' (11.3) – in each case enlarging the scope of his definition.

The raison d'être of I Kings 12.21–24 seems evident; the account of the schism leaves the reader with some unanswered questions: how is it possible that Rehoboam, with the enormous army and unrivalled military force bequeathed him by his father, did nothing, outside the sending of the ill-fated Adoram (v. 18), to secure or restore his sovereignty? Some sign of resolution is certainly expected from a ruler who declared 'my little finger is thicker than my father's loins' (v. 10). The passage in question, then, purports to explain Rehoboam's failure, by showing that Rehoboam planned military action against the rebels, only to be prevented from doing so by a 'word of God'. The apologetic here emphasizes the divine origin of the schism: 'for this thing is from me' (I Kings 12.24) – a view not in full harmony with the Chronicler's own views, expressed in II Chron. 13.7: 'Rehoboam was young and irresolute and could not withstand them'. It is therefore more plausible that the apology for Rehoboam in I Kings 12. 21–24, although not original to the schism narrative in vv. 1–20, was already part of the Chronicler's *Vorlage*, repeated in 11.1–4 with only few changes and adaptations.

We may reconstruct the literary process as follows: an original story to be restored in I Kings 12.1–20, in which Jeroboam was summoned only after the failure of the negotiations; a secondary supplement to this story in I Kings 12.21–24; a Chronistic revision in II Chron. 10.1–11.4, and the final contamination of the original narrative by the Chronistic revision, evidenced by the present text of I Kings 12.

2. The principal narrative in vv. 1–19 (I Kings 12.1–20) is a wisdom story, probably deriving from court circles (cf. I. Plein, 'Erwägungen zur Überlieferung von 1 Reg. 11.26 – 14.20', *ZAW* 78, 1966, 8–15). It is replete with aphorisms and characteristic of a milieu in which the role of the wise courtiers is highlighted. It is obvious, however, that the perspective is hostile to Rehoboam: the schism is portrayed as the result of the king's inept handling of the situation; stupidity, impetuousness, and the attendance of unworthy advisors lead the king into unpardonable errors. He is presented as a master of pretence: he speaks the harshest words while failing to possess any resolution. Rehoboam's foolhardiness is emphasized against the background of his father's wisdom; indeed, the confrontation, even the contest, between these two generations is the underlying theme of the narrative. Huram had congratulated Solomon with the words: 'Blessed be the Lord ... who has given to David a wise son' (I Kings 5.7; MT 5.21); no one, however, would ever bless Rehoboam in like terms. While Solomon's diplomacy is reflected in the advice of 'the old men, who had stood before Solomon his father' (v. 6), Rehoboam's own limitations prevent him from heeding them.

Notwithstanding this hostile attitude toward Rehoboam, it is hardly likely that the story originates in the northern kingdom. All the political presuppositions reflect a Judaean point of view, and even the moderate 'old men' do not justify the demands of the 'assembly of Israel', but merely advise Rehoboam to handle them with cunning. We conclude that the story was composed in the same circles rejected by Rehoboam: the counsellors of the court of Judah, who were probably also responsible for 'the book of the acts of Solomon'.

The wisdom motif and apparently secular spirit of this story place it in some tension with I Kings 11.29–39, where the prophet Ahijah the Shilonite explains the schism as God's punishment for Solomon's sins. It is only v. 15 which links the two views of the schisn, suggesting an excellent example of 'double causality' (cf. I. L. Seeligmann, 'Menschliches Heldentum und göttliche Hilfe – die doppelte Kausalität im alttestamentlichen Geschichtsdenken', *ThZ* 19, 1963, 385ff.). At first sight this conflict is brought about by human factors – Rehoboam's blind arrogance countered the people's disappointment and resolution; in fact, however, God has directed the events in accordance with his plans for the history of Israel.

3. To what extent is this story an authentic reflection of Rehoboam's character? It is difficult to say. Although the counsellors 'who had grown up with him' are called 'young men' (literally 'boys'), his age at accession is given as forty-one (I Kings

14.21). His behaviour is described as that of a spoiled child, exhibiting the mannerisms of power but in fact equivocal and feeble. Some of these features seem dependable, especially the way in which his attitude reveals the gap between the royal court and the people. The hostility which the king displays vis à vis his own subjects is indeed characteristic of certain known oriental rulers. The fact of schism, an irreparable breach between the two parts of the nation, seems to support the authenticity of the king's figure as portrayed in the wisdom story.

4. The narrative itself consists of very few acts, the series of aggressive acts at its end being concisely related. After the gathering of the people at Shechem, the story is presented as a series of progressively lengthening dialogues, with abundant repetitions, developing as follows:

(a) 1–3aα Proposition: the situation
——(b) 3aβ–5. First encounter: the people and Rehoboam
————(c) 6–7 Second encounter: Rehoboam and the old counsellors
————(d) 8–11 Third encounter: Rehoboam and the young counsellors
——(e) 12–16 Fourth encounter: Rehoboam and the people
(f) 17–19 Conclusion: acts leading to the schism.

D. Commentary

[1] The main problem posed by this verse concerns the historical background: why did Rehoboam proceed to Shechem for his enthronement? Underlying this journey is the assumption that the mere inheriting of kingly status from his father Solomon was not enough; some additional affirmation of sovereignty was required. This is a subject which has prompted much discussion and inspired many conclusions about the nature of the Israelite monarchy (cf. A. Alt, 'The Monarchy in Israel and Judah', Essays on Old Testament History and Religion, 1966, 245–6.).

Even if we assume, as many scholars have, that the sovereignty of the Davidic monarchs over the northern tribes was based on a personal union, certain points should be made:

1. Our sources do not indicate that any separate confirmation of kingship was demanded of Solomon, whose accession to the throne took place only in Jerusalem. One may explain this by questioning the state of the extant sources, or by conjecturing that the anointing of Solomon during David's lifetime made their reigns a continuum with no real hiatus in authority. However, the striking difference between Solomon and Rehoboam in this respect cannot be ignored.

2. The covenant between David and all the tribes of Israel was established in Hebron, David's capital at the time, with a convocation 'before the Lord' of the elders of all the tribes of Israel, who came to David of their own accord (II Sam. 5.1–3//I Chron. 11.1–3).

The comparison of Rehoboam to his two predecessors leads to the inevitable conclusion that however we conceive of the bond between the Davidic kings and the northern tribes, the very fact that Rehoboam journeyed to Shechem – for either some kind of negotiation or approval – is already a telling sign either of weakness or of political ineptitude and probably of both.

[2] When did Jeroboam return from Egypt? On the face of the matter, v. 2 indicates that this was when he heard of Rehoboam's journey to Shechem, but this does not allow a realistic time for the journey from Egypt. It seems more likely that the words 'and when Jeroboam heard' refer rather to Solomon's death, after which Jeroboam left Egypt. Accordingly, some scholars would reverse the order of vv. 1 and 2 in I Kings 12 (cf. Montgomery, *Kings*, 248), a proposal not applicable in our passage, since the Chronicler clearly found the Kings text as it now stands. Rudolph (p. 226) therefore suggests that the words 'that Solomon had died' should be added in v. 2 – a very plausible restoration which, unfortunately, cannot be verified. The reading of this verse, 'and Jeroboam returned *from* Egypt', compared to I Kings 12.2, 'then Jeroboam dwelt *in* in Egypt' (changed by the RSV *ad loc*, cf. note), is one of the numerous instances where Chronicles preserves the better reading.

This verse refers to Jeroboam's flight from Solomon, that is, to information which appeared in I Kings 11.40 but is missing from Chronicles. This is one more example among many (cf. the reference to the 'House of the Forest of Lebanon', the building of Solomon's palace, Solomon's marriage to the daughter of Pharaoh, etc.) of the ease, even nonchalance, with which the Chronicler refers to matters which he did not specifically deal with. His editorial procedure caused him to omit certain episodes, but not casual references to them elsewhere; these matters, then, lose in significance but are not completely obliterated. Another example is the reference in II Chron. 13.6 to Jeroboam's rebellion, the original account of which is not, as I have said, to be found in Chronicles.

[3–5] The Chronicler presents Jeroboam as the leader of the Israelite delegation which demanded that Rehoboam lighten the people's burden. The phrasing here is carefully chosen. On the one hand, this is not a request but a demand, since the people's future obedience is conditional on Rehoboam's acquiescence: 'lighten the hard service ... and we will serve you'. On the other hand, the condition is not formally phrased (the formula would be '*if* you lighten ... *then* we will serve'); only a positive *scenario* is explicitly envisaged, and no corresponding negative contingency ('*if* you do not ... *then* ...') is formulated. The implications of Rehoboam's probable refusal are not really expressed. The ensuing events indicate clearly that this very diplomatic tone allowed Rehoboam to conclude erroneously that all the options were still open.

According to our information in Kings, the demand of the people was well justified, and in view of the earlier rebellion of Jeroboam (I Kings 11.29–40) should not have come as a surprise. Chronicles, however, puts a very different face on the matter. The heavy yoke of service which Solomon imposed on the people is a point which the Chronicler systematically suppressed (cf. I Kings 5.13–14 [MT 27–28]; 'and this is the account of the forced labour which king Solomon levied' in I Kings 9.15 – all omitted in Chronicles). Even administrative arrangements for the supplying of food for the royal table by twelve officers (I Kings 4.7–19) are absent from Chronicles, as well as the extravagant descriptions of Solomon's provisions (I Kings 4.22–23). If we base ourselves on the history of Solomon as told in Chronicles, the people's complaint has no basis whatsoever and is merely a false provocation, an excuse for rebellion which should never have been humoured. Indeed, this is the situation described in the Chronicler's own account through Abijah's speech in II Chron. 13.6–7.

The chain of events which seems so logical in the context of Kings, i.e. a heavy yoke – a demand for relief – refusal – rebellion, loses credibility in Chronicles, where there was no burden to justify the people's behaviour. At this point, we begin to expect more thorough reworking of the narrative: Rehoboam should deny the people's accusation of Solomon's harsh ways. Here, however, the adaptation ceases, and even in the Chronistic version Rehoboam bases his reply on this presumption: 'my father made your yoke heavy, but I will add to it' (v. 14). These literary and historical tensions and inconsistencies cannot be reconciled to our full satisfaction, as they are the inevitable results of the logic and dynamic of adapting existing material to the framework of a new historical philosophy.

The stylistic quality of the people's address is also noteworthy: their lengthy statement uses emphatic repetition to render their message obvious: the words 'your father', 'yoke', 'heavy' are all repeated twice; in addition there is a play on the root for 'serve/service' (*'bd*): 'lighten the hard service of your father ... and we will serve you'.

Rehoboam does not respond immediately but instructs the people to return in three days time. From a psychological point of view this postponement is in itself a sign of acquiescence, or at least consideration. A negative answer, which would change nothing in the situation, could have been given on the spot – and would have been, had Rehoboam known his own mind and acted wisely. Having raised the people's expectations by this implied readiness to be magnanimous, the answer which Rehoboam eventually comes back with had, even disregarding practical repercussions, the most demoralizing effect. Already at this early point the narrator exposes Rehoboam's lack of resolution, his inability to cope with any kind of difficulty.

[6–7] Rehoboam turns first to the 'old men' (or 'elders'), who served his father. The message and form of their response should be considered before and after its rephrasing in Chronicles. In I King 12.7 the 'old men' focus their answer on the key words of the people's demand: 'we will serve you'. They have recognized that this demand is actually an ultimatum; the urgent question now is not whether or not to lighten the people's yoke, but rather how to secure the continuation of the Davidic rule of the northern tribes. Their answer to Rehoboam, therefore, does not relate to the people's direct request but applies to the preliminary matter: should the king grant the people's request or deny it? The advice of the elders, then, is definitely affirmative, playing on the same root: 'if you be their servant today – they will be your servants for ever'.

The Chronicler retains the spirit of this response but changes the form in two ways. First, he reduces the use of the root 'serve', especially in reference to Rehoboam; the elders do not advise the king to be the people's 'servant', even metaphorically – this in contrast to the later reference to Jeroboam as 'Solomon's servant' (II Chron. 13.6). The Chronicler likewise replaces the contrasting theme of 'today' – 'for ever' with an emphasis on 'kindness' (*ṭōb*): 'if you will be kind (*lᵉṭōb*) to this people ... and speak good words (*dᵉbārīm ṭōbīm*) to them ...'. The elders' advice of leniency represents not only an interim tactic to overcome a pending crisis, but a regular policy – no doubt the Chronicler's own view of proper rule. (For a more technical interpretation of these terms, and the dialogues in general, cf. M. Weinfeld, 'The Counsel of the "Elders" to Rehoboam and its Implications', *Maarav* 3, 1982, 27–53; id., 'The King as the Servant of the People', *JJS* XXXIII, 1982, 189–94).

[8–9] Rehoboam's dissatisfaction with the elders' response stems not only from its mildness but from its failure, in his view, to address the actual issue raised by the people's demand. He therefore turns to another group of counsellors: 'the young men who had grown up with him'. Here he phrases his query in a way no longer eliciting a general opinion on 'how to answer this people', but as a specific policy in response to the demand: 'lighten the yoke ...' Strikingly, Rehoboam omits from the people's address the hidden ultimatum in the key phrase 'we will serve you'. Indeed, the word 'serve' now disappears, to be replaced by 'yoke', repeated five times in vv. 8–14.

How are we to understand the status of these two groups of counsellors? The narrative assumes that they are part of the royal retinue accompanying Rehoboam to Shechem, i.e regular court officials. Should the designations 'old' and 'young' be seen as merely distinguishing two age-groups, with an implication, in wisdom circles, of an *a priori* preference for the 'old' and criticism of the 'young', or do the terms represent two formal bodies? Malamat claimed the latter, eliciting support from Sumerian parallels (A. Malamat, 'Kingship and Council in Israel and Sumer: a Parallel', *JNES* 22, 1963, 247–53; id., 'Organs of Statecraft in the Israelite Monarchy', *BA* 28,

1965, 34–65); cf. the critique of his view by D. G. Evans, 'Rehoboam's Advisers at Shechem and Political Institutions in Israel and Sumer', *JNES* 25, 1966, 273–9).

[10–11] The words of the 'young men' are a direct response both to Rehoboam's question and to his psychological disposition. These young contemporaries may lack the experience and sound judgment of their elders, but there is no 'generation gap' between them and the king. In short, sharing his inclinations and knowing his preferences, they offer him the advice he is hoping to hear. When quoting the people (now the third version of the request), they omit the crucial 'we will serve you', as if the problem of 'lightening the yoke' was raised in a political vacuum. While the old men answered in straightforward prose, the young men speak in elevated aphorisms. Their reply seems to meet every requirement of professional counselling: it repeats and redefines the question; it relates precisely to the point at hand; it is adequately presented with metaphors and rhetorical acumen. However, from a political and psychological point of view, lacking a deeper evaluation of the situation in its entirety, the counsel of the 'young men' must lead to disaster.

The rephrasing of the people's request here uses a completely antithetic parallelism:

your father made our yoke *heavy*
but you   *lighten* it.

There is also a word play: 'our yoke' (*'ullēnū*) – 'for us' (*mē'ālēnū*) – indeed some scholars propose as a reading *mē'ullēnū*, 'from our yoke' (cf. Curtis, 258).

The 'young men' 's proposed reply opens with an aphoristic saying intending to assert Rehoboam's firm resolution: 'My little finger' (this is the accepted interpretation of the unique *qotonī*, but cf. Dillard, 87) 'is thicker than my father's loins', i.e., for the same act for which Solomon had to 'gird up his loins', Rehoboam only had to move his little finger. This boast is intended more to bolster Rehoboam's own self-confidence than to be repeated in public; indeed, it is not repeated by Rehoboam when he finally delivers his reply to the assembly; at least here he displays some discernment.

The proposed address to the people gives a direct negative answer followed by a literary metaphor. The young men's inclination to extremes attributes to Solomon a greater cruelty than was so far suggested: 'My father chastised you with whips'. This is described as mild in comparison to what the people should expect in the future: 'but I will chastise you with scorpions'. Not only is the people's appeal to be dismissed out of hand, but their demand is shown to aggravate the situation by provoking the king's hostility. This attitude provides an interesting parallel to Exod. 5.7–8, where

Pharaoh's answer to the request of Moses and Aaron follows the same lines: 'You shall no longer give the people straw to make bricks ... let them go and gather straw for themselves. But the number of bricks ... you shall by no means lessen.' The similarity between Pharaoh's attitude and that of Rehoboam's young counsellors is the most striking demonstration of the enstrangement of the king from his people; this is tyranny unmasked.

[12–14] The fourth and last encounter is between Rehoboam and the people, who have returned to him after three days. Here is the climax of the story, of which the practical dénouement is already implied. When the confrontation is over, all that remains for the author is to compile a concise record of the subsequent, concluding events. This is also the place for a comment which will transpose the whole narrative to a different level of meaning (in v. 15, cf. below).

The introduction of this scene repeats Rehoboam's initial order that the people should return in three days. This note provides the background for v. 13: the people, fully expecting leniency, now bear the brunt of the king's implacability. The word 'harshly' (*qāšāh*) is well chosen: it is from the same root as 'heavy' and 'hard' (*haqqāšāh, hiqšāh*) in v. 4; Solomon burdened his subjects with heavy labour, while here Rehoboam his son treats them harshly with the utterances of his mouth. Moreover, 'harshly' is the opposite of 'softly', advised by the book of Proverbs as the correct behaviour in time of anger (Prov. 15.1; 25.15). Rehoboam does more than accept the young men's advice; he recites their formulas with no addition of his own.

There is no reference to God throughout the entire narrative; events are guided entirely by human motives. Verse 15 has the only exception, a single exposé of the hidden meaning of the events, mentioning the name of God and his prophetic word for the first time. While the events have apparently unfolded in accordance with human nature and logic, they were actually dictated by the Lord, to fulfil Ahijah's earlier prophecy. Rehoboam's choices now become inevitable, almost predestined, and his figure is touched with a tragic colour, which nevertheless does not mitigate or atone for the arrogance of his behaviour.

The genre and function of v. 15 parallel perfectly Gen. 50.20, 'you meant evil against me but God meant it for good'; here, however, the turn of events is in the opposite direction. Whether this note originates in the same contemporary wisdom circles, or reflects the final Deuteronomistic intervention (cf. G. von Rad, 'The Deuterononistic Theology of History in I and II Kings', in *The Problem of the Hexateuch and Other Essays*, Edinburgh and New York 1966, 216–21), is an open question. In the context of I Kings 12, v. 15 is perfectly placed to unite all the separate stories into one variegated theological construct. In Chronicles its appearance presents a literary and theological problem.

Of these, the literary crux seems the easier. The Chronicler omitted from his record all of I Kings 11 and therefore any antecedent reference to Ahijah's prophecy to Jeroboam – another example of the Chronicler's reference to material he has actually omitted in its original context. The theological problem is more difficult. The heart of Ahijah's prophecy is the tearing of 'the kingdom from the hand of Solomon' and the giving of 'ten tribes' to Jeroboam (I Kings 11.31). The legitimate reign of Jeroboam is seen as established by God, predicted and encouraged by his prophet. According to the Chronicler's own view, however, 'the Lord God of Israel gave the kingship over Israel for ever to David and his sons'; Jeroboam was little more than a rebellious slave (II Chron. 13.5–6). The real problem, then, is the essential contrast between the Chronicler's view and Ahijah's view of the schism. If so, why did the Chronicler not omit this verse, as he does in other cases? It is convenient to assume that the verse was indeed omitted, but secondarily introduced by a later hand. Such an assumption is, however, methodologically unsound and will be avoided here.

No satisfactory theological solution has been suggested so far (cf. recently Williamson, 239). In fact, ch. 12 as a whole presented the Chronicler with a theological dilemma which he really did not solve. According to the Chronistic view of divine justice, every calamity is God's punishment for some transgression. From the point of view of theodicy, the Deuteronomist has solved the problem of the schism (I Kings 12) rather neatly: it is the punishment for Solomon's sins described in detail in I Kings 11. Moreover, the continuation of a limited Davidic rule is God's reward for David's righteousness. All this is stated in a prophetic utterance, which grants divine sanction to Jeroboam's rebellion and presents him as a legitimate heir of the Davidic dynasty (I Kings 11.38). For unrelated reasons, the Chronicler has omitted Solomon's sins, thus depriving the schism of a theological anchor in Chronistic historiosophy. A solution of sorts is provided by the fact that in Chronicles Jeroboam's rebellion is conceived not as divinely sanctioned but as an ungrateful rebellion of a slave against his master. Nevertheless, from the point of view of the southern kingdom, it still remains an event not satisfactorily explained.

Here again we are confronted with the limits of the Chronicler's historiography. He could not avoid the event of schism, and had no better description of it than I Kings 12; yet there could be no mention of Solomon's sins. The schism thus remains problematical, not fully adjusted or integrated into the Chronicler's philosophy of history.

[16a] The people's reaction is now expected. From a literary point of view it is noteworthy that they answer Rehoboam in the same coin – with an aphorism. The people of the north make use of a standard formula, which calls for the annulment of the bond between Israel and the house of David

(for a similar set of phrases see also Josh. 22.25, 27 and Gen. 31.14). The third line in the verse, 'Each of you to your tents, O Israel', seems like a conflation of the earlier II Sam. 20.1 and I Kings 12.16.

[16b–17] In structure and content, these clauses should be regarded as parenthetical. The immediate continuation of the narrative is in v. 18: when the people proclaimed the rebellious catchword, the king sent against them the man who had exercised authority over them until now, Hadoram the taskmaster, while Rehoboam himself fled for his life to Jerusalem. Verses 16b–17, then, seem to be the Chronicler's insertion to the story, after he had omitted I Kings 12.20 (and secondarily transferred to I Kings 12). The Chronicler refrains from presenting the actual enthronment of Jeroboam, and sees the whole event as a defection of the 'people of Israel': 'all Israel departed to their tents', while Rehoboam ruled the 'people of Israel who dwelt in the cities of Judah'.

The terminology here is significant. 'All Israel' in this context is undoubtedly the people of the north, who are called by the same title also in vv. 1, 3, 16. In v. 18 they are described as 'the children (RSV 'the people') of Israel' – a title which in v. 17 refers to the people of the Judaean kingdom. Thus, the people is an essential unity, and each of its parts may be termed 'Israel', 'the children of Israel' or 'all Israel' – as the literary unit and the context may require.

'The cities of Judah' is one method of providing a geographical definition of the extent of the kingdom of Judah. The phrase is quite common in Chronicles (thirteen times: II Chron. 14.4; 17.2, 7, 9, etc.), but most frequent in Jeremiah, where it appears almost thirty times (1.15; 4.16, etc.).

[18–19] The conclusion of this episode, unlike the narrative up to this point, is portrayed as a series of hasty acts. The contrast to the feigned confidence of vv. 1 and 12–13 is ironic – the man who came to Shechem to be hailed king by the whole people barely succeeds in escaping with his life. Here, too, Rehoboam's irresolute character, lack of initiative and poor understanding of the situation are displayed. Even when he delegates others to handle the crisis, he chooses, surprisingly, not the commanders of the army but an official – Hadoram; even now Rehoboam is blind to any but the most limited perspective of the problem. Only with the actual stoning of the taskmaster does Rehoboam finally understand his position and take to his heels. The death of the taskmaster is of course the first sign that the task is now over, a symbolic act of liberation.

The final result is 'rebellion'; the term used in the final verse ($p^e\check{s}a$‘) is employed elsewhere both for 'revolt' and 'liberation from a foreign conqueror' (II Kings 8.20, 22; R. Knierim, *Die Hauptbegriffe für Sünde im Alten Testament*, [2]1967, 150–1).

While the Chronicles story ends here, I Kings 12.20 goes on to describe how the rebellion was followed by the enthronement of Jeroboam 'over all Israel', excepting the tribe of Judah.

[11.1–4] The last episode of the schism, recorded in I Kings 12.21ff., is a secondary addition there, but this addition was already found in the Chronicler's *Vorlage*. Its purpose is obviously to account in some reasonable way for Rehoboam's unthinkable passive reaction to Israel's rebellion, and his easy surrender of the greater part of his kingdom with no attempt to assert his sovereignty. The explanation offered here is that Rehoboam did not fight back because he was restrained by a 'word of God'.

I Kings 12.21 first defines the people as 'the house of Judah and the tribe of Benjamin', then (v. 23) 'all the house of Judah and Benjamin'; the Chronicler changes these to 'the house of Judah and Benjamin' and 'all Israel in Judah and Benjamin'. 'The house of Israel' (I Kings 12.21) is also changed, to 'Israel'. Indeed, 'the house of Israel', a term occurring frequently in the prophecies of Jeremiah and Ezekiel (but also elsewhere), is absent from Chronicles, and in its few occurrences in parallel verses is always changed (cf. Japhet, *Ideology*, 271 n. 21). 'The house of Judah' is also quite rare, found elsewhere only in I Chron. 28.4 and II Chron. 22.10, in both cases in connection with the royal family.

While an army of 180,000 'chosen warriors' seems extravagant, it is much smaller than the numbers usually introduced by the Chronicler – cf. II Chron. 13.3 for a similar situation.

In the book of Kings, the present episode is the only appearance of 'Shemaiah the man of God'; in Chronicles, on the other hand, his role is broadened: he appears again before Rehoboam during the campaign of Shishak (II Chron. 12.5, 7), and he is designated as Rehoboam's historiographer (II Chron. 12.15). In these places he is called 'prophet', while here he is given the less frequent title 'man of God' (also I Chron. 6.49 [MT 34]; 23.14; II Chron. 8:14; 24.9; 30.16), reserved for Moses, David, and an anonymous prophet in the reign of Amaziah (II Chron. 25.7, 9).

'All Israel in Judah and Benjamin' is a suitable expression of the Chronicler's concept of the people of Israel. 'All Israel' is the designation of the people, in whatever territory they may be settled: the kingdom of Judah was never occupied only by people from the tribes of Judah and Benjamin (cf. I Chron. 9.3) – a fact which will be further recorded in II Chron. 11.16 (for the significance of 11.3 for von Rad's different view, cf. *Geschichtsbild*, 31; G. A. Danell, *Studies in the Name Israel in the Old Testament*, 1946, 275. Cf. also Japhet, *Ideology*, 273–4; Williamson, *Israel in the Book of Chronicles*, 1977, 99ff.).

Shemaiah's prophecy affirms that the rebellion was the will of God – the same attitude as the narrator had expressed in his own words in 10.15 (I Kings 12.15). As frequently in the biblical narrative, and in contrast to the stylistic quality of the earlier story, excessive repetition is avoided by the passing over of certain phases of the story. Here we read that 'the word of the Lord came to Shemaiah ...', and immediately that the people paid heed and obeyed, the intermediate phase in which Shemaiah actually transmitted the message to Rehoboam and his army being passed over as self-evident.

The Rehoboam of this passage is very different from the protagonist of the preceding section. The impetuous, arrogant, timid, and not overly wise character of I Kings 12.1–20 is also referred to later in the Deuteronomistic description as one of the most sinful monarchs of Judah; in his time 'Judah did what was evil in the sight of the Lord, and they provoked him to jealousy with their sins' (I Kings 14.22–24). These Deuteronomistic appraisals accord well with the international atmosphere which Solomon had introduced into Jerusalem, and with Rehoboam's birth from an Ammonite mother. By contrast, the episode here, in which Rehoboam first takes military initiative, and then bows immediately to 'a word of God', abandoning his original plans and sending the army home, is completely unexpected. The courage, flexibility and humility which were so urgently needed in the preceding episode suddenly appear here in full bloom. The character of the prophecy as 'post-eventum' is indeed obvious. This portrait of Rehoboam is much more in accord with that sketched elsewhere in Chronicles: Rehoboam's reign is heralded by a period of hearkening to the Lord's word: 'they walked for three years in the way of David and Solomon' (II Chron. 11.17), and even later Rehoboam was ready to heed the prophets sent to him by God (cf. especially 12.5–6). (On the figure of Rehoboam in Chronicles cf. also G. N. Knoppers, 'Rehoboam in Chronicles: Villain or Victim?', *JBL* 109, 1990, 423–40.)

As the section comes to a close, some words should be said about its place in the Chronistic historiographical scheme. I Kings 12 constitutes a turning point in the Deuteronomistic historiography, as a new reality created by the schism, of two parallel kingdoms of Israel and Judah, demands a new literary pattern. The histories of the kingdoms are presented from now on in a synchronic pattern until the destruction of the northern kingdom, after which a unilinear, but similar, history of Judah continues to its end. In Chronicles, the section also represents an important phase, if to a lesser and different degree. Since Chronicles describes the history of the northern kingdom only through the perspective of Judah, the literary pattern here is of one uninterrupted narrative rather than a synchronic one, and no new literary pattern is introduced with the schism. Chapter 10 marks the transition from a perfect kingdom – of all Israel united under Solomon – to a damaged kingdom under Rehoboam, in which only 'the people of Israel in the cities of Judah' are ruled by the legitimate heir, while the others are led by a rebellious usurper. This change in the status of the monarchy demanded a different theological approach. In the histories of David and Solomon the

Chronicler attempted to erase the negative points: if the period was to display unparalleled achievements, it also had to exemplify perfection of conduct. The period of the later kings claims lower standards, having sin as a constant factor. From now on, the historical narrative attempts to explain transgressions and difficulties, not ignore them. The author's effort is directed towards the forging of a new theological logic underlying the historical process.

11.5–23

11   5 Rehoboam dwelt in Jerusalem, and he built cities for defence in Judah. [6] He built Bethlehem, Etam, Tekoa, [7] Beth-zur, Soco, Adullam, 8 Gath, Mareshah, Ziph, [9] Adoraim, Lachish, Azekah, [10] Zorah, Aijalon, and Hebron, fortified cities which are in Judah and in Benjamin. [11] He made the fortresses strong, and put commanders in them, and stores of food, oil, and wine. [12] And he put shields and spears in all the cities, and made them very strong. So he held Judah and Benjamin.

13 And the priests and the Levites that were in all Israel resorted to him from all places where they lived.[14] For the Levites left their common lands and their holdings and came to Judah and Jerusalem, because Jeroboam and his sons cast them out from serving as priests of the Lord, [15] and he appointed his own priests for the high places, and for the satyrs, and for the calves which he had made. [16] And those who had set their hearts to seek the Lord God of Israel came after them from all the tribes of Israel to Jerusalem to sacrifice to the Lord, the God of their fathers. [17] They strengthened the kingdom of Judah, and for three years they made Rehoboam the son of Solomon secure, for they walked for three years in the way of David and Solomon.

18 Rehoboam took as wife Mahalath the daughter of Jerimoth the son of David, and of Abihail the daughter of Eliab the son of Jesse; [19] and she bore him sons, Jeush, Shemariah, and Zaham. [20] After her he took Maacah the daughter of Absalom, who bore him Abijah, Attai, Ziza, and Shelomith. [21] Rehoboam loved Maacah the daughter of Absalom above all his wives and concubines (he took eighteen wives and sixty concubines, and had twenty-eight sons and sixty daughters); [22] and Rehoboam appointed Abijah the son of Maacah as chief prince among his brothers, for he intended to make him king. [23] And he dealt wisely, and distributed some of his sons through all the districts of Judah and Benjamin, in all the fortified cities; and he gave them abundant provisions, and procured wives for them.

A. Notes to MT

[18] בן ירימות, read בת ירימות with the Qere; אביהיל, read ואביהיל; [23] וישאל המון, read וישא להם.

B. Notes to RSV

[12] 'So he held Judah and Benjamin', NEB 'Thus he retained the possession of Judah and Benjamin'; [13] 'from all places where they lived', better NEB and JPS 'from all their territories'.

C. *Structure, sources and form*

1. II Chron. 11 and 12 relate the history of Rehoboam after the schism. In order to understand fully the structure and composition of these chapters, we should first analyse the story as developed in I Kings 12ff. The story of the schism is followed by the descriptions of each of the now separate states: first the northern kingdom of Israel under Jeroboam (I Kings 12.25–14.20), and then Judah under Rehoboam (I Kings 14.21–31). The continuity between the account of the schism and the further history of Rehoboam is thus interrupted by a large block relating to Jeroboam. When the Rehoboam material resumes, it is structured as follows:

(a) I Kings 14.21–24 Deuteronomistic introduction with an emphasis (vv. 22–24) on Rehoboam's transgressions
(b) I Kings 14.25–28 Shishak's campaign and its consequences
(c) I Kings 14.29–31 Deuteronomistic conclusion.

In the Chronicler's extensive reworking, the structure is wholly altered, and the scope of the material is almost tripled.

(a) The material taken from I Kings 14 is relegated to the end; the Deuteronomistic introduction is merged with the conclusion (II Chron. 12.13–14, 15–16); the record of Rehoboam's transgressions is shortened to one verse (II Chron 12.14); and the story of Shishak's campaign is greatly elaborated (12.1–12).

(b) The beginning of the story (11.5–23) is built of original material, not paralleled in Kings. It is placed in the context preceding Shishak's campaign and providing a smooth sequence with the episode of the prophet Shemaiah (11.1–4) which concludes the story of the schism.

A comparison of the new composition with I Kings 12–14 reveals a surprising literary fact: II Chron. 11 fills the space originally created by the omission of the story of Jeroboam (I Kings 12.25–14.20). It is a commonly accepted view that the placing of this chapter in its present position was due exclusively to theological considerations. These, however, while no doubt valid (cf. also below), cannot be regarded as exclusive. Literary-compositional aspects also play a role, as the new story of Chronicles is structured to retain as faithfully as possible the original sequence, with a new chapter on Rehoboam replacing the story of Jeroboam (for a similar view, see J. Goldingay, 'The Chronicler as a Theologian', *BTB* 5, 1975, 102–4).

The themes of the new material in II Chron. 11 are: building projects (vv. 5–12), aspects of religious life (vv. 13–17), wives and sons (vv. 18–23) – which in the Chronicler's concept of history are signs of God's blessing. These are precisely the topics around which the excised story of Jeroboam in I Kings revolves: Jeroboam's constructions (I Kings 12.25), religious reforms and reactions to them (12.26–13.14), and Jeroboam's wife and son (14.1–18). Moreover, in each case there is an antithesis: the transgressions of Jeroboam are noted by the Chronicler only for the benefit incurred by Judah with the influx of emigrant faithful Israelites; in contrast to the death of Jeroboam's son and the dire prophecy of the extinction of his line, Chronicles enlarges on the superlative blessing of Rehoboam. This element of literary counterpoint is in itself a theological statement, probably making a more profound impression than explicit comment.

2. In addition, there is a peculiar philosophy of history which determines the structure of Rehoboam's history. As the correlation between circumstances and religious conduct is taken to be absolute, the course of history must bear this out. The theologically motivated reconstruction has two points of departure: I Kings 12.24, 'So they hearkened to the word of the Lord', and I Kings 14.25, 'Shishak king of Egypt came up against Jerusalem'. The beginning of Rehoboam's reign is marked by obedience to God's word, while its continuation is marked by an enemy invasion. Since it is the Chronicler's understanding both that Rehoboam's obedience should be properly rewarded and that Shishak's campaign is God's punishment for transgression, the intermediate period, from the first to the fifth year of Rehoboam, in Chronicles becomes an interim of transition, from three years of following 'in the ways of David and Solomon' (11.17) to the fourth year in which Rehoboam 'forsook the law of God' (12.1). Then, in full accord with the Chronicler's theology, all the landmarks of success and well-being are placed in these first three years.

3. In view of the Chronicler's literary inclination and theological suppositions, the problem of historical authenticity seems doubly perplexing. How far can one rely on the data which are peculiar to Chronicles? Is this material sheer composition, or did the Chronicler rely on other sources, and how authentic and reliable could these sources have been? No general statement on this matter would be adequate, but each literary unit should be examined in its own right.

It seems that since the thorough study of Beyer in 1931 ('Das Festungssystem Rehabeams', *ZDPV* 54, 113–34), the list of the fortified cities is generally taken at face value, as an authentic list of fortifications constructed in the period of the monarchy. The main debate over this list revolves around its chronological assumptions: should it indeed be attributed to Rehoboam or to some other period in the history of Judah? For more details cf. the commentary.

There is also a general acceptance of the authenticity of the list of Rehoboam's wives and sons, based on several considerations:

(*a*) There are only very few similar notes in the book of Chronicles (cf. II Chron. 13.21; 21.2–3); this kind of information, while conforming well with the Chronicler's general views, is not really characteristic of his writing.

(*b*) There is nothing in the passage that would indicate artificiality. Even the late linguistic features may testify to a late linguistic reworking, or even to a later phrasing of earlier data.

By contrast, the intermediate passage of vv. 13–17 is more often than not regarded as the Chronicler's own composition, reflecting his language, style and views.

4. We may sum up as follows. 'The story of Rehoboam' in Chronicles is a new work, composed by the Chronicler, in which he strives first of all to present in Rehoboam an equivalent to the history of the two kingdoms of Israel as presented by his Deuteronomistic predecessor in I Kings 12–14. The theological goal is to lay bare the divine principles which determine the course of the history of Israel. The building-blocks of the new composition – whether borrowed or original – are not only juxtaposed but structured along literary and theological lines. The Chronicler's language and style are manifest to a certain degree in the passages he takes from his sources, and of course even more so in the passages he composed. The result is not only a new literary work but a new figure of Rehoboam, which greatly differs from that portrayed in the book of Kings.

D. Commentary

[5–12] The passage is clearly composed of three parts:

5: Introduction
6–10aα: The list of cities
10aβ–12: Conclusion.

Both the introduction and conclusion show stylistic Chronistic features; only the list itself, consisting of a series of unadorned names, shows no features identifiable as Chronistic.

This list of fortified cities has no parallel in biblical sources; however, its geographic-strategic logic is generally taken to reflect authentic historical circumstances; it can hardly be a literary fiction. All of the fifteen cities mentioned, with the exception of Adoraim, are known from other references and are located within Judaean territory. Zorah and Ayalon are more familiar as Danite, but were eventually, probably in different periods, regarded as Judaean (cf. Josh. 15.33; I Chron. 2.53; II Chron. 28.18). All the cities are situated at strategic points along major routes leading to the heart of the Judaean hills, and the greatest attention is given to the western approaches, as the most common routes to Judah, from which danger was most imminent. The north is almost absent; the historical considerations summoned to explain this fact are determined by the time and circumstances to which the list is attributed.

There are four groups of fortifications; the first four cities, from north to south, Bethlehem, Etam, Tekoa and Bethzur, form a clear line of defence on the east. The next four, Soco, Adullam, Gath and Maresha, form the western line, also in a north-south direction. From a geographical point of view, two more cities on the western line should be included, Lachish and Azekah, but in the present structure of the list Lachish is grouped with the southern cities of Ziph and Adoraim while Azekah is attached to the north-western line of defence joining Zorah and Ayalon. The only city which stands outside its geographical context is Hebron, in the southern Judaean hills, mentioned at the end.

The main problem about the list is its chronological context: may we accept the Chronicler's assertion that it reflects the time of Rehoboam? Alternative ideas include the periods of Josiah (A. Alt, 'Festungen und Levitenorte', *Kleine Schriften* II, 1953, 306–15; V. Fritz, 'The "List of Rehoboam's Fortresses" in 2 Chr 11:5–12 – A Document from the Time of Josiah', *Eretz Israel* 15, 1981, 46*–53*), and Hezekiah (N. Na'aman, 'Hezekiah's Fortified Cities and the LMLK Stamps', *BASOR* 261, 1986, 5–21). It does not seem that any unequivocal literary or archaeological evidence can be brought forward in favour of any one view (but for Lachish, cf. D.

Ussishkin, 'Excavations at Tel Lachish', *Tel-Aviv* 5, 1978, 27–31; cf. also Dillard, 94). Certainly, this material does not reflect the full fortification system at any one period (this is certainly the case for the time of Rehoboam, in the wake of Solomon's great enterprises), nor the actual boundaries of the kingdom (cf. Z. Kallai, 'The Kingdom of Rehoboam', *Eretz Israel* 10, 1971, 245–54*), and would not reflect the full scope of the political reality. Conclusions, then, cannot be definite; but since it seems likely that the new king followed his father's policy in fortifying Judah, I am inclined, pending further evidence, to accept the association of this list with Rehoboam.

It remains, then, to inquire whether the fortifications were erected before or after Shishak's invasion (cf. Y. Aharoni, *The Land of the Bible*, 1979, 330–2; Kallai, ibid., 245–7; id., *Historical Geography of the Bible*, 1986, 79–83). It seems that in choosing the earlier context the Chronicler was guided by literary and theological considerations. It is difficult to see how Rehoboam, immediately after the national trauma of schism, could have undertaken and completed such a grand project in three years, only to sit idle after Shishak's campaign had revealed the vulnerability of his kingdom. The Chronicler ascribes to the Egyptian king the actual conquest of 'the fortified cities' (12.4), a claim not confirmed by Shishak's famous inscription at Karnak (cf. K. A. Kitchen, *The Third Intermediate Period in Egypt*, 1973, 294–300, 432–77 and below). In this, too, the literary-theological motif seems obvious: when Rehoboam had gone astray, Shishak's hordes came as a divine punishment, to deprive him of all that he had achieved during the good years when he had walked 'in the ways of the Lord' – the actual record of the campaign being influenced by that of Sennacherib (II Kings 18.13; cf. below). All this indicates that it is more probable that Rehoboam built fortifications both before and after the Egyptian invasion and that the list is a summary of this activity, its present position in the text determined by theological considerations.

[5] The verse begins with the words 'Rehoboam dwelt in Jerusalem' – a connecting link to the preceding passage. The same technique is also found in connection with Jehoshaphat (19.4), upon his return from his joint military campaign with Ahab. The second part of the verse, 'and he built, etc.', is a heading for what follows.

Evidently this verse, at least in its present phrasing, is Chronistic. The term for 'fortified cities' is the unique *'ārīm lᵉmāṣōr* (RSV 'cities for defence'); further similar terms, almost exclusively Chronistic, are *'ārē māṣōr* (II Chron. 8.5), *'ārē mᵉṣōrōt* (II Chron. 14.6 [MT 5]), *'ārē mᵉṣūrāh* (II Chron. 11.10, 11, 23; 12.4; 21.3, and *mᵉṣurōt* (II Chron. 11.11). These terms appear throughout the passage (vv. 5, 10, 11, 23; 12.4) and form a unifying *motif* of the Rehoboam story.

The derivation of this term, however, has been variously conceived. It may be regarded as deriving from *ṣwr* (cf. *BDB*, 848–9) – in which case the Chronicler would illustrate well the semantic development from *'ārīm lᵉmāṣōr*, 'cities for siege', to *'ārē māṣōr*, 'cities of siege', and then in the later form of the plural *'ārē mᵉṣurōt* and *mᵉṣurōt*. Alternatively, it may be derived from *nṣr* or be regarded as a loan-word from the Accadian *maṣṣarātu*, which probably found its way into Hebrew *via* the Aramaic, and gradually assimilated in meaning and usage to the original *māṣōr* (cf. Baumgartner, 589).

[6–10aα] The first four cities – Bethlehem, Etam, Tekoa and Beth-zur – are located on the north-eastern flank of Judah, occupying strategic points on the main north-south road and on the principal routes leading from the east to the hill country. The next four, Soco, Adullam, Gath and Maresha, are almost parallel in latitude to the first four, but on the west side. There is unanimous agreement on the identification of all these cities with the exception of Gath. It is hardly likely that the Philistine city of that name is intended; Gath was ruled by its own king even during the early days of Solomon's reign (I Kings 2.39–40), and was not an integral part of the kingdom of Judah. There is no reason to assume that its status changed thereafter. Geographically, the Philistine Gath would be at the western extreme of the line of fortifications, inside Philistine territory and practically isolated. The list must, then, intend a different Gath, between Adullam and Mareshah. Ziph and Adoraim are clearly in the south; together with Hebron they control the main roads leading from the south into the Judaean hills. Lachish and Azekah (also mentioned together in Jer. 34.7 and Neh. 11.30) were probably the most important strongholds on the western side in the Shephelah. In this list, Lachish is joined to the southern line of fortifications on its western edge, while Azekah is connected with the north-western cities of Zorah and Aijalon, situated on the routes leading to the northern parts of the Judaean hills from the west. The importance of Aijalon on the border between Judah and the Philistines may be illuminated by additional references to its history. It is included in the territory of Dan (Josh. 19.42), conquered by the Amorites (Judg. 1.35); it is a point of controversy between its Bejaminite residents and the people of Gath (I Chron. 8.13); and it is in fact a border point with the Philistines (I Sam. 14.31). Its recapture is referred to in the time of Ahaz (II Chron. 28.18), and it is also designated as a levitical city (Josh. 21.24).

Hebron, as the most important centre of the Judean hill country, is listed last, outside the geographical context.

[10aβ–12] Here the list ends, with the general situation of the cities 'in Judah and Benjamin', and a description of their provision with food and arms 'to make them very strong'. As far as one may gather from such a short unit, the vocabulary and style are characteristic of the Chronicler. The double reference to 'Judah and Benjamin', first as the geographical location of the cities (v. 10b), and then as a military/political unit under Rehoboam's control (v. 12b), is not supported by the list itself, which contains no Benjaminite city. The assertion that Rehoboam 'held Judah and Benjamin' is even more dubious historically, when we note how the territory of Benjamin comprised disputed territory between the two kingdoms (II Chron. 13.19; I Kings 15.17).

Like the phrase 'cities for defence' ('ārē mᵉṣurōt) noted above, here too 'shields and spears' (ṣinnōt ūrᵉmāḥīm; cf. on I Chron. 12.8) is attested only in Chronicles, occurring only here in the plural form. ḥizzēq ('to make strong') in the piel conjugation, while not limited to Chronicles, is a favourite usage there (fourteen times) and nāgīd ('commander') is also very frequent in the Chronicler's vocabulary – over twenty times. The phrase lᵉharbēh mᵉʾōd occurs once more, also in Chronicles (II Chron. 16.8). One may regard these verses, then, as the Chronicler's own composition, adding political 'body' and significance to the simple list of names.

[13–17] This unit is joined to the former passage by means of their common interest: v. 12b ends with the loyalty to Rehoboam of 'Judah and Benjamin'; the passage emphasizes the faithfulness of those members of the northern tribes who fled Jeroboam's rule to side with Judah:

(a) 13–15 the priests and the Levites
(b) 16–17 Israelite individuals.

[13–15] These verses are part of the general topic of 'priestly and levitical cities', which appears throughout the book. In the Chronicler's view, the priests and Levites actually dwelt in their allotted cities throughout the land (cf. I Chron. 6.54 [MT 6.39]; 13.2). What the Chronicler describes here is a major emigration of priests and Levites from all parts of the land, leaving their possessions to resettle in 'Judah and Jerusalem'.

Here for the first time (following I Kings 12.28ff.) the Chronicler alludes to the new cult established in the northern kingdom by Jeroboam, a theme resumed later in 13.8–9. In v. 15, the 'high places, satyrs and calves' (in 13.8 'golden calves') are a reasonable summary of I Kings 12.26–33, which indeed speak of 'calves of gold' (12.28) and 'houses on high places' (v. 31; also 13.33–34). The only reference added here is 'satyrs', known to us as the object of some cult only in Lev. 17.7. This addition is carefully considered. Jeroboam's transgression in establishing his new cult is placed within the frame of reference determined by Lev. 17 – the forbidding of sacrifices not offered with the proper blood-rite before 'the tent of meeting' (cf. Y. Kaufmann, History of the Religion of Israel, I, 1960, 130–1, 542–4*). Such offerings are regarded as 'sacrifices for satyrs'. The full identification of the Temple in Jerusalem with the 'tent of meeting' makes the entire sacrificial institution of the northern kingdom just such a 'cult of satyrs'.

The second of Jeroboam's undertakings, also emphasized in I Kings 12.31–32; 13.33, is the reorganization of the priesthood. This was a sound political step; considering the power of the sacerdotal class, Jeroboam had to ensure the loyalty of the officiating priests, and therefore recruited them from among his followers. This aspect of his reform is mentioned here in v. 15, 'and he appointed his own priests', and is further detailed in 13.9. It seems, however, that the topic of the priesthood is differently presented in the contexts of Kings and Chronicles. According to I Kings 12.26ff., Jeroboam initiated two separate religious innovations, not in principle automatically connected: the cult of the calves and the reorganization of the clergy. The Chronicler regards the two issues as one. Viewed from the perspective of the centralization of the cult, the legitimate priests and Levites could serve only in Jerusalem; against the background of the Second Temple system of rotating divisions, this opportunity was now denied them by the schism, since to dwell in the northern kingdom prevented their free communication to Jerusalem. Their only chance to realize their privilege to serve God was to move to the kingdom of Judah. And as is clear from the words 'Jeroboam *and his sons* cast them out', 'his sons' referring to all the following kings of northern Israel, the very separate existence of this kingdom will continue to prevent the priests and Levites from realizing their privilege and duty.

In Chronicles the word *migrāš*, 'common land', and especially 'a city of common land' (*'ir migrāš*), denotes not only the common grazing lands around a city but the levitical cities themselves (cf. Japhet, *VT* 18, 348–50). The Levites held no 'inheritance' but only 'cities'; these they now leave in order to emigrate to Judah.

In this context (as elsewhere in Chronicles), 'Levites' has two meanings: in the narrow sense, those of the tribe of Levi who were not priests (v. 13), and more broadly, all members of the tribe of Levi, including priests (v. 14).

[16–17] These verses are also associated with I Kings 12: 'and if this people go up to offer sacrifices in the house of the Lord at Jerusalem, then the heart of this people will turn again to their lord, to Rehoboam king of Judah' (v. 27). While in Kings this is a dangerous possibility, which Jeroboam takes every measure to prevent, in Chronicles it is presented as a historical fact: 'and those who had set their hearts to seek the Lord God of Israel came after them from all the tribes of Israel to Jerusalem to sacrifice to the Lord ... They strengthened the kingdom of Judah ...' Nevertheless, Jeroboam's greater fear, that 'the kingdom will turn back to the house of David' (I Kings 12.26), is not realized, even in Chronicles.

The phrasing of these verses leaves ambiguous the purpose of this move of members of 'all the tribes of Israel to Jerusalem'. On the one hand it seems that the reference is only to a one-time pilgrimage 'to sacrifice to the Lord', in contrast to the priests and Levites who 'left ... their holdings'. Yet the phrase 'they strengthened the kingdom of Judah' would imply a permanent migration. Whatever the case, this population movement was limited to the first three years of Rehoboam's rule, as determined by the Chronicler's theological views (above p. 664). These people 'set their heart to seek the Lord', and follow 'the way of David and Solomon' – again regarding David and Solomon as equals.

[18–23] This reference to Rehoboam's wives, concubines and children is an exceptional document: only for king David has Chronicles recorded his wives and their sons by name. There is a somewhat similar record, of Jehoshaphat's sons, in II Chron. 21.2–4, while of Abijah we read that he had fourteen wives, twenty-two sons and sixteen daughters, with no record of their names (13.21). Of David's wives, seven are registered by name with their fifteen sons, while his concubines and their children remain anonymous (I Chron. 3.1–9; 14.3–7). Solomon's extraordinary harem is not mentioned in Chronicles. Rehoboam, then, with his eighteen wives, sixty concubines, twenty-eight sons and sixty daughters, surpasses all.

Two of Rehoboam's wives and their seven sons are mentioned by name. His first wife, Mahalath, was his cousin, herself of royal descent: her father was 'Jerimoth, the son of David' – probably one of the sons of David not mentioned by name in our records – and her mother was in turn Jerimoth's cousin, the daughter of David's brother, Eliab. Through Mahalath's detailed affiliation one may get a glimpse of the marriage customs of either the period in general or the royal court in particular: strict consanguinity.

It has been suggested that 'Abihail' was another wife of Rehoboam rather than his mother-in-law; this seems unlikely. Verses 19–20 continue the account in the singular: '... and she bore him sons ... After her he took. ...' (cf. Rudolph, 230), referring throughout to Mahalath. Most unusually, then, mention is made, not only of Mahalath's father but also – probably because of her distinguished pedigree – of her mother as well.

An apparently innocent detail concerning Rehoboam's second wife identifies her as 'Maacah the daughter of Absalom', Abijah's mother. This creates a famous crux, for which several solutions have been suggested. The relevant texts are as follows. In I Kings 15.2 the mother of Abijah/Abijam is introduced as 'Maacah the daughter of Abishalom'. In I Kings 15.10, Maacah is Asa's mother, as confirmed by I Kings 15.13 ('He also removed Maacah his mother from being queen'). These texts may be harmonized by assuming that Abijah and Asa were brothers, both sons of Rehoboam by Maacah – but this solution would contradict the statement of I Kings 15.8, that when Abijah died 'Asa *his son* reigned in his stead'.

The difficulty is further complicated by II Chron. 13.2. Deviating from its synoptic text in I Kings 15.2, Chronicles here introduces Abijah's mother as 'Micaiah the daughter of Uriel of Gibeah', while in II Chron. 15.16

(//I Kings 15.13) the name of Asa's mother is Maacah. These data by themselves would suggest a reasonable solution to the problem: Abijah's mother was indeed 'Micaiah the daughter of Uriel', while Asa's mother was 'Maacah, the daughter of Absalom' (I Kings 15.10, 13; II Chron. 15.16). I Kings 15.2 would then be regarded as a corruption.

Against this very plausible solution, however, we have our present passage, which repeats the name of Maacah three times as Rehoboam's wife, and tells how for love of her he chose her son Abijah, although not his firstborn, to be his heir.

Thus, no one solution can encompass all the evidence. Either this passage (vv. 20–22) or II Chron. 13.1 is authentic, but not both. As no satisfactory solution has been offered so far, we may add a few more observations. It is quite probable (although impossible to prove) that 'Absalom', Maacah's father, is the famous son of David; this would mean that Maacah, too, was Rehoboam's cousin. On the other hand, we might summon the evidence of II Sam. 14.27, that Absalom had only one daughter: Tamar. If we were to follow this line of reasoning, we would claim that Maacah was not actually Absalom's daughter but his granddaughter, through Tamar and her husband 'Uriel of Gibeah' – Maacah's father. 'Maacah' and 'Micaiah' could then be regarded as interchangeable. The proposed line would be as follows:

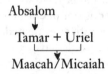

This possible genealogical reconstruction would still not solve all the difficulties. We would have to assume – in spite of I Kings 15.1 – that Asa and Abijah were brothers, or – in spite of I Kings 15.10, 13 – that Maacah was Asa's grandmother rather than mother.

Verse 22 refers to a particular procedure of succession, which in this form is not attested elsewhere: Rehoboam appoints his successor during his lifetime, explicitly because 'he loved Maacah above all his wives and concubines'; the heir-apparent is thus the first-born son of the beloved queen rather than of the king himself. In some respects the precedent of this is the succession of Solomon, for which an explicit oath sworn to Bath-sheba his mother is repeatedly referred to as the justification (I Kings 1.13 etc.).

Abijah is appointed by Rehoboam 'as chief prince among his brothers', either a title implying certain official responsibilities and probable co-regency, or merely a general, unbinding appellation – an alternative which cannot be decided in the absence of relevant data. A similar procedure is described by the Chronicler in the case of Jehoram, who inherited rule from

Jehoshaphat (II Chron. 21.2–4, cf. below). Verse 23 then elaborates on Rehoboam's measures to ensure a smooth and unproblematical succession. He distances from Jerusalem either all or some of his sons, setting them in other areas of his kingdom, and providing for all their needs, while the kingdom is left for Abijah.

The last clause *wayyiš'al hᵃmōn nāšīm* (literally 'and sought many wives') is rather strange. A new division of the text, reading *wayyiśśā' lāhem nāšīm* (RSV 'and procured wives for them'), was suggested by Ehrlich (*Randglossen zur Hebräischen Bibel* VII, 1914, 361), and generally accepted.

The language and style of vv. 22–23 reflect some of the usages known generally in Late Biblical Hebrew (e.g. the use of the verb *nś'*, in place of *lqh* for taking a woman in marriage, cf. v. 21), or the increase in the use of nominal elliptic clauses, as in 'to make him king' (v. 22), while some are more strictly Chronistic (e.g. the frequent use of *lārōb* for 'abundant', in v. 23).

Does the certainly late phrasing of the passage also reflect on the origin and authenticity of the information it contains? A connection between this passage and vv. 5–12 is provided by the reference to 'fortified cities' in both. If we deny the authenticity of the earlier list, this would affect the evaluation of the present passage as well, but even if we regard the list as authentic, we may still attribute the present passage to the Chronicler's hand.

Nothing in the content of the passage would lead us to doubt its authenticity. The subject presented is not one which the Chronicler finds himself obliged to include in his narrative; evaluated on its own terms the information is quite probable. One would have expected that after the problematical precedents of the past, in the chain of succession from David to Solomon and from Solomon to Rehoboam, some kind of standard transfer of the kingship would be devised. It is possible that such measures were indeed taken by Rehoboam, following his own bitter experience. If we regard the procedure presented here as becoming standard, this would account for the fact that it is not recounted in the history of the monarchy; the fact that it is raised in the case of Jehoram (21.1–4) is because, in spite of Jehoshaphat's precautions, Jehoram massacred all his brothers after his accession. It would seem likely, therefore, that this passage contains authentic material, couched in the Chronicler's late idiom.

12

12 When the rule of Rehoboam was established and was strong, he forsook the law of the Lord, and all Israel with him. [2] In the fifth year of King Rehoboam, because they had been unfaithful to the Lord, Shishak king of Egypt came up against Jerusalem [3] with twelve hundred chariots and sixty thousand horsemen. And the people were without number who came with him from Egypt – Libyans, Sukki-im, and Ethiopians. [4] And he took the fortified cities of Judah and came as far as Jerusalem. [5] Then Shemaiah the prophet came to Rehoboam and to the princes of Judah, who had gathered at Jerusalem because of Shishak, and said to them, 'Thus says the Lord, "You abandoned me, so I have abandoned you to the hand of Shishak."' [6] Then the princes of Israel and the king humbled themselves and said, 'The Lord is righteous.' [7] When the Lord saw that they humbled themselves, the word of the Lord came to Shemaiah: 'They have humbled themselves; I will not destroy them, but I will grant them some deliverance, and my wrath shall not be poured out upon Jerusalem by the hand of Shishak. [8] Nevertheless they shall be servants to him, that they may know my service and the service of the kingdoms of the countries.'

9 So Shishak king of Egypt came up against Jerusalem; he took away the treasures of the house of the Lord and the treasures of the king's house; he took away everything. He also took away the shields of gold which Solomon had made; [10] and King Rehoboam made in their stead shields of bronze, and committed them to the hands of the officers of the guard, who kept the door of the king's house ... [11] And as often as the king went into the house of the Lord, the guard came and bore them, and brought them back to the guardroom. 12 And when he humbled himself the wrath of the Lord turned from him, so as not to make a complete destruction; moreover, conditions were good in Judah.

13 So King Rehoboam established himself in Jerusalem and reigned. Rehoboam was forty-one years old when he began to reign, and he reigned seventeen years in Jerusalem, the city which the Lord had chosen out of all the tribes of Israel to put his name there. His mother's name was Naamah the Ammonitess. [14] And he did evil, for he did not set his heart to seek the Lord.

15 Now the acts of Rehoboam, from first to last, are they not written in the chronicles of Shemaiah the prophet and of Iddo the seer? There were continual wars between Rehoboam and Jeroboam. [16] And Rehoboam slept with his fathers, and was buried in the city of David; and Abijah his son reigned in his stead.

B. Notes to RSV

[1] 'when the rule ... was established and was strong', better 'and *he* was strong' (NEB); [3] 'Sukkiim', better 'Sukkites' (NEB); 'Ethiopians', MT 'Cushites' (NEB; JPS); [10] 'kept the door', better NEB 'guarded the entrance'; [12] 'conditions

were good in Judah', better 'good things were found in Judah' (JPS; cf. II Chron. 19.3); [13] 'established himself', MT 'grew strong' (NEB 'increased his power', cf. v. 1); [15] 'from first to last', cf. on 9.29; 'the chronicles ... of Iddo the seer', RSV margin adds, with MT, 'to enrol oneself', JPS 'in the manner of genealogy'.

C. Structure, sources and form

1. The chapter contains the Chronicler's thorough reorganization and adaptation of I Kings 14.21–31:

II Chron. 12.2 + 9–12 = I Kings 14.25–28
II Chron. 12.13–14, 15–16 = I Kings 14.21–24, 29–31

The order of the material has been changed, certain parts are omitted (I Kings 14.22b–24) and some additions are made in Chronicles (esp. 12.2b–8, 12–13a); various changes are also introduced into the synoptic sections.

2. The literary method employed by the Chronicler here is familiar to us from earlier parts of his work. His new introduction (v. 1) provides the necessary transition from the preceding unit, as well as a theological basis for the understanding of the following narrative. Then comes a citation of the text of I Kings 14.25ff., the flow of which is interrupted for the insertion of six additional verses. Following this, the source text is resumed from exactly the point where it left off, and is adhered to faithfully to its conclusion. As we have seen many times, this could be illustrated as follows:

I Kings 14.25		I Kings 14.26ff.
II Chron. 12.1–2	3–8	9ff.

In a variation on this technique, v. 9 introduces the original sequence of I Kings 14.25–26 with the words 'So Shishak king of Egypt came up against Jerusalem', a resumptive repetition of v. 2aβ, necessary here because a direct continuation with I Kings 14.26 would not have afforded a smooth, coherent sequence (cf. I.L. Seeligmann, 'Hebräische Erzählung und Biblische Geschichtsschreibung', ThZ 18, 1962, 315). The chapter, then, is composed of two parts:

(a) 1–12 The story of Shishak's campaign
(b) 13–16 Biographical and chronological summary.

3. The most comprehensive reworking, from both a theological and historical point of view, is in the description of Shishak's campaign (vv. 2–12). The Chronicler attempts to conform the narrative to his general philosophy of history, as an expression of God's providential attributes and the determination of Israel's fate by religious conduct.

In addition to this theological stand, and quite independent of it, the Chronistic version also presents some new historical details (all found in v. 3) which conform to our knowledge of the period, and pass the test of historical probability. It is therefore generally (though certainly not unanimously) accepted that in the elaboration of the description of Shishak's campaign the Chronicler may have used an additional source.

This passage is thus a weave of various elements:

(a) 2a, 9–11, taken from I Kings 14.25–28;
(b) 3, probably reflecting an extra-biblical source;
(c) The introduction and conclusion (vv. 1, 12), a broad insert (vv. 4–8), and an explanatory gloss (v. 2b) – all composed by the Chronicler.

4. Verses 13–16 reflect quite faithfully the Deuteronomistic framework and tone of the Kings source:

13–14 = the introductory part of I Kings 14.21–22a (rephrased; 22b–24 omitted)
15–16 = the concluding part of I Kings 14.29–31 (with alterations).

The Chronicler's own contribution is sensed in the middle, in vv. 14 and 15. The whole passage parallels 9.29–31; it employs the standard Chronistic formulas and brings to a conclusion the history of Rehoboam.

D. Commentary

[1–12] I Kings 14.25–28 describes most concisely Shishak's invasion of Jerusalem and his looting of the treasures. For the Chronicler this story represents a theological difficulty, since no motive is indicated for the attack, nor a reason for the specific date, 'in the fifth year of ... Rehoboam', nor any explanation for the relatively mild consequences. Accordingly, the Chronicler supplies the narrative with a theologically coherent substructure: the invasion was a punishment; it was preceded by a transgression in Rehoboam's fourth year; in the course of the campaign some turn of events caused the moderation of its aftermath. The chronological sequence of the event is thus developed along these lines. For three years Rehoboam and the people 'walked in the way' of the Lord (11.17); in the fourth year they sinned (12.1); in the fifth they were punished (12.2–4). At the climax of the threat to Jerusalem, a prophet succeeded in bringing the people to repentance, and the actual damage was minimized (12.5–8). From this point on, the Chronicler feels free to cite the original conclusion of the story.

It should be noted that also in Kings the description of Rehoboam's sins – a major part of the Deuteronomistic opening – comes prior to Shishak's campaign and is in fact much more severe than any of the Chronicler's statements regarding Rehoboam. However, while in Kings the causal relationship between 'sin' and 'punishment' is only implied, the Chronicler makes it as explicit as possible: in his preface (v. 1), in his explanatory gloss (v. 2b: 'because they had been unfaithful to the Lord'), and, finally, in his conclusion (v. 12).

[1] The two principal terms of this verse literally 'with the establishment' ($k^e h \bar{a} k \bar{\imath} n$) and 'at his strengthening' ($u k^e h e z q \bar{a} t \bar{o}$), are characteristically

Chronistic. The two are infinitives, each prefaced by a preposition to become a nominal clause. All the components of this usage: the preposition k^e in this specific function, its conjunction with the infinitive to signify an indefinite temporal clause, and the placement of this temporal clause at the beginning of the sentence, are all common phenomena in Chronicles (cf. Curtis, §125, p.35). The two roots, in their various forms, are also Chronistic 'favourites'.

'Strength' is indeed a leading *motif* in the context of Rehoboam's reign. The constant reference to the king's 'strengthening' of his sovereignty or being 'strengthened' by the support he received reflect the Chronicler's constant awareness of the impact of the schism (11.17; 12.13; also 11.11, 12, and, negatively, 13.7). However, this very self-reliance prompts Rehoboam and his people to forsake 'the law of the Lord'. This view of human psychology is found several times in Chronicles, based on the classical formulation of Deut. 8.11–17: 'Take heed lest you forget the Lord your God ... lest when you have eaten and are full and have built goodly houses ... then your heart be lifted up and you forget the Lord your God ... Beware lest you say in your heart: My power and the might of my hand have gotten me this wealth', and the succinct metaphor of Deut. 32.15: 'But Jeshurun waxed fat and kicked'. What is posed in Deuteronomy as a possible dangerous psychological turn is described in Chronicles as having come to pass several times during the period of the monarchy. This is particularly true of Uzziah (26.16: 'But when he was strong he grew proud'), but also of that most righteous king after David and Solomon, Hezekiah (32.25–26).

Material strength and security make the people confident and tempt them to assert their own powers and to deny any debt to transcendental factors. Rehoboam's sin is not specified, but it is said of him that he 'forsook' ('*zb*) the law of the Lord' – the same verb '*zb* which becomes the theme of Shemaiah's rebuke in v. 5: 'You abandoned me'. The phrase 'all Israel with him' prepares the way for the meting out of the divine punishment not only to the king himself, but to the people as well (vv. 4, 5, 6).

[2] To the opening phrase of the story, taken from I Kings 14.25, the Chronicler adds the explicit explanation of the invasion as well-deserved; the root *m'l* (RSV 'unfaithful') has here, as elsewhere in Chronicles, the broadest connotation (I Chron. 10.13; II Chron. 26.18, etc).

Shishak's campaign has been dealt with in great detail in scholarly literature (cf. K. A. Kitchen, *The Third Intermediate Period in Egypt*, 1973, 294–300; 432–47; D. Redford, 'Studies in Relations between Palestine and Egypt during the First Millenium BC', *JAOS* 93, 1973, 7–13). It is one of the few pre-Assyrian incidents which is supported and elucidated by extra-biblical epigraphic sources. The context here is very different from that of I Kings 14.25–28, which is focussed more on the question how the kingdom of Judah lost the precious 'golden shields' made by Solomon than on military issues.

Shishak's royal inscription at Karnak, which provides a detailed topographical list of over 150 localities captured by Shishak during his campaign, reveals that Shishak's targets were mostly in northern Israel and in the non-fortified areas of the Negeb, rather than in Judah. It is therefore possible that even the limited perspective of I Kings 14.25–28 is not strictly accurate, and that the kingdom's treasures, rather than being looted, were in fact offered by Rehoboam to keep Shishak from invading Judaean territory. Our biblical sources supply us with no information at all on the course of Shishak's main offensive in northern Israel, and its military and political consequences.

One of the important aspects of this event is that once the date of Shishak is determined by reference to Egyptian data (c. 945–924 BC; cf. Kitchen, 287ff.), a relatively solid comparative point is available for the Israelite chronological system.

[3–4] Here the Chronicler presents details of the campaign not found in Kings: the number of the chariots (1200) is usually regarded as plausible, and therefore '60,000 horsemen' may be a textual corruption of an original 6000 (cf. Williamson, 247; but cf. Kitchen, who regards the number 60,000 as 'not totally impossible', ibid., 295). The composition of the army is given as 'Lybians, Sukkites and Cushites (RSV Ethiopians)' – a combination which cannot be regarded as of a literary biblical origin. 'Lybians and Cushites' appear together only once in a pre-Chronistic source (Nahum 3.9, as part of the Egyptian force, and differently phrased; again later in II Chron. 16.8 and Dan. 11.43). The 'Sukkites' are not mentioned elsewhere in the Bible at all, but are known from Egyptian history, in particular from the 13–12th centuries BC, and were probably related to the Lybians (cf. Kitchen, 295). Their appearance in this connection, while perhaps reflecting the Chronicler's own circumstances, is more likely to derive from some authentic source. The fact that Shishak himself was a Nubian ('Cushite' in the Bible) gives added credibility to this information, regarded by scholars as authentic (cf. inter al. Williamson, 246–7; Dillard, 99–100).

Verse 4 ascribes to Shishak the conquest of the 'fortified cites' of Judah, 'as far as Jerusalem'. Is this historically reliable? While the term used to denote these cities is certainly Chronistic, this consideration is not conclusive, as this may have been the Chronistic replacement of some other usage. More decisive is the fact that there is a real contrast between this verse and the independent evidence of the inscription of Shishak, in which all the locations indicated in Judah are in fact the *unfortified* settlements of the Negeb; of the list of Rehoboam's cities (11.6–10), only Aijalon is mentioned. It would seem, then, that the note in v. 4 has no historical basis; it may have been prompted by the following motives:

(a) The theme of 'fortifed cities' is employed as a unifying factor in the Rehoboam pericope and serves the literary role of *Leitmotif.*

(b) From a theological point of view, v. 4 illustrates very concretely how the achievements of the days of faithfulness were to be lost when the people 'forsook the law of the Lord'.

(c) The Chronicler might have had a historical difficulty: how could Shishak have come as far as Jerusalem? His conclusion is that Shishak must first have overpowered all the fortified cities on the way.

(d) Lastly, this verse draws a parallel between the two major campaigns into the land of Judah: Shishak's and Sennacherib's (II Kings 18.13ff.). This point should be further elucidated.

The main point of Sennacherib's invasion, according to both biblical account and the Assyrian records, was the conquest of all the fortified cities and the complete isolation of Jerusalem (cf. M. Cogan and H. Tadmor, *II Kings*, 1988, 246–51). Shishak's campaign, according to I Kings 14.25ff., had no such disastrous effects on the land of Judah; damage was limited to property in Jerusalem. Although different in scope and consequences, the two events are introduced in similar terms, and in both the foreign invader makes off with the Temple treasures:

> I Kings 14.25: 'In the fifth year of king Rehoboam, Shishak king of Egypt came up against Jersualem; he took away the treasures of the house of the Lord ...'
> II Kings 18.13: 'In the fourteenth year of King Hezekiah Sennacherib king of Assyria came up against ... Judah ... And Hezekiah gave him all the silver ... in the house of the Lord ...'

The Chronicler's reworking uses this similarity as a point of departure. He further develops the common features, attributing to both Rehoboam and Hezekiah the flaw of arrogance and the grace of subsequent humility (cf. 12.1, 6–7 and 32.24–25); for both monarchs 'the wrath of the Lord' was mitigated. On the other hand, the Chronicler reverses the evaluation of the invasion in each case to conform better with his theological convictions. The categorical statement of II Kings 18.13, 'Sennacherib ... came up against all the fortified cities of Judah *and took them*', is changed in Chronicles to read '... *thinking to win them for himself*' (32.1). Thus the danger in Hezekiah's time is greatly moderated, while the threat to Rehoboam is depicted, quite without basis in I Kings 14.25ff., as dire indeed: 'Shishak ... took the fortified cities of Judah' (v. 5). The Chronicler's account thus emphasizes the contextual similarity: the two monarchs become strong and self-confident; both are threatened by the invasion of a foreign emperor and 'humble themselves' in time; their treasures are taken, but Jerusalem is saved. However, since both Rehoboam and the people, who 'forsook ... the Lord ... with him', are held in lower esteem, Rehoboam lost to the conqueror the fortified cities of Judah, while in the time of Hezekiah they were saved.

[5–8] The two-stage encounter between the prophet Shemaiah and the king and princes of Judah is described in vv. 5–6 and 7–8. Here, too, parallel lines are drawn to Sennacherib's invasion, as the princes of Judah 'had gathered at Jerusalem because of Shishak', i.e. because of Shishak's presumed conquest of the fortified cities, immediately calling to mind the similar circumstances (although differently presented) at the time of Hezekiah. The involvement of a prophet is also a shared element, although here Shemaiah takes the initiative (like many of the prophetic figures in Chronicles), while Isaiah was approached by Hezekiah's delegation (II Kings 19.1–2). In both episodes, finally, we find acts and words of repentance (cf. II Kings 19.2–4), answered by God's averting the danger announced by the prophet (cf. II Kings 19.21–34). Thus the Chronicler has formulated the story of Shishak's campaign in analogy to Sennacherib's invasion in II Kings 18–19, even though his own version of the latter takes a much shorter form (cf. II Chron. 32.9–21).

While the gathering of 'the princes of Judah' in Jerusalem shows first of all the destruction caused by Shishak's campaign, it also serves another purpose: the prophet addresses not only the king himself but also the leaders of the people, who also 'forsook the law of the Lord' and now repent together with the ruler – a characteristic feature of the Chronicler's 'democratized' view of the monarchy and systematized view of divine justice. The appellation 'princes of Judah' (v. 5) refers to a geographical perspective, while 'princes of Israel' (v. 6) emphasizes their role as representatives of their people.

Shemaiah's aphorism ('You abandoned me, etc.') combines laconic facts, causal dynamic, and a poignant *double-entendre* of the one verb *'zb*. In the first clause, this indeed denotes 'abandon'; in the second, God is seen not merely as 'abandoning' Israel, but as *'delivering'* them into the hands of Shishak (cf. also Ps. 37.33; Neh. 9.28). Shemaiah's simple declaration of fact is actually understood by the people as a call for repentance, and rightly so. The dynamic of cause and effect is even now reversible: repentance will bring a new outcome.

The new spiritual disposition of the 'princes of Israel and the king' is described by the term 'humbled themselves' – another key word in this story (vv. 6, 7 (bis), 12), and important to the Chronicler's concept of religious experience. 'Humility', countering man's conceited trust in his own power, is a precondition of any true repentance. Here it entails the recognition that 'the Lord is righteous'. This then is the response of both king and people to the prophet's declaration of the cause-effect principle of judgment: a spontaneous surrender to divine righteousness found quite often in the Bible: 'God is just – and we are in the wrong' (cf. e.g. Neh. 9.33; Ezra 9.15, etc.).

God's response to this humility is an immediate second prophetic message declaring a new decision, directly reflecting the people's conduct: 'They have humbled themselves, I will not destroy them'. It is only here, in the words 'my wrath shall not be poured out upon Jersualem' (v. 7b), that the imminent danger to Jerusalem is spelled out, and in much more severe terms than in I Kings 14.25ff., where even the words 'Shishak came up against Jerusalem' do not convey a sense of mortal peril. In Chronicles, Jerusalem under Rehoboam was facing total destruction, averted only by the people's recognition and repentance. This, too, brings our narrative closer to the threats to Jerusalem during the reigns of Hezekiah (when Jerusalem was spared), and Zedekiah (when it was indeed conquered and destroyed). Even the term 'my wrath shall not be poured out', used by the Chronicler here, belongs to the idiom of Jeremiah (Jer. 7.20; 42.18; 44.6), clearly referring to the destruction of the first Temple.

In the present pericope, this danger has been mitigated, but not entirely removed, as is clear from the continuation of God's words in v. 8. The Chronicler includes an element not attested elsewhere: the 'servitude' to be imposed on Rehoboam by Shishak of Egypt. There is no indication of the supposed duration of this forced service, and we can only conjecture whether the Chronicler knows of it from some source no longer extant, or produced the idea himself.

This part of God's words is also phrased as a word-play on one root: 'serve' ('bd). God makes the people serve Shishak in order that they may know the difference between the service of God and the enslavement to earthly powers. Here, again, we find an implied causality: to avoid the Lord's service leads to slavery, while to serve God – the source of human well-being – is liberation.

This second phase in the encounter between Shemaiah and the people is one-sided and lacks the dramatic literary balance of the first: we have to assume that the prophet indeed addressed the prophecy to the people, and their reaction is not recorded.

[9–11] The original narrative sequence now resumes from where it was interrupted in v. 2. In order to bridge the lengthy gap, the Chronicler repeats the note concerning Shishak's approach. The choice of words even reflects the steady progress of the Egyptian force, which in v. 4 'came as far as Jersualem', and here already 'came up against Jerusalem', only to return, however, after looting the sacred and royal treasures, including the golden shields of Solomon.

While the loss of these treasures is the focus of the story in I Kings 14, here it is only the reduced form of divine punishment. The Chronicler, however, has left the story of the shields unchanged (except for some linguistic alterations), causing a certain roughness between Shemaiah's prediction of serving 'the kingdoms of the countries' and the results of Shishak's invasion as actually described.

The shields serve what is primarily a ritual function, carried by the guard accompanying the king when passing from his own palace to the Temple. In one matter only do the new bronze shields differ from the gold ones: after this procession, they were returned for safekeeping not to the House of the Forest of Lebanon (I Kings 10.17; II Chron. 9.16), but to the guard's chamber.

[12] The moral of the event is summarized by the Chronicler with the terminology of the prophet's words. 'They have humbled themselves; I will not destroy them' is echoed in the Chronicler's concluding observation: 'when he humbled himself ... so as not to make a complete destruction'. This solitary verse is pregnant with the Chronicler's views, idioms and style. In order not to be too technical, I shall refer briefly to two matters only. The verse opens with *ūbᵉhikkānᵒō*, one word in Hebrew which is in fact a nominal clause comprising an infinitive, the final possessive suffix, a preposition and a conjunctive *waw*, serving as a temporal or causal clause. As in v. 1, it is placed at the beginning of the sentence and may be rendered 'and when he humbled himself' (RSV, literally 'and at his humbling himself'). The second is the expression *lᵉhašḥīt lᵉkālāh*), another nominal clause comprised of two infinitives prefixed by prepositions, the one serving as an conjugated verb and the other as its adverb, rendered by RSV 'so as not to make a complete destruction'. Moreover, both roots in their specific conjugations, 'humble onself' and 'destroy', are Chronistic 'favourites'. Thus, while each of the verse's peculiarities may not be exclusively Chronistic, their concentration in one short passage leaves no doubt concerning its authorship.

Beyond the repentance of Rehoboam, the verse ends with an emphasis of the idea that the people of Judah had 'some good in them' (not reflected in RSV, but cf. II Chron. 19.3). This last statement is needed for the theological consistency of the story: the king's conduct determines his fate, and the people's determines theirs; there is no substitution or vicarious responsibility.

[13–16] Coming to the end of the history of Rehoboam, the Chronicler here gleans from the two parts of the Deuteronomistic framework all the relevant biographical information, intergrating it into the context of the preceding passages with his own note: 'So King Rehoboam established himself (*wayyithazzēq*, NEB 'increased his power') in Jerusalem and reigned'. Two severe blows have marred Rehoboam's reign: the schism, which ended with the defection of northern Israel, and Shishak's invasion, which threatened the very existence of Judah. Rehoboam's very survival, then, is evidence of a 'strengthening'; here the same verb which signalled the beginning of the king's transgression (v. 1) now marks a positive establishment of his rule: the Davidic line survives and Jerusalem is spared.

The details of Rehoboam's reign now presented follow first of all the data of I Kings 14.21, where we already find a specific affirmation of the choice of

Jerusalem, not a common element in the standard Deuteronomistic framework. The Chronicler takes a stronger stance, using repetition to emphasize a gradual increase in attachment: 'Rehoboam dwelt in Jerusalem' (11.5); '... established himself in Jerusalem' (12.13a); and '... reigned ... in Jerusalem, the city which the Lord had chosen' (v. 13b).'

In the general evaluation of Rehoboam as an evildoer (v. 14), the Chronicler agrees with I Kings 1.22–24; the enumeration of his sins, however, is drastically abbreviated and completely rephrased. The appraisal 'he did not set his heart to seek the Lord' certainly expresses reservations about his religious attitudes, but not downright condemnation. This characteristic Chronistic phrase adequately expresses an ambivalence over Rehoboam. He is presented as a king who twice humbled himself before the Lord and heeded his prophets: in refraining from fighting Israel (11.4) and in repenting during Shishak's invasion (12.6). On the other hand, his reign was also the occasion of the tragic schism between Judah and Israel, and the invasion of Shishak, who threatened Jerusalem and looted its treasures. Rehoboam's history is, then, a complex mixture of good and evil, success and failure; his rule is sketched in moderate contrast to the severely negative view of I Kings 14.22–24, and the final verdict, 'he did evil', is delivered as briefly as possible.

In v. 15–16, the Deuteronomistic conclusion of I Kings 14.29–31 is rephrased and altered. The Kings formula, 'Now the rest of the acts of Rehoboam, and all that he did', is represented by the standard Chronistic form 'Now the acts of Rehoboam, from first to last' (cf. on I Chron. 29.29). Here, too, as with other kings, the sources to which the Chronicler refers his readers are different.

It is not immediately clear whether 'the chronicles of Shemaiah ... and of Iddo ...' indicates one source or two. In previous such references for the histories of David and Solomon, the Chronicler gives a separate title to each work (cf. I Chron. 29.29 and, especially, II Chron. 9.29: 'the history of Nathan ... the prophecy of Ahijah ... the visions of Iddo'). In this passage we should look to the word *l^ehityaḥēś* (RSV margin 'to enrol oneself') as an indication of the type of document attributed to the seer Iddo, i.e. a composition like that mentioned in Ezra 2.62: 'The book of their enrolment' (differently RSV), or assumed in I Chron. 9.1.

The two works, then, which the Chronicler mentions as sources, are 'the chronicles of Shemaiah the prophet' and 'the genealogical enrolment of Iddo the seer'. The two names are hardly coincidental: Shemaiah is presented in Chronicles as accompanying all the crises of Rehoboam's life (11.2; 12.5, 7), and Iddo has been associated with Jeroboam (9.29), and will be mentioned again in reference to Abijah in 13.22. As usual in the Chronicler's citations of 'source titles', the exact intention here is not clear; we may be expected to understand that the 'genealogical enrolment' (v. 15) is the source for all the details of Rehoboam's family (11.18–22). It is noteworthy, however, that Iddo's composition is termed in 13.22 'the story (*midraš*) of the prophet Iddo', and in 9.29 'the visions of Iddo the seer'. It is hardly likely that the same Iddo wrote three different works; the various titles, and even the prophet's alternative title of 'seer', point to a strong literary element, which renders the historicity of these remarks higly questionable.

The 'chronicles of Shemaiah' present a somewhat more complex problem. We have noted the probability that the Chronicler had some extra-biblical source for Rehoboam's reign; but whether this was some kind of 'prophetic source' (so B. Mazar, 'Ancient Israelite Historiography', *World Congress of Jewish Studies* I, 1952, 360–1*) or a limited section of a more comprehensive history of Judah cannot be ascertained.

The note about 'continual wars between Rehoboam and Jeroboam' is taken from I Kings 14.30, with the collective singular 'war' becoming 'wars' – a common feature in the Chronicler's idiom (cf. Kropat, 9–10). This ongoing conflict, the almost inevitable result of the schism, continued during the reigns of Abijah and Asa (I Kings 15.7, 16; II Chron. 13), and ceased only under Jehoshaphat. Since Rehoboam refrained from launching a major campaign against Jeroboam immediately after the schism, these references are probably limited skirmishes on the common boundary of the two kingdoms, in the territory of Benjamin (cf. further on ch. 13).

Verse 16 differs from I Kings 14.31 in that it lacks the repetition of 'with his fathers' and the note 'his mother's name was Naamah the Ammonitess'. Since the same two portions are missing from the Peshitta of Kings, and the mention of Naamah from some LXX MSS, they may be textual corruptions, with Chronicles preserving the better version. A third difference regards the name of Rehoboam's successor, which in I Kings is always Abi*jam* (I Kings 14.31; 15.1, 7bis, 8), and in Chronicles – Abi*jah* (I Chron. 3.10; II Chron. 12.16; 13.1, 2, 3, 4, 15, 17, 19, 22, 14.1 [MT 13.23]) or Abi*jahu* (II Chron. 13.20, 21, RSV Abijah).

The form Abijam is unique, while Abijah is quite common throughout the biblical period; one might therefore consider the first authentic and the other a variant tradition or a Chronistic alteration. Some scholars have proposed that the name Abijam contains the theophoric element 'Yam', which the Chronicler wished to avoid (Dillard, 101). Malamat would go further and, following Albright (*Archaeology and the Religion of Israel*, 158, 219), propose that Abijam was a Phoenician name, pointing to the Phoenician origin of his mother Maacah (A. Malamat, *Israel in Biblical Times*, 1983, 208–9*). Such a process, however, while theoretically possible, is not supported by the source material itself. No other such replacement is attested in the Chronicler's onomasticon; a name like 'Miriam', which may contain the same component, appears in I Chron. 4.17; 6.3 [MT 5.29]. One may note, too, that the

Chronicler had no objection to names with other theophoric elements like Baal and Moth (Eshbaal, Ahimoth, Jeremoth, etc.).

There is an alternative consideration: in I Kings 14.1 the name Abijah is given to Jeroboam's son, who did not survive; the name of Rehoboam's heir may have been changed, to distinguish between the two. This suggestion, too, lacks textual support; whatever form was original, the consistency of neither of the sources is affected by the other.

13 In the eighteenth year of King Jeroboam Abijah began to reign over Judah. [2] He reigned for three years in Jerusalem. His mother's name was Micaiah the daughter of Uriel of Gibe-ah.

Now there was war between Abijah and Jeroboam. [3] Abijah went out to battle having an army of valiant men of war, four hundred thousand picked men; and Jeroboam drew up his line of battle against him with eight hundred thousand picked mighty warriors. [4] Then Abijah stood up on Mount Zemaraim which is in the hill country of Ephraim, and said, 'Hear me, O Jeroboam and all Israel! [5] Ought you not to know that the Lord God of Israel gave the kingship over Israel for ever to David and his sons by a covenant of salt? [6] Yet Jeroboam the son of Nebat, a servant of Solomon the son of David, rose up and rebelled against his lord; [7] and certain worthless scoundrels gathered about him and defied Rehoboam the son of Solomon, when Rehoboam was young and irresolute and could not withstand them.

8 'And now you think to withstand the kingdom of the Lord in the hand of the sons of David, because you are a great multitude and have with you the golden calves which Jeroboam made you for gods. [9] Have you not driven out the priests of the Lord, the sons of Aaron, and the Levites, and made priests for yourselves like the peoples of other lands? Whoever comes to consecrate himself with a young bull or seven rams becomes a priest of what are no gods. [10] But as for us, the Lord is our God, and we have not forsaken him. We have priests ministering to the Lord who are sons of Aaron, and Levites for their service. [11] They offer to the Lord every morning and every evening burnt offerings and incense of sweet spices, set out the showbread on the table of pure gold, and care for the golden lampstand that its lamps may burn every evening; for we keep the charge of the Lord our God, but you have forsaken him. [12] Behold, God is with us at our head, and his priests with their battle trumpets to sound the call to battle against you. O sons of Israel, do not fight against the Lord, the God of your fathers; for you cannot succeed.'

13 Jeroboam had sent an ambush around to come on them from behind; thus his troops were in front of Judah, and the ambush was behind them. [14] And when Judah looked, behold, the battle was before and behind them; and they cried to the Lord, and the priests blew the trumpets. [15] Then the men of Judah raised the battle shout. And when the men of Judah shouted, God defeated Jeroboam and all Israel before Abijah and Judah. [16] The men of Israel fled before Judah, and God gave them into their hand. [17] Abijah and his people slew them with a great slaughter; so there fell slain of Israel five hundred thousand picked men. [18] Thus the men of Israel were subdued at that time, and the men of Judah prevailed, because they relied upon the Lord, the God of their fathers. [19] And Abijah pursued Jeroboam, and took cities from him, Bethel with its villages and Jeshanah with its villages and Ephron with its villages. [20] Jeroboam did not recover his power in the days of Abijah; and the Lord smote him, and he died. [21] But Abijah grew mighty. And he took fourteen wives, and

had twenty-two sons and sixteen daughters. [22] The rest of the acts of Abijah, his ways and his sayings, are written in the story of the prophet Iddo.

14 So Abijah slept with his fathers, and they buried him in the city of David; and Asa his son reigned in his stead. In his days the land had rest for ten years.

A. Notes to MT

[1] וַיִּמְלֹךְ, I Kings 15.1 מלך; מיכיהו, LXX, Peshitta, and I Kings 15.2 מעכה; [9] כעמי, LXX מעמי.

B. Notes to RSV

[5] 'by a covenant of salt', cf. commentary; [9] 'the sons of Aaron, and the Levites', better 'the sons of Aaron and the Levites' (JPS, also v. 10); 'or seven rams', MT '*and* seven rams' (NEB, JPS); [11] 'the table of pure gold', MT 'the pure table' (NEB 'a table ritually clean'); 'care for ... that its lamps may burn', MT 'kindle the lamps' (so NEB, cf. JPS).

C. Structure, sources and form

1. Chapter 13 is devoted to the reign of Abijah, Rehoboam's son, and is more than three times longer than the parallel in I Kings 15.1–8, a quantitative factor already indicating that Abijah has a different position in Chronicles from that in the Deuteronomistic historiography. The text in Kings follows the standard Deuteronomistic framework: introduction (vv. 1–5[6]), followed by conclusion (vv. 7–8), with no additional information barring the general note that 'there was war between Abijah and Jeroboam' (v. 7). Only in the introduction is there any elaboration, as the negative appraisal of Abijah is augmented by a rather long allusion to David (vv. 4–5).

The Chronicler applies himself to the Deuteronomistic material, but makes it only a point of departure for his own composition. He first divides the material into its two components and places the introductory elements at the beginning of his story (II Chron. 13.1–2//I Kings 15.1–2), and the concluding material at the end (II Chron. 13.22–14.1 [MT 13.22–23]//I Kings 15.7a, 8). The lengthy religious appraisal (I Kings 15.3–5) is omitted, but more than compensated for by the Chronicler's central narration of the history of Abijah (vv. 3–21). Thus in Chronicles Abijah becomes one of only two Judaean kings whose rule is not given a formulaic theological appraisal (the other is Jehoahaz, II Chron. 36.1–4); his conduct and attitudes are rather expressed in the Chronicler's own words (cf. in particular vv. 10–12).

2. The Chronistic material in vv. 3–21 comprises a lengthy and detailed description of a war between Jeroboam and Abijah (vv. 3–20), and a short remark about the latter's wives and children (v. 21). The pericope as a whole is well-structured:

(*a*) 1–2a Introduction
(*b*) 2b–20 The war between Judah and Israel

(c) 21 Abijah's wives and children
(d) 22–23 Conclusion.

The heart of the chapter is, of course, the war narrative, with the military circumstances and events forming the framework (vv. 2b–3, 13–20) for Abijah's lengthy speech (vv. 4–12). The two parts – almost equal in length – give expression to some of the Chronicler's central theological and historical views.

3. Even a superficial reading of vv. 3–21 reveals that they reflect not only the Chronicler's own language and style, but some of his most significant attitudes as well; about this there is practically no controversy, not only in the more obvious case of Abijah's speech, but also the description of the actual battle. The question of the 'origin' of this material therefore applies only to the core and motive of the story.

That there was 'war between Abijah and Jeroboam' is explicitly stated in I Kings 5.7b, an observation which may be employed from two alternative perspectives: either that the whole account in Chronicles is a literary elaboration on a single authentic verse, or that the Chronicler here preserves the lost details of a military episode, to which the Deuteronomist preferred to refer by a mere general statement. The focus of this debate is certainly in vv. 4 and 19, which contain some concrete historical data with relevant geographical coordinates. In refuting any historical nucleus for v. 19, one might claim either that the place-names reflect nothing more than the Chronicler's own circumstances, basically the claims of the province of Judah against its neighbouring province to the north (cf. Welten, 116–29), or that an authentic town-list was employed in a non-historical manner (cf. R. W. Klein, 'Abijah's Campaign Against the North (2 Chr 13) – What were the Chronicler's Sources?', ZAW 95, 1983, 210–17). However, in order to avoid circular argumentation, we must consider both the details and the general character of Abijah's history.

Verse 19 relates the conquest of Bethel, Jeshanah and Ephron/Ephraim; together with 'Mount Zemaraim' in v. 4, these form a coherent and logical geographic unit, also mentioned together in Josh. 18.22–23 ('Beth-arabah, Zemaraim, Bethel ... Ophrah' – for their identification cf. Williamson, 252, 254–5). Klein has recently claimed that 'Jeshanah' should be restored here in the MT of Joshua, as it is still reflected in the LXX version (ibid., 212–16). All the locations are on the northern border of the kingdom of Judah; although the Joshua text assigns them to the tribe of Benjamin, they may have been regarded in different historical constellations as Ephraimite, hence 'Mount Zemaraim ... in the hill country of Ephraim' (v. 4). As the Deuteronomistic history in I Kings makes clear, continual war was waged between the first Judaean kings and northern Israel (I Kings 14.30; 15.6; 7b, 16ff.), and the frontier between the two kingdoms would naturally have been the focus of the fighting (cf. also I Kings 15.16ff.). Thus, the authenticity of v. 19 is supported by both historical probability and geographical sense.

4. Another consideration, however, now claims our attention. The overall history of Abijah in Chronicles leaves us with the distinct impression that while the reign of Rehoboam was just an unsuccessful digression, it was Abijah who was the true successor of Solomon. The Davidic 'kingship of the Lord', so emphasized in the histories of David and Solomon (I Chron. 17.14; 28.5; 29.11, etc., cf. von Rad, Geschichtsbild, 125–6), is introduced once more in the figure of Abijah (v. 5). Even the proper service conducted in the Jerusalem Temple accords with the arrangements made by Solomon (compare vv. 10–11 to II Chron. 8.12ff.). Like his dynastic

forebears, Abijah, too, addresses the people with a speech, highly charged with devout faith. However, the portrait of Abijah as a righteous king who fights and wins the Lord's battles and observes his commandments to the letter poses an acute theological problem for the Chronicler, contradicting not only the assessment suggested by I Kings 15.2–5, but also some of the Chronicler's most basic theological principles. One of these is the strict correlation between righteousness and success, a marked feature of which is long life. The longevity of a wicked king (like Manasseh) and the untimely death of a just monarch (like Josiah) demand explanation and theological justification. Abijah, who ruled only three years, is certainly an exception to this rigorous rule. The Chronicler's own philosophy of history should have inclined him to see Abijah's untimely death as a punishment and, choosing the easiest course, to follow the Deuteronomistic verdict of I Kings 15.3–5. Yet the Chronicler in fact deviates from that source and describes Abijah quite contrary to his own theological concepts as a righteous leader who earned an impressive victory over the northern kingdom's superior force. The only possible conclusion is that the Chronicler had access to authentic historical details, upon which he bases his account, in spite of the inherent theological difficulties (cf. further in the commentary). I therefore tend to join those scholars who see the chapter as based on some authentic historical source (cf. Williamson, 250; Dillard, 105–6; D. G. Deboys, 'The Chronicler's Portrait of Abijah', *Biblica* 71, 1990, 48–62).

D. Commentary

[1–2a] In v. 1, the Chronicler transmits the text of I Kings 15.1, omitting only the words 'the son of Nebat' and changing the tense of the verb *mlk* (unexpectedly becoming *wayyimlōk*), probably under the influence of 12.16b. The synchronistic chronology of the northern and southern kingdoms is stated here for the first time; in Kings it becomes a permanent element of the Deuteronomistic historiography (I Kings 15.9, 25, 33; 16.8, etc.), but is systematically omitted in Chronicles. By retaining its first appearance, the Chronicler establishes the principle of synchroneity, thereafter to be avoided throughout the historical narrative.

It is noteworthy that although the Chronicler regards the kingship of Israel as usurpation, he nevertheless uses the title 'king' for its rulers, not only here, where 'king' is somewhat emphasized by the syntax, but also later (II Chron. 15.1, 3, 5; 18.3, 4, etc.).

Another consistent element is the retention of the chronological datum. Although the short duration of Abijah's reign must have been a problem for the Chronicler, he does not take the liberty of changing it. This fidelity to chronological detail cannot be estimated too highly as a key to the Chronicler's historiographical methods.

On 'Abijah' replacing 'Abijam', cf. on 12.16; on the difficulties posed by the name 'Micaiah the daughter of Uriel ...' cf. on 11.20.

[2b–3] Verse 2b is taken from I Kings 15.7b. There, in the original context of a Deuteronomistic summary of Abijah's reign, 'war' is to be interpreted as a collective noun, referring to a constant state of conflict throughout the time of Rehoboam and into the reign of his son. The Chronicler takes this word to refer to and introduce a single confrontation, which he now proceeds to describe.

The initiative is attributed to Abijah. The rare idiom 'begin the battle' (*wayye'sōr 'et-hammilḥāmāh*, again only in I Kings 20.14), literally 'bind the battle', probably derives from the 'binding of horses' in preparing the chariots for battle (cf. Gen. 46.29; Exod. 14.66, etc.).

No immediate cause for this war is suggested; it must be adduced from Abijah's lengthy speech to be a delayed attempt to restore the Davidic sovereignty over the defecting northern Israelites. 'Ought you not to know that the Lord God of Israel gave the kingship over Israel for ever to David and his sons (v. 5) ... do not fight ... for you cannot succeed' (v. 12). Here, then, is the practical antithesis of the unrealized intentions of Rehoboam (I Kings 12.21–24//II Chron. 11.1–4), who refrained from taking military action against the northern tribes because of the divine command: 'you shall not go up or fight against your brethren' (11.4). Although no prophetic message has altered that command, Abijah marches to just such a war.

The sharp contrast between Abijah's exhortation and Shemaiah's prophecy and, as a result, the lack of historiographical and theological continuity, is an inherent feature of the Chronicler's work. Any attempt to harmonize this contrast by claiming that Abijah was forced by Jeroboam into a war in defence of the border territories will not be supported by the actual depiction of the war or the spirit of Abijah's address. The alternative is to realize fully the conflicting attitudes to the schism which find their place in the Chronicler's work, as a result of his historiographical method. Moreover, it is even possible that in describing Abijah's campaign in spite of the evident theological incongruity, the Chronicler is transmitting reliable historical data, emphasizing the apologetic tone of the episode of I Kings 12.21–24 (II Chron. 11.1–4), in which Rehoboam's failure to act is 'excused' by divine intervention. It is quite likely that Abijah, deviating from his father's policy, did indeed make this delayed effort to restore his rule, a military initiative which may in fact have been the cause for Abijah's short reign, completely unaccounted for in Kings (cf. by contrast the fates of Ahaziahu, Amon, Jehoahaz, etc., and further on v. 20).

The troops themselves are numbered typologically: four hundred thousand of Judah, eight hundred thousand of Israel, the two-to-one ratio obviously intended to illustrate that this is a confrontation between the 'righteous few' and the 'hosts of evildoers' – a *motif* characterizing defensive rather than offensive wars. In this case the numbers may also reflect some actual military advantage of Israel over Judah.

[4–12] The heart of the chapter is Abijah's exhortation; its careful, rhetorical structure opens with a forceful second person address, 'Hear me' and 'ought you not to know', and ends in the same way: 'do not fight against the Lord ... for you cannot succeed'. Each of the exhortation's three parts is marked with an expression of rhetorical emphasis: 'Ought you not' (v. 5), 'And now' (v. 8), and 'Behold' (v. 12). In each of the units there is an antithetical dialectic, 'we' and 'you', first one camp, then the other. The three parts relate chiastically to one another; there is also a movement from the monarchs in the first unit to the people in the next two, and from the past in the first unit, through the present in the second, to the imminent future; thus:

we (past): 5 'The Lord ... gave the kingship ... for ever to David'
you (past): 6–7 Jeroboam ... rose up and rebelled
you (present): 8–9 you have 'no gods' and 'false priests'
we (present): 10–11 'we keep the charge of the Lord'
we (future): 12a 'God is with us'
you (future): 12b 'do not fight ... for you cannot succeed'.

While the two camps drawn up for battle are Judah and Israel, the underlying theme developed throughout the speech is that the Israelites are in fact preparing to fight the Lord, defying their God by rebellion against the king he chose, and establishing a false cult; Judah on the other hand represents God's rule through his chosen king and proper worship. This being the true essence of the war, the people of Israel have absolutely no chance of success.

Further rhetorical devices in the speech are intended to weaken one side and encourage the other, each argument introducing a new and detailed antithesis: we – you, few – many, true God – no gods, keep – abandon, etc. Abijah's thorough knowledge of his opponents' circumstances and religious procedures gives credibility to his pejorative description. And in contrast to the antithetical structure, an integral theological principle underlies Abijah's address: both Israel and Judah owe obedience and allegiance to the same 'God of their fathers'.

[4] The staging here is very dramatic: Abijah climbs to a lofty summit, addresses the fighting camps, and bids his opponents surrender without battle. Unrealistic as this setting is, it provides the Chronicler with an opportunity to take a belated but categorical stand on the issue of the schism.

The tone and even some details of this scene resemble the address of Jotham, son of Gideon, to Abimelech and the Shechemites (cf. Judg. 9.7: 'he went and stood on the top of Mount Gerizim, and cried aloud and said to them, "Listen to me, you men of Shechem ..."'. Note, however, the late Hebrew phrasing here in *wayyāqom mē'al*, denoting simply 'stood up' (cf.

various other usages of this phrase in Gen. 23.3; II Sam. 11.2; II Chron. 24.20).

'Zemaraim' is found elsewhere only once, as a town in Benjamin near Bethel (Josh. 18.22); 'Mount Zemaraim', then, bears the name of the nearby town, or *vice versa*. In any event, the location is in 'the hill country of Ephraim', a sound definition, referring to geographical rather than tribal boundaries.

The address 'Hear me' (*šᵉmā'ūnī*) is characteristic of Chronicles, occurring elsewhere only once (Gen. 23.8). The personal address to the rival leader ('O Jeroboam') as well as to 'all Israel' is ironic, as the speech actually intends to turn the people *against* Jeroboam.

[5] After the initial 'Ought you not to know', Abijah declares his dynastic credo: the kingdom of Israel is the Lord's, granted to David and his sons. As an axiomatic statement of faith, the whole speech is fortified with divine epithets, of which the Chronicler's favourites include 'The Lord God of Israel' here and 'the Lord, the God of your fathers' in v. 12.

This passage is a striking adaptation of Num. 18.19: 'All the holy offerings … I give to you, and to your sons and daughters with you, as a perpetual due; it is a covenant of salt for ever before the Lord, for you and for your offspring with you.' The parallelism is clear: a divine grant (holy offerings//kingship) to a favoured beneficiary (Aaron//David) sealed by an eternal commitment. 'A covenant of salt' denotes, in both passages, not a 'means' of the conferral of the offerings or kingship, but rather a metaphor for a binding and immutable obligation (cf. Rudolph, 237; Japhet, *Ideology*, 454–5). This verse thus introduces Abijah's address admirably, not only in its theological tone but in its stylistic affinities as well: the priestly terminology will characterize the speech throughout.

[6] Since the material relevant to Jeroboam's rebellion against Solomon (I Kings 11.26–40) has been omitted in Chronicles, the reference to the subject here is entirely unexpected. The use of the rivals' patronyms ('Jeroboam the son of Nebat' *versus* 'Solomon the son of David') emphasizes the nondescript lineage of the first as against the legitimate claim of the 'son of David' to 'rule over Israel'. Then, too, Jeroboam's relationship to 'his lord' Solomon is defined in the Hebrew *'ebed*; this word may in fact mean 'servant' (so RSV), but the context of wanton revolt against 'his lord', clearly indicates that Jeroboam is to be seen more as a 'rebellious slave'. The Chronicler, then (echoing I Kings 11.26), places the initial stage of the revolt in Solomon's time, a correct realization that the seeds of schism had been sown before Rehoboam's accession.

This verse's categorical understanding of Jeroboam's revolt as an uprising of a slave against his lord removes any shred of legitimacy it may have claimed, and thus sharply contradicts the views which accept the schism as a fulfilment of God's will: I Kings 12.15 (II Chron. 10.15): 'it was a turn of affairs brought about by the Lord'; I Kings 12.24 (II Chron. 11.4): 'for this thing is from me.'

[7] The revolt is described as a continuum, the next stage being in the time of Rehoboam. What began as a personal plot against Solomon now escalates as Jeroboam is joined by 'worthless scoundrels' whom Rehoboam could not withstand (the object of 'about him' is Jeroboam, against Williamson, 252–3). The verse thus adopts a new view of I Kings 12//II Chron. 12: what is seen there as a justifiable complaint presented by 'the people' here becomes the irresponsible act of a handful of blackguards, whose only wish is to defy the divinely chosen king.

The portrait of the 'young and irresolute' Rehoboam matches well the spirit of I Kings 12, where the king's harsh boasts are given the lie by his actions, when he chooses to send his taskmaster to confront the people, and then runs for his life. It is interesting to note that the phrase used here resembles the opinion of Solomon in I Chron. 22.5 and 29.1, *na'ar wārāk* ('young and inexperienced'), with the crucial difference that Solomon was at that time really young (*na'ar*) and therefore inexperienced (*rāk*), while for Rehoboam the terms 'young' and *rak-lēbāb* (literally 'soft of heart') are metaphors for a moral disposition having nothing to do with age, i.e. an immature, submissive personality.

Stylistic characteristics of this verse include its late Hebrew and the double appellations: the people gathered around Jeroboam are 'worthless' and 'scoundrels', Rehoboam who faces them is 'young' and 'irresolute'. Note also the stylistic quality effected by the use of two synonymous verbs, *ḥzq* and *'mṣ*, both denoting 'strength', in an antithetical way: '[they] defied (*wayyit'ammṣū*) Rehoboam ... when Rehoboam was young ... and could not withstand (*hithazzaq*) them'. Moreover, the verse clearly refers back to II Chron. 11.7, where the same two verbs are used, this time synonymously.

[8–9] Having established the historical proposition, the second part of the speech opens with 'and now', thus moving to present time. What began as a limited uprising of Jeroboam against Solomon then broadened to defy the authority of Rehoboam has now escalated into a full-scale war – 'a great multitude ... with the golden calves' pitted against 'the kingdom of the Lord in the hand of the sons of David'. Viewed thus, the schism is an ongoing process rather than a *fait accompli*, and the present war is only the latest stage in Israel's long revolt.

Echoing Solomon's patronym (*ben-dāwīd*) in v. 6, here his successors are also designated *b^enē dāwīd* (RSV 'sons of David'). This title should perhaps be rendered 'Davidides', like the parallel *b^enē 'ah^arōn* in v. 9 ('Aaronides', the priestly order of Aaron's descendants). Here, God has given his kingdom to David and the Davidic dynasty (v. 5); the revolt was first directed against

Solomon the son of David (v. 6), and is now against his 'Davidide' successors, Rehoboam and Abijah.

Verse 8b begins with a clear definition of the opposing camps: an emphatic 'you' in v. 8b, contrasted by an equally emphatic 'but we' in v. 10, an antithesis summed up in v. 11b: 'we keep the charge of the Lord our God, but you have forsaken him'. The focal point here is the question of orthodox, legitimate worship. Two aspects of northern religious practice are scrutinized: (*a*) 'the golden calves, which Jeroboam made you for gods' but which are 'no-gods', and (*b*) the officiating priests, who are not the legitimate Aaronides and Levites but unauthorized personnel, appointed 'like the peoples of other lands'. In choosing these two elements of the cult, the text is completely dependent on I Kings 12.27–32; 13.33 – with the attendant emphasis on a new priesthood as a major step in Jeroboam's 'reform' (cf. II Chron. 11.13–15). All this is seen in the context of the defection from the house of David. The elaborate cult of the north has 'no-gods' and 'no-priests', and has 'forsaken the Lord'; only in Judah, under the Davidic king, is proper worship still observed.

It is clear throughout the harsh condemnation of the northern cult that not the slightest ethnic/national distinction is made between the opposite sides. Abijah approaches the people of the north as 'all Israel' (v. 4); they are expected to serve the same 'Lord, God of Israel' as their southern brothers, the same 'God of their fathers' (v. 12). Although they have forsaken him (v. 11), they are still unquestionably members of the one people.

In v. 9, an interesting apposition sheds important light on the Chronicler's view of the clergy. The term 'priests of the Lord' is explicitly interpreted as referring to two major orders: 'the sons of Aaron' ('priests' in the strict sense) and 'the Levites' (all other members of the tribe of Levi). The same semantic duality has already often been noted in the use of the term 'Levites', which may refer to all members of the tribe (including the priests) or more specifically to the non-priestly order. The return in this passage to the wider, non-technical usage of the word 'priests' draws, in effect, an equation between 'priests of the Lord' and 'Levites'; in their narrow meanings, the two terms complement each other, while the broader meanings have become synonymous:

Priests of the Lord = sons of Aaron (priests) + Levites;
Levites = Levites + sons of Aaron (priests).

For '*like* the peoples of other lands' LXX reads '*from* the peoples ...' This interpretation develops the implication of MT, and harmonizes it with I Kings 12.31: 'appointed priests from among all the people ...'. Anyone, even a foreigner, may conduct the unorthodox worship of the North; God's election of the priesthood is circumvented and ignored.

Reference has already been made to the term *māllē' yād* (translated here 'to consecrate himself', cf. on I Chron. 29.5b); its occurrence in the description of Jeroboam's reforms in I Kings 13.33 draws our attention again to the fact that the Chronicler draws heavily on the relevant source-texts even when he does not cite them in his story. His brief references to Jeroboam's innovations are based on I Kings 12.28; 12.31, and in particular, 13.33, 'any who would, he consecrated to be priests of the high places', to which compare the present verse in Chronicles: 'whoever comes to consecrate himself ... becomes a priest of what are no gods'.

[10–11] 'But as for us' introduces a polemical contrast with 'you' of the preceding verse. The statement 'the Lord is our God and we have not forsaken him' not only refers back to all the northern practices, now defining them as apostasy, but also anticipates the final emphatic antithesis of v. 16. This declaration of loyalty is followed by a detailed description of the meticulous observance of God's worship, as carried out in the Temple. It is noteworthy, however, that there is no specific reference to either Jerusalem or the Temple, as if the whole cult exists as some kind of abstraction.

Following v. 9, the description – in chiastic order – opens with the clergy, 'We have priests ministering to the Lord', who (as in v. 8) include the Aaronide priests and the Levites. The concrete experience of regular daily service follows, including the morning and evening burnt offerings, incense, the showbread and the kindling of the lamps on the golden lampstand every evening. The more remote annual services of the special days are not included.

This specific portrait of the cult is unique, differing from II Chron. 2.4 [MT 3] and 8.12ff., which include the regular yearly offerings but lack the detail found here. The most proximate text is probably Exod. 40.22–29, where Moses initiates the Lord's service: he erects the tabernacle, sets out the bread, lights the lamps of the lampstand, burns incense upon the golden altar, and makes burnt offerings and cereal offerings on the altar. The present text, then, although formulated in distinctly priestly terms, is not taken *in toto* from any extant priestly source. It reflects in fact the actual context of the speech, which is an apologetic for precise, even pedantic, daily orthodoxy.

The Late Hebrew idiom which expresses 'every morning / every evening' by repeating the noun (*babbōqer babbōqer / bā'ereb bā'ereb*, cf. Curtis, 35, no. 124), is found three times in v. 11, giving particular emphasis to the regularity of the performance.

That the service as described here conforms more to the desert tabernacle than to Solomon's Temple is evidenced mainly by one detail, the lampstand. According to I Kings 7.49 and II Chron. 4.7, Solomon fashioned *ten* lampstands; here, the Chronicler presents a model of worship in Solomon's Temple using only one lampstand, following the pattern of the Mosaic tent (Exod. 25.31, 38). The attitude to the sources, then, is here legal and homiletic, and not preoccupied with historical accuracy; emphasis is on continuity between the Mosaic prescriptions and models, and the actual cult of Judah.

[12] The final antithesis, 'we keep the charge of the Lord ... but you have forsaken him', is now applied to the actual situation of imminent war. Abijah's uniquely positive declaration, 'God is with us at our head', means that the opponents of Judah have absolutely no chance. This presence of God at the head of the army is expressed in the most concrete way in the person of priests bearing battle trumpets.

More than in any other biblical book, in Chronicles the 'trumpets' are a regular component of the musical context of Temple liturgy (I Chron. 13.8; 15.24, 28; 16.6, 42; II Chron. 5.12, 13; 7.6; 15.14; 20.28; 23.13; 29.26, 27, 28). Chronicles is the only book where we find also the denominative verb ḥṣṣr ('blow the trumpet', v. 14, and I Chron. 15.24; II Chron. 5.12; 7.6; 29.28). However, the 'battle trumpets' of the present verse, with their specific military role, are mentioned again in only one other biblical context: the book of Numbers.

Numbers 10.2–10 prescribes the fashioning of these trumpets and their intended use for 'summoning the congregation and for breaking camp' (v. 2), 'when you go to war' (v. 9) and 'on the day of your gladness' (v. 10). The employment of the trumpets in wartime is illustrated once, in the conflict between Israel and the Midianites: 'And Moses sent them to the war ... together with Phinehas ... the trumpets of the alarm in his hand' (Num. 31.6). The actual sounding of the trumpets is described by two distinct terms, 'blow' (tq'), and 'alarm' (hry'), the latter limited to two occasions: the breaking of camp (Num. 10.5–6; cf. 10.7) and in time of war (v. 9).

In accordance with this distinction, in Num. 31.6 the trumpets are also called 'the trumpets of the alarm', and this is the term the Chronicler employs here in v. 12. In the continuation of this verse, the translation 'to sound the call to battle against you' (RSV) is a weak representation of the Hebrew, literally 'to sound the alarm against you', and obscures the tight link between this passage and the Numbers texts. On the role of the trumpets in the battle, cf. on vv. 14–15.

Abijah's address concludes with a fervent exhortation: 'Do not fight against the Lord, the God of your fathers ...' This is a very forceful statement. In biblical literature, the wars of Israel are in fact quite frequently called the Lord's wars, just as other gods are seen as fighting for their peoples (cf. II Sam. 7.23). Here, however, the imagery is especially concrete and immediate, and the people of Israel are seen as taking up arms against their own God. The power which they esteem as the greatest will be turned against them.

[13–20] This second unit is devoted to a very precise description of the main stages of the ensuing battle, and is formulated along lines parallel to the speech of Abijah.

13–15 From the first engagement to the turning point
16–17 Judah overpowers its opponents
18–20 The submission of Israel, conquest of cities, death of Jeroboam.

[13–15] The transition here is abrupt. No literary link is provided with the preceding speech, no indication of verbal response, or even that Abijah has been heard at all. Jeroboam's response is in action, which brings a dangerous turn to the course of the war: 'And Jeroboam sent an ambush around ...' The juxtaposition of the opening in v. 4 ('Abijah stood up on mount Zemaraim ... and said') and the emphasized opening of v. 13, 'And (not in RSV) Jeroboam had sent an ambush ...', creates the impression that while Abijah was earnestly moralizing from the mountain, Jeroboam had been sharpening his weapons; the military initiative is now in the northern camp.

Jeroboam employs the tactic of ambush, quite familiar from battles in the Bible, especially as described from the point of view of the attacker and related to the conquest of fortified cities: Ai (Josh. 8) and Gibeah (Judg. 20). Another example of 'a battle before and behind', described from the point of view of the attacked force, is Joab's engagement with the Ammonites (II Sam. 10.9). A comparison between this last and the present passage may highlight the peculiar features of Abijah's war.

When Joab realizes that the battle 'was set against him both in front and in the rear', he takes practical measures, by dividing his fighters into two units, each facing one rank of the attacking forces. He is thus able to continue the struggle along two parallel fronts, each having one objective. Abijah's troops, on the other hand, when they realize that 'the battle was before and behind them', react differently: the men of Judah cry to the Lord, the priests sound the trumpets, and the people raise a battle cry (v. 14–15). Now the two battles may not in fact have differed so greatly; the measures described, at least in part, may be conceived as complementary, not mutually exclusive. The real distinction is in the narrator's point of view: in contrast to Joab's strictly military action, Abijah's war is described exclusively in religious, even ritual terms. And the next act is accordingly not initated by Abijah's warriors, but by God: 'And when the men of Judah shouted, God defeated Jeroboam and all Israel before Abijah and Judah.' This divine intervention, although it brings about a sudden turning point in the course of the war ('the men of Israel fled before Judah', v. 16), does not itself take any concrete military form. It is an abstract, absolute miracle.

It is in this context that the function of the alarm trumpets should be viewed. While they may have been originally conceived as having immanent, magical power, probably still to be sensed in the phrase 'to sound the alarm against you' (v. 12), in the present texts this aspect of their function has been completely spiritualized, in the context of normative Israelite monotheism: cf. Num. 10.9, 'And when you go to war ... then you shall sound an alarm with the trumpets, that you may be remembered before the Lord your God', and here, 'And when the men of Judah shouted, God defeated Jeroboam.'

From now on the actual fighting is in the hands of human agents: Abijah and his forces 'pursuing', 'slaying', 'prevailing', as 'the men of Israel fled' and 'were subdued'. All this, however, was determined by God's miraculous, unexplained and utterly abstract intervention.

It has been pointed out by many scholars that the description of Abijah's war contains several motifs of what is defined in biblical scholarship as 'holy war' (recently, Dillard, 105). However one may regard this supposed institution, it should be noted that the Chronicler's records of war, illustrated primarily by the battles of Abijah, Asa (II Chron. 14.8–14) and Jehoshaphat (II Chron. 20.1–30), do not reflect any living institution. They are literary works, composed – with varying degrees of detail and elaboration – of eclectic, spiritualized motifs, expressing first of all the Chronicler's religious attitudes and views (cf. further on II Chron. 20.1–30, and Japhet, *Ideology*, 126–32).

[16–17] The course of the war and its outcome is thus a proper response to and confirmation of Abijah's speech. The people rashly tried to 'withstand the kingdom of the Lord' (v. 8), but 'God defeated Jeroboam and all Israel' (v. 15); they were fighting 'against the Lord' (v. 12), and 'God gave them into their (Judah's) hands' (v. 16).

The 'five hundred thousand' casualties would be more than half of the whole Israelite army and more than all the Judahite force together; clearly all these numbers are to be taken typologically.

[18–20] The moral of the story, an epitome of Chronistic philosophy, is summarized in v. 18: those who relied on God gained the upper hand. However, this verse in fact introduces a historical problem which becomes more acute in vv. 19–20. The end of the war is presented in three points: the men of Israel were subdued (v. 18), Abijah captured cities from Jeroboam (v. 19), and the Lord smote Jeroboam so that he died (v. 20). Now, the impression arising from vv. 18 and 20 is that Abijah's objectives, i.e. to quell the northern rebellion and ensure the Davidic sovereignty, were in fact achieved: 'the men of Israel were subdued ... and Jeroboam did not recover his power'. It is hardly necessary to mention that this view contradicts historical realities, attested not only in the book of Kings, but also in subsequent Chronistic texts (cf. II Chron. 16.1, etc.), as well as by the scope and dimensions of the military enterprise reflected in v. 19, which are different from those of the main story (vv. 3–18). Rather than a full-scale war, aiming to return the Israelites to obedience to Davidic rule, v. 19 describes the occupation of limited Benjaminite territory on the border of Ephraim.

Moreover, while vv. 13–18 are vague and schematic, v. 19 supplies some concrete details for Abijah's gains: three towns recorded by name, with the villages around them. The implications of this contrast may be viewed from alternative perspectives. One may see here the limited results of what was intended as a major campaign against the North, and link this outcome with the untimely death of Abijah, or, conversely, regard v. 19 as representing the original kernel from which the story grew: a limited military action which was developed into a comprehensive confrontation between 'south' and 'north'.

Of the three place-names, the most interesting is Bethel, the site of Jeroboam's shrine of the golden calf (I Kings 12.28–29). If authentic, this record would imply that the boundary between Judah and Israel moved considerably northward and the central shrine was taken by Judah. The precise fate of this area is unknown to us, but it would seem that Baasha already restored it to the north and moved the boundary further south, at least initially, as far as Ramah (I Kings 15.16//II Chron. 16.1). The central role of Bethel for the north is again attested in the time of the second Jeroboam, the son of Joash (Amos 7.13).

Verse 20 concludes with the death of Jeroboam – apparently during Abijah's lifetime, thus posing a chronological problem. According to the synchronistic data in I Kings 15.1//Chron. 13.1, Abijah reigned in the eighteenth year of Jeroboam, and Asa succeeded Abijah on the throne 'in the twentieth year of Jeroboam' (I Kings 15.9). Jeroboam, then, having ruled for twenty-two years (I Kings 14.20), survived Abijah. Since the length of Jeroboam's rule is not recorded in Chronicles, the discrepancy in this verse is not as glaring when Chronicles is studied in isolation. There can be no doubt, however – as is generally accepted – that the claim that Abijah outlived Jeroboam lacks historical basis and is introduced to serve the Chronicler's theological aims.

This precedence of theological message over historical fact raises anew the problem of the Chronicler's methods. For a plain statement of facts as the sources reflect them, this verse needs only to be reversed: 'And Abijah did not survive in Jeroboam's day, but died.' One may venture the opinion that this was indeed the original text of the Chronicler's source, transposed into its present form for obvious theological reasons. That the Chronicler was capable of such a reversal is evidenced in the episode of the cities which Solomon gave to Huram (or *vice versa*, I Kings 9.11–12//II Chron. 8.2), the story about Jehoshaphat's journey with Ahaziahu (I Kings 22.49//II Chron. 20.35–36), to mention only two. While these parallels increase our reservations concerning the historicity of the data, they also remind us that the Chronicler's literary procedure may entail – even in these extreme cases – not an entirely fictitious composition, but the reversal of a given source. One may consequently conclude that Abijah's successful military compaigns against Jeroboam came to an abrupt halt with Abijah's untimely death.

[21] In contrast to Jeroboam, who in v. 20 'did not recover', 'Abijah grew mighty'. The literary sequence (obliterated by RSV's punctuation) seems to imply that the text reflects the actual order of events; in fact, however, the two texts are better understood as originally unconnected. The 'growing mighty' of Abijah, exemplified by the number of his wives and children, is a general summary of Abijah's whole career.

Although the passage reflects Chronistic idiom (*wayyithazzēq* ... *wayyiśśā'*), and conforms to the Chronicler's view that children are a sign of blessing, these are hardly sufficient reason to doubt the information itself. The similar accounts for Rehoboam (II Chron. 11.18–21) and Jehoshaphat (II Chron. 21.2–4) indicate that systematic family records were kept for all the Davidic kings (except Asa) who reigned before the major crisis in the days of Athaliah. One wonders whether the Chronicler had access to a source with this genealogical information, which the Deuteronomistic author of Kings simply ignored, or whether these were fragmentary records which somehow survived to the Chronicler's time. It may well have been the threat of extinction of the Davidic house with the execution of Ahaziah and the murder of the whole royal family (cf. on II Chron. 22) which inspired the systematic recording of the main genealogical facts of the house of David.

[22–23 or 14.1] The Chronicler now returns to his source in I Kings 15.7 and to the concluding section of the Deuteronomistic framework. The general similarity reflected in themes, structure, sequence and actual citations, is in fact balanced by differences in many of the details.

The recurring formula of Kings, 'and all that he did' (also I Kings 14.29; 15.23, 31; 16.14; 22.39 etc.), is never repeated in Chronicles, but has been replaced in the cases of David, Solomon and Rehoboam by the Chronistic formula 'first and last'; here, sensitive to the context, the Chronicler uses the unique 'his ways and his sayings' (somewhat differently, II Chron. 28.26; but cf. JPS 'his conduct and his acts'). The rhetorical formula of Kings, 'Are they not written', is also completely absent from Chronicles. It is either paraphrased, or replaced by simple, indicative statements such as 'are written', or 'behold they are written'.

Finally, the source for Abijah's history is termed 'the story (*midrāš*) of the prophet Iddo'. Iddo was mentioned earlier in connection with Solomon (as prophesying to Jeroboam), and Rehoboam (II Chron. 9.29; 12.15), with a different title (seer – *ḥōzeh*) and a different genre of his work. Given the Chronicler's strong tendency to variation and the probable chronological limits, we may conclude that the same prophet is intended in all these cases (cf. also on 9.29). Iddo is in fact the only prophet whose works appear three times as sources for the histories of kings. He is also the only prophet to figure in these conclusions of reigns, but never in the narratives themselves. We can thus say that there clearly was a persistent tradition about a prophet by that name, who was active at the time of the schism, although nothing of his doings have reached us.

About the nature of Iddo's writings we know even less. The word *midrash* makes here its first appearance in biblical Hebrew (found again only in II Chron. 24.27) and it is generally accepted that it should be understood in the context of Biblical Hebrew rather than of rabbinic usage – the common translation 'story' (RSV; NEB; JPS) being a probable representation.

To the standard formula, taken verbatim from I Kings 15.9, relating the king's death, burial and succession by his son Asa, the Chronicler adds one more sentence: 'In his days the land had rest for ten years'. With this, a direct transition is made to the reign of the new king, making the standard Deuteronomistic opening redundant. The Chronicler thus skips I Kings 15.9–10 and moves directly to I Kings 15.11, in 14.2 (cf. below). One detail will be gleaned from I Kings 15.10 – the length of Asa's reign – to be incorporated into the concluding formula, II Chron. 16.13.

14.2–15

14 2 And Asa did what was good and right in the eyes of the Lord his God. 3 He took away the foreign altars and the high places, and broke down the pillars and hewed down the Asherim, 4 and commanded Judah to seek the Lord, the God of their fathers, and to keep the law and the commandment. 5 He also took out of all the cities of Judah the high places and the incense altars. And the kingdom had rest under him. 6 He built fortified cities in Judah, for the land had rest. He had no war in those years, for the Lord gave him peace. 7 And he said to Judah, 'Let us build these cities, and surround them with walls and towers, gates and bars; the land is still ours, because we have sought the Lord our God; we have sought him, and he has given us peace on every side.' So they built and prospered. 8 And Asa had an army of three hundred thousand from Judah, armed with bucklers and spears, and two hundred and eighty thousand men from Benjamin, that carried shields and drew bows; all these were mighty men of valour.

9 Zerah the Ethiopian came out against them with an army of a million men and three hundred chariots, and came as far as Mareshah. 10 And Asa went out to meet him, and they drew up their lines of battle in the valley of Zephathah at Mareshah. 11 And Asa cried to the Lord his God, 'O Lord, there is none like thee to help, between the mighty and the weak. Help us, O Lord our God, for we rely on thee, and in thy name we have come against this multitude. O Lord, thou art our God; let not man prevail against thee.' 12 So the Lord defeated the Ethiopians before Asa and before Judah, and the Ethiopians fled. 13 Asa and the people that were with him pursued them as far as Gerar, and the Ethiopians fell until none remained alive; for they were broken before the Lord and his army. The men of Judah carried away very much booty. 14 And they smote all the cities round about Gerar, for the fear of the Lord was upon them. They plundered all the cities, for there was much plunder in them. 15 And they smote the tents of those who had cattle, and carried away sheep in abundance and camels. Then they returned to Jerusalem.

A. Notes to MT

[7, MT 6] דָּרָשְׁנוּ ... כִּי דָרָשְׁנוּ, proposed. דְּרָשֻׁנוּ ... כְּדָרְשֵׁנוּ, cf. commentary; [10, MT 9] צַפְתָה, LXX צְפוּנָה; [13, 14, MT 12, 13] גרר, LXX^{AB} גדר.

B. Notes to RSV

[3, MT 2] 'Asherim', NEB 'sacred poles', JPS 'sacred posts'; [3, 5, MT 2, 4] 'took away, took out', NEB 'suppressed', JPS 'abolished'; [9, MT 8] 'the Ethiopian', MT 'the Cushite' (so NEB), also vv. 12, 13; [11, MT 10] 'there is none like thee to help, between the mighty and the weak', better 'to help [men], whether strong or weak' (so NEB; cf. JPS, 'it is all the same to you to help the numerous and the powerless'); [13,

MT 12] 'until none remained alive', JPS 'wounded beyond recovery', cf. commentary; [15] 'the tents of those who had cattle', NEB 'herdsmen'.

C. Structure, sources and form

1. The history of Asa is subjected in Chronicles to a thorough reworking: literary, historical and theological. The textual scope is tripled by an elaboration of and additions to the source material in Kings. As we have seen in the Chronistic presentation of Rehoboam's history, which is made to equal in length the material on both Rehoboam and Jeroboam (I Kings 12–14), here too the Asa narrative is made to equal the Kings' history of his period, that is, his own story (I Kings 15.9–24) and that of his contemporaries in northern Israel: Nadab, Baasha, Elah, Zimri, Tibni and Omri (I Kings 15.9–16.28).

2. In I Kings 15, the history of Asa is composed as follows:

(a) 9–14 Deuteronomistic introduction, including Asa's reform (vv. 12–13)
(b) 15 Votive gifts brought to the Temple
(c) 15–22 War between Asa and Baasha
(d) 23–24 Deuteronomistic conclusion.

The Chronicler cites this source material almost in its entirety, with only minor changes and omissions (I Kings 15.9, 11b, 12a). The composition as a whole, however, is greatly changed, and the editorial method follows the lines of the history of Rehoboam:

(a) All the material taken from the book of Kings is placed at the end of the narrative, from II Chron. 15.16 to 16.14.
(b) In its new position, this parallel material is elaborated by various longer and shorter additions, in 15.19; 16.7–10, 12, 14.
(c) The parallel material is preceded by a long section, original to Chronicles, in 14.1 [MT 13.23]–15.15.

The structure of Asa's history may finally be viewed as follows:

(a) 14.2–8 [MT 1–7] General introduction
(b) 14.9 [MT 8]–15.19 War with Zerah the Cushite and its consequences:
  14.9–15 [MT 8–14] the war
  15.1–18 the ensuing covenant
  15.19 conclusion
(c) 16.1–10 War with Baasha and its consequences
  16.1–6 the war
  16.7–10 encounter with a prophet
(d) 16.11–14 Conclusion.

Asa's history thus focusses on two wars and their different results, and the diverse material is integrated into one coherent chronological framework.

3. This extensive elaboration, which makes Asa's history one of the most impressive among the Judaean kings (exceeded in scope only by Rehoboam, Jehoshaphat, Hezekiah and Josiah), raises the question whether the Chronicler had any non-biblical source for his additional material.

A study of the synoptic sections in the history of Asa (II Chron. 15.16–16.14) reveals the Chronicler's method in their composition: the use of a source-text (I Kings 15.13–24), with an elaboration of the chronological system (15.19; 16.1, 12), the introduction of a new scene – the encounter between Asa and a prophet (16.7–10), the addition of details of Asa's illness and burial (vv. 12aβ–b, 14aβ–b), and some minor linguistic and stylistic changes. While the whole unit is now marked by the Chronicler's style and theology, there is no doubt that it is based on the text still available to us in Kings.

No such parallel is of course in evidence for the material in 14.2–15.15; moreover, it seems that the Chronicler's language, literary technique and views are more marked here than in the parallel section. Nevertheless, given the Chronicler's methods of composition, it is unlikely that these portions are pure fiction. We have already noted that the scope of the Chronicler's reworking depends very much on the literary form of his source. A fully developed narrative might receive some adaptative treatment, but evidence of the Chronicler's peculiar traits would generally be limited to additions and changes to the source-text. Conversely, a strong imprint of the Chronicler's literary stamp may imply that he was basing himself on more basic material – a short chronicle, a list, an elementary tradition, etc. – the final literary formulation being his own. These two principal modes of work are attested in the Chronicler's treatment of biblical material and they may be assumed for the non-biblical sources as well.

In the present passage, assuming that such a source existed, it must have been of a documentary rather than a narrative nature. Parts which have not been so marked by the Chronicler's editing still have an 'authentic' ring. Tensions between the Chronicler's own views and those of his sources may sometimes be felt not only with biblical sources but also with the assumed extra-biblical ones.

The additional material in question contains several subjects which should be examined separately: the chronological system, the data about Asa's building projects and army, the war with the Cushites (RSV 'Ethiopians'), and Asa's extensive reforms. We will deal with the first of these here, while the others will be better left to the commentary.

4. Asa's reign is provided with a comprehensive chronological framework, the most elaborate provided for any monarch, either in Kings or Chronicles:

(i)   14.1 [MT 13.23] In his days the land had rest for ten years
(ii) 15.10 They were gathered ... in the third month of the fifteenth year of the reign of Asa
(iii) 15.19 And there was no (RSV + more) war until the thirty-fifth year of the reign of Asa
(iv) 16.1 In the thirty-sixth year ... Baasha ... went up against Judah
(v)   16.12 In the thirty-ninth year ... Asa was diseased
(vi) 16.13 And Asa slept ... dying in the forty-first year of his reign.

Of all these details, only one is found in Kings: the standard note fixing the length of Asa's reign, forty-one years (I Kings 15.10); we may also ascribe some chrono-logical value to the general remark 'in his old age' (I Kings 15.23).

This chronological system does not in itself raise difficulties – although some tension is formed by the juxtaposition of 14.1 [MT 13.23] and 15.10. However, the system conforms well with the literary and theological restructuring of Asa's history.

The war with Baasha – together with all the material taken from I Kings 15 – is placed at the end of Asa's history, in the thirty-sixth year of his reign. This date is also theologically reasonable: the evils of Asa's history are all relegated to the end of his career. This very conformity of chronology and literary and theological objectives immediately raises questions about its authenticity, and our doubts are considerably increased by a comparison with the chronological data found in the book of Kings. We infer from I Kings 15.33 and 16.8 that Baasha died in the twenty-sixth year of Asa's reign; how then could they have waged war ten years later, in Asa's thirty-sixth year? Clearly the question here concerns our interpretation of the dates in Chronicles.

As lucidly presented by Williamson (256–8) and R. B. Dillard 'The Reign of Asa (2 Chr 14–16): An Example of the Chronicler's Theological Method', *JETS* 23, 1980, 207–18, and in his commentary, 122–5, biblical research has proposed two alternative approaches to the problem: one, presented in full by Rudolph, regards the entire chronological framework of Asa's reign as a theological structure, having little to do with historical realities (W. Rudolph, 'Der Aufbau der Asa-Geschichte (II Chr 14–16)', *VT* 2, 1952, 367–1, and in his commentary, 239–40). The other, represented by W. F. Albright on one hand ('A Votive Stele Erected by Ben-Hadad I of Damascus to the God Melcarth', *BASOR* 87, 1942, 23–9; 'The Chronology of the Divided Monarchy of Israel', *BASOR* 100, 1945, 16–22) and E. R. Thiele on the other ('A Comparison of the Chronological Data of Israel and Judah', *VT* 4, 1954, 185–91, and in particular *The Mysterious Numbers of the Hebrew Kings*, [3]1983, 57ff.) sees the chronology as fully authentic, suggesting, however, different interpretations. Following Thiele, Williamson would take the dates in 15.19 and 16.1 – the thirty-fifth and thirty-sixth years – as authentic, but base their calculation not from Asa's accession but from the schism between the two kingdoms, a calculation which would make the 'thirty-fifth year' the fifteenth year of Asa – in fact the date of the war with Zerah (II Chron. 15.10). The war with Baasha, then, was in the sixteenth year of Asa's reign. The phrase 'of the reign of Asa' in 15.19 and 16.1 would be a gloss, representing the Chronicler's misunderstanding of the text, while the same note in 15.10 would be authentic.

Williamson's own note of caution concerning the theoretical nature of his proposition should be repeated. We have no hint in Israel's history of a reckoning based on the schism; it is hardly likely that the Chronicler, who did not really regard the schism as a turning point in history, would have been the only historiographer to introduce it, especially as this would mean that he was using two different chronological systems, with each date determined on different grounds. Cf. for example Williamson's own evaluation of 15.10 (the fifteenth year of Asa) as fully authentic; 15.19 and 16.1 as partly so, with the authentic figures calculated to the schism; the note 'to the reign of Asa' as a Chronistic gloss; 14.1b [MT 13.23b] as a 'somewhat arbitrarily chosen round number' (259) and 16.12 (thirty-ninth year of Asa) as 'indecisive'.

The alternative view would focus on the Chronistic development of the full theological meaning of Asa's reign through an overall restructuring of the historical processes, illustrating major tenets in the Chronicler's philosophy of history. This view is supported by the Chronicler's inclination to conceive chronological data in religious terms, and in certain cases to imbue them with a theological message; cf. the treatment of Rehoboam (above) and (below) Hezekiah (cf. also M. Cogan, 'The

Chronicler's Use of Chronology as Illuminated by Neo-Assyrian Royal Inscriptions', in J. Tigay, *Empirical Models for Biblical Criticism*, Philadelphia 1985, 197–210). In view of the literary effort involved and the careful and consistent way in which the events of Asa's reign are dated (compare 11.17; 12.2), I am inclined (at least until further data is produced) to regard the orientation of this chronology as basically theological rather than historical.

5. Chapter 14 itself comprises two parts:

(a) 2–8 [MT 1–7] Introduction to Asa's reign
(b) 9–15 [MT 8–14] The war with Zerah.

The second of these introduces a larger unit ending in 15.19.

D. Commentary

[2–8] (MT 1–7) 1. Verse 1b has already made the smooth transition from Abijah to Asa, in whose days 'the land had rest for ten years'. This will be the leading *motif* of the present introduction, the emphasis on 'peace' and 'rest' repeated in six statements in which the root *šqṭ* appears three times, *nwḥ* twice (and again in 15.15), and once 'there was no war': 'the land had rest ... and the kingdom had rest under him ... for the land had rest. He had no wars ... for the Lord gave him peace ... he has given us peace on every side.'

This is an interesting phenomenon. The title of 'a man of rest', in whose reign peace and quiet will prevail (I Chron. 22.9), is given in Chronicles to Solomon. In the actual description of Solomon's reign, however, Chronicles does not make a single reference to the realization of this potential; all the passages which feature this idea, like I Kings 4.21–22 [MT 5.4–5]; 5.4 [MT 5.19]; 8.56, are for one reason or another not found in the Chronicles text. By contrast, 'peace' is a persistent theme during the greater part of Asa's reign, repeated for Jehoshaphat in 17.10; 20.29–30.

The introduction is devoted to three subjects: religious reform (vv. 2–5), construction (vv. 6–7) and the army (v. 8).

[2–5] (MT 1–4) Having by-passed the Deuteronomistic introduction of I Kings 15.9–10, the Chronicler opens with an evaluation of Asa, following I Kings 15.11: 'Asa did what was good and right in the eyes of the Lord his God'; consistent in his way, the Chronicler omits the comparison with David. I Kings 15.12–13 gives three concrete proofs of Asa's character: he put away the male cult prostitutes, removed the idols, and removed Maacah from her position as queen-mother and destroyed the image she had made. Of these, the Chronicler retains only the last, which he recounts much later in 15.16. The reforms here in v. 2 are described differently: he abolished the 'foreign altars' and 'high places', 'broke down the pillars and hewed down the Asherim' (v. 3); in v. 5, an additional reference to 'high places' with incense altars.

These alterations are neither incidental nor merely stylistic. The 'male cult prostitutes' (*qādēš*), mentioned several times in the books of Kings (I Kings 14.24; 15.12; 22.46; II Kings 23.7, cf. M. I. Gruber, 'The *Qades* in the Book of Kings and in other Sources', *Tarbiz* 52, 1983, 167–76*), are presented there not as innovations but as a prevalent institution ('and there were ... male cult prostitutes in the land'); they are prohibited in Deut. 23.18. The Chronicler omits every reference to the initial existence and eventual abolition of this cult – not, certainly, from ignorance but rather from the strongest conviction that its existence should be silenced altogether.

The 'idols' (*gillūlīm*) appear quite frequently in the Bible, especially in Ezekiel. In the Chronicler's sources in Kings they are mentioned six times (I Kings 15.12; II Kings 17.12; 21.11, 21, 26; 23.24). Although four of these passages are paralleled in Chronicles, the specific reference to idols is completely avoided. The Chronicler relates to idolatry, and even its abolishing, in less extreme terms, referring to 'altars', 'high places', 'pillars' and 'Asherim', probably following the spirit of the Deuteronomic precept in Deut 7.5.

The double reference to 'high places' in this context may indicate a distinction between places for idolatrous worship (v. 3) and *loci* dedicated to the worship of the Lord. While the existence of 'high places' was known to the Chronicler, they played a less significant role in his religious outlook than in that of the Deuteronomist (for details cf. on 15.17, and Japhet, *Ideology*, 217–21).

What are the *ḥammānīm*? Traditional exegesis derives the name from the noun *ḥammāh* (sun), and sees it as signifying 'pillars' for sun worship (cf. *BDB*, 329). The general view in recent times is that, following ancient semitic parallels, it should be explained as 'incense altars' (Baumgartner, 315). Recently, however, it has been suggested that the word denotes a small cultic building, for which 'shrine' would be an adequate rendering (cf. Williamson, 260, following von Fritz). This interpretation would suit the conjunction of *ḥammānīm* with 'high places' in this text, and their 'abolition', but would hardly be appropriate for Ezek. 6.6 and II Chron. 34.4, 7, where the verb used for their removal is *gd'* ('hew down'). These 'pillars', not mentioned in the Chronicler's sources in Kings, appear in only a few passages in Leviticus, Isaiah and Ezekiel (Lev. 26.30; Isa. 17.8; 27.9; Ezek. 6.4, 6).

To the annihilation of prohibited cultic practices which is already mentioned by the Deuteronomist, the Chronicler adds a complementary positive aspect of Asa's deeds (v. 4 [MT 3]): 'he ... commanded Judah to seek the Lord'. While such positive guidance is credited by the Deuteronomist only to Solomon and Josiah (I Kings 8.61; II Kings 23.3, 21), the Chronicler goes back further and attributes it already to David (I Chron. 22.19; 28.8) and later to Asa, Jehoshaphat, Hezekiah and Josiah; all these kings initiate positive measures to encourage correct worship in Judah (II Chron. 17.7–9; 30.6–9; 34.29–32).

This verse in Chronicles is composed of standard Chronistic phrases: the title 'the Lord, the God of their fathers', 'to seek the Lord', and 'law and commandment' (in the collective singular) – one of the designations of the entire scope of God's precepts (Exod. 24.12; II Kings 17.34, 37; II Chron. 19.10; 31.21). Asa's general exhortation will be followed by the more specific actions taken by Jehoshaphat, in II Chron. 17.7–9.

The Chronicler thus credits Asa with quite a comprehensive religious reform, similar to that attributed to Hezekiah (II Chron. 31.1), but less thorough than that of Josiah. However, in the context in which it is here presented, Asa's reform lacks a solid historical logic. In the Deuteronomistic history, the end of Solomon's reign, and especially the period of Rehoboam, saw the infiltration into Judah of every kind of idolatry, symptoms of a 'religious cosmopolitanism', described in Deuteronomistic terminology in I Kings 11.1–6; 14.22–24. The short reign of Abijah did not effect any change, and Asa may be regarded as the 'first reformer', each of his actions well accounted for. The matter is presented differently in Chronicles; here there is no mention of Solomon's transgressions, Rehoboam is described very briefly and vaguely as having done 'evil' (II Chron. 12.14), and Abijah's observance of Temple worship is cited as a model of fidelity (13.10–12). Whence, then, come all these altars, high places, pillars, Asherim and 'abominable idols' (15.8)? While the exhortation of v. 4 may be applicable to any time, there is virtually no justification in the Chronicler's context for the accompanying comprehensive anti-idolatry reform.

This is, then, one more example of the tensions created by a lack of full integration between history and theology in the Chronicler's historiographical method. Certain matters are presented as serving separate and distinct functions, with no overall harmonization. While the modern reader looks for a systematic line of logic, the Chronicler works with smaller units, editing them along lines he considers relevant both to the material itself and to his historical and theological guidelines. Asa is a righteous king, and is presented in I Kings 15 as having undertaken relgious reform, and this feature is probably so well-anchored in history that even the Chronicler's emphasis and elaboration have an authentic ring. However, Asa's reform as here described contradicts the broader context of Chronicles, because of the reworking of the histories of Solomon, Rehoboam and Abijah, motivated by other aspects of the Chronicler's view of history.

[6–7] (MT 5–6) The second topic of the introduction is Asa's building of cities with 'walls and towers, gates and bars'. These verses are redolent of the Chronicler's style and views, including his usual term for fortified cities, and their detailed description, the frequent use of 'seek' (*drš*)) and 'prospered' (*hislīah*) and the chain of causative clauses (with *kī*, 'for', v. 6). There is an obvious theological point to the conjunction of the building projects with days of rest and prosperity: a righteous person is rewarded by God with success, one aspect of which is 'building' (cf. Welten, 42ff.). The role of the people also reflects an attitude found often in Chronicles: the king does not bear the responsibility for ensuring the people's welfare alone (cf. Japhet, *Ideology*, 416ff.); he needs the support of his subjects and turns to ask for it. Here, too, the granting of 'rest round about' depends not only on Asa's conduct, but on that of the people of Judah; even the building enterprises themselves are realized through the cooperation of the people – gained not by command but through persuasion (v. 7) – as expressed in the plural verb 'and they built and prospered'.

The passage, then, was undoubtedly written by the Chronicler; what in that case is its historical value? Welten strongly suggests that the information is fictitious, regarding 'building' as a 'topos', exclusively theological in function (Welten, ibid.). In support of this opinion one may point to the very general reference to the fortified cities, with no concrete names given (cf. Williamson, 260). A less extreme view would regard this passage as a general elaboration of the note about the building of Geba and Mizpah, cited from I Kings 15.22 in II Chron. 16.6. On the other hand, it should be noted that for the Deuteronomist as well, Asa was distinguished for his 'building': he is the only Judaean king who merits the reference to 'the rest of all the acts of Asa ... and *the cities which he built* ...' (I Kings 15.23; for a similar remark about Ahab cf. I Kings 22.39). Unlike the Deuteronomistic historiographer, the Chronicler shows great interest in the theme of building, as a significant component of any enterprising reign (cf. Japhet, *Ideology*, 436f.). For Asa, Chronicles includes this item here in the general introduction, but omits it from his own conclusion (16.11); unfortunately, our evaluation of this matter is hampered by lack of further details.

Verse 7 repeats *dārašnū* ('we sought') twice; this is avoided by LXX, which renders the second appearance as 'he sought us' (*dᵉrāšanū*). This reading has been regarded by several scholars as original, and has prompted the emendation of the clause to *kᵉdoršēnū ... dᵉrāšanū*, 'because we sought the Lord ... he sought us' (cf. Rudolph, 240, following earlier commentators; Williamson, 261; and also NEB). The verse seems to allude to Deut. 11.12: *'ereṣ 'ᵃšer yhwh 'ᵉlōhēkā dōrēš 'ōtāh*, 'a land which the Lord your God cares for' (cf. also Isa. 62.12).

[8–9] (MT 7–8) Asa's army has two major components: three hundred thousand Judeans 'armed with bucklers and spears' and two hundred and eighty thousand Benjaminites 'that carried shields and drew bows'. This is the first of the Chronicler's notices on the kingdom's army; the historicity of these notes should be discussed along similar lines to the issue of building (cf. E. Junge, *Der Wiederaufbau des Heereswesen des Reiches Juda unter Josia*, 1937, 37–45; Welten, 79–114).

At first glance, the fact that this information is found only in Chronicles seems to weigh heavily against its authenticity. As a matter of fact, however, the complete absence of such detail in the Deuteronomistic history indicates nothing but a lack of interest in military topics; their appearance in Chronicles is a welcome historiographical complement. In any case, the information as it stands cannot reflect the Chronicler's own circumstances, when Judah had no army and the tribal separation of 'Judah and Benjamin' was obsolete. If these details are Chronistic compositions, they may be either purely theoretical, or literary reflections of Persian or other foreign military models (according to Welten, 110–11, Hellenistic). On the other hand, except for the exaggerated numbers, there is nothing improbable in the organization of the monarchical army – most probably the conscript forces – on the principle of a territorial distinction between 'Judah' and 'Benjamin' or their alternative specialization. While these data cannot be confirmed for lack of supporting evidence, to reject them outright would clearly be a case of circular argumentation.

[9–15) (MT 8–14) The discussion of Asa's military encounter with Zerah the Cushite is shaped to a great extent by each interpreter's preconceived stand concerning its historicity. The long history of research into Chronicles seems to exclude a *bona fide* starting point of its historicity and to demand a more qualified attitude. A 'non-historical' verdict for the story may view it either as a projection of the Chronicler's own age (H. Winckler, *Bemerkungen zur Chronik als Geschichtsquelle*, 1892, 166), or a complete fiction (Wellhausen, 208). If the latter, this passage should be discussed along literary and theological lines alone, eschewing all historical considerations; if the former (i.e. historical), then the circumstances, details and contextual significance of the story should first be studied, before proceeding to its literary and theological aspects.

While the schematic style, exaggerated numbers and theological orientation of the passage are unmistakable, there are also details which clearly point to a realistic and concrete episode (cf. below). The context of this episode would be more plausibly the pre-exilic monarchy, i.e. Asa's reign, than the Chronicler's own situation, when Judah was a province of the Persian (and then Hellenistic) empire (cf. Curtis, 382, etc.).

'Zerah the Cushite' is here presented as the ruler of a major world power, launching a military offensive on the grandest scale, with an army of a million soldiers. This prompts us to seek this king among the Egyptian Pharaohs, and Osorkon I, whose name has some phonetic affinity to Zerah, has been regarded as the best candidate (cf. Kitchen, 767). However, the details of this encounter, in particular its results, i.e. the plundering of 'the cities round about Gerar', and of herdsmen's property ('sheep ... and camels', vv. 14–15), all point rather to a much more limited engagement. The scope and nature of this local skirmish, on the southern border of Judah, remind the reader of I Chron. 4.39–41, 42–43; 5.10. 'Zerah' would be a dark-skinned leader, one of those referred to in I Chron. 4.39–41 as 'belonging to Ham', who infiltrated the southern territories of Judah probably in the wake of (and exploiting) Shishak's major invasions. The Chronicler elaborated this limited skirmish into an event of significant theological implications to Asa's career; the literary reworking is very similar to that of II Chron. 13: the basic historical facts are in the beginning (vv. 9–10, cf. 13.3–4) and again at the end (vv. 14–15; cf. 13.19).

The war is described in three stages. The two narrative sections (vv. 9–10 [MT 8–9], the setting, and vv. 12–15 [MT 11–14], the victory) serve as an action-framework for the rhetorical passage of v. 11 [MT 10]: Asa's prayer, which represents the turning point in the conflict.

[9] (MT 8) The name 'Zerah' is quite common in the Bible. It is represented in three Israelite tribes: the son of Judah who lost his superior position to his brother Perez (Gen. 38.30 etc.); the son of Simeon (Num. 26.20; I Chron. 4.24, introduced in Gen. 46.10 and Exod. 6.15 as 'Zohar'); and a Levite, one member of the genealogical line of the Gershonites (I Chron. 6.21, 41 [MT 6.6, 26]). Zerah is also a major group of the Edomite tribal system (Gen. 36.13, 17, 33; I Chron. 1.37; 44). 'Cush', which is generally associated with Egypt and regarded (in spite of RSV's insistence on 'Ethiopia') as the biblical designation of Nubia (Gen. 10.6; Isa. 20.3; Ps. 68.31, etc.), may also be linked to Midian, as in Hab. 3.7 and possibly Num. 12.1 (cf. J. Liver, 'Cush', *Encyclopedia Biblica* 4, 1951, 69*). All these indicate the southern parts of the land; it is here, then – without attempting a precise ethnic affiliation or ascribing absolute weight to names – that we should probably seek Zerah's origins.

The depiction of Zerah's army, with its 'million' troops and a disproportionately small unit of chariots, can hardly be accepted as historical. These extraordinary features should be seen as part of the schematic-theological interpretation of the actual battle. In fact, nothing further is said about the deployment of the fighters, and the chariots disappear altogether.

[10] (MT 9) The venue of the battle is the vicinity of Mareshah, one of the cities fortified by Rehoboam (II Chron. 11.8); the 'valley of Zephathah' however, is not known from any other source. A Canaanite city called 'Zephath', conquered by a joint foray of Judah and Simeon, is known from Judg. 1.17, but its precise location is not specified there. The change from 'Zephath' to 'Zephathah' is quite possible; the use of the lengthened form as an alternative form for place-names is well attested in Chronicles (cf. Tim-

nathah, Ephrathah, Hamathah, Baalathah, etc.). The identification of the city with the valley of our verse is however doubtful. The LXX reading 'north of' is preferred by some; it accords well with the preposition l^e in $l^e m\bar{a}r\bar{e}\check{s}\bar{a}h$, 'of/at Mareshah' – certainly rather difficult in MT as it stands (cf. Curtis 383; Rudolph, 240). This reading probably reflects a Hebrew variant in which the מ is represented by ח; since this interchange is possible in either direction, the original reading cannot be determined.

[11] (MT 10) When the two armies have drawn up their battle lines, Asa turns to address the Lord. His prayer reflects not only a Chronistic vocabulary but also the Chronicler's views.

In this short prose prayer, the progression of structure and argument is noteworthy. Of the three addresses to the Lord, the first makes a declaration, phrased as a nominal clause in a negative mode, 'O Lord, there is none like thee to help ...'; the second is a cry for aid, 'Help us, O Lord our God'; and the third opens with the declarative nominal phrase, 'O Lord thou art our God' ($yhwh\ {}^{?e}l\bar{o}h\bar{e}n\bar{u}\ {}'att\bar{a}h$), and ends with an entreaty 'let no man prevail'. The last clause clearly counters the first, in the repetition of 'with you' ($'imm^ek\bar{a}$), the negative formulation and particle ($'al/\ '\bar{e}n$), and the assonance of $la'z\bar{o}r/\ ya'\dot{s}\bar{o}r$.

The theme of the whole is divine rule and omnipotence: God's unrivalled power will inevitably determine the outcome of human conflict. At the same time, the self-presentation of the people of Judah is that of the people of the Lord: they act in God's name and rely on his help; with the emphatic declaration 'O Lord, thou art our God' they claim their God's exclusive protection.

The syntax and precise semantic nuances here are difficult. The first clause begins with $'\bar{e}n\ 'imm^eka\ la'z\bar{o}r$ (RSV 'there is none like thee to help ...'), literally 'there is none *with thee* to help'. Also, the next clause, rendered literally '*between* the mighty and the weak', is rather a poor sequel. Given the reference to the enemy as a 'multitude', one might suggest that the first clause should be seen not as a general aphorism, but as related to the specific context: the people of Judah are in fact 'weak' (literally 'powerless'). The words $'\bar{e}n\ 'imm^ek\bar{a}\ la'z\bar{o}r$ may then be understood as 'there is none *except* you to help' (cf. Pseudo-Rashi and Kimhi), and the context seen as elliptical, 'there is none except you to help [in a conflict] between the strong and the weak'.

The last clause is also not fully clear. We may understand the verb $ya'z\bar{o}r$ to denote 'rule' (e.g. Kimhi), in which case the clause would mean 'may no mortal be a ruler at your side'. However, the verb is more often understood as an elliptical representation of the fuller expression $ya'z\bar{o}r\ k\bar{o}ah$, denoting 'muster strength', 'be capable of', etc. (cf. I Chron. 29.14; II Chron. 2.6 [MT 5]; 13.20; 22.9; Dan. 10.8, 16; 11.6; and cf. also II Chron. 20.37). $'imm^ek\bar{a}$

would then mean, as in many other instances, not 'with you' but 'against you'; thus RSV, 'Let no man prevail against you'.

Asa's address is in the plural: he speaks in the name of the whole people, of whom he is merely a representative (cf. I Chron. 20.6–12).

[12] (MT 11) The answer to Asa's prayer is an immediate divine action: 'So the Lord defeated the Cushites before Asa and Judah', a formula which echoes the divine response to Abijah in his war against Jeroboam (13.14–15). The enemy then 'fled' (also 13.16) and Asa and his army had only to pursue them, smite their cities and plunder their possessions. The message could not be more clearly brought home: 'reliance on God results in victory'.

Again, as in the war between Abijah and Jeroboam, the turning point in the battle is not recorded in military terms; there is not a word about concrete tactics, nor about the million soldiers and the hundreds of chariots; they have no function whatsoever. The turning point of the war is entirely a divine act, not embodied in any visible expression; an absolute – but abstract – miracle.

[13] (MT 12) The pursuit of the routed Cushites pinpoints the geographic location of the war in the vicinity of Gerar. The LXX 'Gedor' is also a possibility, but while 'Gedor' may be viewed as a more general name, 'Gerar' offers a specific geographical setting. More evidence of the interchangeability of *gdr/grr* is interestingly illustrated in I Chron. 4.39, where LXX reads 'Gerarah' and MT Gedor. All things taken into consideration, I would regard MT as the better version.

No numbers are here given, as they are in other such passages, and the magnitude of the victory is expressed by a series of adverbs and adjectives: 'beyond recovery' (*le'en miḥyāh*, cf. Ezra 9.8 and Rudolph, 242), 'very much booty', 'much plunder' (v. 13); 'sheep in abundance' (v. 14)' the three-fold use of 'much' (*lārōb, harbēh, rabbāh*) echoing the words of Asa in his prayer: 'There is none like thee to help, between the mighty (*rab*) and the weak' (v. 11).

'Before the Lord and his army' cannot be taken to refer to a supernatural host, as some commentators would have it (cf. G. von Rad, *Holy War in Ancient Israel*, Grand Rapids 1991, 130). Very much as in II Chron. 13.12, the intent is to describe the Lord as standing at the head of the Judaean army, 'Asa and the people … with him'. While God is indeed a warrior-champion, all the concrete features of the war – smiting, plundering, spoiling etc. – are seen as the role of his human agents.

[14] (MT 13) After the initial victory, the conflict now escalates to the plundering of the 'cities'; it should be noted that these are said to be 'round about Gerar', but not 'Gerar' itself, and that the verb 'they smote' does not indicate the conquest of the cities. All these are probably echoes of the actual features of the episode.

During this confrontation, then, the stages of Asa's victory are carefully defined: the first blow is God's: 'The Lord defeated the Cushites'; Asa pursues and kills the routed troops, taking much spoil. Then, Asa comes into the cities and sacks them, smiting the people around the cities and the herdsmen living in tents, and plundering their property. Even in the last stage, Asa's success is attributed not to human valour but to God's intervention, again portrayed in abstract spiritual terms. 'The fear of the Lord' which paralysed the enemy is taken from the vocabulary of earlier biblical literature (cf. von Rad, *Holy War*, 46–7), and is also an important factor in the Chronicler's political lexicon. Its use, however, is restricted to three kings: in the most limited way for Asa, more broadly for David (in the Chronicler's addition of I Chron. 14.7), and in the most emphasized form for Jehoshaphat (II Chron. 17.10; 20.29).

[15] (MT 14) In addition to the cities, Asa and his people smite the *'oh°lē miqneh* – an uncommon phrase usually viewed as elliptical for 'tents of those who had cattle' (RSV); or, in analogy to the Arabic usage, *'ōhel* is taken to mean 'people', the phrase denoting herdsmen (cf. NEB). The same phrase may also designate a certain type of settlement, consisting of tents (cf. I Chron. 4.41). The plundering is emphasized by repetition, but it is no coincidence that the only specified items taken are 'sheep and camels'.

In conclusion, no conquest of any kind is mentioned; the story has a suitable narrative ending, 'Then they returned to Jerusalem', but the fate of Zerah, with whom the story began in v. 9, is passed over in silence.

15 The spirit of God came upon Azariah the son of Oded, [2] and he went out to meet Asa, and said to him, 'Hear me, Asa, and all Judah and Benjamin: The Lord is with you, while you are with him. If you seek him, he will be found by you, but if you forsake him, he will forsake you. [3] For a long time Israel was without the true God, and without a teaching priest, and without law; [4] but when in their distress they turned to the Lord, the God of Israel, and sought him, he was found by them. [5] In those times there was no peace to him who went out or to him who came in, for great disturbances afflicted all the inhabitants of the lands. [6] They were broken in pieces, nation against nation and city against city, for God troubled them with every sort of distress. [7] But you, take courage! Do not let your hands be weak, for your work shall be rewarded.'

8 When Asa heard these words, the prophecy of Azariah the son of Oded, he took courage, and put away the abominable idols from all the land of Judah and Benjamin and from the cities which he had taken in the hill country of Ephraim, and he repaired the altar of the Lord that was in front of the vestibule of the house of the Lord. [9] And he gathered all Judah and Benjamin, and those from Ephraim, Manasseh, and Simeon who were sojourning with them, for great numbers had deserted to him from Israel when they saw that the Lord his God was with him. [10] They were gathered at Jerusalem in the third month of the fifteenth year of the reign of Asa. [11] They sacrificed to the Lord on that day, from the spoil which they had brought, seven hundred oxen and seven thousand sheep. [12] And they entered into a covenant to seek the Lord, the God of their fathers, with all their heart and with all their soul; [13] and that whoever would not seek the Lord, the God of Israel, should be put to death, whether young or old, man or woman. [14] They took oath to the Lord with a loud voice, and with shouting, and with trumpets, and with horns. [15] And all Judah rejoiced over the oath; for they had sworn with all their heart, and had sought him with their whole desire, and he was found by them, and the Lord gave them rest round about.

16 Even Maacah, his mother, King Asa removed from being queen mother because she had made an abominable image for Asherah. Asa cut down her image, crushed it, and burned it at the brook Kidron. [17] But the high places were not taken out of Israel. Nevertheless the heart of Asa was blameless all his days. [18] And he brought into the house of God the votive gifts of his father and his own votive gifts, silver, and gold, and vessels. [19] And there was no more war until the thirty-fifth year of the reign of Asa.

A. Notes to MT

[8] עדד הנביא, proposed gloss, (to v. 1), or insert עדד הנביא [בן עזריהו בן] אשר נבא עזריהו [אשר נבא עזריהו בן] עדד הנביא, cf. commentary; [9] וממנשה, read וממנשה (haplography).

B. Notes to RSV

[6] 'They were broken in pieces, nation against nation and city against city', JPS 'nation was crushed by nation and city by city'; [8] 'the vestibule of the house of the Lord', better 'the house of the Lord' (cf. commentary); [16] 'his mother', so I Kings 15.13, MT 'the mother of king Asa'; 'King Asa removed', MT 'he removed'.

C. Structure, sources and form

1. Chapter 15 is in content and form a direct sequel to the preceding description of the war with the Cushites. The structure of the chapter, if viewed from the perspective of its sources, seems to reflect two distinct units: the second of these (vv. 16–19) is adopted from I Kings 15.13–16, while the first (vv. 1–15) is peculiar to Chronicles. This view of the structure is supported by the stylistic quality of the first section, where the Chronistic stamp is more clearly marked, and the character of v. 15b as conclusion: 'and the Lord gave them rest round about.'

However, a different view of the chapter arises from its intrinsic nature. The theme of Asa's reform is common to both vv. 8–15 and their appropriate sequel in vv. 16–18. Verse 19, on the other hand, referring to the issue of 'war', concludes the pericope which began in 14.9 [MT 8]. From this point of view, one may analyse the chapter as follows:

(a) 1–18 Asa's reform
    1–7 prophecy
    8–18 reform
        8 removal of idolatry
        9–15 covenant
        16–17 removal of the 'abominable image'
        18 bringing the votive gifts
(b) 19 Conclusion.

The alternative approaches to the question of structure well illustrate the Chronicler's historiographic method: his new composition displays a great measure of literal adherence to its sources, the wholesale integration of which affects – and sometimes mars – the final literary product.

2. The prophecy of Azariah the son of Oded is a characteristic example of what has been wrongly termed by von Rad (and since) 'Levitical sermon' (cf. G. von Rad, 'The Levitical Sermon in the Old Testament', in *The Problem of the Hexateuch and Other Essays*, 1966, 267–80; D. Mathias, '"Levitische Predigt" und Deuteronomismus', *ZAW* 96, 1984, 231–5; R. Mason, *Preaching the Tradition*, Cambridge, 1990, 137–44). In fact, the origin and function of this prophecy parallel the rhetorical pieces in

the Deuteronomistic historiography. Here too, the pieces are composed by the Chronicler, while their formulation as prophecy, oration, prayer, etc., is dictated by the literary requirements of the various contexts.

This prophecy is marked as Chronistic by certain literary and theological features, already displayed in its opening: the plural address 'Hear me' (I Chron. 28.2; II Chron. 13.4 etc.), the definition of the people as 'Judah and Benjamin', and their direct association with the king. There are also the Chronicler's favourite theological epigrams: 'The Lord is with you, while you are with him', employing the typical verbs 'seek', 'find' and 'forsake'; cf. further in the commentary.

Most strikingly, this prophecy is one of the best of several examples in Chronicles of an 'anthological style' – a mosaic of longer or shorter citations from existing prophetic texts, slightly altered and sophistically interwoven, to serve the new context and form a coherent statement of the Chronicler's views. This use of citations is common throughout the Chronicler's work, but is considerably more evident in rhetorical pieces, where the goal is a poetic and eloquent level of expression. The familiar 'building blocks', while enriching the new prophecy with their original associations, are adroitly woven into a new context with its own theological goals.

The texts cited or alluded to in the present prophecy are: Hosea 3.4; 5.15–6.1; Ezek. 38.21; Haggai 2.22; Zech. 14.13–14; Amos 3.9; Isa. 9.18–20; Zech. 8.10b; 11.6; Zeph. 3.16; Jer. 31.16b; cf. the commentary for details.

3. Since vv. 1–7 were in all probability composed by the Chronicler, and vv. 16–19 derive from I Kings 15.13–16, the question of sources is limited to vv. 8–15, dealing with Asa's removal of idols, the repairing of the altar, and the 'covenant' undertaken by Asa and the people of Judah. This passage too bears clear Chronistic marks: the favourite idiom פזחתה, 'took courage', the unification of 'Judah and Benjamin', the recurring phrase 'the Lord his God was with him', the motif of 'seeking', the phrase 'with all their hearts and with all their souls', the emphasis on 'rejoicing', and more. Also characteristic of the Chronicler are the predilection for describing ceremonies and the participation of crowds, the joining of northern Israelites to the kingdom of Judah, the importance of sacrifices, the full co-operation of king and people, the significance of 'joy', and 'rest' as the ultimate achievement. Not all of these, of course, are exclusive to Chronicles, but their massive accumulation surely points here to Chronistic authorship.

A discussion of sources should, therefore, distinguish between two levels: the final literary work, which is Chronistic, and the core of the information which is incorporated into it, and for which the question of earlier sources is relevant. The new data provided by the passage are as follows: removal of idolatry; repairing of the altar; the conquest of Ephraimite cities; the celebration of a 'covenant' in Jerusalem with the chronological note the fifteenth year of Asa's reign.

That Asa was in fact a great reformer, the first among the Judaean kings who took active steps against prevalent or newly introduced institutions, is already attested in I Kings 15.13, where his zeal prompts him to the unconventional step of removing Maacah from her position as 'queen mother'. While the exact details of further acts of reform, especially the rebuilding of the altar, cannot be verified, the tone of this passage certainly matches what we know of the historical Asa. On the other hand, the chronological remark 'the third month of the fifteenth year' is best explained as one component of a theoretical system. For the additional points, cf. the commentary.

D. *Commentary*

[1–7] After a short narrative introduction of Azariah and his prophetic call (1a–2aα), this passage is devoted to the content of his message. After the address (v. 2aβ), the three parts of the prophecy gradually broaden in scope: statement of principle (v. 2b); historical precedent (vv. 3–4); and analogy of past and present (vv. 5–7).

The theological maxim laid down in v. 2b opens with a nominal statement, 'The Lord is with you while you are with him', followed by two specific conditional clauses: 'If you seek him ... if you forsake him ...'. The review of the historical precedent progresses from a negative situation (v. 3) to a positive one (v. 4). The analogical climax (vv. 5–7) opens with an emphatic reference to the past, 'in those times', countered by an equally emphatic exhortation for the present: 'But you take courage'.

[1] Of all the prophets whose words are cited in Chronicles, only for four is there a description of direct inspiration by the 'spirit': 'the spirit of God/the Lord came upon ...' (also II Chron. 20.14), and 'the spirit [of God] took possession of ...' (*lābᵉšāh*, I Chron. 12.18 [MT 19]; II Chron. 24.20); both these idioms are otherwise known in the context of actions rather than prophetic utterances (Judg. 3.10; 6.34; 11.29; I Sam. 19.20; etc.). It should be noted that the four prophetic figures who share this specific charisma – Azariah, Amasai, Jahaziel the Levite and Zechariah the priest – are lesser-known personalities. The more familiar prophets like Nathan, Gad, Jehu, etc. are never described in this way. Possibly, then, the Chronicler employs these idioms to mark an initiation: the first (or only) utterance of the 'non-professional' prophets.

While 'Azariah/u' is very common in the biblical onomasticon, a prophet by that name is not known elsewhere. Oded, however, is the name of another prophet peculiar to Chronicles, whose calling was in the days of Ahaz (II Chron. 28.9; on the etymology, form and probable meaning of the name Oded cf. Willi, 225 n. 23; also Rudolph, 245 n. 1). It seems that while the prophecy of Azariah is itself distinctly Chronistic, the figure of the prophet may be based on authentic tradition (cf. on 9.29 for Iddo).

The emphatic syntax (a *casus pendens* opening with the object, 'Azariahu the son of Oded – the spirit of God came upon him', not reflected in translation) not only especially marks Azariah's appearance, but also sees it as a continuation and sequel of the preceding words 'they returned to Jerusalem'.

[2] The scene of a prophet going out to meet the returning king is also repeated in Chronicles for Jehoshaphat (II Chron. 19.1–2) and Ahaz (28.9); the unusual phrase used here, *yāṣā' lipnē*, elsewhere denotes the act of leading an army to battle (Judg. 4.14; II Sam. 5.24; I Sam. 8.20, etc.; also I Chron.

14.8; II Chron. 14.8 [MT 9]; etc.). For the prophet, the victory in the present war, and the huge amounts of spoil, represent only one stage of the historical event. The more important stage is now brought to Asa's attention: the demand for spiritual accounting in the aftermath of military success, the recognition of the material victory as an opportunity for spiritual renewal. One may say that for Azariah the war was a trial which Asa and the people passed successfully; now they are asked to apply the correct conclusions to the organizing of their everyday life. His excited oration is an urgent call to repentance and reform.

After addressing the king and the people, 'Hear me, Asa and all Judah and Benjamin', Azariah states an axiom which for him is the underlying principle of all history. The detailed formulation here employs various rhetoric techniques.

The opening two-colon nominal epigram is the most general declaration: 'The Lord is with you, while you are with him'. The four words in Hebrew consist of the repeated element *'im* ('with you'/'with him'), and the repetition of the verbal root *hwh/hyh* in the divine name (*yhwh*) and the infinitive *bihyōtᵉkem*. Each colon also chiastically balances second person and third: 'the Lord ... you'; 'you ... him'.

What follows is a perfectly paralleled sequence of two conditional clauses, with their pending results. In each case the subject of the condition is the people, while the subject of the apodosis is God. The conditions reflect two alternatives: the positive 'if you seek him' and the negative 'but if you forsake him'; it is probably for the sake of this structure that a passive verbal form is chosen in the first apodosis, 'he will be found by you'.

The first condition is built on the complementary verbs 'seek' (*drš*) and 'find'. While this word-pair is quite common in biblical literature, one cannot fail to recognize here some similarity to Jer. 29.13–14, and a special affinity to Isa. 65.1 and 55.6 (with the passive verb-form). The second condition uses only one verb, 'forsake', emphasizing the principle of 'measure for measure'.

Through this fine structure the Chronicler gives fullest expression to a major tenet of his philosophy of history, also found elsewhere (II Chron.12.5; 24.20; I Chron. 28.9, etc.): man's fate is determined by his own conduct.

[3–4] Having laid down this principle, the prophecy now turns to what may be the closest the Chronicler comes to a 'historical review'. By illustrating the validity of the axiom in the past, the ground is laid for reference to the present in v. 7. The attempt to illustrate the idea with historical examples follows the model of Nathan's prophecy (II Sam. 7.6–11//I Chron. 17.5–10). This rather vague reference to 'a long time' (literally 'for many days') has led some commentators to follow the interpretation implied by the LXX and explain it as indicating the future (cf. Curtis, 384), or to restructure the passage entirely (cf. Rudolph, 242).

The period which the Chronicler chooses as an example is not clearly defined, but its features imply the pre-monarchical age (cf. *inter al.*, Rudolph, 245), generally called (although not by the Chronicler) the 'period of the Judges'. This time is characterized here by cycles of distress – repentance – relief, and by a negative religious context (v. 3) corresponding to social/political distress on an international scale (vv. 5–6), which may be seen as a foreshadowing of the present circumstances. By contrast, the positive correct attitude of the people in the past (v. 4) is expected to be emulated now (v. 7).

The dependence of v. 3 on Hosea 3.4 has been recognized by earlier commentators (cf. I. L. Seeligmann, 'The Beginnings of Midrash in Chronicles', *Tarbiz* 49, 1979–1980, 20–1*). Both passages relate to a lengthy state of anarchy, marked by the lack of elementary institutions. In both, there is an opening reference to a 'long time for Israel' – for Hosea in the future, for the Chronicler in the past – when three elements are absent in Israel. For Hosea, there are three couplets: 'king or prince ... sacrifice or pillar ... ephod or teraphim', the parallel structure emphasized by the five-fold repetition of *'ēn*, 'without', while the three elements in Chronicles are single rather than couplets (but two of them are in fact phrased in two words) and there is a three-fold negative expressed by another particle, *l'lō'*, 'without': 'Without the true God, without a teaching priest, and without law'. While Hosea defines anarchy as the absence of both political and religious (cultic) institutions – king, sacrifice and guiding oracles – the Chronicler sees it exclusively in religious terms, which in turn are defined as spiritual rather than cultic. The only element which is shared by Hosea and the Chronicler is the priestly function – but even this is defined from two different perspectives: 'ephod and teraphim' as opposed to 'teaching priest'. While the exact forms *'elōhē 'emet*, 'true God' and *kōhēn mōreh*, 'teaching priest', are unique, similar phrases may be found in Jer. 10.10; Ps. 31.5 [MT 31.6] and II Chron. 17.28.

The overall impression is of a complete dearth of knowledge of the true God, because of the absence of teachers and instruction.

Verse 4 is a natural sequel, in the light of both Hosea 3.5a and the Chronicler's own conviction: when distress became unbearable, Israel 'turned to the Lord'. This echoes v. 2, as well as Hosea 3.5, with a change of tense to the past rather than the future: 'they turned' (*wayyāšob*, Hosea *yāšūbū*), and 'they sought him' (*wayy'baqušu*, Hosea *ūbiqšū*). Even at the worst of times, when all seemed hopeless, repentance was possible, and 'the Lord God of Israel' was found by those who truly sought him.

This statement seems to have crystallized the idea, and one would expect v. 7 to follow, with an explicit lesson for the present: 'But you, take courage!' Instead, we find a return to 'those times' (vv. 5–6), now considered from a different angle. All this has led Rudolph to suggest a reconstruction of the passage, placing v. 4 after vv. 5–6 (242). This proposed sequence, while according well with modern logic, ignores the original structure of the passage, disturbs the integrity of vv. 3 and 4, weakens the introductory force of 'In those times' (v. 5), and disregards the forceful juxtaposition of past and present in vv. 5–6 and 7 (cf. above).

Verse 4, too, is influenced by earlier texts. Although the phrase 'in my/your/their distress' is found in the Bible in several contexts (Deut. 4.30; II Sam. 22.7 = Ps. 18.6 [MT 18.7] ; Ps. 107.6, *et passim*), the nearest to this passage is Hosea 5.15–6.1. Note how all the same elements appear in a chiastic order:

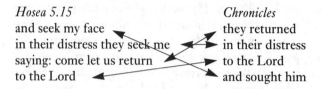

Hosea 5.15
and seek my face
in their distress they seek me
saying: come let us return
to the Lord

Chronicles
they returned
in their distress
to the Lord
and sought him

Thus the theological principle of vv. 3–4 is built in both its parts on models from Hosea.

[5–7] Making an emphatic transition, the prophecy now reverts to the earlier past, in order to lay the foundation for the most important conclusion of v. 7. The structure, which establishes an analogy between past and present, is built as an antithesis: 'In those times'/'But you ...'.

The universal anarchy of 'those times' was marked by three features: lack of security on the highways, 'great disturbances', and strife between cities and nations. Each of the parallel sentences describing this situation is composed of two clauses: indicative and causative; in the first instance both are nominal, 'there was no peace ... for (*kî*) great disturbances afflicted ...', and in the second verbal, 'they were broken in pieces ... for (*kî*) God troubled them'.

This balanced structure includes a series of citations, taken from various prophecies. The concise phrase *ē'n šālōm layyōṣe welabbā'* (cf. JPS 'no wayfarer was safe', better than the too-literal RSV) is a chiastic quotation of Zech. 8.10, *layyōṣe' welabbā' 'ēn šālōm*, a prophecy which will be echoed again in v. 7, and the similarity with which is somewhat obscured by the translations. 'Great disturbances' is an idiom borrowed from Amos 3.9 (RSV 'great tumults'); the Hebrew (*mehōmōt rabbōt*) is unique, although a similar idiom in the singular is in Zech. 14.13. The unique plural form 'the inhabitants of the lands' (*yōšebē ha'arāṣōt*) is a characteristic late Hebrew development of the more common *yōšebē hā'āreṣ*. The context calls to mind many parallel passages, such as Jer. 6.12; 10.18; 25.30; Ezek. 7.7; Joel 2.1; Zeph. 1.18, etc.).

'They were broken in pieces ($w^{e}kutt^{e}t\bar{u}$), nation against nation' is reminiscent of Zech. 11.6: 'I will no longer have pity on the inhabitants of the land ... I will cause men to fall each into the hand of his shepherd (MT neighbour) ... and they shall crush ($w^{e}kitt^{e}t\bar{u}$) the earth'. Interfraternal strife is depicted in similar terms several times in the Bible, but the closest text to this may be found in Hag 2.22; cf. also Isa. 19.2.

The climax of the prophecy is found in v. 7. The development has been from general principles to third-person descriptions, and now the prophet returns to a second person imperative: 'But you, take courage!'; this is the true sequel to the opening address, 'Hear me, Asa, and all Judah and Benjamin'.

The prophet is again using ready citations and standard idioms: 'take courage' is common (Deut. 31.6; II Sam. 13.28, etc.), but the specific context here recalls Zech 8.9, 13. 'Do not let your hands be weak' is a literal quotation of Zeph. 3.16, with a shift to the plural; the final clause 'for your work shall be rewarded' has been long recognized as a citation of Jer. 31.6, again in the plural.

As in the previous passage, here too the message is only very generally stated; the prophet gives no practical instructions. Nonetheless, his demand must be abundantly clear to his audience: the analogy to 'those days' leaves no doubt that a return to God is imperative.

[8–18] Asa stands the test. He understands what is demanded of him and acts promptly. The immediate nature of Asa's response is expressed both in the explicit statement 'when Asa heard ...', better translated 'As soon as Asa heard ...', and also in the repetition of the leading motif: Asa was exhorted to 'take courage', and indeed, 'he took courage'.

In complying so wholeheartedly with the prophet's expectations, Asa is faithful to the religious integrity he displayed in the earlier episode, the war with the Cushites. In Chronicles, heeding the prophets is second only to trusting in God (II Chron. 20.20); these are in fact two facets of the same faith. For Asa, full trust in God's help has won him a war, and obedience to a prophetic command will now grant him and his people 'rest round about' (v. 15). By contrast, Asa's conduct in the following trial will be the antithesis of the present case: there he will mistrust God's help (16.7) and fail to heed a prophet's rebuke (16.9), and for both lapses will be heavily punished.

Although Azariah has not made any specific demands, Asa initiates a comprehensive reform, the first aspect of which is the removal of the 'abominable idols' from all the territory under his hegemony. This rather general reference is the only occurrence of *šiqquṣīm* in Chronicles; other appearances in parallel texts (II Kings 23.13, 24) are not reproduced in Chronicles.

Asa's territorial expansion is described as 'the land of Judah and Benjamin and ... the cities which he had taken in the hill country of Ephraim'. The latter note is not recorded in I Kings, which immediately raises the question of its authenticity. Some commentators see here an anachronistic reference to Geba and Mizpah, which are mentioned after the retreat of Baasha (I Kings 15.22//II Chron. 16.6; cf. Rudolph, 245). However, although the Benjaminite cities of Geba and Mizpah may be very generally referred to as situated in 'the hill country of Ephraim', they were not 'taken' but only 'built' by Asa. Moreover, the conquest of cities from the northern kingdom, Bethel, Jeshanah and Ephrain/Ephron is mentioned in the time of Abijah (13.19), and the reigns of Abijah and Asa are viewed in Chronicles as actually a single unit. The victory of Abijah granted rest to the land 'for ten years' during Asa's reign (14.1 [MT. 13.23]), and Asa brought to the house of the Lord his father's votive gifts as well as his own (v. 18//I Kings 15.15) – all of which indicates that Abijah died unexpectedly (13.20) and Asa continued from what he had begun. In a later context, the cities conquered by Asa are mentioned in his son's reign: 'He [Jehoshaphat] ... set garrisons ... in the cities of Ephraim which Asa his father had taken' (17.2). The expansion of Judah northwards during the reign of Asa/Abijah is thus a constant feature of the Chronicler's view; there are no concrete data for determining its authenticity. Our present clause is too short to reveal any Chronistic peculiarities, and even if Chronistic language and style were found here, this would be no sure sign of inauthenticity.

Historical probability may support the Chronicler's claim. The internal situation of the northern kingdom in the time of Asa, and the pressure of the Aramaeans in the north and the Philistines in the west (cf. I Kings 15.25 – 16.29), contributed to an extremely unstable situation; Asa himself witnessed the accession of seven kings (Nadab, Baasha, Elah, Zimri, Tibni, Omri and Ahab), of five different houses. It is quite possible that this state of affairs was exploited for 'adjustments' on the northern border of Judah (cf. Z. Kallai, *The Northern Boundaries of Judah*, 1960, 59–62*). On the other hand, a tendentious interest in depicting the territory of the Judaean kings as constantly expanding northwards is attested in the Chronicler's narrative (cf. Japhet, *Ideology*, 355–6); a final decision on this matter cannot be made.

The next stage in Asa's reform is the 'renovation' (RSV 'he repaired') of the altar 'before the vestibule' (cf. already 8.12, '*ullām* in both cases is a metonym for the Temple). Here again, no verdict may be given on authenticity. The book of Kings refers only to Temple repairs in general, and then only twice, in the days of Joash and Josiah; never to specific repairs of the altar. The construction of a *new* altar is, however, recorded in the time of Ahaz (II Kings 16.10–16). The Chronicler, by contrast, refers here to an altar 'renovation', in Hezekiah's time to a 'purification' (29.18), and in Manasseh's time to a 'restoration' (33.16); the new altar of Ahaz is passed over in silence.

While it is certainly reasonable to assume that the altar was periodically renovated, there is no way for us to ascertain whether these renovations can be dated to these specific kings, as claimed by the Chronicler.

The short clause $w^e hann^e b\bar{u}'\bar{a}h\ {}^c\bar{o}d\bar{e}d\ hann\bar{a}b\hat{i}'$ (cf. RSV margin 'the prophecy Oded the prophet') is difficult, both in its naming of the prophet 'Oded' rather than 'Azariah the son of Oded', and in its lack of the construct case for the noun 'prophecy', problems overcome in RSV by assuming the construct 'the prophecy of' and inserting the words 'Azariah the son of', following the Vulgate. We should probably accept the proposal to insert a relative clause: 'the prophecy [prophecied by Azariah son of] Oded the prophet' (cf. already Kimhi, ad loc; Curtis, 387; Rudolph, 244, and others).

[9–15] The third step of Asa's response to the prophet's call is the covenant, celebrated in Jerusalem by a great assembly. While public ceremonies are common in Chronicles, and certain stylistic and linguistic features mark this passage as Chronistic, the ceremony itself as described here has many peculiar features, and some favourite Chronistic elements are conspicuously absent. All the signs of Temple ritual – burnt offerings, liturgical music, priests, Levites or singers – are missing, and in fact it is not to the Temple but simply to 'Jerusalem' that the people are gathered (v. 10). Finally, there is no rhetorical address attributed to king, prophet or priest; only the warning of v. 13 seems to quote an explicit decree. This non-stereotypical character may indicate that the ceremony had a historical model; a discussion of the details may lead us to a better appreciation of the problem.

[9] The supposed historical context of the Jerusalem convocation creates a certain discrepancy: the general narrative sequence presupposes a certain lapse of time for Asa's acts depicted in v. 8, and yet the specific setting of v. 11, especially the reference to 'the spoil', implies that the gathering was held promptly after the war.

Differently from most ceremonies in Chronicles, the multitude here is not described by social or official status ('princes', 'heads of fathers' houses', 'elders of Israel', etc.), but only by tribal origin: 'all Judah and Benjamin' are summoned according to their tribes (cf. similarly in the ceremony of Hezekiah, II Chron. 30). In addition to the main tribal elements of Judah and Benjamin (already mentioned in vv. 2 and 8), additional representatives came to Jerusalem from three tribes: Ephraim, Manasseh and Simeon, 'who were sojourning with them'. The presence of these elements in Asa's kingdom is immediately explained: these people 'had deserted to him ... when they saw that the Lord his God was with him'. The Chronicler's historical and theological views are very distinctly expressed: the claim of the kings of Judah to rule over 'all Israel' did not expire with the establishment of the northern kingdom; the faithful from Israel kept joining Judah. We saw the same phenomenon in the reign of Rehoboam, when people from 'all the tribes of Israel' joined him to strengthen his kingdom (II Chron. 11.16–17). In both cases, the motive was religious: in 12.16, the people 'set their hearts to seek the Lord', and here they realize that Asa's 'God was with him' – an illustration of the axiom established in v. 2.

The names of the tribes reflect the artificial nature of the list: Ephraim and Manasseh, Judah's nearest neighbours to the north, and Simeon to the south. Assuming that the kingdom of Judah comprises 'Judah and Benjamin', these other three tribes would be outside the southern kingdom. This is of course in accord with learned geographical concepts, but in geo-political reality Simeon was at a very early date absorbed into Judah. (For the possibility of a 'northern' affinity for Simeon, cf. M. Noth, *Das System der Zwölf Stämme Israels*, 1930, 77 n. 2; Japhet, *Ideology*, 295 n. 124.) According to Chronicles, then, the realm of Judah expanded in two ways: by the annexation of cities conquered in the hill country of Ephraim, and by accepting northerners who attached themselves to the righteous and prosperous southern kingdom.

[10] 'The third month of the fifteenth year' is a relatively precise date, but it does not give the exact day of the month. The 'third month' is associated with two major events according to the chronological framework of the Pentateuch: the Sinai theophany and the Feast of Weeks. The first is determined by several statements of date: the Exodus and the Feast of Passover were in the first month (Exod. 12.1–42), and the people of Israel encamped 'before the mountain' and there received the Sinai theophany, in the third month (NEB; RSV 'third new moon'), cf. Exod. 19.1. Independently, the Feast of Weeks (Pentecost) is to be held 'seven full weeks ... after the sabbath' (Lev. 23.15–16), i.e. in the third month. The biblical traditions nowhere attest the combination of these two events, and the designation of the Feast of Weeks as the anniversary of the law-giving at Sinai is explicitly attested in rabbinic literature no earlier than the second century CE, although some scholars would find it already among the Pharisees (L. Jacobs, 'Shavuot', *EJ* 14, 1320–1).

Does this text point to an earlier identification of the Feast of Weeks 'in the third month' with the Sinai revelation? This seems hardly to be the case. While the significance of 'the third month' in the cultic calendar could hardly have escaped the Chronicler's attention (cf. the explicit rendering in the Targum), none of the conventional Torah terminology ('commandments', 'precepts', 'keep', 'hear', etc.) appears in this context.

The connection between the Feast of Weeks and Asa's festival should be sought, then, in another direction, as already suggested by earlier commentators (cf. E. Lohse, 'πεντηκοστή', *TDNT* VI, 1971, 48 n. 28). The Hebrew name of the feast, *ḥag haššābu'ōt*, may be seen as derived from *š^ebū'āh*, 'oath', rather than *šābū'a*, 'week', i.e 'Feast of Oaths'. Indeed, according to the book of Jubilees, elaborating on Gen. 9.9–16, Pentecost as commanded to Moses is a re-enactment of the covenant with Noah, made 'with an oath' (Jubilees 6.11, 17; cf. 6.1–20). While in the Genesis context neither the term 'oath' nor oath-phraseology are to be found, the understanding of covenant as 'oath' forms the basis for the development in Jubilees. The term šᵉbūʻōt does not itself appear in this passage, but the axis of the convocation is the covenant (v. 12) and the oath (vv. 14–15), with the verb šbʻ repeated three times.

The implication, then, is that this gathering in the third month is an observance of the 'Feast of Oaths', but there is no hint of the identity of the covenant re-enacted here. Is it, as in the tradition of Jubilees, the covenant between the Lord and Noah (Gen. 9), or rather a reliving of the Sinai covenant (Exod. 24)? The idiosyncratic terminology of the text, devoid of any affinity to either text, prevents us from pin-pointing more precisely its role in the development of these concepts.

In the context of the Chronistic narrative, the 'fifteenth year of the reign of Asa' is somewhat difficult. According to the sequence of events, there was no war in Asa's reign for ten years (14.1 [MT 13.23]), and then, i.e. in Asa's eleventh year, the war with Zerah broke out. Since the events described in this chapter follow the victory (vv. 2, 8), and the festive sacrifices are offered from 'the spoil' (v. 11), this convocation must be placed in the twelfth year of Asa at the latest. These data may lead us to two opposite conclusions: if the reference to the fifteenth year is a reliable piece of information drawn from some other source, and therefore not fully integrated into the narrative (e.g. by changing the date of the war with Zerah), then Asa's acts of reform are given an authentic ring. On the other hand, the date may be totally artificial, based on the schematic number 'five': 'ten years' (14.1 [MT 13.23]), 'fifteen' (15.10), 'thirty-five' (v. 19); if the Chronicler assumed the reader's familiarity with this numerical symbolism, he would not invest effort in harmonizing the narrative details.

[11] Quite unexpectedly, sacrifices open, rather than close, the event. The very general terminology, and the absence of specific terms like 'burnt offerings', serve to underline the role of the sacrifice as thanksgiving offerings; they are not, then, an integral element of the following covenant. In fact, most of the covenants depicted in the Bible – with the marked exception of the Sinai covenant – do not relate to sacrifices at all (Josh. 24; II Kings 23.1–3; Neh. 10). The numbers of the beasts are certainly typological: the basic symbolic numeral seven is again connected with the root/concept 'oath'; the proportion of cattle to sheep is one to ten (cf. also II Chron. 35.7, 9).

The syntax of the second clause is somewhat obscure. On the basis of the MT accents, hēbīʼū is a relative clause without the relative particle, appropriately added by the RSV: '[which] they had brought'. Another way of understanding the verse, putting the Ethnah under haššālāl, is as two separate clauses: 'They sacrificed to the Lord on that day from the spoil; they brought seven hundred oxen and seven thousand sheep' (cf. JPS).

[12] The making of the covenant is defined by the less usual 'enter into a covenant' (*wayyābō'ū babbᵉrīt*) rather than by the more common *wayyikrᵉtū bᵉrit*. The goal of this commitment is also described in very specific Chronistic terms: to 'seek the Lord, the God of Israel' (v. 13). This terminology may be appreciated by comparison with II Kings 23.3 (repeated with small changes in II Chron. 34.31): 'made a covenant (*wayyikrōt 'et habbᵉrīt*) before the Lord, to walk after the Lord and to keep his commandments and his testimonies and his statutes, with all his heart and all his soul, to perform the words of this covenant that were written in this book'. From these Deuteronomistic phrases the Chronicler borrowed only 'with all their heart and with all their soul', subsequently adapted and recast in v. 15.

Who are the partners 'entering into the covenant'? Is it a reciprocal commitment between the people and the Lord? Such an understanding is supported neither by the linguistic usage nor by the context; in Chronicles the term 'covenant' in reference to the Lord has lost its reciprocal connotation and denotes a unilateral obligation by the people alone (cf. Japhet, *Ideology*, 115–16). There is therefore a full parallel between 'entering into a covenant' here, and 'taking an oath' in v. 15.

This covenant terminology reveals a process of shift in connotation: in Ezek. 16.8, where the 'making of a covenant' is described by an idiom similar to that of Chronicles: 'I entered into a covenant with you', reciprocal relationship between the human and the divine partners is meant (cf. also I Sam. 20.8; Ezek. 20.37), while for the Qumran sect 'those entering the covenant' (*bā'ē habbᵉrīt*) are those who undertake a unilateral human obligation to adhere to a certain code (cf., *inter al.*, the Damascus Covenant II.2; VIII.48, etc.). The Chronicler's usage seems nearer to – and earlier than – that of the sectarians: the people bind themselves to 'seek the Lord the God of their fathers'.

[13] The sanctions dictated here are unexpectedly severe: capital punishment is decreed for breaching the general and rather vague obligation 'to seek the Lord', and this without consideration of age or sex, as is indicated by the double merismus: 'whether young or old, man or woman'. While capital punishment is decreed in the Pentateuch for very grave transgressions of religion, specifically idolatry or incitement to idolatry (cf. mainly Deut. 13), in this Chronistic context 'seeking the Lord' may include almost everything. Moreover, since in the specific narrative context Asa and his people are entering whole-heartedly into the covenant, what could be the reason for these dire threats?

The phrasing here, beginning with 'and that whoever did not seek' (*wᵉkōl 'ᵃšer lō' yidrōš ...*) is in fact known as the mark of a severe warning in other contexts of the Persian period. Cf. Ezra 10.8: 'and ... if any one did not come (*w^{e}kōl ^{a}šer lō' yābō'* ...) within three days ... his property should be forfeited and he himself banned' (the similarity to this passage is obscured by the RSV); cf. also the Aramaic of Ezra 7.26: 'Whoever will not obey the law of your God ... let judgment be strictly executed upon him ...' So, the sanction in all its aspects – idiom, most general address, and extreme harshness – is typical of warning statements from the Persian period, i.e. is of the Chronicler's own provenance.

[14] The climax of the passage is the actual oath-ritual: ratified 'with a loud voice, and with shouting, and with trumpets, and with horns'. This passage is unusual in several ways. The concept of 'taking an oath to the Lord' is attested only three other times: in Zeph. 1.5; Isa. 19.18 and 45.23. Roughly similar is the covenant of Nehemiah's time, when the people 'enter into a curse and an oath to walk in God's law' (Neh. 10.29; [MT 10.30]). Here the manner of swearing is unique; every conceivable acoustic means is employed: 'loud voice, shouting, trumpets and horns'. Each of these elements is attested elsewhere, with certain combinations of some of them (in particular 'shouting' and 'horn', cf. II Sam. 6.15; Amos 2.2 etc.), but only here do we find all four at once. This is also the only place (except the parallel text of I Chron. 15.28) where the Chronicler includes a 'horn' among his instruments! A 'loud voice' is a sign of public and absolute commitment to an explicit declaration, involving full absorption in the vocal expression. These aspects too receive an extreme expression here.

[15] The very vocal oath-ritual has its counterpart in the people's spiritual disposition of whole-hearted devotion. This is emphasized by a repetition of Chronistic phrases. First is 'joy', which for the Chronicler is the peak of faithfulness, the true sign of a 'whole heart'. This theme is repeated by a statement formed in parallel colons: the base is 'with all their heart and with all their soul' (v. 12), and the two colons in the verse also open with 'with all'; in addition, they have a matched rhythm of three words, and a rhyming pattern:

with all their heart they had sworn (*b^{e}kol l^{e}bābām nišbā'ū*)//
and with all their desire they had sought him (*ūb^{e}kol r^{e}ṣōnām biqšuhū*).

All poetical details are lost in translation.

God's reaction to this whole-hearted address is immediate, and, in the context, self-evident. 'He was found by them and ... gave them rest round about.'

Thus the passage concludes with a full confirmation of Azariah's prophecy. The axiom 'If you seek him he will be found by you' (v. 2), demonstrated in times of old (v. 4), is now proved by the generation of the living: 'they sought him ... and he was found by them'. 'Rest', the desired counterpoint to the 'great disturbances' (v. 6), is achieved.

[16] Asa is the only king of the Davidic dynasty who is known to have demoted his 'queen mother' from her special royal status. This seems to have been a major political decision, expressing the reform he represents *vis à vis* earlier monarchs and in particular his own father, who is represented after his death by his wife, the present king's mother. (On the role and position of the queen mother, cf. N. Andreasen, 'The Role of the Queen Mother in Israelite Society', *CBQ* 45, 1983, 179–94.) Together with the removal of the queen mother, Asa eradicates her 'abominable image' by cutting, crushing and burning it – a series which symbolizes complete annihilation. I Kings 15.13 speaks only of 'cutting and burning'; the addition 'crushing' establishes an analogy to Josiah's treatment of the image of the Asherah, in the course of his thorough reform (II Kings 23.6).

The unique *mipleṣet* has not been satisfactorily interpreted, but the context surely requires some kind of an image (cf. Baumgartner, 584).

[17] This is the first reservation about Asa's devotion. His reform knows limits: the high places in Israel continue to function. The verse is taken (with the addition of the words 'out of Israel') from I Kings 15.14, and does not in itself raise a problem. However, it is in direct tension with the earlier statement of 14.3 [MT 14.2], that Asa 'took away ... the high places'. This famous *crux* has invited various responses: 'Israel' may be seen to refer exclusively to the northern kingdom (Curtis, 386), a weak solution which does not explain why then those high places could be held against Asa, nor solve the very same difficulty in the account of the days of Jehoshaphat (cf. II Chron. 17.6; 20.33). A more drastic proposition is to regard this verse (and the entire passage vv. 16–18) as portions omitted by the Chronicler and interpolated back into the text by a later hand (Rudolph, 241). This approach ascribes to the Chronicler a fully consistent adaptation of his sources, a matter which, however, cannot be proved from his actual procedures, and can be considered only by positing extreme literary-critical steps, thus turning the argument into a vicious circle. I have shown elsewhere that the theme of high places is much less significant for the Chronicler than for his Deuteronomistic predecessor (Japhet, *Ideology*, 217–20), a fact which may account for his lack of consistency in handling this theme. Nevertheless, these contradictions – so glaring to the modern reader – remain an issue which has not yet been adequately clarified.

In the context of Chronicles, 'all his days' (taken from I Kings 15.14) should be qualified and understood as 'most of his days' or 'all of his days up to the present'. Asa's last years, as presented in the Chronicler's version, did not pass the test of 'blamelessness'.

[19] The conclusion of this unit is based on the parallel in Kings, but has

been completely transformed. According to I Kings 15.16 (and cf. I Kings 14.30; 15.7), the kings of Judah and Israel warred continually. The verse thus presents a general situation: 'And there was war between Asa and Baasha ... all their days', and then goes on to describe in detail one, and probably the last, of these conflicts. For the Chronicler, the rule of continual warring is certainly true for Rehoboam and Abijah (II Chron. 12.15; 13.2), but in the case of Asa the statement is utterly altered, and with it the literary function and theological message of our verse. Here the war with Baasha (16.1ff.) is not a continuation and illustration of a permanent state of hostility, but a new, completely different stage in Asa's reign. This verse states that 'there was *no* war' until the thirty-fifth year of Asa, and thus concludes the first, extremely positive stage of Asa's reign, confirming what has already been said in v. 15, that the Lord gave him 'rest round about'.

Here is another example of how the Chronicler, when he feels that necessity dictates it, can turn a source-text upside-down. Given the strongly negative theological significance of 'war' in Chronistic terms, the Chronicler could hardly accept the existence of conflicts during the reign of Asa the just king. Accordingly, his version reads: 'there was *no* war'!

16

16 In the thirty-sixth year of the reign of Asa, Baasha king of Israel went up against Judah, and built Ramah, that he might permit no one to go out or come in to Asa king of Judah. [2] Then Asa took silver and gold from the treasures of the house of the Lord and the king's house, and sent them to Ben-hadad king of Syria, who dwelt in Damascus, saying, [3] 'Let there be a league between me and you, as between my father and your father; behold, I am sending to you silver and gold; go, break your league with Baasha king of Israel, that he may withdraw from me.' [4] And Ben-hadad hearkened to King Asa, and sent the commanders of his armies against the cities of Israel, and they conquered Ijon, Dan, Abel-maim, and all the store-cities of Naphtali. [5] And when Baasha heard of it, he stopped building Ramah, and let his work cease. [6] Then King Asa took all Judah, and they carried away the stones of Ramah and its timber, with which Baasha had been building, and with them he built Geba and Mizpah.

7 At that time Hanani the seer came to Asa king of Judah, and said to him, 'Because you relied on the king of Syria, and did not rely on the Lord your God, the army of the king of Syria has escaped you. [8] Were not the Ethiopians and the Libyans a huge army with exceedingly many chariots and horsemen? Yet because you relied on the Lord, he gave them into your hand. [9] For the eyes of the Lord run to and fro throughout the whole earth, to show his might in behalf of those whose heart is blameless toward him. You have done foolishly in this; for from now on you will have wars.' [10] Then Asa was angry with the seer, and put him in the stocks, in prison, for he was in a rage with him because of this. And Asa inflicted cruelties upon some of the people at the same time.

11 The acts of Asa, from first to last, are written in the Book of the Kings of Judah and Israel. [12] In the thirty-ninth year of his reign Asa was diseased in his feet, and his disease became severe; yet even in his disease he did not seek the Lord, but sought help from physicians. [13] And Asa slept with his fathers, dying in the forty-first year of his reign. [14] They buried him in the tomb which he had hewn out for himself in the city of David. They laid him on a bier which had been filled with various kinds of spices prepared by the perfumer's art; and they made a very great fire in his honour.

A. Notes to MT

[4] אבל מים, I Kings 15.20 אבל בית מעכה; מסכנות ערי, I Kings 15.20 כנרות על; [12] ויחלא, read ויחלה or ויחל (dittography).

B. Notes to RSV

[2] Damascus, MT 'Darmesek'; [2, 7] 'Syria', MT 'Aram' (so NEB, JPS); [3] 'Let there be', not in MT, NEB 'There is'; [4] 'conquered', NEB 'attacked', JPS 'ravaged' (MT ויכו); [9] 'show his might', better 'give support', cf. I Chron. 11.10; 'more', not in MT; [12] 'sought help', not in MT.

C. Structure, sources and form

1. Whereas in ch. 15 only four verses were taken from the parallel record of Kings and interwoven into a wider literary context, in the present chapter we find an entirely different procedure. The parallel material from I Kings 15.17–24 is taken as a basis and elaborated to form a comprehensive literary and theological unit.

I Kings 15.17–24 comprises two sections: vv. 17–22 describe the conflict between Asa and Baasha, and vv. 23–24 consist of the Deuteronomistic conclusion of Asa's reign. These two sections are adopted from Kings almost verbatim, and are further elaborated with longer and shorter additions. To the first section (vv. 1-6) the Chronicler adds Asa's encounter with a prophet and its implications (vv. 7–10), while the second (vv. 11, 12a, 13a) is broadened by the addition of vv. 12b, 13b and 14. Most – although certainly not all – of these changes have as common denominator the Chronicler's need to provide full theological and historical coherence for the events described in his sources.

2. We have already had occasion to observe the methodology of these additions. The text follows the sources faithfully to the end of v. 6 and is then interrupted by the insertion of a whole new passage, after which the original sequence is resumed, with no connecting aids of any kind:

I Kings 15.17–22		23–24
II Chron. 16.1–6	7–10	11–17.1

In the adaptation of I Kings 15.23–24, v. 23a is reproduced in a standard Chronistic rephrasing in v. 11. The main landmarks and sequence of the Kings text are then preserved nearly verbatim, but interspersed by the Chronicler with additions, omissions and rephrasing, as follows:

I Kings 15.23a	23b		24aα		24aβ		24b
II Chron. 16.11	12a	12b	13a	13b	14aα	14aβ–b	17.1a

The resulting structure of the chapter is basically parallel to that of I Kings 15.17ff., as follows:

(a) 1–10 The war between Asa and Baasha
    1–6 the war and its outcome
    7–10 the encounter with a prophet and its outcome
(b) 11–14 Asa's illness and death; summary

3. Furthermore, within Chronicles itself a new literary and historical antithesis is established vis à vis the themes of 14.8–15.19, thus:

(a) The war	14.9–15 [MT 8–14]	16.1–6
Threat of war	14.9 [MT 8]	16.1
Asa's initial reaction	14.10–11 [MT 9–10]	16.2–3
Course of war and results	14.12–15 [MT 11–14]	16.4–6
(b) Encounter with a prophet	15.1–19	16.7–10
Prophet's appearance and words	15.1–7	16.7–9
Asa's reaction	15.8–18	16.10

(c) Conclusion   15.19   16.11–14

This parallel structure carries a theological message: Asa's fate is determined by his initial response to the prophet, positive in the first instance, negative in the second (cf. the commentary).

4. The Chronicler's additions illustrate his peculiar language, style, literary method and theology (cf. below); their composition is authentically Chronistic. Here, as in many similar cases, the question of outside sources pertains only to the new information, i.e. the following details: a prophet by the name of Hanani (vv. 7–9); his fate (v. 10a); Asa's cruelty towards some of the people (v. 10b); the date of Asa's illness (v. 12) and his recourse to physicians (v. 12b); and the funeral bier and fire (v. 14). As will be shown in the commentary, these details are in full accord with the Chronicler's theological assumptions and literary methods; it is hardly likely that they derive from any authentic source.

D. Commentary

[1–6] According to I Kings 15, these verses relate one of the incidents between Asa and Baasha; here it is viewed as the only one. There are three protagonists: Israel, Judah and Aram (RSV, 'Syria'); while the initial threat is against Judah, the actual military encounter is between Aram and Israel, with the latter suffering heavy losses in its northern districts.

This war is already described in the book of Kings from the point of view of the history of Judah, and more so here; the outcome for Israel is not given the same perspective. However, the rise of Aram which began in the days of Solomon (I Kings 11.23–25) seems to continue unhindered until the days of Ahab, when Benhadad actually lay siege to Samaria (I Kings 20). Only the major defeat of the Aramaeans in this war restricts the threat of their expansion for some time.

[1] Baasha's belligerent action, when he 'built Ramah', in fact signified a major expansion southwards, into the heart of Benjaminite territory, cutting off important territory from the hold of the kings of Judah, in particular after the apparently short-lived victories of Abijah (cf. on 13.19). The presence of Baasha only thirteen kilometers from Jerusalem constitutes a serious threat to its rulers.

To the virtually literal citation of his source, the Chronicler has added only the date, the thirty-sixth year of Asa. The difficulty inherent in this date has long been recognized. The assumption of a textual error, and the restoration of 26 or 16 for 36 (cf. Curtis, 387f.), resolves neither the tension with the Deuteronomistic chronology, as Baasha died in the twenty-sixth year of Asa (I Kings 16.8), nor the contradiction with the Chronicler's statement in 15.19, that there was no war until the thirty-fifth year of Asa. (On the various approaches to this data, cf. above, pp. 703–5)

[2] In the face of Baasha's threat, Asa avoids any direct encounter, military

or political, but turns instead to a third party. The facts of the matter, basically derived from I Kings 15.18, are presented by the Chronicler more concisely: Ben-hadad's patronym is shortened, and a significant change is made in the scope and definition of the money sent by Asa. I Kings 15.18 reads: '*all* the silver and the gold that *were left* in the treasures of the house of the Lord, and the treasures of the king's house' – in short, everything found in the state's treasuries. With minimal textual intervention, the Chronicler reads: 'silver and gold from the treasures of the house of the Lord and the king's house', that is, a certain fraction of the content of each. Also, in I Kings 15.19 the money is defined as a 'bribe' (*šōḥad*, RSV 'present'; cf. Cogan-Tadmor, *Kings* II, 188), a pejorative word which is omitted in Chronicles.

[3] Asa's message to Ben-hadad is diplomatic, alluding to three assumed leagues. The gift now being offered is intended to confirm the treaty between Asa and Ben-hadad, based on a former agreement between their fathers, and to void the existing league between Ben-hadad and Baasha. The 'breaking' of this latter will upset the balance of power, forcing Baasha to withdraw.

This series of agreements, however, is not attested in the sources; allusion to it in this specific historical situation raises several doubts. Why, and under what terms, would Abijah, for example, have contracted a *liaison* with Damascus? Also, the MT (followed by NEB, JPS) sees the league between Asa and Ben-hadad as a *fait accompli* ('there is a league'), not a proposal, as in RSV: '*Let* there be a league between me and you *as* between my father and your father'. It would seem that all reference to 'leagues' is just diplomatic language representing the present situation of Aram's non-involvement. To the request 'break your league with Baasha', the response then is not political but military – an assault against the northern parts of Israel, the territories of Dan and Naphtali.

[4–5] Ben-hadad's offensive is launched against some of the major Israelite cities in Dan and Naphtali, Ijon, Dan and Abel(-mayim), as well as against other parts of the land of Naphtali. The general term used in MT, *wayyakkū* ('they struck'), is rendered by the RSV more explicitly, 'they conquered'. Baasha's immediate reaction is to discontinue the building of Ramah; since the event is viewed from the perspective of Judah, we are left without information about Baasha's measures to repulse the forces of Aram, the final outcome of the encounter, or its wider impact on the northern kingdom.

The territory affected by the Aramaean invasion is described in I Kings 15.20: 'Ijon, Dan, Abel-beth-maacah and all Chinneroth with all the land of Naphtali', i.e. a large territory from the north-east limits of the land, as far south as the Sea of Galilee (Chinneroth). In the Chronicler's version Abel-beth-maacah appears as 'Abel-mayim' ('Abel on the water'), and 'Chinneroth' is replaced by the obscure 'the store cities', probably an attempt to simplify a difficult text.

[6] Asa takes full advantage of the new situation: delivered from the siege, he now exploits the stones and timber prepared by Baasha to fortify two Judaean cities – Geba and Mitzpah – in the land of Benjamin, probably anticipating future Israelite initiatives, and basing his claim to the territory of Benjamin on solid military fact.

Asa's strategy was at best short-sighted. At least according to the present account, he did not even attempt independent action, and his appeal to foreign aid catalysed the greatest enemy the people of Israel would know for many years. A similar plot, with different protagonists, is followed years later by Ahaz (II Kings 16.7ff.), whose appeal to Tiglath-pileser serves to strengthen the Assyrian foothold in the west (cf. Cogan-Tadmor, *Kings* II, 190–1). While the Deuteronomistic history refrains from passing explicit judgment on Asa's action, the Chronicler expresses severe criticism. Although this is enunciated by a prophet, in religious rather than political (or even moral) terms, the long-range political implications of the event evidently did not escape the Chronicler's attention.

[7–9] Following the Chronicler's standard procedure, the theological conclusions are drawn by a prophet, who also warns of imminent consequences. We saw so far that the position of theological interpretation in the course of the narrative may vary: Shemaiah approaches Rehoboam during Shishak's campaign, and the king's reaction determines the outcome of the invasion (II Chron. 12.5–8); Jehu appears before Jehoshaphat after the war in Ramoth-gilead (II Chron. 19.2), and Eleazar confronts the same king in the midst of the 'ships' project (II Chron. 20.37), etc. In this case, the political event follows without interference the original lines of I Kings 15, the prophetic response acting as a bridge between this and the future history of Asa.

This passage has the only appearance of 'Hanani the seer'. While there is in principle no apparent reason to deny his authenticity, the prevalent scholarly view is that he was not historical. His figure should be viewed in the perspective given explicit expression in rabbinic literature. Post-biblical sages, in an attempt to explain irregularities in the presentation of biblical prophets, coined the axiom 'every prophet whose patronym is recorded – both he and his father were prophets' (Leviticus Rabbah 6.7). 'Hanani' is of course the father of 'Jehu', a prophet appearing in Israel in the time of Baasha (I Kings 16.1, 7), and according to Chronicles also active under Jehoshaphat (II Chron. 19.2; 20.34). Although this principle is articulated only in rabbinic literature, the very appearance of the prophet 'Hanani' in the time of Asa may be regarded as its earliest intimation; of course the historicity of 'Hanani' is then strongly suspect.

Hanani's message follows a progression of three parts, or stanzas: a direct critique of Asa's policy (v. 7), an antithetical precedent (v. 8), and a definition of the principle which will determine Asa's future (v. 9). The prose prophecy nevertheless employs parallelism, repetition of phrases and *motifs*, and even rhymes, all to some extent lost in translation.

The first part has three colons:

(1) 'Because you relied on the king of Aram (2) and did not rely on the Lord your God (3), the army of the king of Aram has escaped you.'

(1) and (2) comprise an antithetic parallel, while the synthetic third colon presents the causal conclusion. The theme is 'reliance', repeated three times, and a contrast is drawn between 'the king of Aram' and 'the Lord your God'; the last two colons of this part are rhymed: *'elōhēkā – b^{e}yād^{e}kā*.

The second part, contrasting Asa's present with his earlier conduct, is again structured in three colons:

(1) 'Were not the Cushites and the Libyans a huge army (2) with exceedingly many chariots and horsemen? (3) Yet because you relied on the Lord, etc.'

(1) and (2) are synonymous parallels, (3) their synthetic sequel.

The theme of 'relying' is repeated, and there is an element of rhyming with the third part (*b^{e}yōd^{e}ka/miyyād^{e}kā*). This part brings up the theme of 'many', and prepares the conclusion of the final section.

The third part is structured in four colons:

(1) 'For the eyes of the Lord... (2) to show his might ... (3) You have done foolishly ... (4) for from now on...'.

Poetical rhythm is employed, but no conventional parallelism.

Like other rhetorical pieces in Chronicles, the prophecy of Hanani makes use of biblical citations. 'For the eyes of the Lord run to and fro ...' (v. 9) is a paraphrased quotation after Zech 4.10b (the similarity is somewhat lost in translation, cf. NEB, etc.). The declaration 'you have done foolishly in this' immediately evokes Samuel's warning to Saul, 'You have done foolishly ... your kingdom shall not continue' (I Sam. 13.13–14); the reference to a 'blameless heart' relates to the earlier description of Asa himself (15.17), and the final statement 'from now on you will have wars' (*yēš 'imm^{e}kā milḥāmōt*)is an almost literal antithesis to 14.6 [MT 5]: 'He had no war' ('*en 'immō milḥāmāh*) . The moral of Hanani's speech is self-evident: whatever the danger or threat, the only correct conduct is reliance on God; the details of the passage, however, are of great interest.

The accusation of reliance on a foreign king is well known from Isa. 31.1: 'Woe to those who go down to Egypt for help and rely on horses, who trust in chariots because they are many.' The result of this vain trust, as presented by the prophet in this context, is unexpected: 'the army of the king of Aram has escaped you'. How could this be, when Aram was not Asa's opponent in this affair, and there were no hostilities between them? Rudolph accordingly suggests (248) that the text should read, with one Greek MS, 'the army of the king of Israel' (so BHS, already followed by NEB). However, this too contradicts the context, where there is no record of an actual military encounter between Judah and Isreal. Hanani's words should be understood from a broader perspective, as acknowledging the true danger to the existence of Israel and Judah. In his weakness and lack of faith, Asa's apparent success has brought upon his people the constant threat of war with Aram, and has turned Israel into a battlefield; the negative consequences of this incident still lie ahead.

There is an explicit antithesis between Asa's earlier trial (14.9–14) and the present one. In the war against Zerah, with his multitude of troops and chariots, the odds were entirely against Asa, who nevertheless, through his total reliance on God, prevailed. In this other conflict, Asa's inferior conduct already determined his further fortunes.

The punishment meted out to Asa is very much in accord with his previous reward (14.6 [MT 5]) and with the general view of his reign as alternating periods of war and peace. War is here defined as punishment, contrary to the blessing of 'peace' and 'rest'. This theological axiom is, however, also historically sound: the present period sees the beginning of an incessant Aramaean pressure and continuous warfare. Although the protagonists will be for the most part Aram and Israel, for the Chronicler, with his global view of history and his concept of the unity of Israel, this too is Asa's responsibility.

The Chronicler's late idiom and peculiar style are very distinct in this passage. The following features, *inter alia*, may be mentioned: (*a*) the use of the infinitive prefixed by a preposition as a temporal/causal clause, and its position at the beginning of the sentence (vv. 7, 8: $b^e hišša'en^e k\bar{a}$), literally 'at your relying', RSV 'because you relied'); (*b*) the intensive use of the preposition l^e in various functions – five times in v. 8; (*c*) the use of the relative clause without the relative particle and governed by a preposition; $l^e hithazzēq$ '*im* $l^e b\bar{a}b\bar{a}m$, 'to support [those whose] heart, etc.' (cf. Gesenius §155n, p. 488, and I Chron. 15.12; II Chron. 1.4); (*d*) the abundance of causative clauses opening with $k\bar{\imath}$, 'for' (v. 9); and (*e*) the distinctive vocabulary.

[10] Asa does not heed Hanani's words. On the contrary, he imprisons the prophet, not for transgression but solely because of the king's anger, a *motif* repeated twice. Here Asa proves beyond doubt that his infidelity was not a momentary weakness but a wilful disposition, which will countenance no criticism. Thus, the prophet is more than an oracle; his very appearance becomes a criterion for testing the king's religious conduct. Asa's reaction is added to the roster of his sins, and the expected punishment soon follows.

The word *mahpeket* (RSV 'stocks') is mentioned three times in connection with Jeremiah (Jer. 20.2, 3; 29.26), the context implying some kind of detention: 'over every madman who prophesies, to put him in the stocks and collar'. The present context, which probably follows the model of Jeremiah, is the only occurrence of *bet hammahpeket*.

Asa's arbitrary anger also affected the people, on whom he 'inflicted cruelties' (literally 'crushed'). *rṣṣ* is several times parallel to *'ṣq* (I Sam. 12.3, 4; Amos 4.1; Hosea 5.11), but it generally governs an object and not the preposition *min*. How and why Asa would have punished the people for the prophet's rebuke is not made clear; we can only say that the general and vague phrasing may preserve some historical memory, but no more. The passage concludes with the same words used in v. 7 as an opening: 'at that time' (RSV 'at the same time'), which form a fine *inclusio*.

[11] The Chronicler here returns to the sequence of his source (I Kings 15.23–24) for the concluding remarks on Asa's reign. The standard rephrasing of 'Now the rest of the acts of Asa ... all that he did' to 'The acts of Asa, first and last' is followed by the statement 'are written', replacing the question 'are they not written?'. The Deuteronomistic summary of more specific acts of Asa, 'all his might ... and the cities which he built', is omitted. For the first time, the record cited is not a prophetic work but (in closer similarity to Kings) 'the Book of the Kings of Judah and Israel' – a work dedicated to the history of the two kingdoms which will now reappear under several, slightly variant, titles. For the possible nature of this work, cf. the introduction.

[12] Following but rephrasing I Kings 15.23b, the Chronicler now records the disease which afflicted Asa's feet in his old age. The judgmental note which may be heard in the Kings presentation, '*But* in his old age he was diseased in his feet', here becomes a direct statement including the date, the severity of the illness, and Asa's misconduct during his sickness. In the Chronicler's philosophy of history, every misfortune is regarded as a chastisement, and since the punishment for his recourse to Aramaean help against Baasha has been explicitly defined as impending wars, Asa's present illness must be due to another specific error, i.e. his treatment of the prophet. The deterioration in Asa's general disposition is now confirmed for the third time: even in his sickness he did not seek the Lord. This is the last proof, if one were necessary, that he surely deserved whatever ill fate befell him.

The first elaboration in Chronicles is the providing of a precise date for the disease, rather than the general 'old age' of Kings. There is no way to validate the reference to the 'thirty-ninth year' of Asa's reign; one's attitude to its authenticity is naturally influenced not only by its possible logic, but by the other dates in the pericope. In fact, the literary pattern of the pericope is based on even three-year intervals between the encounter with the prophet (in the thirty-sixth year of Asa), Asa's disease (in the thirty-ninth) and his death. This typological pattern and its theological implications make it unlikely that any of these dates are historical.

The second Chronistic elaboration is the emphasis on the severity of the disease, implying that this was the cause of Asa's eventual death. On the various suggestions for the identification of the illness, cf. Williamson, 276–7.

Finally the third note: 'even in his disease he did not seek the Lord but sought help from physicians'. This is the only categorical statement in the Bible warning against eliciting human medical advice in case of illness, and making a man's conduct during his sickness a touchstone of his attitude towards God. The view that God is the supreme physician ('I am the Lord your healer', Exod. 15.26) is prevalent throughout the Scriptures, as well as the conviction that illness is divinely inflicted. The turning to God for cure is attested abundantly throughout the Bible; nowhere, however, do we find a negative attitude towards human medicine or human attempts to heal. The Chronicler follows his views to their extreme conclusion – a demand of absolute exclusivity. In any case of distress, public or personal, the relief is in seeking the Lord's help. Anything else is transgression.

This was not, most probably, a personal opinion. Testimony to an ongoing debate on this issue can be found in the eulogy of the physician's role in Ecclus. 38, as well as in the rabbinic dictum from the school of R. Ishmael: 'From this we learn that permission has been given to the physician to heal' (BT, Berachoth 60a; cf. also Midrash Shemuel, ch. 4). One should note, however, that the Chronicler, in spite of his views of retribution, does not regard Asa's recourse to medicine as a sin deserving punishment. A common Chronistic expression of judgment on a king is the manner of his burial – the absolutely final opportunity of reward or punishment, in which an unworthy king may be denied the last grace of an honourable burial (cf. Rudolph, XX). While the description of Asa's burial differs in Chronicles from Kings, it is quite the contrary of disgraceful (cf. further on v. 14). The implication is – in the Chronicler's theological lexicon – that Asa's last misconduct is not held against him.

Even in such a small unit as this one verse, there is the clear mark of the Chronicler's style and late Hebrew. The Chronistic literary methods are illustrated both by elaboration (the inserting of new material into the source-text, cf. above, and by the use of Asa's name as the basis for the note on his resort to physicians; in the midrashic interpretation, the name is viewed as derived from 'sy', medicine (cf. Jastrow, 92–3, and below).

[13] The note on Asa's death parallels the original sequence of I Kings 15.24a. Again, the Chronicler proceeds to divide the text and insert a short note, 'dying in the forty-first year of his reign', necessary to complete the basic chronological information about the king. In the Deuteronomistic

framework of Kings, the length of a king's reign is found among the introductory remarks (in the case of Asa, in I Kings 15.10), a pattern often followed by the Chronicler as well (II Chron. 13.2; 22.2; 24.1; 25.1, etc.). In the case of Asa, the Chronicles text has restructured these opening remarks, so that his history proceeds in a more narrative style, as a direct sequel to the story of Abijah his father (cf. the same phenomenon for other monarchs, e.g. Jehoshaphat in 17.1). Pedantic about chronological data, the Chronicler carefully introduces the length of Asa's reign here at the end, as (differently phrased) for Rehoboam and Jehoshaphat (12.13ff.; 20.31ff.).

[14] The description of the king's burial shares one basic element with the Deuteronomistic source: Asa was buried 'in the city of David'. As on several other occasions, Chronicles omits the phrase 'buried with his fathers'; the passive 'he was buried' is changed to the active 'they buried him'; for other examples of this usage cf. II Chron. 12.16 with I Kings 14.31; II Chron. 21.20 with II Kings 8.16, etc. (in regard to Reboboam, Jehoram, Ahaziahu, Joash, Jotham and Ahaz).

Next, however, we find a funeral description which is the longest recorded for any king, and a description of the 'fire of spices' in his honour, a custom otherwise known only by implication in the Chronistic note on Jehoram ('his people made no fire in his honour like the fires made for his fathers', II Chron. 21.19), and once again in Jer. 34.5: 'And as spices were burned for your fathers, the former kings who were before you, so men shall burn spices for you and lament for you ...' (for a different interpretation of the 'fire', cf. now W. Zwickel, 'Über das angebliche Verbrennen von Räucherwerk bei der Bestattung einer Königs', *ZAW* 101, 1989, 266–77).

Both Asa and Jehoram were severely diseased at their death – Jehoram in his bowels and Asa in his feet – and one wonders whether the notes about the fire are related to this fact. Of Jehoram it is said that when he died 'in great agony' he was not mourned, there was 'no fire in his honour' and his body was not buried in the royal tombs. Asa, on the other hand, in spite of his illness, had an honourable death and burial. It is possible that an explanation for this difference is hinted in 'which he filled' (*'ªšer millē'*, RSV 'which had been filled'): Asa probably made all the extravagant preparations in his lifetime.

Whatever the historical origin of the custom of 'spice-fire', the special elaboration on the idea in Asa's case may have yet another reason. *'āsā'* in Aramaic also denotes 'myrtle' (cf. Jastrow, 88; for its possible Accadian origin, see von Soden, *Akkadisches Handwörterbuch*, 1965, 76a), which was celebrated for its scent. Could the reference to 'various kinds of spices' be based on a midrashic interpretation of Asa's name, parallel to the derivation from *'sy'* (medicine) already mentioned? If this is true, we find here two alternative midrashic interpretations of the name Asa, both connected with the story of his death. The ways of the midrash are not always obvious, but it is possible that these interpretations were motivated by Asa's name – the only one among the kings of Judah which has a distinct Aramaic form.

The story of Asa now concludes (in 17.1) with the standard statement 'Jehoshaphat his son reigned in his stead' (cf. I Kings 15.24b).

We have seen that the history of Asa is elaborated in Chronicles to almost three times its scope in Kings; not only is nearly all the information of I Kings 15.9–24 repeated, but lengthy Chronistic additions appear at every point. The result is a much more detailed picture of the historical period and of the king's figure. In Kings, the appraisal of Asa is explicitly positive and general: 'Asa did what was right in the eyes of the Lord as David his father had done … But the high places were not taken away. Nevertheless the heart of Asa was wholly true to the Lord all his days' (I Kings 15.11, 14). As far as there is guilt in his days it refers only to the existence of the high places, but nevertheless does not diminish from his 'wholeheartedness' throughout 'all his days'.

This portrait is greatly altered in Chronicles. Here the emphasis is on the inconsistency of Asa's personality and career. On the one hand he is depicted as a greater reformer than in Kings: the high places which stood to his discredit there are here destroyed by his zeal (14.2, 4). The Chronistic Asa is an outstanding ruler, a builder, organizer, warrior, and religious leader, conspicuous for his absolute trust in the Lord and his prophets, and his comprehensive steps in reforming the faith of his people. On the other hand, all this represents only one facet of his character. In his old age, after thirty-five years of positive rule, Asa displays clear signs of a weakened faith. Although he is not accused of practising idolatry or forsaking his God, his blameless trust in divine help is shaken. He turns to foreign kings, refuses the counsel of a prophet, acts cruelly toward his people, and consults physicians rather than seeking God. He cannot meet the measure of the Chronicler's severe criteria for a 'righteous king'.

The fulcrum of this reappraisal, as has been claimed by many scholars, is the war with Baasha, which the Chronicler views in a most negative light. The historiographical choice which the Chronicler made at this point is of the highest significance for understanding his historical outlook. In the framework of his philosophy of history, Asa's conduct during this war was bound to be punished, and his guilt was compounded by his rejection of the prophet Hanani. This negative development, juxtaposed to the high initial esteem accorded to Asa by the Chronicler, surely posed a major historical and theological problem. A possible solution was to delete the story altogether – a procedure adopted by the Chronicler several times during the histories of David and Solomon – by which the Chronicler could have produced an 'undamaged' image of Asa, without losing much in the scope of his story.

Another way, however, was chosen: not only is the narrative transmitted in full, but the theological and historical implications are given a much sharper tone than in the sources.

The inevitable conclusion is that this particular story was essential to the Chronicler's historical presentation, and to his concept of 'Israel'. Indeed, in the course of the narrative are included all the events which relate to the relationship – positive or negative – between Judah and Israel. Even the eventual necessity of denouncing his admired kings does not deter the Chronicler from presenting these events in full, the only concession being their positioning at the very end of Asa's reign, during his 'old age'. In appraising the Chronicler's historical concepts, the reader should take into account both his view of divine justice, in all its aspects, and his attitude toward the northern people as an organic part of Israel throughout its history.

Although it is clear that this reappraisal of Asa derives from theological considerations, it nevertheless also displays the Chronicler's realistic appreciation of human nature. The Chronistic history, based on the most rigid principles, is very far from naive idealization, even of the Davidic kings.

17

17 Jehoshaphat his son reigned in his stead, and strengthened himself against Israel. ² He placed forces in all the fortified cities of Judah, and set garrisons in the land of Judah, and in the cities of Ephraim which Asa his father had taken. ³ The Lord was with Jehoshaphat, because he walked in the earlier ways of his father; he did not seek the Baals, ⁴ but sought the God of his father and walked in his commandments, and not according to the ways of Israel. ⁵ Therefore the Lord established the kingdom in his hand; and all Judah brought tribute to Jehoshaphat; and he had great riches and honour. ⁶ His heart was courageous in the ways of the Lord; and furthermore he took the high places and the Asherim out of Judah.

7 In the third year of his reign he sent his princes, Ben-hail, Obadiah, Zechariah, Nethanel, and Micaiah, to teach in the cities of Judah; ⁸ and with them the Levites, Shemaiah, Nethaniah, Zebadiah, Asahel, Shemiramoth, Jehonathan, Adonijah, Tobijah, and Tobadonijah; and with these Levites, the priests Elishama and Jehoram. ⁹ And they taught in Judah, having the book of the law of the Lord with them; they went about through all the cities of Judah and taught among the people.

10 And the fear of the Lord fell upon all the kingdoms of the lands that were round about Judah, and they made no war against Jehoshaphat. ¹¹ Some of the Philistines brought Jehoshaphat presents, and silver for tribute; and the Arabs also brought him seven thousand seven hundred rams and seven thousand seven hundred he-goats. ¹² And Jehoshaphat grew steadily greater. He built in Judah fortresses and store-cities, ¹³ and he had great stores in the cities of Judah. He had soldiers, mighty men of valour, in Jerusalem. ¹⁴ This was the muster of them by fathers' houses: Of Judah, the commanders of thousands: Adnah the commander, with three hundred thousand mighty men of valour, ¹⁵ and next to him Jeho-hanan the commander, with two hundred and eighty thousand, ¹⁶ and next to him Amasiah the son of Zichri, a volunteer for the service of the Lord, with two hundred thousand mighty men of valour. ¹⁷ Of Benjamin: Eliada, a mighty man of valour, with two hundred thousand men armed with bow and shield, ¹⁸ and next to him Jehozabad with a hundred and eighty thousand armed for war. ¹⁹ These were in the service of the king, besides those whom the king had placed in the fortified cities throughout all Judah.

A. Notes to MT

[3] דויד, probably omit, with several MSS and LXX^AB; [8] וטוב אדוניה, omit, dittography; בלוים (second), proposed omit; [13] היה, several MSS היתה; [16] גבור, Sebirin and many MSS גבורי.

B. Notes to RSV

[1] 'strengthened himself against Israel', better, 'strengthened himself over Israel' (JPS 'took firm hold of Israel'); [2] 'garrisons', or 'officers' (NEB); [3] 'his father' MT 'his father David' (cf. A above); [4] 'the ways of Israel', better 'the practices of

Israel'; [5] 'Therefore', not in MT; [6] 'his heart was courageous', NEB 'he took pride'; [8] 'and with these Levites, the priests', ignores the punctuation and syntax of the MT, better 'the Levites; with them were ... the priests'; [11] 'Some of the Philistines', NEB 'Certain Philistines'; [13] 'great stores', NEB 'much work'; [14] 'This was the muster of them', NEB 'enrolled'.

C. Structure, sources and form

1. In the story of Jehoshaphat, like that of Asa, Chronicles introduces the material from I Kings together with extensive additions. The Deuteronomistic historiography relates the story of Jehoshaphat in three different contexts: in its proper position as determined by the standard Deuteronomistic pattern (I Kings 22.41–51), and twice in the context of the northern kingdom, as a partner in the wars of Ahab against Aram (I Kings 22.1–35), and Jehoram against Moab (II Kings 3.4–27).

The Chronicler reproduces the first two pieces (I Kings 22.41–51 and 22.1–35) in 20.31–21.1 and ch. 18 respectively. This parallel material is complemented by chs. 17, 19, and 20.1–30, doubling the original scope of the Jehoshaphat story and making it one of the most detailed in Chronicles, second only to that of Hezekiah (II Chron. 29–32) among the post-Solomonic kings of Judah. This certainly is an indication of how important this 'period of Jehoshaphat' is in the Chronicler's view.

In the book of Kings, the focus of this same period is rather the history of Ahab and his house. The Ahab narratives (I Kings 16.29–22.40) encompass the prophetic stories of Elijah, while the history of his sons Ahaziah and Jehoram is interwoven with the stories of Elisha (II Kings 1–9). The Chronicler strives for the same scope with the history of Judah alone, focussing his attention on the two contemporary monarchs – Asa and Jehoshaphat.

2. Adhering to the sequence of the Kings narrative, the Chronicler here preserves the Deuteronomistic framework as the final section (20.31–41), rather than separating its introductory and concluding parts, as for Abijah (II Chron. 13), Joash (II Chron. 24), Amaziah (II Chron. 25), etc. A special Chronistic introduction is provided, and the whole Jehoshaphat narrative now reflects the Chronicler's careful attention to composition, and his peculiar philosophy of history.

The structure of the broad section of II Chron. 17–20 is as follows:

(a) 17.1–6 General introduction
(b) 17.7–9 Teaching the law of the Lord
(c) 17.10–19 Jehoshaphat's political and military status
(d) 18.1–19.3 War in Ramoth-gilead
(e) 19.4–11 Judicial reform
(f) 20.1–30 War against Ammon
(g) 20.31–21.1 Conclusion, including the episode of the ships.

At the centre of Jehoshaphat's history are the detailed descriptions of two wars (18.1–19.3; 20.1–30), and two reforms, one concerning the teaching the law, the other entailing judiciary authority (17.7–9; 19.4–11). There is a great similarity here, in both the topics and their order, to the history of Asa, which is also centred upon two wars and religious reforms (cf. the details in the commentary). Here, however, there is no systematic chronological framework, with only one date specified: 'the third year of his reign' (17.7).

3. As most of the material is not paralleled in Kings or elsewhere in the Bible, the question of sources and authenticity is naturally of great significance. Over the years, scholars have proposed every possible answer, and I, too, have dealt with these questions several times.

Most of the additional material is written in late Biblical Hebrew, with distinct Chronistic features – leaving no doubt as to the ultimate literary origin of the composition. One should, however, distinguish between the present literary format and its historical content, and examine possible sources for the data themselves. Since in each case a conclusion depends on a thorough analysis of the text, we shall return to this question in the commentary.

4. Chapter 17 is composed of three parts, distinguished by their style and subject-matter: the middle section, vv. 7–9, is a narrative piece marked by a specific date and telling of one event in the history of Jehoshaphat; the other two, vv. 1–6 and 10–19, are a summary-style introduction, presenting general facts about Jehoshaphat's reign, as well as political and religious characterizations and evaluations. One may regard vv. 1–6 and 10–19 as a lengthy general introduction, providing a 'Chronistic' replacement of the Deuteronomistic opening which was shifted to form part of the Chronistic conclusion (20.31–33). This text sequence was then interrupted to introduce an important event, with a specific date early in Jehoshaphat's reign. This 'theological core' (vv. 7–9) has themes which are referred to elsewhere (cf. in particular the Chronistic introduction to the reign of Asa, 14.1–7), but it is not stereotyped and well adjusted to its specific context.

With the exception of the verses about the teaching of the law (vv. 7–9) and only three more verses devoted to Jehoshaphat's religious undertakings and attitudes (vv. 3, 4, 6), the chapter as a whole deals with political matters – Jehoshaphat's domestic and international position, military administration, building projects, etc.

5. Of the details of style and language which will be addressed in the commentary, one feature should be mentioned here. The name 'Judah' is, as one would expect, extremely common in Chronicles, occurring well over one hundred times. Still, we are struck by the unusual density of its appearance in this chapter, twelve times altogether, in every form: the cities of Judah (vv. 2, 7, 9, 13); the land of Judah (v. 2); all Judah (vv. 5, 19); out of Judah (v. 6); in Judah (vv. 9, 12); of Judah (v. 14); 'Judah' alone (v. 10); and the final words of the chapter: 'throughout all Judah' (v. 19). Considering that the subject of the chapter, king Jehoshaphat, is himself mentioned by name only six times (vv. 1, 3, 5, 10, 11, 12), one wonders whether this stylistic feature is not carefully calculated to highlight the true scene of the events, and the significance of people and land as protagonists on the stage of history.

D. Commentary

[1] In I Kings 15.24b the Asa narrative concludes with the words 'Jehoshaphat his son reigned in his stead'; the story then moves to the history of Nadab, the son of Jeroboam (15.25ff.). The same verse serves here to introduce Jehoshaphat's story, an example of how the Chronicler adheres to the sequence of his source, extracting every possible section, and remodelling

the material in keeping with the new historiographical context. Skipping over I Kings 15.25–22.1 and replacing them with his ch. 17, the Chronicler will then come to I Kings 22.2ff. and introduce it in ch. 18.

'Strengthened himself' (*wayyithazzēq*) is not only a favourite Chronistic phrase but an astute historical statement as well. According to RSV's interpretation, 'Israel' denotes the northern kingdom, and *'al* means *against*, the clause referring to Jehoshaphat's status *vis à vis* Israel (also NEB, cf. Dillard, 133). This interpretation, however, does not do justice to the verbal connotation, the Chronistic historical method, or the context. The same phrase is translated in II Chron. 1.1 correctly as 'established himself in his kingdom' (or, with a more literal rendering of *'al* by NEB: 'King Solomon … strengthened his hold on the kingdom'; cf. Dillard 'to consolidate one's power over'), echoing the parallel in I Kings 2.12b and 46b: 'So the kingdom was established in the hand of Solomon'. In this context, the statement that Jehoshaphat 'strengthened himself over Israel' is in fact followed by v. 5: 'the Lord established the kingdom in his hand'. 'Israel' should be understood in its general connotation as 'the people', or 'the kingdom'.

It is therefore clear that the Chronicler views the last years of Asa's reign as a time of unrest, with internal uprising and opposition – as hinted in 16.10b. The new king found it necessary to make a purposeful effort to stabilize the kingdom, and restore it to a track of peace and stability (cf. also for Rehoboam in 11.17; 12.1, and Amaziah in 25.3).

[2] The Chronicler now specifies some of Jehoshaphat's actions aimed at establishing his rule. The military measures are of course only one aspect; others soon follow in vv. 3 and 5: correct religious practice and attitudes, blessed with God's approval. In a military reorganization, Jehoshaphat places forces (*hayil*) in the fortified cities of Judah and sets garrisons (or 'officers', *n*e*ṣibim*) in all the territory under his hegemony; this verse distinguishes clearly between the two. The note, from another point of view, will be repeated in v. 19 which concludes this unit.

Unfortunately, we cannot judge which of Jehoshaphat's actions are routine and which are innovative. The Chronicler attributes the building and fortifying of cities to all the Judaean kings until this point, except for the short-lived Abijah: Solomon (8.5–6, paralleling I Kings 9.17–18), Rehoboam (11.5–11), and Asa (14.5–6), and later to Jehoshaphat himself (17.12). He also attributes to Rehoboam the administration, arming and provisioning of these cities (11.11–12, 23). On the other hand, until the days of Manasseh, we find nowhere a specific reference to military personnel stationed in these fortresses (cf. 33.14), and this is the only mention of *hayil* in this context. The text probably describes some kind of administrative military reform, perhaps entailing a greater centralization of the royal authority, and more reliance on the armed forces.

The word *nᵉṣībīm* may be interpreted alternatively 'officers' (cf. I Kings 4.5, 27 [MT 5.7], 5.16 [MT 5.30]; 9.23 – in all these cases in the form *niṣṣābīm*), or 'garrisons' (II Sam. 8.6, 14, etc.). In II Chron. 8.10 we have *niṣṣābīm* (*Kethib*) and *nᵉṣībīm* (*Qere*), which may indicate a transition from one form to the other. Following the reference of 'forces' in the first clause of the verse, one tends to prefer 'garrisons' for the second.

Several features are specific to this context. The fortified cities are not termed *'ārē māṣōr*, etc, according to 'Chronistic' usage (cf. 8.5; 11.5, 11, 23; 12.4; 14.6 [MT 5]; 21.3), but *'ārē yᵉhūdāh habᵉṣurōt* (also 19.5; differently 17.19), a phrase repeated only in the time of Hezekiah – Manasseh (32.1; 33.14). Although possibly nothing more than a stylistic feature peculiar to our context, this usage may in fact indicate a source different from the above references. The term *'ereṣ yᵉhūdāh* is also not very common in Chronicles: only in I Chron. 6.55 [MT 40] (the parallel in Josh. 21.11 reads *har yᵉhūdāh*), and II Chron. 9.11; there is no other mention in Chronicles of the stationing of *nᵉṣībīm*. Noting that the only specifically 'Chronistic' element in this verse is the apparent interest in military topics, one may well surmise that some source was here employed by the Chronicler, serving as a basis for several other passages in this pericope (cf. Rudolph, 249; Williamson, 278, 280–4).

[3–4] These verses present the complementary side of Jehoshaphat's success: divine approval, well justified by the observation that 'he walked in the earlier ways of his father' (for the omission of 'David' in v. 3, cf. Dillard, 132). Jehoshaphat's right conduct is presented in a way different from all the preceding kings of Judah, for the first time by comparison with the practices of northern Israel: Jehoshaphat 'did *not* seek the Baals'. The Chronicler shows awareness of the actual circumstances of the introduction of the Tyrian Baal into Israel: it is the first mention by the Chronicler of the Baal cult. (The deity Baal in Chronicles is always plural, 'Baals', except in II Chron. 21.17, parallel to II Kings 11.18; see II Chron. 24.7; 28.2; 33.3; 34.4.) Jehoshaphat is then compared first to his own father: he successfully follows the positive 'earlier' ways of Asa, not the failings close to his own time. On the other hand, he is compared to the neighbouring northern kingdom; here, again, the contrast is complimentary: he is not tempted by the newly-introduced cult.

The passage shows Chronistic features. The opening statement is almost a declaration of the final situation: 'The Lord was with Jehoshaphat'. The explanation which follows is built on the parallel use of the causative *kī* ('because'), and the negative particle *wᵉlō*:

'*because* he walked (*kī hālak*) ... and *did not seek* (*wᵉlō' dāraš*) ...

because (*kī*, RSV 'but') he *sought* and *walked* ... and *not* (*wᵉlō'*).'

The second *kī* is not dependent on the main statement, but is adjacent to the first *kī* forming a chain of explanatory clauses, positive and negative. The special balance of this series is largely lost in translation.

One should also note the antithesis formed by the use of the Chronistic favourite *dry*: 'he did not seek the Baals, for he ('but') sought the God of his fathers', and the chiastic alternation of 'walk' and 'seek': he walked and did not seek ... he sought and walked. The statement ends emphatically with a nominal clause: 'and not according to the ways of Israel'.

[5] The former statement, 'Jehoshaphat strengthened himself over Israel', is here paraphrased 'the Lord established the kingdom in his hand'. The consequences are political/economic (v. 5b) and religious (v. 6).

'All Judah brought tribute (*minḥāh*) to Jehoshaphat' is an unusual statement, the only instance in fact of a people bringing tribute to their own king. Only of Saul is it said: 'they despised him and brought him no present' (*minḥāh*, I Sam. 10.27). On the other hand, bringing tribute was standard procedure between rulers and their subordinate states (cf. Judg. 3.15; II Sam. 8.2, 6; I Kings 4.21 [MT 5.1]; II Kings 17.3, 4, etc.). One wonders whether it is merely coincidental that such a tribute exacted by a monarch from his own people is never mentioned elsewhere, whether this does indicate an exceptional arrangement or innovation in the time of Jehoshaphat, or whether *minḥāh* should in fact be interpreted in this text in the more general sense of 'present' or 'gift' (NEB, JPS) – the basis for Jehoshaphat's 'riches'.

'Riches and honour', or 'riches and wealth' (*'ōšer wᵉkābōd*, cf. NEB), as royal qualities have been mentioned so far only for David and Solomon (I Chron. 29.28; II Chron. 1.12), and will appear again for Hezekiah (32.27). The double use of this note for Jehoshaphat (also 18.1) should be taken as an indication of the Chronicler's esteem for this king.

[6] Not only does the syntax of this verse link it with the preceding (v. 5), but the tension created there is here subtly relaxed. 'Riches' and 'strength' – although of great positive significance in the Chronicler's appraisal of Judean kings – are also a hidden test and may lead to disaster. This is shown in Chronicles by the examples of Rehoboam: 'When the rule of Rehoboam was established and he was strong he forsook the law of the Lord' (12.1), and even more of Uzziah: 'But when he was strong he grew proud ... For he was false to the Lord' (26.16). Even Hezekiah did not withstand temptation (32.25). Both Uzziah and Hezekiah, when they waxed strong, fell into the pitfall of pride. Although the same phrase is used for Jehoshaphat, he alone escaped the moral danger of conceit. 'His heart was proud (*wayyigbah libbō*, RSV 'courageous')', not in his own achievement but 'in the ways of the Lord'; what might have been a curse became a blessing.

The Chronicler here highlights a basic psychological intuition, which has strong roots in biblical tradition: material prosperity has inherent dangers, expressly warned against in the impressive admonition of Deut. 8.11–18 (cf.

on 12.1). For the Chronicler, this admonition was given living reality in the figures of the Judaean kings. At the one end, David and Solomon were above and beyond temptation; at the other end, Uzziah and Hezekiah succumbed to the pride emanating from strength; Jehoshaphat, who was led to pride by his strength, riches and honour, turned it into 'positive' pride, 'in his ways of the Lord'.

The practical result of Jehoshaphat's attitude was the taking of 'the high places and Asherim out of Judah'. The difficulties inherent in this statement have been amply pointed out, in particular in view of 20.33, which states that under Jehoshaphat 'the high places, however, were not taken away'. We have already noted how difficult and contradictory the Chronicler's statements about the high places are (cf. II Chron. 14.2, 4, later contradicted by 15.17). It seems that these difficulties cannot be solved by logical arguments, and even the literary-historical solutions are not convincing (cf. Rudolph, 263). We tend to regard the 'high places' as a typological stigma rather than a historical observation. In Chronicles this problem, which constituted a major factor in the Deuteronomistic view of the cult, lost its central position and became something of an abstract measure for the righteousness of a king.

The abundant Chronistic phraseology of verses 5–6 includes the already mentioned 'riches and honour' and pride of heart (*gbh lēb*), and also *lārōb* (represented by 'great'), and the late syntax of w^e'*ōd hēsīr* (w^e'*ōd* followed by a verb in the perfect, cf. Eccles. 3.16; 12.9 and in II Chron. 20.33; 27.2; 28.17; 32.16).

[7–9] This short passage relates an unusual and unique episode in the history of Israel: the mission composed of five royal officers, eight Levites and two priests, sent to travel about the cities of Judah and teach the people the law of the Lord. The story is based on some very interesting and significant sociological, political and religious assumptions.

As in texts of Deuteronomistic provenance, the narrative assumes the existence of a 'book of the law of the Lord' (variously defined in Deut. 28.61, Josh. 1.8; II Kings 14.6; Neh. 8.8, etc.). It is also presumed that the people are expected to know (and therefore *learn*) the laws in order that they may keep them (cf. Deut. 5.1, 'and you shall learn them and be careful to do them'). However, this is the only instance in which the teaching of the law is described not in the future but as a specific historical event.

The teaching is entrusted to a royal commission composed of royal officers (RSV 'princes'), Levites and priests. This composition is unusual. Biblical evidence ascribes specifically to the priests the task of transmitting and teaching God's law, so that 'instruction' is by definition a priestly function (cf. Jer. 18.18; Haggai 2.11; Ezek. 7.26; Lev. 10.11, to mention only a few). This commission, by contrast, includes only two priests; the thirteen other members are Levites and laymen. While the Pentateuchal sources do not ascribe any teaching function to the Levites, the Levites do act in this capacity in post-exilic circumstances; cf. Neh. 8.7: 'the Levites expounded (NEB; RSV "helped the people to understand") the law to the people'. Whatever view we take of the origin and development of the levitical order, their function as teachers of the law is confined in the biblical testimony to the Second Temple period. As for the king's officers, they may be scribes (although this is not stated), but no evidence whatsoever connects them with the teaching of the 'Law of the Lord'.

The original initiative and responsibility for this teaching is attributed in this passage to the king – an unusual fact in view of the biblical testimony. Deut. 17.18–20 is the only context which links the king with the book of the law, but more as a recipient than as a 'dispenser' of the teaching: 'and when he sits on the throne of his kingdom, he shall write *for himself* in a book a copy of this law, from that which is in charge of the Levitical priests, and it shall be with him, and he shall read in it all the days of his life, that he may learn to fear the Lord his God ...'

The concept of a ruler teaching the people is paralleled only, it seems, in the practice of the Persian period. This is attested by the letter of Artaxerxes, authorizing Ezra to undertake, among other things, two missions: 'And you Ezra ... appoint magistrates and judges who may judge all the people ... all such as know the laws of your God; and those who do not know them, you shall teach' (Ezra 7.25). This is an astonishing parallel to Jehoshaphat's activity – the introduction of a judicial reform (19.4ff.), juxtaposed with an organized policy of 'teaching the law of the Lord'. The basic presupposition in both cases is that the people must know the law; they therefore must be taught, and this is the responsibility of the king.

Taking all this into account, it would seem that the precise terms of the Chronicler's account here reflect a post-exilic reality, anachronistically projected back to the age of the monarchy.

A few words about language and style: the stylistic unity of the passage is created by the repetition of 'and with them' (*w^e'immāhem*): 'he sent his officers (RSV princes) and *with them* the Levites ... and *with them* (RSV and with these Levites) the priests ... and *with them* (RSV having) the book of the law', and by the prevalence of the verb *lmd* (teach), once at the opening clause, and twice at the end, a repetition emphasized by the fact that these are the only occurrences in Chronicles of this root in verbal forms (cf. in I Chron. 5.18; 25.7, 8).

[7] The teaching commission is sent by Jehoshaphat 'in the third year of his reign' – a very early date. The exact number is no doubt typological, illustrating the idea of 'as soon as possible', the first two years having been devoted to the consolidation of his rule. (For the probability that the 'third year' was in fact his first, cf. Williamson, 282; Dillard, 132.)

Of the five officers ('princes') in the commission, four have very common names, while the first, Ben-hail, is unique. It is understood by LXX as an attribute ('able men/men of valour', cf. I Chron. 26.7, 9, 30, 32; II Chron. 26.17; 28.6); the hyphenated form possibly supports this view (cf. by contrast Abihail in Num. 3.35, etc.). If this term in fact originally described all the officers, the commission would have comprised two priests, four officers, and eight Levites – a proportion which might indicate some hierarchical division of respective tasks.

[8] The name 'Tobadoniah' should probably be omitted, as a dittography of the preceding two names; there are then eight Levites, and two priests. The specific reference to the Levites as coming 'with' the officers, and the priests 'with' the Levites, might suggest a descending order of authority: officers, Levites, priests. It is not likely, however, that the lowest status would be represented by only two individuals; we see here rather an ascending hierarchy of the three classes of the Second Temple period: laity, Levites, and – in the position of supervision and guidance – two priests.

[9] This verse, the climax of the passage, adopts an emphatic, repetitive style, stating first the general task and then the details. Most interesting is the way in which these 'wandering professors' circulated 'through all the cities of Judah and taught among the people', a description which deviates from all known traditional forms of instruction. The teaching is provided to the community in its most general form, 'among the people', by outsiders, as a one-time experience; it has no explicit connection to public holidays (cf. Deut. 27.1ff.; Neh. 8.1–8, 13–18; 9.3), or family circles (cf. Prov. 4.3ff. etc.; Exod. 13.8, 14; Deut. 6.20). The only parallel is found in the figure of Samuel, who acted as an 'itinerant judge': 'he went on a circuit year by year … and he judged Israel in all these places' (I Sam. 7.16). How much the Chronicler's description of folk-education is a reflection of a reality at any period of Israel's history and not merely a literary imitation of the image of Samuel is impossible to say. Compare, however, the antithetic centralized form of education practised in the time of Ezra (Neh. 8.8, 12, 13, 18), which may also have been a unique event.

[10–11] With these verses, the chapter returns to the general introduction of Jehoshaphat's rule, specifically to the first of the three subjects: international status, building projects, and the army.

The historical information, as distinct from the theological garb in which it is presented, is that Jehoshaphat succeeded in establishing his control not only within his kingdom but also at its borders. The terms are carefully chosen: 'the kingdoms of the lands that were round about Judah … made no war against Jehoshaphat'. The text then refers specifically to Judah's western and southern neighbours – Philistines and Arabs, who brought tribute of 'silver' and 'rams and he-goats' respectively. Only later will it be related how Jehoshaphat established peace with the kingdom of Israel on his northern border (18.1), while hostilities were to continue to the east with Aram (ch. 18), and Ammon and its allies (ch. 20). All these statements (regardless of the alleged quantities of tribute) are in fact reasonable, and in accord with the historical circumstances. Jehoshaphat is portrayed as a dynamic king, who brought stability and prosperity to his country.

Jehoshaphat's contribution to these achievements, however, is only indirect; according to the Chronicler's view, the true reason for prosperity was 'the fear of the Lord' which 'fell upon all the kingdoms of the lands'. This in turn is certainly a result of Jehoshaphat's righteousness and fidelity (vv. 3–4).

After the preoccupation with the Philistines in the time of Saul and David, only cursory remarks give us an idea of their relationship with Judah and Israel. 'The land of the Philistines' is designated as Solomon's border (I Kings 4.21 [MT 5.1]), and the continual struggles with them are mentioned *à propos* other matters: 'Baasha struck him [Nadab] down at Gibbethon, which belonged to the Philistines; for Nadab and all Israel were laying siege to Gibbethon' (I Kings 15.27; also 16.15, 17). It is therefore quite possible that while there were struggles between Israel and the Philistines, Judah under Jehoshaphat continued to enjoy the *status quo* of David's and Solomon's days, a situation later interrupted in the time of Jehoram (II Chron. 21.16–17). This last text also mentions the Arabs in connection with the Philistines: 'the Arabs who live near the Cushites' (NEB; RSV 'who are near the Ethiopians'). Three items concerning the Arab tribes on the south-western border of Judah thus unite to form a probable historical sequence: they were defeated by Asa, paid tribute to Jehoshaphat, and assumed their independence during the depressed times under Jehoram.

[12–13] The touch of the Chronistic style is introduced at the beginning of v. 12 with 'Jehoshaphat grew steadily greater' ('*ad lᵉmā'lāh*, a favourite idiom, cf. *VT* 18, 1968, 357). Yet Jehoshaphat's building enterprises are given only cursory attention and are relatively limited in scope: 'fortresses and store-cities'. The first appear again in the time of Jotham together with 'towers' (27.4) and the latter in Hezekiah's time (32.28).

A line of highway forts in the Jordan Valley near the Dead Sea have been dated by their excavator to the time of Jehoshaphat (cf. M. Kochavi [ed.], *Judea, Samaria and the Golan*, 1972, 93–4*). This opinion may have been affected by the present text, but clearly fortifications were raised on the eastern front of the kingdom around this time.

While v. 13 is ostensibly a continuation of v. 12, it also complements matters raised earlier in v. 2; the reference in 13b to Jehoshaphat's military forces in Jerusalem provides a transition to the next topic, the army. In 13a, RSV's use of 'stores' for the Hebrew *mᵉlā'kāh* is probably influenced by 'store-cities' of v. 12, and is much too specific (cf. JPS 'he carried out extensive works', similarly NEB).

[14–19] This is a description of Jehoshaphat's conscript army, warriors 'in the service of the king' (v. 19). For this definition, cf. NEB 'men who served the king' (ham⁽ᵉ⁾šār⁽ᵉ⁾tīm 'et hammelek) and I Chron. 27.1; 28.1, in the framework of the 'divisions'. The implication of v. 19 is that this conscript army supplemented the professional forces, 'those whom the king placed in the fortified cities', also mentioned in v. 2. Here, as in the conscript force of Asa, the composition is along tribal lines: three units of Judah and two of Benjamin, with registration of recruits consistently referred to by 'fathers' houses', i.e. by family affiliation. Classification by weapon-type applies only for one unit of Benjamin: 'men armed with bow and shield' (v. 17; cf. by contrast 14.8 [MT 7]).

The individual commanders are given the general rank 'commanders of thousands', but four out of the five bear titles of their own: 'commander' (vv. 14, 15), 'volunteer for the service of the Lord' (v. 16) and 'mighty man of valour' (v. 17). The recruits are termed either 'mighty men of valour' (vv. 14, 16), or 'armed for war' (v. 18). Whether or not these are technical terms is impossible to say,

The presentation of the organisation of the units is consistent: the first commander of the tribal group is introduced first, and then the others, 'next to him': 'Adna of Judah' (v. 14b), and 'next to him' Jehohanan (v. 15) and Amariah (v. 16); Eliada of Benjamin (v. 17), and 'next to him' Jehozabad (v. 18). Thus, although each of these officers is commander of his own troops, it seems that the first in each tribal group exercises authority over the others.

The peculiar phrasing 'X the commander' is also peculiar to one other context in Chronicles (I Chron. 15.5–10); if not merely coincidental, this may also reflect some stylistic or linguistic inclination of the time (cf. Z. Talshir, 'Linguistic Development and the Evaluation of Translation Techniques in the Septuagint', *Scripta Hierosolymitana* 31, 1986, 311–14).

The systematic portrait which emerges may be commended in every way except for two features: the unlikely numbers (over one million armed men) and the fact that this note echoes other notices of this nature, all of which appear in Chronicles only in the histories of the 'righteous' kings. The second question has been addressed in regard to Asa; a few words will be in order here on the problem of numbers (cf. also J. W. Wenham, 'Large Numbers in the Old Testament', *Tyndale Bulletin* 18, 1967, 19–53).

That the number of troops is highly exaggerated seems certain enough (cf. the detailed discussion of Dillard, 135). We should, however, take note of the consistent system, whereby the units are listed in descending order according to their numbers, the first two units of Judah comprising respectively

300,000 and 280,000 men. These were the exact figures for the two units of King Asa: 300,000 of Judah, and 280,000 of Benjamin (14.7). The other three units of Jehoshaphat also amount together to 580,000 men; Jehoshaphat's army is then exactly twice as large as that of Asa, and the greatest army documented in Chronicles, except for the military census of David (I Chron. 21.5). Amaziah will regard his army of 300,000 as too small, requiring the hiring of a troop from Ephraim (25.5–6); Uzziah's force is somewhat larger (307,555 + 2,600). David's reserves are calculated as twelve times 24,000, that is, 288,000 (I Chron. 27.1–15) – a figure which lacks only 12,000 (1,000 per unit) to become 300,000. In conclusion, although quantitatively probably too high, these numbers seem to reflect some method, the basis of which for the time being we may not be able to clarify.

18 Now Jehoshaphat had great riches and honour; and he made a marriage alliance with Ahab. ² After some years he went down to Ahab in Samaria. And Ahab killed an abundance of sheep and oxen for him and for the people who were with him, and induced him to go up against Ramoth-gilead. ³ Ahab king of Israel said to Jehoshaphat king of Judah, 'Will you go with me to Ramoth-gilead?' He answered him, 'I am as you are, my people as your people. We will be with you in the war.'

4 And Jehoshaphat said to the king of Israel, 'Inquire first for the word of the Lord.' ⁵ Then the king of Israel gathered the prophets together, four hundred men, and said to them, 'Shall we go to battle against Ramoth-gilead, or shall I forbear?' And they said, 'Go up; for God will give it into the hand of the king.' ⁶ But Jehoshaphat said, 'Is there not here another prophet of the Lord of whom we may inquire?' ⁷ And the king of Israel said to Jehoshaphat, 'There is yet one man by whom we may inquire of the Lord, Micaiah the son of Imlah; but I hate him, for he never prophesies good concerning me, but always evil.' And Jehoshaphat said, 'Let not the king say so.' ⁸ Then the king of Israel summoned an officer and said, 'Bring quickly Micaiah the son of Imlah.' ⁹ Now the king of Israel and Jehoshaphat the king of Judah were sitting on their thrones, arrayed in their robes; and they were sitting at the threshing floor at the entrance of the gate of Samaria; and all the prophets were prophesying before them. ¹⁰ And Zedekiah the son of Chenaanah made for himself horns of iron, and said, 'Thus says the Lord, "With these you shall push the Syrians until they are destroyed."' ¹¹ And all the prophets prophesied so, and said, 'Go up to Ramoth-gilead and triumph; the Lord will give it into the hand of the king.'

12 And the messenger who went to summon Micaiah said to him, 'Behold, the words of the prophets with one accord are favourable to the king; let your word be like the word of one of them, and speak favourably.' ¹³ But Micaiah said, 'As the Lord lives, what my God says, that I will speak.' ¹⁴ And when he had come to the king, the king said to him, 'Micaiah, shall we go to Ramoth-gilead to battle, or shall I forbear?' And he answered, 'Go up and triumph; they will be given into your hand.' ¹⁵ But the king said to him, 'How many times shall I adjure you that you speak to me nothing but the truth in the name of the Lord?' ¹⁶ And he said, 'I saw all Israel scattered upon the mountains, as sheep that have no shepherd; and the Lord said, "These have no master; let each return to his home in peace."' ¹⁷ And the king of Israel said to Jehoshaphat, 'Did I not tell you that he would not prophesy good concerning me, but evil?' ¹⁸ And Micaiah said, 'Therefore hear the word of the Lord: I saw the Lord sitting on his throne, and all the host of heaven standing on his right hand and on his left; ¹⁹ and the Lord said, "Who will entice Ahab the king of Israel, that he may go up and fall at Ramoth-gilead?" And one said one thing, and another said another. ²⁰ Then a spirit came forward and stood before the Lord, saying, "I will entice him." And the Lord said to him, "By what means?" ²¹ And he said, "I will go forth, and will

be a lying spirit in the mouth of all his prophets." And he said, "You are to entice him, and you shall succeed; go forth and do so." [22] Now therefore behold, the Lord has put a lying spirit in the mouth of these your prophets; the Lord has spoken evil concerning you.'

23 Then Zedekiah the son of Chenaanah came near and struck Micaiah on the cheek, and said, 'Which way did the Spirit of the Lord go from me to speak to you?' [24] And Micaiah said, 'Behold, you shall see on that day when you go into an inner chamber to hide yourself.' [25] And the king of Israel said, 'Seize Micaiah, and take him back to Amon the governor of the city and to Joash the king's son; [26] and say, "Thus says the king, Put this fellow in prison, and feed him with scant fare of bread and water, until I return in peace." ' [27] And Micaiah said, 'If you return in peace, the Lord has not spoken by me.' And he said, 'Hear, all you peoples!'

28 So the king of Israel and Jehoshaphat the king of Judah went up to Ramoth-gilead. [29] And the king of Israel said to Jehoshaphat, 'I will disguise myself and go into battle, but you wear your robes.' And the king of Israel disguised himself; and they went into battle. [30] Now the king of Syria had commanded the captains of his chariots, 'Fight with neither small nor great, but only with the king of Israel.' [31] And when the captains of the chariots saw Jehoshaphat, they said, 'It is the king of Israel.' So they turned to fight against him; and Jehoshaphat cried out, and the Lord helped him. God drew them away from him, [32] for when the captains of the chariots saw that it was not the king of Israel, they turned back from pursuing him. [33] But a certain man drew his bow at a venture, and struck the king of Israel between the scale armour and the breastplate; therefore he said to the driver of his chariot, 'Turn about, and carry me out of the battle, for I am wounded.' [34] And the battle grew hot that day, and the king of Israel propped himself up in his chariot facing the Syrians until evening; then at sunset he died.

19 Jehoshaphat the king of Judah returned in safety to his house in Jerusalem. [2] But Jehu the son of Hanani the seer went out to meet him, and said to King Jehosaphat, 'Should you help the wicked and love those who hate the Lord? Because of this, wrath has gone out against you from the Lord. [3] Nevertheless some good is found in you, for you destroyed the Asherahs out of the land, and have set your heart to seek God.'

A. Notes to the MT

[13] אלהי, proposed insert אלי, with I Kings 22.14 and the Versions, haplography; [19] אמר (first), omit, cf. I Kings 22.20; [29] התחפש ובוא, already in I Kings 22.30; proposed אתחפש ואבוא, cf. commentary. [30] את הגדול, read ואת הגדול with I Kings 22.31 and the versions.

B. Notes to RSV

[3] 'my people as your people', thus in I Kings 22.4, MT 'your people as my people'; [10, 34] 'Syrians', 'Arameans' (NEB, JPS); 'push', literally 'gore' (NEB; JPS); [18] 'standing', better 'standing in attendance' (JPS; cf. also NEB); [24] 'you shall see on that day', or 'you see that day ...'; [29] 'I will disguise myself and go', cf. A

above; [30] 'Syria', 'Aram' (NEB, JPS); [32] 'for when', MT 'when'; [33] 'battle',
so LXX, MT 'camp' (NEB 'line').

C. Structure, sources and form

1. Chapter 18 is one of the units which the Chronicler adopts in its entirety from his
source in I Kings 22, with no internal alterations of content, and only very few
deviations of a linguistic, stylistic, literary and theological nature. The Chronicler's
main contribution is the integration of this story into the overall framework of
Jehoshaphat's history, by the addition of a new introduction and conclusion (vv. 1–2;
19.1–3), balanced by the omission of the original introduction and conclusion of
I Kings 22.1, 35bβ–38.

2. In Kings, this narrative appears in the context of the history of northern Israel,
specifically as one stage in the long war between Israel and Aram during Ahab's reign.
'For three years Aram and Israel continued without war' (I Kings 22.1), until the king
of Israel decides to reclaim Ramoth-gilead. Ahab's death in battle is explained at
length as the fulfilment of an unheeded word of God, and the story deals with major
theological problems concerning prophecy. How may a true divine revelation be
identified? Is warning given to man? What is the measure of human free choice?

In Chronicles, the context is completely changed to relate to the southern kingdom
of Judah. It is not the purpose of this chapter to account for Ahab's end; his whole
career, in fact, including the prophetic prediction of his death (I Kings 20.42, etc.), is
absent from Chronicles. The war with Aram here is not one in a series but a unique
event, and the focus of the chapter is on the figure and conduct of Jehoshaphat, which
in Kings are unquestionably secondary – in spite of his important role in introducing
the 'prophetic theme' (I Kings 22.5., 7). Thus one may sense a certain tension
between the original story, with its focus on the figure of Ahab – which is transferred
to Chronicles basically as it stands – and the new context, the history of Jehoshaphat.

3. The new introduction and conclusion make absolutely clear the Chronicler's
negative judgment of Jehoshaphat's action as described in this chapter. According to
18.2, he succumbs to the evil influence of Ahab's 'incitement', and the words of the
prophet in 19.2 rebuke him explicitly for helping 'the wicked'. This is the first
deviation of Jehoshaphat from his hitherto highly commendable conduct. One
wonders, therefore, why the Chronicler has not taken the option of omitting this
chapter, thus saving Jehoshaphat and himself the need of apology; this problem is
emphasized by the retaining of negative material in the parallel of 20.36–37. The
Chronicler's motive here is clarified by his historiographical and theological policy:
to incorporate all of the material found in his Deuteronomistic source on the relations
between Judah and Israel. This applies where the point of view is both that of Judah
(as in the wars between Asa and Baasha, or between Amaziah and Jehoash, I Kings
16.1–6; II Kings 14.8–14), and that of Israel, as in the present pericope. In all these
cases, the Chronicler integrates the Deuteronomistic material in full into the context
of the Judaean kingdom, even when the consequences for the figures and appraisal of
the Judaean kings is, as in many cases, negative (cf. also Japhet, *Ideology*, 311–18, and
above, on ch. 16). Thus, although he chooses not to tell the independent history of
the northern kingdom, the Chronicler has a profound interest in that history, views it
as one aspect of the destiny of Judah, and does not miss an opportunity to include it.

4. The pericope is a highly refined piece of literature. Attempts have been made to discern two main stages in its development (cf. E. Würthwein, 'Zur Komposition von 1. Reg 22.1–38', *Festschrift L. Rost*, BZAW 105, 1967, 245–54; also S. DeVries, *I Kings*, 1985, 263–6), but this may be relevant only to the version in Kings. The structure of the Chronicles format should be discussed on its own merits.

As in many of the best examples of biblical narrative, here too there is rapid change of scene and a significant component of dialogue, lending a dramatic quality to the story. One may actually gauge the preponderance of dialogue by counting the phrases which serve to introduce direct speech, and the great number of citations in the various scenes: the roots אמר (say), נבא (prophesy) הגיד (speak), etc., appear in this unit around fifty times!

The narrative comprises an introduction, followed by three comprehensive parts, each containing several, sometimes simultaneous, scenes:

(*a*) 1–2 Introduction: general background
(*b*) 3–11 Part one: setting and problem
(*c*) 12–27 Part two: encounter, prophet versus king; prophet versus prophet
(*d*) 28 – 19.3 Part three: unfolding and conclusion.

Each part has two central protagonists, with the other figures – individual or collective – playing auxiliary roles. The main figures in the first and third parts are Ahab and Jehoshaphat, in the second, Ahab and Micaiah. In the second part Jehoshaphat recedes into the background almost completely, while in the third part the prophet's fate becomes entirely irrelevant.

Although the changes introduced in Chronicles at the beginning and end of the narrative, and in particular the new conclusion, cause a certain shift in the relative importance of these protagonists, the main lines of the story remain the same in both versions.

D. Commentary

[1–2] In the original introduction of I Kings 22.1–3, Jehoshaphat appears in the context of the Aramaean wars and the initial scene between the king of Israel and his servants. The new introduction opens with the reign of Jehoshaphat, and sets the scene between Jehoshaphat and Ahab on a different plane.

Verse 1 portrays Jehoshaphat's achievements and status, as well as his marriage alliance with Ahab, and v. 2 proceeds to tell of one specific event, Jehoshaphat's visit to the northern king. Thus the relationship between the two monarchs, in which in the context of I Kings 22 Jehoshaphat seems to have inferior status (cf. J. M. Miller – J. H. Hayes, *A History of Ancient Israel and Judah*, 1986, 278–9), is presented here differently, as an expression of the Chronicler's systematic effort to describe the kings as equals.

In mentioning the 'marriage alliance', the Chronicler refers to what is related in the Deuteronomistic narrative only later (II Kings 8.18, 27). With

Jehoshaphat taking Ahab's daughter for his heir-apparent Jehoram, a *de facto* unification of the two dynasties is formed, the disastrous consequences of which for the Davidic dynasty will come to light only in the next generation, with Athaliah's rule and policy (cf. on ch. 22).

The Chronicler's attitude towards this marriage may seem at first glance neutral, even positive: an aspect of Jehoshaphat's achievements in addition to 'riches and honour'. Considering, however, Jehu's words in 19.2, and the Chronicler's axiom that material prosperity may become a trap even for the most righteous king, a more critical evaluation is intended. Jehoshaphat became rich, and stumbled; only because of the 'good things' which were found in him did he eventually escape the hazards which this alliance entailed.

Following the omission of I Kings 22.1, with its reference to 'three years', the Chronicler also replaces 'in the third year' with the general 'after some years'. He then elaborates the way Ahab receives Jehoshaphat in a manner worthy of an equal monarch, and describes Ahab's intentions as 'incitement' (*wayyᵉsîtēhū*, NEB). With this verb, a negative perspective is set for the whole ensuing expedition. Since 'incitement' implies that a certain (wrong) act is encouraged by false arguments, Ahab's motives are thus defined; the war will not be waged on the basis of a legitimate claim, 'Ramoth-gilead belongs to us' (I Kings 22.3), but simply because Ahab desires 'to go up against Ramoth-gilead'.

[3] From this point, the narrative resumes the sequence found in Kings. In the first dialogue between Ahab and Jehoshaphat, the presentation of the protagonists is of interest. The full emphatic ceremonial introduction, 'Ahab king of Israel said to Jehoshaphat king of Judah', is an interesting change from the source in Kings. In I Kings 22 Jehoshaphat is usually called by his name alone (vv. 4 [twice], 5, 7, 8 [twice], 18, 30, 32 [twice], and three times given his full title: 'Jehoshaphat king of Judah' (vv. 2, 10, 29), while Ahab is consistently called 'the king of Israel' (vv. 2, 3, 4, and twelve more times in this chapter), or simply 'the king' (vv. 6, 8, and ten more times), his proper name being mentioned alone only once, in God's words (I Kings 22.20). Most striking is the juxtaposition in vv. 2, 10 and 29 of 'Jehoshaphat king of Judah' with the nameless 'king of Israel' (for literary-critical conclusions from these titles, cf. Würthwein, 246–8).

While the Chronicler does not interfere with this terminology in the narrative itself, he takes care to change it in the introduction. In the first two verses he mentions Ahab by name three times, and creates a fully-balanced introduction of the two kings: 'Ahab king of Israel and Jehoshaphat king of Judah'. To the single occurrence of the name Ahab in the story, he adds 'king of Israel' (compare v. 19 with I Kings 22.20).

The dialogue between the two kings is quoted with several alterations. In

I Kings 22.4 Jehoshaphat's response is a conventional epigram of three parallel parts: 'I am as you are, my people as your people, my horses as your horses'. The Hebrew has obvious stylistic features: an equal number of words in each unit; an alliteration created by the six-fold repetition of k^e, 'as', and the final rhyming possessive suffix *-kā* (cf. also II Kings 3.7). This epigram is generally also preserved in our text in Chronicles, but the form is disrupted, and a new message emerges.

The Chronicler first omits the reference to 'horses', making the three-part formula into a two-part one, to which a simple answer is now added: 'we will be with you in the war'. The main point of Ahab's query 'Will you go *with me* (*'immī*, I Kings 22.4 *'ittī*)' is here repeated literally: 'we will be *with you*' (*wᵉ'immᵉkā*). Clearly, if any superiority was implied for Ahab in the form of the dialogue in Kings, not so here: Jehoshaphat speaks as an equal.

[4–5] Having given his consent, Jehoshaphat now stipulates that Ahab seek counsel of the Lord, an aspect of the plot which will remain his initiative. Ahab's response is in action rather than words: he promptly summons the prophets, 'four hundred' in number (I Kings 22.6: 'about four hundred'), to confront them with one question, whether or not to go to battle.

The Chronicler slightly rephrases the question in the plural: 'Shall *we* go' (so also in v. 14); the war is seen as a joint enterprise of Ahab and Jehoshaphat, although the reworking in this vein is far from consistent. For the conventional answer of the prophets, cf. especially II Sam. 5.19.

The plethora of prophets, certainly typological, emphasizes the theme of 'one' versus the 'many', the individual against the multitude. It is an organic *motif* of the story, immediately calling to mind the struggle of the lonely Elijah with the 'four hundred and fifty' prophets of Baal and the four hundred prophets of Asherah (I Kings 18.19). However, if viewed from a historical perspective, this passage clashes with the notes of I Kings 18.4, 13, according to which only one hundred prophets, hidden by Obadiah, survived Jezebel's massacre. This problem does not, of course, apply when Chronicles is considered on its own, without reference to the preceding Elijah stories.

[6] Jehoshaphat's reaction to the prophets' unanimous reply seems strange: in spite of the magnanimity of Ahab in gathering the four hundred prophets, Jehoshaphat is not satisfied with their unequivocal answer, but demands 'one more prophet'. The obvious question disturbs the commentators: why did Jehoshaphat distrust these prophets? Even Ahab seems to realize that Jehoshaphat's request is justified; while he tries to avoid it, he does not argue in the end. The mistrust seems to be inherent in the very description of mass prophetic unanimity. Post-biblical sages were of the opinion that 'no two prophets prophesy in precisely the same way' (BT, Sanhedrin, 89a); here four hundred have a single voice – could this be the voice of truth?

[7] Ahab admits the existence of 'one more' prophet, but resists consulting him. Ahab's resentment of Micaiah may be explained as an elementary result of a long history of personal animosity, or as a reflection of doubts Ahab may have had regarding the reliability of a seer prejudiced by an attitude of ill-will. In fact, however, the motive for Ahab's reluctance should be sought precisely in his basic faith in the prophet and his power. The king clearly subscribes to the concept that the prophetic utterance not only unveils what has already been determined, but actually gives form to future events (cf. G. von Rad, 'History in I and II Kings', in *The Problem of the Hexateuch and Other Essays*, 1966, 208–13). This being so, Micaiah's attitude may effect a negative turn of the events – a prospect Ahab wishes to avoid.

Several differences between the parallel texts illustrate well the process of linguistic modernization; some of these may be pointed out: *(a)* the consistent character of the prophet's attitude is expressed in I Kings 22.8 by an imperfect, *yitnabbē'*, negated by *lō'* (translated adequately 'he never prophesies …'). The Chronicler, intending to make this message clear to his contemporaries, expresses the continuous action/attitude by a participle of the same root, negated by *'ēn* (*'ēnennū mitnabbē'*). Moreover, the aspect of repetition is given a lexical expression by the addition of *kol yāmāyw* (RSV 'always'); *(b)* the nouns 'good' and 'evil' (in their feminine form) are both preceded by a preposition; *(c)* the prophet is introduced with the addition of a demonstrative: *he* is Micaiah.

[8] The individual summoning of Micaiah by a special messenger, with their subsequent dialogue (vv. 12–13), is also a way of singling him out, in contrast to the other prophets whom 'the king of Israel gathered' (v. 5), without further detail. Thus the minutest elements of the narrative highlight the difference between the multitude and the individual.

[9–11] This relatively lengthy vignette provides a broad literary pause at the end of the first part, and at the same time prepares the background for the prophetic vision of vv. 18ff. The scene is sketched with a series of participles: 'were sitting', 'arrayed', 'were prophesying'. Contrasting with the static posture of the seated monarchs is the constant motion implicit in the phrase: 'all the prophets were prophesying before them'. We do not know whether this 'prophesying' is only vocal, or involves mantic actions, as in I Sam. 19.20–24 or I Kings 18.29. In any case, within this homogeneous crowd one prophet is singled out, a soloist in the chorus, by the indication of three features: his name, Zedekiah the son of Chenaanah; his symbolic act involving horns of iron; and the individual prophecy he utters. The promotion of Zedekiah to the position of leader places Micaiah in a situation of double confrontation: as one in the face of many, and as true prophet against false prophet.

The apparently superfluous note, 'arrayed in [their] robes', in fact prepares the reader for the function which 'robes' will later have in the story. At this stage, each of the kings is clothed in his own attire; later, Ahab's change of garments will be his way of testing the reliability of God's word, and will also put Jehoshaphat in danger (cf. on v. 29).

[12–13] From the perspective of narrative continuity, this dialogue seems an unnecessary elaboration: the plot moves smoothly to v. 14. However, the exchange here between Micaiah and the king's messenger in fact serves several purposes: introducing a parallel and simultaneous context, it delays development of the main plot, increasing the reader's suspense. Further, it introduces the new figure of Micaiah himself, a chief protagonist of the next part; and in the messenger's effort to moderate the prophet's zeal is a foreshadowing of the encounter between king and prophet and a highlighting of the moral issue involved. The king's messenger, surely inspired by the courtly aspiration to settle this affair smoothly, pleasing the king and leaving the prophet unharmed, advises Micaiah to 'speak favourably'. The unexpected vehemence of the response, 'what my God says, that I will speak', is a telling sign. In this early encounter between the messenger of the king and the messenger of the Lord, it is already clear that the issue is not whether 'good' or 'evil' tidings are given to the king, but whether the word of the Lord is faithfully transmitted. This principle is articulated by Micaiah's emphatic oath, 'As the Lord lives …', and the root *dbr* ('word') is repeated five times.

The dynamic tension introduced here reaches its climax with the vision of vv. 18–22, and the last scene outlines the final test of the fidelity to the authentic divine inspiration, of which Micaiah is very conscious: 'If you return in peace, the Lord has not spoken by me' (v. 27).

The insights into Micaiah's attitudes provided in this dialogue make the next scene all the more surprising: to the king's question, Micaiah will answer just as the messenger has advised him: 'Go up and triumph'. The insincerity of this assurance, however, will not escape the informed reader any more than it convinces King Ahab himself.

[14] Micaiah's first response is a faithful echo of the voice of the crowd: '… they will be given into your hand'. In the text of Kings, the similarity is complete (cf. I Kings 22.12 and 15), which is certainly the intention. In the present version, two changes are introduced deliberately by the Chronicler: the shift from singular to plural, making both Ahab and Jehoshaphat the addressees of his words, and, more important, the change of the active form 'the Lord will give' to the passive general form 'they will be given'. Although it is obvious that Micaiah speaks ironically, the Chronicler will not countenance his uttering an outright false prophecy, invoking the name of the Lord.

[15] Just as v. 6 did not specify why Jehoshaphat doubted the message of the many prophets, so here we are not told how it was that Ahab saw the

mockery in Micaiah's words so immediately and clearly that he actually adjured him to tell the truth. Was there an assumed intonation, or gestures which the written text cannot communicate, or was it enough that Micaiah chose 'precisely the same' words as his rivals? For whatever reason, Ahab is not misled, and courageously and insistently demands the truth.

[16] Forgoing the conventional opening 'Thus says the Lord' (cf. v. 10), and also avoiding giving a direct answer to Ahab's original question, Micaiah now answers promptly and to the point. In very brief, stark phrases, he describes a scene of abandonment and confusion, evoking a statement of divine pity: 'These have no master ...' The original query, 'shall we go up ... or shall I forbear', is not given an easy resolution, as in the encouragement of the other prophets, but is left to the king's own discretion. And yet, in a veiled but vivid image, the vision tells Ahab that he alone will be slain in the coming battle: the apparently comforting words, 'let each return to his home in peace', bear a hidden warning, as they refer only to the 'sheep', not to the 'master' or 'shepherd'. There is a fine irony to the prophet's message: he appears to speak 'favourably', but he in fact utters Ahab's doom.

Micaiah has expressed the axis of the whole encounter: 'return in peace'. Ahab, in his angry reaction, continues the theme: 'Put this fellow in prison ... until I return in peace' (v. 26), and the prophet's 'last word' is: 'If you return in peace the Lord has not spoken by me' (v. 27).

Finally, one should note the characterization of Micaiah's prophetic activity as presented here. Most striking is the fact that he is never referred to as a 'prophet' or by any of the other common designations. 'Prophets' in this context refers only to the crowd (vv. 5, 9, 11, 12, 21, 22), or the hypothetical 'another prophet' of v. 6. Micaiah himself is referred to either by name, or as 'one man' (v. 7). Micaiah is not a prophet of much 'doing'; he does not act in conventional mantic ways (cf. v. 9), or undertake symbolic feats (v. 10). He is principally a man of vision, a quality referred to in each of his three main prophecies. Here he opens with 'I saw all Israel'; in v. 18ff., 'hear the word of the Lord' is in fact an invitation to the kings to join his own 'visual' experience: 'Therefore hear the word of the Lord: I saw the Lord... .'; in v. 24, his retort to Zedekiah is also based on vision: 'Behold, you shall see (hinn^ekā rō'eh) on that day ...' (v. 24). Micaiah, then, is a concrete example of a 'seer', although this title itself is never used.

[17] Ahab's reaction here is interesting. From this point on, he will no longer address Micaiah directly, as he has done (vv. 14, 15). His rebuke, meant for the prophet, is couched in an almost triumphant remark to Jehoshaphat: 'Did I not tell you ...?'

This is the third time the narrative raises the issue of prophesying 'good' or 'evil' (cf. vv. 7, 12); the repetition through identical phrasing is more obvious in I Kings (22.8, 18). Ahab's reaction reveals his problematical situation: he has courageously demanded that the prophet speak nothing but the truth; now, confronted with a personally unacceptable divine warning, he chooses to see it as additional confirmation of his *a priori* judgment of Micaiah as a harbinger of only evil tidings.

In spite of his secondary role, Jehoshaphat's presence here, as addressee for the king's response, is important, and his own reaction is instructive: he now keeps silent, no longer trying to correct Ahab's conclusions (cf. v. 7). His subsequent actions seem to indicate that he has complied with Ahab's attitude, rather than with the prophet's advice.

[18–22] Micaiah correctly understands Ahab's words as an accusation, and feels that he should explain his position. This he endeavours to do first by assuring Ahab that his prophetic message is not motivated by personal prejudice but is 'the truth in the name of the Lord', and then (and this is more difficult still) by broaching the question of reliability: he and the other prophets, pronouncing opposite verdicts, were all speaking under divine inspiration; who is the messenger of truth?

Much has been written on Micaiah's vision, its similarity to Isa. 6, and the problem of the two levels of the prophecy, reality and vision (cf. M. Kaplan, 'Isaiah 6.1–11', *JBL* 45, 1926, 255–9); I will refer to these matters only briefly.

The visionary portrait of God sitting on his throne with 'all the host of heaven standing on his right hand and on his left' is a reflection of the earthly scene which Micaiah sees before his eyes: king Ahab is seated on his throne surrounded by his servants, and just as Ahab consults the prophets about the war on Ramoth-gilead, so God summons his 'counsellors' to the same end. The outcome of the expedition, which is hidden from the earthly advisors, i.e. Ahab's imminent death in battle, serves as a point of departure for the heavenly consultation. While various suggestions are made there, only the last, proposed by 'a spirit', is spelled out, given divine confirmation and delegated to the 'spirit' for execution.

With the pivotal phrase 'Now, therefore' (vv. 22), Micaiah moves from vision to the level of present reality, and from the meeting of these two planes of experience derives the inevitable conclusion: all the other prophets are prophesying falsely!

The theological problem posed by this vision, and Ahab's practical dilemma, are far from simple. Micaiah, while not denying that the other prophets are authentic messengers of the Lord, nevertheless wants to estab-lish that their pronouncement is false; his goal is to disprove their message without denying their call. To this end, he transfers the origin of the conflict to the heavenly plane, giving rise to yet another problem, of a theological nature. The divine decree is that Ahab should be slain in battle, if he chooses to go to war – and yet there remains the theological imperative that he should be granted an element of free choice. Divine guidance thus takes two simultaneous courses: while through the four hundred prophets Ahab is incited to go to war, another messenger is simultaneously commissioned to inform him of the true situation and warn him to desist. Ahab, then, faces the impossibly difficult choice between two opposing revelations of God.

Ahab's decision is determined by his character, his disposition, and the immediate practical situation. In the end, overruling Jehoshaphat's scruples, Ahab heeds those prophets who demand no change of policy and go along with his original intention of making war. From this final perspective, Ahab's concession to Jehoshaphat's stipulation that he 'inquire first' was nothing more than insincere lip-service to the 'word of the Lord'; in truth he was ready to accept only what suited his plans.

The idea presented here by Micaiah, that a *bona fide* prophet of the Lord may declare a false inspired message, is daring in the extreme. On the one hand, we find here a very strong emphasis on the understanding of the prophet as an unresisting channel for God's own purposes, even if this means allowing inspiration by a 'lying spirit'. Neither Micaiah nor the four hundred prophets may express their own preferences or views, but only transmit what they are told. On the other hand, by this same obedience a prophet may be an instrument of false action, and the credibility of the prophetic vocation on the human plane greatly shaken.

The same set of problems is also raised in Deut. 13.1–5 [MT 2–6]: the hypothetical prophet who incites the people to idolatry. There, however, the people have a very clear measure for judging a prophet's word, in the content of his message. Idolatry is so absolutely evil that it must always be shunned, even when encouraged by a prophet. This is not the case in the present context, where the issue is neutral from a religious point of view, and the problem of discernment between 'true' and 'false' remains unsolved.

Another interesting point in this passage is the concept of 'the spirit', a neutral and independent entity, which may in fact serve as God's messenger in the role of either 'true spirit' or 'lying spirit'. Verse 23, however, stresses a different aspect: 'the Spirit of the Lord' is seen as divine inspiration, speaking through the prophet.

I shall conclude the discussion with some points of a literary and linguistic nature.

(*a*) The heavenly vision is portrayed along precisely the same lines as the narrative preceding it, most of it taken by dialogues through which the plot develops. Only short clauses in v. 18 and 20a serve to introduce the new speakers. So distilled is the dialogue that towards the end of the scene the identification of the speaker is omitted, the discourses being introduced simply by 'and he said'. Opening with the Lord's question 'who will entice Ahab..?', it also ends with God's words. The dialogue thus alternates six times between God, the heavenly host and 'the spirit', ending with the commission 'go forth and do so'.

(*b*) As in many other narratives, this passage is built around several leading key-words: repetition of 'the Lord' and 'say' establish the general context of dialogue in heaven; the specific message, however, is expressed by the careful use of 'spirit' (three times, vv. 20, 21, 22), and 'entice' (also three times, vv. 19, 20, 21).

(*c*) We have seen above that Ahab views the problem as one of prophetic orientation, defined as either 'good' (RSV 'favourable') or 'evil' – cf. vv. 7, 12, 17. Micaiah's address emphatically ends with the word *rā'āh* (NEB 'disaster'), and it is clear that what is meant is not the prophet's own attitude but an unveiling of what 'the Lord has spoken' (NEB 'decreed').

(*d*) A last point concerns who is addressed throughout the vision. While Micaiah opens with a conventional formula, 'Therefore hear the word of the Lord' (v. 18), he does not in fact deliver any verbal divine message to Ahab, but rather moves immediately to describe a heavenly scene in which Ahab is the passive object of discussion. After the vision, with no further address formula except the single word *wᵉ'attāh*, 'and now', which signifies a turning point, Micaiah turns to Ahab directly, not with the expected oracle, but simply with an explanation of the vision.

(*e*) Some of the minimal changes introduced by the Chronicler should be mentioned. As already remarked, the singular 'hear' (*šᵉma'*) of I Kings 22.19 is replaced here by the plural (*šimᵉ'ū*), addressing both Ahab and Jehoshaphat. The idiom *'ōmēd 'ālāyw* (I Kings 22.19), which emphasizes the idea of serving (RSV, 'standing *beside* him' is too weak; cf. NEB 'in attendance') is probably not recognized by the Chronicler, who omits the preposition *'ālāyw*, leaving the heavenly host simply 'standing'. Note also the addition, already discussed, of the title 'king of Israel' to Ahab's name in v. 19 (also in the Versions of I Kings 22.20).

[23–24] The first reaction to Micaiah's words comes not from the king but from the rival prophet, Zedekiah the son of Chenaanah. This might be expected in view of the fact that Micaiah's main point is the reliability of the prophets. Zedekiah, the only individual in the opposite camp, now steps forward to respond to the challenge, a development which also satisfies the narrative structure: just as Micaiah was introduced through a dialogue with a messenger (vv. 12–13), so his exit is heralded by an encounter with a prophet.

Zedekiah's reaction in word and deed is patently aggressive. The blow he strikes Micaiah 'on the cheek' is not merely an act of physical violence, but certainly contains an element of insolence and insult (cf. Job 16.10; also Isa. 50.6; Lam. 3.30). His ironic rebuke in the form of a rhetorical question attacks Micaiah's integrity as a prophet, an attitude which Micaiah himself has avoided with the other prophets.

Micaiah's response to this accusation is interesting, in that it does not answer Zedekiah's challenge by attempting to establish his own prophetic authenticity. In fact, he deflects the attack by turning his rival's attention to his own fate: 'Behold, you see'.

RSV ('you shall see') obscures the implication of the Hebrew, that Micaiah in fact evokes Zedekiah's own vision of his future: 'Behold, you see that day, when you will hide yourself . . .'. Rather than denying Zedekiah's credibility, Micaiah volunteers to interpret for him his own personal vision of flight and concealment, clearly inconsistent with the optimistic forecast of v. 10.

[25–27] In this scene Micaiah leaves the stage. King Ahab, acting on his earlier assumption that Micaiah was motivated only by personal antagonism, now determines not only to punish the prophet for his malicious intentions, but to put his words to the test as well. The issue now becomes whether or not Ahab will in fact 'return in peace'.

In the book of Kings, the imprisoning of Micaiah is the first and only incident of this kind; in Chronicles it is preceded by Asa's detention of Hanani (16.10). Micaiah does not react to this undeserved sentence, nor complain of its injustice; he does not even point out, as well he might have after Ahab's cynical remark in v. 17, that he had known beforehand what Ahab's insincere demand for the truth might cost him. Rather, the prophet responds to the main point: the test of an authentic warning. Although Ahab is still refusing to speak to him directly, Micaiah addresses the king point-blank: 'If you do return in peace, the Lord has not spoken by me'.

The final words of v. 27, 'Hear, all you peoples!', are a citation of Micah 1.2, generally regarded as a secondary gloss, intended to identify Micaiah the son of Imlah with 'Micah of Moresheth' (Curtis, 398–9, but cf. E. Ball, 'A Note on I Kings XXII:28', *JTS* 28, 1977, 90–4). For the Chronicler, however, who found this exhortation in his *Vorlage*, it strikes the final chord for Micaiah's exit: the whole world must witness his authenticity as a prophet. With this declaration Micaiah disappears from the narrative; his future fate and actions remain unknown.

[28–34] The passage in I Kings 22.29–38 has a single focus, Ahab's end; in Chronicles this last part is restructured in two sections, the first relating to Ahab (28–34), the second to Jehoshaphat (19.1–3).

We have seen how Ahab rejects Micaiah's advice, and even Jehoshaphat, who insisted on consulting 'one more prophet', complies with his ally's instructions. Ahab's own conduct is interesting: while he seems to defy the prophet's warning by going out to war, he nevertheless takes careful precaution against injury, as if aware of the impending danger. He thus behaves as if he could fool the enemy by his disguise, not realizing that it is not the Aramaean army but the Lord himself he seeks to confuse, an impossible conceit. Ahab's comportment also illustrates his essential character as a warrior, whose motivation to fight and win takes precedence over his fears. This indeed is the portrait even as he dies, standing erect facing the army of Aram all day long, until the bitter end of the battle (v. 34; I Kings 22.35). Ahab chooses to conceal his identity by changing his attire (v. 29). The two infinitives (*hithappēś, wābō'*) may reflect a textual error, but if so the error was already in the Chronicler's *Vorlage* (cf. Rudolph, 255). Again, the singular '[he] went into battle' of I Kings 22.30 is changed to the plural: 'they went into battle'. Although Ahab's ruse now endangers the regally-clad Jehoshaphat, the latter voices no reservations when Ahab orders him to wear his kingly robes (note the imperative). From this point the narrative sequence leads to v. 31; the intervening v. 30 introduces an earlier scene expressed by a perfect tense, and is correctly translated by the past perfect, '*had* commanded'.

We have noted that Ahab's disguise is not only an attempt to avoid danger, but also his way of testing the prophetic warning, and through it, God's decree. From this point the plot unfolds on two parallel planes: the overt, military confrontation, and the hidden divine guidance behind the scenes. Although God is explicitly mentioned in I Kings 22.29–39 only at the end, and the Chronicler's version adds only one direct divine intervention (v. 31), it is clear throughout that not one of these events is incidental. Each stage of the battle thus has a theological significance.

For instance, while the practical or political motive of the command of the king of Aram – 'fight … only with king of Israel' – is not spelled out, its theological significance is obvious. Even the enemy's policy is dictated by the divine plan: Ahab alone must die, and the people will 'return in peace'. Next, in Ahab's attempt to outwit his fate by fooling the enemy, the ruse of disguise seems at first to succeed, not indeed by rendering Ahab immune but at least by drawing the danger towards the king of Judah. As his royal attire attracted the captains of the chariots in his direction, 'Jehoshaphat cried out' (v. 31). In the context of Kings, this cry seems to be one of distress or desperation, which in some unspecified way informs the Aramaean warriors that Jehoshaphat is not the man they seek. The Chronicler gives this scene new significance: Jehoshaphat's cry is directed to God, who hears him, helps him and draws the enemy captains away from him, not through any decision of theirs but by direct intervention of the Lord. Not only, then, does royal attire fail to endanger Jehoshaphat, but Ahab, concealing himself from the Aramean captains who seek him, is struck down by the random arrow of an anonymous archer. No human scheme or counter-plot can withstand the Lord's purpose.

Certain stylistic and linguistic details should be noted. Verse 31 constitutes a tidy illustration of the Chronicler's mode of interpolation. Following his source step by step, he pauses to divide the text, insert his own comment – this time extremely brief – and then proceeds where he left the source sequence:

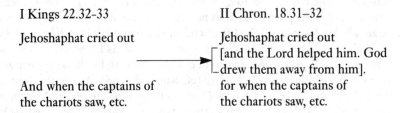

I Kings 22.32-33	II Chron. 18.31–32
Jehoshaphat cried out	Jehoshaphat cried out
	[and the Lord helped him. God drew them away from him].
And when the captains of the chariots saw, etc.	for when the captains of the chariots saw, etc.

In v. 31, *wayyāsobbū* in place of *wayyāsurū* (I Kings 22.32) probably reflects a better reading, since *sūr 'al* is never attested in biblical Hebrew. The meaning of the unique *d^ebāqīm* is not clear. The translations usually follow the European armour forms; cf. Rudolph, 255, for the rendering of the Ancient Versions.

[19.1–3] In I Kings 22.35–38 the story ends with a disbanding of the army of Israel, 'Every man to his city', followed by an elaborate description of Ahab's death, burial and disgrace. The Chronicler cites from his source only the first verse (v. 34 = I Kings 22. 35a), replacing 'at evening' with 'at sunset', from I Kings 22.36. The omitted portion of the Kings text is replaced by a Chronistic addition concerning Jehoshaphat.

19.1 follows Micaiah's prophecy (18.16) to the letter: the prophet's words 'let each return to his home in peace' are here used of Jehoshaphat, who 'returned ... to his house in peace' – a textual echo which is lost in the RSV translation.

Jehu the son of Hanani comes to meet Jehoshaphat, just as Azariah the son of Oded came out to meet Asa and his returning army upon their return to Jerusalem (14.14–15.1). Although certainly a rebuke, Jehu's message does not require any specific action of Jehoshaphat: this is rather an evaluation of his conduct and its theological significance.

Jehu opens his address with a rhetorical question, structured in synonymous parallel colons (the metric value of which is lost in translation): 'Should you help the wicked, and love those who hate the Lord?' No specific proscription concerning 'those who hate the Lord' is found in the Bible. The Pentateuch makes clear demands regarding idolatry (Exod. 23.24; 34.12–14; Deut. 12.2–3, etc.), and attitudes toward the 'seven nations' of Canaan (Deut. 7.2–5; 20.16–17). Here, however, the terms 'wicked' and 'those who hate the Lord' seem to have a much broader connotation than idolatry. Biblical historiography in general does not single out cooperation with 'the wicked' as sinful. The Chronicler, however, does espouse a vision of 'walking in the ways of the Lord' which entails non-cultic matters, not found explicitly in the legal corpus of the Pentateuch. In terms similar to Ps. 139.21, 'Do I not hate them that hate thee, O Lord? I hate them with perfect hatred ... Search me, O God and know my heart', the Chronicler expects of the pious an absolute and exclusive loyalty to the Lord, so that extending aid to 'those who hate the Lord' is a transgression. Jehoshaphat, then, has aroused God's anger ('Because of this, wrath has gone out against you from the Lord'); if he was not in fact punished, it was because the final balance of good behaviour was in his favour. These rather obscure statements seem to refer to the specific danger which faced Jehoshaphat during the battle; his eventual rescue signified the withdrawal of 'wrath' (cf. also II Chron. 32.25–26).

The 'good things' (RSV 'some good') found in Jehoshaphat are specifically two: destroying the Asherahs and setting his heart to seek God. The conjunction of these two is instructive of the Chronicler's view: true worship of the Lord is not fulfilled by the annihilation of idolatry; it must be founded on 'preparation of the heart' – a characteristic idiom in the Chronicler's theological vocabulary (cf. Japhet, *Ideology*, 251–2).

Jehu's words do not require an answer, nor does Jehoshaphat offer one; the pericope ends with the words 'to seek God'. Seeking the Lord's advice was the starting point of the story (18.4, 6, 7), but this idiom has here a broader meaning: 'seeking God', according to Chronicles, is the essence of religious disposition and orientation.

Even in the quite brief address of Jehu, the signs of late Biblical Hebrew and the Chronicler's terminology are unmistakable. Of the latter, I have already mentioned 'seek' (*drš*) and 'prepare the heart' (*hākīn lēb*). The late Hebrew idiom is evident, *inter alia* in the preponderance of nominal clauses, the use of the infinitive with *lamed* in the capacity of an inclined verb, and the placement of explanatory clauses after the main statement rather than *vice versa*.

19 4 Jehoshaphat dwelt at Jerusalem; and he went out again among the people, from Beer-sheba to the hill country of Ephraim, and brought them back to the Lord, the God of their fathers. [5] He appointed judges in the land in all the fortified cities of Judah, city by city, [6] and said to the judges, 'Consider what you do, for you judge not for man but for the Lord; he is with you in giving judgment. [7] Now then, let the fear of the Lord be upon you; take heed what you do, for there is no perversion of justice with the Lord our God, or partiality, or taking bribes.'

8 Moreover in Jerusalem Jehoshaphat appointed certain Levites and priests and heads of families of Israel, to give judgment for the Lord and to decide disputed cases. They had their seat at Jerusalem. [9] And he charged them: 'Thus you shall do in the fear of the Lord, in faithfulness, and with your whole heart: [10] whenever a case comes to you from your brethren who live in their cities, concerning bloodshed, law or commandment, statutes or ordinances, then you shall instruct them, that they may not incur guilt before the Lord and wrath may not come upon you and your brethren. Thus you shall do, and you will not incur guilt. [11] And behold, Amariah the chief priest is over you in all matters of the Lord; and Zebadiah the son of Ishmael, the governor of the house of Judah, in all the king's matters; and the Levites will serve you as officers. Deal courageously, and may the Lord be with the upright!'

A. Notes to MT

[8] ולריב וישבו ירושלים, read ולריב ישבי ירושלים, cf. commentary.

B. Notes to RSV

[8] 'and to decide disputed cases. They had their seat at Jerusalem', reconstructed, cf. above A, and commentary; [10] 'you shall instruct them,' better NEB 'you shall warn them', cf. commentary; 'that they may not incur guilt', better 'that they may not be guilty', cf. commentary. [11] 'upright,' MT 'good'.

C. Structure, sources and form

1. This section, which has no parallel in the Deuteronomistic history, has been intensively discussed in scholarly literature, in particular in respect of its significance for the juridical history of early Israel, and the light it sheds on the goals and reliability of Chronicles. (As only a sample of the whole list of studies, cf. C. Machholz, 'Zur Geschichte der Justizorganisation in Juda,' *ZAW* 84, 1972, 314–40;

A. Rofé, 'The Law about the Organization of Justice in Deuteronomy', *Beth Mikra* 65, 1976, 199–210, esp. 204ff.*; M. Weinfeld, 'Judges and Officers in Ancient Israel and in the Ancient Near East', *Israel Oriental Studies* VII, 1977, 65–88; K. Whitelam, *The Just King*, JSOTS 12, 1979, 185–206; H. Reviv, 'The Traditions Concerning the Inception of the Legal System in Israel', *ZAW* 94, 1982, 566–75; R. Wilson, 'Israel's Judicial System in the Pre-exilic Period', *JQR* 74, 1983, 229–48). In interpreting this unit, then, the commentator is faced with the prior need to establish its authenticity and clarify its sources; the discussion of these questions will be facilitated by first examining its structure and form.

2. The unit is devoted first to Jehoshaphat's effort to 'bring the people back' to God (v. 4), and then to his judicial reform (vv. 5–11); these may be regarded as the king's response to the prophet's rebuke in vv. 1–3, a new initiative in his 'seeking the Lord'. The two different issues of v. 4 and vv. 5ff. are presented as a single linguistic-syntactic sequence.

The description of the judicial reform is composed of two entirely symmetrical paragraphs, uniformally patterned, each having one topic, relating first an action and then an admonition. The formulative force of this pattern is so binding that in the second paragraph some of the reform measures are included, for the sake of literary symmetry, as part of Jehoshaphat's exhortation (v. 11). The structure of this section may be illustrated as follows:

(i) 5–7 – Judges in the cities
    (*a*) 5 the appointment
    (*b*) 6–7 Jehoshaphat's address to the judges
(ii) 8–11 Judges in Jerusalem
    (*a*) 8 the appointment
    (*b*) 9–11 Jehoshaphat's address to the judges.

This transparent structure in itself indicates a distinction between the actual appointment of local court officials in the fortified cities of Judah and a central court in Jerusalem, presented rather briefly in vv. 5, 8, 11a, and the more lengthy citation of Jehoshaphat's elaborate instructions and admonitions to the judges (vv. 6–7, 9–10, 11b).

3. Wellhausen, in his critical discussion of the possible historical reliability of this unit and its derivation from some source, reached a categorically negative conclusion: the judicial system reflects realities contemporary to the Chronicler himself, and any anachronistic attribution to Jehoshaphat is no more than a midrash on the root *špṭ* ('judge') in Jehoshaphat's name, 'the Lord is judge' (cf. Wellhausen, 191).

Further arguments against the authenticity of Jehoshaphat's reform may be summarized as follows:

(*a*) This judicial system, with its distinction between priests and Levites, cannot be ascribed to such an early date; the position of the chief priest as the highest legal authority (v. 11) reflects the realities of the post-exilic period, and the dichotomy between 'matters of the Lord' and 'king's matters' is contrary to the concept of law in the monarchic period.

(*b*) The proposed reform is greatly influenced by the laws of Deuteronomy (Deut. 16.18–20; 17.8–13); it must then be later than the promulgation of this book, and cannot therefore be attributed to Jehoshaphat.

(*c*) The description is replete with characteristic Chronistic language, style and views, and the tendency to extol Jehoshaphat is shared by the related portions of the king's history in Chronicles; only the Chronicler could have written these passages.

4. A response to this negative appraisal of the authenticity of Jehoshaphat's reform and to its understanding in terms of post-exilic legal circumstances and thought was eventually developed. The initial steps should be attributed to Albright's discussion ('The Judicial Reform of Jehoshaphat', in *A. Marx Festshcrift*, 1950), in which a comparison of this text with Near Eastern parallels, in particular the reform of king Haramheb of Egypt in the fourteenth century BCE, and a recognition of the 'matters of the Lord' and 'the king's matters' as an early distinction, led to the conclusion that Jehoshaphat's reform should be viewed as entirely authentic. Albright also indicated other ancient elements in the passage, e.g. the institution of 'governor of the house of Judah', which would be meaningless in the Chronicler's time.

5. It is clear, then, that the discussion of this matter involves general controversial issues of biblical scholarship, such as the development of the clerical orders, the administration of the kingdom, and the history of biblical literature. Nor should we ignore the involvement here of such imponderable elements as respective attitudes of either trust or suspicion towards the Chronicler's work.

Without discussing all the aspects of this debate, let us summarize it as follows:

(*a*) The Chronicler must be the author of the passage as it stands, as it bears the signature of his language, literary method and basic views – elements concentrated principally in Jehoshaphat's two addresses (vv. 6–7, 9–11):

(i) The interweaving of rhetoric and admonition into the narrative sequence;

(ii) The distinctly anthological composition of these addresses, juxtaposing adopted biblical texts with the author's own formulas;

(iii) The expression of fundamental Chronistic philosophy and attitudes, for which cf. the commentary.

(*b*) No one can deny that this reform is fully integrated into the Chronistic portrait of Jehoshaphat and certainly furthers the Chronicler's interests. However, perhaps for this very reason one should pose the question of authenticity in clear terms: is the fact that the Chronicler wrote this passage in his own language, and adapted it to the coherent context of his own views, sufficient proof that the content is purely imaginative or, at best, a projection of data from the Chronicler's own period? Not if we take the overall evidence of Chronicles and the specific case of the passage into account. As a matter of fact, there are many passages in Chronicles – such as the accounts of Shishak's campaign (12.1–12), Asa's disease (16.12), or the deeds of Joash (chs. 23–24) – which, if they were to be analysed without the benefit of reference to a parallel Deuteronomistic source, that is, without the possibility of distinction between earlier Deuteronomistic material and Chronistic adaptation, would be judged by some, I am sure, as complete fabrications. Rather, the accentuated Chronistic character of this unit is more an indication of the nature and literary format of the Chronicler's sources than of their utter absence.

In discussing authenticity, then, we should differentiate between the two components of the unit: the orations – which are definitely Chronistic – on one hand and the basic narrative facts on the other; the latter should be examined in the light of the relevant criteria for the historical context they presuppose.

6. The political crisis which accompanied the division of the united kingdom under David and Solomon into two separate monarchies could hardly have failed to catalyse administrative adjustments. In fact, such adjustments would be needed in

the course of time even without such drastic political changes. There is an inherent historical logic to reform in Jehoshaphat's day, when there is a process of stabilization after many years of military encounters, and the striking finally of a certain political balance with the northern kingdom – a dominant feature of the Deuteronomistic history of the period.

The probability of such reform is moreover enhanced by the figure of Jehoshaphat himself in the Deuteronomistic material: a monarch of great vitality, who contracts international alliances, undertakes military expeditions, and initiates both economic projects and religious renewal. The additional data provided by Chronicles have already noted the placing of troops and garrisons (or officers) in the fortified cities (17.2), the provisioning of store-cities (17.13), military organization (17.14, 19), arrangements for his succession by Jehoram, and provision for the position of his other sons (21.2–3). All these indicate an enterprising restructuring of administrative matters, of which the legal system would be one aspect.

Several specific details of this judicial reform should also be pointed out:

(i) The reform begins in the 'fortified cities', which play a key role in Jehoshaphat's administration, as we have noted above. The establishment of these cities as centres of royal authority was implemented by the positioning there of the king's sons, officers, troops and courts. Such intense activity around the fortified cities is not related by Chronicles to any other Judaean kings.

(ii) Not only is the distinction between 'matters of the Lord' and 'matters of the king' reasonable, but it is in fact attested by earlier sources. Already in the Deuteronomistic presentation we find a consistent division between 'the treasures of the house of the Lord' and the 'treasures of the king's house' (I Kings 14.26; 15.18, etc.); these were no doubt administered independently. The pragmatic distinction between a man's obligations towards his king and towards his God is not neutralized by the theological concept that the Lord is the only lawgiver. The citizen's obligation is a dual respect (Exod. 22.28) and a dual loyalty (cf. I Kings 21.10, 13); separate legal procedures for each of these realms in Jehoshaphat's time is therefore a reasonable assumption.

(iii) The court in Jerusalem serves a double role: regular court for the Jerusalemites, and court of higher appeal for people in the provinces. This may reflect a development from the independent authority of the local courts to a central court in Jerusalem supervised by the king.

It should be noticed that the reform as presented here is not an accurate realization of the law of Deuteronomy 16–17. Thus, for example, Deuteronomy stipulates 'judges and officers in all your towns' (Deut 16.18), while in this context only judges (with no 'officers',) are appointed, and only in the fortified towns. Also, according to Deut. 17.8–9, in cases of doubt 'you shall ... go up to the ... levitical priests and to the judge who is in office', and it is clear that either 'the priest' or 'the judge' will handle the appeal (v. 12). In Chronicles, we have a court with Levites, priests and 'heads of families of Israel' presiding. If the reform were merely a reflection of the law of Deuteronomy, there would be a much greater conformity between the texts. Similar considerations apply to the view that Jehoshaphat's reform reflects the system of the Sanhedrin, the courts of the Second Temple. Unfortunately, our information regarding these institutions comes from much later sources; the details of their constitution, however, do not conform to the picture drawn by this chapter (cf.

H. Mantel, 'Sanhedrin', *EJ* 14, 1971, 836–39). The idiosyncratic features of Jehoshaphat's judicial reform thus mark it as distinct both from the law of Deuteronomy and from the legal system of the Chronicler's time.

7. In sum, the fact that the Deuteronomistic historiographer did not refer to Jehoshaphat's reform – a corollary to his lack of interest in royal administration in general (cf. Japhet, *Ideology*, 432ff., 510–11) – should not influence our attitude towards the Chronicler's presentation. It would seem that the Chronicler did in fact use some sort of source for his report; judging from the Chronistic features of the text, that source must have been a brief, undetailed and basic record of changes in the legal administration, amplified by the Chronicler with an introduction and rhetorical pieces, and integrated into his own view of Jehoshaphat's reign. The only detail which raises doubts and is difficult to evaluate into a historical perspective is the role and position of the Levites – which may reflect the Chronicler's wish to further their interests (cf. further the discussions of Machholz, Whitelam, Weinfeld and Reviv).

D. *Commentary*

[4] The subject-matter of v. 4, 'Jehoshaphat dwelt (NEB 'had his residence') in Jerusalem', is a direct continuation of the preceding reference to the king's 'return' to Jerusalem: the implication is that the city was his permanent base of activity, and no more visits to the northen kingdom were undertaken.

Jehoshaphat now sets out on a campaign of religious reform throughout his kingdom, an initiative attributed in the book of Kings only to Josiah, who heads north – probably to the hill country of Ephraim – in a comprehensive offensive against idolatry and illegitimate cult forms (II Kings 23.15–20). The Chronicler, besides transmitting Josiah's reform (II Chron. 34.6–7), views in a similar manner the cultic purge of 'all Israel' in the time of Hezekiah (31.1). In the time of Jehoshaphat there is really no need for such radical measures. The text describes Jehoshaphat's voyage as very different from Josiah's: he travels not only in the north but throughout his realm, the borders of which – 'from Beer-sheba to the hill country of Ephraim' – are well in accord with the map of his kingdom presented earlier (17.2). Jehoshaphat 'went out ... among the people' (*wayyēṣē bāʿām*), a term which evokes the earlier teaching commission of his delegates who '... taught among the people' (17.9). In this policy, Jehoshaphat is unique among all the kings of Judah.

Do we have here a historical memory of Jehoshaphat's activity, or a literary response to the prophet's admonition, developed by the Chronicler under the influence of Josiah's reform? The verse is composed as a paranomastic play on the roots *šwb/yšb* (cf. the forms *wayˤšībēm/wayyāšob/ wayyēšeb*), which creates a literary link with v. 1, and even a phonetic assonance with 'Beer-sheba'. Also, the divine title 'the God of their fathers' is one of the Chronicler's favourites. Thus, although the idiom is not specifically Chronistic, this verse is very much in accord with the Chronicler's methods and views.

[5] This verse, while introducing a new topic, continues the syntax of the preceding passage. This syntactical structure might lead to the conclusion – otherwise rather unlikely – that the appointment of judges was carried out during Jehoshaphat's journey.

Attention has already been given above to the affinity between the legal arrangements of Jehoshaphat and the law of Deut. 16.18. This passage in Deuteronomy is in fact the only Torah precept which deals with appointment of judges, just as the present verse is the only narrative on the subject. However, barring their common topic, the texts differ in many details. The term used here for appointing judges is the *hiphil* form of '*md* (a common usage of late Hebrew), while Deuteronomy has *ntn*. Deuteronomy stipulates that judges be placed 'in all your towns', while Chronicles specifically limits the appointment to the 'fortified cities'. The 'officers' (*šoṭˤrîm*) of Deuteronomy are in Chronicles confined to the Jerusalem court, and the division of Deut. 16.18, 'according to your tribes', is altered here: 'he appointed judges *in the land*', implying the entire territory without tribal distinction. Concerning the identity of these judges, and the precise composition of their courts, we are given no information at all.

[6–7] The legal appointments are accompanied by theological admonitions, notably the dogmatic statements 'you judge ... for (or "of") the Lord' and 'he is with you in giving judgment'. The first implication is that the Lord is both the source and the authority of the law; it is to him that the human magistrate is responsible, as human deputy of the supreme judge of the universe. The king's exhortation, 'let the fear of the Lord be upon you', reflects this sober responsibility: the presence of the Lord makes every legal judgment a religious act, to be observed with proper awe of the divine presence.

It is noteworthy that the attributes of divine justice as models for judges' conduct are defined in negative terms: 'For there is no perversion of justice with the Lord our God, or partiality, or taking bribes'. We have noted before (cf. to I Chron. 29.11) how the Chronicler struggles with the limitations of language in his effort to express the abstract nature of divine attributes. Here, in describing the attribute of God's justice – a cornerstone of his religious outlook – the Chronicler chooses to formulate his expression in a negative way, by the absence of certain qualities rather than the existence of any. He also avoids active verbs which might imply any 'doing' on God's part; only nouns are used.

The same three stumbling blocks to the exercise of justice are listed in Deut. 16.19, 'You shall not pervert justice; you shall not show partiality; and you shall not take a bribe ... Justice, and only justice, you shall follow'; in spite of light differences in terminology (not reflected by RSV), the similarity to the present verse cannot be denied. However, what in Deuteronomy are direct exhortations to the judges, appear here as divine attributes, upon which human behaviour should be modelled. This tenet is expressed explicitly by post-biblical sages: man should 'stick to the Lord's ways' – 'Just as he is gracious and compassionate, so be thou gracious and compassionate' (BT, Shabbath 133b; also Sota 14a; Leviticus Rabbah 24,4 etc.).

Several linguistic and stylistic features are worthy of note. The late idiom is evident in the use of the participle *'ōśīm* (v. 6), preceded by an explicit pronoun, to denote present tense. Compare *r^e'ū māh 'attem 'ōśīm*, 'consider what you do', to Judg. 18.14, where the same is phrased with an imperfect: *d^e'ū mah ta'^aśū* (RSV literally 'consider what you will do'). That the present text represents a transitional linguistic period is manifest in the appearance immediately afterwards of the classical form *tišp^eṭū* ('you judge', literally you will judge), instead of the possible late form *'attem šōp^eṭīm* (the difference between the alternative expressions cannot be fully represented by the translation).

Note also the stylistic symmetrical alternation of imperative opening verbs followed by an explanation of persuasive tone: 'consider ... for you judge not for man' (v. 6), 'take heed ... for there is no perversion of justice with the Lord' (v. 7). Each admonition also concludes with an emphatic nominal clause: '[He is] with you in giving judgment' (v. 6); '[There is] no perversion ... with the Lord our God' (v. 7). Lastly, I should mention the preponderance of the root *špt* in the first verse, in three forms: judges, judge (verb) and judgment.

[8] The second stage of the reform is the establishment of the court in Jerusalem. While the information here and in v. 11a gives some portrayal of the composition and responsibilities of this court, many questions still remain unanswered.

The court is composed of an unspecified number of Levites, priests and 'heads of fathers' houses of Israel', responsible, according to v. 11, for 'matters of the Lord' and 'king's matters', the chief priest presiding supreme for the first realm, the governor of Judah for the second. It is not clear whether the court was actually divided into two separate legal sections, each dealing with one of these realms, or whether the presiding high judge alone was exchanged according to the matter at hand, with no institutional consequences in the composition of the court. Also, one wonders whether the definition of Levites as 'officers' (v. 11) indicates that the actual function of magistrate is confined to priests and 'heads of families' (v. 8).

Our view of the precise authority of the Jerusalem court depends in great measure on the interpretation of the verse's conclusion. RSV here reflects textual emendation of the Hebrew, which in fact reads 'to give judgment for the Lord and dispute; and they returned to Jerusalem'. In this text as it stands, there are two categories of authority: 'judgment of the Lord' and 'dispute'. The apparent balance between these two categories is misleading, since 'judgment of the Lord' is a very general heading, referring in fact to every matter brought before the judges, while 'dispute' is a specific category. In addition, 'they returned to Jerusalem' is completely out of context; the grammatical subject is still 'Jehoshaphat', not an unspecified plural, and the context has already been set 'in Jerusalem', not elsewhere. RSV overcomes the difficulty by assuming a corrupt text and rendering (with no footnote) *wayyāšubbū*, 'they returned', as *wayyeš^{e}bu*, 'they had their seat in Jersualem' (also Dillard, 146). Another reading, following the Versions, is very generally adopted (cf. Curtis 404, Rudolph 256, Williamson, 290–1; also J. Heller, 'Textkritisches zu 2 Chr 19:8', *VT* 24, 1974, 371–3): the *waw* is taken to be a corruption of *yod* and belonging to the first word (or a dittography), and *yšbw* is pointed as *yōš^{e}bē*, thus: 'for the dispute (or law-suits) of the inhabitants of Jerusalem' (in this vein, NEB). The dual responsibility of the court may thus be viewed as the general administration of the 'judgment of the Lord', and the specific hearing of the legal cases of the Jerusalem residents.

A command to establish a high court of justice in 'the place which the Lord your God will choose' is found in Deut. 17.8ff. The cases to be tried there are those 'too difficult' for the provincial courts referred to earlier (16.8). It is to be presided over by clerical and lay figures: 'levitical priests' and 'the judge' (17.9), the latter being probably the supreme authority nominated by the king. The text in Chronicles has priests *and* Levites, and adds to them 'the heads of fathers' houses', headed by the 'governor of the house of Judah'. While the separation of Levites from priests may reflect a later development or a different view of the court's composition, 'the heads of fathers' houses' cannot be regarded as developed from Deut. 17. While the term itself is certainly a favourite of the Chronicler, it may represent relatively early arrangements, and we might ask whether the text might reflect circumstances in which not only military but also legal authority was still held by these tribal leaders.

[9–10] Jehoshaphat's second admonition, like the first, echoes earlier texts, while still stating the Chronicler's peculiar views in his own language. Jehoshaphat requires of the judges as a moral starting point that they act in the 'fear of the Lord, in faithfulness and with your whole heart', all characteristic terms in the Chronistic lexicon. The parallel to 'the fear of the Lord' of v. 7 is overshadowed here by the emphasis on 'whole-heartedness': there is no doubt that the act of judgment is regarded as a form of worship, demanding utter piety and devotion.

Verse 10 shows close affinity to Deut. 17.8. Both texts refer to cases brought to the court from the provinces ('any case within your towns'; or here, 'a case for your brethren who live in their cities'). More important, both texts emphasize the need for discernment. Deuteronomy presents three categories of cases requiring distinction, using the stereotyped formula 'between x and x' – 'between one kind of homicide and another, one kind of legal right and another, one kind of assault and another'. Chronicles opens with exactly the same form and the same first doublet, which should be translated, as in Deuteronomy, 'between one kind of homicide and another' (RSV obscures the identity of the texts). In the continuation of the present verse, the same structure is preserved but with different categories: 'between instruction or commandment, or statutes or ordinances'. The discernment required is thus not between different legal cases, but between different kinds of *written law*, the terms *mišpāṭīm, ḥuqqīm, miṣwāh, tōrāh* being assumed to represent different categories of commandments.

The structural affinity of these texts (notwithstanding the changes in terminology) should not distract us from the essential conceptual difference between them. The main point of the law in Deut. 17 is to ensure the power and authority of the central court in Jerusalem – a fact which may point to the innovative nature of that institution. Obedience to the court is given the highest priority: 'Then you shall do according to what they declare to you from that place which the Lord will choose; and you shall be careful to do according to all that they direct you; according to the instructions which they give you, and according to the decision which they pronounce to you, you shall do; you shall not turn aside from the verdict which they declare to you, either to the right hand or to the left' (vv. 10–13). Jehoshaphat's admonition is focussed elsewhere. He addresses himself to the instruction of the judges themselves, focussing on three terms which are known from other Chronistic contexts: guilt, wrath and warning (NEB; RSV's 'instruct' misses the point). The combination of these three presents one of the major tenets of the Chronicler's concepts of law and justice: the clear distinction between wilful and inadvertent transgression (cf. Japhet, *Ideology*, 184–91; L. Schiffman, *Sectarian Law in the Dead Sea Scrolls*, Chico, Ca 1983, 89–109). Culpability is incurred only for wilful transgression, and the distinction is made through the provision of 'warning'. Since many people are unaware of their acts, or do not understand their meaning, a primary obligation is to warn them. This warning may lead either to repentance, if the individual warned turns away from error, or – if he nevertheless persists wilfully in wrongdoing – to a state of 'guilt' and 'wrath'. The primary obligation of the judges is that of 'warning'; by fulfilling it, 'guilt and 'wrath' may be averted, and they themselves will be free of guilt: 'that you may not be guilty' (cf. NEB; RSV wrongly 'you will not incur guilt').

[11] As already noted, while this verse forms part of Jehoshaphat's admonition, its first, longer, part actually refers to further arrangements regarding the court (cf. above on v. 8).

Amariah as a 'chief priest' in the time of Jehoshaphat is not mentioned elsewhere, but the name is very common among the priests (cf. I Chron. 6.7, 11, 52 [MT 5.33, 37; 6.37]; Ezra 7.3; Neh. 11.4; 12.2, 13, etc.), and is probably connected with the house of Immer, known from the end of the monarchy and the beginning of the Second Temple (Jer. 20.1; Ezra 2.37, etc.). Both the name and patronym of the 'governor' of Judah are very common in the biblical onomasticon. More specifically in Judah is of course 'Ishmael the son of Nethaniah' of the royal family (II Kings 25.25), but nothing can be deduced from these names.

Jehoshaphat mentions that the Levites will serve 'as officers' in the court. These 'officers' (*šoṭᵉrîm*), juxtaposed with the judges, appear in the Bible on several occasions and probably reflect the form of the judicial system (cf. Deut. 1.15; 16.18; Josh. 8.33, etc.). The delegating of this position to the Levites, however, is peculiar to Chronicles (cf. I Chron. 23.4; 26.29; II Chron. 34.13). In two more appearances of *šoṭᵉrîm*, their levitical affiliation is not specified (I Chron. 27.1; II Chron. 26.11).

It is difficult to determine conclusively whether this text reflects a certain historical reality, relevant to some time in the monarchic period (cf. R. de Vaux, *Ancient Israel*, 1968, 153–4), or the Chronicler here expresses his personal view that Levites were entrusted with juridical positions (cf., in particular, I Chron. 23.4). In any case, the Levites clearly form only one contingent of the court personnel. Jehoshaphat concludes his words with spirited encouragement, cf. I Chron. 28.10, 20; II Chron. 25.8; also Ezra 10.4.

Two stylistic features which convey a unified character to the pericope should now be noted. A major element in Jehoshaphat's admonitions is the verb *'śh*, do, repeated five times: 'consider what you do' (v. 6), 'take heed what you do' (v. 7), 'thus you shall do' (vv. 9, 10), and 'have courage and do' (v. 11; RSV 'deal courageously'). This *motif* in fact serves as a framework for the two addresses of Jehoshaphat, as well as for vv. 9–10, where 'thus you shall do' is repeated in an archaic, emphatic form. From all this it is clear that the administration of justice is 'doing', one way of 'doing the word of the Lord'.

The second feature is in the special frequency of the divine name, already extremely common in Chronicles. The name of the Lord is not missing from a single verse, and it is referred to from every possible point of view, each time with a different phrase: 'brought them back to the Lord their God' (v. 4); 'for you judge ... for the Lord' (v. 6); 'let the fear of the Lord be upon you' (v. 7); 'there is ... no perversion with the Lord' (v. 7); 'to give judgment for the Lord' (v. 8); 'in the fear of the Lord' (v. 9); 'incur guilt before the Lord' (v. 10); 'matters of the Lord' (v. 11); 'may the Lord be with the good' (v. 11, RSV 'with the upright'). The concept that 'judgment is of the Lord' here receives full expression, in substance as well as form.

20 After this the Moabites and Ammonites, and with them some of the Me-unites, came against Jehoshaphat for battle. [2] Some men came and told Jehoshaphat, 'A great multitude is coming against you from Edom, from beyond the sea; and, behold, they are in Hazazon-tamar' (that is, En-gedi). [3] Then Jehoshaphat feared, and set himself to seek the Lord, and proclaimed a fast throughout all Judah. [4] And Judah assembled to seek help from the Lord; from all the cities of Judah they came to seek the Lord.

5 And Jehoshaphat stood in the assembly of Judah and Jerusalem, in the house of the Lord, before the new court, [6] and said, 'O Lord, God of our fathers, art thou not God in heaven? Dost thou not rule over all the kingdoms of the nations? In thy hand are power and might, so that none is able to withstand thee. [7] Didst thou not, O our God, drive out the inhabitants of this land before thy people Israel, and give it for ever to the descendants of Abraham thy friend? [8] And they have dwelt in it, and have built thee in it a sanctuary for thy name, saying, [9] "If evil comes upon us, the sword, judgment, or pestilence, or famine, we will stand before this house, and before thee, for thy name is in this house, and cry to thee in our affliction, and thou wilt hear and save." [10] And now behold, the men of Ammon and Moab and Mount Seir, whom thou wouldest not let Israel invade when they came from the land of Egypt, and whom they avoided and did not destroy – [11] behold, they reward us by coming to drive us out of thy possession, which thou hast given us to inherit. [12] O our God, wilt thou not execute judgment upon them? For we are powerless against this great multitude that is coming against us. We do not know what to do, but our eyes are upon thee.'

13 Meanwhile all the men of Judah stood before the Lord, with their little ones, their wives, and their children.

14 And the Spirit of the Lord came upon Jahaziel the son of Zechariah, son of Benaiah, son of Je-iel, son of Mattaniah, a Levite of the sons of Asaph, in the midst of the assembly. [15] And he said, 'Hearken, all Judah and inhabitants of Jerusalem, and King Jehoshaphat: Thus says the Lord to you, "Fear not, and be not dismayed at this great multitude; for the battle is not yours but God's. [16] Tomorrow go down against them; behold, they will come up by the ascent of Ziz; you will find them at the end of the valley, east of the wilderness of Jeruel. [17] You will not need to fight in this battle; take your position, stand still, and see the victory of the Lord on your behalf, O Judah and Jerusalem." Fear not, and be not dismayed; tomorrow go out against them, and the Lord will be with you.'

18 Then Jehoshaphat bowed his head with his face to the ground, and all Judah and the inhabitants of Jerusalem fell down before the Lord, worshipping the Lord. [19] And the Levites, of the Kohathites and the Korahites, stood up to praise the Lord, the God of Israel, with a very loud voice.

20 And they rose early in the morning and went out into the wilderness of Tekoa and as they went out, Jehoshaphat stood and said, 'Hear me, Judah and inhabitants of Jerusalem! Believe in the Lord your God, and you will be established; believe his

prophets, and you will succeed.' ²¹ And when he had taken counsel with the people he appointed those who were to sing to the Lord and praise him in holy array, as they went before the army, and say,

'Give thanks to the Lord,
for his steadfast love endures for ever.'

22 And when they began to sing and praise the Lord set an ambush against the men of Ammon, Moab, and Mount Seir, who had come against Judah, so that they were routed. ²³ For the men of Ammon and Moab rose against the inhabitants of Mount Seir, destroying them utterly, and when they had made an end of the inhabitants of Seir, they all helped to destroy one another.

24 When Judah came to the watchtower of the wilderness, they looked toward the multitude; and behold, they were dead bodies lying on the ground; none had escaped. ²⁵ When Jehoshaphat and his people came to take the spoil from them, they found cattle in great numbers, good clothing, and precious things, which they took for themselves until they could carry no more. They were three days in taking the spoil, it was so much. ²⁶ On the fourth day they assembled in the Valley of Beracah, for there they blessed the Lord; therefore the name of that place has been called the Valley of Beracah to this day. ²⁷ Then they returned, every man of Judah and Jerusalem, and Jehoshaphat at their head, returning to Jerusalem with joy, for the Lord had made them rejoice over their enemies. ²⁸ They came to Jerusalem, with harps and lyres and trumpets, to the house of the Lord. ²⁹ And the fear of God came on all the kingdoms of the countries when they heard that the Lord had fought against the enemies of Israel. ³⁰ So the realm of Jehoshaphat was quiet, for his God gave him rest round about.

31 Thus Jehoshaphat reigned over Judah. He was thirty-five years old when he began to reign, and he reigned twenty-five years in Jerusalem. His mother's name was Azubah the daughter of Shilhi. ³² He walked in the way of Asa his father and did not turn aside from it; he did what was right in the sight of the Lord. ³³ The high places, however, were not taken away; the people had not yet set their hearts upon the God of their fathers.

34 Now the rest of the acts of Jehoshaphat, from first to last, are written in the chronicles of Jehu the son of Hanani, which are recorded in the Book of the Kings of Israel.

35 After this Jehoshaphat king of Judah joined with Ahaziah king of Israel, who did wickedly. ³⁶ He joined him in building ships to go to Tarshish, and they built the ships in Ezion-geber. ³⁷ Then Eliezer the son of Dodavahu of Mareshah prophesied against Jehoshaphat, saying, 'Because you have joined with Ahaziah, the Lord will destroy what you have made.' And the ships were wrecked and were not able to go to Tarshish

2 1 Jehosaphat slept with his fathers, and was buried with his fathers in the city of David; and Jehoram his son reigned in his stead.

A. Notes to MT

[1] מהעמונים, read מהמעונים, cf. LXX^AB; [2] מארם, probably read מאדם; [19] מן בני הקרחים, dittography? [25] בהם, read בהמה with LXX; ופנרים read ובנדים with several MSS.

B. Notes to RSV

[1] 'After this', better NEB 'Some time afterwards'; [6] 'Dost thou not rule', better NEB 'Thou rulest'; [8] 'they have dwelt in it', NEB 'they lived in it'; [13] 'all the men of Judah', MT 'all Judah' (thus NEB); [15] 'Fear not', MT 'Fear you not'; [16] 'east of', JPS 'in the direction'; [18] 'bowed his head, etc.', NEB 'bowed his face to the ground' (MT ויקד); [20] 'believe his prophets', better NEB 'have faith *in* his prophets'; [20] 'in holy array', NEB 'the splendour of his holiness' (cf. also JPS); [24] 'watchtower', better 'lookout' (JPS, MT מצפה); [27] 'every man', better 'all the men' (NEB, JPS); [35] 'After this', better 'Some time afterwards' (cf v. 1); [36] 'He joined him', better 'He joined with him' (cf. v. 35).

C. Structure, sources and form

1. Chapter 20 has two distinct parts:

    (a) 1–30 War with Moab and Ammon
    (b) 31–37 (21.1a) Concluding summary of Jehoshaphat's reign.

The second part is based on I Kings 22.41–47, while for the first no biblical source is extant.

2. The campaign against the eastern coalition of Moab and Ammon is the most lengthy and intricate war story in Chronicles. While the genre resembles II Chron. 13.3–20 and 14.9–15 [MT 8–14], here we find the most thorough development of all the characteristic literary features.

    (*a*) A major part of the Chronistic war narratives is taken by the rhetorical passages uttered by the protagonists, not only where the whole story can be attributed to the Chronicler, but also as additions to accounts adapted from his sources. Thus, for example, the war of Abijah and Jeroboam includes Abijah's long speech (II Chron. 13.4b–12); Asa's prayer is set in his war with Zerah the Cushite (14.11 [MT 10]); a prophetic word of rebuke is appended to Asa's war with Baasha (16.7b–9) and to Jehoshaphat's joint expedition to Ramoth-gilead (19.2b–3); and so on. The present chapter contains the greatest number and broadest variety of rhetorical passages: Jehoshaphat's prayer before the campaign (vv. 6–12); Jahaziel's prophecy of encouragement (vv. 15–17); the king's exhortation to battle (v. 20b); and the singers' doxology (v. 21b). In addition, the narrative makes oblique references to a blessing of the Lord (v. 26) and a song of thanksgiving (v. 28).

    (*b*) In the actual record of the battle, too, the narrative supplies abundant detail, including the following scenes: the enemies' attack (v. 1); how news of it reaches Jehoshaphat (v. 2); the gathering of the people in Jerusalem (v. 4); precise tactical instructions (v. 16); the army's march (v. 20ff.); the enemies' defeat (vv. 22–24); the spoils (v. 25); the ingathering after the combat (v. 26); and the return to Jerusalem (v. 28).

    (*c*) Expressions of piety, in the form of prayers, liturgical music, author's appraisals, etc., are also important features of this genre, and they are so numerous in this pericope as practically to dominate the story: Jehoshaphat determines 'to seek the Lord' (v. 3) and proclaims a fast (v. 3); Judah assembles 'to seek help from the Lord' (v. 4); the king prays (vv. 6ff.); both ruler and people bow low and fall down, 'worshipping the Lord' (v. 18), while the sacerdotal groups 'praise the Lord' (v. 19);

Jehoshaphat makes a declaration of faith (v. 20) and appoints singers 'to the Lord' (v. 21); the people bless the Lord after the battle (v. 26) and return 'to the house of the Lord' (v. 28).

3. The extreme literary elaboration of every possible aspect of the narrative has its counterpart in the representation of the war as an event of the grandest proportions, and this without the recourse to numbers found in similar war narratives. Here, it is emphasized that the enemy comprises three peoples rather than one (v. 1, etc.), a 'great multitude' (vv. 2, 12, 15, 24), while the people of Israel involved in the event include not only the men of all Judah (v. 4), but also 'their little ones, their wives and their children' (v. 13). The destruction of the enemy is complete: 'they were dead bodies lying on the ground; none has escaped' (v. 24), and the spoil was so great that 'they could carry no more' (v. 25). Likewise, the war has the most significant political results: 'And the fear of the Lord came on all the kingdoms of the countries' (v. 29).

4. The concept of 'holy war' as a form-critical term, implying both a sociological *Sitz im Leben* and a literary genre, has been suggested by many scholars as a framework for understanding the Chronicler's war narratives (cf. G. von Rad, *Holy War in Ancient Israel*, Grand Rapids 1991; Dillard, 154–61; also in the literary connotation of the concept, Williamson, 291–301 passim). The application of this concept, however, is qualified by a clear differentiation between the strict literary genre and broader theological presuppositions. The tenet that human wars and their outcome are in fact determined by divine intervention is common to all literary strata in the Bible, whether or not a war is presented within the genre-framework of a 'holy war'. Notwithstanding this general tenet, biblical war narratives in general display an intertwining of divine and miraculous aspects with realistic record, in varying measures. Thus, although victory or failure may be ascribed to God, the military terms employed enable the reader to adduce some information concerning the fighting forces, the course of the battle, the tactics, the scope of victory or failure, and so on.

For the Chronicler, 'war' is by definition God's domain: 'the battle is not ours but God's' (v. 15). For man, armed conflict is a divine test, one more arena demanding concrete expression of religious integrity. The Chronicler's main interest lies in the degree to which man has passed the test, his religious stature deciding the war's results; the concrete aspects of the confrontation are in fact of marginal significance. For the modern historian, interested in pragmatic data, the Chronistic stories are therefore unattractive; their overwhelmingly religious approach invites a verdict of imaginative fiction. (For an alternative presentation of this disposition, cf. Wellhausen, 191–2, and Welten, 140–53.)

5. As so often in Chronicles, the questions of source and authenticity are here of major importance and have been extensively discussed (cf. D. L. Petersen, *Late Israelite Prophecy*, 1977, 70–1). By now it is clear that the narrative is characteristically Chronistic: details of language, style, literary formulation and theology will be discussed in the commentary. The question of sources applies, then, only to the framework of basic data, around which the broader composition is built. Were these data invented freely by the Chronicler to serve his own theological purposes, or was he working with existing material?

It has been long recognized that this chapter displays a solid geographical logic (cf. Z. Ilan, 'Jehoshaphat's Battle against Ammon and Moab', *Beth Mikra* 53, 1973, 205–11*, and the critique of R. North, 'Does Archeology Prove Chronicles' Sources?', in

Festschrift J. M. Myers, 1974, 382, 392). The locations, which are either precisely or approximately identifiable, provide a clear setting for the assumed events: 'the sea' (i.e. the Dead Sea) and Hazazon Tamar/En-gedi (v. 2), the wilderness of Tekoa (v. 20) and the ascent approaching it from the rift valley (v. 16). This geographical setting, however, even when appreciated as authentic, has received various historical interpretations: as reflecting a Nabataean invasion in the third century (cf. M. Noth, 'Eine palästinische Lokalüberlieferung in 2 Chr 20', *ZDPV* 67, 1944/5, 45–71), or an authentic encounter during the monarchic period (Rudolph, 258–9, followed by Myers, Williamson and Dillard).

6. Postponing detailed arguments until the commentary, I shall here briefly summarize my attitude:

(*a*) The concrete details reflected in the story are clearly weighty enough to indicate the existence of a source utilized by the Chronicler. In view of the Chronistic work as a whole, this was most probably a source concerning the history of the Judaean kings, with information of a political, economic and administrative nature.

(*b*) In contradistinction to the Deuteronomistic historiography, this source seems to have comprised only short chronicles, not developed literary compositions. The Chronicler has either preserved the dry economic form of this material (for wars – cf. for example II Chron. 21.16–17; 26.6–7; 27.5), or, alternatively, elaborated the material in comprehensive narratives, bearing distinctly the marks of Chronistic composition. Again, for wars, we have, in addition to this chapter, the confrontation between Abijah and Jeroboam, Asa and Zerah, and Ahaz and Israel.

(*c*) While the new literary formulation has rendered it impossible to establish with any precision the scope and wording of the text which the Chronicler was using, we may still establish with relative confidence the relevant concrete facts, and, keeping in mind the Chronicler's literary and theological methods, reach some conclusions about the historical nucleus.

7. The structure of the chapter's first part is as follows:

A. 1–4 Introduction: the background
   1–2 the invasion
   3–4 the people assemble in Jerusalem
B. 5–19 The assembly in Jersualem
   (*a*) 5 Jehoshaphat in the midst of the congregation
      6–12 Jehoshaphat's address
      13 the people's prayer
   (*b*) 14 Jahaziel's inspiration
      15–17 the prophecy
      18–19 response: worship and thanksgiving
C. 20–28 The war
   (*a*) 20a going forth to battle
      20b Jehoshaphat's address
      21 the singers and their doxology
   (*b*) 22–24 the victory: the enemies fight and destruction
      25 the spoiling
   (*c*) 26 end of the war: the blessing of the Lord
      27–28 return to Jerusalem
D. 29–30 Conclusion

8. In vv. 31ff. the Chronicler returns to his source, using the Kings' record of Jehoshaphat's entire reign (I Kings 22.41–47) as a concluding summary (cf. above). Although the Chronicler's adaptation is clearly distinguishable in this section as well, neither the information nor the implications concerning Jehoshaphat's figure are fully integrated into the narrative which precedes.

The reworking of the passage is apparent: some of the elements in Kings were omitted, some are enlarged, elaborated or changed in various ways. The mode of reworking reflects the peculiar combination of servile adherence to the source-text and constant change and adaptation. The order of the source is followed step by step, with the Chronicler handling each unit in its turn:

| I Kings 22.41a | (41b synchronism) 22.42 | 22.43 | 22.44a | 22.44β (change) |
| II Chron. 20.31a | (omitted) | 20.31b | 20.32 | 20.33a | 20.33b |

| 45 | 46aα | 46aβ | 46b | 22.47, 48 | 22.49, 50 (change) | 22.51 |
| (omitted) | 34aα | 34aβ | 34b | (omitted) | 20.35–37 | 21.1 |

9. The function in Chronicles of 21.1 should be further noted. The parallel in I Kings 22.51 concludes Jehoshaphat's record, with the next verse moving to the record of Ahaziah, king of Israel. In Chronicles, the reference to Jehoshaphat's death and burial certainly pertains to this pericope. However, from a literary-syntactical point of view, it also serves to introduce the next unit, referring to Jehoram, as a grammatical continuum: 'He (Jehoram) had brothers, the sons of Jehoshaphat ...' (21.2). We have seen the same literary phenomenon elsewhere, in verses which, like two-faced Janus, both conclude the preceding unit and introduce the next (cf. 14.1 [MT 13.23]; 17.1; 19.4, etc.). In this way, pericopes are linked one to the other, rather than being clearly distinct.

D. Commentary

[1] The formulaic opening 'It happened some time afterwards' (NEB; RSV 'After this') is common in biblical narratives to signify a continuation of the story when the events are not really connected (Judg. 16.4; I Sam 24.6; II Sam 2.1, etc.). It is found, *inter alia*, in II Samuel, and in the parallels in Chronicles (II Sam. 8.1; 10.1; 21.8//I Chron. 18.1; 19.1; 20.4), in II Chron. 24.4, and with variations in II Chron. 20.35; 32.1. This literary convention is thus still a living function of the Chronicler's literary repertoire.

Jehoshaphat is attacked by the Moabites and the Ammonites and 'with them of the Ammonites' (MT; RSV 'some of the Meunites'). The MT is certainly corrupt; *mēhā'ammōnîm* may be viewed either as representing a gloss or conflation, or a textual corruption, easily explained, of an additional third name: Meunites (*mᵉ'ûnîm*). The latter is generally accepted (already Kimhi *ad loc*; also RSV), mainly because of the LXX rendering as Μιναίων, which points to a different reading from MT, and because of the consistent reference to three components of the enemy's fighting forces, the third element being 'the men/inhabitants ... of mount Seir' (vv. 10, 23).

The 'Meunites' are found elsewhere in Chronicles, in II Chron. 26.7 for the time of Uzziah, and with a variation of the *Qere* and *Kethib* in I Chron. 4.41, for the time of Hezekiah. They are also mentioned as a family of temple servants with the alternation of *Kethib* and *Qere* in Ezra 2.50, and as 'Meunim' in the parallel of Neh. 7.52.

The exact ethnic and geographical identification of 'the Meunim' is a matter of controversy (cf. I. Ephal, *The Ancient Arabs*, 1982, passim; Williamson, 293–294; Dillard, 156), but if the Chronicler's information is to be taken seriously, they constitute a nomadic group living on the southern borders of Judah, mentioned in I Chron. 4.41 together with the Hamites, and in II Chron. 26.7 with the Arabs. It may be only coincidental that the first of these references juxtaposes the 'Meunim' with the Simeonites' expedition to Mount Seir – a connection which may be confirmed by the present context. The connection with the Arabs, occupying the southern border-territories of Palestine, recurs in Tiglath-pileser's inscription, from the second half of the eighth century (Eph'al, 79–80, but cf. E. A. Knauf, 'Mu'näer und Meuniter', *WO* 16, 1985, 114–22). All in all, there is a quite impressive uniformity of references, while their precise location – on the east or the west side of the Arabah – cannot be conclusively determined, and may have actually shifted through the years. Here they are connected with 'Mount Seir', but it is clear throughout that they are distinct and separate from the Edomites. The link with Moab and Ammon (cf. also v. 10) may indicate some eastern region, south of the Dead Sea (but cf. Williamson's arguments for a western identification of 'Mount Seir', 294 and bibliography, and Dillard, 155–6).

A war of the kind presented here is most plausible in view of the historical background supplied by both biblical and extra-biblical evidence (II Kings 1.1; 3.5 and Mesha's inscription). After the death of Ahab, the Moabite revolt probably succeeded in establishing Moab's independence from Israel since the campaign launched against it ended indecisively (II Kings 3.27). The waxing of Moab's strength during the active rule of Mesha may have catalysed a military expedition against Jehoshaphat, Israel's ally. It should be noted that Edom does not join this war, since at this time it is still a dependency of Judah (I Kings 22.48; II Kings 8.20–22); it is only 'of the Meunites', 'inhabitants of Mount Seir' who actually participate. Moreover, the unsettled situation on Judah's eastern border may be already implied in 17.10–11, in which only peoples on Jehoshaphat's southern and western borders are mentioned, later complemented by a reference to his alliance with the northern kingdom (18.1). Nothing is said about the eastern border, which had long been the focus of all the military efforts of both Judah and Israel: Aram in the north (I Kings 22 – II Chron. 18), Moab to the south (II Kings 3), and then a coalition of Moab and Ammon.

An invasion of Judah from the direction of the Dead Sea also has a certain military logic, although in the end it seems to have been disastrous for the invading armies. Only three of the fortified cities ascribed to Rehoboam are situated in this area: Bethlehem, which is quite in the interior of the hill-country, Etham and Tekoa. Despite the difficult terrain, this weakness in the fortification system along the available east-west routes may have encouraged the invaders, and actually determined their course.

[2] The report which reaches Jehoshaphat contains several precise details. The direction of the invading host is 'from beyond the sea', that is, from the territories east of the Dead Sea (MT 'from Aram' should probably be restored to 'from Edom', as already RSV, but cf. Williamson, 294). The invaders have already forded the water, are camped in 'Hazazon-tamar' and are preparing to invade the hill country of Judah. The location of En-gedi is well known, while 'Hazazon' may reflect what is known as the 'valley of Hazazah' (Ilan, 206), with the descriptive 'tamar' referring probably to an oasis of palm-trees there. All these details provide a solid geographical background for the narrative.

Contrary to other elaborate stories in Chronicles, no numbers are reported, either of the invading force or, later, of the Judaean army. The enemy is constantly referred to as a 'multitude' (*hāmōn*, vv. 1, 12, 15, 24), and the attribute *rāb* ('great, many') is used to qualify not only the host of the attackers but the spoil as well (v. 25). One wonders whether the term *hāmōn* may designate not only great numbers, but also the manner of their attack – a 'horde' (thus NEB) rather than an organized military array.

[3] Jehoshaphat's reaction is absolutely non-military. In a psychological state of great fear, he is reluctant to take any tactical initiative, and his attitude of total resignation is expressed best in his own words: 'We do not know what to do' (v. 12). At the same time, he is not utterly passive; he bestirs himself to ask help of the Lord, and even proclaims a fast throughout his kingdom – the strongest expresson of human soul-searching and complete surrender to God. In both of these aspects, Jehoshaphat's behaviour bears a distinct Chronistic stamp. I have noted above that in both the Deuteronomistic historiography and Chronicles itself, Jehoshaphat is seen as a keen and active fighter (cf. in particular, I Kings 22.45); his passive attitude in the present context is certainly tendentious and, since the army is all ready for battle (v. 21), contrary to the historical context itself (cf. below).

[4] The phrasing of this verse is instructive for the Chronicler's ideals: the people 'assembled … from all the cities of Judah' without actually having been summoned! Not only Jehoshaphat, but his subjects as well, handle the situation precisely as they should, responding spontaneously to the emergency by gathering in Jerusalem 'to seek the Lord'.

[5–19] This larger unit is composed of two smaller sections (vv. 5–13 and 14–19), each with a rhetorical focus: Jehoshaphat's prayer and Jahaziel's prophecy, respectively. Each section has a narrative framework (vv. 3 and 13;

vv. 14 and 18–19); vv. 18–19, with their longer formulation, also conclude the whole unit.

[5] The 'new court' is not mentioned elsewhere, so we cannot know its place or provenance. The juxtaposition 'Judah and Jerusalem' is very common in Chronicles, repeated emphatically in the present narrative in various phrases (cf. vv. 15, 17, 18, 20, 27). The people are also designated by the more general terms 'Judah' (vv. 4, 24) or 'all Judah' (vv. 3, 13), the term 'Israel' appearing in this context only four times, vv. 7, 10, 19 and 29. Thus, the Chronicler's inclination to variation is well evidenced, even within the framework of a uniform terminology.

[6–12] Jehoshaphat's long prayer bears the stamp of a Chronistic literary piece. Its dominant feature is its persuasive tone – an emotionally forceful rhetoric, aiming to convince the Lord that the situation requires his intervention. This plea, however, appeals neither to God's compassion nor to his favour; rather, it demands justice. Jehoshaphat emphasizes the treacherous nature of the invasion and the rightness of Israel's cause, and ends with the call 'wilt thou not execute judgment upon them' (v. 12). The prayer is in fact built on antithesis: powerful and treacherous invaders against a powerless but righteous Israel; helpless humans pleading with an omnipotent Lord.

The argument is developed in three stages, a rhetorical device which also determines the literary structure of the prayer. These stages are of gradually decreasing length, with the climax in the last and shortest. Verses 6–9 establish a general theological basis for the argument, vv. 10–11 define the nature of the threat, and v. 12 presents the plea for intervention.

The invocation which opens vv. 6–9 has characteristically Chronistic phrasing, perfectly suited to the occasion: 'O Lord, God of our fathers'. This is followed by two passages, formulated as rhetorical questions. The first, beginning with 'Art thou not God ...?', is in fact a series of four nominal statements of divine attributes (v. 6). The second, 'didst thou not... drive out? etc. (v. 7), in a narrative style, defines the relationship between the Lord and his people, and guarantees the people's privilege to appeal to God for help.

Verses 10–11 move on to the second stage of Jehoshaphat's argument, with the characteristic formula 'and now'. Here, too, the description of the enemy threat is phrased in two parts (vv. 10 and 11), each beginning with the introductory term 'Behold'. The topic is the scope and inherent injustice of the attack.

The final chord of the prayer is struck in v. 12, the actual supplication. It opens again with an invocation ('O our God'), followed by a rhetorical question ('Wilt thou not execute judgment?'), concluding with an explanation ('For we are powerless').

The structure of the prayer may be illustrated as follows:

O Lord, the God of our fathers
   Art thou not... .
   Didst thou not... .
And now
   behold...
   behold
O, our God ...
   Wilt thou not ...
   For we are ...

[6] After the characteristic invocation, Jehoshaphat establishes a series of divine attributes, most relevant to the occasion. Within the limits of language, he strives for maximum abstraction, by defining these attributes with nouns (the most proximate verbal form being the participle *mōšēl*, ruler), and formulating a series of nominal rather than verbal clauses. The theological assumptions of this passage are that God alone rules over the world, he alone determines the fortunes of every single nation, and no one can withstand him.

The first clause, 'Thou art God in heaven' (RSV preserves the question form), expresses a common biblical concept (cf. Ps. 2.4; 115.3; Eccl. 5.2 [MT 5.1], etc.). However, the verse as a whole is closest to another text by the Chronicler himself; cf.

v. 6: 'Art thou not God in heaven / thou rulest (NEB) over all the kingdoms of the nations / In thy hand are power and might / none is able to withstand thee.'

I Chron. 29.11–12: 'For all that is in the heavens and in the earth is thine ... / thou rulest over all / in thy hand are power and might / in thy hand it is to make great.'

The affinities are unmistakable, but so are the differences. The final statement in this context refers to the specific crisis at hand (cf. also II Chron. 14.11 [MT 10]), while the phrasing 'thou rulest over all the kingdoms of the nations' provides an explicit basis for Jehoshaphat's eventual appeal. The echoes of the text associated with the great David his ancestor, and with the preparations and free-will offerings for the Lord's Temple, provide an implicit undercurrent for Jehoshaphat's appeal.

[7] The second paragraph takes the argument of the first one step further. As God is all-powerful, he drove out the inhabitants of the land before his people. The shift from an ontological to a historical statement is effected by a new introduction, 'Didst thou not ...', and by the transition from nominal to verbal clauses: 'drive out ... give, dwelt, built, comes, stand, cry, hear and save'.

In the gift of the land to the people of Israel, the specific terminology creates a close affinity between this text and Isa. 41.8, cf: 'Israel my servant / Jacob, whom I have chosen / the offspring of Abraham, my friend'.

That Israel inherits the land because of kinship to Abraham 'the Lord's friend' is a concept expressed even more emphatically in Ezek. 33.24, although with no literal affinity to the Isaiah context. This is also the main theme of I Chron. 1–9: the occupation of the land from of old, beginning with the patriarchs.

The terminology of this verse, with the two dominant verbs 'drive out' and 'give', is clearly based on Deuteronomy, with its recurring formulaic reference to the giving of the land (Deut. 1.8, 21; 4.1, 5, 21–22, etc.). The conceptual framework, however, differs from Deuteronomy in the addition of 'for ever', which is not applied in Deuteronomy to the inheritance of the land, and in the different historical context: where Deuteronomy refers it to Joshua and his generation, this context extends it to the offspring of Abraham.

[8–9] Jehoshaphat now moves directly to the next major historical reference point, the building of the Temple, basing himself directly on the phraseology and concepts of Solomon's prayer. Here, the true culmination of the people's settlement in their land is the construction of the Temple, which in turn ensures a constant line of communication through which the people may plead for and secure God's saving aid.

Jehoshaphat conceives of his present situation as a concrete illustration of Solomon's prayer, the main elements of which are then summarized in these verses: 'building the house', 'for the name', 'if evil comes', 'stand before this house', 'before thee', 'cry', 'hear' and 'save'. It is noteworthy, however, that even this faithful epitomization of Solomon's appeal still introduces some change in the concept of prayer. While Solomon stresses repeatedly that the people will pray 'toward the house' and that God will hear 'in heaven, his dwelling place' (I Kings 8.30 etc.), Jehoshaphat emphasizes the Lord's presence within the Temple: 'We will stand before this house, and before thee, for thy name is in this house.' In what may seem redundant language (cf. the suggestion of BH to omit *lᵉkā*, 'thee', in v. 8), Jehoshaphat makes very clear that the Temple built 'for thy name' is built 'for thee', with the implication that to 'stand before this house' means to stand before God himself. The image of the Lord hearing 'from heaven', a major aspect of Solomon's prayer, is passed over in silence.

Note also the literary technique employed in vv. 8–9, replacing an objective, third-person, statement with a direct speech in the first person: 'If evil comes upon *us*, *we* will stand ... etc.' The effect of this manner of quotation is not only a tone of authenticity, but a level of identification with those who in fact built the Temple for our sake: they are 'us' and we are 'they'.

Of the various circumstances listed in Solomon's prayer, Jehoshaphat refers only to calamities, of which he mentions three or four. The more common triad is 'sword, famine and pestilence' (cf. *inter al.* Lev. 26.25–26; Jer.14.12; 27.8; Ezek. 6.11–12, etc.). However, the unique *šᵉp̄ōṭ* (of which *šᵉp̄uṭīm* of Ezek. 23.10 may be a plural) could be taken as the designation of a fourth calamity (so RSV), in the light of Ezek. 14.21: 'I send upon Jersualem my four sore acts of judgment'. The distribution of the conjunctive *waw* in this verse would support a reading 'the sword of judgment' (RSV margin).

[10–11] With a clear change of tone, indicated by 'and now', Jehoshaphat now moves from the declaratory statements of vv. 6–9 to the present, with its impending calamity. This is the 'evil', the 'affliction', which the ancient generation has foreseen; it is this which forces him to apply the right of Israel to make an urgent appeal to the Lord. The attack is described, not as a common campaign for a limited military victory or territorial gains, but as a total war, a threat to the very existence of Israel in its land (cf. A. Rofé, 'Eretz Israel at the Beginning of the Second Commonwealth', *Cathedra* 41, 1986, 5*). Jehoshaphat recalls events from the past, when these same three peoples were left unharmed because the people of Israel obeyed the commandments of the Lord. They owe their very survival to God's providence and Israel's piety, and should have been, if not grateful, at least compliant with God's plans. Instead, they repay the Israelites (Jehoshaphat uses the very term – *gōmᵉlīm*, RSV 'reward'), by threatening to do what the Israelites themselves, following God's instruction, refrained from doing. The ingratitude of the invaders is also a direct affront to God's plans for the world. In 'coming to drive us out of thy possession' they violate the Lord's designs when he established 'the bounds of peoples' (Deut. 32.8). The argument is based on Deut. 2; there is a close affinity to the phrasing in that context: 'because I have given mount Seir to Esau as a possession' (Deut. 2.5); 'because I have given Ar to the sons of Lot for a possession' (v. 9 referring to Moab, v. 19 to Ammon), and to Jephthah's words in Judg. 11.15–27.

It is noteworthy that the Chronicler, moved perhaps by a sense of special significance, deviates here from his general practice when he makes reference to a precedent from the past, the Exodus. Several points should be made about this reference:

(*a*) The Exodus is not presented as the constitutive event in Israel's history, but merely as a chronological marker, for the events here recorded.

(*b*) The passage deviates from the two common formulas, 'bring up out of Egypt', or 'go forth from', and applies the more neutral phrase 'come from'.

(*c*) The inheritance of the land is not connected to the Exodus, but to the 'descendants of Abraham' on the one hand and to the building of the Temple on the other.

[12] The last part of Jehoshaphat's prayer, the appeal, opens again with an

invocation. The king asks not for victory in battle but for vindication of his claims: that God may 'judge them' (NEB). The unique use of *špṭ*, 'judge', with the preposition *bᵉ* (*tišpoṭ bām*), in place of the common accusative, probably informed the RSV's rendering 'execute judgment against them' (JPS 'punish them'). Even with this semantic nuance, the root *špṭ* is well chosen to carry the whole burden of the plea.

There is a literary bond with preceding passages: Jehoshaphat refers to his own position, 'for we are powerless' creating a perfect antithesis to v. 6, 'In thy hand are power and might'. 'Against this great multitude that is coming against us' clearly refers back to 'a great multitude is coming against you' (v. 2), completing the circle.

Jehoshaphat's petition is a long sentence, with clear stylistic marks. On the one hand, it is a chain of clauses, linked by various particles: 'wilt thou not ... for we are powerless ... and we do not know ... for our eyes ...' This seemingly monotonous chain, which is broken in translation into three independent sentences in order to render it more dramatic, is very carefully structured. The sentence opens with an emphatic vocative ('O, our God'), and closes with an emphatic nominal clause, 'our eyes [are] upon thee'; these two phrases sum up the spirit of the appeal. The long sentence is further structured in two parts, each ending with a causative clause beginning with *kī*:

'O Our Lord, wilt thou not ... for (*kī*) we are powerless
and we do not know ... for (*kī*, RSV but) our eyes are upon thee.'

Jehoshaphat acknowledges his weakness: he has neither power nor knowledge of what course he should take. He approaches the Lord with a double request: to execute judgement upon the enemy, and to instruct his own people in the right path.

We have seen several times that there is a set procedure for 'inquiring of the Lord' before going forth to war. For example, David asks 'shall I go up against the Philistines' (II Sam. 5.19), and the Lord either confirms his plan, denies it, or gives him further instructions (II Sam. 5.23; cf. also I Kings 22.6, 15 and the parallels in Chronicles). The assumption is that the king knows his own wishes and asks for approval and instructions. Jehoshaphat's expressions of humble helplessness are a striking contrast.

The whole attitude of Jehoshaphat's prayer summarizes one of the interesting paradoxes of the Chronicler's thought. As I have amply shown, the Chronicler's historiography attributes military power and activity to righteous kings. Jehoshaphat himself was earlier described as equipping and manning the fortified cities (17.2, 12, 19) and recruiting an army of over a million warriors (17.14–19). At the same time, the pious king is expected not only to possess military strength but to forego its use and to rely only on God for protection. This paradox may illustrate the comprehensiveness of the religious element in the Chronicler's historical philosophy.

[13] This verse returns to the description of the ceremony in v. 5; the 'assembly of Judah' is a gathering of the entire families. This is a practical fulfilment of the situation described in the king's prayer: 'If evil comes upon us ... we will stand before this house and before thee' (v. 9); here, indeed, 'all Judah ... stood before the Lord'. One wonders if the root *'md*, especially in its conjunction with *lipnē yhwh*, 'before the Lord', had already acquired at this stage the specific connotation of 'standing in prayer', from which the later term for the regular daily prayer was derived ('Amidah', cf. *EJ* II, 1971, 839).

[14] The statement that 'the Spirit of the Lord came upon Jahaziel' may imply that Jahaziel was not a regular prophet, but a singer inspired spontaneously in the midst of the assembly, to bring God's message to the king and people. The figure of Jahaziel has many artificial features: his name, 'the one who sees God', his affiliation with the singers, who are conceived in Chronicles as prophets (I Chron. 25.1, 2, 3, 5), and his direct descent from Asaph, the assumed head-singer of David's time, all point to the 'literary' nature of his figure. With this affiliation he is linked to the Temple, and more specifically to the Temple's music – both of which play significant roles throughout the narrative.

The name 'Jahaziel' is unique; a lineage of five generations links him, through a series of common levitical names, to Mattaniahu 'of the sons of Asaph', a name affiliated with Heman (I Chron. 25.4, 16), and with Asaph in all other instances (cf. Neh. 11.17//I Chron. 9.15; II Chron. 29.13; Neh. 11.22; 12.35; 13.13).

[15–17] Jahaziel's prophecy, a Chronistic composition, is modelled on what may be defined as a 'salvation oracle' (cf. in detail Williamson, 297–9, who seems to regard it as an authentic sample of the genre; also Dillard, 154–5). It is a perfect response to all the significant points of Jehoshaphat's prayer, each point repeated twice: there is encouragement of people and king, as an opening and concluding address (vv. 15, 17), a declaration that 'the war (RSV battle) is God's' (vv. 15, 17), and accurate instructions on how to proceed (vv. 16, 17). This repetition may be schematized as ABC-B'A'C', that is, a chiasm for the first two elements ('fear not', 'the battle is not yours'), and a concluding place for the third: 'tomorrow go out against them'. On the anthological style of the address, cf. on v. 17.

[15] The style here shows deviations from previous prophetic declarations. Jahaziel addresses first the people – in their longer definition as 'all Judah and the inhabitants of Jerusalem' – and only then the king (cf. by contrast 13.4 and 15.2). Also, Jahaziel opens with 'hearken' (*haqšību*) rather than the more common 'Hear me' (*šᵉmāʿûnî*), which is reserved for Jehoshaphat's exhortation in v. 20. In this the verse depends on prophetic and poetic

precedents: 'hearken' often comes after, and parallel to, 'hear' (Isa. 34.1; 49.1, Hos. 5.1, etc.), but may also appear, although more rarely, first (cf. Isa. 51.4; Jer. 18.19 etc.; RSV renderings confuse the issue).

The direct second person address is very much emphasized throughout Jahaziel's speech. The opening formula 'thus says the Lord' is broadened by the addition of 'to you', and the prophetic formula 'Fear not' is preceded by an emphatic 'you' (omitted by the translation). *lākem* ('for you') is then repeated twice more in 15b and 17a, together with *'immākem*, with you (17a, 17b).

Jahaziel's message first gives the Lord's response to Jehoshaphat's over-whelming fear. The Chronicler here employs the common formula of which he also makes use elsewhere (I Chron. 22.13; 28.20; II Chron. 32.7), so well-suited for the present military context. It will become clear presently that the text is an adaptation of Moses' exhortation at the crossing of the Sea, in Exod. 14.13–14. The tone of confidence is not due to an under-estimation of the danger; Jahaziel in fact repeats literally Jehoshaphat's description of the enemy armies: 'this great multitude'. Hope stems rather from the conviction that God, responding to Israel's appeal, regards this war as his own, an attitude repeated five times in this short prophecy, in both negative and positive expressions: 'the battle is not yours but God's', 'you will not need to fight', 'the victory of the Lord on your behalf', 'the Lord will be with you'. Notice the emphatic conclusion of the first verse with a nominal explanatory clause, and the succession of two particles *kī*, the second serving in place of *kī 'im*: 'for (*kī*) the battle is not yours but (*kī*) God's'.

[16] To Jehoshaphat's last cry 'we do not know what to do', Jahaziel responds with detailed instructions. The enemy will be approaching Judah *via* the 'ascent of Ziz', and Jehoshaphat and the people are told to meet them 'at the end of the valley, facing (RSV east of) the wilderness of Jeruel'. Although these place-names are unique and therefore cannot be pin-pointed, they portray an accurate view of the terrain.

The position of Jehoshaphat 'at the end of the valley', and the assumed march of only one day from Jerusalem, seem to allow the invaders a substantial progress into the Judaean hills – a strategy demanding considerable restraint of the Israelites. Eventually, however, the enemy's hard climb of over one thousand metres in altitude from the Dead Sea up difficult paths into the Judaean wilderness would give Jehoshaphat the natural strategic advantage of a superior topographical position and a rested army ready to confront an exhausted and disorganized crowd. These realistic tactical details, which probably reflect the original setting of the battle, are now put in Jahaziel's oracle. They are soon to become immaterial, since – as the story proceeds – there is really no need for Jehoshaphat to fight at all.

Although neither 'the ascent of Ziz' nor 'Jeruel' is explicitly attested in biblical sources, the latter may be implied as the aetiological basis of Gen. 22 (cf. H. Gunkel, *Genesis*, 1910, 241–2). Much of the story of the binding of Isaac seems to be phrased as a popular etymology of some name like Jeruel, employing the verbs *r'h* (see) and *yr'* (fear), and referring repeatedly to 'God':

> Gen. 22.4 'Abraham ... saw (*wayyar'*) the place far off'; v. 8: 'God will provide himself (*'elōhīm yir'eh lō*) the lamb for burnt offering'; v. 12: 'I know that you fear God' (*y'rē' 'elōhīm*); v. 13: 'Abraham ... looked' (*wayyar'*); v. 14: 'Abraham called ... that place "The Lord will provide" (*yhwh yir'eh*), as it is said: on the mount of the Lord it shall be seen (*b'har yhwh yērā'eh*)'.

[17] This verse, continuing as it does the statement of v. 15, has long been recognized as a paraphrase of Moses' exhortation:

Exod. 14.13–14	*II Chron. 20.17*
Fear not, stand still	Take your position, stand still,
and see the salvation	and see the salvation
of the Lord which he	of the Lord
will work for you today.	on your behalf.
The Lord will fight for you	Fear not
and you have only to be still.	and be not dismayed.

While v. 16 implied active military measures ('Tomorrow go down against them'), this verse counsels a total passivity: 'stand still and see'. The unmistakable echoes of the crossing of the Red Sea, and the repetition of the verb 'stand', probably referring back to vv. 9 and 13, highlight the Chronicler's view of this battle as a pure miracle. Finally, just as 'Israel saw the Egyptians dead upon the seashore' (Exod. 14.30), the present battle ends with a similar sight: 'behold ... dead bodies lying on the ground; none had escaped' (v. 24).

Jahaziel's oracle concludes with a final vocative, containing the central elements of the speech: 'Fear not, go out against them', and with a final assurance: 'the Lord will be with you'.

[18] Jehoshaphat's reaction fits perfectly not only the circumstances but his own character as portrayed in our context; both he and 'all Judah' fall down, bowing themselves before the Lord, an act which the Levites accompany with a united voice of thanksgiving. The whole structure is a perfect chiastic conclusion to the scene begun in v. 14: there Jahaziel the Levite/ singer stands up in the crowd to address 'all Judah and the inhabitants of Jerusalem', and the king; here, the response follows the opposite order with precisely the same participants, defined in precisely the same terms: first the king, then 'all Judah and the inhabitants of Jerusalem', and finally, the Levites with their song.

Jehoshaphat's reaction here is a powerful gesture of piety: he does not delay his praise and thanksgiving until the battle has proven God's promise. His trust in the Lord is such that he is content with the prophetic assurance that his prayer has been heard. Whatever follows will be the inexorable consequence of the divine response.

In v. 13, neither Levites nor priests were specifically mentioned, but the inclusive phrase 'all Judah' and the location of the assembly in the Temple courts certainly presume their presence.

This verse describes the singers as 'Levites, of the Kohathites and the Korahites'. The term *min bᵉnē haqqᵉhatīm* (literally, 'of the sons of the Kohathites'), is found elsewhere only in II Chron. 34.12; other expressions of affiliation to Kohath are much more common (I Chron. 6.33 [MT 6.18]; 9.32; 15.5, etc.). *min bᵉnē haqqoḥīm*, 'the sons of the Korahites', is unique, the more common form being either 'the sons of Korah' or 'the Korahites' (Ps. 87.1; I Chron. 9.19, 31; etc.). While the Korahites are better attested as gatekeepers (I Chron. 9.19, 31; 26.1, etc.), the reference to the 'sons of Korah' in the titles of numerous psalms surely reflects historical circumstances (Ps. 42.1; 44.1; etc.). In Chronicles, 'Korah' as a singer represents one stage in the genealogical line connecting the head-singer Heman to the house of Kohath (cf. on I Chron. 6.22, 37 [MT 6.7, 22]). The separate appearance of the 'Korahites' is difficult, and may be due to textual corruption, a dittography of *min bᵉnē haqqᵉhatīm* (differently, in the constructions of J. M. Miller, 'The Korahites of Southern Judah', *CBQ* 32, 1970, 58–68; H. Gese, 'Zur Geschichte der Kultsänger am Zweiten Tempel', in *Von Sinai zum Zion*, 1974, 147–58; also Dillard, 158).

The reference to a segment of the singers accords well with the arrangement of the liturgical music of the Second Temple, with the service rotating among the divisions.

[20–28] This third section of the narrative describes the actual battle as engaged within the framework of a religious procession. Of the story's four parts, the first and the last form the setting: the going out to war (vv. 20–21) and the return (vv. 27–28); the inner two scenes describe the actual events on the battlefield: the actions of the enemy (vv. 22–23), then those of Judah (vv. 24–26). Although basically a narration, involving many verbal expressions of action, even this part contains two rhetorical passages: Jehoshaphat's final address to the people (v. 20b) and the singers' praise (v. 21b).

[20] Jehoshaphat acts out Jahaziel's prophecy to the letter. His instructions were 'tomorrow go out', and here, indeed, we read 'they rose ... and went out'. The king in fact goes beyond literal obedience: 'he rose in the morning'. This is not only an authentic way to act in desert conditions (cf. Gen. 19.2; Josh. 6.15; Judg. 7.1; I Sam. 29.10, etc.), but also a literary sign of his vigilance (cf. Gen. 22.3). Jehoshaphat's words of encouragement to the army

are also beyond what the prophet counselled; they are a firm declaration of trust, and attest to the profound transformation wrought in Jehoshaphat as a result of the Lord's intervention. The fearful and bewildered victim of circumstances has become a decisive leader.

It has been long recognized that the king's exhortation is based on the words of Isaiah to Ahaz in Isa. 7.9: 'If you will not believe, surely you shall not be established.' And yet there are several differences between the two utterances. Isaiah's demand for complete faith is phrased as a warning, with a negative condition: 'If you will not believe ...'. Here, there is a positive admonition: 'Believe ... and you will be established.' Isaiah's brief statement is elaborated into a two-colon parallel passage, in which the play on the root *'mn* is continued in 'believe in (NEB) his prophets', and climaxes with 'you will succeed'. Most important of all is this addition of faith in the prophets to trust in God; while strictly related to the context, it nevertheless reflects a major tenet of the Chronicler's attitude towards prophecy: the prophets themselves are objects of faith.

This short passage bears abundant marks of the Chronicler's hand: the anthological composition, the characteristic address 'hear me', the favourite reference to 'success', the threefold *'mn*, and the context-related definition of the people as 'Judah and the inhabitants of Jerusalem'.

[21] Another step taken by Jehoshaphat on his own initiative is the appointment of 'singers to the Lord', not merely accompanying the army, but leading in the vanguard. This feature of the story is unique, and Jehoshaphat's procedure is highly instructive. The Chronicler's familiar 'democratizing' tendency has already been amply illustrated in this story, with its constant reference to the active participation of the people. Here, however, this tendency is epitomized, with the king actually taking counsel with the people in a matter of military tactics, or cultic activity, ordinarily defined as a kingly prerogative. After having been made his full partners in his initiative and responsibility, his subjects will deservedly share the reward of victory.

[22–24] These verses present the realistic-military aspect of the war: they describe how in fact the foe was defeated and the victory won. In essence, the enemy forces utterly annihilated one another: first the people of Moab and Ammon rose against those of Mount Seir, and then they turned against each other, until all were destroyed.

We find similar descriptions of self-destruction in several other biblical contexts. In II Kings 3.23, the Moabites assume – mistakenly – that in the Israelite camp 'the kings have surely slain one another', and this is also the picture in Judg. 7.22; I Sam. 14.20. In this case, the fatal confusion is attributed to an anonymous 'ambush' which the Lord set against the invading army – interpreted by some scholars as meaning the intervention of superhuman entities (cf. for references Japhet, *Ideology*, 130 and n. 373; Williamson, 300). This idea does not accord with the available evidence and common linguistic usage. The Chronicler never claims the intervention of super-human forces in human enterprises. As for $m^{e^,}ar^eb\bar{\imath}m$, this always means 'people in ambush'; the most similar passage to the present text is Judg. 9.25: 'And the men of Shechem put men in ambush against him on the mountain tops, and they robbed all who passed by them along that way.' This story should be interpreted in a similar manner: as they approached the wilderness of Judah, the enemy armies were set upon by people in ambush. Caught off-guard, the invaders were easily defeated, their rout followed by mutual suspicion and self-destruction. In the end, the war itself is executed by human agents, first the men in ambush, then the invading forces destroying one another.

This realistic report, which certainly seems likely to anyone familiar with the difficult terrain between the Dead Sea and the Judaean hills, is obfuscated by the Chronicler, who sees the ambush as a miraculous event, motivated by the Lord at the very moment when the singers began to praise him.

The Chronicler has chosen a series of strong verbs to express the destruction. First 'they were routed' and then 'destroying utterly', 'made an end', 'destroy'. It is therefore only to be expected that when Jehoshaphat and his people come to the 'watchover' (*miṣpeh*) overlooking the desert, they find the invading host a heap of lifeless bodies.

[25–26] All energies are now turned to the spoiling, which lasts for three full days. However, even the excitement of victory and the enormous spoil do not turn the people from the path of faith and devotion. On the fourth day they all gather again to bless the Lord.

This last clause, 'therefore the name of that place has been called the 'Valley of Beracah (=blessing) to this day', is a rare case of marked aetiological phrasing in Chronicles. Although the Chronicler favours homiletical interpretations of names, there are only few instances of explicit derivations (I Chron. 11.7; 14.11//II Sam. 5.20), and only one other narrative is of an aetiological nature (I Chron. 4.9). The term 'aetiological' implies a certain literary process in which an existing name inspires a secondary tradition intended to establish the supposed origin of the name. In this case, however, the role of 'blessing' is only marginal, and it is certainly not the motivative force of the narrative (cf. B. O. Long, *The Problem of Etiological Narrative in the Old Testament*, 1968, 10–11). It would seem, rather, that this uncharacteristic passage belongs to the stratum of the Chronicler's source-material. Whether in that context the aetiology in fact inspired the tradition of the great victory or was added to an essentially historical story is beyond our power to determine.

[27–28] The people assembled in the house of the Lord before going out to battle; now they return to the same place. The march is characterized by music and, above all, by 'joy', the perfect expression of whole-heartedness.

[29–30] These verses conclude the narrative with a description of the broad ramifications of the event for Jehoshaphat and his people. While v. 29a is almost a repetiton of 17.10, there are several differences. According to 17.10, 'the fear of the Lord fell on all the kingdoms ... *round about Judah*', and according to the Chronicler's portrait, Jehoshaphat could boast peace only on three sides of his kingdom. In the present chapter, these limitations are no longer necessary, so we read 'the fear of God came on all the kingdoms of the countries', an awe inspired by the Lord's battle 'against the enemies of Israel'. Now, after the victory on the eastern frontier, Jehoshaphat's kingdom reaches the blessed state of 'peace' and 'rest round about' – the ideal to which every generation aspires.

It may be appropriate to add at this point some general remarks about the chapter's language. On the whole, the Chronistic linguistic idiom may be best characterized as a mixture of 'classical' syntax – of a rather 'archaized' nature – with a multitude of non-classical forms and syntactic usages. This mixture may be best illustrated by the regular use of 'the' biblical narrative tense, imperfect with *waw* consecutive, shifting all along to the use of perfects, together with the increased usage of the infinitive with various prepositions. We should also note the ample use of causative clauses, appearing after the main clause, which have been discussed above (cf. vv. 8, 10, 12, 15, 26, 27, 29), and of course, the peculiar vocabulary.

[31–37] With this last section of Jehoshaphat's history, the Chronicler returns to his source in I Kings 22.41–47, with certain omissions, additions and changes of detail. The unit is composed as follows:

31 Biographical summary (I Kings 22.41a, 42)
32–33 General religious appraisal (I Kings 22.43–44)
34 Reference to additional sources (I Kings 22.46)
35–37 The shipping enterprise (I Kings 22.48–49 [MT 49–50])
21.1 Jehoshaphat's death and his successor (I Kings 22.50 [MT 51]).

[31] The note in Kings, synchronizing Jehoshaphat's reign with that of the king of Israel, is omitted, as always in the Chronicler's historiographical system; that Jehoshaphat and Ahab were contemporaries is still abundantly clear from the story in ch. 18.

[32–33] The appraisal of Jehoshaphat's reign from a religious, specifically Deuteronomistic point of view, is also taken verbatim from I Kings 22, with the final clause replaced. This appraisal is centred upon two themes: the comparison of Jehoshaphat's piety with that of his father Asa, and the issue of the high places. In the specific handling of both these themes, a certain tension arises between the data peculiar to Chronicles and that deriving from his Deuteronomistic source.

The comparison with Asa is problematical. In the Deuteronomistic historiography Asa is regarded as a blameless king, with the one reservation that the high places were not removed in his day (I Kings 15.11–14). The comparison of Jehoshaphat with his father (I Kings 22.43) is therefore very positive, over-shadowed only by this one failure. By contrast, in Chronicles, Asa is not as perfect, and there is a clear tension between the great piety which marked most of his reign and the increasing guilt of his old age. Jehoshaphat, on the other hand, is in Chronicles a righteous king throughout; the single transgression of joining northern Israel (ch. 18) is pardoned because of his overall merit (19.3). Chapters 19–20, which depict the aftermath of that transgression, are a tribute to Jehoshaphat's uprightness and devotion. The comparison with Asa his father at this point is in fact detrimental to his positive appraisal. The Chronicler pointed to the difference between the two kings in his remark in 17.3: 'he walked in the *earlier ways* of ... his father'. All this may illustrate how the Chronicler's dependence on a variety of sources, and his inclination to verbatim citations, prevent the achievement of an overall textual harmony.

The same feature is also attested by the issue of the high places. The reservation 'the high places, however, were not taken away' is a faithful reflection of the situation as related in Kings, but is rather meaningless in Chronicles. We were told in 17.6 that Jehoshaphat 'took the high places out of Judah', while here we hear the opposite. It is hardly likely, given Jehoshaphat's exemplary conduct, that he restored the local cults himself in the interim. Nevertheless, the note (taken verbatim from I Kings 22.43 [MT 44]) remains, with uneasy consequences for the modern reader.

The only change that the Chronicler does introduce here is in the second colon of the verse in Kings, 'the people still sacrificed and burned incense on the high places', a cultic observation which the Chronicler replaces with a more spiritual judgment: 'the people had not yet set their hearts upon the God of their fathers'. This explanation of motive is characteristic of the Chronicler and contains two of his favourite idioms, 'God of their fathers' and 'set their hearts' (*hēkīnū lᵉbābām*) , and follows the typical technique of opening a sentence with a citation from the Chronicler's source (*wᵉ῾ōd hā῾ām*, 'and still the people'), only to supply a different continuation.

Even after this reworking, v. 33 still creates a certain tension with what comes before. Throughout Jehoshaphat's history, and especially in ch. 20, the people – who play an important role in the historical record – are very favourably portrayed. Jehoshaphat sent envoys who 'taught among the people' (17.9), and he himself 'went out among the people' (19.4) to instruct and guide them. The people's conduct in the war with Ammon and Moab was above reproach. And yet, the passage still claims that the people did not achieve the desired moral standard. We discern here, behind the textual inconsistency arising from the method of adaptation, the Chronicler's realistic awareness of the difficulty of complete devotion. For the people to 'set their hearts' purely on their Lord is an extremely difficult goal, and even after all the efforts of Jehoshaphat, it has not been completely achieved.

[34] The reference in Kings to Jehoshaphat's 'peace with the king of Israel' was transferred to an earlier passage in Chronicles (18.1–2). The Chronicler now cites the reference to sources, introducing two changes. In the Kings text, the individual characterization of Jehoshaphat with 'his might that he showed and how he warred' (I Kings 22.45), which highlights his figure as a warrior king, is replaced by the standard formula 'from first to last'. As for the source to which the reader is referred, it is described in more length: 'the chronicles of Jehu the son of Hanani, which are recorded in the Book of the Kings of Israel'.

This allusion, together with II Chron. 32.32, provides an important indication of the actual source which the Chronicler used. So far the Chronicler has defined his sources as either books written by prophets (for the reigns of David, Solomon, Rehoboam and Abijah), or a work bearing a general title 'the book of the Kings of Judah and Israel', for the reign of Asa (16.11) – which will be referred to in similar titles for some of the succeeding kings. In this verse (and in 32.32), the 'chronicles' of a prophet are viewed as a specific section of the overall 'Book of the Kings of Israel'. If we take these notices seriously, we may conclude that the source which the Chronicler was using was some kind of a 'chronicle' from the monarchical period, which he conceived as having been written by successive generations of prophets.

[35–37] Again omitting the references to male prostitutes and the exact political status of Edom at that time (the latter serving in I Kings 22 as a background for the following passage), the Chronicler now turns to the episode of the ship-building. This is in fact the only episode from Jehoshaphat's reign which the Deuteronomist historiographer recounts in the context of his 'Jehoshaphat pericope'; typically, it appears in I Kings 22 as an 'appendix', just before the record of Jehoshaphat's death. The date of the event may be established with no difficulty, since Ahaziah the king of Israel ascended the throne in the seventeenth year of Jehoshaphat and ruled over Israel for only two years (I Kings 22.51 [MT 52]). It is interesting that the Chronicler, who elaborated the story of Jehoshaphat extensively, does not lift this item from its original context and reintegrate it into his own narrative.

The general topic of the story in both contexts is the same: the initiative of Jehoshaphat in a maritime expedition to Ophir, and the wreck of the vessels before setting sail. The book of Kings has added another matter: the proposition of Ahaziah to join Jehoshaphat in this enterprise, and Jehoshaphat's refusal. This story presents the Chronicler with both a historical and a theological problem. In I Kings 22.49–50 Ahaziah's proposal to join the expedition comes – illogically enough – after the ships have been wrecked. Furthermore, there is no effort to interpret these events in the light of any general theoligical system.

The Chronicler adapts the existing elements of this brief story from several angles. The wreck of the fleet is interpreted as punishment, the reference to Ahaziah as an allusion to sin, and the whole is reorganized into a meaningful theological sequence. Where I Kings 22.50 claims that Jehoshaphat refused to co-operate with Ahaziah, the Chronicler presents Jehoshaphat as having in fact initiated the joint ship-building enterprise. In the present version, then, the sequence of sin – prophecy – punishment is exemplified: Jehoshaphat joins with Ahaziah in an 'evil' project; he is warned by the prophet; and finally all his work was destroyed.

This is not the first case in which the Chronicler utterly reverses an existing text. His motivation seems to be his own sense of 'probability' – the conviction that this was indeed the correct order of the events, and thus forms a 'better' literary, historical and theological sequence.

Although, following his source, the Chronicler places this passage within the concluding summary of Jehoshaphat's reign, it is nevertheless given a measure of narrative autonomy by the conventional opening formula: 'Some time afterwards' (NEB of v. 1; RSV 'After this'). The theme of the story is indicated, in the Chronicler's stylistic strategy, by a repetition of 'join' (*ḥbr*) three times: 'joined with Ahaziah' (v. 35), 'joined him in building' (v. 36) '… because you have joined' (v. 37); 'make' or 'do' (*'śh*) four times (in vv. 35–37 this root is rendered by 'did', 'building', 'built', 'made'); and lastly, 'ships' three times (vv. 36, 37).

There is also a difference between the two versions in the definition of the ships. 'The ships of Tarshish' of I Kings 22.49 are clearly a particular type of vessel; the destination of the expedition was to be 'Ophir', in an attempt by Jehoshaphat to repeat his great-grandfather's achievement (I Kings 9.26–28; 10.11, 22). For the Chronicler, 'ships of Tarshish' denotes a fleet sailing to Tarshish (cf. also II Chron. 9.21: 'for the king's ships went to Tarshish'); this explains the Chronicler's omission of 'to go to Ophir', which is replaced by 'to go to Tarshish'. 'Tarshish' may originally have been a Medtereranean port, but for the Chronicler it is certainly somewhere along the shores of the Red Sea, according to the generally accepted location of the more common 'Ezion-geber' near to 'Eloth on the shore of the sea, in the land of Edom' (II Chron. 8.17; cf. I Kings 9.26).

The sinful nature of Jehoshaphat's co-operation with Ahaziah is spelled out for the reader, first of all in the Chronicler's own parenthetic comment 'he did wickedly' – a judgment which prepares the reader for the consequences. Then there is an explicit statement of Eliezer, phrased as a 'prophetic perfect': 'because you have joined ... the Lord *destroyed*', translated properly (but less decisively) 'the Lord will destroy'.

Although very brief, the prophecy of Eliezer the son of Dadavahu is phrased in a recognizable late, Chronistic idiom. The syntax is marked by the use of the infinitive with the explicative or temporal preposition, and a pronominal suffix. These repesent a complete clause: $k^e hith abberk\bar{a}$ (literally 'as your joining', RSV 'because you have joined'). The prophetic word is organically linked to the narrative framework by the phrase 'join ... with' (*'thbr*), which in this specific declension and preposition is peculiar to Chronicles. It is thus clear that one hand is responsible for the little story throughout, including the prophecy.

The fulfilment of the prophecy is immediate: the ships are unable to proceed.

The prophet Eliezer is not known from any other place, and his patronymic, Dodavahu, is unique. This is probably the full form of the hypocoristic Dodai or Dodo (Judg. 10.1; II Sam. 23.9, 24; I Chron. 11.12, 26; 27.4); one man by this name was the father of two of David's warriors, of whom one was named Eleazar.

I have already referred to the historiographical significance of the inclusion of this and similar stories in Chronicles. Jehoshaphat's failure to imitate Solomon casts a negative reflection on the king's ability, and yet the brief note in I Kings 22.49–50 does not draw any further theological conclusions. This is where the Chronicler felt a difficulty and a need for reformulation. However, the theological coherence gained through adaptation is obtained at the price of Jehoshaphat's moral reputation: the failure of his enterprise is explained as the result of religious misconduct. Considering the stature of Jehoshaphat in Chronicles, the contradiction thus created poses a greater dilemma than the original difficulty of I Kings 22.49–50. One wonders, therefore, why the Chronicler did not follow the simple procedure of omitting the story altogether. There seems to be only one response: the Chronicler considered it imperative to include in his history every item of information regarding the northern kingdom, presented from the perspective of Judah. This should then be regarded as a major motivation in his historiographical scheme.

[21.1] In full parallelism with I Kings 22.51, the story of Jehoshaphat's reign ends with his death, burial and the accession of his son, Jehoram. The citation from Kings is verbatim (with the omission of one word). On the literary function of this verse as a transition from Jehoshaphat to Jehoram, cf. above, p. 785.

21 Jehoshaphat slept with his fathers, and was buried with his fathers in the city of David; and Jehoram his son reigned in his stead. [2] He had brothers, the sons of Jehoshaphat: Azariah, Jehiel, Zechariah, Azariah, Michael, and Shephaniah; all these were the sons of Jehoshaphat king of Judah. [3] Their father gave them great gifts, of silver, gold, and valuable possessions, together with fortified cities in Judah; but he gave the kingdom to Jehoram, because he was the first born. When Jehoram had ascended the throne of his father and was established, he slew all his brothers with the sword, and also some of the princes of Judah. [5] Jehoram was thirty-two years old when he became king, and he reigned eight years in Jerusalem. [6] And he walked in the way of the kings of Israel, as the house of Ahab had done; for the daughter of Ahab was his wife. And he did what was evil in the sight of the Lord. [7] Yet the Lord would not destroy the house of David, because of the covenant which he had made with David, and since he had promised to give a lamp to him and to his sons for ever.

8 In his days Edom revolted from the rule of Judah, and set up a king of their own. [9] Then Jehoram passed over with his commanders and all his chariots, and he rose by night and smote the Edomites who had surrounded him and his chariot commanders. [10] So Edom revolted from the rule of Judah to this day. At that time Libnah also revolted from his rule, because he had forsaken the Lord, the God of his fathers.

11 Moreover he made high places in the hill country of Judah, and led the inhabitants of Jerusalem into unfaithfulness, and made Judah go astray. [12] And a letter came to him from Elijah the prophet, saying, 'Thus says the Lord, the God of David your father, "Because you have not walked in the ways of Jehoshaphat your father, or in the ways of Asa king of Judah, [13] but have walked in the way of the kings of Israel, and have led Judah and the inhabitants of Jerusalem into unfaithfulness, as the house of Ahab led Israel into unfaithfulness, and also you have killed your brothers, of your father's house, who were better than yourself; [14] behold, the Lord will bring a great plague on your people, your children, your wives, and all your possessions, [15] and you yourself will have a severe sickness with a disease of your bowels, until your bowels come out because of the disease, day by day."'

16 And the Lord stirred up against Jehoram the anger of the Philistines and of the Arabs who are near the Ethiopians, [17] and they came up against Judah, and invaded it, and carried away all the possessions they found that belonged to the king's house, and also his sons and his wives, so that no son was left to him except Jehoahaz, his youngest son.

18 And after all this the Lord smote him in his bowels with an incurable disease. [19] In course of time, at the end of two years, his bowels came out because of the disease, and he died in great agony. His people made no fire in his honour, like the fires made for his fathers. [20] He was thirty two years old when he began to reign, and he reigned eight years in Jerusalem; and he departed with no one's regret. They buried him in the city of David, but not in the tombs of the kings.

22 And the inhabitants of Jerusalem made Ahaziah his youngest son king in his stead; for the band of men that came with the Arabs to the camp had slain all the older sons. So Ahaziah the son of Jehoram king of Judah reigned.

A. Notes to MT

[2] ישראל, Sebirin, MSS and Versions יהודה; [6] בת, proposed: אחות; [11] בהרי, probably read בערי with Sebirin, MSS and Versions; [22.1] למחנה, proposed למלחמה.

B. Notes to RSV

[3] 'king of Judah', MT 'king of Israel', cf. A above; [4] 'had ascended the throne of his father', better 'rose against the kingdom of his father', cf. commentary; [9] 'and his chariot commanders', MT differently; [14] 'people', better 'family'; [16] 'stirred up ... the anger', MT 'stirred up the spirit' (JPS), cf. I Chron. 5.26; II Chron. 36.22; 'Ethiopians', MT 'Cushites' (so NEB); [20] 'with no one's regret', cf. commentary.

C. Structure, sources and form

1. The history of Jehoram is based on the material found in II Kings 8.16–24, which the Chronicler adopts with light changes and the omission of two verses (16, 23). Rather than presenting it in a single sequence (as, e.g., 20.31–37), the Chronicler places the borrowed material at the beginning, middle and end of the present story (vv. 1, 5–10a, 20a and 22.1b). The addition of the intermediate sections, in vv. 2–4, 10b–19, 20b and 22.1a, brings the Jehoram narrative to three times its original scope. The interesting interweaving of the various elements into one coherent structure differs from all the preceding histories of individual kings.

2. The formulation of the pericope adheres closely to the framework of the Deuteronomistic source. The opening reference to Jehoram's accession is taken literally from I Kings 22.50b [MT 51b], but is similar in content to II Kings 8.16b; the conclusion of the passage (22.1b) represents II Kings 8.24 and 25b. The intervening material comprises three blocks: vv. 5–10a are taken from Kings, while vv. 2–4 and vv. 10b–22.1a (with the exception of 20a) are original. The structure of this new pericope, however, cuts across these units and should be seen as follows:

1b-5   Jehoram's accession, and the establishment and length of his reign
6–7   Religious appraisal
8–10   Political disturbances:
    8–9 Edom
    10 Libnah
11   Jehoram's further sins
12–15 Elijah's epistolary prophecy
16–17 Further disturbances
18–20 Jehoram's disease, death and burial
22.1   Ahaziah's accession.

3. The literary structure of the chapter is determined throughout by its underlying theological logic. The tight sequence (sin – punishment – further sin – warning – realization of warning – conclusion) reflects the almost iron-bound theological system of the Chronicler's most basic convictions; there is no doubt here about the Chronistic composition of the pericope. The question of sources should be discussed within this framework: did the Chronicler have any sources for the non-synoptic material?

4. This non-paralleled material includes: (*a*) religious admonitions and appraisals (found in one block in vv. 10b–15), and (*b*) various historical data referring to Jehoram's character and the events of his reign (vv. 2–4, 16–20, 21.1a). Both categories may be characterized as 'negative': the history of Judah, from the moment of Jehoram's accession until his death, is cast in black. This negative tone is marked with exceptional emphasis at the two ends of Jehoram's reign: his first steps as ruler (v. 4) and last illness (vv. 18–20) are unparalleled in the entire history of the monarchical period.

This enhancement and the addition of negative material in the portrayal of Jehoram is certainly as Chronistic a technique as the antithetical attribution of numerous positive traits to kings appraised *a priori* as 'righteous' rulers. It is no wonder, then, that scholars have questioned the authenticity of both categories of additional material (cf. Welten, 173–4). Could the Chronicler have derived his data from actual sources, or are they not to be traced to the circumstances of the author's time, and, especially, to his theological convictions and creative imagination?

5. In dealing with the new material, the rhetorical sections and religious appraisals which give direct expression to the Chronicler's attitudes should be distinguished from his historical facts. Regarding the latter, one should take into consideration the principle of 'choice' in the Chronicler's method: even when he applies himself to the Deuteronomistic history, the choice of material is governed by clear priorities. Thus, even had 'positive' elements about Jehoram been available in his sources, it is doubtful whether he would have cited them. Furthermore, the integration of his source material into the narrative is also in accordance with his own views. Taking all this into consideration, I would hesitate to categorize all the new material as stemming from the Chronicler's 'creative imagination' before scrutinizing its historical probability. In fact, even the highly tendentious material added to the history of Jehoram fits well with the data of Kings. With all due caution, the suggestion that the Chronicler had some source for his history of Jehoram provides the better starting point for understanding the present passages (cf. further in the commentary).

6. One further literary note: 22.1 serves a function similar to that of 21.1, linking the histories of Jehoram and Ahaziah by concluding one and introducing the other. Since, however, 22.2 has its own distinct subject, 22.1 properly belongs to the passage which it concludes.

D. *Commentary*

[1] Cf. above.

[2–4] The procedure of royal succession is a problem dealt with in the Deuteronomistic history on only two occasions: Solomon's accession (I Kings 1–2) and the challenge to the Davidic dynasty in the time of Ahaziah –

Athaliah – Joash (II Kings 11). In addition to these cases, the Chronicler also treats of the subject in regard to the succession of Rehoboam by Abijah (II Chron. 11.21–23) and, here, of Jehoshaphat by Jehoram.

The passage refers to events during the reign of Jehoshaphat and the early years of Jehoram. Like his great-grandfather Rehoboam (11.22–23), Jehoshaphat already during his lifetime addresses himself to the question of succession: he appoints his firstborn Jehoram as heir-apparent, and at the same time disperses his other sons throughout the fortified cities of Judah. The authenticity of these actions is conceded by virtually all scholars (cf. Welten, 193–4).

Besides Jehoram, v. 2 records only six more sons of Jehoshaphat; this is unlikely to be the full total of his male offspring. The names cited in the record probably represent only the 'firstborn', similar to the list of David's sons in II Sam. 3.2–5 (and parallels). The view that each of the names here stands for the firstborn son of one of Jehoshaphat's wives, each holding a privileged status, with certain prerogatives, may explain some of the features of the following events.

The period spanned by Jehoram, Ahaziah and Athaliah brought with it the most severe crisis in the history of the Judaean monarchy – excepting only the Destruction itself. Facing utter extinction (cf. below), the Davidic dynasty is saved only by the intervention of Jehoshabeath, the daughter of Ahaziah, on behalf of her brother Joash, and by the revolt led by the priest Jehoiada (II Kings 11//II Chron. 22–23). The threat felt in Judah emanated from the northern dynasty established by Omri and known as 'the house of Ahab' – pressing now for the inclusion of Judah as one component, or a secondary partner, of northern Israel, under the rule of an 'Omride'. The tensions within the royal household of Judah are best interpreted against this background of dynastic rivalry and competition. What may have begun as a friendly alliance between Jehoshaphat and Ahab now threatens to annihilate the Davidides and their followers in Judah.

In II Kings, these same facts are connected almost exclusively with the reign of Athaliah and her planned effort to extinguish all survivors of the house of David (II Kings 11.1). The material added in Chronicles places the beginning of the struggle almost ten years earlier, with the death of Jehoshaphat and the accession of Jehoram.

The rather peculiar phrasing of v. 2 refers to Jehoram's brothers not from his own point of view, but as 'sons of Jehoshaphat' (cf. the same tone in v. 13: 'you have killed your brothers, of your father's house'). The implication may be that these were only half-brothers of Jehoram, whose different mothers – unlike Jehoram's – were affiliated with Judaean families of long standing.

Two of the brothers have the same name: 'Azariah/u'; one of these may be a corruption (cf. II Chron. 22.6, where the MT *^{a}zaryāhū* is certainly wrong –

corrected in RSV: Ahaziah), or the same name may have been given to sons of two different mothers (cf. the sons of David, I Chron. 14.5, 7).

[3] There is clear emphatic antithesis between all the other brothers, who received 'great gifts', and Jehoram himself, who inherited the kingdom 'because he was the first-born'. From the earlier account (II Chron. 11.21–22) in which Rehoboam chose Abijah to rule after him, although Abijah was explicitly *not* the king's first-born, one may deduce that between Rehoboam and Jehoshaphat the right of primogeniture had become normative. We have no specific information on subsequent generations of Davidic kings, but it seems that this norm was eventually taken for granted.

The transfer of the royal offspring to the fortified cities seems to serve several purposes: the crown prince Jehoram is spared the presence in the capital of possible rivals, and a smooth, controlled succession is assured; at the same time, the placement of personages representing the royal interest is thus effected in key-points throughout Judah. According to the Chronicler, Jehoshaphat made the fortified cities key administrative, economic, military and juridical centres, and the appointment of his sons there as commanders or governors is part of the same policy.

[4] Jehoram's reign is ushered in with systematic bloodshed; his accession is marked by the peculiar phrase *wayyāqōm ... 'al mamleket 'ābīw*. The term *qūm 'al* is used throughout the Bible as 'rise against' (cf. Deut. 19.11; Judg. 9.18; I Sam. 17.35; Amos 7.9, etc., Baumgartner, 1016, 3c). This is the only case where this idiom is used of a king *vis à vis* his own kingdom; to consolidate his control, Jehoram 'rose *against* the kingdom of his father and slew all his brothers ... and also some of the princes of Israel'. The animosity of this usage is ignored in the translations' neutral renderings: 'When Jehoram had ascended the throne of his father' (RSV); 'Joram was firmly established on his father's throne' (NEB). Jehoram's destructive tendency in his own realm is later emulated by his wife Athaliah upon the death of her son (II Kings 11.1//II Chron. 22.10); we may detect here the seeds of a movement which was to reach its climax a hundred years later in the time of Ahaz (cf. Isa. 7.5–6).

[5] In the following verses the Chronicler returns to his source in Kings, faithfully presenting II Kings 8.17–22. Contrary to the Deuteronomistic routine so far, the standard reference to the king's mother is not included, and she is later referred to by her patronymic 'the daughter of Ahab' (v. 6).

[6] The religious crisis connected with Jehoram's rule is emphatically portrayed in the Deuteronomistic historiography. After his two predecessors, Jehoshaphat and Asa, the new era beginning in Judah with Jehoram is marred by the introduction of Baal-worship, at the initiative of the royal family itself. This form of paganism, termed consistently 'the way of the kings of Israel', was imputed to 'the house of Ahab', and was introduced into

Judah – according to the Deuteronomist – through a marriage alliance: 'for the daughter of Ahab was his [Jehoram's] wife' (II Kings 8.18, 27; cf. also 16.3; 21.3).

The same alliance is referred to in II Chron. 18.1; the Israelite partner in that union, i.e. Athaliah, is 'the daughter of Ahab' in II Kings 8.18, probably by his wife Jezebel. This note, however, contradicts the assertion of II Kings 8.26 (and the parallel in II Chron. 22.2), that Athaliah was the 'daughter of Omri' (MT *bat 'omri*), that is, Ahab's sister. The Peshitta accordingly renders in this verse 'the *sister* of Ahab', a reading preferred by some commentators (cf. Rudolph, 264). However, while chronological considerations are perhaps not conclusive, a general historical perspective nevertheless prompts me to accept the Massoretic version. The RSV rendering 'grand-daughter of Omri' reflects a legitimate interpretation of *bat* as 'grand-daughter'. Along the analogy of 'the house of Omri', we should probably regard *bat 'omri* as meaning 'an Omride'. The thorough penetration of Baal-worship into Judah and the attempt at a political and religious coup can only be explained if Athaliah was indeed Ahab's daughter by Jezebel, and not merely his sister.

[7] The wording of this verse differs somewhat from II Kings 8.19, and the two versions should be examined carefully. The Kings text reads: 'The Lord would not destroy *Judah* for the sake of David his servant', a difficult reading from several angles. 'For the sake of David' is characteristic of a specific Deuteronomistic stratum; it occurs several times in the book of Kings in the context of the survival of the Davidic kingdom and dynasty (I Kings 11.12, 13, 32, 34; 15.4; also II Kings 19.34; 20.6; Isa. 37.35). This text is the only instance in which the divine motive 'for the sake of David' applies to providential care of 'Judah' rather than the preservation of the monarchy. Moreover, the narrative setting does not imply any danger to 'Judah'; one can understand 'the Lord would not destroy *Judah*' only in a very general and indirect way. The version of Chronicles, by contrast, 'The Lord would not destroy *the house of David*', is in full accord with both linguistic/stylistic evidence and the historical context; for the first time since the division of the kingdom, the existence of the 'house of David' is seriously threatened by a confrontation with 'the house of Ahab'. In political and religious circum-stances such as these, one expects the Deuteronomistic recollection of God's promise to David. In terms of textual originality, then, Chronicles takes priority over II Kings 8.19; the verse enunciates a major historiosophical and theological statement: God's promise to David will determine future developments in defiance of human schemes.

This verse contains the only mention in Chronicles of 'the covenant ... made with David'. Its essence is a fundamental divine obligation 'to give him and his sons a lamp for ever'. The explicit interpretative clause of I Kings

15.4 makes it clear that here, too, this metaphor means 'to set up his son after him', establishing a continuous, unbroken Davidic dynastic line.

[8–10] The political disasters of Jehoram's reign begin with the Edomite revolt, a clear-cut antithesis to the brief note from Jehoshaphat's reign: 'There was no king in Edom; a deputy was king' (I Kings 22.47). As would be expected, Jehoram undertakes a military campaign against the Edomites, but the difficult, probably corrupt, version of II Kings 8.21 (cf. v. 9) permits no conclusive reconstruction of the encounter.

According to II Kings 8.21 Jehoram (RSV Joram) goes forth with a chariot force to subdue the Edomite insurrection. Two contradictory statements follow: 'he (Jehoram) smote the Edomites' (RSV), and 'the people fled to their tents' (NEB). Then in the following verse it is stated that Edom's revolt has become a *fait accompli*. The questions are self-evident: if Jehoram smote the Edomites, why did the people flee? And how did the Edomites succeed in their revolt? This contradiction seems to arise from a minor textual corruption. An original *wayyakkeh 'ōtō 'ᵉdōm* ('The Edomites smote him', cf. BH, BHS, also NEB) has been corrupted into the present MT by the omission of one letter (*'tw* → *'t*). In the original story, then, it was the Edomites who routed Jehoram's chariot force in a surprise night raid, causing the total failure of his expedition.

The Chronicler's *Vorlage* was the present text of II Kings 8.21; he introduced two changes, omitting 'his army (or: the people) fled home (literally 'to their tents')', and replacing 'to Zair' by 'with his commanders' (cf. further below). According to the Chronicler's portrayal, Jehoram indeed smote the Edomites who had surrounded him, but could not put down the revolt; Edom's independence became a fact 'to this day'.

The Kings' text 'to Zair' (*ṣā'īrāh*) becomes in Chronicles 'with his commanders' (*'im śārāw*), a change which may be explained as initially of an orthographic nature. An original *ś'īrāh* ('to Seir') may have been corrupted to *'im śārāw*, although some scholars would propose *ṣo'arāh* = 'to Zoar', as an original reading (cf. Cogan/Tadmor, *II Kings*, 96). Be this as it may, the Chronicler's reading accords well with his inclination to limit the royal exclusivity of action by positing an explicit co-operation between the king and the people or their representatives.

[10] The phrase 'to this day' views Edomite independence from a certain distance; Amaziah's campaign against the Edomites, not too many years later (II Kings 14.7), was once again to reverse the situation.

The revolt of Libnah is seen as a result of the Edomite uprising, and a continuation of the Judaean kingdom's increasing loss of control on all fronts. The case of Libnah is of particular interest, as it was a Canaanite city-state, mentioned in Josh. 10.29–30 as one of Joshua's conquests in the Shephelah, between Makkedah and Lachish. Its king is duly recorded among the thirty-

one Canaanite rulers subdued by Joshua (Josh. 12.15). It is also presented as a
levitical town (Josh. 21.13; I Chron. 6.57 [MT 6.42]), and as one of the towns
of Judah (Josh. 15.42). The allusion to revolt may imply that Libnah kept its
Canaanite character and was not absorbed into the Judaean kingdom; its
inhabitants regarded Judaean rule as foreign, and were ready, when the
opportunity was right, to seize their independence. This single recorded
episode may raise far-reaching questions regarding the absorption and integration of Canaanite cities into Judah, and the meaning of their inclusion in
the lists of Judaean and levitical cities. Unfortunately we do not have enough
information to answer these questions, nor even to determine whether such
an incident was characteristic or exceptional.

With the last clause of v. 10b, the Chronicler again takes up the pen,
explaining all the disasters of Jehoram's time within a theologically meaningful framework, as punishment for royal sins. Both the introduction of Baal
worship and Jehoram's political failures are already found in the Deuteronomistic source; the Chronicler's contribution is to link them into a meaningful chain of cause and effect.

[11] The general statement of v. 10, 'because he had forsaken the Lord', is
here made more specific: 'he made high places in the hill country (or the
towns) of Judah'. There follows a solemn statement of two pregnant phrases
in parallel (wayyezen 'et yošᵉbē yerūšālayim / wayyaddaḥ 'et yᵉhuddāh) , the
stylistic solemnity of which is lost in translation (but cf. JPS).

In general, 'high places' are less central in Chronicles than in the Deuteronomistic historiography, and their construction was certainly a lighter sin
than 'walking in the ways of the kings of Israel', an accusation previously
levelled against Jehoram (v. 6). In the present context, however, the worship
at high places plays a specific and theologically significant role. In the book of
Kings this is essentially a transgression of the people. In the case of six of
Judah's righteous kings, their integrity is challenged by the reservation: 'the
people were still worshipping on the high places' (I Kings 22.43 [MT 44];
II Kings 12.3 [MT 4]; 14.4; 15.4, 35; also I Kings 15.14). This is the basis for
the Chronicler's statement: Jehoram's special guilt was in his wilful and
malicious incitement of the people to the wrong way. More than any other
king – even Manasseh (cf. II Chron. 33.9) – Jehoram is presented as
intentionally leading the people astray. Of the two causative verbs wayyezen
and wayyaddaḥ, the first is found in Chronicles only in the present context,
where it is repeated three times (also v. 13), and the second appears only once
more (II Chron. 13.9). The RSV rendering of wayyezen, 'led … into
unfaithfulness', is a circumlocution for the idea of 'incitement to whoredom',
an expression used especially by Hosea, Jeremiah and Ezekiel to express
Israel's unfaithfulness (Hos. 1.2; 2.7; 4.10, 15, 18; 9.1; Jer. 2.20; 3.1, 3, 9; etc;
Ezek. 16.35; 23.3; etc.). ndḥ in the causative mode is the characteristic theme

of Deut. 13, where 'enticement' is a crime punishable by death (vv. 5, 10, 13 [MT 6, 11, 14]). Jehoram's actions are diametrically opposed to the deeds of his father, who made an extraordinary effort to bring the people 'back to the Lord, the God of their fathers' (19.4).

The present text, while emphasizing Jehoram's guilt, makes no explicit allusion to the people's transgression, although this is surely implied by the causative form of the verbs.

[12–15] The letter from Elijah is a direct response to Jehoram's transgressions. The king has sinned; now the prophet is commissioned to warn him, to confront him with the gravity of his crimes and offer him the opportunity to avert destruction. Jehoram does not react to the letter, nor move toward repentance. His punishment, then, is inevitable.

The choice of Elijah for the task of warning is almost self-evident. Just as Jehu the son of Hanani, who rebuked Baasha, king of Israel (I Kings 16.1, 7), is presented in Chronicles as also approaching Jehoshaphat in Jerusalem (II Chron. 19.2), so too with Elijah. The renowned 'troubler of Israel' (I Kings 18.17), zealously engaged in combating Baal worship in Ahab's realm, is also Jehoram's contemporary. The gravity of Jehoram's sins demands a prophetic figure of Elijah's calibre, and the Chronicler is not deterred by the geographical or political borders between the two kingdoms.

Two difficult points, however, remain. The first is chronological: were Jehoram and Elijah indeed contemporaries? According to the possible sequence of events in Kings, Elijah's death/disappearance (I Kings 2) preceded the accession of Jehoram or occurred during the early years of his reign; at the date assumed by the present context, Elijah had already made his mysterious departure. The second question regards the extraordinary form of a letter for communicating prophecy (but cf. Jer. 29.1ff.); why did the Chronicler not have Elijah appear before Jehoram in person? Some scholars would combine both difficulties and explain that the letter was written before Elijah's death and sent in due course, or even transmitted as 'a letter from heaven' (cf. Rudolph, 267 for the various suggestions).

The last suggestion is not supported by the text, which refers simply to 'a letter' and implies that Elijah has been an eye-witness of the situation. Nor does Chronicles ever posit a movement between this world and the next. As for the chronology, it is in fact difficult to date with any precision any of the traditions of Elijah and Elisha as presented in II Kings 2, and most especially the moment when Elisha 'saw him no more'. It seems more probable that the Chronicler had a different view of the chronological pattern, which in any case implies a difference of a very few years. The last question, concerning the use of a letter rather than a personal appearance, is not raised in the narrative; one opinion is as good as another.

Elijah's letter is a characteristic Chronistic rhetorical piece, intrinsically linked to the context of the present pericope, where its central structural position is some indication of its role and meaning. After the conventional (somewhat modified) introduction, the letter is structured in two parts: vv. 12b–13 present the cause, Jehoram's sins, and vv. 14–15 predict the effect, Jehoram's fate. In both phrasing and subject, a close literary bond is developed between the preceding passage (vv. 1–11) and the first part of the letter, and a corresponding link between the second part of the letter and what is to follow (vv. 16–19). This thematic development, and the strategic literary position of this rhetorical piece, make it an explicit expression of the Chronicler's view of history, not only providing the necessary clear 'prophetic warning' but weaving all the details of Jehoram's reign into a theological unit.

A synopsis of the respective sections may highlight the similarities, and the chiastic ordering of the individual elements:

The letter	The narrative
Because you ... have walked in the way of the kings of Israel ...	v. 6: And he walked in the way of the kings of Israel ...
and have led Judah and the inhabitants of Jerusalem into unfaithfulness ...	v. 11: he ... led the inhabitants of Jerusalem into unfaithfulness and made Judah go astray
and you have killed (hārāgtā) your brothers ...	v. 4: he slew (wayyahᵃrōg) all his brothers with the sword
the Lord will bring ... on your people, your children (banēkā) your wives, and all your possessions	v. 17: and they came up ... and carried away all the possessions ... and also his sons (bānāw) and his wives
and you yourself will have severe sickness with a disease of your bowels until your bowels come out because of the disease.	vv. 18–19: the Lord smote him in his bowels with an incurable disease ... his bowels came out because of the disease.

Elijah's message is one long sentence; its protasis opens with the formulaic phrase 'in return for', or 'in equivalence to' (cf. Num. 25.13; Deut. 21.14, etc., *BDB*, 1065–6; the rendering 'because' reflects the meaning only in a general way), and the apodosis opens with the resultative *hinnēh* (behold).

Let us now turn to the details:

[12] The address opens with the standard formula 'Thus says the Lord', but with the added emphatic reference 'the God of David your father'. This is already an indication of some of the prophecy's salient points; an antithesis is immediately evoked between 'the house of David', Jehoram's affiliation

through his father, and 'the house of Ahab', his affiliation through his mother. Moreover, 'David your father' is followed by 'Jehoshaphat your father', and 'your brothers of your father's house' (v. 13) – a point of great significance (cf. on the next verse).

Jehoram's sin is characterized by the term 'to walk', repeated three times in vv. 12–13; this usage establishes a contrast between 'the ways ... of Judah' and 'the ways ... of Israel', and an ideological confrontation between Jehoshaphat and Ahab.

[13] Jehoram's three sins are now recorded: 'walking in the ways of the kings of Israel', enticing Judah and the inhabitants of Jerusalem to whoredom, and murdering his brothers. Note the emphatic familial context of Jehoram's transgression: they are first and foremost a betrayal of his own family, represented by no less than three of his predecessors: 'David his father', 'Jehoshaphat his father', and 'Asa the king of Judah'. The most elementary of a man's obligations, loyalty to his own kindred, his 'father's house', has been abandoned by Jehoram in favour of the 'house of Ahab' – a foreign allegiance, resulting in the terrible massacre of his brothers and the violating of his own people.

[14–15] The predicted punishment, like the sin, is described in family, personal terms: your sons, your wives, your possessions. I am therefore inclined to see in *'amm^eka* a reference not to 'your people', since they have no part in Jehoram's downfall (cf. v. 17), but to 'your family' (cf. Baumgartner, 792 (*b*)). The crimes committed by the king against his 'house' are punished by injuries to his body, his possessions and his near kin. Of all retributions recorded in Chronicles, this passage has the most personal, almost limited to the king himself.

[16–17] The following verses reveal the way in which Elijah's prophecy is fulfilled. First, 'the Lord stirred up against Jehoram the spirit (RSV 'the anger') of the Philistines and of the Arabs'. We have encountered these two peoples together in 17.11, bringing Jehoshaphat tribute, and they are later seen as allies against whom king Uzziah wages war (26.6–7). We thus acquire a quite coherent picture of Judah's relationship with its neighbours on the western and south-western borders, defined in this period as 'Philistines' and 'Arabs'.

'The Arabs who are near the Cushites (RSV Ethiopians)' probably defines their geographical situation: in Asa's time the 'Cushites' were affiliated to the vicinity of Gerar (14.13), that is south-west of Judah. The point is that all these details combine into a plausible historical continuum, from the days of Asa on. The sharp decline of Judah's power with the death of Jehoshaphat, and the revolt of Edom and Libnah, catalysed a series of aggressive assaults from the west and south-west. The phrasing of 22.1 makes it clear, however, that this was not a major military campaign, but a raid of smaller bands, invading Judah with the intention of looting and taking captives, as described in v. 17 (cf. similar events in I Sam. 30.1–2; I Chron. 4.38ff., etc.).

Similar incursions, at approximately the same time, are also recorded in northern Israel, cf. I Kings 5.2: 'Now the Aramaeans (RSV Syrians) on one of their raids had carried off a little maid from the land of Israel', or II Kings 13.20: 'Now bands of Moabites used to invade the land in the spring of the year'. In these periods of instability, mutual invasions of local marauders, killing the males, taking the women and children captive and looting possessions, were probably common.

So far, the chronological, geographical and social aspects of this raid seem authentic. However, the peculiar point of the passage is that the invaders strike exlusively against king Jehoram: 'all the possessions ... that belonged to the king's house, and also his sons and his wives'. Is it possible that such bands could have breached the defences of Jerusalem, entering the king's palace, abducting his family and spoiling his possessions? It is much more likely – as the text indeed states – that 'they came up against Judah', i.e. invading the Judaean hill country in the proximity of their own settlements. In this case, even if we assume that the raiders actually attacked one or several of the 'fortified cites', staffed by some of Jehoram's sons (cf. v. 3), the riddle still remains: how could *all* of the sons and wives of the royal family have fallen together into the marauders' hands? Doubts are also raised by reference to Jehoahaz (Ahaziah) as 'his youngest son' (vv. 17; 22.1). Ahaziah was in fact twenty-two years old when his father Jehoram died at the age of forty (II Kings 8.17, 26); he seems rather to have been the *oldest* son, by Jehoram's wife Athaliah.

The solution to these difficulties lies in the clear distinction between two different components: a short chronicle about the raid of a local Arab band on one hand, and on the other, the particular Chronistic touch which turned this attack into a punitive expedition against the king and his household. The Chronicler's adaptation highlights several points:

(*a*) The marauders' strike, seemingly incidental, was in fact divine punishment of Jehoram.

(*b*) The blow of retribution, falling upon the king's family alone, accurately fits the crime of his massacre of his brothers.

(*c*) The house of David is in danger of extinction. This chapter reports the first two stages: the murder of all of Jehoshaphat's sons, except Jehoram (v. 4), then the death by sword of all Jehoram's sons, except Jehoahaz. In the third stage, still to come, all the royal family is extinguished, except Joash (22.10). In less than ten years, a negative process of 'election' has singled out Joash as the sole survivor, the 'lamp' of David's house.

The name of the only survivor is given here as Jehoahaz, but as the more common Ahaziah in 22.1. This is one more example of the flexibility in the structuring of theophoric names, with the theophoric element placed either before or after the verbal phrase. Another well-known example is that of Jeconiah/Jehoiachin (cf. e.g. I Chron. 3.16–17; II Chron. 36.8–9).

[18–20] The last passage of Jehoram's history, relating his death and burial, should be seen as the Chronistic parallel to the conventional Deuteronomistic conclusion of II Kings 8.23–24a. Two features characterize the Chronicler's version: the unparalleled elaboration of the king's last agony, and the omission of the usual reference to a source for 'the rest of the acts of Joram' (II Kings 8.23).

Such source-references are in fact missing in Kings in the case of several rulers: Ahaziah, whose reign lasted only one year; Athaliah, who was not really considered a legitimate ruler; and three of the last kings of Judah, who were exiled, Jehoahaz, Jehoiachin and Zedekiah. To this list the Chronicler adds two more: Ammon (II Chron. 33.21–25) and here, Jehoram. None of these omissions are coincidental. The fact that a king's history is, or is not, properly recorded, expresses the historian's judgment. Not only did Jehoram die in disgrace and agony, to be buried outside the tombs of the kings (cf. below); even the details of his reign were not put on record for the memory of coming generations.

Although vv. 18ff. is an obvious continuation, describing one more step in the realization of Elijah's prophecy, we nevertheless find here an emphatic chronological statement, 'And after all this', which here has a qualitative ring. We are about to read of the final, most derogatory stage of Jehoram's fall. The beginning of v. 19, with the three-fold repetition of *yāmīm* (literally 'days'), echoes Elijah's prediction 'day after day' (v. 15). Throughout v. 19, however, the word *yāmīm* denotes 'a year' (cf. Judg. 17.10; II Sam. 14.26 etc.; Baumgartner, 383), not only in its final occurrence (so RSV 'at the end of two years') but also in the initial expression denoting 'from year to year'. Jehoram suffered from his disease continually, and at the end of the second year he died in great pain.

The expressions for 'disease' in this context are varied – $ḥ^oli$ and its plural $ḥ^olāyīm$ (vv. 15, 18, 19), $taḥ^alu'īm$ (v. 19), and the unique $maḥ^aleh$ (v. 15) – six times altogether – with emphatic effect.

What was Jehoram's disease? Considering the king's early death, after reigning only eight years, there is no reason to doubt that he was in fact gravely ill, although there is no mention of this in the parallel record of II Kings 8. The present text, however, hardly provides us with data for a clinical diagnosis (cf. also Williamson, 308). Bowel disease was probably a not uncommon health hazard at the time, and kings are no exception. The Chronicler's specific contribution to the account is the dramatic repetition of the symptoms – both in the prophet's warning and later in actual fact – and the great literary elaboration.

The verse includes the telling comment: 'his people made no fire in his honour, like the fires made for his fathers'. We have already seen (16.12–14) that in the case of king Asa, the sickness of his old age did not prevent the making of a funeral fire. In Jehoram's case, then, the omission of the traditional rite is another aspect of his bitter fate. The king who denied the righteous ways of his ancestors (v. 12) is himself denied the least sign of respect by his subjects: the funerary rites which all of his fathers had received.

[20] This verse deals with the king's death and burial (II Kings 8.23), but each of the original phrases is reformulated. The Chronicler also repeats at this point the chronological data of v. 5. The standard formulas found in Kings, 'Joram slept with his fathers and was buried with his fathers in the city of David', are changed. The first assertion is sometimes also missing in the book of Kings, when a monarch comes to a violent end (cf. II Kings 12.20ff.; 14.19; 21.23; 23.29–30, for Joash, Amaziah, Amon and Josiah). To these the Chronicler adds the case of Jehoram, probably intending that the fatal suffering brought on by his disease cannot be considered a natural death. Consequently, although he was buried in the city of David, he was not interred in the royal tombs.

Note the stylistic repetition of negations and reservations in the description of Jehoram's death: 'His people made *no* fire ... he departed with *no one*'s regret ... They buried him ... *not* in the tombs of the kings'.

The unique phrase *bᵉlō'ḥemdāh* has been usually translated, on the basis of the common understanding of *ḥmd*, as 'without being wanted', rendered by various idioms like 'with no one's regret' (RSV), 'unsung' (NEB), 'unpraised' (JPS), etc. It has been recently proposed that the root *ḥmd* should be interpreted – as in several rabbinic texts – as 'heat' or 'fire', the phrase being a restatement of v. 19 (cf. S. Abramson, '2 Chr 21:20', *Beth Mikra* 33, 1988, 381–2*).

[22.1] The beginning of the verse repeats 21.16–17, explaining again why Ahaziah, the youngest of Jehoram's sons, was enthroned by the inhabitants of Jerusalem. The language is somewhat obscure: the difficult *habbā' bā'arbīm* is rendered 'the band ... that came *with* the Arabs' (cf. Baumgartner, בוא 2e, 109), or, less literally, 'joined the Arabs' (NEB), probably referring to the Philistines (v. 16). The 'camp' could be that of the Arab marauders, or that of Jehoram himself, for some reason in the field with his troops when ambushed. It has been proposed that the MT *lammaḥ ᵃneh* should be regarded as a corruption of *lammilḥāmāh* (cf. BHS), but the same textual difficulty in II Chron. 18.33 may imply that *maḥ ᵃneh* is in fact also, in addition to the common 'camp' and 'host', a partial synonym for *milḥāmāh* 'battle' (so NEB; cf. II Sam. 1.2, 3, 4).

The peculiar point of this verse is the assertion that Ahaziah was made king by 'the inhabitants of Jerusalem'. There are several kings enthroned by the initiative of citizen groups, 'the people of Judah' or 'the people of the land' (Joash, Uzziah, Josiah and Jehoahaz, II Kings 11.12–20; 14.21; 21.24; 23.30; cf. parallels in II Chron. 23.1ff; 26.1; 33.24; 36.1) – all following the violent death of their predecessors. The similar treatment of Ahaziah is another indication of the Chronicler's view that Jehoram's death should not be regarded as natural. This is the only instance in which 'the inhabitants of Jerusalem' in particular take the corporate responsibility for the stability and continuation of the kingly line.

With the last clause, 'So Ahaziah ... reigned', the Chronicler returns to a strict reproduction of his source. This conflation of II Kings 8.24 and 25 serves in its double capacity of concluding one pericope, the history of Jehoram, and opening the next, the Ahaziah narrative.

22 2 Ahaziah was forty-two years old when he began to reign, and he reigned one year in Jerusalem. His mother's name was Athaliah, the granddaughter of Omri. [3] He also walked in the ways of the house of Ahab, for his mother was his counsellor in doing wickedly. [4] He did what was evil in the sight of the Lord, as the house of Ahab had done; for after the death of his father they were his counsellors, to his undoing. [5] He even followed their counsel, and went with Jehoram the son of Ahab king of Israel to make war against Hazael king of Syria at Ramoth-gilead. And the Syrians wounded Joram, [6] and he returned to be healed in Jezreel of the wounds which he had received at Ramah, when he fought against Hazael king of Syria. And Ahaziah the son of Jehoram king of Judah went down to see Joram the son of Ahab in Jezreel, because he was sick.

7 But it was ordained by God that the downfall of Ahaziah should come about through his going to visit Joram. For when he came there he went out with Jehoram to meet Jehu the son of Nimshi, whom the Lord had anointed to destroy the house of Ahab. [8] And when Jehu was executing judgment upon the house of Ahab, he met the princes of Judah and the sons of Ahaziah's brothers, who attended Ahaziah, and he killed them. [9] He searched for Ahaziah, and he was captured while hiding in Samaria, and he was brought to Jehu and put to death. They buried him, for they said, 'He is the grandson of Jehoshaphat, who sought the Lord with all his heart.' And the house of Ahaziah had no one able to rule the kingdom.

A. Notes to MT

[2] ארבעים, read עשרים with II Kings 8.26; [5[הרמים, read ארמים with II Kings 8.28 and some of the Versions, LXX הרמֹים or הֹמֹרים; [6] כי, read מן with II Kings 8.29; ועזריהו, read ואחזיהו with II Kings 8.29 and the Versions; [7] תבוסת, proposed נסבת.

B. Notes to RSV

[2] 'granddaughter', MT 'daughter', or 'descendant' (בת); [5] 'Syria', 'Aram' (so NEB), also v. 6; 'the Syrians', 'the Aramaeans' (so NEB); [9] 'grandson', MT 'son', or 'descendant' (בן); 'had no one able to rule', better 'could not muster the strength to rule' (JPS).

C. Structure, sources and form

1. This small unit, devoted to Ahaziah's single year of reign, marks one more step in the decline of Judah under the Ahab branch of the Davidic dynasty. With the death of Ahaziah, and Athaliah's massacre, the fortunes of the royal house and the kingdom will reach their nadir.

This continuous record is composed of two passages: vv. 2–6 are a literal reproduction of II Kings 8.26–29, with slight changes and several of the Chronicler's additions; vv. 7–9, a concise but accurate summary of II Kings 9, are composed by the Chronicler, following a method which so far we have encountered only rarely (cf. on I Chron. 12.1, 19–20).

2. As seen so far, it is the Chronicler's practice, when basing himself on Deuteronomistic sources, to cite them, in full or with abbreviations, verbatim or slightly rephrased. Thus the Chronicler's version may be shorter or longer than its source because of the process of selection, omission and elaboration, all based on the cited texts. A different method altogether is followed in 22.7–9. Here the Chronicler completely rewrites the story of II Kings 9–10, using his own words, and ordering the events in a new way. The result is a concise summary of the source texts, with the minor differences accounted for by Chronistic priorities.

3. While this pericope clearly parallels II Kings 8.26–9.28, different details appear for the place and manner of Ahaziah's death; the question of the possible source of this new information will be dealt with in the commentary.

D. Commentary

[2] Taken literally from II Kings 8.26, the verse provides the conventional Deuteronomistic opening. In this text, however, Ahaziah is 'forty-two' rather than 'twenty-two' years of age. As this is the only instance in Chronicles where chronological information of this kind deviates from the source material, there seems to be no doubt that 'forty-two' is a textual error (but cf. Myers, 125). Obviously, if Jehoram was forty years old at his death (21.5, 20), his son was not forty-two at that time.

We have already noted above (p. 809) that the phrase *bat 'omrī* in the description of Ahaziah's mother (following II Kings 8.26) should be understood to mean 'of the house of Omri, an Omride'; in fact she was the daughter of Ahab. RSV actually translates *bat* as 'granddaughter', a somewhat misleading rendering.

[3–4] Here (and in v. 5a) is an interesting reproduction of II Kings 8.27. The original verse is divided into independent components and each of these (with the exception of one clause, 'for he was son-in-law to the house of Ahab') is cited separately and complemented by a Chronistic interpretative or causative phrase. This phrase is followed directly, in each case, by the continuation of the source text from the point where it was left:

Source: **He also walked in the ways of the house of Ahab,**
Chron.: *for his mother was his counsellor in doing wickedly.*
Source: **He did what was evil in the eyes of the Lord, as the house of Ahab had done;**
Chron.: *for after the death of his father they were his counsellors, to his undoing.*

Chron: *He even followed their counsel*
Source: **and went with Jehoram**, etc.

The dominant theme of all three additional clauses is to be found in the three-fold repetition of *y'ṣ*, counsel. A major difference is thus formulated between the Chronicler's view of Ahaziah and that of Kings. In the latter, Ahaziah's actions are entirely the results of his own free initiative. The biographical fact of his affiliation with 'the house of Ahab', which has been made clear in the conventional mention of his mother in v. 26, is emphasized three times in the single brief verse of II Kings 8.27, and his voluntary decision to affiliate himself with his mother's family is expressed in a concrete way by his imitation of the 'ways of the house of Ahab'. In the Chronistic version, Ahaziah indeed perpetuates all these evils, but the weight of responsibility shifts first of all to his mother Athaliah, and also to the treacherous 'counsellors' of the 'house of Ahab', all of whom acted to lead him astray. The great sin of Ahaziah's father Jehoram was that he 'made Judah go astray'; the same kind of evil influence is associated with the new king, but Chronicles sees him as a victim rather than as an instigator. Even the war at Ramoth-gilead – a neutral decision in II Kings 8.28 – is here conceived as a result of heeding wrong advice. While not completely denying Ahaziah's personal responsibility, the Chronicler's rendering certainly mitigates it. One wonders whether the formulation of this text might not echo the tone of the following pericope, in which the infant Joash is saved and guided by the good counsel of Jehoiada and Jehoshabeath. Ahaziah, too, was the 'youngest son' (21.17; 22.1), a theme peculiar to Chronicles.

[5–6] These verses, a slightly altered citation of II Kings 8.28–29, serve in both contexts as a preparation and proposition for Jehu's revolt; here, however, the account goes only as far as the death of Ahaziah.

The struggle with the Aramaeans for Ramoth-gilead, beginning with Ahab's joint campaign with Jehoshaphat (I Kings 22.3ff.//II Chron. 18.2ff.) did not end with Ahab's death. At the time of his son Jehoram, the third king in succession, battles were still being waged. The wording of II Kings 9.14, 'Now Joram with all Israel had been on guard at Ramoth-gilead against Hazael king of Aram', may imply that by that time the city had been reconquered by Israel, with the Aramaeans trying to win it back. Ahaziah is said to have co-operated with Joram in this war, just as his grandfather Jehoshaphat had joined with Ahab. However, the movements and actual involvement of the forces of Judah in the expedition are not made clear; even Ahaziah's visit to the sick Joram seems to proceed from Jerusalem rather than from the battlefield.

Whatever the actual historical circumstances, in this literary pericope Ramoth-gilead is the scene of Ahab's doom and the extinguishing of his dynasty. Ahab himself fell in the battle of Ramoth-gilead (I Kings 22.34–35 //II Chron. 18.33–34); his son Joram was injured there (II Kings 8:28)// II Chron. 22.5), and there too Jehu was anointed to 'strike down' the house of Ahab (II Kings 9.1–7).

In v. 5, Jehoram is given his full title, 'son of Ahab the king of Israel' (cf. II Kings 8.28, 'Joram the son of Ahab'). It can be argued that this minor change reflects the Chronicler's *Vorlage*, the words 'king of Israel' being subsequently omitted in II Kings 8.28; on the other hand, we have already encountered the same addition in II Chron. 18.19 (cf. I Kings 22.20).

[7] From this point the Chronicler goes his own way, extracting the main narrative details from the record of II Kings 9. A preliminary theological comment establishes the terms of reference for all the succeeding events: 'it was ordained by God that ... Ahaziah should come ...'

The word *t^ebūsat* is unique; the root *bws*, denoting 'trampling, down-treading' (cf. BDB, 100–1), appears exclusively in biblical poetic passages, never in prose. As a term for Ahaziah's end it seems somewhat laboured (cf. BDB's shift to 'ruin, downfall'), and the syntax of v. 7a is also awkward – although the possibility of an unusually constructed nominal clause cannot be excluded. It has therefore been proposed by Rudolph to follow the Targum and render *n^esibat* for *t^ebūsat*, similar to 10.15 (Rudolph, 268, also BHS): 'it was a *turn of affairs* brought about by God ...'. Once the divinely-ordained circumstances had brought Ahaziah to visit Joram, the fatal consequences were inevitable.

Following this comment, the Chronicler continues to record the events, beginning with II Kings 9.21 and using the same verb: 'he went out'. The whole narrative in II Kings 9.1–10 is distilled here in a relative clause of several words: 'Jehu ... whom the Lord had anointed to destroy the house of Ahab'.

[8] This verse may be regarded as the Chronistic parallel to II Kings 10.12–14, where Ahaziah's brothers are slain during a systematic purge of the house of Ahab. This verse first shifts the scene from the first encounter between Jehoram and Jehu (alluded to in v. 7) to the latter's massacre of 'the house of Ahab in Jezreel' (II Kings 10.1–11) and his arrival in Samaria. Its dependence on the Kings text is also evident in the phrasing; the Chronicler's main changes are the replacement 'of the brothers (*'aḥē*, RSV 'kinsmen') of Ahaziah' with 'the sons of the brothers of Ahaziah' (*b^enē 'aḥē*), and the addition of 'the princes of Judah'.

In Kings, 'the brothers of Ahaziah' are slain during Jehu's total bloody purge of all branches of the house of Ahab: 'all his great men and his familiar friends and his priests, until he left him none remaining' (II Kings 10.11). According to Chronicles, however, all of Ahaziah's brothers were killed by the Arab raiders during their father's lifetime (21.17); this explains the rendering here – '*the sons* of Ahaziah's brothers'. The Chronicler's addition of 'the princes of Judah' probably stems from his general tendency to present 'the princes' as active participants in every aspect of political life. Thus, according to Chronicles, while Jehoram of Judah had killed 'the princes of Israel' who opposed him and his 'house of Ahab' policy (21.4–6), Jehu now slays 'the princes of Judah' who had supported this same policy.

[9] Unlike the narrative of II Kings 9–10, where the death of Ahaziah precedes the slaying of his brothers, the Chronicler places it at the end of his story. It is the different context which prompts this shift: in Kings, Ahaziah's fate is one theme in the comprehensive framework of Jehu's revolt; here, Ahaziah is the focus of the passage – his death is both the climax and the point of transition to the next passage: 'Now when Athaliah ... saw that her son was dead' (v. 10).

There are also different details in the present version. According to II Kings 9.27–28, Ahaziah succeeded in escaping from Jehu on their first encounter; he was pursued by Jehu's men, who wounded him 'at the ascent of Gur which is by Ibleam'. Even then, Ahaziah managed to flee to Megiddo, only to die there; finally he was taken by his servants to Jerusalem for burial. According to the Chronicler's version, Ahaziah was hiding in Samaria where he was apprehended, brought before Jehu, and executed.

Did the Chronicler have a different tradition concerning Ahaziah's end, or did he introduce these changes himself? The main argument in support of a different tradition is the fact that the present version, while independent of II Kings 9.27–28, does not display any obvious Chronistic motives (cf. Rudolph, 269). There are, however, several considerations making a stronger case for the opposite alternative (cf. Williamson, 311–12; Dillard, 172–3). According to the course of events in II Kings 10.17, having killed the brothers of Ahaziah, Jehu finally arrives in Samaria: 'when he came to Samaria he slew all that remained to Ahab in Samaria, till he had wiped them out, according to the word of the Lord which he spoke to Elijah'. Since the Chronicler has moved the execution of Ahaziah to the end of the story, it was natural for him to assume that it took place in Samaria. Moreover, in the record of II Kings we find a great similarity between Ahaziah's death and that of Josiah (cf. II Kings 9.28 with 23.29–30). The Chronicler's conviction that the manner of a man's death and burial are important indicators of his fortunes as decreed by God would lead him to make a clear distinction between the righteous Josiah and the wicked Ahaziah, who is then depicted here as a coward, hiding from Jehu who eventually executes him.

Unlike his partner Joram, whose body was 'cast ... on the plot of ground belonging to Naboth' (II Kings 9.25–26), Ahaziah is afforded a proper burial, the details of which are not recorded (and cf. II Kings 9.28). This last gesture of respect was entirely due to his kinship to 'Jehoshaphat, who sought the

Lord with all his heart'. The irony of this remark is obvious. Ahaziah's evil fortunes were determined by his voluntary affiliation with 'the house of Ahab'; and yet, at the moment of his departure, it was the merit of David's house which secured for him the last grace of burial.

It seems that in the Chronicler's view Ahaziah was buried somewhere in Samaria ('he was brought to Jehu and put to death. They buried him for they said ...'), and not, as claimed in II Kings 9.28, 'in his tomb with his fathers in the city of David'. For Chronicles, then, none of the Judaean rulers affiliated with the Ahab line was buried in a manner proper to descendants of the house of David: Jehoram was buried in the city of David but 'not in the tombs of the kings' (21.20); Ahaziah was buried in an anonymous grave, probably in Samaria; and the burial of Athaliah, the wife of the one and mother of the other, is not recorded at all.

The story is summed up with another characteristic idiom; the 'house of Ahaziah' was not able (*w^e'ēn ... la'ṣor kōaḥ*, cf. 2.5; 13.20; 20.37; etc.) to rule the kingdom.

One more word should be said about the significance of the last passage in bringing to light some of the Chronicler's underlying historiographical principles. The circumstances of Ahaziah's downfall are certainly a necessary part of the history of the southern kingdom's dynasty. The Chronicler could, however, have summarized this matter in one short sentence relating Jehu's search for and execution of Ahaziah, adding the last clause of v. 9 as a transition to vv. 10ff. And yet, the Chronicler composes a concise summary of II Kings 9–10, with all the important details of Jehu's revolt: his full name, his being anointed by the Lord, his 'anointing' to destroy the house of Ahab, his encounter with Jehoram, his execution of judgment on the house of Ahab, his coming to Samaria and his search for Ahaziah in order to execute him. Such a detailed summary, ostensibly unnecessary for the history of the Judaean kingdom, reveals the Chronicler's profound interest in the history of the northern kingdom, and illustrates his consistent attempt to describe as much of it as possible, through the exclusive perspective of the history of Judah.

22 10 Now when Athaliah the mother of Ahaziah saw that her son was dead, she arose and destroyed all the royal family of the house of Judah. ¹¹ But Jeho-shabe-ath, the daughter of the king, took Joash the son of Ahaziah, and stole him away from among the king's sons who were about to be slain, and she put him and his nurse in a bedchamber. Thus Jeho-shabe-ath, the daughter of King Jehoram and wife of Jehoiada the priest, because she was a sister of Ahaziah, hid him from Athaliah, so that she did not slay him; ¹² and he remained with them six years, hid in the house of God, while Athaliah reigned over the land.

23 But in the seventh year Jehoiada took courage, and entered into a compact with the commanders of hundreds, Azariah the son of Jeroham, Ishmael the son of Jeho-hanan, Azariah the son of Obed, Ma-aseiah the son of Adaiah and Elishaphat the son of Zichri. ² And they went about through Judah and gathered the Levites from all the cities of Judah, and the heads of fathers' houses of Israel, and they came to Jerusalem. ³ And all the assembly made a covenant with the king in the house of God. And Jehoiada said to them, 'Behold, the king's son! Let him reign, as the Lord spoke concerning the sons of David. ⁴ This is the thing that you shall do: of you priests and Levites who come off duty on the sabbath, one third shall be gatekeepers, ⁵ and one third shall be at the king's house and one third at the Gate of the Foundation; and all the people shall be in the courts of the house of the Lord. ⁶ Let no one enter the house of the Lord except the priests and ministering Levites; they may enter, for they are holy, but all the people shall keep the charge of the Lord. ⁷ The Levites shall surround the king, each with his weapons in his hand; and whoever enters the house shall be slain. Be with the king when he comes in, and when he goes out.'

8 The Levites and all Judah did according to all that Jehoiada the priest commanded. They each brought his men, who were to go off duty on the sabbath, with those who were to come on duty on the sabbath; for Jehoiada the priest did not dismiss the divisions. ⁹ And Jehoiada the priest delivered to the captains the spears and the large and small shields that had been King David's, which were in the house of God; ¹⁰ and he set all the people as a guard for the king, every man with his weapon in his hand, from the south side of the house in the north side of the house, around the altar and the house.

11 Then he brought out the king's son, and put the crown upon him, and gave him the testimony; and they proclaimed him king, and Jehoiada and his sons anointed him, and they said, 'Long live the king.'

12 When Athaliah heard the noise of the people running and praising the king, she went into the house of the Lord to the people; ¹³ and when she looked, there was the king standing by his pillar at the entrance, and the captains and the trumpeters beside the king, and all the people of the land rejoicing and blowing trumpets, and the singers with their musical instruments leading in the celebration. And Athaliah rent

her clothes, and cried, 'Treason! Treason!' [14] Then Jehoiada the priest brought out the captains who were set over the army, saying to them, 'Bring her out between the ranks; any one who follows her is to be slain with the sword.' For the priest said, 'Do not slay her in the house of the Lord.' [15] So they laid hands on her; and she went into the entrance of the horse gate of the king's house, and they slew her there.

16 And Jehoiada made a covenant between himself and all the people and the king that they should be the Lord's people. [17] Then all the people went to the house of Baal, and tore it down; his altars and his images they broke in pieces, and they slew Mattan the priest of Baal before the altars. [18] And Jehoiada posted watchmen for the house of the Lord under the direction of the Levitical priests and the Levites whom David had organized to be in charge of the house of the Lord, to offer burnt offerings to the Lord, as it is written in the law of Moses, with rejoicing and with singing, according to the order of David. [19] He stationed the gatekeepers at the gates of the house of the Lord so that no one should enter who was in any way unclean. [20] And he took the captains, the nobles, the governors of the people, and all the people of the land; and they brought the king down from the house of the Lord, marching through the upper gate to the king's house. And they set the king upon the royal throne. [21] So all the people of the land rejoiced; and the city was quiet, after Athaliah had been slain with the sword.

A. Notes to MT

[22.10] ותדבר, II Kings 11.1 ותאבד; [11] יהושבעת, II Kings 11.2 יהושבע; [23.7] וְהָיוּ, read וְהָיוּ with MSS and Versions; [13] עמדו, proposed עָמְדוּ; והשרים, several MSS and LXX of II Kings 11.14 והשרים; [14] ויוצא, read ויצו with II Kings 11.15 and some Versions; [18] הלוים, read והלוים with MSS and Versions; insert הכהנים מחלקות את ויעמד והלוים with LXX.

B. Notes to RSV

[11] 'who were about to be slain', better 'who were being slain' (JPS; cf. NEB); [23.3] 'Behold the king's son! Let him reign', MT differently; better 'The son of the king shall be king' (JPS); [4] 'who come off duty on the Sabbath', better 'who come on duty on the Sabbath' (MT באי השבת); cf. JPS 'who are on duty for the week'; [8] 'who were to go off duty ... who were to come on duty', better the other way round, 'who were to come on duty (באי השבת) ... who were to go off duty' (יצאי השבת; so NEB); [9] 'captains', MT 'commanders of hundreds'; [10] 'around the altar', JPS 'at the altar'; [11] 'he brought out ...', thus II Kings 11.12, MT '*they* brought out' (so NEB); 'and put the crown upon him, and gave him the testimony', MT 'and put upon him the crown and the testimony'; 'the testimony', JPS 'the insignia'; [13] 'by his pillar', MT '*on* the pillar' (cf. NEB); 'leading in the celebration', JPS 'leading the hymns'; [15] 'they laid hands on her', better 'they cleared a passage for her' (JPS); [18] 'posted watchmen for the house of the Lord', thus II Kings 11.18; better NEB, 'committed the supervision of the house of the Lord to the charge of ...'; 'and the Levites', not in MT (cf. A above); [21] 'after Athaliah', better 'as for Athaliah' (JPS).

C. *Structure, sources and form*

1. 22.10–24.27, which parallels II Kings 11–12, tells the history of Joash, son of Ahaziah. The pericope, about thirty per cent longer than its Deuteronomistic source, has been thoroughly edited, and comprises two lengthy sections:

(a) 22.10–23.21 From the death of Ahaziah to the accession of Joash
(b) 24 The reign of Joash.

2. Unlike the sections on Asa and Jehoshaphat, where the narrative of the Deuteronomist is completely restructured (chs. 13–16; 17–20), this pericope adheres faithfully to the original composition and course of events. It begins with Athaliah's rule, Jehoiada's uprising and the crowning of Joash; the history of Joash opens with the Deuteronomistic introduction (24.1), proceeds with the repairing of the Temple, and ends with the attack of Aram and the Deuteronomistic conclusion, which also includes Joash's violent death. The Chronicler's adaptation is thus manifestly not in the order of the events but in their careful reformulation:

(*a*) The whole narrative of Joash is cast in a theologically meaningful and coherent framework, a sequence of cause and effect. This involves not only the addition of details concerning the sins of Joash and the appearance of a prophet, but the minute re-organization of isolated items into the causal chain. It is no wonder that the history of Joash was chosen first by de Wette and then by Wellhausen as a paradigm of the Chronicler's historiographical method, highlighting his figure as a theologian and editor (cf. de Wette, *Beiträge*, 91–5; Wellhausen, 195–200; cf. also Japhet, *Ideology*, 173–5).

(*b*) Another major line of reworking concerns the role of the Temple and the clergy in Jehoiada's revolt. Most significant is the appearance of the Levites, who are completely ignored in the story of II Kings 11–12, and the careful attention to ritual matters.

(*c*) The Chronicler gives a distinctive position to the history of Jehoiada himself, who in some respects occupies a place similar to that of the kings.

(*d*) The Chronicler's literary method entails changes of detail and additions of various length, but practically no omissions from the source text in II Kings 11–12. Nevertheless, almost all the topics are to some degree conceived and presented differently.

3. As mentioned above, the first unit (22.1–23.21) is devoted to the intermediate period between the death of Ahaziah and the accession of Joash, composed of three parts:

(a) 22.10–12	The threat to Joash and his rescue
(b) 23.1–15	The enthronment of Joash
	1–7 Jehoiada's preparations
	8–11 the crowning
	12–15 Athaliah's end
(c) 23.16–21	The covenant and its consequences
	16 establishing the covenant
	17 eradication of Baal worship
	18–19 reorganization of the Temple cult
	20–21 the king is enthroned.

4. Most of the changes introduced into the pericope may be satisfactorily explained by the Chronicler's literary methods and theological concepts. The principal informative additions concern the high priest Jehoiada – notes of a biographical nature including the name of his son, his age, death and burial. These details amount to a short chronicle and may have been drawn from an extra-biblical source (cf. also Dillard, 179). On the different details of the Aramaean campaign, cf. on ch. 24.

D. Commentary

[22.10–12] With the reign of Athaliah the threat to the house of David reaches a climax. Ironically indeed, the royal houses in the two kingdoms are facing extinction: the house of Ahab in Israel and the house of David in Judah; the last stronghold of the Ahab dynasty is Athaliah ruling in Jerusalem, with Baal-worship as its religious regime.

Just as in Kings, Athaliah's reign is not recorded along the usual Deuteronomistic pattern, undoubtedly because her rule is not counted as legitimate. Apparently two features disqualify her for rule, being a woman and a scion of the house of Ahab; although the text does not elucidate the matter, the first seems to be her decisive shortcoming. (For a different interpretation cf. H. Reviv, 'The Period of Athaliah and Joash', *Beth Mikra*, 47 1971, 541ff.*)

Verse 10 is cited from II Kings 11.1; the Chronicler adds the words 'of the house of Judah' to emphasize that no legitimate candidate remains, and the verb *watt^{e}dabbēr* replaces *watt$^{e\prime}$abbēd*. There is no necessity to restore the Kings reading.

In v. 11, the Chronicler cites II Kings 11.2. The changes introduced focus greater attention on the figure of Jehosheba/Jehoshabeath: she is called 'wife of Jehoiada the priest' in addition to her other titles (daughter of king Joram, sister of Ahaziah), and the oblique reference in Kings (MT 'they hid him') is understood specifically: 'Jehoshabeath ... hid him'.

The strong association of Jehosheba with the Temple is also apparent from the Deuteronomistic version, especially II Kings 11.3, 'and he remained with her six years, hid in the house of the Lord'. That Jehosheba was also wife of the high priest may be considered theoretical (Curtis, 422–3), but if we accept this note as historical we will in fact gain a better explanation for the story as it stands (already H. Ewald, *The History of Israel*, London 1869, IV, 135; Williamson, 315; Dillard, 179). Her position as wife of the high priest explains her easy access to the royal palace (v. 11), since the palace and Temple were an architectural unit, as well as her permanent presence in the Temple precinct (v. 12), and the subsequent involvement of Jehoiada the priest (23.1), not mentioned in the initial rescue of Joash. That the Deuteronomist passed in silence over this detail is no indication that it is inauthentic.

It seems appropriate to note at this point the role of women at this critical hour in the history of Israel (cf. the similarities between this chapter and Exodus 1–2). Commentators have given great attention to the role of Jezebel in northern Israel, but much less has been said about Athaliah, who so severely threatens the house of David in her desperate attempt to secure the hegemony of the house of Ahab. The scheming Athaliah, 'the wife of Jehoram', is confronted by another woman of the royal house, 'the daughter of Jehoram', who decides at the greatest personal risk to save the future of the dynasty of David. One may surmise – although this is not explicitly stated – that Jehosheba was Jehoram's daughter by another wife, therefore identified as 'the sister of Ahaziah' and 'the daughter of Jehoram'. Although a member of the 'house of David', she was left unharmed by Athaliah's purge, probably because, as a woman, she was not regarded as a candidate for the throne.

Verse 12 is taken verbatim from II Kings 11.3, with the change of 'with her' to 'with them', implying the full collaboration of Jehoiada already at this early stage. This verse sums up the dramatic confrontation, palace versus Temple: 'Athaliah reigned over the land', at the very time when, in closest proximity, the child who was to disinherit her 'hid in the house of God'.

[23.1] Since the pioneer analysis of de Wette, all commentators have noted that the Chronicler's understanding of Jehoiada's *coup* is different from that of II Kings 11. A limited conspiracy between the high priest and the king's guard is here presented as a popular uprising, with the people themselves as essential partners. It is they, not Jehoiada, who restore the scion of David to his kingdom, not in secrecy but with open publicity, and the various units of the king's guard are replaced here by the Levites. The Chronicler emphasizes more than Kings that Athaliah was a foreign ruler, who had never received the people's blessing; the very knowledge that a Davidide was still alive was enough to prompt the people to join loyally the effort to remove her.

The description of the revolt offers an interesting opportunity to trace the Chronicler's literary methods. While the sequence of the source is faithfully adhered to, the material is nevertheless transformed to a great extent. Verse 1 begins with a literal citation of II Kings 11.4, with the verbs 'sent and took' (*šālaḥ ... wayyiqqaḥ*) changed to 'strengthened himself and took' (*hithazzaq ... wayyiqqaḥ*; RSV paraphrases). After 'the commanders of the hundreds', instead of recording the titles of the units ('the Carites and the guards') and their summoning to the Temple, the Chronicler elaborates by giving the names, five commanders altogether, with whom the high priest 'entered into a compact'. The first act of Jehoiada is to gather the five commanders and send them through the cities of Judah, to gather the Levites and the heads of fathers' houses to Jerusalem.

Some commentators (cf. Rudolph, 271; Williamson, 315) suggest that the 'commanders of the hundreds' are viewed by the Chronicler as Levites, but the text does not support this interpretation. This particular title and the system of organization it presupposes are never attested in Chronicles in regard to the Levites (not even in the context of I Chron. 12.24–39). Although the Levites play an important role in the pericope, the 'commanders of the hundreds' have their own distinct place in Jehoiada's arrangements (vv. 9, 20). The names recorded are much too common to serve as the basis for any levitical identification (cf. also Dillard, 180–1).

[2–3] In addition to the covenant made with the commanders of the guards, the text has another covenant: 'And all the assembly made a covenant with the king in the house of God', transferred to this initial position from II Kings 11.17. In the original version Jehoiada first secures the loyalty of the captains by placing them under oath, and then shows them the living heir. He subsequently gives them strict instructions on how to proceed with the uprising, focussing mainly on absolute secrecy in order to take the queen utterly by surprise. All the necessary preparations are made in the limited space between the Temple and the palace. When Athaliah eventually hears the noise of the assembly, she still does not realize the danger she is in, and falls into the trap. The covenant between the people and the king is made much later, after the execution of Athaliah. A sense of authenticity pervades the entire course of the narrative.

The scope of the Chronicles version is different. The first task of the captains is to go out through Judah and gather the people to Jerusalem. All the people of Israel, both Levites and heads of fathers' houses, gather at the Temple, where a covenant is ratified, already at this stage, between the people and the king. This whole description is rather improbable: it is hardly possible that Athaliah could have been unaware of such a popular assembly gathered at her very doorstep, and yet she is still described as going 'into the house of the Lord to the people' (v. 12). Her reaction of total suprise (v. 13), natural enough in II Kings 11, is hardly credible in the context of Chronicles. Here we again notice the limitations of a literary presentation of this kind: in the Chronicler's reworking of his source, some of the details are better dealt with than others.

The content of the covenant is presented in Jehoiada's proclamation: 'The son of the king shall be king' (JPS; the rendering of RSV ignores both the syntax and accents of the MT). This addition is required by the different emphases in this version of the uprising. Affirmations of the kingly prerogative of the Davidic line are found in Chronicles in three contexts. The first is the initiation of the dynasty through God's promise to David, confirmed by Solomon's succession to the throne (I Chron. 22.10; 28.7). As David's line was destined to endure 'for ever' (II Sam. 7.16//I Chron. 17.4), there was no need for a repetition of this promise – except at times of serious threat to the continuation of the kingdom or the very survival of the dynasty. Two such cases were to come in Jeroboam and in the 'house of Ahab', and in both contexts the Davidic right is again explicitly stated: in Abijah's speech (13.5) and here in Jehoiada's proclamation.

Jehoiada's orders, 'This is the thing that you shall do', are now addressed not to the limited body of guards, but to the whole assembly, gathered in the Temple court.

[4–5a] In II Kings 11.5–8, it is not entirely clear how Jehoiada proposes to ensure the safety of the king until his actual crowning; the difficulty lies in v. 6, which is regarded by many as a secondary elaboration (cf. BH, BHS *ad loc.*; also RSV). Without this verse, a much clearer picture emerges. The king's guard seems to comprise three units: one third 'who come on duty on the Sabbath' and two thirds 'who come off duty on the Sabbath' (inexplicably, RSV has reversed these terms; this is rightly corrected by NEB).

The third part of the guard who were on duty on the Sabbath were expected to perform their regular function while keeping watch lest anything happened from the direction of the palace; the other two-thirds, ordinarily on leave, were now summoned to protect the king in the Temple, surrounding him on all sides with a human wall, ready to slay whoever might approach. Verse 6, with its reference to details of the regular guarding system, is no more explicable (but cf. Dillard, 182).

The Chronicler takes as his point of departure the description of II Kings 11.5–8 (repeating some of its clauses verbatim), but he understands Jehoiada's strategy very differently. Most importantly, the three-part division is conceived as applying not to the king's guard but to the people in general. Accordingly, the reference to those 'who come off duty on the Sabbath' is omitted. However, the division into 'thirds' (*haššᵉlišīt*, similar to II Kings 11.5–6) is retained. The first of these divisions is identified by the Chronicler as 'the gatekeepers' (*šō'ᵃrē hassippim*), i.e. those guarding the Temple, where the young king is hiding. Since entrance into the sacred precinct is permitted only to the clergy, the gatekeepers are only 'priests and Levites'. The second third of the multitude is stationed at the palace, and the last third 'at the Gate of the Foundation', a term which, like its parallel 'Gate of Sur' in II Kings 11.6, is unique and not possible to identify.

The words 'all the people shall be in the courts …' signal a new aspect of Jehoiada's arrangements; the punctuation of MT, followed by RSV, should be slightly modified, with the final accent placed after 'the Gate of the Foundation', and vv. 5b–6 seen as a parenthetic comment. The arrangements for the king's safety continue in v. 7.

[5b–6] This parenthetic passage is an elaboration of II Kings 11.7b. Chronicles structures the passage within a literary frame: 'all the people shall be in the courts …' (5b), and 'all the people shall keep the charge of the Lord' (6b). This latter phrase (*hišmᵉrū mišmeret yhwh*) is in fact a reinterpretation of 'guard the house of the Lord' (*wᵉšāmᵉrū 'et mišmeret bēt yhwy*) in Kings; the finesse of the rendering is lost in translation. The Chronicler here addresses one of the most difficult problems posed by the Deuteronomistic narrative: the presence of laymen within the Temple. The statement of v. 3, 'all the assembly made a covenant with the king in the house of God', is clarified here: 'all the people' remain in the Temple courts, while only 'the priests and ministering Levites' are entitled to enter the Temple building itself.

[7] To the literal citation of II Kings 11.8 the Chronicler introduces two important changes. First, 'you shall surround the king' is rendered: 'The Levites shall surround the king'. This is a significant change in the light of the context, as it makes absolutely clear that the king's bodyguard is chosen from only that third of the people who are entitled to enter the Temple, i.e. of the tribe of Levi. They are to 'stay with the king (cf. NEB) when he comes in and when he goes out'.

The other change is even more significant. The Kings version 'Whoever approaches the ranks' presumably refers to interference from outside the conspiracy, especially the intervention of Athaliah's entourage. In Chronicles, 'whoever enters the house' indicates laymen from the participating throng, who might trespass the bounds of the Temple precincts. In Kings the trespasser is to be slain for political reasons, because of the danger he may pose to the success of Jehoiada's *coup d'état*; in Chronicles the same penalty has religious motives – to prevent the desecration of the Temple.

This line of adaptation raises a major question relating to the Chronicler's method: how should we define the addition of vv. 5b–6 and the changes introduced into v. 7? Do they represent some unlimited '*Tendenz*' to ascribe to the Levites as many roles as possible, with the practical-political goal of supporting their actual demands (cf. *inter al.* de Wette, *Beiträge*, 80–92; Wellhausen, 197–8; for Willi, 198, they form part of the 'cultic' post-Chronistic elaboration of the book)? This is a rather narrow understanding of the story, and of the Chronicler's work. The role of the Levites during the uprising in fact remains rather limited; they are entrusted only with the protection of the young prince inside the Temple. It is not a magnification of the levitical role which prompts this version, but rather a *bona fide* dilemma facing the Chronicler as he records the events of II Kings 11 (cf. Rudolph, 271). One of his most elementary convictions is the absolute validity of the prohibition limiting entry into the Temple to priests and Levites only – and 'any outsider ... shall be put to death' (Num. 1.51; 3.10; 18.7, etc.). We thus witness the Chronicler's ambivalent attitude towards his source as he strives to follow it in his presentation as closely as possible, while at the same time changing it in accordance with what are for him basic principles of 'historical probability'.

[8] This same ambivalence also influences the Chronicler's alterations to II Kings 11.9. There we read: 'The commanders of the hundreds' (RSV

'captains') did according to all that Jehoiada the priest commanded'; here the single group of 'commanders of the hundreds' is changed to read 'the Levites and all Judah'. The actions of these two groups are then recorded separately: v. 8b refers only to the Levites, 'who were to come on (and go off) duty on the Sabbath', while 'all Judah' is represented in vv. 9–10. Not only is the scope of the event much broader, but the original king's guard is completely removed; the Levites are responsible for whatever happens in the Temple, while 'all Judah' are in charge of the military activity.

The note that 'Jehoiada ... did not dismiss the divisions' is relevant only for the levitical group: the entire clerical order was present in Jerusalem; whether actually on duty or not, they were all to remain on active alert.

[9] In this verse, the literal citation of II Kings 11.10 in fact represents a different grouping. In Kings, the 'commanders of hundreds' (RSV 'captains') command 'the Carites and the guards' (v. 4), but here they command the people of 'all Judah'.

The spears and shields 'that had been king David's', delivered by Jehoiada to the people, would seem to have reached the Temple as 'votive gifts' (*q^odāšim*, cf. I Chron. 26.26; II Chron. 5.1; 15.18). These ancient weapons, kept among the Temple sacred gifts, were probably tactically unusable, and their help in an actual confrontation would be dubious at best. While the text does not enlarge on this point, one wonders whether Jehoiada even planned an armed struggle. From another point of view, Jehoiada's use of 'votive gifts' for political purposes would seem risky indeed, as 'devoted things to the Lord' (*ḥ^erem l^eyhwh*, Lev. 27.28) were forbidden for use. Theologically speaking, however, it is certainly significant that king David's arms now serve, if only symbolically, to secure the survival of the Davidic dynasty. Have such considerations directed Jehoiada's tactics?

[10] The Chronicler is bound by his own view of the events to omit the mention of 'the guards' (II Kings 11.11) and to read instead 'all the people'. In both versions a 'human wall' is formed, to ensure the king full protection.

[11] The ground is now prepared for the crowning and anointing of the new king. In the LXX version of II Kings 11.12, all the actions of the verse are expressed by singular verbs, with Jehoiada himself as subject, with the one exception of 'they clapped their hands and said ...'; in MT the first two actions are ascribed to Jehoiada, while the rest, including the anointing of Joash, are in the plural. This verse in Chronicles has plural verbs throughout (reverted for some reason in RSV back to the singular), and the subject of 'they anointed him' is explicitly 'Jehoiada and his sons', thus avoiding any implication of anointing by any unauthorized person. These slight changes, while they do not materially effect the course of the events, do shift the emphasis from Jehoiada to the people in general (implied in the pronoun 'they'). Even the single action which is an exclusive priestly prerogative – i.e.

anointing – is in fact done by a group ('Jehoiada and his sons') rather than by an individual.

The 'clapping of the hands', a phrase which appears elsewhere only in Ezekiel (6.11; 21.14 [MT 19], 17 [MT 22]; 22.13) in a variety of 'negative' connotations (resentment, anger, etc.), is omitted in Chronicles.

[12–15] Joash has been successfully enthroned, and now it remains to depose Athaliah. Jehoiada's preparations were directed largely towards this phase, which will end Athaliah's rule and seal her fate. This passage follows, with the change of minor details, the record of II Kings 11.3–16.

Verse 12 parallels II Kings 11.13. The obscure (and probably corrupt) *hārāṣîn hā'ām* (interpreted by RSV to mean 'the guard *and* the people') is here rendered 'the people running' (*hā'ām hārāṣîm*) followed by 'and praising the king' in full accord with the description so far.

Verse 13 has two examples of the fine nuances which the Chronicler has introduced into his *Vorlage*. According to II Kings 11.14, the king was 'standing on the pillar (RSV by the pillar) according to the custom' (*kammišpāṭ*). This 'custom' is changed and interpreted in the present version as 'at the entrance' (*bammābō'*), in full accord with the Chronicler's view that no one, not even the king, was allowed into the Temple. II Kings 16.18 explicitly refers to 'the outer entrance for the king', and some kind of entrance, at which Jeremiah meets king Zedekiah, is mentioned in Jer. 38.14. It is therefore possible that this change reflects concrete facts which were passed over in silence in the Chronicler's source.

The second alteration is the addition of 'the singers with their musical instruments leading in the celebration (or hymns)'. For the Chronicler, no joyful ceremony is complete without music; here, then, the singers and instruments supplement the rejoicing and the blowing of trumpets already found in the Kings version.

Athaliah's reaction contrasts diametrically with the aggressive manner which marked her seizure of the throne. The rending of clothes is a symbolic act with several meanings in biblical times. First and foremost, it is an expression of mourning (cf. M. I. Grubber, 'Mourning', *EJ* 12, 485), but it also expresses submission and repentance (cf. II Kings 19.1), fear of disaster (II Kings 5.7, 8), or utter despair (Num. 14.6). Athaliah resorts to this symbolic gesture in lieu of any concrete action: she does not flee, and her cry of 'Treason' goes unheard – because of Jehoiada's precautions.

[14] Jehoiada commands that Athaliah be led out 'between the ranks', preventing anyone from following her (cf. II Kings 11.15). Here, just as in II Kings 11.8, the point is a complete isolation of Athaliah from any support. The uprising is presented as a classic *coup d'état*; with the exception of Athaliah's execution, there is no bloodshed.

[16] II Kings 11.17 refers to two different covenants: one 'between the

Lord and the king and people', a commitment initiated and mediated by Jehoiada, and a different covenant 'between the king and the people'. The consequences of the first covenant are described in II Kings 11.18 as entailing the eradication of Baal worship, established in Jerusalem by king Jehoram. II Kings 11.19–20 relate the ramifications of the second covenant in the renewal of Davidic rule.

While the Chronicler cites some parts of his source practically verbatim, he has a different view of the covenant and its effects. He has transposed the solemn agreement 'between the king and the people' to the beginning of the chapter (v. 3), where it establishes the basis for all the subsequent actions. Now that Joash has been crowned and Athaliah executed, another covenant signifies the beginning of the next stage: the people undertake to 'be the Lord's people' (v. 16). Both the covenant and its consequences are differently conceived.

The reading of II Kings 11.17, 'between the Lord' (*bēn yhwh*), is rendered in Chronicles as 'between him' (*bēno*, restored to the Kings text by some commentators, cf. BH). The result of this seemingly minor change is that the Lord is no longer a partner to the covenant; this is a 'firm undertaking' of the people themselves, including the high priest and the king, to be 'the Lord's people', with broader implications including both 'religious/ritual' (vv. 17–19), and 'political' aspects (vv. 20–21).

The outcome of the covenant according to II Kings 11.18 is the eradication of Baal worship. We thus learn that Jerusalem has not only 'the house of the Lord', but also 'a house of Baal', with its 'altars and images' and an officiating priest, all of which are destroyed after the ratifying of the covenant. According to Chronicles, the religious/cultic aspect of the covenant involves, in addition, the restoration of a full and proper cult in the Temple (vv. 18–19), which is altogether missing from Kings. It thus includes the absolute exclusivity of the Lord's worship, a wholehearted repentance and eradication of any form of idolatry.

[17] This verse is a literal repetition of II Kings 11.18a. The Chronicler introduces only one change: he attributes the acts of wiping out 'Baal worship' to 'all the people' rather than 'all the people of the land'. It is difficult to say whether the Chronicler is motivated by some awareness of the limited institutional connotation of the term 'the people of the land'. In any event, he continues as before to augment the role of the people.

[18–19] Jehoiada's arrangements in the Temple include first the appointment of the divisions of priests and Levites. That the Chronicles version originally mentioned 'divisions' specifically is still attested by the LXX text; the clause *wayya'ᵃmēd 'et maḥlᵉqōt hakkōhᵃnîm wᵉhalᵉwiyyim* ('he appointed the divisions of priests and Levites') was probably omitted by homoioteleuton (cf. Rudolph, 272; Dillard 178). In fact, MT also preserves an echo of the noun *maḥlᵉqōt* ('divisions') in the relative clause 'whom David had organized', literally 'divided' (*ḥalaq* cf. I Chron. 23.6; 24.3, etc.). The priests and Levites are appointed to handle the sacrificial and liturgical cult, while the gatekeepers are positioned to guard the Temple's gates. This concise record of the major cultic aspects also alludes explicitly to their respective source of authority: the 'divisions' which 'David had organized', the sacrificial cult 'as it is written in the law of Moses', and the music 'according to the order of David'. The specific context is clarified in the final statement: 'He stationed the gatekeepers ... so that no one should enter who was in any way unclean'.

The Chronicler's literary method in supplementing his source has been demonstrated many times. He takes the text of II Kings 11.18b–19 as his starting point, cuts it after v. 18b, and introduces a lengthy insertion. He then takes up the thread of the original text from the point where it left off, unaltered. This may be illustrated as follows:

II Kings 11.18b		II Kings 11.19
II Chron. 23.18aα	18aβ–19a	II Chron. 23.20

As a result of the insertion, the original phrase *wayyāśem hakkōhēn pᵉquddōt 'al bēt yhwh* (RSV 'and the priest posted watchmen over the house of the Lord') is in fact reinterpreted. In II Kings 11.18b it refers to the stationing of 'watchmen', whose role is to ensure the full accomplishment of Jehoiada's plans and the safe entrance of Joash into the palace; in Chronicles it refers to the functions which Jehoiada re-establishes in the Temple at the charge of the priests and Levites. Unfortunately, RSV conforms its translation to the reading of II Kings 11 and fails to recognize the new meaning.

The extensive record at this juncture of the establishment of the cult should not be viewed simply as the result of the Chronicler's 'cultic inclination', his wish to magnify the Temple or his stylistic penchant for repetition. Rather, allusions to the Temple arrangements recur in Chronicles at specific junctures in the history of Israel, and always in response to necessity. According to the Chronicler's understanding of the events, Athaliah's actions (and probably also those of Jehoram and Ahaziah before her) entailed the actual discontinuation of the Temple worship, as is explicitly stated in 24.7: 'For the sons of Athaliah, that wicked woman, had broken into the house of God; and had also used all the dedicated things of the house of the Lord for the Baals.' For the Chronicler, both Israel's worship and idolatry are exclusive; 'evil' rulers introduced 'other gods' not as optional additions to, but as actual replacements of, God's worship. Thus, a commitment to be 'the Lord's people' could not be fulfilled only by the eradication of Baal from Jerusalem. It also demanded a renewal of Temple orders, and eventually – the restoration of the sanctuary, to be handled in ch. 24.

[20–21] The thread of the story is now picked up where it was left in II Kings 11.19. Jehoiada organizes his forces for the last stage: the young king is brought from the Temple to the palace, there to be enthroned. According to Kings, those who accompany the king to the palace are 'the commanders of the hundreds (RSV captains), the Carites, the guards', i.e. the military force which was responsible for the *coup d'état*, and the additional 'people of the land' who represent popular support. Consistent with his different view, the Chronicler omits 'the Carites' and 'the guards' and replaces them by 'the nobles'(*hā'addīrīm*) and 'the governors of the people' (*hamōšᵉlīm bā'ām*). Both titles are rare and attested mainly in the poetic parts of the Bible; for the first, see in particular Neh. 3.5; 10.29 [MT 30].

The 'gate of the guard' of II Kings 11.19 is here rendered 'the upper gate'. These may have been different names for the same gate, but a corruption of the Kings text should not be ruled out. 'The upper gate of the house of the Lord' is mentioned in II Kings 15.35 (II Chron. 27.3); Ezek. 9.2; and probably also in Jer. 20.2.

Verse 21 sums up the various aspects of the event in three concluding clauses. 'The city was quiet' indicates the return of daily routine after the agitations; it may also imply that, notwithstanding appearances, there was some kind of resistance either from Athaliah's supporters or the Baal devotees. The emphatic 'all the people of the land rejoiced' (cf. also v. 13) is an expression of their active participation. According to Kings, the people entered the plot at a rather late stage (II Kings 11.14, 18, 19, 20), a fact which has prompted the suggestion that an original version of the story was reworked in this vein (cf. Gray, *Kings*, 565–9). In Chronicles the *coup* was the people's enterprise from the very beginning.

24 Joash was seven years old when he began to reign, and he reigned forty years in Jerusalem; his mother's name was Zibiah of Beer-Sheba. [2] And Joash did what was right in the eyes of the Lord all the days of Jehoiada the priest. [3] Jehoiada got for him two wives, and he had sons and daughters.

4 After this Joash decided to restore the house of the Lord. [5] And he gathered the priest and the Levites, and said to them, 'Go out to the cities of Judah, and gather from all Israel money to repair the house of your God from year to year; and see that you hasten the matter.' But the Levites did not hasten it. [6] So the king summoned Jehoada the chief, and said to him, 'Why have you not required the Levites to bring in from Judah and Jerusalem the tax levied by Moses, the servant of the Lord, on the congregation of Israel for the tent of testimony?' [7] For the sons of Athaliah, that wicked woman, had broken into the house of God; and had also used all the dedicated things of the house of the Lord for the Baals.

8 So the king commanded, and they made a chest, and set it outside the gate of the house of the Lord. [9] And proclamation was made throughout Judah and Jerusalem, to bring in for the Lord the tax that Moses the servant of God laid upon Israel in the wilderness. [10] And all the princes and all the people rejoiced and brought their tax and dropped it into the chest until they had finished. [11] And whenever the chest was brought to the king's officers by the Levites, when they saw that there was much money in it, the king's secretary and the officer of the chief priest would come and empty the chest and take it and return it to its place. Thus they did day after day, and collected money in abundance. [12] And the king and Jehoiada gave it to those who had charge of the work of the house of the Lord, and they hired masons and carpenters to restore the house of the Lord, and also workers in iron and bronze to repair the house of the Lord. [13] So those who were engaged in the work laboured, and the repairing went forward in their hands, and they restored the house of God to its proper condition and strengthened it. [14] And when they had finished, they brought the rest of the money before the king and Jehoiada, and with it were made utensils for the house of the Lord, both for the service and for the burnt offerings, and dishes for incense, and vessels of gold and silver. And they offered burnt offerings in the house of the Lord continually all the days of Jehoiada.

15 But Jehoiada grew old and full of days, and died; he was a hundred and thirty years old at his death. [16] And they buried him in the city of David among the kings, because he had done good in Israel, and toward God and his house.

17 Now after the death of Jehoiada the princes of Judah came and did obeisance to the king; then the king hearkened to them. [18] And they forsook the house of the Lord, the God of their fathers, and served the Asherim and the idols. And wrath came upon Judah and Jerusalem for this their guilt. [19] Yet he sent prophets among them to bring them back to the Lord; these testified against them, but they would not give heed.

20 Then the Spirit of God took possession of Zechariah the son of Jehoiada the priest; and he stood above the poeple, and said to them, 'Thus says God, "Why do

you transgress the commandments of the Lord, so that you cannot prosper? Because you have foresaken the Lord, he has forsaken you."'' [21] But they conspired against him, and by command of the king they stoned him with stones in the court of the house of the Lord. [22] Thus Joash the king did not remember the kindness which Jehoiada, Zechariah's father, had shown him, but killed his son. And when he was dying, he said, 'May the Lord see and avenge!'

23 At the end of the year the army of the Syrians came up against Joash. They came to Judah and Jerusalem, and destroyed all the princes of the people from among the people, and sent all their spoil to the king of Damascus. [24] Though the army of the Syrians had come with few men, the Lord delivered into their hand a very great army, because they had forsaken the Lord, the God of their fathers. Thus they executed judgment on Joash.

25 When they had departed from him, leaving him severely wounded, his servants conspired against him because of the blood of the son of Jehoiada the priest, and slew him on his bed. So he died; and they buried him in the city of David, but they did not bury him in the tombs of the kings. [26] Those who conspired against him were Zabad the son of Shime-ath the Ammonitess, and Jehozabad the son of Shimrith the Moabitess. [27] Accounts of his sons, and of the many oracles against him, and of the rebuilding of the house of God are written in the Commentary on the Book of the Kings. And Amaziah his son reigned in his stead.

A. Notes to MT

[7] בניה, read, probably, ובניה with LXX and V; [12] עושה, read עושי with several MSS and the Versions, cf. v. 13; [22] וכמתו, many MSS ובמתו; [25] בני, LXX and V בן; [26] זבד, II Kings 12.22 יוזבד, or B יוזכר, probably read זכר.

B. Notes to RSV

[4] 'decided', MT 'wished'; [5] 'from year to year', better 'annual tax' (NEB), 'repair' (JPS); 'did not hasten it', NEB 'did not act quickly'; [6] 'on the congregation', MT 'and the congregation' (RSV margin); [11] 'until they had finished', better NEB 'until it was full'; [14] 'continually', better 'regularly' (JPS); [15] 'But Jehoiada', MT 'Jehoiada'; [19] 'testified against them', better 'warned them'; [23, 24] 'the Syrians', MT 'the Aramaeans' (so NEB); 'Damascus', MT Darmesek; [24] 'They executed judgment', better JPS 'they inflicted punishment' (cf. also NEB); [27] 'the Commentary', NEB, JPS 'the story'.

C. Structure, sources and form

1. Chapter 24, the reign of Joash, parallels II Kings 12. The general lines of the composition of this chapter do in fact follow the Kings source, preserving the Deuteronomistic framework of introduction and conclusion (II Kings 12.1–3 [MT 4], 19–21 [MT 20–22]//II Chron. 24.1–2, 26–27), with all the topics of the source

material in their original order. Within this basic plan, however, the story is thoroughly reworked and a series of theological problems, which the Chronicler could not leave unresolved, leads to the emergence of a new history and portrayal of Joash.

2. The Kings narrative has four parts: Deuteronomistic opening (vv. 1–3 [MT 1–4]): Restoration of the Temple (vv. 4–16 [MT 5–17]); Hazael's invasion (vv. 17–18 [MT 18–19]); Deuteronomistic conclusion, with the assassination of Joash (vv. 19–21 [MT 20–22]). Even without examining details, this outline alone is, for the Chronicler, fraught with difficulties – in fact, historically impossible. His most basic convictions would not permit him to see the Temple restoration followed by the invasion of Jerusalem by a foreign king and the violent assassination of Joash by conspirators, especially given the Deuteronomistic appraisal that 'Jehoash did what was right in the eyes of the Lord all his days' (II Kings 12.2 [MT 3]). The simple recording of these incidents posed no difficulty for the Deuteronomist, but for the Chronicler, any calamity is conceived as a punishment and must be preceded by some sin; the Kings narrative, then, lacks the necessary historical and theological logic.

In dealing with this problem the Chronicler had more than one alternative. He could, for example, have preserved the positive view of Joash and readjusted the last part of his reign by omitting or changing the 'negative' elements: Hazael's campaign and the king's violent death. Such an adaptation would have been quite simple, from either angle, literary or theological, as illustrated in the histories of David and Solomon. The Chronicler, however, chose the more difficult alternative of keeping the negative information and complementing the necessary lacunae. He views the reign of Joash as composed of two completely distinct periods. In the first, Joash indeed does 'what was right in the eyes of the Lord' and fares well (vv. 1–16); then comes a turning point, the death of Jehoiada. Joash now forsakes the way of the Lord, for which he is justly punished (vv. 17–27). The Chronicler's reworking bears fruit in a lucid, theologically coherent composition.

3. The main feature of the adaptation is therefore the lengthy addition of vv. 15–22, which draws the line between the two periods, accompanied by extensive changes in detail. The resulting structure may be illustrated as follows:

(a) 1–16 The first period of the king's reign
     1–3 introduction
     4–14 restoration of the Temple
     15–16 Jehoiada's death and burial
(b) 17–27 The second period of the reign
     17–18 transgression
     19–22 warning: Zechariah and his fate
     23–24 Hazael's campaign
     25–27 conclusion: Joash's death and burial.

4. The chapter consists mainly of a narrative, but it also has several clearly Chronistic rhetorical sections: the short address of Joash to the Levites and his admonition of the high priest (vv. 5, 6–7), and Zechariah's prophecy and proclamation (vv. 20, 21). These give a more emphatic religious sense to the record of the events.

D. Commentary

[1–2] The biographical details of Joash follow II Kings 11.21–12.2 [MT 12.1–3], with the usual omission of synchronism with northern chronology. However, the religious appraisal of the Chronicler deviates from the source in two ways. While II Kings 12.2 [MT 3] describes Joash as doing 'what was right in the eyes of the Lord *all his days* because Jehoiada the priest instructed him', the Chronicler makes this final clause a reservation: Joash indeed did what was right, but only '*all the days* of Jehoiada the priest'. With this minor orthographic change (*ymyw/ymy*), the foundation is laid for the different periodization of the reign of Joash. The second change is the complete omission of II Kings 12.3 [MT 4] with its own reservations concerning the continued worship on the high places. This criticism, which, with slight variations, in the Deuteronomistic version characterizes the rule of six kings, is omitted in Chronicles for Joash and his three successors, Amaziah, Uzziah and Jotham (cf. also Japhet, *Ideology*, 219–20).

[3] In the Hebrew *wayyiśśā' lō* the prepositional phrase *lō* may be regarded as reflexive ('got for himself'), referring back to Jehoiada (so LXX), or dative 'for him', referring to Joash (RSV, *et al.*). The latter rendering is more probable (cf. 11.23 as commonly reconstructed) and serves to illustrate the role of the priest in Joash's life: taking upon himself the absent father's responsibilities, the priest not only guides the young king but chooses for him worthy wives. The 'sons and daughters' born of these unions give concrete expression to both the physical renewal and the moral blessing of the Davidic line.

The origin and value of this information are matters of question: I have pointed out several times that the Chronicler may have had additional sources about the royal family and administration, the late idiom being due to his formulation of that earlier material. On the other hand, the very general tone of the verse might indicate that these biographical data are the Chronicler's own surmises.

[4–14] The theme of the restoration of the Temple follows II Kings 12.4–15 [MT 5–16]. While certain phrases and details recur in both versions, the similarity is primarily in the broad lines of the narrative: (*a*) the general topic; (*b*) the record of two attempts to collect money for the restoration; (*c*) after the first, unsuccessful attempt, the collection is made in a 'chest'; (*d*) the king's reproach of the priests; (*e*) undertaking a comprehensive restoration in the Temple.

The Kings version relates the collection of funds and the subsequent restoration in two stages. First, Joash approaches the priests with the demand to collect for the building project all the money brought to the Temple: '*all the money brought as holy gifts* (NEB; RSV: holy things) ... and the money which a man's heart prompts him to bring to the house of the Lord' (12.4 [MT 5]). By the twenty-third year of the reign of Joash, however, nothing has been done. The king then initiates a different strategy: the priests are relieved of the duty of restoring the Temple, but at the same time are also deprived of the privilege of receiving the funds (v. 8 [MT 9]). This change is effected by Jehoiada's placing of a chest beside the altar, for the deposit of contributions. The responsibility for the money is shared by the high priest and the king; when enough is collected, it is appropriated for the restoration (vv. 9–12 [MT 10–13]).

These steps of Joash should be viewed in the perspective of the status and authority of the priests. Joash's new initiative implies the king's intervention in the Temple's financial administration – a realm initially seen as a priestly prerogative – and the establishment of the royal responsibility for the restoration of the Temple.

Two more notes of reservation are added: the accumulated money should be used exclusively for restoration – none of it for the making of vessels (12.13–14 [MT 14–15]); and a specific portion of the contributions, 'guilt offerings and ... sin offerings', was to be appropriated directly to the priests, and not used for restoration (v. 16 [MT 17]).

While the Chronicler also records a two-stage attempt to collect funds, one that ended in failure (vv. 4–5) and the other involving a chest (vv. 8–10), with the transition between these two marked by the king's admonition (vv. 6–7), the details are very different from the Kings version, as will soon become evident.

[4] The Chronicler opens the pericope with the common formula 'Some time after this' (NEB; RSV 'After this'), which not only serves explicitly as introduction, but establishes a literary link between matters not initially connected, and states that Jehoash wished (RSV 'decided', *hāyāh 'im lēb* cf. I Chron. 22.7; 28.2; II Chron. 6.7, etc.) to restore the Temple.

For the restoration, the term used here is *lᵉhaddēš* (literally: 'renovate', also v. 12), juxtaposed to 'repair (*lᵉhazzēq*) the house' (vv. 5, 12). These idioms completely replace the original terminology of II Kings 12, with its seven-fold emphasis on the construct *bedeq habbayit* (literally 'the damage of the house') – a term which is absent from Chronicles.

[5] The first stage of the project as presented in Chronicles is already more limited than in II Kings 12.4–5 [MT 5–6]. Here the king charges the priests only with the collection of funds, not with the actual restoration (cf. II Kings 12.5 [MT 6]: 'now let them repair'). Joash summons the priests and Levites, and sends them to 'gather from all Israel money to repair the house', urging them to make haste. In this address, some features of the Chronicler's view are introduced: the collection of funds is an *active role* of the clergy; they are to go out of Jerusalem and circuit the cities of Judah; the clergy comprises not

only the priests, as in II Kings 12, but also the Levites; and the money in question is not from random donations brought to the Temple, but is designated from the outset for the purpose of restoration.

The title 'Levites' is used in this verse in its double connotation: together with 'the priests', it has the narrower meaning of those members of the tribe of Levi who are not priests; in its second occurrence it refers to all the members of the tribe, priests and Levites alike.

The words 'from year to year' seem almost an afterthought. Their position in the syntax makes it difficult to decide whether they reflect an annual restoration (JPS), an annual circuit of the clergy, or an annual tax (NEB); the last seems the most probable – although Liver would regard this as a gloss (cf. J. Liver, 'The Ransom of Half Shekel', *Y. Kaufmann Jubilee Volume*, ed. M. Haran, Jerusalem 1960, 59–60*). These words (and the following vv. 6 and 9) have been connected with the regulations of Nehemiah's covenant: 'We also lay upon ourselves the obligation to charge ourselves yearly with the third part of a shekel for the service of the house of our God' (Neh. 10.32 [MT 33]). Reflecting the actual situation of the Chronicler's time, they were seen as anachronistically retrojected to the monarchical period. Liver, however, argued very strongly against this common view, pointing to the basic differences between the 'half-shekel' contribution of the Second Commonwealth, reflected in Nehemiah and other sources, and the Chronicler's concept of Joash's demand (ibid, 57–60).

The *motif* of 'going out to the cities of Judah' thus characterizes two of the major events in the history of Joash: Jehoiada sent the commanders to gather 'the Levites ... and the heads of fathers' houses ... to Jerusalem' (23.2) as the initial step in overthrowing Athaliah's rule; here Joash himself is sending forth the priests and Levites in a similar way. In both cases the Chronicler's predilection for decentralization and democratization is distinctly reflected.

[6] As the Levites do not accomplish their mission promptly, Joash summons Jehoiada and rebukes him for negligence. The king's criticism of the Levites is a major argument in Williamson's claim (following Welch) that vv. 5b–6 are a secondary, post-Chronistic gloss. As the detailed commentary will show, the difficulties are somewhat overstated in Williamson's presentation (320–1) and 'may not be so great as to require positing a later author for the section' (Dillard, 190). However, while in II Kings 12.7 [MT 8] Joash reproaches 'Jehoiada ... and the other priests', here the rebuke is for Jehoiada alone, as primarily responsible. The content and tone of the admonition are also completely different. I Kings 12.7 [MT 8] consists of a rhetorical question and a subsequent command: 'Why are you not repairing ... Now therefore take no more money... .' In the present context, the king's exhortation is not only longer, but more full of rhetorical emphases intending to convince and affect, by explaining first of all why the money was needed, and

what was the basis for the king's demand. By failing to supervise the fund-raising project, Jehoiada has neglected to fulfil not only the king's command, but also an ancient obligation set by 'Moses the servant of the Lord'.

The rather long definition of the people's contribution (repeated with slight variation in v. 9) is 'the tax levied by Moses, the servant of the Lord and (RSV on) the congregation of Israel for the tent of testimony'. This illustrates the Chronicler's view of the right and obligation exercised by Joash in collecting the money. The word *maś'at*, meaning essentially 'a contribution, gift' (cf. Gen. 43.34; II Sam 11.8; Jer. 40.5; Esther 2.18, and Baumgartner, 605), is found here and in v. 9 in the unique phrase 'the contribution of Moses', which probably denotes 'the contribution which Moses has decreed'. The explicit context of the 'tent of the testimony' (*'ōhel ha'ēdūt*) refers us to the context of the wilderness, and the exacting of 'half a shekel ... as an offering to the Lord' (Exod. 30.13), eventually allocated 'for the service of the tent of meeting' (*'ōhel mō'ēd*, v. 16), from 'each who is numbered in the census'. The identification of 'tabernacle' and 'Temple' and the application by the Chronicler of the laws pertaining to the former to the latter have been pointed out several times. In the context of the wilderness, however, this atonement offering is regarded as a one-time donation, while in this text it is more of a yearly tax (cf. on v. 5). The point being made in the present text is that Joash is not issuing an arbitrary command; he was simply enforcing an old statute, in response to an urgent need in the particular circumstances of his time, following a severe threat to the Temple divine worship.

Is this view exclusively Chronistic? Its foundations are already visible in II Kings 12: the funds allocated for the repairs are defined in II Kings 12.4 [MT 5] as 'the money for which each man is assessed', and 'the money from the assessment of persons'. Although difficult, these terms show unmistakable affinity to Exod. 30.13; 38.26 and Lev. 27.2ff., and may reflect early procedures of atonement (cf. also E. A. Speiser, 'Census and Ritual Expiation in Mari and Israel', *BASOR* 149, 1958, 17–25). The Chronicler's definition in this verse may therefore represent his exegesis of the older difficult texts: reducing the various categories into one, he links the initiative of Joash with Moses' ancient decree.

It is also of interest that this verse attributes the levying of the tax to 'Moses *and* the congregation' (RSV *on* the congregation). This view is more in line with Neh. 10.32 [MT 33], where the people actually take upon themselves this obligation, and the Chronicler's general attitude toward the people as full partners in any decision and undertaking.

[7] The persuasive tone which marks many rhetorical parts of Chronicles is most obvious in this verse, as Joash endeavours to convince Jehoiada that his demand is justified. The view that Athaliah and 'her sons' broke into the Temple is, as has already been pointed out, a novel idea of the Chronicler.

Accordingly, it was not a natural process of decline, in particular during the reigns of Jehoram, Ahaziah and Athaliah, that necessitated a restoration. Rather, the Temple was 'broken into' and all its 'sacred objects' were taken for Baal worship.

[8] The king's admonition to Jehoiada receives no reply, and the initiative still lies with Joash. Contrary to II Kings 12.9 [MT 10], where 'Jehoiada the priest took a chest, etc.', here Joash simply decides to introduce a different method of collection and he himself implements it. In principle, this is the same solution suggested in Kings, but for Chronicles, where Joash has been more involved in the matter from the very outset, his continuing to take the lead does not reduce the priests' responsibility. There is also a change in the location of the chest: not 'beside the altar on the right side', but 'outside the gate of the house of the Lord'; the implication is probably that the money was deposited directly by the people, without mediation by the priests (II Kings 12.9b [MT 10b]).

[9–10] The successful completion of the undertaking emphasizes three aspects of the event: first, the people's contribution is not a single response to an arbitrary royal demand, but rather the fulfilment of an age-old obligation. Further, in order that *all* the people may be aware of their obligation, a proclamation is made throughout the kingdom 'in Judah and Jerusalem', and subsequently 'all the princes and all the people' make their offerings. Thirdly, the whole-hearted good will and enthusiasm with which the money is donated are expressed by the reference to 'rejoicing' and by the fact that the chest is filled 'to the brim' (*'ad l^ekalleh*, RSV 'until they had finished'). This will be more emphasized in the next verse, where the emptying of the chest is a daily procedure.

The proclamation itself is expressed in the phrase *wayyit^enū qōl*, literally 'they gave a voice', the more common meaning of which is 'to raise the voice' (Prov. 1.20; 8.1; Lam. 2.7), or, with the preposition *'al*, 'to shout against' (Jer. 4.16; 12–8); it should here be interpreted as synonym of *ha^{"a}bīr qōl*, 'word was proclaimed' (Exod. 36.6; Ezra 1.1; 10.7; II Chron. 30.5).

[11–14] In v. 11, the literal similarity to II Kings 12.19 [MT 11] is more apparent than in the preceding verses, but the passage has undergone several reformulations of both language and emphasis. First, the role and responsibility of the king are greatly augmented. While Kings 12.10 refers to the king's secretary at the beginning of the verse, all the following actions are related in a general plural form (vv. 11–12, 14–15 [MT 12–13, 15–16]), or in the passive (vv. 13, 16 [MT 14, 17]). In this context, the king is mentioned much more often, before or replacing Jehoiada. Thus, although in the broader context of Joash's history the priest Jehoiada is afforded more attention and praise in Chronicles than in Kings, so far as the actual work on the Temple restoration is concerned, Jehoiada is first rebuked by Joash for his negligence (vv. 6–7, as elaboration of II Kings 12.7 [MT 8]), and during the restoration project itself, the priest is overshadowed by the king. These 'intersecting' lines in the reworking of the narrative are characteristic of the Chronicler's many-faceted guidelines, and should warn the reader against too dogmatic a view of his objectives.

The actual appropriation of the money is viewed as comprising three different stages. The precise understanding of the whole process depends on how we read the phrase *p^{e}quddat hammelek b^{e}yad hal^{e}wiyyim*. The translations render the abstract noun *p^{e}quddāh* as a concrete plural, i.e. 'the king's officers'. However, there is no support for this unusual rendering, and the usual sense of 'charge, task, commission' (cf. Baumgartner, 902) should be retained. The first stage would then be 'the commission of the king to the Levites' (*b^{e}yad hal^{e}wiyyim*), 'Levites' probably denoting the clergy in general, as in v. 5. The responsibility for emptying the chest and counting the money is entrusted to the 'king's secretary and the officer of the chief priest' (cf. II Kings 12.10 [MT 11], the high priest himself), and the allocation of the money is then carried out by the king and the high priest jointly.

Although it is clear that the emptying of the chest was a recurring event, the Kings text does not specify how often this occurred. The present verse is explicit: the *daily* collection yielded 'money in abundance'. The whole situation calls to mind the free-will offerings and great enthusiasm of David's days (cf. I Chron. 29.6–9).

Verses 12–14 are even farther from the source text, illustrating how thoroughly the Chronicler has reformulated the Kings version while still adhering to its theme and sequence. In II Kings 12.11–12 [MT 12–13] the workmen include only 'carpenters' and 'masons', the emphasis being on the basic materials of 'timber' and 'stone' needed for the repairs. There follows an explicit reservation that no cultic vessels are to be made (II Kings 12.13–14 [MT 14–15]). In Chronicles the description is made to include not only 'workers in iron and bronze' (v. 12), but also the use of funds for 'utensils for the house of the Lord ... vessels of silver and gold' (v. 14).

There are two reasons for these changes. While the Kings narrative gives the impression of economic dearth, the Chronicler's version emphasizes that 'they ... collected money in abundance' (v. 11), so much so that when the building was completed, money remained for other purposes. More importantly, according to the Chronicler's view, the replacement of the cultic vessels was imperative, since the Temple had been broken into and defiled by Athaliah. If the prohibition of II Kings 12.13 were followed, no ritual would be possible! The end of v. 14 confirms this view: after the restoration was completed and the new vessels provided, 'they offered burnt offering in the house of the Lord, regularly' (RSV 'continually').

From a literary point of view, the Chronicler's version of the restoration narrative is much more complete than the story of II Kings 12, which has neither a proper introduction (Kings 12.4 [MT 5] opens directly with Joash's instruction to the priests) nor a conclusion (12.15–16 [MT 16–17] closes with two notes about the honesty of the workers and the money which was exempt from use in the restoration). Chronicles, by contrast, provides an explicit introduction: 'Some time after this Joash decided to restore the house of the Lord', and has two successive conclusions. The first (v. 13) relates at length, with an inclination to parallelism and poetic idiom, that the restoration was successfully accomplished. The words 'the repairing went forward' (RSV) actually stand for the Hebrew poetic idiom of 'healing' (*watta'al '"rūkāh*, cf. Jer. 8.22; 30.17; 33.6; Isa. 58.8). The use of this idiom in reference to a building (cf. also Neh. 4:7 [MT 4.1]), together with the rare word *matkōnet* (RSV 'proper condition'; cf. Exod. 5.8; 30.32, 37; Ezek. 45.11), the unique *way°'amm°ṣuhū* as synonym for 'strengthen', the repetition of *m°lā'kāh*, 'work', and the consistent use of the imperfect consecutive all add to the concluding force of the verse. Verse 14, with its final reference to the renewed Temple ritual, ends with 'all the days of Jehoiada', clearly referring back to v. 2: these were the days when 'Joash did what was right in the eyes of the Lord', and it is in this way that the Chronicler epitomizes the positive period of Joash's reign, now ended.

[15–16] The significance of this completely new passage for the Chronicler's narrative is twofold: in the immediate context, the death of Jehoiada marks the end of the first period of Joash's career; in the broader context, this is the only case of the Chronicler reporting the death and burial of someone other than a king, and in fact, the terms used here are those regularly employed for the kings (cf. in particular I Chron. 29.27–28). The chronological note regarding the length of a king's reign is replaced here by the priest's age.

We have noted several times that for the Chronicler, the circumstances of burial are a significant component of God's reward. The fact that Jehoiada is honoured by being laid to rest 'in the city of David among the kings' points to his exceptional worth, and should of course be contrasted with the burial of Joash himself, 'in the city of David', but 'not in the tombs of the kings' (v. 25). For Jehoiada the priest, the unique gesture of royal respect is fully explained by the 'good' he had done, first 'in Israel', by ensuring the survival of David's house, and also 'toward God', by renewing regular Temple worship in all its aspects.

Did the Chronicler have any extra-biblical source for the information contained in this passage? The evidence does not seem to be conclusive. The pericope as a whole contains several scattered data about Jehoiada which were not recorded in Kings: the facts that Jehosheba, king Jehoram's daughter, was Jehoiada's wife (22.11), and that Jehoiada took wives for the young monarch (24.3), Jehoiada's great age and his entombing among the kings (24.15–16), and the name and fate of his son (24.20–22), all items which may have been drawn from some outside tradition. However, the specific notes recorded in this passage – concerning Jehoiada's longevity, and his burial in the city of David – seem to be of a homiletic rather than a historical nature.

[17–22] This long Chronistic addition serves as a necessary preamble to the events recorded from v. 23. Here is a description of the king's sin (v. 17–18), a prophetic warning (vv. 19–20), and the king's murder of the prophet (vv. 21–22) – all of which provide the causal background for the indicated punishment in vv. 23ff.

[17–18] The description of the transgression of Joash fully parallels the first part of his reign. Then, Joash was guided by the wisdom of Jehoiada, but now, just like his father Ahaziah, he is misled by an evil counsel (cf. also 22.3–5). The difference between the two parts of his reign is thus due to the different sources of advice and guidance: Jehoiada in the first, the 'princes of Judah' in the second.

The sin of the king and his advisors is described with the unique phrase: 'forsook the house of the Lord (*bēt yhwh*) the God of their fathers'. LXX^AB omits the word 'house', and Rudolph, following one Hebrew MS (two, according to BHS), would read instead 'the covenant of the Lord' (*bᵉrīt yhwh*, Rudolph, 276). However, 'the house' has been the focus of 'doing what is right' for Joash, and moreover plays an essential role in his life: he was concealed 'in the house of God' (22.12), he was crowned there (23.3, 6, 11, etc.), and the restoration of the Temple was his major undertaking (ch. 24). The forsaking of the Lord, under the anti-priestly influence of evil advisors, is viewed primarily as abandoning God's house (cf. also S. Zalevski, 'The Problem of Reward in the Story of the Sin of Jehoash and his Punishment', *Beth Mikra* 21, 1975/6, 279*).

The definition of idolatry given here is unique. 'Asherim' is quite a common term in Chronicles (II Chron. 14.2; 17.6; etc.), but the specific term for 'idols' (*ᵃṣabbīm*) occurs only once more, in I Chron. 10.9//I Sam. 31.9.

The passage ends with a distinctively Chronistic statement, with the characteristic 'wrath' and 'guilt' and more references to 'Judah and Jerusalem' (cf. v. 9). This condemnation betrays the theological origin of the entire passage: the Chronicler's need to substantiate and justify the imminent disasters.

[19] It is difficult to overestimate the significance of this verse for understanding a major facet in the Chronicler's concept of prophecy: its task as 'warning'. I have already referred to this matter several times (cf. on II Chron. 19.9–10, and Japhet, *Ideology*, 176–91); but it is in this context that warning is presented both as a general phenomenon (v. 19) and with a particular example (v. 20). This verse is an accurate presentation of the

warning, with the root *ʿwd* in the *hiphil* conjugation and the preposition *bᵉ* used in this early connotation: 'The Lord sent prophets among them to bring them back to him, they warned them (*wayyāʿîdū bām*) but they would not give heed' (the RSV rendering 'testified against them' misses the sense). A warning is a measure of an individual's 'wilfulness' and so of his liability to punishment. A similar general reference to the prophetic warning is found again in Chronicles only in the context of the destruction of Jerusalem (36.15), where this opportunity for repentance is presented as the ultimate expression of God's compassion for his people.

[20] Following the general statement, a specific example is reported in full: the appearance of Zechariah the son of the priest Jehoiada, inspired on this very occasion, apparently for the first time: 'The spirit of the Lord took possession of Zechariah' (cf. also on I Chron. 12.19). The dramatic effect of this episode highlights the complex dynamic of the situation, some of which is expressed explicitly in v. 22: 'Joash ... did not remember the kindness which Jehoiada ... had shown him, but killed his son'. However, Zechariah's intervention and his fate should be viewed in a political and historical context broader than the personal relationship between Joash and Jehoiada (cf. also H. Reviv, 'The Times of Athaliah and Joash', *Beth Mikra* 16, 1971/2, 541–8*).

We have noted above that the death of Jehoiada marks a turning point in Joash's reign; now, from the same family, comes admonition against the king's new cults. In a more general perspective this may illustrate the conflict between the priests and the bureaucracy, presented here in terms of religious loyalty. The fact that Joash was eventually assassinated by his 'servants' (v. 25) may indicate more than the Chronicler's historiosophical inclinations: an echo of actual tensions within the Judaean court under Joash.

Did 'Zechariah the son of Jehoiada' succeed his father as high priest? This would certainly sharpen the historical irony of the episode; however, the text does not support the inference. Nor do we find Zechariah's name in the priestly genealogies (I Chron. 6.4ff. [MT 5.30ff.]; Ezra 7.1–5), although this is far from compelling, as Jehoiada too is missing from these lists.

Zechariah's prophecy exemplifies in both phrasing and content the Chronicler's rhetorical method: it opens with a rhetorical question ('why ...') and ends with an explanatory statement ('because ...'); the immediate bond between a man's actions and his fate is described with a literary application of the 'measure for measure' principle (cf. also Zalevski, 279): 'Because you have forsaken the Lord, he has forsaken you'.

[21] The short note about the killing of Zechariah raises several questions. Most immediately striking is the gross lack of proportion between Zechariah's admonition and his execution. His brief prophecy was couched in the most general terms, with no specific threats. When compared, for

example, with the harsh words of Jeremiah and his contemporaries during the time of the destruction (Jer. 26, etc.), the much earlier prophecy of Amos (Amos 7.7–17), or even the words of Micaiah the son of Imlah (I Kings 22.28//II Chron. 18.27), the unprovocative character of Zechariah's prophecy is all the more obvious. Are these words deserving the death penalty?

The second problem regards the manner of Zechariah's killing: this is not a private business, limited to the king's court (cf. Jer. 26.20–23). The prophet is stoned openly, *coram populo*, in the Temple courtyard. This desecration of the sacred precinct is even more glaring in light of Jehoiada's orders regarding Athaliah: 'Do *not* slay her in the house of the Lord' (II Chron. 23.14//II Kings 11.15). The particular effect of stoning is first and foremost in its public character; it is always executed by a crowd, whether as lynching by an angry mob (I Kings 12.18; Exod. 8.22; 17.4; Num. 14.10), or as an organized act, expressing the extinguishing of evil within the community. The decree of stoning is explicitly related to this public effect: 'all Israel shall hear and fear' (Deut. 13.10–11 [MT 11–12]), and 'you shall purge the evil from the midst of you' (Deut. 17.5–7; 21.21; 22.21; etc.). Some cases of actual stoning are described in the biblical narrative; the best-known are the stoning of Achan (Josh. 7.25) and Naboth the Jezreelite (I Kings 21.8–16).

A third question is raised by the choice of words: 'they conspired against him (Zechariah)'; this idiom is usually used in the opposite sense, i.e. the individual conspiring against the state (cf. Amos 7.10). The exceptional nature of this story and its analogy to the case of Naboth, against whom a royal conspiracy is indeed initiated, may imply that the prophet Zechariah is considered a traitor – an understanding which is confirmed by the next verse.

[22] The Chronicler's evaluation of the cruel deed of Joash is, again, quite mild. Zechariah's death is attributed to the ingratitude of Joash, who forgot the kindness shown him by Jehoiada. In fact, the prophet's dying words are themselves indecisive; they express Zechariah's subjective claim of innocence but leave the avenging of his death to the Lord's discretion. There is every indication that Zechariah's intervention is interpreted as treason: this explains the mode of his execution, the lack of balance between his prophecy and fate, the fact that Joash is not accused of 'shedding innocent blood' but only of ingratitude, and Zechariah's last words. Is there any connection with the eventual death of Joash by the conspiracy of 'his servants' (v. 25)? One wonders if the story about Zechariah does not preserve echoes of a tradition about the intricate relationship between king, priesthood and bureaucracy during the critical days of Joash and continuing into the reign of Amaziah. The Chronicler has employed this tradition on another plane: within the framework of his own philosophy, presenting a prophet who delivers a divine warning to the king, whose response determines his future fortunes.

[23–25] The punishment meted out to Joash is described in two stages: for his first sin, the idolatry he shared with the princes of Judah and the people (vv. 17–18), comes the invasion of the Aramaean army, affecting 'Judah and Jerusalem', killing 'the princes' and wounding the king (vv. 23–25aα). For the slaying of Zechariah, a sin imputed to Joash alone, he now must pay 'measure for measure', with his own life (v. 25aβ–b). This unequivocal accord between the sins and their consequences is not the speculation of a modern commentator, but is explicitly stated in these verses: the Aramaeans attacked Jerusalem and Judah 'because they had forsaken the Lord, the God of their fathers' (v. 24, cf. the use of the verb *'zb* in v. 19 and 24, and then again in v. 25), and Joash met a violent end 'because of the blood of the son (MT sons) of Jehoiada' (v. 25).

[23–24] The theme of the Aramaean invasion is common to this chapter and to II Kings 12; however, the two versions differ in every respect. In Kings, Hazael the king of Aram had conquered Gath and was making preparations to attack Jerusalem, only to withdraw upon receipt of a heavy tribute from Joash – the entire treasury of Jerusalem. In military and political terms, this would imply an Aramaean conquest of certain territories in Judah or on its borders, but no general incursion into the kingdom, and certainly not to Jerusalem.

In Chronicles, the details of the narrative are almost the opposite. The attack of the Aramaean army is not led by the king Hazael in person, a fact emphasized by the explicit statement that the commanders 'sent all their spoil to the king of Damascus' (v. 23); the army does not stay on the frontiers of Judah but invades the kingdom as far as Jerusalem, 'destroying' the princes, striking the forces of Joash a severe blow, and taking great spoil. Moreover, king Joash himself is 'severely wounded' (v. 25aα).

The scope of Joash's defeat is emphasized by the statement that the Aramaean army came 'with few men'. This is probably the reason that the invasion is described here as a raid of a small band rather than a campaign conducted by the Aramaean king. Although few in number, the Lord 'delivered into their hands a very great army'. That the few and weak prevail against the strong and many is a common feature in Chronicles (and elsewhere); it gives concrete proof that 'the war is of the Lord'. However, until now this principle has described Israel's victories over its powerful enemies; here the tables are turned: when Israel sins, no amount of military might can avail, for the Lord strengthens the hand of their enemies.

The two versions of this episode share nothing but the general topic. Did the Chronicler have an alternative source for his version, a description of another Aramaean campaign, different from the one described in the Deuteronomistic material in Kings (cf. Williamson, 325–6)? Or, is this pericope the Chronicler's own adaptation of II Kings 12.17–18 [MT 18–19]? The latter alternative is more likely, for several reasons:

(a) The historical assumptions of the story, that the Aramaean raiders succeeded in invading Jerusalem, even injuring the king, are not supported by any source and are hardly probable. There is no evidence that the forces of Aram reached so far, especially at the very time in their history when their previous increasing pressure on Israel was beginning to diminish (II Kings 13.7, 22–25).

(b) There are points of similarity between this narrative and the Chronicler's version of Shishak's campaign against Jerusalem (II Chron. 12.2–12); these indicate the probability of literary reformulation in this case.

(c) The full accord in the Chronicles narrative between sin and punishment highlights its theological nature, and its function in the more comprehensive theological composition.

It would seem, therefore, that although Hazael's attack against Judah is described in terms entirely different from the Kings' version, we are still dealing with an adaptation of the basic data, with thorough adjustment of the details.

Several points of language and style should be pointed out. Characteristic Chronistic vocabulary is evident in 'the Lord the God of their fathers', the rather unusual and broad connotation of the root *šḥt*, and the preference for 'Judah and Jerusalem'. The peculiar syntax presents us with one long sentence composed of a series of clauses, in a complex parenthetic and causal sequence: 'They came to Judah and Jerusalem ... and sent all their spoil to the king of Damascus – *for* (*kī*, RSV 'though') the army of the Aramaeans (RSV 'Syrians') had come with a few men, the Lord delivered ... a very great army, *because* (*kī*) they had forsaken the Lord ... and (RSV 'thus') they inflicted punishment on Joash.' Cf. also the parenthetic/causal clause of v. 25 – 'for (*kī*) they left him severely wounded' – and the specific use of the temporal infinitive *ūbᵉlektām*, 'at their departure' (RSV 'when they had departed'); for the latter, cf. in this chapter: *wᵉkir'ōtām* (v. 11, literally 'at their seeing'), *ūkekallōtām* (v. 14, literally 'at their completing'), *ūkᵉmōtō* (v. 22, literally 'at his dying').

[25–26] The last episode, Joash's death, is reported in great detail and with many changes from the source in II Kings 12.20–21 [MT 21–22]. With the exception of Athaliah, who was regarded as a usurper, Joash was the first Judaean king whose death was brought about by conspirators; he will be followed by his son Amaziah (II Kings 14.19–20//II Chron. 25.27–28) and, much later, Amon the son of Manasseh (II Kings 21.23//II Chron. 33.24). In all of these cases the dynasty is not adversely affected by the conspiracy, as it is always the son of the assassinated king who succeeds him on the throne. The causes of these conspiracies are probably to be sought in the kings' internal and international policies, the details of which are no longer available. It is nevertheless no coincidence that the unrest and general lack of stability which characterize the days of Jehoram – Ahaziah – Athaliah continue during the reigns of the succeeding kings, Joash and Amaziah; only under Uzziah does political stability return to Judah, and although tensions and opposing political forces are certainly attested for the time of Ahaz (cf. Isa. 7.3–9), this stability will endure almost to the end of the Judaean monarchy.

The description of the death of Joash both adheres to the Deuteronomistic source and deviates from it in many ways. In both versions, the narrative follows two stages: first the assassination (II Kings 12.21 [MT 20])/II Chron. 24.25), and then details of the conspirators (II Kings 12.21, [MT 22]//II Chron. 24.26). Of the differences between the two versions, I would mention the following:

(a) The position of the passage in the context has been changed; it is here seen explicitly as a direct sequel to the Aramaean invasion: 'When they had departed from him ... his servants conspired ...'. The intervening reference in II Kings 12.19 [MT 20] to further sources for the reign of Joash is transferred to the end of the chapter, where it is also differently phrased. These changes in literary structure are in fact the results of a theological adaptation of the whole pericope.

(b) Some of the details are either different or altogether new. According to II Kings 12.20 [MT 21] Joash was assassinated 'in the house of Millo, on the way that goes down to Silla' – an extremely obscure designation. The text in Chronicles is much simpler on this point: they 'slew him on his bed'; this change too is indicated by the new sequence, since Joash has already been 'severely wounded' by the Aramaeans.

II Kings 12.21 [MT 22] states that Joash was buried 'with his fathers in the city of David', while the present text expresses the reservation 'they buried him in the city of David, but they did not bury him in the tombs of the kings'. There is an intentional and significant contrast to the burial of Jehoiada (v. 16) who, although not of royal lineage, was laid to rest 'in the city of David among the kings'.

A third change in detail is the variation in the names of the conspirators, and their presentation as of foreign origin. The patronymic elements have here feminine forms: 'Shimeath' (so also II Kings 12.21 [MT 22]) and 'Shimrith' (II Kings 12.21, 'Shomer'), referring to the conspirator's mothers, an 'Ammonitess' and a 'Moabitess'. The ostensibly feminine ending (th) is in fact also attested in masculine proper names (cf. Goliath in I Sam. 17.4 etc.; Kohath, in Gen. 46.11, etc.; cf. Gesenius, §80f-g, 223); thus the renderings in II Kings 11.22 (Shimeath, Shomer) may be understood as patronymic. In Chronicles, by contrast, the form 'Shimrith' for 'Shomer' and the feminine titles 'Moabitess' and 'Ammonitess' surely indicate that the Chronicler himself identifies the two names with the mothers of the conspirators (cf. also his change of 'Jehosheba' to 'Jehoshabeath' in 22.1). Genealogical affiliation through the mother is quite rare in the Bible, yet not unknown – cf. in particular the affiliation of Joab and Abishai through their mother Zeruiah (I Sam. 26.6; II Sam. 2.18, etc.).

There is no conclusive answer to the difficult question of sources in this case. It is hard to see why the Chronicler would 'invent' this unique information, identifying ministers in the Judaean court as of foreign origin; it seems more likely that the identification was found in his source and was subsequently omitted in Kings.

(c) A last difference between the two versions is the addition of: 'because of the blood of the son (MT sons) of Jehoiada'. This explanation is both historical and theological; it reflects the conflicting political currents in the royal court and also makes the punishment meted out to Joash fit his crime: he who instigated a conspiracy against Zechariah (v. 21) now falls victim to conspirators.

[27] This reference to additional sources is unique in Chronicles. The common Chronistic formula, 'now the rest of the deeds of X from first to last', which appears with slight variations for most of the Judaean kings, is here replaced by three specific subjects: 'his sons', 'the many oracles against him', and 'the rebuilding of the house of God' (cf. specifics like these for Manasseh, in II Chron. 33.18–19). We have no way of confirming the Chronicler's references here. The account of the Temple building is already found in Kings, and the Chronicler's deviations can be fully explained without the assumption of additional sources. Certainly the very general allusion to 'sons' (v. 3), and the generally phrased prophecy (v. 20), cannot be used as supporting evidence.

Even the title of the source referred to in this remark is unique: 'the Commentary on the Book of the Kings' (*midraš sēper hammᵉlākīm*, cf. 13.22 *midrāš hannābīʾ ʿiddō*), and has received great attention in scholarly works, with a growing awareness that the sense of 'midrash' here cannot be learned from the much later rabbinic usage. Following the sense of the root *drš* in biblical Hebrew ('search', 'seek', and then 'study'), one may conceive of this work as one in which the acts of the king were recorded in more detail. More than this would be conjecture. For the importance of this title to the general question of sources in Chronicles, cf. the Introduction.

25 Amaziah was twenty-five years old when he began to reign, and he reigned twenty-nine years in Jerusalem. His mother's name was Jeho-addan of Jerusalem. ² And he did what was right in the eyes of the Lord, yet not with a blameless heart. ³ And as soon as the royal power was firmly in his hand he killed his servants who had slain the king his father. ⁴ But he did not put their children to death, according to what is written in the law, in the book of Moses, where the Lord commanded, 'The fathers shall not be put to death for the children, or the children be put to death for the fathers; but every man shall die for his own sin.'

5 Then Amaziah assembled the men of Judah, and set them by fathers' houses under commanders of thousands and of hundreds for all Judah and Benjamin. He mustered those twenty years old and upward, and found that they were three hundred thousand picked men, fit for war, able to handle spear and shield. ⁶ He hired also a hundred thousand mighty men of valour from Israel for a hundred talents of silver. ⁷ But a man of God came to him and said, 'O king, do not let the army of Israel go with you, for the Lord is not with Israel, with all these Ephraimites. ⁸ But if you suppose that in this way you will be strong for war, God will cast you down before the enemy; for God has power to help or to cast down.' ⁹ And Amaziah said to the man of God, 'But what shall we do about the hundred talents which I have given to the army of Israel?' The man of God answered, 'The Lord is able to give you much more than this.' ¹⁰ Then Amaziah discharged the army that had come to him from Ephraim, to go home again. And they became very angry with Judah, and returned home in fierce anger. ¹¹ But Amaziah took courage, and led out his people, and went to the valley of Salt and smote ten thousand men of Seir. ¹² The men of Judah captured another ten thousand alive, and took them to the top of a rock and threw them down from the top of the rock; and they were all dashed to pieces. ¹³ But the men of the army whom Amaziah sent back, without letting go with him to battle, fell upon the cities of Judah, from Samaria to Beth-horon, and killed three thousand people in them, and took much spoil.

14 After Amaziah came from the slaughter of the Edomites, he brought the gods of the men of Seir, and set them up as his gods, and worshipped them, making offerings to them. ¹⁵ Therefore the Lord was angry with Amaziah and sent to him a prophet, who said to him, 'Why have you resorted to the gods of a people, which did not deliver their own people from your hand?' ¹⁶ But as he was speaking the king said to him, 'Have we made you a royal counsellor? Stop! Why should you be put to death?' So the prophet stopped, but said, 'I know that God has determined to destroy you, because you have done this and have not listened to my counsel.'

17 Then Amaziah king of Judah took counsel and sent to Joash the son of Jehoahaz, son of Jehu, king of Israel, saying, 'Come, let us look one another in the face.' ¹⁸ And Joash the king of Israel sent word to Amaziah king of Judah, 'A thistle on Lebanon sent to a cedar on Lebanon, saying, "Give your daughter to my son for a wife"; and a wild beast of Lebanon passed by and trampled down the thistle. ¹⁹ You say, "See, I

have smitten Edom," and your heart has lifted you up in boastfulness. But now stay at home; why should you provoke trouble so that you fall, you and Judah with you?'

20 But Amaziah would not listen; for it was of God, in order that he might give them into the hand of their enemies, because they had sought the gods of Edom. [21] So Joash king of Israel went up; and he and Amaziah king of Judah faced one another in battle at Beth-shemesh, which belongs to Judah. [22] And Judah was defeated by Israel, and every man fled to his home. [23] And Joash king of Israel captured Amaziah king of Judah, the son of Joash, son of Ahaziah, at Beth-shemesh, and brought him to Jerusalem, and broke down the wall of Jerusalem for four hundred cubits, from the Ephraim Gate to the Corner Gate. [24] And he seized all the gold and silver, and all the vessels that were found in the house of God, and Obed-edom with them; he seized also the treasuries of the king's house, and hostages, and he returned to Samaria.

25 Amaziah the son of Joash king of Judah lived fifteen years after the death of Joash the son of Jehoahaz, king of Israel. [26] Now the rest of the deeds of Amaziah, from first to last, are they not written in the Book of the Kings of Judah and Israel? [27] From the time when he turned away from the Lord they made a conspiracy against him in Jerusalem, and he fled to Lachish. But they sent after him to Lachish and slew him there. [28] And they brought him upon horses; and he was buried with his fathers in the city of David.

26 And all the people of Judah took Uzziah, who was sixteen years old, and made him king instead of his father Amaziah. [2] He built Eloth and restored it to Judah, after the king slept with his fathers.

A. Notes to MT

[3] עליו, MSS, Versions and II Kings 14.5 בידו; [4] כי, proposed omit; [6] גבור, Sebirin גבורי; [8] למלחמה, probably add למה; [20] ביד, proposed בידו; [23] הפונה, read הפינה with MSS, Versions and II Kings 14.13; [24] התערבות, add לקח, cf. II Kings 14.4 and the Peshitta; [26] הלא, omit?; [28] יהודה, MSS, Versions and II Kings 14.20 דוד; [26.1] עזיהו, II Kings 14.21ff. עזריה.

B. Notes to the RSV

[2] 'blameless heart', MT 'whole heart' (NEB 'whole-heartedly'); [3] 'in his hand', thus II Kings 14.5, cf. A above; [4] 'be put to death', thus II Kings 14.6, MT 'die' (thus NEB and JPS); [8] 'But if you suppose, etc.', better JPS 'But go by yourself and do it; take courage for battle', cf. commentary; [14] 'the slaughter', MT 'defeating' (JPS); [17] 'let us look one another in the face', JPS 'let us confront each other', cf. also v. 21; [19] 'I have smitten', MT 'you have smitten'; [23] 'Ahaziah', MT 'Jehoahaz'; 'Corner Gate', cf. A above; [24] 'and Obed-edom with them', better 'in the care of Obed-edom' (NEB; cf. also JPS); [28] 'David', MT Judah.

C. Structure, sources and form

1. The history of Amaziah is based on the parallel Deuteronomistic material (II Kings 14.1–22), which is preserved in its entirety, in precisely the same order, with only very slight changes. At the same time, however, the borrowed material is adapted by

means of various Chronistic additions into a new historical and theological composition.

2. We would do well to open with an outline of II Kings 14.1–22, the Deuteronomistic source on which the structure of the present narrative depends:

14.1–12 Conventional Deuteronomistic opening
14.5–6 A note on the execution of the conspirators
14.7 War with Edom
14.8–14 Amaziah's war with Jehoash, king of Israel
14.17–22 Conclusion, including Amaziah's death and the accession of Uzziah.

This general structure informs the Chronicler's narrative as well, from the Deuteronomistic opening formula and the note on the execution of the assassins (vv. 1–4) to the concluding formula, with all its details (25.25–26.2). The description of Amaziah's war with Joash, the king of Israel, is taken from II Kings 14.8–14 with only slight changes, the most important of which is the addition of v. 20. The war with Edom, however (vv. 5–16), while derived essentially from the brief account of II Kings 14.7 (which forms the basis for the central description of the battle in vv. 10–11), becomes, through the Chronicler's lengthy additions (vv. 5–10; 13–16), the focus of a series of significant events, both political and religious.

3. The structure of the Chronicles version may be illustrated as follows:

(a) 1–4 Introduction
        1–2 opening formula
        3–4 execution of Joash's assassins
(b) 5–16 War against Edom
        5–10 preparations for the war
            5 mustering of the Judean army
            6–10 hiring of an Israelite band
        11–12 the battle
        13–16 the aftermath
            13 the Ephraimite raid in Judah
            14–16 Amaziah's worship of the Edomite gods
(c) 17–24 War against Joash king of Israel
        17–20 preparations
            17 challenge
            18–19 the response
            20 theological comment
        21–22 the battle
        23–24 the aftermath
(d) 25.25–26.2 Conclusions
        25.5–28 the record of the remainder of Amaziah's life, and the account of his death
        26.1 –2 the accession of Uzziah

4. As in so many cases, the change of structure reflects the theological difficulties posed for the Chronicler by the Deuteronomistic version. In Kings, the righteousness of Amaziah – 'he did what was right in the eyes of the Lord' (II Kings 14.3), followed appropriately by his victory over Edom (v. 7), is then succeeded by a serious

military defeat (vv. 12–14) and Amaziah's violent assassination (vv. 19–20). This sequence, for the Chronicler, utterly lacks historical and theological probability. There must be a missing link, a change in the king's conduct which would account for his later evil fortunes. This change is provided by Chronicles in vv. 14–16: Amaziah's transgression and his refusal to heed the Lord's warning – a development very similar to the history of Joash (cf. 24.17–22). Once established, the king's sudden apostasy is referred to as the plot unfolds, e.g. v. 20: 'because they had sought the gods of Edom', and v. 27: 'From the time when he turned away from the Lord'.

The similarity with the Joash pericope is one of motive and basic historiographical procedure; our attention is drawn, however, to the differences in the methods of adaptation. In both narratives the Chronicler employed the topics and material of the Deuteronomistic parallel, and yet the themes of Jehoiada's revolt, the restoration of the Temple and the Aramaean invasion are presented with very few actual citations from II Kings 11–12; the adaptation is really a transformation of the source-texts. At the same time, only very few verses in the Joash pericope (especially in the second part) are pure additions. In the Amaziah narrative the situation is different: not only is most of the material cited literally (or almost so) from II Kings 14, but the Chronicles text (especially for the early part of the story) contains many additions.

5. The question of divine justice may account for some features of the new section of the text, vv. 5–13. Since Amaziah's reign is conceived as composed of two periods, the first (righteous) years must be portrayed in some way parallel to the later apostasy, when he worshipped the gods of Edom. Amaziah's success in the first part of his reign is thus augmented to include a note on his army (v. 5) and an elaboration of his military exploits in the Edomite war (vv. 11–12). However, principles of divine justice, or a system of retribution, are not sufficient to explain the story about the 'Israelite band', a major literary component of the first part of the king's reign. In fact, from a theological point of view, especially for the Chronicler, the integration of this story into the pericope leaves a number of unsolved questions. The prophet's response to Amaziah, 'The Lord is able to give you much more than this', implying the recovery of the lost 'hundred talents', is not confirmed by the events as told. Although Amaziah is victorious in his campaign against Edom, there is no mention of any material gain (quite unlike Asa and Jehoshaphat, 14.13–15 [MT 12–14]; 20.25). In fact, Amaziah's loss of the hundred talents is aggravated when the dismissed Israelites spoil and damage the cities of Judah. Thus, in terms of the Chronistic theory of divine retribution, Amaziah is actually punished for his proper conduct in heeding the prophet's demand. We look in vain here for some account of transgression by Amaziah, or by the inhabitants of the spoiled cities. And finally, it is precisely the Ephraimites, of whom the prophet said 'The Lord is not with Israel, with all these Ephraimites', who have the upper hand in their encounter with Judah.

There is lack of integration, then, on two planes: the prophet's promise to the king concerning the 'hundred talents' is not fulfilled, and the narrative as a whole remains in some tension with the Chronicler's theological system. The resulting literary and thematic tension has several implications. First, we can rule out the possibility that the Chronicler wrote the passage himself (cf. Rudolph, 281; Williamson, 328; Dillard, 197, and also below); further, the Chronistic motive of a 'divine retribution system' is not a sufficient explanation for the inclusion of the story in Chronicles. This, then, must be due to the Chronicler's interest in northern Israel and its people. The Chronicler systematically relates all the encounters between the northern kingdom and the people of Judah, and this pericope is particularly significant as it elucidates an otherwise obscure aspect of these complex relationships. It attests to a reality of local animosity and unrest between North and South during the monarchic period.

6. Did the Chronicler have extra-biblical sources for his story? The question is relevant to the data about Amaziah's army, the hiring of the Israelite band and its aftermath, and the course of the Edomite war. These notices have as their common topic the military circumstances of Israel and Judah, but the different nature of each of these reports requires us to discuss them separately.

(a) I have already briefly referred to the hiring of the Ephraimite band, which is not merely a historical note but a multi-faceted narrative with clear stages of development. It is best defined as the literary elaboration of a short chronicle, originally concerning the raiding of Judahite cities by an Ephraimite band formerly loyal to the king of Judah. The elaboration is found mainly in the explanatory part of the story – the causes for the dismissal of the band, presented in a dialogue between prophet and king (vv. 7–9).

The unique quality of the story is to be found not only in its details, but in its general historical presuppositions. As I have already demonstrated, this passage could not have been the composition of the Chronicler himself; a source of some kind must be posited: for a detailed discussion, cf. the commentary.

(b) There is no serious reason to dismiss out of hand the information about the organization of the army in the days of Amaziah, unless we assume that the Chronicler could not have had at his disposal any additional sources from the monarchical period (cf. Wellhausen, 222 etc.), or that all the data regarding the organization of the army were, at most, retrospected (Welten, 105ff.). In fact, there is nothing impossible or improbable in the account as it stands, except for the numbers – a problem endemic in Chronicles, for which no satisfactory solution has been offered (cf. above on II Chron. 17.14–19). It should be noted, however, that the difficulty with the numbers cannot really be dispelled by claiming that the whole passage is fictitious or retrospective. Historically, the war with Edom must as a matter of course have been preceded by a mustering and preparation of the army, similar to the Chronicles account, even if the book of Kings chose to relate only some final facts about this war. The conscription according to 'father's houses', in divisions of hundreds and thousands, is confirmed elsewhere, and even the total is not as extravagant as numbers given in other cases – considering the fact that we are dealing with a conscript army.

A weighty argument against the authenticity of these data is the claim that the Chronicler systematically attributes 'military facts' to the 'positive' kings, implying that military notes of this kind are *de facto* tendentious and unreliable (cf. Wellhausen, 209; Welten, 98ff.). Even this argument does not stand too stoutly in the present case, as Amaziah cannot be regarded particularly as a 'positive' king, a category more relevant to Asa, Jehoshaphat, etc. The commentators may feel uneasy about the Chronicler's material in this passage because it is not paralleled in earlier historiographical works, but there is no rational argument against its credibility.

(c) The differing details of the Edomite war are best accounted for as a misunderstanding (or reinterpretation) of II Kings 14.7, combined with the drive to augment Amaziah's victory for theological reasons. For the details, cf. the commentary.

7. The shortcomings of the overall theological integration (above p. 858) should not blind us to the literary effort invested in the composition of the new passage of vv. 5–16. Its three components, just outlined above, originally of different genres and sources, are not only juxtaposed, but skilfully intertwined into a cohesive composition with clear literary guidelines. Two of these components, the story of the Israelite band and the account of the Edomite war, are arranged in parallel, sometimes synchronic lines; the third – the mustering of the army – is presented as an introductory proposition. The whole composition may be defined as an account of 'the war against Edom', but its focus shifts from 'the hired Israelites' (vv. 6–10) to 'the war' (vv. 11–12), then the Israelite band again (v. 13), and Edom again (vv. 14–16). Moreover, each of the individual components is in itself a literary complex, composed of two elements: a narrative and a dialogue. The dialogues, each involving the king and a prophet, follow the same three-phase pattern: moving from prophet to king and leaving the final word with the prophet. Furthermore, both dialogues have the same literary and theological role, and the king's response to the prophet's warning – acceptance in the first case, denial in the second – dictates the subsequent course of events. The pattern may be sketched as follows:

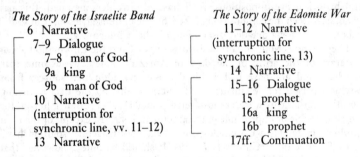

The Story of the Israelite Band
6   Narrative
   7–9   Dialogue
      7–8   man of God
      9a   king
      9b   man of God
   10   Narrative
   (interruption for
   synchronic line, vv. 11–12)
   13   Narrative

The Story of the Edomite War
11–12   Narrative
   (interruption for
   synchronic line, 13)
   14   Narrative
   15–16   Dialogue
      15   prophet
      16a   king
      16b   prophet
   17ff.   Continuation

This structure elucidates the problem of sources from another angle. The Chronistic influence is most evident in the rhetorical sections – the very literary phenomenon as well as the style and content – while the narrative portions are in each case dependent on some biblical or exterior source. The situation may be compared, e.g. with the story of Shishak's campaign (12.2–12), where the basic source narrative (I Kings 14.25–28) is elaborated by the appearance of a prophet and his dialogue with the king (12.5–8), as well as the addition of some actual information.

8. Finally, the status of 26.1–2 should be examined: do these verses conclude the history of Amaziah, or open the reign of Uzziah? In Kings the question does not arise, as the very next verses (II Kings 14.23ff.) turn to the history of the northern kingdom: clearly the accession of Uzziah is seen as concluding the reign of Amaziah. In Chronicles, however, there is no intervening material. The note about Uzziah becomes a connecting link between the two units.

D. Commentary

[1–2] The Deuteronomistic introduction to Amaziah's reign is cited from I Kings 14.1–4 with the routine changes in style and content: the synchronism is omitted, and the people's worship in the high places is replaced by a reservation applying to the king himself: 'he did what was right ... yet not with a blameless heart'. There is another difference between the two versions: in Kings, Amaziah's religious behaviour is compared, first positively to the conduct of his own father Joash, then, with reservations, to that of his illustrious forefather, David. This element of comparison is not preserved in Chronicles; after a token literal adherence to his source – 'he did what was right in the eyes of the Lord' – the Chronicler proceeds in his own way, representing II Kings 14.3–4 with one short clause.

[3–4] Amaziah's purge of his father's assassins follows literally II Kings 14.5–6, including the legal foundation for the particular procedure. There are, however, slight linguistic changes between the two versions, and one of these is of theological significance. The Kings text follows Deut. 24.16, the legal basis for the king's decision, 'the fathers shall not be put to death for the children, etc.'; the verbal form is the *hophal yūm^etū*, correctly translated as 'be put to death'. This is changed in the Chronicles version to the more general statement, in the *qal* conjugation *yāmūtū* (to be rendered 'die'), a reading already implied once in the *Kethib* of II Kings 14.6. This linguistic variant is ignored altogether by RSV (which simply reproduces II Kings 14.6), but for the Chronicler this is a key to a different theological principle: vicarious punishment is to be avoided not only in the sphere of human judicial procedure, but also in the divine management of the world; the strictly individual character of retribution is a universal and absolute rule (cf. M. Greenberg, 'Some Postulates of Biblical Criminal Law', *Y. Kaufmann Jubilee Volume*, 1960, 20–7).

RSV follows the text of II Kings 14.6 in v. 4 as well, ignoring the specific nuance of the word *kī* in the MT. It is of interest that the Chronicler retains the reference to 'the book of Moses', although his phrasing already in fact reflects his own exegesis of the original law in Deut 24.16.

[5] The Chronicler's additions open with a description of Amaziah's mustering of the combined forces of Judah and Benjamin. The term 'Judah' thus serves a double role in this verse: first, the entire southern kingdom, then the particular tribal or geographical element.

References to the organization of an army and details about its size and equipment are found in Chronicles also regarding Asa (14.8 [MT 7]), Jehoshaphat (17.14–19) and Uzziah (26.11–13). Unlike these notes, which are confined to relating simply the composition of each king's forces ('Asa had an army ...'; 'He had soldiers, mighty men'; 'Uzziah had an army ...'), this passage also narrates the method of recruitment: 'Amaziah assembled the men of Judah, and set them by fathers' houses ... He mustered those twenty years old, etc'. The assumed context is an assembly for the purpose of some type of a military census. A comparable picture may be found in the census of David, on the one hand (cf. II Sam. 24.2, 5–8; I Chron. 21.1, 4), and of Moses in the wilderness, on the other (Num. 1ff.); even these parallels, however, do not enable us to draw decisive conclusions.

The number of the warriors here is the smallest of all the armies just mentioned, very close to that given for the forces of Uzziah.

[6–10] The next step in Amaziah's preparations is the hiring of Israelite mercenaries. This passage is our only biblical evidence for this phenomenon, although the existence of foreign units in the regular army on the one hand, and the activity of 'bands' on the other, are both attested on several occasions (for the first, cf. II Sam. 8.18; 15.18 etc.; II Kings 11.4, 19; for the latter, cf. I Sam. 27.1–3; 29.2–3; I Kings 5.2; 13.20, etc.). In this specific case, however, the historical and sociological context is far from clear. If we accept the implication of the text, that the Israelite fighters were already an organized body when hired by Amaziah, our conclusion concerning the contemporary social reality in the kingdom of Israel will be that there existed irregular paramilitary groups on the local level, in the most central parts of the kingdom, not controlled by the central government – a rather extreme picture which is not supported by our information concerning the kingdom at that time. So I am inclined to understand the matter differently: individuals from northern Israel, after the military force of Judah was exhausted, were recruited by Amaziah himself to form *ad hoc* auxiliary units.

The numbers seem exaggerated; not only for the warriors (cf. I Sam. 27.2; II Sam. 15.18), but also for the wages. A hundred talents equal 300,000 shekels, and given an average of 11.4 grams per shekel, the total weight would be 3420 Kilograms (cf. Exod. 38.25–26)! If there was an authentic source for this item, it cannot now be restored.

[7–8] In this brief unit, there are three references to 'a man of God', an attribute which appears several times in Chronicles: for Moses (I Chron. 23.14; II Chron. 30.16), David (II Chron. 8.14) and Shemaiah (II Chron. 11.2). This passage is the only case where the 'man of God' is anonymous, as is the 'prophet' of v. 15. These two are the only individual prophets not named in the book of Chronicles; the reference to 'seers', 'prophets' and 'messengers' in II Chron. 33.18 (and probably v. 19); 36.15, 16, are all general and plural. The Deuteronomistic history (I Kings 13.1ff.; 20.13–43, etc.), by contrast, has many anonymous individual prophets. An extreme conclusion which might be drawn is that the figures of the two anonymous prophets are fictitious (Williamson, 328), introduced by the Chronicler to serve his own purpose, i.e. a necessary theological coherence. However, the two anonymous references might in fact reflect the Chronicler's reluctance to supplement arbitrarily details for which he had no authentic tradition (cf. Dillard, 197). This would imply that for all the other prophets mentioned by name the Chronicler was drawing on some historical tradition.

The syntactic structure of vv. 6–7 is clearly emphatic. The transition from

v. 6 to v. 7 is not achieved through a usual series of imperfect consecutives (cf. vv. 14–15), but places the subject of v. 7 at the beginning of the verse: 'But a man of God came to him. . . .' (the emphatic syntax is largely lost in transla-tion). The phrasing of the prophet's words is also of emphatic quality: first a straightforward vocative, 'O King!' (cf. I Sam. 24.8–9; for a less stressed vocative cf. Judg. 3.19), followed by a prohibition: 'Do not let the army of Israel go with you'. Three consecutive explanatory sentences follow, each opening with the explanatory particle *kī*. Two of the sentences, of concluding force, are nominal, phrased antithetically with 'there is not' (*'ēn*) and 'there is' (*yēš*; the nuances of the Hebrew text are lost in RSV).

The prophet's message is simple: defeat or victory are decided by God, who helps or hinders the rival forces. If you fight alone, God will be on your side; if you seek the assistance of those Israelites, you will fail. This idea, however, is formulated in general, nominal clauses, rather than specific statements: 'The Lord is not with Israel, etc.'; 'God has the power to help or to cast down.'

Here a question arises: does v. 7 comprise a general denunciation of northern Israel independent of its immediate context? Many scholars would say yes: 'The Lord is not with Israel' is a declaration of principle, even dogma (cf. among others, von Rad, *Geschichtsbild*, 29ff.; Rudolph, IX; Mosis, 171, 200–201), and therefore the most emphatic expression of the Chronicler's alleged 'anti-Israel' attitude (cf. Japhet, *Ideology*, 308–24; Willi, 190–3; R. L. Braun, 'A Reconsideration of the Chronicler's Attitude toward the North', *JBL* 96, 1977, 59–62).

I take a different view of the matter (cf. also Williamson, 329). 'The Lord is with …' or 'not with' are characteristic expressions of the Chronicler's religious evaluation. However, this judgment is always conditional, as ex-pressed so clearly by another prophet's address: 'The Lord is with you while you are with him: if you seek him, he will be found by you, but if you forsake him, he will forsake you' (15.2). The Lord's absence is not an existential declaration; God withdraws his presence only from those who are not 'with him', that is, those who sin (cf. also I Chron. 22.11–13, 17–19; 28.9, 20; II Chron. 1.1, etc.). The context of II Chron. 28.10 makes it clear that the northern Israelites are guilty of transgression, 'Have you not sins of your own against the Lord your God?', and therefore cannot expect, *at present*, that the Lord should be with them; but this is not an irrevocable condemnation.

There is a two-fold definition here, 'Israel' (vv. 6, 7a, 7b, 9b) and 'Ephraimites' (literally 'the children of Ephraim'). The name Ephraim is quite common in Chronicles, in various idioms and usages, but usually with a tribal connotation (I Chron. 7.20; 9.3; 12.30; 27.10, 14, 20). In reference to the people of the Northern Kingdom, it is also found in the context of II Chron. 28.7, 12 (where it parallels the more general 'Israel' or 'children

of Israel' in vv. 8, 13; cf. also the definition 'Ephraim and Manasseh' in
II Chron. 30.1; 31.1, etc), but is very common in several biblical sources,
e.g. Isaiah, Jeremiah and Hosea. This designation may be dependent of the
Chronicler's source.

The difficulty in the phrasing of 8a stems primarily from the apparently
conditional syntactic link between 'If you ...' and 'God will cast you down'.
Consulting the MT, we find that the first clause is a series of imperatives,
joined to the vocative 'you': literally, 'come, do, take courage'; we expect the
second clause to state a positive outcome, but instead we find the dire threat
'God will cast you down before the enemy'. This incoherent sequence has
inspired a series of propositions: one, suggested by Kittel on the basis of the
Septuagint, is represented by RSV (cf. BH); another is adopted by NEB (cf.
also Curtis, 443; Rudolph 278 and BHS). Of these, I prefer to follow
Rudolph's suggestion (adopted also by the JPS), to restore the word *lāmāh*
('why') after *lammilḥāmāh*: 'Why should God cast you down?' (= 'lest God
cast you down', cf. Gen. 27.45; 47.19 etc., and Gesenius, §150e, p. 474). This
restoration, besides being orthographically probable, also accords well with
the style of the prophetic address: it unveils one more rhetorical element in
the form of a rhetorical question.

For the nominal statement 'God has power to help or to cast down' cf.
similar declarations, in I Chron. 29.12; II Chron. 20.6, etc.

[9] In the short dialogue between king and prophet, Amaziah is described
as a petty merchant. In view of the risks, he is ready to consider favourably
the prophet's advice but he is troubled by the unnecessary expenditure:
'What shall we do about the hundred talents?', that is, 'How shall I recover
my investment?' The prophet's answer follows the same line of reasoning but
is rather vague: 'The Lord is able to give you much more . . .'.

There is also an element of stylistic repetition in this passage: 'which came
to him' recurs in v. 7 and in v. 10; 'the band' (RSV 'the army') is a repetition
from v. 9; there is double reference to 'anger' with the idiom *hārāh 'ap*; and
the root 'come' (*bw'*) is repeated three times in vv. 7–8, once in v. 10, and
twice again in vv. 12 and 14.

[11–12] Here the story returns to the war with the Edomites, elaborating
on II Kings 14.7; the differences between the two versions are quite comprehensive. From a literary point of view, the Kings text states a fact, in the
perfect tense: 'He killed ... and took'. Chronicles presents a narrative, a
detailed series of imperfects: 'Amaziah took courage, and led out his people
and went to the valley ... and smote ... etc.'. At first the king is the subject,
but soon the protagonists become 'the men of Judah'. Further, the original
'Edom' is here 'men of Seir' – probably a stylistic preference for variety,
based on various biblical sources (cf. the preference for 'Seir' in
Deuteronomy, 2.4, 5, 8, 22, 29, etc., 'Edomite' only in Deut. 23.8), as

opposed to Numbers with its exclusive use of 'Edom' (except Num. 24.18). For Chronicles, the two terms are clearly synonymous (cf. v. 14).

The picture of the war is elaborated in Chronicles by the addition of the details in v. 12. The reference to the 'top of the rock' (or 'the rock') is to be seen as a misunderstanding – or an interpretation – of the word 'Sela' (thus Rudolph, 281–3). In II Kings 14.7 Sela is a specific place, usually regarded as the ancient name of Petra (but cf. the discussion and bibliography in Dillard, 200; Tadmor-Cogan, *II Kings*, 155). The general description of the Kings version is thus transformed into a dramatic presentation of the Edomites' fate – a tradition probably reflected in the obscure passage of Ps. 141.6–7 – and the number of the enemy slain is doubled.

[13] The narrative is developing two lines of plot simultaneously, a synchronicity not expressed in so many words but rather through the syntax: v. 13 is clearly juxtaposed to v. 12 by the opening use of a *casus pendens*: 'but (as for) the men of the army ... [they] fell upon, etc.'. While Amaziah was fighting far away, a massacre was being carried out in the 'cities of Judah'.

Again, the stylistic unity of the passage is expressed by the preference for the ethnic designation 'the sons of' (*bᵉnē*). Cf *bᵉnē 'eprāyim* in v. 7 (RSV Ephraimites); *bᵉnē śeʿīr* in vv. 11, 14 (RSV men of Seir); *bᵉnē yᵉhūdāh* in v. 12 (RSV the men of Judah); *bᵉnē haggᵉdūd* in v. 13 (RSV the men of the army); and *bᵉnē hattaʿᵃrubōt* in v. 24 (RSV hostages). One wonders if this preference should not be combined with the topic 'sons/children' (*bānīm*), dealt with in vv. 4 and 18, for an overall perspective of stylistic uniformity.

The problematical point of this verse is geographical: neither 'Samaria' nor even 'Beth-horon' can be regarded as 'cities of Judah'. Several unconvincing harmonizing interpretations led Rudolph to propose a textual emendation, reading 'Migron' for 'Shomron' (Rudolph, 279, also BHS). However, the method of overcoming problems of content by arbitrary (although cautiously proposed) orthographical corrections, not otherwise warranted or supported, cannot be recommended. So while still cautious in my turn, I would consider another approach: a rather peculiar geographical and political presupposition, that within the very territory of Ephraim, 'from Samaria to Beth-horon', there were also cities which belonged to Judah. This is supported by the phrasing of 17.2, 'the cities of Ephraim which Asa ... had taken', and possibly also 19.4. The Ephraimite band, avoiding the risk of actually raiding Judaean territory, may have fallen upon the 'cities of Judah' scattered in Ephraim; the looting of their Judean neighbours was to be some compensation for not joining in the spoil of the Edomites.

[14] As in the days of Joash, so also for Amaziah, a drastic change takes place in the king's religious conduct. The turning point for Joash was the death of Jehoiada and the negative influence of the princes of Judah (24.17–18); for Amaziah, it is his victory over Edom. In spite of (or perhaps *because*

of) his success, as he 'becomes strong' (cf. 12.1), Amaziah turns to the 'gods of the men of Seir', a transgression which from now on plays a decisive role in the fate of Amaziah and his kingdom.

The war against Edom and the war with Israel are thus linked even more closely. The first indication of this will be in the northern king's reply to Amaziah's challenge: 'You have indeed smitten Edom, and your heart has lifted you up' (v. 19//II Kings 14.10). The narrator sees the impact of the Edomite war on Amaziah's psychological state – an unwarranted boldness. The Chronicler interprets this link and Amaziah's 'lifting of the heart' in a more concrete religious sense (as in 26.6ff.; 32.25) – a sinful pride which leads not only to self-confident attack but to idolatry and destruction.

[15–16] The episode with the prophet has an unusual beginning: 'The Lord was angry with Amaziah', the phrase *wayyiḥar 'ap* appearing again only in I Chron. 13.10//II Sam. 6.7 (and a similar phrase in I Chron. 13.11//II Sam. 6.8). Although there is no theological connection between the 'anger' of the Ephraimite mercenaries (v. 10) and the Lord's 'anger' against Amaziah, this idiom, repeated three times, serves as a stylistic element giving a certain unity to the various sections of the pericope. (Another phrase for 'anger', *ḥ^{a}rōn 'ap*, occurs in Chronicles four times in a coherent context, cf. 28.11, 13; 29.10; 30.8 – probably designating the Assyrian threat to both Israel and Judah.)

The divine anger is followed not by punishment, as one might have expected, but by a prophetic warning – again paralleling the sequence in the history of Joash: sin, wrath and the sending of prophets (24.17–19). The prophet's admonition is phrased in a rather sophisticated form as a rhetorical question: 'Why have you worshipped (RSV 'resorted to') the gods ...?' The implication is that Amaziah lacks both sense and gratitude, but there is no explicit allusion to impending punishment. What can be perceived here is a substratum of popular concepts. The whole point of the prophet's rebuke is to show that Amaziah has done wrong by worshipping gods who are worthless since they could not help their own people in battle. What if Amaziah had lost the war? Would the worship of Edomite gods then be justified? This popular implication cannot, it seems, be taken at face value, nor should it be regarded as a general theological tenet, but rather as an address tailored to the specific circumstances.

The RSV 'resort to gods' renders a very common Chronistic idiom, 'seek the gods'. Coming after 'he ... worshipped them, making offerings to them', the verb is better rendered 'worship' (cf. JPS). This is another example of the broad semantic range of the verb *drš* ('seek') in Chronicles.

[16] The dialogue between the prophet and the king has two more stages: the king's reaction and the prophet's final word. The king phrases his answer in three short clauses, all rhetorical; the first and last are rhetorical questions:

'Have we made you a royal counsellor'?, 'Why should you be killed?' (or: 'be hit'; RSV 'be put to death' renders the Hebrew *yakkūkā* too specifically); the intermediate clause is an emphatic imperative: 'Stop!'

The prophet reacts to all these points; indeed he falls silent, but not before having the last word: 'God has counselled (RSV determined) to destroy you', a verdict which may be implied in his first address but is now stated explicitly. Thus the king's ironic rebuke, describing the prophet as an unwanted 'counsellor', is taken up by the prophet and reversed to fall upon the king himself: since he has refused counsel, the Lord has 'counselled' (RSV 'determined') his death.

The stylistic quality of the passage is obvious not only in the series of rhetorical questions ('why'? vv. 15, 16), but also in the three-fold repetition of the verb 'counsel', which will also open the next passage (v. 17), and the series of explanatory clauses opening with *kī*: 'That (*kī*) God has determined ...', 'Because (*kī*) you have done this.'

[17–24] From this point to the end of Amaziah's history the Chronicler resumes the Deuteronomistic source, citing the Kings text literally except for small changes of linguistic and stylistic nature and short theological comments. What is noteworthy here, however, is the very fact that this story is included in the Chronistic history. From several points of view it poses a theological problem: since Amaziah was basically a righteous king, properly rewarded by his great victory over the Edomites, how are we to understand his subsequent severe defeat, the damage to the wall of Jerusalem, the rout of the Judaeans, and the spoiling of the royal treasuries (cf. above, pp. 857–8)? Moreover, the narrative is told entirely from a 'northern' point of view. The geographical designation 'Beth-shemesh which belongs to Judah' (v. 21//II Kings 14.11) is only one expression of the 'Israel-orientated' disposition of the passage. Joash is portrayed as a capable and sensible ruler who tries to avoid the war, while Amaziah is seen as presumptious and arrogant, unaware of his limitations and overly belligerent.

Yet, in spite of all these problems the Chronicler still chooses to include this pericope, cited directly from II Kings 14.8–14. Rather than reworking the narrative in favour of the Judaean king, or omitting it altogether, the theological problem of Amaziah's defeat is explained by introducing the cultic transgression. It is clear that, of the Chronicler's historiographic principles – the system of divine justice, the inclusion of all mutual contacts between the kingdoms of Judah and Israel, and the glorification of the Davidic monarchs – it is the first two which take priority at the expense of the last.

[17] To the beginning of the story the Chronicler adds only the words 'took counsel' (*wayyiwwā'aṣ*). This addition serves a literary function in the present unit, unifying it with the larger pericope, as it continues the theme of

'counsel' in v. 16: the king did not accept God's advice through a prophet, but himself 'takes counsel' to go out to war; and through this war the Lord's counsel will be realized: Amaziah's destruction.

From the more general perspective of Chronistic theology, 'counselling' is a major factor in the king's status and behaviour (cf. Japhet, *Ideology*, 422–8). The exclusivity of the king's authority is limited by the need to include other factors in the state's management. This same idea of shared responsibility also serves to account for the scope of the disaster: it is not the king alone who will suffer, as will become clear; the sin must then have involved more than the guilt of the king alone.

[18] A matter of great literary interest in this parable is the relationship between the fable and its moral. There are three protagonists, all 'of Lebanon': the thistle, the cedar and the wild beast. The thistle proposes a marriage alliance with the cedar, which disdains even to reply; before long the thistle is trampled by a passing animal. This parable does not reflect a real situation, nor does it seem to correspond to the answer given by Joash in v. 19. Amaziah does not in fact propose peace but war, Joash does answer him, and Amaziah's downfall is not effected by a third party (the 'wild beast') but by Joash himself. The only relevant lesson which can in reality be derived from this parable is that Joash sees himself as a cedar, while Amaziah is a presumptuous thistle!

Joash's parable is a demonstration of confidence, even arrogance, and the conventions of courtly wisdom are here peppered with a mocking tone. The two monarchs – Amaziah and Joash alike – share the same traits of stubborn arrogance, and war is inevitable: Amaziah will never retreat from his initiative after such a mocking challenge.

We should note the stylistic triple repetitions of 'send' (vv. 17, 18), and 'of Lebanon' (RSV 'on Lebanon'), emphasizing not only the neighbourhood of cedar and thistle, but also the unfathomable presumption on the part of the thistle in the presence of this lofty 'cedar of Lebanon'.

[19] The main difference between this verse and II Kings 14.10 is the seemingly minor change of form, position and meaning of *hikkābbēd*. In the original version it follows the rhetorical question as the beginning of a new clause: 'Be content with your glory'. In Chronicles, this word is seen as a continuation of 'your heart has lifted you up', and the *niphal* form becomes a *hiphil* infinitive: *lᵉhakbīd*. English translations render variously 'in boastfulness' (RSV), 'Enjoy your glory' (NEB), 'to get more glory' (JPS). It seems, however, that these translations follow too closely the spirit of II Kings 14. In the framework of Chronistic theology, the words of Joash should be seen as a divine warning, following the earlier admonition of the prophet (vv. 15–16) and comparable to the words of Pharaoh Neco to Josiah in 35.21–22. Joash is telling Amaziah that 'your heart has been hardened', immediately recalling

the precedent of Pharaoh (Exod. 7.14; 8.15 [MT 11]; 8.32 [MT 28]; 9.34, etc., all using different conjugations of *kbd*). It is because of this that 'Amaziah would not listen' (v. 20; cf. Exod. 8.15, etc.).

The form *hakkēh hikkītā* ('You have indeed smitten') is represented in this version with *hinnēh hikkītā* ('See, you have smitten'), expressing two of the Chronicler's linguistic inclinations: to avoid the infinitive absolute in conjunction with the finite verb, and to replace one word with another that is orthographically similar (הנה for הכה).

[20] This verse contains the most significant addition to the Kings citation; we have encountered the method many times: the literal quotation of the text is broken and a Chronistic note is interpolated into the place of the cut, to be followed by a precise continuation of the original text; thus:

II Kings 14.11aα		II Kings 14.11aβ–b etc.
II Chron. 15.20aα	II Chron. 25.10aβ–b	II Chron. 25.21 ff.

Following the parallel clause, 'But Amaziah would not listen', the Chronistic interpolation occupies all of v. 20, and the thread of the original narrative is picked up again in v. 21 'So Joash king of Israel went up'.

This obviously Chronistic note is a signficant indicator of the Chronicler's style and theology. It accounts in the most straightforward way for the introduction of Amaziah's idolatry, and provides the missing cause for his serious military defeat. It also gives another turn to the parable of Joash: it is not merely a courtly fable, an answer to Amaziah, but a divine warning, making the Judaean king liable to punishment. Finally, the fact that 'Amaziah would not listen' no longer means only that he disregarded the sensible advice of Joash, but that he was once again deaf to divine counsel and warning (as in v. 15). However, even this inability to listen is the Lord's doing, for Amaziah must be punished for his earlier idolatry.

The late, Chronistic language and style are evident even in this short sentence. The series of three clauses, all causative or final, is introduced by three consecutive particles, *kī*, *l^ema^{'a}n*, *kī*: 'for ... in order that ... because'. The first two clauses are nominal; the infinitive of the second represents an abstract idea, literally: 'for the sake of their deliverance into hand' (JPS 'in order to deliver them up'). Another stylistic note is the favourite *dār^ešū* ('sought'), which alludes back to the prophet's rebuke in v. 15; the singular form here becomes plural, in preparation for the forthcoming defeat: 'and *Judah* was defeated' (v. 22).

[21] 'Beth-shemesh which belongs to Judah' clearly betrays the northern point of view of the narrator (Curtis, 445). Most probably the reference is to the town in the Shephelah, on the border between Judah and Dan (cf. Josh. 15.10), at a considerable distance from the boundary between Israel and

Judah. Whether or not Beth-shemesh was considered a border town, its very mention seems to imply a major offensive by Israel into traditional Judahite territory.

[23] Amaziah is utterly defeated. The details of this verse, however, raise several questions: if Joash had 'captured' Amaziah before approaching the city, why are we told that he 'broke down the wall of Jerusalem for four hundred cubits'? We may either assume that the city was resisting Joash in spite of the fact that he held the king hostage, or that these were punitive measures, to establish superiority. It is generally agreed that Amaziah was taken captive to Samaria, together with the other hostages, and his son Azariah/Uzziah was appointed as regent, under Israelite hegemony (cf. Tadmor-Cogan, 159). This would give adequate explanation for the unique statement of v. 25, and a reasonable starting point for the co-regency of Uzziah. It may also account – although the details are unclear – for Amaziah's eventual assassination.

Joash is unique in that he succeeded where the great Assyrian king Sennacherib with all his forces failed – in breaching the wall of Jerusalem. Pinpointing the exact segment 'from the Ephraim Gate to the Corner Gate' depends on archaeological considerations, but the names themselves are well-attested (Neh. 8.16; 12.39; Jer. 31.38, probably also Zech. 14.10). The restoration of the Corner Gate by Uzziah (26.9) probably signalled the renewal of Judaean independence.

Amaziah's grandfather in II Kings 14.13 is 'Ahaziah'; here he is called (in the MT) 'Jehoahaz'. RSV circumvents the problem by rendering 'Ahaziah' here as well, but MT cannot be regarded as a simple orthographic corruption. Rudolph (280) has proposed that the title 'son of Jehoahaz' originally described the other Joash (RSV Jehoash), the king of Israel (cf. BHS of II Kings 14.13), the two kings mentioned in this verse having equally long titles. The patronymic was secondarily transposed to another place in the same verse, and applied to Joash of Judah, king Amaziah's father, disturbing the original balance; this was the text which served as the Chronicler's *Vorlage*. Later a scribal correction was made to the Kings text, changing 'Jehoahaz' to 'Ahaziah', which is the present MT. Although the proposal may account for both the unusual name and the lack of symmetry, it should be noted that Ahaziah king of Judah is also called 'Jehoahaz' in another Chronistic passage (Chron. 21.17). This may, then, be a textual change introduced by the Chronicler himself.

[24] Joash spoils Jerusalem; looting (RSV correctly supplies the missing verb 'he seized', but there is no need to repeat it) all the treasures of gold and silver from the palace and the Temple. He also takes hostages into captivity in the north, for reasons not spelled out. The Chronicler adds one small detail: the treasures of the house of the Lord were under the care of Obed-

edom (RSV wrongly 'and Obed-edom with them', cf. NEB). This name is associated in the Chronistic texts with a family of gatekeepers (I Chron. 26.15), but according to the registers of I Chron. 26 they were not in charge of the treasuries. Moreover, while the spoiling of the treasuries, or their use as ransom, is mentioned in Chronicles several times, nowhere is their guardian mentioned (cf. II Chron. 12.9; 16.2; etc.). All of this has prompted the view that this note is a post-Chronistic addition (cf. Rudolph, 280; Williamson, 331). However, the mention of Obed-edom in this context is of theological rather than historical significance. It highlights the 'poetic justice' of the situation: Amaziah's sin was that he 'worshipped (*'bd*) the gods of Edom' (v. 14) – he himself may be described as 'Obed (*'ōbēd*) Edom'! When the treasures kept with 'Obed-edom' are now looted by his enemy, the name is the code-word for the common Chronistic principle of 'measure for measure' in divine punishment.

[25] This unique note, correlating the lifetime of the king of Judah to that of the king of Israel, seems to imply a dependent relationship between the two kingdoms, probably a result of the preceding war. Rudolph claims that this note must be either a mechanical repetition of the Kings text, or a later interpolation into Chronicles by a later harmonizer (Rudolph, 280). Neither of these solutions is necessary; the context accords with the Chronicler's interest in the fortunes of northern Israel, whenever seen from the perspective of Judah. In fact, the exclusion of this verse from Chronicles would have been more exceptional than its inclusion.

[26] The reference to an additional source for the king's history basically follows the regular Chronistic pattern. 'The book of the Kings of Judah and Israel' is also mentioned for Ahaz (28.26) and Hezekiah (32.32), and with the names reversed ('Israel and Judah'), for Jotham (27.7), Josiah (35.27) and Jehoiakim (36.8). Thus this title, mentioning the names of both kingdoms, is used for most of the Judaean kings after Amaziah, even for those who reigned after the northern kingdom had already ceased to exist.

[27–28] The literal quotation of II Kings 14.19 is prefaced here with a Chronistic temporal clause: 'From the time when he turned away from the Lord'. The point of this note, however, seems to be to indicate cause rather than time. The conspiracy against Amaziah is viewed by the Chronicler as a result of his transgression; every event has a reason, and sin is the root of all evil.

The conspiracy itself is described with a series of general plural verbs: 'they made ... sent ... slew ... brought'. We are told nothing of the motives or identity of the conspirators themselves. The dynasty is not threatened; Amaziah is succeeded by his son just as he himself succeeded his assassinated father (24.27); here, however, the fate of the conspirators is not recounted (cf. vv. 3–4).

The note about Amaziah's place of burial is unusual already in II Kings 14.20: the usual reference to the 'city of David' is augmented by 'Jerusalem'. This can be explained by the context: the king was killed in Lachish; nevertheless he was brought to Jerusalem and properly buried in the 'city of David' (cf. also II Kings 9.28 for Ahaziah). The Chronicler omits 'Jerusalem', and 'the city of David' is changed to the unique 'a city of Judah'. This last reference is taken by many to be a textual error (also RSV, which restores 'the city of David'; cf. Curtis, 447; Rudolph, 280, *et al.*). This view is supported by the fact that the text retains 'with his fathers', regularly associated with royal burial in Jerusalem. However, as Dillard points out, 'it is far easier to account for the correction [of 'Judah' to 'David'] than to explain a change to Judah' (197). Moreover, considering the role which burial plays in the Chronicler's system of retribution, the reference to an anonymous tomb in 'a city of Judah' seems to be the final stage of a progression of punishment, through conspiracy and assassination, all determined by Amaziah's initial transgression 'when he turned away from the Lord'.

[26.1–2] Cited from II Kings 14.21–22, these verses form a transition between the reigns of Amaziah and Uzziah. In the Deuteronomistic version they clearly conclude the history of Amaziah; the next section refers to the northern king, Jeroboam (14.23ff.), and the history of Judah is resumed only in II Kings 15.1. Here in Chronicles, the position of these verses *before* the conventional Deuteronomistic introduction for Uzziah creates a somewhat repetitive text, but highlights the continuity of the narrative, as illustrated for earlier kings as well.

The only difference in v. 1 is in the king's name: Uzziah rather than Azariah. The Kings version certainly prefers the latter, but also has the form Uzziah four times (II Kings 15.13, 30, 32, 34); the Chronicler's usage is more consistent, with 'Azariah' appearing only once (I Chron. 3.12 – a different context altogether). This alternation has been presented as an outstanding example of 'regnal names' (A. Honeyman, 'The Evidence for Regnal Names among the Hebrews', *JBL* 67, 1948, 13–25, esp. 20: 'the most conspicuous set of variants to which the hypothesis of throne names affords an explanation', cf. also Dillard, 205). A more phonetic/semantic understanding of the variation is followed by others (cf. Curtis, 448, Williamson, 333–4, and in particular G. Brin, 'The Roots עזר – עזז in the Bible', *Lešonenu* 24, 1959/60, 8–14*).

Uzziah is enthroned by 'the people of Judah', a unique term in Kings and Chronicles, and quite uncommon elsewhere (cf. II Sam. 19.41, in juxtaposition to 'the people [RSV men] of Israel'; Jer. 25.1, 2; 26.18; and Ezra 4.4, juxtaposed to 'the people of the land'). The precise connotation in this context is not clear; it may imply independence from the northern kingdom of Israel upon the death of Amaziah (cf. also II Kings 21.24//II Chron. 33.25).

The content of v. 2 is clear; not so the precise historical circumstances. Does 'He built Eloth' refer to Uzziah or to Amaziah his father? And who is the king whose death is used as a chronological anchor? Curtis is of the opinion that in this context the builder is certainly Uzziah, following the death of Amaziah, but in II Kings 14.22 the builder would be Amaziah himself (Curtis, 448).

We should also note that for the Chronicler the name of the town is always 'Eloth' (cf. II Chron. 8.17), while earlier sources have both this form (II Kings 9.26) and the alternative 'Elath' (Deut. 2.8; II Kings 14.22; 16.6).

Reflected in these isolated details is the continual struggle between the Israelites and Edom over the control of the Red Sea port, a significant gateway of international trade (cf. M. Haran, 'Observations on the Historical Background of Amos 1.2–2.6', *IEJ* 18, 1968, 207–12). There are glimpses of this struggle in the time of Jehoshaphat (I Kings 22.48–49), Jehoram his son (II Kings 8.20), Amaziah (II Kings 14.7), and now in this text. Elath reverts to Edomite control during the time of Ahaz (II Kings 16.6, where the MT three times has 'Aram', but many scholars prefer to read 'Edom', cf. BHS).

26 3 Uzziah was sixteen years old when he began to reign, and he reigned fifty-two years in Jerusalem. His mother's name was Jecoliah of Jerusalem. [4] And he did what was right in the eyes of the Lord, according to all that his father Amaziah had done. [5] He set himself to seek God in the days of Zechariah, who instructed him in the fear of God; and as long as he sought the Lord, God made him prosper.

6 He went out and made war against the Philistines, and broke down the wall of Gath and the wall of Jabneh and the wall of Ashdod; and he built cities in the territory of Ashdod and elsewhere among the Philistines. [7] God helped him against the Philistines, and against the Arabs that dwelt in Gurbaal, and against the Me-unites. [8] The Ammonites paid tribute to Uzziah, and his fame spread even to the border of Egypt, for he became very strong. [9] Moreover Uzziah built towers in Jerusalem at the Corner Gate and at the Valley Gate and at the Angle, and fortified them. [10] And he built towers in the wilderness, and hewed out many cisterns, for he had large herds, both in the Shephelah and in the plain, and he had farmers and vinedressers in the hills and in the fertile lands, for he loved the soil. [11] Moreover Uzziah had an army of soldiers, fit for war, in divisions according to the numbers in the muster made by Je-iel the secretary and Ma-aseiah the officer, under the direction of Hananiah, one of the king's commanders. [12] The whole number of the heads of fathers' houses of mighty men of valour was two thousand six hundred. [13] Under their command was an army of three hundred and seven thousand five hundred, who could make war with mighty power, to help the king against the enemy. [14] And Uzziah prepared for all the army shields, spears, helmets, coats of mail, bows, and stones for slinging. [15] In Jerusalem he made engines, invented by skilful men, to be on the towers and the corners, to shoot arrows and great stones. And his fame spread far, for he was marvellously helped, till he was strong.

16 But when he was strong he grew proud, to his destruction. For he was false to the Lord his God, and entered the temple of the Lord to burn incense on the altar of incense. [17] But Azariah the priest went in after him, with eighty priests of the Lord who were men of valour; [18] and they withstood King Uzziah, and said to him, 'It is not for you, Uzziah, to burn incense to the Lord, but for the priests the sons of Aaron, who are consecrated to burn incense. Go out of the sanctuary; for you have done wrong, and it will bring you no honour from the Lord God.' [19] Then Uzziah was angry. Now he had a censer in his hand to burn incense, and when he became angry with the priests leprosy broke out on his forehead, in the presence of the priests in the house of the Lord, by the altar of incense. [20] And Azariah the chief priest, and all the priests, looked at him, and behold, he was leprous in his forehead! And they thrust him out quickly, and he himself hastened to go out, because the Lord had smitten him. [21] And King Uzziah was a leper to the day of his death, and being a leper dwelt in a separate house, for he was excluded from the house of the Lord. And Jotham his son was over the king's household, governing the people of the land.

22 Now the rest of the acts of Uzziah, from first to last, Isaiah the prophet the son

of Amoz wrote. [23] And Uzziah slept with his fathers, and they buried him with his fathers in the burial field which belonged to the kings, for they said, 'He is a leper.' And Jotham his son reigned in his stead.

A. Notes to MT

[5] בראת, some MSS and the Versions ביראת; [6] ויבנה ערים, proposed ויבז ערים; [7] בגור–בעל והמעונים, read ועל המעונים (בנרר or) בגור; [8] העמונים, proposed המעונים; [10] ובמישור אכרים..., read ובמישור אכרים; [11] משרי, LXX משנה; [21] בית, Sebirin בבית; [23] עם אבתיו, (second) difficult, omit?

B. Notes to RSV

[5] 'in the fear', cf. A above; [6] 'broke down the wall', JPS, 'breached the wall' (MT פרץ); [11] 'secretary', NEB, 'adjutant general'; [16] 'to his destruction' or, 'he acted corruptly' (NEB margin JPS); 'For he was false to the Lord', JPS; 'he trespassed against his God'.

C. Structure, sources and form

1. The very brief Deuteronomistic history of Uzziah – only a few lines – comprises mostly the conventional framework (II Kings 15.1–4, 6–7). The very few additional details include Uzziah's enthronement by 'the people of Judah'; the building of Eloth and its restoration to Judah, both still in the framework of Amaziah's history (II Kings 14.21–22), and the king's leprosy, resulting in Jotham's co-regency (II Kings 15.5). This narrative brevity is odd, in view of Uzziah's long reign, surpassed only by Manasseh's, and the fact that this period was one of great changes for Uzziah's northern neighbours. The northern kingdom, Israel, enjoyed extensive territorial expansion during Uzziah's earlier years (II Kings 14.25, 28), and suffered sharp decline and great domestic instability near the end of his reign (II Kings 15.8–31). At the same time, the relatively dormant Assyrian empire was again beginning actively to extend its western frontiers (cf. II Kings 15.19, 29, and Cogan-Tadmor, *II Kings*, 163–4; 176–8). Is it possible that all these developments had no impact on Judah? Moreover, the prophecies of Isaiah attest to great economic prosperity (*inter al.* Isa. 2.7, 15–16; 3.18–23), which does not fit the time of Ahaz and probably should be dated earlier, that is, to the period of Uzziah-Jotham. The brevity of the Deuteronomistic story seems to stem not from any lack of data but from historiographical inclinations, such as a limited interest in certain aspects of political life, and the generally laconic attention given to the kings of Judah during the period of the divided kingdom.

2. The Chronicler cites, with very slight changes, all the Deuteronomistic material for Uzziah, excepting two verses: II Kings 15.1 (superfluous in the new context) and 15.4 (a reference to the people's worship in the high places). The arrangement of the remaining material in principle follows the Deuteronomistic structure: the introductory part is placed at the beginning of the story (vv. 3–4), and the concluding part at the end (vv. 21–23); between them, an extensive section of the Chronicler's own is

inserted (vv. 5–20), three times the scope of the Deuteronomistic material, just as in the earlier histories of Abijah, Joash and Amaziah (chs. 13, 24, 25).

The new material belongs to two different genres: a collection of notes concerning various aspects of military, diplomatic and development activity (vv. 6–15a), and a priestly narrative, of great dramatic impact, concerning Uzziah's leprosy (vv. 16b–20). These two literary components are given distinct contexts: the informative material at the beginning of Uzziah's history, the dramatic narrative at its end, and both are accompanied by evaluative explanatory statements (vv. 5b, 7a, 15b, 16a). This specific structure is adopted by the Chronicler for both literary and theological reasons.

The original note about Uzziah's leprosy (II Kings 15.5) is cited near the end of the chapter (v. 21). It is natural that the narrative attributing this illness to sacrilege should come before. This, in turn, is preceded by the various other data. These literary considerations are, however, outweighed by theological ones, which in fact determine the order of the events.

From the Chronicler's particular point of view the Deuteronomistic story is theologically incoherent. Uzziah 'did what was right in the eyes of the Lord' (II Kings 15.3), a positive evaluation supported by his exceptionally long rule (fifty-two years). And yet, the shameful leprosy inflicted by the Lord (II Kings 15.5) must, in the Chronicler's terms, be regarded as a punishment. The story lacks mention of Uzziah's sin, a gap duly filled by the account of the king's sacrilege (vv. 16–20).

Another outstanding lacuna in the Deuteronomistic history (from the Chronicler's perspective) is the absence of an adequate reward for the king's righteousness. This the Chronicler also supplies, by the generous data about Uzziah's enterprises; these, then, must be placed during the early years, before the king's transgression. These lines of adaptation are brought to the attention of the reader with an explicit statement, 'as long as he sought the Lord, God made him prosper' (v. 5), and the description of the leprosy as an immediate outcome of transgresion (vv. 19, 21aβ).

The dichotomy of Uzziah's reign – like that of Joash and Amaziah before him – is portrayed as an organic development, a dynamic of opposites, righteousness – reward, sin – punishment, bound together in a causal chain. As in the case of Rehoboam (12.1), and implicitly of Amaziah (25.14), it is pride and over-confidence which in the end destroy Uzziah: 'But when he was strong he grew proud, to his corruption' (RSV 'to his destruction'). The transition between the two stages of Uzziah's reign is then not merely chronological; it is essential.

3. The structure of Uzziah's history may be illustrated as follows:

(*a*) 3–5 Introduction
(*b*) 6–15 Uzziah's enterprises
        6–8 military and international activity
        9–10 construction and economic activity
        11–15a organization and equipment of the army
        15b conclusion
(*c*) 16–21 Uzziah's sin and punishment
(*d*) 22–23 Conclusion

4. Did the Chronicler have extra-biblical sources for his story? All that has been said so far about the exemplary theological harmony of Uzziah's history raises serious doubts about the authenticity of this material. Could the Chronicler have found in his

sources material so perfectly suited for his purposes? Moreover, the late, Chronistic language and style of the added material (cf. below) surely betray its author. Nevertheless, these indications alone are not sufficient for denying the material's authenticity; the very same phenomena are to be found in material taken from the Deuteronomistic history as well, for which the existence of sources is self-evident. One should detach the information itself from its present theological context, as well as from its chronological presentation. Viewed on their own merits, the data themselves are neither unrealistic nor imaginary. Moreover, the accumulating archeological evidence can no longer be disregarded. The many excavated sites (for an impressive selection of references cf. Williamson, 336–7) show building activity and an expansionist policy which must be dated somewhere around this period. Uzziah's long rule must certainly have been the climax of a longer process, which will come to an end in the time of Ahaz.

I thus tend to agree with the many scholars who regard the information found in vv. 6–15 as basically authentic, in spite of the undeniable Chronistic idiom and theological tone (cf. *inter al.* H. Tadmor, 'Azriyau of Yaudi', *Scripta Hierosolymitana* 8, 1961, 232–71; G. Rinaldi, 'Quelques Remarques sur la Politique d'Azarias (Oziahs) de Juda en Philistie', *VTS* 9, 1963, 225–35; Dillard, 206). Whether or not the Chronicler cited *all* the material found in his sources is beyond our knowledge; he certainly succeeded once again in producing a controlled selection of data suiting his needs. At the same time, the Chronicler's composition cannot be seen as an 'objective' or a 'complete' portrayal of Uzziah's history.

5. The narrative of Uzziah's leprosy belongs to a different genre and has another objective. The story's theological motive, religious presuppositions, content, literary method and late language have all been taken to indicate the Chronicler as its author (cf. recently Williamson, 338–9). There is, however, another possibility. The narrative represents two stages of literary development, in which the principal line of reworking transforms an encounter between Uzziah the king and Azariah the high priest into a full-scale confrontation between the king and the entire priestly class (v. 17, and later). Since this development may be easily identified as 'Chronistic', with its 'democratizing' guidelines and the increased involvement of crowds and groups, the original story must be a priestly homily on Uzziah's leprosy predating the Chronicler but reworked and integrated by him into his overall history (cf. also Rudolph, 286–7, and below).

6. A stylistic feature of the Uzziah pericope is the unifying elements. The Chronicler repeats various forms of the verb עזר ('help') – the root of Uzziah's name in its Deuteronomistic form (II Kings 14.21ff. also I Chron. 3.12), as well as its partial synonym חזק – 'be strong', altogether seven times (עזר, vv. 7, 13, 15, חזק, vv. 8, 9, 15, 16). The story of Uzziah's leprosy is given literary unity by the sevenfold recurrence of the root קטר (vv. 16, 18, 19), and the five-fold reference to 'leper/leprosy' (vv. 19, 20, 21, 24).

D. Commentary

[3–4] After the standard omission of the synchronism (II Kings 15.1), the Chronicler presents the Deuteronomistic introduction, with only slight changes in the original phrasing. Nevertheless, the comparison of Uzziah to

Amaziah his father, found in both texts, here has a somewhat different meaning. In Kings, this comparison is essentially positive: in doing 'what was right in the eyes of the Lord', Uzziah followed the example of his father Amaziah: the fact that the people continued to worship at the high places, common to both reigns, does not seem to affect the general positive tone. In the Chronicler's context, comparison to Amaziah is no longer a compliment, because the latter sinned in worshipping the gods of Edom (II Chron. 25.14) and was severely punished. The Uzziah of Chronicles, although in general more positive than Amaziah, is also not a blameless figure: for both monarchs we find a major turn for the worse at a crucial point in their career: idolatry for Amaziah and sacrilege for Uzziah (26.16ff., cf. Rudolph, 284). In the last analysis, however, the description of Uzziah's reign is more similar to that of Joash his grandfather than to that of his father Amaziah (cf. below).

[5] The reference of II Kings 15.4 to worship in the high places is replaced by a more emphatic reference to Uzziah's religious conduct. The literary and theological function of this change is quite clear: as long as the king sought the Lord he prospered; Uzziah's devotion is a solid theological basis for his great achievements. The Chronicler's need to elaborate on Uzziah's righteousness is another indication (if such is needed) that he possessed information about Uzziah's enterprises, for which he felt that a more convincing theological basis must be provided.

Zechariah is introduced as an 'instructor' (*mēbīn*) of 'the vision (MT $r^{e'}\bar{o}t$) of God'. RSV's rendering 'in the fear of God' follows some of the Hebrew MSS and the Versions, and is assumed by the commentary of Pseudo Rashi (*ad loc.*). MT implies that Zechariah was a prophet (cf. Kimhi *ad loc.*) or, more precisely, a 'seer' (*ro'ēh*), which immediately recalls the figure of Zechariah the son Berechiah the son of Iddo, prophet of the Restoration period (Zech. 1.1), who may have been anachronistically identified with Zechariah the son of Jeberechiah of Isa. 8.2. In Chronicles, however, prophets do not function as instructors, and the content of his teaching would be rather unusual. The reading $b^{e}yir'at$ ('in the fear of God') is much more appropriate referring to a king's education, in particular when viewed as a synonym for 'worship' (cf. II Kings 17.25, 28, 32, 33), or even for keeping the Lord's commandments (cf. in particular Ps. 19.7–10, where 'the fear of the Lord' [v. 19] is parallel to 'the law', 'the testimony', 'the precepts', 'the commandments' and 'the ordinances'). Zechariah thus fulfils the same task described in II Kings 12.2 and II Chron. 24.2; he may in fact have been a priest.

We have noted that when the Chronicler does not have any personal tradition about a prophet, he refers to him anonymously as simply 'a prophet' or 'a man of God' (II Chron. 25.7, 9, 15); the implication for this context would be that the Chronicler did have some kind of tradition regarding this Zechariah. The verse also supports the existence of 'educators' in the royal court, whose influence during the king's childhood could continue into his adult years (cf. also I Chron. 27.32). No further evidence on this matter is extant.

The langauage of v. 5 is clearly late and Chronistic, in both syntax and vocabulary; besides these features note the interchangability of the divine names: MT has 'God' ($'^el\bar{o}h\bar{\imath}m$) three times and $yhwh$ once. LXX, for example, attests to the Tetragrammaton in all four cases.

[6–9] The passage deals with Uzziah's military and international achievements, all restricted to the western and south-western frontiers of his kingdom (but cf. further on v. 8):

(*a*) Campaigns against the Philistines in the west, and the breaking into three of their cities (v. 6a)
(*b*) Expansion into Philistine territory through construction enterprises (v. 6b)
(*c*) Success against Arabs and Meunites (v. 7)
(*d*) Tribute from the 'Ammonites' (v. 8, cf. below).

The inevitable need for expansion, and the specific geographical and political circumstances, led to Judaean pressure towards the west, and occasional conflicts with the Philistines, a few of which are attested in our sources (cf. also to 17.11). This verse is of interest for its precise description of the Philistine fortified cities, two of which – Gath and Ashdod – are familiar Philistine centres, while Jabneh is unique (perhaps 'Jabneel' of Josh. 15.11, situated in the vicinity of Ekron). The text does not speak of actual conquest, but only of 'breaking into' the walls of these cities (RSV 'breaking down' is too strong for the Hebrew *prṣ*). There are two more details concerning Uzziah's relationship with the Philistines: 'he built cities in the territory of Ashdod and elsewhere among the Philistines' and 'God helped him against the Philistines' (v. 7). The total portrait is an altogether reasonable one of expansion of Judaean settlement into territories which were before under Philistine control, and – although this is not stated in so many words – a certain dependency of the Philistines on Uzziah.

The mention of 'Ashdod' as apparently distinct from the 'Philistines' (v. 6b) has prompted the suggestion that it is a gloss (cf. Curtis, 451), or that all of v. 6b is secondary (cf. Williamson, 335, for all the arguments). It is possible, however, that Ashdod did have some particular status at this period (for a later time cf. Isa. 20.1); our knowledge does not permit either a positive or a negative conclusion.

[7] The irregular absence in MT of the preposition *'al* ('against') before the last name, 'the Meunites', together with the fact that this is the only appearance of a place by the name 'Gurbaal' (*gūr-ba'al*), and the different rendering of this name in the Ancient Versions, support the reading *w^e'al*

(against) for *baʿal* (-baal, the second component of the name; cf. Versions, assumed by RSV). The remaining place name, Gur, has been identified as *Gari* of the Amarna letters (cf. among others, Curtis, 451–2; Rinaldi, 'Remarques sur la Politique', *SVT* 9, 1963, 229–30; Williamson, 335), an area east of Beer-sheba; others would follow the reading of the Targum *gᵉrar* ('Gerar', cf. Rudolph, 282). While the first reading would assume a broader scope for Uzziah's expedition, the latter would put this verse in the general historical picture emerging from II Chron. 14.8ff. and 21.16, with black Arab tribes in the southern territories, on the border between Judah and Philistia. The linking of the Meunites to the same area is found also in I Chron. 4.39–41, in an episode related to the time of Hezekiah.

The phrasing of Uzziah's success as 'God helped him against the Philistines' is too vague to indicate whether the scope of Uzziah's achievement was actual conquest, or only temporary military success which halted the further expansion of these tribes and delineated their territory. Our understanding of this issue is dependent also on our interpretation of the next verse.

[8] The unexpected reference to 'Ammonites' who paid tribute to Uzziah does not seem convincing. Wars with the Ammonites are referred in Chronicles to the time of Jehoshaphat (II Chron. 20) and of Jotham (II Chron. 27.5). The first reference has the Ammonite attack on Judah end with their complete destruction, and no further influence on the relationships between the two states is mentioned; the second reference is still in the future. Since the general context is the southern and western borders of Judah, and since the LXX attests to a reading different from MT, many commentators render 'Meunites' (*mᵉʿūnīm*) for 'Ammonites' (*ʿammōnīm*), cf. Dillard, 206, and H. Tadmor, 'The Meunites in the Book of Chronicles in the Light of an Assyrian Document', *Festschrift J. Liver*, 1972, 222–30*. The passage as a whole thus attests to a gradual strengthening and stabilization of Judah under the leadership of Uzziah, after the severe decline in Jehoram's time. Following Amaziah's expedition to Edom, Uzziah is subduing the west; Jotham his son will eventually turn his attention to the east (II Chron. 27.5).

The word-play dominating the entire pericope is well illustrated by the framework of vv. 7–8, beginning with *wayyaʿzᵉrēhū* and ending with *hᵉʿĕḥᵉzīq ʿad lᵉmāʿlāh*. The Chronicler expresses here in his own words an evaluation of Uzziah's achievements; it will be repeated with the same terms – 'fame' (*šēm*), 'help' (*ʿzr*) and 'strong' (*ḥzq*) – and with a similar syntax, in v. 15b.

Although the phrasing is certainly Chronistic, one should note that the insistence on 'fame' is peculiar in Chronicles to Uzziah out of all the kings of Judah (somewhat differently in regard to Jehoshaphat in II Chron. 20.29, and Hezekiah, in II Chron. 32.23); the wording of v. 15b is similar to the same reference about David (I Chron. 14.17, not found in the parallel of II

Samuel). One wonders whether this highlighting of Uzziah's 'fame', besides being a literary unifying *motif*, may not also attest to the king's involvement in international politics.

[9–10] Uzziah's economic enterprises and his extensive building projects are presented systematically: the repairs to the walls of Jerusalem are mentioned first (v. 9), and then various military and developmental undertakings in the country (v. 10).

The work in Jerusalem is intended first to repair the damage caused by Jehoash of Israel during the reign of Uzziah's father (II Kings 14.13//II Chron. 25.23), as indicated by the mention of the 'Corner Gate' in all these texts (but cf. Williamson, 336, for reservations about the precise location of the damaged wall). The fact that Jeroboam of Israel does not interfere with these works may imply that Judah had regained its independence. The 'Valley Gate' is also mentioned in Neh. 2.13, 15; 3.13, but there is no reason to deny its existence during pre-exilic times (cf. mainly, Neh. 2.13).

The precise division of v. 10 is not entirely clear (cf. also NEB and JPS); it seems that the *Ethnah* accent should be moved for a reading: 'and farmers in the Shephelah and the plain' (thus JPS). The 'cisterns' would seem to be located in the 'wilderness' where the 'large herds' were to be grazed. The farmers were probably located both in the 'Shephelah' ('lowlands', 'foothills') and the plains, while the vinedressers worked the hills and the 'Carmel' (RSV 'fertile lands'). RSV's general rendering for this last term should be preferred here, since the more famous region of 'Carmel' was certainly under the control of northern Israel, and the Judaean 'Carmel' (I Sam. 25.2) was an area of grazing and some farming, certainly not of vineyards. For these three – herds, farming and vineyards – as the major factors in the agriculture of the land, cf. Isa. 61.5 (for partial elements, cf. Jer. 14.3–4; 31.24; Joel 1.10–12).

The title attributed to Uzziah (literally 'lover of the soil') is not used to describe any other person in the Bible, although agricultural development was certainly a common enterprise of the Judaean kings (cf. I Chron. 27.25–31 for David, and A. F. Rainey, 'Wine from the Royal Vineyards', *BASOR* 245, 1982, 57–62; J. N. Graham, 'Vinedressers and Plowmen', *BA* 47, 1984, 55–8). Uzziah's unusual title is highlighted by its appearance in an emphatic causal nominal clause at the end of the passage.

[11–15] Two specific military topics are brought up in this passage: the army (vv. 11–13) and its equipment (vv. 14–15). Each of these sections is concluded by a Chronistic evaluative phrase, using recurring elements of the pericope. Verse 13 ends with a short statement: 'to help the king against the enemy', and v. 15b has a longer conclusion, which also summarizes the whole first part of Uzziah's reign: 'And his fame spread far, etc.'.

Information on the army and its fitting out is given in Chronicles for four Judaean kings (also Asa, Jehoshaphat and Amaziah); this passage is the most detailed, including the registration of the troops, and more details of equipment.

The description of the army itself includes 1. the military census (RSV 'muster') and the people in charge of it (v. 11); 2. the number of fathers' houses (v. 12), and 3. the actual number of troops. The inventory of military equipment is composed of 1. a detailed list of arms issued to the fighting units (v. 14), and 2. the special 'devices' on the towers of Jerusalem (v. 15a), referring back to v. 9.

[11] Three persons are given charge of the military registration: a scribe or a secretary (*sōpēr*) and an adjutant (*šōṭēr*, RSV 'officer'), supervised by 'one of the king's officers' (RSV 'commanders'). This only appearance of this general title, which may in fact refer to any officer, makes the LXX 'second to the king' (τοῦ διαδόχυ LXX = Hebrew *mišnēh*) rather attractive. This is also the only occasion in which *šōṭēr* is found in the singular; the plural, sometimes with 'judges', is quite common (cf. Deut. 16.18; 20.5, 8, etc.).

[12] As elsewhere in Chronicles, both the census and the organization of the army are based on the tribal system of 'fathers' houses' (cf. I Chron. 23.24; II Chron. 17.14; 25.5); the number of 'heads of fathers' houses' (2,600) is given first, and then the troop count. Conspicuously absent is the actual division of the army into two major tribal (or territorial) units, Judah and Benjamin. This distinction has undergone a long process of deterioration: for Asa we find not only the two tribal units, but also their respective arms (II Chron. 14.7–8); for Jehoshaphat, the units are still tribal, but a specific weapon is given only for the Benjaminite troops (II Chron. 17.14–19); the army of Amaziah is 'of all Judah and Benjamin', with no distinction between the tribal units (II Chron. 25.5); finally, in this context, the distinction has disappeared entirely.

These facts may have some role in the consideration of historicity. The data here have been repeatedly questioned, and regarded as characteristic Chronistic 'topoi', of theological significance only. The textual differences in the tribal composition of the army could be attributed to the Chronicler's inclination to literary variety, but this would hardly account for their systematic nature. It would be better to assume an authentic tradition of registration, based on 'fathers' houses', with a gradually declining affiliation of these units to larger 'tribal' or territorial entities.

[13] The size of the conscript army seems reasonable enough: units are of about 120 warriors (the traditional 'hundred') – the internal organization is not specified.

[14] The military equipment comprises three doublets: shields and spears, helmets and coats of mail, bows and sling-stones (the doublet structure is lost in RSV). In spite of the designation 'for all the army', it is possible that different units are intended.

[15] In addition to general armaments, this passage dwells upon peculiar installations which Uzziah prepared for the protection of Jerusalem: 'on the towers and on the corners', clever devices for launching arrows and large stones. These 'engines' are certainly regarded as so innovative that, for want of a familiar definition, they are described with the unique and amazing pleonasm: *ḥiššᵉbōnōt maḥªšebet ḥōšēb*, (literally 'devices, the devising of devisers', RSV 'engines invented by skilful men'), a threefold repetition of the root *ḥšb* ('scheme, device'), emphasizing their inventive design.

The reference to these devices plays a significant role in the discussion of the origin of the Chronicler's military data. Assuming that the Chronicler is referring to catapults transformed into defensive weapons, and a possible history of the catapults, Welten concludes that our verse has a Hellenistic context 'of the first half of the third century B.C.' (111–14). However, Welten's basic assumptions are not so certain (cf. Williamson, 338 for references). The origin of the catapults may be earlier and different from that posited by Welten, and – more importantly – the general, unspecified term *ḥiššᵉbōnōt* and the description of its purposes do not necessarily point to catapults, but may refer to other implements (cf. Y. Sukenik [Yadin], 'Engines Invented by Cunning Men', *BJPES* 13, 1946–7, 19–24; id., *The Art of Warfare in Biblical Lands*, London 1963, 325–7). It is hardly likely that one device would shoot both 'arrows and large stones'. Either 'large' is a secondary gloss, in which case the *ḥiššᵉbōnōt* are similar to 'bows and slings' (cf. also I Chron. 12.2), or two different devices are meant, indicating the 'modernization' of ancient tactics (cf. Judg. 9.53; 20.16). Yadin is of the opinion that the text refers not to 'instruments' but to 'special structures built on the towers and battlements ... to facilitate the firing of arrows and the casting down ... of "great stones"' (*The Art of Warfare*, 326).

I have already referred to the Chronistic idiom of v. 15b, which contains all the elements of the pericope: the two roots '*zr* and *ḥzq*, the reference to Uzziah's 'fame', and the specific use of prepositions. Here the section of Uzziah's achievements concludes; the account of his transgression follows. A stylistic and theological link between the two is supplied by the last word of v. 15, *ḥāzāq*, and the first of v. 16, *ukᵉḥezqātō*: the 'strength' of a king may determine his fate.

Attention has increasingly been given to the historical ground of the figure of Uzziah as outlined in this pericope (cf. H. Tadmor, 'Azriyau of Yaudi', *Scripta Hierosolymitana* 8, 1961, 232–72; J. Milgrom, 'Did Isaiah Prophesy During the Reign of Uzziah?', *VT* 14, 1964, 164–7. A critique of the Assyrian documentation is found in N. Na'aman, 'Sennacherib's Letter to God on his Campaign to Judah' *BASOR* 214, 1974, 25–38). The Uzziah portrayed here is not a great conqueror who succeeded in extending considerably the borders of his kingdom and was active in the international arena; here his military exploits are restricted to the determination of the state's borders and some territorial expansion to the south and west. He is an efficient ruler, a diligent administrator and, in particular, a man of strong economic initiative, who brought his realm to prosperity and affluence.

[16–21] The topic of this unit is Uzziah's leprosy; from the point of view of sources, it is clear that v. 21 and the last two words of v. 20 are taken from II Kings 15.5, while the preceding story is peculiar to Chronicles and has no biblical parallel. The structure of the unit may be viewed as follows:

16a Evaluative introduction
16b–20 An account of the appearance of Uzziah's leprosy
21 Conclusion.

The dreadful verdict of v. 21, 'King Uzziah was a leper to the day of his death', is now the focus of the narrative. The task of v. 16a is to provide the literary and theological link between the first part of Uzziah's reign and this unexpected development. Material prosperity led the king to pride, which in turn prompted transgression. It is the Chronicler's conviction that the integrity to withstand this fatal *hybris* was a virtue with which only very few kings were blessed; Uzziah cannot be counted among them.

The story has great dramatic force. The entrance of Uzziah into the Temple with 'a censer in his hand to burn incense' (v. 19) is seen as concrete sacrilege – intrusion into the most sacred precinct, with the intention of performing the most exclusive priestly function. He is immediately followed by the priests who, before taking any action, make clear to Uzziah the gravity of his deed. Their rebuke is caustic: 'Go out of the sanctuary; for you have done wrong (or 'trespassed', cf. below).' Even more dramatic is the moment when, as Uzziah insists on his right and becomes angry with the priests, still holding the censer in his hand, his forehead reddens with leprosy – the utmost impurity in the midst of the sanctuary. From this point all is done in extreme haste: the priests push him out, and he himself hastens to depart; the king's confident entrance into the Temple now ends in panic and flight.

Several points should be noted:

(a) Although the story ends with the words 'the Lord had smitten him' (an adaptation of II Kings 15.5), there is still a strong impression that the king's infliction was brought upon him by an automatic, almost magical process, catalysed by contact with the holy censer at the moment of his 'anger'. The tabu of Temple sanctity and the absolute impurity of leprosy are thus causally connected.

The intense priestly concern with the various forms of impurity caused by leprosy, and the rituals of its detection and purification (Lev. 13–14), are evidence of a basically magical concept of leprosy. This would account for the emergence of this tradition in Israelite lore, as an explanation for the phenomenon of a leper-king (for similar themes, cf. Num. 12.10 and I Kings 13.4, suggested by A. Zeron, 'Die Anmassung des Königs Usia im Lichte von Jesajas Berufung', *TZ* 33, 1977, 65–8, and amplified by Williamson, 338–40). In this story the terrible sacrilege also involves the tabu against burning 'foreign (RSV 'unholy') incense', already prohibited in Exod. 30.9 and punished by the instant death of Aaron's sons in Lev. 10.2.

(*b*) I have already mentioned my view of the secondary adaptation of our story (cf. above, p. 877). The central drama of the narrative seems to lie in the confrontation of King Uzziah/Azariah, as head of state, with the high priest Azariah, head of the clergy. The Temple is the sanctified arena of this confrontation, in which the legitimate activity of the priest is trespassed by the king, effecting dangerous impurity. There is no physical conflict; the priest's word of rebuke, and the king's refusal to concede, are enough to activate the power of Temple sanctity. It is significant that the resultant contamination makes its appearance on the forehead, the most conspicuous place on the king's body, announcing his impurity to the world.

This scene is adapted by the addition of 'with eighty priests of the Lord who were men of valour' in v. 17, the resulting plural in v. 18 ('and they withstood … and said'), and the addition of 'and all the priests' in v. 20. These weaken the dramatic power of the confrontation, as such a large body of priests already constitute a physical threat to the king; the suspense of a face-to-face challenge is lost when the possibility exists for the priestly group forcibly to remove the king. This line of adaptation expresses the Chronicler's inclination to extricate historical events from the realm of the individual, and to make them public (cf. Japhet, *Ideology*, 416–27). It would therefore seem that an original story was secondarily adjusted by the Chronicler, whose hand is also evident elsewhere in the story.

[16] The first half of the verse is extraordinary in that each of its elements reflects something of the Chronicler's idiom. In its eight words in Hebrew we find three roots which are Chronistic 'favourites': *ḥzq* (strong), *m'l* (trespass, RSV 'false') and *šḥt* in the hiphil conjugation (RSV 'destruction'). Also found here are the phrase *gābāh lēb* (RSV 'proud'), the preposition *'ad l*ᵉ (reflected in 'to his'), and the temporal use of the infinitive with preposition and suffix (literally: 'at his strengthening', RSV 'when he was strong') at the beginning of the sentence. All these, however, are restricted to v. 16a; the second half of the verse ('he entered the temple of the Lord', etc.) presents common priestly usage.

The RSV rendering of *lᵉhašḥīt* as 'to his destruction', while possible, does not reflect the predominant Chronistic usage of the *hiphil* as intransitive. It would seem that NEB's margin and JPS 'acted corruptly' better represent the Chronicler's idiom as well as his line of thought.

Note also the more specific usage of *m'l* in this context as 'trespass' (RSV 'he was false'), in particular in v. 18, for which cf. J. Milgrom, *Cult and Conscience*, Leiden 1976, 16–35, in particular 17–18.

[17] 'Eighty' priests seems a rather high number. We have no data regarding the size of the priestly 'division' (cf. I Chron. 24); the number of an officiating division of singers was twelve (I Chron. 25.7–31). If anything may be deduced from I Chron. 12.28–29 (which is doubtful), a division of priests would be about 168 persons, about twice the number of our text. 'Eighty' is in any case a large body of priests, but far from impossible.

[18] Although in the present context the priestly address of v. 18 is represented as if spoken by a chorus ('eighty priests' headed by the high priest), it in fact should be understood as the rebuke of Azariah alone. The verse's structure is framed by a double repetition of *lō' l^{e}kā* (represented in RSV by different renderings), and by an interchange of statements and causative (or restrictive) clauses, in a chiastic format: *kī ... kī ... lō' l^{e}kā ... lo l^{e}kā ...* The declarative style is realized in the nature of its clauses: three out of the five are nominal (in two cases the infinitive *l^{e}haqṭīr*, 'to burn incense', serving in place of a finite form of the verb), while the central position of the verse is occupied by a firm imperative. An additional nominal clause concludes the whole. In accord with Chronistic style, the particle *kī* serves as the opening of both the causative and the restrictive clauses, the latter in place of *kī 'im*, thus:

> '*It is not for you*, Uzziah, to burn incense *to the Lord*
> *but* (*kī*) for the priests ...
>> *Go out of the sanctuary*
> *for* (*kī*) you have done wrong;
> *It is not for you* (*lō' l^{e}kā*), to have honour *from the Lord*'

[19] The circumstances of the appearance of the leprosy are precisely described. The king's reaction to the priests' rebuke concerning his burning of incense is a stubborn anger (*za'ap*), twice repeated. He is standing just next to the 'altar of incense', and at that very moment, as he stood holding the censer, 'in front of (*lipnē*', RSV 'in the presence of') the priests', the leprosy 'shone' (*zārḥāh*, RSV 'broke out') on his forehead.

This is the only use of the verb *zrḥ* in connection with leprosy; the implication is probably both its sudden appearance and its red colour (cf. Gen. 38.30; Lev. 13.12–15; II Kings 3.22, and *Thesaurus of the Language of the Bible*, III, 1968, 64; already Rashbam on Gen. 38.30). I have already mentioned the prominent position of the forehead: this leprosy is a 'branding', as it were, of the sacrilegious monarch. For the 'sign of Cain' (Gen. 4.14), the biblical text is not so specific, but it is generally taken to have been placed on the forehead (cf. Midrash Tanhuma, Genesis, sections 10–11).

This is certainly so for the priest's 'plate of pure gold' (Exod. 28.36–38), and 'the mark' of the grieving people in Ezek. 9.4–6.

This verse concludes the theme of 'burning incense' with the words 'censer' (*miqṭeret*), 'burn incense' (*lᵉhaqṭīr*) and 'altar of incense' (*mizbaḥ haqqᵉṭōret*), bringing the total of the repetitions of the root *qṭr* in the pericope to seven. It also introduces the theme of 'leprosy', which will be repeated from now on, altogether five times.

[20] The story, which began with impertinent sacrilege, ends with an abrupt, undignified rush from the Temple. The two verbs of haste in the verse are *wayyabhilūhū*, 'thrust him out quickly', and *nidḥap*, 'hastened'; the latter is evidenced only in Esther (3.15; 6.12; 8.14), while the first has broader distribution, but in this form and connotation is also probably late (cf. Esther 6.14; also in the *piel* form in Eccles. 5.2 [MT 5.1]; 7.9 etc.).

[21] The narrative now resumes the wording of its source in II Kings 15.5, with slight variations in phrasing and a short addition, introducing 'leprosy' for the third time, and stating again its cause: 'for he was cut off (JPS; RSV 'excluded') from the house of the Lord'.

The designation of the king's quarters (*bēt haḥopšīt*) is unclear; it is rendered by RSV 'a separate house', and is reconstructed by NEB. The literal sense 'house of freedom' may be regarded as a euphemism, describing in fact a 'house of confinement' (Rudolph, 284; also id., 'Ussias "Haus der Freiheit"', *ZAW* 89, 1977, 418; Cogan-Tadmor, *II Kings*, 166–7).

[22–23] The conclusion of Uzziah's reign generally follows the Deuteronomistic source of Kings 15.6–7; there are some standard variations, while others are peculiar to this context. The attribution to the prophet Isaiah of the writing of Uzziah's history uses the direct statement 'wrote', rather than the more common passive verb. This reference is also unique in another respect. Isaiah is the only classical prophet to whom the Chronicler ascribes historiography. Only one more of the classical prophets, Jeremiah, is mentioned in Chronicles (II Chron. 35.25; 36.12, 21, 22), but it is as a 'mourner' of Josiah (II Chron. 35.25), not as his biographer. It is not clear why Isaiah occupies this different position in Chronicles (cf. also the writing of Hezekiah's history in II Chron. 32.32).

Another change concerns Uzziah's burial. The usual 'in the city of David' (II Kings 15.7) is replaced in this verse by 'they buried him with his fathers in the burial field which belonged to the kings'. This wording seems inconsistent, since the reference 'with his fathers' implies the 'kings' tombs' and not a separate 'burial field'. Although 'with his fathers' is absent from some MSS, the Vulgate and the Peshitta, it seems to be original to this text, a mechanical repetition of II Kings 15.7; 'in the burial field ...' provides the necessary reservation. According to Chronicles, then, Uzziah was buried in a separate grave, in the general area of the kings' tombs.

The term *sᵉdēh qᵉbūrāh* ('burial field') is attested in the Bible only here, but we find a constant reference to 'the field' as part of a burial precinct in the story of the Machpelah (Gen. 23.11, 13, 17, 19, 20; cf. S. Yeivin, 'The Sepulchres of the Kings of the House of David', *JNES* 7, 1948, 31–2). For the Aramaic tomb inscription 'Here were brought the bones of Uzziah king of Judah. Not to be opened', cf. E. L. Sukenik, 'To the Epitaph of Uzziah', *Tarbiz* 2, 1931, 288–92*; J. N. Epstein, 'To the Epitaph of Uzziah', ibid., 293–4*.

The form of Uzziah's burial is not depicted as a punishment, but simply as the ritual consequence of his disease. In the Bible there are no regulations pertaining to the burial of lepers, but only to their exclusion from the camp during their lifetime (Lev. 14.3–8; Num. 12.14–15; II Kings 7.3). Whether or not this verse reflects specific customs in this matter is not clear (cf. R. K. Harrison, 'Leprosy', *IDB* 3, 1962, 111–113).

27

27   Jotham was twenty-five years old when he began to reign, and he reigned sixteen years in Jerusalem. His mother's name was Jerushah the daughter of Zadok. [2] And he did what was right in the eyes of the Lord according to all that his father Uzziah had done – only he did not invade the temple of the Lord. But the people still followed corrupt practices. [3] He built the upper gate of the house of the Lord, and did much building on the wall of Ophel. [4] Moreover he built cities in the hill country of Judah, and forts and towers on the wooded hills. [5] He fought with the king of the Ammonites and prevailed against them. And the Ammonites gave him that year a hundred talents of silver, and ten thousand cors of wheat and ten thousand of barley. The Ammonites paid him the same amount in the second and the third years. [6] So Jotham became mighty, because he ordered his ways before the Lord his God. [7] Now the rest of the acts of Jotham, and all his wars, and his ways, behold, they are written in the Book of the Kings of Israel and Judah. [8] He was twenty-five years old when he began to reign, and he reigned sixteen years in Jerusalem. [9] And Jotham slept with his fathers, and they buried him in the city of David; and Ahaz his son reigned in his stead.

A. Notes to MT

[5] בשנה ההיא, proposed transpose before ובשנה in 5b.

B. Notes to RSV

[2] 'did not invade', better 'did not enter' (NEB, JPS, cf. II Chron. 26.16); [5] 'in the second', MT '*and* in the second', cf. A above; [6] 'he ordered his ways', JPS 'he maintained a faithful course'.

C. Structure, sources and form

1. The history of Jotham in II Kings 15.32–38 comprises almost exclusively a unification of the two parts of the Deuteronomistic framework, with the additional information that Jotham 'built the upper gate of the house of the Lord' (II Kings 15.35b), and a remark about the deterioration of the contemporary political situation (II Kings 15.37). Chronicles adopts this story in its entirety, with certain changes and omissions. Further elaborations are introduced in the same manner as is employed for the history of Uzziah, and elsewhere: the Chronicler dissolves the two components of the Deuteronomistic framework and separates them (vv. 1–3a; 7–9), inserting into the gap his own (in this case rather limited) additional material (vv. 3b–6); thus:

II Kings 15.32–35		II Kings 15.36–38
II Chron. 27.1–3a	II Chron.27.3b–6	II Chron. 27.7–9

In an interesting development of this technique, the last parallel section is also adopted in Chronicles by means of omission and substitution:

II Kings 15.36   = II Chron. 27.7
II Kings 15.37   = – – – – – – –
– – – – – –   = II Chron. 27.8
II Kings 15.38   = II Chron. 27.9.

For the precise method of adaptation of v. 2b, cf. below.

2. The new Chronistic material comprises a brief record of Jotham's enterprises (vv. 3b–5) and a few further words of appreciation for Jotham and his reign (v. 6). Although the Jotham narrative is thus somewhat longer than in Kings, it is still the most laconic and least developed of all the 'positive' histories of Judaean kings. Some light may be shed on the Chronicler's methods of adaptation by comparing this chapter with the Uzziah pericope.

In the Deuteronomistic history, both of these kings are given equal scope. For Uzziah, the account of his leprosy and its consquences is included in his own story, and some further notes are found in the context of Amaziah's history, referring to his enthronement and the building of Elath (II Kings 14.22 – assuming, with Chronicles, that this building was achieved by Uzziah). In the same way, the information about Jotham in the context of his own history is supplemented in the history of his father by the account of his regency (II Kings 15.5). Even more significant is the Deuteronomistic evaluation of these monarchs (Azariah in II Kings 15.3–4; Jotham in II Kings 15.34–35a), which is precisely the same: 'And he did what was right in the eyes of the Lord, according to all that his father … had done. Nevertheless the high places were not taken away; the people still sacrificed and burned incense on the high places.'

In spite of this original similarity, the Chronicler has portrayed these monarchs differently. The history of Uzziah is considerably broadened by additional material lauding his achievements; at the same time, the king's figure is shadowed by negative features and sin. Jotham's history, by contrast, is only very little developed, while the king's figure remains positive throughout.

One may claim, of course, that a different adaptation reflects nothing more than the dictates of the basic facts of the Deuteronomistic story: the length of Uzziah's reign requiring the 'reward' of material prosperity, and his serious disease indicating an element of transgression (cf. above, p. 876), while for Jotham, by contrast, no facts of his personal or public career have this binding quality. This argument, although correct to some degree, is not sufficient. Thus, for example, although the note 'the people were still sacrificing and burning incense on the high places' is shortened in Chronicles to 'the people were acting corruptly' (v. 3), it still reflects the people's religious conduct; nevertheless, it has no consequences in an expected form of failure or punishment. At the same time, the political note on the Rezin/Pekah alliance against Judah (II Kings 15.37), which would clearly have been seen by the Chronicler as a punishment, inviting the introduction of the necessary transgression, is omitted altogether. We may thus conclude that a positive view of Jotham does not derive automatically from the Chronicler's sources, but is a historiographical decision. At the same time, however, no great enterprises, reforms, colourful victories or military information are given for Jotham's reign.

The only logical explanation seems to lie in the state of the Chronicler's sources: unlike the case of Uzziah, for Jotham there were no adequate data for editing. This conclusion may have broader ramifications, indicating that the Chronicler's historiographical method was conditioned by his sources to a much greater degree than some modern scholars would admit.

3. The above observations on sources are balanced by the Chronicler's general view of the two kings Uzziah and Jotham. The explicit statement of II Kings 15.5//II Chron. 26.21 that Jotham ruled as regent during his diseased father's last years is supported by all chronological calculations. How many years, however, passed thus before Jotham began to rule alone, is still debated. Some scholars would see Jotham's independent reign as quite short, even non-existent (cf. the comparative picture provided by H. Tadmor, 'Chronology', *Encyclopaedia Biblica* IV, 1962, 261*). The distinction between these monarchs is thus not too obvious; while Jotham continued Uzziah's policy, his own activities may have been ascribed to his father. Compare, for instance, the 'enrolment' or 'muster' which in II Chron. 26.11 is ascribed to Uzziah, and in I Chron. 5.17 to Jotham. They may have been one and the same.

D. *Commentary*

[1–2] The Deuteronomistic opening is cited from II Kings 15.32–33, with several changes. First, as usual, the synchronism with the contemporary ruler in Israel is omitted. Since in the new sequence the history of Jotham follows that of Uzziah without interruption, II Kings 15.32 becomes superfluous and is left uncited.

The evaluation of the king's religious merits is cited verbatim from Kings up to a certain point; the standard Deuteronomistic criticism of the popular cult, 'Nevertheless the high places were not removed, etc.', is then altered to include two reservations, one touching on the comparison between Jotham and his father, and the other concerning the people. The manner of this adaptation – which also affects the linguistic usage – is obscured by the contingencies of translation, but may be clearly seen in the Hebrew.

II Kings 15.35 רק הבמות לא סרו עוד העם מזבחים ומקטרים בבמות
II Chron. 27.2 רק לא בא אל היכל יהוה עוד העם משחיתים

The note concerning the 'corrupt practices' of the people in the Chronicles text can be explained only in light of this mode of editing, with its firm anchor in a given source text. The reference to sinful practices is not in fact followed through during Jotham's reign, nor is the expected punishment forthcoming. The note is thus a textual 'remnant', with no literary or theological consequences.

[3–4] From the Book of Kings the Chronicler cites Jotham's building 'the upper gate of the house of the Lord', and adds renovations to the wall of the Ophel, construction of cities in the hill country of Judah, and fortifications in the wooded areas of the kingdom. These clear definitions of the sites and projects are reasonable and plausible, but not specific enough for their authenticity to be confirmed or denied (cf. by contrast the list of Rehoboam's fortified cities in II Chron. 11.6–10). Note, however, that these additions do not represent standard Chronistic idiom: 'Ophel' appears elsewhere in Chronicles only once (II Chron. 33.14); the plural $h^o r\bar{a}\check{s}\bar{i}m$ for 'woods' is *hapax legomenon* in the Bible, and the usage of the collective singular *har y^ehūdāh* for 'the hill country of Judah' is unique in Chronicles and quite rare elsewhere (cf. Josh. 11.21; 20.7; 21.11).

The Chronicler's general position is that Jotham's enterprises are a sequel to his father's; this may be confirmed by historical considerations. The breaching of Jerusalem's wall in the days of Amaziah (II Kings 14.13//II Chron. 25.23) revealed the vulnerable points of these defences. The work of restoration was begun by Uzziah (II Chron. 26.9), very probably continued by Jotham, in sections not completed by his father, and will continue later, as demonstrated by II Chron. 33.14.

Jotham's further building activities are different from Uzziah's. His 'forts and towers' are not in the 'wilderness' (cf. 26.10) but in the forests, probably thickening the network of lookouts and highway fortifications, not only on the frontier but also inside the kingdom. Most vague is the note concerning the entirely unspecified cities in the hill country of Judah.

[5] Here the Chronicler also ascribes to Jotham one specific military exploit (although 'all his wars' will be mentioned in v. 7). In the campaign against the Ammonites, there is nothing impossible or extraordinary; even the tribute, while its quantities are certainly too high, represents a probable combination: silver, wheat and barley, The note is carefully phrased, Jotham campaign is limited, with no miraculous victory or conquest of Ammonite territory. The Chronicler's familiar tendency to add 'positive' information for the righteous kings, especially victorious wars, may incline the reader to doubt the authenticity of our note. However, its inclusion may be more the fruit of careful selection than of imagination on the part of the Chronicler. While it is unfortunate that the information is so vague, there is still no reason to doubt the facts themselves.

[6] A general statement gives an evaluation of Jotham's conduct and fortune: 'Jotham became mighty, because he maintained a faithful course (JPS) before the Lord his God'. Although Chronistic, the note is far from stereotypical. The common Chronistic idiom *wayyithazzē*, rendered variously in RSV 'established himself' (II Chron. 1.1; 12.13), 'strengthened himself' (II Chron. 17.1) etc., generally implies some internal or external problems which needed to be overcome before the kingdom could be 'estab-

lished'. In our case, no concrete background is given (hence, probably, the RSV 'became mighty'), but it may refer to the war with the Ammonites, or to the note of II Kings 15.37 which the Chronicler omitted. Because of his good deeds, Jotham succeeded in maintaining and establishing his reign.

Also unusual is the unique phrase *hēkīn dᵉrākāw* (literally 'prepared his ways', RSV 'he ordered his ways'). The more common usage, not exclusively Chronistic but certainly one of the Chronicler's favourite idioms, is *hēkīn lēb* (prepare the heart; cf. II Chron. 12.14; 19.3; 30.19, etc.), while the expression 'prepare the way' is quite rare (cf. Deut. 19.3 with a different connotation; Prov. 21.23). In this context there is a clear contrast between Jotham and Uzziah; of the latter we read 'when he was strong (*ukᵉḥezqātō*) he grew proud' (26.16), but the 'strengthening' of Jotham does not result in sinful pride. Even more striking is the contrast with Rehoboam (12.1): 'When the rule of Rehoboam was established (*kᵉhākīn*) and he was strong (*ukᵉḥezqātō*), he forsook the law of the Lord and all Israel with him' (II Chron. 12.2). The juxtaposition in this passage of the same two roots may be an intentional allusion.

Jotham is thus a positive ruler from every point of view. Nevertheless, the dull record of his rule, the scarcity of material, and the absence of elaborate descriptions of battles, religious reforms or even the presence of prophets, render his reign unimpressive and routine.

[7] The 'rest of the acts of Jotham' is not described with the Chronistic convention 'from first to last' (II Chron. 9.29; 12.15; etc.), but with a more individual reference to 'all his wars, and his ways'. This unique formula refers back to vv. 5 and 6, and may have been chosen to add some colour to Jotham's history.

The alleged source, 'The Book of the Kings of Israel and Judah', is mentioned (with slight variations) for other Judaean kings as well (cf. II Chron. 28.26, etc.).

[8–9] Verse 8 concludes Jotham's reign with a repetition of the chronological information already found in v. 1. This is not the only case in which chronological data are found in the concluding part of a king's history; cf., for Rehoboam (II Chron. 12.13), Jehoshaphat (II Chron. 20.31), and, to a certain degree, Asa (II Chron. 16.13). In all these cases, however, the details are not recorded earlier in the story because of the specific structure of the narrative; their record at the end is accompanied by more details taken from the Deuteronomistic opening formula. This case is different, for it is a simple repetition. It has thus been seen as a dittography, or a gloss to 28.1 (cf. Rudolph, 286, Dillard, 213). In my opinion it is more likely an intentional repetition, designed to lengthen somewhat the history of Jotham.

The description of Jotham's death and burial, and the succession of his son, follow the usual formulas.

28 Ahaz was twenty years old when he began to reign, and he reigned sixteen years in Jerusalem. And he did not do what was right in the eyes of the Lord, like his father David, ² but walked in the ways of the kings of Israel. He even made molten images for the Baals; ³ and he burned incense in the valley of the son of Hinnom, and burned his sons as an offering, according to the abominable practices of the nations whom the Lord drove out before the people of Israel. ⁴ And he sacrificed and burned incense on the high places, and on the hills, and under every green tree.

5 Therefore the Lord his God gave him into the hand of the king of Syria, who defeated him and took captive a great number of his people and brought them to Damascus. He was also given into the hand of the king of Israel, who defeated him with great slaughter. ⁶ For Pekah the son of Remaliah slew a hundred and twenty thousand in Judah in one day, all of them men of valour, because they had forsaken the Lord, the God of their fathers. ⁷ And Zichri, a mighty man of Ephraim, slew Maaseiah the king's son and Azrikam the commander of the palace and Elkanah the next in authority to the king.

8 The men of Israel took captive two hundred thousand of their kinsfolk, women, sons, and daughters; they also took much spoil from them and brought the spoil to Samaria. ⁹ But a prophet of the Lord was there, whose name was Oded; and he went out to meet the army that came to Samaria, and said to them, 'Behold, because the Lord, the God of your fathers, was angry with Judah, he gave them into your hand, but you have slain them in a rage which has reached up to heaven. ¹⁰ And now you intend to subjugate the people of Judah and Jerusalem male and female, as your slaves. Have you not sins of your own against the Lord your God? ¹¹ Now hear me, and send back the captives from your kinsfolk whom you have taken, for the fierce wrath of the Lord is upon you.' ¹² Certain chiefs also of the men of Ephraim, Azariah the son of Johanan, Berechiah the son of Meshillemoth, Jehizkiah the son of Shallum, and Amsa the son of Hadlai, stood up against those who were coming from the war, ¹³ and said to them, 'You shall not bring the captives in here, for you propose to bring upon us guilt against the Lord in addition to our present sins and guilt. For our guilt is already great, and there is fierce wrath against Israel.' ¹⁴ So the armed men left the captives and the spoil before the princes and all the assembly. ¹⁵ And the men who have been mentioned by name rose and took the captives, and with the spoil they clothed all that were naked among them; they clothed them, gave them sandals, provided them with food and drink, and anointed them; and carrying all the feeble among them on asses, they brought them to their kinsfolk at Jericho, the city of palm trees. Then they returned to Samaria.

16 At that time King Ahaz sent to the king of Assyria for help. ¹⁷ For the Edomites had again invaded and defeated Judah, and carried away captives. ¹⁸ And the Philistines had made raids on the cities in the Shephelah and the Negeb of Judah, and had taken Beth-shemesh, Aijalon, Gederoth, Soco with its villages, Timnah with its villages, and Gimzo with its villages; and they settled there. ¹⁹ For the Lord brought

Judah low because of Ahaz king of Israel, for he had dealt wantonly in Judah and had been faithless to the Lord. [20] So Tilgath-pilneser king of Assyria came against him, and afflicted him instead of strengthening him. [21] For Ahaz took from the house of the Lord and the house of the king and of the princes, and gave tribute to the king of Assyria; but it did not help him.

22 In the time of his distress he became yet more faithless to the Lord – this same King Ahaz. [23] For he sacrificed to the gods of Damascus which had defeated him, and said, 'Because the gods of the kings of Syria helped them, I will sacrifice to them that they may help me.' But they were the ruin of him, and of all Israel. [24] And Ahaz gathered together the vessels of the house of God and cut in pieces the vessels of the house of God, and he shut up the doors of the house of the Lord; and he made himself altars in every corner of Jerusalem. [25] In every city of Judah he made high places to burn incense to other gods, provoking to anger the Lord, the God of his fathers. [26] Now the rest of his acts and all his ways, from first to last, behold, they are written in the Book of the Kings of Judah and Israel. [27] And Ahaz slept with his fathers, and they buried him in the city, in Jerusalem, for they did not bring him into the tombs of the kings of Israel. And Hezekiah his son reigned in his stead.

A. Notes to MT

[1] עשרים, proposed add וחמש; [16] מלכי, Versions מלך; [19] ישראל, Sebirin, some MSS and the Versions יהודה.

B. Notes to RSV

[5, 23] 'Syria', MT 'Aram' (so NEB, JPS); 'Damascus', MT 'Darmesek'; [5] 'who defeated him with great slaughter', better 'who inflicted a severe defeat on him' (NEB, cf. also JPS); [7] 'commander of the palace', NEB 'comptroller of the household' (JPS 'chief of the palace'); [12–13] 'stood up against' NEB, 'met', JPS 'confronted'; [14] 'left', JPS 'released'; [15] 'all that were naked among them', MT 'all their nakedness'; [17] 'For the Edomites ...', MT 'Again the Edomites ...'; [19] 'he had dealt wantonly', JPS 'he threw off restraint' (similarly NEB, cf. commentary); [20] 'instead of strengthening him', better 'he did not overcome him', cf. commentary.

C. Structure, sources and form

1. The Deuteronomistic history of Ahaz (II Kings 16.1–20) provides the basis and the framework for the Chronicler's passage. The general portrait of the king is similar in both versions; it may be epitomized with the words: 'he did not do what was right in the eyes of the Lord' (v. 1//II Kings 16.2). However, the Chronistic reworking is so comprehensive, even drastic, that the resultant picture is different in many details.

2. The Chronicler's attitude to his Deuteronomistic source and his mode of editing are of interest. At first it seems that only the Deuteronomistic framework is cited, with its respective parts faithfully placed at the beginning and end of the story (vv. 1–4, 26–27), while the main body of the Ahaz story (vv. 5–25) seems to be an

original composition, containing new, sometimes contrasting, information. A more careful study of the parallel chapters reveals a much greater affinity; while there are indeed significant differences in historical portrayal and theological judgment, the two versions are connected by themes, literary order, and sometimes verbal presentation.

A synopsis of the respective structures may illustrate their affinity:

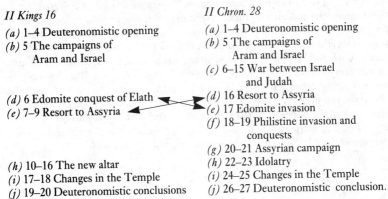

II Kings 16	*II Chron. 28*
(a) 1–4 Deuteronomistic opening	*(a)* 1–4 Deuteronomistic opening
(b) 5 The campaigns of Aram and Israel	*(b)* 5 The campaigns of Aram and Israel
	(c) 6–15 War between Israel and Judah
(d) 6 Edomite conquest of Elath	*(d)* 16 Resort to Assyria
(e) 7–9 Resort to Assyria	*(e)* 17 Edomite invasion
	(f) 18–19 Philistine invasion and conquests
	(g) 20–21 Assyrian campaign
(h) 10–16 The new altar	*(h)* 22–23 Idolatry
(i) 17–18 Changes in the Temple	*(i)* 24–25 Changes in the Temple
(j) 19–20 Deuteronomistic conclusions	*(j)* 26–27 Deuteronomistic conclusion.

Clearly, some of the parallel passages have precisely the same topic, mostly in the same position in the narrative, with the Chronicler providing his own equivalent for the Kings material. Thus, for example, Ahaz' visit to Damascus and the resulting construction of a new altar is interpreted in Chronicles as worship of the gods of Aram; the reference to alterations in the Temple 'because of the kings of Assyria' is interpreted to imply both an actual Assyrian campaign (vv. 20–21) and the closing of the Temple with the rise of idolatry (vv. 24–25). Only two items in the Chronicler's presentation have no equivalent in II Kings 16: the war between Ahaz and Pekah (vv. 6–15) and the Philistine invasion and conquests (v. 18). The question of sources and authenticity will be addressed mainly to these, in the context of the commentary on each of these units.

3. The Chronicler's Ahaz pericope itself, independently of its parallels, is seen to be composed of simple lines, resulting in a chiastic structure:

> *(a)* 1 Introduction
>> *(b)* 2–4 Ahaz' transgressions
>>> *(c)* 5–21 Political and military afflictions
>> *(d)* 22–25 Ahaz' further transgressions
> *(e)* 26–27 Conclusion

The story is thus focused on two themes, sin and punishment; the connection between them is stated explicitly several times: 'Therefore the Lord his God gave him into the hand of the king of Aram (RSV Syria) ... because they had forsaken the Lord' (vv. 5–6); 'For the Lord brought Judah low because ... (Ahaz) had been faithless to the Lord' (v. 19); 'But they were the ruin of him and of all Israel' (v. 23). The main units of Ahaz' history follow a simple line of development, with the transition points discernible in the paraenetic comments of vv. 5–6 and 22. The groundwork is provided by the initial disposition of transgression suggested in vv. 2–

4. The subsequent disasters are an inevitable and deserved consequence, as clearly stated in vv. 5–6. After a long series of failures and chastisements, two alternative sequels are in principle possible: a recognition of guilt and an attitude of repentance (cf. II Chron. 33.12), or a stubborn persistence in evil, in spite of all. Verse 22 makes clear which choice Ahaz made: 'In the time of his distress he became yet more faithless to the Lord'. Here, then, comes the climactic act of Ahaz' reign – the final closing of the Temple doors.

Unlike the kings who precede him, Ahaz enjoys no change of fortunes; the script is uniformly black, moving toward a climax of evil. The severe gloom of the history of Ahaz is matched only by that of Jehoram before him and Zedekiah after him. Interestingly, the only ray of light in this period is provided in the contemporary northern kingdom, where a prophet appears and is heeded by the people, who are then guided by a spirit of repentance.

4. Most of the Ahaz pericope comprises short informative notes, peppered occasionally with evaluative or explanatory remarks (vv. 6b, 19, 22, 23b). These are interrupted by a longer section of different genre – a narrative of the Judah-Israel war (vv. 6–15). Opening in an informative vein (vv. 6–7), this soon becomes a dramatic narration, with rhetorical qualities (vv. 8–15). The unusual content of this story not only contrasts with its immediate context, but is also unique in the Bible as a whole.

The structure is simple and transparent. There are four parts, almost equal in length:

(a) 6–8 The actual details of the battle and its aftermath
(b) 9–11 Oded's prophecy
(c) 12–13 Address of the Ephraimite chiefs
(d) 14–15 Restoration.

The narrative sections (*a*) and (*d*) thus encompass two rhetorical pieces, (*b*) and (*c*); the whole structure may be seen as either chiastic or circular. The first narrative section establishes a situation of captivity; Oded's prophecy is a call to restore liberty to the captives. The chiefs' address is both a response to the prophet's words and a further command to the people; the last narrative section relates the accumulated impact of the addresses, in a series of actions intended to reverse the original situation.

The actions of the narrative sections are described at first (vv. 6–8) as moving slowly: 'slew ... took captives ... brought'. The verbal density and rhetorical force increase toward the end (v. 15); cf. the series of seven consecutive imperfects with the accusative suffix (not so obvious in translation) 'they clothed them, gave them sandals, provided them with food and drink, and anointed them, and carrying all the feeble among them ... they brought them to their kinsfolk'.

The parallel references to Samaria in both v. 8 and v. 15 underline the link between these narrative sections; cf. the commentary.

D. Commentary

[1] As already mentioned, the Deuteronomistic opening is cited in Chronicles with only one omission: II Kings 16.1 with its repetitious reference to Ahaz' accession, and the synchronism with northern Israel. This

verse is thus a quotation of II Kings 16.2, with minor changes. The biographical data for Ahaz pose a problem when compared with those of his son
Hezekiah (II Kings 18.2). According to this verse, when Ahaz died at the age
of thirty-six, his son and successor Hezekiah was twenty-five; this certainly
makes Ahaz the youngest father in the Bible! The difficulty has prompted
suggestions that the verse is corrupt, Ahaz' age at his accession ('twenty')
needing some supplement (cf. Curtis, 457). Indeed, there is some textual
evidence to this effect in the Chronicler's version ('twenty-five', cf. BHS),
although not for the parallel text of II Kings 16.2.

Ahaz is one of the Judaean kings whose mother's name is not recorded in
Kings; the missing information is not provided in Chronicles.

[2–4] These verses elaborate on the transgressions of Ahaz, the tone being
set by the phrase 'he walked in the ways of the kings of Israel'. This
evaluation characterizes the kings of Judah affiliated with the Israelite Om-
rides (II Kings 8.8; II Chron. 21.6, 13; also II Kings 8.27; II Chron. 22.3–4),
defining the Baal apostasy as distinguished from the 'way of Jeroboam' (I
Kings 15.34, etc.). In this technical connotation it is also referred to Ahaz of
all the kings of Judah (differently from Manasseh, II Kings 21.3), and its
specific meaning is clear in the Chronicler's addition: 'He even made molten
images for the Baals' (v. 2). Thus the Deuteronomist and, following him, the
Chronicler distinguish clearly between the 'sins of Jeroboam' which involved
resorting to cultic 'calves' in the context of worshipping the God of Israel and
the Canaanite worship of Baal and Asherah, limited to the kings specifically
mentioned.

The book of Kings also ascribes to Ahaz 'abominable practices of the
nations', in particular 'passing his son through the fire'. It is still debated
whether this practice, imputed to Ahaz and Manasseh (II Kings 21.6//II
Chron. 33.6), was actually child sacrifice; there is no doubt, however, that
this is the meaning of the text of the Chronicler, who reads 'he burned'. He
also has the plural 'his sons' instead of the singular, and adds the burning of
'incense in the valley of the son of Hinnom' (added also for Manasseh, cf. II
Chron. 33.6). It is noteworthy that while the Deuteronomist ascribes to
Josiah the defilement of the valley where this cult had been practised (II
Kings 23.10), he does not mention the site of this cult under the other kings.
This fact may be learned from the relevant texts in Jeremiah (Jer. 7.31, 32;
19.2–6; 32.35).

In addition, to Ahaz are ascribed cultic practices on the high places. He is
preceded in this, in the context of Kings, by Rehoboam (I Kings 14.23), and
in the context of Chronicles by Jehoram. For the significance of this note in
the Chronistic theological context, cf. on 21.11.

The picture emerging from the Deuteronomistic text is that after a
relatively long period of religious stability in Judah, with exclusive faithful-

ness to the Lord's worship established by Joash and maintained by his successors Amaziah, Uzziah and Jotham, there is a significant change of orientation during the reign of Ahaz. The data just cited, as well as the building of the new altar for the Temple cult (II Kings 16.10–16), present Ahaz as an active religious innovator, who made a consistent effort to introduce into Judah religious forms of various kinds, revoking the hegemony of the Lord's worship. From now on we will find a constant struggle between absolute allegiance to the Israelite religion – as in the reforms of Hezekiah and Josiah – and syncretism, foreign influence and strange cults, as under Ahaz and Manasseh-Amon (cf. M. Smith, *Palestinian Parties and Politics that Shaped the Old Testament*, London [2]1987, 38–40).

Although the Chronicler has cited his Deuteronomistic source in full, his own view is different. While Ahaz is indeed portrayed as one of the greatest sinners, it is clear that none of his predecessors (except Jotham his father) was entirely free of fault; some of his transgressions are different in degree, but not in principle, from those of kings like Joash and Amaziah.

[5] As mentioned above, this verse parallels in topic II Kings 16.5, but presents an opposite picture of this episode. According to the Kings text, the rulers of Aram and Israel attacked Ahaz and besieged him, but could not conquer him. A version of this campaign is also reflected in the more detailed description of Isa. 7, where the combination of details provides a clear picture of how Israel and Aram tried to compel the Judaean king to take arms against Assyria, or to give up the throne of Jerusalem to a supporter of their policies (Isa. 7.6). It is in this context that II Kings 16.7 anchors the appeal made by Ahaz to the king of Assyria, resulting in the conquest of Damascus and many parts of the Galilee and northern Transjordan (II Kings 15.29; 16.9; cf. Cogan-Tadmor, *II Kings*, 176–9; 190–2). By contrast, Chronicles describes the defeat of Ahaz by the kings of Aram and Israel. The Chronicles record differs from that of Kings in every detail: the two kings are described as acting, not in co-operation, but each as a separate enemy of Ahaz, who meets them in separate battles; Jerusalem is not mentioned, and Ahaz is 'defeated with great slaughter' – although the Kings version claims that he could not be conquered.

One might attribute this contradictory situation to the Chronicler's theological reworking, simply inverting the data of Kings and Isaiah (cf. Wellhausen, 206; also Dillard, 221). It is possible, however, that the Chronicler is telling different incidents, related to the text of Kings only by their topic (cf. Rudolph, 289–90). Within the framework of the relationship between Judah and her two northern neigbours in those troubled days of crisis one would assume that there were frequent incidents of conflict, only one of which, the attempt to conquer Jerusalem, is mentioned in Kings.

[6–15] These verses tell in more detail of the war between Ahaz and his opponent, Pekah, the son of Remaliah. Although the story is a self-contained unit, in the present context it is phrased as a direct continuation of v. 5b, and illustrates the measure of Ahaz' defeat.

As I have already indicated, this story is exceptional; unlike other Chronistic war tales, its focus is not at all on the military aspects of grand victory or degrading defeat. Some of the Chronicler's most common theological principles, usually illustrated in these contexts, are either absent or secondary. These include the portrayal of the war as an unequal conflict, the reliance on God as the only way to ensure victory, the miraculous divine intervention, etc. In fact, nothing is said about the locale, circumstances or number of fighting troops in the actual battle. Even the assumption that the righteous must win is not confirmed in this encounter: according to the prophet's address, both parties have sinned gravely (vv. 9, 10). The main point of the story as a whole is the *brotherhood* of Judah and Israel, with unifying elements being highlighted against the background of religious vice and political separation, and the conduct of the northern Israelites being seen as a corollary of this unity. This conduct is a model of moral integrity, guided by recognition of sin and a desire for repentance, and withstanding human greed and political animosity.

The informative details in vv. 6–8a illustrate the scope of Ahaz' defeat as a result of his transgression; the rest of the story, however, does not serve the Chronicler's objectives in the history of Ahaz, and in fact seems to contradict them. Verses 9–15 attribute the reversal of the initial defeat, the return of the captives and spoil to Judah, not to any repentance on the part of Ahaz or the people of Judah, but to the unparalleled fraternal generosity of the Israelites.

Two conclusions seem pertinent: this story cannot be seen as the Chronicler's creation, but must have been taken from one of his sources; secondly, its inclusion in the present pericope serves different objectives from the portrayal of Ahaz. These may be seen in two characteristic features which we have already encountered: the Chronicler's consistent effort to incorporate into his story, and from a Judaean perspective, every piece of information concerning the history of the kingdom of Israel; and the firm emphasis on the kinship between Judah and Israel. They are all 'the children of Israel' and 'the people of the Lord', and it is only their political circumstances, not any difference in national or religious identity, which estrange them.

[6–8] These verses provide basic information concerning the war: when the army of Pekah the son of Remaliah smote Ahaz the king of Judah, 120,000 people were slain 'in one day', and 200,000 were taken captive. In addition, three personages nearest to the king were all slain by 'Zichri, the champion of Ephraim' (JPS): the king's son, the 'chief of the palace' and the 'next in authority'.

One need hardly point out that this record, in its present form and with all its details, is historically impossible. No army in ancient times would kill 120,000 in one day – certainly not in the circumstances here described – and the taking of 200,000 captives is utterly unrealistic. Above all, the didactic purpose of these descriptions is more than clear; the question is therefore whether any historical nucleus can be sought behind the numerical exaggerations and tendentious tone.

It seems that in weighing the possibilities we should pay special attention to the concrete details of vv. 7 and 15. The three people mentioned here bear the titles the 'king's son', the 'palace comptroller' (NEB; $n^e g\bar{\imath}d\ habb\bar{a}yit$), and 'the second to the king' (JPS; $mi\check{s}n\bar{e}h\ hammelek$). Of these, only the first is attested elsewhere as having an official role (cf. I Kings 22.26; II Chron. 11.22, etc., cf. A. F. Rainey, 'The Prince and the Pauper', UF 7, 1959, 427–32). The precise title (RSV 'commander of the palace') is not found in other biblical sources, but is similar to $n^e g\bar{\imath}d\ b\bar{e}t\ h\bar{a}'^e l\bar{o}h\bar{\imath}m$ (Neh. 11.11//I Chron. 9.11; II Chron. 31.13; 35.18), $hann\bar{a}g\bar{\imath}d\ l^e bet\ y^e h\bar{u}d\bar{a}h$ (II Chron. 19.11), etc. It is therefore quite possible that $n^e g\bar{\imath}d\ habbayit$ is the equivalent of the more common $'^a\check{s}er\ 'al\ habbayit$ found in various biblical sources (I Kings 16.9; 18.3; II Kings 10.5; 18.18, 37; 19.2, etc.; compare II Kings 15.5 to II Chron. 26.21; cf. also S. C. Layton, 'The Steward in Ancient Israel: A Study of the Hebrew ('Asher) 'Al-Habbayit in its Near Eastern Setting', JBL 109, 1990, 636). As for the title 'second to the king', we have no evidence that such a function was indeed to be found in Israel, although it is known from Persia (Esther 10.3) and is suggested as a possibility in Jonathan's words to David (I Sam 23.17; cf. also the LXX of II Chron. 26.11). None of these titles, including the 'mighty man of Ephraim', belongs to the standard Chronistic vocabulary, and the recorded details do not really contribute to the development of the Chronistic story. I am thus inclined to regard them as authentic reflections of some unknown incident from Ahaz' times.

Spoiling and the taking of captives are regular features of the war stories in Chronicles, with the quantity of the spoil and the number of prisoners indicating the extent of the victory (cf. I Chron. 5.21; II Chron. 14.13–14; 20.25). However, here the theme of 'captives' may be regarded as central to the chapter as a whole; the root is repeated nine times in both verbal and nominal forms (vv. 5, 8, 11, 13, 14, 15 and 17), together with $\check{s}ll$ (vv. 8 and 15) and $bzh/bzzw$ (vv. 8, 14). The word $\check{s}iby\bar{a}h$, 'captives', repeated here five times, is restricted in Chronicles to this context.

No information is given in the story as to where this battle was fought, but the spoil and captives are brought to the capital Samaria, emphatically referred to three times (vv. 8, 9, 15). It is also to be noted that from this point on, the events take place outside the royal court. The king and his counsellors are entirely absent, the protagonists being 'the armed men', 'the chiefs', 'the princes' and 'the assembly'. This tension between vv. 6–7 and 8–15 may result from the use of different sources for the respective passages; for Reviv this is one of the major arguments for a specific historical understanding of the whole episode (H. Reviv, 'The Historical Background of II Chronicles 28.8–15', in *Nation and History*, ed. M. Stern, Jerusalem 1983, 11–16*). For another interpretation cf. Williamson, 347 (on v. 12).

[9–11] After the somewhat elaborate presentation 'But a prophet ... was there, whose name was Oded', his address is cited. It is very clearly constructed of two parts, each with a proposition and conclusion:

(*a*) 9 'behold ...'   10a 'And now'
(*b*) 10b 'Have you not ...?'   11 'And now ...'

The first part describes the present circumstances: the theological reason for the defeat of the Judaeans is their sin, now incurring divine punishment. The second part offers suggestions for necessary action, emphasizing that the same condition of transgression prevails among the people of northern Israel whom he addresses. Thus the two sections beginning with 'And now' present two opposite alternatives: one the intention of the victors to subjugate their kin, the other a command to set them free.

The prophecy is also framed by the repeated theme of 'anger', moving from 'Judah' to 'you'. It opens with a causative, 'because of the *fury* of the Lord God of your fathers against Judah' (JPS; RSV reverses the syntax), and also ends emphatically with a causative: 'for the *fierce wrath* of the Lord is upon you'. 'Anger' also characterizes the Israelites' vehemence in battle: 'you have slain them in *a rage* that reached the heaven', the reference to heaven serving not only to describe the enormity of this anger (cf. Ezra 9.6), but also to emphasize that it has reached the Lord's attention (cf. II Chron. 30.27), revealing that the people of Israel have overstepped their mandate (cf. Ackroyd, 176).

The speech has three references to God, all different: 'the Lord, the God of your fathers' (v. 9); 'the Lord your God' (v. 10); and 'the Lord' (v. 11). This is not only a stylistic feature which aims at variety of expression; it is also a theological statement, identifying 'the Lord' as 'your God' and 'the God of your fathers' (cf. Japhet, *Ideology*, 14–19). Note as well the progressive designation in the prophet's words: 'Judah' (v. 9), 'the people of Judah and Jerusalem' (v. 10), and the climax 'your brothers' (v. 11 *'aḥēkem* (RSV 'kinsfolk').

The prophet's argument is the development of a *motif* also found in II Kings 6.22, which may have reflected a legal custom: 'Did you take them captive with your sword and bow that you would strike them down? Rather, set food and drink before them, and let them ... return to their master' (JPS).

That is, in the present context, the people of Israel have no *right* to enslave the Judahites, since it was not they, but God himself, who defeated them in battle! The prepositional phrase 'to yourselves' (*lākem*) has an emphatic position which is ignored by the translation. It is not you who smote them, you have no right to subjugate them! In order not to aggravate their own guilt, the Israelites should now let the captives free.

These words are already of great significance for understanding the Chronicler's view of northern Israel. Whatever our perspective on this story, it is clear that the northerners are an organic part of the people of Israel. There is in Samaria 'a prophet of the Lord' who addresses the 'men of Israel' in God's name; like prophets in Judah addressing their people, he too argues that they bear 'guilt' against the Lord and have incurred God's wrath; both they and the people of Judah have the same Lord, who for all alike is 'the God of your fathers'; in sum: Judah and Israel are brothers. This message is not delivered after the people have given heed to the prophet, but before; it is a fundamental presupposition of this address.

[12–13] The response to this prophecy is presented first in words and then in deeds. Four persons of the northern leadership, specifically designated as Ephraimites (for this detail cf. Reviv), have been aroused, and now address the returning army. They respond to the prophet's words in a chiastic order, making his last item their first. While the prophet concluded his address with an appeal, 'Now hear me and send back the captives ...', these leaders open with a straightforward command: 'You shall not bring the captives in here'. However, the point which they see as most relevant in the prophet's words is the characterization of their own situation as that of 'guilt' and 'sin'. While the prophet did not explicitly state that for the Israelites to enslave their Judaean brothers is a sin, this may certainly be understood from the juxtaposition of vv. 10a and 10b. Certainly, for the 'chiefs of Ephraim' this is the primary issue: guilt is too great already, and should not be increased. Thus, following the imperative tone of the first words, most of their address is persuasive, centring on the themes of 'guilt' (three times), 'sin' and 'anger'.

The chiefs' address may thus be seen as an ascending structure of three parts, moving from the concrete to the general. It opens with a short command, responding decisively to the prophet's final appeal. Two explanatory statements follow, defining the taking of Judaean captives as a sin, which will be added to the already grave transgressions of Israel. The conclusion is a full and general confession: 'our guilt is already great, and there is fierce wrath against Israel'.

[14–15] Here the story reaches its climax, with the cooperation of all parties concerned. The 'armed men' renounce their claim, not only to the captives they have taken, but also to the spoil, leaving both 'before the princes and all the assembly'. Now the leadership takes the initiative, proving that they have the integrity to practise what they preach. The determination and energy with which they turn to their task is appropriately conveyed by the intensive series of verbs: having begun the work, they do not desist until all is accomplished.

Among the concrete details of the passage, note the repeated reference to the captives as needing to be clothed. This may indicate not only the extent of the spoiling of the Judahites, but also a reflection of ancient customs: the naked shame of captivity exchanged for raiment of respect.

Another point is the choice of Jericho as the place of return (cf. Williamson, 347). This city is indeed described in biblical sources as being on the border between Ephraim and Benjamin (Josh. 16.1; 18.12), but the town itself is included in the inheritance of Benjamin (Josh. 18.21). Its political affiliation during the period of the divided monarchy may only be surmised (cf. I Kings 16.34; II Kings 2.4, 5, 15, 18, which may imply that it belonged to northern Israel, cf. Y. Aharoni, *The Land of the Bible*, 1979, 255–6). On the frontier between north and south there were certainly points nearer to Samaria, and much easier of access. Thus the mention of Jericho may provide an anchor for the story's provenance and historicity. As elsewhere in Chronicles, here too it is possible that an event of limited scope, originating in border-conflicts between Judah and Ephraim, and resulting in the taking of Judaean captives, was secondarily elaborated into the present narrative. The valley of Jericho, as a flourishing oasis at a main crossroads between the two kingdoms, is a very plausible locus for such conflicts. The Chronicler, basing himself on this tradition, gave this local incident the broad national dimensions reflected in the present text. (For a different view of the war, and a suggestion to identify the prophet Oded with Hosea, cf. P. M. Arnold, 'Hosea and the Sin of Gibeah', *CBQ* 51, 1989, 457–60.)

[16–21] Here begins a new unit in the history of Ahaz, containing a series of afflictions. The passage opens and closes with 'the king(s) of Assyria' (vv. 16, 20–21), but also refers to friction with Edom (v. 17) and Philistia (v. 18). The opening narrative time-formula is quite a common method in Chronicles (I Chron. 21.28, 29; II Chron. 13.18, etc.) for synchronizing events. This synchronism is further continued in the next passage, 'In the time of his distress ...' (v. 22).

The first issue is Ahaz' request of help from Assyria (v. 16). In II Kings 16, the major part of Ahaz' reign is portrayed under the shadow of the Assyrian empire. Reacting to the imminent Israel-Aram threat, Ahaz sends a gift to the Assyrian king with a plea for help. The response is an Assyrian campaign against Aram, the conquest of Damascus and execution of its ruler (II Kings 16.7–9). Ahaz then journeys to Damascus to pay homage to the king of Assyria; here the Kings narrative focusses on the consequent building of a new altar for the Jerusalem Temple to replace the bronze altar made by

Solomon (II Kings 16.10–16). Thirdly, Ahaz dismantles certain of the Temple utensils and makes changes in the Temple 'because of the king of Assyria' (v. 17), probably for completing his tribute in metals.

In Chronicles, this comprehensive structure is not preserved, and the role of Assyria diminishes greatly. Ahaz' visit to Damascus is not recorded, and the imitation of the Aramaean altar is conceived as influence of the cults of Aram (v. 23). The changes in the Temple (v. 24) are also viewed differently, without reference to Assyria. All of Ahaz' 'Assyrian connections' are limited to the present pericope, and are viewed in two stages: Ahaz' turn for help (v. 16) and the Assyrian response (v. 20–21), which is seen as the climax of the blows inflicted on Ahaz.

[16] Why did Ahaz send for Assyrian aid? In the Kings version (16.7), the reason is very precisely expressed: 'rescue me from the hand of the king of Aram (RSV Syria) and from the hand of the king of Israel'. The same circumstances seem to prevail in Chronicles, the statement 'at that time' referring back to the defeats of vv. 5ff. Verse 17, with its new opening, 'Moreover', introduces new problems for Ahaz.

[17] Following II Kings 16.6, this verse turns to the Edomite threat. According to the Kings text, the Edomites took advantage of Ahaz' situation to regain control of and resettle Elath. In Chronicles, this information is replaced by an account of an Edomite incursion into Judean territory, slaying and taking captives, in the same terms used earlier for Aram and Israel (v. 5).

The account is vague; no localities or specific circumstances of the battle are given. On the other hand, just such invasions of Edomite bands into Judah were most likely precisely when the political situation in Judah had deteriorated. The detailed description by the Deuteronomist of the time of Jehoiakim, 'And the Lord sent against him bands of the Chaldaeans and bands of Aramaeans (RSV 'Syrians', I would propose 'Edomites') and bands of Moabites and bands of Ammonites, and sent them against Judah to destroy it' (II Kings 24.2), certainly does not reflect an isolated or unprecedented incident.

As already mentioned, this verse is loosely connected to the preceding by the general 'Moreover' ($w^{e'}\bar{o}d$); the RSV rendering ('For') establishes an unnecessary causal connection between vv. 16 and 17.

[18] The record of the Philistine invasion uses the more specific term 'raids', and the Judaean cities attacked are pinpointed in the 'Shephelah and the Negeb of Judah'. In the subsequent conquest and occupation of six towns, the first three – Beth-shemesh, Aijalon and Gederoth – are mentioned alone, and the other three – Soco, Timnah and Gimzo – with their 'villages' (literally 'daughters'). Most of the names are familiar, and their locations imply quite a deep invasion into extensive tracts of Judaean territory, in particular in the Shephelah; none of the identifiable towns is in the Negeb.

The balance of power with the Philistines as described here is the opposite to that prevailing during the earlier reign of Uzziah (26.7) and the later reign of Hezekiah (II Kings 18.8), and represents one more aspect of the constant struggle between these two peoples.

How reliable is this information? The Philistine campaign took a serious bite of Judean territory, as far as the foothills, and took control of several key positions on the main lines of communication: the city (and valley) of Aijalon, Beth-shemesh and Timnah guarding the valley of Sorek, and Soco on the way through the valley of Elah. In principle, there is nothing improbable in such an incursion; it could have resulted from the military decline of Ahaz because of the constant pressure on the northern and eastern borders. The list of cities is not stereotyped in any way; Gimzo is unique, Gederoth appears only once more (Josh. 15.41, as a town in the Shephelah), and the other four names never appear as a group. On the other hand, it may be inferred from Isaiah that matters were different: 'In the year that king Ahaz died came this oracle: "Rejoice not, O Philistia ... that the rod which smote you is broken"' (Isa. 14.28–29). This prophecy confirms the constant animosity between Judah and Philistia at this period, but describes Ahaz as the 'rod which smote' – not the opposite. Should we accept the testimony of Chronicles, which is both specific and probable, although integrated into a theological context, or the evidence implied by Isaiah's prophecy? Without additional data, no conclusive answer may be given.

[19] The series of historical notes is now interrupted by a theological comment, consisting of two explanatory clauses: 'For ... the Lord brought ... for he had dealt ...' The message is clear: the dramatic decline of the political and military state of Judah in the days of Ahaz is a result of one thing only: Ahaz' sins. The precise phrasing, however, needs clarification. The chapter implies, and our verse explicitly states, that the punishment included not only Ahaz but all Judah as well: 'For the Lord brought Judah low because of Ahaz'. In the context of the Chronicler's theology, which insists on the separate responsibility of the people for their fate (cf. Japhet, *Ideology*, 163–4), this is a difficult statement. Indeed, in order to obviate any misunderstanding, the Chronicler goes on immediately to explain that the corruption of Ahaz had infected Judah as well. The rare verb *hiprīʿa* (RSV 'dealt wantonly', found in the *hiphil* form only once more, in Exod. 5.4), is already in its *qal* conjugation a transitive verb: cf. Exod. 32.25: 'Aaron had let them break loose'. The *hiphil* form designates not only 'allowing' but actually directing and instigating the people into error (cf. Baumgartner, 913). It is therefore possible that both Ahaz and Judah are the subject of the next nominal clause *ūmāʿōl maʿal* (note that *maʿal* is a noun, not – as the translations imply – a verbal form), referring in the most general way to an attitude of infidelity to the Lord. The Hebrew *maʿal* is in fact stronger and more

active than 'be unfaithful'; I would therefore read: 'For he made Judah act wildly, and sin against the Lord.'

[20–21] The last in the list of disasters is the Assyrian attack: 'Tiglath-pilneser came (NEB 'marched') against him, and afflicted him.' The meaning is unequivocal: the Chronicler takes II Kings 16.9 (Tiglath-pileser's campaign against Damascus) and reverses it to make the Assyrian king attack Ahaz. (For the specific form of the name, peculiar to Chronicles, cf. also I Chron. 5.26.)

A more precise understanding of the Assyrian campaign in Chronicles depends on the interpretation of the phrase *weʾlōʾ ḥazāqō*. The rendering of the RSV, 'instead of strengthening him', assumes the common connotation of this verb in the *piel* conjugation, while the actual form in the verse is the *qal*. Moreover, this interpretation ignores the explanatory statement of the next verse, forcing it, as it were, to explain nothing: 'For Ahaz took from the house of the Lord ... and gave tribute to the king of Assyria.' The form *ḥazāqō* should, then, be understood as the common usage, 'overcome', 'overpower' (cf. BDB, 304; Baumgartner, 290), while the objective pronoun should be interpreted as representing a preposition i.e., 'he did not overcome him'. (For a similar use of the accusative pronoun, cf. Jer. 20.7, *ḥazaqtanī* 'You overpowered me', JPS). The statement is then fully coherent: the king of Assyria marched against Ahaz but did not conquer him, because Ahaz 'gave tribute'.

The last nominal clause, repeating the *motif* of help (cf. v. 16), ends with the comment that Ahaz' tribute was to no avail. The concrete results of this Assyrian campaign are not, however, recorded. The laconic style allows only a surmise, that the Chronicler has transferred to the time of Ahaz the gist of an incident which in the Deuteronomistic history belongs to the period of Hezekiah, and in the parallel of II Chron. 32 is in fact omitted (compare II Chron. 32.1–9ff. to II Kings 18.14–17ff.).

The phrasing of v. 21 is probably based on II Kings 16.8; the reference is to the sources from which Ahaz drew the money he needed. However, the verb *ḥālaq* (RSV 'took') is not clear, this being the only illustration of this use (cf. Baumgartner, 310, suggesting a textual emendation). While the Chronicler abbreviates the Kings version, he adds to 'the house of the Lord and the house of the king' also 'and of the princes', a characteristic feature of his adaptation.

[22–25] The accumulated afflictions, defined as 'distress', could have inspired Ahaz to turn to the Lord, as illustrated e.g. in the Psalms (II Sam. 22.7//Ps. 18.6 [MT 7]; Ps. 107.6, 13, 19, 28, etc). In Chronicles this 'turning in distress' is a characterization of proper behaviour (II Chron. 15.4; cf. Hosea 5.15), and in a text so similar to this marks the turning point in Manasseh's career: 'And when he was *in distress* he entreated the favour of the

Lord his God and humbled himself' (II Chron. 33.12). The stubborn wilfulness of Ahaz is such that this very distress induces him to further sin. Note the emphatic phrase 'this same king Ahaz', concluding v. 22.

[23] Ahaz' guilt involves the worship to the 'gods to Damascus' (the only occurrence of this title), later explained as 'the gods of the kings of Aram (RSV Syria)', illustrating the complete identification of 'Damascus' with 'Aram'. Various gods were named by their cities rather than by their peoples, and there are several examples in the Bible ('the god of Ekron', II Kings 1.2; cf. II Kings 17.31; 18.34, etc.). In Chronicles is found also the unique 'the God of Jerusalem' (II Chron. 32.19), identified explicitly as the God of 'the people of Jerusalem' (32.18).

This verse has three parts: Ahaz's actions, his theological arguments, and the author's comment on both. Popular stances predominate: Ahaz' defeat is attributed to the 'gods of Damascus', and Ahaz is described as reasoning that since Aram overpowered him, he might do well to worship the gods of Aram. These considerations show basic similarity to the rebuke levelled at Amaziah when he worshipped the gods of Edom (II Chron. 25.15) – conduct held up by the prophet as a model to stupidity, since those gods could not save their own people. Ahaz is following the same reasoning, indeed worshipping gods who have demonstrated their superiority by helping their own people against him. The Chronicler's denunciation of this logic in this context, based on his general theological view that 'the Lord his God gave him into the hand of the king of Aram (RSV Syria)' (v. 5), may clarify his general stand on such arguments. In the case of Amaziah, the prophet's admonition cannot be taken as a theological statement, but only as a rhetorical argument.

We have already noted that v. 23 is probably the Chronicler's interpretation of II Kings 16.10–16; there the theme is 'the altar' (*mizbēaḥ*, repeated in every verse) built in Jerusalem in imitation of an Aramaean model. The Chronicler understands this as reference to actual idolatry, but retains the root 'sacrifice' (*zbḥ*) twice.

The closing comment 'but they were the ruin of him' addresses a leading *motif* in Ahaz' reign. The king repeatedly asks for help (cf. vv. 16, 21), but always from the wrong quarter. Instead of help comes ruin, because he does not turn to the one who alone can aid him, the 'God of his fathers'.

[24–25] This is the nadir of Ahaz' sins: 'he shut the doors of the house of the Lord'. II Kings 16.17 refers to a 'cutting in pieces' (*wayeqaṣṣēṣ*) rendered there by RSV 'cut off') of Temple vessels, and to some changes introduced in the Temple 'because of the king of Assyria'. These references receive an entirely new meaning in Chronicles, referring to the most serious of transgressions: the wilful abolition of the Temple worship and the wanton destruction of sacred vessels. The gravity of this deed is highlighted by Hezekiah's words in 29.7: 'They also shut the doors of the vestibule and put out the lamps, and have not burned incense or offered burnt offerings in the holy place to the God of Israel.' Replacing the worship of the Lord, Ahaz installs altars 'in every corner of Jerusalem', and high places 'in every city of Judah'.

The concluding words summarize Ahaz' sin: 'He provoked the anger of the Lord, the God of his fathers' (NEB). After such a statement, familiar as we are with the Chronicler's principles of theological reworking, we would expect a mention of Ahaz' punishment. That none is forthcoming is probably due to the state of the Chronicler's sources: he did not possess a tradition of any such punishment – in contrast to the cases of Asa, Jehoram, Amaziah and Uzziah. Thus the Chronicler will provide his own description of Ahaz' burial, contradicting the Kings text (cf. on v. 27).

[26] The Deuteronomistic concluding formula appears here with the standard changes. It is interesting that while the writing of the history of Uzziah and Hezekiah is attributed to the prophet Isaiah, this is not the case for the intervening kings, Jotham and Ahaz. There is no obvious reason for this preference, as chronological considerations are not of course applicable here. If we suppose that only kings mentioned in the book of Isaiah were seen as chronicled by the prophet, then why not Ahaz (cf. Isa. 7 *passim*; 14.28)? And if only righteous rulers, why not Jotham (cf. II Chron. 27.6)?

[27] II Kings 16.20 employs the common formula for Ahaz' demise: 'And Ahaz slept with his fathers, and was buried ... in the city of David', but the Chronicler states explicitly that 'they buried him in the city, in Jerusalem, for they did not bring him into the tombs of the kings of Israel'. As I have observed many times, the Chronicler viewed a person's burial as a theologically meaningful event, the last opportunity for recompense according to his deeds. It was almost to be expected, given the Chronicler's description of this king, that the text would deprive Ahaz of the honourable burial deserved by his righteous predecessors.

29 Hezekiah began to reign when he was twenty-five years old, and he reigned twenty-nine years in Jerusalem. His mother's name was Abijah the daughter of Zechariah. [2] And he did what was right in the eyes of the Lord, according to all that David his father had done.

3 In the first year of his reign, in the first month, he opened the doors of the house of the Lord, and repaired them. [4] He brought in the priests and the Levites, and assembled them in the square on the east, [5] and said to them, 'Hear me, Levites. Now sanctify yourselves, and sanctify the house of the Lord, the God of your fathers, and carry out the filth from the holy place. [6] For our fathers have been unfaithful and have done what was evil in the sight of the Lord our God; they have forsaken him, and have turned away their faces from the habitation of the Lord, and turned their backs. [7] They also shut the doors of the vestibule and put out the lamps, and have not burned incense or offered burnt offerings in the holy place to the God of Israel. [8] Therefore the wrath of the Lord came on Judah and Jerusalem, and he has made them an object of horror, of astonishment, and of hissing, as you see with your own eyes. [9] For lo, our fathers have fallen by the sword and our sons and our daughters and our wives are in captivity for this. [10] Now it is in my heart to make a covenant with the Lord, the God of Israel, that his fierce anger may turn away from us. [11] My sons, do not now be negligent, for the Lord has chosen you to stand in his presence, to minister to him, and to be his ministers and burn incense to him.'

12 Then the Levites arose, Mahath the son of Amasai, and Joel the son of Azariah, of the sons of the Kohathites; and of the sons of Merari, Kish the son of Abdi, and Azariah the son of Jehallelel; and of the Gershonites, Joah the son of Zimmah, and Eden the son of Joah; [13] and of the sons of Elizaphan, Shimri and Jeuel; and of the sons of Asaph, Zechariah and Mattaniah; [14] and of the sons of Heman, Jehuel and Shime-i; and of the sons of Jeduthun, Shemaiah and Uzziel. [15] They gathered their brethren, and sanctified themselves, and went in as the king had commanded, by the words of the Lord, to cleanse the house of the Lord. [16] The priests went into the inner part of the house of the Lord to cleanse it, and they brought out all the uncleanness that they found in the temple of the Lord into the court of the house of the Lord; and the Levites took it and carried it out to the brook Kidron. [17] They began to sanctify on the first day of the first month, and on the eighth day of the month they came to the vestibule of the Lord; then for eight days they sanctified the house of the Lord, and on the sixteenth day of the first month they finished. [18] Then they went in to Hezekiah the king and said, 'We have cleansed all the house of the Lord, the altar of burnt offering and all its utensils, and the table for the showbread and all its utensils. [19] All the utensils which King Ahaz discarded in his reign when he was faithless, we have made ready and sanctified; and behold, they are before the altar of the Lord.'

20 Then Hezekiah the king rose early and gathered the officials of the city, and went up to the house of the Lord. [21] And they brought seven bulls, seven rams, seven

lambs, and seven he goats for a sin offering for the kingdom and for the sanctuary and for Judah. And he commanded the priests the sons of Aaron to offer them on the altar of the Lord. [22] So they killed the bulls, and the priests received the blood and threw it against the altar; and they killed the rams and their blood was thrown against the altar; and they killed the lambs and their blood was thrown against the altar. [23] Then the he-goats for the sin offering were brought to the king and the assembly, and they laid their hands upon them, [24] and the priests killed them and made a sin offering with their blood on the altar, to make atonement for all Israel. For the king commanded that the burnt offering and the sin offering should be made for all Israel.

25 And he stationed the Levites in the house of the Lord with cymbals, harps, and lyres, according to the commandment of David and of Gad the king's seer and of Nathan the prophet; for the commandment was from the Lord through his prophets. [26] The Levites stood with the instruments of David, and the priests with the trumpets. [27] Then Hezekiah commanded that the burnt offering be offered on the altar. And when the burnt offering began, the song to the Lord began also, and the trumpets, accompanied by the instruments of David king of Israel. [28] The whole assembly worshipped, and the singers sang, and the trumpeters sounded; all this continued until the burnt offering was finished. [29] When the offering was finished, the king and all who were present with him bowed themselves and worshipped. [30] And Hezekiah the king and the princes commanded the Levites to sing praises to the Lord with the words of David and of Asaph the seer. And they sang praises with gladness, and they bowed down and worshipped.

31 Then Hezekiah said, 'You have now consecrated yourselves to the Lord; come near, bring sacrifices and thank offerings to the house of the Lord.' And the assembly brought sacrifices and thank offerings; and all who were of a willing heart brought burnt offerings. [32] The number of the burnt offerings which the assembly brought was seventy bulls, a hundred rams, and two hundred lambs; all these were for a burnt offering to the Lord. [33] And the consecrated offerings were six hundred bulls and three thousand sheep. [34] But the priests were too few and could not flay all the burnt offerings, so until other priests had sanctified themselves their brethren the Levites helped them, until the work was finished – for the Levites were more upright in heart than the priests in sanctifying themselves. [35] Besides the great number of burnt offerings there was the fat of the peace offerings, and there were the libations for the burnt offerings. Thus the service of the house of the Lord was restored. [36] And Hezekiah and all the people rejoiced because of what God had done for the people; for the thing came about suddenly.

A. Notes to MT

[12] ועדן, read ועדו, cf. I Chron. 6.21 [MT 6.6]; [18] פנימה, dittography? [21] כבשים שבעה, proposed add לעולה, cf. v. 24; יהודה, LXX ישראל, cf. v. 24; [25] ביד יהוה, read מיד יהוה? [36] לעם, read לבם.

B. Notes to RSV

[3] 'In the first, etc.', the emphatic syntax of MT is lost, cf. JPS: 'He, in the first year, etc.'; [4] 'in the square on the east', 'in the east square' (JPS); [5] 'holy place', better 'sanctuary'; [7] 'of the vestibule', cf. commentary; [10] 'make a covenant with the

Lord', NEB 'pledge ourselves to the Lord'; [11] 'burn incense', better 'burn sacrifices' (NEB), similarly JPS; [12–15] 'Then the Levites arose ... They gathered ...', better 'Then the Levites set to ... and gathered' (cf. JPS); [22, 24] 'killed', literally 'slaughtered' (cf. NEB, JPS); [25] 'was from the Lord', better 'is from the Lord'; [27] 'accompanied by', NEB 'led by'; [28, 29] 'worshipped', better 'prostrated themselves' (NEB, JPS); [28] 'the singers sang, and the trumpeters sounded', MT 'the song was sung and the trumpets sounded'; [30] 'princes', 'officers' (NEB, JPS); [33–35] for the parenthetical nature of v. 34, cf. commentary; [34] 'upright in heart', NEB 'scrupulous', JPS 'conscientious'; [36] 'had done for the people', JPS 'had enabled the people to accomplish', cf. commentary.

C. Structure, sources and form

1. The story of Hezekiah is the most extensive among the Chronicler's reports concerning the kings of Judah. The quantitative weight of the story, covering four long chapters (about seventy per cent more than the parallel version in Kings), is certainly no accident. Moreover, its importance becomes even more evident when we examine the precise relationship between the two parallel accounts and the manner in which the Deuteronomistic material has been adapted and integrated into the Chronistic story. The space which the Chronicler has devoted to Hezekiah's story is one way of expressing that Hezekiah is the greatest Judaean monarch after David and Solomon.

2. In reworking II Kings 18–20 to create his own composition, the Chronicler followed several different methods of adaptation.

(a) All the material found in II Kings 18–20 has been used for the new account, but only two short passages are presented in Chronicles with literal similarity (but nevertheless with many alterations) to their source in Kings: the Deuteronomistic introduction (II Kings 18.2–3 = II Chron. 29.1–2), and conclusion (II Kings 20.20–21 = II Chron. 32.33–34). The Chronicler's dependence on II Kings is thus indicated by his utilization of the Deuteronomistic framework to contain his own story.

(b) Notwithstanding the fact that the literal similarity is limited, the dependence of the Chronicler's story on II Kings 18–20 is abundantly clear. With the exception of very few verses which deal with other matters, II Kings 18–20 is devoted to three topics: Sennacherib's campaign against Judah (II King 18.13–37), Hezekiah's illness (II Kings 20.1–11), and the visit of the Babylonian envoys (II Kings. 20.12–19). These three incidents, in the same order, are also treated in the last chapter of the Chronicler's pericope, but in an abbreviated and reworked form: Sennacherib's campaign, II Chron. 32.1–21; Hezekiah's illness, II Chron. 32.24–26; the visit of the Babylonian envoys, II Chron. 32.31. This placing of material taken from II Kings at the end of his own account has already been encountered in the Chronicler's reports on Rehoboam and Asa (II Chron. 12.2–16; 15.16ff.), and thus constitutes one of the Chronicler's standard literary techniques. Contrary, however, to his presentation of Rehoboam and Asa, the borrowed material about Hezekiah is not reproduced with literal accuracy but rather in a very condensed epitomization, which transmits only the main points of the story – for which cf. in particular the precedent of II Chron. 22.1–9.

(c) Certain isolated elements of the Kings material are positioned differently in the new description: the Deuteronomistic religious appraisal of Hezekiah and the reference to his reform (II Kings 18.4–6) are offered in II Chron. 31.1, 20–21, while II Kings 18.7–8 may be represented – in a very reworked form – in II Chron. 32.22–23. Only II Kings 18.9–12, which deals with the northern kingdom and refers to the conquest of Samaria and the exile of the Israelites, has no parallel in the Chronicler's version – again following standard Chronistic procedures. These events are alluded to, however, from a Judaean perspective, in II Chron. 30.6–7.

(d) To the material taken from Kings, the Chronicler adds extensive chapters which have no basis in Kings, either in their subjects or in the details of their descriptions: II Chron. 29.3–36, the purification of the Temple and the restoration of its service; II Chron. 30.1–27, the celebration of the Passover; II Chron. 31.2–19, the organization of the clergy and provision for the maintenance of the Temple and clergy; and II Chron. 32.27–30, Hezekiah's prosperity.

3. Taking as our point of departure the Deuteronomistic structure of Kings, the synopsis of Kings=Chronicles presents the following picture:

II Kings 18.1–3	= II Chron. 29.1–2
———	II Chron. 29.3–36
———	II Chron. 30.1–27
II Kings 18.4	= II Chron. 31.1
———	II Chron. 31.2–19
II Kings 18.5–6	= II Chron. 31.20–21
II Kings 18.7–8	II Chron. 32.22–23
II Kings 18.9–12	———
II Kings 18.13–19.37	= II Chron. 32.1–21
II Kings 20.1–11	= II Chron. 32.24–26
———	= II Chron. 32.27–30
II Kings 20.12–19	= II Chron. 32.31
II Kings 20.20–21	= II Chron. 32.32–33

This synopsis illustrates a faithful adherence by the Chronicler to the structure and composition of the original story; it may be sketched according to the same model which applied to shorter passages: one parallel continuum, broken along the line for omissions or additions, with only one passage – II Kings 18.7–8 – being differently placed, represented as it is by II Chron. 32.22–23.

II Kings	18.1–3		18.4		18.5–6	18.7–8
II Chron.	29.1–2	29.3–30.27	31.1	31.2–19	3.20–21	32.22–23

II Kings	18.13–19.37	20.1–11		20.12–19	20.20–21
II Chron.	32.1–21	32.24–26	32.27–30	32.31	32.32–33

In spite of this fidelity to his source, the weight of the additional sections has pushed the centre of Hezekiah's history elsewhere, producing a shift in the portrayal of his reign.

4. The difference in the Chronicler's presentation has yet another aspect. Most of Hezekiah's story in II Kings is recounted in the framework of a 'prophetic story' (II Kings 18.13–20.19), which also appears, with only negligible variants, in Isa. 36–39.

The problem of its original position in either Isaiah or Kings is irrelevant to the present discussion, but as determined by the genre, the prophet Isaiah is as much the protagonist of the story as Hezekiah, and even the more 'political' part of this story, the account of Sennacherib's campaign, bears clear signs of its prophetic genre. In the portrayal of the two protagonists, there is an obvious preference for Isaiah – a firm, directing, encouraging and rebuking messenger of the Lord, confronting a frightened, confused, sick and impulsive king. This literary genre of 'prophetic story' may also account for the prevalence of rhetorical sections, linked to one another by short, narrative sections. The major rhetorical units are the speeches of the Rabshakeh (II Kings 18.19–25, 27, 28b–35), the letter of the Assyrian king (19.10–13), Hezekiah's words to Isaiah (19.3–4) and his prayer (19.15–19), and Isaiah's prophecies and messages (19.6–7, 20–34). Moreover, each of the narrated events includes a prophetic address (in addition to the above, also 20.1b, 5–7, 9, 16b–18). The version found in the book of Isaiah also contains a thanksgiving psalm by Hezekiah, in Isa. 38.10–20.

The literary genre of the Chronicler's story is altogether different, and Isaiah is definitely not the main figure. In fact, the whole of II Kings 20 is transmitted in very short passages (32.24–26, 31) in which Isaiah is not even mentioned, while the story of Sennacherib's campaign is greatly abbreviated, the figure of Isaiah becoming much more vague (32.20) and his prophecy omitted. The 'prophetic story' of II Kings has been transformed into a historical account.

To state this conclusion more generally, we may say that in spite of the enormous significance of prophets, and their varied roles in the history of Israel in the Chronicler's historiography, the prophets are not its protagonists. The centre of the historical stage for the Chronicler is taken by the king and people: here, Hezekiah and the people of Jerusalem rather than the prophet Isaiah.

5. Each of the additional chapters, 29, 30, and 31, consists of a lengthy, self-contained narrative dedicated to one topic, and all three constitute a continuous composition, revolving around the topic of Hezekiah's restoration of the Lord's worship. Integrating fully the material taken from II Kings, this composition may be outlined as follows:

(a) II Chron. 29.3–36   opening the Temple, purification and dedication
(b) II Chron. 30.1–27   Passover
(c) II Chron. 31.1   removal of idolatry
(d) II Chron. 31.2   appointment of the cult personnel
(e) II Chron. 31.3–19   Temple and clergy's maintenance
(f) II Chron. 31.20–21   conclusion

This complex composition follows the analogy of other Chronistic comprehensive pericopes, such as I Chron. 15–16; 23–29 and others.

6. What were the Chronicler's sources for Hezekiah's history? At the outset, a scholarly distinction is often made between the additions to II Chron. 32 (vv. 22–23, 27–30), which contain details of a political and economic nature, and chs. 29–31, which are devoted to religious matters. Although the 'Chronistic idiom' is found throughout, the Chronicler's language, style, and historical and religious views are more strongly felt in the latter. Nevertheless, even within these chapters, the picture is not monolithic; various sections receive different answers to the problem of their possible sources. We will therefore deal with this source problem as we proceed.

7. After its Deuteronomistic introduction, ch. 29 is a long story, revolving in great detail around one topic: purification of the Temple and its rededication. Its protagonist is king Hezekiah, who actually initiates and directs every step and stage of the process. Two of his addresses, a longer one to 'the Levites' (vv. 5–11) and a shorter one to the people (v. 31), are actually cited, complemented by a report of the Levites (vv. 18–19). The structure of the chapter appears to be:

(*a*) 1–2 Introduction
(*b*) 3–19 Purification of the Temple
  3 introduction: initial steps
  4–11 Hezekiah's address to the Levites
  12–17 purification
  18–19 Levites' report
(*c*) 20–30 Temple's dedication
  20 Introduction
  21–24 preparation of sacrifices
  25–26 stationing of the musicians
  27–30 sacrifices, worship and thanksgiving
(*d*) 31–36 Popular celebration
  31a Hezekiah's address
  31b–35 sacrifices
  36 conclusion

D. *Commentary*

[1–2] Having omitted the synchronism with northern Israel and the statement of Hezekiah's reign (II Kings 18.1), the Chronicler takes over the Deuteronomistic introduction of II Kings 18.2–3 with a few slight alterations. Although the comparison of Hezekiah with David is taken from the Chronicler's source, it does not function merely as 'a stereotyped expression of commendation' (Williamson, 352); rather, the Chronicler has systematically omitted all comparisons to David found in Kings, in either positive or negative terms, except for the stories of Hezekiah here and Josiah in 34.2 (for II Chron. 17.3, cf. there). This comparison with David, then, confirmed and intensified by the various details of the story, is a significant element of the Chronicler's portrayal of Hezekiah.

A few words should be said about the name of the king, 'Hezekiah'. The name appears in the biblical material in four alternate forms, with shorter or longer representations of its first and last elements. Its initial element may be either the perfect form of the verb *ḥzq*, or the imperfect *yḥzq*, and the final element may be represented with the longer *yāhū* or the shorter *-yāh*. The four variations would be 1. *ḥizqīyyāh*, 2. *yᵉḥizqīyyāh*, 3. *ḥizqiyyāhū*, 4. *yᵉḥizqiyyāhū*. Although the distribution is not consistent, a few general guidelines may nevertheless be noted. The most common form of the name in II Kings is 3.; second to it is 1., and 4. appears only once, in II Kings 20.10.

The most common form appearing in Chronicles is 4.; Chronicles also contains very few occurrences of 3. 1. does not appear in Chronicles at all, and 2. is missing from both II Kings and Chronicles, being found only in Hos. 1.1 and Micah 1.1. It is clear that the Chronicler has followed his own rules, independently of the Deuteronomistic usage, and the preference of the longer forms is unequivocal. The common rendering of the name in the translations, therefore, represents only one of the forms, and not necessarily the most common one. For Chronicles, in fact, it is really a misrepresentation.

[3] At first glance the Chronicler appears to continue here in the same direction as II Kings 18, which moves in v. 4 to Hezekiah's reform. In fact, however, II Kings 18.4 has its parallel in II Chron. 31.1, while here the Chronicler turns his attention to Hezekiah's most urgent task: the reopening of the Temple gates, the necessary reaction to his father's acts (28.24). Hezekiah's dispatch in fulfilling this task is expressed in Chronicles not only by referring to it first, but by emphasizing it through a detailed formulation of the date ('in the first year of his reign, in the first month'), and an emphatic syntax, opening the sentence with the personal pronoun, 'He' (overlooked by RSV).

[4] One would naturally expect the task of purifying the Temple to fall to the priests or the clergy in general. As the story is told in Chronicles, however, although the cult personnel indeed carry out the work of purification, both the initiative and responsibility remain with the king. Consistent with the Chronicler's method elsewhere, the first step in this initiative is a speech in which the king sets forth his plan; cf. the words of Asa (II Chron. 14.6), and of Jehoshaphat (19.6–7, 9–11).

[5–11] The speech is comprised of two elements.

(a) Verses 5 and 11 are the framework; the first contains the command to the Levites to proceed with the undertaking, and the latter consists of Hezekiah's final encouraging words, including an explicit reference to the Levites' election. The two parts of the framework may thus be combined into one continuous sequence, dealing with the immediate issue of the purification of the Temple.

(b) The main body of the speech, vv. 6–10, contains Hezekiah's reflections, presenting a cause-and-effect relationship between the cultic state of affairs and the political situation. It is thus composed of three parts: sin (vv. 6–7); resulting punishment (vv. 8–9); and conclusion (v. 10), and by establishing the principle of causality as a 'sin – punishment' sequence the necessary expiatory steps become self-evident.

The speech as a whole is constructed with a series of formulaic markers. The two parts of the framework open with a second-person invocation of the Levites, 'Hear me, Levites' (v. 5), and 'My sons' (v. 11). Each of the invocations is followed by the introductory 'now', continued by a command, 'sanctify yourselves ...' (v. 5) and 'do not be negligent' (v. 11). The main body of the speech has three opening formulations: the causative *kī* introducing its beginning, and the two concluding markers, 'behold' (v. 9 RSV 'For lo'), and 'Now' (v. 10). A sketch of the passage reveals the following structure:

> 5 Hear me, O Levites! Now ... (+ command)
>   6 For ...
>   9 Behold ...
>   10 Now ...
> 11 My sons! Now ... (+command)

As very often occurs in Chronicles, the dominant feature of Hezekiah's address is that of persuasion. Although he formally employs imperatives, his tone is one of explanation, attempting to persuade his listeners of the truth of his position. He first explains to the Levites the considerations lying behind his own initiative, and then, when encouraging them for their work (v. 11), he points out that the care of the Temple is not merely their responsibility, but indeed the task for which they were chosen.

[5] The speech opens with a characteristic Chronistic formula, 'Hear me, X', this time addressed to the Levites. The term 'Levites' is used here in its broader connotation, referring to the two groups mentioned in v. 4 ('Levites' in its narrow sense and 'priests'), that is, all the members of the tribe of Levi, constituting the clergy at large. The flexible connotation of this term is a common feature in Chronicles, cf. for example, I Chron. 15.11 and 12.

The key term in Hezekiah's command is 'sanctify', the root *qdš* being repeated three times in this one verse. ('Holy place' would be better rendered by 'sanctuary' in view of the context.) The Levites are to sanctify themselves, sanctify the house and take out the filth from the 'sanctuary'. This is also the leading theme in the process of restoration described later: the Levites sanctify themselves (v. 15), purify the house of the Lord and sanctify it (v. 17), and in their report state that 'We have cleansed all the house of the Lord ... All the utensils ... we have made ready and sanctified' (vv. 18–19).

To designate the uncleanness the Chronicler employs a very strong word, *niddāh* ('filth'), which appears nowhere else in the book.

[6–7] In these verses Hezekiah summarizes the religious state of affairs he found upon ascending the Israelite throne: utter abandonment of the paths of righteousness. This situation is presented in two forms. First, in a series of intensive idioms, Hezekiah describes this abandonment with no specification of the exact sin ('... our fathers have been unfaithful... have done what was evil ...; they have forsaken him and have turned away their faces ... and turned their backs'). Then, beginning in v. 7, Hezekiah presents a detailed description of the fathers' major crime, the cancellation of the Lord's service in the Temple: they shut the doors of the Temple, put out the lamps, and stopped the burning of incense and the sacrificing of burnt offerings.

The passage as a whole, and in particular v. 7, is phrased with some attention to metre and with a certain parallelism of members. Verse 6 has six cola, while v. 7 has five, the first four being of equal length, and the fifth, shorter one, consisting of a kind of conclusion to the whole. Not surprisingly, this metrical quality is not reproduced in translation.

As in several other places, the Chronicler uses the word *'ūlām* (literally vestibule or porch) as a metonym for the Temple at large (cf. II Chron. 8.12; 15.8; cf. also further in v. 17), rendered correctly by LXX ναός. The three verses (5–7) have four different designations for the Temple: the house of the Lord (v. 5), the dwelling of the Lord (v. 6, *miškan yhwh*), Temple (*'ūlām*), and sanctuary (*qōdeš*).

Does this description of a lapse in the Temple service reflect any concrete historical reality? A situation like this was hardly possible according to the Deuteronomistic history, and none of the Judaean kings, not even Manasseh, is accused of such a deed. For the Second Temple period, although our information is very scant, the possibility of a total cancellation of the Temple service, initiated by the people themselves or their leaders, seems even less likely. There may have been a cessation of the Temple service during the period when the Temple lay in ruins (but this is not quite certain, in view of Jer. 41.5), but that is certainly no case of literally 'shutting the doors'. Rather, the description reflects a peculiar Chronistic view of the vicissitudes of the Lord's worship, which diverges considerably from that of the Deuteronomist. Its leading principle is that of the mutual exclusivity of idolatry and the worship of the Lord, and entails the complete cancellation of the one during the prevalence of the other (cf. also on II Chron. 24.7, and Japhet, *Ideology*, 203–16). The accounts of the closing down of the Temple in Ahaz' time and its reopening, purification and the restoration of the Lord's service in Hezekiah's time are all the work of the Chronicler, their ultimate origin lying in his own view of the history of the cult, rather than in historical facts.

[8–9] With the common idiom 'the wrath of the Lord came', the self-evident result of transgression is now introduced; God's anger, always justified, marks the beginning of punishment. The description of the punishment is also comprised of two parts. Verse 8 refers to the devastation in a general formula, 'he has made them an object of horror, of astonishment, and of hissing', formulas probably borrowed from the Deuteronomistic layer of Jeremiah where they are most frequently found (cf. in particular Jer. 29.18). This general phraseology is made concrete by the second-person witness-statement 'as you see with your own eyes', followed by specific references to two evils: death in war and captivity (v. 9). The literary movement from the general to the specific is parallel to that of vv. 6–7, thus granting a formal expression to the sequence 'sin – punishment'.

Both the sin and the punishment refer to the days of Ahaz, with the details of punishment hearkening back to 28.6–8: 'For Pekah ... slew a hundred and twenty thousand in Judah ... because they had forsaken the Lord ... the men of Israel took captive two hundred thousand of their kinsfolk, women, sons and daughters.' This chain of events, which links so strongly the stories of Ahaz and Hezekiah, now demands a change.

[10] Having laid the groundwork for his action with this theological interpretation of history, Hezekiah's conclusion is self-evident: he decides to reverse the unfolding process by causing the Lord's anger to 'turn away'. This change of orientation the Chronicler describes as $lik^erōt\ b^erīt\ l^eyhwh$. Although it includes the term 'covenant' ($b^erīt$), no true covenant-making is intended, and no facile comparison with the time of Josiah should be made. Hezekiah speaks of his wish ('it is in my heart to make a covenant'), but there is no allusion to a ceremony of covenant-making among the many acts ascribed to him. The linguistic usage is also unusual; the use of krt with the prepositional l^e which originally indicated a position of superiority – the superior making a covenant to the inferior (see Japhet, *Ideology*, 112–15) – would yield an impossible sense in this context, as if Hezekiah were making 'a covenant *to* the Lord'. The whole idiom, then, should be interpreted as an expression of absolute loyalty, of making a complete commitment (cf. also Ezra 10.3), represented well by the NEB: 'pledge ourselves to the Lord'.

[11] Having described the general background and then stated his intentions, Hezekiah turns to the Levites with words of encouragement, the address 'my sons' creating a feeling of great intimacy and partnership between Hezekiah and the clergy; they are to be the vanguards, the leaders of the change. This is in fact the only case in the Bible where a group of people is addressed with this intimate appellation. While the singular 'my son' is very common, the plural vocative appears only in Eli's address to his two sons (I Sam. 2.24). Indeed, both LXX and V avoid the phrase altogether.

The terminology describing the election of the Levites is similar to other statements on the same matter in Deuteronomy and Chronicles (Deut. 10.8; 18.5; 21.5; I Chron. 15.2; 23.13), but it is nevertheless well adapted to the particular situation. Addressed to the tribe of Levi as a whole, it entails the general 'serving of the Lord' as well as the more specific 'burn sacrifices', directed at the priests among the 'Levites'. The root qtr, which is often used as a specific term for 'burning incense', actually has the more general connotation of 'making sacrifices smoke' (BDB, 882–3; Baumgartner, 1022–3), and this is its usage here. The comprehensive service of the clergy is thus described by the most general terms: 'serve' ($šrt$) and 'burn sacrifices' (qtr).

[12–17] The Levites do not answer the king in words but in deeds. Verses 12–14 mention by name fourteen leaders of the Levites, two for each family, who immediately set about to perform the necessary tasks. The levitical families represented by these leaders are Kohath, Merari, Gershom, Elizaphan, Asaph, Heman, and Jeduthun.

The enumeration of levitical families gives the initial impression that only 'Levites' in the strict sense of the term are intended, that is, those of the tribe who are not priests. The description of their acts in vv. 16–19, however, clearly implies that there were priests among them as well, who alone were permitted to enter the Temple. They are explicitly mentioned in v. 16, and implied in v. 18. This apparent 'unsmoothness' may be approached in several ways. The problem may be pursued along textual-critical lines with the conclusion that 'the priests' represent a secondary stratum in this pericope, while the Chronicler himself included only the 'Levites' proper (cf. Petersen, *Late Biblical Prophecy*, Missoula 1977, 79ff.). As Rudolph and Williamson point out, this would create more difficulties than it solves, since the logic of the situation demands that the priests participate in it (cf. Rudolph, 293–4; Williamson, 351–60 *passim*). Alternatively, it may be posited that in his preference for the Levites, the Chronicler chose to mention them only, while still assuming the sanctification of the priests. It is possible, however, that the priests are indeed included among the 'sons of the Kohathites' – to whom they belong by descent – without a more specific note of their descent (e.g. 'the sons of Aaron') being necessary at this point (but cf. v. 21). In that case, the term 'Levites' in v. 12 (similar to v. 5) would have the broader connotation, designating all the clergy, while in v. 16 the division into two groups, priests and Levites, would indicate 'Levites' in its limited sense.

The composition of the list of levitical families is peculiar. Traditionally the tribe is conceived as being composed of three major families, Gershon, Kohath and Merari; these are then divided into sub-units, as in Exod. 6.16–25. The present list likewise begins with these three families, but moves Gershon to the third position (cf. I Chron. 15.5–7). This change was no doubt derived from the prominence of the Kohathites, to whom the priests were affiliated. The leaders of these families, two for each family, are listed in a systematic, almost uniform manner, each being identified by his patronym: 'X the son of Y'. Then four other families are mentioned, Elizaphan, Asaph, Heman and Jeduthun, with their leaders, two for each family, mentioned only by their proper name. The last three, of course, represent the singers.

The combination of the three levitical families with the three sub-units of singers is also attested in the lists of I Chron. 6, the present context having two representatives for each family rather than one. The unusual feature in the text is Elizaphan, who occupies the middle position between these two groups. 'Elizaphan' appears once more as a group of its own (I Chron. 15.8), but is joined with Hebron and Uzziel, all three being descendants of Kohath.

Given the highly conventional and standardized nature of this material, it is difficult to view it as a reflection of any historical situation (Dillard, 235); it seems rather that the key to its understanding lies in this very conventionality. The number seven is a dominant feature in the whole context: the purification of the Temple is carried out in two phases, devoting seven days for the first stage, seven+one for the second (v. 17). The enumeration of sacrifices is also dominated by this number: 'seven bulls, seven rams, seven lambs and seven he-goats' (v. 21), and it is 'seven' which necessitated the addition of one more branch to the six traditional ones. This consistency is probably related to the concept of 'wholeness', making a full, complete, round purification and sin-offering. The list of levitical leaders, then, in its specific construction and in its use of the broader connotation of 'Levites', is an integral part of the Chronicler's composition.

The list of names constitutes a parenthetic element in the passage, the verb *wayyāqumū* having an adverbial function rather than a verbal one (cf. Gesenius, §120d, p. 386), and therefore being inadequately represented by RSV, 'arose'. The syntax is best represented by JPS: 'So the Levites set to [names] and gathered ...' (cf. also NEB). Given this syntax, the list may be easily excised, and this, together with its peculiar composition, has prompted some scholars to regard is as secondary (cf. Willi, 199). Its relatedness to the context, however, as pointed out above, is well established.

The names of the first group, except for the second among the Merarites, appear in other levitical lists. For the Kohathites Mahath the son of Amasai and Joel the son of Azariah, cf. I Chron. 6.35 and 36 [MT 6.20, 21]; for the Merarite Kish the son of Abdi, cf. I Chron. 6.44 [MT 6.29]; and for the Gershonites Joah the son of Zimmah and Eden (probably read *'iddō* for *'eden*), the son of Joah, cf. I Chron. 6.20–21 [MT 6.5–6]. Among the singers, for the Asaphites Zechariahu (also Zaccur) and Mattaniahu cf. Neh. 12.35; I Chron. 16.5; 24.10 and I Chron. 9.15; 24.16 respectively. The names of the others, the Hemanites Jehiel and Shimei, Shemaiah and Uzziel of Jeduthun, and Shimri and Jeiel of Elizaphan, are very common levitical names, appearing throughout the various families.

[15–17] The levitical leaders follow the king's orders with great precision: they organize their 'brethren', sanctify themselves, and prepare to work. The 'sanctification' of the Temple will be described in detail in the following passages; what their own sanctification entails is not made explicit, and must be inferred from either II Chron. 30.15 (cf. there) or Ezek. 44.26–27.

Even here, the Chronicler emphasizes the king's initiative, presented as being 'by the words of the Lord'. This is a very interesting interpretation of the king's acts; what has been presented very clearly as the king's own initiative and will – 'Now it is in my heart' (v. 10) – is designated as 'the king has commanded by the words of the Lord', without any explicit 'word of the Lord' actually cited or referred to. The king, then, is the transmitter of the Lord's will and represents his authority.

The preparation of the Temple is described by two terms: 'purify' (*ṭhr*) and 'sanctify' (*qdš*). Notwithstanding some unclarity at the beginning of v. 17, 'purify' denotes the cleansing, the deliverance of the Temple from a state of 'pollution', the removal of an essentially negative condition; 'sanctify' or 'hallow' goes beyond 'purity' and brings the Temple to the elevated state of sanctity. Although it is not fully specified, a certain distinction also seems to obtain between the tasks of the priests and Levites. Since entrance into the house is restricted to the priests, all the chores related to the interior of the house are their responsibility. Once all the 'impurity' had been taken out to 'the court of the house of the Lord', it was handled by the Levites, who brought it to the Kidron valley. The same valley is mentioned elsewhere as the depository for all the refuse from Jerusalem probably eventually to be carried away by the water (cf. the burning of the 'abominable image' in the days of Asa, I Kings 15.13//II Chron. 15.16, and the reform of Josiah, II Kings 23.4, 6, 12. The Chronicler omits this reference for Josiah but adds another one for Hezekiah in II Chron. 30.14).

While the direction of the cleansing was from the house into the court, and from the court to the valley of Kidron, the sanctifying process applied mainly to the house, but also included the altar located in the court. The sanctification began on the eighth day, when the priests entered the house. The statement that 'on the first day of the first month' they began 'to sanctify' seems to employ this verb in a more general sense, denoting the process as a whole, similar to its use in v. 4.

Verse 17 relates precise details of chronology, continuing the preoccupation of the story with this matter, as already seen in v. 3. The affinity between these two verses, however, raises a question regarding the precise meaning of 'the first month'. In v. 3 we assumed that 'the first month' referred to Hezekiah's accession, highlighting his zeal for the Lord's worship; 'the first month' of v. 17, however, is counted according to the calendrical year, as confirmed by II Chron. 30.2. Because of the long time required for the sanctification, and its completion 'on the sixteenth day of the first month', Passover had to be postponed. This date is also supported by the prescription of Ezek. 45.18, indicating that the date reflects a longer-standing priestly tradition. The combination of the two would imply either that Hezekiah actually began to reign on the first month of the year – a fact which seems rather artificial – or that the 'first year' is considered to be his first 'full year' as king, implying that some time has elapsed from the beginning of his actual rule. In this case, however, Hezekiah's zeal would be much less prominent, and the beginning of the cleansing of the Temple more in line with priestly injunctions. It seems that a complete reconciliation of this tension is impossible, a price to be paid for the Chronicler's literary methods.

Another point of chronology involves the length of the sanctification: eight full days. While one may take this unusual duration to be a neutral temporal unit, this seems to me unlikely in this context. Taking 'the first day of the first month' as the date prescribed by Ezek. 45.18, the length of the consecration of the Temple seems to reflect a prevalent concept, connected with the Temple ritual maintenance, for which we have further evidence only much later in the Hasmonaean period. After the desecration of the Temple by Antiochus Epiphanes, its restoration required eight days, and in the context of the Maccabaean revolt this length of time is explained as either following the example of Solomon (II Macc. 2.12), or that of the Feast of Tabernacles (II Macc. 10.6). One wonders if both instances may not reflect a longstanding tradition, which may go back even to the monarchic period, but this must be left to further study.

[18–19] Having finished their task, the Levites now go back to Hezekiah to report its completion. The story, however, is not satisfied with merely indicating this fact but grants the Levites the right to speak, announcing to the king that his orders have been carried out. This unusual course of events not only expresses the importance of the clergy in the Chronicler's view, but imbues the procedure with the character of an ongoing ritual. With the Levites' declaration 'We have cleansed', all is ready for the next step.

Verse 18 begins as a direct continuation of the foregoing with no specification of subject. 'They' would then refer to the leaders of the levitical families, those who had been commanded by the king and were responsible for the work (vv. 4, 12–14). They first declare that they have purified 'all the house of the Lord', and then go on to mention two objects in particular: the altar of the burnt offering and the table for the showbread. The separate reference to the altar is well justified by the fact that the altar was placed in the Temple court and not inside the house, and was the site of the sacrificial rites. As we have noted before, both for the wilderness tabernacle and for Solomon's Temple, the dedication of the altar is recounted as a separate narrative (cf. on II Chron. 7.1–3), and a discrete consecration of the altar is also suggested by Ezek. 43.18–27. However, from among the objects inside the Temple proper, only the table of the showbread is mentioned explicitly, while the lampstand and the altar of incense, with all their utensils, are probably included in the summary of v. 19: 'and all the utensils ... we sanctified'. This special attention paid to the table is unusual, and there is no ready answer for it.

According to the phrasing of v. 18, the Levites came 'inside' (p^{e}nīmāh) to king Hezekiah. While the use of the same word in v. 16, where the priests are said to have entered 'inside' (RSV 'into the inner part of') the house of the

Lord, may be required by that context, this emphasis is superfluous when referring to Hezekiah. RSV renders it 'when they went *in* to Hezekiah', NEB 'then they went *into the palace*'. The word may be a dittography, influenced by v. 16.

In v. 19, a tone of reproach enters the address of the Levites, as their rather laconic report is suddenly broadened to include events of the past: 'the utensils which king Ahaz discarded in his reign when he was faithless'. This is, in fact, the first explicit reference to Ahaz in the present context as the person responsible for the desecration of the Temple, since Hezekiah himself referred only in general terms to 'our fathers' (v. 6).

The last detail in the Levites' report, that all the utensils were brought 'before the altar of the Lord', also merits comment. The altar mentioned here is the altar of burnt offerings (cf. vv. 18 and 21ff.), while 'the utensils' are those of the sanctuary – the utensils of the altar were expressly mentioned in v. 18. Although not specified, it seems that the ritual of sin-offering (vv. 21ff.) also included the sanctification of the Temple utensils, for which they were taken out to the court and placed 'before the altar'.

[20–30] The ceremony is now very carefully described, step by step, in two main phases: vv. 21–26, the preparations, and vv. 27–30, the ritual. The ceremony as described is different from anything prescribed or described elsewhere in the Bible. For one, it is a multi-purpose ceremony: even the included sin-offering is designated 'for the kingdom and for the sanctuary and for Judah' (v. 21). The ceremony also functions as a dedication of the altar, which bears some similarity to Num. 7 (cf. in particular vv. 87–88), and Ezek. 43.18–27. Nevertheless, the differences between this ceremony and the others are quite extensive, involving the selection, number and characterization of the sacrificial animals, the duration of the ceremonial rites, and the character of the ritual itself. Most prominent among these differences is the introduction of music, which is never attested in any of the priestly material, including Ezekiel. How much of these details reflect actual procedures of the Second Temple, and how much is the Chronicler's own innovation, cannot be determined.

[20] Hezekiah begins to prepare for the actual ceremony by 'rising up early'. The early morning is the time for many acts in the Bible (cf. Gen. 19.27; 20.8; 21.14; 22.3, etc.), and is certainly a reflection of local customs. It also emphasizes, however, Hezekiah's diligence in promptly carrying out all the necessary actions – an appropriate sequel to v. 3.

His second act is the gathering of the 'officers of the city' (*śārē hā'îr*). This designation of municipal officials is another unique feature of the Chronicler. While a 'city officer' in the singular is mentioned a few times in the Bible (Judg. 9.30; I Kings 22.26//II Chron. 18.25; II Kings 23.8; II Chron. 34.8), we never find such 'officers' in the plural. Moreover, one would expect

Hezekiah to gather the people's leadership, as in I Chron. 28.1 or II Chron. 1.2, and not a particular body of officials. Since the same group is later presented as 'the assembly' (v. 23), representing the people as a whole, *śārīm* in the plural may designate the dignitaries of Jerusalem rather than a limited body of officials. A rendering like 'the nobles of the city' would probably be preferable.

With this act, a change in the narrative pattern is introduced. Until this point, Hezekiah acted alone; from this point on, the king will be accompanied by 'all his company' (v. 29, NEB), who will share with him some of the responsibility for conducting the ceremony (cf. in particular v. 30).

[21–24] The preparations for the sacrificial ritual are described in three stages: bringing forth the sacrificial animals and commanding the priests to perform the rite (v. 21); preparation of the burnt-offering (v. 22); preparation of the sin-offering (vv. 23–24). There are four kinds of sacrificial animals, seven of each, bulls, rams, lambs and he-goats, the first three for burnt offerings, the he-goats for the sin-offering. Consequently, Rudolph suggests adding the word *le'ōlāh* before the mention of the he-goats, providing more balance to the verse: 'x for burnt offering and y for sin offering' (Rudolph, 296, cf. BHS). This attractive proposition, however, is not supported by the Versions, and the assumed omission is not fully accounted for by orthographical causes.

This particular combination of sacrifices – bulls, rams and lambs for burnt offering and he-goats for sin-offering – is prescribed in the priestly literature for 'the dedication of the altar when it was anointed' (Num. 7.88, NEB), as well as for the additional sacrifices of the holidays (Num. 28.11–15, 19–22, 27–30; 29.2–5, 8–11, 12–37). They are also mentioned in the dedication of the second Temple (Ezra 6.17), and again in Ezra 8.35. The numbers vary from case to case, but the typological element remains constant in each context. Most similar to the present combination is the dedication of the altar in Num. 7.87–88, with the main difference being the one-day length of the sacrifice rather than the twelve days upon the dedication of the wilderness altar. See also the dominance of the number twelve in all other instances except Ezek. 43.18–27, which nevertheless shares with Num. 7 the prolonged duration of the ritual (seven versus twelve days), as against the one-time ceremony of our context.

The purpose of the sacrifice is stated very clearly: for a sin-offering for the kingdom, the sanctuary and the people. It is interesting to note how a distinction we have observed throughout Chronicles – between the king and people – here receives explicit expression by the presentation of 'the kingdom' and 'Judah' as distinct entities. As will become clear in v. 23, 'the kingdom' is represented by the king, while the people are represented by 'the assembly'; neither of them stands for the other.

[22] The major stages in the preparation of the sacrifices are carefully listed, with a threefold repetition of the whole procedure for 'the bulls', 'the rams', and 'the lambs'; only the 'reception of the blood' is mentioned just once.

While the 'reception of the blood' is conducted by the priests, the actions that precede it, including the slaughter of the animals and their flaying (not mentioned here), are done by laymen, referred to by the non-specific 'they'. This, then is a concrete example of the procedure later codified in rabbinic literature as: 'From reception and onward it is the task of the priesthood' (BT, Yoma, 27a). The change of performers, introduced for 'the bulls', is not made explicit for the two further classes of sacrificial animals, but the non-specific verbs would be rendered better by the passive: 'the rams were slaughtered, and their blood was flung against the altar, etc.' (NEB; similarly JPS).

[23–24] The sin-offering is described in even greater detail: the sacrificial animals are brought to the king and the assembly, who 'laid their hands upon them', and the priests slaughter the goats and perform a purgation-rite on the altar. These features are attested in the priestly literature; for the symbolic act of 'laying of the hands' upon the sacrifice (which is not restricted to the sin-offering, cf. Lev. 1.4), cf. Lev 4.15; for the slaughtering of the sin-offering by the priests rather than by laymen, cf. among others Lev. 9.15; 16.15. The particular purgation-rite, indicated by the verb *way^{e}ḥaṭṭ$^{e\prime}$ū*, is prescribed in varying detail and with some nuances of ceremony in Lev. 4.4–12, 14–21 and elsewhere. This is, then, the 'sin-offering for all Israel', the people as such.

[25] Now the story moves to the other aspect of the preparation, that of the music accompanying the sacrifices, but the main interest of the verse lies neither in the enumeration of the participants – which is accomplished by the short 'he stationed the Levites' – nor in the stages of preparation. The verse centres on the problem of authority, presented in two stages. The initial command by which music was made an integral part of the sacrificial ritual is attributed to David and the prophets of his time: 'the commandment of David, and of Gad the king's seer, and of Nathan the prophet'. Then comes a general statement, the significance of which cannot be overestimated, addressing in general terms the problem of authority: 'for the commandment is (RSV was) from the Lord through his prophets'.

The phrasing of this statement needs some clarification. 'The hand of the Lord' is one of several biblical idioms for divine inspiration (e.g. I Kings 18.46; II Kings 3.15, and in particular in Ezekiel – 1.3; 3.22; 8.1, etc.). 'As the Lord has commanded/spoken by the hand of (RSV 'through') a prophet' (Exod. 9.35; 35.29, etc.) is again a recurrent idiom, describing the intermediary role of the prophet in announcing the divine will. The precise phrasing of this verse combines the two idioms 'by the Lord's inspiration' and 'by the hand of the prophet'. (The first *b⁵yad*, 'by the hand', is probably a corruption by analogy of *miyyad*, as recognized by practically all commentators, including RSV: *'from* the Lord'; cf. I Chron. 28.19.) They are both related to *miṣwāh* (commandment or ordinance), a term which eventually became the overarching term for all the Pentateuchal injunctions. Here it occurs in the determinate singular, an abstract noun denoting the phenomenon of 'commandment' as such.

This statement contains several elements which, taken together, constitute an important plank in the Chronicler's theological platform. The plural 'prophets', its coming after the explicit mention of Nathan and Gad, and the causative 'for' (*kī*), press the point that the Lord's commandments are delivered to the people not exclusively by Moses, but by 'the prophets' in general. Thus, according to the Chronicler, it is not only messages of rebuke or encouragement which are delivered in *ad hoc* situations by the prophets after Moses; the prophets after Moses also deliver the 'commandment', with its broad sense of legal obligatoriness. This general statement is linked to an institution which is presented clearly and explicitly as an innovation, established for the first time by David. This, then, represents an expression of the view that legislation did not cease with Moses; even within the sacred realm of the cult there was room for change, indicated by the Lord's continuing inspiration through the prophets. One is tempted to speculate here on the implications of this view for the Chronicler's view of 'Law' and 'canon', but these conjectures would carry us far beyond the evidence.

This verse is phrased in common Chronistic style, as a nominal clause, which reinforces its already general quality. By rendering it in the past ('the commandment *was*'), with 'commandment' denoting an ordinary singular, RSV limits its scope to the actual contemporary situation. Even so, however, it does not eradicate its basic meaning. A general rendering 'is', or 'commandments are', would better represent the original.

Note that Gad is called 'seer' and Nathan 'prophet', their common titles in Chronicles, and in juxtaposition to the priests, the singers are systematically called 'Levites' (vv. 25, 26, 30).

[26] With this verse the preparations are complete. In contradistinction to v. 25, where the Levites alone are mentioned, this verse refers to two groups of musicians: Levites and priests. This distinction is precisely made: the 'cymbals, harps and lyres', which are 'the instruments of David' (cf. I Chron. 23.5, II Chron. 7.6, and somewhat differently, Neh. 12.36), are alone the innovation introduced by David; the priests are to sound the trumpets, the age-old components of the ritual, which contrapuntally respond to the song of the Levites. This is a recurrent feature in Chronicles, in all its descriptions of ritual: the sounding of the trumpets remained throughout the prerogative

of the priests; the trumpets are not included among 'the instruments of David' and they are never sounded by Levites.

[27–28] These verses describe the actual rite of sacrifice. At a signal given from the king, the service of sacrifice begins, and with it the music, the sounding of trumpets, and the prostrating of the crowd present. The precise timing and the grand ensemble are indicated by temporal markers, 'and when the burnt offering began, the song to the Lord began ...' (v. 27), and then by the use of the present tense to record the proceedings, in a series of participles: 'the whole assembly were prostrating themselves, and the song was being sung and the trumpets were sounding ... until the burnt offering was finished' (v. 28; RSV differently).

'The assembly', which had been mentioned for the first time in v. 23, is clearly distinguished here from 'the king and his company' (v. 29). Without any explicit introductory comment being made, the narrative indicates that the ceremony is attended by a large crowd, referred to again in vv. 31 and 32 as 'the assembly' and in v. 36 as 'the people'. Although the term *qāhāl* is quite common in Chronicles, it is most frequent in the Hezekiah pericope, thirteen times in all (II Chron. 29.23, 28, 31, 32; 30.2, 4, 13, 17, 23, 24 [twice], 25; 31.18).

[29–30] The ritual is not over when the burnt offering has been offered; it is then time for the king and his entourage to prostrate themselves, followed by the singing of hymns by the Levites and accompanied by their own prostrating and bowing. The praising by the Levites is presented as the execution of the command of 'the king and his officers', which indeed makes Hezekiah the master of ceremonies.

We have already noted the significance of 'joy' in the Chronicler's theological vocabulary; it is the conclusive expression of the fact that a deed has been executed with the whole heart. This whole-heartedness is of special significance in this context, for the ceremony is that of sin-offering and atonement, in which Hezekiah and the people repent with a full 'commitment of the heart' (cf. v. 36). The specific idiom, however, is not 'with joy' (*bᵉśimḥāh*) as in I Chron. 15.25; 29.22, and others, but the unique *'ad lᵉśimḥāh*, constructed with the favourite Chronistic prepositional phrase *'ad lᵉ* (e.g. II Chron. 16.12, 14; 24.10). Its rendering with the adverbial phrase 'with gladness' (RSV) or 'joyfully' (NEB) fails to capture its full force; the expression is better represented by JPS, 'rapturously'.

This passage places great emphasis on the role of David and the precedents he established. David is mentioned four times in vv. 25–30, the most condensed distribution of Davidic references outside his own story. Reference is made to 'the commandment of David' (v. 25), 'the instruments of David' (vv. 26, 27), and 'the words of David', invoking the tradition which attributed to David everything pertaining to the Temple song: its initiation, the appointment and organization of the singers, preparation of the instruments and the composition of psalms. As already noted, Hezekiah is the first king for whom the Chronicler retains from his source the comparison with David (above, v. 2); with the emphasis on David, Hezekiah's acts are here presented as a full revival of David's institutions.

[31] The formal ceremony of the Temple rededication is now followed by another celebration, of a more popular nature, centred upon the offering of sacrifices by the people themselves. This is in fact the first and only event in which the Chronicler ascribes to the people active participation in the contribution of sacrifices. The people's participation is highlighted when compared with the original dedication of the Temple by Solomon (II Chron. 7.5), or his trip to Gibeon (II Chron. 1.6), and may be juxtaposed with the Passover, which is from the outset a popular feast, and it is rather the contribution of the king and his officers which is emphasized in its descriptions (II Chron. 30; 35). Popular participation as such, however, is a constant feature in the Chronicler's view of history; in the enthronement of David all the people supplied the food (I Chron. 12.40–41), and in the enthronement of Solomon they made free-will contributions for the building of the Temple (I Chron. 29.6–9). The thrust of the Chronicler's presentations is the transformation of the royal/courtly events into public and popular ones, not merely by the physical presence of crowds, but by the people's active participation in the events themselves.

The different character of this celebration from the prior ritual is expressed first of all by the different kinds of sacrifices. As over against burnt offerings and sin-offerings, the people are asked to offer 'sacrifices' (z^{e}ebāhim) and 'thank offerings', that is, sacrifices which are eaten by their owners and express the festive atmosphere of thanksgiving.

The term zebah, although of a general connotation, is more strictly defined as 'a general name of all sacrifices eaten at feasts' (BDB, 257–8, also Baumgartner 251–2). It is often qualified as zebah or z^{e}bah š^{e}lāmim, translated as either 'peace-offering' (cf. RSV to II Chron. 7.7, etc.), or 'offering of well-being' (JPS). All these terms are interchanged in Chronicles (e.g. I Chron. 16.1; 29.21; 30.22).

The people's response exceeds Hezekiah's request. He proposed offering 'sacrifices of well-being and thank-offerings', of which their owners partake, but the people brought not only these but burnt offerings as well, in which the owners have no share. These people are explicitly described as being 'of a willing heart', a term which brings to mind the great precedents of the contributions for the tabernacle (Exod. 35.21–29), and the Temple (I Chron. 29.5–9).

The phrasing of Hezekiah's address is interesting; 'consecrate oneself to the Lord' is a term used most often in priestly contexts, including

Chronicles. Here, as in I Chron. 29.5, it has lost its concrete sense and is used metaphorically (cf. Williamson, 359): you have made a pledge to the Lord, and have thus consecrated yourselves; you should now take part in the joy of the day.

[32–33] The enumeration of the popular sacrifices begins in a chiastic order with the more elevated contribution, the sacrifices of burnt offering being mentioned first. The narrator's surprise and delight in this spirit of free-will contribution is expressed by his repetition of the theme 'burnt offerings' – twice in v. 32, again in v. 34 and twice in v. 35. It thus becomes a leading theme of the pericope (cf. also vv. 7, 18, 21, 24, 27, 28, 29). The other sacrifices, mentioned earlier as $z^eb\bar{a}h\bar{i}m$ and designated here by the general term 'consecrated offerings' ($qod\bar{a}\check{s}\bar{i}m$), amount to 3,600 bulls and sheep. All these form an enormous collection of sacrifices, the spontaneous response to Hezekiah's request.

[34] This verse, with its unequivocal praise of the Levites at the expense of the priests, plays a prominent role in many commentaries on Chronicles, as well as in the history of Chronicles research. It serves as the ultimate proof of the Chronicler's negative view of the priesthood, and his clear favouritism of the Levites (cf. Rudolph, 298). In the immediate context, however, it underlines the unexpectedness of the events: 'for the thing came about suddenly' (v. 36). What had been planned as a limited ritual for the Temple dedication became a popular event of a grand scale, and the clergy that had been designated in advance to officiate could not cope adequately with these new dimensions: 'the priests were too few'. In this unexpected emergency, two measures were undertaken: the addition of more priests – who had to prepare themselves for the task – and the employment of non-priests for some of the chores urgently needed.

This second measure, deriving from the exigencies of the situation, is significant for the matter of the personnel of the Temple cult in its broader context. It provides an explicit legitimation for the penetration of non-priests into spheres of the cult which had previously been the exclusive charge of the priests. It is presented, however, as an *ad hoc* measure, of temporary application: 'until the work was finished', and 'until other priests had sanctified themselves'.

The specific role for which the Levites replace the priests is the flaying of the sacrificial animals for the burnt offering, that is, their treatment after the slaughter. According to the MT of Lev. 1.5–6, both the slaughtering and the flaying were done by laymen, while the levitical role in this verse is supported also by II Chron. 35.11. The participation of laymen in the preliminary preparation of sacrifices seems to have been a controversial issue, on which this verse makes a very clear statement.

The syntax of the verse is parenthetical, as the main sentence, enumerating the large amounts of burnt offerings, proceeds directly from v. 33 to v. 35. It is probably because of the length of this parenthetical statement that the translations ignore it. The main sentence should read: 'And the consecrated offerings were six hundred bulls and three thousand sheep (v. 33), besides the great number, etc.' (v. 35), and v. 34 should therefore be put in parentheses.

The feature of unexpectedness, of reality surpassing original expectations and necessitating *ad hoc* solutions, also characterizes the Chronicler's portrayal of Hezekiah elsewhere. The celebration of the Passover demanded several *ad hoc* adjustments (cf. on II Chron. 30), and the call to the people to give the clergy's portion surpassed all expectations and forced Hezekiah to prepare 'chambers' to accommodate it (II Chron. 31.11). These notices serve a double function: they highlight the spontaneity and religious enthusiasm which characterize all of Hezekiah's activities, and show the concomitant full commitment of the people to whatever is proposed and undertaken. At the same time, these responses of the people call for and actually legitimize various *ad hoc* arrangements, initiated and carried out by the king.

[35] After the parenthetical statement of v. 34, v. 35 returns to the main issue introduced in vv. 32–33: the enormous quantity of burnt offerings. In addition to the 'burnt offerings' proper, mentioned in v. 32, there was the offering of the fat of the peace-offering and the libations – everything exceeding expectations! The clause 'besides the great number of burnt offerings there was also' is an appropriate interpretation of the verse but not its translation, and the different renderings of the NEB or JPS are likewise more interpretative than translational.

At this point the purpose of all the preceding is again explicitly stated: 'The service of the house of the Lord was established' (RSV 'restored'). The verb *wattikkōn* is used here for the second time, after the reference to Solomon (II Chron. 8.16) and before Josiah (II Chron. 35.16). In all three cases it is related to Temple service, and should best be rendered by a uniform idiom: 'The service of the Lord has been established.'

[36] The clause *hahēkīn hā'elōhīm lā'ām* presents a double difficulty, in syntax and contents. The syntax of *hahēkīn* reflects the use of the article as a relative pronoun, which also functions as a demonstrative (cf. Gesenius, §138i, p. 447). The content is rendered literally as 'because of what God has done for the people', but this seems completely out of context; the people and Hezekiah rejoice because everything was so surprising and unexpected, but what God does for the people is never mentioned anywhere in the story. In the face of this difficulty, several emendations have been proposed, the best of which seems to be that of Ehrlich (*Randglossen*, VII, 376), who reads *libbām* in place of *lā'ām*: 'because God had prepared their heart'. This minor change reveals a common Chronistic idiom and concept, which is especially appro-

priate for the occasion: Hezekiah and the people rejoice at the expression of 'whole-heartedness' which characterizes their activity; this readiness and enthusiasm, however, could only have been the result of a 'preparation of the heart', which God has granted to the people (cf. e.g. II Chron. 30.12). In parallelism to the first stage (v. 30), and as befits the occasion, the event concludes in rejoicing.

30 Hezekiah sent to all Israel and Judah, and wrote letters also to Ephraim and Manasseh, that they should come to the house of the Lord at Jerusalem, to keep the passover to the Lord the God of Israel. ² For the king and his princes and all the assembly in Jerusalem had taken counsel to keep the passover in the second month – ³ for they could not keep it in its time because the priests had not sanctified themselves in sufficient number, nor had the people assembled in Jerusalem – ⁴ and the plan seemed right to the king and all the assembly. ⁵ So they decreed to make a proclamation throughout all Israel, from Beer-sheba to Dan, that the people should come and keep the passover to the Lord the God of Israel, at Jerusalem; for they had not kept it in great numbers as prescribed. ⁶ So couriers went throughout all Israel and Judah with letters from the king and his princes, as the king had commanded, saying, 'O people of Israel, return to the Lord, the God of Abraham, Isaac, and Israel, that he may turn again to the remnant of you who have escaped from the hand of the kings of Assyria. ⁷ Do not be like your fathers and your brethren, who were faithless to the Lord God of their fathers, so that he made them a desolation, as you see. ⁸ Do not now be stiff-necked as your fathers were, but yield yourselves to the Lord, and come to his sanctuary, which he has sanctified for ever, and serve the Lord your God, that his fierce anger may turn away from you. ⁹ For if you return to the Lord, your brethren and your children will find compassion with their captors, and return to this land. For the Lord your God is gracious and merciful, and will not turn away his face from you, if you return to him.'

10 So the couriers went from city to city through the country of Ephraim and Manasseh, and as far as Zebulun; but they laughed them to scorn, and mocked them. ¹¹ Only a few men of Asher, of Manasseh, and of Zebulun humbled themselves and came to Jerusalem. ¹² The hand of God was also upon Judah to give them one heart to do what the king and the princes commanded by the word of the Lord.

13 And many people came together in Jerusalem to keep the feast of unleavened bread in the second month, a very great assembly. ¹⁴ They set to work and removed the altars that were in Jerusalem, and all the altars for burning incense they took away and threw into the Kidron valley. ¹⁵ And they killed the passover lamb on the fourteenth day of the second month. And the priests and the Levites were put to shame, so that they sanctified themselves, and brought burnt offerings into the house of the Lord. ¹⁶ They took their accustomed posts according to the law of Moses the man of God; the priests threw the blood which they received from the hand of the Levites. ¹⁷ For there were many in the assembly who had not sanctified themselves; therefore the Levites had to kill the passover lamb for every one who was not clean, to make it holy to the Lord. ¹⁸ For a multitude of the people, many of them from Ephraim, Manasseh, Issachar, and Zebulun, had not cleansed themselves, yet they ate the passover otherwise than as prescribed. For Hezekiah had prayed for them, saying, 'The good Lord pardon every one ¹⁹ who sets his heart to seek God, the Lord the God of his fathers, even though not according to the sanctuary's rules of

cleanness.' [20] And the Lord heard Hezekiah, and healed the people. [21] And the people of Israel that were present at Jerusalem kept the feast of unleavened bread seven days with great gladness; and the Levites and the priests praised the Lord day by day, singing with all their might to the Lord. [22] And Hezekiah spoke encouragingly to all the Levites who showed good skill in the service of the Lord. So the people ate the food of the festival for seven days, sacrificing peace offerings and giving thanks to the Lord the God of their fathers.

23 Then the whole assembly agreed together to keep the feast for another seven days; so they kept it for another seven days with gladness. [24] For Hezekiah king of Judah gave the assembly a thousand bulls and seven thousand sheep for offerings, and the princes gave the assembly a thousand bulls and ten thousand sheep. And the priests sanctified themselves in great numbers. [25] The whole assembly of Judah, and the priests and the Levites, and the whole assembly that came out of Israel, and the sojourners who came out of the land of Israel, and the sojourners who dwelt in Judah, rejoiced. [26] So there was great joy in Jerusalem, for since the time of Solomon the son of David king of Israel there had been nothing like this in Jerusalem. [27] Then the priests and the Levites arose and blessed the people, and their voice was heard, and their prayer came to his holy habitation in heaven.

A. Notes to MT

[9] יסיר, probably read יסתר; [11] ומנשה, probably read וממנשה (haplography); [18–19] MT punctuation is contrary to syntax, read as one sentence; [21] בכלי עז, proposed בכל עז; [22] ויאכלו, LXX ויכלו; [27] וישמע, proposed שמע; ויהוה הכהנים הלוים; proposed, with MSS and Versions הכהנים והלוים.

B. Notes to RSV

[3] 'in its time', MT 'at that time' (NEB, similarly JPS); [5] 'not ... in great numbers', JPS 'not often', cf. commentary; [9] 'if you return', or 'when you return'; [11] 'only', better 'however' (NEB, JPS); 'a few', MT 'some' (JPS); [15–17] 'killed', MT 'slaughtered' (JPS); [15] 'were put to shame', better 'were ashamed' (JPS); [16] 'sprinkled', NEB 'flung', JPS 'dashed'; [18] 'a multitude of the people', NEB 'a majority of the people' (similarly JPS); 'cleansed', better 'purified' (JPS); [19] 'not according to the sanctuary's rules of cleanness', cf. commentary; [22] 'the people', literally 'they'; [23] 'agreed together', MT 'took counsel'; [25] 'sojourners', JPS, NEB 'resident aliens'; [27] 'the priests and the Levites', MT 'Levitical priests', cf. A above.

C. Structure, sources and form

1. Chapter 30 presents the second phase in the restoration of the Lord's worship in Jerusalem, the celebration of the Passover in the first year of Hezekiah's reign. Taken on its own, Hezekiah's Passover may be regarded as an independent episode, not necessarily related to Hezekiah's early days. In the present composition, however, it is a continuation of the Temple's rededication, finally completed in II Chron. 31.2.

2. One of the most engaging issues of this chapter is the problem of origin and

historicity (for a summary of the discussion cf. Williamson, 361–4; Dillard, 240–1): what is the source, if any, of the Chronicler's story?

There is practically no question that the story as it stands has been composed by the Chronicler; language, style, literary technique, theological and historical views – all are stamped by his literary personality. The question of 'source' or 'origin' is restricted to the facts and data which form the narrative's basis. Do they represent an authentic event of Hezekiah's time, do they reflect the Chronicler's own time and circumstances (or maybe even later), or are they a sheer invention, devoid of any historical basis?

The clear stamp of the Chronicler's hand makes the attribution of the chapter to his creative talent a very tempting and convincing proposition. A certain view of the history of the cult, dominated by the evidence of II Kings 22–23 and Deut. 16.1–8, makes Hezekiah's centralized celebration of Passover a clear case of anachronism. Together with the assumption that the Chronicler has modelled the figure of Hezekiah on that of Josiah, the conclusion that 'it is probably a purely imaginative occurrence' (Curtis, 471) seems largely incontestable. Yet, the question of 'origin' keeps cropping up, and this 'easy' solution is faced with some difficult questions. Not only are the basic presuppositions being questioned – the unimpeachable reliability of the Deuteronomistic portrayal of both Josiah and Hezekiah and the assumed history of the Passover – but the evidence of the chapter itself seems incompatible with this view.

The major problem lies in some unconventional and non-standard features of the story, for which the Chronicler seems forced to account and apologize. If the whole thing was a reflection of an accepted reality, or alternatively, a free creation, why would it be composed along unusual and non-conventional lines instead of accepted, legitimate principles? Moreover, if it were indeed modelled on the figure and deeds of Josiah, a stronger accord would be expected between Hezekiah's Passover and that of Josiah, which is also not the case. These general considerations are supported by the fact that some of the data easily pass the test of historical probability for the very period to which they are ascribed.

It is therefore quite likely that the story is based on some authentic tradition concerning a celebration of Passover in Jerusalem during the time of Hezekiah. Two elements in particular may reflect authentic Hezekianic circumstances: the date, the second month of the year rather than the first, a fact which the story makes an effort to justify, and the scope, the fact that people from the northern tribes of Israel were included in the celebration, which constitutes the major theme of the story.

The issue of 'date' actually has two components: the month and the year. While the celebration of the passover in the second month may be regarded as a *bona fide* feature of the tradition, the first year of Hezekiah's reign can hardly be accepted as authentic. The Chronicler joins the Passover to the rededication of the Temple in the first year of Hezekiah's reign, and at the same time presents the Passover as having taken place after the destruction of Samaria (30.6, 9). A date after the fall of Samaria has much historical logic to commend it; it is doubtful, however, if this had occurred before Hezekiah's accession. This is of course dependent on the view we take of the chronology of Hezekiah's rule – one of the most debated issues in the reconstruction of biblical chronology (cf. recently, Tadmor – Cogan, *II Kings*, 228f.). If Hezekiah's ascent to the throne is placed at 727 BCE (cf. Tadmor – Cogan, ibid.), the fall of Samaria could only have occurred several years later, while the date 715/714

BCE (R. E. Thiele, *Mysterious Numbers of the Hebrew Kings*, 1983, 174–5) would agree with the Chronicler's statement, but leave difficult questions about a possible pilgrimage to Jerusalem under a well-organized Assyrian suzerainty. According to biblical tradition at least, 'In the sixth year of Hezekiah, which was the ninth year of Hoshea king of Israel, Samaria was taken' (II Kings 18.10). Thus, while a conclusive statement on this issue would be inadvisable, it seems that the Chronicler was here carried away by his wish to attribute all the aspects of Hezekiah's religious reform to the king's first year, and exceeded the evidence of his sources.

As for the 'second month', it is very difficult to believe that the Chronicler would freely invent something which condemns Hezekiah, the king among the post-Solomonic monarchs he glorifies more than any other. The force of this consideration may be illustrated by later rabbinic exegesis, which finds Hezekiah's change of date a serious transgression, for which he was punished (BT, Sanhedrin, 12a–12b; Berakoth, 10b; JT, Nedarim, 6.13). This is indeed a major issue in the story (vv. 2–5, 13, 15), and seems to constitute an important component of the tradition which the Chronicler used. For the possible origin of this date, cf. the commentary on v. 2.

3. Even when we postulate that an existing tradition formed the basis for the story of Hezekiah's Passover, it is doubtful whether any of its original literary features can still be uncovered (but cf. the attempt of H. Haag, 'Das Mazzenfest des Hiskia', *Festschrift K. Elliger*, 1973, 87–94). There is no way of isolating any literary core in the present composition, which is written as an integral whole and is certainly the work of the Chronicler.

4. The chapter is constructed of two large sections of equal length, yet in its syntax there is a continuous flow of narrative. While the second section begins in v. 14, the subject is explicitly mentioned in v. 13, which thus may serve in a double capacity as conclusion and introduction.

I. 1–13 Preparations
    (*a*) 1–5 decision to celebrate the Passover
    (*b*) 6–9 the king's letter to the northern Israelites
    (*c*) 10–13 reaction to the letter, gathering in Jerusalem
II. 14–27 Celebration
    (*a*) 14 removal of idolatry
    (*b*) 15–20 Passover sacrifice
    (*c*) 21–22 feast of unleavened bread
    (*d*) 23–27 seven days of rejoicing.

The chapter contains a major rhetorical component (vv. 6–9), and several rhetorical features, but in contrast to chapter 29, on the one hand, and the description of Josiah's Passover, on the other (35.7–16), it shows very little interest in the actual sacrificial ritual. The various aspects of the ritual receive scant attention, while the focus of the chapter clearly lies elsewhere.

D. *Commentary*

[1–5] The literary structure of this unit displays some roughness at the outset. It is structured backwards, beginning with a reference to the sending of letters ('Hezekiah sent to all Israel and Judah, and wrote letters ...'), but continuing with matters which actually preceded this dispatching of letters (vv. 2–5). This 'flashback' construction is not signalled by any syntactical indications, prompting RSV to supply the omission by the use of the past-perfect verbal form in v. 2: 'for the king ... *had taken* counsel'. The only indication of this inverted structure is a partial repetition in v. 5 of some of the phrases of v. 1, bringing the story to the same point:

> 1 'Hezekiah sent ... that they should come to ... Jerusalem to keep the passover to the Lord the God of Israel
> [2–4 For the king ... had taken counsel ... and the plan seemed right ... so they decreed to make a proclamation]
> 5b that the people should come and keep the passover to the Lord the God of Israel at Jerusalem [for they had not kept it ... as prescribed].'

This is a peculiar form of resumptive repetition; the similar clauses in vv. 1 and 5b reflect their intended overlapping and continuation, while the intervening section in vv. 2–5a precedes v. 1. The 'logical' structure which would arrange the temporal sequence as vv. 2–5, 1, 6, is abandoned in favour of an emphatic literary structure which places the most important, declarative statement at the beginning.

[1] According to the literal wording of the verse, Hezekiah addressed the various constituents among the people in different ways: 'he sent to all Israel and Judah' and 'wrote letters to Ephraim and Manasseh', but as is made clear from vv. 5 and 6, it was the same couriers who carried the letters throughout the entire land. The apparent discrepancy reflects a stylistic feature, more common in poetry than in prose, in which the two parts of the verse act as parallel members, the elements of the one also relating to the other. The phrasing 'Hezekiah sent to all Israel and Judah // and wrote letters to Ephraim and Manasseh' should be understood as, 'Hezekiah wrote letters and sent to all Israel and Judah, including Ephraim and Manasseh', which is then continued by a second pair of parallel members: 'That they should come to the house of the Lord at Jerusalem // to keep Passover to the Lord the God of Israel.'

The passage is constructed to reflect a clear process of rhetorical persuasion: consultation and its topic (v. 2); arguments (v. 3); consent (v. 4); and decision (v. 5). The persuasive tone of the passage, with its arguments couched to appeal to the better judgment of the people, characterizes the Chronicler's tone in general; cf. in particular I Chron. 13.1–5.

The theme of 'couriers with letters' seems to be of great significance in the present context, being repeated in vv. 1, 6, and 10. The same announcement is described in v. 5 with 'make a proclamation' attesting to a combination of written and oral messages, borne by the same couriers. E. J. Bickerman has claimed ('The Edict of Cyrus in Ezra 1', *JBL* 65, 1946, 251–3; 272–5) that this should be seen as a practice of the Persian empire, with analogies to the Hittites on the one hand and to the Roman *edictum* on the other. The peculiar feature of this practice is the addition of 'posters' to the more common Near Eastern procedure of announcement by heralds, and it should be distinguished, according to Bickerman, from the employment of letters in regular diplomatic communication. Indeed, the similarity between the procedure described here and the one described in Ezra 1.1 is unmistakable. Is this, then, a reflection of the Chronicler's circumstances, attesting to practices introduced by the Persians (cf. also Esther 1.22; 3.13; 8.8–10, etc.), or does it represent an authentic Hezekianic feature of the story? Given the present state of our information, the only sound conclusion appears to be the first.

[2–3] Going backwards, v. 2 now describes the manner in which the decision was made, illustrating the Chronicler's distinct habit of making the people partners not only in the events, but also in the decision-making process, and thereby sharing responsibility with the king. The Chronicler employs his frequently-used term 'take counsel', to which not only the 'officers' (RSV 'princes') are asked, but also 'the assembly'. Reviv would see here an authentic piece of evidence for the existence during the monarchic period of a social institution along the lines of a 'general assembly', having specific status and roles in the state's administration (H. Reviv, 'The Pattern of the Whole-Kingdom's Assembly in Israel', *Eretz Israel* 15, 1981, 308–11*). It is more generally accepted that if any social or political reality is to be observed here, it would more probably be that of the post-exilic period.

As the narrative presents them, the issues on which the assembly is to make a decision concern two aspects of the Passover celebration: the postponement of the feast to the second month and its announcement throughout Israel. As determined by the context of 'counsel taking', each of these decisions is buttressed by a rational argument. Both arguments are phrased along similar lines: a causative clause in the negative, concerning the 'keeping' of the feast: 'for they could not keep it in its time' (v. 3); 'for they had not often kept it as prescribed' (v. 5).

The first issue in turn, the postponement of the feast, is again supported by two arguments, also cast in the negative: 'the priests had not sanctified themselves in sufficient number', and the people 'had not assembled in Jerusalem'. Both arguments are connected with the preceding story: the first recalls the notice that 'the priests were too few' (29.34), while the second goes back to 29.3, positing that Hezekiah began his activities 'in the first year of his reign in the first month', and lacked sufficient time to assemble the people. This last explanation is based on the unspoken assumption that the cele-

CHAPTER 30 939

bration of the Passover in Jerusalem was a standing custom, and only the
brevity of the interval between Hezekiah's accession and Passover's normal
date prevented its performance.

It is clear from the arguments that the Chronicler's view on the matter
bears the marks of apologetic. The postponement of the Passover is not
presented as a positive feature but as an evil, which must be justified by the
exigencies of the time, and this would make the 'second month' an essential
component of the ancient tradition. Since the arguments the Chronicler
adduces are intimately related to the present context and to the celebration of
the feast in Hezekiah's first year, and since from a historical point of view this
was hardly an appropriate time, if an actual historical event is to be postulated, the question of an original motive for the postponement obviously
arises: what was, then, the original motive for the celebration of the Passover
in the second month?

The most comprehensive answer to this question has been given by S.
Talmon, who takes as his point of departure the correct observation that a
change of the cultic calendar is a matter of enormous consequences, and
should be justified by commensurably weighty arguments. Talmon claims
that Hezekiah's change of date is one aspect of his attempt to extend his
influence to the northern parts of the land after the Assyrian conquest, and to
bring about a closer union of the two separate parts of the kingdom. In
pursuit of this goal he makes a courageous attempt to reunite the separate and
divergent calendars of Judah and Israel by giving up the Judaean calendar in
favour of the Israelite one (S. Talmon, 'Divergences in the Calendar Reckoning in Ephraim and Judah', *VT* 8, 1958, 58–63, reprinted in *King, Cult and
Calendar*, Jerusalem 1986), thus making it possible for the whole people to
celebrate the feasts at the same time. This would bring together all the
particular aspects of the story: the peculiar date and the force of Hezekiah's
address to the north against the background of the destruction of the
northern kingdom. It would also grant the details a solid political motivation.
Its shortcoming is of course the absence of decisive support, which is the flaw
of many a brilliant hypothesis (cf. also F. L. Moriarty, 'The Chronicler's
Account of Hezekiah's Reform', *CBQ* 27, 1965, 399–406). A more limited
conjecture, and one still within the context of a political effort by Hezekiah to
extend his influence to the north, might propose an emergency situation – a
military campaign or the like – as the cause of the change, which then
remained as an established detail in the people's collective memory.

How is Hezekiah's Passover related to the law of Num. 9.6–13, which
regulates the keeping of a 'second Passover'? As the texts stand, there is really
no connection between them. Hezekiah does not point out that a postponement of the Passover has already been provided by the Law, nor is there any
literal affinity between the two texts. The assumption that Num. 9.6–13 was

motivated and justified by Hezekiah's precedent is difficult, precisely because of this lack of similarity between the two texts. Num. 9.6–13 deals with the problem of individuals who are precluded from keeping the feast at its regular time by two specific reasons: being unclean because of the death of a relative and being far away from home. The present chapter deals with the people at large, and is motivated by different considerations. In fact, Hezekiah's Passover is not a 'second Passover' but a general postponement of the main feast. What both texts have in common is the possibility *in principle* of postponing the Passover ceremony, but no closer connection between them may be demonstrated.

On the other hand, we do not find anywhere in the context what might have been the strongest argument for the postponement – that on the prescribed date, on the fourteenth day of the first month, the Temple was not yet purified and ready to function, since it was only on the 'sixteenth day of the first month' (29.17) that the purification was finished. This is additional evidence supporting the assumption that from the outset there was no organic connection between the purification of the Temple and the Passover; the Passover story had a source of its own, and even though the two have been arranged as a sequential narrative, the connection remains rather superficial.

[4] The consultation is summarized by the people's consent, 'and the plan seemed right to the king and to all the assembly', which is a clear parallel of an earlier occasion during David's time, depicted along very similar lines: 'for the plan seemed right to the whole people' (I Chron. 13.4; the RSV's different translations obscure the similarity).

[5] The subject of 'they' in 'they decreed' is of course the antecedents mentioned earlier, 'the king and all the assembly', the dominant tone of the passage being that the decision is not only the king's but also the assembly's, a good illustration of the Chronicler's democratizing inclinations. The people have a voice not only in the general decision to celebrate and postpone the Passover, but also in the details of carrying it out.

The territory to which the messengers are sent is defined in both ethnic and geographical terms: 'all Israel' and 'from Beer-sheba to Dan', with the Chronistic reversal of the more common 'from Dan to Beer-sheba' (cf. I Chron. 21.2). More than being a precise geographical delineation, it expresses the idea of 'all Israel' which will later be conveyed by naming various tribes to represent the whole (v.v. 10, 11, 18).

The phrasing of the last argument is difficult, because of the obscure meaning and function of the adverb *lārōb*; when we excise the adverb, the sentence becomes clear: 'for they did not keep it as prescribed' (literally 'as written'). *lārōb* is rendered by RSV (following BDB) 'in great numbers', supplying a more concrete reason why a proclamation throughout the land was necessary, but it is doubtful whether this is the correct rendering of the adverb. *lārōb* is a favourite term in the Chronicler's language and generally means 'in respect to abundance, abundantly', and therefore also 'many' (cf. BDB, 914). The translation 'in great number' is therefore a circumlocutory interpretation which would better suit the form *bᵉrōb*. Moreover, RSV's rendering would make the focus of Hezekiah's interest the celebration of the feast in 'great numbers'; although this certainly constitutes a feature of the story, Hezekiah's main point is different: to celebrate the Passover *in Jerusalem*, and to encourage the people to come there from all over the land. It seems, then, that the rendering of JPS, 'many [times]', that is, 'often', should be preferred, leaving the meaning of the clause general, with no precise indication as to which aspect of the holiday the proclamation was intended to set right.

The only law which explicitly prescribes the centralized celebration of Passover is Deut. 16.2–7, which expresses this demand in argumentative, even polemical terms: 'you shall offer the Passover sacrifice ... at the place which the Lord will choose ... You may not offer the Passover sacrifice within any of your towns ... but at the place which the Lord your God will choose ... there you shall offer the Passover sacrifice.' However, in the present text we find no actual literal allusions to the law as phrased in Deut. 16; although the Chronicler ascribes to Hezekiah the wish to celebrate 'as prescribed', he does not colour his arguments with Deuteronomic idioms. The connection with Deuteronomic legislation may raise yet another question, namely, whether this was Hezekiah's original intent, i.e. whether he was instigating a 'Deuteronomic' reform with a more general view towards centralization of the cult. Since it is the Chronicler's voice rather than Hezekiah's that comes to the surface here, and he, of course, regards the entire Pentateuch as fully authoritative from the time of Moses onwards, the question can hardly be answered on the basis of this chapter.

Whether purposefully or not, there is some hidden irony in Hezekiah's desire to celebrate the Passover 'as prescribed', for this is precisely the opposite of what would eventually happen, when the people 'ate the passover otherwise than prescribed' (v. 18).

[6–9] The execution of the public decision is related in detail, together with the contents of the letters delivered by the king's messengers. Verse 6 contains an unclear conflation: the letters are from 'the king and his princes', but the messengers depart 'as the king has commanded'. Rudolph assumed that 'the command of the king' refers to some additional act which dropped out by textual corruption (Rudolph, 300, cf. BHS), but it is also possible that the two statements express two somewhat conflicting features in the Chronicler's attitude. They highlight the 'democratic' nature of the kingdom's administration by referring to the 'princes', while simultaneously restating Hezekiah's function and authority. The command is the king's, but the letters are sent from the king and his officers.

In presenting the addressees of the letter the text returns to the terminology of v. 1, in which a clear distinction is drawn between 'Israel' and 'Judah', the two parts together qualified by 'all'. Although much of the content may apply also to Judah after the days of Ahaz (cf. 29.8–9, and Williamson, 366–7), the primary addressees are nevertheless the people of the North, for whom alone the Assyrian threat has become a devastating reality.

The letter itself represents an outstanding example of the Chronicler's literary methods and theological positions. Its literary structure is determined by clear rhetorical considerations. It opens with a vocative, 'O people of Israel', itself phrased with the ancient coin 'children of Israel', followed by an immediate statement of purpose, in the imperative 'return to the Lord'. The positive declaration is continued in two ways: immediately (vv. 7–8), and essentially (v. 9). With this structure, vv. 6 and 9 form one sequence. In the best rhetorical style, it is these two focal points which get the maximum attention (cf. also 29.5–11). Support for the main address is found in the argumentative middle section, which also has a rhetorical structure, constructed as it is of a series of contrasts designed to carry persuasive force. Verse 7 presents a contrast to v. 6, also in the imperative 'Do not be like your fathers', etc., while v. 8 moves from the past to the present with the introductory 'Now', again followed by a negative imperative with a positive message (RSV misses the structure here by placing 'now' later in the sentence). Verse 9 provides the explanation, opening with 'for', and including the theological basis as well as the impending results of correct conduct. These verses may be sketched as follows:

6 vocative ('O people of Israel'), imperative ('return'), result ('that he may return')
7 negative imperative with a look to the past, 'do not be'
8 negative imperative with a positive message 'do not stiffen'
9 explanation and goal 'For …'.

The sequence of vv. 6 and 9 may also be seen in a different way. The leading theme of the passage is the root *šwb* and the phonetically similar *šbh*, strongly emphasized at the beginning and end of the letter. These two can be read as one sequential movement, presenting the main message:

Opening (v. 6): 'return (*šūbū*) to the Lord … that he may turn (*weyāšōb*) …'

Conclusion (v. 9): 'For if you return (*bešūbekem*) … your brethren … will find compassion with their captors (*šōbēhem*) and return (*lāšūb*) to this land. For the Lord … will not turn away his face … if you return (*tāšūbū*) to him.'

The letter is written in an elevated prose style, with a certain metrical rhythm and occasional parallelism. It also provides a very good example of the Chronicler's anthological style, being based on extant texts and ready expressions. Verses 6–7 may be seen as being based on, or drawing from, Zech. 1.3–4 (and Mal. 3.7). The focus of the letter is an echo of the theme of this prophecy: 'Return to me (*šūbū 'ēlay*) ... and I will return to you (*w^e'āšūb '^{a}lēkem*)'. 'Be not like your fathers' of Zech. 1.4 is broadened in the present verse to 'Do not be like your fathers and your brethren', the addition marking the direction in which the letter departs from Zechariah's call for repentance: it is not the distant past which is referred to, but the very near one.

'The remnant of you who have escaped' reflects the phrase of II Kings 19.30//Isa. 37.31, with the necessary change of addressees. Verse 9 is based on the theme of Solomon's prayer, in its Deuteronomistic phrasing, missing from its parallel in Chronicles: 'if they repent (*w^{e}šābū 'ēleykā*) ... grant them compassion in the sight of those who carried them captive that they may have compassion on them' (I Kings 8.48–50). The concrete result of the captors' compassion, not found in I Kings 8.50, is added by the Chronicler: 'and return to this land'.

One may also feel in the phrase *wayyitt^{e}nem l^{e}šammāh* the dependence on another prophecy, Jer. 18.16–17, with its dominant theme 'making their land a horror' (*lāśūm 'arṣām l^{e}šammāh*).

The gist of the letter is a call for repentance, with a strong element of theodicy. It opens with a general call for repentance, 'Return to the Lord ... that he may turn ...', a phrasing in positive terms of the admonition repeated in Chronicles: 'Because you have forsaken the Lord he has forsaken you' (II Chron. 24.20). The repentance called for will affect 'the remnant of you who have escaped from the hand of the kings of Assyria', that is, those who remained in the land after the catastrophe, and those who have been exiled: 'your brethren and your children will find compassion ... and return to this land' (v. 9). The theological root of this call for repentance is a firm conviction of the Lord's justice and the people's own responsibility for their fate, which grants them the power to change it: they 'were faithless to the Lord ... so that he made them a desolation ... yield yourselves to the Lord ... and serve the Lord your God that his fierce anger may turn away from you'. The sin of north Israel is defined here with the common, general term 'they were faithless to the Lord', but its precise nature may be inferred from the proposed remedy: 'Do not now be stiff-necked ... yield yourself to the Lord and come to this sanctuary ... and serve the Lord your God.' It is the abandonment of the Lord's sanctuary in Jerusalem which constitutes Israel's faithlessness.

Thus, although the letter is connected by its narrative context to one limited event – the celebration of the Passover – it actually has a broader purpose: to bring the people of the North back to the Jerusalem Temple. In fact, the celebration of Passover is not even mentioned in it. The letter takes us back in time about two hundred years, when (according to I Kings 12) the division of the monarchy expressed itself in two institutions: the establishment of a separate monarchy and the establishment of a separate cult. Hezekiah's letter is based on the same historical presuppositions as II Chron. 13, where these two institutions are conceived as Israel's sin; the destruction of the northern monarchy is the Lord's punishment for the people's abandonment of his worship, that is, the Jerusalem cult.

The Chronicler's view that a threat of such magnitude as the Assyrians is the Lord's response to the abandonment of the Temple is also expressed in other historical contexts. The Chronicler attributes to Judah in Ahaz' time the sin of abandoning the Lord's Temple (II Chron. 28.24; 29.6–7), and accounts for the Babylonian assault in Zedekiah's time through reference to the same sin: 'they polluted the house of the Lord ... in Jerusalem' (II Chron. 3.14). Hezekiah takes upon himself the necessary preparations for restoration, first by re-establishing the Temple service (ch. 29), and then by affiliating the northern Israelites to the Jerusalem Temple; with these steps completed, the anger of the Lord will be removed. The age of Zedekiah, with its consistent rebellion, will have no such opportunity.

Viewed from a historical and political perspective, such a move on the part of Judah seems both probable and adequate. The question is one of timing: after the conquest by the Assyrians, northern Israel had become an Assyrian-controlled territory, comprising several provinces; one must assume either a preliminary or gradual weakening of this system to make an initiative by Hezekiah (or for that matter, any of the Judaean kings) possible. Our knowledge of the general and particular details of the political system and balances of the time appear too scant to provide a definitive answer, or to propose what might have been the right moment for such an initiative.

[6] In the beginning of his address Hezekiah employs a rather rare divine epithet 'the God of Abraham, Isaac and Israel', which appears elsewhere only in I Kings 18.36 and I Chron. 29.18; its more common parallel, 'The God of Abraham, the God of Isaac, and the God of Jacob', appears three times in the context of the revelation of the Lord's name to Moses (Exod. 3.6, 15; 4.5 and, abbreviated, in 3.16). The use of this rare and solemn epithet is well-advised on Hezekiah's part, as it evokes the unity of the northern and southern tribes, their common faith stemming from one revelation and one tradition. As is his practice, the Chronicler prefers the name 'Israel' to 'Jacob', drawing a closer identification between the patriarch and his eponymous descendants.

The reference to 'the king of Assyria' in this text is in the plural, 'the kings of Assyria', a phenomenon repeated in Chronicles three times, when the king's proper name is not recorded; the singular is found only once (II Chron. 28.21). This is probably a plural of abstraction, which presents 'the kings of Assyria' as a historical phenomenon rather than any particular royal figure. This usage is more emphasized in II Chron. 28.16; 32.4, where the identity of the Assyrian king is known from the context. Understandably, the Versions in all these cases convert it to the singular.

[7] As already pointed out, the reference to 'fathers and brothers' presents the catastrophe alluded to as a contemporaneous fact: the people of this very generation are those who sinned and were punished. The Chronicler here evokes the force of self-witnessing, 'as you see', similar to the earlier 29.8, 'as you see with you own eyes'. In both cases the self-witnessing serves to emphasize the here-and-nowness of the events: the reality described is the Israelites' own reality, which they have the power to change.

[8] The idiom 'stiff-necked' (also 30.13) is probably borrowed from the Deuteronomistic lexicon; a similar expression, *wayyitt^enū 'ōrēp* (RSV 'turned their back'), characterizes the attitude of Ahaz' time (II Chron. 29.6). This, then, is another expression of the comparison between the times of Ahaz and Hezekiah on the one hand, and the Assyrian and Babylonian threats on the other. The opposite of stiffening the neck is the idiom 'give the hand' (*t^enū yād*, RSV 'yield yourselves'), the precise meaning of which is not clear; it may refer to an expression of loyalty as part of an oath, cf. mainly Ezek. 17.18; Lam. 5.6; 1 Chron. 29.24.

After this general statement come the details. The appropriate way for the people to express their loyalty to the Lord is to worship him in his Temple. With the same phrases that marked his reflections on the sins of Ahaz, Hezekiah now describes how God's anger applies to the Israel of his own time, the phrase *ḥ^arōn 'ap* being peculiar to this historical context (28.11, 13, 29.10; 30.8).

[9] Hezekiah supports his call for repentance by referring to the Lord's epithets 'gracious and merciful', peculiar in Chronicles to this context. If the people return to the Lord, the Lord in his mercy will forgive their sins, and will dispose their captors to have compassion on them, so that they may return to the land. References to God's compassion are not especially common in Chronicles, and are distinctly connected to situations of extreme danger. Thus, at the very last days of the kingdom, the Lord delayed the deserved punishment and called for repentance because of his compassion: 'The Lord ... sent persistently by his messengers ... because he had compassion on his people' (II Chron. 36.15). This is another point of comparison between this period of Ahaz-Hezekiah and that of Zedekiah; Hezekiah's call for repentance was heeded, that of the prophets in Zedekiah's days was not.

I have already pointed to the difference between I Kings 8.50 and this verse. There we read: 'grant them compassion in the sight of those who carried them captive, that they may have compassion on them', but no mention is made of return, which constitutes the main point in the text. What had happened between the composition of these two texts was the actual event of the return, the realization of the possibility that captors may relinquish captivity, and that exiles may return.

The phrase 'turn away the face' (*yāsīr pānīm*) is unique. Its literal meaning is 'remove the face' and the rendering of the RSV actually assumes another idiom, *yāssēb pānīm*, which, although more frequent with a concrete connotation (cf. Judg. 18.23; I Kings 8.14; II Kings 20.2, etc.), may also be used metaphorically, 'face' probably denoting 'good will, grace' (Ezek. 7.22). It may have the same connotation as the more common metaphor *histīr pānīm* (cf. Deut. 31.17, 18; Isa. 59.2; Ezek. 39.29; Ps. 38.8 etc.), or this may actually have been the original reading.

[10–13] This passage describes the manner in which 'the king's command' was actually executed and how it was received. The couriers go 'from city to city', but their route is described only with reference to the northern tribes, of whom three representatives are mentioned: Ephraim, Manasseh, and 'as far as Zebulun'. This seems to be a synecdochic reference by the Chronicler, just as in the following we hear about Asher (v. 11) and Issachar (v. 18), after the whole has been indicated as 'from Beer-sheba to Dan' (v. 5).

The people's acceptance of the message assumes three forms: rejection, partial acceptance and full acceptance. The general attitude of the northern Israelites is negative, rejecting the invitation with mockery and scorn. Certain individuals from among these tribes, however, respond favourably and come to Jerusalem. Only Judah responds in the spirit of the address; they all come, for they were of 'one heart'. This variation in the people's response is quite unexpected, there being no obvious reason why the Chronicler would describe the response of northern Israel as essentially negative. A prejudice against the North is certainly not an aspect of the Chronicler's overall view, as evidenced on the one hand by the basis of Hezekiah's address being the assumption that his call will be properly responded to, and on the other by the demonstration already in ch. 28 of the Israelites' capacity and favourable disposition toward full repentance. It would seem, therefore, that this detail is a reflection of the historical facts underlying the original narrative, and originally may have stemmed from not only spiritual but also political and practical causes; Hezekiah kept the Passover as he planned, but his success with the North was not unqualified.

[10] As already noted, each time the Chronicler mentions the northern tribes, he cites a representative selection, thus producing a varied literary effect. His umbrella term is 'all Israel from Beer-sheba to Dan', or 'all Israel and Judah'.

The response is scorn and mockery. The two verbs *mashīqīm, mal'igīm* provide an interesting example of the Chronicler's late Hebrew. They are both in the *hiphil* rather than in the more common *qal* conjugation; this is the only occurrence of *šhq* in this conjugation, while *l'g* is attested several more times (Job 21.3; Ps. 22.8, which might be a matter of vocalization; Neh. 2.19; 3.33). The two synonymous verbs, frequently employed as a 'word-pair' in parallel lines (Jer. 20.7; Ps. 59.9; Prov. 1.26; etc.), here serve as hendiadys, being put in conjunction with a copulative *waw*. Cf. also the unique preposi-tional phrase *mal'igīm bām* replacing the more common *l^e* (II Kings 19.21; Jer. 20.7; Ps. 2.4, etc.).

[11] The positive response of the few is described with the common Chronistic verb 'humbled themselves'. This was, then, not only an external act of making the trip to Jerusalem, but an internal one as well: these people recognized the need to repent and to bring to fruition the implications of repentance. They will be referred to again as 'everyone who sets his heart to seek God, the Lord the God of his fathers' (v. 19).

[12] In contrast to the ambivalent reaction of the majority of the North, the Judaeans have made a full commitment. This verse places an unusual em-phasis on the divine origin of human initiative, with the two phrases 'the hand of God' and 'the word of the Lord'. The call to celebrate the Passover, which in v. 1 is described as Hezekiah's own initiative, and in v. 6 as 'the king's command' or the command of 'the king and his princes', and is further supported by rational arguments in v. 3, is here defined as the king's and the princes' command 'by the word of the Lord'. This is an exceptionally broad understanding of the origin of the king's authority (cf. J. D. Newsome, 'Toward a New Understanding of the Chronicler and his Purposes', *JBL* 94, 1975, 204; Japhet, *Ideology*, 234–9) and a widening of the idea of the 'word of the Lord' acting through the king and the political system.

Divine inspiration, 'the hand of the Lord', is also posited as the source of Judah's 'one heart'. Only one other act is described in Chronicles with this same idiom 'one heart' – the enthronement of David: 'all the rest of Israel were of a single mind (literally 'one heart') to make David king' (I Chron. 12.38 [39]). The phrase itself is found only once more in Ezek. 11.19, but its originality there is doubtful (cf. BH and the commentaries). The view that a complete commitment to keep the Lord's command is beyond human power and needs God's help is stated elsewhere in Chronicles in David's prayer: 'Grant to Solomon my son a whole heart that he may keep your command-ments' (I Chron. 29.19; RSV somewhat differently), and reflects the Chronicler's awareness of the complexity of human choice. The Chronicler posits an absolute moral responsibility, and never tires of repeating that a man is responsible for whatever befalls him; at the same time he knows that the attainment of this perfect 'one heart' or a 'whole heart' may be beyond human power, and both the individual and the community need God's help.

[13] The first part of the chapter is here summarized, with the note that a large crowd is assembled in Jerusalem. Their purpose, however, is 'to keep the feast of unleavened bread', which has not been mentioned up to this point. We should note the parallel between this statement, 'to keep the feast of unleavened bread in the second month', and the phrasing of v. 2: 'to keep the Passover in the second month', to realize that a full identification of the two has taken place, with the 'feast of unleavened bread' containing the Passover as its beginning. This terminological identification is not found elsewhere in the Bible, not even in II Chron. 35, where 'Passover' and 'the feast of unleavened bread' are mentioned in the same verse, but are clearly separated (cf. II Chron. 35.17). Nor are they to be identified in Ezra 6.19–22, where the two feasts – although celebrated sequentially – are nevertheless separate. From the point of view of terminology and the ultimate identification of 'Passover' as contained within 'the feast of unleavened bread', this verse represents the most advanced stage of the liturgical calendar in the Bible.

[14] The story now moves to its second part, the celebration. Yet, as already pointed out, this new beginning is not indicated by the syntax, since the verse begins with no mention of a subject. This structure has been noted earlier, for example at 21.1–2.

The first step of the assembling crowd is to purify the city. This is a necessary extension of Hezekiah's earlier initiative which centred upon the purgation of the Temple; the third stage of purification will take place after the Passover, when 'all Israel' will take it upon themselves to purify the whole country from its idolatrous objects (31.1). The objects to be removed are the altars and the incense altars/stands, which are probably related to each other. Thus, in the same way as Hezekiah's purification of the Temple was an antithesis to Ahaz' works, the people, too, set about to remove Ahaz' installations, described earlier as 'he made himself altars in every corner of Jerusalem' (II Chron. 28.24).

[15–16] In distinct contrast to the dedication ceremony on the one hand, and Josiah's Passover on the other, the actual sacrifice is described with great brevity, with no enumeration or the detailing of the sacrifices. Those details which are mentioned, therefore, are of special significance. These include, now for the third time, a remark that the feast is being celebrated in the second month, a point of great significance within the event; the affinity between vv. 15 and 13 (as between 13 and 2) highlights the point that the 'Passover' is just one aspect of 'the feast of unleavened bread' and not a discrete entity.

The second point noted is the sanctification of priests and Levites, prompted by their 'shame' – fully understandable in view of their earlier 'non-sanctification' which caused the postponement of the feast (v. 3). The preceding remarks to this effect, however, referred only to the priests, while expressly commending the Levites (29.34; 30.3), a fact which prompted Rudolph to suggest the omitting of the copulative *waw* before 'Levites', to read 'the levitical priests', similar to v. 27 (Rudolph, 302; cf. BHS). One may also detect here a general comment about the clergy's prompt sanctification, reacting to their earlier failure to do so, with the 'priests and Levites' denoting the 'all'.

The process of sanctification involves sacrificing burnt offerings, an element of the sanctification ceremony which has not been mentioned so far (cf. I Chron. 15.12, 14; II Chron. 5.11; 29.15, 34; 35.6). The phrasing 'they ... brought' would indicate that these were their own offerings (cf. for example, Lev. 2.8; 4.4; 5.12; Deut. 12.6, 11), but the precise liturgical context in which these 'burnt offerings' are made is not clear, since the situation is neither the inauguration of the priests (Exod. 29; Lev. 8), nor a general sin-offering (Lev. 4.3–12), nor a return to office after having been defiled by the death of a relative (Ezek. 44.27), which also requires a sin-offering. The nature and function of these 'burnt offerings' thus remain obscure.

The syntax of these verses is somewhat complex. As pointed out by Williamson (369), the act of 'sanctification' must have preceded the present tense of the narrative, and therefore must be regarded as a pluperfect act, while the narrative chronology would flow directly from v. 15a to v. 16a. Although this is certainly the meaning of the text, it is not constructed with the necessary syntax, which should have had an uninterrupted sequence from v.15a to 16a. Rather, the subject of 16a is 'the priests and the Levites' of v. 15b, and not the 'they' of v. 15a. While not being an exact translation of the text, a rendering such as 'and the priests and Levites – who had been ashamed and had sanctified themselves – took their accustomed posts, etc.' would represent the present structure.

It is not specified who the subject of 'they slaughtered' is, but the statements of vv. 16 and 17 make it clear that 'they' refers to laymen, each person slaughtering his family's Passover lamb.

Verse 16 describes only one aspect of the sacrificial procedure: the dashing of the blood against the altar. On the face of the matter this is a regular aspect of the ritual, prescribed in detail with regard to the burnt offering and the well-being sacrifice (Lev. 1.5, 11; 3.2, 8, 13), and one may only wonder why this element alone was singled out for mention. In fact, however, this feature of the sacrifice introduces an innovation, at least in view of the available sources. The question is if and when the Passover sacrifice came to be regarded as a regular *zebaḥ*. This is not the case in the instruction of Exod. 12.6–11, 21–22, nor is it referred to anywhere else, and it is precisely the peculiar rite of the blood which constitutes the specific object of the Passover sacrifice in Exod. 12. With the transfer of the Passover sacrifice first to the local sanctuaries and then to Jerusalem, it gradually became analogous to a well-being sacrifice, assuming all the features of a regular sacrifice. The precise chronology of this development, however, is debated. Haran, for example, claims that the phrasing of Exod. 34.25 (*zebaḥ ḥag happāsaḥ*) already indicates the identification of 'Passover' as a 'sacrifice' (M. Haran, *Temples and Temple Service in the Old Testament*, 1978, 341–3). This verse, however, is the first instance where this transformation is clearly attested, repeated in a more obscure way in II Chron. 35.11.

Related to the preceding is the remark that the priests 'receive the blood' from the Levites. The identity of those from whom the priests 'receive the blood' is left unspecified in II Chron. 29.22, and II Chron. 35.11 is ambiguous. This again is an innovation when compared with the sacrificial laws of Leviticus 1ff. While the slaughtering is executed by laymen and the dashing of the blood on to the altar is the task of the priests, the responsibility of 'carrying' the blood is not specified (e.g. Lev. 3.2: 'he shall lay his hand upon the head of his offering and kill it … and Aaron's sons the priests shall throw the blood against the altar round about'), allowing one to assume that it was executed by the same laymen. The prescription of the burnt offering includes one more sentence: 'and Aaron's sons the priests shall present the blood, and throw the blood round about against the altar' (Lev. 1.5). This may suggest that the bringing of the blood, termed here 'present', is the priests' task, and this is indeed the rabbinical dictum: 'From reception and on it is the task of the priesthood' (Yoma 27a). This procedure is stated very specifically elsewhere in rabbinic literature regarding the Passover sacrifice: 'a layman should slaughter and a priest should receive' (Mishnah Peshahim, 5.6). This verse introduces the Levites as intermediaries between the people and the priests in the rite of dashing the blood. While in principle this is a logical position, well in accord with the general functions of the levitical class, in fact, neither the Pentateuchal laws nor rabbinical customs as illustrated by the Mishnah provide for this procedure. It is therefore all the more surprising when the Chronicler states in this very verse that all this is done according to both 'custom' (*kᵉmišpāṭām*) and 'to the law of Moses the man of God'.

This tension may be resolved in several ways. One may assume that the Chronicler had in his possession a version of the Pentateuch which was different from the MT, but there is no other support for this assumption than the difficulty which prompted it, and this would then be a circular argument. It seems more likely that the Chronicler did not refer to the written word as it stands, but rather to the way it was understood and interpreted, either by him or at his time (cf. S. Japhet, 'Law and "the Law" in Ezra-Nehemiah', *Proceedings of the Ninth World Congress of Jewish Studies* (panel sessions), 1985, 99–115). This would lead to the conclusion that the procedure he posits was to some degree different from that prescribed in the Mishnah, and the concomitant conclusion that the Mishnaic law was a final stage of a conflicting development.

[17–20] This section is constructed as a chain of apparent causative clauses, all beginning with the causative particle *kī* ('for'). The passage is also marked by a series of negatives: 'Had not sanctified themselves' ... 'every one who was not clean' (v. 17); 'had not cleansed themselves'... 'otherwise than as prescribed' (v. 18); 'not according to the sanctuary's rules' (v. 19). These stylistic features, together with Hezekiah's prayer in vv. 18b–19, lend the whole passage a strong apologetic tone of heightening tension, which is finally resolved in the positive statement of v. 20. The topic of the passage is also highlighted by repetition, the roots *ṭhr* (pure) and *qdš* (sanctify) each being repeated three times, and appearing together as one phrase at the end of the prayer.

In spite of the dense repetition of 'for' (*ki*), not all the clauses are genuinely causative or explanatory, and this particle should be variously rendered, according to context. It may be omitted at the beginning of v. 18, where it serves as a regular conjunction; in v. 18aβ it may be rendered 'yet' (already RSV; NEB 'therefore'), and should probably be translated by 'therefore' in 18b (NEB 'but'). Its repetition thus serves as a stylistic feature which unifies the passage.

Another point of noteworthy syntax is the Massoretic division of vv. 18–19, which contradicts the actual syntax of the sentence and cannot be followed. The beginning of v. 19, when read on its own, may be understood as referring to Hezekiah: 'He set all his heart to seek the Lord'. However, this reading renders difficult both the end of v. 18 which precedes it, and the second part of v. 19 which follows it. At the end of v. 18 the phrase *yᵉkappēr bᵉʿad* (= 'atone for', RSV 'pardon') is left as an abstract conclusion with no object, while the end of v. 19 ('not according to the ... rules of cleanness') is left with no antecedent, since it certainly does not refer to Hezekiah. A better understanding of the sentence structure is to see in the first clause of v. 19 a relative clause with no relative particle – a common feature of the Chronicler's idiom (cf. Curtis, 34; already Kimhi, *ad loc*) – rather than a beginning of a new sentence, which has been rendered correctly by RSV and others: 'everyone [who] sets his heart'. This is then the object of the Lord's atonement mentioned at the end of v. 18. As presented by the translations (e.g. RSV, NEB, JPS), the clause which begins in v. 18b finds its ending at the end of v. 19.

[17] This concludes the discussion of 'sacrifice'. The fact that the priests received the blood from the Levites (v. 16b) is qualified and explained; it was necessary because there were so many people who were unclean. The logical corollary follows immediately: since these people could not perform their own slaughtering, the Levites undertook both the slaughtering and the

presentation of the blood that accompanies it. These, however, provide only a partial remedy for the problematical situation, as it leaves unsolved another issue, that of 'eating', the topic of vv. 18–20.

Verse. 17b is phrased as a nominal clause, which turns it into a type of declaration: 'The Levites were in charge of slaughtering the paschal sacrifice for everyone who was not clean' (JPS). As argued above, transfer of lay functions to the Levites is the most reasonable procedure in the circumstances of the narrative, since their status as an intermediate clerical class makes them serve both the priests and the people. These unexpected but urgent needs may have greatly promoted the status and claims of the Levites, a development which need not be seen as the peculiar position of the Chronicler.

[18–19] The possibility that an unclean person would partake in the Passover sacrifice is explicitly rejected in the Pentateuchal law, and indicates the provision of the 'second passover' (Num. 9.10). However, the instructions to begin the preparations for the sacrifice four days earlier (cf. Exod. 12.3ff.), would reduce to the minimum the cases of regular 'uncleanness'. The circumstances of Hezekiah's Passover present a problem which is discussed in the Pentateuchal laws, with no solution suggested: the problem of the pilgrims. Because of the journey and the lack of time and facilities, these people were ritually unclean, unable to perform the sacrifice for which they made this pilgrimage. The partaking of the sacrifice by the ritually unclean is unequivocally prohibited by an explicit law: 'All who are clean may eat flesh, but the person who eats of the flesh of the sacrifice of the Lord's peace offerings while an uncleanness is on him, that person shall be cut off from his people' (Lev. 7.19–21). The dilemma facing Hezekiah is obvious, and in principle he could have followed any of three options. At the two extremes, he could have denied the pilgrims the right to both slaughter and to eat of the sacrifice, or he could have fully permitted these acts; in the middle would be some compromise between the extreme poles. Hezekiah opted for the third possibility, prohibiting these people the act of slaughtering but allowing them to partake in the sacrifice. Indeed, the problem of the pilgrims' purity was a major issue in the second commonwealth, and the inclination to alleviate the strict demand for purity characterized the post-biblical attitude in general (cf. S. Saphrai, *Pilgrimage at the Time of the Second Temple*', Tel Aviv, 1965, 135–141*) and the statement: 'The impurity of laymen in the pilgrimage – the Lord had purified it' (ibid., 139). It is thus very probable that Hezekiah's decision, which in this context is presented as utterly unexpected and unprecedented, reflects the regular customs and the general atmosphere of the festivals.

Hezekiah's dilemma is presented in his prayer with unequivocal clarity, as it presents a clear-cut contrast between 'body' and 'soul' – the internal disposition and will described as 'setting the heart', and the physical situation of impurity, caused by inevitable circumstances. The divine decision, which is described as 'and the Lord heard Hezekiah, and healed the people' (v. 20), is an explicit pronouncement that 'the setting of the heart' is of greater value than ritualistic purity. Contrary to v. 2, however, the decision is taken by Hezekiah alone, with no consultation or involvement of either clergy or prophets; he takes upon himself the full responsibility. Being aware of the severity of his decision, he prays to the Lord that he may atone for what is done in goodwill but in violation of the letter of the law.

Two further points should be clarified.

(a) According to the exact wording of Hezekiah's prayer, he does not ask 'pardon' (RSV, NEB), for this is not the issue at hand. Transgression of cultic impurity is an act which cannot be 'taken back' or pardoned. Rather, Hezekiah asks that the Lord in his goodness 'provide atonement' ($y^ekapp\bar{e}r$) for those whom he, Hezekiah, allowed to commit this transgression. The concrete expression of the Lord's 'atonement' is 'healing'.

(b) Although the general sense of the last clause $k^etoh^orat\ haqq\bar{o}de\check{s}$ is clear, its literal meaning is less so. It is rendered by RSV as 'the sanctuary's rules of cleanness', but in fact there is no reference to 'rules', and the problem is not that of the 'sanctuary' but of the people. I therefore tend to see here a more general statement, like 'holy purity'; the people had 'set their hearts', but were not in the state of purity demanded by 'holiness'.

[20] Should we infer from the cure, 'and the Lord healed the people', that there was some sort of plague among the people which needed to be healed? The context does not endorse such an inference, and, considering that the statement follows the prayer for 'atonement', we must understand 'heal' as a preventative rather than corrective measure (cf. Ehrlich: 'he did not plague them', *Randglossen*, VII, 377). The immanent danger involved in the desecration of the holy by eating it in a state of uncleanness was averted, and it did not result in a plague among the people.

[21–22] These verses describe the feast of unleavened bread, celebrated in Jerusalem after the Passover sacrifice. At the centre of this feast we find, not the sacrifices but the great joy expressed by the liturgical music in the Temple, and the people's eating of 'peace offerings' and giving thanks to the Lord. The special sacrifices of the festival as prescribed in Num. 28.19–24, are not even mentioned.

Rejoicing as a component of a festival is mentioned explicitly in Deuteronomy in reference to two of the three festivals: the Feast of Weeks (Deut. 16.11: 'you shall rejoice before the Lord your God ...'), and the Feast of Booths (Deut. 16.14: 'you shall rejoice in your feast'), but not in reference to either Passover or the Feast of Unleavened Bread. In Ezra 6.22 it is mentioned as part of the Feast of Unleavened Bread, but the rejoicing is related to the historical circumstances: 'and they kept the feast of unleavened bread ... with joy; for the Lord had made them joyful, and had turned the heart of the king of Assyria to them'. In Hezekiah's feast, 'rejoicing' is a major element of the feast itself, continuing into the festivities which follow it (vv. 23, 25, 26).

The liturgical expression of the rejoicing is music, performed by both the priests and Levites, but its details, surprisingly, are not recorded by the Chronicler. Only the instruments are mentioned, with the uncommon term 'powerful instruments' *(biklē-'ōz)*. Although both RSV and NEB regard the term as a corruption (cf. also BHS), the originality of the reading is defended by I. L. Seeligmann, 'Researches into the Criticism of the Masoretic Text of the Bible, *Tarbiz* 25, 1955/6, 137*.

Verse 22 comprises two independent sentences. Verse 22b depicts the actions of the people but with no specification of subject; it is duly supplemented by RSV: 'the people ate the food of the festival, etc'. Verse 22a has Hezekiah as subject and tells about his address to the Levites, stating that Hezekiah 'spoke encouragingly to all the Levites'. At this point, an address to the 'Levites' in the strict sense of the term would be surprising, since the chores of the festival were not exclusively their responsibility, and in contrast to ch. 29, they are not preferred to the priests; rather, the priests and Levites are mentioned together all along in their respective roles (cf. vv. 15, 16, 21, 25). 'The Levites' should be understood in this context in the more comprehensive connotation of the term, referring to all the 'descendants of Levi' including the priests (cf. 29.5 and elsewhere), accentuated by the explicit 'all'. Contrary to what one might expect, Hezekiah's words to the Levites are not cited, and the same applies to the prayer mentioned in v. 27; except for the letter in vv. 6–9, no other rhetorical examples are included in this pericope.

The people celebrate the feast for seven days, dedicating themselves to the offering of peace-offerings, eating the food of the festival, and praying to the Lord to the accompaniment of the Temple's music 'day by day'. This is in fact the first pilgrimage to Jerusalem actually described in the Bible.

Two linguistic matters require some clarification. The second clause begins with *wayyo'k^{e}lu 'et hammō'ēd*, translated as 'they ate the food of the festival'. While *mō'ēd* is certainly a term for 'festival' (cf. Hos. 2.13; Ezek. 46.11; Lam. 1.4; 2.6, etc.), it never denotes the festival's sacrifice or food, except here. The other point of note is the rendering of *mitwaddīm*, which is literally 'making confession' (thus NEB) or 'confessing' (JPS). The RSV's 'giving thanks' takes the Hebrew to be *mōdīm* rather than the actual MT.

[23–27] The last paragraph of the chapter recounts a very unusual event – an additional feast. After the people have celebrated the Passover and seven days of the festival of unleavened bread, they 'take counsel' (*wayyiwā'^{a}ṣū*,

RSV 'agreed together') to celebrate one more festival, defined as 'rejoicing' (*śimḥah*). This festival, decided upon by the people themselves, has no background or precedent, and no apparent historical or religious motive except for the people's wish to continue their festivities. This constitutes, then, the premier example of 'spontaneous popular religiosity' which finds expression in voluntary additions to existing customs and obligations. In a certain way it resembles the time of Solomon, when the festivities continued for two weeks, and this comparison is explicitly drawn (v. 26). The festival depicted in the present passage is different from that of Solomon's time, however, in that it springs from no cultic or ceremonial source. Solomon had celebrated first the dedication of the Temple, and then 'the feast', that is, 'the feast of booths' in the seventh month (I Kings 8.65//II Chron. 7.8–9), while the celebration described in this chapter is not a part of the cultic calendar, is not prescribed anywhere, and does not follow any established rubrics or customs. Indeed, the Chronicler does not ascribe a religious character to it; the sacrificial animals are not defined as 'sacrifices', and the only hint of their being so is the reference to the priests. Even the constant feature in the Chronicler's description of celebrations – song and music by the levitical singers – is not mentioned here. Thus, it is as close to a 'secular' celebration as anything connected with the Temple might be. It expresses the wish of the pilgrims to stay in Jerusalem after the official festival was over, probably reflecting the actual customs of the pilgrimages of the Second Temple.

[23–24] 'Rejoicing' involves sacrifices of well-being, and these are made possible by the generous contribution of the king and his officers – the contribution of the princes somewhat exceeding that of the king. The numbers are round, but add up to 2,000 bulls and 17,000 sheep. Considering the distribution of the festival over seven days, and the great numbers of pilgrims during the Second Commonwealth, this may not be an impossible number (cf. Safrai, 71–4).

The second requirement for carrying out the festivities is the availability of priests, without whom the offering is impossible. Their participation brings to a happy conclusion the process of their full integration: 'the priests sanctified themselves in great numbers'. Their performance became gradually better, eventually becoming completely satisfactory.

[25] What this passage does emphasize instead of the actual sacrificing are two other elements: the rejoicing and the scope of the festivities. Not only is the feast itself defined as 'rejoicing' (the RSV 'with gladness' reads the noun *śimḥāh* as an adverb': *bᵉśimḥāh*), but the reference to rejoicing is repeated twice more: 'the whole assembly ... rejoiced' (v. 25), and 'so there was great joy in Jerusalem' (v. 26). The second emphasis is the scope of the celebration. Here the Chronicler takes care to enumerate all the sectors of the people who participate in the celebration, and this detailed listing is of great significance.

II CHRONICLES

It is constructed concentrically, moving from those at the centre to those on the periphery. First in the list are the citizens of the kingdom of Judah, who are composed of three groups: 'the whole assembly of Judah, and the priests and the Levites'. Then the people of north Israel are listed: 'the whole assembly that came out of Israel'. At the end there are two groups of originally non-Israelites, mentioned chiastically: 'the sojourners who came out of the land of Israel', and 'the [sojourners] who dwelt in Judah'. This unfolding description from the centre outwards is a portrayal of 'Israel' in its broadest constituency, which includes the foreign elements in the land of Israel whom the Chronicler defines as 'sojourners' (*gērīm*), or even possibly 'proselytes', and 'residents' (*yōš^ebīm*). These two terms may reflect the earlier priestly hendiadys *gēr w^etōšāb* (Lev. 25.35, 47; Num. 35.15), and may imply that the status of these people as an integral part of the community entitled them to partake in the Passover sacrifice (Exod. 12.43–49).

I have already discussed the fact that the Chronicler does not recognize the existence of true foreigners within the land of Israel (cf. Japhet, *Ideology*, 328–34). According to his view, all those who dwelt in the land of Israel were part of the people of Israel, either as 'the people of Israel' proper, or as *gērīm*. This definition is of particular significance at the time of Hezekiah, when according to our historical information, the contingent of foreigners living in the land of Israel had increased in number and power, because of the Assyrian importation of these peoples into the land (II Kings 17.24). The Chronicler does not specify who are the people whom he regards as 'resident aliens', but this general, comprehensive view of the people is all-inclusive.

[26] The comparison of Hezekiah to Solomon which is apparent in many aspects of the story (cf. H. G. M. Williamson, *Israel in the Book of Chronicles*, Cambridge 1977, 119–25; M. A. Throntveit, *When Kings Speak*, 1987, 121–5) is now drawn explicitly: 'Since the time of Solomon ... there had been nothing like this in Jerusalem.' The focus of the comparison is on the grand celebration, which first consumed one week and was then prolonged for a second. The inspiring sensation of unity, of the whole people assembling in Jerusalem and participating in the Lord's worship, and the pervasive mood of great rejoicing, all combine to express an optimistic climax in the history of Israel. Now, after the abolition of a separate monarchy in northern Israel and with the accession of Hezekiah, the king of Judah, a new 'correct' beginning in the history of Israel is possible. It is no wonder then, that Solomon is given his full title: 'Solomon the son of David king of Israel' – an appropriate expression of this feeling of completeness and grandeur.

[27] The celebration is brought to its close with a benediction: the priests bless the people. This is indeed their role, as defined by various biblical passages (e.g. Num. 6.23–27; Deut. 10.8; 21.5; I Chron. 23.5, etc.), and a full presentation of the priestly benediction is given in Num. 6.23–27: 'Thus

you shall bless the people of Israel ... So shall they put my name upon the people of Israel, and I will bless them.' However, the actual blessing of the people by the priests is described in the Bible only on the occasion of the inaugural dedication of the altar (Lev. 9.22), and may possibly be implied for the ceremony on Mount Ebal (Josh. 8.33; cf. Deut. 27.12–14). In the monarchical period, as far as our historical sources indicate, the 'blessing of the people' is made by the king (II Sam. 6.18; I Kings 8.14, 54–56).

This verse consists of a clear reflection of the literary tradition expressed in Deut. 27.9 and its parallel in Josh. 8.33. In both these texts, the priests are designated 'the levitical priests', and this literary affinity is the origin for the occurrence of this title in the present context. The affinity with Deuteronomy is illustrated by the end of this verse also; compare Deut. 26.15, 'Look down from thy holy habitation, from heaven', with the present 'and their prayer came to his holy habitation in heaven'. According to Deuteronomy 26.15, the Lord 'looks down from his holy habitation' to bless his people Israel; this is indeed the meaning of the statement that the priests' blessing 'was heard'. As we shall see shortly, 'the Lord has blessed his people' (31.10), a climactic conclusion to the celebrations.

31 Now when all this was finished, all Israel who were present went out to the cities of Judah and broke in pieces the pillars and hewed down the Asherim and broke down the high places and the altars throughout all Judah and Benjamin, and in Ephraim and Manasseh, until they had destroyed them all. Then all the people of Israel returned to their cities, every man to his possession.

2 And Hezekiah appointed the divisions of the priests and of the Levites, division by division, each according to his service, the priests and the Levites, for burnt offerings and peace offerings, to minister in the gates of the camp of the Lord and to give thanks and praise. [3] The contribution of the king from his own possessions was for the burnt offerings: the burnt offerings of morning and evening, and the burnt offerings for the sabbaths, the new moons, and the appointed feasts, as it is written in the law of the Lord. [4] And he commanded the people who lived in Jerusalem to give the portion due to the priests and the Levites, that they might give themselves to the law of the Lord. [5] As soon as the command was spread abroad, the people of Israel gave in abundance the first fruits of grain, wine, oil, honey, and of all the produce of the field; and they brought in abundantly the tithe of everything. [6] And the people of Israel and Judah who lived in the cities of Judah also brought in the tithe of cattle and sheep, and the dedicated things which had been consecrated to the Lord their God, and laid them in heaps. [7] In the third month they began to pile up the heaps, and finished them in the seventh month. [8] When Hezekiah and the princes came and saw the heaps, they blessed the Lord and his people Israel. [9] And Hezekiah questioned the priests and the Levites about the heaps. [10] Azariah the chief priest, who was of the house of Zadok, answered him, 'Since they began to bring the contributions into the house of the Lord we have eaten and had enough and have plenty left; for the Lord has blessed his people, so that we have this great store left.'

11 Then Hezekiah commanded them to prepare chambers in the house of the Lord; and they prepared them. [12] And they faithfully brought in the contributions, the tithes and the dedicated things. The chief officer in charge of them was Conaniah the Levite, with Shime-i his brother as second; [13] while Jehiel, Azaziah, Nahath, Asahel, Jerimoth, Jozabad, Eliel, Ismachiah, Mahath, and Benaiah were overseers assisting Conaniah and Shime-i his brother, by the appointment of Hezekiah the king and Azariah the chief officer of the house of God. [14] And Kore the son of Imnah the Levite, keeper of the east gate, was over the freewill offerings to God, to apportion the contribution reserved for the Lord and the most holy offerings. [15] Eden, Miniamin, Jeshua, Shemaiah, Amariah, and Shecaniah were faithfully assisting him in the cities of the priests, to distribute the portions to their brethren, old and young alike, by divisions, [16] except those enrolled by genealogy, males from three years old and upwards, all who entered the house of the Lord as the duty of each day required, for their service according to their officers, by their divisions. [17] The enrolment of the priests was according to their fathers' houses; that of the Levites from twenty years old and upwards was according to their officers, by their divisions. [18] The priests

were enrolled with all their little children, their wives, their sons, and their daughters, the whole multitude; for they were faithful in keeping themselves holy. [19] And for the sons of Aaron, the priests, who were in the fields of common land belonging to their cities, there were men in the several cities who were designated by name to distribute portions to every male among the priests and to every one among the Levites who was enrolled.

20 Thus Hezekiah did throughout all Judah; and he did what was good and right and faithful before the Lord his God. [21] And every work that he undertook in the service of the house of God and in accordance with the law and the commandments, seeking his God, he did with all his heart, and prospered.

A. Notes to the MT

[2] ולהלל, insert והשוערים; [4] ליושבי ירושלם, gloss? [6] transfer the pause (Atnaḥ) under הביאו; ומעשר, proposed add כל תבואת השדה; [10] והנותר, proposed והנה נותר; [15] בערי, read על יד with LXX; [16] transfer the final pause (Soph Pasuq) to אבותיהם in v. 17a; [17] זאת, read זאת with LXX.

B. Notes to RSV

[2] 'to minister in the gates, etc.' MT differently, cf. commentary; [3] 'contribution', MT 'share, portion' (NEB; JPS); [15] 'in the cities', cf. A above and commentary; [18] 'The priests', not in MT.

C. Structure, sources and form

1. From the point of view of composition, ch. 31 is a direct continuation of ch. 30, with vv. 1–2 concluding the preceding units, and vv. 3–20 presenting the new topic of the chapter. Verse 1 has a topic of its own, the abolition of idolatry throughout the land of Israel, presented as the final consequence of the Passover celebrations. It ends with the formula of 'return': 'Then all the people of Israel returned to their cities', an established concluding formula of biblical narrative (cf. I. L. Seeligmann, 'Hebräische Erzählung und Biblische Geschichtsschreibung', TZ 18, 1962, 314ff.), in v. 2 brings the two preceding chapters, 29–30, to a final conclusion. The full rehabilitation of worship in the Temple culminates in the appointment of priests and Levites to their respective offices.

Verses 3–20 are devoted in the main to one topic: the arrangements for the support of the Temple service and its personnel. The structure emerges in the following outline:

(a) 1 Abolition of idolatry
(b) 2 Appointment of priests and Levites
(c) 3–19 Support of the Temple
    3–4 the king's and people's portions
    5–7 bringing of tithes
    8–13 storage

14–19 distribution
(*d*) 20–21 Conclusion.

2. While verse 1 is based on II Kings 18.4 and vv. 20–21 reflect II Kings 18.5–6, the main body of the chapter is peculiar to Chronicles. What are its sources?

We should first distinguish between v. 2 and what follows. Verse 2 is entirely governed by the Chronicler's concepts concerning the history of the Temple service, and reflects his peculiar view that the full liturgical system has to be re-installed every time it has been suspended. The verse is a final conclusion of the events described in II Chron. 29, and a continuation of 29.35: 'thus the service of the house of the Lord was established (RSV 'restored')'. In both its aspects – subject matter and phrasing – this verse is the work of the Chronicler.

Verses 3–19 introduce an entirely new topic, which has not been dealt with so far either by the Deuteronomistic historian or by the Chronicler himself: the economic basis for the maintenance of the Temple. This general topic is then divided into four sub-topics: a very brief reference to the regular obligation of the king for the burnt offerings (v. 3); a notice of the similar obligation of the people for the support of the clergy (v. 4); a detailed description of the bringing and storing of the people's contribution (vv. 5–13); and a programme for its distribution (vv. 14–19). While vv. 3–13 are presented in the immediate context of Hezekiah's reign, vv. 14–19 seem to introduce more general practices and to reflect a source of their own.

3. Does the chapter reflect, as it claims, the reality of the monarchical period, the reality of the Second Temple, or is it an artificial work, with no concrete historical basis at all? We have no direct or specific evidence about the way in which the practical maintenance of the sanctuaries in the monarchical period was organized, and even the Pentateuchal laws and instructions are not sufficient to draw an accurate picture. As for the Temple in Jerusalem, nothing about its maintenance is mentioned in the book of Kings except for the passing remark that 'the money from the guilt offerings and the money from the sin offerings ... belonged to the priests' (II Kings 12.16 [MT 17]). Since the Temple was basically a 'king's sanctuary', part of the complex of royal buildings, it may be inferred that its maintenance was the king's responsibility, and if this was the case, it must also have included full responsibility for the support of the officiating clergy.

In laying down the 'blueprint' for the new Temple, Ezekiel prescribes that 'it shall be the prince's duty to furnish the burnt offerings, cereal offerings and drink offerings, at the feasts, the new moons and the sabbaths, all the appointed feasts of the house of Israel; he shall provide the sin offerings, cereal offerings, burnt offerings and peace offerings to make atonement for the house of Israel' (Ezek. 45.17). The maintenance of the clergy is not included, and the people's contribution for the priests is prescribed in Ezek. 44.29–30; the provision for the Levites is not referred to by Ezekiel.

It is impossible to judge how accurately Ezekiel's picture reflects the actual circumstances of the Temple during the last days of the monarchical period, and to what degree it introduces new ordinances intended to change and complement the old ones. In principle, however, these are the guidelines which underlie the picture presented by our chapter: the king provides for the sacrifices, the people are responsible for the sustenance of the clergy. In fact, the same division of responsibility is also followed by the Persian rulers. In his decree, Darius states that all the expenses for the regular sacrifices should be paid from the state treasury: 'whatever is needed – young bulls, rams, or sheep for burnt offerings ... wheat, salt, wine, or oil ... let that be given to them day by day without fail' (Ezra 6.9–10). Darius does not refer to the clergy, and while Artaxerxes explicitly exempts them from the regular taxes (Ezra 7.24), he does not make any provisions for their support.

This uniform picture is contradicted by the 'firm covenant' of Neh. 10.32–39 [MT 33–40], according to which all the expenses for the maintenance of the Temple, including the regular sacrifices, are to be covered by the people's tax for the Temple – 'the third part of a shekel', the wood offering, and the various tithes and first fruits. These obligations are repeated in part in Neh. 12.44, and the difficulty in carrying them out is illustrated by Neh. 13.10 and Mal. 3.8–10. The circumstances which brought about this change are not specified, and one may conjecture that the contribution of the Persian rulers was either short-lived or in practice less comprehensive than Darius' original instructions.

Whatever the precise historical development, the general picture of chapter 31 corresponds to that of Ezekiel and the Second Temple situation following Darius' instructions, and not to that of Neh. 10, which lays the exclusive and comprehensive responsibility on the people alone. The main interest of the chapter, however, does not lie with the king's portion, but with the collection and distribution of tithes and first fruits. It may reflect the arrangements and problems of the Chronicler's time.

4. As for the form of the chapter, two literary elements may be clearly distinguished. Most of the chapter is cast as a narrative, describing the one-time events of Hezekiah's reign, and relating the matter of tithes and first-fruits to the context of Hezekiah's first-year reform (vv. 3–13). The following passage (vv. 14–19) is an administrative document, which deals in general terms with the registration of priests and Levites for the purpose of distribution of tithes. Its topic is stated in v. 14: 'to apportion the contribution reserved for the Lord and the most holy offerings', and its leading themes are 'enrolment' (התיחש), repeated in vv. 16, 17, 18, 19, and 'apportion' (לתת), repeated in vv. 14, 15, 19. In the absence of comparative material, the meaning of some details remains debated, but there seems to be no doubt that an actual document of the Second Temple period has been used and retrojected by the Chronicler to the context of Hezekiah.

D. Commentary

[1] This verse goes back to the main framework of the pericope in II Kings 18.4 (cf. above, pp. 912f.), and is connected to its present context in two ways. It opens with the transitional clause 'Now when all this was finished', identifying the removal of idolatry as a continuation of the Passover, and it adds the introductory statement 'all Israel who were present went out to the cities of Judah'. The result is a major shift in the position and message of the passage. II Kings 18.4 serves as a concluding summary for all Hezekiah's efforts to remove idolatry and illegitimate forms of the cult, illustrating the earlier statement that 'he did what was right in the eyes of the Lord' (18.3). According to Chronicles, this is a one-time event, undertaken throughout the land at one historical point. Moreover, what had been attributed to the king

alone is here presented as the people's undertaking. One may infer that the people were acting with the king's encouragement and blessing, but it is the only instance in the Bible where a popular religious reform is indicated. Thus, in the division of labour between the king and the people, the present story attributes to Hezekiah only the purification and sanctification of the Temple; the same acts regarding the city of Jerusalem (30.14) and the land were the contribution of the people.

The significance of this division is very clear in the context of the Chronicler's world-view, where the people occupy a dominant position both politically and theologically. This full rapport between people and king may be contrasted to other cases when the two are explicitly juxtaposed; statements that the king did what was right in the eyes of the Lord, but the people were doing wrong are found mainly in Kings (I Kings 22.43–44, etc.), but appear also in Chronicles; cf. in particular II Chron. 20.32–33. Here, by contrast, with no coercion or even intimation from the king, the people themselves undertake the reform. By way of contrast, one may compare it to the Chronicler's phrasing regarding the period of Josiah: 'and Josiah ... *made all* who were in Israel *serve* the Lord' (II Chron. 34.33). The 'unity of heart' during the reform of Hezekiah is another echo of the Chronicler's longing for a return to the days of David and Solomon.

Another difference between II Kings 18.4 and this verse are the geographical dimensions of the reform, another corollary of the Chronicler's stand on the matter. The Deuteronomistic history does not dwell on this point, and therefore the text implies that the reform is limited to Judah. The Chronicler refers explicitly to 'All Israel who were present', and then to 'Judah and Benjamin and in Ephraim and Manasseh', that is, including the territory of the northern kingdom. This is a direct sequel to the atmosphere which permeated ch. 30: the people of north Israel are integrated into the move to centralize the cult in Jerusalem, and make Jerusalem their only Temple.

Last to be noted is the omission of any reference to the 'bronze serpent', and the addition of 'the altars'. It seems that what was still a matter of significance for the Deuteronomist has become an obsolete reference for the Chronicler, with no need for repetition.

Thus, although the facts related in this verse are drawn from the Chronicler's source in II Kings 18.4, the spirit of the passage is very much in harmony with its present context. The people returning from Jerusalem, having remained for some time at the Temple and its service, are filled with the inspiring experience of pilgrimage, and, imbued with religious enthusiasm and dedication, give concrete expression to their renewed conviction by totally removing all vestiges of idolatry. Later the same enthusiasm will be manifested in the generous contributions for the Temple.

[2] The final establishment of the Temple service demands that the clergy

be properly installed in their prescribed offices. What may seem on the face of the matter to be a superfluous repetition of well-known facts is in fact indicated by the course of events as the Chronicler understands them. Until this point, only temporary arrangements for the clergy were taken care of, in the context of the purification of the Temple and the celebration of the Passover. Now, when all the excitement is over, it is time to establish the regular service of the Temple personnel, with full rehabilitation of the damage done by Ahaz.

In its subject matter, the present passage parallels II Chron. 8.14–15 and 23.18–19, but it is phrased more succinctly, the most conspicuous absence being any of those references to David which play such a prominent role in the other two passages. This silence is abundantly compensated for by earlier references to David in this pericope, in particular II Chron. 29.25–30.

In the present MT, only two categories of Temple personnel are mentioned, priests and Levites, and the Levites are divided 'each according to his service'. The Temple functions mentioned are the sacrifices on the one hand, and music and the guarding of the gates on the other. According to the syntax of the last clause, the giving of thanks and praising is conducted – contrary to all that we know about the Temple music – 'in the gates of the camp(s) of the Lord', a fact which is never mentioned in Chronicles. It has therefore been suggested that, following the Septuagint, the word 'to minister' should be moved before 'the gates' (Rudolph, 304, and BHS), or, differently, that the words 'at the gates ... of the Lord' should be moved after 'to minister' (RSV). However, either one of these reconstructions would make the general term 'minister' refer in a very unusual way to the limited service of the gate-keepers. Rather than assuming a 'somewhat awkward style' (Dillard, 248), I propose to see the text as somewhat corrupt, and to restore the word *wᵉhaššoᵃrim* before *bᵉšaᵃrē*, omitted by haplography. This structure, with the mention of priests, Levites and gatekeepers, has several parallels in Chronicles (cf. II Chron. 8.14; 23.18–19), the whole being a concise description of all the roles involved in the regular service.

[3–4] The topic of this short passage is 'portion' (*mānāh*): the king's portion is described in v. 3, the people's portion in v. 4. While the former is stated as an established fact, the latter is presented as the king's order to the people. According to the Chronicler's presentation, neither is an innovation, but both represent the re-instatement of ancient customs and ordinances which had been abolished by Ahaz.

The unity of the passage is illustrated not merely by the repeated theme (these are the only two occurrences of *mānāh* in Chronicles, the plural *mānōt* occurring once, in v. 19 of this chapter), but by the syntax, which has no explicit subject in v. 4, and the identical conclusion, 'in the Law of the Lord', which establishes both the purpose and authority of these arrangements.

The definition 'portion' (cf. Baumgartner, 567, and Ecclus. 26.3) means that this is no goodwill contribution, but an obligation. Following the general statement that 'the portion (RSV 'contribution') of the king from his own possession was for the burnt offering', we find an accurate list of all the burnt offerings which constitute the regular cult: the daily sacrifice, and the additional ones for the Sabbaths and festivals, as prescribed by the Law.

In the phrasing of v. 4 there is some difficulty. 'The people' are unexpectedly qualified by the apposition 'the inhabitants of Jerusalem' (RSV 'who lived in Jerusalem'). This limitation is strange in itself, and creates a certain discrepancy with the following verses, since the response to the king's command comes from 'the people of Israel' (v. 5), that is, those of the northern territories, and 'the people of Israel and Judah who lived in the cities of Judah' (v. 6), but not from 'the inhabitants of Jerusalem'. Those who have been approached do not respond, and those who contribute so generously have not been approached. It seems that the words 'the inhabitants of Jerusalem' are a gloss, intended to supplement this apparently missing group; its excision brings all the difficulties into order.

The last clause of v. 4 is clear, and may be rendered literally as: 'that they may be strong (*yeḥezqū*) in the law of the Lord'. It is often taken to refer to the 'priests and Levites', describing the goal of the king's command, and represented as 'that they might give themselves to the law of the Lord' (RSV), or more emphatically in the NEB 'that they might devote themselves entirely'. Thus already Pseudo Rashi *ad loc.*: 'that they may occupy themselves with the Law even more willingly'. Although not impossible, this interpretation of the verb *yeḥezqu* is quite uncommon, and presses the limits of its usual usage. It is thus possible that the purpose clause refers not to the 'priests and Levites' but to 'the people', to whom the king's command was delivered. The king's motivation is presented as directing the people to be strong in the law, in fulfilling its ordinances. With this understanding the clause may be compared to a similar statement 'if he continues resolute (*'im yeḥᵉzak*) in keeping my commandments' (I Chron. 28.7), referring to Solomon.

[5–6] In relating the people's contribution, two different groups are mentioned. Verse 6 refers to 'the people of Israel and Judah who lived in Judah', portraying the citizens of the kingdom of Judah in the Chronicler's terms as including both 'Judaeans' and 'people of Israel' (cf. in particular, I Chron. 9.3; II Chron. 10.17; 11.16–17, etc.). The other group is 'the people of Israel' (v. 5), which, in view of v. 6, would refer to the people of the north. The contribution of each of these groups seems, however, to comprise different items. The people of Israel bring 'the first fruits of grain, wine, oil, honey and all the produce of the field, and ... the tithes of everything', while the people of Judah bring 'the tithe of cattle and sheep and the tithe of the dedicated things'. If we take 'the tithe of everything' to be all-inclusive, then the people of Israel contributed both tithes and first fruits, while the people of Judah contributed only tithes, and even here, not in all its varieties. In view of the Chronicler's opinion of the Judahites (cf. II Chron. 30.12), this would hardly seem likely. It seems that the text should be interpreted from a literary point of view rather than with a too literal legal precision. Between Israel and Judah, everything possible was contributed, as a sign of prosperity and blessing. This generous contribution is also expressed by the repeated reference to abundance: 'the people... gave in abundance... and they brought in abundantly ... and laid them in heaps'.

Among the contributions of Judah, the text mentions the obscure 'tithes of the dedicated things'. The tithe itself is called 'holy' or 'dedicated', and so are all the priests' gifts, defined as 'holy offerings' (Num. 18.19), but nowhere is there a tithe of 'holy/consecrated/dedicated things'. The phrase is interpreted by Kimhi as an extreme sign of goodwill: 'they brought tithes even from the dedicated things which are exempt from it'. RSV's rendering assumes a dittography of 'tithe' and omits it, while Rudolph suggests the opposite, the addition of a few words to read 'tithes of all the produce of the field' (304, also BHS). Both suggestions give a smoother text.

Two items in the list deserve special attention.

(a) The 'first fruits' of honey is not mentioned explicitly in the Pentateuchal regulations for tithes (cf. Num. 18.12), or the covenant in Nehemiah's time (Neh. 10.39, [MT 40]); it may, however, be implied from the text of Lev. 2.11–12. While the preparation of the cereal offering designated for the Lord with any kind of leaven, including honey, is forbidden, these are allowed as 'first fruits', which are given directly to the priests and are not brought as offerings.

(b) 'The tithes of cattle and sheep' are mentioned in the Pentateuch only in Lev. 27.32–33, in the context of redemption laws, and are missing in Neh. 10. They are mentioned in the Apocrypha (Jub. 13.25–26; 32.15, and more), but are not found in rabbinic sources (cf. Mishnah, Zebahim, 5.8, and M. Haran, 'Tithe', *Encyclopedia Biblica* V, 207, 210–11*).

[7] The chronology of the contributions is an authentic reflection of both the Pentateuchal laws and the agricultural calendar. The third month, when the 'feast of harvest' (or 'the feast of weeks') is celebrated, marks the beginning of the harvest and is connected with the presentation of 'a cereal offering of new grain' (Lev. 23.16–17), while the seventh month, containing the celebration of 'the feast of ingathering' (Exod. 23.16), marks the end of the agricultural year.

[8] Having given a command to the people, Hezekiah proceeds to ascertain its execution, and, as is often the case in Chronicles, does so 'with his officers' (RSV 'princes'). Their reaction is natural: they bless the Lord for the prosperity which he granted to his people, and they bless the people for their

enthusiasm in fulfilling the king's command. Again, the blessing, too, is said to issue not merely from the king but also from his officers.

[9–10] The priest's answer to the king's question is an adequate expression of the blessing which prevails everywhere. Although certainly in prose, the answer displays some metre which is naturally lost in translation. It is constructed of four colons of equal length; the first three have five words each, while the last has now (cf. above A) only four words. For the purpose of heightened literary expression and emphasis, there is a prevalence of nominal forms.

I have already mentioned that Hezekiah's reign is described with enthusiasm and unrestrained optimism. Here it is expressed in the agricultural exuberance. The people contribute good-naturedly and their contribution provides more than that necessary for the clergy's sustenance. The priests have eaten to satiety, and this great store is left.

The genealogy of the high priests mentions several priests by the name Azariah(u) (I Chron. 6.9, 10, 13–14 [MT 5.35, 36, 39–40]), and this is also the name of the high priest in the time of Uzziah (II Chron. 26.17), but none of these may be related to the time of Hezekiah. Azariah's title is 'the chief priest' (*hakkōhēn hārō'š*), and later he is called 'the chief officer of the house of God' (v. 13), both terms reflecting the Chronicler's language and terminology. Uniquely, however, Azariahu is defined as 'who was of the house of Zadok'. Although descent of the high priests from 'Zadok' is presupposed by the constitutive genealogy of the priests (I Chron. 6.1ff. [MT 5.27ff.]), this is never explicitly stated for any high priest. This unusual reference brings to mind another person by a similar name: 'Azariah(u) the son of Zadok ... the priest' of Solomon's time (I Kings 4.2). One may take this lead in regarding this person as a literary rather than a historical figure; or one may claim simply that the name was common in the house of Zadok.

[11–13] Hezekiah's reaction takes the form of two practical measures. He issues orders to prepare store chambers, attached to the Temple, for the preservation of the surplus, and he appoints the Temple staff to supervise and manage it. The bringing of contributions to 'the chambers, to the storehouse' is mentioned several times in Nehemiah; cf. 'For the people of Israel and the sons of Levi shall bring the contribution of grain, wine and oil to the chambers' (Neh. 10.39 [MT 10.40]; also in Neh. 10.37, 38 [MT 10.38, 39]; 12.44), but in that context, the tithes are collected by the Levites themselves in the provinces: 'for it is the Levites who collect the tithes in all our rural towns' (Neh. 10.37 [MT 38]). This passage reflects a process of increasing centralization in the administration of the tithes, and probably reflects a specific development of the Second Temple period (cf. also M. Haran, *Encyclopedia Biblica* V, 210*).

The various categories of gifts are clearly defined in this context: contribution (*t͏ᵉrūmāh*), tithe (*ma͏ʿᵃśēr*), and dedications (*q͏ᵒdāšîm*). All three reflect priestly terminology (cf. Num. 18.8, 11, 19, 21; RSV's terminology is somewhat different), but their precise connotation should be determined by the present context. The 'contribution' would refer to the 'first fruits', and the 'dedicated things' to various gifts which have not been specified before and may include firstborns (Num. 18.15–17), 'vows' (Lev. 27.2–13), 'dedications' (Lev. 27.14–25), and 'devoted things' (*ḥērem*, Num. 18.14; Lev. 27.14–25).

The administrative hierarchy is portrayed very precisely: the upper authority is that of the king and the chief priest, and they appoint two administrators: Conaniah and his brother Shimei, who in turn appoint ten more officials by the authority granted them by the king and high priest. This is, then, 'a charge of the Levites by the king' as defined in II Chron. 24.11 (RSV differently). The context of the repair of the Temple under Joash, in which this general term is found, is the other context in Chronicles in which the same kind of co-operation between king and high priest is manifest; together they take responsibility for the management of the Temple (cf. II Chron. 24.11, 12, 14).

This co-operation of king and high priest may reflect, at least to a certain degree, the situation of the Second Temple period. However, the relative significance of king and priest, with the latter playing a rather secondary role, would be surprising, since 'the king' would then be represented by the governor, appointed by the Persian ruler. While this kind of relative significance is attested also for the period of Nehemiah, it is doubtful whether this was the common balance between the two representatives of authority, especially in matters of the cult. It seems to reflect the Chronicler's own view and inclinations, projected to the monarchical period.

The actual staff in charge of the contributions are thus the Levites, who are appointed by the king and high priest. This is another broadening of the levitical responsibilities, probably of the gatekeepers, to a role which is presented as new, an *ad hoc* decision in the specific historical and religious circumstances: the storage and supervision of the surplus. The number of appointed persons is not incidental. It is repeated, for instance, in the number of musical performers at the tent of the ark (Asaph the chief and Zechariah his second, conducting eight Levites and two priests; cf. I Chron. 16.5–6), and constitutes the general membership of each division (I Chron. 24.9–31). This repetition of the number twelve does not necessarily point to its artificiality, but rather to the opposite: to the fixed patterns of administrative bodies. The names are more or less common levitical names, but as a group they do not appear elsewhere.

Finally we should note the adverb 'faithfully' (*be͏ʾᵉmūnāh*) which qualifies the 'bringing of the contribution' and is repeated in this chapter with regard to the distribution of the gifts (v. 15), and the registration of the Levites in the context of distribution (v. 18). This insistence on 'faith' or 'trust' is manifest in Chronicles in very specific contexts. It is repeated three times in another context dealing with the gatekeepers (I Chron. 9.22, 26, 31), once in the context of the Temple repairs (II Chron. 34.12; cf. also II Kings 12.16; 22.7), and only once again in a more general address to the judges (II Chron. 19.9). This emphasis on 'trust' in all matters concerning safe-keeping, measurements and allocation, is not incidental, and is explicitly mentioned by Nehemiah in his choice of administrators: 'and I appointed as treasurers over the storehouse ... for they were counted faithful' (Neh. 13.13).

[14–19] While v. 14 is technically a continuation of the former passage, proceeding with the names of the appointed Levites, the topic of the passage changes from 'storage' of the contribution to 'apportioning'. It introduces a general administrative document, which lays down some principles for the distribution of the gifts collected in Jerusalem.

The administration of the distribution was quite involved from the outset because of the complexity of the clergy organization during the Second Temple period. The great number of priests eligible for service gave rise to the 'division system', a mechanism by which the majority of priests and Levites dwelt in the provincial towns, while small groups came to Jerusalem, in rotation, for short terms of office. There must also have been a certain permanent, non-rotating section of the clergy, stationed in Jerusalem at all times. This division system was further complicated by the fact that according to the Pentateuchal laws, all the members of the tribe of Levi were entitled to 'portions', but these were different for 'priests' and 'Levites'. Since the contributions were collected in Jerusalem, the logistics of their distribution was rather complicated, and the standards of eligibility had to be clearly formulated. Accurate registration, and rules governing the status of officiating versus non-officiating, capital versus provincial clergy, had to be established.

The text of the passage evidences some textual disruptions, and consequently some details may be differently interpreted (cf. below), but the general principles are nevertheless clear:

(a) The 'portions' are distributed to both priests and Levites, in both Jerusalem and the provincial towns.

(b) The eligibility for the portions is determined by 'enrolment', based on genealogy, age, and place of residence.

(c) The priests receive their portions according to personal registration applying only to males, from three years onwards.

(d) The Levites receive their portions according to registration of households, including women and children, the head being from twenty years and older.

(*e*) The distribution is in the charge of the senior gatekeeper, assisted by an administrative body of six persons; the distribution for the provincial clergy is conducted in the towns by appointed administrators.

As for the structure of the passage, it has already been mentioned that v. 14 identifies as the topic 'to apportion', and gives the name of the person in charge. Verses 15–18 are devoted to the priests and Levites who serve in the Temple, each group being defined by the same terms: 'in their offices by their divisions'. In v. 16 these refer to the priests, in v. 17 to the Levites. Since the section dealing with the Levites begins in 17aβ ('The Levites, from twenty years old and upwards, in their offices by their divisions'; RSV differently), the first clause of v. 17a should be regarded as the conclusion of the passage dealing with the priests. The structure of the passage would thus be:

14 the person in charge and the topic of the passage
15–17aα distribution to the officiating priests
17aβ–18 distribution to the officiating Levites
19 distribution to the priests and Levites in the province.

An interesting feature of the passage is its peculiar syntax. It is built throughout of nominal clauses, with the verbal aspects of the sentences consistently expressed by infinitives. In the whole section there are only two declined verbs, and both appear in subordinate clauses, the one in a causative clause (v. 18), the other in a relative one (v. 19). This extreme non-narrative (or even anti-narrative) style underlines the character of the passage as a document of general applicability, but aggravates our difficulty in fully comprehending its details.

[14] Here the people's contribution for the clergy is defined with three terms: the more general 'freewill offerings to God' (*nid^eḇōt hā'^elōhīm*); what is probably the more specific 'the contribution reserved for the Lord' (*t^erūmat yhwh*); and 'the most holy offerings' (*qod^ešē haqq^odāsīm*). This terminology is different from that of v. 12, and the relationship between the two sets is unclear. Two of the terms reflect more precisely the priestly terminology of Num. 18.8ff., which distinguishes between 'the most holy things' (18.9) and the 'contribution' (18.11); the third, however, is peculiar to this text. In Num. 18, both categories relate to strictly priestly gifts, which later rabbinical law defines as 'most holy' and 'light holy' (cf. M. Haran, 'Priestly Gifts', *Encyclopedia Biblica* IV, 39*). In this context, the terms include also levitical gifts, and the procedures for their disposition is different from both Num. 18 and the rabbinic practice (cf. below).

The man in charge is 'Kore ... the Levite, keeper of the east gate'. The 'east gate', also called 'the king's gate' (I Chron. 9.18), was the charge of the primary family of gatekeepers (I Chron. 26.14), and was guarded by a larger contingent of sentinels (I Chron. 26.17). This makes Kore *primus inter pares* in the security force. The name 'Kore' is attested elsewhere among the gatekeepers (I Chron. 9.19; 26.1).

[15–17] The passage related to the priests is obscured because of a textual corruption which should be restored at the outset. The phrase 'in the cities of the priests' is impossible at this point in the text because (*a*) it creates a contradiction within the passage itself, ascribing to the priests 'in the cities' (v. 15) the office actually executed in the Temple – 'all who entered the house of the Lord as the duty of each day required, for their service according to their office by their division' (v. 16); (*b*) it also creates an unnecessary doublet to v. 19, where the priests in their cities are explicitly referred to, with the full designation of these cities: 'their towns with their adjoining fields' (JPS); (*c*) finally, with this rendering, the passage overlooks the most important constituent of the priesthood, the priests of Jerusalem.

The original version is still preserved in the LXX, where 'in the cities' (*b*ᵉ*'ārē*) is represented by διὰ χειρός (literally 'at the hand'), which clearly reflects the Hebrew idiom *b*ᵉ*yad* or *'al yad* (I Chron. 26.28; 29.8; II Chron. 23.18, etc.), rendered variously by the translations according to the various contexts: 'by', 'under', 'in the care of', etc. (cf. RSV of I Chron. 24.19; II Chron. 23.18; I Chron. 26.28). When this slight error is restored, the contradiction and the doublet disappear, and the passage refers to the priests who actually officiate in the Temple.

As Rudolph has observed (306), v. 16a consists of a parenthetical clause. Contrary to his suggestion, however, the parenthesis should begin with the parenthetical particle *mill*ᵉ*bad*, here having its common connotation 'besides, in addition to' (cf. BDB, 94; *Thesaurus*, II, 18). The parenthetical clause should read 'besides those enrolled [by genealogy], males from three years old and upwards'. The statement is made necessary by the fact that the passage deals with the *officiating* priests, describing their entire body with the term 'old and young alike' (cf. I Chron. 25.8; 26.13). In order to include all eligible priests, the note mentions those who are too young to qualify for service.

As just mentioned, according to v. 16 the priests who are entitled to shares in the 'holy offerings' are 'those who enter the house of the Lord', and 'males from three years old and upwards'. This very clearly includes the entire male constituency of the priestly body, with the concomitant exclusion of any other person. This view is very different from the Pentateuchal priestly regulations, according to which there is indeed one category of gifts (later defined by rabbinic law as 'most holy offerings') that is restricted to the male priests and should be consumed within the Temple precincts; these include 'every cereal offering ... every sin offering ... and every guilt offering' (Num. 18.9–10; cf. Ezek. 46.20). All the other gifts, however (later defined as 'light holy offerings'), may be consumed not merely by the female members of the priestly families, but by the entire households, including slaves. Cf. Num. 18.11: 'I have given them to you, and to your sons and daughters with you ...; everyone who is clean in your house may eat it', and Lev. 22.11–13: '... the slave may eat of it; and those that are born in his house may eat of his food'.

In order for the Chronicler's regulations in v. 16 to be in accord with the Pentateuchal laws, they need to be supplemented by two items: a clear indication that v. 16 applies only to the 'most holy offerings', and an additional regulation which should apply to the priests' households. Neither of these rulings is found in the present context, and they are actually refuted by it. Verse 14 includes all categories of priestly gifts, and v. 18, which refers to entire households, is clearly related to the Levites. It is probably this straightforward contradiction with priestly law which has motivated scholars to see v. 18 as relating to the priests (so also RSV), and occasionally to read v. 17b as a parenthesis; but the 'male only' rule regarding the priests and the 'general enrolment' rule for the Levites are repeated again in v. 19 in unequivocal terms: 'to every male among the priests and to every one among the Levites who was enrolled'.

This passage is thus another illustration of the Chronicler's deviation from the spirit of the Pentateuch's laws, while employing similar terminology. The two categories of eligibility are determined, according to the Chronicler's view, not by the different kinds of offering, but by the clerical class which receives them: male only for the priests, all who register for the Levites.

The passage mentions by name six persons who are in charge of the distribution, without identifying their affiliation. It is the Chronicler's view that the administration of the treasuries is the responsibility of the Levites, who are mentioned in I Chron. 26.20–26 after the gatekeepers, and this is probably assumed here as well. This is somewhat different from the view of Neh. 13.13, where the charge of the treasuries is held by 'Shelemiah the priest, Zadok the scribe, and Pedaiah of the Levites', the three assisted by Hannan, whose descent from 'Zaccur, son of Mattaniah' marks him as one of the singers. The arrangements attested by the present text may be later than those of Neh. 13.

The age of the eligible priests, 'three years old and upwards', is easily accounted for by the social customs of the ancient world. It is the age of weaning, and implies that a priest is entitled to receive his sustenance from public resources his entire life, from the very moment of his weaning.

A last point relates to the first clause of v. 17. Contrary to the present division of MT, it seems that this clause actually functions as a conclusion to the earlier passage. I would also prefer the reading of LXX, $z\bar{o}'t$, to MT $w^e'et$, introducing the concluding statement 'this is the enrolment of the priests ($z\bar{o}'t$ = 'this') according to their fathers' houses'. This demonstrative particle is extremely common in priestly documents, in either headings (cf. *inter al.* Exod. 12.43; Lev. 6.2, 7, 18; 7.1, etc.) or conclusions (cf. Lev. 7.35, 37; 11.46, etc.), and here it brings to a close the first item of the passage (cf. also I Chron. 4.33).

[17aβ–18] Moving now to the officiating Levites, 'according to their offices, by their divisions', the registration for eligibility is entirely different from that of the priests, which is probably to be explained by the rigorous rules pertaining to purity of descent, which govern the priests but not the Levites (cf. Lev. 21.7–9, 13–15; Ezek. 44.22; also Ezra 2.61–63). The Levites register 'from twenty years old and upwards', that is, from the beginning of their active service; an alternative age of qualification for service, thirty years old, is attested in some texts (cf. I Chron. 23.3). On the other hand, the registration of the Levites includes entire households, described in the most comprehensive manner: 'with all their little children, their wives, their sons, and their daughters, the whole multitude'. Since, however, the decisive criterion is that of genealogy, it seems that slaves would not be included. Thus, while the priests get their shares personally, allocated by name to each of the priests from the age of three, the Levites provide for their families through the registration of households.

RSV incorrectly interprets v. 18 as referring to the priests, and therefore marks v. 18 the beginning of a new sentence, and adds the assumed subject 'The priests'. I find no need to deviate from the original reading.

[19] After the registration of priests and Levites in Jerusalem, and in order to complete the picture, the last passage deals in very general terms with the clergy in the provincial towns. It actually lays down only the principles of distribution: every male among the priests and everyone registered among the Levites. Appointed persons ('men ... who were designated by name'), whose names or affiliation are not stated, are in charge of this task. It seems, however, that the fuller title of the priests at this point, 'the sons of Aaron, the priest', serves to emphasize the need for an accurate registration, to identify priests whose descent from Aaron is undisputable, although they dwell in their towns.

[20–21] Basically parallel to II Kings 18.5–6, these verses place a highly positive evaluation on Hezekiah's reign, rephrased completely in a series of Chronistic idioms. The first clause, with its rather nondescript statement, serves the function of connecting this passage to the preceding one: 'Thus Hezekiah did throughout all Judah.'

Hezekiah is described as having done 'what was good and right and faithful before the Lord his God' – the only king of Judah to be characterized by this three-fold epithet, and the one who possesses 'faith' (*'emet*) among his merits, repeated again in 32.1. Hezekiah succeeded in everything that he undertook because he performed it all 'with all his heart'. The areas to which he devoted his attention are detailed: the service of the house of the Lord, the Law, the commandments, and seeking his God. Note also that the leading theme of the passage is the root *ʿśh*, repeated four times, and underlining Hezekiah's active 'doing'. This is an appropriate summary of the three preceding chapters.

To the formulas found in II Kings 18.5–6 the Chronicler adds the phrase 'with all his heart', which is very common in Deuteronomy but reserved in the book of Kings for David (I Kings 14.8) and Josiah (II Kings 23.25). In Chronicles it is omitted from the evaluation of Josiah, but is added to two other monarchs: Jehoshaphat (II Chron. 22.8) and Hezekiah. In Chronicles, the figure of Hezekiah overshadows all other Judaean kings, including Josiah.

32 After these things and these acts of faithfulness Sennacherib king of Assyria came and invaded Judah and encamped against the fortified cities, thinking to win them for himself. [2] And when Hezekiah saw that Sennacherib had come and intended to fight against Jerusalem, [3] he planned with his officers and his mighty men to stop the water of the springs that were outside the city; and they helped him. [4] A great many people were gathered, and they stopped all the springs and the brook that flowed through the land, saying, 'Why should the kings of Assyria come and find much water?' [5] He set to work resolutely and built up all the wall that was broken down, and raised towers upon it, and outside it he built another wall; and he strengthened the Millo in the city of David. He also made weapons and shields in abundance. [6] And he set combat commanders over the people, and gathered them together to him in the square at the gate of the city and spoke encouragingly to them, saying, [7] 'Be strong and of good courage. Do not be afraid or dismayed before the king of Assyria and all the horde that is with him; for there is one greater with us than with him. [8] With him is an arm of flesh; but with us is the Lord our God, to help us and to fight our battles.' And the people took confidence from the words of Hezekiah king of Judah.

9 After this Sennacherib king of Assyria, who was besieging Lachish with all his forces, sent his servants to Jerusalem to Hezekiah king of Judah and to all the people of Judah that were in Jerusalem, saying, [10] 'Thus says Sennacherib king of Assyria, "On what are you relying, that you stand siege in Jerusalem? [11] Is not Hezekiah misleading you, that he may give you over to die by famine and by thirst, when he tells you, 'The Lord our God will deliver us from the hand of the king of Assyria'? [12] Has not this same Hezekiah taken away his high places and his altars and commanded Judah and Jerusalem, 'Before one altar you shall worship, and upon it you shall burn your sacrifices'? [13] Do you not know what I and my fathers have done to all the peoples of other lands? Were the gods of the nations of those lands at all able to deliver their lands out of my hand? [14] Who among all the gods of those nations which my fathers utterly destroyed was able to deliver his people from my hand, that your God should be able to deliver you from my hand? [15] Now therefore do not let Hezekiah deceive you or mislead you in this fashion, and do not believe him, for no god of any nation or kingdom has been able to deliver his people from my hand or from the hand of my fathers. How much less will your God deliver you out of my hand!"'

16 And his servants said still more against the Lord God and against his servant Hezekiah. [17] And he wrote letters to cast contempt on the Lord the God of Israel and to speak against him, saying, 'Like the gods of the nations of the lands who have not delivered their people from my hands, so the God of Hezekiah will not deliver his people from my hand.' [18] And they shouted it with a loud voice in the language of Judah to the people of Jerusalem who were upon the wall, to frighten and terrify them, in order that they might take the city. [19] And they spoke of the God of Jerusalem as they spoke of the gods of the peoples of the earth, which are the work of men's hands.

20 Then Hezekiah the king and Isaiah the prophet, the son of Amoz, prayed because of this and cried to heaven. [21] And the Lord sent an angel, who cut off all the mighty warriors and commanders and officers in the camp of the king of Assyria. So he returned with shame of face to his own land. And when he came into the house of his god, some of his own sons struck him down there with the sword. [22] So the Lord saved Hezekiah and the inhabitants of Jerusalem from the hand of Sennacherib king of Assyria and from the hand of all his enemies; and he gave them rest on every side. [23] And many brought gifts to the Lord to Jerusalem and precious things to Hezekiah king of Judah, so that he was exalted in the sight of all nations from that time onward.

24 In those days Hezekiah became sick and was at the point of death, and he prayed to the Lord; and he answered him and gave him a sign. [25] But Hezekiah did not make return according to the benefit done to him, for his heart was proud. Therefore wrath came upon him and Judah and Jerusalem. [26] But Hezekiah humbled himself for the pride of his heart, both he and the inhabitants of Jerusalem, so that the wrath of the Lord did not come upon them in the days of Hezekiah.

27 And Hezekiah had very great riches and honour; and he made for himself treasuries for silver, for gold, for precious stones, for spices, for shields, and for all kinds of costly vessels; [28] storehouses also for the yield of grain, wine, and oil; and stalls for all kinds of cattle, and sheepfolds. [29] He likewise provided cities for himself, and flocks and herds in abundance; for God had given him very great possessions. [30] This same Hezekiah closed the upper outlet of the waters of Gihon and directed them down to the west side of the city of David. And Hezekiah prospered in all his works. [31] And so in the matter of the envoys of the princes of Babylon, who had been sent to him to inquire about the sign that had been done in the land, God left him to himself, in order to try him and to know all that was in his heart.

32 Now the rest of the acts of Hezekiah, and his good deeds, behold, they are written in the vision of Isaiah the prophet the son of Amoz, in the Book of the Kings of Judah and Israel. [33] And Hezekiah slept with his fathers, and they buried him in the ascent of the tombs of the sons of David; and all Judah and the inhabitants of Jerusalem did him honour at his death. And Manasseh his son reigned in his stead.

A. Notes to MT

[5] עַל הַמִּגְדָּלוֹת, read מִגְדָּלוֹת; עָלֶיהָ; הַחוֹמָה אַחֶרֶת, irregular, read חוֹמָה אַחֶרֶת (dittography) or הַחוֹמָה הָאַחֶרֶת (haplography); [22] וַיְנַהֲלֵם, probably read וַיָּנַח לָהֶם; [24] וַיֹּאמֶר, probably read וַיֵּעָתֶר; [28] עֲדָרִים לָאֲוֵרוֹת, probably corrupt, read וַאֲרָוֹת לַעֲדָרִים; [29] וְעָרִים, proposed וַעֲדָרִים, cf. v. 28.

B. Notes to RSV

[3] 'he planned', better 'he consulted' (NEB, JPS); [5] 'raised towers upon it', cf. above A; [7] 'one greater', better 'more' (NEB, JPS), cf. commentary; [22] 'his enemies', not in MT; 'and he gave them rest', MT 'he provided for them' (JPS), cf. above A; [24] 'he answered him', MT 'he said to him', cf. above A; [28] 'sheepfolds', MT differently, cf. above A; [33] 'ascent', NEB 'uppermost', JPS 'upper part'.

C. Structure, sources and form

1. Chapter 32 is a thorough reworking of II Kings 18.13–20.21, dealing with Sennacherib's campaign, Hezekiah's illness, the visit of the Babylonian envoys and

Hezekiah's grandeur. Its dependence on the Deuteronomistic source is evident throughout, and the technique by which it adapts this source constitutes an instructive example of two aspects of the Chronicler's literary method: the employment of the Deuteronomistic story of Kings as his point of departure on the one hand, and the extensive reworking through omissions, additions, rephrasing and epitomization on the other. The Deuteronomistic material has undergone a drastic abbreviation – about 50 lines replacing about 150 – but, as a detailed synopsis may show, most of the issues presented in II Kings 18–20 are also included in the Chronicler's version, and their original order is carefully followed.

Because the general tendency of the Chronicler is to abbreviate, the Chronistic additions are all the more significant. These include a short speech by Hezekiah (vv. 7–8); several passages describing practical matters absent from the prophetic story: military and administrative preparations for the war (vv. 3–6, 30); Hezekiah's political and economic achievements (vv. 23, 27–29); and some theological comments (vv. 25–26, 31b).

2. Overall, the main body of the chapter comprises two unequal parts, the first dedicated to Sennacherib's campaign, and the second to 'the rest of Hezekiah's reign'. The structure of the chapter may be sketched as follows:

    A. 1–23 Sennacherib's campaign
      (*a*) 1 introduction
      (*b*) 2–8 preparations for war
        2 the threat
        3–6a practical preparations
        6b–8 spiritual preparations
      (*c*) 9–15 Sennacherib's delegation
        9 the delegation
        10–15 the address
      (*d*) 16–19 varia
      (*e*) 20–21 prayer and delivery
      (*f*) 22–23 conclusion
    B. 24–31 Further information on Hezekiah's reign
      (*a*) 24–26 Hezekiah's illness
      (*b*) 27–30 Hezekiah's enterprises
      (*c*) 31 the Babylonian visit
    C. 32–33 Conclusion.

3. The adaptive character of the chapter will become abundantly clear in the commentary, but it may be anticipated by a synopsis of the two parallel pericopes:

II Kings 18.13//II Chron. 32.1;
II Kings 18.17–18//II Chron. 32.9;
II Kings 18.19–25, 28–35//II Chron. 32.10–15;
II Kings 18.26–27, 36//II Chron. 32.18;
II Kings 19.1–4; 14–19//II Chron. 32.20;
II Kings 19.9b–13//II Chron. 32.17, 19;
II Kings 19.35–37//II Chron. 32.21;
II Kings 20.1–11//II Chron. 32.24–26;

II Kings 20.12–19//II Chron. 32.31;
II Kings 20.20–21//II Chron. 32.32–33.

Entirely absent from the Chronicler's presentation are several passages concerning political matters: the rebellion (II Kings 18.7–8); the tax (II Kings 18.14–16); the move of the Assyrian force from Lachish to Libnah, and the intermediate episode with the Cushite Tirhaka (II Kings 19.8–9). These were all omitted for the sake of creating a simpler and more unified account, and to some degree may have been influenced by the parallel account of Isa. 36–39, which does not contain the first two.

The comprehensive epitomization is achieved by the omission of various details and extensive rhetorical passages such as Hezekiah's prayers (II Kings 19.3–4, 15–19) and Isaiah's prophecies (19.6–7, 20–34; 20.5–6, 16–18), as well as the whole interaction of king and prophet. The Chronicler's version of Sennacherib's campaign is much simpler, with all the unclear features, mostly of a political nature, omitted, and its course is straightforward, with no deviations: invasion – military and psychological preparations – [siege] – call for surrender – prayer – delivery. Although the other two episodes – Hezekiah's illness and the visit of the Babylonian envoys – are represented in Chronicles in drastically abbreviated passages, both are accompanied by theological commentary.

4. Since the main body of the chapter is an adaptation of II Kings 18–20, the question of 'sources' applies only to the material without parallels: did the Chronicler rely on any sources for these sections? We have already noticed that the additions are of three kinds: oratorical disquisitions, theological comments and various details about matters of state.

(a) Hezekiah's address to the people (vv. 7–8) can be easily recognized as the Chronicler's work. Its inclusion conforms to the Chronicler's method of adding passages of a persuasive, rhetorical nature at various crucial points in the story, and the people's response, making them full partners in the situation ('the people took confidence from the words of Hezekiah') is a major feature in the Chronistic historiography.

The style, language and contents of the address also reflect characteristic Chronistic features. One must mention phrases like 'be strong and of good courage', 'do not be afraid or dismayed', 'horde' (המון), 'to help us' (לעזרנו) as recurrent Chronistic elements. The style is marked by the more general rhetorical technique of juxtaposition and opposition, 'with us – with him', and the more specific anthological style: the re-integration of existing phrases and formulas into a new texture. Also to be mentioned is the constant repetition of one theme, that of 'with': 'with him ... with us ... with him, with him ... with us'. The theme itself belongs to the general biblical thesaurus, but it is especially common in Chronicles, where it has two aspects: the idea that the Lord fights for Israel (e.g. II Chron. 20.15–17), and the juxtaposition of the human king with the divine one (cf. in particular II Chron. 12.8). The theological comments, of which vv. 25–26 are the more conspicuous, may serve as a model for Chronistic style and theology.

(b) Verses 3–6 are of a different genre, and describe Hezekiah's tactical preparations in the face of Sennacherib's invasion. Their style, phrasing and some subjects include definite Chronistic favourites: 'he took counsel', 'they helped him', the massive popular participation, and the rhetorical element in the question. 'Why should the kings of Assyria ... find much water?' However, beyond these, the content of this passage does not reflect common Chronistic themes; the matters discussed have no parallel in Chronicles, they do not belong to any 'topos', traditional or idiosyncratic, and they are very relevant and perfectly suited to the situation at hand. The stopping of 'all the springs' and 'the brook that flowed through the land', and the building of another wall – specific to this context – have nothing exaggerated, miraculous or aggrandized about them.

In trying to evaluate these data, a preliminary remark is indicated. The story of II Kings 18.13–19.37 is characterized by an interesting feature: the absolute silence about any practical steps taken by either Hezekiah or his people in the face of Sennacherib's threat or during the siege. Only at the conclusion of Hezekiah's reign – which does not form part of the 'prophetic story' – do we hear about Hezekiah's 'might', and how 'he made the pool and the conduit and brought water into the city' (II Kings 20.20). The omission of these facts in II Kings should therefore be regarded as a significant feature of the prophetic story and should alert us against evaluating its evidence as conclusive.

A different picture emerges from some of Isaiah's contemporary prophecies. In the first place, Isaiah describes the actual preparations: 'and you counted the houses of Jerusalem, and you broke down the houses to fortify the walls. You made a reservoir between the two walls for the water of the old pool' (Isa. 22.10–11a). Secondly, it is specifically these practical steps which evoke Isaiah's anger, as he rebukes Hezekiah and his people for trusting in these for their security and not turning to the Lord for help: 'But you did not look to him who did it, or have regard for him who planned it long ago' (Isa. 22.11b).

As there is no reason to doubt the probability or authenticity of the data itself, the question becomes rather one of the Chronicler's historiographical method: did he cull these data from some extra-biblical source, or did he compose them himself, drawing on what he found in the books of Isaiah and Kings? As will become clearer in the commentary the passage is not dependent on the texts of either Kings or Isaiah in subject-matter, language or terminology, but goes its own way; it is best accounted for as being based on an additional independent source.

Summing up vv. 1–8, we may conclude the following. In writing this unit, the Chronicler made use of two sources, the Deuteronomistic history, from which he utilized II Kings 18.13, and an extra-biblical source, from which he drew the subject matter of vv. 2–6. These two were joined, retouched with the Chronicler's language, and modified to match his particular views and aims. To these, the Chronicler added Hezekiah's address and the people's response in vv. 7–8, establishing the background and framework for Sennacherib's campaign. Having omitted II Kings 18.14–16, he returns in v. 9 to the parallel text of II Kings 18.17ff., which describes the Assyrian delegation's encounter with the people of Judah.

(c) The next addition from the realm of events is the passage in vv. 27–30, which describes Hezekiah's constructional and economic enterprises and achievements. We have already encountered the Chronicler's view that a king's worldly success is a corollary of his righteousness, leading him to attribute such worldly achievements only to the righteous kings. Should we see this theological concept as the *actual source* of this data, or merely as the guide, which directed the Chronicler to choose from his sources?

In discussing the problem of historicity, two aspects should be distinguished:

subject-matter as such and chronology. Although the data of vv. 27–29 are quite general, the passage is not a stereotyped record, and it is only lightly retouched by Chronistic language. It is focussed on one topic, 'construction', depicting Hezekiah's various building projects, while ignoring other concerns of state administration, such as the military, or even building for military purposes. Nor is it exaggerated in any way, and the items listed in it belong to common and expected matters of royal menage. These arguments are supported by extra-biblical evidence. Archaeological discoveries attest to increased economic activity during this period (cf. N. Na'aman, 'Sennacherib's campaign to Judah', *VT* 29, 1979, 70–86). The central role of Hezekiah in the anti-Assyrian league attests to considerable power and also may have involved more intensive political and economic activity. The unprecedented increase in the population of Jerusalem (cf. M. Broshi, 'The Expansion of Jerusalem in the Reigns of Hezekiah and Manasseh', *IEJ* 24, 1974, 21–6), even if not itself caused by economic factors, certainly had economic consequences, and the extraordinary record of booty in Sennacherib's Rassam cylinder (cf. Cogan–Tadmor, *II Kings*, 339) may also bear on this matter. Although the latter's extraordinary detail may have served the purpose of Assyrian propaganda, there must have been at least some truth to it.

As for v. 30, the principal question concerns the relationship between this material and II Kings 20.20: does the Chronicler relate these details on the basis of some source, or does he merely re-adapt the Deuteronomistic material? Furthermore, should the 'Siloam tunnel' be connected to this historical context of Hezekiah's times, or should it be separated from it? The general consensus – although not without challenge (cf. R. North, 'Does Archeology Prove Chronicles' Sources?', *Festschrift J. M. Myers*, 1974, 375–9) – is that the Siloam tunnel should be attributed to the time of Hezekiah, and that the evidence of Chronicles is independent of Kings, and supported by archaeological evidence. Summing up all these pieces of evidence, we may attribute to Hezekiah's time a period of economic prosperity, reflected to some extent in this passage.

The other aspect to be considered is that of the chronology of this passage, connected to the more basic problem of the reconstruction of Hezekiah's chronology in general. Three chronological factors come into play here: the generally (but not unequivocally) accepted date of Sennacherib's campaign as 701 BCE; the date of Hezekiah's reign, alternately determined as either between 727 and 698 BCE (cf. Tadmor, *Encyclopedia Biblica* 4, 1962, 262* for a comparative table), or 716/15–687/86 BCE (E. R. Thiele, *Mysterious Numbers of the Hebrew Kings*, 1983, 135–6, 174–7), to cite only the two most common; and, if the Chronistic literary structure is interpreted as having chronological implications, whether the date of this prosperity is posterior to the withdrawal of the Assyrian army. If Hezekiah's reign is placed between 727 and 698 BCE, the Chronicler's dating would be very unlikely; it would be quite reasonable, on the other hand, if Hezekiah's reign is placed between 716–687 BCE. It seems, however, that the chronological issue should be approached as an aspect of the Chronistic historiography. For the Chronicler, the placing of Hezekiah's prosperity and economic activity where they are was more likely determined by literary and theological considerations, but they may nevertheless reflect Hezekiah's economic and building activity in various periods of his reign. While the data itself may have derived from authentic sources, their chronology must be determined by non-Chronistic considerations.

5. To sum up: the Chronicler has reworked the history of Hezekiah in a comprehensive sweep, and ch. 32 occupies a special place in this reworking. In summary fashion, the Chronicler represents in this chapter the broad pericope of II Kings 18–20, with all the major events recorded but greatly abbreviated. The Chronicler has also used another source, from which he drew such details as the actualities of the reign of Hezekiah, which are missing from the Deuteronomistic record. All this material has been cast in a new framework, and several passages were added to it, resulting in a new portrait of Hezekiah himself and his reign.

D. Commentary

As I claimed above and will demonstrate extensively throughout the commentary, the Chronicler's version of Sennacherib's campaign, Hezekiah's illness and the Babylonian visit is basically an adaptation, along literary and theological lines, of the Deuteronomistic account. Therefore problems of a historical nature, pertaining to the chronology of these events, the composition and historicity of the Deuteronomistic account, the relationship between the biblical material and the Assyrian evidence and, consequently, the historical re-construction of the events against their international background, all arise from the original account of II Kings 18–20, and are of only secondary relevance for its Chronistic reworking. Our interest should thus focus on the Chronicler's historiographical endeavour; for the ongoing debate on all these historical matters, the reader may consult Cogan–Tadmor, *II Kings*, 223–63.

[1] While dependent on II Kings 18.13, v. 1 opens the story of Sennacherib's campaign not by the date ('the fourteenth year of king Hezekiah'), but by a general conjunctive formula: 'After these things'. The conventional phrasing of this formula is subtly changed by the addition of the word $w^e h\bar{a}'^e met$ (RSV 'and these acts of faithfulness'), immediately linking the story to the earlier conclusion of Hezekiah's enterprises: 'Hezekiah did what was good and right and faithful ($w^e h\bar{a}'^e met$) before the Lord his God' (32.20). Since 'the way the Chronicler introduces a narrative is often a key to his primary purpose in using it' (Dillard, 256), the sequence between Sennacherib's campaign and the earlier account points to its specific perspective. According to the Chronicler's view, in the divine order of the world the most common purpose of wars and invasions is punishment for human transgression. The attribution of such a role to Sennacherib's invasion, however, is absolutely out of the question, since Hezekiah's unparalleled righteousness has just been so enthusiastically acclaimed (31.20–21). The link between chs. 31 and 32 must therefore be interpreted differently, as a case of a divine test, and one wonders whether the similar beginning of this verse and Gen. 22.1 does not serve as a clue to the correct interpretation. The depth of Hezekiah's uprightness will be plumbed by the foreign invasion, and will demonstrate to

what level of faith he may rise in difficult moments. His response to this challenge will determine his fate and the well-being of his kingdom.

According to the record of II Kings 18.13 and Sennacherib's inscriptions, Sennacherib conquered all the fortified cities of Judah, forty-six in all. The siege of Jerusalem marked the conclusion and climax of this conquest; Hezekiah, according to Sennacherib's very famous metaphor, remained in Jerusalem 'like a bird in a cage' (Tadmor–Cogan, *II Kings*, 338). This, however, is not the picture which one takes from the Chronicler's presentation. According to his account, Sennacherib did not actually conquer the cities of Judah but only *thought* 'to win them for himself'. Therefore, the move against Jerusalem is not the end but the beginning of this campaign, part of his plans for the whole of Judah.

The theological significance of this change is transparent. According to the Chronicler's most basic theological principles, the conquest of the Judaean cities would constitute a divine punishment. Cf. II Chron. 12.2–4: 'In the fifth year of king Rehoboam, because they had been unfaithful to the Lord, Shishak king of Egypt came up against Jerusalem ... And he took the fortified cities of Judah and came as far as Jerusalem', which includes the telling Chronistic addition 'because they were unfaithful to the Lord'. At this point in Judah's history, any kind of punishment would be quite inappropriate, and thus all we have is Sennacherib's 'plan' to take over these cities. The change of the historical picture is so very clearly the result of theological considerations that hardly any historical value should be assigned to it.

[2–6] Hezekiah's reaction is immediate. As he realizes Sennacherib's destination, that he 'intended to fight against Jerusalem', Hezekiah organizes all available resources. His first steps are all on the practical, military plane; his prayer to the Lord is mentioned only in v. 20, and even then with great concision. We should note this feature against, for instance, the initial reaction of Jehoshaphat in the face of the Ammonite invasion, which is portrayed as fear on the one hand and excited invocation of the Lord on the other: 'Then Jehoshaphat feared, and set himself to seek the Lord, and proclaimed a fast', etc. (20.3ff.). His military preparations are postponed until after the Lord's answer is delivered through a prophet (II Chron. 20.20). Hezekiah acts with confidence and resolution as he attends to three essential matters: water (vv. 3–4), fortification and weapons (v. 5), and the military organization of the people (v. 6). Yet his words to the people (vv. 7–8a) disclose that the true source of his confidence is not his own might but his trust in the Lord, who is the source of all strength.

This is a very clear illustration of the Chronicler's theological stand with regard to divine aid. God's help is provided to those who trust him, and he often grants to the few and weak victory over the many and strong. This decision, however, is absolutely at God's discretion and is not to be presumed upon by man. The Lord's miraculous intervention does not exempt man from taking all necessary steps demanded by the concrete situation. As illustrated by our pericope, Sennacherib's failure was brought about by the angel of the Lord (v. 21) and not by Hezekiah's military force, but it was Hezekiah's primary duty on his part to undertake all possible human measures.

[3–4] The issue of 'water' is dealt with in the Hezekiah pericope in three places: here, in II Kings 20.20, and in v. 30 below, but the actions described here approach this issue from a particular perspective. Verse 30 and II Kings 20.20 deal with the supply of water to Jerusalem: 'He … brought water into the city' (II Kings 20.20), or 'directed them down to the west side of the city of David' (II Chron. 32.30), a matter of enormous significance for a city in siege, in particular Jerusalem. This passage deals with another matter: denying Sennacherib's army access to water, cast as a rhetorical question: 'Why should the kings of Assyria come and find much water?' This is in fact the only case in the Bible where this topic is referred to – the active diversion of a water supply from an invading enemy. This goal determines the course of action: stopping the springs out of the city and the brook that flows through the land. (For the acuteness of the problem cf. II Kings 3.9ff., and for the practice implied, Gen. 26.15, 18; II Kings 3.19, 25.)

Great emphasis is laid in this passage on the co-operation of the people. Hezekiah 'takes counsel' with his staff, 'they helped him', the act of stopping the springs is carried out by 'a great many people', and – as on many other occasions – the purpose of the project is explained with clear arguments and a tone of persuasion. This is a popular undertaking in its full sense, and the people are taking action because they are convinced of its necessity.

The actual mechanics themselves are less clear. It has been taken as a matter of fact that these verses deal with the same projects described in the other two passages; the plural 'springs' has been understood as a generalized reference to the Gihon, while the 'flowing stream' was seen as the Kidron (cf. among many others, J. Simons, *Jerusalem in the Old Testament*, 1952, 186; P. R. Ackroyd, 'The Chronicler as Exegete', *JSOT* 2, 1977, 11; Williamson, 380–1). This interpretation may have already inspired the LXX rendering 'through the city' in place of the MT 'through the land'. Since no names are provided, it is difficult to pinpoint the precise terrain or measures to which the Chronicler is referring, and the wording, speaking of springs in general and their 'stopping', with no similarity at all to the other passages, makes unambiguous identification rather doubtful. If indeed 'stopping' of the springs and not 'redirecting' is intended, this must be regarded as a temporary expedience, as it may severely affect the local population as well. Nevertheless, one may still consider a temporary stopping of the springs within the realm of possibility, especially if the occlusion refers to the small springs of the Judaean hills; it is more difficult to see how the 'brook which flows through the land' is stopped. The rendering 'brook' for *naḥal* seems to represent one attempt to overcome this difficulty, since the same word may also be rendered 'river' (Ezek. 47.6, 7, 9, etc. and many more), 'stream' (regularly), or even 'torrent', in particular when qualified by *šōṭēp* (cf. Jer. 47.2: 'waters are rising out ... and shall become an overflowing torrent'; see also Isa. 30.28; 66.12; etc.). On the other hand, the Chronicler may have chosen to employ a more elevated term (as he occasionally does), while still having a very particular 'stream' in mind. Since no names are given, and the 'flowing stream' cannot be identified, the precise steps remain obscure.

[5] Hezekiah's preparations inside the city, this time ascribed to him alone, are devoted to two matters: fortifications of the city and the supply of weapons. Four projects referring to fortifications are mentioned laconically:

1. Repair of the breaches in the existing wall. This undertaking belongs to the regular maintenance of the wall, not necessarily indicating a previous breaching of the wall or particular negligence.

2. Construction of towers on the wall, the role of which is not specified.

3. Building of a new wall outside the old one. The succinct text does not include any detail regarding the line or length of this wall, but some data may be gathered from Isa. 22.10–11, the two texts supporting each other. Isaiah 22.11 testifies that there were indeed two walls around Jerusalem, and that at some point the ground between them was inundated to create a reservoir, either for extra protection, or as part of the water system. It is also clear that this building project was launched under the pressure of wartime; the stones were taken from houses inside the city, broken down for that very purpose. (For the possible archeological identification of this wall and its tentative line, cf. N. Avigad, 'Excavations in the Jewish Quarter of the Old City Jerusalem 1969/1970, Preliminary Report II', *IEJ* 20, 1970, 129–34.)

4. A specific strengthening of the Millo of the city of David, which also conforms to Isa. 22.9: '... and you saw that the breaches of the city of David were many'.

This, then, together with the provision of 'weapons and shields in abundance', is a systematic strengthening of the city and a complementing of its fortification system. It accounts well for the difficulties which Sennacherib encountered in his attempt to conquer the city, and may have contributed to his eventual withdrawal.

[6] The final step in Hezekiah's preparation is directed to the human factor, the organization of a military force (v. 6) and the bolstering of their morale (vv. 7–8). This passage does not belong to the category of notices about the army which we found concerning the days of Asa, Jehoshaphat, Amaziah and Uzziah (II Chron. 14.7; 17.13–19; 25.5; 26.11–13). In contrast

to these reports, no details are supplied here: no names, numbers, or the division of the army by tribes or families. Hezekiah prepares the people by appointing 'combat commanders over the people'; it is an *ad hoc* step which does not refer to the regular or even the conscript army, but probably includes the whole citizenry of Jerusalem, a comprehensive organization of all the military power of the city, in view of the impending danger.

[7–8] Hezekiah's address to the people is concise and entirely appropriate to the occasion, neither undervaluing nor exaggerating the danger. It juxtaposes the two forces, 'the king of Assyria and all the horde that is with him', with the stronger force of the Lord, which is the source of Hezekiah's confidence. This juxtaposition is made in two ways, first in general terms: 'we have more (JPS; RSV 'one greater') with us than he has with him'. The decisive point is 'more' (*rab*) – the king of Assyria has got 'all the horde with him', and yet, there is more with us! This 'more' is then presented for what it is: he has 'an arm of flesh', and we have, says Hezekiah, 'the Lord our God, to help us and to fight our battles'. The conclusion to be drawn from this reasoning is stated at the beginning: 'Be strong and of good courage'.

The Lord's 'being with' individuals or the whole people, particularly in battle, is a common biblical theme (cf. Num. 14.43; Deut. 20.4; Judg. 6.12–16, etc.), but it is specifically in the context of the Assyrian threat that it is epitomized by Isaiah as Immanuel, 'God is with us', to become a token of faith (Isa. 7.14; 8.8, 10). It is probable that the Chronicler is here drawing specifically upon these prophecies of Isaiah (Ackroyd, 192).

In both contents and phraseology, Hezekiah's address is very similar to the prophecy in ch. 20 of Jahaziel to Jehoshaphat and his people before the war with Ammon (the similarity, however, being somewhat obscured by the different translations):

vv. 7–8	*20.15*
Do not be afraid or dismayed before ... all the horde that is with him;	Do not be afraid or dismayed at this great horde;
with us is the Lord our God, to help us and to fight our battles.	for the battle is not yours but God's.

However, Jahaziel's words are defined as a prophecy, the Lord's answer to Jehoshaphat through inspiration; Hezekiah's words issue from the force of his own faith.

Inserted at this point, Hezekiah's address serves several purposes. The very approach of the king turns the people into active partners in the battle against Sennacherib. This feature is greatly highlighted when compared with the people's role and stance in the prophetical story in II Kings 18–19, with the very famous request of Hezekiah's representatives to the Assyrian delegation demanding surrender: 'Pray, speak to your servants in the Aramaic language, for we understand it; do not speak to us in the language of Judah within the hearing of the people who are on the wall' (II Kings 18.26). The officials wish to keep the people as far as possible from the Assyrians' threats and flattery, while the Assyrians themselves seek to create a conflict of interests between the people and the king. Using the argument of 'incitement', blaming Hezekiah for misleading his people by empty promises, the Rabshakeh attempts to seduce the people to turn against Hezekiah and surrender. The reaction of the audience to all this may be described as 'controlled passivity': 'But the people were silent and answered him not a word, for the king's command was: "Do not answer him"' (II Kings 18.36). Not so in Chronicles. Here Hezekiah shares his great faith in the Lord with his people, and does so in preparation for the assault and not as a result of it. It thus becomes the faith of the whole people.

The address also presents Hezekiah himself in a different light from the prophetic story of Kings. Although he appears there as a person of strong faith in the Lord, praying to him and sending a delegation to Isaiah to seek his word, the general tone is one of despair and loss of direction: 'This day is a day of distress, of rebuke, and of disgrace' (II Kings 19.3). In Chronicles, Hezekiah is a man of faith and resolution, and he is fully capable of leading and inspiring his people.

[9–15] Sennacherib's address to Hezekiah and his people is a careful and concise summary of II Kings 18.17–37. According to the Kings version, Sennacherib's approach follows several stages: a delegation sent from Lachish meets with Hezekiah's representatives (vv. 17–18); the latter hear the Rabshakeh's words (vv. 19–25), which are interrupted by an argument regarding the language (vv. 26–27); then comes a second address of the Rabshakeh, this time to 'the people on the wall', and their reaction (vv. 28–36); the account ends with the officers' return to Hezekiah (v. 37).

All this the Chronicler summarizes into eight verses, with drastic changes in presentation. All the secondary figures – the Rabshakeh and his entourage on the one side, Hezekiah's princes and officers on the other – are removed from the scene. The name 'Rabshakeh' appears eight times in Kings, and Hezekiah's officials are mentioned by name in II Kings 18.18, 26, 37; 19.2; they are all ignored in Chronicles. Sennacherib sends 'his servants' and they relate what they were told 'to Hezekiah king of Judah and to all the people of Judah that were in Jerusalem' (v. 9). The two speeches are combined into one as a kind of anthology, the Chronicler quoting complete sentences or fragments and adding very little of his own, and the intermediate negotiations regarding the language are hinted at later, in v. 18. Ultimately, however, the new speech has its own emphases.

While the Rabshakeh's two addresses in Kings challenge Hezekiah's trust in the Lord, the details of his argument are different in each case. His address to Hezekiah is a direct bid for surrender (18.19–25), departing from the rhetorical question, 'On what do you rest this confidence of yours?' (v. 20). To Hezekiah's possible reply he has ready counter-answers. If you imagine that you will rely on military force, either your own or that of Egypt, you have none of yourself (vv. 23–24), and Egypt is 'a broken reed of a staff' (v. 21); if you rely on your God, you have forfeited your claim to his help by removing his high places and altars (v. 22). Moreover, it is precisely in the service of your God that Assyria has come upon the land: 'the Lord said to me, Go up against this land, and destroy it' (v. 25).

The Rabshakeh uses a different set of arguments in his approach to the people sitting on the walls of Jerusalem (II Kings 18.29–35). Since his goal is to incite the people against their king, he claims that Hezekiah forfeited the people's trust, has made empty promises, and neither he nor his God will save the expectant people. The prudent way out of the dilemma is to surrender, a move which will also carry with it material profit (vv. 31–32). There is none greater, stronger or better than the king of Assyria (vv. 33–35).

From all these lines of argument the Chronicler picks only one, and in contrast to his own introduction (v. 9), addresses it to the people alone, speaking of Hezekiah in the third person (vv. 11, 12, 15). Sennacherib, in Chronicles, reacts only to Hezekiah's claim that the Lord will save Israel from the hands of Assyria and his arguments rest on the following points: the Lord will not help, because Hezekiah has removed his high places and altars; he will not help, because he is unable to help. None of the gods could withstand Assyria, and the God of Israel is no exception. This last point is clearly Sennacherib's most important claim; it is repeated twice within this address, with almost the same phrases (vv. 13–14, 15b), consumes the larger part of the speech, and is repeated again in v. 17.

Another major change in the Chronicler's adaptation is the explicit expression of ideas which in II Kings 18.33–35 are merely implied. Although the Rabshakeh states repeatedly that the Lord 'will not save' in the same way that the gods of the nations did not save (II Kings 18.33, 34, 35; 19.12), he never expresses doubts in the Lord's *ability* to save, his only reference to 'ability' being directed to Hezekiah (18.29). One may even infer from his careful rhetoric that he does concede the Lord's potency, but Jerusalem will not be saved because the Lord himself acts against her: did he not send the king of Assyria to destroy the land (18.25)?

In rephrasing the Rabshakeh's words, the Chronicler emphasizes the Assyrians' claim that the Lord is *unable* to save his people (cf. Williamson, 384). His version of the Assyrian address is composed of a series of key words, insistently repeated and juxtaposed: be able, vv. 13, 13, 14, 14, 15; save, vv. 11, 13, 14, 14, 15, 15; mislead, vv. 11, 15, 15; the nations, the nations of the lands, vv. 13, 13, 14, 15; Lord, God, god, vv. 11, 11, 13, 14, 14, 15, 15; I, me, my fathers, vv. 13, 13, 14, 14, 15; you, vv. 11. 14. 15.

[9] According to the precise phrasing of this verse, no siege of Jerusalem actually takes place. Sennacherib stays in Lachish (also II Kings 18.17), with 'all his forces', and from there he sends a modest delegation for the purpose of negotiating with Hezekiah and his people. Later, he will also send Hezekiah letters (v. 17). This is very different from the story of II Kings 18, where Sennacherib's military commanders are sent to Jerusalem 'with a great army' (II Kings 18.17), and the siege is the central point of the whole event. Notwithstanding this change, we find an allusion to this siege also in Chronicles, included in Sennacherib's address: 'On what are you relying, that you stand siege in Jerusalem?' (v. 10). This disharmony is a direct result of the Chronicler's literary method. While carefully reworking the story in contents and phrasing, the Chronicler still insists on producing an adaptation of an existing text and not a new composition; the price to be paid is the unavoidable tension between old and new.

[10–11] In II Kings 18.19–20, Sennacherib's first challenge is expressed as a series of rhetorical questions: 'On whom do you now rely, that you have rebelled against me?' This reference to 'rebellion', which alludes to the political context of the event (also II Kings 18.7, 14), has been omitted in Chronicles entirely, together with other notes of political interest, such as Hezekiah's feats against the Philistines (II Kings 18.8), and in particular the league with Egypt (II Kings 18.21, 24), which is referred to also in the words of Isaiah (Isa. 30.2–5; 31.1–3). Preserving the form of a rhetorical question, the political allusion is replaced by a description of the situation in Jerusalem based on other excerpts from the pericope, in particular II Kings 18.27.

[12] Sennacherib's claim that Hezekiah had removed the Lord's altars and high places is cited in full from II Kings 18.22 but contains one further emphasis. In place of 'you shall worship before *this* altar in Jerusalem' the Chronicler reads 'before *one* altar' (LXX, however, here displays the reading of II Kings 18.22). The significance of this statement for the history of the Israelite cult has been pointed out repeatedly; notwithstanding its actual source, it proves that the movement for the centralization of the cult was initiated by Hezekiah, and it is only the Deuteronomist's preference for Josiah which made him the almost exclusive hero of this cultic revolution.

[13] The example of the world at large constitutes an important element in II Kings as well (18.33–35 and 19.11–13). This argument gains in rhetorical force by the listing of the names of the conquered peoples, including Samaria: 'Where are the gods of Hamath and Arpad? Where are the gods of Spharvaim, Hena and Ivva?' (18.34). The list is repeated in 19.12 to include over ten names altogether. The Chronicler remains in the general sphere, referring repeatedly to 'peoples, nations, lands, kingdoms'. Furthermore, in

the Rabshakeh's addresses, the hero of these conquests is Sennacherib himself (II Kings 18.29, 30, 31, 32, 33, 34, 35), and it is only in a different context that his predecessors are mentioned (19.12: 'the nations which my fathers destroyed'). By contrast, the Chronicler emphasizes that these wide conquests are the work of many Assyrian kings, referred to in the mouth of Sennacherib as 'I and my fathers' (vv. 13, 14, 15). For the Chrounicler, then, 'Assyria' is not one single king, but an existential threat to the world of nations.

[16–19] The actual continuation of the story comes in v. 20, with Hezekiah's prayer to the Lord in response to the Assyrian threats. The intervening vv. 16–19 stand out as a separate block, illustrating the Chronicler's literary methods. The passage consists of a group of summary statements, superfluous in the present context; they are fully understood only against the background of their source.

In v. 16 the Chronicler himself accounts for the literary method which he has just employed by stating explicitly that what has been cited of Sennacherib's words constitutes only a fraction of his addresses: 'his servants said still more against the Lord God and against his servant Hezekiah'. Verse 17 refers back to II Kings 19.9–14, which recounts the dispatch of a second Assyrian delegation to Hezekiah. While the Chronicler presents the contents of the 'letters' as repeating some of the themes already addressed, the precise phrasing of v. 17 is influenced by Hezekiah's words that Sennacherib sent his messengers 'to mock the living God' (II Kings 19.4, 16).

In v. 18 the Chronicler picks another element from the text of Kings: the Rabshakeh's direct address to the people sitting on the wall, in their own language – both a summary of II Kings 18.26–27, and a commentary on it. The sophisticated weave of incitement, seduction and threats, designated to ease the Assyrian conquest of Jerusalem, is seen for what it is: 'to frighten and terrify them, in order that they might take the city'. The precise synopsis is thus:

18a	And they shouted it with a loud voice in the language of Judah	II Kings 18.28
18b	to the people of Jerusalem who were upon the wall	II Kings 18.27
	to frighten … take the city	summary and commentary

Verse 19 concludes this series of notes with an epitome of all the Assyrian addresses: they compare the God of Israel to the gods of the other nations. Taken from Hezekiah's prayer in II Kings 19.18, it serves the Chronicler as a concluding summary.

The Chronicler's stylistic inclinations are also manifest in other details. The juxtaposition of the king of Assyria and 'his servants' with 'the Lord

God and Hezekiah his servant' (v. 16), is sufficient to make the reader understand what course the events may take. The Chronicler also employs alternating titles for the God of Israel. In these four verses the Lord is designated as 'the Lord God' (v. 16), 'the Lord the God of Israel', 'the God of Hezekiah' (v. 17), and finally 'the God of Jerusalem' (v. 19). All these should be understood in their very specific context: this major threat to the people of Israel, to king Hezekiah, and to the city of Jerusalem, will come to nothing because the Lord is very specifically their God.

[20] Now comes Hezekiah's awaited reaction to all that Sennacherib has done so far – the delegation, the letter, the mockery, etc. Quite unexpectedly, however, his reaction is recounted in an extremely brief statement: 'Then Hezekiah the king ... prayed because of this and cried to heaven.' This extreme brevity becomes even more noticeable when compared to the Chronicler's source on the one hand, and his own description of other Judaean kings on the other. We find in Kings a long reference to Hezekiah's deeds: 'he rent his clothes, and covered himself with sackcloth, and went into the house of the Lord. And he sent ... to the prophet Isaiah' (II Kings 19.1–2), and his words and prayers are cited twice (II Kings 19.3–4, 15–19). The Chronicler himself describes Asa and Jehoshaphat in similar circumstances; faced with severe threats, their behaviour and excited prayers are conveyed in detail (II Chron. 14.11 [MT 10]; 20.3–20]). Concerning Hezekiah, however, the Chronicler not only refrains from elaborating on his reaction, but actually omits what already exist in his source. In the light of the Chronicler's high opinion of Hezekiah, and the miraculous divine response to Hezekiah's prayer (v. 21), this unusual brevity should be seen as a tribute to Hezekiah. His devoted behaviour so far, and his address to the people on this very occasion (vv. 7–8), are such a perfect expression of faith and trust in the Lord that nothing more need be said about it. A mere statement of his prayer suffices to initiate the Lord's response – expected and foreseen – in view of all that preceded it.

An interesting feature of this verse is the role of the prophet Isaiah. As already noted, in the 'prophetic story' of II Kings 18–20, the central figure is the prophet, who either stands by the king or confronts him. Only after Isaiah's great reassuring prophecy, cited in full (II Kings 19.20–34), does the Lord's deliverance come to Jerusalem. In the Chronicler's version of the story, Hezekiah alone has been the protagonist so far; Isaiah is much less significant, and even his appearance in this verse is unexpected. His role is also changed: he does not deliver to the king the word of the Lord, but prays to the Lord together with the king. It seems that Hezekiah does not really need the prophet's encouraging words; they are part of his own conviction no less than that of the prophet's.

[21–23] This passage concludes the story of Sennacherib's campaign,

relating the fate of Sennacherib himself (v. 21), the deliverance of Jerusalem
(v. 22), and the consequent great fame and glory of Hezekiah (v. 23). While
the first element of this conclusion is based on II Kings 19.35–37, although
the actual phrasing is very much revised, the other two elements are the
Chronicler's own addition, and bring the story to its proper end. From a
literary point of view they balance the one-sided presentation of II Kings
20.35–37 and describe the political and military repose in Judah and the
international ramifications of the Assyrians' retreat. Whether there is a
source for these two verses is not very clear. On the one hand, the supplementary passage does not really introduce any new data but basically contains
words of appreciation and praise, which by themselves are quite probable.
On the other hand, their historical presupposition is that of a disastrous end,
for whatever reason, of Sennacherib's invasion. If this fact is accepted as
authentic (cf. e.g. Montgomery, who regards the biblical story as a 'development of popular legend based on historical fact', *Kings*, 497), there would be
no reason to doubt the Chronicler's appraisal; if the account is considered
historically unfounded (cf. Cogan–Tadmor, *II Kings*, 240–50), no authentic
source or historical merit may be assigned to it.

[21] The Lord's reaction to Hezekiah's prayer is direct and immediate.
It is not proclaimed by a prophet, nor have its details been previously
announced. The Lord intervenes directly in the historical process and puts
an end to Sennacherib's enterprise.

In conformity with the general literary style of the passage, the report of
II Kings 19.35–37 is abridged, the three original verses contracted into one,
with the subject changing three times: 'The Lord sent an angel ... he
[Sennacherib] returned ..., some of his own sons ...' The 'Assyrian' colouring of the report in Kings, created mostly by the pedantic listing of names, is
leached out: Nineveh, Nisroch, Adramelech, Sharezer, the land of Ararat
and Esar-hadon are all omitted. All that remains is a bare skeleton of facts:
Sennacherib was murdered by his own sons while coming to the house of his
god. Even here, however, the Chronicler adds a touch of his own, having
Sennacherib return 'with shame of face to his own land' (there is a pun:
wayyāšob – bᵉbōšet), preparing the way for the statement concerning the
honour of Hezekiah, who 'was exalted in the sight of all the nations' (v. 23).

Another Chronistic adaptation is found in the reference to the 'angel of the
Lord'. According to II Kings 19.35 'the angel of the Lord went forth', while
here we read: 'And the Lord sent an angel'. Any possibility of attributing
autonomy to the angel is absolutely excluded; the 'angel' is nothing but a
messenger (cf. also on I Chron. 21.15).

Regarding the scope of the plague, the Kings text reports that the angel
slew 'a hundred and eighty-five thousand in the camp of the Assyrians'
(19.35). The present text avoids the sensational number and carefully lists

the slain: 'all the mighty warriors and commanders and officers in the camp of the king of Assyria' – that is, all the military leadership, without whom any further action would be impossible. This is followed by another omission. II Kings 19.35 has a precise chronology, which underlines the miraculous dimensions of the plague by the emphasis on its short duration – one night: 'And that night, the angel ... went forth ... and when the men arose early in the morning ...' The two time markers are omitted in Chronicles, and thus, in contrast to other military encounters, the scope of the enemy's disaster is mitigated. It seems that in his attitude to the plague-story, the Chronicler anticipated modern rationalistic reservations. Since he does not himself refrain from extraordinary numbers (cf. in particular II Chron. 13.17; 14.8, 12 [MT 9, 13]), the different attitude in this case may derive from the particular nature of the disaster – the fact that it is an act of 'the angel' and not a military encounter of human combatants. Not only is it presented as an unequivocal action of the Lord, but its demonic and autonomous features are removed.

[22–23] The destruction of the Assyrian camp is the first step towards Israel's deliverance and eventual rest. The Chronicler emphasizes by repetition that the Lord saved Hezekiah and Jerusalem, and he brought them 'rest round about'. This turn of events also has political and religious ramifications: 'many brought gifts to the Lord ... and precious things to Hezekiah'.

The passage reflects well the political ambiance of the time. Regardless of any rational attempt to explain Sennacherib's retreat from Judah after a lengthy siege of Jerusalem (cf. Montgomery–Gehman, *Kings*, 498; Tadmor–Cogan, *II Kings*, 239, 249), the arresting of his progress at the walls of Jerusalem was an event of international consequences, with implications for all the neighbouring states. In this context, however, it is presented as a reaction to Sennacherib's boasting. The quintessence of this boasting was the comparison of the Lord, God of Israel, with the gods of the other nations, with the conclusion that he was unable, like all the others, to save his people. Now, not only did the Lord save his people and cause the death of Sennacherib 'in the house of his god', but the recognition of the Lord's superiority, of which Hezekiah and his people were aware all along, became international common knowledge, accepted by all the nations around Israel.

The MT of 22 reads 'so the Lord saved Hezekiah ... and provided for them on all sides' (*way^{e}nah^{a}lēm missābīb*, JPS). This translation is actually a way out of a very unusual idiom, as *nāhal* usually means 'lead, guide' (BDB, 624), a connotation which would be awkward in this context, particularly with the adverbial/descriptive 'around' (JPS 'on all sides'). It has therefore been suggested, in the light of the LXX, to read MT *way^{e}nah^{a}lēm* as *wayyannah lāhem* ('gave them rest'), which involves a very slight orthographic change (cf. Curtis, 490). This idiom is a major theme in the

Chronicler's theology; it represents the final expression of peace and well-being which very few kings in the history of Israel – conspicuously not David – achieved (cf. on I Chron. 17.1; also 22.17[18]; II Chron. 14.6–7 [MT 5–6]; 15.15; 20.30; Japhet, *Ideology*, 391–3). This reading is already adopted by RSV.

[24–26] The account continues in the track of its Deuteronomistic source, coming now to II Kings 20, to recount its first episode, Hezekiah's illness (vv. 1–11). This illness is presented in Kings as initially a neutral fact, with no implications regarding its causes: 'In those days Hezekiah became sick ...' It further serves to illustrate Hezekiah's piety and faith, his prayer bringing a change in the Lord's decision. This theological framework is unacceptable to the Chronicler, for whom 'illness' is by definition a 'punishment', and therefore an implication of sin. Considering the degree of perfection which Hezekiah achieved in the Chronicler's portrayal, one would expect this episode to be omitted altogether, but this is not the case. Rather, the Chronicler includes the episode and, bound by his own philosophy, introduces it with its full theological implications; the only allowance he makes is the extensive abbreviations: '... for his heart was proud. Therefore wrath came upon him and Judah and Jerusalem' (v. 25). Thus, in spite of the extensive reworking of his source, the Chronicler maintains a remarkable adherence and fidelity to what he regards as the historical facts. These are retained even at the expense of the tension which they create with his own theological inclinations.

[24] The beginning of the verse is a literal repetition of II Kings 20.1, with a minor change of preposition. Although the story is abridged, the sequence conforms perfectly with that of the Kings' source: 'and he prayed to the Lord' (II Kings 20.2–3), 'and he answered him (II Kings 20.4–7), and gave him a sign' (II Kings 20.8–11). It should be noted that RSV's reading 'he answered him' already assumes a reconstruction of MT (cf. II Chron. 33.13).

The omission of Isaiah, who stands at the centre of the Kings narrative, should be accounted for not only by the general abbreviation, but as intentional in itself. Even this short account retains an allusion to Isaiah's miracle, with the clause 'and the Lord ... gave him a sign' (II Kings 20.8–11); yet no mention is made of the person who was the mediator responsible for bringing 'the sign' about. It is thus again established that the communication between Hezekiah and the Lord is direct, with no need of an intermediary.

[25–26] The Chronicler's commentary on and evaluation of Hezekiah's illness is twice as long as the depiction of the illness itself. It is composed of Chronistic key terms: 'pride of heart' (twice), 'wrath' (twice), and 'humble', but their phrasing is very general, verging on the obscure. It illustrates the serious theological problem which confronted the Chronicler when faced with the fact of Hezekiah's illness, his struggle to understand the profound meaning of the historical events even to their smallest details, and his constant attempt to discover the divine causality and theological logic of history.

The point of departure of these comments is the theological meaning in the Chronicler's philosophy of history of the two aspects of this illness. A disease being a punishment implies the existence of sin, while the healing demands that the sin was forgiven, implying in turn a necessary repentance. From this set of theological principles, the general comments of vv. 25–26 become abundantly clear: '... his heart was proud ... wrath came upon him ... but Hezekiah humbled himself ... so that the wrath of the Lord did not come upon them'.

There are, however, other matters to be considered here. First is the context. The story is placed here in the same relative position as in II Kings, that is, immediately following the story of Sennacherib's invasion and as synchronous with it. This synchronization is expressed in the prophetic story of Kings in two ways: the statement that 'in those days Hezekiah became sick' (II Kings 20.1), and the internal chronology of the two events. According to the illness story, Hezekiah was at this point granted fifteen more years of life (II Kings 20.6), a fact which places his sickness at the fourteenth year of his reign, and this is also the explicit dating of Sennacherib's invasion (II Kings 18.13). While this synchronization and the resulting date of Sennacherib's campaign are accepted as authentic by some modern scholars and rejected by others (cf. Montgomery, *Kings*, 483; Cogan–Tadmor, *II Kings*, 228), for the Chronicler, of course, they constitute the actual historical sequence, a proximity which makes the theological difficulty even greater. The sin ascribed to Hezekiah thus follows the most glorious example of the Lord's help. This concatenation determines the phrasing of the present verse: 'But Hezekiah did not make return according to the benefit done to him', that is to say, his sin is to display gross ingratitude. This context also determines the nature of the sin as 'pride of heart', the greatest danger a prosperous king may encounter (cf. for Rehoboam and Uzziah, II Chron. 12.1; 26.16).

It is not made clear in this passage what exactly in Hezekiah's actual conduct is conceived of as the evidence of his 'pride'; it is perhaps his behaviour during the visit of the Babylonians (II Kings 20.13), which may be interpreted as boasting, but this story appears separately in the Chronicler's composition, and is accompanied by its own theological commentary. (For a different view, which regards the two stories as merged into one theological composite, cf. Williamson, 386–7.) It is also unspecified what the 'wrath' was which first 'came upon him' and then was removed. Since the sources did not supply the Chronicler with more concrete data, and since he did not add anything of his own, it all remains as vague generalizations.

Another element is the consistent conjunction of Hezekiah and the people: 'wrath came upon him and Judah and Jerusalem. But Hezekiah humbled himself..., both he and the inhabitants of Jerusalem, so that the wrath of the Lord did not come upon them ...' This material is not drawn from the story in Kings, where Hezekiah's illness remains an absolutely personal matter. It may be explained in two different ways: as a reflection of II Kings 20.6, 'and I will add fifteen years to your life. I will deliver you and this city ..., and I will defend this city ...', to be understood as a constant waiving of the still impending Assyrian threat; or as a retrojection from the next story, which will then become an organic part of the 'illness narrative' (cf. Williamson, ibid.). We find there an allusion to a possible affliction of Jerusalem, postponed for the time being; cf. the words of Isaiah in II Kings 20.17–18 and Hezekiah's response: 'If there will be peace and security in my day' (II Kings 20.19).

[27–30] This addition to the history of Hezekiah deals with one topic: Hezekiah's economic projects and achievements, mainly in the realm of 'construction'. It is composed of two parts. Verses 27–29 form a round literary unit, with formal structural features revolving around the topic of the treasuring of Hezekiah's property. Verse 30 is an addendum, with a different topic, its own opening, and an additional conclusion. The conjunction of the two passages is indicated by literary features: the similarity of topic, the positive light in which Hezekiah's worldly achievements are portrayed, and the fact that also in Kings the remark about the water project appears at the end of Hezekiah's story (II Kings 20.20).

The structure of vv. 27–29 is as follows:

(a) 27a introduction, general statement of Hezekiah's wealth
(b) 27b–29a constructions
    27b treasuries for precious items
    28a storehouses for the agricultural yield
    28b stalls for the cattle
    29a towns for the herds
(c) 29b conclusion: God has given him possessions.

The stylistic character of this passage – in such contrast to the preceding – is its detail. It conveys the feeling of luxury not only by mentioning the contents, but also by listing meticulously all the items. Thus we have silver, gold, precious stones, spices, shields, costly vessels, yield of grain, wine and oil, cattle, sheep and herds. This abundance is also expressed by the repetition of the adjectives 'many' and 'every'.

Although the description of Hezekiah's wealth falls far short of the opulence described of Solomon, it nevertheless resembles it in several aspects. It comes at the end of Hezekiah's story (cf. on II Chron. 9–10), includes 'shields' among the 'costly vessels' rather than among the military objects (II Chron. 9.15–16; also 12.9), and refers to 'spices', which are among Solomon's most valued treasures (II Chron. 9.9, 24). One may regard these touches as an intentional enhancement of the comparison between these two great monarchs.

Verse 30 describes Hezekiah's water project in a clear and straightforward manner, including names and directions: the closing of the upper outlet of the Gihon spring, and the directing of the waters downwards, to the west of the city of David. It shares with II Kings 20.20 the same general purpose, to bring water to the city, but in its phrasing and terminology it is independent of Kings. According to II Kings 20.20, Hezekiah 'made the pool and the conduit and brought water into the city', joining other data about 'pools' in this historical context. Isaiah 7.3, with 'the end of the conduit of the upper pool', relates the 'pool' and 'conduit' already to the time of Ahaz, and these are again mentioned for the time of Hezekiah (II Kings 18.17 = Isa. 36.2). An 'upper pool' certainly implies a 'lower pool', mentioned explicitly in Isa. 22.9: 'you collected the waters of the lower pool'. Isaiah also refers to the 'old pool' (22.11), which implies the existence of a 'new pool', but how these are related to the 'lower' and 'upper' pools is not made clear. This verse in Chronicles is phrased in different terminology, outlining the general plan of Hezekiah's project with no indication of the various implements, either 'pool' or 'conduit'. Thus, although the data seems authentic and reliable, much is left unclear and inconclusive when translated into concrete, 'archaeological' facts. For the whole problem, cf. among many others P. L. H. Vincent, *Jérusalem de l'ancien Testament*, 1954, 260–84; J. Simons, *Jerusalem in the Old Testament*, 1952, 157–92; M. Avi-Yonah, *Encyclopedia of Archeological Excavations in the Holy Land*, 1976, 591–7, 642–7.

Verse 30 ends with a conclusion: 'Hezekiah prospered in all his works', parallel to that of II Chron. 31.21: 'And every work that he undertook ... he did ... and prospered'. This 'prosperity' is the mark of several other kings in Chronicles, but it is most conspicuous with regard to Solomon (I Chron. 22.11, 13; 29.23; II Chron. 7.11); for Hezekiah it marks the two realms of his activity: the religious (chs. 29–31) and the earthly (ch. 32); these two are certainly connected.

[31] Again, in a very laconic fashion, this verse reflects a longer passage in II Kings 20.12–19, recording the visit of the Babylonian envoys with some comments on its theological significance. Its introduction, with the non-specific 'And so', points to the artificial link between the passages, and indicates that its position is determined by the order of its source.

The purpose of the visit is briefly stated: 'to inquire about the sign that was (JPS; RSV: that had been done) in the land', as against the purpose stated in II Kings 20.12: 'for he heard that Hezekiah had been sick', referring to the same event from different perspectives. The Chronicler chooses to view 'the visit to the sick' as a response of amazement, or even a 'scientific inquiry' of the sign, the change often being ascribed to his awareness of the Babylonian interest in astronomy (cf. Curtis, 493). Neither the story nor the Chronicler's theological inclinations suggest a better motivation.

The divine purpose of this visit is 'a test', the only case in Chronicles where 'test' appears explicitly as a principle of divine intervention in the history of Israel. Defined as a 'test', it is not a 'result' but a 'cause', related to what is to follow rather than reacting – as either punishment or reward – to what preceded it. The object of the test is not Hezekiah's actions, but 'to know all that was in his heart', a citation of Deut. 8.2: 'testing you to know what was in your heart'. The text of Deut. 8.2 goes on to specify this purpose: 'whether you would keep his commandments, or not'. In the present context there is no sequel: Hezekiah is tested for his faith and trust. Although this is the only case in Chronicles where 'test' is found as the explicit description of a historical phenomenon, it indicates the Chronicler's inclusion of 'testing' in his theological vocabulary. Other events as well belong to this category (cf. Japhet, *Ideology*, 191–8).

Did Hezekiah 'pass the test'? While II Kings 20.12–19 does not allude to the concept of 'test', some elements of the story may have encouraged the Chronicler in this direction. To the divine message by Isaiah, Hezekiah responds with: 'the word of the Lord which you have spoken is good' (II Kings 20.19), an expression of absolute resignation to the divine will. In its spiritual disposition this statement may be compared to that of Job, in his famous words 'the Lord gave and the Lord has taken away; blessed be the name of the Lord' (Job 1.21), or further on, 'Shall we receive good at the hand of God, and shall we not receive evil?' (2.10). If this is how the Chronicler interpreted the story, then Hezekiah indeed passed the test.

[32–33] Like II Kings 20, where the Deuteronomistic conclusion follows the story of the Babylonian delegation, now comes the concluding passage concerning Hezekiah's rule, with most of the details of its source rephrased along standard lines.

In place of Hezekiah's 'might' the Chronicler mentions 'his good deeds' ($h^a s\bar{a}d\bar{a}w$), a feature repeated only for Josiah (35.26). As the document on which 'the rest of his acts' is recorded, 'the vision of Isaiah ..., in the Book of the Kings of Judah and Israel' is cited. This citation is interesting in both its phrasing and contents. We have already noted that the Chronicler indicates his sources as *either* prophetic books *or* a general historical source, designated by several titles. There are, however, two passages that constitute exceptions to this rule, in which the prophetic work is regarded as part of the general work: this one, and II Chron. 20.34. It is these references which prompt the view that the Chronicler regards the general historical work as being composed of smaller units, each having been written by a contemporary prophet.

In this specific context, however, these references suit very well the canonical book of Kings, where the specific pericope of II Kings 18–20 might well be described as 'the vision of Isaiah' included in 'the Book of the Kings of Judah and Israel'. Such an understanding of these designations would have broad consequences for the question of 'sources' in two respects: its implication for the meaning of all the other Chronistic references to sources, and the resulting absence of a reference to the Chronicler's extra-biblical source, from which he may have drawn some of his information. These broader implications incline me to adhere to the accepted view and see these terms as references to the 'general' work of history mentioned repeatedly in the Chronicler's concluding remarks.

As we have observed several times, the figure of Isaiah diminishes considerably in the Chronicler's version of this historical period; nevertheless, the basic Chronistic view that the history of Israel has been recorded by contemporary prophets is expressed here by the assignment of this task to Isaiah. This is a significant choice, since Isaiah is the only one among the 'classical prophets' who is given such a role in Chronicles, the choice certainly to be accounted for by Isaiah's unique position in biblical traditions. Isaiah appears in the Bible as both a 'classical prophet', whose prophecies are cited in the book bearing his name, and a messenger-prophet, whose acts and words are included in the Deuteronomistic history. His being assigned the role of historian for Hezekiah's time thus points out the clear distinction between the two prophetic categories. Although the distinction is never explicitly stated or defined, it underlies the Chronicler's historiographical decisions.

[33] To the brief reference in II Kings 20.21, which does not even mention Hezekiah's burial, the Chronicler now adds an extensive description of his death and burial. It is similar in scope to the passage devoted to Asa's burial (II Chron. 16.14), but unlike that of Asa, the ceremonious burial of Hezekiah is not initiated by the king but by the people. Hezekiah is the only king whose burial is 'on the upper part (JPS; RSV 'ascent') of the tombs of the sons of David', and although this may be merely a description of location, it is likely that *ma᷍ᵃlēh* is also an expression of distinction. Moreover, although this was probably the conventional custom (cf. Jer. 22.18), he is the only one of all the kings of Judah, this time including David and Solomon, of whom it is explicitly stated that 'all Judah ... did him honour at his death'. Hezekiah thus receives the most elaborate and distinguished burial description of all of Judah's kings, a sign of exceptional distinction in the particular Chronistic theological lexicon (cf. P. R. Ackroyd, 'The Death of Hezekiah – A Pointer to the Future?', *Festschrift H. Cazelles*, 1981, 221–6).

In recent scholarship we find an ongoing debate: does the Chronicler view Hezekiah as a 'second David' (cf. in particular Mosis, 189–92), or a 'second Solomon' (cf. in particular, Williamson, *Israel in the Book of Chronicles*, 119–25, and his commentary, *passim*)? Or does he portray him as a combination of the two, David and Solomon (cf. Ackroyd, 179–89; M. Throntveit, *When Kings Speak*, Atlanta 1987, 124; Dillard, 228–9, and in his commentary, *passim*.)? Neither seems to be the case. As has been abundantly shown by other commentators and throughout the pericope, in many of their traits Hezekiah's figure and period resemble those of David, to whom he is also explicitly compared (II Chron. 29.2). In many others he resembles Solomon, to whom also there is an explicit comparison (II Chron. 30.26). His figure, however, and that of his reign, are idiosyncratic, with their own specific features and contours, determined by Hezekiah's personality, specific historical position, and the data from which his portrait is structured. Certain of the deeds attributed to Hezekiah – such as the celebration of Passover or the organization of the contributions – have not been mentioned before him, and the description of his burial surpasses all his predecessors. There are clear similarities between him and Josiah – the Passover, the reform, and their 'good deeds'. The purification of the Temple after its desecration by Ahaz bears some resemblance to the acts of Joash. The Assyrian threat has its parallels in the invasion of Shishak in Rehoboam's time – in particular after the latter has been reworked by the Chronicler – and to some degree in the threat of the eastern enemies in the time of Jehoshaphat. Hezekiah's 'pride' has its most conspicuous precedent in Uzziah. One might go on with this list, showing points of resemblance and dissimilarity, but it is not intended for that purpose. The Chronicler shaped Hezekiah's history from the materials he had at his disposal and in line with his theological and historical principles. The figure that emerges is that of the greatest Judaean king after David and Solomon, a figure who should be seen in the lively particulars of his person, deeds and historical circumstances, rather than in the generals of a stereotypical 'type'.

33 Manasseh was twelve years old when he began to reign, and he reigned fifty-five years in Jerusalem. [2] He did what was evil in the sight of the Lord, according to the abominable practices of the nations whom the Lord drove out before the people of Israel. [3] For he rebuilt the high places which his father Hezekiah had broken down, and erected altars to the Baals, and made Asherahs, and worshipped all the host of heaven, and served them. [4] And he built altars in the house of the Lord, of which the Lord had said, 'In Jerusalem shall my name be for ever.' [5] And he built altars for all the host of heaven in the two courts of the house of the Lord. [6] And he burned his sons as an offering in the valley of the son of Hinnom, and practiced soothsaying and augury and sorcery, and dealt with mediums and with wizards. He did much evil in the sight of the Lord, provoking him to anger. [7] And the image of the idol which he had made he set in the house of God, of which God said to David and to Solomon his son, 'In this house, and in Jerusalem, which I have chosen out of all the tribes of Israel, I will put my name for ever; [8] and I will no more remove the foot of Israel from the land which I appointed for your fathers, if only they will be careful to do all that I have commanded them, all the law, the statutes, and the ordinances given through Moses.' [9] Manasseh seduced Judah and the inhabitants of Jerusalem, so that they did more evil than the nations whom the Lord destroyed before the people of Israel.

10 The Lord spoke to Manasseh and to his people, but they gave no heed. [11] Therefore the Lord brought upon them the commanders of the army of the king of Assyria, who took Manasseh with hooks and bound him with fetters of bronze and brought him to Babylon. [12] And when he was in distress he entreated the favour of the Lord his God and humbled himself greatly before the God of his fathers. [13] He prayed to him, and God received his entreaty and heard his supplication and brought him again to Jerusalem into his kingdom. Then Manasseh knew that the Lord was God.

14 Afterwards he built an outer wall to the city of David west of Gihon, in the valley, to the entrance by the Fish Gate, and carried it round Ophel, and raised it to a very great height; he also put commanders of the army in all the fortified cities in Judah. [15] And he took away the foreign gods and the idol from the house of the Lord, and all the altars that he had built on the mountain of the house of the Lord and in Jerusalem, and he threw them outside of the city. [16] He also restored the altar of the Lord and offered upon it sacrifices of peace offerings and of thanksgiving; and he commanded Judah to serve the Lord the God of Israel. [17] Nevertheless the people still sacrificed at the high places, but only to the Lord their God.

18 Now the rest of the acts of Manasseh, and his prayer to his God, and the words of the seers who spoke to him in the name of the Lord the God of Israel, behold, they are in the Chronicles of the Kings of Israel. [19] And his prayer, and how God received his entreaty, and all his sin and his faithlessness, and the sites on which he built high places and set up the Asherim and the images, before he humbled himself, behold,

they are written in the Chronicles of the Seers. [20] So Manasseh slept with his fathers, and they buried him in his house; and Amon his son reigned in his stead.

21 Amon was twenty-two years old when he began to reign, and he reigned two years in Jerusalem. [22] He did what was evil in the sight of the Lord, as Manasseh his father had done. Amon sacrificed to all the images that Manasseh his father had made, and served them. [23] And he did not humble himself before the Lord, as Manasseh his father had humbled himself, but this Amon incurred guilt more and more. [24] And his servants conspired against him and killed him in his house. [25] But the people of the land slew all those who had conspired against King Amon; and the people of the land made Josiah his son king in his stead.

A. Notes to MT

[14] וסבב, probably read וסביב (cf. LXX and V); [16] read ויבן with the Kethib; [19] חוזי, proposed חוזיו (haplography); [20] ביתו, read בגן ביתו with II Kings 21.18.

B. Notes to RSV

[9] 'seduced', better 'misled' (NEB), or 'led astray' (JPS); [11] 'therefore', or 'so' (NEB, JPS); 'took', literally 'caught'; [23] 'he incurred guilt more and more', better 'he was exceedingly guilty' (cf. also NEB).

C. Structure, sources and form

1. Chapter 33 is devoted to two topics, unequal in length: the reign of Manasseh (vv. 1–20) and the reign of Amon (vv. 21–26), which parallel respectively II Kings 21.1–18 and 19–25. Each of these constitutes a unit in its own right, but certain themes and phrases provide a common unity.

2. The first impression gained by the comparison of the Manasseh pericopes in the two parallel histories is the fact that their length is almost equal, with Chronicles being somewhat shorter. The larger part of the unit is repeated verbatim, a phenomenon which we last encountered to this degree of fulness for the reign of Amaziah (II Chron. 25). Yet the Deuteronomistic passage has undergone much reworking, with great literary and theological consequences.

3. Manasseh is described in II Kings 21, very uniformly and unambiguously, as the most wicked of all the kings of Judah, his transgression being the leading theme of his reign. The pericope is structured along conventional Deuteronomistic guidelines, but is more emphatically cast in Deuteronomistic terminology and theology, and employs a greater variety of Deuteronomistic genres. Without going into the problem of its possible literary history, its present structure may be sketched as follows:

   (a) II Kings 21.1–9 Deuteronomistic introduction, exceptionally elaborated
   (b) II Kings 21.10–15 Deuteronomistic prophetic speech
   (c) II Kings 21.16 special reference to the shedding of 'clean blood'

(d) II Kings 21.17–18 Deuteronomistic conclusion, which again refers to Manasseh's sin.

The Chronistic reworking is expressed first of all by the fact that the period of Manasseh loses its absolute one-sidedness and its definitive Deuteronomistic stamp. The history of Manasseh is composed of two eras: the sin, and the repentance. While the former is fully anchored in the Deuteronomistic source of II Kings 21, the latter, as well as the transition between them, is peculiar to Chronicles. In principle, this pattern of reworking may also be found for the reigns of Rehoboam, Joash, Amaziah and Uzziah, where a uniform Deuteronomistic portrayal is reshaped to depict the king's reign as composed of two opposite periods, the hiatus marked by a decisive transformation. However, while in the four earlier cases the change is from 'good' to 'bad', from 'righteousness' to 'sin', Manasseh illustrates the opposite development, from 'sin' to 'repentance'. Thus, although in principle Manasseh's reign is portrayed along familiar Chronistic principles, his reign nevertheless has a stamp of its own, illustrated also by several of its details.

4. The literary procedure of the Chronistic adaptation also follows earlier examples. The Chronicler cites from II Kings all of the Deuteronomistic framework, both 'introduction' and 'conclusion', and contains his own story within the same framework (II Kings 21.1–9; 21.17–18//II Chron. 33.1–9; 33.18–20). This procedure is of special importance in this case, since the introduction is exceptionally elaborated, but is nevertheless recorded in full. A different procedure, however, is employed for the passages which do not belong to the framework. II Kings 21.10–15 is summarized in one verse (33.10), and II Kings 21.16 is omitted, the two sections being replaced by a new passage (vv. 11–16). The Chronistic record thus represents all of the Deuteronomistic source except for one verse; its first part is cited almost verbatim, its middle part epitomized, and its conclusion rephrased. However, what in II Kings 21 is a general view of Manasseh's reign, devoted exclusively to his religious miscreance, is presented in Chronicles as one part of his reign. It is followed by a dramatic change (vv. 11–13), and its consequences (vv. 14–17). This is all new, with no parallel either in the Bible or outside it.

5. The structure of the Chronistic pericope, as much as that of the Deuteronomistic one, reflects the author's theological presuppositions and may be sketched as follows:

(a) 1 Introduction: Manasseh is king
  (b) 2–8 Manasseh's transgressions
    (c) 10–11 Punishment: exile to Assyria
      (d) 12–13 Repentance and delivery
    (e) 14 Manasseh's earthly enterprises
  (f) 15–17 Religious restoration
(g) 18–20 Conclusion: death and burial.

The chiastic principle of this structure is transparent, the pivot being represented by vv. 12–13, Manasseh's repentance and delivery, marking the turning point of his career.

6. Because of the central position of Manasseh in Deuteronomistic theology, the significance of his dissimilar portrayal is far greater than that of the other figures just mentioned. In certain Deuteronomistic strata, the 'sins of Manasseh' are regarded as

the 'cause' for the final destruction of the Judaean kingdom and the burning of the Temple (cf. II Kings 23.26–27; Jer 15.4; Japhet, *Ideology*, 158–60). This Deuteronomistic theologoumenon comprises two elements: a picture of Manasseh as a king who introduced into Judah every form of idolatry and syncretistic cult, thereby threatening the true Israelite religion with extinction, and the theological evaluation of this fact as the cause for Judah's undoing. The Chronistic portrait of Manasseh as a 'convert' undermines the basis for the whole argument as it casts into doubt not merely the theological conception, but its factual basis. Moreover, the change in the figure of Manasseh also affects that of Josiah, who is presented by the same Deuteronomistic theology as the great reformer. According to the Chronicler's picture, Manasseh himself has already cancelled at least some of his religious innovations, leaving much less for the time and effort of Josiah – a conclusion which is indeed followed in the Chronistic history of Josiah in II Chron. 34–35.

7. It is thus natural and almost self-evident that the problem of sources and historicity of the Chronicler's picture of Manasseh would engage the interest of many scholars: What are the sources of the new material? What are the motives of this new picture? And how authentic is it?

The peculiar Chronistic figure of Manasseh has long been explained as motivated exclusively by theological considerations (cf. Wellhausen, 206–7). Since the Chronicler perceives any positive aspect of a king's history as a reward for his good deeds, and since a long rule and longevity clearly represent the more outstanding signs of 'blessing', the fact that Manasseh reigned for fifty-five years – more than any other king of Judah – and reached the age of sixty-seven poses difficult theological questions for the Chronicler. Not only is any mention of Manasseh's merits missing in the Deuteronomistic description, but its very plausibility is utterly excluded by the manner in which he is portrayed in II Kings 21. Thus the Chronicler was forced – by what he conceived to be the most binding principles of historical causality – either to account for the length of Manasseh's rule or to change this fact altogether. Although the latter would involve only a negligible literary and textual change, the Chronicler never avails himself of this expedient, and systematically refrains from tampering with these hard-core chronological data, even in the face of the most embarrassing theological questions. His only alternative, then, was to find the causes which enabled Manasseh to remain so long on his throne. This is accomplished by Manasseh's repentance. Since, however, the Chronicler's theological need and his way to cope with it are so transparent, his picture of Manasseh has been regarded as having absolutely no historical credibility.

8. Yet, in spite of the weight of these theological considerations, the issue of historical probability for the given facts persists; it is in fact one of the more insistent topics in the extreme critical approach to the Chronicler's historicity (already H. Winckler, *Alttestamentliche Untersuchungen*, 1892, 159–60, commentators like Kittel and Curtis, 496, and others, cf. in particular E. L. Ehrlich, 'Der Aufenthalt des Königs Manasse in Babylon', *TZ* 21, 1965, 281–6). It seems that several other factors should be considered, first and foremost the data themselves.

The additional data in vv. 11–17 fall into three categories: (*a*) a note on Manasseh's exile to Assur and his return to his kingdom (vv. 10–13); (*b*) notes on Manasseh's building projects, particularly in Jerusalem (v. 14); and (*c*) notes on the changes in Manasseh's religious policy, and the restoration of the Temple's cult (vv. 15–16). These details are now structured into a comprehensive theological conspectus:

Manasseh's exile is a punishment for his sins; his distress is the motive for acknowledgment of the sovereignty of the Lord, for humility and prayer, and these in turn bring about his eventual reinstitution on his throne. With this, a new era begins, marked by enterprises of statecraft and religious reforms. However, when separated from their theological framework, the historical data themselves have many points to commend their probability and reliability.

The first point is their unconventional character. Manasseh's exile and return is an exceptional event, for which the Chronicler had no biblical model, and hardly any contemporary one. If regarded as unhistorical, it would have to be an absolutely 'pure' invention – a procedure which is not supported by the Chronicler's historiographical methods. The historical likelihood of the Chronicler's information is supported also by the example – mentioned often – of the exile and return of the Egyptian Necho, who was brought to Assur by Assurbanipal as a prisoner and then restored to his kingship (*ANET*, 295), an example which presents the story of Manasseh as a possibility, especially in this period and in this very historical context. Moreover, Manasseh's exile does not really represent an adequate solution for the Chronicler's theological problem. In view of the gross transgression of both Manasseh and his people, the exile of the king alone seems a rather mild divine response, which may be explained only on the assumption of its historicity.

Should we also accept as historical the Chronicler's chronology of Manasseh's reign, and his view that the exile prompted Manasseh's repentance and reform? This sequence is so much an integral part of the Chronicler's philosophy of history and the way in which he understands the historical process that it can hardly be accorded a reliability on its own. Thus, while the events themselves may be historical, the theological structure in which they are embedded is a construction, which turns the isolated data into an architectonic structure, historical and theological.

The same line of reasoning should also be applied to Manasseh's projects in Jerusalem and 'the fortified cities'. As a general consideration it is very difficult to assume that such a long reign of fifty-five years would be dedicated exclusively to religious innovations, with no initiatives whatsoever for the public good in any other field. More specifically, Manasseh's building of the wall may be seen as a direct continuation of his father's efforts to strengthen the fortifications of Jerusalem, the need certainly being implied by both Isa. 22.9 and II Chron. 32.5. It seems that Hezekiah's 'other wall' did not surround the 'city of David', the latter having been only strengthened. The precise line of the wall, 'an outer wall ... west of Gihon, in the valley, to the entrance by the Fish gate ... round Ophel ... to a very great height', may indicate that Manasseh found a new solution for the engineering problems of these fortifications. There is also no reason to doubt that Manasseh took care to strengthen the fortified cities; one may even assume that the present text does not include the entire range of his activities in this area. The fortified cities suffered the greatest damage during Sennacherib's invasion, and although we have no explicit reference to this topic, their restoration would have been a major project already for Hezekiah, and later for Manasseh. The brief clause 'He also put commanders of the army in all the fortified cities of Judah' makes good historical sense, and there is no reason for it to be doubted.

9. My conclusion may be phrased as follows. The change in the figure of Manasseh certainly answers the Chronicler's urgent theological need to account for Manasseh's long reign and longevity. Theoretically, however, a 'repentance' could have followed

any calamity – illness, a family disaster, famine, drought, plague, military invasion, and so on. The Chronicler's specific historical data should be seen as authentic, therefore, but with the caveat that they have been integrated into a new theological framework with marked Chronistic features.

10. The history of Amon is presented with great concision already in its Deuteronomistic version, and even more so in Chronicles. In its Deuteronomistic presentation Amon's reign is portrayed as a mere extension of that of his father. In adhering to the negative picture of Amon, the Chronicler views him rather as a regression, for 'he did not humble himself before the Lord, as Manasseh his father had humbled himself' (v. 23). Thus in the reworking of his Deuteronomistic source, the two significant changes are the replacement of II Kings 21.22 by v. 23, and the omission of II Kings 21.25–26. While the former is clearly the Chronicler's contribution, the latter may be viewed as a result of homoioteleuton, but cf. further in the commentary.

D. Commentary

[1] The Chronistic introduction of Manasseh follows that of II Kings 21.1, with the omission of the name of Manasseh's mother. This datum is already unusual in its original appearance, for the designation of this particular queen mother deviates from all others. All the queen mothers mentioned in Kings (absent for Joram and Ahaz) are identified by some affiliation: their descent (I Kings 15.2, 10; 22.42; II Kings 8.25, etc.), their ethnic or geographic origin (I Kings 14.21; II Kings 12.2; 14.2) or both (II Kings 21.9; 22.1; 23.1, 36; 24.8, 18). Manasseh's mother is the only queen mentioned only by her proper name, and moreover she seems to have been one of the younger wives of Hezekiah, since Manasseh was born to his father when he was forty-two years of age (cf. on II Kings 18.2). This irregularity, however, would not be the reason for the Chronicler's omission, since from this point to the end of his story, the Chronicler systematically omits the names of the queen mothers. Beginning with Manasseh, he introduces a new principle of adapting his source and follows it systematically, with no concern for the origin of the queen mother, or discrimination between 'good' and 'bad' kings. I therefore find unconvincing the claims of J. W. McKay (*Religion in Judah under the Assyrians*, 1973, 23–5; also Williamson, 390), who views this omission for Manasseh and Amon alone, in isolation from the more general historiographical phenomenon. The motive for this new procedure may not be obvious, but cf. further on the three last kings of Judah.

[2–9] The religious evaluation of Manasseh, an unprecedented listing of religious transgressions, covers eight verses and is cited in full from II Kings. Contrary to what may appear to be a random conglomeration of everything evil, it is structured very carefully. Its framework is laid down in vv. 2 and 9, placing the transgressions of Manasseh and his generation in the context of the comparable evils of the nations, establishing not only a historical context but also a theological one: 'He did what was evil ... according to the abominable practices of the nations whom the Lord drove out before the people of Israel' (v. 2), and '. . . they did more evil than the nations whom the Lord destroyed before the people of Israel' (v. 9). While v. 2 refers to Manasseh alone, v. 9 includes 'Judah and the inhabitants of Jerusalem'.

Contained within this framework are two sections. Verses 3–6 include a systematic list of all Manasseh's projects, summarized with its own conclusion in v. 6b: 'he did much evil in the sight of the Lord, provoking him to anger'. Verses 7–8 describe a special item as the peak of abomination, accompanied by a lengthy commentary: the installations of the Asherah in the Temple. Verses 3–6 in turn are systematically structured as a series of actions: (a) cancellation of Hezekiah's reform by rebuilding the high places (v. 3a); (b) building of various installations for idolatry (v. 3b); (c) building of altars inside the Temple and its courts (vv. 4–5); and (d) human sacrifice and sorcery (v. 6). Some of these reflect standard Deuteronomistic prohibitions, while others are peculiar to this context. The whole, however, is strongly marked by Deuteronomistic nomenclature and concepts.

[2] The phrase 'abominations of the nations' characterizes in Deut. 18.9 the series of forbidden practices in the realm of sorcery and human sacrifice: 'any one who burns his son or his daughter as an offering, any one who practices divination, a soothsayer, or an augur, or a sorcerer, or a charmer, or a medium, or a wizard, or a necromancer' (18.10–11) – a list partially repeated in v. 6 below. In the Deuteronomistic stratum of Kings, 'the abominations of the nations' characterizes the practices of three kings: Rehoboam (I Kings 14.24), Ahaz (II Kings 16.3) and Manasseh, with 'the nations' being further qualified: 'according to all the abominations of the nations which the Lord drove out before the people of Israel'. More than a comparison of facts, or a neutral description of the nations, this statement combines Deut. 18.9 and 12: 'Because of these abominable practices the Lord your God is driving them out before you.' Therefore, the practice of the same 'abominations' by the people of Israel will likewise lead to their undoing. It is also a very acute indictment of Israel's ingratitude. What the Lord receives in return for his gracious acts on behalf of his people is that they abandon him, provoke his anger, and adopt the ways of the same peoples he disinherited for Israel's sake.

[3] The first move towards the cancellation of Hezekiah's reform attributed to Manasseh is his rebuilding of the high places. Rather than being an innovation, it is a conservative act of counter-reform, returning to earlier forms of the cult which the Deuteronomistic school finds so undesirable. It seems, however, that the list progresses from the least egregious to the most, beginning with practices still within the religion of Israel.

Manasseh's next step is the introduction into Judah of Canaanite cults: building altars to the Baals, making 'Asherahs', and worshipping the host of heaven. The combination of these three elements is repeated in the record of Josiah's reform (II Kings 23.4, 5), as well as in the retrospective review of II Kings 17.16, but, except for Manasseh, the worship of the 'host of heaven' is not ascribed to any other king. The scope and detail of these practices are made even clearer by the specifics of Josiah's reform, in particular in II Kings 23.4–7, 10–12. For the deep entrenchment of this cult in Jerusalem and its impact, cf. for instance Zeph. 1.5; Jer. 8.2; Ezek. 8.16, etc.

In this context the Chronicler introduces a few slight changes: he makes the single 'Asherah' into a plural, and omits the reference to Ahab king of Israel. Since the Chronicler does not refrain from mentioning Ahab's sins in connection with Joram and Ahaziah (II Chron. 21.6; 22.3–4), it seems that he omits it here because he perceives it to be immaterial.

[4–5] Both verses deal with the building of altars in the courts of the Temple, the general information of v. 4 being made more precise in v. 5. The effrontery of Manasseh's rebellion is expressed by v .4b: to the very house which has been dedicated to the worship of the Lord, Manasseh introduced the foreign altars! The removal of these altars is attributed to Josiah in II Kings 23.12, but according to Chronicles, it was Manasseh himself who was responsible for their removal: 'all the altars that he had built ... he threw them outside the city' (v. 15).

[6] This verse is a clear reflection of Deut. 18.10: to Manasseh is attributed the trespassing of almost all of the expressed prohibitions, which was never attributed to any other monarch in such accumulation. For partial items cf. I Kings 14.22–24 and II Kings 16.3–4. These matters refer to the realms of human sacrifice and various practices of sorcery.

The Chronicler transmits the verse as it is with three changes. He turns the singular 'son' into the plural 'sons', and the name of the place in which this abominable cult was performed, 'the valley of the son of Hinnom', is added, taken from the record of Josiah's reform in II Kings 23.10. And thirdly, to the pair 'soothsaying and augury', the Chronicler adds 'sorcery', in closer similarity to Deut. 18.10.

[7–8] Verse 7 begins a new unit, dedicated to the installation of the Asherah idol in the house of the Lord. With this step Manasseh reached the extreme negative pole of the principle of the Lord's exclusivity, laid down by the concept of 'jealousy': 'For I the Lord your God am a jealous God' (Exod. 20.5). The significance of this act may be elucidated by comparing it to the practices of 'the house of Ahab'. Those of Judah's kings who affiliated themselves to the house of Ahab established a fully-fledged cult for the Baal in Jerusalem, by building a temple and altars to him and by appointing the requisite clergy (cf. II Kings 11.18//II Chron. 23.17). They kept the cult of Baal separate from the Temple, however, which was left to whom it was originally consecrated. Manasseh installed the Asherah image in the Lord's

Temple itself, without the text elucidating whether this was conceived as a change of the Temple's dedication, making the Lord's Temple into a temple for the Asherah, or whether it involved a syncretistic concept, which either identifies the Lord with the Asherah, or regards them as a 'pair', a god and his consort goddess, residing in the same house. The record of II Kings 21 does not make us privy to Manasseh's religious beliefs which may have prompted this unusual act, but the recent, and much quoted, references to 'YHWH and his Asherah' (cf. e.g. Z. Meshel, *Kuntillet 'Ajrud. A Religious Centre from the Time of the Judean Monarchy on the Border of Sinai*, Israel Museum Catalog 175, 1978; A. Lemaire, 'Les Inscriptions de Khirbet El-Qôm et l'Ashérah de YHWH', *RB* 84, 1978, 595–608; J. A. Emerton, 'New Light on Israelite Religion: The Implications of the Inscriptions from Kuntillet 'Ajrud', *ZAW* 94, 1982, 2–20; P. Kyle McCarter, 'Aspects of the Religion of the Israelite Monarchy', in *F. M. Cross Festschrift*, Philadelphia 1987, 143–9), may point to the religious presuppositions and background of Manasseh's cult. According to II Kings 23.7, where Josiah is credited with the breaking down of 'the houses of the cult prostitutes which were in the house of the Lord, where the women wove hangings for the Asherah', this involved further cultic installations, the precise ritualistic and religious significance of which is not clarified.

It is clear why this act represents the culmination of Manasseh's abominations, rousing the Deuteronomist to set down his entire 'Temple theology'. The Lord's presence in the Temple was the consequence of his decision to 'put his name there', and together with the people's keeping of the commandment was to ensure Israel's well-being and their very occupation of the land given to them by the Lord. Manasseh desecrated the one and forfeited the other. Without explicitly saying so, this theology implies the people's doom.

This passage is cited in full from II Kings 21.7–8, including all its specific Deuteronomistic phraseology, with only minor changes in detail; some of these may be pointed out here. The Chronicler changes 'the graven image of the Asherah (*pesel hā'ªšērāh*) to 'the image of the idol (*pesel hasemel*)', the term 'idol' being repeated in v. 15. These are the only occurrences of the term *semel* in Chronicles, which in the Bible generally is a rare word (occurring also in Deut. 4.16, and Ezek. 8.3, 5). On the other hand, 'Asherah', particularly in the plural, is quite common in Chronicles (II Chron. 14.2; 15.16; 19.3, etc.), and is also found in this context (v. 3; 34.3, 4, 7). The term is attested in Phoenician and Punic inscriptions (cf. McKay, 22–3), but its origin is still unresolved (cf. Baumgartner, 717). It is thus possible that the Chronicler distinguished between these cultic forms, and under the influence of Ezek. 8.3, 5, chose a different term for the present context.

The Chronicler also reads 'your fathers' instead of 'their fathers' (v. 8), a reading which is syntactically inferior, since Israel is spoken of in the third person. The Chronistic alteration to the second person thus conveys a stronger attachment to the land, which the Lord 'appointed for your fathers'.

[9] The conclusion of the passage sums up the nadir which the people of Israel have reached: they were led not only to follow the abominations of the nations, but even to exceed them. While the people are certainly partners to these evils, in both II Kings 21 and in Chronicles, the centre of the stage is occupied by the king, who 'leads the people astray', similar to Joram (II Chron. 21.11, 13), and Ahaz (II Chron. 28.19). The participation of the people, however, is emphasized in Chronicles more than in Kings, by the replacement of the accusative pronoun in 'he led them' with the explicit 'Manasseh misled Judah and the inhabitants of Jerusalem'.

Nothing explicit is said in the whole passage about the unavoidable consequences of these transgressions. Although the deeds themselves and the accompanying comments (vv. 2, 4, 7–8) are not given to any equivocal interpretation and certainly imply the impending punishment, its explicit pronunciation is delegated in Kings to the prophetic speech (21.10–15); it is avoided altogether in the Chronicler's presentation.

[10] Rather than citing the prophetic speech of II Kings 21.10–15, the Chronicler sums it up in one verse: the Lord rebuked Manasseh and his people, but they would not listen. The introduction of this summary follows a common Chronistic literary procedure: beginning his own presentation with the very same words of his source, and then going his own way. Thus compare:

II Kings 21.10: 'And the Lord spoke [by his servants the prophets ...]'

II Chron. 33.10: 'And the Lord spoke [to Manasseh and to his people ...]'

(for another example cf. II Chron. 32.24 with II Kings 20.1; etc.).

In telling of the existence and ineffectualness of the prophetic speech rather than citing it, the Chronicler expresses two aspects of his historical philosophy. On the one hand, he refrains from citing Deuteronomistic theology which in many aspects contrasts with some of his most basic views. The historical causality as established by II Kings 21.10–15 is foreign to his whole world view, according to which 'divine justice' excludes both 'delayed punishment' and 'cumulative sin' (cf. Japhet, *Ideology*, 156–65). Therefore, the destruction of the Temple could not have been caused by the sins of Manasseh, nor by the cumulative sins of many generations (II Kings 21.15), but is a result of the misdoings of the generation coeval with its destruction, that of Zedekiah. On the other hand, the existence of a prophetic speech provides the 'warning' which is, according to the Chronicler's view, a major principle in the Lord's ordering of his world (cf. Japhet, *Ideology*, 176–91). By keeping a reference to the prophecy, and to the fact that it was not heeded, the Chronicler has reshaped the Deuteronomistic account in his own theological cast.

[11] Following the unheeded warning, the imminent punishment is presented by the Chronicler's own addition to the earlier account: the exile of Manasseh to Assur. The explicit sequence makes this meaning of the event absolutely clear, but in contrast to the explicit linkage, no true accord exists between 'sin' and 'punishment'. The repeated emphasis that the sin encompasses not merely the king but also the people (vv. 9–10) is not followed up by the punishment of exile which affects Manasseh alone, with no damage to the people, the land, or the city of Jerusalem. Moreover, in view of the extraordinary and unprecedented transgressions, this arresting of Manasseh presents a relatively mild reaction of the Lord, disproportionate to the immensity of sin (cf. for instance, the fate of Joram, in II Chron. 21.16–19, or that of Amon in v. 24). The only answer to these discrepancies in the Chronicler's theological system may be found in his historiographical method. Rather than imaginatively 'inventing' a catastrophe which would be theologically adequate and proportionate, the Chronicler chose to appropriate the historical facts which he found in his extra-biblical sources for this purpose.

The possible historical event has been debated in biblical scholarship, since no mention of it is found in Assyrian documents. The implication of the text is that Manasseh was punished by the Assyrians for some reason, and together with the mention of 'Babylonia' as the place to which he was taken, this fact prompted its connection with the rebellion of Shamash-shum-ukin, Assurbanipal's brother, in 652–648 BCE (already Curtis, 498: Rudolph, 316–17; cf. in particular Ehrlich, *TZ* 21, 1965, 281–6, followed by many others). As far as our sources go, the two references to Manasseh in Assyrian documents (cf. *ANET*, 291, 294) seem to present him as a loyal vassal, but this scant and random evidence cannot by any means be regarded as conclusive. We are thus left feeling more or less certain regarding the historicity of this event, but not very enlightened regarding its actual circumstances.

The phrase 'they caught (RSV 'took') Manasseh in hooks' may seem strange, since 'catching with hooks' belongs very specifically to the semantic field of hunting and fishing, and is used metaphorically in prophecy (Ezek. 19.4, 9; 29.4; 38.4; also II Kings 19.28//Isa. 37.29). The Chronicler employs this metaphor in prose (cf. NEB 'they captured ... with spiked weapons'), and may well have reflected Assyrian custom, as illustrated by the Assyrian reliefs (cf. for instance, *ANEP*, 447).

[12–13] A 'distress' may serve in principle in two ways: it may harden the sinner, make him more stubborn in his way (thus, for example, Ahaz; II Chron. 28.22), or it may open his eyes to recognize his mistakes. Manasseh's case is the latter, the turn of affairs described by the Chronicler in an intensive series of verbs: 'he entreated ... and humbled himself ... He prayed ... and God received his entreaty and heard ... and brought him ... Then Manasseh knew ...', ending with a declaration: 'the Lord is God'. These verbs are all put in the third person singular, moving from Manasseh as subject to the Lord as subject, with no explicit mention of Manasseh until the very last clause. They may serve as a perfect expression of the Chronicler's philosophy of history, in which the appropriate reaction to 'distress' is 'humility' and 'prayer', prompting an immediate and direct response of the Lord, displayed instantly by a concrete change of the historical course (cf. also II Chron. 32.20–21).

[14–17] The two aspects of the turn in Manasseh's orientation, the earthly and religious, are now presented in sequence, first his building enterprises (v. 14) and then the consequent cultic reform (vv. 15–17). With this structure, vv. 15–17 form the counter-paragraph to vv. 2–9, the restoration of the religion of Israel to a more sober practice.

Of Manasseh's worldly undertakings the Chronicler mentions two: the building of an outer, exceptionally high wall for the city of David, and the manning of the fortified cities with commanders of the army. Both these projects are of military significance, and are aimed at strengthening the kingdom's power to resist. It is possible – especially in regard to the fortified cities of Judah – that this presents only a part of Manasseh's activity, indicated by the state of his kingdom following Sennacherib's invasion, and in particular towards its end, with the weakening of the Assyrian hold in Judah (for a possible discovery of Manasseh's wall in Jerusalem, cf. D. Bahat, 'The Wall of Manasseh in Jerusalem', *IEJ* 31, 1981, 235–6).

Manasseh's spiritual repentance is expressed in a concrete reform: the cancellation of his earlier cultic innovations and the restoration of the Lord's worship. It begins with the removal of the foreign gods, the taking out of the idol from the Temple and the altars from its courts (v. 15), and continues with the building of the Lord's altar and resuming its cult (v. 16). This is a relatively brief account, and it does not present a full reversal of the installations described in vv. 2–9. The abolition of the high places is explicitly excluded by v. 17, and the practices recounted in v. 6 are not mentioned. The removal of these installations is left for Josiah's reform.

The passage is phrased in non-Deuteronomistic terminology, and reflects the Chronicler's view. As elsewhere, he regards the building of altars for foreign gods not as an addition to the Lord's worship, but as its replacement, and the removal of the foreign altars thus necessitates the rebuilding of the altar of the Lord. However, in stark contrast to the similar report from Hezekiah's reign, the dedication of the altar is recorded only in a few words: 'He ... offered upon it sacrifices of peace offerings and of thanksgiving'; the change in the people's attitude, similar to v. 9, is also ascribed to the king's initiative: 'And he commanded Judah to serve the Lord'. No ceremonies or festivities accompany these acts.

[17] The reservation established in this verse about the imperfection of the people's worship is interesting in several ways. In content and phrasing it is similar to the Deuteronomistic statements that 'the high places were not taken away; the people still sacrificed and burned incense on the high places', repeated with slight variations, for six of the Judaean kings (I Kings 15.14; 22.43; etc.). We saw, however, that the Chronicler tends to omit these statements, and keeps them, with variation, in only two cases (II Kings 15.17; 20.33). Here he adds this reservation of his own, leaving the removal of the high places explicitly for the reform of Josiah, and turning it into the principal aspect of this reform. This is not the impression gained from either the Deuteronomistic record of Josiah's reform (II Kings 23.4–20) or its Chronistic adaptation (II Chron. 34.3–7), but it is certainly a correct inference from the Chronicler's record of Manasseh's acts. So it is quite interesting that the emphasis on the centralization of the cult and the abolition of the high places as the focus of Josiah's reform, which has been showcased by scholarly research since the time of de Wette, was conceived for the first time by the Chronicler, in his record of Manasseh's reign.

Another point of interest is the specific wording of this reservation. It offers the clearest biblical expression of the distinction between two kinds of high places: for idolatry and for the worship of the Lord. Although any worship in the high places is undesirable, there is nevertheless room to distinguish between them.

[18–20] The conclusion of Manasseh's reign, basically a reworked citation of the Deuteronomistic one, contains a reference to the additional sources for the king's history, details about his death and burial, and a statement of the reign of his son. Rather unusually, however, the first of these items is greatly elaborated in our passage and repeated twice. A synopsis with II Kings 21.17–18 will clarify the situation.

Verse 18 on the one hand, and v. 20 on the other, constitute the common Chronistic representation of II Kings 21.17–18, with either standard variations or alterations indicated by the new account:

> II Kings 21.17: 'Now the rest of the acts of Manasseh, and all that he did, and the sin that he committed, are they not written in the Book of the Chronicles of the Kings of Judah?'
>
> II Chron. 33.18: 'Now the rest of the acts of Manasseh, and his prayer to his God, ... behold they are [written] in the Chronicles of the Kings of Israel.'

Thus in place of 'the sin that he committed' we find here, in conformity with the story, a reference to Manasseh's prayer and the words of the seers who spoke to him; the historical source for the rest of his acts is, as always, differently designated.

The similarity is even greater in the next verse. Cf.

II Kings 21.18: 'And Manasseh slept with his fathers, and was buried in the garden of his house, in the garden of Uzza; and Amon his son reigned in his stead'
II Chron. 33.20: 'So Manasseh slept with his fathers, and they buried him in [the garden of] his house; and Amon his son reigned in his stead.'

The intermediate v. 19 consists of a parallel to v. 18; it provides a fuller list of 'the rest of his acts', and another source for Manasseh's reign. To the mere 'and his prayer to his God', v. 19 now adds a full list: 'and how God received his entreaty, and all his sin and his faithlessness, etc.' More than an elaboration, v. 19 presents a different spirit from both the story and the preceding v. 18. While the latter places emphasis on Manasseh's repentance, v. 19 – in similarity to II Kings 21.17 – underscores his transgressions 'before he humbled himself'. The mention of two separate sources one next to the other, a general source and a prophetic one, is also unusual. All these considerations lead to the conclusion that v. 19 is basically a gloss to v. 18, intended to complement or even reverse the 'positive only' statement of v. 18, more in accord with the Deuteronomistic estimate of Manasseh.

The prophetic source is presented in v. 19 as 'the words of Hozai'. The unknown name, its root (hzh = see), and the evidence of one LXX MS, has prompted the change of the proper name to the general 'his seers', the final letter having been dropped through haplography (cf. Curtis, 500). This rendering has already been followed by the RSV and NEB. It is possible, however, that this is a reflection of 'the words of the seers' (*dibrē hahōzīm*) of v. 18, which was misinterpreted by the glossator to be the title of a prophetic work. Cf. the common titles: 'the words of Amos' (Amos 1.1), 'the words of Jeremiah' (Jer. 1.1), etc. Thus, although deriving from *hōzīm*, *hozāy* is probably the original reading (for a different approach cf. W. M. Schniedewind, 'The Source Citations of Manasseh in History and Homily', *VT* XLI, 1991, 450–61).

[20] Manasseh's burial place is described in II Kings 21.18 with a double designation: 'in the garden of his house, in the garden of Uzza'. The second part was omitted in Chronicles, and the first then corrupted by the omission of *b^egan*.

Although the precise relationship between 'the tombs of the kings' in 'the city of David' and the house garden is not clear, it seems that in this matter also Manasseh introduced a new practice, deviating from all his predecessors. According to the conventional notes of Kings, all the kings of Judah up to Ahaz were buried in 'the city of David' (cf. I Kings 2.10; 11.43; etc., down to

II Kings 16.20). For whatever reason, the note on Hezekiah's burial is absent from the Deuteronomistic conclusion (II Kings 20.21), but is supplemented in II Chron. 32.33. Of the kings following Hezekiah, their burial place is indicated only for three – Manasseh, Amon, and Josiah – with different designations: 'in the garden of Uzza' for the first two, 'in his own tomb' for Josiah (II Kings 23.30). The systematic difference in the Deuteronomistic comments certainly assumes that Manasseh provided for a new burial place, which was to become the royal tombs from this point onward.

[21] As was the case with Manasseh, and as will be the common procedure from now on, the name of Amon's mother is omitted; other than that, the verse is an accurate reproduction of II Kings 21.19.

[22–23] Amon's religious evaluation begins with a verbatim repetition of II Kings 21.20: 'He did what was evil in the sight of the Lord as Manasseh his father had done'. However, the detailed description which follows in II Kings 21.21–22 is changed, to suit better the earlier account of Manasseh and the following one of Amon himself. The Chronicler rephrases II Kings 21.21 in a way that is less incriminatory of Manasseh; by omitting the statement that Amon 'walked in all the way in which his father walked', he avoids a general characterization of Manasseh's 'way'. Only the fact that he 'served the idols that his father served' is retained, but somewhat rephrased. In place of II Kings 21.22 the Chronicler introduces his own interpretation of the figure and fate of Amon, by pinpointing the fact that Amon did not repent like his father, but 'was exceedingly guilty'. This statement, a perfect example of the Chronicler's language and views, forms the transition from 'sin' to 'punishment': Amon's assassination in his house. The Chronicler's presentation of Amon's fate as punishment is a good example of how the historical facts as dictated by his sources take the primary position in the Chronicler's attempt to understand historical causality. After many years of intensive transgression, Manasseh was exiled to Babylonia and given a chance to repent and return, while two years of evil-doing had sufficed to determine Amon's fate. It is this sense of theological disproportion, caused by the facts of his sources, which leads to the explicit decree, even in this short record, that Amon was 'exceedingly guilty'.

[24–25] The conspiracy against Amon, the execution of the conspirators by the 'people of the land', and the enthronement of Josiah, all follow precisely II Kings 21.23–24, with slight linguistic variations. Amon's assassination was clearly a *coup d'état*, the king having been killed 'in his house' by his officials; the identity of these conspirators, however, their motives and objectives, are not specified. In a quick counteraction, 'the people of the land' undo the conspirators' plan and enthrone Amon's son, eight years of age, in his place.

These aggressive developments in the royal court were viewed by

Malamat as reflecting contrasting political currents in Judah, taking a stand
in the Assyrian-Egyptian antagonism of the time, while Nielsen ascribes
them to internal differences of a religious nature (cf. A. Malamat, 'The
Historical Background of the Assassination of Amon, King of Judah' *IEJ* 3,
1953, 26–9; E. Nielsen, 'Political Conditions and Cultural Developments in
Israel and Judah during the Reign of Manessah', in *Selected Essays*, Copen-
hagen 1983, 129–37). However, except for the explicit juxtaposing of court
officials on the one hand, and 'the people of the land' on the other, and the
latter's support of the royal dynasty, the evidence is much too scant to
support any of these conjectures. Whatever the reasons, with the backing of
the 'people of the land' it is the legitimate heir who succeeds his father on the
throne. How much his eventual religious policy and political alliances reflect
these earlier stages remains unknown.

The concluding formula of Amon's reign, which contains the common
data about the source for 'the rest of his story', his death, burial and the
reigning of his son, are found in II Kings 21.25–26 but absent in Chronicles.
This absence may be interpreted as either a result of a textual corruption, an
omission due to homoioteleuton (Rudolph, 316), or an intentional abbreviation by the Chronicler. The reference to the historical source for the king's
reign is omitted also in regard to Joram, the son of Jehoshaphat (II Chron.
21.20), and in that context it is doubtless intentional. The omission of a king's
burial place is found also in regard to some other kings, in particular at the
end of the Judaean kingdom, such as Jehoahaz, Jehoiachin, Jehoiakim and
Zedekiah (and cf. below, p. 1064), and the fact that 'Josiah reigned in his
stead' has been recorded anyhow in v. 25. Although the possibility of textual
corruption should not be excluded, I tend to see here an intentional omission,
with the view of presenting as short a description of Amon as possible. For
the Chronicler this would be an expression of disgust at a king the length of
whose rule and the manner of whose death attest to his lack of stature.

34 Josiah was eight years old when he began to reign, and he reigned thirty-one years in Jerusalem. [2] He did what was right in the eyes of the Lord, and walked in the ways of David his father; and he did not turn aside to the right or to the left. [3] For in the eighth year of his reign, while he was yet a boy, he began to seek the God of David his father; and in the twelfth year he began to purge Judah and Jerusalem of the high places, the Asherim, and the graven and the molten images. [4] And they broke down the altars of the Baals in his presence; and he hewed down the incense altars which stood above them; and he broke in pieces the Asherim and the graven and the molten images, and he made dust of them and strewed it over the graves of those who had sacrificed to them. [5] He also burned the bones of the priests on their altars, and purged Judah and Jerusalem. [6] And in the cities of Manasseh, Ephraim, and Simeon, and as far as Naphtali, in their ruins round about, [7] he broke down the altars, and beat the Asherim and the images into powder, and hewed down all the incense altars throughout all the land of Israel. Then he returned to Jerusalem.

8 Now in the eighteenth year of his reign, when he had purged the land and the house, he sent Shaphan the son of Azaliah, and Ma-aseiah the governor of the city, and Joah the son of Joahaz, the recorder, to repair the house of the Lord his God. [9] They came to Hilkiah the high priest and delivered the money that had been brought in to the house of God, which the Levites, the keepers of the threshold, had collected from Manasseh and Ephraim and from all the remnant of Israel and from all Judah and Benjamin and from the inhabitants of Jerusalem. [10] They delivered it to the workmen who had the oversight of the house of the Lord; and the workmen who were working in the house of the Lord gave it for repairing and restoring the house. [11] They gave it to the carpenters and the builders to buy quarried stone, and timber for binders and beams for the buildings which the kings of Judah had let go to ruin. [12] And the men did the work faithfully. Over them were set Jahath and Obadiah the Levites, of the sons of Merari, and Zechariah and Meshullam, of the sons of the Kohathites, to have oversight. The Levites, all who were skilful with instruments of music, [13] were over the burden bearers and directed all who did work in every kind of service; and some of the Levites were scribes, and officials and gatekeepers.

14 While they were bringing out the money that had been brought into the house of the Lord, Hilkiah the priest found the book of the law of the Lord given through Moses. [15] Then Hilkiah said to Shaphan the secretary, 'I have found the book of the law in the house of the Lord'; and Hilkiah gave the book to Shaphan. [16] Shaphan brought the book to the king, and further reported to the king, 'All that was committed to your servants they are doing. [17] They have emptied out the money that was found in the house of the Lord and have delivered it into the hand of the overseers and the workmen.' [18] Then Shaphan the secretary told the king, 'Hilkiah the priest has given me a book.' And Shaphan read it before the king.

19 When the king heard the words of the law he rent his clothes. [20] And the king

commanded Hilkiah, Ahikam the son of Shaphan, Abdon the son of Micah, Shaphan the secretary, and Asaiah the king's servant, saying, [21] 'Go, inquire of the Lord for me and for those who are left in Israel and in Judah, concerning the words of the book that has been found; for great is the wrath of the Lord that is poured out on us, because our fathers have not kept the word of the Lord, to do according to all that is written in this book.'

22 So Hilkiah and those whom the king had sent went to Huldah the prophetess, the wife of Shallum the son of Tokhath, son of Hasrah, keeper of the wardrobe (now she dwelt in Jerusalem in the Second Quarter) and spoke to her to that effect. [23] And she said to them, 'Thus says the Lord, the God of Israel: "Tell the man who sent you to me, [24] Thus says the Lord, Behold, I will bring evil upon this place and upon its inhabitants, all the curses that are written in the book which was read before the king of Judah. [25] Because they had forsaken me and have burned incense to other gods, that they might provoke me to anger with all the works of their hands, therefore my wrath will be poured out upon this place and will not be quenched. [26] But to the king of Judah, who sent you to inquire of the Lord, thus shall you say to him, Thus says the Lord, the God of Israel: Regarding the words which you have heard, [27] because your heart was penitent and you humbled yourself before God when you heard his words against this place and its inhabitants, and you have humbled yourself before me, and have rent your clothes and wept before me, I also have heard you, says the Lord. [28] Behold, I will gather you to your fathers, and you shall be gathered to your grave in peace, and your eyes shall not see all the evil which I will bring upon this place and its inhabitants."' And they brought back word to the king.

29 Then the king sent and gathered together all the elders of Judah and Jerusalem. [30] And the king went up to the house of the Lord, with all the men of Judah and the inhabitants of Jerusalem and the priests and the Levites, all the people both great and small; and he read in their hearing all the words of the book of the covenant which had been found in the house of the Lord. [31] And the king stood in his place and made a covenant before the Lord, to walk after the Lord and to keep his commandments and his testimonies and his statutes, with all his heart and all his soul, to perform the words of the covenant that were written in this book. [32] Then he made all who were present in Jerusalem and in Benjamin stand to it. And the inhabitants of Jerusalem did according to the covenant of God, the God of their fathers. [33] And Josiah took away all the abominations from all the territory that belonged to the people of Israel, and made all who were in Israel serve the Lord their God. All his days they did not turn away from following the Lord the God of their fathers.

A. Notes to MT

[6] ובהר בתיהם, difficult, probably read בער בתיהם; [7] להדק, read והדק or להדק; [9] וישבו/וישבי, read וישבי with the Kethib; [10] עושי, read לעושי with II Kings 22.5; [12/13] for the MT division of verses, cf. commentary; [12] כל מבין בכלי שיר, gloss? [13] על, read ועל; [20] עבדון, probably read עכבור (cf. II Kings 22.12; Jer. 26.22; 36.12); [22] ואשר read ואשר צוה or ואשר שלח (with some of the Versions); [32] ובנימן, read בברית, cf. II Kings 23.3.

B. Notes to RSV

[6] 'in their ruins', reconstructed; NEB 'he burned down their houses', cf. A above and commentary; [9] 'the remnant', or 'the rest'; [10] 'and the workmen who were working ... gave it ...', better 'and they gave it to the workmen who were working, etc.' (cf. A above); [11] 'beams', MT 'make roof-beams' (JPS); 'had let go to ruin', MT 'had damaged', cf. commentary; [12] 'all who were skilful with instruments of music', JPS 'all the master musicians'; [15] 'Hilkiah said', thus II Kings 22.8, MT 'Hilkiah spoke up and said' (JPS); [17] 'they have emptied out', MT 'they have melted down' (NEB, JPS); [18] 'he read it', thus II Kings 22.10, MT 'he read from it' (JPS); [25] 'burned incense', better NEB 'burnt sacrifices'; [32] 'stand to it', NEB 'keep the covenant', cf. A above, and the commentary; [33] 'all who were', better 'all who were present', cf. v. 32.

C. Structure, sources and form

1. While the Chronistic story of Josiah is built on the basis of the Deuteronomistic one and contains all its essential elements, it has undergone comprehensive reworking, in content as well as in structure. The result is a different portrait of the period and king, and a different theological perspective. The present Deuteronomistic story of Josiah is structured in a standard, uncomplicated way, in four blocks: (a) II Kings 22.1–2 Introduction; (b) 22.3–23.23 The events of 'the eighteenth year', including repairs of the house, finding the book, the covenant, the great reform, and the celebration of the Passover; (c) 23.24–27 Deuteronomistic summary and reflections; and (d) 23.28–30 Conclusion.

As in many other cases, the Chronicler encapsulates his own story within the Deuteronomistic framework, thereby pointing to his source and the overall context; he structures his own narrative, however, along different paths – literary, chronological and theological. The broader lines of the synopsis may be sketched as follows:

(a) 34.1–2	Introduction	II Kings 22.1–2
(b) 34.3–7	Josiah's eighth and twelfth years	– – – –
(c) 34.8–33	The eighteenth year: repairs of the house, finding of the book, covenant and reform	II Kings 22.3–23.23
(d) 35.1–19	Passover	
	– – – –	II Kings 23.24–27
(e) 35.20–25	The battle of Megiddo and Josiah's death	
(f) 35.26–36.1	Conclusion	II Kings 23.28–30 (including Josiah's death)

2. The restructuring of the Chronicler's story mainly affects the chronology and scope of Josiah's reform and its relationship to the celebration of the Passover. According to II Kings 22.3ff., the reform is a one-time, all-embracing event, which took place at Josiah's eighteenth year as a result of the 'finding of the book'. In Chronicles, the reform is seen as a prolonged process, beginning in the eighth year of

the king's reign, with the main phase of the purge of the land belonging to the twelfth year of his reign. These stages of the reform predated the finding of the book and may have been seen as its cause. The reform is concluded by the events of the eighteenth year: the making of a covenant and the celebration of Passover.

This restructuring of the narrative also gives different weight to two rather secondary elements in the Deuteronomistic story, by placing them in a more prominent position in our narrative: the celebration of the Passover, and the circumstances of Josiah's death.

The Passover is narrated in Kings in three verses, mostly of an evaluative nature (II Kings 23.21–23), while the story of Josiah's death is included as a note within the Deuteronomistic conclusion (II Kings 23.29–30a); both are dealt with in Chronicles on their own, in much greater detail and elaboration (35.1–19; 20–25).

3. In introducing these changes, the Chronicler follows literary methods which have been illustrated in this commentary time and again. The source text is used as a basis, with some passages excised from it and other passages interpolated into it. Both procedures are methodologically the same. Additions are made by cutting the basic text at a certain point, interpolating the new passage, and continuing the text from the precise point of the cut as if nothing had happened. Deletions are made in the same way from the opposite direction: a passage is taken out, and the two ends are then spliced into a sequence. Only occasionally, when the new sequence (after either interpolation or deletion) is extremely unclear, is some connecting element provided to fill the gap. The same technique is employed for larger blocks or smaller passages, (including even short clauses or a few words), and thus the original continuity is strictly preserved. In the case of this pericope, only at one point at the end of the story is a short passage (II Kings 23.29–30a) taken out from its original position and placed earlier. Seen at first only with regard to the large blocks, this may be sketched as follows:

II Kings 22.1–2	----	22.3–23.3	23.4–20	23.21	-----
II Chron. 34.1–2	3–7	8–32	33	35.1	1b–17

23.22–23	24–27	29–30a	28, 30b
35.18–19		20–25	26–36.1

With respect to the smaller passages, the same technique may be observed, cf. for instance:

II Kings 22.6–7	-----	8
II Chron. 34.11–12a	12–14	15, etc.

but then, within the parallel verses 11–12a, some clauses are again inserted and a few changes introduced. A comparison of the synoptic texts may thus lead to either of two opposite conclusions: an omission in the one or an addition in the other.

4. Since the result of the Chronicler's restructuring is a very different picture of the reform, the question of historicity is particularly important: should the Chronicler's picture be regarded as authentic and preferred to the Deuteronomistic one, or is it motivated entirely by his philosophy of history and theology and should, therefore, be dismissed?

The story of II Kings 22–23 indeed presents the Chronicler with severe theological problems.

(*a*) The intensity of the reform as presented in II Kings 23 is incredible, the list of cultic objects having been removed from the Temple being almost bewildering. Without referring for the moment to the other aspects of the reform, the Temple is portrayed as having been overloaded with idolatrous objects: 'vessels made for Ba'al, for Asherah, and for all the host of heaven' (23.4); 'the Asherah' (v. 6); 'houses of the male cult prostitutes ... where the women wove hangings for the Asherah' (v. 7); 'the horses ... dedicated to the sun, at the entrance to the house of the Lord' (v. 11); 'the altars which Manasseh had made in the two courts of the house of the Lord' (v. 12).

(*b*) Yet, again according to the Deuteronomistic record, this situation obtained in the kingdom of Judah not merely in the days of Manasseh and Amon, but also during seventeen long years of Josiah's reign, that is, the greater part of his reign. The high priest during all these long years may have been the same Hilkiah who later played an important part in the reform. When one considers the Chronicler's judgment on Amon, whose assassination after two years of reign is accounted for by his transgression (33. 23–24), this lassitude on the part of Josiah becomes even more embarrassing.

(*c*) Moreover, II Kings 22.3ff. describes the plan to repair the Temple as a routine procedure, with no thought of reform. The eventual impulse for reform comes from the book which is handed to Shaphan during his visit (22.8). This course certainly implies that when Josiah was making preparations for the repair of the Temple, at the eighteenth year of his reign, he was accepting the situation of the Temple as it was, with the Asherah and all the cultic objects intact.

(*d*) In spite of all these facts, Josiah is described in the book of Kings with the most lavish superlatives: 'He did what was right in the eyes of the Lord, and walked in all the way of David his father, and he did not turn aside to the right hand or to the left' (22.2), and: 'Before him there was no king like him, who turned to the Lord with all his heart ... nor did any like him arise after him' (23.5).

From the Chronicler's theological perspective, this adds up to an impossible situation. Has Josiah ruled seventeen years in sin and not been punished? Was he not even reprimanded? Did Hilkiah the priest find the book of the Law of the Lord inside a Temple filled with idolatrous objects? How could one even conceive of the existence of the Lord's cult in such a Temple, and of Hilkiah as a priest?

5. The Chronicler's efforts to provide this period with more solid theological cohesiveness already begin in the change of Manasseh's figure (cf. to ch. 33), but their principal expression is in this restructuring of Josiah's history.

(*a*) Josiah did not wait until the eighteenth year of his reign. The change of disposition occurred in the eighth year of his reign 'while he was yet a boy' (34.3). It is before his majority – which determines his accountability – that he repented, and during all his adult years he was walking in the ways of his father David.

(*b*) Josiah's reform did not apply to the Temple but only to the land. The Deuteronomistic passages which so elaborately link the idolatry with the Temple are absent from Chronicles. It is said that Josiah 'began to purge Judah and Jerusalem' (34.3), and that he 'purged Judah and Jerusalem' (v. 5). He then moved to 'the cities of Manasseh, Ephraim and Simeon, and as far as Naphtali' (v. 6) and 'throughout all the land of Israel' (v. 7). After he has purified the land, he returns to Jerusalem to repair the Temple but not to 'purge it', and finally, after making the covenant, he 'took away all the abominations from all the territory that belonged to the people of

Israel' (34.33). Nothing is said about cleansing the Temple – this aspect had already been taken care of by Manasseh himself (33.15–16).

(*c*) The impulse for reform did not come from the finding of the book but from the king's own religious conviction. His wish to purge the land led him to make repairs in the Temple (34.8), and it was on the occasion of the restoration that the book was found (34.14). The finding of the book is not the cause for the reform, but incidentally resulted from the repairs of the house.

(*d*) At the same time, the Chronicler tempers the praise of Josiah. The most extravagant verse, II Kings 23.25, is omitted altogether. Josiah is still a very worthy king, but less extolled in Chronicles than in the Deuteronomistic picture.

6. As the general outlines of the story are so well accounted for by the Chronicler's theological considerations, scholars have tended to deny it any historical value (cf. Curtis, 502–3; Rudolph, 319–21, denying the Chronicler's story both coherence and historical probability). Yet the view that Josiah's reform was prior to the finding of the book has been advocated by many scholars (cf. for example the works listed by Rudolph, 321, or by Williamson, 397–8), even to the point of regarding the Chronicler's presentation as reflecting the precise chronology of the time, in full accord with the stages of the Assyrian decline (cf. in particular, S. Smirin, *Josiah and his Age*, 1952, 53–8*; F. M. Cross – D. N. Freedman, 'Josiah's Revolt against Assyria', *JNES* 12, 1953 56–8). This latter view, however, has been strongly criticized, because of a new understanding of Assyrian chronology, in particular the dating of Assurbanipal's death at 627 BCE.

It seems that the point is not so much the acceptance of the Chronicler's precise chronology as the scholarly discomfort with the Deuteronomistic one. The telescoping of all of Josiah's enterprises into one year – and even less if we count the year as beginning in the month of Tishri and the reform concluding with the celebration of the Passover – seems difficult from any perspective. No preparation for the reform is assumed, either practical or spiritual, but the whole stems rather from the accidental discovery of a book, the effect of its presentation being nothing less than a shock. The Chronicler's picture, which dissociates the reform from the book and presents the change as a gradual process, seems much more balanced and of sounder inner logic (cf. Michaeli, 241). It also supports scholarly opinion that the circles which composed the book had exerted influence on Josiah before its formal 'finding', a picture which may be based on social and political conventions (cf. Cogan–Tadmor, *II Kings*, 294).

The inevitable conclusion seems to be that while the Chronicler's picture does seem more plausible and less 'frozen' than that of the Deuteronomist, his dependence on the Deuteronomistic source, the absence of any indication of an additional source, and the theological thrust of the Chronistic reworking also cast doubt on its authenticity. In the end, neither source presents an accurate picture of the time. 'Lacking firmer evidence ... exact dates for the various stages of Josiah's reform cannot be fixed' (Tadmor–Cogan, *II Kings*, 299).

7. The structure of ch. 34 may be sketched as follows:

(*a*) 1–2 Introduction
(*b*) 3–7 Purging the land
    3a Change
    3b–5 Judah and Jerusalem
    6–7 The rest of the land of Israel

(c) 8–33 The covenant
    8–13 Repair of the Temple
    14–21 Finding the book
    22–28 Huldah's prophecy
    29–33 Making the covenant and consequences.

The structure of section *(c)* follows that of II Kings 22.3–23.3, but there is some difference in the scope and proportion of the sub-units. In II Kings 22.3–23.3 there is no apparent balance between the sections, except that the first and the last are of similar length; because of the Chronicler's omissions and additions, the four sections are almost equal in length, except for the last, which is somewhat shorter.

D. Commentary

[1–2] These verses are an accurate citation of II Kings 22.1–2, except that, as is the case of Manasseh and Amon, the name of the queen mother is omitted. The comparison of Josiah to David is left in its place – a comparison which is retained in Chronicles only for Josiah and Hezekiah. The only linguistic change is the alteration of the collective singular ('all the way'), to the regular plural – 'in the ways'.

[3–7] The cultic purification of the land and the restoration of the Temple are described in Chronicles in two stages, preceded by the king's spiritual re-orientation 'in the eighth year of his reign'. The cleansing of the land, in turn, is presented in two parts, formally delimited: vv. 3b–5 record the cleansing of Judah and Jerusalem, vv. 6–7 the rest of the country. The first part is defined by a formal framework, 'he began to purge Judah and Jerusalem' (v. 3b), and 'he ... purged Judah and Jerusalem' (v. 5b), while the whole is concluded by a third reference to Jerusalem: 'Then he returned to Jerusalem' (v. 7). There is also an interesting parallelism between the two parts in the list of cultic objects and the manner of their removal. The objects are high places (v. 3), Asherim (vv. 3, 4, 7), graven images (vv. 3, 4, 7), molten images (vv. 3, 4), altars (vv. 4, 7), and incense altars (vv. 4, 7); they are removed by 'breaking down' (vv. 4, 7), 'hewing down' (vv. 4, 7), and 'breaking down and making them into dust' (vv. 4, 7).

In both cases, the statements are very general, and the objects are described in the plural with no specification. They are basically the same objects repeated in Chronicles on several occasions, a fact which blurs the uniqueness of Josiah's actions. Cf. for instance the record of Asa's reform: 'He took away the foreign altars and the high places, and broke down the pillars and hewed down the Asherim ... He also took out of all the cities of Judah the high places and the incense altars' (II Chron. 14.3–5 [MT 2–4]; cf. also II Chron. 17.6 and 31.1). There is, however, one difference between what Josiah did in Jerusalem and what he did in the provinces, which also distinguishes Josiah from all other reformers: the connection he made between 'purification' and 'defilement', effected by the inclusion of 'graves' and 'bones' in the purgation (cf. below).

[3a] The turning point in Josiah's career is attributed to the 'eighth year of his reign, while he was yet a boy'. This sudden change in Josiah's orientation is not explained and has no parallel. It is true that the Chronicler portrays the figures of the Judaean kings with fluctuations and changes of conduct, in contrast to the Deuteronomistic history, where the kings are described in a unified form, each of them stigmatized for the whole length of his career. Yet these changes always occur in the king's adulthood, and often under the influence of some powerful external event. For Josiah, neither an external event nor any purposeful educational experience account for his re-orientation (cf. II Chron. 24.2, 14, 17; 26.5). After the first seven years of his reign in which he followed the ways of his predecessors, he suddenly begins 'to seek the God of David his father', and it is doubtful whether the change may be accounted for by political factors, such as his having been freed from the influence of his regents. The designation of the Lord as 'the God of David his father' is influenced and determined by the preceding v. 2, the whole statement actually being a qualification, and even a correction, of this verse, cited from II Kings 22.2.

[3b–5] Although the names of the cultic objects mentioned in this passage are very common, debate continues over their precise nature. The high places are among the items which are mentioned for 'Judah and Jerusalem' alone, and there is no indication whether these were regarded as idolatrous, or intended for the Lord's service. The clearest distinction in this respect is found in the context of Manasseh's reform: 'Nevertheless the people still sacrificed at the high places, but only to the Lord their God' (33.17). Taking this remark into consideration, 'the breaking down of the high places' would refer to the completion of Manasseh's beginnings. On the other hand, since all the other items in the context are clearly idolatrous, this may have been the common denominator of the list, including the high places; the matter remains inconclusive.

Asherim, and graven and molten images, are mentioned as a group twice in this passage, and as the transliteration rather than translation may indicate, the precise nature of the 'Asherim' is not fully clear. Their present joining with 'images' may imply some kind of statues or poles for the Asherah (NEB 'sacred poles', similarly JPS, and cf. R. Hestrin, 'The Cult Stand from Taanach and its Religious Background, Phoenicia and the Mediterranean', *Studia Phoenicia* V, 1987, 61–77). For the Hamanim (RSV 'incense altars'), cf. on II Chron. 14.5 [MT 4].

In order to finalize the eradication of these objects, Josiah performs two more acts, both confined to 'Judah and Jerusalem': he casts the dust of the broken images on the graves of their worshippers, and burns the bones of the priests on their altars. Since the 'pollution of the dead' was regarded as the utmost form of defilement, this treatment of the cultic objects represents the greatest degradation possible; it desecrated them for ever.

As the rest of the record is so unspecific, the introduction of these precise elements surely must have a specific reason, which seems to be found in their relation to the Deuteronomistic record. There we read that 'He brought out the Asherah from the house of the Lord ..., to the brook of Kidron, and burnt it at the brook Kidron, and beat it to dust and cast the dust of it upon the graves of the common people' (II Kings 23.6). This reference to 'the graves of the common people' is qualified in Chronicles to yield a more appropriate theological statement: 'the graves of those who had sacrificed to them'. Similarly, the text in Kings records that 'he ... took the bones out of the tombs, and burned them upon the altar, and defiled it' (II Kings 23.16), and then, 'he slew (literally 'sacrificed') all the priests of the high places who were there, upon the altars, and burned the bones of men upon them' (23.20). To these remarks the Chronicler reacts with a polemical statement, making one issue out of the two; the slaying of the priests on the altars is omitted, and only the burning of 'the bones' of the priests remains; all are now limited to 'Judah and Jerusalem'.

[6–7] One of the most emphasized points in the Chronistic story of Josiah's reign is the extension of his acts to cover all the land of Israel. This point is treated in a systematic way, throughout the pericope; it is repeated six times, all found in the Chronicler's own contributions. Some of these have no basis whatsoever in the book of Kings, while for others a certain anchoring may be found in the Deuteronomistic account. Their wording and phraseology are systematically diversified, attesting to the Chronicler's stylistic inclination to variety of expression. Thus:

(a) 34.6 'in the cities of Manasseh, Ephraim and Simeon, and as far as Naphtali'
(b) 34.7 'throughout all the land of Israel'
(c) 34.9 'from Manasseh and Ephraim and from all the remnant of Israel and from all Judah and Benjamin and from the inhabitants of Jerusalem'
(d) 34.21 'Go inquire of the Lord for me and for those who are left in Israel and Judah'
(e) 34.33 'And Josiah took away ... from all the territory that belonged to the people of Israel, and made all who were in Israel serve the Lord their God'
(f) 35.17–18 'the people of Israel who were present kept the passover ... Josiah, and the priests and the Levites, and all Judah and Israel who were present, and the inhabitants of Jerusalem.'

It is also evident from II Kings 23 that the reform reached beyond the traditional boundaries of the kingdom of Judah, given in II Kings 23.8 as 'from Geba to Beer-sheba'. Thus we find a detailed reference to 'the altar at Bethel...' (II Kings 23.15–17), and 'all the shrines also of the high places that were in the cities of Samaria' (23.19–20). The farthest point, 'the cities of Samaria', may apply to the whole territory of the former northern kingdom, without its precise borders being delineated. The Chronicler presents this aspect with clearer geographical terminology, and as encompassing the whole land of Israel, from Simeon in the south to Naphtali in the north. He also indicates it both at the beginning of the story (34.6) and at the end (34.33). This territorial scope is defined, among others, by two comprehensive terms: 'the land of Israel' (*'ereṣ yiśrā'ēl*), a term connected only to the times of David, Solomon and Hezekiah and depicting the greatest expansion of Israel (I Chron. 22.2; II Chron. 2.17 [MT 16]; 30.25), and the unique phrase in the plural: 'the lands (*hā'ᵃraṣōt*) of the people of Israel' (34.33), rendered by RSV as 'the territory that belongs to the people of Israel'.

Thus, according to the Chronicler, Josiah's rule expands to the whole of the land, similar to the days of David and Solomon. In the present passage, this territorial expansion is described first by selected names of tribes: Manasseh and Ephraim representing the northern kingdom, Simeon and Naphtali marking the two most extreme tribes, Simeon in the south and Naphtali in the north. This expansion, however, covers only the western side of the Jordan; the eastern side has been lost for ever with the exile of the two-and-a-half tribes (I Chron. 5.26).

How authentic is this view? The considerations that apply to this matter are similar to those applied to the chronological issue. As mentioned above, the expansion of Josiah's rule is implied also by II Kings 23. The international political situation, with the gradual decline of the Assyrian empire after Assurbanipal's death (627 BCE) to its final collapse in 610 BCE (cf. Tadmor–Cogan, *II Kings*, 291–3), and before the consolidation of the rising Babylonian power, would make this expansion a 'natural' policy for an energetic Davidide. The picture described in Chronicles is thus very probable in general terms. On the other hand, the Chronicler's historical and theological views must not be overlooked; the authenticity of the details, such as the full expansion of Josiah's rule already in his twelfth year (628 BCE), cannot be verified.

As illustrated above, there is really no difference between the kind of idolatry which is practised in 'the land of Israel' and that practised in 'Judah and Jerusalem', except perhaps that the latter is more extensive. This is very different from the Deuteronomistic account, in which Josiah directs his efforts against the particularly northern irregularities, and treats them with exceptionally thorough and cruel sanctions (II Kings 23.15–20). The unity of the people, according to Chronicles, is also illustrated in the similar forms of their transgression, necessitating the same reformatory measures.

One of the famous textual cruces is found in the obscure interchange of the Kethib *bāhar bāttēhem* and the Qere *bᵉharbōtēhem*. The difficult Kethib would read 'their houses on the mountain(s)', the relevance of 'mountain' (*bāhar*) in the context being attested in II Kings 23.16, while the Qere would read 'with their swords'. A different vocalization of the Qere form is represented by RSV's rendering, following several commentators, 'in their ruins'. It has been suggested that both readings are corrupt, and there have been several propositions for reconstruction.

The words 'and he returned to Jerusalem' are cited from II Kings 23.20, and constitute the 'narrative conclusion' of the passage. They present Josiah as personally responsible for all these activities. All the abominable cultic installations were actually 'broken down ... in his presence' (v. 4), the king's involvement being the profoundest expression of devotion.

[8–13] Although the Chronicler's story of the Temple repair is strongly dependent on that of II Kings 22, he introduces to it major and minor alterations which grant it its particular character. Rather than an incidental or routine procedure (cf. II Kings 22.3), the repair is presented as part of the general plan to purify the land, stated explicitly in the Chronicler's two additions to the introduction of the passage: 'Now, in the eighteenth year of his reign, *when he had purged the land and the house*, he sent Shaphan ... *to repair* the house of the Lord' (v. 8). According to the Kings narrative, Josiah sent his scribe Shaphan to the house of the Lord to deliver his commands to the priest Hilkiah, with the contents of this command clearly set out: that 'Hilkiah ... may reckon the ... money which has been brought in to the house ...; and let it be given into the hand of the workmen ... repairing the house' (II Kings 22.4–5). According to this version, then, the initiative to repair the Temple is the king's, but his actual involvement is rather limited; he gives an order to Hilkiah to take care of the repair, and directs him to the source of the remuneration.

The picture is different in Chronicles. The king's delegation to the priest (which consists of three persons rather than one, cf. below) does not come to transmit the king's commands but to administer the whole project, which has as its professed goal 'to repair the house of the Lord his God' (v. 8). Hilkiah is not asked 'to reckon the money' but rather the opposite: the delegation brings the money with it and delivers it directly 'to the workmen who had the oversight of the house of the Lord' (v. 10). This is, then, a topic of its own, further elaborated by some details referring to the administration of the work, in the Chronicler's addition of vv. 12–13.

The Chronicler also presents in a different manner the sources of the money which underwrite the cost of the repair. According to II Kings 22.4, the money is collected at the house of the Lord itself. While adhering to the same terminology, 'the money that had been brought into the house of God/the Lord' (II Kings 22.4; II Chron. 34.9, 14), the Chronicler sees in a different way both the source of the money (v. 9) and its function in the story (v. 14). According to v. 9, the money is collected by the Levites, as they circulate in all Israel, encompassing 'Manasseh and Ephraim and from all the rest (or remnant) of Israel and from all Judah and Benjamin, and from the inhabitants of Jerusalem' – in short, the whole people, Judah and Israel alike, in their places of residence. What the Chronicler describes here is an established institution, to which he referred already at the time of Joash (II Chron. 24.5). Contrary to that occasion, however, when the Levites failed to perform their task and another procedure was provided for the collection of the money (II Chron. 24.6–9), this present chapter reflects the proper functioning of this arrangement. As may be inferred from the text, the Levites deliver the collected money to the king, who eventually sends it to the Temple, its original destination.

[8] The delegation which Josiah sends to the Temple comprises not only Shaphan the son of Azaliahu, but three dignitaries: 'Shaphan ... Maaseiah the governor of the city, and Joah the son of Joahaz, the recorder'. Were these names extant in the Chronicler's *Vorlage*, having dropped out in the MT of II Kings 23.4 (Rudolph, 321; Williamson, 400), or were they added by the Chronicler? There is nothing in the names or the titles that would point to a conclusive answer. The names Maaseiahu and Joah are both common, Joah ('the son of Asaph') being the recorder for the time of Hezekiah (II Kings 18.18, 26, 37), and the titles are also attested elsewhere: for 'the governor of the city' (*śar hā'îr*), cf. in particular II Kings 23.8. On the other hand, throughout the following story, even in its Chronistic version, only 'Shaphan the secretary' is referred to (vv. 15ff.), which again may be seen as deriving from the particular context of 'a book'. A delegation of three is also sent by Hezekiah to meet the Rabshakeh, (II Kings 18.18, 26, 37), and a larger one to Isaiah (II Kings 19.2) and to the prophetess Huldah (II Kings 22.12//II Chron. 34.20). It is also possible that 'Asaiah the king's servant' (II Kings 22.12, 14) is the same as 'Maaseiah the governor of the city' of this verse.

In the phrasing of the verse, Shaphan's original longer genealogy is abridged and his title is omitted, but it is abundantly attested in vv. 15, 18 and 20.

[9] This verse is a nice illustration of the Chronicler's method of adaptation, taking the base text and reworking it along the way. Compare:

II Kings 22.4 'Go up to Hilkiah the high priest, that he may reckon (*wᵉyattēm*)'.

II Chron. 34.9 'They came to Hilkiah the high priest and delivered (*wayyittᵉnū*)'.

II Kings '... the money which has been brought into the house of the Lord'.

II Chron. 'the money that had been brought to the house of God'.

II Kings 'which the keepers of the threshold have collected from the people'.

II Chron. 'which the Levites, the keepers of the threshold had collected from Manasseh and Ephraim ... and the inhabitants of Jerusalem'.

Except for slight variations in translation, there are four points of change; two are determined by the different view of the delegation's task: 'go up' and 'reckon' are changed to 'they came' and 'delivered', the second illustrating the Chronicler's manner of replacing his source with a very similar word (*wytm-wytnu*). 'The keepers of the threshold' becomes very specifically 'the Levites, the keepers of the threshold'. Although left unidentified in II Kings 22.4, these 'keepers of the threshold' were most probably priests (cf. II Kings 12.9 [MT 10]: 'the priests who guarded the threshold'; also II Kings 23.4; 25.18; Jer. 35.4; 52.24). In Chronicles, here and in general, this task is entrusted to the Levites (cf. I Chron. 9.19–22; II Chron. 23.4). And last, 'the people', which in the context of Kings probably refers to those who had come to the Temple where the money had been collected, are now described in the most detailed picture: each and every constituent of the people, throughout the land, contributed via the circulating Levites to the repair of the Temple.

The people of Israel are described here with the peculiar idiom *šeʾērīt yiśrāʾēl*, a term which is never found in biblical prose except in Chronicles (cf. also I Chron. 12.38 [39]). RSV's rendering 'the remnant of Israel' colours it with a specific theological nuance, which may not be implied by the Chronicler's usage. Its other occurrence in Chronicles is in the context of David's enthronement, where the same term is correctly rendered 'the rest of Israel'. The comparison of David and Josiah, expressed in this pericope in various forms, should lead to the use of the same term here also, referring to the people in its most general composition: those mentioned, 'and all the rest'.

[10] What in II Kings 22.5 is a continuation of the king's command – the execution of the repair is not actually recorded except partially in the secretary's report to the king (22.9) – is here changed to the record of doing, followed systematically throughout the passage. 'And let it be given' (*weyittenū*, literally 'that they may give') becomes 'and they gave' (*wayyittenū*, RSV 'they delivered'), twice here and then again in v. 11.

The people working on the Temple repair consist of two groups, mentioned hierarchically: those in charge, to whom the money is given first, and those who actually do the work, carpenters, builders, etc. This distinction, very clear in II Kings 22.5–6, is obscured here by a slight textual corruption – the omission of l^e before $l^{e'}\bar{o}s\bar{e}$, and the repetition of 'and they gave' in v. 11. The restoration of $l^{e'}\bar{o}s\bar{e}$, 'to those who do the work', in v. 10b turns v. 11 into an apposition to v. 10b, the whole reflecting a very clear hierarchy also supported by the Chronicler's own alteration in v. 17.

The goal of all this, the repair of the house, is defined in the parallel texts in similar yet divergent terms. II Kings 22.5 reads $l^e\d{h}azz\bar{e}q$ $bedeq$ $habb\bar{a}yit$ (reconstructed also for 22.6), with the common construct $bedeq$ $habbayit$ and the verb $\d{h}\bar{a}zaq$ in the *piel* conjugation. These are attested in the two contexts of the repair of the Temple (cf. also II Kings 12.6, 7, 8, 9), while in Chronicles this phrase has disappeared. Its replacement here is provided by a verbal form $libd\bar{o}q \ldots habbayit$ (RSV, NEB 'repairing'; JPS 'examining'), which is unique in the Bible but well attested in later rabbinic Hebrew.

[11] In listing the works planned for the Temple, the Chronicler introduces two changes. He states more precisely the function of the timber, and explains why these repairs were necessary in the first place. The timber is to be used for two purposes: 'binders' , found in the plural only once again (I Chron. 22.3), and being a rather general term (cf. in the singular and for different materials, Exod. 26.4, 5; 28.7, etc.); and for 'making roof-beams for the building' (for the plural form 'buildings' cf. also I Chron. 15.1; 29.4.). This latter function is then explicitly explained: 'the buildings which the kings of Judah damaged'. This blunt causative $hi\d{s}\d{h}\bar{\imath}t\bar{u}$, literally 'ruin, damage' (cf. BDB, 1008), is taken by many commentators to be too aggressive: 'The kings of Judah did not damage the Temple with their own hands; they were simply not doing anything and the house was getting damaged' (Ehrlich, *Mikra Kipheshuto*, 468*; *Randglossen*, 383, also referring to II Chron. 24.7). This position is followed by many (cf. for instance Rudolph 322; Michaeli, 238, etc.), and is reflected also in the RSV rendering 'which the kings of Judah had let go to ruin'.

Both lexical and contextual considerations do not support this view. I have observed several times that for the Chronicler, every repair or purification of the Temple presupposes an actual damage to the Temple (Japhet, *Ideology*, 216), attested in the days of Joash, Hezekiah and now of Josiah. The non-specific language in the plural probably implies the two kings preceding Josiah, Manasseh and Amon, who are not mentioned by name because of the change which occurred in Manasseh's conduct. $hi\d{s}\d{h}\bar{\imath}t\bar{u}$ should be understood for what it literally means: damaged.

[12–13] This Chronistic addition takes as its point of departure II Kings 22.7b, 'for they deal honestly', and provides a broader record of the administration of the work, highlighting the role of the Levites as the supervisors of all its different aspects. They have the oversight of the work, and serve as secretaries, clerks and gatekeepers. The hierarchy is again clearly set. The upper charge and supervision is entrusted to four persons, two of Merari and two of Kohath, of quite common levitical or other names; beneath them is a larger body of Levites, who were over the porters and those 'who did the work'. There are, however, several points of detail which must be clarified.

Only two families of Levites are represented in the upper supervision: Merarites and Kohathites, mentioned in a reversed order relative to their traditional rank. If two other names of the Gershonites have fallen out, we have no way of restoring the omission. Note the rare designation 'the sons of the Kohathites', repeated only in II Chron. 20.19, clearly presenting them as an order.

The Levites in charge of the burden bearers are qualified as 'skilful with instruments of music', with no explanation why the supervision of the manual work should be entrusted to 'master musicians'. In order to avoid this puzzling identification, the NEB transposes these words; they are more probably a gloss, added to complete the series of 'Levites, scribes, officers and gatekeepers' by the only class of Levites missing, the singers (cf. Curtis, 507; differently Rudolph, 323; Dillard, 280).

[14–21] This passage tells about the finding of the book of the Law, its conveyance to the king, the king's reading of it and his reaction. From a literary point of view, it is fuller than the parallel of II Kings 22.8–13, with the addition of the introductory v. 14 which sets the narrative backdrop, and other small elements. Except for these additions, the passage follows almost literally the parallel passage of Kings, and I shall deal with the major differences at the appropriate points in the commentary.

[14] The story in Kings does not relate to the finding of the book on its own, nor to the circumstances under which it was found. Already during Shaphan's first visit to the Temple, he is told by the priest that he has 'found the book of the law in the house of the Lord' (II Kings 22.8). Unless an earlier commencement of the repair is assumed, the finding of the book would be prior and unrelated to it. The Chronicler's account is different in both contents and literary presentation. He makes a specific note of the finding, and of the circumstances in which the book was found: 'While they were bringing out the money that had been brought into the house of the Lord, Hilkiah the priest found the book.' The finding is a direct result of the repair and, more importantly, it is not found '*in* the house of the Lord'. If 'the money that had been brought into the house of the Lord' is the money collected by the Levites from all Israel (v. 9), and the book was found 'while they were bringing out the money', then the book reached the Temple from some place outside it which the Levites visited in their circulation, and Hilkiah's statement in v. 15, cited from II Kings 22.9, would be correct only in general terms. Is it only for literary purposes that the Chronicler makes

this change, or is it also of theological significance that the book was brought to the Temple from outside? Or does it still preserve the echo of some ancient tradition of the actual origin of the book? These questions must remain unanswered.

Can 'the book of the Law' be identified? Since de Wette's epoch-making *Dissertatio Critica* (1805), it has been generally accepted by biblical scholarship that the book which prompted Josiah's reform was Deuteronomy, either in its canonical form or some variation of it, with the arguments for and against to be found in the vast literature dedicated to the topic (cf. Eissfeldt, *The Old Testament – An Introduction*, Oxford 1974, 171–6). Although this question does not seem to have bothered the Chronicler, his presentation indicates that he assumed the recovered book to be the entire Pentateuch. The 'book' is defined in II Kings 22–23 in several ways, of which the significant ones are 'the book of the law' (22.8, 11), or 'the book of the covenant' (23.2), but nowhere is it ascribed explicitly to Moses or defined as 'the Law of the Lord'. The Chronicler preserves the above titles (34.15, 30), but in his initial presentation of the book makes its identity absolutely clear: 'The book of the Law of the Lord, given through Moses' (v. 14). Moreover, the slight alteration is v. 18, 'and Shaphan read *in it*', rather than 'and Shaphan read *it*' (II Kings 22.10; RSV does not reflect the change, as it follows in Chronicles the reading of Kings), and in v. 24, 'all the curses that are written in the book' rather than 'all the words of the book' (II Kings 22.16), seem to lead in the same direction. The 'covenant' and the 'curses' are some, not all, of 'the words' of a more comprehensive document.

[15] Hilkiah tells Shaphan that he found the book of the Law in the house of the Lord – note the Chronicler's introduction using the elevated narrative formula 'Hilkiah spoke up and said' – and hands over the book to Shaphan. At this point, II Kings 22.8 explicitly mentions that Shaphan read the book; the absence of this remark from Chronicles probably reflects a more original version. As presented in the sequence in Kings, Shaphan's early reading of the book has no consequences, his non-reaction being rather surprising in view of the influence which the book exerted on the king. Nor does he disclose to the king that he had already read the book. The Chronicler displays a more harmonious, and probably more original, literary development: Shaphan received the book from Hilkiah but read it for the first time in the presence of the king.

[16–17] Shaphan conducts his steps with bureaucratic precision: he first tells the king that his order was carried out, and only then relates the news, the finding of the book. The intransitive language of Kings 'and Shaphan the secretary came ...' (*wayyābō' šāpān hassōpēr*) is rendered in a transitive form in Chronicles: 'Shaphan brought the book' (*wayyābē' šāpān hassēper*) – a very slight orthographical change, which may have been caused by either textual or linguistic factors, by the Chronicler or his *Vorlage*.

Shaphan opens his address to the king with a general statement: 'All that was committed to your servants they are doing', an addition perhaps motivated by considerations of literary perfection. II Kings 22.9 (and its parallel in 34.17) refers to the execution of only one of the tasks commissioned by the king; the Chronicler anticipates this detail with a general clause which informs the king that all his orders have been carried out. The Chronicler also changes the designation of the workers, by rendering 'the workers who have the oversight' to refer to two different groups, 'the overseers' and 'the workmen', in full accord with the preceding division in v. 10.

In both II Kings 22.9 and v. 17, the treatment of the money/silver is described as 'melting' (cf. NEB). In both places RSV renders the verb with 'empty out', probably under the influence of the *nifal* conjugation of the same root.

[18] After bringing the book to the king, Shaphan reads from it, the Chronicler replacing 'read it' with 'read in it'. Although only a minor change of preposition, it may be based on the silent assumption that Shaphan could not have read the whole book, but only 'in it'.

[19–21] An almost literal citation of II Kings 22.11–13, these verses describe the king's dramatic reaction, beginning with the spontaneous expression of mourning and remorse, that of rending the clothes. Although certainly a conventional act, it gives the sharpest and most forceful expression to the king's feelings. In what follows, the prophetess Huldah will regard this reaction of the king as the most authentic expression of his repentance and humility: 'because your heart was penitent and you humbled yourself before God ... and have rent your clothes and wept before me' (v. 27). Although put in conventional terms and actions, this is an emotional outburst which may throw some light on Josiah's personality.

The spontaneous reaction is followed by an organized response. Josiah arranges for a delegation of high officials to approach the prophetess Huldah. The delegation is comprised of five persons: the high priest and the secretary mentioned by their names and titles; another official by the name of Asaiah and the general title of 'the king's official' (RSV 'servant'); and two more, Ahikam and Abdon (or better Achbor, cf. II Kings 22.12), whose titles are not given. While it is not clear whether Ahikam, too, was a scribe or a secretary, like Shaphan his father, his major position in the royal court is well attested (cf. also Jer. 26.24), and it is his son Gedaliahu who was to be appointed by the Babylonians as governor of Judah (II Kings 25.22). Achbor is mentioned as the father of Elnathan (Jer. 26.22; 36.12), also of the well-established dignitaries in the royal court. This is, then, a very distinguished group, and the very sending of such high-ranking royal representatives is already a sign of the king's 'humbling himself' before the Lord.

Josiah commissions the delegation to 'inquire of the Lord ... concerning the words of the book'. He thus expresses his full acknowledgment of the authority of this book, and of the demand of this book that its prescriptions be followed. This is not a self-evident conclusion. As far as the story goes, this is a newly found book, the authority of which is not sanctioned by tradition; yet, Josiah immediately concedes its claim to authority, with all the ensuing implications. He recognizes the fact of sin, 'our fathers have not kept the word of the Lord, to do according to all that is written in this book', and they deserved punishment. Josiah blames only the previous generations, a clear expression of the Deuteronomistic view of retribution which the Chronicler did not change to include the present generation as well: 'great is the wrath of the Lord that is poured out on us, because our fathers have not kept ...' (v. 21).

Josiah opens his words of commission by 'go, inquire' (*l^ekū diršū*), but this phrasing requires examination. 'Inquiring of the Lord' by means of a prophet was originally the seeking of guidance, enabling the inquirer to take the right action in matters personal or public (cf. among many others, I Kings 22.5ff. //II Chron. 18.4 ff.). The same verbal root came to denote any 'seeking of the Lord', and in Chronicles it is used with the broadest connotations, expressing any form of religious loyalty and piety (cf. for example, II Chron. 22.9). However, its use with the preposition *b^e'ad* ('for, on behalf of') is extremely rare and attested only in Jer. 21.2. By contrast, *b^e'ad* is the common preposition attached to verbs of supplication, denoting the other role of the prophet: praying on behalf of his people (I Sam. 12.19; I Kings 19.4, very often in Jeremiah, etc). The idiom *dāraš b^e'ad* expresses the prophet's double role, and uses the conventional *dāraš* to denote 'pray for'. The scene described in Jer. 21.2 from the days of Zedekiah shares this new coinage. Josiah sends the delegation not merely 'to inquire' but also to 'pray', that the imminent 'wrath of the Lord' be averted.

Two changes in the Chronicler's presentation should be noted. According to II Kings 22.13, Josiah seeks the Lord 'for me, and for the people, and for all Judah' – a somewhat conflated reading in which the last phrase (if original) may be seen as apposition: 'for the people, that is, for all Judah'. The Chronicler rephrases this address to become more comprehensive, and to include the two major components of Israel: 'for me, and for those who are left in Israel and Judah' (for *hanniš^eār*, cf. also the term *š^e'ērît* in v. 9). Secondly, the more neutral phrasing 'our fathers have not obeyed the *words of this book*, to do according to all that is written concerning us' is rephrased with a more explicit referent: 'our fathers have not kept the *word of the Lord*, to do according to all that is written in this book'.

[22–28] Again with some literary ellipsis, the Deuteronomistic account records the delegation's departure to Huldah (II Kings 22.14//v. 22), but only very briefly its return (v. 28b), and the focus of the passage is devoted to the prophetic address itself. This is even more accentuated in Chronicles, where the second listing of names is replaced by 'Hilkiah and those whom the king [had sent]'.

The prophecy of Huldah is a characteristic Deuteronomistic speech, full of Deuteronomistic expressions (cf. for example, M. Weinfeld, *Deuteronomy and the Deuteronomistic School*, 1972, 25–6), its main point being an outright rejection of Josiah's plea. His recognition of the book's authority and claim for obedience, and his whole-hearted humility before the Lord, are met with the answer that the verdict is final and cannot be changed. The most that he can secure from the prophetess is that the final catastrophe will be somewhat delayed and will not come in his own lifetime, and that he himself will die in peace. Although this prediction did not come true in the end, some of it – 'your eyes shall not see all the evil which I will bring upon this place' (v. 28) – was indeed fulfilled.

Even within the Deuteronomistic context, Huldah's prophecy presents some difficult literary and historical questions. As the prophecy stands, Huldah does not answer Josiah's address: she does not tell him what to do, and does not demand anything from him. On the contrary, she tells him that the fate of the people, the land and the city, has been sealed, and the policy that may be implied from her words is, 'Sit down and do nothing, for whatever you do would be futile'. This unusual reaction may be compared to the many inquiries by the kings and people of Judah of Jeremiah, who always responded with some pointer to the correct path that should be followed, whether or not the people were willing to take it (cf. Jer. 37.7–10; 38.2; 42.1–22, etc.). Josiah's reaction is the opposite of what Huldah suggests. He assembles the people, makes a covenant with the Lord, and conducts the most comprehensive reform in the history of Israel – steps which, from the perspective of Huldah's prophecy, are already of no effect.

There is thus some obvious gap, both of a narrative nature and of a theological one, between the prophecy and the overall context. The theological gap is further alluded to by the highly apologetic remark of II Kings 23.26, which follows this reform. In spite of everything that Josiah had done, 'still the Lord did not turn from the fierceness of his great wrath, by which his anger was kindled against Judah, because of all the provocations which Manasseh had provoked him'.

There is thus no escape from the conclusion that Huldah's prophecy is a secondary element in its Deuteronomistic context. The question becomes that of the scope of the addition. Does it encompass all the 'Huldah episode' (II Kings 22.12–20), the original sequence having led from 22.1, 'And when the king heard the words of the book of the law, he rent his clothes', to 23.1, 'Then the king sent, and all ... were gathered to him, etc.', with the coherence of the story preserved from every point of view, or is the present prophecy alone a secondary replacement of an original one? The general consensus seems to be that 'This is so developed by the Deuteronomistic redactor, that the original oracle is no longer distinguishable' (Gray, *Kings*, 727). The fact that Huldah's prediction of Josiah's personal fate – 'you shall be gathered to your grave in peace' (II Kings 22.20) – did not come true is taken to suggest that this part of the prophecy is authentic, and has not been changed after historical developments proved it wrong (II Kings 23.29–30; cf. Cogan–Tadmor, *II Kings*, 295).

The Deuteronomistic story, including Huldah's prophecy and the summarizing reflections in II Kings 23.25–26, presents the Chronicler with difficult theological problems. Although Manasseh is described in II Kings 21 as the most evil king in the history of Judah, and Josiah is presented as the best of kings, the final balance should have favoured Josiah, whose 'good deeds' greatly superceded Manasseh's 'bad deeds'. Josiah removed from the land of Israel not only the idolatry which had been introduced by Manasseh, but each and every form of idolatry which had been introduced by any king of Judah or Israel: 'the horses that the kings of Judah had dedicated to the sun' (23.11); 'the altars on the roof of the upper chamber of Ahaz, which the kings of Judah had made' (v. 12); 'the high places ... which Solomon ... had built' (v. 13); 'the altar at Bethel ... erected by Jeroboam the son of Nebat' (v. 15); 'And all the shrines ... which kings of Israel had made' (v. 9). Nevertheless, all these actions were not potent enough to change the impending judgment against Judah, implying that no human act could have changed it, and there was no possibility of repentance! This theological imbalance is probably the reason why a theodicy which attempted to make sense of the catastrophe of the exile was eventually reconceived: it was not only the sins of Manasseh but the sins of the people of Israel ever since the exodus from Egypt which caused the destruction of the Temple and the kingdom (II Kings 2.15).

Although the Chronicler cites this pericope almost literally, his comprehensive reworking has taken away some of the edge of the literary and theological problems. Josiah's reform does not follow the words of Huldah but precedes them, the consequences of the book being only the making of the covenant and the celebrating of the Passover. The Deuteronomistic remarks of II Kings 23.25–26, which compare Manasseh with Josiah, are omitted, as are other words of theodicy in II Kings 21; 23. As for the death of Josiah 'in war', contrary to the prediction that he would die 'in peace' (v. 28), the Chronicler provides a different solution. Such a prediction assumes as a matter of course that Josiah would not commit any sin; since, according to the Chronicler's story, Josiah did sin, the prophecy could not have been fulfilled.

[22] The prophetess Huldah is identified very carefully, by her own name and title, the name of her husband, his descent listed for three generations

and title, and their place of residence. The precise 'in Jerusalem, in the Second Quarter', may convey some particular information which is no longer evident (for her identification as being of northern origin, cf. R. R. Wilson, *Prophecy and Society in Ancient Israel*, Philadelphia 1980, 219–33).

The names in the genealogy are slightly different in the two parallel versions. The unique form 'Harhas' may point to its bearer's non-Israelite origin. Also the title 'the keeper of the wardrobe' appears here for the only time (but cf. II Kings 10.22). For 'the second quarter', cf. also Zeph. 1.10, and N. Avigad, *The Upper City of Jerusalem*, 1980, 54–60*.

[24] The Chronicler refers differently to 'the book' read to the king; he replaces 'all the words of the book' (II Kings 22.16) with 'all the curses that are written in the book', thus avoiding the implication that it was 'a book of doom' from beginning to end. He also replaces 'which the king of Judah has read' with 'which was read before the king of Judah', referring more precisely to the detail of v. 18.

[27] By way of illustration, two changes of the Kings text may be pointed out. The Chronicler omits the harsh words 'that they should become a desolation and a curse', and replaces them with a second reference to the king's humility: 'and you have humbled yourself before me'. These light changes contribute to the change of tone in the Chronicler's version.

[29–33] Josiah responds to Huldah's rebuke with a major undertaking: a new covenant, pledging himself and the whole people to the Lord. The king's central role in this event is also apparent in II Kings 23.1–3, but inasmuch as this is possible, the Chronicler emphasizes it even more, the whole passage being structured as a series of third person singular acts, with occasional active references to the people.

The passage is composed of three parts: v. 29, assembly of the people to Jerusalem; vv. 30–32a, the making of the covenant; vv. 32b–33, the consequences of the covenant. While the first two are practically a literal citation of II Kings 23.1–3 with slight changes, the third is the Chronicler's epitomized representation of II Kings 23.4–20. The lengthy description of the reform is replaced in Chronicles with an elaborate record of the Passover (35.1–19).

The centrality of the king may already be observed in the first verse. The Deuteronomistic version reads: 'Then the king sent, and all the elders ... were gathered to him' (II Kings 23.1). This passive voice may be seen as being either an English rendering of the non-specific plural of the MT (*wayya'as^epū*, they gathered), or based on the assumption that the MT represents an incorrect vocalization of an original *wayyē'ās^epū*, 'were gathered'. The rendering of Chronicles is active and straightforward: 'Then the king sent and gathered all the elders ...'

[30] The people gathered to the Temple are listed in detail: all the men of Judah, the inhabitants of Jerusalem, the priests and the Levites, summarized

as 'both great and small'. Among the changes introduced into this verse, the omission of 'with him' and of *wᵉkōl* ('and all') before 'the inhabitants of Jerusalem', and the reversal of the merism 'both small and great', are stylistic. The change which has attracted considerable attention is that of 'the priests and the *prophets*' to 'the priests and the *Levites*' (cf. von Rad, *Geschichtsbild*, 114). The Chronicler's interest in the Levites has been illustrated many times and may be regarded as one of his major tenets; yet the significance of the present change should not be overestimated. While 'the priests and the Levites' is common coin, repeated in Chronicles alone almost thirty times, and the joining of priests and Levites in numerous other ways is extremely frequent, the combination of 'priests and prophets' is characteristic of Jeremiah (4.9; 13.13; 26.16; 29.1, etc.) and appears rarely elsewhere, sometimes under the influence of Jeremiah (Zech. 7.3; Lam. 2.20; 4.13; Neh. 9.32, etc.). This phrase belongs almost exclusively to a specific historical context, the close of the monarchical period, and it comes as no surprise that the Chronicler would replace the rare phrase with a more common one.

[31–32a] The ceremony is portrayed in clear, brief lines. A large crowd assembles in Jerusalem, the king (or an unspecified agent) reads the book to them, the king stands in his place and makes the covenant before the Lord, including in this covenant the whole people.

So much literature has been written on 'covenant' in general, and Josiah's covenant in particular, that there is no need for me to elaborate here on this concept. One point, however, should be clarified and emphasized. The covenant as described in this context, in both its versions, is 'a covenant *before* the Lord' and not 'a covenant *with* the Lord' (cf. I Sam. 23.18; II Sam. 5.3; Jer. 34.15, 18), and therefore indirectly only reflects the meaning of 'covenant' as the conceptual context of the relationship between the people and the Lord, or its ceremonial forms. Inasmuch as there are two partners to the covenant, these are not 'the people and the Lord', but the king on the one hand and the people on the other, pledging themselves to the Lord, 'to walk after the Lord and to keep his commandments ..., to perform the words of the covenant that were written in this book'. 'The covenant' is already represented by the book and 'the words of the covenant' are the terms which place the king under obligation; when Josiah 'makes the covenant', he undertakes to keep what is written in the book.

The ceremony is concluded in II Kings 23.3 with the notice 'and all the people joined in (*wayyaᵃmōd*; NEB pledged themselves to) the covenant'. This is rendered in the causative in the Chronistic presentation, making the king its subject: 'Then he made all who were present ... stand to it'. However, the MT seems slightly corrupt; the phrase 'Jerusalem and Benjamin' is unique, and stands in contrast to the earlier reference to the assembling crowd as 'the men of Judah and the inhabitants of Jerusalem'

(v. 30). Also, the causative 'and he made stand' has only a direct object, and the awkwardness of this phrase in the present context is glossed by RSV's rendering 'stand *to it*, which has no basis in the MT. I therefore adopt the often suggested reconstruction of 'and Benjamin' to $b^e b^e r\bar{\imath}t$, reading the Chronistic text as a reworked formulation of his source.

II Kings 23.3: *wayya^{ca}mōd   kol hā'ām   babb^{e}rīt*
II Chron 34.32: *wayya^{ca}mēd 'et kol hannimṣā' bīrušalāyim   babb^{e}rīt*.

(Differently M. K. Hauge, 'On the Sacred Spot: The Concept of the Proper Localization before God', *SJOT* 1/1990, 38–41).

The Chronistic clause thus displays two changes: the subject is not 'the people' but the king, who 'makes them enter into the covenant', and the people are designated with 'all who were present in Jerusalem'. This qualification of the original 'all the people' is noteworthy, particularly when joined by the following reference to 'all who were present in Israel' (v. 33). These refinements seem to imply a distinction between the people who were present in person at the making of the covenant and were made personally responsible for its terms, and those who were made to follow its injunctions by the king's order and guidance.

[32b–33] The consequences of the covenant are recorded in chiastic order following the statement of its institution, referring first to 'the inhabitants of Jerusalem' and then to Josiah. Verse 32b does not detail how 'the inhabitants of Jerusalem did according to the covenant of God', but there is a broader description of the king's undertaking concerning 'all who were in Israel'. In line with the whole description, we find here the broadest territorial encompassment, defined by the unique term in the plural: 'the lands (RSV 'the territory') of the people of Israel' (cf. the similar usage of II Chron. 11.23). The pericope is concluded by a stylistic return to the beginning, forming a complete circle. Josiah 'took away (*wayyāsar*) all the abominations', and the people 'all his days ... did not turn away (*lō' sārū*); they verify and validate the initial statement that Josiah 'did not turn aside (*lō' sār*) to the right or to the left' (34.2).

35 Josiah kept a passover to the Lord in Jerusalem; and they killed the passover lamb on the fourteenth day of the first month. [2] He appointed the priests to their offices and encouraged them in the service of the house of the Lord. [3] And he said to the Levites who taught all Israel and who were holy to the Lord, 'Put the holy ark in the house which Solomon the son of David, king of Israel, built; you need no longer carry it upon your shoulders. Now serve the Lord your God and his people Israel. [4] Prepare yourselves according to your fathers' houses by your divisions, following the directions of David king of Israel and the directions of Solomon his son. [5] And stand in the holy place according to the groupings of the fathers' houses of your brethren the lay people, and let there be for each a part of a father's house of the Levites. [6] And kill the passover, and sanctify yourselves, and prepare for your brethren, to do according to the word of the Lord by Moses.'

7 Then Josiah contributed to the lay people, as passover offerings for all that were present, lambs and kids from the flock to the number of thirty thousand, and three thousand bulls; these were from the king's possessions. [8] And his princes contributed willingly to the people, to the priests, and to the Levites. Hilkiah, Zechariah, and Jehiel, the chief officers of the house of God, gave to the priests for the passover offerings two thousand six hundred lambs and kids and three hundred bulls. [9] Conaniah also, and Shernaiah and Nethanel his brothers, and Hashabiah and Je-iel and Jozabad, the chiefs of the Levites, gave to the Levites for the passover offerings five thousand lambs and kids and five hundred bulls.

10 When the service had been prepared for, the priests stood in their place, and the Levites in their divisions according to the king's command. [11] And they killed the passover lamb, and the priests sprinkled the blood which they received from them while the Levites flayed the victims. [12] And they set aside the burnt offerings that they might distribute them according to the groupings of the fathers' houses of the lay people, to offer to the Lord, as it is written in the book of Moses. And so they did with the bulls. [13] And they roasted the passover lamb with fire according to the ordinance; and they boiled the holy offerings in pots, in cauldrons, and in pans, and carried them quickly to all the lay people. [14] And afterward they prepared for themselves and for the priests, because the priests the sons of Aaron were busied in offering the burnt offerings and the fat parts until night; so the Levites prepared for themselves and for the priests the sons of Aaron. [15] The singers, the sons of Asaph, were in their place according to the command of David, and Asaph, and Heman, and Jeduthun the king's seer; and the gatekeepers were at each gate; they did not need to depart from their service, for their brethren the Levites prepared for them.

16 So all the service of the Lord was prepared that day, to keep the passover and to offer burnt offerings on the altar of the Lord, according to the command of King Josiah. [17] And the people of Israel who were present kept the passover at that time, and the feast of unleavened bread seven days. [18] No passover like it had been kept in Israel since the days of Samuel the prophet; none of the kings of Israel had kept such a

passover as was kept by Josiah, and the priests and the Levites, and all Judah and Israel who were present, and the inhabitants of Jerusalem.[19] In the eighteenth year of the reign of Josiah this passover was kept.

20 After all this, when Josiah had prepared the temple, Neco king of Egypt went up to fight at Carchemish on the Euphrates and Josiah went out against him.[21] But he sent envoys to him, saying, 'What have we to do with each other, king of Judah? I am not coming against you this day, but against the house with which I am at war; and God has commanded me to make haste. Cease opposing God, who is with me, lest he destroy you.'[22] Nevertheless Josiah would not turn away from him, but disguised himself in order to fight with him. He did not listen to the words of Neco from the mouth of God, but joined battle in the plain of Megiddo.[23] And the archers shot King Josiah; and the king said to his servants, 'Take me away, for I am badly wounded.'[24] So his servants took him out of the chariot and carried him in his second chariot and brought him to Jerusalem. And he died, and was buried in the tombs of his fathers. All Judah and Jerusalem mourned for Josiah.[25] Jeremiah also uttered a lament for Josiah; and all the singing men and singing women have spoken of Josiah in their laments to this day. They made these an ordinance in Israel; behold, they are written in the Laments.[26] Now the rest of the acts of Josiah, and his good deeds according to what is written in the law of the Lord,[27] and his acts, first and last, behold they are written in the Book of the Kings of Israel and Judah.

36 The people of the land took Jehoahaz the son of Josiah and made him king in his father's stead in Jerusalem.

A. Notes to MT

[3] תנו, probably read נתנו; [4] בכתב, probably read ככתוב בכתב (haplography); והכינו/ והכונו, probably read והכונב with the Kethib; [5] והתקדשו, probably read והקדשים; [11] מידם, read הדם מידם with LXX; [15] חוזה, proposed יחזיו.

B. Notes to the RSV

[6, 11] 'kill/ed', MT 'slaughter/ed' (JPS); [3] 'who taught all Israel', NEB 'the teachers of Israel'; 'put the holy ark', cf. A above and commentary; 'no longer', MT 'not'; [4] 'following the directions ... and the directions ...', better JPS 'as prescribed in the writing of ... and in the document of ...'; [5] 'and let there be for each', not in MT; 'a part of a father's house of the Levites', MT 'According to the division of the Levites by fathers' houses'; [7, 8, 9] 'bulls', JPS 'large cattle'; [8] 'willingly', better 'free-will offering' (JPS): [8, 9] 'lambs and kids', not in MT; [11, 13] 'passover lamb', MT 'passover sacrifice' (cf. 7, 8, 9: passover offering); [11] 'sprinkled' NEB 'flung', JPS 'dashed'; [12] 'they set aside the burnt offerings', better 'they removed the parts to be burnt' (JPS, similarly NEB); [21] 'God ... God', 'or god ... god', cf. commentary; [22] 'joined the battle', literally 'came to fight' (JPS).

C. Structure, sources and form

1. As sketched above, ch. 35 comprises three sections:
(a) 1–19 Celebration of the Passover
(b) 20–25 Josiah's death

(c) 26–36 Conclusion.
Each major unit of the chapter contains a rhetorical element of major significance: Josiah's address to the Levites in the first (vv. 3b-6), and Neco's address to Josiah in the second (v. 21). The addresses establish the premises on which the unit is founded: Josiah's address to the Levites provides a legal basis; Neco's address a theological one. They both attest to the Chronicler's literary and theological effort to present history within a plausible theological context.

2. The story of Josiah's Passover is an elaboration of the note in II Kings 23.21 and the following comment in vv. 22–23. Following his common practice, the Chronicler uses the Deuteronomistic narrative as his point of departure and framework but greatly elaborates it, and even the verses cited from II Kings are reformulated: II Kings 21.21 = 35.1a (with alterations); II Kings 23.22–23 = 35.18–19 (with alterations). The intermediate section of vv. 1b-17 is the Chronicler's own. This affinity with the Deuteronomistic source also determines the structure of the passage: (a) Verse 1, heading; (b) v. 2–9, preparations; (c) v. 10–17, celebration; (d) v. 18–19, summary and evaluation. These are juxtaposed and interconnected by repeated elements and parallel structures, which grant them a certain sense of balance. There is thus a parallelism between the heading and conclusion of the Passover story, each containing the three leading themes, 'Josiah', 'keep', 'passover', the two actually forming a kind of sequence: 'Josiah kept a passover to the Lord in Jerusalem' (v. 1a); 'In the eighteenth year of the reign of Josiah this passover was kept' (v. 19). Another type of parallel structure is illustrated by the presentation of the sub-units, in which the recurrent themes are placed in a progressive development: 'He appointed (ויעמד) the priests to their offices ...' (v. 2); 'When the service had been prepared for (ותכון העבודה), the priests stood (ויעמדו) in their place ...' (v. 10); 'So all the service of the Lord was prepared (ותכון כל עבודת יהוה) ... to keep the passover' (v. 16).

The story is also reinforced by constant repetition of key terms and phrases, giving a high degree of uniformity by focussing attention on the central points of interest. This can already be seen in the treatment of the two major protagonists, Josiah and the clergy. It is because of Josiah's initiative, command, provision and supervision that this Passover has been performed in Jerusalem. Although Josiah is not referred to by his name or title very often, they appear together eight times (the name five times, vv. 1, 7, 16, 18, 19; the title three, vv. 7, 10, 16), and all the third-person singular verbs have him as subject. The priests and Levites are referred to constantly, in both explicit and implicit references; the Levites are mentioned ten times (vv. 3, 5, 8, 9 [twice], 10, 11, 14, 15, 18), and the priests eleven (vv. 2, 8 [twice], 10, 11, 14 [five times], 18), in two of which they are designated 'the sons of Aaron' (v. 14). The people, on the other hand, are a less prominent and more passive participant, referred to by the common titles 'Israel', 'people of Israel' and 'the people' (vv. 3 [three times], 4, 7, 8, 17, 18 [three times]), as well as the unusual title 'the lay people' (literally 'the children of the people', vv. 5, 7, 12, 13), which is peculiar to this context.

Another insistent theme of the pericope is the concept of authority, the view that everything has been done 'according to order and prescription'. Various statements to this effect are repeated six times, including the king's command (vv. 10, 16), the word of the Lord by Moses (v. 6), as written in the book of Moses (v. 12), and as prescribed in the writing of David and in the document of Solomon (v. 4).

This repetitious character is evidenced even more clearly in the smaller units. In vv. 3–4 the phrase 'David the king of Israel' is repeated twice – as against only three other times in the whole book (II Chron. 8.11; 29.27; 30.26) – and Solomon is also mentioned twice. In v. 3, 'Israel' is mentioned three times: 'all Israel', 'king of Israel', and 'his people Israel', while in v. 14 the priests are mentioned five times; note also the parallel structure of vv. 7–9, etc.

3. How historical is this description and what exactly does it reflect? There seems to be little reason to doubt the historicity of the festival itself; it is already recorded in the book of Kings. A central administrative effort must also be taken for granted, although the Deuteronomistic account provides no details in this regard. The question of historicity, then, relates only to the specific details. Do they reflect the time and arrangements of Josiah or someone else?

Although infallible critical tools have not yet been provided, as far as scholarly consensus goes, some aspects of the Passover certainly have the second Temple period as their provenance: the existence of defined classes of singers and gate-keepers, the organization of the clergy by divisions, the parallel organization of the lay people by divisions, the affiliation of the singers to Asaph, Heman and Jeduthun, the attribution of their establishment to David, and so on. Together with the Chronicler's language and style, the details are best accounted for as basically reflecting the Chronicler's own circumstances, or at least his peculiar view of the matter.

4. The unit of vv. 20–25 is parallel to II Kings 23.29–30a in subject-matter, with its literary structure entirely dependent on this source. Nevertheless, it is restructured and reformulated to play a different role in the overall context. In the Deuteronomistic account, Josiah's death is not recounted as an independent narrative, but constitutes a part of the final conclusion which begins II Kings 23.28 and continues through v. 30b to the end. This historiographical technique – the relating of a significant detail of a king's reign as an off-hand remark within the Deuteronomistic conclusion – belongs to the Deuteronomistic historiographical pattern (cf. I Kings 15.7, 23; 22.39, etc.), and in this case is even more understandable as the note refers to Josiah's death and is introduced just before the concluding formula referring to his burial. From a literary point of view, however, this method detaches the note from the main narrative of Josiah's history.

The story is recast in Chronicles into a new frame, extracted from the concluding section and put in the actual story of Josiah's reign. Since the Chronicler also refrains from citing the Deuteronomistic evaluative and apologetic remarks which follow the account of the Passover (II Kings 23.24–26), the story of Josiah's death becomes a direct sequel to the account of the Passover, creating a more narrative and historical sequence. This new context is further highlighted by the explicit connecting clause, 'after all this, when Josiah had prepared the house' (v. 20).

The Chronistic passage is also much longer than the Deuteronomistic one – over four times the length – and contains many more elements. Rather than a laconic chronicle, it is formulated as a story, with a series of protagonists, changing scenes, two monologues, and a plot developing through a dramatic turn of events to a tragic conclusion.

5. In spite of all the clear differences in context and genre between the parallel passages, it is apparent that the Chronistic story is erected on the Deuteronomistic one; the original passage is fully represented in Chronicles, with all its textual elements utilized, and the new elements are woven into the borrowed ones along the original continuum. A synopsis reveals the following relationships:

II Kings 23.29a	29b	30a		30b
II Chron. 35.20	21–23	24a	24b–26	36.1

Since the 'cutting and pasting' is so obvious, the question of sources is all the more engaging: did the Chronicler 'paste in' the additional elements of his own, did he incorporate materials which he found in other sources, or does the story as it is antedate the Chronicler altogether?

Although the language of the additional sections displays a few late features, they are not specific enough to be defined as Chronistic, and even if this were the case, the Chronicler might still have transmitted in his own language some existing document, biblical or extra-biblical. The proposition that the Chronicler's passage represents a different, 'post-MT' version of II Kings has been suggested by Williamson and gained attention through his discussion with C. T. Begg (cf. Williamson, 408–11; 'The Death of Josiah and the Continuing Development of the Deuteronomistic History', VT 32, 1982, 242–8; VT 37, 1987, 9–15; C. T. Begg, 'The Death of Josiah in Chronicles: Another View', VT 37, 1987, 1–8; Dillard, 288–9). It is my contention, however, that the new passage should be ascribed to the Chronicler, as it clearly reflects his literary techniques and theological tendencies. As for the sources of this composition, cf. further below.

6. The different or additional elements in the Chronicler's story are concentrated at two points of the story and belong to two different categories. The first focus is the description of the battle (vv. 20–24a), and the other is the mourning over Josiah's death (vv. 24b–25). The different literary categories are narrative elements and rhetorical passages, illustrated by Pharaoh's address to Josiah (v. 21), and Josiah's words to his servants (v. 23b).

Josiah's death at Megiddo is described in Kings by the laconic statement: 'And Pharaoh Neco slew him at Megiddo, when he saw him. And his servants carried him dead ... from Megiddo' (23.29–30). This may be interpreted as implying that there was no battle at all, a lead which was taken by some scholars to conclude that the encounter between Josiah and Neco began as the latter's summons of Josiah for an interview (cf. in particular, A. C. Welch, 'The Death of Josiah', ZAW 43, 1925, 255–60). The Chronicler postpones the death of Josiah, and interrupts the above course by inserting Neco's warning to Josiah through his messengers, an actual battle, the king's severe wounding, and his death in Jerusalem. How should this difference be explained?

Within the framework of the Chronicler's historical philosophy, the untimely death of Josiah must be conceived as punishment and be preceded by some sin. Moreover, it must be a wilful sin, committed after an expressed warning has been delivered (cf. Japhet, *Ideology*, 176–91). The address of the Egyptian king provides all the missing elements. God has warned Josiah to refrain from fighting; by going to battle in spite of this warning, Josiah acted wilfully against God's expressed command, an element which is strongly emphasized: 'Nevertheless Josiah would not turn away from him ... but joined battle in the plain of Megiddo' (v. 22). The actual battle thus becomes Josiah's concrete defying of God's will. The addition of these elements does not prove 'that the Chronicler knows the subject better' (Rudolph, 333), but that he had 'good reasons' to change the description.

Moreover, many scholars have pointed out that several elements of the story either cite or intimate the description of Ahab's death (I Kings 22.30, 34–37), and contain some echoes of those of Saul and Ahaziah (I Sam. 31.3–4; II Kings 9.27–28, cf. Dillard, 292). The common elements are: (*a*) the change of clothes; (*b*) the wounding of the king in battle; (*c*) by shooters; (*d*) his dying of this injury; (*e*) the king's request 'take me away, for I am badly wounded'; and (*f*) the role of the 'carriage' in the story. This similarity is further enhanced by the literal borrowing of the present passage from II Kings 22.30ff.; cf.:

I Kings 22.30 (II Chron. 18.29)	II Chron. 35.22
'I will disguise myself and go into battle ... And the king ... disguised himself and went into battle'	Josiah disguised himself in order to fight with him
I Kings 22.34	II Chron. 35.23
'Turn about, and carry me out of the battle, for I am wounded'	'Take me away, for I am badly wounded'

This similarity is emphasized by the fact that the motive of 'disguise', which is essential to the story of Ahab's last war, is completely out of context in the case of Josiah, and the form החליתי (חלה in the *hophal* conjugation) is exclusive to these two contexts. For other elements, cf. also v. 23a with II Sam. 11.24; v. 24 with II Kings 9.27–28 and Gen. 41.43.

The affinity between this story and that of Ahab's death is in fact much greater than merely a literary stylistic borrowing, and relates to the more profound theological substructure. Josiah, like Ahab, received the Lord's warning to refrain from going to battle and, like him, ignored the warning. For both kings the warning came after they had already gone into battle, and both were put in a situation in which they were practically unable to recognize the divine message. The prophets who addressed Ahab pronounced a false prophecy: 'I will ... be a lying spirit in the mouth of all his prophets' (I Kings 22.22//II Chron. 18.21), and Josiah heard the divine message from an Egyptian king, who was also his opponent in battle. Ahab accepted the prophets' words, and Josiah did not attend to Pharaoh Neco, but both were deceived by appearances. It is probably this basic affinity which caused the extensive borrowing from Ahab's story to formulate the present episode.

Did the Chronicler use other sources for the mourning over Josiah's death (vv. 24b–25)? Did he possess the book of 'the Laments', or did he witness ceremonies of lamentation, to which he refers by the words 'they made these an ordinance in Israel'? While all these are possible, the opposite might also be the case. A connection between Josiah and Jeremiah is self-evident in view of the biblical evidence; Jeremiah began his mission in the time of Josiah, and outlived him (Jer. 1.1). The mourning over the death of Josiah is attested in Jeremiah's prophecy concerning Jehoahaz: 'Weep not for him who is dead, nor bemoan him' (Jer. 22.10). As illustrated by Ezek. 17 and 19, the fate of Josiah and his sons became a subject for dirge and lament in Israel. As for 'the Laments', the reference in v. 25b indicates that a known book is intended, and this may be identified with the canonical book of Lamentations which bears the same name (*qînôt*) in rabbinic tradition (e.g. BT, Baba Bathra 14b), the reading of which has indeed become 'an ordinance in Israel'. The tradition that the canonical scroll of Lamentation was composed by Jeremiah, attested by the canon of the Septuagint and the express statement of the Talmud (ibid.), may have been earlier. It is thus possible that vv. 24b–25 are an elaboration of biblical and traditional elements, with no additional sources.

There are two elements of 'historical fact' in which Chronicles deviates from Kings, the circumstances of Neco's expedition and the place of Josiah's death, the first of which is of the greater historical significance. According to II Kings 23.29 'Pharaoh Neco ... went up against (RSV 'to') the king of Assyria to the river Euphrates', while v. 20 reads: 'Neco ... went up to fight at Carchemish on the Euphrates'. The Chronistic account has a plus and a minus: a more detailed description of Pharaoh's destination – not merely 'the Euphrates', but 'at Carchemish on the Euphrates' – and an omission of the words 'against the king of Assyria'. The Chronicler's credibility, then, lies not so much in the addition of correct information, but in the omission of an incorrect datum. While the location of the battle at Carchemish could be learned from Jer. 46.2 and does not necessarily imply an additional source, the correct presentation of the political situation cannot be deduced from biblical sources alone. As has been learned from the Babylonian Chronicles (Gadd, 1923; cf. A. K. Grayson, *Assyrian and Babylonian Chronicles*, 1975, 100), Neco indeed came on behalf of Assyria and not against it. We must either conclude that the words 'against the king of Assyria' are a misleading later gloss in the Deuteronomistic story and were absent from the Chronicler's *Vorlage*; or that the Chronicler did have some extra-biblical source, a view favoured by a number of scholars (cf. Rudolph; 331, Myers, XXX, and others; also A. Malamat, 'Josiah's Bid for Armageddon', *JANES* 5, 1973, 267–78). As for the alternating tradition about the place of Josiah's death – Megiddo or Jerusalem – the Chronicler could have either reinterpreted the story along the lines of his earlier presentation, or used a divergent tradition on Josiah's death, but no conclusive statement may be made.

D. Commentary

[1–19] The first part of the chapter is an elaborate account of Josiah's Passover, departing from II Kings 23.21 and going its own way. There is an inverse correlation between the relative significance of the Passover in the Deuteronomistic and Chronistic accounts and the scope of the passages devoted to them. Josiah's Passover is presented in Kings as of the greatest significance, 'For no such Passover had been kept since the days of the judges ... or during all the days of the kings of Israel or the kings of Judah' (II Kings 23.22). Yet it is recorded in one terse verse (v. 21), followed by these evaluative statements. In Chronicles, by contrast, Josiah's Passover was preceded by that of Hezekiah, and differed from it in details rather than in principle. Nevertheless, the Chronicler devotes a long paragraph to it, composed with earnest literary and theological effort.

A comparison of this passage with II Chron. 30 may provide the explanation for this phenomenon. Hezekiah's Passover is portrayed as a spontaneous initiative, the main purpose of which was to provide a cultic-religious framework for the integration of the people of the North into the Jerusalem cult; the approach to these Israelites, and the effort to bring them to Jerusalem, consume the major part of ch. 30. Hezekiah's Passover is thus presented as an *ad hoc* undertaking, with the resulting difficulties of the situation entailing a series of *ad hoc* decisions: the postponement of the date (v. 2), a hasty organization of the priests and Levites (v. 15), the recruitment of the Levites to perform the many chores (v. 17), and a last-minute permission to some of the people to partake in the sacrifice without the necessary purification, accompanied by the king's propitiatory prayer (vv. 18–19). The foundations of Hezekiah's Passover, with the additional feast following it (v. 23) – in both administration and cult – are found in the king's own command (30.6), his taking counsel with his officers (30.12), or the people's decision (30.2, 4, 23), all sanctioned by the Lord. There are only two references to a written prescription (vv. 16, 18), the latter referring to the deviation from the prescribed protocol rather than to its fulfilment. Hezekiah's spontaneous act conforms well with the general nature of his whole enterprise, which the Chronicler says 'came about suddenly' (II Chron. 29.36). Josiah's Passover is a different matter altogether. Josiah works to establish a permanent institution, built on solid administrational and organizational foundations, with a clear division of roles and an undisputed legal basis.

In establishing the centralized Passover as a permanent institution, Josiah is faced with several problems. As it is no longer possible to leave the responsibility for the slaughter of sacrifices with all the accompanying rites to the individual families, the setting up of a central cultic administration is indicated, built around the experienced body of the Temple personnel. Within their ranks, the role of the priests is not only the most established and defined, but also absolutely exclusive; they preside over the various aspects of sacrifice at the altar and attend to the inside of the Temple, and they are irreplaceable. The roles of the singers and gatekeepers are also well defined, and so the group with the least articulated position is that of the 'Levites', who constitute a kind of corps of intermediaries between the cult and the people. In v. 3 they are presented as both 'the teachers of Israel' and 'holy to the Lord', and are asked to 'serve the Lord your God' on the one hand 'and his people Israel' on the other. Except for the acts which are exclusively priestly, everything connected with the Passover sacrifice is now transferred to the Levites: slaughter, flaying, conveyance of the blood, removal of the fat parts, roasting of the Passover sacrifice, and its distribution according to fathers' houses.

Josiah's second problem is to establish a legal basis for the new arrangements, the solution of which is suggested by v. 3. Following the principles laid down in the book of Numbers, which depict the Levites as a mediating body between the people and the 'holy', and taking the lead from David's precedent of regarding the cancellation of their initial role of carrying the ark (Num. 3.6–9; 8.19) as justifying a change in their role (I Chron. 23.26), Josiah appoints them to the same kind of intermediate service, a 'go-between' between the people and the 'holy'.

The problem of economics involved in the Passover festival is also solved with a centralized administration of the feast. The obligation to provide the Passover animals is laid on the king, who would provide for the people, and the heads of the clerical classes, who would provide for their members. As is commonly his manner, the Chronicler also relates the officers' assistance: they volunteered to contribute from their own possession 'to the people, to the priests, and to the Levites' (v. 8).

[1] The introduction of the Passover with 'Josiah kept a Passover to the Lord in Jerusalem' deviates in three principal points from its parallel in II Kings 23.21. According to Kings ('And the king commanded all the people, "Keep the Passover ..."'), the initiative is Josiah's but its performance is the people's. In practical terms this would imply that everyone would care for his own Passover sacrifice, the only innovation being the location, celebrating in Jerusalem rather than in the provinces. According to Chronicles, however, everything concerning this festival has been left to Josiah. The Chronicler also omits the clause 'as it is written in this book of the covenant'. Although the reference to the date at the end (35.19) will connect the celebration of the Passover with the finding of the book and the ensuing covenant, this is greatly played down. On the other hand, the Chronicler emphasizes more than the Deuteronomist the fact that the Passover is 'in Jerusalem'; these words are moved from the conclusion (II Kings 23.23) to the beginning of the account.

The story begins with the general statement that 'they slaughtered ... on the fourteenth day of the first month'. In presenting this detail so early, before the preparations for the festival have been recorded, the point being made is that of the date: 'the fourteenth of the first month' rather than the fourteenth of the second month. Already at this point we are given to understand that Josiah's Passover would be observed with strict adherence to the Law.

[2–9] The preparations are divided into two parts: organization of the personnel, who will carry out the laborious projects (vv. 2–6), and the provision of sacrificial animals (vv. 7–9). The organization of the clergy, in turn, comprises two unequal sections: the priests (v. 2) and Levites (vv. 3–6), the second part constituting a second-person address of Josiah to the Levites, in which the role of the Levites, presented as an innovation, is accounted for and defined.

[2] The appointment of the priests should present no problem; the king takes care that they are present in their regular offices, and encourages them

to perform the Temple's service. The latter statement, however, is somewhat disturbing. Why should the priests 'be encouraged' in the performance of their regular tasks? It seems to be a part of Josiah's systematic preparation; in view of earlier precedents (cf. II Chron. 29.34; 30.2), he takes supererogatory precautions to avoid any unnecessary disturbances.

[3–6] While the priests are merely 'encouraged', without any indication of an actual audience with the king, Josiah's long address to the Levites is now cited. The existence of such an address is characteristic of Chronicles, where the king's command is substantiated and very clearly defined. Yet, although Josiah presents the legal basis for the new arrangements (v. 3), the general tone of the address is more of command than of rhetorical persuasion. It opens with no vocative, and after the proposition has been laid down, the adverb 'Now' introduces one long sentence, composed of a series of imperatives – serve, prepare, stand ... etc. – to the end of v. 6.

[3] The Levites are identified with two appellations: 'the teachers of (*m^e bînîm*) (RSV 'who taught') all Israel', and 'holy to the Lord', both relevant to the present situation. The view of the Levites as teachers betrays the late date of the address; the role of 'teaching' had originally been that of the priests, who are almost by definition 'teaching priests' (II Chron. 15.3); *tôrāh*, which is their inheritance, literally denotes 'teaching'. This role is also evidenced during the Persian period, as illustrated by Hag. 2.11; Zech. 7.3, and Mal. 2.7. It seems, however, that in this realm as well as the cultic sphere, a new class – a class of 'teachers' (*m^e bînîm*) – gradually emerged, mediating between 'the teaching', i.e. the Law, and the people. Their position and role are well-illustrated by the reading of the law as described in Neh. 8. While the person reading the law and conducting the ceremony is the priest Ezra (Neh. 8.1 ff.), a whole group of Levites – thirteen according to Neh. 8.7 – 'teach the people of the law' (RSV 'help the people to understand the law'; also vv. 9, 11–12). Rather than replacing the priests (Rudolph, 325), the Levites become an auxiliary class in this role, too; the priests keep the law and study it, but the Levites are the teachers of 'all Israel'.

The term 'holy to the Lord' is of more widespread usage. It is used in reference to individuals such as the priests (Lev. 21.7–8, etc.) and the Nazirite (Num. 6.8), as well as to the people at large (Lev. 19.2 etc.; Num. 15.40; Deut. 7.6, etc.), and even to abstract entities like 'the Sabbath' (Isa. 58.13). The attribution of this title specifically to the Levites is peculiar to the present verse.

The proposition offered by Josiah is that the Levites are in fact 'unemployed', since their major task of carrying the ark had been nullified with the building of the Temple. His statement has a clear affinity with the story of Numbers, where the role of the Levites is limited to 'carrying' (Num. 3–4), their normative role and the *raison d'être* of their existence as a clerical order.

It is, then, not an actual contemporaneous situation to which he is referring, but a legal one: the consequences for the levitical class of the permanent placing of the ark in the Temple. The mention of the ark alone and not the entire tabernacle with its furnishings conforms neatly with the Chronicler's general view. The ark was certainly the most important object in the sanctuary, but it is in Chronicles that the Temple is explicitly defined as 'a house of rest for the ark' (I Chron. 28.2).

As the MT now stands, Josiah describes the situation with an imperative, 'Put the holy ark in the house', as if a concrete situation in the present moment is assumed. This phrasing gave rise to suggestions that the ark had been taken out of the Temple in the time of Manasseh and was returned in the time of Josiah (cf. Pseudo-Rashi and Kimhi), or that it had been removed to be concealed (Kimhi), or even destroyed (M. Haran, 'The Disappearance of the Ark', *IEJ* 13, 1963, 46–58). However, the description of the Temple as 'the house which Solomon ... king of Israel built', with the sudden and only reference outside the Solomon pericope to Solomon as the builder of the Temple, is to be linked to this matter. Solomon was not only the builder, but the one who installed the ark in the Temple, a fact which was seen as the basis for all the changes in the roles of the Levites. The Chronicler sees the origin of the Levites' legitimization in the time of David and Solomon: David defined their new roles and formed their divisions (I Chron. 23.25–32; also 6.31 [MT 16]), while in Solomon's days these were fully consolidated. I therefore prefer to see the imperative form of the MT *t^enū* ('put') as a textual corruption. Of the various suggested restorations – *nāt^enū* ('they put, placed'), *m^enūḥat* (the rest of'), and *hinnēh* '(behold') – all assuming minor orthographic changes, the former is best accounted for (cf. also I Esdras 1.4). It should be rendered: 'The holy ark was placed in the house which Solomon ... built ... you need no longer carry it.'

[4] Now comes a detailed order to the Levites in a series of imperatives: 'prepare yourselves ... and stand in the holy place ... and slaughter the passover, and sanctify yourselves and prepare for your brethren ...'

The references to 'the writing (RSV directions) of David' and 'the document (RSV directions) of Solomon', raise one of the more salient features of this pericope – the author's constant effort to root all the features of Josiah's Passover in earlier prescriptions and authority, referring in fact to all the recognized sources of authority: the Law of Moses (vv. 6, 12), the prescriptions of David and Solomon (v. 4), or David and the chief singers (v. 15), the authority of the ruling king (vv. 10, 16), and 'the ordinance' (v. 13). This is the most variegated and comprehensive appeal to authority in any single pericope, with very clear delineations of the various aspects of ritual and their respective sources of authority. It is noteworthy, however, that the division of the clerical personnel into divisions, the attribution of which to David is a common feature in Chronicles, is regarded here as having been found in a written document. This is another point of comparison between the authority of David and that of Moses, both established by 'books'.

[5] The two words p^e*luggāh* and h^a*luqqāh* are unique. The former derives from the quite rare root *plg* denoting 'divide', while the latter comes from its common synonym *ḥlq*, the ordinary word for 'division' being *maḥ*^{a}*lōqet*, also found in this chapter (vv. 4, 10). The meaning of these terms is clarified by their synonyms, attested in v. 12 for the one and v. 10 for the other. The unique p^e*luggāh / miplaggāh* refer to the 'father's house' of the lay Israelites, while h^a*luqqāh / maḥ*^{a}*lōqet* refer to the Levites (or more generally, the clergy). It seems that we have here the same division known from late Second Temple literature, in which these groups were called 'Ma'amad', deriving from '*md*, also attested in this verse. By analogy to the priests and Levites, the lay people of Israel ('Israelites') were divided into twenty-four divisions, each represented in its turn at the daily sacrifice in the Temple (cf. Mishnah, Taanit 4.2, etc.), and this division was also maintained during the pilgrimages, when the service was not limited to any specific division (cf. O. Sperber, 'Mishmarot and Ma'madoth (Priestly and Levitical Divisions)', *EJ* 12, 90–1). Although the terminology is different, the arrangements reflected here are well attested by later literature.

Another term peculiar to the pericope is the designation of the people as b^e*nē hā'ām*, repeated in vv. 7, 12, 13, and correctly rendered as 'the lay people'. It appears elsewhere only in II Kings 23.6 and Jer. 26.23 in the reference to 'the graves of the lay people' (RSV 'of the common people'), and in 'the gate of the lay people' (Jer. 17.19; RSV differently). This is another illustration of the Chronicler's use of 'unifying motifs' for the particular pericopes, but may also reflect his attempt to provide a clearly differentiated cultic terminology.

[6] Although an explicit demand to 'sanctify themselves' would be expected within the Chronicler's strong emphasis on sanctification (cf. chs. 29–30), its appearance at this late stage is rather awkward. It is also not supported by the following record of the actual ceremony, where we find no mention that the priests or the Levites have sanctified themselves. This aspect, then, should probably be seen as already included in the general 'prepare yourselves ... and stand in the holy place' (vv. 4–5), and the form *hitqaddᵉšu* ('sanctify yourselves') of v. 6 a corrupt reading, arising by analogy to the series of imperatives in the passage. Of the possibilities suggested, the one most attractive from orthographic and contextual considerations is w^e*haqq*^{o}*dāšîm* – 'and the holy sacrifices' (cf. also v. 13). The verse would then read: 'and kill the Passover lamb and the holy sacrifices, and prepare for your brethren etc.'.

[7–9] The provision of sacrifices is also managed from a centralized standing point. While in Exod. 12 this remains each family's concern, while Deut. 15 is silent on the matter, and II Chron. 30 is not fully clear, the present chapter presents it as fully institutionalized, the provision of sacrifices having been taken care of prior to the ceremony itself, the responsibility having been divided between Josiah and the chiefs of the priests and Levites. In addition, there is also the voluntary contribution of the 'officers' for 'free will offerings' (*n^{e}dābāh*, RSV 'willingly').

The contributed animals are allocated for two purposes: small cattle (lambs and goats) for the Passover sacrifice; large cattle (*bāqār*) for 'holy (or: sacred) offerings', adding up to 37,600 Passover sacrifices and 3,800 large cattle. The latter constitute as a rule one tenth of the small cattle, although for the priests the numbers are not round; if the lambs and goats were allotted one per family, then the large cattle was calculated to provide for ten families.

What are the large cattle for? According to the Pentateuchal sources, the Passover sacrifice itself is taken only from the small cattle: 'you shall take it from the sheep or from the goats' (Exod. 12.5), probably deriving from the original character of the feast as a shepherds' sacrifice. On the other hand, Deut. 16, which is not especially precise in ceremonial details, establishes a general rule: 'And you shall offer the Passover sacrifice to the Lord your God from the flock (*ṣo'n*) or the herd (*bāqār*), at the place which your Lord will choose' (16.2). This may imply that, contrary to tradition and all other sources, the Passover sacrifice itself includes large cattle also, and this may, on the face of the matter, be supported by our text.

Rudolph has correctly pointed out that this can hardly be the case, and has suggested that the 'large cattle' are intended for the peace offerings of the feast of unleavened bread, which are mentioned here too early (327). Since the feast of unleavened bread, however, plays only a secondary role in this context (cf. v. 17b), such a reference would be premature and much too elaborate. These sacrifices, then, may belong to the category defined in rabbinical terminology as '*Shalmei Hagigah*', that is, peace-offering sacrifices offered during the festivals. These were offered at the eve of Passover together with the Passover lamb (Mishnah, Hagigah, ch. 1); they thus belong to the Passover, but were not 'the' Passover sacrifice.

The term 'Passover' (*pesaḥ*), basically referring to the particular sacrifice (Exod. 12.21, etc., 43, etc.; Deut. 16.2, etc.), has also become the name of the festival (Lev. 23.4–5; Num. 28.16, etc.). The Chronicler attests its use in the plural for the first time (II Chron. 30.17; 35.7, 8, 9), making it an exclusive term for the sacrificial animals.

The three heads of the priests are designated 'the chief officers (*n^{e}gīdē*) of the house of the Lord' (v. 8), while the heads of the Levites are referred to by the more general 'the officers (*śārē*) of the Levites'. The term *nāgīd* is very common in Chronicles, used for the king himself (I Chron. 11.2//II Sam.

5.2), but also as a title for any officer, head, leader, etc. Among the priests we find this title used of the head of the priests, that is the high priest (cf. I Chron. 9.20; 12.27), but also of the 'chief officer of the house of God' (II Chron. 31.13; also I Chron. 9.11//Neh. 11.11). Is 'the chief of the house of God' also the high priest? Although this would seem to be the case, this title is shared here by three priests, among whom we also find 'Hilkiah', who is known to be the high priest at the same time (34.9ff.).

The names of the others are extremely common; there is no hint of their exact position and role, nor are there any other data to clarify the issue more precisely.

Among the six officers of the Levites, the first three are designated 'brothers', which presents them as belonging to the same levitical sub-order (I Chron. 15.17–18; 16.37, 38, 39; etc.). This may imply that the six Levites represent respectively the two major components of the non-priestly clergy: 'Levites' in general, and 'singers', similarly to the concept of I Chron. 6, where two different genealogical constructions lead separately to the three heads of the Levites (vv. 15–30 [MT 1–15]), and three heads of the singers (vv. 31–47 [MT 16–32]). The names being so common and no genealogy being provided, it is not possible to pursue this further.

Verses 7–9 again illustrate the feature of 'democratization', one of the staples of the Chronistic presentation (Japhet, *Ideology*, 416–28). Although Josiah occupies the central place in the event (cf. above p. 1040), nevertheless, the provision of the sacrificial animals is not attributed to him alone (cf. by contrast I Kings 8.63//II Chron. 7.5), but is broadened in several directions. Next to Josiah we find the heads of the clerical orders, who provide for the clergy; the king himself is reinforced by the contribution of his officers. Even among the clergy, the responsibility is not that of the high priest alone, but of a larger body: three priests and six Levites, who, together with the king, form a body of ten, supported by an even larger body of 'officers'.

[10–17] The celebration of the Passover is framed very clearly with an introduction and conclusion:

10 'When the service had been prepared for'
16 'So all the service of the Lord was prepared'.

The passage may be divided by content into two sections, indicated formally by the temporal adverb 'and afterward' (v. 14). In the first series of continuous actions, the Levites complete the preparation of the sacrifices for all the lay people (vv. 10–13). These are followed by the listing of the Levites' colleagues who are dependent on the Levites for the proper performance of their own chores (vv. 14–15). Because the Levites took upon themselves the preparations of the Passover sacrifices for the entire body of officiating clergy, the ceremonies could proceed successfully.

[11] The slaughtering of the sacrifices is expressed in a non-specific third person plural, no subject being indicated, 'And they slaughtered ...', followed by a specific reference to the priests and then to the Levites in regard to 'flaying': '... the Levites flayed the victims'. It might be supposed that the non-specific 'they slaughtered' alludes to 'the people', the role of the Levites beginning with the flaying. In view of v. 6, however, and the fact that the priests dashed the blood 'from their hand' (cf. on II Chron. 30.16), this could hardly be the case. The beginning of v. 11 should therefore be seen as a direct continuation of v. 10, referring to the Levites: they slaughtered the sacrificial animal, flayed it, and passed the blood to the priests.

The 'dashing (RSV 'sprinkling') of the blood' is one of the points in which the Passover sacrifice becomes similar to the regular peace-offering (cf. on II Chron. 30.16). However, a major difference still remains between the two, since nothing is said about the priests receiving any share in this sacrifice ('breast and thigh' according to Lev. 7.34; 'shoulder, two cheeks and stomach', according to Deut. 18.3); the priests, like the Levites, have their own Passover sacrifices.

[12] The term *'ōlāh*, repeated in vv. 12, 14 and 16, seems to denote various aspects of 'burnt offerings'. Verse 16 represents the general meaning of the term. Mentioned next to the Passover sacrifice, the 'burnt offering' refers to the regular daily sacrifice and the additional offerings of the festival of the same category (Num. 28.3ff.). The same applies also to v. 14, where 'burnt offering' is mentioned next to 'the fat parts', the latter having been removed from all the other sacrifices. Verse 12 presents a different usage of the term. It occurs in the phrase 'they removed (RSV: set aside) the burnt offerings', the verb 'remove' (*hāsīr*) being the common term for the treatment of the fat parts of the sacrifices (Lev. 3.4, 10, 15, etc.). It therefore denotes part of the preparation of the Passover sacrifice itself and not any separate sacrifice, private or communal. The fat parts removed from the lambs are offered on behalf of the lay people as 'burnt offering', according to their fathers' houses (cf. NEB, JPS).

Like the slaughter, so also the removal of the fat parts is here entrusted to the Levites who replace the laymen (Lev. 3.3–5, 9–11, etc.). The Levites hand the fat parts to the representatives of the respective fathers' houses in whose name the sacrifices are made, thence to be consumed on the altar, and the same applies to the large cattle, the 'peace-offerings of the festival'. The plural pronoun in 'to distribute *them*' (literally 'to give them') is somewhat difficult, but may be accounted for by the collective meaning of the noun.

[13] All the necessary preparation having been completed, the time for the cooking of the meat has come. Since two kinds of sacrifices are involved, the Passover offering and the 'holy offerings', there is also a difference in the manner of their preparation: roasting for the Passover, boiling in pots,

cauldrons and pans for 'the holy sacrifices'. The awkward phrase 'cook with fire' (*way'baššelū bā'ēš*) has been noted by all commentators. It is rightly regarded as a harmonistic Midrash which tries to reconcile Exod. 12.8–9, 'They shall eat the flesh ... roasted ... Do not eat any of it raw or boiled with water but roasted', with Deut. 16.7, 'and you shall boil it (*ūbiššaltā*) and eat it'. The problem lies in the precise interpretation of *biššaltā* in Deut 16.7, which the Chronicler solved by a kind of 'linguistic compromise'; in his text, *bšl* has the general sense of 'cook', used here for the roasting over fire.

[14] Moving to the next stage of the Levites' functions, the preparation of the Passover sacrifice for all the officiating clergy, the Chronicler does not repeat the various phases of preparation but subsumes them under one general term 'prepared' (*hēkīnū*), a key term repeated three times (vv. 14, [twice], 15). The strongest emphasis is laid on the fact that the Levites prepared the sacrifice for the priests, who were thus able to perform their own chores. This emphasis takes two forms: a two-fold repetition of the issue, at the beginning and end of the verse, and a special designation for the priests ('the sons of Aaron'), the only ones in the chapter.

[15] The picture of the ceremony is completed by the mention of the other clerical orders, again from the perspective of the Levites. The singers and gatekeepers were able to devote themselves to their duties because of the Levites' dedication. The manner in which the text refers to the singers' role is a brief but pointed indicator of the degree to which the description of Josiah's Passover is centred on the sacrificial ceremony. When compared, for example, with the events of Hezekiah's time, where the prominence of the singers and that of 'rejoicing' in general is immediately evident (II Chron. 29.25–30; 30.21), the contrast becomes very distinct. The present text is satisfied with the note that 'the singers ... were in their place', while the whole vocabulary of 'song' is missing from Josiah's Passover.

The phrasing of the verse is peculiar. The singers are identified as 'the singers, the Asaphides (literally: the sons of Asaph)', but at the same time the source responsible for their establishment is David and the three chief singers, Asaph, Heman and Jeduthun, with either the latter alone or all the three defined as 'the king's seer'. This reference thus recalls I Chron. 25.1–6, in which David's establishment of the Temple song is described. The designation of *all* the singers as 'Asaphides' (*b'nē 'āsāp*) is generally regarded as an earlier stage in the development of the singers' class (cf. Ezra 2.41 //Neh. 7.44; Ezra 3.10), before diverging into three distinct groups. In this text, in which the three head singers are explicitly mentioned, 'Asaphites' should be seen as a 'frozen' term, encompassing all the branches of the singers.

[16–17] The conclusion is found in v. 16, which refers meticulously to all the aspects of the feast: service of the Lord, prepared, that day, keep the passover, offer burnt offering, the command of king Josiah. Verse 17, which follows it, stands as a kind of reprise of v. 1, bringing the story to its final conclusion:

1 'Josiah kept a Passover to the Lord ...'
17 'And the people of Israel ... kept the Passover ...'

It is only at this ultimate point, at the very end of the story, that 'the people of Israel' are referred to as an active participant. Although they were mentioned all along in one capacity or another, this is the only reference to them as subject: 'the people of Israel ... kept'. This is also the place where a very brief reference is made to the feast of unleavened bread – a fact which is not recorded at all in II Kings 23.21–23. While certainly constituting a 'corrective' to the Deuteronomistic account, this short note also indicates that for the present context the feast of unleavened bread is of secondary significance, and not a single detail is provided for it. This is very different from the portrayal of Hezekiah's Passover, where this feast is referred to in much greater detail, and is followed by another seven days of 'rejoicing' (30.21–27). The interest of the chapter remains in the Passover proper.

[18–19] Taken from II Kings 23.21–23 with various alterations, this passage serves in the present context as a kind of 'addendum'; it provides some details of the Passover and puts it in a broader historical perspective. With the move from the Chronicler's account to the cited Deuteronomistic one, we also move from an intensive, active phraseology to a passive one: 'No passover like it had been kept ... In the eighteenth year ... this Passover was kept.' The passive style is interrupted by the Chronicler's own statement in v. 18: 'none of the kings of Israel had kept ...'. There is thus a measure of tension between the Chronicler's wish to present his source as literally as possible and his own inclination to rephrase it in his own style.

Several points of difference between the two texts may be pointed out. First, the different syntax. II Kings 23.22–23 consists of one long explicatory sentence, with a protasis beginning with 'for' (*ki*) and an apodosis with 'but' (*kī 'im*). In Chronicles it loses both its explicative nature and its complexity, and is presented in three simple statements of fact: no Passover like it was celebrated since the days of Samuel; none of the kings of Israel had kept such a Passover; this Passover was kept in the eighteenth year of Josiah. Secondly, the historical horizon is delimited differently: 'Since the days of the judges who judged Israel' becomes 'since the days of Samuel the prophet'. While Samuel may be regarded as the last of the judges, this replacement signifies more than simply designating the period by its last representative. As already observed, the Chronicler's historical narrative skips the period of the judges, the only allusions to this period being I Chron. 17.6, which is a citation of II Sam. 7.7, and possibly II Chron. 15.3–6; and even these are rather general.

On the other hand, Samuel is a person of stature in the book of Chronicles, mentioned by name seven times in different contexts, all of which are peculiar to Chronicles. Outside the book bearing his name, Samuel appears in the Old Testament only twice (Jer. 15.1; Ps.99.6) and seven times in Chronicles (I Chron. 6.28, 33 [MT 6.13, 18]; 9.22; 11.3; 26.28; 29.29 and this verse). Among other things, according to Chronicles, he wrote the history of David, and together with him established the role of the gatekeepers. As may be implied from I Chron. 26.28, Samuel represents the period of Saul and also what preceded it. By mentioning Samuel in this text, then, the Chronicler avoids the reference to the period of the judges while still keeping the historical context of 'pre-David'.

'The kings of Israel and the kings of Judah' of II Kings 23.22 become 'the kings of Israel'. In all of the Passover pericope, Judah is mentioned only once (v. 18), as one component of the people of Israel. The people at large and the kingdom are 'Israel' (vv. 3 [three times], 4, 17, 18), and both David and Solomon are designated as 'the king of Israel' (vv. 3, 4). A reference to 'the kings of Israel' includes them all, in the more comprehensive sense of the term.

The change from the passive voice of his source to an active one (cf. above) is also expressed by the detailed listing of the people who did keep the Passover: 'Josiah, and the priests and the Levites, and all Judah and Israel who were present, and the inhabitants of Jerusalem'. This standard listing has one peculiar feature, the qualification 'who were present'. This quite common expression (cf. Deut. 20.11; Judg. 20.48; I Sam. 13.16, etc.), which also occurs occasionally in Chronicles, serves in the Josiah pericope as a kind of 'unifying motif', repeated three times in the Passover story (vv. 7, 17, 18) and twice earlier (34.32, 33). It is also found three times in Hezekiah's pericope (II Chron. 29.29; 30.21; 31.1) with no specific limitation, and may also be translated neutrally as 'who were'.

Verse 19, which functions as the counterpart to 34.8, concludes the story with an independent and decisive statement of date: 'in the eighteenth year of his reign'.

[20] The Chronicler opens the new episode with a narrative formula, providing a literary bridge between the individual units: 'After all this, when Josiah had prepared the temple, Neco ... went up'. It has a similar function to II Chron. 32.1: 'After these things ... Sennacherib ... came ...' This literary conjunction, however, brings to the fore the theological problem with which the Chronicler is confronted in the story of Josiah, very much in the same way as for Hezekiah (cf. above on II Chron. 32.1). How should we account for the untimely death of a king who 'prepared the temple'? The similarity between this verse and II Chron. 32.1 prompted Pseudo-Rashi to state that 'the verse laments Josiah, for whom no miracle was performed, since a

miracle was performed for Hezekiah of whom it is written: "after these things Sennacherib came"'.

Neco's expedition to Carchemish was long explained according to the data of Kings as a step taken against Assyria. Since the publication of the Babylonian Chronicles (by Gadd, 1923, and see A. K. Grayson, *Assyrian and Babylonian Chronicles*, 1975, 100), it has become clear that Neco was going to support Assyria against the rising power of Babylon and not oppose it, and that the army stationed at Carchemish managed to hold out until 605 BCE. Josiah's intervention did not take place at one of the locations along the 'sea route', although (as learned from the ostracon of Hashabiahu) the kingdom of Judah had expanded to the west, but rather near Megiddo, in the narrow pass of the Iron valley. Josiah arrived at this location by marching through the hill country, the former territory of the northern kingdom, which after its fall was under Assyrian dominion. Josiah's march against Pharaoh Neco on his way to support Assyria may be explained by his fear that a stronger Assyria might be a threat to his newly gained freedom and territorial expansion (cf. Malamat, 'Josiah's Bid', *JANES*, 1973, 274–8).

[21–22] The theological burden of the passage is borne by Neco's address to Josiah and the latter's response, which aim to put the whole event in a particular theological perspective. At the outset, Josiah's departure for battle is presented differently. According to II Kings 23.29, 'Pharaoh Neco... went up... King Josiah went to meet him'. According to the Chronicler's version, after Josiah 'went out against him' (v. 20), Neco sent messengers to him to interrupt him on the way; Josiah would not desist, but 'joined battle in the plain of Megiddo'. This was, then, a very deliberate challenge of Neco's warning, for which the latter was prepared in every way. In theological terms, the presentation of Neco's address as the Lord's warning to Josiah makes the latter's march to battle a strong-headed, wilful act against the Lord.

Neco's address is structured as a rhetorical progression in four stages: a vocative embedded in a rhetorical question ('What have we to do with each other, king of Judah?'); a very concise statement of the true situation ('I am not coming against you...'; 'God has commanded me to make haste'); an imperative ('Cease!'); and a threat ('lest he destroy you'). It is thus a series of very short clauses, the first ones being nominal.

Neco raises two arguments, followed by a threat: You are not my destination, and I must hurry on my way at the command of my god. The inclusion of the god at whose command Neco was proceeding is also the basis of the threat: do not challenge my god lest he ruin you. The seemingly straightforward address actually places Josiah in an impossible situation. Neco's words appropriately refer to his own god, 'god who is with me', and may suggest that the statue of his deity was physically 'with him', carried into the battlefield. According to v. 22, however, when this address is qualified as coming 'from the mouth of God', the reference is certainly to the one God, with a capital G. This presents a major theological difficulty. Although it is true that foreign emperors were seen as the Lord's instrument in the history of his people, this case is different, since Neco threatens Josiah by the name of his own god, the god of Egypt. It is only to be expected that Josiah would not pay heed – specifically because of his piety. How could Josiah accept Neco's claim that his revelation from his own god was actually a message to Josiah from the Lord? For Josiah to accept Neco's words by refraining from war would imply the acknowledgement of the validity of the Egyptian god!

This, then, is a position from which there is no escape – Josiah cannot listen to Neco, but his not-listening is interpreted as sin. Formally, however, the Chronicler did construct *the mise-en-scène* necessary for the theological coherence of the situation. Josiah's battle, fought in spite of an explicit divine warning, is a transgression.

The theological problem embedded in the text has already been faced by the earliest commentators on the book. In I Esdras, for instance, the situation is changed to a great degree, with all references to the divine being explicitly and repeatedly phrased as 'the Lord God' (1.27) or 'the Lord' 1.27, 28). This is, in fact, the position taken by RSV, where the rendering is systematically 'God', even when the context demands 'god' (cf. also the rephrasing and restructuring of Neco's statement in NEB and JPS). The 'messenger' who delivered the Lord's word to Josiah is, according to I Esdras, the prophet Jeremiah, so that Josiah could not have mistaken the authentic divine message. With these adjustments and at the expense of the historical aspects of the episode, the rough theological edges are polished a bit.

Verse 21 has the unique phrase 'the house with which I am at war' (*bēt milḥamātī*), in a somewhat elliptical nominal clause, in which 'I am coming' may be implied (thus RSV). This phrase was interpreted by Malamat to denote an actual 'house', that is, an Egyptian stronghold in Megiddo ('Josiah's Bid', *JANES* 5, 1973, 278), with ensuing conclusions regarding the general political situation and the choice of Megiddo as the site of battle. Although attractive, there is no support for this interpretation of the term. The location of the war is given as 'the plain of Megiddo' (also Zech. 12.11), which may have been the actual place of the battle.

[23–24] The record of the battle, the king's injury, his death and burial, is a mosaic of borrowed motifs and complete citations, culled from various biblical contexts, illustrating the Chronicler's anthological style (cf. also above, pp. 1042f.). 'And the archers shot' is a quotation of II Sam. 11.24 (with *mōrīm*) changed to *yōrīm*, as in I Chron. 10.3 in comparison to I Sam. 31.3); the king's request to his servants, 'Take me away, for I am badly wounded', is very similar to the words of Ahab in I Kings 22.34, while the change of carriage is expressed in words cited verbatim from Gen. 41.43, from another context altogether. The account deals exclusively with Josiah's own fate, with no particulars about the battle or the more general consequences of its outcome.

Josiah is said to have died in Jerusalem, where he was buried 'in the tombs of his fathers'. Both statements deviate from II Kings 23.29–30, where he is said to have died in Megiddo, carried dead to Jerusalem, and buried 'in his own tomb'. The motive for these changes is not made clear, but the dramatic effect is certainly greater in the Chronistic presentation.

[25] The mourning over Josiah is described in the most elaborate manner, and includes an accumulation of all possible components: all Judah and Jerusalem mourn; Jeremiah uttered a lament; all the singing men and women have spoken of Josiah in their laments; to this day; they made them an ordinance in Israel; they are written in the laments. The short passage contains a three-fold repetition of 'lament' and 'for Josiah' (vv. 24b, 25), highlighting these two as the leading themes. A similar occasion of mourning, which became 'an ordinance in Israel', was that for the daughter of Jephtah; cf. the similar statement of Judg. 11.39.

[26–36.1] With the removal of the account of Josiah's death to an earlier position, this part of the Deuteronomistic conclusion (taken from II Kings 23.28, 30b) now refers to two matters only: to the additional sources for Josiah's reign, and to the reign of his son. In a fashion similar to his handling of other parallel texts, the Chronicler begins and ends the passage with his Deuteronomistic source, but replaces the middle clause 'and all that he did' with a longer statement, referring to 'his good deeds according to what is written in the law of the Lord, and his acts, first and last'. *ḥ^{a}sādīm* in the plural as an expression of 'good deeds' has also been mentioned for Hezekiah (32.32), but, in contrast to Hezekiah, the Chronicler emphasizes that all Josiah's good deeds were 'according to the law of the Lord'. 'His acts, first and last' is a standard Chronistic phrase, repeated regularly in the conclusions of his pericopes.

[27] The Deuteronomistic 'The Book of the Chronicles of the Kings of Judah' is replaced by 'The Book of the Kings of Israel and Judah', a designation similar to that for Jotham and Jehoiakim (II Chron. 27.7; 36.8), and, with a reversal of 'Israel' and 'Judah', for Amaziah, Ahaz and Hezekiah (II Chron. 25.26; 28.26; 32.32). The specific phrasing and contents of this reference may equally imply the canonical book of Kings or an extra-biblical source; no conclusive statement may therefore be made on the basis of this citation alone.

[36.1] The state of emergency which is created by the unexpected death of the king in battle is responded to by 'the people of the land', who make Jehoahaz king in his father's place. The intervention of 'the people of the land' in times of political crisis, managing with promptness the 'political vacuum' and providing for continuation of government, is also attested in the enthronement of Josiah himself after the assassination of his father (II Kings 21.24//II Chron. 33.25). 'The people of the land' are also a partner in the restoration of the Davidic rule in the time of Joash (II Kings 11.14–20//II Chron. 23.13–21), while a body by a different designation, 'the people of Judah', is responsible for the enthronement of Uzziah after the assassination of his father (II Kings 14.21//II Chron. 26.1). Whether 'the people of the land' is a strictly defined body, or a more general term for the rural gentry (cf. in particular II Kings 23.35; 24.14, 25.19), the enthronement of Jehoahaz is certainly a political statement. It demonstrates a claim for independence on the part of the people of Judah, and by making a younger son of Josiah follow his father rather than the firstborn, a specific political orientation is also declared. These will all be reversed by a direct intervention of the Egyptian Pharaoh Neco (cf. 36.3–4).

The Chronicler omits the statement that the people of the land 'anointed' Jehoahaz (II Kings 23.30b). The cause for the omission may be seen in the Chronicler's wish to avoid the implication that 'anointment' can be exercised by laymen. It is also illustrated by the change of the non-specific 'they ... anointed him' (II Kings 11.12) to 'and Jehoiada and his sons anointed him' (II Chron. 23.11; Curtis, 519). It is also possible that the Chronicler refuses to ascribe being anointed to a king whose kingship did not last, and who ended his short career in deportation to a foreign land. On the other hand, the Chronicler emphasizes more than his source that the enthronement of Jehoahaz was in Jerusalem: he began his short rule in the city of Jerusalem, but did not survive to end it there.

36 2 Jehoahaz was twenty-three years old when he began to reign; and he reigned three months in Jerusalem. [3] Then the king of Egypt deposed him in Jerusalem and laid upon the land a tribute of a hundred talents of silver and a talent of gold. [4] And the king of Egypt made Eliakim his brother king over Judah and Jerusalem, and changed his name to Jehoiakim; but Neco took Jehoahaz his brother and carried him to Egypt.

5 Jehoiakim was twenty-five years old when he began to reign, and he reigned eleven years in Jerusalem. He did what was evil in the sight of the Lord his God. [6] Against him came up Nebuchadnezzar king of Babylon, and bound him in fetters to take him to Babylon. [7] Nebuchadnezzar also carried part of the vessels of the house of the Lord to Babylon and put them in his palace in Babylon. [8] Now the rest of the acts of Jehoiakim, and the abominations which he did, and what was found against him, behold, they are written in the Book of the Kings of Israel and Judah; and Jehoiachin his son reigned in his stead.

9 Jehoiachin was eight years old when he began to reign, and he reigned three months and ten days in Jerusalem. He did what was evil in the sight of the Lord. [10] In the spring of the year King Nebuchadnezzar sent and brought him to Babylon, with the precious vessels of the house of the Lord, and made his brother Zedekiah king over Judah and Jerusalem.

11 Zedekiah was twenty-one years old when he began to reign, and he reigned eleven years in Jerusalem. [12] He did what was evil in the sight of the Lord his God. He did not humble himself before Jeremiah the prophet, who spoke from the mouth of the Lord. [13] He also rebelled against King Nebuchadnezzar, who had made him swear by God; he stiffened his neck and hardened his heart against turning to the Lord, the God of Israel. [14] All the leading priests and the people likewise were exceedingly unfaithful, following all the abominations of the nations; and they polluted the house of the Lord which he had hallowed in Jerusalem.

15 The Lord, the God of their fathers, sent persistently to them by his messengers, because he had compassion on his people and on his dwelling place; [16] but they kept mocking the messengers of God, despising his words, and scoffing at his prophets, till the wrath of the Lord rose against his people, till there was no remedy.

17 Therefore he brought up against them the king of the Chaldeans, who slew their young men with the sword in the house of their sanctuary, and had no compassion on young man or virgin, old man or aged; he gave them all into his hand. [18] And all the vessels of the house of God, great and small, and the treasures of the house of the Lord, and the treasures of the king and of his princes, all these he brought to Babylon. [19] And they burned the house of God, and broke down the wall of Jerusalem, and burned all its palaces with fire, and destroyed all its precious vessels. [20] He took into exile in Babylon those who had escaped from the sword, and they became servants to

him and to his sons until the establishment of the kingdom of Persia, [21] to fulfil the word of the Lord by the mouth of Jeremiah, until the land had enjoyed its sabbaths. All the days that it lay desolate it kept sabbath, to fulfil seventy years.

22 Now in the first year of Cyrus king of Persia, that the word of the Lord by the mouth of Jeremiah might be accomplished, the Lord stirred up the spirit of Cyrus king of Persia so that he made a proclamation throughout all his kingdom and also put it in writing: [23] 'Thus says Cyrus king of Persia, "The Lord, the God of heaven, has given me all the kingdoms of the earth, and he has charged me to build him a house at Jerusalem, which is in Judah. Whoever is among you of all his people, may the Lord his God be with him. Let him go up."'

A. Notes to MT

[3] בירושלם, read ממלן בירושלם with II Kings 23.33 (Qere); [9] שמונה, add עשרה with II Kings 24.8; ועשרת ימים omit, cf. commentary; [10] אחיו, II Kings 24.17 דדו, proposed אחי אביו; [14] שרי הכהנים, probably read שרי יהודה והכהנים; [19] וכל כלי, probably omit כלי, dittography; [23] יהוה אלהיו, read יהי אלהיו or with Ezra 1.3 יהי יהוה אלהיו.

B. Notes to RSV

[3] 'laid ... a tribute', thus II Kings 23.33; MT 'fined' (NEB); [6] 'to take him', NEB 'and took him'; [8] 'against him', or 'about him'; [10] 'In the spring of the year', MT 'At the turn of the year' (NEB, JPS); [14] 'the leading priests', MT 'the officers of the priests' (JPS), cf. A above; [17] 'in the house of their sanctuary', better 'in their sanctuary' (NEB, JPS); [19] 'precious vessels', cf. commentary; [20] 'escaped', MT 'remained' JPS, 'survived'.

C. Structure, sources and form

1. Chapter 36 is a defined and well-structured literary unit, dedicated to the topic of the last kings of Judah. When it is compared with its Deuteronomistic source (II Kings 23.31–25.30), the fact which immediately strikes the eye is the great brevity with which this period is described. This quantitative feature is one of the Chronicler's historiographic means to render his evaluation of a topic, and in the 'last kings of Judah' it appears most distinctly: from fifty-seven verses in II Kings 23–25 to only twenty-three in Chronicles, less than half the scope, by any method of measurement. While he strictly adheres to the original narrative sequence, the Chronicler disregards the following sections: II Kings 23.31b–32, 35; 24.1b–4, 7, 11–16a, 20, and all of ch. 25. Unable to ignore this period altogether, he chooses to portray it in the briefest possible terms.

This dearth of quantity has its counterpart in the different view of this period, in particular with respect to the destruction of Jerusalem, its stages, scope and aftermath. As will become clear in the commentary, the Chronicler has a very specific picture of the final days of the monarchy, and his omissions are well-calculated.

These include not only isolated matters, phrases and passages of his source, but some recurrent elements, which are systematically deleted:

(a) The names of the queen's mother (vv. 2, 5, 9, 11 as compared to II Kings 23.31, 36; 24.8, 18);

(b) The comparable element in the description of the kings' transgressions (vv. 2, 5, 9, 12 as compared to II Kings 23.32, 37; 24.9, 19);

(c) The record of the kings' deaths (vv. 4, 6–8, 17ff. as compared to II Kings 23.34; 24.6; 25.6–7//Jer. 52.11);

(d) The Deuteronomistic theological reflections (II Kings 24.3, 20);

(e) The details of the destruction (II Kings 23.35; 24.2, 10–16; 25.1–21).

2. The formulation of the Chronistic pericope is accomplished not merely by abbreviation of the Deuteronomistic source, but also by alteration of some of its details, as well as two additions: a long passage in vv. 12b–21, which displays very clearly the Chronicler's composing hand, and the conclusion of the chapter (vv. 22–23) by a passage borrowed from another source, Ezra 1.1–3 (the most common literary technique in the book). While so much is being taken out, changed and added, the underlying structure remains parallel to that of II Kings 24–25, not only in the history of the kings, but also beyond it. Just as the conclusion of Kings goes beyond the destruction, recording first the governorship of Gedaliahu the son of Ahikam (II Kings 25.22–26) and then the release of Jehoiachin from prison (vv. 27–30), the Chronicler, too, ends his story with the edict of Cyrus which announces the restoration (vv. 22–23), and concludes the book with a pointer to the future. Taking the omissions, alterations and additions into account, the synopsis would appear as follows:

II Kings 23.31a	31b–32	33–34	35	36–24.1a	1b–4	5–6
II Chron. 36.2		3–4		5–6a	6b–7	8

7	8–10a	11–16	17	18–19	20, 25.1–30	
	9–10a		10b	11–12a		12–23b

3. Chapter 36 is composed of five parts, four of which are very short and almost equal in length. Only the days of Zedekiah and, more precisely, the destruction of Jerusalem receive a broader treatment:

(a) 2–4 Jehoahaz
(b) 5–8 Jehoiakim
(c) 9–10 Jehoiachin
(d) 11–21 Zedekiah, and the destruction
(e) 22–23 Turning point for redemption.

D. Commentary

[2–4] The record of Jehoahaz's kingship follows that of II Kings 23.31–34, the differences in detail being peculiar to the pericope as a whole. The attempt of 'the people of the land' to assert Judah's independence by placing on the throne of Judah a person of their choice – the second among Josiah's sons – foundered. Pharaoh Neco intervened immediately, deposed the new king, and installed his older brother Eliakim in his place.

[2] The Chronicler omits two details from the introduction to Jehoahaz's reign: the name of his mother and the evaluation of his religious conduct, 'and he did what was evil in the sight of the Lord' (II Kings 23.32). While the former is a constant feature for all the kings since Manasseh, the latter is unusual. The description of a king's religious behaviour is a consistent element in the Deuteronomistic framework of Kings and, followed in principle if not in detail, also in Chronicles. It is in fact absent only in two cases: Abijah (II Chron. 13.1–2), where the chapter as a whole provides the missing information, and Jehoahaz. Since this omission deviates from the Chronicler's practice throughout, including the specific pericope of the last kings, the most likely explanation seems to be its evaluation as a scribal error, a result of *lapsus oculi*.

[3] With the absence of information about the scope of Josiah's defeat and its full political consequences, the circumstances of Neco's intervention are not fully clear. Some clues given by II Kings 23.33–35 may imply a more active role of Jehoiakim in this matter than explicitly stated. The fact that Neco elevates to the throne the late king's firstborn, the person who was probably the heir apparent but who had been skipped by the 'people of the land', and the fact that the penalty laid upon the land by Neco is exacted from 'the people of the land' (II Kings 23.35), point to Jehoiakim's co-operation in this matter. Indeed, Jehoiakim maintained his pro-Egyptian policy throughout his reign.

Three matters of detail should be pointed out. (*a*) As part of the general tendency to abbreviate his source, the Chronicler omits the geo-political detail 'at Riblah in the land of Hamath', thus making the whole scene much simpler. (*b*) The reading *wayᵉsirēhū ... bīrušālayim* (RSV 'deposed him in Jerusalem') is difficult, since the verb actually means 'removed', and the resulting 'removed him in Jerusalem' simply makes no sense. I would therefore join the many commentators who insert the infinitive *mimmᵉlōk* (literally 'from reigning') attested by the parallel text of II Kings 23.33 (cf. Curtis, 520; Rudolph, 334, etc.). Rendered literally, the phrase would be: 'he removed him from reigning in Jerusalem.' (*c*) On the other hand, 'talent of gold', which is probably a corruption of a text where the number of talents had been originally mentioned, was already in the Chronicler's *Vorlage*, as attested by II Kings 23.33, and should not be amended.

[4] The emphatic phrasing 'Eliakim the son of Josiah ... in the place of Josiah his father' (II Kings 23.34) emphasizes Jehoiakim's right to kingship; it implies the legality of Neco's procedure and the 'penalty' laid on the land. This emphasis is avoided in Chronicles, where Eliakim is described simply as 'his brother', and the clause 'in the place of Josiah his father' is replaced by 'over Judah and Jerusalem'. Since the details of the collecting of the tribute (II Kings 23.35) are also omitted, what remains in Chronicles are the minimal facts: the king of Egypt removed Jehoahaz, imposed a penalty on the land, enthroned Jehoiakim, changed his name, and took Jehoahaz with him to Egypt.

Two matters need special attention.

(*a*) Two of the last kings of Judah, Jehoiakim and Zedekiah, were imposed on the throne by the foreign rulers who invaded the country, Jehoiakim by Pharaoh Neco and Zedekiah by the king of Babylon; in both cases the Chronicler states that each was made king 'over Judah and Jerusalem' (cf. also v. 10). While the appellation clearly delineates the territory of their rule, it also implies an obvious contrast to the days of Josiah, when 'Judah and Jerusalem' constituted only one part of the kingdom (cf. 34.3–5, 6–7, 9, 33; 35.18). How did the Chronicler conceive of the rest of the land during the time of the last kings? Although he does not provide an answer to this question, it certainly means that all the vicissitudes of the last period affected only Judah and Jerusalem, sparing the outlying areas of the country.

(*b*) In contrast to II Kings 23.34, the fact of Jehoahaz's death is not mentioned. The Chronicler simply omits the short clause 'and died there'. Since this omission is maintained consistently for all the last kings, it cannot be regarded as coincidental. Cf. also for Jehoiakim (v. 8), where the clause 'so Jehoiakim slept with his fathers' (II Kings 24.6) is not cited, and further the records of Jehoiachin and Zedekiah, which have no reference to their end. According to the Chronicler's presentation, all these kings share the fate of having died outside the land of Israel, and this may be the cause of the change. From the moment a king crosses the borders of the land of Israel, he leaves the orbit of the Chronicler's interest. Even Jehoiachin's favourable fortune and his rehabilitation in Babylon (II Kings 25.27–30) are of no interest to the Chronicler. This consistent line of adaptation, executed with different techniques and with a varying degree of intervention in his source material, is a telling expression of the centrality of the land in the Chronicler's overall view of history: the arena of the history of Israel is the land of Israel; whatever happens outside it is beyond the Chronicler's purview.

[5–8] In the history of Jehoiakim, the Chronicler retained only the most rudimentary framework of the king's history, omitting most of the historical details (II Kings 24.1b–2a), and the theological reflections (II Kings 24.2b–4). The record of Jehoiakim's history thus contains two elements: the Deuteronomistic framework in vv. 5 and 8, cited from II Kings with several alterations, and a core description of Jehoiakim's fortunes in vv. 6–7, which is the Chronicler's contribution.

[5] Jehoiakim was Josiah's son from a different wife and probably his first-born. According to the extant biblical chronology, Josiah fathered Jehoiakim when he was fourteen years of age (cf. II Chron. 34.1), a very young but not

impossible age. Since all these are round figures, the inclusion of some partial years may make this age somewhat higher. The Chronicler omits the name of the king's mother, in this case obscuring the fact that Jehoiakim was Jehoahaz's half-brother, and the comparative element in the description of his sins, leaving out the words 'according to all that his fathers had done'. Since 'his father' implies first and foremost his own father Josiah, the omission of the standard but inaccurate formula is well justified.

[6–7] The events of Jehoiakim's reign begin in II Kings 24.1 with 'In his days Nebuchadnezzar king of Babylon came up', and go on to tell how Jehoiakim 'became his servant three years', how he 'rebelled against him', and how bands of the neighbouring peoples invaded the land of Judah. In keeping with his customary technique, the Chronicler begins very similarly: 'Against him came up Nebuchadnezzar king of Babylon', but in place of all the details just mentioned, two other facts are recorded: 'and [Nebuchadnezzar] bound him in fetters to take him to Babylon. Nebuchadnezzar also carried part of the vessels of the house of the Lord to Babylon.'

Since the Deuteronomistic and Chronistic records do not actually seem to be mutually exclusive, one could regard the Chronicler's report as complementing rather than superseding the earlier one, and some scholars would indeed see Jehoiakim's arrest and exile, also repeated in Daniel 1.1–2, as a historical datum (cf. W. Baumgartner, 'Neues keilschriftliches Material zum Buche Daniel', *ZAW* 44, 1926, 51–5, see also M. K. Mercer, 'Daniel 1:1 and Jehoiakim's Three Years of Servitude', *AUSS* 27, 1989, 179–92). In view of the statement that 'Jehoiakim slept with his fathers' (II Kings 24.6), however, others would see the specific phrasing 'to take him to Babylon' as denoting intention and threat rather than actual exile, contrary to the explicit statement of Dan. 1.2 (already Pseudo-Rashi; cf. Dillard, 299). This consideration is supported by the record of Manasseh, where his actual deportation is referred to unambiguously: 'who ... bound him with fetters ... and brought him to Babylon' (II Chron. 33.11).

Three different but interrelated matters should be discerned in the discussion. (*a*) The precise meaning of the Chronistic phrasing: does 'to take him' mean actual deportation or only an unrealized intention'? (*b*) The historicity of the Chronicler's view of Jehoiakim's fate, against the evidence of II Kings 24.6 on the one hand and Dan. 1.2 on the other. (*c*) The Chronicler's historical views as reflected in the reworking of the history of Jehoiakim. It is this last which provides the key to the understanding of the pericope, and I shall begin with the Chronicler's view, as juxtaposed with that of the Deuteronomist.

The Deuteronomistic view of the destruction is that it was a gradual process, beginning with the death of Josiah. One may even say that Josiah died in order that Huldah's prophecy 'your eyes shall not see all the evil which I will bring upon this place' (II Kings 22.20) might be fulfilled. Jehoahaz's kingship did not last, and the first stages of the decline are to be found in the reign of Jehoiakim, when the target is the land of Judah, afflicted in two ways: by the penalty imposed by the king of Egypt 'upon the land' (II Kings 23.33, 35) and the marauding of the bands of Aram, Moab and Ammon, 'against Judah to destroy it' (II Kings 24.2).

This is not so in Chronicles, where the land of Judah is not scourged at all. The measures of the Babylonian king affect only king Jehoiakim himself, and part of the Temple's vessels. The Deuteronomistic 'in his days' ($b^e y\bar{a}m\bar{a}w$) is rendered in Chronicles 'against him' ($'\bar{a}l\bar{a}w$), which makes Jehoiakim himself very clearly the target of Nebuchadnezzar's expedition.

The specific phrasing of Chronicles, 'to take him', should be explained as denoting actual deportation, as has been explained already by Kimhi, in analogy to Exod. 21.14 ('to kill him'; cf. P. Joüon, *Grammaire de l'Hébreu Biblique*, Paris 1947, §124e, pp. 362–3). It is difficult to see how the passage in Chronicles can be separated from the parallel tradition of Daniel 1.2, which states clearly that Nebuchadnezzar brought Jehoiakim to Babylon, and this is supported by the fact that the Chronicler actually omits the statement of II Kings 24.6, that 'Jehoiakim slept with his fathers', joining him to the kings who did not end their life in the environment of their capital. The unavoidable conclusion seems to be that II Kings 24.1–6 and the Chronicler's view are not complementary but deliberately exclusive, expressing alternative views of the fortunes of king and land at the time.

Together with the king, some of the Temple vessels are also taken to Babylon, to be deposited in Nebuchadnezzar's palace in Babylon. This aspect of the tradition differs from that of Ezra 1.7, Dan. 1.2 (and probably also Ezra 5.14), according to which the vessels were brought to 'the house of his god'. This version may be regarded as a general statement rather than a different tradition (cf. also v. 10).

[8] To the conclusion of Jehoiakim's reign the Chronicler introduces several changes. 'All that he did' (II Kings 24.5) becomes 'the abominations which he did, and what was found about (RSV against) him', the only occasion where a reference to a king's 'abominations' is found in the final summation. The Chronicler may be referring (thus Kimhi) to the severe reproof of Jeremiah, 'But you have eyes and heart only for your dishonest gain, for shedding innocent blood, and for practising oppression and violence' (Jer. 22.17). Other details relating to Jehoiakim in Kings and Jeremiah, and additional prophecies against him (cf. Jer. 36.29ff.), may be implied by 'what is found about (or: against) him'. I have already referred to the omission of 'so Jehoiakim slept with his fathers', which certainly expresses the Chronicler's different view on the matter. The last change refers to the title of the source for Jehoiakim's history, 'the Book of the Kings of Israel and

Judah' rather than 'the Book of the Chronicles of the kings of Judah', similar to that of his father Josiah and others (II Chron. 35.27).

[9–10] Together with all the details pertaining to the international backdrop of the period (for which, cf. Cogan – Tadmor, *II Kings*, 305–9), the Chronicler omits the important remark that 'the king of Egypt did not come again out of his land, for the king of Babylon had taken all that belonged to the king of Egypt...' (II Kings 24.7), and moves directly to the history of Jehoiachin. He borrows and alters the introductory Deuteronomistic formula (II Kings 24. 8–9) and the final verse of his record (II Kings 24.17), thus adhering to his common procedure of preserving the general framework of his source. The core of the description, however, reporting the coming up of Nebuchadnezzar, the siege of Jerusalem, and the details of the king's deportation, is replaced by a single sentence. In both literary method and historiographical results, the record of Jehoiachin's reign is fully parallel to that of his father Jehoiakim.

As already mentioned, the Chronicler omits from the introductory formula the name of the queen mother and the comparative clause 'according to all that his father had done'. However, the difference in the chronological data – the age of the king upon his ascent to the throne ('eight' instead of 'eighteen'), and the length of his reign ('three months and ten days' instead of 'three months') – seems to derive from a scribal error (as generally accepted). After the word *'śrh* had fallen out and had been reinserted into the text at the wrong place, the word 'days' was added as hyper-correction. The correct reading is II Kings 24.8.

The drastic abbreviation of Jehoiachin's story results in a new perspective on the destruction. The days of Jehoiachin, according to the Deuteronomistic picture, witness the penultimate stage before the final destruction of Jerusalem, while in Jeremiah's prophecy they are portrayed as a 'sample' of what the final disaster may be, a last warning to the people of Judah. These include Nebuchadnezzar's own march against Jerusalem (II Kings 24.11), the siege of the city (24.10–11), the deportation of Jehoiachin, his family and entourage (24.12), the spoiling of the treasuries (of the house of God and of the king's, as well as all the golden vessels, 24.13), and the exile of 'all Jerusalem' – the officials, the warriors, the craftsmen (v. 14). The city and the Temple themselves, however, remain unharmed. As for the inhabitants of Jerusalem, only 'the poorest people of the land' (v. 14) remain.

This is all omitted in Chronicles. In its place the Chronicler has one laconic sentence, according to which Nebuchadnezzar did not 'come to the city' but 'sent' for Jehoiachin and brought him to Babylon. It is the king alone – no one of his family, entourage, or the people of Judah – who is affected by this act. As for the spoiling, only the 'precious vessels' are brought to Babylon with the king.

The accession of Zedekiah is also presented differently, the principal change referring to the king's descent. Rather than being listed as Jehoiachin's uncle (II Kings 24.17), the full brother of Jehoahaz (cf. II Kings 23.31) and half-brother of Jehoiakim, Zedekiah is presented as Jehoiachin's elder brother, the accompanying change of his name from Mattaniah to Zedekiah becoming inappropriate and being omitted. The omission of his mother's name in the next verse would conform well with this change. This divergent view of the king's affiliation may be linked to the Davidic genealogy, where two persons by the name of 'Zedekiah' are listed: Zedekiah the son of Josiah, and Zedekiah the son of Jehoiakim (I Chron. 3.15–16). According to the data of Kings, the king by that name was the son of Josiah; according to Chronicles, he was the son of Jehoiakim.

This understanding of the situation presents Zedekiah as Jehoiachin's elder brother, and thus most probably the legitimate heir to his father's throne. A closer parallelism is thus formed between the circumstances of his enthronement and those of Jehoiakim his father. Just as Jehoahaz, the first successor of Josiah, who had been anointed by 'the people of the land' contrary to the strict line of succession, reigned for three months, and was removed by the king of Egypt in favour of his older brother, Jehoiakim, who then reigned eleven years, so too was Zedekiah. Jehoiakim's younger son Jehoiachin, who ascended the throne after his father's deportation, reigned for three months and was removed by the king of Babylon, who replaced him by his elder brother, Zedekiah. Zedekiah would also reign for eleven years (v. 12).

It is difficult to assess how much of this is fact and how much is 'construction'. There is no reason to doubt the Deuteronomistic statement that the king who followed Jehoiachin was his uncle, Josiah's youngest son, but there is also no reason to doubt the possibility that Jehoiakim had a son by the name of Zedekiah, as attested by the genealogy of I Chron. 3.16. On the other hand, it is also difficult to accept that the Chronicler's version, with its 'parallelistic' view of the last kings, is nothing but a scribal error (cf. Rudolph, who suggests the reading 'his father's brother' for the MT 'his brother', 334, also BHS). Since the Deuteronomist is closer in time to the events recorded, and since the Chronicler shows such propensity for 'structured narrative', the evidence of II Kings should be preferred in terms of historicity, but the Chronicler's view should be retained as a variant tradition, with its specific features.

For the emphasis 'over Judah and Jerusalem', cf. above.

[11–21] From the history of Zedekiah in Kings the Chronicler borrows only the introductory formula (vv. 11–12a//II Kings 24.18–19a), into which he introduces all the standard changes of this chapter: omission of the name of the queen mother and the comparative clause 'according to all that

Jehoiakim had done'. From this point on, however, the Chronicler writes his own version of the destruction, a passage of great significance for his historiographical method and particular view of history.

At the heart of this change is the Chronicler's disagreement with the Deuteronomistic theodicy, attributing the destruction to the sins of Manasseh or to the accumulating sins of many generations (cf. Japhet, *Ideology*, 156–65) and his different view of the end of the monarchy and the destruction of the Temple. According to his most basic convictions, no 'postponed' punishment is conceivable; the responsibility for the destruction, therefore, must lie exclusively with the contemporary generation, that of Zedekiah. He thus describes *in extenso* the transgression of this generation, and not having a ready source for it in the Deuteronomistic account, he composes his own, unfettered by the usual Deuteronomistic formulas. As for the destruction, while isolated elements are used from various biblical sources, the result is a peculiar Chronistic picture. The most distinct stylistic element of this passage is its aspiration to elevated prose, characterized by an anthological style with extensive borrowing from other books, the use of metaphors and other literary embellishments, and occasional use of parallelism of members, in imitation of poetic diction.

The passage is composed as one lengthy exposition, containing the following elements presented seriatim, toward its final climax: vv. 12–14, sin; vv. 15–16, warning and the response to it; vv. 17–21, destruction and exile. The passage is followed by the chapter's climax and conclusion in vv. 22–23, revival.

[12–13] The description of sin is an extensive list of various offences, referring first to the king himself (vv. 12–13) and then to the people (v. 14). Zedekiah is indicted of the following:

(a) 'He did what was evil in the sight of the Lord his God', a very general statement, cited from II Kings 24.19, with the omission of the comparative clause.

(b) 'He did not humble himself before Jeremiah the prophet, who spoke from the mouth of the Lord.' The refusal to listen to the Lord's prophets is the most emphasized transgression in this list, repeated again in vv. 15–16. It expresses more than anything else the wilful and obstinate rebellion, perceived as the opposite of 'humility'. The Chronicler may be alluding here to the accounts of the book of Jeremiah, where the prophet's continuous warnings and exhortations fall upon deaf ears. Although they are all in the political realm, Zedekiah's misdeeds illustrate his consistent defiance of the Lord's word.

(c) 'He also rebelled against king Nebuchadnezzar, who had made him swear by God.' This, again, is a political act. The neutral statement of Kings, 'And Zedekiah rebelled against the king of Babylon' (II Kings 24.20b), is seen here as religious malfeasance: an oath by the Lord's name was defied. This view of the matter has been dramatically expressed by Ezekiel: 'Therefore thus says the Lord God: As I live, surely my oath which he despised, and my covenant which he broke, I will requite upon his head' (Ezek. 17.19), a viewpoint on which the Chronicler is probably drawing, using different terminology.

(d) 'He stiffened his neck//and hardened his heart
against turning to the Lord// the God of Israel.'

This last sin of Zedekiah, which sums up all the preceding ones, is also the worst: refusal to return to the Lord, revealing his obstinacy and malice. This culmination of sin is expressed in an elevated style, created by the use of consecutive forms of the verb (*wayyekeš*, *way*ᵉ'*ammeṣ*) after more common simple perfects (*lōʾ niknaʿ*, *mārād*), a balanced structure of parallel cola as illustrated above, and the employment of conventional metaphors with broad literary associations (cf. in particular Deut. 2.30; Jer. 7.26; 17.23, etc.).

It is noteworthy that in all this there is not even one reference to the cultic transgressions or idolatry which characterized earlier kings such as Jehoram, Ahaz and Manasseh (II Chron. 21.6, 10b–11; 28.2–4, 22–25; 33.3–7 following its Deuteronomistic source). The apogee of the king's transgression, according to this view, is his unwillingness to listen to the Lord's word, the wilful spurning of the Lord's authority.

[14] According to the MT, only two constituents are mentioned among the people: 'the officers of the priests (*śārē hakkohᵃnīm*)', and the 'people'. The former seems rather awkward in this context, and following the LXX and I Esdras 1.47, I accept the proposal of many (cf. BHS) to read here *śārē yᵉhūdāh wᵉhakkohᵃnīm*, indicating that among the people there were three strata: the often-mentioned 'princes' (*śārīm*), the priests, and the people. The enumeration of these classes is vital, since according to the following record they are participants in the events and to that extent share the responsibility for their unfolding. Their accountability should therefore be apparent. It is certainly no coincidence that at this crucial point the Levites are absent. They do not share the people's responsibility for its most terrible catastrophe.

The people's sins are described as follows: (*a*) they were 'exceedingly unfaithful, following all the abominations of the nations'; (*b*) 'they polluted the house of the Lord which he had hallowed in Jerusalem'. While it may be assumed that the Chronicler has in mind specific idolatrous practices, no details are given; the Chronicler chose to express himself with these broad generalizations, drawing on conventional terms. The most specific among these, and rather unusual, is the 'pollution of the house' (cf. Jer. 7.30; 32.34; Ezek. 5.11; 23.38). Although the existence of 'pollution' in the Temple has been mentioned in Chronicles in the context of Hezekiah's extensive purifications (II Chron. 29.5, 16), this is the only case in which the cultic installations are defined as an active 'polluting' of the Temple, an act which by its nature and malice determines the fate of the Temple for destruction.

[15–16] The chain leading from 'sin' to 'punishment', according to Chronicles, is not inevitable; there is still one more stage, that of 'warning', which would disclose the sinners' true disposition and attitudes. The sending of messengers is the last opportunity for repentance, and the expression of God's compassion. However, not only did the people not turn back to the Lord their God, but their obstinacy surpasses their king's who 'stiffened his neck, and hardened his heart'. The people take an active and aggressive stand against the Lord's messengers, mocking the word of the Lord. This is the gravest sin, for which there is no forgiveness.

The prophets are designated in the present passage not merely by this title, but also as 'messengers of God' (mal'ªkē hā'ᵉlōhīm) and 'his messengers' (mal'ākāw). This is the only use of this terminology in Chronicles, but it is attested in other works of the same period (e.g. Isa. 42.19; Hag. 1.13). mal'āk, the term used here, denotes not the super-human messengers of the Lord but the human ones: his prophets.

The solemn message of this passage is appropriately expressed in an elevated style and diction, characterized by several features. In v. 15 we find a strong paranomastic quality, built on the repetitive sounds of ע and מ. Verse 16 is characterized by a very careful parallelistic structure, in five cola. Although its rhythm is less pronounced in translation, the parallelistic syntax is apparent:

'they kept mocking the messengers of God//and despising his words// and scoffing at his prophets;
till the wrath of the Lord rose against his people//till there was no remedy'.

This structure is enhanced by the conclusion of the passage with two nominal clauses, both beginning with 'till' ('ad). The passage also contains some borrowed phrases with their original associations adhering. This is obvious with 'sent persistently', cited from Jeremiah (7.25; 25.3–4; 29.19, etc.), and less so with 'till there was no remedy' (cf. Jer. 14.19; Prov. 6.15; 29.1; II Chron. 21.18).

[17–21] In the description of the punishment, the Chronicler was constrained by certain 'hard facts' which could not be eclipsed, such as the end of the monarchy, the burning of the Temple, the destruction of the city and the exile. It is therefore of great interest to observe how these 'data' of the history of Israel were formulated in this context to present a very distinct picture and message.

The first fact to notice is that Zedekiah disappears. The punishment is described in collective terms, while the king himself, his actions and fate, are left out. This is very much in contrast to II Kings 25, where the end of Zedekiah is related in great detail (II Kings 25.4–7; cf. also Jer. 39.4–7; 52.7–11), followed by the whereabouts of Jehoiachin in Babylon (II Kings 25.27–30). It seems as if the Chronicler has reserved his judgment on the issue of the Davidic dynasty, an aspect of Israel's history which has not reached its culmination. Combined with his genealogical list of I Chron. 3.17–21, where the Davidic house is traced to the latest generations, probably his own contemporaries, this reticence may point to one of his most compelling convictions: an expectation of the renewal of the Davidic monarchy.

Secondly, the genre of the passage is different from that of II Kings 25. The detailed narrative, which covers a period of three years and tells its story in accurate and dramatic detail, including the siege, the famine, the surrender of the city, the flight of the king and his warriors, their capture and tragic end and so on, is replaced by a summary notice, which could be described as a 'chronicle' were it not for its poetic style. With this transition of genre, some of the 'hard core' facts disappear, such as the date, the siege and its aftermath, the flight of Zedekiah and his fate, the details of the Temple's vessels and the detailed listing of all the officials who were exiled and executed. The impression gained from the description in Chronicles is of a discrete punitive expedition, rather than a long-term project which spanned three years, exhausted the vital energy of land, and ended in the cruellest treatment of the city and people. The Chronicler devotes one sentence to each of the aspects of the catastrophe: the slaying of the young men 'in the … sanctuary' (v. 17); the spoiling of the treasuries (v. 18); the burning of the Temple and the destruction of the city (v. 19); and the exile (vv. 20–21).

Last is the Chronicler's insistence that everything was the work of the Lord. This is, of course, also, the underlying assumption of the Deuteronomistic presentation in II Kings 23–25, but the events themselves are recounted in a dispassionate narrative manner, with no interruptions for historiosophical reflections, and – except for the introductory verse in II Kings 24.20 – without the explicit presentation of the Lord's role in these events. The Chronicler expresses this view in the actual phrasing of the passage: compare 'he brought up against them the king of the Chaldaeans …; he gave them all into his hand' (v. 17), with 'Nebuchadnezzar king of Babylon came' (II Kings 25.1), or 'Nebuzaradan … came' (25.8, etc.). The Chronicler also concludes with the explicit statement of the underlying motive of the divine act: 'to fulfil the word of the Lord by the mouth of Jeremiah' (v. 21).

[17] In place of the proper name of the Babylonian king, the Chronicler chooses a unique and more poetical form, 'the king of the Chaldaeans', based on the data of II Kings 24–25, but immediately displaying his stylistic inclinations.

The first aspect of Jerusalem's undoing is the slaughter of its sons: '[he] slew their young men ... in their sanctuary'. This verse draws very clearly on Ezek. 9.5–7, employing not merely its contents but actual phrases: 'Pass through the city ... and smite; your eye shall not spare, and you shall show no pity, slay old men outright, young men and maidens, little children and women ... And begin at my sanctuary' (cf. also Lam. 2.20–21). In Chronicles the vision of terror has become a historical fact.

[18] The spoiling of Jerusalem begins with the most precious vessels of the Temple and also includes its treasuries and those of the king and his officials. The reference to the vessels is an extremely concise summary of II Kings 25.13–17; the two other paragraphs are almost a literal citation of II Kings 24.13: 'and carried off all the treasures of the house of the Lord and the treasures of the king's house'. Two points are to be noticed. The first is the addition of the treasures of 'his princes' to those of the Temple and the palace. The 'princes' have thus been included in both the list of transgressors (v. 14) and those who suffered the hand of punishment. We have often noticed how the Chronicler's 'democratizing' inclination does not leave the king in his splendid isolation; even in unexpected contexts and with minute alterations of the sources, he is joined by 'his princes'.

The second fact to be noted is that in the book of Kings this record is dated to the time of Jehoiachin. Already at that early stage the king of Babylon had taken away all the treasures of Jerusalem, with none – except for the Temple's vessels – remaining for the time of Zedekiah (cf. II Kings 25.13–17). In Chronicles all the aspects of the destruction are consigned to the time of Zedekiah, with only a minimal precedent in the context of Jehoiachin's exile (v. 10).

[19] The passage is built on II Kings 25.9, where the fate of the house of the Lord, the royal palace, and all the houses of Jerusalem is described as 'burning', that of the wall of Jerusalem as 'breaking down'. The Chronicler does not refer specifically to the king's palace, however, and casts the whole in a more poetic diction. The destruction of the city is portrayed in a chiastic parallelism, with a changing order of verb-object between the two first and the two last cola. Before presenting this structure, however, one textual issue should be examined.

The phrase $k^e l\bar{e}\ mah^a madd\bar{e}h\bar{a}$ (rendered 'precious vessels') is unique, and seems to have arisen from a dittography. While the term $mahm\bar{a}d$ or the construct $mahmad\ 'ēnayim$, found in several biblical contexts, may equally denote objects (I Kings 20.6; Joel 4.5) or persons (Ezek. 24.16; Hos. 9.16; Lam. 2.4), in the literature of the period it often denotes the Temple itself (cf. in particular Isa. 64.11 [MT 10]; Ezek. 24.21; Lam. 1.10), while the term for precious vessel is the similar $k^e l\bar{\imath}\ hemd\bar{a}h$ (Jer. 25.34; Hos. 13.15; Nahum 2.10; II Chron. 32.37; 36.10). Considering the strong dependence of the

Chronicler on these texts, *maḥmaddēhā* may refer to the Temple itself, the word *keˡlē* being a dittography of *kol*. With this reading the verse would display not merely a chiastic change of the internal order (cf. above), but a full chiastic alternation of subject: 'Temple – city – city – Temple':

'They burned the house of God//and broke down the wall of Jerusalem; all its palaces they burned with fire//and all its delight they destroyed.'

[20–21] The last stage is deportation: 'He took into exile in Babylon those who remained (RSV 'had escaped') from the sword'. The exile also constitutes the final aspect of the destruction in Kings (II Kings 25.21), before the story continues with the fate of the people who remained 'in the land of Judah' (vv. 22–26). The phrasing of this verse, however, is dependent on II Kings 25.21 only in its position and basic contents; it deviates from its wording in almost every possible detail. Verse 20 is more similar to II Kings 25.15–16, with the mention of 'to Babylon', and the causative conjugation of the verb *wayyēgel* having the king of Babylon as subject. This literary affinity and choice of phrasing may reflect not only a linguistic or literary disposition but an essential aspect of the Chronicler's conception of the destruction. A general expression like 'Judah was taken into exile out of its land' (II Kings 25.21) is not found in Chronicles, in the same way that the references to 'the poorest of the land' (II Kings 25.12) and 'the people who remained in the land of Judah' (II Kings 25.22) are avoided. In fact, according to the Chronicler's own description, the destruction fell upon Jerusalem alone, its people, its buildings and the house of the Lord; there is no hint in the passage itself of any damage to the land of Judah or to its people. A similar picture, depicting damage to Jerusalem alone, characterizes the period of Jehoiachin in the Deuteronomistic history. It is from this section, then, that the Chronicler derives the terminology of exile.

The phrase 'those who remained from the sword' is peculiar to this verse, but its inverse is found in Jeremiah's prophecy 'And the rest of them I will give to the sword' (15.9). The idiom 'remain from' itself, rendered by the RSV 'escape from', is also found elsewhere; cf. Exod. 10.5; II Chron. 30.6; and in particular Neh. 1.2–3.

The servitude to the king of Babylon 'and his sons' brings to mind another text from Jeremiah, 'all the nations shall serve him and his son and his grandson, until the time of his own land comes' (Jer. 27.7), 'his sons' referring to his successors. Writing from a perspective in which Jeremiah's prophecy has been realized, the Chronicler replaces 'until the time of his own land comes' with its specific historical realization: 'until the establishment of the kingdom of Persia'. The sensation of 'exile' expressed in this verse, then, does not carry the same tragic finality delivered by II Kings 25.21. Quite the contrary, the servitude to the Babylonian oppressor is clearly limited and delineated; when the prescribed date arrives, everything will return to normal. The expected turn in the historical course is already alluded to here, but the actual beginning of the new era will be presented in the last passage, concluding the book.

The explanatory remarks of v. 21 account for two matters: the very fact of exile and its length. The specific Chronistic understanding of 'exile' as a historical phenomenon can best be elucidated against its background in other biblical works. In biblical thought the phenomenon of exile – deportation and loss of homeland – receives several theological interpretations, which stem from different views of the relationship between the people, the land, and the God of Israel. According to the book of Deuteronomy, for example, the land is the greatest gift which the Lord gave his people, and it is the people's obligation to keep and guard it by keeping the commandments: 'You shall ... keep all the commandment ..., that you may be strong, and go in and take possession of the land which you are going over to possess, and that you may live long in the land which the Lord swore to your fathers to give to them and to their descendants' (Deut. 11.8–9). Exile is deprivation of the gift, caused by the non-observance of the commandments. The nature of this loss is expressed as either a final loss (e.g. Deut. 28.63–68) or a temporary one (e.g. Deut. 4.7–31).

Another view of the exile is found in Lev. 18 and 20, where the land itself, induced by its inhabitants' pollution, turns malevolent: 'lest the land vomit you out when you defile it' (Lev. 18.28; also vv. 24–27; 20.22). Still another view, of priestly origin, conceives of the exile in terms of the Sabbath laws: 'And your land shall be a desolation ... As long as it lies desolate it shall have rest, the rest which it had not in your sabbaths when you dwelt upon it' (Lev. 26. 33–35). This concept views the fact of 'desolation' from a positive perspective, the land receiving through exile the restitution its inhabitants denied it. Moreover, this may also imply – and in a secondary stratum of the same priestly context it is explicitly stated – that this desolation is limited in time, a period which may even be calculated: 'But the land shall ... enjoy (*tēreṣ*) its sabbaths while it lies desolate ...; and they shall make amends (*yirṣū*) for their iniquities' (Lev. 26.43). This viewing of 'destruction and exile' as restitution of the 'land's sabbaths' implies no final loss of the right to the land – either in the sense of certain passages in Deuteronomy, or in the concept of the land's 'vomiting out' its inhabitants – but from the outset raises the expectation of a limited exile. Exile only creates a necessary hiatus, after which life will return to its regular course; with the conclusion of the 'land sabbaths' the time will come for its 'redemption'.

This is the view which the Chronicler adopts for his own explanation of exile, taking one further step beyond the general concepts of Lev. 26. In a perfect example of midrashic exegesis, he combines the view of Lev. 26 with

Jeremiah's prophecy to form one statement. While the view of exile as 'the land's sabbaths' demands that it is limited in time, Leviticus does not allude to its duration, either actual or theoretical. Even in the secondary layer of Lev. 26.43–45, with its view that after the land has enjoyed its Sabbaths, and the people have served their time and have repented, the Lord will forgive and renew the covenant, there is no hint regarding the chronological terms of these expectations. Jeremiah's prophecy, by contrast, which focusses on the nations' subordination to the king of Babylon, views this subordination as of seventy years' duration. It is beyond our interest to deal with the literary development of Jeremiah's prophecy and its diverse layers, but it is clear that its theological foundations are to be found in another context. It is a prophecy to the nations at large and not specifically to the people of Israel, linked to the concepts of the transient and cyclical nature of mundane power (cf. Jer. 25.11–14; 27.6–7; 29.10). The Chronicler combines these two different concepts, stemming from such different theological schools, to express one view. The 'seventy years' of Jeremiah are the necessary time for the land 'to keep its deserved sabbaths'. For the Chronicler, then, 'seventy years' is not a chronological datum which may be explained by various calculations, but a historical and theological concept: a time limit for the duration of the land's desolation, established by a divine word through his prophet.

The literary procedure by which this midrash is formed is also of interest. The sentence is constructed as an *inclusio*: 'to fulfil the word of the Lord by the mouth of Jeremiah ... to fulfil seventy years'. Into this framework the Chronicler inserts the explanation, taken almost verbatim from Lev. 26.34–35 (the similarity being somewhat obscured by the different translations), 'until the land had enjoyed its sabbaths. All the days that it lay desolate it kept sabbath.' The major difference between the two texts is the change of the future-orientated warning 'then the land shall enjoy ...' to a fact of the past.

[22–23] The book concludes in the way it began: the citation of an existing source (Ezra 1.1–3a) and the beginning of a new era. This is indeed the only case in Chronicles in which the Lord's title is the one common in texts of the Persian period, 'the God of Heaven', an epithet never used by the Chronicler himself (cf. Japhet, *Ideology*, 25–6).

This final passage of the book is both the continuation and the reversal of what went before. Verses 17–21 recorded the calamity of Jerusalem around two major pivots: destruction of Temple and city, and exile. Verses 22–23 are a reversal of both, citing Cyrus' message that 'The Lord ... has charged me to build him a house at Jerusalem ... Whoever is among you ... Let him go up.'

This reversal of historical fortunes is also expressed by close affinity of literary detail. In the same way that the destruction was brought about by a foreign king, Nebuchadnezzar king of Babylon, so its reversal is initiated by a foreign king, the successor to world power – Cyrus the king of Persia. The work of these world powers is part of the divine plan in the history of Israel: 'he brought up against them the king of the Chaldeans' (v. 17), and he 'stirred up the spirit of Cyrus king of Persia' (v. 22). As the catastrophe came 'to fulfil the word of the Lord by the mouth of Jeremiah' (v. 21), so the revival comes 'that the word of the Lord by the mouth of Jeremiah be accomplished' (v. 22).

We find here a salient feature of the Chronicler's historiography, viewing the course of history as moving in extremes of thesis and antithesis, in a constant swing of the historical pendulum. The edict of Cyrus is the beginning of a new era in the history of Israel, pointing with hope and confidence toward the future.